Semiramis' Legacy

EDINBURGH STUDIES IN ANCIENT PERSIA

Dealing with key aspects of the ancient Persian world from the Achaemenids to the Sasanians: its history, reception, art, archaeology, religion, literary tradition (including oral transmissions), and philology, this series provides an important synergy of the latest scholarly ideas about this formative ancient world civilization.

SERIES EDITOR
Lloyd Llewellyn-Jones, Cardiff University

EDITORIAL ADVISORY BOARD
Touraj Daryaee
Andrew Erskine
Thomas Harrison
Irene Huber
Keith Rutter
Jan Stronk

TITLES AVAILABLE IN THE SERIES

Courts and Elites in the Hellenistic Empires: The Near East After the Achaemenids, c. 330 to 30 BCE
By Rolf Strootman

Greek Perspectives on the Achaemenid Empire: Persia through the Looking Glass
By Janett Morgan

Semiramis' Legacy: The History of Persia According to Diodorus of Sicily
By Jan P. Stronk

ReOrienting the Sasanians: East Iran in Late Antiquity
By Khodadad Rezakhani

Sasanian Persia: Between Rome and the Steppes of Eurasia
By Eberhard Sauer

FORTHCOMING TITLES

The Bactrian Mirage: Iranian and Greek Interaction in Western Central Asia
By Michael Iliakis

Plutarch and the Persica
By Eran Almagor

Visit the Edinburgh Studies in Ancient Persia website at
edinburghuniversitypress.com/series/esap

Semiramis' Legacy
The History of Persia According to Diodorus of Sicily

Jan P. Stronk

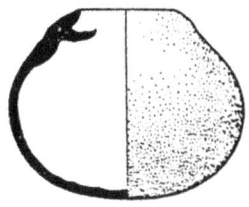

EDINBURGH
University Press

For Anne;
for Merel and Lars;
and for Clio

Edinburgh University Press is one of the leading university presses in the UK. We publish academic books and journals in our selected subject areas across the humanities and social sciences, combining cutting-edge scholarship with high editorial and production values to produce academic works of lasting importance. For more information visit our website: edinburghuniversitypress.com

© Jan P. Stronk, 2017

Edinburgh University Press Ltd
The Tun – Holyrood Road
12(2f) Jackson's Entry
Edinburgh EH8 8PJ

Typeset in 11/13pt Sabon by
Servis Filmsetting Ltd, Stockport, Cheshire

A CIP record for this book is available from the British Library

ISBN 978 1 4744 1425 8 (hardback)
ISBN 978 1 4744 1426 5 (webready PDF)
ISBN 978 1 4744 1427 2 (epub)

The right of Jan P. Stronk to be identified as the author of this work has been asserted in accordance with the Copyright, Designs and Patents Act 1988, and the Copyright and Related Rights Regulations 2003 (SI No. 2498).

Contents

List of Figures and Tables	viii
Preface	ix
Abbreviations	xii
Series Editor's Preface	xvi
Introduction: Diodorus' Work and Our Sources	1
A. Introduction	1
B. Diodorus' life	3
C. The Βιβλιοθήκη ἱστορική ('Historical Library')	5
D. Diodorus' method	10
E. Diodorus' views	13
F. The structure of the *Bibliotheca*	14
G. Final observations	16
H. Summary	17
I. Our primary sources for Diodorus: manuscripts and relevant editions	18
Manuscripts of books 1–5	18
Manuscripts of books 11–20	20
The *Excerpta Constantiniana*	22
Manuscripts of the *Excerpta Constantiniana*	23
Photius' *Bibliotheca*	27
Manuscripts of Photius' *Bibliotheca*	28
Some editions of Diodorus' *Bibliotheca*	28
1 Diodorus' Sources	31
A. Preliminary remarks	31
B. Books 1–5	33
C. Fragments books 6–10	41
D. Books 11–20	44
E. Fragments books 21–32	60
F. Fragments books 33–40	72

	G. Diodorus and his source-authors	81
	H. Diodorus' use of his sources	83
2	Ancient History: Assyrians, Chaldeans, and Medes	86
	A. The Assyrian History	86
	B. The Chaldean History	131
	C. The Median History	135
3	The Persians and the Greek Wars	142
	A. The Arians and general customs of the Persians	142
	B. Cyrus the Great (c. 576/5–530)	143
	C. Cambyses II (?–523/2)	149
	D. Darius the Great (c. 550–486)	151
	E. Xerxes I (c. 519–465)	156
4	Revolt and Sedition	194
	A. Artaxerxes I (?–424)	195
	B. Xerxes II (?–423)	202
	C. Sogdianus (?–423)	202
	D. Darius II (?–404)	203
	E. Artaxerxes II *Mnemon* (c. 436–358)	210
	F. Artaxerxes III *Ochus* (425–338)	254
5	Alexander the Great Defeats Darius III	275
	A. Darius III *Codomannus* (c. 380–330)	275
	B. Alexander's expedition up to the end of the Battle of Issus	279
	C. From Issus to Gaugamela	301
	D. From Gaugamela to Persepolis	323
6	From Persepolis to Babylon	334
	A. Alexander pursues Bessus	334
	B. Alexander's Indian adventure	345
	C. The final phase of the expedition	364
7	The Period of the Diadochs: The Rift Opens	383
	A. The years 323/2–318/17	383
8	The Period of the Diadochs: The Rift Deepens	418
	A. The years 317/16–311/10	418
9	The Vicissitudes of the Diadoch Kingdoms: The Final Years of Diodorus' Persian Account	
	A. The years 311/10–260/79	473
	B. The years after 280	497

10 Semiramis' Legacy	525
Conclusion	543
Bibliography	546
Index of Classical Sources	578
Index of Modern Authors	595
General Index	599

List of Figures and Tables

Map Some geographical features of the ancient Near East. xviii
Fig. 2.1 The Neo-Assyrian Empire, c. 824–c. 650 BC. 88
Fig. 2.2 Plan of Nineveh. 91
Fig. 2.3 Plan of Babylon. 105
Fig. 3.1 The tomb of Cyrus the Great at Pasargadae. 148
Fig. 3.2 The Bisitun inscription of Darius the Great. 154
Fig. 3.3 The Achaemenid Empire. 156
Fig. 5.1 The expedition of Alexander the Great, 334–323 BC. 280
Fig. 5.2 The River Granicus. 282
Fig. 5.3 The River Payas (ancient River Pinarus), site of the Battle of Issus. 297
Fig. 5.4 Persepolis: panoramic view. 330
Fig. 6.1 The River Jhelum Rive (ancient River Hydaspes). 350
Fig. 9.1 The Seleucid Empire, c. 200 BC. 493
Fig. 10.1 Τρυφή and Βίος 539

Table 9.1 List of Seleucid kings 494
Table 10.1 The peoples bringing tribute depicted on the *apadāna* reliefs of Persepolis 532

Frontispiece and Figures 2.1–2.3, 3.3, 5.1, and 9.1 © Clio Stronk; Figures 3.1–3.2, 5.2–5.4, and 6.1 © Jona Lendering, <http://www.livius.org>; Figure 10.1 © Royal Ontario Museum, Toronto.

Preface

Composing the present book, I had to make several choices. First of all, of course, was the choice of which parts of Diodorus' work to include, which parts to leave out. The second choice involved the problem of how to translate the selected parts. I have opted to follow the original as closely as possible, but to apply a freer approach wherever I could or occasionally even had to. This way, I hope to have done the talents of Diodorus as much justice as he – in my view – undoubtedly deserves. The next choice was the most difficult one. To be of optimum use to the reader, the text at several places needs clarification, elaboration, and/or additional literature to get a wider (sometimes a better) perspective on the story as Diodorus relates it to us. This goal could partly be achieved in the Introduction, Chapter 1 (providing some general background), and Chapter 10 (providing some more background and the beginning of a synthesis), partly in the footnotes of the chapters that contain the translation of Diodorus' account.

However, a full commentary on Diodorus' text was obviously impossible within the framework of this book, and not only because it would require a book at least thrice as voluminous. It would, moreover, involve the risk that Diodorus' very account in its context would be overlooked: at this stage of reassessment of his work I found this risk unacceptable. Regrettably, this decision meant that much (recent and less recent) literature had to be left out. On the other hand, providing too little information (part of which may well have been more or less general knowledge among the *pepaideumenoi* in Diodorus' days) would also do no justice to Diodorus' account, which should – as indicated – be the most important feature of this book. I hope that the choices I have made in the comments will, on the one hand, make the reader realise what problems Diodorus faced and how he coped with them, and, on the other, make the notes serve as an incentive to explore the world of Persian history further.

It may be clear that the composition of a book like the present one is not a task one can perform alone, but requires the help of many. First of all I need to mention Lloyd Llewellyn-Jones. From the days when each of us worked on his own edition of Ctesias' *Persica* (he together with James Robson) we have been in contact, discussing elements of both Ctesias' and Diodorus' text. He encouraged me to continue to work on Diodorus' account (within the framework of my preparation of a historical commentary on Ctesias' *Persian History*) and invited me to publish this book in the *Edinburgh Studies in Ancient Persia* series, of which he is the Series Editor. I am very grateful for his friendship and his support, as well as the opportunity he has offered to me. I am also grateful for both the friendship and support of my friend Jona Lendering, 'Altertumswissenschaftler', driving force behind the unsurpassed website <http://www.livius. org> (even though he himself emphatically believes students should look for their information in libraries and not on the internet), and editor of the recent periodical *Ancient History Magazine*. He was also so kind as to provide me with several photos from his rich archive, photos that were taken during numerous journeys, *inter alia* following the trail of Alexander the Great. The Royal Ontario Museum of Toronto, Canada, was prepared to license reproduction of a photograph of a fourth-century AD wall-mosaic from Syria, depicting the couple Luxuriousness (Τρυφή) and Life (Βίος).

I am equally grateful to Clio Stronk, not only for finding interesting websites, like the one on James Tappern blowing Tut-ankh-amun's trumpets (<http://io9.com/5793270/hear-king-tutankhamuns-trumpets-played-for-the-first-time-in-3000-years>), but also for drawing the maps and plans for this book, and for demonstrating several times to my computer, whenever it tried to prove otherwise, that (wo)man still masters machine. I am (obviously) also indebted to several colleagues who have provided me, one way or another, with useful information during the past years: they include Reinhold Bichler (Innsbruck), Carsten Binder (Düsseldorf), Shane Brennan (Exeter), Pierre Briant (Paris), John Dillery (Charlottesville, VA), Dominique Lenfant (Strasbourg), John Ma (Oxford/New York), Robert Rollinger (Innsbruck), and Josef Wiesehöfer (Kiel). In the same category are the anonymous first and second reader of my original proposal for this book to Edinburgh University Press: their comments were both a stimulus and helpful, for which I would like to thank both cordially.

As stated, I could rely on the knowledge of many. Some of them I have already referred to above. Some books or series, however, are so fundamental that it is hardly possible to mention them everywhere where they (may) have, one way or another, influenced my thinking on places, situations, and/or people. Nevertheless, they too obviously merit the credits they are entitled to: they are volumes in the *CHI*, notably volumes I and II; the *CAH*²; and the two volumes of Amélie Kuhrt's *The Persian Empire: A Corpus of Sources from the Achaemenid Period*.

I regret that a draft of Matt Waters's *Ctesias's Persica and its Near Eastern Context: Case Studies* reached me too late to be able to include in this book: it seems, though, an asset, not merely for students of Ctesias' work but also for the interested readers of Diodorus' account of Semiramis. The edition of book XVI of Diodorus in the 'Les belles lettres' series also appeared too late to be considered. The same goes for Michael Rathmann (2016), *Diodor und seine 'Bibliotheke': Weltgeschichte aus der Provinz* (Berlin: De Gruyter).

I am indebted to the head of my Department of Ancient History (Universiteit van Amsterdam), Emily Hemelrijk, for her continued support for my position as a research associate. I am grateful as well to Carol Macdonald, Ellie Bush, Rebecca Mackenzie, and James Dale (all of Edinburgh University Press), and to Fiona Sewell (freelance editor), who each in her or his own way and/or capacity guided me expertly, competently, and in a friendly way through the whole process that publishing a book like the present one appears to require, as well as to the other members of the staff of EUP for producing this book.

Last but by no means least, I owe an immense debt to the love of my life, my wife Anne Keverkamp, to my elder daughter, Merel, and her husband Lars, and to my younger daughter, Clio (already glancingly referred to above), for their continued support to me in every imaginable way. Without these four pillars of strength in my life this book could not have been written. It is therefore only appropriate that I dedicate it to them.

Nieuw-Vennep, the Netherlands, August 2016
Jan P. Stronk

Abbreviations

For the names of authors of classical literature and their works, the abbreviations used are primarily according to the *LSJ* and Glare, P. G. W. (ed.) (1985), *The Oxford Latin Dictionary*, Oxford: Clarendon; if not found there, abbreviations are used according to the *OCD*[4].

Further abbreviations used in this volume are:

ABC   Grayson, A. K. (ed.) (1975), *Assyrian and Babylonian Chronicles*, Locust Valley, NY/ Glückstadt: J. J. Augustin (repr. Winona Lake: Eisenbrauns, 2000).

AchHist   Sancisi-Weerdenburg, H. W. A. M. et al. (eds) (1987–94), *Proceedings of the Achaemenid History Workshops* (various primary titles), Leiden: Nederlands Instituut voor het Nabije Oosten.

ANET   Pritchard, J. B. (ed.) (1955[2]), *Ancient Near Eastern Texts relating to the Old Testament*, Princeton: Princeton University Press (with a supplementary volume).

ARAB   Luckenbill, D. D. (ed.) (1989), *Ancient Records of Assyria and Babylonia*, 2 vols, London: Histories & Mysteries of Man (repr. of the 1926–7 edition, Chicago: University of Chicago Press).

BM   British Museum Inventory Number.

BNJ   Worthington, I. (ed.), *Brill's New Jacoby*, online-version: <http://referenceworks.brillonline.com/browse/brill-s-new-jacoby>, Brill-online.

CAH[2]   Edwards, I. E. S. et al. (eds) (1970–), *The Cambridge Ancient History*, 14 vols in 19,

	Cambridge: Cambridge University Press (most volumes in 2nd edn, vols 1 and 2 in 3rd edn).
CHI	Boyle, J. H. et al. (eds) (1968–91), *The Cambridge History of Iran*, 7 vols in 8, Cambridge: Cambridge University Press.
CLeO	*Classica et Orientalia*, Wiesbaden: Harrassowitz.
Dittenberger *Syll.*³	Dittenberger, W. (ed.) (1898–1900), *Sylloge Inscriptionum Graecarum*, 2 vols, 3rd edn, Leipzig: Hirzel.
D.-K.	Diels, H. and W. Kranz (eds) (2004), *Die Fragmente der Vorsokratiker: Griechisch und deutsch von H. Diels, herausgegeben von W. Kranz*, Zurich: Weidmann (repr. of 5th edn, 1951).
DNP	Cancik, H. and H. Schneider (eds) (1996–2003), *Der Neue Pauly: Enzyklopädie der antike: das klassische Altertum und seine Rezeptionsgeschichte*, Stuttgart/Weimar: J. B. Metzler.
EI	Yarshater, E. and A. Ashraf (eds) (1982–), *Encyclopædia Iranica*, London: Routledge and Kegan Paul; later New York: Bibliotheca Persica Press.
FCG	Meineke, A. (1847), *Fragmenta Comicorum Graecorum*, vol. 1, Berlin: Reimer.
FGrH	Jacoby, F. (ed.) (1923–58), *Die Fragmente Griechischer Historiker*, vols I–III, Berlin: Weidmannsche Buchhandlung; from 1955 onwards Leiden: Brill.
FHG	Müller, C. [= K.] and T. (eds) (1841–78), *Fragmenta Historicorum Graecorum*, 5 vols in 6, Paris: Firmin-Didot.
GGM	Müller, K. (ed.) (1855–61), *Geographi Graeci Minores*, vols I–III, Paris: Firmin-Didot (repr. Hildesheim: Georg Olms, 1990).
IG	Wilamowitz-Moellendorf, U. von, et al. (eds) (1902–2013), *Inscriptiones Graecae*, 49 vols, Berlin: Reimer; from 1927 onwards De Gruyter (some vols are revised edns, esp. for Attic inscriptions).

Kirchner *PA*	Kirchner, J. (1901–3), *Prosopographia Attica*, 2 vols, Berlin: Reimer (repr. with additional material 1966 Berlin: De Gruyter, ed. S. Lauffer).
LGPN	Fraser, P. M. and E. Matthews (eds) (1987–), *A Lexicon of Greek Personal Names*, 5 vols in 7, Oxford: Oxford University Press.
LSJ	Liddell, H. G. and R. Scott (eds) (1983), *A Greek-English Lexicon*, revised and augmented throughout by H. Stuart Jones with the assistance of R. McKenzie, with a supplement, Oxford: Oxford University Press.
Migne *PG*	Migne, J. P. (ed.) (1857–66), *Patrologiae cursus completus, sive bibliotheca universalis, . . . series graeca*, 161 vols, Paris: Imprimerie catholique (*Patrologia Graeca*; repr. Turnhout: Brepols, 1959–80).
Migne *PL*	Migne, J. P. (ed.) (1841–55), *Patrologiae cursus completus, sive Bibliotheca universalis, . . . series latina*, 221 vols, Paris: Siroune (*Patrologia Latina*; repr. Turnhout: Brepols, 1956–75).
OCD[4]	Hornblower, S., A. Spawforth, and E. Eidinow (eds) (2012), *The Oxford Classical Dictionary*, 4th edn, Oxford: Oxford University Press.
OGIS	Dittenberger, W. (ed.) (1903–5), *Orientis Graeci Inscriptiones Selectae: supplementum sylloges inscriptionum graecarum*, 2 vols, Leipzig: Hirzel (repr. 1970, Hildesheim: Georg Olms).
OP	Old Persian.
RE	Pauly, A., G. Wissowa, and K. Ziegler (eds) (1894–1980), *Real-Encyclopaedie der classischen Altertumswissenschaft*, 84 vols, Stuttgart: Metzler.
RIMA 3	Grayson, A. K. (1996), *Royal Inscriptions from Mesopotamia: Assyrian Periods*, vol. 3: *Assyrian Rulers of the Early First Millennium* BC *(858–745* BC*)*, Toronto: University of Toronto Press.

RLA	Ebeling, E. et al. (eds) (1929–), *Reallexikon der Assyriologie und Vorderasiatischen Archäologie*, Berlin/New York: De Gruyter.
RSV	*The Bible, Revised Standard Version* (Old Testament, 1952), Swindon: Bible Society.
SEG	various editors (1923–), *Supplementum Epigraphicum Graecum*, Leiden: Sijthoff; Amsterdam: Gieben; Leiden: Brill.
TGF	Nauck, A. (vol. 1), B. Snel (vol. 2), S. Radt (vols 3, 4), and R. Kannicht (vol. 5), (eds) (1856–2004), *Tragicorum Graecorum Fragmenta*, 5 vols, Leipzig: Teubner (vol. 1)/ Göttingen: Vandenhoeck & Ruprecht (vols 2–5).
TLG	Pantelia, M. et al. (eds), *Thesaurus Linguae Graecae*: <http://stephanus.tlg.uci.edu/>.

Series Editor's Preface

Edinburgh Studies in Ancient Persia focuses on the world of ancient Persia (pre-Islamic Iran) and its reception. Academic interest in and fascination with ancient Persia have burgeoned in recent decades and research on Persian history and culture is now routinely filtered into studies of the Greek and Roman worlds; Biblical scholarship too is now more keenly aware of Persian-period history than ever before; while, most importantly, the study of the history, cultures, languages, and societies of ancient Iran is now a well-established discipline in its own right.

Persia was, after all, at the centre of ancient world civilisations. This series explores that centrality throughout several successive 'Persian empires': the Achaemenid dynasty (founded c. 550 BCE) saw Persia rise to its highest level of political and cultural influence, as the Great Kings of Iran fought for, and maintained, an empire which stretched from India to Libya and from Macedonia to Ethiopia. The art and architecture of the period both reflect the diversity of the empire and proclaim a single centrally constructed theme: a harmonious world-order brought about by a benevolent and beneficent king. Following the conquests of Alexander the Great, the Persian Empire fragmented but maintained some of its infrastructures and ideologies in the new kingdoms established by Alexander's successors, in particular the Seleucid dynasts who occupied the territories of western Iran, Mesopotamia, the Levant, and Asia Minor. But even as Greek influence extended into the former territories of the Achaemenid realm, at the heart of Iran a family of nobles, the Parthian dynasty, rose to threaten the growing imperial power of Rome. Finally, the mighty Sasanian dynasty ruled Iran and much of the Middle East from the second century CE onwards, proving to be a powerful foe to Late Imperial Rome and Byzantium. The rise of Islam, a new religion in Arabia, brought a sudden end to the Sasanian dynasty in the mid-600s CE.

These successive Persian dynasties left their record in the historical, linguistic, and archaeological materials of the ancient world, and Edinburgh Studies in Ancient Persia has been conceived to give scholars working in these fields the opportunity to publish original research and explore new methodologies in interpreting the antique past of Iran. This series will see scholars working with bona fide Persian and other Near Eastern materials, giving access to Iranian self-perceptions and the internal workings of Persian society, placed alongside scholars assessing the perceptions of the Persianate world from the outside (predominantly through Greek and Roman authors and artefacts). The series will also explore the reception of ancient Persia (in historiography, the arts, and politics) in subsequent periods, both within and outwith Iran itself.

Edinburgh Studies in Ancient Persia represents something of a watershed in better appreciation and understanding not only of the rich and complex cultural heritage of Persia, but also of the lasting significance of the Achaemenids, Parthians, and Sasanians and the impact that their remarkable civilisations have had on wider Persian, Middle Eastern, and world history. Written by established and up-and-coming specialists in the field, this series provides an important synergy of the latest scholarly ideas about this formative ancient world civilisation.

Lloyd Llewellyn-Jones

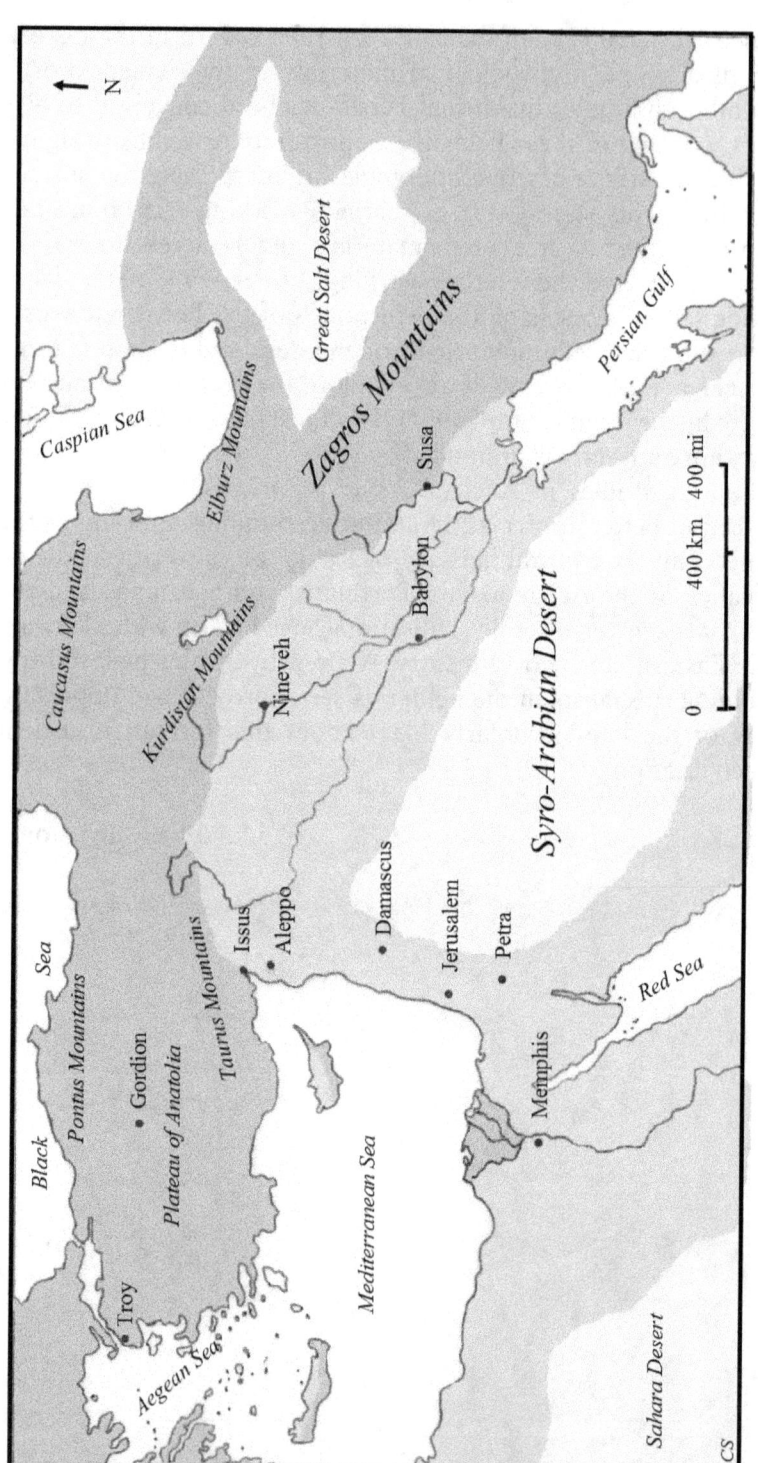

Some geographical features of the ancient Near East.

Introduction:
Diodorus' Work and Our Sources

A. INTRODUCTION

There are few detailed histories of Persia in ancient Greek historiography that have survived. Herodotus presents us with an account of the so-called Persian Wars and the periods before them, Ctesias wrote a much more comprehensive (and disputed!) account of Persian history down to about 390,[1] unfortunately only fragmentarily preserved, while Arrian's (c. AD 90–c. AD 165) history of the expedition of Alexander the Great is, despite its date, as yet a main testimony for Alexander's period.[2] Diodorus of Sicily, however, is the only author whose work has been, to some extent, transmitted to us to have written a comprehensive history (the Βιβλιοθήκη ἱστορική (Bibliotheca historica)) in which more than cursory attention is paid to Persia. Even though Diodorus' work has not survived in its entirety, it nevertheless presents us with a view on Persia's development. The Bibliotheca (as we shall further refer to this work) covers the entire period from Persia's prehistory (in fact a history of Assyria, as it appears predominantly based upon Ctesias) until the arrival of the Parthians from the East and that of Roman power throughout Asia Minor and beyond from the West, some 750-odd years or more later. Diodorus' contribution to our knowledge of Persian history is

---

[1] All three-, two-, and one-digit dates in the text are BC, unless stated otherwise.
[2] Naturally, there have been more classical authors who have written, one way or another, a *Persica* or *Persian History*. Many of these are lost, some have been fragmentarily preserved. For an overview of these see, for example, *FGrH*, vol. IIIC: 364–547: 'V: Babylonien, Assyrien, Medien, Persien', listing most authors of whom a *Persica* is known either by name or even through (a) surviving fragment(s). For a review of Greek literature on Persia see also, for example, Stevenson 1997; Lenfant 2011; Harrison 2011; Lenfant 2014; and Morgan 2016.

I

therefore, though again far from uncontested, as yet of great value for the modern historian of the ancient Near East.

Many, or even most, ancient authors were not primarily interested, let alone equipped, to provide us with accurate historical data as we would like to have them today (see Stronk 2014/15). They were, however, interested to provide their audience, one way or another, with their views of how societies worked, and, perhaps related thereto, with examples of proper conduct. For *our* purpose, these examples include, for example, tales of Persian expansion, effeminacy, depravity, and so on.[3] Because most authors, at least from Herodotus onward, saw Assyrian, Median, and Achaemenid history – which may be stretched to 304 following the views of Depuydt (Depuydt 2008: 1,3) – and post-Achaemenid history as a continuous line, it was self-evident for these authors – and therefore also for Diodorus – that such examples could be found in each of these periods. It therefore should not surprise us that, like Alexander the Great or Darius the Great, Ninus and Semiramis are also described as making an expedition to the East, Semiramis even invading India. To describe such an expedition, impossible in our views and according to our evidence, only served to complete a picture, a picture coloured by wars and expansion as much as by the effeminacy of Ninyas' successors down to Sardanappalus, by Semiramis' depravity, by the treason committed by kings and/or courtiers, and by Alexander's irascible behaviour: they all figure in Diodorus' account. It seems, therefore, right to focus on these wondrous tales and unveil this author and his account to a modern audience.

To do so, we shall first briefly discuss what we know of Diodorus and his works and aims. In the Introduction some general issues will be dealt with, as well the more specific matter of *our* primary sources for Diodorus' work. In the first chapter a much more complicated issue is at stake, namely the sources Diodorus (may have) used composing his *Bibliotheca*. After that exercise, we will let Diodorus take the stage, to entertain and instruct us with his narrative. Though I have tried to avoid making this an edition with a full commentary, as indicated in the Preface, I have nevertheless found it necessary to comment on several remarks in Diodorus' account. In Chapter 10, finally, I will try to make clear for the modern reader how I see Diodorus' work in a wider context of Persian history. As regards the latter term, a caveat is in place: the story does not deal merely with

---

[3] For references to Persian vices, like τρυφή ('luxuriousness'), see below and Chapter 10, and Stronk 2014/15 note 81.

Introduction: Diodorus' Work and Our Sources 3

Persia proper. Persia proper, *Pārsā* or Persis, is a relatively small territory, nowadays called Fārs, near the Zagros Mountains in modern Iran. We will discuss Persian history here as the vicissitudes of all empires or reigns of which, one way or another, either real, alleged, or implicated, the area of Persis and/or Iranian tribes was/were a part. Acting like this, I believe, I will do Diodorus the best service I can.

B. DIODORUS' LIFE

Almost all that is known about Diodorus personally comes from allusions within his own work.[4] Born and raised in the Sicilian town of Agyrium (D.S. 1.4.4),[5] he visited Egypt in 60/59 and may have remained there until 56. Although he claims to have travelled throughout Asia and Europe, there is no further indication that he actually did so. At least it is certain that he, for instance, never visited the place where Nineveh once stood (Sacks 1990: 161 and note 2). The only other specific reference to a foreign journey is to Rome. Diodorus may have gone there directly from Egypt, in or around 56. The inclusion of a minor detail, which is possibly based upon personal observation, indicates that he may have been in Rome by 46 or 45. In that year, he probably started to write the preface to the *Bibliotheca*.

He remarks, in 12.26.1, that the bronze tables were affixed to the *rostra* 'then' in front of the Curia: in 45/4, new *rostra* were planned and completed by Caesar at the west end of the Forum. Diodorus may have witnessed this event. He notes that he remained in Rome a long while. The *Bibliotheca* was probably finished in about 30. Sacks assumes that it is unlikely that Diodorus survived much past the turn of the century (Sacks 1990: 161). Chamoux and Bertrac (1993: viii) think he may have died by about 30. It is perhaps a coincidence that a funeral stele (of unknown date) was found in Agyrium, bearing the text Διόδωρος · Ἀπολλωνίου ('Diodorus, son of Apollonius': *IG* XIV.588).[6] Though the editors of the *IG* were originally tempted to attribute the stele to our author, we must, if only upon the basis

---

[4] This and following parts of the Introduction rely heavily upon the material I collected for and presented in Stronk 2010: 60–72. I also used Ambaglio's contribution from Ambaglio et al. 2008: 3–7.
[5] Chamoux and Bertrac 1993: viii estimate that Diodorus was born about 90. In the rest of this book I shall, referring to the *Bibliotheca*, omit the letters D.S.
[6] See, for example, <http://epigraphy.packhum.org/inscriptions/main → IG XIV → 567–713 → 586–605 → 588>.

of the register of the *SEG*, acknowledge that Diodorus was quite a common name and that the attribution cannot be certain.

Diodorus' remark that he originated from Sicilian Agyrium does not help us much further either. Like many Sicilian *poleis* and towns during the late Republic, it may well have been on the decline. It was situated at what is now Agira, on the northern ridge of the exceptionally fertile eastern plain, watered by the River Chrysas (modern Dittaino). The site was well located for commerce, situated on the central route from Catana to Panormus (= Palermo) and connected by road to Morgantina. Timoleon of Corinth is said to have settled, διὰ τὸ μέγεθος καὶ κάλλος τῆς χώρας ('because of the extent and quality of the region'), 'ten thousand' Greek colonists in Agyrium (in 339/8: 16.82.5, 83.3; Sacks 1990: 165). This number may well be exaggerated by Sacks and fellow translators: it might perhaps be more appropriate to read for μυρίοι 'very many' instead of 'ten thousand' (see Stronk 1995: 80 for a similar situation at Calpes Limen in Xenophon's *Anabasis*).

Diodorus himself is likely to have been quite well off. He travelled to Egypt and met there with priests and embassies (3.11.3) and remained for a prolonged period at Rome. Nothing suggests that, while in Rome, he earned himself a living by tutoring, as most other Greek intellectuals had to do. His criticism of the middle class (1.74.7) also suggests wealth, though his attitude towards democracy is still under debate. It was, however, his prejudice that in democracies masses – as they are easily swayed – facilitate the rise of demagogues (Sacks 1990: 167 and note 39). Sentences like 'In fact, the multitude becomes exacting when it remains under the same authority and every group that is not preferred welcomes change' (19.81.3), 'the masses welcomed, because of the obsequiousness of the ever succeeding kings, the dynastic changes' (33.4.4), or 'some of the citizens of Antioch ... stirred up the masses and proposed that the king should be banished from the city' (40.1a.1) illustrate this view.

Both his travels and his political sentiments at least *suggest*, therefore, that Diodorus enjoyed independent wealth. Despite this, he does not appear to have socialised with Romans of his (alleged) social class. A similar position was held by Nicholas of Damascus, a near contemporary of Diodorus, who had easy access to the most powerful men of the early Principate, but was criticised for maintaining a philosophical distance from Roman society (see *FGrH/BNJ* 90 F 138).

During his stay at Rome, Diodorus may well have kept in touch with Sicily and Sicilians. He may even have returned there incidentally,

Introduction: Diodorus' Work and Our Sources 5

as 16.70.6, a detail possibly referring to the *ius Latii* that is to be dated between 44 and 36, might suggest (see also Sacks 1990: 162 and note 6). By that time, Sicily had become a cultural backwater. It had been the major battleground during the First Punic War and by degrees had become a Roman province. Apart from the payment of a yearly tithe and harbour and pasture taxes, no doubt collected through tax contractors (*publicani*), during the late Republic, Sicily suffered from bloody slave revolts (Diodorus describes them in some detail), uneven administration, and finally the excesses of Verres (Diodorus grew up during the rule of Verres). Octavian's sustained campaign to establish his power over Sicily, where Sextus Pompeius Magnus opposed him with great military skill, and Octavian's harsh conquest and punishing measures, finally, were particularly devastating. Some anti-Roman bias on Diodorus' part would be, therefore, understandable. In this he would resemble Philinus (one of Diodorus' sources; see Chapter 1), who went anti-Roman after the destruction by the Romans of his town of Acragas during the First Punic War. If, however, Diodorus harboured anti-Roman feelings, he had, living in Rome as he did, to be extremely careful. It may have been one of the reasons that he may have stopped his historical narrative at 60, as is generally assumed nowadays, instead of pursuing it to about 45 as he (may have) indicated in his introduction.[7]

C. THE Βιβλιοθήκη ἱστορική
('HISTORICAL LIBRARY')

As far as we know, the *Bibliotheca* was the only work written by Diodorus. It probably consisted originally of forty books, of which fifteen have been transmitted (nearly) completely to us, the remaining

---

[7] See also the Introduction by Oldfather 1968: xv, xix. Diodorus enumerates the years of the periods he sets out to describe in 1.5.1. From the first Olympiad to the events described at the end of his work he counts 730 years: it means that he might relate events as late as 46/5. However, in this same *caput* he states that he will end his story with the beginning of the Celtic campaign (Gallic War) of Julius Caesar, that is, in 60/59. This also seems to be the point of view of Goukowsky 2014: vii, though nuancing it in the following pages. The problem is further complicated by remaining fragments. If we look at the summary of Diodorus in Photius' *Bibliotheca*, especially in *codex* 244, lines 393a12–b5, we see that these lines summarise events after 60. It appears that Diodorus continued his story after all until at least 45 – as the reference to Cleopatra in Tzetzes' *Chiliades* also seems to indicate (Tz. H. 2.34 *sqq*.: such a reference may not have been part of book 40, but possibly in a book 41 or even 42: the reference on Diodorus in the *Suda* [delta, 1151], which emphatically states the work was in 40 [μ'] books, pleads against this idea). These fragments have been omitted from modern editions because Wesseling has ruled them to be not authentic. The discussion on whether he was right to do so was reopened by Botteri 1983; see also Botteri 1992: 25. See also Chamoux and Bertrac 1993: cxxxiii. For Wesseling see below. See also Rubincam 1998. Notable in 4.21.2 is the reference to the deification of Julius Caesar, dating the writing or revision of this book to 42 or later.

fragmentarily. Its book 2, *capita* 1–34, has (allegedly; see below) preserved most of what we know about the first six books of Ctesias' *Persica*, containing the history of what Ctesias called the Assyrians[8] and the Medes. Diodorus relates in those *capita* part of Ctesias' record of the fabulous origins of Nineveh and Babylon and the establishment of an Assyrian Empire. He continues with *capita* on the Chaldeans, the Median revolt, followed by the destruction of Nineveh and its sequel in a Median Empire, and the defeat of the Medes by the Persians. In later books, Diodorus discusses with some regularity events in the Near East, instructing his audience regarding events involving the Achaemenids – including Alexander and his direct relatives – and the Diadochs, whether or not in relation to their neighbours.[9] In this way he presents a surprisingly comprehensive account of Persian history, if, at least as discussed above, we use that term generously.

> The real value of Diodorus Siculus' βιβλιοθήκη ἱστορική has been debated by scholars for many years. The very title of the work indicates that little more is to be expected than a convenient compilation of earlier historical writings. And in spite of the noble declarations in his introduction, Diodorus seems generally to have achieved little more than this. Scarcely ever is he credited with any originality. (Burton 1972: 1)[10]

This verdict reflects the judgement on Diodorus in the *Real-Encyclopädie* by Schwartz, who states: 'Nur ein günstiger Zufall kann einem solchen Buch zur Fortdauer verhelfen. Kein gebildeter Heide citiert D[iodor] jemals; Plinius erwähnt nur den Titel; erst die Christen waren anspruchslos genug, ihn heranzuziehen' (Schwartz 1903a: cols. 663–4).[11] Here are quite a number of value judgements in only a few sentences.[12] Schwartz's opinion appears to have been

---

[8] Many ancient (Greek) historians did not distinguish between Babylonians and Assyrians: see also Forsdyke 1956: 70. Certainly Herodotus did not (Hdt. 1.106, 178), Ctesias occasionally did (see, for example, Ctes. *Pers.* F. 1b = 2.1.7), as is shown by that passage. As it appears, Diodorus (Ctesias) here intends, in all likelihood, primarily the Neo-Assyrian kings. For the Greeks' general lack of knowledge of Assyrian and/or Babylonian history, see Heller 2015.

[9] For a more detailed account of the content per book, see below, Chapter 1. See also Ambaglio in Ambaglio et al. 2008: 8–10.

[10] The most important books and articles on Diodorus are presented in Chamoux and Bertrac 1993: vii–viii: note bibliographique. A more extensive bibliography may be found in Sacks 1990: 213–30 and in Ambaglio et al. 2008: 85–102, 113–15, 129–30. For more recent literature, the online databases of, for example, *Gnomon* and/or *L'Année Philologique* provide excellent information, and a search in the *JStor* database also reveals many interesting and rewarding papers.

[11] Schwartz's judgement is echoed, *inter alia*, in the works of Laqueur 1936 and 1958. See also below.

[12] Schwartz was not the only one who thought so negatively on Diodorus. Chamoux and Bertrac 1993: xxi and notes 47 and 48 quote some nasty remarks on Diodorus by Mommsen

Introduction: Diodorus' Work and Our Sources 7

based upon the *Quellenforschung* as it had been applied to Diodorus by Niebuhr and his successors.[13] Their work made it fashionable to depict Diodorus as a naïve 'Dummkopf', a fashion one encounters even today (see, for example, Hornblower 1981: 19; see also Stylianou 1998: 132, who considers the *Bibliotheca* as 'a work of compilation, one hastily and incompetently carried out'). It reflects a question put forward by Edwin Evers: 'ob Diodor wirklich nur eine atmende Copiermaschine gewesen ist, der 30 Jahre gebraucht hat, um aus anderen Werken das seine gedankenlos zusammen zuschreiben [*sic*!]' (Evers 1882: 244). Evers himself answered the question as follows: 'dass Diodor doch wohl mehr gethan hat, als allein abzuschreiben' (Evers 1882: 289) and 'dass Diodor's Arbeit ein grössere gewesen sein muss, wie man annimmt' (Evers 1882: 290), a position he elaborates somewhat further on (Evers 1882: 291–2). I share his views on this point and therefore totally disagree with the view expressed by Stylianou 'that Diodorus was an epitomator, one of limited abilities too, and as such ... would always seek to simplify his task' (Stylianou 1998: 51). I hope that the review of Diodorus' sources in Chapter 1, below, will elucidate my point.

Of the (as we now generally accept: see, though, Rubincam 1998) forty books of which Diodorus' *Bibliotheca* originally consisted, only fifteen are (nearly) completely extant (books 1–5 and 11–20), with most of the others surviving in various fragmentary states, fragments that were notably preserved in the *Excerpta Constantiniana* (see below), but also elsewhere. It is reported by Constantine Lascaris (1434–1501) that he had seen a copy of the complete *Bibliotheca* of Diodorus, perhaps (one of) the last remaining, in the imperial library before Constantinople fell to the Turks in 1453.[14] The *Bibliotheca*'s claim to universality is established by its range, both geographic and chronological. Along with the myths of the 'foreigners'[15] and the

---

(commented upon by Chamoux and Bertrac as a 'jugement cruel') and Wilamowitz, who describes Diodorus as 'ein so miserabeler Skribent'.
[13] Eduard Schwartz and, for example, Felix Jacoby primarily focused on two particular and partly overlapping fields of research, that is, '*Quellenforschung*' and, less important in this context, '*Textkritik*', all in line with the type of approach to classical sources and their authors that had been shaped by Gottfried Hermann (1772–1848), Barthold Georg Niebuhr (1776–1831), Franz Leopold Ranke (1795–1886; from 1865: von Ranke), Hermann Alexander Diels (1848–1922), and their followers (see Green 2006: 33–4 regarding criticism on Diodorus). See notably Maas 1960 for the content of that specialism.
[14] Lascaris 1866: c. 198; see Reynolds and Wilson 1991: 72. See also <http://www.rogerpearse.com/weblog/2008/12/06/the-last-complete-copy-of-diodorus-siculus-part-2/>. Goukowsky 2014: xxxiv note 139 refers to the view of Bertrac, who believed that Lascaris was mistaken.
[15] Throughout my translation, I have tried to translate Greek βάρβαρος/βάρβαροι as specifically as possible, namely as 'Persians', 'Indians', and so on. Whenever this approach

Greeks, it covers the affairs of mainland Greece, Sicily, Rome, and surrounding areas, from before the Trojan War until 60 (supposedly; see above, note 7; and see Sacks 1990: 3). In some respects Diodorus' work resembles the *Deipnosophistae* (*Learned Banqueters*) by Athenaeus of Naucratis (late second–early third century AD), a work preserved in fifteen books, albeit that both scope and intention in the latter work are (entirely) different from those of Diodorus' work. However, like Athenaeus', many of the sources Diodorus refers to or uses are also now (sadly) lost.

Diodorus' important contribution to our knowledge is, thus, that he preserved various historical traditions. Though Unger is less than complimentary as regards Diodorus, he gives him at least some credit for his choice of sources: 'Diodoros von Agyrion, ein schlechter stilist und noch schlechterer historiker, ist dadurch für uns von hohem werthe, dass er den stoff seiner weltgeschichte fast lauter guten, uns verlorenen geschichtschreibern entlehnt' (Unger 1880: 305; *sic*, without capitals!). A complication is, however, that in his later books Diodorus appears to reveal himself as an inaccurate and uncritical excerpter, using his sources without judgement (see, for example, Hammond 1937: 79: 'a careless and unintelligent compiler'; 81: 'his habitual laziness'), and occasionally duplicating events and information (Burton 1972: 2; *contra*: Oldfather 1968: xxi, xxiii).[16] Moreover, certainly in his later books, Diodorus often represents, regarding Greek history and relations, an Athenophile tradition. That might probably be best explained by his dependence for that part of his work on Ephorus, historian and pupil of the Athenian rhetor Isocrates (see Barber 1935: *passim*; see also below, Chapter 1; for the relation between Ephorus and Isocrates see also Stronk 2014/15: 192, 203 note 54): nevertheless, it remains a problem. It may also have happened that Diodorus plainly and completely misinterpreted and/or misrepresented his sources, as may have been the case in 1.80.1–2.[17] Worse still, he may even occasionally, whenever appropriate in his view, have *created* a historical tradition. The practice of enabling the search for *ta genomena*

---

seemed textually inappropriate, I have favoured the general word 'foreigner(s)', with the same slightly pejorative implication it has in English as βάρβαρος probably had in Greek.

[16] Oldfather 1968: xxiii even states: 'when he errs [,] in fact the fault is not so much his as that of his source'. I believe this statement goes beyond what it is responsible to uphold. As regards duplicating the narrative: we will encounter some instances where Diodorus does so and point out the duplication in a note.

[17] My attention was drawn to this example through a paper by Stijnen 2002: 35; see also Lutz 1937: 239–40. A different view is held by Vycichl 1984–5.

('wie es eigentlich gewesen')[18] proved, thus, to be more difficult for Diodorus than he claimed: τὸ δ'ἀναγραφῆς ἀξιῶσαι τὰ διαφωνούμενα παρὰ τοῖς συγγραφεῦσιν ἀναγκαῖον, ὅπως ἀκέραιος ἡ περὶ τῆς ἀληθείας κρίσις ἀπολείπηται τοῖς ἀναγινώσκουσιν after (and yet, the differences among writers must be recorded, in order to make judgement on the truth with an open mind possible for the readers': 1.56.6).

In the introduction to his historical commentary on Diodorus' fifteenth book, Stylianou pays, very rightly, much attention to the work of one of Diodorus' main sources, namely Ephorus of Cyme (in Asia Minor). Regrettably that work is largely lost. What remains are the fragments, *inter alios* collected by Felix Jacoby (*FGrH/BNJ* 70), and a, by now, almost obsolete monograph by Barber (1935: the second edition by Miller took care of some updating).[19] One of Stylianou's discussions of the work of Ephorus focuses on whether he dedicated separate books to the history of Persia (Stylianou 1998: 92–3). It is a relevant question, especially because Jacoby argues that separate regions were treated by Ephorus in separate books, a view – as Stylianou rightly remarks – that used to be widely shared (Stylianou 1998: 89 and note 236). Stylianou concludes, and I believe he is right, that Persian matters at least were not discussed by Ephorus in separate books, but appeared 'just as they do in those of Diodorus' (Stylianou 1998: 92), even though 'Ephorus' method was flexible and made to serve the themes he wanted to emphasize' (Stylianou 1998: 93).

Apart from giving his audience what we would call nowadays some solid historical information, Diodorus' treatise seems to a large extent to be guided by his ambition to present examples, specifically moral examples. This is most clearly expressed in the opening *caput* of book 15:

> παρ' ὅλην τὴν πραγματείαν εἰωθότες χρῆσθαι τῇ συνήθει τῆς ἱστορίας παρρησίᾳ, καὶ τοῖς μὲν ἀγαθοῖς ἀνδράσιν ἐπὶ τῶν καλῶν ἔργων τὸν δίκαιον ἐπιλέγειν ἔπαινον, τοὺς δὲ φαύλους, ὅταν ἐξαμαρτάνωσιν, ἀξιοῦν δικαίας ἐπιτιμήσεως, διὰ τοῦ τοιούτου τρόπου νομίζομεν τοὺς μὲν εὖ πεφυκότας πρὸς ἀρετὴν τῷ διὰ τῆς δόξης ἀθανατισμῷ προτρέψεσθαι ταῖς καλλίσταις ἐγχειρεῖν πράξεσι, τοὺς δὲ τὴν ἐναντίαν ἔχοντας διάθεσιν ταῖς ἁρμοττούσαις βλασφημίαις ἀποτρέψειν τῆς ἐπὶ τὴν κακίαν ὁρμῆς
> ('Throughout our entire treatise our practice has been to employ the customary freedom of speech enjoyed by history, and we have added just praise of good men for their fair deeds and meted out just censure upon bad men

---

[18] The phrase coined by Ranke 1885: 57.
[19] See also my discussion on Ephorus and references to more modern scholarship on him in Stronk 2014/15: 203–5.

whenever they did wrong. By this means, as we believe, we shall lead men whose nature fortunately inclines them to *aretē*[20] to undertake, because of the immortality fame accords them, the fairest deeds, whereas by appropriate obloquies we shall turn men of the opposite character from their impulse to evil.')[21]

It looks here as if Diodorus presents himself above all as a teacher of morality, essentially using Clio as his handmaiden. It also raises the question whether it is right to view Diodorus primarily as a historian, a question we shall further discuss below.

D. DIODORUS' METHOD

Originally, it was believed that Diodorus invariably followed a single author for many *capita* at a time, changing his source as infrequently as possible: a position recently still held, *inter alios*, by Stylianou (1998). Many, however, now accept that, although Diodorus *perhaps* drew primarily upon a single source for the main line of the different sections of his work, he certainly also incorporated extracts from other writers.[22] In Chapter 1 I will try to present, as stated before, as comprehensive an account as possible of Diodorus' sources.

Various scholars have speculated widely on the sources of opinions and facts presented in the *Bibliotheca*, without even making an attempt to investigate what Diodorus' own contribution was: 'Thoroughly cannibalized, with parts assigned to a variety of authors and traditions of the previous four centuries, the Bibliothêkê has lost its integrity as a unified work and its place within the history of ideas' (Sacks 1990: 4; also Chamoux and Bertrac 1993: xxvi–xxviii). In his turn Sacks argues: 'that Diodorus himself, influenced by contemporary political and aesthetic considerations, is responsible for much of the nonnarrative material and determined the overall shape and main themes of the history' (Sacks 1990: 5; see also Oldfather 1968: xvii; Bigwood 1980: 199). Wherever Diodorus' expressions are not original, and this may be the case quite often, they are, nevertheless, generally compatible with his own beliefs. As Sacks points out, sentiments throughout the *Bibliotheca* are consistent and

---

[20] Both here and in the translation of the fragments of the *Bibliotheca* I have left the word '*aretē*' (or its plural '*aretae*') untranslated, as the traditional translation 'virtue' does not suffice in my view. '*Aretē*' does not merely imply the moral component that is usually stressed in translations, but frequently also has other connotations: see, for example, Stronk 1995: 83 on X. *An.* 6.4.8 and note 21.
[21] See also Sinclair 1963.
[22] Burton 1972: 1; also: Oldfather 1968: xvii, and, eloquently, Green 2006: 24–31; for this particular part of Diodorus' history, see Bigwood 1980: 202 *sqq*.

Introduction: Diodorus' Work and Our Sources

intertwined (see also Chamoux and Bertrac 1993: xxxii *sq.*). Such could not, probably, be the case if the work were merely a random compilation of older traditions.

Surviving fragments from Diodorus' sources serve as controls on his method of excerption. These outside checks prove that, while paraphrasing factual narrative fairly faithfully, Diodorus freely invents asides on politics, philosophy, and historiography (Sacks 1990: 6; *contra*: Oldfather 1968: xxiii). Oldfather's view appears to fit in with Diodorus' own ideas:

> δεῖ γάρ, οἶμαι, τοὺς συγγραφεῖς ἐν μὲν τοῖς ἀγνοήμασι τυγχάνειν συγγνώμης, ὡς ἂν ἀνθρώπους ὄντας καὶ τῆς ἐν τοῖς παροιχομένοις χρόνοις ἀληθείας οὔσης δυσευρέτου, τοὺς μέντοι γε κατὰ προαίρεσιν οὐ τυγχάνοντας τοῦ ἀκριβοῦς προσηκόντως κατηγορίας τυγχάνειν, ὅταν κολακεύοντές τινας ἢ δι' ἔχθραν πικρότερον προσβάλλοντες ἀποσφάλλωνται τῆς ἀληθείας

('For historians should, in my opinion, be granted pardon for faults of ignorance, because they are humans and because the truth of past ages is hard to discover, but those [historians] who are deliberately imprecise should properly be open to censure, whenever they stray from the truth, flattering some people or attacking others through too bitter animosity.' 13.90.7)

In spite of this starting point, checks indicate that Diodorus was an all but flawless excerpter. A comparison, for example, between *P.Oxy.* 1610, a fragment of Ephorus, and the relevant part of the *Bibliotheca* (part of book 11 on Themistocles), suggests several omissions, faults, vagaries, and confusions in Diodorus' work – assuming *P.Oxy.* 1610 is a true reflection of Ephorus' *History* (see for the title Str. 13.3.6/622).[23] Moreover, Diodorus only infrequently quotes Ephorus' text *verbatim* but (as indicated above) mostly paraphrases it, sometimes adding personal observations as well (see also Stylianou 1998: 132–3).

The *Bibliotheca* does not only preserve a 'history' covering what we might call the historical era, but deals with the 'prehistoric' period as well (notably in books 1–6). According to Diodorus, history πολλὰ συμβάλλεται τοῖς ἀνθρώποις πρὸς εὐσέβειαν καὶ δικαιοσύνην ('contributes greatly to piety and justice among men': 1.2.2), and for him this 'prehistoric period' was both an integral part of history and a collection of moral examples. A striking aspect of Diodorus' treatment of 'prehistory' is, nevertheless, that the first three books, covering the eastern lands and the major part of the 'prehistoric period', *at first sight* appear to bear no obvious relationship to the 'historical'

---

[23] In my references to Strabo, I present both the conventional order of book, *caput*, and paragraph and the still frequently used pagination according to Isaac Casaubon's 1587 edition of the *Geographica*, separated by a forward slash.

portion of the *Bibliotheca*. However, the territory that Ninus and after him Semiramis (allegedly) ruled essentially coincides with the extent of the later Achaemenid Empire: I shall later (notably in Chapter 10) return to this issue and show its essential function.

As regards his sources, Diodorus states that he had (had) access to research materials in Alexandria and Rome (1.4.2–4; 3.38.1; 17.52.6), where travelogues and local histories were certainly available.[24] The histories of eastern lands were, at the time Diodorus composed the *Bibliotheca* (namely the first century BC), becoming fashionable, as the works of Alexander Polyhistor, Timagenes, and Pompeius Trogus show, and it looks, therefore, natural that Diodorus somehow incorporated such histories into his work. Nevertheless, in spite of his attention to the 'prehistoric period' of the east, Diodorus is relatively silent as regards eastern peoples after book 3, except when – as we shall see – they are somehow (directly) involved with Greeks or Romans (see Sacks 1990: 55–6) or their interests. Stylianou phrases it as follows: 'there was no connected history of Persia as such, only a series of events which bore directly on Greek history, and my contention is that these were juxtaposed with the Greek events to which they were related' (Stylianou 1998: 90; see also above, the discussion on Ephorus). As it will turn out, however, not only does Persian involvement with the Greek world appear to have occurred quite often but 'Persian history' also played another role in Diodorus' account: Stylianou's statement appears, therefore, to be too absolute.

As we have argued above, Diodorus' claim to universality might appear, to some extent, empty boasting, as he limits himself – certainly as regards the historical period – essentially to Greece, Rome, and Sicily, a view I myself have expressed before (Stronk 2010: 68): 'We also observed that the regions of Egypt and Mesopotamia, the subject of Diodorus' books I and II, hardly recur in the sequel of his *Bibliotheca*.' However, they do recur, sometimes even prominently, though not always independently, but frequently somehow incorporated into greater developments which were more important to Diodorus. Sacks is, therefore, ultimately largely right to state that an investigation into Diodorus' view of progress reveals that books 1–3 are philosophically connected to the rest of Diodorus' work and that they do help to establish the universalism of the *Bibliotheca*. We shall, however, argue below in Chapter 10 that Diodorus' books 1–3

---

[24] Access to these sources must not, though, have been an easy task: see Chamoux and Bertrac 1993: xx–xxi and note 44. See also Stronk 2014/15: 207.

are not only *philosophically* but also *historically* connected to the rest of his work.

Frequently it will also become clear that material traditionally ascribed to Diodorus' sources might, in fact, well be of his making. His treatment of eastern mythologies and his view of progress are intricately connected with other themes in the *Bibliotheca* already recognised as being his own (Sacks 1990: 56). Sacks elaborates this theory for Diodorus' book 1, but not really for the other books. Discussing Semiramis, though, one of the main characters of Diodorus' book 2, Sacks postulates that 'what is especially thematic about the early books is the emphasis on female rulers' (Sacks 1990: 76 and note 100). A substantial part of *capita* 1–34 of book 2[25] is indeed devoted to Queen Semiramis. As regards these *capita*, however, it has been suggested that the author who really focused on the position of women at the court was Ctesias (Sancisi-Weerdenburg 1987a: 40-3), apparently Diodorus' main source for these *capita*. According to Heleen Sancisi-Weerdenburg, the vindictive queen may very well have been a mainly literary character, stemming from an oral storytelling tradition. This observation is likely to be correct, but does not necessarily exclude Sacks' conclusion. Though female rulers occasionally return in Diodorus' later books (or even in book 2 in the person of Queen Zarina(ea): 2.34.3-5), we shall see that they feature much less prominently there – even though, for example, the figures of Olympias and Sisyngambris (as Diodorus writes her name) do play a noticeable role in the Alexander story, as does Eurydice during the so-called Triparadisus conference after Alexander's death, acting as authoritative queens. How should we, then, value *their* roles? It is a minor problem, but it underlines the challenges we may meet in determining how Diodorus used his sources in connection with his views.

E. DIODORUS' VIEWS

We noticed above that, in spite of all the criticism the *Bibliotheca* has met, the work shows a remarkable cohesion (see also below). Sacks remarks that Diodorus has constructed the *Bibliotheca* around his programme for moral living, which we have already cited above. Again and again, Diodorus judges individuals and nations by how

---

[25] In fact almost two thirds of chapters 1–34 of book 2 are, in one way or another, dealing with Semiramis and her exploits. It shows, in my view, that Diodorus preferred an elaborate example to a balanced rendering of the story as presented by his source, in this case Ctesias.

benevolently they act while enjoying good fortune, awarding praise to those contributing civilising gifts in the arts and sciences and in politics (Sacks 1990: 205; also Oldfather 1968: xx–xxi). In the account of the 'Persian history' below, we will encounter several expressions of Diodorus' moral views. Though they are of little or no value for an account of Persian history, I have retained some of them, as they present us with a clear view of Diodorus' intentions.[26] These also show very clearly (though the actors fall outside of the scope of the present account) in Diodorus' attitude towards Caesar (32.27.3), Pompey (38/9.20),[27] and Octavian. The last of these he left out of the text almost completely (as far as we are able to judge on the basis of the remaining generally accepted text), except for a short remark that Octavian expelled the inhabitants of Tauromenium, originally a Greek *polis* in Sicily, in 36 after his defeat off Tauromenium against the younger son of Pompey (16.7.1; see also App. BC 5.109 *sqq.*). What actually happened there was not benevolent at all. This view, it should be stressed, is based upon the fragmentary account we have today: we cannot be sure whether (and if so, how) Diodorus discussed Octavian in the parts of the *Bibliotheca* we do *not* have, the parts, as Ambaglio phrases it, 'la tradizione diretta ha lasciato naufragare' (Ambaglio in Ambaglio et al. 2008: 10).

Another element that frequently pops up in Diodorus' account and merits being mentioned in this context is his emphasis on or fascination with (Persian) τρυφή, commonly translated as 'luxuriousness'. As recent studies show (Gorman and Gorman 2014; Morgan 2016), this emphasis was not 'typically Greek', but rather an 'innovation' from the period of the late Roman Republic (see also Chapter 10). As such, Diodorus appears to have understood (and adapted to) the fashion of his times and – by doing so – shows himself to have been (much) more than a simple breathing copying-machine.

F. THE STRUCTURE OF THE *BIBLIOTHECA*

Reading through the *Bibliotheca*, notably from book 11 onwards, it becomes clear that Diodorus arranges his material basically in a very tight structure. As regards time, he uses three 'pegs' on which to mould his account: first, the cycle of Olympiads, naming its number and (frequently) the winner of the *stadium* race; second, the

---

[26] In the translation I have placed these views between double square brackets ([[ ]]).
[27] I have maintained the combination of these books, following the Teubner and Loeb Classical Library editions, even though the edition by Les Belles Lettres convincingly advocates separating them.

Athenian *archon* list, mentioning the eponymous *archon* of the year; and third, the chief Roman magistrate list, usually giving the names of the consuls (or, occasionally the *tribunes*) of the year. As regards the latter method, Diodorus' counting of the years is slightly at variance with the more or less accepted Varronian chronology.[28] At first, Diodorus is sometimes up to seven years ahead of the Varronian chronology, and for a long time three or four years ahead of it, but in his later books Diodorus' years run parallel with those in the Varronian chronology. In the notes to my translation I shall point out how the two chronologies relate.[29] There is, however, an occasional hitch in this structure. At times, Diodorus seems to have lost track of the date for the events he describes, assembling a cluster of, more or less, related events into one year, and not always the right one at that. However, because the coherence of his account is so strong, it more than compensates, in my opinion, for this disadvantage. Nevertheless, I also shall mention in the notes where Diodorus is at fault as regards his dates.

I have already referred to the fact that Diodorus' attempt to apply structure in his account coincides, or nearly so, with the efforts of Varro to structure Roman chronology itself. They were, however, obviously not the only ones attempting to construct a framework for what we would call historical research and/or historiography.[30] In this respect, they were following in the footsteps of Timaeus of Tauromenium (c. 350–c. 260) as well.[31] Based upon all the evidence, Baron (2013: 17–42) distinguishes three works that can be attributed to Timaeus: a chronographic treatise, called the *Olympic Victors*; a history of the Greeks in the western Mediterranean to the death of Agathocles in 289, known as the *Histories*; and a work on the wars of Pyrrhus in Sicily and Italy in the 270s, the *Pyrrhus*. Evidence shows that Timaeus in the *Histories* (a title of convention, as the official title is unknown) uses numbered Olympiads (Timaeus' *Olympic Victors* related a list of victors of the *stadium*) to date historical

---

[28] The compilation by M. Terentius Varro (116–27; he was, therefore, an almost exact contemporary of Diodorus) of the so-called Varronian chronology was an attempt to determine an exact year-by-year timeline of Roman history up to his time. It is based on the traditional sequence of the consuls of the Roman Republic, eked out, where that did not fit, by inserting dictatorial and anarchic years. It has become a widely accepted chronology in spite of its errors, in large part because it was inscribed on the Arch of Augustus in Rome, even though Livy's chronology is demonstrably more accurate. Though Augustus' arch no longer stands, a large portion of Varro's chronology has survived under the name of *Fasti Capitolini*.
[29] To do so, I shall use Broughton 1951 as my main reference.
[30] The most notable example naturally being Thucydides' arrangement of affairs in 'summers' and 'winters'.
[31] See now for this author Baron 2013.

events. Though embroidering on a theme already treated previously, Timaeus appears to have been (one of) the first to use such a list, augmented by lists of magistrates, kings, and priestly office-holders, as a chronological backbone for his work (see Plb. 12.11.1–2). In practice, Diodorus uses a very similar backbone, his 'pegs' as I have called them, for his work. Whether or not he had any contact with Varro during his time in Rome eludes us, and is not directly relevant to this study.

Though his effort to provide his audience with a chronological framework was, in my opinion, the most important structural feature of Diodorus' account, at least as regards the 'historical period', it was not the only one. Diodorus also applies a geographical divider. He walks his public, as it were, along stage after stage to describe what happened on it, sometimes to draw attention to some particularities, frequently adding a moral judgement on affairs, essentially focusing on things (and notably people) μνήμης ἄξια ('worthy to remember').[32] Subsequently he pays attention to the Asian theatre, the Greek, the Sicilian, Egyptian, Carthaginian, Roman, Gallic ones – whatever was applicable and/or of interest in his view – to return in the following year to the then predominant theatre (only book 17, largely devoted to the vicissitudes of Alexander III the Great, deviates from this schedule). Using both structural elements, chronology and geography, simultaneously, combined with his consistent morality, Diodorus creates the strong cohesion in his account we have already referred to above.

G. FINAL OBSERVATIONS

Schwartz's remark that Diodorus was held in high regard only by the Christian writers (and typically not by more learned pagan contemporaries) is not correct. We know that the *Bibliotheca* was available for and used by the elder Pliny, Athenaeus of Naucratis, and later legal and textual scholars (see also Sacks 1990: 162 and note 9). Pliny (*Nat*. Preface, 25) even praises Diodorus for the straightforward title of his work. It may also have been used by Plutarch and Cassius Dio (Sacks 1990: 162 and note 10), and finally the notoriously fraudulent Cephalion wrote, in Hadrian's time, a history that, as writers then noted (see Sacks 1990: 162 and note 11), resembled

---

[32] See, for example, Diodorus' phrase καὶ τοὺς ἀγαθοὺς ἄνδρας ἀξίους λόγου προσαγορεύομεν ('and we discuss great men worthy to speak of': 1.2.6); see also his position expressed in 1.45.3 and 1.63.1.

an epitome of Diodorus. On the basis of these observations I think Schwartz's judgement cannot be maintained in its absoluteness.

On the other hand, it cannot be established with any degree of certainty that Diodorus' work was widely read either. There is, unfortunately, no way of knowing how common Diodorus' *Bibliotheca* still was in, for example, the early ninth century AD. Access to it after antiquity initially largely depended on whether a complete manuscript of the *Bibliotheca* was ever copied into a parchment *codex*, which probably only made any sense if the work was sufficiently widely read. Evidence shows that this, indeed, most probably did occur. Even then, however, its continuity after the early or middle ninth century was not assured. It is only likely that the *Bibliotheca* was sufficiently important to survive the following major divide, namely the transition (around the beginning of the ninth century) of texts written in the earlier majuscule into later minuscule, as shown by the quite extensive excerpts of some of Diodorus' now lost books in Photius' *Library* (Phot. *Bibl.* [244]). However, the fact that the *Excerpta Constantiniana* present us, as we shall see below, with substantial relevant direct *verbatim* fragments[33] of the *Bibliotheca* is a very strong indication that Diodorus' work not only did survive until the tenth century AD, but was even believed to be sufficiently important to serve imperial purposes. It is, therefore, in spite of the doubts expressed by Bertrac (see above, note 14), perhaps not too far-fetched to believe that Lascaris did indeed see a complete copy of the *Bibliotheca* as late as 1453 (as believed by Casevitz and Jacquemin 2015: ix). Certainty about that, obviously, is absent, nor does it answer the question on the *general* accessibility of Diodorus' work.

H. SUMMARY

Reviewing the material on Diodorus we see that:

- he perhaps drew primarily upon a single source for a section of his work, but also certainly incorporated extracts from other writers;
- he appears an uncritical, and sometimes inaccurate, excerpter, occasionally using his sources without judgement;
- the sources he used were generally of high quality;
- he freely invented asides on politics, philosophy, and historiography,

---

[33] To be exact: in total 949 of such fragments of Diodorus have been preserved in the *Excerpta Constantiniana*: see below.

occasionally adding material of his own under the name of his (alleged) source;
- he was responsible for the overall shape and main themes of his work;
- he maintained a strong cohesion throughout his work, aimed at a central theme, and constructed it around a programme for moral living;
- the work survived more or less complete until at least the tenth century AD.

I. OUR PRIMARY SOURCES FOR DIODORUS: MANUSCRIPTS AND RELEVANT EDITIONS

The text of the fifteen preserved books of Diodorus' *Bibliotheca* has been transmitted by in total fifty-nine manuscripts.[34] Apart from some special cases, none of them involving so-called prototypes, the manuscripts of books 1–5 on the one hand and books 11–20 on the other form two distinct groups.

Manuscripts of books 1–5

Books 1–5 of Diodorus' *Bibliotheca* are transmitted to us through twenty-eight manuscripts, of which four, thanks to the benefits of *Textkritik*, can be considered as prototypes. The first of these prototypes is the *codex Neopolitanus suppl. gr.* 4 (in the *Biblioteca Nazionale Napoli*), formerly the *Vindobonensis suppl. gr.* 74 (from the *Österreichische Nationalbibliothek, Wien*), (with the signature D in the editions) written on parchment. It dates from the beginning of the tenth century, probably originating from Constantinople. Some parts have been restored. A new collation of this manuscript, by Wilhelm Richard Bergmann (1821–70),[35] was used in the Diodorus edition by Friedrich Vogel (1856–?), published at Leipzig (Teubner), 1888–1906 (Teubner's so-called third edition; see below; the last three volumes of this edition were edited by Carl Fischer), in six volumes.

---

[34] Unless mentioned otherwise, the information on the manuscripts is based upon Chamoux and Bertrac 1993: lxxvii–cxxiii. See also Bravi in Ambaglio et al. 2008: 120–8.

[35] Though the *Allgemeine Deutsche Biographie* reports Bergmann died in 1871, both his obituary, probably by Imhof, in Fleckeisen and Masius 1871, and a commemorative tombstone at Palermo, where he died, state he died on 24 December 1870 (see <https://cimiteripalermo.wordpress.com/2011/10/14/stele-di-richard-bergmann/>). Therefore, 1870 is taken as the correct year of Bergmann's death.

The second prototype is the *codex Vaticanus gr.* 130 (C in the editions), from the middle of the tenth century, also written on parchment and kept in the *Biblioteca Apostolica Vaticana (Palatina)*.[36] The text of this manuscript has been the object of numerous scrapings and corrections, which generally concern orthography (the accentuation was very poor in the text by the first hand). The quite insufficient collations of this manuscript that have been used by Petrus Wesseling (1692–1764), who in or about 1745 published an edition of the *Bibliotheca* in two volumes at Amsterdam (combined with the 1604 translation into Latin by Laurent Rhodoman (1546–1606)),[37] were, unfortunately, followed without modification by succeeding editors.

The third manuscript, another *Vaticanus*, *codex Vaticanus gr.* 996 (V in the editions), at present bound in two volumes and kept at the same library as the preceding prototype, is written on Arabic paper. This kind of paper, without a watermark, is of a format that is attested in Spain as well, albeit at a later date (thirteenth century). It goes back to the eleventh–twelfth century, as far as may be judged on the basis of the writing; because of the paper, however, a later date (the thirteenth century) has also been advocated. The beginning and the end of the manuscript are mutilated and were restored in the fourteenth century. The original, but much damaged, paper has been covered with a protective sheet: the sheet has since yellowed and reading the manuscript is sometimes difficult. Wesseling only offers a few readings from this manuscript; it has not been collated by later editors.

The fourth manuscript, *codex Laurentianus* 70,1 (L in the editions), is written on paper and may, tentatively, be dated to about 1330; it rests in the *Biblioteca Medicea Laurenziana* in Florence. The manuscript contains Arrian's *Anabasis Alexandri* and *Indica*, the treatise *De Alexandri magni fortuna aut virtute* (*On the fortune of Alexander*) by Plutarch (Plu. *Mor.* 326D–345B), an abridged version of books 1–3 and 5 of Diodorus (from which the copyist left out the mythological passages as far as he could), and at the end, in another hand, a text mainly consisting of fragments of Plutarch. This manuscript has not been used by editors of Diodorus' *Bibliotheca*.

From these four manuscripts of Diodorus' books 1–5, twenty-four direct or indirect *apographa* are known. The complete *stemma* is presented in Chamoux and Bertrac (1993: xcvii) and by Bravi in Ambaglio et al. (2008: 125).

---

[36] See also, for this MS and others from the Vatican library, Pitra and Stevenson 1885.
[37] Rhodoman 1604.

Apart from the manuscripts proper there is also, finally, as a source for books 1–5, Bracciolini 1472 (indicated as P in the editions). It is a (quite faulty) translation of the first five books of Diodorus by Giovanni Francesco Poggio Bracciolini (1380–1459). Its first printed edition was published in Bologna in 1472, after it had been reproduced initially by manuscript tradition, and was reprinted several times both in Venice and in Paris. It provides, in spite of its faults, some alternative readings. Unfortunately, Poggio Bracciolini's manuscript itself, completed in 1449 (Eck 2003: lxv), is lost.

Manuscripts of books 11–20

As regards books 11–20, they have been transmitted through a total of thirty-four manuscripts, of which three are in common with books 1–5.[38] However, as indicated before, the latter remark does not apply to any of the prototype manuscripts. Of these there are, here again, four.

The first prototype is *codex Marcianus gr.* 375 (M in the editions), a parchment from the middle of the tenth century in the *Biblioteca Marciana* in Venice, containing books 11–15. At some time it was in the possession of Basilius, Cardinal Bessarion (1403–72), who left his collection to the San Marco library in Venice in 1468. Though the manuscript is fundamental for books 11–15, it has never been collated completely: Wesseling, for example, only had a selection of lectures provided by Blasius Caryophilus (= Biago Garafolo, 1677–1762) at his disposal. In Wesseling's edition this manuscript was provided with the siglum 'Ven.' and, confusingly (see below), with the siglum 'R' in the (so-called second Teubner) edition by Ludwig August Dindorf (1805–71).

The second prototype is from the Patmos library (in full: the Βιβλιοθήκη της Μονής του Αγίου Ιωάννη του Θεολόγου ('Library of the monastery of St. John the Theologian'), the *codex Patmiacus* 50 (P in the editions), a parchment from the end of the tenth or the beginning of the eleventh century, mutilated at its beginning and end; at a much more recent date, six more folios (containing the text from 14.101.2–114.5) have been lost. The mutilated folios (1 and 309) have been replaced, as it appears, sometime during the fourteenth century. This *codex* contains the (majority of the) text of books 11–16. It has been collated by Bergmann in 1866 during his stay at

---

[38] These paragraphs are predominantly based upon Chamoux and Bertrac 1993: ci–cxxiii.

Patmos, a collation used for the first time in the Teubner edition by Friedrich Vogel and Curt Theodor Fischer (1869–?).

The third prototype is *codex Parasinus gr.* 1665 (R in the editions), dating to the middle of the tenth century. This *codex* is on parchment and it contains books 16–20, lacking *capita* 17.79.2–81.2 and from 20.112.2 to the end of book 20. It contains, *in margine*, some corrections and notes from various dates. Before it entered the *Bibliothèque du roi* (now *Bibliothèque nationale de France*), the manuscript had been in the possession of Janus Lascaris (1445–1535, the younger brother of Constantine Lascaris, whom we have encountered before), nicknamed *Rhyndacenus*; of Niccolò, Cardinal Ridolfi; and of Catherine de'Medici. For his edition, Wesseling (attributing siglum '*Reg. 2*' to this manuscript; Dindorf siglum 'T') used a collation made by Denis François Camusat (1695–1732). For the Teubner edition, Fischer made a new collation of the *Parisinus*.

The final prototype of this series of manuscripts is the *codex Laurentianus* 70,12 (F in the editions) from the *Biblioteca Medicea Laurenziana* in Florence. It is a manuscript on paper, dating to the second quarter of the fifteenth century, and contains all of books 11–20. With the exception of book 17 and part of book 18 (up to halfway, 18.49.2), which were written by a copyist whose name I have been unable to retrace, the whole manuscript was written by Isidore of Kiev (1385–1463), 'Metropolitan of Kiev and Moscow and all Rus' from 1437 onwards, later also cardinal presbyter and papal legate.

The text of books 11–15 in this manuscript goes back, through an intermediary, to manuscript M (discussed above),[39] after the first hundred-odd pages of book 13 diverges in the direction of MS P, while book 16 appears to be based upon MS R. Books 17–20, finally, go back to a now lost prototype (called 'Φ' by Chamoux/Bertrac 1993: civ). In fact, *Laurentianus* 70,12 can, therefore, only count as a prototype for books 17–20, even though it contains important variants and corrections for the other books. In 1491, this *codex* was bought by Janus Lascaris for Lorenzo de'Medici. A collation by Francesco Del Furia (1777–1856) was used for the editions by Dindorf and Vogel, but Fischer collated the manuscript again for books 16–20 of the Vogel and Fischer edition at Teubner's.

In total, we can name MSS M and P as the basis for books 11–15, MSS P and R for that of book 16, and MSS R and F for that of books 17–20. A complete *stemma*, with all *apographa*, thirty in number, can

---

[39] See Chamoux and Bertrac 1993: ciii and note 73.

be found in Chamoux and Bertrac (1993: cxxi) and Ambaglio et al. (2008: 126). As regards an *archetype* for all manuscripts together, if it existed at all, nothing can be stated with any degree of certainty.

The Excerpta Constantiniana

As already discussed above, quite a number of fragments from the missing books of Diodorus, some of them pertaining to Persian history, have been preserved in the *Excerpta Historica iussu Imperatoris Constantini [VII] Porphyrogeniti Confecta*,[40] originally catalogued in fifty-three sections (of which only four have survived: Boissevain et al. 1903–10), a work compiled in the second quarter of the tenth century on the orders of Constantine VII *Porphyrogenitus* (AD 912–59). The Constantine excerpters in Byzantium had little interest in history as such. Their main concern was with practical and moral lessons. The lessons were divided into rubrics under which they filed excerpts from the writers on historical subjects. Selection was made on the basis of moral edification rather than on the context of the subject matter. Consequently, the context is frequently missing, sometimes making passages incomprehensible (see, for example, Wacholder 1962: 8).

The preserved sections are:

- Vol. 1: Parts 1–2: De Boor 1903: these volumes preserve in total 35 fragments of Diodorus;
- Vol. 2: Parts 1–2: Büttner-Wobst and Roos 1906–10: these volumes preserve 380 fragments of Diodorus;
- Vol. 3: De Boor 1905: providing in total 54 fragments of Diodorus;
- Vol. 4: Boissevain 1906: preserving 480 fragments of Diodorus.

In fact, only four manuscripts, one for each volume, form the basis of the present edition of the *Excerpta Constantiniana*: for the *Excerpta de legationibus* it is an *Escorialensis*; for the *de virtutibus* … a *Turonensis*; for the *de insidiis* another *Escorialensis*; and for the *de sententiis* a *Vaticanus*. Common to all volumes is that a fragment typically starts with the word ὅτι. In the translation I have, generally, neglected this construction and translated each fragment as a normal sentence. Occasionally the fragments of the *Excerpta* as used in the

---

[40] Naturally, the *Excerpta Constantiniana* not only cover Diodorus' lost books, but also preserve quite a number of fragments of books 1–5 and 11–20 and offer sometimes interesting alternative readings.

Teubner and Loeb editions of Diodorus comprise more than one fragment of the *Excerpta* series as rendered by Boissevain, De Boor, and Büttner-Wobst. For clarity's sake I shall, therefore, indicate in the translation with an asterisk where the beginning is of each fragment as presented in the latter series.

Manuscripts of the *Excerpta Constantiniana*

The manuscript from El Escorial (in full: *Real Biblioteca del Monasterio de San Lorenzo del Escorial*) of the *Excerpta de legationibus*, *codex Escorialensis* I.Θ.4, like other manuscripts, probably came from the legacy of the Jesuit priest and, one might say, spiritual father of the Escorial library, Juan Páez de Castro (1512–70). This manuscript, which may have been dated to between the tenth and twelfth centuries, was lost during a fire that struck the El Escorial library on 7 June 1671.[41] Fortunately, the scribe and trader Andreas Darmarios (a Venetian of Greek origin, 1540–after 1587) and his companions had made an *apograph* of this manuscript as well as several other copies of it during their occasionally interrupted stay in Spain between 1570 and 1587. Though several of these have been lost partially or totally as well, four have been preserved completely:[42]

- a copy in three volumes at El Escorial (E in the editions), brought there after the fire. Of these volumes, Darmarios wrote two volumes himself, the third only partially;
- a copy in two volumes at the Brussels *Bibliothèque royale de Belgique/Koninklijke Bibliotheek van België* (B in the editions). Of these volumes one may have been written by Darmarios, the other was certainly written by him;
- a copy in two volumes at the Monaco library (*Bibliothèque Louis Notari*) (M in the editions). Both volumes are certainly written by Darmarios, one by name, the other by adscription.
- a copy in four volumes at the Vatican library (P in the editions). These were partly written by Darmarios.

Of these manuscripts De Boor remarks that '*In* legationibus Romanorum *solum librum E ex ipso codice Scor. I.Θ.4 fluxisse constat*' ('It is certain that … only book E derives directly from

---

[41] See, for example, Revilla 1936: xviii–xix. See also Kresten 1980: 413 note 3, and 409–11 for Darmarios' time in Spain. An invaluable source of information on the Greek manuscripts in the Escorial library is Graux 1880.
[42] See De Boor 1903: viii–xvii.

codex Scor. I.Θ.4').[43] It serves, therefore, as the prototype for the *Excerpta de legationibus*.

The Tours manuscript containing the *Excerpta de virtutibus* ..., *Codex Turonensis* 980 in full (the name *codex Peirescianus* also occurs, after its one-time owner Nicolas-Claude Fabri de Peiresc (1580–1637), who acquired it, with two other MSS, through a middleman at Cyprus),[44] dates from the middle of the tenth century (or, less precisely, tenth–eleventh century) and shows all the characteristics of a manuscript manufactured on parchment at the imperial scriptorium.[45] Fabri de Peiresc described the manuscript as follows to a friend:

> Ce livre est intitulé ΠΕΡΊ ΑΡΕΤῆΣ ΚΑῚ ΚΑΚΊΑΣ et contient des extraicts ou collections sur cette matiere tirées de quattorze differants autheurs des meilleurs que l'on eust en Constantinoble au temps de Constantin Porphyrogenete qui a faict ou faict faire cette compilation.[46]

To obtain an edition of the fragments going back to Nicholas of Damascus, Fabri de Peiresc sent the manuscript to Hugo Grotius in Leyden in Holland, where it was also seen by, *inter alios*, Josephus Justus Scaliger (1540–1609) and Claude Saumoise (Salmasius, 1588–1653). Notes by the latter on the folia containing fragments of Diodorus have been used by Pieter (Petrus) Wesseling in his edition of Diodorus' works (Büttner-Wobst 1906: xv). Another who published (parts of) the manuscripts was Henri Valois (Valesius, 1603–76), who had the manuscript at his disposal in Paris (Valois 1634). The history of the manuscript between 1634 and 1716 is obscure. In the latter year it appears in the library of Marmoutiers monastery (*Abbaye de Saint Martin de Marmoutiers*) near Tours, whence it takes its customary name. Though the manuscript, or parts of it, has/have been edited several times, there are no known other manuscripts of the *Excerpta de Virtutibus et vitiis*.

The manuscript from El Escorial of the *Excerpta de insidiis*, *codex Escorialensis* Ω.I.11 (*olim* I.K.3 *et* I.Z.2), like many of the other manuscripts of this library, probably came from the legacy of Juan Páez de Castro as well. This manuscript dates to somewhere in the sixteenth century and is written by two hands. The history of the manuscript of the *Excerpta de insidiis* before it came into De Castro's possession is largely unknown, but at least part of it

---

[43] De Boor 1903: xvi. On the same page a *stemma* is presented.
[44] Büttner-Wobst 1906: ix–x.
[45] See Irigoin 1959: 177–8; see also Büttner-Wobst 1906: xx–xxi.
[46] See Büttner-Wobst 1906: x.

may have belonged to the library of Didaci de Mendoza of Venice in 1543. Fortunately, this *codex*, written on parchment, was not destroyed by the fire that struck El Escorial in 1671 and destroyed so many other manuscripts. The text of the *Excerpta de insidiis* is complemented by *Codex Parisinus Graecus* 1666, especially for the parts relating to Johannes Antiochenus: for Diodorus the latter manuscript has no relevance. The two manuscripts are independent from each other.

In the Escorial library the manuscript remained virtually unnoticed for a long time. It was first mentioned by Carl Christoph Plüer (1725–72) in a posthumously published book from 1777, suggesting this manuscript might well contain the *Excerpta de insidiis* (Plüer 1777: 84). Plüer's remark was noticed by Miller, who mentioned it in his 1848 catalogue on Greek manuscripts from the Escorial library (Miller 1848). In the same year Carl August Ludwig Feder (1790–1856) was the first to publish fragments from this manuscript.[47] After him, Carolus (Karl) Müller also used fragments in several of the later volumes of the *Fragmenta Historicorum Graecorum* (Paris: Didot, 1841–83), but the 1905 publication by De Boor is, to the best of my knowledge, the first integral publication of the *Excerpta de insidiis*.

As regards the *Excerpta de sententiis*, codex *Vaticanus (rescriptus) gr. 73* is the only surviving manuscript: it is written on parchment, in fact a palimpsest, resting in the *Biblioteca Apostolica Vaticana (Palatina)*. Like the *Turonensis*, '*cui Vaticanus simillimus est*' ('to which the Vaticanus is very similar': Boissevain 1906: vii), the Vatican manuscript dates to the tenth–eleventh century. It is mainly written by a single hand, occasionally augmented by a second hand. It is remarkable that almost on every page of excerpts of Diodorus this second hand has been active. Unfortunately the manuscript is not at all complete. As regards the folia containing the fragments of Diodorus, Boissevain remarks: '*Diodori quaterniones qui nunc septem sunt, olim decem fuerunt*' ('the quires of Diodorus, which are now seven, once were ten': Boissevain 1906: xvi). One quire holds eight folia, written on on both sides. It has been established that, for example, not only are excerpts from book 12 *caput* 13 through to the end of book 14 lacking, but also folia are missing from other books, notably books 1–10.

---

[47] Feder 1848–55.

Physically, the manuscript is at present in a very bad condition;[48] numerous leaves were discarded and the others disarranged when it was overwritten. This second writing, from the fourteenth century, consisted of Plato's *Gorgias* and speeches by Aristides (Boissevain 1906: vii). Angelo, Cardinal Mai, who first published these *Excerpta*, employed chemical reagents (Boissevain 1906: vii calls them '*venena*' ('poisons')) to bring out the letters of the *Excerpta* and even then had to despair of many passages.[49] Since his (ab?)use of the manuscript, the letters have faded still more due to the reagents used, and parts of some leaves, moreover, have been covered in the work of repair.

The first edition of parts of the *Codex Vaticanus 73* was in 1827 and was, as stated, published by Angelo Mai (1782–1854).[50] At that time, he was the librarian of the Vatican library and had detected the *codex* about seven years before. After the publication of excerpts of Polybius from this *Vaticanus* by Theodor Friedrich Heyse (1803–84) in 1840,[51] Henricus van Herwerden (1831–1910) started another investigation in 1854 into the excerpts uncovered by Mai, notably including fragments by Diodorus (Herwerden 1860). Though some others have since ventured into parts of the *Excerpta de sententiis*, the edition by Boissevain is the one to be preferred. As noted by Goukowsky (2006: xii): 'Là où les lectures de T. Büttner-Wobst [*sic*!] diffèrent de celles d'Angelo Mai, la verification se révèle aujourd'hui impracticable, si bien que P. Bertrac avait jugé l'entreprise illusoire dans l'état actuel des techniques d'investigation.' It is a sad conclusion.

Apart from those in the *Excerpta Constantiana*, fragments of Diodorus may also be found in other collections, like the *Excerpta Hoescheliana* (by David Hoeschel, 1556–1617),[52] providing fragments of books 21–6; the *Suda*;[53] the *Florilegium Vaticanum*;[54]

---

[48] These remarks are based on the introduction to the edition by Boissevain, and also upon E. Cary's introduction to Cassius Dio in Cary 1968–70: xxi.

[49] Nowadays, of course, ultraviolet light and/or X-rays are used to make underlying texts of a palimpsest visible. In the case of the Herculaneum papyri (for clarity's sake: these are not palimpsests but charred scrolls), alternating light sources, light frequencies, and CT tomography are also applied. These all are non-invasive techniques and keep the manuscripts maximally intact.

[50] Mai 1846. See also Németh 2010: 127–34.

[51] Heyse 1840. In the 1846 edition of the work the *codex* number has been corrected.

[52] Hoeschel 1603. The work was an appendix to a part of the *Excerpta Legationum* that had been left aside by Fulvio Orsini. In the Loeb edition of Diodorus by Walton, in total fifty-seven fragments from the *Excerpta Hoescheliana* figure: see Chamoux and Bertrac 1993: cxxxvii–cxxxviii, note 174.

[53] For the *Suda*, I use the Adler edition. It includes at least sixty-four quotes from the *Bibliotheca*: see Chamoux and Bertrac 1993: cxxxviii–cxl.

[54] This is the name given in his second Diodorus edition by Dindorf to *codex Vaticanus gr. 739*, dating to the eleventh century and published by Mai 1827 (the series was published

Photius' Bibliotheca

Finally, another work should be mentioned as a source for Diodorus' *Bibliotheca*, namely the *Bibliotheca* of the ninth-century Byzantine patriarch Photius (before AD 828–891/7).[56] In this work, a collection of 279 (280) reviews (called *codices*) of works belonging to various genres, varying in length from two lines to seventy pages,[57] Photius discusses Diodorus' work in two places, that is, in *codex* 70 (35a1–39), presenting a rough outline of the *Bibliotheca*, and in *codex* 244 (377a25–393b5), in which Photius states: Ἀνεγνώσθη τῆς Διοδώρου βιβλιοθήκης ἄλλοι τε λόγοι καὶ ὁ λβ καὶ λδ, καὶ ὁ μ́ καὶ ὁ λή, καὶ ὁ λά καὶ ὁ β καὶ δ, καὶ ς, καὶ ὁ λζ καὶ ὁ λή. Ὧν ἐκλογὴν ἡ παροῦσα ἔκδοσις περιέχει ('Read from the Library of Diodorus, amongst other books, the thirty-second, thirty-fourth, the fortieth, thirty-eighth, thirty-first, thirty-second, thirty-fourth, thirty-sixth, thirty-seventh, and thirty-eighth.[58] The present publication provides a choice of these': Phot. *Bibl.* 377a25–28). Though Photius is not always the perfect excerpter one would wish (see Stronk 2010: 143–4), it has to be acknowledged that the reliability of his excerpts increases as the excerpt is longer and more specific. *Codex* 244 meets both these requirements. Therefore this *codex* is potentially an important contribution to our knowledge of the specific books of Diodorus' *Bibliotheca* Photius refers to in the sentence quoted above. Whether Photius has actually seen the complete work of Diodorus eludes us, though we may surmise the work was still more or less complete in Photius' days: at least, of the books he states he has excerpted in this *codex* only fragments remain today.

---

between 1825 and 1838 and numbers ten volumes): it includes sixteen fragments of Diodorus (see Chamoux and Bertrac 1993: cxl).
[55] For Tzetzes, I use the edition by Leone 1968.
[56] For a fuller account of both author and work, see Stronk 2010: 107–48.
[57] Originally the work consisted of 279 *codices*: that we now count 280 *codices* arises from a misconception, separating *codex* 88 (on the Synod of Nicaea) into two different *codices*, 88 and 89: see Ziegler 1941: 692.
[58] One notices that three books occur twice. Reading this quite lengthy *codex*, one observes that Photius indeed did go back to books previously discussed and that the seemingly confused list is in fact correct.

Manuscripts of Photius' *Bibliotheca*

The *Bibliotheca* of Photius is preserved in twenty-five manuscripts and a number of others with excerpts from it.[59] Only two manuscripts are independent: *Marcianus gr.* 450 (A in the editions), completed for the missing end by its *apograph*, *Parisinus gr.* 1266 (B in the editions), thirteenth century, and *Marcianus gr.* 451 (M in the editions), both preserved in the *Biblioteca Marciana* at Venice. Manuscript A dates to the tenth century and is the work of a not very educated but scrupulously conscientious copyist. During recent research the date for the copy has been narrowed down to the years AD 910–20, hardly (if at all!) three quarters of a century after the completion of the *autograph* and only some two or three decades after Photius' death. During the following centuries, from the eleventh to the fifteenth, four different correctors' hands are recognisable (Schamp 1987: 27 and note 2). The other main manuscript, M, dates to the twelfth century and is the co-production of three successive contemporaneous hands. Some corrections here, by five different hands, were also made between the twelfth and fifteenth centuries (ibid.). For Photius I use the edition by Henry (1959–78).

Some editions of Diodorus' Bibliotheca

The *editio princeps* of the Βιβλιοθήκη ἱστορική (*Historical library*) was prepared by Henri Estienne (1528–98),[60] and is dedicated to Ulrich Fugger. On the basis of this text, Laurent Rhodoman published his edition of the *Bibliotheca* in two volumes at Hanover, mentioned above. A major landmark in the publication of Diodorus – and one with far-reaching consequences as to what was to be considered as Diodorus proper and what as spurious – was the edition of Wesseling, mentioned above (discussing MS C; see also above, note 7).[61] Wesseling had not seen the manuscripts themselves, but with help on many sides had assembled a documentation that was as complete as possible. After Wesseling some less complete editions appeared. The first edition that was as complete as the sources allowed after Wesseling's was published by Ludwig August

---

[59] Martini has shown that the two main manuscripts, A and M, represent independent branches of the tradition, and that all manuscripts derive, directly or indirectly, from these two: Martini 1911.
[60] Estienne 1559.
[61] Wesseling 1745.

Dindorf:[62] it was, nevertheless, as yet almost completely dependent on Wesseling's work. This was not the case for Dindorf's following edition of Diodorus, Leipzig 1828–31: for the time, that edition was up to date.

An edition in four volumes, published in 1853–4 at Leipzig (Teubner) by Immanuel Bekker (1785–1871), brought little that was new (publisher Teubner later treated it as their first edition of Diodorus' work). Also the edition in five volumes by Dindorf, 1866–8, brought little news (publisher Teubner's so-called second edition). The next major step forward was Teubner's so-called third edition (already mentioned) by Vogel (volumes 1–3) and Fischer (who edited the last three volumes), Leipzig 1888–1906. It presents the Greek text with an *apparatus criticus* limited to the readings of the main manuscripts. However, Vogel (who published books 1–15) did not examine any manuscript and remained, through Dindorf, mainly tributary to Wesseling's work. Fischer, on the other hand, did collate some manuscripts again. Moreover, these editors could also rely on Bergmann's collations, mentioned above. My references to Diodorus' *Bibliotheca* are – unless mentioned otherwise – based upon this edition.

The edition by Les Belles Lettres (Collection Budé) is based on a new collation of the fundamental manuscripts. Though, regrettably, all books have not yet been published, the majority of them are now accessible in this new edition, comprising the text and a translation in French. It offers several new readings, provides the reader with a sufficient *apparatus*, and is, therefore, very much worthwhile to use next to (and sometimes to be preferred to) the traditional Teubner edition. However, because the Teubner Leipzig edition as yet is the only *complete* edition provided for the larger part with an *apparatus* (only volume 6 – in fact merely a reprint of Dindorf's second edition for Teubner, with Fischer's name added – regrettably lacks such an asset: for the fragments of books 21–40 one should, therefore, *textually* ideally use the three volumes by Paul Goukowsky in the Budé edition dedicated to these books),[63] I opted for the Teubner. Apart from the Teubner edition, I also frequently consulted the Loeb edition (with, regrettably, a bare minimum of textual remarks), including the translation, and, obviously, the editions of books 1–3,

---

[62] Dindorf 1826. This still is an edition without *apparatus*, like, regrettably, the others I have seen of Dindorf's editions.

[63] Published in 2006 (books 21–6), 2012 (books 27–32), and 2014 (books 33–40).

5, 11–12, 14–15, 17–20, and the fragments (four volumes) of the Collection Budé Diodorus.

All these works together contributed, in one way or another, to my translation. Sometimes my translation will, inevitably, be similar, or almost so, to an existing translation, sometimes it will deviate substantially from such translations: in all cases, however, it will ultimately be my translation, based upon my (textual) choices and, therefore, I alone am responsible for the mistakes it, surely, contains. Because the term 'fragment' has, in classical studies, a narrowly defined meaning (that is: 'piece of an untransmitted text': see Stronk 2010: 3 and note 7), I have opted to indicate in this book the passages of Diodorus detailing the history of Persia (though some of them might qualify as fragments proper as well) as 'sections' (abbreviated as S.). The names of the people featuring in this account I have Latinised as much as possible, unless provided with a name familiar in English.

1 *Diodorus' Sources*

A. PRELIMINARY REMARKS

Diodorus generally seems extremely reticent about revealing his sources. Even in the first books, where he enlightens his readers most frequently about the authors he used, their names appear only relatively sporadically. It appears certain at least that Diodorus used Ctesias to compile his second book (Diodorus used specifically Ctesias' books 1-3, notably featuring Semiramis, and used books 4-6 considerably less), and possibly he also used parts of Ctesias' books 19-23 (on the reign of Artaxerxes II: see Stronk 2010: 184-8). Whether Diodorus also used other books of the twenty-three constituting Ctesias' *Persica* cannot, regrettably, be determined with certainty, though Haillet believes he did (Haillet 2002: xi). Though I was, for reasons of method, unable to include these passages in the text in my edition of Ctesias' *Persian History* (Stronk 2010), I concur on this point with Haillet and will discuss such passages in the historical commentary on Ctesias' *Persica* I am preparing. Ctesias might well, therefore, be one of the more prominent sources Diodorus used, directly or indirectly (for example through Ephorus), to compile his chapters and paragraphs on the East until c. 390, the year Ctesias concluded his *Persica*.

To a large extent Diodorus' sources can only be found through scrutiny of his text (see Haillet 2002: x). Even for our purpose, this seems to be insufficient to determine the sources Diodorus relied on to compose his view on the events in the Assyrian and Median Kingdoms and especially in the Achaemenid Persian Empire (which may be stretched to 304, the year Alexander's last direct relative died: Depuydt 2008: 1, 3) and its successors, the Seleucid,

Antigonid, and Arsacid Kingdoms. Pascale Giovannelli-Jouanna and Christine Maisonneuve (in Lenfant 2011: 120–43) argued that Diodorus relied for those parts in his work dedicated to Greece, Asia Minor, and Persia on the works of Herodotus (11.37.6),[1] Thucydides, Xenophon (15.76.4 and 15.89.3), Ctesias of Cnidus (for example, 14.46.6), Ephorus of Cyme (14.11.1 (indirect reference) and 16.76.5), Clitarchus of Alexandria, Hieronymus of Cardia (book 17, *passim*), the *Hellenica Oxyrhynchia*, and Polybius. To the major sources regarding the region we are interested in, we should perhaps add Isocrates of Athens, Hellanicus of Lesbos (Mytilene), and chronographic sources (Haillet 2002: xi) as well. By restricting ourselves to those sources, we lose insight into 'what made Diodorus tick': it is, therefore necessary to determine as many of his sources as we can.

Diodorus occasionally refers to some of his sources more or less explicitly throughout the *Bibliotheca*. Regrettably, the works of most of these authors are lost, making it hard to establish whether they would have added to our knowledge of the East. It seems hardly likely that the authors he mentions were Diodorus' only sources. We are, thus, forced to look further into Diodorus' work to try to determine the sources he used. To do so we shall have to look book by book – as far as they have been transmitted (more or less) completely to us – into the *Bibliotheca*, largely relying on the observations made by the respective editors of volumes of Diodorus for Les Belles Lettres/Collection Budé, série grecque (regrettably at the time still lacking some volumes) and the Loeb Classical Library. Obviously, there is room for conjecture in this process, but I hope to keep my method – and thereby the conjectures – as transparent as possible. Inevitably it will not always be possible to observe the distinction Klaus Meister made (Meister 1990: 178). He distinguishes three levels in Diodorus' work, namely a principal source (for most books I would prefer to distinguish several principal sources), one or several secondary sources, and Diodorus' additions. This inability to observe Meister's distinction is not only because such levels are often difficult to distinguish and/or separate, but also because I firmly believe that Meister's distinction does not (always) do right by Diodorus' way of writing (Stronk 2010: 67 and note 10), which increasingly seems to me more complex than it is (or has been) generally credited to be, as

---

[1] As indicated in the Introduction, I will not use the letters D.S., as the list in the *LSJ* does, in references to the *Bibliotheca*, but only the combination of numbers denoting respectively book, *caput*, and paragraph. For other authors the references will be preceded by the letters customary for them in the *LSJ* or Glare's *Oxford Latin Dictionary*.

I have already mentioned in the Introduction. Especially as regards the transmitted fragments, Meister's distinction is generally hard to establish.

Regrettably, only fifteen of the original forty books of the *Bibliotheca* have been transmitted (nearly) completely, adding thereby to our problem. In the books that have been transmitted fragmentarily, it is difficult to detect a source-author more or less certainly (more conjecture may be needed there), which might leave us with a more limited amount of text to work with. The definition of a source-author I shall use is: any author of whom it seems likely, either through direct reference, by context, or by implication, that his work has contributed to the text of the *Bibliotheca*. Perhaps it is not the best of definitions, but it seems to me a definition that may yield at least some verifiable results.

B. BOOKS 1-5

As discussed in the Introduction, the preserved books of Diodorus fall into two groups, namely books 1-5 and books 11-20. A third group, we might say, is that of the fragments, which also fall in two groups, namely those of books 6-10 and books 21-40. Obviously, we must, as discussed above, examine all of them for the references we need. In the last groups we are, *de facto*, dealing with data at third hand (regarding the original author as the first hand, Diodorus – in the three levels as outlined by Meister (see above) – as the second, and the work(s) preserving Diodorus' therefore necessarily the third), adding to our problem in finding Diodorus' sources.

In their introduction to book 1, Bertrac and Vernière observe for Diodorus' proem (1.1-5) the philosophical influence of the Stoic philosopher Posidonius of Apamea in Syria (Bertrac and Vernière 1993: 3-4), and the historical influence of Thucydides, Ephorus of Cyme, and Polybius (Bertrac and Vernière 1993: 4). To the last group it might also be possible to add the name of Anaximenes of Lampsacus (Oldfather 1968: 14 note 1). Here I already find it hard to apply Meister's criteria: eventually I would rank all of them, one way or another, as principal sources. For Diodorus' 'Genesis of the universe' and prehistory of man (1.6-10)[2] he was influenced by Hecataeus of Abdera and/or Democritus of Abdera (Bertrac and Vernière 1993: 5-6), who would presumably have been principal sources, and by

---

[2] This part shows characteristics similar to *De rerum natura* (*On the Nature of Things*), notably book 5, by his slightly older contemporary Lucretius.

(as it then would seem as his secondary sources) Anaximander, Empedocles, and Anaxagoras.³ Another major source of inspiration for Diodorus for this part was the Stoic *'Thesistheorie'* (Bertrac and Vernière 1993: 7; see also Burton 1972: 49–50),⁴ just as it influenced M. Terentius Varro, slightly older than Diodorus. I would evaluate this 'Thesistheorie' as a principal source as well, because in fact Diodorus' whole work is imbued with Stoic values. Probably Stylianou (1998: 68, *inter alia*) would argue that Diodorus took such views from Ephorus (Stylianou's crediting of Diodorus as an original author is extremely low), but I firmly believe that Stylianou's position does insufficient justice to the whole of Diodorus' *oeuvre* as we have it. Next to these, we find the odd reference to other sources (of undetermined but most likely secondary level, possibly partly retraceable to Diodorus' education), such as those to Homer (1.1.2) or Euripides (1.7.7), or the cryptic remark ἡ γὰρ ταύτης τῆς πόλεως ὑπεροχή ... ἑτοιμοτάτας καὶ πλείστας ἡμῖν ἀφορμὰς παρέσχετο ... ἐκ τῶν ... ὑπομνημάτων ἐκ πολλῶν χρόνων τετηρημένων ('the supremacy of this city [Rome] ... has provided us ... with copious resources in the most accessible form ... from the records which have been carefully preserved ... over a long period of time': 1.4.3–4). In the description of his method (*caput* 1.5), Diodorus also remarks that he attributes a prominent position in his work to the *Chronology* of Apollodorus of Athens (1.5.1), reason for Oldfather to suspect that Diodorus may well have also used the *Chronology* of Castor of Rhodes, namely for the period after the date where Apollodorus stopped.⁵ Observing the structure and contents of Castor's work,

---

³ In his method on these issues Diodorus' work shows a striking likeness as well to that of Ovid, who was about half a century younger than Diodorus: 'ces deux auteurs reflètent non pas telle source servilement suivie, mais le syncrétisme de leur temps': Bertrac and Vernière 1993: 6.

⁴ Unlike Aristotle and the early Peripatetics, who believed, *inter alia*, that the universe, earth, and man were eternal, Stoicism believed in a development of these entities (see also the discussion below, Chapter 2, note 192). For the arguments of the Peripatetics as used by Theophrastus, see Philo Judaeus (Ph. *Aetern. Mun.* 23–7). Ancient Stoicism, founded (if such a term applies) by Zeno of Citium on Cyprus (c. 334–c. 262), is originally a theory on the universe and a form of logic. It defines wisdom as 'knowing divine and human matters', that is, as knowledge of the laws that regulate the entire universe and not only human conduct. It provides a unified account of the world, consisting of formal logic, monistic physics, and naturalistic ethics (which should be the main focus of human knowledge). Later Stoicism was more centred on man, on the effort and the intention to do well: wisdom becomes an attempt to acquire *aretē* (generally translated as 'virtue', but as the contexts in which the word is used show, *aretē* is a complex concept: see my remarks above, Introduction note 20). It underlines the evolution of Stoic doctrine (as all things must evolve, as Stoicism itself underlines), moving from a physical to a moral basis. It seems that Diodorus is more or less moves on the hinge of this development.

⁵ See Oldfather 1968, 21 note 3; for Castor of Rhodes see also Christesen 2007: 418–32. For Apollodorus of Athens see, for example, Hornblower 1996 (an entry lacking in *OCD*⁴).

I might add that Diodorus may well have used Castor's work for those parts of books 4 and 5 dealing with the times before the Trojan War as well. In fact, the strict chronological order Diodorus tries to maintain, though not always completely successfully, in most of the *Bibliotheca* (see above, Introduction) suggests he used the chronographical method, if not also the data, expounded and/or collected by Apollodorus, Castor, and especially Timaeus of Tauromenium throughout his entire work.[6] All these works should, therefore, in one way or another, certainly be marked as principal sources.

The remainder of book 1 (1.11–98) is taken up by Diodorus' description of Egypt, alluded to by the editors of book 1 of the edition for Les Belles Lettres as 'une monographie très complète et la plus intéressante qui soit intégralement parvenue jusqu'à nous depuis le livre II d'Hérodote (Bertrac and Vernière 1993: 8). As it seems, it was inspired primarily by Hecataeus of Abdera (who wrote an *Aegyptiaca*; Bertrac and Vernière 1993: 5, 13), Stoic outlooks (Bertrac and Vernière 1993: 9), Herodotus (either directly or through an intermediary: Bertrac and Vernière 1993: 10–13), and Agatharchides of Cnidus (either directly or through Artemidorus of Ephesus: Bertrac and Vernière 1993: 11). Next to these (as secondary sources, thus) Ctesias of Cnidus is also referred to (1.56.5), and possibly one paragraph (1.55.8) may have been derived from Manetho of Sebennytus (Bertrac and Vernière 1993: 13; see also Dillery 2015 for this author). Naturally, Diodorus himself also contributed information (Meister's third level), if only because he had autoptic knowledge of Egypt. Finally, there are some authors whose work has not been transmitted at all or too fragmentarily to be of service to us on this point, but who as yet might be credited with some influence on Diodorus: they are Lynceus of Samos, one Athenagoras (obviously not the Christian philosopher), Eratosthenes of Cyrene, and Alexander Polyhistor (Bertrac and Vernière 1993: 17): all of these appear to me to be authors of Meister's secondary level as well. The same may be true of 'undetermined' or vague assertions like φασὶ Αἰγύπτιοι ('the Egyptians tell'): such references really do not help to establish a source for the information Diodorus provides.

As regards Diodorus' book 2, Eck (2003: xi–xii) has made a good job of distinguishing the various levels. The principal source for

---

Stylianou 1998: 25, 43 believes that the (not consistently flawless) chronographic sources Diodorus uses for Greece were the works of Eratosthenes (the *Chronographies*) and Apollodorus (the *Chronica*) and that he may have found the Roman colleges he uses in the work of Castor.

[6] See, for Timaeus' contributions to chronography, Baron 2013.

capita 2.1.4–34.6 was, no doubt, Ctesias of Cnidus (books 1–6 in general, but predominantly books 1–3). As secondary sources Eck discerns at least Hieronymus of Cardia (2.1.5–6); Clitarchus and the companions of Alexander (2.7.3); 'Athenaeus and certain other historians', in which 'Athenaeus' may equally be a proper name or an *ethnicon*, 'of Athens' (for example, referring to Apollodorus; it certainly was not Athenaeus of Naucratis, who should be dated to the second–third century AD), after an unrecorded lacuna or a mistake in the early phases of the copying process (2.20.3–5); and Herodotus (2.32.2–3). I would add to this list Megasthenes, who (I believe) was Diodorus' source for the remark on the River Ganges (2.11.1, whether or not in combination with Hieronymus of Cardia: see Bosworth 1998: 186–200; or possibly even with Scylax of Caryanda, the explorer who was referred to by Strabo as Σκύλαξ ὁ παλαιὸς συγγραφεύς ('Scylax [of Caryanda], the ancient author': Str. 14.2.20/653)) and, I think, for the observations on India (2.16.3–4, 17.5).[7] Whether, and if so to what extent, Diodorus was familiar with the work of Berossus (see Dillery 2015 for this author as well) eludes us. Naturally, Diodorus himself also adds a few remarks and provides the occasional vague phrases in the vein of φασί or λέγεται ('they tell'), thus not disclosing any real information at all.

I feel compelled to refer here to some of the observations I wrote down in 2010 (Stronk 2010: 64–5), discussing whether or not Diodorus was familiar with Ctesias' actual work (for a useful review of those holding that he was not, see Bigwood 1980: 196 and note 5). Krumbholz (1886; 1895; 1897) argued at length that Diodorus must have used Ctesias' work itself. This view was shared by Schwartz (1903a), Jacoby (1922; though he had initially taken another view in the *FGrH*), Drews (1973), and Bigwood (1980: 196). I believe that Diodorus' remark in 14.46.6, recognising the end of Ctesias' project, makes it clear that Diodorus did know the *Persica* directly.

However, if we accept that as a fact, we are obliged to explain how Diodorus' account of Semiramis shows elements similar to, or perhaps even drawn from, the (reports on the) campaigns of Alexander, for example regarding the expedition against India.[8] These elements obviously cannot have been derived from Ctesias,

---

[7] See, for an elaborate appreciation of the relation between Megasthenes' work and Diodorus, Muntz 2012. The works by Scylax himself are now lost. What remains under his name dates to the fourth century BC or even later and is rightly referred to as Pseudo-Scylax.

[8] Note also my observation on 2.6.8 on Ninus' campaign against Bactra, below, Chapter 2, note 44.

even though Diodorus asserts he based this part of the *Bibliotheca* on Ctesias, both by references and by use of indirect speech. The use of an intermediary, notably Clitarchus, also referred to by Diodorus as one of his sources (for later books), might be an explanation. Like his father Dinon, who used Ctesias' work extensively (see below), Clitarchus too might well have adapted Ctesias' original and have thus become (the chief person) responsible for the transformation of Assyrian Ninus and Babylonian Semiramis into the central figures of a popular cycle of Greek stories. In that case, we should conclude that in writing his Assyrian and Babylonian history Diodorus used both Ctesias and Clitarchus, but without reference to the latter for this book (see Gardiner-Garden 1987: 8–9 and notes 39 and 40). I shall, necessarily, return to this issue in Chapter 10.

Let us, however, return to the analysis of book 2, still based on Eck (2003). *Capita* 2.35–2.42 provide the reader with an account of India. Its principal source is the work of Megasthenes (see Muntz 2012), while Eck distinguishes as secondary sources an unknown author (for 2.35.2), Nearchus (2.35.2), Onesicritus and/or Aristobulus and/or Eratosthenes (2.36.1–3), Clitarchus or Hieronymus of Cardia (2.37.2–3), and possibly Aristobulus (2.37.5–6), again with some remarks by Diodorus himself. *Capita* 43–7 present an incoherent picture. The source(s) for *capita* 43–4 on the Scythians is/are unknown,[9] as are those of *capita* 45–6 on the Amazons. The observations of *caput* 47 on the Hyperboreans are, as Diodorus acknowledges, based upon Ἑκαταῖος καί τινες ἕτεροί ('Hecataeus [of Abdera] and certain others': the latter without further specification). Of course, Diodorus does add some observations of his own to these *capita* as well, for example indicated by the words ἡμεῖς ... φασιν ('we say'). *Capita* 2.43–7 discuss Arabia, with Posidonius of Apamea as principal source and Hieronymus of Cardia, probably Agatharchides, and an unknown author as secondary sources. The 'voyage' of Iambulus (2.55–60) concludes this book. Its source is, obviously, the more or less utopian novel by Iambulus, disguised as a report of his travels near the 'Ethiopian coast' (apparently located by Diodorus in the region of either Arabia or India), and on this topic as well as on Arabia Diodorus also inserts observations of his own (for the terms 'Arabs' and 'Arabia', see also below, Chapter 2, note 2).

---

[9] I believe that Herodotus may well have been among Diodorus' secondary sources for these *capita*: see Hdt. 4.8–12 and Hdt. 1.105. Part of 2.43.6 is reflected in the work of Diodorus' younger contemporary Strabo of Amasia (in Pontus), namely in Str. 12.3.9/544.

Book 3 recounts the history of Africa minus Egypt and consists of two parts. The first part, consisting of *capita* 3.1–48, is essentially devoted to the ethnography and geography of, in order, Ethiopians, *ichthyophages* ('fish-eaters'), and other peoples living in the southern parts of Ethiopia, the fauna of these regions, concluded by a *Periplous* (≈ round trip) through the Persian Gulf. The second, shorter, part (3.49–74) deals with 'Libyan' mythology. The principal sources for the first part appear to have been the second book of the *Affairs in Asia* (Τὰ κατὰ τὴν Ἀσίαν or probably preferably Περὶ Ἀσίας or Περὶ τῆς Ἀσίας: see Burstein, *BNJ* 86, commentary on T2) by Agatharchides of Cnidus, a work in ten books, as well as the eighth book of the *Geographic Descriptions* (Γεωγραφούμενα) by Artemidorus of Ephesus, a work in eleven books (see Banchich, *BNJ* 438, F1 and Biographical Essay).

For the second part Diodorus mentions Dionysius of Mytilene (also known as Dionysius *Scytobrachium* ('leather-arm')), *BNJ* 32, the author of a *Libyan Stories* (*Libyca*) amongst other works, and, as secondary source, Antimachus of Colophon. Moreover, Diodorus remarks that he used τινες ἕτεροι τῶν ἐν Αἰγύπτωι κατοικούντων, ἱστορηκότες τὰ πλεῖστα τῶν προειρημένων ('some others, who lived in Egypt, and who are the sources for most of the previous account': 3.11.2). However, as Bommelaer (2002: xi) underlines: 'ces indications sont à la fois imprécises et insuffisantes'. She believes that Diodorus was also inspired by another work of Agatharchides of Cnidus for *capita* 12–48 of book 3, namely the fifth and final book of Περὶ τῆς Ἐρυθρᾶς θαλάσσης (*On the Erythraean Sea* (Persian Gulf)). This is a work, as Burstein phrases it, that

> treated in five books the history, ethnography, and geography of the southern portion of the *oecumene*, and unlike his other two histories, which, like other universal histories, were primarily syntheses of the works of earlier historians, the *On the Erythraean Sea* was based on the reports of Ptolemaic military officers and explorers that were preserved in the royal archives in Alexandria.[10]

What we know about this work is due to the epitome of it by Photius (Henry, vol. vii (1974): 135–89, *codex* 250), epitomising its books 1 and 5.

Next to these sources, it appears that Diodorus also consulted (royal) archives in Alexandria (3.38.1, possibly 3.40.8, discussing the πρόσταγμα βασιλέως ('king's order'): Bommelaer 2002, xvi–xvii) and, perhaps, talked to eyewitnesses, priests, and ambassadors he

---

[10] Burstein, *BNJ* 86, 'Biographical Essay'.

met to add to his account.[11] As regards Bommelaer's comparison of Photius' epitome with that of Diodorus, I totally disagree with her premise 'Photius n'a jamais être convaincu d'erreurs graves.' As I have indicated before, 'abridgements by Photius show some disbalance where we can compare them with their transmitted originals' (Stronk 2010: 146; see also 143–4 for criticism on Goossens 1950, who holds a similar view to that of Bommelaer). Nevertheless, Bommelaer's examples clearly show that Diodorus is all but flawless as regards his excerpts (see also above, Introduction). In the second part of Diodorus' discussion of Africa, he occasionally weaves into the account references to Dionysius *Scytobrachium* (see, for example, 3.52.3 and 3.66.5), probably one of 'those who lived in Egypt'. Diodorus provides us with no further references, but Bommelaer (2002: xiv, xxxi–xxxv) suggests that Diodorus' debt to Dionysius is probably far more considerable than he makes it appear, that in fact Dionysius was likely to have been the only source for Diodorus in this part of book 3. However, it stands to reason that, both in this part and in the first part of this book, Diodorus also inserts his own views into the *Bibliotheca* (Bommelaer 2002: xlii–xlix).

Book 4 of Diodorus is dedicated to Greek myths, apart from *caput* 1 – the introduction – in which Diodorus instructs his audience that he does not intend to follow the examples of Ephorus of Cyme, Callisthenes, and Theopompus, 'who passed over the tales of the old mythology' (4.1.3). Possibly he may have used here the *Chronology* of Castor of Rhodes (Oldfather 1968: 21 note 3), without referring to it. In his catalogue of myths (initially featuring especially Heracles – *capita* 4.8–39 – but also the Argonauts – *capita* 4.40–56 – and several others in less detail – *capita* 4.57–85), Diodorus mentions the following sources: Aratus (4.80.2); Hesiod (4.7.2; 4.85.5); Homer (4.2.4; 4.7.2; 4.32.2; 4.39.3 (not by name but by work); 4.49.7; 4.75.2; 4.85.6; 4.85.7); Timaeus (4.21.7; 4.22.6; 4.56.3); and οἱ δ'Αἰγύπτιοι ('the Egyptians': 4.6.3). Further there are some references, some direct, others by implication, to poets of tragedy, *inter alia* for their desire for the marvellous (see, for example, 4.56.1), or for different versions of a particular myth. Naturally, there are some very general and/or vague remarks as well.[12]

---

[11] See Peremans 1967: 443–55.
[12] I came across the following phraseology: μυθολογοῦσιν οἱ παλαιοί ('the ancients record in their myths'); ἀκολούθως τοῖς παλαιοτάτοις τῶν ποιητῶν τε καὶ μυθολόγων ('in accordance with the most ancient poets and writers of myths'); οἱ δὲ ποιηταί ('the poets'); τὰ μυθολεγούμενα ('the myths relate'); τινὲς δὲ τῶν συγγραφέων ('some of the historians'); ἔνιοι λέγουσιν ('some say'); and several times an undetermined φασί, ἱστοροῦσι, μυθολογοῦσι, or λέγεται (I think generally best translated as 'they say' or 'it is said'), or variations on such expressions.

I admit that many references in Diodorus' text vary from vague to extremely vague and that they help but little to establish Diodorus' sources for these *capita*. We may surmise that among the poets hidden in references in note 12 we could have found the names of both Homer and Hesiod, but equally well those of others whose work is unknown to us. We should, though, think here equally of the work of Greek mythographers, like, for example, Hecataeus of Miletus (notably his *Genealogies*), Acusilaus of Argos, Pherecydes of Athens, the mythographical works of Hellanicus of Lesbos (Mytilene), Antiochus of Syracuse (his *Sicelica*, notably for the story of Cocalus, the king of the Sicans), Andron of Halicarnassus, the pseudo-Epimenides, Herodorus of Heraclea (for the story of Heracles and partly also that of Theseus: see Plu. *Thes. passim*), and many other ancient Greek mythographers.[13]

Part of book 5 of Diodorus' *Bibliotheca* is also devoted to mythology, namely that of 'the islands' (5.2.1; which is why Casevitz and Jacquemin (2015) call book 5 the 'Livre des Îles'), combined with a geography of first the western Mediterranean basin (5.2–20), then some countries in the West (for example Britain,[14] Gaul, Celtiberia, Liguria, Tyrrhenia), some countries in the East (Arabia *Felix* and some utopian islands), concluding with the Aegean islands, Rhodes, and Crete (5.47–84). Diodorus refers many times to Phoenicians and Phoenician discoveries in the first part of book 5, but fails to mention any source(s). The same is true for the data Diodorus provides for the circumference of Britain (5.21.3–4), as it appears to be based upon the work of Pytheas of Massilia, who circumnavigated Britain c. 300, but remains unmentioned. Posidonius of Apamea also remains unmentioned (Oldfather 1970a: 196–7 note 2; for Posidonius see also below, on books 33–40), as does Euhemerus of Messene (allegedly the origin of *capita* 5.41–6: Oldfather 1970a: 210 note 1). I believe that the stories of the utopian islands near Arabia *Felix* (= Yemen) are largely inspired by Iambulus, an author we have already encountered in the sources for book 1, though Diodorus fails to refer to him as well. Casevitz and Jacquemin (2015: xii) refer to Prontera's words

---

[13] Fowler 2001: xxvii–xxxviii gives a succinct but good review of the field, certainly in combination with the introduction to Fowler 2013: xi–xxi. Fowler's is, I think, currently by far the best edition of Greek mythographical texts. See also Wendel 1935, still always a valuable starting point for the subject.

[14] Diodorus refers here (5.21.2) to Caesar's invasion in 55–54, stating that he will discuss it ἐν τοῖς οἰκείοις χρόνοις ('at the appropriate moment': see also 5.22.1). This rekindles the argument regarding the period covered in Diodorus' *Bibliotheca*. For this discussion see above, Introduction, note 7.

on this book, the only one provided with a title by Diodorus himself: 's'y mêlent littératures utopique, paradoxographique et mystico-religieuse, mais aussi science ethnographique puisée aux meilleures sources'. Notable throughout the book is Diodorus' positive appreciation for the 'Otherness' of various peoples (Casevitz and Jacquemin 2015: xxxi).

The source-authors Diodorus does refer to in this book are: Carcinas of Acragas[15] (5.5.1); Dosiades (5.80.4); Epimenides of Knossos, the author of a *Cretica* (5.80.4); Ephorus (5.1.4; 5.64.4); Hesiod (5.66.6); Homer (directly or by implication: 5.2.4, 5.7.7; 5.28.4; 5.69.3); Laosthenidas (5.80.4); Philistus of Syracuse (5.6.1); Sosicrates (5.80.4); Timaeus (directly or by implication: 5.1.3; 5.6.1; 5.16.3; 5.17.1); and Zeno (5.56.7).[16] Some of these authors, like the writers on Cretan history Dosiades, Laosthenidas, and Sosicrates, are, apart from their names, hardly if at all known to us. Much more vague are ascriptions like: Αἰγύπτιοι λέγουσι ('the Egyptians tell': 5.69.1); οἱ τὴν Κρήτην κατοικοῦντές φασιν ('the inhabitants of Crete tell': 5.64.1); and all kinds of variations on this theme, which really are not very instructive or helpful at all. As regards direct evidence on Diodorus' sources these references have no value, or an extremely limited value at best, and are (apart from the reference on Cretan authors in 5.80.4) not easy to connect with known authors. Perhaps a thorough comparison with the work of Fowler, referred to above (note 13), *might* yield some viable suggestions. Casevitz and Jacquemin (2015: xxviii–xxx) believe Diodorus' principal sources for this book were, however, Timaeus of Tauromimium, Ephorus of Cyme, Posidonius, and Euhemerus of Messene, the other source-authors being of secondary importance, at various levels of interest.

C. FRAGMENTS BOOKS 6–10

It is outside the scope of this book, let alone this chapter, to present a detailed account of the history (for lack of a better word) of Diodorus' fragments of books 6–10 and 21–40. For those interested, I refer to Cohen-Skalli (2012: ix–lxxvii), though some succinct remarks can be found as well in my Introduction above. Book 6 opens with the only

---

[15] Two writers of tragedies share this name. The elder *floruit* about the beginning of the Peloponnesian War, the younger was his grandson and should, therefore, be dated to the first half of the fourth century BC.

[16] Polybius believed that Zeno was sufficiently important as a historian to criticise him as inaccurate: Plb. 16.14.1–17.11. 'He is largely not so much concerned with an inquiry into facts and proper treatment of material as with elegance of style': Plb. 16.17.9.

clear reference to a source-author, namely Euhemerus of Messene (6.1.1 – and several times further in this fragment; see also Chamoux and Bertrac 1993: xxiii), author of the *Sacred History* (6.1.3). Other writers are also referred to in this fragment, taken from Eustathius' *Commentarii ad Homeri Iliadem*, 19.1190: they are Hesiod, Homer, and Orpheus (all in 6.1.3). Further references are absent, as I do not believe that the reference to Pherecydes (6.4.1) can be attributed to Diodorus with any degree of certainty. Nevertheless, I believe that Cohen-Skalli (2012: xciv) is absolutely right when she observes in the background the deep influence of Ephorus' work on Diodorus, not only for this book but probably for many more.[17] Book 7 rests, according to Chamoux and Bertrac (1993: xxiii), on the work of at least Apollodorus of Athens (7.8.1), Q. Fabius Pictor (7.5.4), and Theopompus (7.17.1). The appearance of the name of Cyme (7.10.1), though, might suggest that Diodorus used Ephorus as a source for this book as well, as Ephorus was known to extol his native city exceedingly (see Str. 13.3.6/622). We may, perhaps, also infer some oracles from Delphi as sources (7.12.1–2, 5, 6; 7.16.1). The reference to a work *On Stones* by Orpheus (7.1.1) – though this author has been mentioned before in 6.1.3 – is most likely to be attributed to the source of this fragment, which is Joannes Tzetzes, the twelfth-century Byzantine poet and grammarian. According to the excerpt by George Syncellus, the Byzantine chronicler and churchman who lived until c. AD 810, Diodorus in this book too displays the vagueness as regards his sources we already encountered in the use of ἔνιοι τῶν συγγραφέων ('some of the historians': 7.5.1).

As regards book 8, Oldfather (1970a: 387 note 2) believes that Diodorus follows the account of Dionysius of Halicarnassus (or his source) closely in the version that is presented of the quarrel between Romulus and Remus.[18] Here, as in the preceding book, some oracles may have been used as a source (8.8.2; 8.13.2; 8.17.1–2;

---

[17] See the remark by Diodorus in 5.1.4: Ἔφορος δὲ τὰς κοινὰς πράξεις ἀναγράφων οὐ μόνον κατὰ τὴν λέξιν, ἀλλὰ καὶ κατὰ τὴν οἰκονομίαν ἐπιτέτευχε· τῶν γὰρ βίβλων ἑκάστην πεποίηκε περιέχειν κατὰ γένος τὰς πράξεις. διόπερ καὶ ἡμεῖς τοῦτο τὸ γένος τοῦ χειρισμοῦ προκρίναντες, κατὰ τὸ δυνατὸν ἀντεχόμεθα ταύτης τῆς προαιρέσεως ('Ephorus, on the other hand, who wrote a *Universal History*, was successful, not only in his style of composition, but also as regards the arrangement of his work. Indeed, each of his books is so constructed as to embrace events which fall under a single topic. Therefore, we also prefer this method of handling our material, and, as far as it is possible, shall adhere to this policy'). Elsewhere (16.76.5), Diodorus emphasises that each of Ephorus' chapters had an introduction.

[18] Oldfather's suggestion appears to overlook the fact that Dionysius of Halicarnassus was a younger contemporary of Diodorus (by about thirty years): I would suggest that both Diodorus and Dionysius of Halicarnassus used the same (unspecified) source for their respective accounts of the alleged quarrel between Romulus and Remus.

8.21.3; 8.23.1–2; 8.29.1). Likewise, Diodorus' vagueness also features again, as is shown by remarks like λέγουσι δέ τινες ('some say') or φασί ('they say') and similar references. A clear reference to a source-author is, however, lacking in this book. As sources mentioned in book 9 we should think, again, of oracles (9.3.1–2; 9.6.1; 9.16.1; 9.31.1–2; 9.33.2; 9.36.2–3), and, perhaps, of Aesop (9.28.1), Euripides (9.10.4), the so-called oath of Plataea (9.10.5), Solon (9.20.2–3), and Plato (9.10.2). Because all passages are, as indicated before, sources at third hand, it is by no means certain that Diodorus did indeed use them as his sources. In the context of the remaining preserved books (and, perhaps, Diodorus' education; see below, section G), however, it does not seem to be totally unlikely, which is why I have included these sources here, albeit with some provisos (applicable to all sources from the fragmentarily transmitted books).

For book 10 too we have to skate on thin ice. The stories of Pythagoras and the Pythagoreans (10.3.1–12.3), for example that on the friendship between Damon and Phintias (10.4), may well go back largely to Aristoxenus of Tarentum's works on Pythagoras and the Pythagoreans.[19] Next to this, Diodorus also may have used the work of Aristoxenus' younger contemporary (a difference of about half a century) Callimachus, as suggested by 10.6.4.[20] If so, it is to the best of my knowledge the only time in the *Bibliotheca* Diodorus refers directly to Callimachus (see also Cohen-Skalli 2012: 372 *ad* note 27). Next to this we encounter in this book a reference to Euripides' *Phoenissae* (10.9.8) and a potential link to Herodotus (Hdt. 3.125) in the story of Polycrates (10.16). Herodotus is certainly the origin of the fragments that constitute 10.24 and possibly even of 10.25.1. The rest of *caput* 10.25 is either loosely based upon Herodotus or, perhaps, an invention by Diodorus (notably the embassy of Hecataeus the Milesian: 10.25.4). Chamoux and Bertrac (1993: xxiv) therefore regard Herodotus as one of the principal sources of this book. The origin of Diodorus' reference to Zeno

---

[19] See Wehrli 1945: 10–20, FF. 11–41; comments on 49–62; see also the remarks by Oldfather 1970b: 58–9 note 1 and Meister 1967: 39.

[20] As indicated by Oldfather, the text as presented by Diodorus according to the *Excerpta Constantiniana* (4), pp. 293–4 (Fr. 77), is quite different from the (original?) lines of Callimachus, retrieved from the damaged *P.Oxy.* 1011 (see Oldfather 1970b: 62–3 note 1). Whereas Oldfather has opted to stick to the lines as presented by the *Excerpta Constantiniana*, Cohen-Skalli 2012: 192 Fr. 11 has opted to adapt the lines, in fact making a combination of the rendering of the words in the *Excerpta* and the papyrus. I find this ultimately an unlucky combination. Finding Callimachus' words in the papyrus and comparing the versions make one wonder (once again) about the reliability of the rest of Diodorus' excerpts. They underline the doubts expressed in connection with his handling of the material in book 3.

of Elea (10.18.1) remains hidden to us. In book 10, too, we find further vague references in the style of φασὶ ('they say') as well as traces of Diodorus' (Stoic) concepts of the right attitude (see 10.12; 10.16.2–3; 10.19.1; 10.21).

D. BOOKS 11–20

With the following books we are again on somewhat more solid ground. Book 11, which covers the years 480–451, largely devoted to Athens/Greece and Sicily, is for Diodorus' story of Greece predominantly based upon Ephorus, Herodotus, and Thucydides (Haillet 2002: x):[21] they would presumably have been Diodorus' primary sources. As secondary sources for this part of the account we may infer Ctesias, Hellanicus, Isocrates, 'chronographic sources' (Haillet 2002: xi), an oracle (see 11.14.4), and, as I have argued elsewhere (Stronk 2014/15: 214–15, 228), the poet Simonides (for example in 11.11.6 and 11.62.3, perhaps also 11.33.2). Perhaps Diodorus also made use of the work of the Athenian logographer Lycurgus for the so-called oath of Plataea (11.29.3; see Lycurg. *Leocr.* 81 and Diodorus' 12.3.3). Naturally Diodorus' Stoic values are also ever present, as in his *laudatio* for the Spartan dead of Thermopylae (11.11.1–6). As for the histories of Sicily, Laqueur and Jacoby believe that an excerpt from Ephorus was Diodorus' principal source (Haillet 2002: xi and note 10), though Volquardsen[22] believes it was Timaeus of Tauromenium, and Manni[23] that it was Silenus of Cale Acte in Sicily.[24] Meister (1967: 41–54), after scrutiny of the text, opts for a mixed solution: Timaeus provided most of Diodorus' source material, but Ephorus was also an important supplier of material, even though Diodorus reverses that order for book 15. Of the chronographic sources, Meister mentions above all Apollodorus of Athens, according to Meister a direct source for Diodorus, but also several other works that are difficult to link with the name of an author (Meister 1967: 5). To what extent the *Sicelica*

---

[21] Haillet 2002: x–xi also provides an analysis of which author was the source-author for which part of Diodorus' Greek account in book 11: at least as regards his analysis of Diodorus' source for the Battle of Thermopylae I disagree with Haillet's view, as I have argued elsewhere at some length (Stronk 2014/15: 193).
[22] Volquardsen 1868: 80–107.
[23] Manni 1957–8.
[24] He was the author of, *inter alia*, a *Sicelica* (*History of Sicily*: see FGrH/BNJ 175; see also Jacoby 1927. However, Walbank 1968–9: 487–97 suggests that Silenus' role was a modest one and that the *Sicelica* (of which only three fragments survive) may well have been a periegetic or paradoxographical work on the wonders of Sicily rather than a work on its history.

of Antiochus of Syracuse and that of Philistus had any influence as sources for this book for Diodorus cannot be determined (Haillet 2002: xiii).

As for Diodorus' use of sources for the history of Rome, we should distinguish between the consular lists and the events described (Perl 1957: 123; also Haillet 2002: xiv). As regards the first element, Perl believes Diodorus worked with the *Fasti* of the following annalists: Q. Fabius Pictor, L. Calpurnius Piso Frugi, Cn. Gellius, and L. Cassius Hemina (Perl 1957: 122). Somewhat later Perl remarks that the description of events and the consular lists did not originate from the same source(s) (Perl 1957: 162). For the descriptions regarding events in Roman history in books 11–20 of Diodorus' *Bibliotheca* combined, Perl discerns fifteen Roman authors as primary sources and some ten Greek authors as secondary sources, adding some for the later books of Diodorus.[25]

As regards Diodorus' use of his sources in book 11 on Greece, Haillet observes that where scholars used to see Ephorus everywhere in Diodorus' text (a tradition advocated at some length most recently by Stylianou), it is at present customary to dissect the work excessively, perhaps because the text contains a fair number of uncertainties (Haillet 2002: xv). To explain these uncertainties Haillet opts for a simpler explication, which he considers to be a more likely one: 'les contradictions et les obscurités de Diodore reflètent celles d'Hérodote, et celles-ci reflètent la réalité historique, à savoir la confusion qui a régné dans le camp grec et les dissensions entre les chefs' (ibid.). I must admit that I quite like this conclusion, albeit that I would like to add an additional cause for confusion, notably in book 11 (and not entirely unrelated to the cause mentioned by Haillet), that is, the disparity between simply describing *ta genomena* (≈ 'wie es wirklich gewesen [ist]') and the wish or the need to retain or even enlarge the ideological charge as regards the role and/or position of Greece in the world that many of the events described in this book have gained in the following centuries (notions in fact starting at least as early as Herodotus, some of them even continuing

---

[25] Perl 1957: 163–4 mentions the following Roman source-authors for Diodorus: Cn. Flavius; Q. Fabius Pictor (Greek); a Latin Fabius; L. Cincius Alimentus (Greek); C. Acilius (Greek); A. Postumius Albinus (Greek); L. Cassius Hemina; L. Calpurnius Piso; an older Latin annalist; the *Annales maximi*; a middle Latin annalist (shortly before Sulla); Q. Claudius Quadrigarius; C. Licinius Macer; a younger Latin annalist; and Cornelius Nepos; as well as the following Greek ones: Theopompus; Philistus; Timaeus; Hieronymus of Cardia; Duris of Samos; Philinus; Polybius; Posidonius; Castor; an author from the beginning of the first century BC. On pp. 164–7 Perl describes the source-authors for Diodorus' Roman history by period, adding as further sources Coelius Antipater; Silenus; and Sosylus.

in the minds of people until the present time).[26] There is, I think, a certain natural imbalance between these two elements, an imbalance reflected in Diodorus' sources and therefore necessarily in Diodorus' text itself. This imbalance, in my view, makes book 11 one of the most interesting of Diodorus'*oeuvre*. Of course this does not necessarily minimise Ephorus' alleged influence on Diodorus, but I believe we should embed Ephorus' influence in a context of developments which may have started before his death but certainly continued more vigorously thereafter inside the Greek world, such as, most notably, the effects of Hellenism. Diodorus was, I believe, certainly aware of the differences between 'his' world and the world, for example, Ephorus lived in, even though Diodorus does not consistently reflect it in his *Bibliotheca*: it shows in 'les contradictions et les obscurités' discussed above. Moreover, consistency in *every* respect is, regrettably, not one of Diodorus' main qualities. I think Stylianou takes historical developments insufficiently into account.

Book 12 deals with events between 450 and 415. As Casevitz (2002: xiii) remarks, it is usual to state that Diodorus in book 12 merely follows Ephorus, though Casevitz underlines that it would be wrong to state that Ephorus was Diodorus' only or even principal source (Casevitz 2002: xiii–xiv). Casevitz also leaves the possibility quite open that Thucydides, Philistus, and Silenus were amongst Diodorus' sources for this book, as was Timaeus (for example 12.11.4: Casevitz 2002: xiv, 100 (note *ad loc.*)) and/or Posidonius (12.11.4: see Casevitz 2002: 100 (note *ad loc.*)). Chamoux and Bertrac (1993: xxiv) add Antiochus of Syracuse to this list of potential source-authors. I believe that several *capita*, though they do not refer to Thucydides by name, do indeed suggest his work was at their origin, probably also as a principal source (see Casevitz 2002: notes *passim*). At least one oracle was among Diodorus' sources as well (12.10.5), some Pythagorean influence perhaps (12.12.1), while 12.13.1 echoes a *topos* familiar from Aeschylus' *Prometheus* (lines 459 *sq.*) onwards and may also show some influence from Isocrates (*Panegyricus* 47–50; Casevitz 2002: 18 note 1). Not only does Aeschylus feature in book 12, but so too does Euripides, where

---

[26] Concepts like Persian effeminacy and the superiority of Greeks and Greek culture and institutions, to name but a few. See also, for example, my remarks on the ideological issue in Stronk 2014/15: 221–2. Just as Sparta, which during the 380s and later traded in its ἀνδρεία ('manliness') and ὁμόνοια ('concord') for τρυφή ('luxury') and ῥαθυμία ('laziness'), consequently lost its superiority, the latter two had also allegedly caused Persia's corruption and were the ultimate cause of its fall. For a much-needed adjustment to these views see Gorman and Gorman 2014; Morgan 2016: *passim*. See Samiei 2014: *passim* for recent Hellenocentric views.

Diodorus (12.14.1) refers to some lines from Euripides' *Phoenix* (Fr. 812, 7–9 [Nauck]), lines frequently quoted in antiquity according to Casevitz, for example by Aeschines (Aeschin. *Timar.* 152) and Demosthenes (see Casevitz 2002: 17 note 1). In the same paragraph (12.14.1) Diodorus also quotes another poet, unknown to us, but allegedly an author of comedies (Casevitz 2002: 17 note 2; Oldfather 1970b: 403 note 2). In the following paragraph Diodorus also quotes Philemon, an author of the New Comedy, from his work *Nothos* (*Bastard*). Old Comedy appears when Diodorus (12.40.6) quotes Aristophanes' *Pax* (lines 603–11) and *Acharnenses* (lines 530–1),[27] as well as Eupolis' *Demes*.[28] Perhaps Diodorus was also aware of epigraphical evidence (for example *IG* I^2, 397, 52, 98–9), as might be suggested by 12.45.7, 12.53.1, and 12.84.1 respectively, but I find that hard to prove beyond doubt. Diodorus probably uses an early but unknown source for his description in 12.36.2 of the new calendar based upon a solar cycle of nineteen years (Casevitz 2002: 110 (note *ad loc.*); Oldfather 1970b: 448–9 note 1). Whether Diodorus, for 12.38.3, also used a work of Aristodemus (*FGrH/BNJ* 104 F 1) cannot be established with any certainty, as the author (and therefore his dates) 'cannot be identified with anyone else of that name'.[29] The preserved fragment (F 1) of Aristodemus shares, though, some elements familiar from Diodorus' account.

Book 13 of the *Bibliotheca* covers the years 415–404 and largely focuses on events in Greece proper and Sicily (prominently), with some minor remarks on events in Asia. Like book 12, this book too appears to rest mainly upon Ephorus and Thucydides (at least to the year 411, that is, 13.42.5), the latter being replaced by Xenophon (namely his *Hellenica*) and the *Hellenica* by Theopompus (for the period from 411 onwards) as principal sources for Greece and by Timaeus for Sicily. Secondary sources that, implicitly or explicitly, come to the fore are Andocides (And. *Myst.*), Aristophanes (Ar. *Lys.* 1094), Timaeus (several times for Greece), perhaps Isocrates (Isoc. *Bigis* for 13.74.3), Empedocles (Emp. *Cath.* = D.-K. 31 [21] F 112 line 3), Polyclitus of Larissa (*Histories*; see *FGrH/BNJ* 128), Philistus (*Sicelica*), and Apollodorus of Athens (*Chronology*).

In book 14, Diodorus discusses the years 404–387, dividing his attention between Greece proper, the Greeks in Asia Minor,

---

[27] As Casevitz 2002: 113 note *ad loc.* indicates, Diodorus quotes Aristophanes' lines with some errors.
[28] See Kock 1880: F. 94, lines 5–7; see also, for example, the previous *FCG*, I, 173: VI (2, 458), lines 5–8.
[29] Pownall, *BNJ* 104: 'Biographical Essay'.

developments in the Persian Empire, Sicily and its relations with the Carthaginians, and finally the capture of Rome by the Gauls. Like the preceding books, this book too mainly rests on the account of Ephorus, supplemented as a principal source predominantly by Xenophon's *Hellenica* (and, partly, his *Expeditio Cyri* or *Anabasis*) and to a lesser extent by the *Hellenica* of Theopompus, for the developments in Greece and Asia; and on Timaeus for Sicily. Secondary sources are perhaps Aristotle (*Ath.* 35–7, for the period of the 'Thirty'), Philistus, Ctesias (as I explained in Stronk 2010: 184, 185, 188, and 191), either directly or through Ephorus, while Diodorus also shows himself knowledgeable about the works of Philoxenus of Cythera, Timotheus of Miletus, Telestus of Selinus, and Polyides – all four makers of dithyrambs – and the orator Lysias (his *Olympiacus*, calling the Greeks to unite against both the Persians and the Sicilian tyrant Dionysius I). Bonnet and Bennett (2002: viii) add to this list the historian of the *Hellenica Oxyrhynchia* (either directly or, more likely, through Ephorus) as well. Bonnet and Bennett (2002: ix) also believe that Ephorus, for his account of the expedition of Cyrus the Younger, based himself not only on Xenophon's description of the events, but also on Sophaenetus' version,[30] a version that, therefore, may also have found its way into Diodorus' *Bibliotheca*. As source for the history of Rome in this book Bonnet and Bennett (2002: xiii) surmise Fabius Pictor. Chamoux and Bertrac (1993, xxiv) add Callisthenes, Thucydides, and Timaeus to the list of Diodorus' source-authors for this book.

Book 15 covers the years 386–361 and concerns almost exclusively events in the realm of the Achaemenids (including Cyprus), in mainland Greece, and in Sicily, but with some attention as well to developments in Carthage. As in the previous books, in this book too Ephorus seems to have been Diodorus' principal source for events taking place in Greece and the East, augmented notably by the *Hellenica* of Xenophon (even though there are significant differences between the accounts of Diodorus and Xenophon, neatly summarised in Vial 2002: xv), that of Theopompus, and as it seems the *Hellenica Oxyrhynchia* – whether directly or through Ephorus. For Sicily, first Ephorus and subsequently Timaeus appear to have been Diodorus' principal sources, even though Hammond believes it was Theopompus.[31] Striking is (in my view) Diodorus' introduction

---

[30] *FGrH/BNJ* 109. See for *BNJ* 109 Stronk, 'Sophainetos Stymphalikos (109)'.

[31] Hammond 1938: 144 maintains that Theopompus is, in fact, the principal source for all of Diodorus' account of Sicilian history, however without adducing convincing evidence. Meister's 1967 study, though, convincingly argues Diodorus' source-author for that part of the

to this book (15.1.1–6), in which he underlines *expressis verbis* the moral guidelines he practised in the *Bibliotheca*, more or less putting a description of *ta genomena* on a secondary level. It is a practice he shows particularly in relation to Sparta throughout book 15 (see his remarks in 15.1.3–4).

As secondary sources in book 15 we might surmise the works of Philoxenus of Cythera for Sicily, Philistus, and perhaps even a Roman source (for example for the description of the *Punica fides* in 15.16.1).[32] For Greece and the East some oracles might be inferred as secondary sources as well as, perhaps, Demosthenes (D. 20.76), Dinarchus (Din. *Demosth.* 39), some epigraphical evidence (like IG.II².40–2, 43, 44, 45, 82, 95–101; IG II³.1.43), Isocrates (Isoc. *Paneg.* 126, 140 sq.; *Pax* 99; *Arch.* 44 sq., 63), Cornelius Nepos (Nep. *Cha.* 1, 2.1; *Iph.* 2.4; *Pel.* 4.2, 5), Polybius (Plb. 4.27.4), and Xenophon (X. *Ages.* 26). Possibly we also might include as Diodorus' sources the works of both Dionysodorus and Anaxis, both Boeotians, both authors of a *Hellenica* (see 15.95.4): as their works are completely lost, we can say nothing final on that point. Of course Stylianou (1998: 49–132) argues that the data of (many of) these authors had not been read by Diodorus himself, but were incorporated into the work of, primarily, Ephorus[33] or, to a much lesser extent, Timaeus: though acknowledging this as a possibility, I am much less adamant in defending this position, especially because of the specific references to authors throughout the several books of Diodorus we still have. Stylianou adds a potential source-author for Diodorus' book 15, namely Dinon (on the trial of Tiribazus), allegedly not a source used by Ephorus (Stylianou 1998: 108–9).[34] To this already extensive list Chamoux and Bertrac (1993: xxiv) add Anaximenes, Athanis of Syracuse, Duris of Samos, and Hermias of Methymna. Nevertheless, I very much doubt whether we can include Athanis in the list of source-authors for this book, because Diodorus

---

Bibliotheca normally is Timaeus supplemented by Ephorus, except as regards book 15: here Diodorus follows primarily Ephorus' account, completed by Timaeus.

[32] Οἱ Καρχηδόνιοι τῇ συνήθει πανουργίᾳ ('The Carthaginians with their customary knavery'): 15.16.1).

[33] Stylianou refers to a number of authors who may have contributed to Ephorus' work (Stylianou 1998: 104–9). In the context of this chapter, I do not believe it to be essential to pursue this inquiry further. Suffice it to refer to his conclusion on Artaxerxes *Ochus*' reconquest of Cyprus, Phoenicia, and Egypt in the 340s (related in Diodorus' book 16): 'Diodorus' narrative is again detailed and it gives the impression of being accurate' (Stylianou 1998: 107). Further on he describes this account as 'impressive' (Stylianou 1998: 128).

[34] Stevenson 1987: 31 states that the story of Tiribazus' trial is a 'pure invention' by Dinon. Stylianou 1998: 109 refers to the majority of the story as 'romantic fiction', but does not dismiss the entirety of the trial as a work of imagination.

makes it unmistakably clear that Athanis' work only started with a prequel beginning in 362/1, the very year Diodorus' limit for this book ends. For the following book, though, Athanis' name certainly merits being mentioned.

The events detailed in book 16 run from 360 to 336 and have Philip II of Macedon as their main character. It is a complex book, or, as Robert Drews phrases it: 'Book XVI is a welter of confusion' (Drews 1962: 389). Hammond too, who devoted two papers to this book, is far from enthusiastic about it: some of his qualifications on Diodorus in particular I have already referred to in the Introduction. However, enthusiasm for Diodorus is not needed in an attempt to identify his sources. For the main part of the Greek and Macedonian events related in this book, Hammond discerns the following possible source-authors: Theopompus, Ephorus, Demophilus, Diyllus of Athens, and Duris of Samos (Hammond 1937: 84). Of these source-authors Hammond rules out Theopompus for Graeco-Macedonian affairs 'because his work in fifty-eight books presented too heavy a task for a compiler such as Diodorus and because the numerous fragments we possess find no echo in Diodorus' (ibid.).

The last part of the argument may have some weight, though I believe it to be not conclusive, even though there still remain 217 fragments of Theopompus' *History of Philip* (Sherman 1963: 245 note 1). As for the first part of the argument, it is rather a sentiment fed by prejudice than a conclusion based upon sound scholarly research, and as such I think we can discard it. If Diodorus refers to Theopompus, one way or another, we have to accept that as a datum (whether we like it or not) and, as matters stand, Diodorus does so twice, in 16.3.8 (announcing the start of Theopompus' *Philippica*) and in 16.71.3 (informing his audience that Theopompus' *Philippica* also included three books dealing with affairs in Sicily). I do not claim that this is decisive evidence that Diodorus used the work of Theopompus, but we certainly cannot exclude the possibility. Sherman recognises this too and even goes a step further, remarking that 'Theopompus' admiration for Philip is reflected by Diodorus, who must have relied heavily on his account' (Sherman 1963: 245 note 1). For this position too there is, however, no conclusive evidence, but at least it looks a *little* less biased.

Next to Graeco-Macedonian matters Diodorus also pays attention to Sicilian matters in book 16. The first candidates as source-authors are, according to Hammond (1938: 141), Ephorus, Theopompus, and Timaeus, augmented by Diyllus of Athens: according to Hammond the final conclusion must be that Diodorus relied for the Sicilian account of book 16 mostly on Theopompus' *Philippica* (Hammond 1938: 144; Hammond does not tell us why this book of Theopompus would have been easier for Diodorus to handle) and to a lesser extent on Timaeus (Hammond 1938: 145). The chart on his p. 150 summarises Hammond's views on the sources of Diodorus' book 16 neatly, though in my view rather unsatisfactorily because it starts from a strong bias against Diodorus and so precludes other sources than the ones Hammond believes feasible, apparently without looking further in the text. My judgement of Hammond is probably unfair, but I believe his bias does not do justice to the source material we have to deal with.

In spite of Hammond's arduous work (no cynicism intended!), he did not (probably, as discussed) cover all of Diodorus' source-authors.[35] He may well have omitted, for example, Aeschines (Aeschin. *De Falsa Leg.* 26-7, 132; *In Ctes.* 85, 97, 107-12), Anaximenes of Lampsacus (Anaximen. Lampsac. *Rh. Al.* 8.3/1429b), almost certainly Athanis of Syracuse (*FGrH/BNJ* 562 F 2; see also the remarks on this author above in connection with book 15), Demades (Demad. *Duod. Ann.* 9-10), Demosthenes (D. 2.14; 4.35; 6.20; 7.32; 8.40; 9.65-6; 10.34; 12.6; 15.26; 18.61, 87-94, 169-78, 237; 19.61, 83, 84, 139, 193-5, 265, 266, 342; 20.80-2; 23.108, 121, 157), Dinarchus (Din. *In Dem.* 14), Homer (Hom. *Il.* 2.517-19, 9.404-5, 13.131-4), Isocrates (Isoc. *Antid.* 129; *Areop.* 8, 10, 81; *Pax* 16; *Phil.* 102; *Paneg.* 161), Cornelius Nepos (Nep. *Di.* 5, 8-10 (using the name of Callicrates instead of Callippus); *Cha.* 4; *Tim.* 3, 5.4; *Iph.* 3.3), Philochorus (*FGrH/BNJ* 328 F 132), Polybius (Plb. 18.28.6; 3.24; <12.4a.2 (referring to Theopompus, apparently used in 16.70.2 by Diodorus)>), Xenophon (X. *HG* 6.4.35-7), and Callisthenes. A speech of Lycurgus is quoted in 16.88.2, but to the best of my knowledge there is no further record of it:[36] therefore, we cannot determine where this fragment originated. Most of these (potential) source-authors are not mentioned by name by Diodorus. However, the works and places referred to above appear to have inspired him (sometimes even more than that, as, for example, in the case of Demosthenes (19.193-5, the story of Satyrus), which is

---

[35] See also the description of Diodorus' sources for books 16.66-95 in Welles 1970: 3-5. The picture Welles paints is much more favourable to Diodorus than Hammond's and comes close to my ideas.

[36] Lycurgus mentions in the *In Leocratem* 23 one Lysicles, possibly a banker but certainly not the general referred to in this *caput*. The passage as Diodorus has it also occurs in the *Exc. Const.* (4): 324 F. 182, but that is taken from Diodorus' *Bibliotheca* and cannot, therefore, serve as conclusive evidence for the correct presentation of a source-author by Diodorus. The same statement applies to Georgius Gemistus' *Adnotationes e Diodoro*, section 20 line 19.

repeated almost *verbatim* by Diodorus) and, therefore, might probably be regarded as secondary sources. To this already impressive list Chamoux and Bertrac (1993: xxiv) add Demophilus, the son of Ephorus. Apart from these authors we also note some oracles and possibly some personal observations by Diodorus (16.83), *inter alia* referring to his home town of Agyrium.

Book 17 essentially recounts the history of Alexander III the Great but stands out in the *Bibliotheca* because Diodorus refers in the text to no source-author at all (see also Chamoux and Bertrac 1993: xxiv). Contrary to, for example, Tarn (1948: 63–91),[37] who states that book 17 is a medley of many sources, Goukowsky (2002a: xii–xiii) believes that some now lost work, commonly known as the *Vulgate*, stood at the origin of this book.[38] Moreover, as Goukowsky remarks, 'on voit mal pourquoi Diodore n'aurait pas inséré dans son livre XVII certaines informations glanées au cours de ses lectures et susceptibles de combler les lacunes de sa source principale'. As for the name of the author who was Diodorus' principal source, there has been (and still is) much debate: Clitarchus of Alexandria (*FGrH/ BNJ* 137) has been especially mentioned.[39] Goukowsky, however, rightly I think, does not believe the case is closed and sealed *completely* (my emphasis) as yet, even though Clitarchus looks for him at the moment the best candidate by far (Goukowsky 2002a: xvi–xix). It is, more or less, the same conclusion he brought forward in a paper from 1969 (Goukowsky 1969). In that paper he also pointed to some remarkable similarities in fragments of Ctesias and Diodorus' account regarding the production of poisons in India (*FGrH/BNJ* 688/Lenfant 2004 FF 45 i and r). However, Goukowsky states in his 1969 work (Goukowsky 1969: 334) that a more serious source than Ctesias was responsible for Diodorus' information and suggests it may have been Theophrastus (whether or not based upon Aristotle).[40] Obviously, Ctesias is absolutely excluded as a principal

---

[37] A critical and succinct review of Tarn's suggestions can be found in Sinclair 1963: 42–5.
[38] The notion of the *Vulgate* goes back to Raun 1868.
[39] This is the position notably taken by Schwartz 1903a, Jacoby 1921, and their pupils. As usual, their influence has been tremendously important for subsequent discussions. Their idea was based upon the similarity of the information provided by Diodorus of Sicily and Q. Curtius Rufus. Though it could be technically possible that Curtius Rufus (first century AD) based himself on Diodorus (first century BC), it is considered to be unlikely and therefore a common source is believed to be necessary: as such Clitarchus seemed to be an obvious choice. See, however, the remarks below on Cn. Pompeius Trogus.
[40] One of Goukowsky's defences in this paper is that it cannot be shown that the information does derive from Clitarchus (p. 336: 'on ne peut démontrer qu'elle provient de Clitarque'). I find this a cheap argument, simply because we do not have Clitarchus' work: all that is left of it is fifty-two fragments (fifty-four if we count F 52 a, b, and c separately) and is, therefore, rather a meagre base for such an overly confident position. Moreover, as Welles 1970: 11

source for this book, but Diodorus may have used his work as a secondary source, for example to add *couleur locale* to his account, just like Megasthenes' work.

In his introduction to Diodorus' sources for book 17, Welles (1970: 6–11) is, I believe, more cautious than Goukowsky. The following remarks summarise his view quite succinctly:

> Lacking any extensive text of any of the primary historians, and in some uncertainty as to the scope and manner and even the date of many of them, it is impossible for us to prove or to disprove that Diodorus used, for example, Aristobulus or Cleitarchus. It seems certain, of course, that he did not use Ptolemy; and specific disagreement with Aristobulus and Cleitarchus makes it unlikely that he used them directly. (Welles 1970: 11)

Some pages further on, Welles, very cautiously, suggests that Diodorus might have used the work of Cn. Pompeius Trogus as his prime source (Welles 1970: 13–14; also 473 at addenda for p. 13). It is a suggestion (as Welles acknowledges) previously made by Otto Seel.[41] I think, though, also this is again a suggestion that can neither be proven nor disproven. What Welles does make clear is that several *capita* of book 17 (primarily through references in third sources) may be linked to a specific source-author or source-authors. They are for *caput* 49 Callisthenes and Aristobulus; for *caput* 50 Callisthenes; for *caput* 52 Aristobulus; for *caput* 72 Clitarchus; for *caput* 75 Onesicritus and Clitarchus; for *caput* 77 Clitarchus, Onesicritus, and others; for *caput* 90 Clitarchus and/or Nearchus, Onesicritus, and Aristobulus; for *caput* 91 Onesicritus; for *caput* 102 Clitarchus; for *caput* 105 Onesicritus, Clitarchus, and Nearchus; for *caput* 106, somewhat variously, Nearchus and Onesicritus (for the celebration after the reunion), and Nearchus (for the whales); and for *caput* 108 Clitarchus and Theopompus. Perhaps we might add to that the work of Megasthenes on India and, with even more reservation, that of Ctesias (possibly for 17.71.7; much less likely for 17.77.6) and

---

note 2 rightly observes: 'It is always hard to prove a negative', after noting in the text that 'it is impossible for us to prove or disprove that Diodorus used, for example, Aristobulus or Cleitarchus'. For clarity's sake: I do not claim Clitarchus was or was not Diodorus' principal source, but I simply plead for more modesty, circumspection, and – above all – sense of reality: we simply do not have the means to prove or disprove any author was Diodorus' principal source.

[41] Seel 1956: 84–119 at 116. I must confess that I am, to some extent, charmed by this suggestion, *inter alia* because Diodorus in this book rather writes of Alexander's φίλοι ('friends') than of his ἑταῖροι ('companions'), the more usual Greek expression (which he does use regularly in book 18: see 18.3.3), even though later in the Hellenistic world φίλοι became a more common way to indicate the circle around the king (see below, note 46). Elsewhere too, Diodorus' choice of words might imply a translation of Roman terminology into Greek: see also Welles 1970: 14 note 1.

Chares of Mytilene (for 17.76.6). A *Fundgrube* may have been the work of Marsyas of Pella, referred to by Diodorus in 20.50.4, on the history of Macedonia, a work that according to the *Suda* described the history up to the return of Alexander in Syria after his journey into Egypt in 331.[42] Naturally, the same work may have been used by Diodorus for previous books as well!

Book 18 describes the events between, largely, 323 and 317, mainly in the Macedonian Empire (the territory formerly dominated by Alexander the Great). According to Goukowsky (2002b: xii–xiii) most scholars agree that Diodorus' principal source for this period was, directly or indirectly, the work of Hieronymus of Cardia (the *History of the Diadochs*; see also Chamoux and Bertrac 1993: xxiv and note 54).[43] Occasionally Duris of Samos has been mentioned as *Zwischenquelle*: this idea has received far less support. As, more or less, secondary sources appear Diyllus (Goukowsky 2002b: xv) and an Alexandrian source (for the expedition of Perdiccas against Egypt: Goukowsky 2002b: xvi), perhaps identical with Agatharchides of Cnidus – even though no preserved fragment of his matches Diodorus' account (see Goukowsky 2002b: xvi note 4). Whether a separate Cyrenaican source was used by Diodorus eludes us. As things stand, Goukowsky strongly stresses the fact that it is extremely problematic to discover the source-authors of Diodorus' book 18, let alone to establish Hieronymus with certainty or confidence as his main source-author for this book: Hieronymus is merely the most likely author we can think of, Goukowsky states (see Goukowsky 2002b: xviii–xix).[44]

In his introduction to book 18, Geer is much less cautious than Goukowsky:

> [t]he chief source of Diodorus in books 18 through 20, except for the material dealing with Italy and Sicily, is the history of Hieronymus of Cardia, a friend and fellow countryman of Eumenes, and after Eumenes' death the companion of Antigonus, Demetrius, and Gonatas. (Geer 1969: vii)[45]

---

[42] See *Suda*, *s.v. mu*,227. See also Chapter 9, below, and note 24.

[43] Some, like Schwartz 1903a and Jacoby 1913, claim a *Zwischenquelle* between Hieronymus and Diodorus. Beloch, 1904, vol. 2: 4–5 also tends to believe that Diodorus uses Hieronymus indirectly, that is, through Agatharchides of Cnidus, a view that has won some support: see Goukowsky 2002b: xiii notes 6 and 7.

[44] 'Hiéronymus était le seul historien qui répondit à la condition requise. Hypothèse vraisamblable, séduisante même. Mais simple hypothèse. Dans l'état actuel de nos connaissances, impossible de percer l'anonymat de l'historien résumé par Diodore' (Goukowsky 2002b: xix–xx).

[45] In this respect, Geer fits into a tradition that easily accepts the relationship between Diodorus and Hieronymus: see, for example, Engel, 1972a.

Geer's argument is circumstantial, not textual – he admits that the latter is impossible (ibid.): the examples he adduces are admittedly strong (notably the eyewitness argument), but are far from accounting for the entirety of book 18. He also adduces (therefore?) a second, anonymous, source, one favourable to Ptolemy I *Soter Lagides*. As for the origin of the Sicilian account in book 18, Geer points to the *History of Agathocles* by Duris of Samos as well as to the work of Timaeus.

Reading through book 18, we see that Diodorus starts it with references to Pythagoras and Homer. A story about Greeks in the upper satrapies (18.4.8; 18.7) is not encountered elsewhere in Greek historiography, though it is referred to in the prologue to book 13 of the *Philippica* by Cn. Pompeius Trogus,[46] the same source we have already encountered in the description of potential sources for book 17. In 18.2.2 and 3 too a slight reminder of Trogus appears (Just. 13.3.1–3), as it does in 18.2.4 (Just. 10.3 and 13.4), 18.3.1 (Just. 13.4.9–23 (partially corrupt: see Seel 1985: 126, *apparatus*)), 18.8.7 (Just. 13.5.4–7), 18.10.5 (Just. 13.5.10), 18.12.1 (Just. 12.12.9), 18.13.5 (Just. 13.5.12),[47] 18.14.1 (Just. 13.6.18), 18.15.3 (Just. 13.5.14–16), 18.15.5 (Just. 13.5.15–16), 18.16.1 (Just. 13.6.1), 18.22.4 (Just. 13.6.1–3), 18.23.1 (Just. 13.6.4–7), 18.29.4–5 (Just. 13.8.3–8), 18.31.2 (Just. 13.8.8), 18.37.2 (Just. 13.8.10), 18.40.1 (Just. 14.1.6–7), 18.42.1 (Just. 14.2.4), 18.52.4 (Just. 14.2.4), 18.61.2 (Just. 14.2.8–12), and 18.72.2 (*Prol. lib.* 14: see Seel 1985: 310). It looks like an impressive number of references/parallels, but it is, as indicated, insufficient to assign a, let alone the most,

---

[46] Just. *Prol. lib.* 13: *Vt veterani, qvi ab eodem lecti erant in colonias, moliti, relictis illis, in Greciam redire, a Pythone sint deleti* ('how the veterans, chosen by him [Alexander] to stay in colonies, having left them, trying to return to Greece, were wiped out by Pytho'). This observation might have implications for the discussion on the source-authors for Diodorus' book 18, looking at the content of the prologues of books 13 and 14 of Trogus' work preserved by Justin: see Seel 1985: 310 (not to be confused with Seel's 1956 work, mentioned above); see also, for example, Yardley 1994: 277–8. The prologues appear to correspond neatly to the general direction of Diodorus' account. Regrettably, Justin's epitome itself, even in combination with Pompeius Trogus' own *Prolegomena*, looks insufficient to serve as a solid base for such an assumption, precisely because of what it is, an epitome: see also below. The more frequent use of ἑταῖροι ('companions') instead of φίλοι ('friends': see, however, for example, 18.2.2), the term Diodorus frequently used in book 17, might also be a complicating factor in ascribing a prominent role to Trogus – or another Latin-writing author – as a principal source for Diodorus in book 18. Of course, Hellenistic kings from at least the early third century BC surrounded themselves with φίλοι ('friends'). Though this practice had already started during the reign of Philip II, it was, to the best of my knowledge, not yet very widespread during Alexander's time. See, for example, Dreyer 2011: 47 and notes 12 and 13. Wherever possible, I will translate both ἑταῖροι and φίλοι as 'companions'.

[47] Diodorus tells us in this paragraph that one Leosthenes was struck on the head by a stone. In his epitome of Trogus, Justin adds: *telo a mvris ... iacto* ('by a projectile shot from the walls': Just. 13.5.12).

prominent role to Pompeius Trogus as source-author for Diodorus, both because Diodorus is also occasionally at variance with this source and because it is not absolutely clear whether the *Epitome* is a wholly reliable reflection of Pompeius Trogus' work.[48]

The origin of the geographical description of the empire left by Alexander (18.5–6) might ultimately go back to Dicearchus of Messana (in Sicily), a pupil of Aristotle, though it is thoroughly possible that Diodorus' main source borrowed it and thus transmitted it to Diodorus (Goukowsky 2002b: xx–xxi).[49] An additional source for large parts of this book may have been Cornelius Nepos' *Life of Eumenes* and for parts perhaps his *Life of Phocion* (2.2; 2.4; 4.1–2, 3–4), admitting that, like Pompeius Trogus', Nepos' date might also pose a problem. In 18.35.6, Theocritus' *Hymn to Ptolemy Philadelphus* (17.5.98) may have had some influence, unless we accept that Diodorus' autoptic knowledge of Egypt pays off in this paragraph. What further surprises is the relatively great number of official documents, like inscriptions, Diodorus appears to have used in this book, a matter looked into by Klaus Rosen.[50] Taken together, book 18 offers a complex picture, and as far as I can see there is no single conclusive and totally satisfactory solution at hand as regards Diodorus' source-authors for this book. As it stands, it seems that Hieronymus of Cardia, used either directly or indirectly, is indeed the least controversial candidate. It is, however, a candidacy that is only acceptable for lack of a more suitable candidate.

Like Chamoux and Bertrac (1993: xxiv), Geer assumes that Hieronymus of Cardia was also Diodorus' principal source-author for book 19 of the *Bibliotheca* (accounting for the years 317–311/0), except for those parts discussing events in Italy and Sicily (Geer 1969: vii). Geer also refers to a second, anonymous, source, favourable to Ptolemy (see, for example, 19.86.3), as source-author for Diodorus as regards events in the East (Geer 1969: viii). As for Sicilian matters, Geer believes Duris of Samos' *History of Agathocles* and the work of Timaeus of Tauromenium were Diodorus' main inspiration (ibid.). For Roman history, Diodorus appears to have

---

[48] In the introduction to Yardley 1994: 5–6, Develin argues that Justin did more than merely excerpt Pompeius Trogus' work: 'There is nothing in this which asserts that his excerpts were taken *verbatim* from Trogus rather than reworked by himself': Yardley 1994: 5.

[49] Geer 1969: 25 note 1 believes that the division of Asia by the Taurus Range follows Eratosthenes and that, therefore, Diodorus founds this account on Eratosthenes. I can only partially agree with this view, because some elements are totally at variance with Eratosthenes' views: see for example Schwartz 1903a: 685; Jacoby 1913: 1555. See also Aristobulus in FGrH/BNJ 139 F 23; Agathemerus in GGM, II: 472 *sub* 5.

[50] Rosen 1967.

mainly used 'one of the earlier Annalists, for example, Fabius Pictor' (Geer 1969: ix) and probably also an unknown 'brief account of Roman history written in Greek' (ibid.), *inter alia* responsible for Diodorus' remark in 19.72.9 on Luceria. How precisely, Geer adds,[51] Diodorus used his sources eludes us (ibid.).

Though Bottin believes that, except for the parts on Rome, Diodorus founds his account of events in Greece and the East as well of those in Sicily on the work of Agatharchides of Cnidus (Bottin 1928), Bizière discerns various parts within book 19, and she believes that Diodorus relies on various source-authors to compose those parts (Bizière 2002: xiv–xv). For Greek and eastern affairs she refers to the fact that 'tout le monde est d'accord pour considerer' that Hieronymus of Cardia was Diodorus' principal source-author (apparently totally neglecting, *inter alios*, Bottin's view), albeit for some parts through an intermediary (Bizière 2002: xv). She accepts that view, at least for that part up to the death of Eumenes, and with the remark that Diodorus uses Hieronymus' work directly, without intermediary (Bizière 2002: xvi); 'ce qui ne l'a ['le' meaning here Diodorus] pas empêché d'ajouter quelques passages, qu'il est d'ailleurs difficile de determiner avec certitude' (Bizière 2002: xvii; also Simpson 1959). As regards Diodorus' Sicilian *logos*, Bizière believes it impossible to decide whether he uses a single ancient source (Duris of Samos), several ancient sources, or an intermediary source (Bizière 2002: xviii). As for the situation on Roman history, she finds it hopeless and refers to Perl for suggestions (see above, note 25): as a matter of fact, Perl does not offer a specific suggestion for source-authors of this book. Bizière's final conclusion on book 19 appears to me overly influenced by the findings on Sicily and Rome: 'Le livre XIX apparaît donc comme un assemblage de textes d'origines et de tendances diverses, que Diodore n'a pas vraiment réélaborés et integrés les uns aux autres' (Bizière 2002: xix). I am not absolutely sure that I share the latter part of her observation.

One merit she credits Diodorus with is the fact that he chose the right sources for this book. As regards Diodorus' secondary sources, we may surmise Eratosthenes in 19.1.9 (for the date of the fall of Troy), perhaps Herodotus (Hdt. 7.27.2) and/or Chares of Mytilene (preserved in Ath. 12.514F) and/or Amyntas the bematist (ibid.) in 19.48.7 (on the golden vine), Diyllus (*BNJ* 73 F 1) in 19.52.5, Homer (Hom. *Il*. 11.236) in 19.53.5, Theophrastus (Thphr. *HP* 9.6.1–4) in 19.98.4 (on balsam). Next to these, Pompeius Trogus may perhaps

---

[51] Referring to the relevant articles in the *RE* as well as to Schubert 1914.

also be included among at least Diodorus' secondary sources, as might be surmised on the basis of 19.2.6–7 (see Just. 22.1.2–6); 19.5.4 (Just. 22.2.1–7); 19.6.4 (Just. 22.2.10); 19.11.1 (Just. 14.5.1–5); 19.11.7 (Just. 14.5.9–10); 19.35.4–36 (Just. 14.6.1–5); 19.43.8–9 (Just. 14.3.11–4.21); 19.49.1 (Just. 14.6.2–5); 19.51.5 (Just. 14.6.9–11); 19.52.1 (Just. 14.6.13); 19.52.4 (Just. 14.6.13);[52] 19.57.1–3 (Just. 15.1.1–5); 19.81.2–85.3 (Just. 15.1.6–9); 19.102.7 (Just. 22.3.1–8); 19.105.2 (Just. 15.2.5); and 19.106.2 (Just. 22.3.6).[53] In the aftermath of the Battle of Gabiene (19.43.7–9) too, we recognise much that resembles Just. 14.3.6–11, even though the story in the *Epitome* (see also 14.4) is, like Nepos' *Life of Eumenes* 10, much more dramatic than Diodorus' account.[54] At the same time (acknowledging and repeating the provisos), we might also point to Cornelius Nepos as a potential secondary source-author for 19.38.2 (Nep. *Eum.* 9). Whether Diodorus also used Aristotle (Arist. *Mu.* 398A30–5) as (additional) source for the use of light beacons cannot be ascertained at all. The same conclusion goes to some extent for Timaeus: his story of the bull of Phalaris (*BNJ* 566 F 28b.4–5, taken from Polybius; see 19.108.1; also Plb. 12.25) strongly suggests that Diodorus does not use him as a source-author for this part of the *Bibliotheca*.[55] Like the previous book, book 19 also offers, thus, a varied picture of potential source-authors, accepting the general idea that Hieronymus of Cardia at least looks like the most likely candidate as principal source-author.

It is assumed that this conclusion also goes for book 20 (ranging from 310–302): Goukowsky (2002b: xii), Bizière (2002: xv), and Geer (1969: vii) at least suggest as much, the last two explicitly, Goukowsky implicitly. Nevertheless, for this book too it is possible to suggest a few additional sources. Among the feasible sources

---

[52] Part of the uproar around the uncovering of the impressive Casta tumulus at Amphipolis in 2013–14 was caused by the fact that some believed that Roxane and/or her son had been interred there. Hephaestion, one of Alexander the Great's companions, was also suggested as the person the Casta tumulus had been constructed for. At the time of writing (February 2016), no certainty whatsoever has been reached regarding the original occupant(s) of this complex, though most details seem to suggest that the tumulus was constructed in the last quarter of the fourth century BC.

[53] There are, however, probably as many instances in this book in which Diodorus deviates from Pompeius Trogus' account as presented by Justin (for example: 19.67.5–6 vs. Just. 15.2.1–2): we cannot, therefore, be certain that Diodorus really used Pompeius Trogus (if we accept that Justin's epitome more or less correctly reflects the *Philippica*). As stipulated before, Diodorus and Pompeius Trogus may have used a, so far unknown, communal source-author.

[54] At the same time Diodorus' account is sometimes much more dramatic than the story in the *Epitome*, like, for example, the story of the rise to power of Agathocles (19.2.2–3.2).

[55] In 13.90.4–7, Diodorus asserts that he himself had seen this bull, returned to Acragas by P. Cornelius Scipio *Africanus* after the sack of Carthage in 202: see also 20.71.3.

(once again: with all possible provisos) is Cn. Pompeius Trogus, for example for the first part of Agathocles' expedition into Libya (ending with 20.18.3; see Just. 22.4.1–7.3). For Agathocles' life and career Diodorus may also have used the works of Timaeus of Tauromenium (not Syracuse, as Diodorus writes in 21.16.5!), Callias of Syracuse (*BNJ* 564; also Ath. 12.542A), and/or Antander of Syracuse (*BNJ* 565), who was Agathocles' brother according to Diodorus 21.16.5.[56] As in previous books, in book 20 too Euripides is referred to again (E. *IT* 625–6 in 20.14.6). Diodorus returns to events in Sicily and North Africa from 20.29.2 to 20.34.7, followed by an account of events in Italy to 20.36.6, resuming his account of Sicily and North Africa in *caput* 38. In these *capita* only relatively little information can be linked, to the best of my knowledge, with known sources,[57] apart from potential connections between 20.41.3–42.5 and Duris of Samos (*FGrH*/*BNJ* 76 F 17); 20.41.6 and again Euripides (*TGF*, Euripides, 922);[58] 20.42.3 and Just. 22.7.5; and 20.43.1–44.6 and Just. 22.7.6–11.

Diodorus resumes the story about the East and Macedonia in 20.19.1 (with a short interlude on Italy in 20.26.3–4). For this story, too, Hieronymus of Cardia should be considered as Diodorus' principal source. Unlike Chamoux and Bertrac (1993: xxiv), I do not think of Marsyas of Pella as a source for this part, though his name and (principal?) work are referred to by Diodorus in 20.50.4. The résumé of Marsyas' work in the *Suda* (*s.v. mu,227*), accepting – as we must, due to lack of evidence to the contrary – that it is correct, makes unmistakably clear that it could add nothing to the events described here.[59] If Marsyas had written additional works, not documented in the *Suda* (and he really could have written a fascinating inside account for this period, being not merely – allegedly – the

---

[56] Roller, *BNJ*, commentary on F 7: 'With at least two apologists at his court (Kallias and Antandros [*BNJ* 565], see F 6) as well as one exceedingly hostile opponent (Timaios [*BNJ* 566]), the tyrant [Agathocles] has been portrayed as unscrupulous, lawless, pious, and humane. These contradictions were established as soon as he died: Diodoros (21.17), aware of these issues, felt that all three historians were hopelessly biased and saw more virtue than fault in Agathokles.' Notably, Diodorus' criticism of Timaeus is very sharply formulated: τὰ πολλὰ κατέψευσται τοῦ δυνάστου διὰ τὴν πρὸς αὐτὸν ἔχθραν ('the majority is lying propaganda against the ruler through his hostility against him': 21.17.1). In itself, Timaeus being one of Agathocles' victims and banished by him from Sicily, Timaeus' attitude to Agathocles is not altogether surprising. Champion's remark in the 'Biographical Essay' (*BNJ* 565), stating Antander wrote a history of Agathocles' career, is not warranted by the evidence he adduces.

[57] However, 20.40.1 seems to contradict Just. 22.7.4 regarding the initiator of the alliance.

[58] The name of the play from which the line that Diodorus refers to originates is unknown.

[59] Though the *Suda* mentions several historians/authors by the name of Marsyas (namely *mu,227* through to *mu,230*), the additional information provided by Diodorus makes clear that only the first of the four mentioned in the *Suda* could be intended by him.

half-brother of Antigonus, but also directly involved in the events), Diodorus would probably have referred to it if he had seen them. On the basis of such indirect proof I, as yet, have to dismiss the work of Marsyas as a source for book 20 (and as a source for books 19, 18, and the second part of book 17, roughly the part after the foundation of Egyptian Alexandria). Here, as well, Trogus (or their communal source) may have inspired Diodorus (see 20.19.1 and Just. 15.2.1; 20.20.1 and Just. 11.10.2, 13.2.7 (not 12.10.9!); 20.28.2-3 and Just. 15.2.3).[60] In *caput* 37 Diodorus briefly resumes his story of the East and again in *caput* 45, ending in 20.53.4. For these parts I could not find any potential additional source-author for Diodorus' account.

The career of Agathocles and his supporters and/or relatives (probably based upon the same sources as Diodorus used for the previous part)[61] is first followed from 20.54.1 onwards to 20.72.5; then from 20.77.1 through to 20.79.5;[62] next from 20.89.1-90.2; and from 20.101.1 to 20.101.4 (to be continued in book 21). At least part of the story of the second Libyan campaign of Agathocles (20.64.1-69.5) seems based upon Pompeius Trogus (see Just. 22.8.4-15). Some of the events in Italy (esp. 20.104.3) appear to be founded on the work of Duris of Samos (*FGrH/BNJ* 76 F 18 = Ath. 13.605E). The East (including Greece) figures in 20.73.1-77.1; next in 20.81.1-88.9; in 20.91.1-100.7; in 20.102.1-103.7; and in 20.106.1-113.5. As regards 20.106.1-2, there seems to be a parallel with Pompeius Trogus (see Just. 15.2.12, 15, 17), but in general there are few firm indications for source-authors used by Diodorus in this book beyond this.

E. FRAGMENTS BOOKS 21-32

These books are, as previously underlined, like books 33-40, only fragmentarily transmitted, most prominently in various books of the *Excerpta Constantiniana*. As Goukowsky observes (Goukowsky 2006: 6-7), it looks probable that part of the sources used for book 20 was also used for the composition of book 21, discussing events

---

[60] Though Just. 15.1.1 mentions the death of Polypercon (*sic*), Yardley 1994: 138 note 1 remarks that this should be the death of Craterus: Polyperchon lived at least until the end of the fourth century BC. See also Heckel 2009: 226-31 *s.v.*

[61] The information that Utica would have deserted Carthage (20.54.2) is contradicted by Polybius 1.82.8.

[62] In the description of the events in the latter paragraph, to be dated to 306, Diodorus acknowledges a difference between the *datum* he provides and the information provided by Timaeus. Just. 22.8.15 provides no exact information, only mentions that an agreement was reached.

between 301 and 281 (Goukowsky 2006: 3–4). We should think of the accounts of the Diadochs and of Agathocles. Diodorus also mentions other source-authors: the *Universal History* in twenty-six books by Diyllus of Athens, continued in thirty books, now completely lost, by his successor Psaon of Plataea (21.5.1; Goukowsky 2006: Fr. 13). In 21.6.1 we are told of information provided by Duris of Samos:[63] as Diodorus is known to have used that author before, we might surmise he served here as source-author as well, even though (as Goukowsky 2006: 10 asserts): '[r]ien ne permet d'affirmer que Diodore utilisait Timée et Douris plus que Callias et Antandros'. As regards Duris, this could be especially true for Agathocles' attitude to democratic institutions: in cols. 2 and 4 of *P.Oxy* 2399, a papyrus dating to the first century BC and believed to preserve part of a history of Sicily under Agathocles,[64] we are informed that Agathocles has never suspended the functioning of democratic institutions (as Diodorus seems to imply). In book 21 we may again find evidence for Diodorus using (the same source-author as) Pompeius Trogus, namely in 21.7.1 (= Goukowsky 2006: 18, Fr. 16; see Just. 16.1.7–8), albeit that the situation there is a little clearer than in the heavily condensed version of Diodorus. Of 21.8.1 (= Goukowsky 2006: 18–19, Fr. 17.5) too, we may find a somewhat fuller account in Trogus (see Just. 23.2.3–4), though here as well the return of Agathocles to Syracuse is discussed. It is surprising, however, that the (long) illness of Agathocles is nowhere mentioned by Diodorus, even at the point of Agathocles' demise in 21.16.4: we may, therefore, rightly wonder whether Diodorus here really uses Pompeius Trogus (or the latter's source). As Goukowsky (2006: 25 note 79) remarks, to include this source would ruin the idea of poisoning that Diodorus brings forward.

Though Diodorus frequently seems to favour melodramatic effects, the melodrama brought forward in the history of Pompeius Trogus as epitomised by Justin on Agathocles' demise, its cause,

---

[63] Duris' account ran no further than the death of Philip, the son of Cassander (see *P.Oxy.* 2082, F. 3 lines 22–3; also 16.76.6). As the remark in 16.14.5 entails that Duris' story treated τὰς ... γενομένας πράξεις περί τε τὴν Ἑλλάδα καὶ τὴν Σικελίαν ('the events regarding Greece and Sicily'), Goukowsky 2006: 17 note 30 believes that it excludes events in Asia (and/or Asia Minor, even though that was part of the Greek world) and that Diodorus, for the story of those areas, had to rely on another source, namely Hieronymus of Cardia. For Duris and his influence, see Naas and Simon 2016: *passim*.

[64] The editor of this papyrus, Eric Turner (in Lobel et al. 1957: 99 *sqq.*), describes this text as written by an anonymous author, adding between brackets that it may have been written by Duris. Manni 1966 suggests the author might have been Antandrus, while Cavallaro 1977: 51–9, believes the text represents a fragment of Callias. Goukowsky 2006: 196 *ad* note 92 appears to discredit the latter suggestions as 'incontrôlable' and 'invérifiable'.

and follow-up was obviously lost on Diodorus (Just. 23.2.3–12, especially paragraphs 9 and 10), just as its logic has been lost on modern hypotheses regarding Agathocles' final political enterprises (Goukowsky 2006: 26 note 88). The return of the Carthaginians described by Diodorus in 21.18 (= Goukowsky 2006: 30 Fr. 32.2) resembles that of Trogus (Just. 23.2.13) much more than one would anticipate after the previous paragraphs. The murder of Agathocles' son, described in 21.16.3 (= Goukowsky 2006: 25, Fr. 29.3.5), also looks to come close to the version preserved in Just. 23.2.5. Viewing the whole picture of book 21, however, the relationship between the works of Diodorus and Pompeius Trogus in this book admittedly seems dimmer than in previous books, perhaps partly due to the fragmentary form in which both works have been preserved.

In this turmoil of possible relationships between works (see Chamoux and Bertrac 1993: xxiv), it should be noted that the sentiments expressed in 21.12d (= Goukowsky 2006: 22 Fr. 24) regarding the frugality and other virtues of certain peoples are a recurring *topos* in Greek literature, starting as early as Homer (Hom. *Il.* 13.6) and certainly very present in the work of one of Diodorus' most prominent principal sources, namely Ephorus (*FGrH/BNJ* 70 F 42). The situation described in 21.18.1 (= Goukowsky 2006: 31, Fr. 32.5–6), where the people of Messana welcomed the mercenaries, only to be put to the sword by them at night, is largely confirmed by Polybius (1.7.2), who adds that the mercenaries were Campanians. Whether Diodorus really used Polybius here, however, eludes us.

For book 22, accounting for the period 280–265 (Goukowsky 2006: 39), Diodorus appears to have used mainly Timaeus and Hieronymus of Cardia and a source not used by many others, that is Proxenus of Epirus (Goukowsky 2006: 41), for the composition of the story of King Pyrrhus of Epirus. Diodorus' source-author(s) for the Celtic invasion elude(s) us: though several authors might qualify, we have no corroborating evidence to guide us. For the period after Pyrrhus too, several source-authors qualify: Philinus of Acragas[65] (either directly or through Silenus), Silenus himself, perhaps Fabius Pictor, and I believe even Polybius may have contributed as source-author to this book of the *Bibliotheca*.[66] Whether Diodorus quotes

---

[65] Occasionally also referred to, for example by Goukowsky, as Philinus of Agrigentum. As Agrigentum is the Roman denomination for Acragas, I believe it to be more appropriate to refer to this author as Philinus of Acragas. It is also the name Diodorus himself uses for this author (see 23.8.1 below).

[66] See Goukowsky 2006: 42–5; see Plb. 3.25.1–5 for the naval clauses in 22.7.5 = Goukowsky 2006: 63 Fr. 15; the surrender by some of the Mamertines at Messana to the Carthaginians

the epigram referred to in 22.11.1 (= Goukowsky 2006: 71 Fr. 23), ascribed to Leonidas of Tarentum (AP 6.130), directly or through another source cannot be established. Further, as might be expected, some local knowledge of the situation in Sicily shines through, as in 22.2.2 (= Goukowsky 2006: 58 Fr. 3.2; see also note 29).

The presents referred to in 22.6.3 (= Goukowsky 2006: 61 Fr. 10) are mentioned, *inter alios*, by Pompeius Trogus (Just. 18.2.7–8): whether Diodorus was influenced in any way by this reference eludes us. The same goes for the remark on the age of the Macedonian King Ptolemy (22.3.1 = Goukowsky 2006: 59 Fr. 5; Just. 24.4.1); the fate of Ptolemy fighting the Celts (22.3.2 = Goukowsky 2006: 59 Fr. 6; Pomp. Trog. *Proleg.* 24; Just. 24.5.5–6); the role of Sosthenes (22.4.1 = Goukowsky 2006: 59 *Testimonium*; Just. 24.5.12–13); Carthage taking the initiative after Agathocles' death (22.8.1 = Goukowsky 2006: 63–4 Fr. 17b.1; Just. 23.2.13); the Syracusans asking the help of Pyrrhus (22.8.2 = Goukowsky 2006: 64 Fr. 17b.2; Just. 23.3.1); the problems facing the Celts under Brennus in Greece, regrettably an account partly lost in a lacuna (22.9.1 = Goukowsky 2006: 66 Fr. 19.1; Just. 24.6.1–4; see also Goukowsky 2006: 211 *ad* p. 66 note 103); the suicide of Brennus at Delphi (22.9.2 = Goukowsky 2006: 66 Fr. 19.2; Just. 24.8.11); and the death of all the Celts during their march through the territory of the Dardanians (22.9.3 = Goukowsky 2006: 67 Fr. 19.3.2; Just. 24.8.16). Naturally, the versions of events presented in Justin's *Epitome* and Diodorus' *Bibliotheca* also regularly differ, but the main point of the exercise we set out to undertake was to look for similarities, not differences.

In book 23 Diodorus treats the years 264–251 (see Goukowsky 2006: 81). As this book is linked to the events discussed in the previous one, most of Diodorus' source-authors for it are the same as for book 22: Philinus of Acragas, perhaps Fabius Pictor, perhaps Polybius (for example, the disheartenment of the Carthaginians in 23.13.1 = Goukowsky 2006: 104 Fr. 13; Plb. 1.31.1–3 – though Polybius puts another emphasis on the events, as he does in Plb. 1.32.4–5 on the Spartan Xanthippus: see 23.14.1 = Goukowsky 2006: 104–5 Fr. 14), perhaps – as a new source-author – the Roman Annalist L. Cincius Alimentus,[67] possibly Silenus of Cale

---

in 22.13.7 = Goukowsky 2006: 75 Fr. 26.7.4–5; see Plb. 1.10.1–2; the agreement between the Carthaginians and Hiero in 22.13.9 = Goukowsky 2006: 75 Fr. 26.9; see Plb. 1.11.7.

[67] A Roman annalist and jurist, *praetor* in Sicily in 209 and captured by the Carthaginians. He spent years as their prisoner, during which he apparently got information from them, and wrote, *inter alia*, an account of his imprisonment, probably as part of his *Annals* (see Liv. 21.38.3–4; Breisach, 2007: 44–5; see also Goukowsky 2006: 85 note 23).

Acte, and probably quite considerable local knowledge and/or sentiments of Diodorus' own (Goukowsky 2006: 82–93). I find it remarkable that there are no straight parallels in Justin's *Epitome* for this book of the *Bibliotheca*, at least none that I could point to.

Book 24 is devoted to the years 250–241 (Goukowsky 2006: 117), ending with the treaty between Carthage and Rome. All preserved fragments are related, one way or another, to the First Punic War, presenting in those very fragments a view that is rather more favourable to the Carthaginians than to the Romans.[68] All the source-authors we have already encountered in book 23 also appear in this book, including Philinus of Acragas – who is even mentioned by name in 24.11.2 (= Goukowsky 2006: 132 Fr. 14.4) – a reference that constitutes an extremely valid counterargument for my idea that he perhaps might have died in 255. Other source-authors, though, have been left anonymous. The same goes for personal observations by Diodorus, like the one on Acellum (24.1.10 = Goukowsky 2006: 128 Fr. 2.10): one merely observes it is there. As in book 23, Justin's *Epitome* does not serve here either as source-author for Diodorus.

In the fragments of book 25 too, which begin with a reference to the *Principal Doctrines* of Epicurus,[69] Carthage, notably its wars and conquests, occupies an important place, but events in Greece proper are also accounted for. The book relates events between 240 and 219. Diodorus' main source-author for the African War has, at least since Dindorf, been credited as Polybius, who follows in his *Histories* here neither Philinus nor Fabius Pictor (see Goukowsky 2006: 141–2). Others believe both Polybius and Diodorus use the same source, be it Philinus, Silenus, or Sosylus (Goukowsky 2006: 142). Goukowsky believes, however, that Diodorus uses Polybius' work, augmented by a second source, probably an Annalist (Goukowsky 2006: 144–5; see also the remarks of Walton 1968: 152–3 note 1, 161 note 2). Schwartz believes that Diodorus follows a 'römische Annalistik schlechtester Sorte' (Schwartz 1903a: 688) for his account of Hamilcar's conquests, a judgement one might expect in view of Schwartz's general opinion of Diodorus' work. Goukowsky argues, however, that Diodorus combines the views of two authors, one focusing on the sequel of the First Punic War, the other on the prequel

---

[68] Goukowsky 2006: 120–1 rightly emphasises the fact that too little remains of book 24 to make final conclusions as regards Diodorus' point of view on the conflict.

[69] The reference is to: ὁ δίκαιος ἀταρακτότατος, ὁ δ'ἄδικος πλείστης ταραχῆς γήμων ('the just man is most free from disturbance, while the unjust is full of the utmost disturbance': Epicur. *Sent.* 17).

of the Second Punic War (Goukowsky 2006: 145–6). Authors that might qualify include Sosylus of Elis (or Lacedaemon) and Silenus of Cale Acte,⁷⁰ and probably here, too, we might include L. Cincius Alimentus among Diodorus' potential source-authors. As for the account of the Second Punic War, Diodorus largely appears to have followed that of an Annalist: Goukowsky again proposes L. Cincius Alimentus here, a convenient source-author for Diodorus because he wrote in Greek, like Fabius Pictor (Goukowsky 2006: 148; also Goukowsky 2002c: lxxix–lxxx).

Book 26 describes the events from 218–207. It opens with a proem in which Diodorus observes that every practitioner of the Arts meets with people who disagree with what he or she has created. Though Diodorus mentions a few names of authors/rhetors, the tenor is, I think, too general to allow conclusions. Most of the remaining transmitted fragments of this book describe the methodical destruction of Italy by the Carthaginian army, but other theatres of war also pass in review: Spain, Africa, and Sicily. Additionally, the conflict between Philip V of Macedon and the Aetolian League is, briefly, paid attention to. As source-authors Diodorus himself mentions Menodotus of Perinthus and Sosylus of Elis (or Lacedaemon).⁷¹ It is remarkable that for this book Diodorus appears to have neglected Polybius (almost) completely, but relies on (an) annalistic source(s). As for the developments in Sicily, Diodorus appears to rely on sources that Polybius describes as excessive (see Plb. 7.7.1, 4), perhaps an author like Bato of Sinope (see Ath. 6.251EF = *FGrH/BNJ* 268 F4), an author who also wrote a now entirely lost *Persica* (*FGrH/BNJ* 268 T1), or possibly even Eumachus of Neapolis, who in his *History of Hannibal* also wrote about the Sicilian ruler Hieronymus (*FGrH/ BNJ* 178 F1; see also Goukowsky 2006: 169). Goukowsky also, rightly I believe, observes that Diodorus in general and certainly

---

⁷⁰ See Nep. *Han.* 13.3: *hvivs belli gesta mvlti memoriae prodidervnt, sed ex eis dvo, qvi cvm eo in castris fvervnt simvlque vixervnt, qvamdiu fortvna passa est, Silenvs et Sosylvs Lacedaemonivs* ('Many have passed on the acts of this war to memory, but two of them, who were with him [Hannibal] in the barracks and lived in the same period, as long as Fate allowed, namely Silenus and Sosylus the Lacedaemonian'). For the work of Sosylus see, for example, *FGrH/BNJ* 176 F 1. See also below, note 71.

⁷¹ Μηνόδοτος δὲ ὁ Περίνθιος τὰς Ἑλληνικὰς πραγματείας ἔγραψεν ἐν βιβλίοις πεντεκαίδεκα, Σώσιλος δὲ ὁ Ἠλεῖος τὰ περὶ Ἀννίβαν ἔγραψεν ἐν βιβλίοις ἑπτά ('Menodotus of Perinthus wrote a work *The Greek Affairs* in fifteen books, Sosylus of Elis a *History of Hannibal* in seven books': 26.4.1 = Goukowsky 2006: 176 Fr. 7a). As a matter of fact, Goukowsky reads, instead of Ἠλεῖος ('of Elis'), Λακεδαιμόνιος ('of Lacedaemon'), referring to Flavius Vegetius (namely *De re milit.* 3.*Praef.*): I find this reference inconclusive, remarkably regarding Nepos (see note 70 above). For Menodotus, see *FGrH/BNJ* 82; for Sosylus *FGrH/BNJ* 176. The reading Ἴλιος ('of Ilium') instead of Ἠλεῖος ('of Elis'), as Hoeschel and Rhodoman suggest, is, to the best of my knowledge, not supported by other literary evidence.

as regards Sicilian matters follows a source that is favourable to Rome and more specifically to Marcellus (Goukowsky 2006: 170). Whether Goukowsky is right to suggest Diodorus' attitude could have risen from some dependency relation (*patronus–cliens*, even?) with great Roman families – like the Marcelli – cannot be proven – or disproven (see Goukowsky 2006: 170 note 25; also Goukowsky 2014: 292: 'le vrai problème ... est ... plutôt de chercher le Romain de haut rang dont il était devenu le client et les cercles qu'il fréquentait'). In this respect I refer to statements I made previously:

> Diodorus himself is likely to have been quite well off. He travelled to Egypt and met over there with priests and embassies (D.S. III.xi.3) and remained for a prolonged period at Rome. Nothing suggests that he earned himself a living in Rome by tutoring, as most other Greek intellectuals had to do. His criticism of the middle class (D.S. I.lxxiv.7) suggests wealth, though he may well have been less hostile to democracy than he is usually portrayed. It is, however, his prejudice that in democracies masses – as they are easily swayed – facilitate the rise of demagogues (Sacks 1990, 167 and note 39). Both his travels and his political sentiments suggest he enjoyed independent wealth. Despite this, Diodorus does not appear to have socialised with Romans of his social class. (Stronk 2010: 61)

Book 27 essentially covers the years 206–201 and ends with the victory of P. Cornelius Scipio *Africanus* at Zama. The book appears, though, not to focus entirely on the Punic War, be it in Spain, Italy, or Sicily, but to pay ample attention to developments in Greece as well – even when this necessitated going somewhat back in time to before 206. It is difficult to assign a principal source-author for the latter part of this book, if only because the relevant period is preserved as fragmentarily in Polybius' *Histories* as in Diodorus' *Bibliotheca*. Wherever both have been transmitted, however, notable differences show, for example between 27.1.1 and Plb. 13.6.1–11, suggesting Diodorus does not use Polybius as a source-author for this book. Because Diodorus showed in previous books too that he frequently uses more than one source-author, I am less adamant than Goukowsky as regards Polybius' role as a source for this book, especially because he features prominently as such in the following books.[72] It is, though, impossible to identify Diodorus' source-author(s) positively: all we can surmise is that they definitely include a source that has not been

---

[72] The use by Diodorus of οἱ καχέκται ('the unsatisfied') in 27.11.1 (= Goukowsky 2012: 24 Fr. 14a) might be an indication that he does indeed use Polybius as one of his sources. Diodorus uses the word καχεξία ('disaffection') only once before in the preserved fragments of the *Bibliotheca* (namely in 13.36.5 on the Athenians' Sicilian disaster), whereas Polybius uses καχέκτης, precisely in the context of 'disgruntled', 'dissatisfied', some four times (see also Goukowsky 2012: 24 note 48).

influenced by the propaganda of the Achaean League at the time of Philip V (see Goukowsky 2012: 3–14).

Regarding the events involving Rhodes (like 27.3.1 = Goukowsky 2012: 19 Fr. 4), however, we may surmise that Diodorus may well have relied upon Zeno of Rhodes (see Goukowsky 2012: ix; also above on book 5). As for the account of the Punic War, Diodorus follows the same source-author(s) as in the preceding book. An additional source for Diodorus may have been the work (a Roman history, precise title unknown, probably written in Greek, now lost) of A. Postumius Albinus (who was a consul in 151), and of which the quite damaged remains of *P.Rylands* III 491 might be a fragment.[73] However, it seems the works of all source-authors Diodorus may have used are lost and any identification is, therefore, impossible (see Goukowsky 2012: 15). Naturally, the preserved fragments also include potential references to other works, like λεγόμενον ἄρρητα ('unutterable'), which might well remind Diodorus' readers of Sophocles' phrase ἄρρητ'ἀρρήτων ('unspeakable'; S. *OT* 465). In these fragments they seem, though, very rare.

In book 28 Diodorus takes up the story of the enmity between Rome and Philip V of Macedon (and, consequently, Antiochus III, due to a secret agreement between those two rulers: see Plb. 15.20.1–8, also Plb. 16.9.8–9) in an account that ranges from 200 to 193. Typical of one of Diodorus' confessed intentions, namely the distribution of 'blame and fame', are *capita* 28.2–3. In this Diodorus differs from Polybius: whereas the latter ascribes much of one's success to Fate, the former believes success primarily follows from morality. Though there seems to be much that Diodorus derives from Polybius, a suggestion advocated, for example, by Schwartz (1903a: 689–90) and repeated as recently as 1999 by Perlman,[74] there are important differences that force us to doubt too direct a connection between these two (see Goukowsky 2012: 38–40). There is, though, a similarity between the accounts of Diodorus and Appian: this leads Goukowsky to surmise an intermediary between Polybius and these two authors, a man like P. Rutilius Rufus (Goukowsky 2012: 43 and note 50).

What remains clear in book 28 is the negative image of Philip

---

[73] See Goukowsky 2012: 15; see also Plb. 39.1.1–4 for an assessment of this man, not quite unbiased, though; for *P.Rylands* see: Hoyos 2001.
[74] Perlman 1999: 132 as regards Diodorus' 27.3.1. Perlman believes Diodorus relies on Polybius, who relies on Zeno for events involving Rhodes, not acknowledging that one of Diodorus' source-authors is this very Zeno of Rhodes, as appears, *inter alia*, from book 5 of the *Bibliotheca* (see also above note 16).

V painted by Diodorus, of which the origin may well lie in Philip's invasion of Attica. This invasion led to a vehement reaction in Athens, such that Livy stated that *Athenienses qvidem litteris verbisqve ... bellvm adversvm Philippvm gerebant* ('the Athenians conducted a war in words and writing ... against Philip': Liv. 31.44.9). This reaction, perhaps suggesting an Attic-inspired source, we find to some extent preserved in Polybius' relatively balanced account. In Diodorus' version the tables are switched: though Philip had received a good education that would have enabled him to become a good king, the influences of bad counsellors changed all that for the worse (see, for example, 28.2.1 = Goukowsky 2012: 50–1 Fr. 2; 28.3.1 = Goukowsky 2012: 51 Fr. 3). Such a set phrase is typical of Hellenistic authors, and I think that in this respect Diodorus is a typical example of the kind.[75] It appears, moreover, that 28.3.1 especially announces a new era or, as Goukowsky phrases it, that:

> La cent quarante-cinquième Olympiade [the period between 200–197] marquait en quelque sorte, pour Diodore, la fin de l'ère des bons héritiers d'Alexandre et le début de celle des bons Romains, leurs affrontements sous le regard sourcilleux de la Justice divine [a typical set phrase for Diodorus] fournissant la matière des livres suivants. (Goukowsky 2012: 48)

Whether this change in subject is reflected in a change of (the type of) source-authors is a matter we will discuss below.

In book 29, the story from the start of the war against Antiochus III up to the brink of the Third Macedonian War, the period 192–181, is related. At least for some fragments of Diodorus a serious investigation makes clear that, though there are several points of correspondence between Polybius and Diodorus, the latter in all likelihood does not always use Polybius directly for his account of the war against Antiochus III, but, as it appears more frequently than not, uses him through an intermediary, possibly an Annalist writing in Greek (see Goukowsky 2012: 63–4). Occasionally the connection between Appian and Diodorus reappears, supporting this suggestion.[76] We can also observe Diodorus' moral views taking the upper hand in some of the fragments, for example in 29.2.1 (= Goukowsky 2012: 80–1 Fr. 2). It makes me believe that Schwartz's suggestion, mentioned above, for the relation between Polybius and Diodorus cannot be maintained in its absoluteness for this part of book 29 either.

---

[75] See Pédech, 1964: 234; see also Goukowsky 2012: 47 and note 68.
[76] See 29.8.1 (= Goukowsky 2012: 84 Fr. 10) and App. *Syr.* 29.146; possibly also 29.10.1 (= Goukowsky 2012: 84–5 Fr. 12) and App. *Syr.* 38.198; see also Goukowsky 2012: 66–7, 69 for a more elaborate analysis.

Regarding the story of the end of the reign of Philip V too, the problems mount. Goukowsky refers to a remark by André Aymard,[77] who compares this part of the *Bibliotheca* with the (preserved) account of Polybius on this period (Plb. 22.7.2–14): 'Si les faits les plus simples sont ainsi déformés, que pouvait-il advenir des details ... relatifs aux institutions?', concluding that it would be 'impossible d'essayer d'utiliser' Diodorus' account. Livy, however, presents us with an account that differs from Polybius', emphasising the importance of the second of two Roman embassies, one in 185, another in 184, to Greece. As it appears, Diodorus has combined the *data* of these two embassies, minimising the importance of the first – which was highlighted by Polybius – and stressing the second: as Goukowsky remarks: 'un annaliste romain ... pourrait avoir procédé à l'amalgame des deux ambassades successives, reproduit ensuite par Diodore'. This picture seems to be reinforced by the account of the embassy of Eumenes II. On this embassy the versions of Polybius and Diodorus vary hugely as well (for an analysis see Goukowsky 2012: 72–4), again suggesting Diodorus does not follow Polybius on this issue either. An identical conclusion goes for 29.17.1–21.1 (= Goukowsky 2012: 88–92 Frr. 21–4; see also 74–5).

Though for 29.22.1 (= Goukowsky 2012: 92 Fr. 25) there are some similarities with Polybius' version (Plb. 24.5.1–2), there are notable differences, too. As for 29.23.1–24.1 (= Goukowsky 2012: 92–3 Frr. 26–7) no definite conclusions are possible, but again in 29.28.1 and 29.26.1 (= Goukowsky 2012: 93–4 Frr. 29–30) a considerable divergency from Polybius' version shows: here some echo of Diodorus' words may be found in Appian's account (App. *Hisp.* 42–3). Reviewing the fragments of book 29 as they are, I can find no support at all for Schwartz's conclusion that Diodorus starts from Polybius' account, and I cannot but agree with Goukowsky's that 'il n'en est qu'un seul que l'on puisse supposer directement inspiré de Polybe' (Goukowsky 2012: 76). As for Goukowsky's suggestion (Goukowsky 2012: 76–8) that the last parts of book 29 actually belong to book 30, I am less sure than he is: it is striking, though, that notably in 29.31.1–34.2 (Goukowsky 2012: 95–7 Frr. 34–8) Diodorus' account appears to be fairly close to Polybius': Goukowsky (2012: 8) also observes 'il le [Polybius] résume sans le défigurer ni rien perdre de ses outrances'. It is, nevertheless, insufficient by far, in my view, to vindicate Schwartz.

---

[77] Aymard 1938: 156 note 4. He, too, starts his comparison from the assumption that Schwartz was right and that Diodorus' account is derived from Polybius' *Histories*.

In book 30, Diodorus guides his readers through the years 180–168, paying most attention to what is known as the Persian War. Goukowsky believes that this book actually started with the succession to the Macedonian throne by King Perseus (in 179: see Goukowsky 2012: 101) and should have included the fragments of book 29 starting with 29.30.1 (= Goukowsky 2012: 95 Fr. 33), but he admits that it would be too confusing to adapt the traditional partition of the books. Another topic discussed in this book is the renewal of the struggle between the Seleucids and the Lagides, the Sixth Syrian War. To this end, Diodorus uses several source-authors. Though it might at first sight seem that he uses Polybius as his source for 30.1.1 (= Goukowsky 2012: 108 Fr. 1), it appears that he actually may well have used the same source as Appian (see App. *Mac.* Fr. 11.9). Though 30.2.1 (= Goukowsky 2012: 108–9 Fr. 2) looks to be an epitome of Polybius, this cannot be stated with certainty regarding 30.3.1 and 30.4.1 (Goukowsky 2012: 109 Frr. 3–4). The latter cannot be linked with any source-author at all; for the former a comparison with Polybius could do, even though the emphases are differing. The same can be stated *a fortiori* regarding 30.5.1 (Goukowsky 2012: 110 Fr. 5), while the following chapter, again, cannot be linked with any other known source.

As for 30.7.1 (= Goukowsky 2012: 111 Fr. 7) the source-author might have been Polybius (but the relevant part of the *Histories* is lost) or an Annalist. For 30.7.2 (= Goukowsky 2012: 111 Fr. 8) there is, again, no known counterpart, just as there is none for 30.8.1 (= Goukowsky 2012: 111–12 Fr. 9), which is an expression of one of Diodorus' own views. In the following fragments of this book too we can discern a mixture of source-authors (see Goukowsky 2012: 104–7): sometimes (strong) links with Polybius emerge, sometimes the same source as Appian uses turns up or the same one as Livy does, occasionally no known source at all is available, and at times Diodorus also expresses his own views, as in 30.21.3–4 (= Goukowsky 2012: 121 Frr. 27–8), 30.23.2 (= Goukowsky 2012: 123 Fr. 31), and perhaps also in parts of 30.22.1 (= Goukowsky 2012: 121–2 Fr. 29). Reviewing this book, it shows again that, with due respect, Schwartz's ideas are not to be followed without question. Goukowsky's conclusion is, therefore, absolutely in line with my own feelings (expressed in the Introduction): 'Il [Diodorus] composait son propre récit, assorti de commentaires personnels' (Goukowsky 2012: 107).

Though book 31 discusses the years 167–151, 31.1.1–2.2

(= Goukowsky 2012: 140–1 Frr. 1–2) appear to review some of the developments of the Sixth Syrian War. The period discussed here by Diodorus is described *in extenso* by Polybius in books 29–35 of the *Histories* (exclusive of book 34, a geography). If the former uses the work of the latter, as seems feasible for about half of the fragments making up what remains of this book, it is at a distance at best, Polybius' work being much too detailed to be of use for Diodorus' purposes. Goukowsky has compared all fragments of Diodorus' book 31, and his findings confirm much of the general impression one gains by reading these fragments and described above (see Goukowsky 2012: 130–5). Occasionally the abstracts of Polybius are – as usual – interspersed with the personal observations (often morally based) of Diodorus (see Goukowsky 2012: 131 on Fr. 14, 132 on Fr. 19). However, there are also a number of fragments for which Polybius is obviously not the source-author (see Goukowsky 2012: 135–8). Analysis of these fragments shows a variety of potential origins, few of them – regrettably – with a good degree of certainty. However, as for Diodorus' reports on the situation in Egypt, I believe we may surmise that he acquired part of his information during his stay there, even though there is no evidence to corroborate this view. As it stands, this book too seems to indicate that the traditional view of Diodorus, namely that of a lazy compiler, indiscriminately following the same source for a long time, a compiler moreover without any imagination, ideas, or personal qualities, needs to be readjusted. Goukowsky phrases it as follows: 'actualisation du modèle permet de redonner un peu de lustre à Diodore, si injustement méprisé' (Goukowsky 2012: 138).

Though the starting point of book 32 was established by Dindorf at 150, the endpoint is less certain, depending on the year of death of Ptolemy VI *Philometor* and Alexander I *Balas*. That year having been established now, we can conclude that the events described in book 32 extend to 145. It is the very year the *Chronicles* of Apollodorus of Athens (dedicated to Attalus II of Pergamum) reach their conclusion (see *FGrH/BNJ* 244). As Goukowsky (2012: 188) acknowledges, this is a work Diodorus is familiar with, as he is with that of Polybius, who discussed the years 150–146 in his books 36–8 (we have no fragment at all of book 37). Diodorus' debt to this/those book(s) is, therefore, hard to establish. Comparison for sources for this period is also impossible with the work of Livy (lost, while its *periochae* (in fact a list of contents) are not helpful at all). In addition, the works of Diodorus' potential direct source-authors, namely the *Histories* by Heraclides *Lembus* of Oxyrhynchus[78] (a contemporary of Ptolemy VI and Antiochus IV and, moreover, as a civil servant, as it seems, actively engaged in the developments of those days) and the work by Posidonius of Apamea, are completely lost (see Goukowsky 2012: 189 and notes 6 and 7).

In a number of fragments of this book Diodorus and Polybius do touch (see Goukowsky 2012: 189–93), sometimes in agreement, sometimes differing, occasionally adducing additional sources (as does Appian: see Goukowsky 2012: 190 *ad* Fr. 6 [= 32.6.1]). As regards the corresponding notions of Diodorus and Appian, Goukowsky expounds that these do not (always and/or necessarily) result from a common use of Polybius' work,[79] but might be the result of the common use of another source as well. As such a common source-author, Goukowsky, as a hypothesis, has suggested P. Rutilius Rufus (ibid.). However, the interpretations of their source(s) by Diodorus and Appian do not always run parallel, as Goukowsky (2012: 194) demonstrates with an example based upon 32.1.1–3.1 (= Goukowsky 2012: 198 Frr. 1 and 2, 200 Fr. 4). It shows, moreover, Diodorus working from a Sicilian point of view as a Roman subject in the latter days of the Roman Republic, a view the blinkered *Quellenforschung* has lost (Goukowsky 2012: 194). Though Goukowsky allows himself to be carried away a little too much on this point, I believe his view is nevertheless essentially right. Diodorus' unmistakable interests and qualities come forward clearly even in the abstract by Photius (Goukowsky 2012: 194–5). As regards this very *epitome* of Diodorus by Photius, I think Goukowsky is probably right in his assessment of some differences between the texts of Appian and Diodorus in the *data* concerning Carthage, pointing to potential scribal errors (see Goukowsky 2012: 195; Phot. *Bibl.* [244] 383b11–16 = 32.14.1 = Goukowsky 2012: 203–4 Fr. 10 *Testimonium*; App. *Pun.* 95–6).

F. FRAGMENTS BOOKS 33–40

As regards Diodorus' source(s) for books 33–40 some persistent positions have been held over the past century or so. I think it is right to discuss the most important of these in order to discuss the source-authors per book more fruitfully afterwards. Goukowsky (2014: x–xi) rightly observes that it is impossible that Diodorus based books

---

[78] See *Suda s.v. eta*,462; see also *OCD*[4] *s.v.* 'Heraclides [4]'.
[79] Goukowsky 2002c: lxxxvii–lxxxviii.

33–40 on Polybius' *Histories* and that the *Quellenforschung* has constructed true and impressive houses of cards in attempts to establish Diodorus' source-authors, in spite of 'the shipwreck of Hellenistic and Roman historiographies'. It has been suggested, most fervently by Georg Busolt,[80] that the work of Posidonius of Apamea (part of it preserved in forty-two fragments in Athenaeus' *Deipnosophists*) was, indeed, the basis for Diodorus' books 33–40. It is true that (to some extent like Diodorus) the Posidonius preserved in Athenaeus appears to have emphasised Eastern τρυφή ('softness', 'luxuriousness', 'daintiness'),[81] but we have no idea how he wrote history. As Goukowsky rightly observes, the mere fact that, like Diodorus, Posidonius was a moralist does not justify the conclusion that Diodorus based himself upon Posidonius (see Goukowsky 2014: xi). Moreover, as Sacks (1990: 22–3) has demonstrated, Diodorus' moral concepts are consistent throughout the *Bibliotheca* and do not (necessarily) rest upon Posidonius.

Nevertheless, even though Schwartz had to admit that only part of Diodorus' account in books 33–40 (namely the part on the First Servile War) appears to have been based upon Posidonius (see Schwartz 1903a: 690), Reinhardt ventured half a century later that Diodorus was largely inspired by Posidonius,[82] a position also vigorously (and, dare I state, quite blindly) defended by, for example, Strasburger[83] and, much more cautiously, by Ludwig Edelstein and Ian Kidd.[84] In the latter edition, Kidd mentions that Diodorus owes much to Posidonius, but nowhere mentions him as a source-author (Edelstein and Kidd 1989: xviii note 3). Though, as Goukowsky rightly observes, at least from 1979 onwards, certainty about the relationship between Posidonius and Diodorus started to falter (see Goukowsky 2014: xv–xviii), later scholars dealt quite sensibly with this. Without denying a *potential* (my emphasis) influence of Posidonius on Diodorus (quite obvious in the early books), they are, rightly, cautious in directly ascribing fragments of Diodorus to Posidonius as a source for this part of the *Bibliotheca*. Though

---

[80] Busolt 1890; see also, for example, Botteri 1992: 73.
[81] See notably Clarke 2007. For a full account of testimonies and fragments of Posidonius see Dowden, *BNJ*. For τρυφή see notably below, Chapter 10.
[82] Reinhardt 1953: 632–41.
[83] Strasburger 1965: 42: 'But the traces in the secondary tradition lead further down, most clearly in Diodoros, who based his universal history on Poseidonios continuously from book 32, that is from where his former source Polybios left off, to the end. As this is a certain and never seriously questioned result of source-criticism, Diodoros is, next to the fragments proper, our most valuable source for discovering what is characteristic of Poseidonios and thus identifying further fragments elsewhere in the secondary tradition.' See also Goukowsky 2014: xiv.
[84] Edelstein and Kidd 1989: xviii note 3.

Emmanuele Vimercati is undoubtedly at the beginning of this movement,[85] I firmly believe (as Goukowsky also suggests (2014: xix)) that Gerhard Wirth defines it best (see, for example, Wirth 2007: 115–16 and note 166). In my view, the direct link between Posidonius and Diodorus, as the evidence stands today, has to be waved aside here, though we should acknowledge the probability of an intellectual connection, as appears in the early books of the *Bibliotheca* (see above).

Another author believed to have influenced Diodorus (indirectly through Posidonius or even directly) for books 33–40 was P. Rutilius Rufus, a Roman patrician. One of the outspoken supporters of the theory that Rutilius Rufus had briefed Posidonius on the situation in Rome – and that in his turn Posidonius had influenced Diodorus – is Jürgen Malitz.[86] P. Rutilius Rufus started his military career in 134, as a member of the staff of P. Cornelius Scipio *Africanus Minor* during the Numantine War. Later on, Rufus was a legate of Q. Caecilius Metellus *Numidicus* in the campaign against King Iugurtha of Numidia of 109, along with C. Marius (whom he is said to have detested: Plu. *Mar.* 28.5). In 105 Rufus was elected to the consulship as a senior partner of Cn. Mallius Maximus. Subsequently, he served as legate to Q. Mucius Scaevola, governor of Asia. In 92, Rufus was charged with extortion, a charge that appears to have been false, but he was, nevertheless, convicted. Accepting the verdict as a Stoic, Rufus retired, first to Mytilene, afterwards to Smyrna, where he spent the rest of his life. Although invited by L. Cornelius Sulla to return to Rome, Rufus refused to do so. It was during his stay at Smyrna that he wrote his autobiography and a history of Rome in Greek. What we know of the style and contents of the work of Posidonius – and, for that matter, Diodorus – at the very least looks inconsistent with the information such a well-informed patrician would provide, even though, here again, we should leave open the possibility –relevant for us – that Diodorus may have taken some information from P. Rutilius Rufus after all (see also Goukowsky 2014: xxi–xxv).

Where I believe Goukowsky to be too critical of Diodorus is about the latter's ability and willingness to do research for his *Bibliotheca* in the libraries and/or archives at Alexandria and Rome (see, for example, the remarks of Diodorus in 1.4.2, 3.38.1). It is a point of underestimation of Diodorus by Goukowsky that returns in Goukowsky's discussion of book 40 (see below). Though we cannot

---

[85] Vimercati 2004.
[86] Malitz 1983: 324, 360–1, 368.

assume that Diodorus was personally acquainted with Agatharchides of Cnidus (the lifespans of the two lie too far apart from each other), the former was obviously well acquainted with the latter's work, as book 3 testifies. Of Agatharchides we know that he used to consult, for a time (see Phot. *Bibl.* [250] 460b11–13), the library of Alexandria. It could suggest Diodorus merely benefitted indirectly from work done in this institution. We simply do not have the ability, though, to check whether Diodorus himself did (some) work there and/or at institutions in Rome as well. We merely have to go where the evidence leads us. Diodorus informs us thrice that he had access to research materials in Alexandria and Rome (1.4.2–4; 3.38.1; 17.52.6), and – even acknowledging that this definitely would not have been an easy task[87] (even though Diodorus possibly was well connected: see above, Introduction), as Chamoux and Bertrac (1993: xx–xxi and note 44) agree –unless *evidence* (my emphasis) to the contrary emerges, we have to accept that as a *datum* for now (though without falling into positivism: accepting the written word as absolute truth), whether we like it or not (see Goukowsky 2014: xxv–xxx, who disagrees with this view).

Having discussed the general problems we face in the discussion of books 33–40 as a distinct group, it is now time to focus on these books one by one. Most of the remaining fragments of book 33 deal with the problems of Rome with the Iberians and Lusitanians, but (*inter alia*) also treat the war of Attalus II against the Thracian Caeni, allies of King Prusias II of Bithynia (see the prologue to book 36 of Pompeius Trogus), the beginning of the reign of Ptolemy VIII *Euergetes II* (*Physco* = 'Potbelly'), and the civil war in Syria. In general we can assume that the description of the events begins with those of about the year 145/4 (with a small excursus to 147) and that the latest events described in this book can be dated to around 137/6. Regrettably I cannot be more precise as regards the dates due to the nature of these fragments and our source material for comparison, though the period itself also created some additional uncertainties (Goukowsky 2014: 7–14). In spite of some similarities of Diodorus' fragments to some ascribed to Posidonius, I must concur with Goukowsky's conclusion (Goukowsky 2014: 16) that the problem of the sources cannot be solved unless a papyrological discovery provides us with sufficient new evidence.

---

[87] See, for example, below, section G, my remarks in Stronk 2014/15: 207 on the problems Plutarch, *inter alios*, faced.

The earliest events in the fragments to be ascribed to books 34/5[88] can be dated to about 135 (though book 34 probably started with the events of 138/7), the last one describing the defeat the Romans suffered at the hands of the Cimbrians at Arausio in 105.[89] The period described in these books was full of meaningful and important events, little known as regards the Hellenistic world, but the fragments from the *Excerpta Constantiana* dedicated to it, regrettably, fail to inform us how much detail Diodorus gave his audience regarding developments in both the East and the West. Luckily, the epitome by Photius (Phot. *Bibl.* [244] 379a35–380a4, 384a31–386b10) presents us, regardless of how disproportionate it may be (see the remarks by Goukowsky 2014: 51–3), in two episodes, with a valuable addition to the Constantinian excerpts, especially as regards the First Servile War in Sicily.[90] The different ways Photius' epitome has been inserted into the editions of Dindorf and Fischer and of Walton on the one hand, into that of Goukowsky on the other, are notable (see also Goukowsky 2014: 68–83). In view of chronological elements I must confess that I prefer the latter approach, though in view of the order of treatment by Photius I can understand the other one.

As already indicated in my introduction to the sources of books 33–40, the question of Diodorus' source-authors for these books is a delicate one. For books 34/5 we may doubt whether Posidonius can be regarded as the genuine source of Diodorus in more than a single case: this concerns a phrase in 34/5.2.34 (= Goukowsky 2014: 93 Fr. 5.1) that *might* be compared with a quote from Posidonius by Athenaeus (Ath. 12.542B; see Goukowsky 2014: 56). However, whether the relation was present in reality remains in the dark, as it does for most other potential sources: almost no solid candidate can be established, though it appears Diodorus uses more than one and quite differing sources (Goukowsky 2014: 57; see for potential sources ibid.: 57–67). All we can safely assume is that Diodorus probably uses an author who was a contemporary of the events

---

[88] I follow the division used by Walton after Dindorf and Fischer, though Goukowsky 2014 treats books 34 and 35 separately. I believe the division Goukowsky applies is a sensible one (see Goukowsky 2014: 43–5).

[89] Goukowsky 2014: 45 suggests book 34 originally covered the years 138–129, book 35 the years 128–105 (Goukowsky 2014: 111). The subject of Walton's Fr. 1 (= Goukowsky book 34 Frr. 36a, Testimony, and 36b) is the siege and taking of Jerusalem by Antiochus VII *Euergetes* (*Sidetes*), which Walton dates to 134 but Goukowsky – with good reason, I believe – to about 131 (see Goukowsky 2014: 43–4).

[90] For this war, notably the Seleucid elements in the slaves' motives (or at least in those of the rebellion's leader, Eunus) for revolt, see, for example, Engels 2011.

he described as his principal source for the Servile War, perhaps, I think, one of the Roman Annalists. Regarding the history of the Roman Republic during the time of the Gracchi one might,[91] possibly and/or hypothetically, also think of the *Histories* by P. Rutilius Rufus (Goukowsky 2014: 113). As for the fragments dedicated to the expedition by Antiochus VII against the Parthians, Pompeius Trogus (his book 38) might – perhaps – come to mind (again) as a *potential* source for Diodorus (a suggestion guarded by all necessary provisos as indicated before, even more because the epitome by Justin does not really match the fragments of Diodorus preserved by the *Excerpta Constantiniana*). As things stand, however, most of the fragments are too short to warrant any possible firm conclusion on Diodorus' sources for books 34/5, apart from the fact that certainly, just as no other source-author can be established, nor can a distinct link with the work of Posidonius be solidly proven.

Book 36 seems to cover the events of eight years, namely the years 104–97 (Goukowsky 2014: 137), characterised within Rome by, *inter alia*, the five consecutive consulships of C. Marius, more or less outside Rome's sphere of influence, and by the invasions of the Cimbrians and Teutons and the Second Servile War (predominantly, again, in Sicily). The preserved fragments, both from the Constantinian excerpts and an extensive one by Photius (386b11–391a28, our main source for the Second Servile War), provide little or no information regarding the Persian East, in spite of Diodorus' proven interest in that very region and the apparent developments there, for instance in Syria.[92] Probably we should, in this case, blame the excerpters for this omission. For this book again, the quality (if not the quantity) of (near) contemporary sources describing the events of these days makes it virtually impossible to recognise Diodorus' source-authors, obviously including (probably, again, only as a secondary source) Posidonius (Goukowsky 2014: 154–5, who describes some attempts to attribute to Posidonius the origin of Diodorus' account). Notably, all that Photius' résumé appears to suggest (in the phrase φασί τινες 'some say': Phot. *Bibl.* [244] 390b28) is that Diodorus uses at least two source-authors as well

---

[91] For a discussion of Diodorus' treatment of the Gracchi see especially Botteri 1992.
[92] See Liv. *Per.* 68.11: *bella praeterea inter Syriae reges gesta continet* ('moreover, the wars waged between the kings of Syria continued'). This refers to the prolonged civil war between Antiochus VIII *Epiphanes Callinicus Philometor* (*Grypus* = 'hook-nose') – he ruled from 125 onwards – and Antiochus IX *Cyzicenus*, who had returned from exile in Cyzicus to Syria in 116. Finally, both contestants were murdered in 96. The conflict considerably weakened the Seleucid kingdom, contributing to its demise.

as his principal source. It seems, moreover, that one of these sources may well have been of Roman origin, as some topographical anomalies may reveal (Goukowsky 2014: 155–6).

Though Photius discusses in his epitome Diodorus' books 37–40 in their entirety, he reveals elsewhere that book 37 ends with the departure of L. Cornelius Sulla for Greece: it provides us with a terminus for this book, namely the period 96–88. As regards other problems in putting a correct date to distinct events, I refer to Goukowsky's introduction to this book (Goukowsky 2014: 178–83). To the important events in the Roman world discussed in book 37 belong both the Social War (91–88) and the antagonism between the *optimates* (Senate party) and the *populares* (seeking support from both *equites* and *plebs*), which appears according to Diodorus to have been an antagonism reinforced by a decline in morals. As Goukowsky rightly observed, it is a theme preluded by Polybius in book 6 of his *Histories* as well,[93] though it also was a more widely felt issue, an issue, moreover, that divided Roman and Greek historians (see Goukowsky 2014: 184–9). For one like Diodorus, who puts moral issues so prominently at the forefront of the events described in the *Bibliotheca*, it may well have been a key issue. For this book too, as might be expected, Posidonius has been presumed to have been Diodorus' principal source-author, and for this book as well there is no single piece of compelling evidence for this presumption, even though Diodorus here too might have borrowed some elements from Posidonius (Goukowsky 2014: 189–91). Sources that might come to mind as well are L. Cornelius Sisenna, P. Rutilius Rufus, P. Sempronius Asellio, L. Licinius Lucullus,[94] Q. Hortensius Hortalus,[95] and Alexander of Ephesus:[96] from their works, however, nothing remains to serve as evidence in favour or to disprove it. In

---

[93] See also Walbank 1979: 500–1 on the decline of Roman morale due to the abandonment of ancestral values and the adoption of those of conquered peoples, notably Greeks and Asians.

[94] See Plu. *Luc.* 1.8: διασῴζεται γὰρ Ἑλληνική τις ἱστορία τοῦ Μαρσικοῦ πολέμου ('there has survived a history in Greek of the Marsic War'), after Plutarch had written earlier in that paragraph that Lucullus as a young man, provoked by Hortensius and Sisenna, had consented to write a poem and a history, either in Greek or Latin, on the Marsic War.

[95] Vell. Pat. 2.16.3: *cuius de virtutibus cum alii, tum maxime dilucide Q. Hortensius in annalibus suis rettulit* ('several [historians] have recorded his merits, but the most extensive and clearest testimony is that of Quintus Hortensius in his *Annals*').

[96] Str. 14.1.25/642: τῶν δὲ νεωτέρων Ἀρτεμίδωρος καὶ Ἀλέξανδρος ῥήτωρ ὁ Λύχνος προσαγορευθείς, ὃς καὶ ἐπολιτεύσατο καὶ συνέγραψεν ἱστορίαν καὶ ἔπη κατέλιπεν ('of the more recent ones [namely from Ephesus] Artemidorus and Alexander the orator, surnamed *Lychnus* ('Lamp'), who was a statesman, and wrote a history, and left behind him poems'). See also, for Alexander Ephesius' history (on the Marsic War), FHG, vol. 3: 344: *bellum illud ipse viderit* ('he himself has seen this war').

Diodorus' Sources

itself this observation does add to the value we should attribute to the *Bibliotheca* as a source for this period as well.

In the same way as for books 33/4, both Dindorf and Fischer and Walton combine books 38/9, unlike Goukowsky (2014), who discusses these books separately.[97] Nevertheless, as before, I shall here follow the traditional pattern (to preserve the cohesion of my review, following the Teubner editions as my main guide), despite the fact that I can fully endorse Goukowsky's solution. Together, books 38 and 39 cover events between 87 and 73: it appears the caesura may well have been the year 78. This is the year L. Cornelius Sulla died, L. Cornelius Sisenna ends his *Annals*, and the *Histories* of C. Sallustius Crispus (Sallust) start.[98] This very year also marks the beginning of book 90 of Livy, as the list of *periochae* makes clear, and both Appian and John of Antioch attribute special significance to this year as well (Goukowsky 2014: 219–20): all this contributes to strengthen the force of Goukowsky's proposal. I can also follow Goukowsky's suggestion of considering 37.30.1–3 in the editions of Dindorf and Fischer and of Walton as in fact the proem to book 38 (= Goukowsky 2014: 250–1, book 38 Fr. 1), in which the verses taken from Euripides' *Danae* underline the moral choices people have to make (see Goukowsky 2014: 222–5). Such choices had to be made by the partisans of Marius and Sulla in Rome, by the supporters of Marius in the war against Mithridates, in behaviour in political life in Rome in general,[99] in the conflict between the consuls for the year 78 (namely M. Æmilius Lepidus and Q. Lutatius Catulus: see Broughton 1952: 85), and during the slave revolt led by Spartacus, to name but a few of the subjects discussed by Diodorus in these books. That Posidonius played a minor role at best – for example, in Diodorus' description of C. Marius' death – was recognised at an early stage, even by Schwartz (1903a: 690–1). Which sources did play a part can, again, not be determined with certainty, but it appears that for those fragments that should be assigned to book 38, the *Tuscae Historiae* may well have been an important source for Diodorus.[100] Moreover, most of these events took place during

---

[97] As we can frequently observe in his volumes dedicated to the fragments, Goukowsky often changes their order. I shall not comment on that aspect of his work.
[98] See McGushin 1992: 65–6.
[99] A conclusion most clearly worded by John of Antioch in his closing sentence (see 38/9.5.1 = Goukowsky 2014: 219 '*testimonium spurium*'), as rightly stipulated by Goukowsky 2014: 226 and note 50; see in general Goukowsky 2014: 225–8, 231.
[100] Goukowsky 2014: 225–48 expounds the role of Etruscan 'prophecies' in classical literature; Diodorus' uses them most clearly on 246–8.

his lifetime, when he was already at an age to be to some extent sufficiently conscious of his surroundings.

The last book of Diodorus that we usually accept – in spite of some potential doubts – as having been transmitted to us[101] is book 40, generally believed to discuss the period from 72 to c. 60. Goukowsky, who – as we discussed above in note 101 – doubts Diodorus' authorship of an extended version, believes that the events included in the *Bibliotheca* that describe events that happened after 60 should be ascribed to an 'update' by Diodorus.[102] As major reasons for his insistence that Diodorus did not extend the *Bibliotheca* proper beyond 60, Goukowsky (2014: 282) adduces that 'il est improbable qu'il ait dépassé le terme fixé par Castor [of Rhodes]' (whose *Chronicle* described events until 61) and that Diodorus may well have been a supporter of Cn. Pompeius Magnus, made that to some extent apparent in the *Bibliotheca*, and only added some *capita* after 44, mainly to appease Octavian. I find Goukowsky's suggestions extremely ingenious, but – to my regret – can find no compelling evidence to support his view. Moreover, the suggestion that Diodorus depended in such measure on the schedule drafted by Castor to construct the *Bibliotheca* that he could not go beyond it I find almost offensive *post tanto*. No matter how useful or practical the steppingstone of Castor's *Chronicle* may have been for Diodorus, and I certainly believe it may have been of major use for him, I also believe that Diodorus must have been able by then to describe the essentials of some fifteen to thirty-odd years he himself witnessed, having had already some practice in the art of writing and composition.

The events described in book 40 relate not merely to the East (for example Crete, Syria, Jewish people), but also to the Catalinarian conspiracy (if it ever existed). As regards Diodorus' account of the history of the Jewish people, he appears to return to a principal source for book 1, namely Hecataeus of Abdera (see also Goukowsky 2014: 285–6 and notes 43–5) as well to 'some other authors', though it

---

[101] Even though there is some suggestion there might have been more books. See, for example, above, Introduction, note 7, and also the discussion in Goukowsky 2014: 275–83. In the latter, Goukowsky suggests there were two versions in circulation: a shorter one (more or less congruous with the 'traditional division') and a longer one (used by Photius, Tzetzes, and others), which in fact he sees as an apocryphal version – as his remark on Tzetzes on 279 testifies. I am much less confident than he shows himself to be that his optimism is supported by the evidence as we have it. He frequently refers to Botteri's 1992 work on the Gracchi in Diodorus' work, and she too has questioned the evidence in a later work more critically than Goukowsky does here (see, once more, Introduction, note 7).

[102] As an example of such an 'update' Goukowsky 2014: 282 note 30 refers to 32.27.3 (= Goukowsky 2012: 213 Fr. 30), in which Diodorus mentions that C. Iulius Caesar had become *divus* ('deified').

Diodorus' Sources 81

remains unclear whether it is Hecataeus or Diodorus who used that terminology. Further, Goukowsky mentions as a potential source one Theophanes of Mytilene and, naturally, the ubiquitous Posidonius (Goukowsky 2014: 291). This must be becoming a tedious phrase for the reader: there is no evidence to support the source-authorship of either of these two in the remaining fragments of the *Bibliotheca*.

G. DIODORUS AND HIS SOURCE-AUTHORS

Reading through Diodorus' *Bibliotheca* we get a glimpse both of the huge amount of source material available to him and of the staggering number of source-authors he (may have) used, some regularly, most incidentally. I cannot hope to be able to present the reader with an elaborate analysis of Diodorus' principal and his secondary sources, but only to remember him or her of the potential, probable, and established sources we encounter reading the *Bibliotheca*. I find the number of, even potential, source-authors we have come across impressive, even if we assume that Diodorus did not read all these works 'from cover to cover', but may well have used instead prepared sets of extracts on various themes.

To quote from a paper on the Battle of Thermopylae (regarding Plutarch's comments on it):[103]

> The number of texts present at Chaeronea itself will, probably, have been limited to those Plutarch and his circle of friends owned themselves. Few works, though, existed in many copies and an ancient scholar/author could only hope to see a few of the works he heard of. Add to this the problem of looking up passages in papyrus rolls and it must become obvious that any writer, but surely a writer dealing with such a variety of topics as Plutarch – or extensive histories like Ephorus, Diodorus, or Pompeius Trogus -, faced a titanic task (see also Reynolds and Wilson 1991, 2). This could only be facilitated by relying whenever necessary on opinions and references at second or third hand (Russell 1973, 42; also Ziegler 1964, 273, 277). To facilitate things further, there also existed prepared sets of extracts on various themes. Apart from these, Plutarch himself also is likely to have collected excerpts and commonplaces – and so are Ephorus, Diodorus, and Pompeius Trogus, to name but a few.

I suggest here, therefore, once more that Diodorus too may well have used such prepared collections of relevant references and/or quotations. Few of the works we encountered going through Diodorus' work will have been used, therefore, in their entirety by him or even served as principal sources. Moreover, many, if not most, of them,

---
[103] Stronk 2014/15: 207.

whether Diodorus had read them entirely or merely in bits and pieces, he probably used as secondary sources. Nevertheless, it is necessary to add yet another matter to consider. Diodorus was a Greek, not merely by descent but also as regards his cultural attitude (in its widest sense) – as the *Bibliotheca* shows. Apparently he was of sufficiently good descent to allow him to travel and indulge in his studies. Those studies alone indicate that Diodorus had enjoyed at least more than a basic education (see also Palm 1955: 13). That very conclusion in its turn (though I am not entirely familiar with the *curriculum* in Diodorus' days) suggests that he was more than likely to have been familiar with the works of Homer, with those of the prominent tragedians and authors of comedies, and with at least parts of the works of historians like Herodotus, Thucydides, and/or Ephorus, all of them works we see surfacing time and again in the *Bibliotheca*. Next to these, being a Stoic, the works and/or teachings of Zeno of Citium and, probably, other philosophers as well may have been familiar to Diodorus. Such an education in itself may very well offer a solid base for such a massive undertaking as the composition (I use this word intentionally) of the *Bibliotheca* undoubtedly was.

Does all this mean Diodorus was a great historian after all? Does it make him a reliable historian? The answer to both questions should be, unequivocally, 'no', I believe, if only because, as he himself admits as a prime goal (see above, Introduction), his determination to focus first and foremost on morality (*aretē*; τρυφή) may well have obscured his view of the facts and, in fact, may cast doubt on whether he should be primarily considered as a historian at all. As to his ability (in terms of time, distance, and personal qualities) to check facts by study and/or inquiry I have serious doubts as well, as I have them also as regards several other classical authors (like, for example, Ctesias of Cnidus). In spite of all these doubts, however, we should constantly bear in mind that for several episodes in ancient history Diodorus' account is the only testimony we have; moreover that he, in some cases, is the only reference to a classical author we have at all: that fact alone does make him an important author and, probably even, historian – a qualification that stands without a judgement on his qualities, which were actually in my view not much less than those of many of his colleagues that we unequivocally qualify as historians. Even if we consider him primarily as a moralist who merely uses, as I phrased it before, Clio as his handmaiden, he does us an excellent service in preserving parts of many authors now lost; moreover, as Unger (1880: 305) acknowledges, differing from Schwartz, these were authors of generally high quality. Therefore, and if only for that reason, Diodorus does not deserve much of the scorn heaped upon him by Schwartz and the latter's followers.[104]

H. DIODORUS' USE OF HIS SOURCES

As I hope to have conveyed, I believe it is fair to state that Diodorus made use, one way or another, of an impressive array of source-authors. One might, therefore, get the impression that Diodorus should after all perhaps be considered as little more than a mere copying machine, slavishly (and perhaps injudiciously) transcribing (parts of) the works of predecessors. I believe that such an impression would be wrong, even though it is in line with the judgement of, notably, Schwartz and many practitioners of *Quellenforschung stricto sensu*. Diodorus certainly achieves more than Athenaeus of Naucratis (irrespective of the latter's achievements in preserving fragments of authors whose works are now lost), whose work today mainly serves as a *Zitatengrube* (after Palm 1955: 11). Even Schwartz (1903a: 669) does acknowledge that Diodorus succeeds in creating, more or less, a unity and a style of his own in his 'collection of excerpts', as do several studies on Diodorus' use of language.[105] However, Palm (1955) sets out to research that suggestion in more depth, as it appears to clash with the (equally commonly held) position that Diodorus is – to put it mildly – not a very original author (a position Palm also admits holding: Palm 1955: 13).

Palm's analysis, worthwhile as it is, is too detailed to epitomise here in great detail. I can only recommend those interested in such extremely detailed linguistic research to consult his work, and shall confine myself to communicating Palm's conclusions. Comparing Diodorus' work with that of his source Agatharchides of Cnidus (Palm 1955: 15–55), Palm observes that Diodorus does not copy Agatharchides literally, but adapts his words to comply with the formal standards of Diodorus' times, even though both use a typical Hellenistic Greek (Palm 1955: 55). A more thorough comparison (Palm 1955: 55–8) with a fragment ascribed to Ephorus of Cyme (*P.Oxy.* 1610) also contradicts the judgement of Grenfell and Hunt that Diodorus 'incorporated whole sentences or even chapters with little or no change'.[106] More to the point is their observation that Diodorus 'at other times merely paraphrased ... his main authority'

---

[104] See also the 'Einleitende Worte' in Palm 1955: 11.
[105] See Bigwood 1980: 199 and note 17 as well as Palm 1955: 12, who refers to examples of such studies: I have paid no particular attention to them in view of the purpose of this work.
[106] Grenfell, and Hunt 1919: 111.

(ibid.), though Palm – rightly – remarks that it shows 'nicht ... dass DS von seiner Vorlage sklavisch abhängich sei' (Palm 1955: 57). The same conclusion goes for a common source of both Ephorus and Diodorus, namely the *Hellenica Oxyrhynchia*. The only similarity between Ephorus and Diodorus is 'dass beide, jeder für sich, ungefähr denselben stilistischen Geschmack gehabt haben' (Palm 1955: 60). In addition, Diodorus' use of Thucydides and Xenophon (Palm 1955: 60–3) shows no cases of 'verbal dependency'.

After establishing this fact, Palm devotes himself to determining whether Carl Wachsmuth was right,[107] who had stated that Diodorus 'die eigene Ausdrucksweise fortwährend versetzt mit der Sprache der verschiedenen Quellen, die er gerade ausnutzt, und so hat das Ganze ein merkwürdig buntes Aussehen angenommen', was right. In itself this conclusion appears to be at odds with Palm's findings described in the preceding paragraph. On the basis of comparisons in the field of grammatical constructions (Palm 1955: 66–101) and phraseology (Palm 1955: 101–9), Palm decides that, indeed, we can establish that there is a coherent and consistent use by Diodorus of a proper *koinē* Greek, not or at worst minimally influenced by his sources. Other stylistic peculiarities (Palm 1955: 110–93) also confirm that Diodorus was a typical, average, Hellenistic author with a proper but very undistinctive style. Only as regards the descriptive and rhetorical parts in his account does he seem to be inclined to lean closer to his sources, but in sum the conclusion should be that 'seine Sprache in den verschiedenen Büchern, die verschiedene Quellen gehabt haben, eine einheitliche Gestaltung erhalten, mit Ausnahme von einigen ziemlich belanglosen Einzelheiten' (Palm 1955: 194). Certainly, Diodorus is stylistically inferior as an author to Thucydides or Polybius, inferior, too, to Herodotus as regards liveliness, but in its own right and taking its distinctive purpose into account, the *Bibliotheca* is definitely a firm and coherent account (see also Palm 1955: 195). It more or less confirms the judgement of Photius:

> Κέχρηται δὲ φράσει σαφεῖ τε καὶ ἀκόμψῳ καὶ ἱστορίᾳ μάλιστα πρεπούσῃ, καὶ μήτε τὰς (ὡς ἂν εἴποι τις) λίαν ὑπερηττικισμένας ἢ ἀρχαιοτρόπους διώκων συντάξεις, μήτε πρὸς τὴν καθωμιλημένην νεύων παντελῶς, ἀλλὰ τῷ μέσῳ τῶν λόγων χαρακτῆρι χαίρων, φεύγων τε τροπὰς καὶ τἄλλα, πλὴν τῶν παρ' Ἕλλησι μυθολογουμένων θεῶν τε καὶ ἡρώων, ὅσα τὸ ποιητικὸν ἔθνος νέμεται
> ('His style is clear, unadorned, and most suited for history. He neither (as one might say) excessively uses Atticisms or archaisms, nor on the other hand does he altogether descend to the level of everyday language but rather takes

---

[107] Wachsmuth 1895: 103.

pleasure in a style midway between the two, both avoiding figures of speech and similar peculiarities, except where he relates the legends of both gods and heroes, after the manner of poets.' Phot. *Bibl.* [70] 36a6–14)

Palm adjusts this view (Palm 1955: 196–8) with some additional comments, *inter alia* pointing at the Isocrates-inspired schematics of Diodorus, his psychologisms, his *Kunstprosa*, and the apparent lack of personal involvement in the events he describes; in short, the *Schreibtischprodukt* Diodorus' style has become. Nevertheless, I think our final conclusion should still be that Diodorus has somehow created a comprehensive account of events in both the East and the West that took place over a prolonged period, preserving relevant parts of many source-authors (many of whose works are by now more or less lost), and presents it in a personal and coherent style. In my view that is, in spite of all the points of criticism that are possible, quite an impressive achievement. I find, therefore, in the end that a judgement like that of Palm, describing Diodorus as an author 'von zweitem oder drittem Rang' (Palm 1955: 208), no matter how well I understand his reasoning, passes over too many elements that should have been taken into account as well. It also underlines that Schwartz's position in all its absoluteness is, in my view, untenable and that Diodorus' position in ancient Greek literary heritage deserves to be reassessed.

2 Ancient History: Assyrians, Chaldeans, and Medes

A. THE ASSYRIAN HISTORY

S. 1:
2.1.4–28.8:

Assyrian expansion under Ninus:
(2.1.4) In ancient times, then, Asia was ruled by native kings, of whom no memory either of a notable deed or of a personal name has been preserved. The first to be transmitted to history and memory for us as somebody who achieved great deeds is Ninus, king of the Assyrians: of him we shall now try to give a detailed account. Since he was by nature a warlike man and eager for *aretē*, he gave arms to the strongest of the young men, and he trained them for a long time to become accustomed to every hardship and all the dangers of war. (5) And after he thus had collected a notable army, he made an alliance with Ariaeus,[1] the king of Arabia,[2] a country which in

---

[1] No Arab king with this or a similar name is known. However, the Persepolis tablets mention a man by the name of *Ha-ri-ya* (Akkadian *Ariya*): Mayrhofer 1973: 155, no. 8.458. Ctesias, Diodorus' source, might have named the man after a friend of Cyrus the Younger, later serving Artaxerxes II, named Ariaeus. For an Arab–Assyrian alliance there is no direct evidence, though there appear to have been casual joint military enterprises of these two powers: see also Eck 2003: 105 *ad* p. 5 note 3.

[2] Macdonald (2015: 12, 13) remarks 'that the term Arab is rarely found in the Semitic inscriptions from this period', meaning the times from the Achaemenid through to the (late) Roman period, and 'We cannot tell whether any of the inhabitants of the [Arabian] Peninsula thought of it as "Arabia", but it seems probable that they did not.' The latter conclusion follows his basic observation that 'The meaning of the term "Arab" in antiquity has been hotly debated for many decades' and that there has been a 'search for a single definition which could be applied to all the numerous references to "Arabs" and "Arabias" in the ancient sources. . . . [T]he vast majority of these sources were written by authors looking at the ancient Near East from the outside. Moreover, when one of them called a group "Arabs", or the place where

Ancient History: Assyrians, Chaldeans, and Medes 87

those times seems to have abounded in brave men. Now, in general, this nation loves freedom and submits on no condition to a Persian ruler. Therefore, neither the kings of the Persians at a later time nor those of the Macedonians, though they were the most powerful rulers of their days, were ever able to reduce this nation to slavery. (6) For Arabia is, in general, a difficult country for an enemy army to campaign in, part of it being desert and part of it waterless and supplied at intervals with wells which are hidden and known only to the natives.[3] (7) Thus Ninus, the king of the Assyrians, went to war with a great force and in alliance with the ruler of the Arabians, against the Babylonians whose country bordered his.[4] In those times the present city of Babylon had not yet been founded, but there were other notable cities in Babylonia. After he had easily subdued the inhabitants because they were inexperienced in the dangers of warfare, he taxed them with the annual payment of fixed tributes. The king of the conquered, however, whom he took captive along with his children, he put to death. (8) Then he invaded Armenia[5] with a large army and after he had ruined some of its cities, he struck terror into the inhabitants. That is why their king, Barzanes,[6] met him and gave Ninus many presents and announced that he would do as he would be told to, because he realised himself that he was no match for Ninus in battle. (9) In return Ninus treated him with great magnanimity, and agreed that Barzanes should not only continue to rule Armenia, but, as his friend, should also furnish a contingent and supplies for the Assyrian army. And while his power continually increased, he made war with Media.[7] (10) The king of this country,

---

they lived "Arabia", he did not cross-check what other peoples or places had been given these names and whether there was any possible connection between them. Thus, by the end of the Hellenistic period, populations from eastern Egypt throughout the Fertile Crescent to the Arab-Persian Gulf, around the edges of the Peninsula, and even in central Iran, had been labelled as "Arabs" and their homeland as "Arabia"' (ibid.; see also p. 14, fig. 1.1).

[3] Eck 2003: 5, note 5, remarks that this resembles a description of the territory of the Nabataeans around Petra. Eck suggests that the source of this description may well have been Hieronymus of Cardia and not Ctesias. Perhaps part of it may also rest on autopsy by Diodorus himself.

[4] Here, it seems, the Assyrians *have* been distinguished from the Babylonians (see Introduction, note 8). For the problems in Greek historiography regarding correct geographical names in the Near East, see De Kuyper 1979.

[5] Possibly an allusion to the kingdom of Urartu, which was at the height of its power in the eighth century BC and regularly in conflict with the Assyrians: see, for example, *ARAB, passim* (see vol. II: 489 *s.v.*).

[6] Apparently the transcription of the Median name *Ú-ar-za-an*: see Eck 2003: 106 *ad* p. 6 note 5.

[7] Between the Assyrians and the Medes too, frequent hostilities have been related: see *ARAB, passim* (see vol. II: 473 *s.v.*); also, for example, Cook 1983: 1–2.

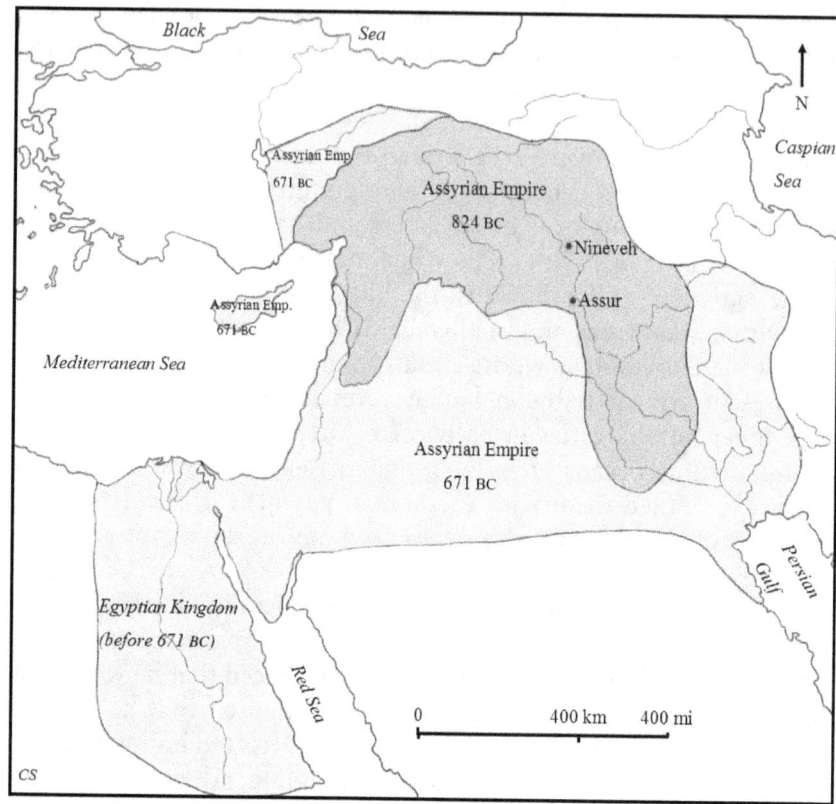

Fig. 2.1. Outlines of the expansion of the Neo-Assyrian Empire, c. 824–c. 650 BC.

Pharnus,[8] opposed Ninus in battle with a formidable force, but he was defeated. He not only lost the larger part of his soldiers, but after he was taken captive along with his seven sons and wife he was personally impaled as well.[9]
(2.2.1) While Ninus' enterprises prospered thus, he had a powerful desire to subdue all of Asia between the Don and the Nile.[10] [[After all, as a rule, when men have good luck, the steady current

---

[8] This name is a *hapax*, probably a transcription of an Iranian name, which may be related to the Median name **farnaka-* 'Glück', in Greek usually rendered by the name of Φαρνάκης: see Hinz et al. 1975: 94–5.
[9] As the reliefs of Assyrian palaces show, impalement was one of the traditional treatments of prisoners of war, next to decapitation and being flayed alive. For impalement Eck 2003: 107 *ad* p. 6 note 8 refers to Barnett and Forman 1958: plates 40–1, 159,d, 163,b, and 167,a.
[10] Whether the Don was the border between Asia and Europe was a matter of contention. In 1.55.4 Diodorus had already stated it as a fact; Herodotus claims the River Phasis in Colchis was this border, though admitting some did believe it was the River Tanaïs (= Don): see Hdt. 4.45; see also Krumbholz 1897: 273–4. For the Nile as border between Asia and Africa, see below, Chapter 7, note 33.

of their success makes them want more.]] Consequently he made one of his close friends satrap of Media,[11] but set himself to the task of subjecting the peoples of Asia. Within a period of seventeen years he became master of them all, except for the Indians and Bactrians. (2) No historian has recorded the specific battles or the number of all the peoples Ninus had waged war against, but we shall venture to run briefly over the most important peoples, as given in the account of Ctesias of Cnidus.[12] (3) Of the lands that lie by the sea or near it, Ninus conquered Egypt and Phoenicia,[13] then Coele Syria, Cilicia, Pamphylia, and Lycia, and also Caria, Phrygia, Mysia, and Lydia. Moreover, he brought under his rule the Troad, Phrygia on the Hellespont, Propontis, Bithynia, Cappadocia, and all the foreign peoples that inhabit the shores of the Pontus as far as the Don. He also made himself lord of the lands of the Cadusians and Tapyres, and also of those of the Hyrcanians and the Drangians; moreover of those of the Derbices, Carmanians, Choromnaeans, and of the Borcanians, and Parthians. He also invaded both Persis and Susis and so-called Caspia, which is entered by exceedingly narrow passes, which are known for that reason as the Caspian Gates. (4) He also brought many other of the lesser tribes under his rule, about whom one could speak at length.[14] But since Bactria[15] was difficult to invade and was full of warlike men, after much vain effort he deferred the war against the Bactrians to a later time. After Ninus had led his forces back into Assyria,[16] he chose a place that was excellently situated to found a great city.

---

[11] The terminology 'satrap' is an anachronism, derived from the Achaemenid Empire. See, for example, Grayson 1991b: 200–1. For the position and duties of a satrap, see Klinkott 2005.

[12] Krumbholz 1887: 272 argues that Diodorus abridged and adapted the original list provided by Ctesias. Most of these names also occur in either Herodotus or Xenophon (or both) and do not provoke the idea that the list was a late invention. Only the term 'Coele Syria' seems more recent.

[13] Assyrian presence and domination in Egypt are attested during the Third Intermediate Period: see, for example, Dodson 2012: 166–71, detailing Assyrian rule in Egypt, which started c. 671 (under Esarhaddon). Assyrian kings ruled Egypt until 555, the ninth year of the rule of Psamtik I, the first ruler of the 26th or Saïte dynasty (even though the Assyrian capital Nineveh had already fallen in 612). See also the *Babylonian Chronicles*, telling how Egypt 'was sacked and its gods were abducted' (ABC 1 Col. 4:25; also in ABC 14:28–9).

[14] The description of the empire allegedly conquered by Ninus resembles the extent reached in the three centuries following Adad-nirari II from 911 onward: see, for example, Roux 1992: 282–336.

[15] The word used here, Βακτριανή ('Bactriane'), is a form typical for Diodorus, or more general the Hellenistic period, as Bigwood 1980: 200–1 argues. As far as we know now Ctesias used the forms Βακτρία ('Bactria') and Βάκτριοι ('Bactrians'), the forms that I also intend to use, even in a translation of Diodorus' work. As for Bactria, an excellent and succinct introduction to it can be found in Holt 1988: 11–51.

[16] Ἀσσυρίαν is used in MS Dᵃ, but the form Συρίαν, preserved in MSS C, V, and L, is also not impossible. Eck 2003: 109 *ad* p. 8 note 3 rightly points to Nöldeke 1871, documenting

Founding of Nineveh:

(2.3.1) Since he had accomplished more glorious deeds than any king before him, Ninus was eager to found such a great city that it would not only be the largest of all those existing in the whole inhabited world, but that likewise no one of his successors, if he would put himself to such a task, should find it easy to surpass him. (2) After Ninus had honoured the king of the Arabians with gifts and rich spoils from his wars, he dismissed him and his army to their own country. He himself, however, after he had gathered men from everywhere and all necessary materials by the River Euphrates,[17] founded a city which was well fortified with walls, giving it the form of a rectangle. The longer sides of the city were each one hundred and fifty *stadia* in length [c. 28 km], the shorter ones ninety [c. 17 km]. (3) Since the total circumference of the city comprised four hundred and eighty *stadia* [c. 88.8 km],[18] he was, therefore, not disappointed in his hope: no one would later found such a city, with respect both to the length of its circuit and to the magnificence of its walls. After all, the wall had a height of one hundred feet [c. 31 m] and its width was sufficient for three chariots abreast to drive upon. The total of all towers was one thousand five hundred, and their height was two hundred feet [c. 62 m]. (4) In it, Ninus settled the most powerful of the Assyrians and those who wished to come from the other tribes.[19] He named the city after himself, Ninus (Nineveh),[20] and he added to the territory of its colonists a large part of the neighbouring countryside.

---

the confusion among Greek authors over how to use 'Assyrians' and 'Syrians': the authors use both words without distinction for the more or less important peoples/tribes of the Near and Middle East. Only Ctesias clearly distinguished between Assyria, Babylonia, and Syria, Nöldeke 1871: 457 asserts. Eck believes the disagreement in the MS tradition forces us to reconsider the latter part of Nöldeke's view; I am much less sure on that issue. See also Herzfeld 1968: 306–8; De Kuyper 1979; Frye 1992; Rollinger 2006a; 2006b.

[17] A clear error, both here and also further: Nineveh was situated by the River Tigris. It is unclear who is to blame for the error, Ctesias or Diodorus (or even a copyist?): see Eck 2003: 109–10 *ad* p. 8 note 4. It is noteworthy that Nicholas of Damascus, as it seems also based on Ctesias, situates Nineveh correctly on the Tigris: see Stronk 2010: 264–5 (*FGrH/BNJ* 90 F 3).

[18] The figures may be exaggerated, but the circumference corresponds to Herodotus' data for that of Babylon: Hdt. 1.178, which Ctesias mentioned as 360 *stadia* (= c. 66.6 km). The *stadium* is not a fixed extent, but varies, depending on the measure of the local foot (a *stadium* measured 600 feet), between c. 177 m and the Olympic *stadium* of slightly over 192 m. I have taken the *stadium* as c. 185 m, being about the length of the *stadium* in Roman-dominated territories and measured not in feet but as 125 double *passus*. See also Eck 2003: 119 *ad* p. 16 note 9 and Boncquet 1987: 72–3 and notes 294–301 for different numbers.

[19] For larger entities, I translate ἔθνη as 'peoples', for smaller entities I use the term 'tribes'. Whenever the distinction is unclear, I usually opt for either 'peoples and tribes' or 'tribes'.

[20] In Akkadian texts, Eck 2003: 110 *ad* p. 9 note 3 argues, the Assyrian capital is mentioned as *Ni-nu-a*^{ki}, Iranian *Ni-nu(w)a*. Eck asserts that the personal name of Ninus has been created in Greek traditions to serve as the eponymous founder of the city. Unlike him, I do not think

Ancient History: Assyrians, Chaldeans, and Medes

Fig. 2.2. Simplified plan of the city of Nineveh.

Youth of Semiramis:

(**2.4.1**) After the founding of Nineveh, Ninus made war against Bactria. In Bactria he married Semiramis,[21] the most renowned

---

the 'creation' was that of Ctesias: 'Ninus the son of Belus' already appears in Hdt. 1.7, though there, admittedly, as the father of the first Heraclid king of Sardis and apparently not connected with Nineveh. See also Eilers 1971: 26–8. For a succinct review of Nineveh, its history, and relevant literature see, for example, Leick 2001: 218–44, 326–8.

[21] For Semiramis, see below, Chapter 10.

of all women we have a record of. We must, therefore, first of all relate how she rose from a lowly fortune to such fame. (2) There is in Syria a city, Ascalon, and not far from it is a large and deep lake full of fish.²² On its shore is a precinct of a famous goddess whom the Syrians call Derceto;²³ this goddess has the head of a woman, but all the rest of her body is that of a fish. The reason for this is something as follows. (3) The story as related by the most learned of the inhabitants of the region runs like this: Aphrodite, who was annoyed at this Derceto,²⁴ inspired in her a violent passion for a handsome youth among her votaries. Derceto had intercourse with the Syrian and bore him a daughter. Next, however, she was filled with shame for her indecency and killed the youth. She exposed the child in a remote and rocky region and from shame and grief she threw herself into the lake:²⁵ the form of her body was changed into that of a fish. Therefore, the Syrians to this day abstain from this animal and honour their fish as gods.²⁶ (4) In the region where she had exposed the baby, a great multitude of doves had their nests.²⁷ They nurtured the child in an incredible and miraculous manner. Some of the doves kept the body of the baby warm on all sides by covering it with their wings. While other doves observed both the cowherds and the other keepers,²⁸ they brought milk in their beaks from the nearby farmsteads and fed the baby by putting the milk between its lips drop by drop. (5) When the child was a year old and in need of more solid nourishment, the doves pecked off bits from the cheeses and supplied the child with sufficient food. And the learned men tell that, when the

---

²² Ascalon, situated on the Mediterranean north of Gaza, only paid tribute to the Assyrians in some periods: Boncquet 1987: 48. During excavations, the existence of a pond there has been demonstrated: see Honigmann 1928; Boncquet 1987: 52 note 181.
²³ This story is reflected in Luc. Syr.D. 14. Derceto was apparently the local name of Atargatis, the so-called Syrian goddess, a fertility goddess, with alternately a fish and a dove as attributes (Boncquet 1987: 50–3), and assimilated with Aphrodite (Hdt. 1.105; Paus. 1.14.7). Atargatis was seemingly one of the aspects of the goddess Astarte, who in her turn is assimilated with the Babylonian goddess Ištar (who also had a fish as an attribute, down to the Achaemenid period: Boncquet 1987: 52). See also Van Berg 1972.
²⁴ The precise relation between Derceto and Aphrodite is not straightforward, as it appears to shift over time: see also Boncquet 1987: 51 and notes 172–7.
²⁵ The exposure story is a well-known and popular theme in many traditions. See Boncquet 1987: 55 note 212, referring to B. Lewis.
²⁶ See also X. An. 1.4.9; Ov. Met. 4.44–51.
²⁷ Du Mesnil du Buisson 1973: 80, states that the dove was first the hypostasis of Astarte, later her attribute. See also Eck 2003: 111 ad p. 10 note 4.
²⁸ καὶ τοὺς ἄλλους νομεῖς <ἀπόντας>. In this phrase ἀπόντας is a conjecture by Ursinus (Fulvio Orsini, 1529–1600), one of the early modern editors. Both Vogel 1985a: 174–5 and Oldfather 1968: 358–9 accept it; Eck 2003: 10 omits it. I support his option, since the conjecture does not add significantly to the meaning of the text.

keepers returned and saw that the cheeses had been nibbled round the edges, they wondered at this strange situation. Accordingly the keepers kept a lookout: they discovered the cause and found the baby, which was of all-surpassing beauty. (6) They brought it at once to their farmstead and turned it over to the keeper of the royal herds, whose name was Simmas.[29] Because Simmas was childless, he gave every care to the rearing of the girl as his own daughter. He called her Semiramis, a name slightly altered from the word that, in the language of the Syrians, means 'doves':[30] since that time all the inhabitants of Syria have continued to honour these birds as goddesses.

Marriage of Onnes and Semiramis; Ninus prepares for an expedition against Bactria:

(2.5.1) Such, then, is essentially the story told about the birth of Semiramis. When she had become a full-grown girl, she surpassed by far all the other maidens in beauty. One day, an official was sent on behalf of the king to inspect the royal herds.[31] His name was Onnes, and he stood first among the members of the king's council and had been appointed governor over all Syria. He stayed with Simmas, and when he saw Semiramis, he was captivated by her beauty. Therefore he earnestly entreated Simmas to give him the maiden in lawful marriage. He took her off to Nineveh and there he married her and begat two sons, Hyapates and Hydaspes.[32]

---

[29] The name of Simmas is a *hapax*. I am not convinced by the rapprochements presented by Boncquet 1987: 57.
[30] Akkadian (not Syrian!) *summatu(m)* means 'dove', but the etymology seems quite farfetched and may have sprung from (Ctesias' (?)) imagination; see also Eilers 1971: 38–46.
[31] I am slightly at a loss as regards Onnes' function. As his duties are related here, the word ὕπαρχος might perhaps best be translated as 'deputy', a civil servant and possibly not even the top administrator. However, a sentence later he is described as 'first among the members of the king's council and ... ὕπαρχος over all Syria', a function that in Diodorus' days, in fact, might better fit that of an ἔπαρχος ('*praefectus*', 'governor'), a primarily military servant, especially manifest in the Hellenistic and Roman periods (though a ὕπαρχος as Herodotus frequently uses the term is what we consider as a satrap; in Assyria it was the *shaknu* 'governor'; see Liverani 2014: 350). For the development of the story, the latter function would seem the more promising one, certainly regarding the way Onnes accompanies Ninus during his campaign against Bactria. As all MSS read ὕπαρχος, I have left it that way and translated it as 'official'. See also Boncquet 1987: 58–9. As it stands, Onnes is probably the right reading of the emissary's name, even though its origin is still contested: see Eck 2003: 11 note 2; Boncquet 1987: 58.
[32] As Boncquet 1987: 59 observes, an acceptable way to transpose a girl from Ascalon to Nineveh to enable her later ascent in hierarchy. Hyapates and Hydaspes are both genuine Persian names: see Justi 1895: 131. In Diodorus' story they do not feature further, but their story (presumably by Ctesias) is continued by Nicholas of Damascus (*FGrH/BNJ* 90 F 1): see also Stronk 2010: 254–7 *ad* F. *1δ [L]. Diodorus presents the conspiracy of the eunuch and Onnes' sons as a conspiracy of a eunuch and Ninus' son (see below, 2.20.1).

(2) Because the other qualities of Semiramis were in keeping with the beauty of her countenance, her husband became completely enslaved by her. Since he, moreover, did nothing without her advice, he prospered in everything. (3) It was at just this time that the king, now that he had completed the founding of the city which bore his name, undertook his campaign against the Bactrians.[33] He was well aware of the great number and the valour of these men. Moreover, he realised himself that the country had many places that could not be approached by an enemy because of their strength. Therefore, he enrolled a great host of soldiers from all the peoples and tribes he ruled. Because he had come off badly in his earlier expedition, he was resolved to appear before Bactria with a force many times larger than theirs. (4) Accordingly, after he had assembled the army from every source, it numbered, as Ctesias has stated in his history, one million seven hundred thousand foot, two hundred and ten thousand cavalry, and slightly less than ten thousand six hundred scythe-bearing chariots.[34] (5) When one hears about it for the first time, the enormity of the army is incredible. It will, however, not seem at all impossible to anyone who takes into account the great extent of Asia and the vast numbers of the peoples and tribes who inhabit it. For if one forgets the campaign of Darius against the Scythians with eight hundred thousand men and the crossing made by Xerxes against Greece with a host beyond

---

[33] Briant 1984: 13–27 discusses the alleged expedition by Ninus against Bactria and states (p. 16): 'aucun récit assyrien ne peut server de référent au texte de Ctésias/Diodore sur une expédition assyrienne à Bactres'. See also Potts 2014: 77–8: 'But perhaps the most intriguing evidence of Assyrian penetration in the east, fleeting though it may have been, dates to the early seventh century B.C., when, according to a text inscribed on numerous clay prisms, Esarhaddon (680–669 B.C.) campaigned against Patušarra (^{kur}Pa-tu-$uš$-ar-ra/ri), "a district in the area of the salt desert, which is in the midst of the land of the distant Medes," on the border of "Mount Bikni, the lapis lazuli mountain, (and) upon the soil of whose land none of the kings, my ancestors, had walked."' Potts refers to remarks on the identification of the salt desert by François Vallat, though he doubts Vallat's identification of Mt Bikni. Normally, the Zagros Mountains were as far east as the Assyrian Empire stretched.

[34] This number is highly overstated (as is true, for example, for Herodotus' figures of Xerxes' army invading Greece: Hdt. 7.60). Jacoby 1922: 2060 is, like Bigwood 1976: 10–16, a confirmation of this assessment. Hignett 1963: 351 remarks that an Oxford scholar (no name is given) remarked to him that Greek writers may have misinterpreted the Persian unit of calculation of a *chiliad* as a *myriad*, so that all figures were automatically multiplied by ten. Perhaps a reduction to 10 per cent of the figures given might be a realistic start. See also note 35 on this issue. On scythed chariots, see Nefiodkin 2004. According to him, we have to deal with an anachronism here: both Xenophon (X. *Cyr.* 6.1.27) and Arrian (Arr. *Tact.* 19.4) attribute (probably mistakenly) the first use of such weapons to Cyrus the Great. As Nefiodkin explains (at 373), scythed chariots were devised to be used against compactly deployed infantry, like (perhaps) Egyptians and, notably, Greeks. It seems feasible to date the actual introduction of scythed chariots between 479 and 401 (the Battle of Cunaxa), when they were reportedly used (Nefiodkin 2004: 376).

number,[35] and looks at the events that have taken place in Europe only yesterday or the day before, one would be readier to come to regard the statement as credible. (6) [[In Sicily, for instance, Dionysius commanded on his campaigns from Syracuse alone one hundred and twenty thousand infantry and twelve thousand cavalry and from a single harbour four hundred warships, some of which were *tetrereis* and *pentereis*.[36] (7) When the Romans foresaw the size of the war, shortly before the time of Hannibal, they enrolled all the men in Italy fit for military service, both citizens and allies, and the total number of them was only slightly less than one million. And yet, as regards the number of inhabitants no one would compare all Italy with a single one of the nations of Asia. Let these facts, then, be a sufficient reply from us to those who try to estimate the ancient density of the populations [in Asia] by today's cities' prevailing desolation.]][37]

Campaign against Bactria; marriage of Ninus and Semiramis: (2.6.1) Because Ninus waged war against Bactria with such a large force, he was compelled to advance his army in divisions, in view of the fact that access to the country was difficult and that the passes were narrow. (2) Though Bactria had many large cities,[38] one was the most famous and the royal palace happened to be there. That city was called Bactra,[39] and in size and in the strength of its acropolis it was by far the first of them all. The king of the country, Zaortes [Zoroaster],[40] had conscripted all the men of military age, and they

---

[35] Normally, the figures presented for Persian armies in Greek literature are hugely exaggerated. The cause for this is a basic misconception of, for instance, the structure of Persian armies: see, for example, Barkworth 1993; Keaveney 2011: 38–3. See also note 34.
[36] If Dionysius I (404–367) is meant, the information relates to a contemporary of Ctesias; if, however (and that is not impossible: see Boncquet 1987: 63), Dionysius II (367–357) is intended, this information is a later addition. As regards *tetrereis* and *pentereis*, I have stuck to the Greek words because, as Morrison and Williams 1968: 3, rightly remark, there is: 'The lack of certainty that the ... *penteres* <was> in fact identical to the ... *quinqueremis*.' In later years, in the case of the equation *trieres–trireme*, Morrison obviously became less dogmatic: see the title of his work *The Athenian Trireme*, Cambridge: Cambridge University Press 1986 [2000²]. Yet, methodologically his 1968 remark remains a correct observation.
[37] These paragraphs indirectly provide some information on Diodorus' aims and method.
[38] Holt 1988: 27–32 asserts that traces of numerous fortified cities dating to the times before Alexander the Great have been recovered in Central Asia and notably in Bactria, where urbanisation went back well into the Bronze Age.
[39] The modern-day city of Balkh, in what is currently northern Afghanistan. As it stands, the description appears largely correct – as Eck 2003: 114 *ad* p. 13 note 3 observes; see also Str. 11.11.3/516 and Boncquet 1987: 65.
[40] The name of the king offers some problems. Eck 2003: 114–15 *ad* p. 13 note 4 explains that the *stemma codicum* forces us to accept the reading Ἐξαόρτης, attested in MSS Dᵃ, V, and L, and that the reading Ὀξυάρτης (also the name of Roxane's father: see, for example, below, 18.3.3, 39.6), attested in MS C, should be rejected on technical grounds (namely

had been gathered to the number of four hundred thousand. (3) So he took this force with him and when he met the enemy at the passes, he allowed a division of the army of Ninus to cross them. However, when he thought that a sufficient number of the enemy had descended into the plain, he deployed his own forces. After a fierce struggle the Bactrians put the Assyrians to flight and pursued them as far as the mountains overlooking the field, killing about one hundred thousand of the enemy. (4) But later, after the whole Assyrian force had crossed the passes, the Bactrians, overpowered by its multitude, withdrew city by city, each group intending to defend its own homeland. And so Ninus easily subdued all the other cities: Bactra, though, he could not take by storm, because it was both strong and well equipped for war. (5) As the siege proved to be a long affair, the husband of Semiramis, who was in love with his wife and was in the king's army, sent for her.[41] And she, smart, daring, and gifted with all distinctive qualities, seized the opportunity to present herself. (6) Because she was about to make a journey of many days, she devised in the first place a garment that made it impossible to distinguish whether its wearer was a man or a woman. This dress was well adapted to her needs, both when she travelled in the heat, to prevent her becoming suntanned, and for her convenience to do whatever she might wish to do. The garment was quite pliable and suitable to a young person, and, in a word, was so attractive that later the Medes, when they were dominant in Asia, always wore the garment of Semiramis, as did the Persians after them.[42] (7) When Semiramis arrived in Bactria she observed the progress of

---

because the combination *ξαόρτης seems certain). Boncquet pays serious attention to other variants, based upon Just. 1.1.9, namely Ζοροάστηρ, Ζαόρτης, or even Ζαθραύστης (all to be translated as 'Zoroaster'); see Boncquet 1987: 65–8. Of these only Ζαόρτης might pass the test (if the ξ/ζ issue could be managed), since Eck 2003: 13, *apparatus ad* l. 11, admits that in V and L ὁ Ξαόρτης *legi potest*: 'Xaortes could be read'). As, however, a passage in Eus. (Arm.) *Chron*. p. 28.28–29.3 (ed. Karst), reads: 'Next he [Ctesias] relates the pedigree of Semiramis [Šamiramay]; and of Zarathustra [Zaravyšt] the *magus, of his war as king of the Bactrians and his being defeated by Semiramis* (my italics); and the years of Ninus' rule, 52 years, and of his demise' (Ctes. *Pers*. F. 1a: Stronk 2010: 202–3), we have a kind of contextual evidence we have to take into account. Because both Eusebius and Diodorus mention Ctesias as their source, and because of the remarks in Eck's *apparatus*, I opt, for the time being, to read here 'Zaortes', first (?) presented in the *Poggii versio librorum I–V* (= P). As a matter of fact, a ζ/ξ-shift is, perhaps, not unique: see below, Chapter 6, note 3.

[41] According to Pettinato 1988: 15–16, it is well attested that the wives of Assyrian functionaries or commanders were allowed to accompany their husbands, including during military expeditions.

[42] Boncquet 1987: 69 and note 279 believes the garment was what the Greeks called the κάνδυς: see X. *Cyr*. 1.3.2, *An*. 1.5.8; see also Hdt. 1.135; X. *Cyr*. 8.1.40; Str. 11.13.9–10/525–6; Just. 1.2.3; also Strommenberger 1980–3; Boncquet 1987: 68–70; Eck 2003: 115 *ad* p. 14 note 2.

the siege.⁴³ She noted that the Assyrian army attacked on the plains and at positions that could be easily assailed. No one, however, ever assaulted the acropolis because of its strong position. Therefore its defenders had left their posts there and had come to the aid of those who were hard pressed on the walls below. (8) Guided by this observation, she took with her those soldiers who were accustomed to climbing rocks. She made her way up through a difficult ravine with this company, seized a part of the acropolis, and gave a signal to those who were besieging the wall down in the plain. Thereupon the defenders of the city, who were struck with terror at the seizure of the acropolis, left the walls and abandoned all hope of saving themselves.⁴⁴ (9) After the Assyrians had seized the city in this way, the king, stunned by the ability of Semiramis, at first honoured her with great gifts. Later on, when he had become infatuated with her because of her beauty, Ninus tried to persuade Onnes to yield her to him of his own accord. He offered Onnes his own daughter Sosane as wife in return for this favour.⁴⁵ (10) When Onnes took his offer with ill grace, Ninus threatened to gouge out his eyes unless he immediately obeyed his commands. And Onnes hanged himself, after he had fallen into a kind of frenzy and madness and had put a noose round his neck, because he at the same time feared the king's threats and was simultaneously consumed by love. Such, then, were the causes of Semiramis' attaining the position of queen.

Accession to the throne of Semiramis; the founding of Babylon:
(2.7.1) Ninus took hold of the treasures of Bactra, which contained a great amount of both gold and silver.⁴⁶ After he had dealt with the

---

⁴³ For sieges and Neo-Assyrian siege techniques, see the comprehensive De Backer 2013.
⁴⁴ Eck 2003: 115–16 *ad* p. 15 note 1 argues that geographical and archaeological evidence makes it clear that the story cannot be dismissed out of hand as pure fantasy. This may well be the case for the position of Bactra (apart from the fact that an Assyrian attack on Bactra should be dismissed to the realm of fantasy), but I think it feasible that this particular story and Arrian's *An.* 4.18.4–19.5 (and Curt. 7.11) have been created as a mirror of each other: similar circumstances, similar result, but in the latter Alexander meets Roxane, as Ninus and Semiramis come together in this episode: see also below, Chapter 10.
⁴⁵ This story to some extent mirrors the history of the wife of Masistes, desired by Xerxes (even though the result differs: see Hdt. 9. 108–13). As regards the name of Ninus' daughter there is a minor problem: if the name is written as Σωσάνην, as MSS C, V, and perhaps Dᵃ suggest (in the latter a letter what might be a *nu* was scraped away), it is a *hapax*; if it is Σωσάννην, as might be the reading to be preferred in MS L, it transcribes the Hebrew name of Suzanne. If so, one might wonder if someone has tried to Iranise a Hebrew name, which was unlikely for an Assyrian girl: see also Eck 2003: 15 note 3. As Boncquet 1987: 70 remarks, the name might have been less out of the ordinary at a Persian court – where Ctesias may have noticed it.
⁴⁶ Eck 2003: 15 note 4 remarks that the so-called Oxus treasure, now in the British Museum, might come to mind as a reminder of the richness of Bactria.

affairs of Bactria, he disbanded his forces. Afterwards he begat by Semiramis a son, Ninyas;[47] when he died he left his wife as queen. Semiramis buried Ninus in the precinct of the palace and erected over his tomb a very large mound. The height of this mound was nine *stadia* [c. 1.7 km] and the width ten [nearly 1.9 km], as Ctesias says.[48] (2) Because the city lay on a plain alongside the Euphrates, the mound was visible for a distance of many *stadia*, like an acropolis. It is said to be visible still, even to this day, even though Nineveh was razed to the ground by the Medes when they destroyed the empire of the Assyrians.[49] Semiramis' nature made her eager for great exploits and ambitious to surpass the fame of her predecessor on the throne [= Ninus]. Therefore she put herself to the task of founding a city in Babylonia.[50] After she had secured the architects and the skilled artisans from everywhere and had made all the other necessary preparations, she gathered from her entire kingdom two million men to complete the work. (3) She drew the River Euphrates into the centre and threw about the city a wall of three hundred and sixty *stadia* [c. 66.6 km] in circumference.[51] This wall she provided with solid and great towers set at frequent intervals. So massive were the works that the walls were sufficiently wide to allow six chariots abreast to drive on it and their height was unbelievable for those who only heard of it,[52] as Ctesias of Cnidus says, but according to the account

---

[47] Eilers 1971: 28 and note 31a remarks that this form is a younger and more correct representation of the Akkadian *Ninua*. See also Weidner 1936.

[48] An explicit reference by Diodorus to Ctesias as his source. Even though I find Eck's remark (Eck 2003: 16 note 1) unnecessarily harsh, it would indeed be pointless to look for such a mound. Whether Diodorus' source had some impressive *tell* in mind is anybody's guess, but it is unlikely that Kuyunjik or Nebī Yūnus – where ancient Nineveh was situated, near modern Mosul – was intended, as the site was unknown to the Greeks: Xenophon (on his retreat after Cunaxa) even passed by without mentioning it, while – as it seems – Ctesias (or Diodorus, naturally) may even have situated it on the wrong river. The reference to Jonah by Eck I do not understand.

[49] Nineveh was destroyed in 612: see also below, *capita* 27–8; also, for example, Liverani 2014: 495 *sqq*.

[50] The name of the city is not mentioned, but there can be no other intended than Babylon. See for this description Bigwood 1978 and Jacobs 2011. See also Eck 2003: 116 *ad* p. 16 note 4. For a succinct review of city and history of Babylon see, for example, Leick 2001: 245–74, 329–30.

[51] Though the River Euphrates did cut Babylon in two, the actual centre of the city was situated east of the river. At its western side, Unger 1970: 80–1 believes the *alu eššu* ('new town') was situated. As Boncquet 1987: 71 remarks, no thorough archaeological survey in that part has been carried through until now: see also ibid.:71 note 291, 72 note 292, 73–4 and notes 302–7. The events after the Third Gulf War of 2003, when parts of Babylon were converted into a military base, make it doubtful whether any meaningful research can be executed in the future: see, for example, Rothfield 2009.

[52] Though according to the MSS these phrases (τηλικοῦτο δ' ἦν ... τοῖς ἀκούουσιν) formed part of the text, Vogel 1985a: 181 (*apparatus ad* line 6) and Oldfather 1968: 372–3 deleted them, following a suggestion by Eichstädt. These lines need, according to Eck 2003: 117–18 *ad* note 7, close scrutiny. Eck's argument is clear and solves the apparent contradictions in this

Ancient History: Assyrians, Chaldeans, and Medes 99

of Clitarchus and certain of those who at a later time crossed into Asia with Alexander, three hundred and sixty-five *stadia* [c. 67.5 km];[53] and these latter add that it was her desire to make the number of *stadia* the same as the days in the year. (4) Fastening baked bricks in bitumen[54] she built a wall with a height, as Ctesias says, of fifty fathoms [c. 92.5 m].[55] Some of the later writers,[56] however, have recorded the walls were fifty cubits [c. 22.5 m] high and wide enough for more than two chariots abreast to drive upon. There were two hundred and fifty towers, sixty fathoms [c. 110 m] high, as some more recent authors write, sixty cubits [c. 27 m].[57] (5) In spite of the great length of the circuit wall one does not need to be surprised that Semiramis constructed a small number of towers. Since the city was surrounded by swamps over a long distance,[58] she decided not to build towers along that space, as the swamps offered sufficient natural defence. And right between the houses and the walls a road was left of two *plethra* [c. 62 m] wide.[59]

(2.8.1) In order to expedite the building of these constructions she apportioned a *stadium* [c. 185 m] to each of her friends. She furnished them with sufficient material for their task and directed them to complete their work within a year. (2) And while they finished these assignments with great speed she gratefully acknowledged their zeal. She herself chose to build a bridge with the length of five *stadia* [c. 925 m], at the narrowest part of the river, after she had skilfully sunk the piers, which stood twelve feet [c. 3.70 m] apart,

---

phrase: there is no need to athetise these lines. I follow his edition here. Eck 2003: 117 *ad* p. 16 note 6 refers to Koldewey 1932: 48–9, believing Ctesias' numbers originally were more precise but were transformed before arriving at Diodorus. Clitarchus might be an appropriate guess, as he is also named explicitly by Diodorus as a source. It appears all measurements provided by Diodorus are 7.5 times greater than the actual ones (see Koldewey 1925: 12), which might, according to Boncquet 1987: 87, indicate a fault in the conversion of Babylonian into Greek measures.

[53] For Clitarchus et al. see, for example, Boncquet 1987: 75–7.
[54] See Boncquet 1987: 77–8, indicating that this phrase represents a frequently occurring expression in Neo-Babylonian texts (*ina kupri u agurri*), with an identical meaning. For books on bitumen, Boncquet 1987: 77 note 318. See also below, note 104.
[55] See also Eck 2003: 119 *ad* p. 17 note 1.
[56] Probably again Clitarchus and some of those who later crossed into Asia with Alexander, referred to before.
[57] The phrase τὸ δὲ ὕψος <ὀργυιῶν> ἑξήκοντα, ὡς δ' ἔνιοι τῶν νεωτέρων φασί, πηχῶν ἑξήκοντα ('sixty fathoms high, as some more recent authors write, sixty cubits') is given in MS D^a. Though it is omitted by the other MSS and Bekker, Vogel, and Oldfather, Eck 2003: 119 *ad* p. 17 note 4 argues that it is a correct addition. I endorse his view. For various views on the width of the walls, see also Boncquet 1987: 79–80. For an archaeological review of the walls: Boncquet 1987: 81–3.
[58] For the surroundings of Babylon see below, 17.116.5; see also Arr. *An.* 7.17.6, 22.1.
[59] Eck 2003: 120 *ad* p. 17 note 6 wonders, with Boncquet 1987: 80, why Ctesias (and Q. Curtius Rufus, Strabo, and – in a way – Herodotus) remains (largely) silent about the gates of Babylon, like the magnificent Ištar- gate, now reconstructed in Berlin's Pergamon Museum.

into the river's bed.⁶⁰ The stones, which were set firmly together, she bonded with iron cramps, and she filled the joints of the cramps by pouring in lead.⁶¹ Again, in front of the piers on the side that would be exposed to the current she constructed cutwaters. The sides of the cutwaters were rounded to turn off the water and gradually accommodated to the width of the pier. This was done to make sure that the sharp points of the cutwaters divided the impetus of the stream, while the rounded sides, yielding to its force, softened the violence of the river.⁶² (3) This bridge was given a floor with beams of cedar, cypress, and palm logs of exceptional size and had a width of thirty feet [c. 9.3 m].⁶³ It is considered to have been inferior to none of the works of Semiramis in technical skill. On each side of the river she built a very costly quay of about the same width as the walls and one hundred and sixty *stadia* [c. 29.6 km] long.⁶⁴ She also built two palaces on the very banks of the river, one at each end of the bridge.⁶⁵ It was her intention to be able both to look down over the entire city from these,⁶⁶ and to hold the keys – as it were – to

---

⁶⁰ Wetzel 1930: 54–7, pl. 78, reports that excavations have revealed a bridge, about 123 m long, c. 5 m wide, constructed on eight very massive piers, two of them on land and six in the water, crossing the Euphrates, which is here about 115 m wide (much less than Ctesias reports), standing about 9 m apart from each other (further than Ctesias reports). They date to either the reign of Nebuchadnezzar II, who ruled from 605 to 562, or that of his father Nabopolassar, who reigned from c. 625 to 605. Hdt. 1.186 ascribes the bridge to another lady, Nitocris, but describes the construction in similar terms. See also Boncquet 1987: 83–4 and note 348.
⁶¹ Rather a Greek technique than a Babylonian, or Assyrian, one. Wetzel 1930: 55 reports that the baked bricks, measuring about 31 × 31 cm, were joined by bitumen. See also Eck 2003: 121 *ad* p. 17 note 9.
⁶² As Wetzel 1930: 55 notices, an apt description of the situation. It leads Eck 2003: 18 note 1 to believe Ctesias' description rests upon autopsy.
⁶³ Though cedar, cypress, and especially palm-wood were typical construction woods in Babylonia (see, for example, below 17.115.2; Str. 16.1.5/739), they have, being quite perishable, obviously not been found on the site.
⁶⁴ Only a quay of 3.5 m wide has been found on the east bank of the river (see Wetzel 1930: 48–9); on the west side of the river there have been found no traces of either a quay or a wall near the site of the bridge (Wetzel et al. 1957: 22), nor is any quay on the west side referred to in Neo-Babylonian inscriptions.
⁶⁵ Koldewey 1931: 124–5 suggests the palaces intended are, on the one side, the southern castle and, on the northern side, the summer palace on the *Babil* hill. Eck 2003: 121–2 *ad* p. 18 note 5 remarks that Herodotus only refers to one palace, the entire *Kasr*, though other authors more or less confirm the situation as described in Diodorus. However, neither palace really sat at either end of the bridge. Here either Ctesias or Diodorus himself was at fault, as Eck 2003: 122 suggests, who offers a suggestion to reconcile story and archaeological evidence. There are reasons to doubt whether Herodotus' description was based upon autopsy: see Rollinger 1993. See also Boncquet 1987: 85–6, who succinctly pays attention to the change in the bed of the Euphrates, making the description of Diodorus (or Ctesias) a more or less correct one of the situation in his times, whereas the situation was altogether different at the time of the (re)construction of the city by Nebuchadnezzar.
⁶⁶ πόλιν ἅπασαν κατοπτεύ<σ>ειν. While all the manuscripts give κατοπτεύειν, κατοπτεύσειν is a conjecture by Hertlein. Like Eck 2003: 18 and 122 *ad* p. 18 note 6, I have followed this

Ancient History: Assyrians, Chaldeans, and Medes

the most important sections of the city. (4) As the River Euphrates runs through the centre of Babylon and flows southward, one of the palaces faced the rising sun and the other the setting sun, and both had been constructed on a lavish scale. In the case of the palace that faced west[67] she made the length of its first or outer circuit wall sixty *stadia* [c. 11.1 km]. She fortified it with lofty walls, which had been built at great cost and were of baked brick. And within this wall she built a second one, annular[68] in form. In the bricks of this wall wild animals of every kind had been engraved before the bricks were baked, and by the ingenious use of colours these figures reproduced the actual appearance of the animals themselves.[69] (5) This circuit wall had a length of forty *stadia* [c. 7.4 km], a width of three hundred bricks,[70] and a height, as Ctesias says, of fifty fathoms [c. 92 m]. The height of the towers was seventy fathoms [c. 129 m]. (6) Within these two walls she built yet a third circuit wall,[71] which enclosed an acropolis,[72] the perimeter of which was twenty *stadia* [c. 3.7 km]. The height and width of the structure, however, surpassed the dimensions of the middle circuit wall. On both the towers and the walls were again animals of every kind, ingeniously executed by the use of colours and the realistic representation of the several species. The whole had been made to represent a hunt of all kinds of wild animals, complete in every detail, more than four cubits [c. 1.8 m] in size. Moreover, Semiramis had also been portrayed, among the animals, on horseback, hurling a javelin at a leopard, and nearby was her husband Ninus, thrusting his spear into a lion at close quarters.[73] (7) In this wall she also set triple gates, two of

---

conjecture. If not, ἕξειν, as the MSS have it now, should be altered into ἔχειν, to make both forms congruent to each other.

[67] That is, the so-called *Südburg*, *de facto* the main palace.

[68] Translated this way on the basis of Koldewey 1914: 130. As Boncquet 1987: 87 notices, this conclusion is not supported by archaeological evidence.

[69] A description that fits the animals on the walls as nowadays displayed in the Pergamon Museum, Berlin.

[70] The most current size of bricks used in Babylon was 33 × 33 × 9 cm: see Eck 2003: 19 note 2.

[71] Koldewey 1931: 124–5 suggests the three walls correspond to (1) the walls directly north of the so-called *Nordburg*; (2) the two walls enclosing the processional road between the *Nordburg* and the so-called *Vorwerk* (decorated with lions, bulls, and dragons like those on the Ištar gate now in Berlin); and (3) the wall of the so-called *Südburg*.

[72] Koldewey 1931: 1 suggests that the structure Diodorus calls the acropolis only describes the so-called *Südburg*, where the actual royal palace was to be found.

[73] Though Koldewey 1931: 125 believes he and Wetzel may have found in the glazed bricks inside the *Südburg* fragments that might confirm Diodorus' description, Haerinck 1973: 122–3, qualifies that picture, stating that the fragment that Koldewey and Wetzel believe depicts a woman is too small to determine the figure's sex, let alone to suggest it might be related to the figures of Diodorus' account. Others again believe in still other inspiration for the figures: see also Eck 2003: 123–4 *ad* p. 19 note 9.

which were of bronze and were opened with a mechanical device.[74] Now this palace surpassed that on the other bank of the river by far in both size and details of execution. The perimeter of the wall of the latter, made of baked brick, was only thirty *stadia* [c. 5.5 km] long,[75] and instead of the ingenious portrayal of animals it had bronze images[76] of Ninus and Semiramis and their lieutenants,[77] and also one of Zeus, whom the Babylonians call Belus.[78] On this wall were also depicted both battle scenes and hunts of every kind,[79] which filled those who looked at it with mixed feelings.

(2.9.1) After she had completed this goal, Semiramis picked out the lowest spot in Babylon and built a square reservoir, which was three hundred *stadia* [c. 55.5 km] long on each side. It was constructed of baked brick and bitumen, and had a depth of thirty-five feet [c. 10.85 m].[80] (2) Then, after she had diverted the river into it, she built an underground passageway from one palace to the other.[81] After she had constructed the vaulted chambers of baked brick, she coated both sides with hot bitumen until she had made the thickness of this coating four cubits [c. 1.8 m]. The side walls of the passageway were twenty bricks thick and twelve feet high [c. 3.72 m], exclusive of the barrel vault, and the width of the passageway was fifteen feet [c. 4.65 m]. (3) After she had completed this construction in only seven days, she let the river back again into its old course. Therefore, because the stream flowed above the passageway, Semiramis could go across from one palace to the other without passing over the river. She also put bronze gates at each end of the passageway, which stood until the time of Persian

---

[74] Eck 2003: 124–5 *ad* p. 19 note 10 believes the description of these gates might well evoke either the famous and colossal Ištar gate of Babylon, or another, thus far unknown, of the main gates of Babylon.

[75] In fact it was no more than 4 *stadia* [c. 740 m] long: see, for example, Boncquet 1987: 87.

[76] As Diodorus expressly uses the word ἄγαλμα for 'statue' (see 2.9.5–6), Eck is, probably rightly, hesitant to translate εἰκόναι as such and opts for a more general term.

[77] Here, it is probably right to translate ὕπαρχος as lieutenant or governor.

[78] See Hdt. 1.181. *Bêl* is an Akkadian word with the meaning 'Lord': it relates here to Marduk, Babylon's main deity: see also Eck 2003: 125 *ad* p. 19 note 14; Boncquet 1987: 89–90.

[79] Apart from ceremonial scenes, battle and hunting scenes were a favourite subject of Assyrian reliefs: Bigwood 1978: 43. See also Amiet 1977: 235, 252, 411–15.

[80] This story shows some similarity with the account of Hdt. 1.185–6 on Nitocris. As a matter of fact, north of the Ištar gate and east of the processional road, traces were found of something that may have been a reservoir: see also Bergamini 1977: 116–18 and note 113. Gullini 1979: 187 suggests this reservoir might match the lake described in Hdt. 1.191. See also Boncquet 1987: 88–9 and Eck 2003: 125 *ad* p. 20 note 2.

[81] As Boncquet 1987: 88 phrases it, we enter, with the description of the tunnel, the realm of fantasy, as no evidence of such a structure has, up to now, been found. See, though, Eck 2003: 125–6 *ad* p. 20 note 3.

Ancient History: Assyrians, Chaldeans, and Medes   103

rule.⁸² (4) Afterwards, she built in the centre of the city a sanctuary for Zeus, whom, as we have said, the Babylonians call Belus.⁸³ As the historians disagree with regard to this sanctuary and since time has caused the structure to fall into ruins, it is impossible to describe it accurately.⁸⁴ But all agree that it was exceedingly high, and that in it the Chaldeans⁸⁵ made their observations of the stars, whose risings and settings they could see accurately because of the height of the structure. (5) After the entire building had been ingeniously constructed at great expense of bitumen and brick,⁸⁶ Semiramis set up three statues of hammered gold at the top of the ascent, of Zeus, of Hera, and of Rhea.⁸⁷ Of these statues that of Zeus represented him upright and striding forward, and, as it was forty feet [c. 12.4 m] high, it weighed a thousand Babylonian talents [c. 30,000 kg].⁸⁸ The statue of Rhea showed her seated on a golden throne. It was of the same weight as that of Zeus: at her knees stood two lions, while nearby were huge serpents of silver,

---

⁸² For an interpretation of this phrase see Eck 2003: 126 *ad* p. 20 note 8.
⁸³ The sanctuary proper of Marduk was called the *Esagila*, dominated by the great ziggurat, the *Etemenanki*, probably the legendary Tower of Babel, situated north of the temple of Marduk in an enclosure. See especially Wetzel and Weissbach 1938. See also Boncquet 1987: 89–90.
⁸⁴ Possibly an addition by Diodorus himself: see also Eck 2003: 21 note 1. As regards his adducing evidence from Herodotus' account (Hdt. 1.181–3), some caution is needed.
⁸⁵ Chaldea was properly the southernmost portion of the valley of the Tigris and the Euphrates (see Ur of the Chaldeans', Genesis 11:28, 31), essentially the region of the Šatt al-Arab (Arvand Rud) in the modern Iraq–Iran border region. Sometimes it is extended to include Babylonia and thus comprises all of South Mesopotamia, as in the Bible. Notably in the Old Testament, the expressions 'Chaldea' and 'Chaldeans' are frequently used as equivalents for 'Babylonia' and 'Babylonians' (see, for example, Daniel 1:4, 9:1). It is, *inter alia*, apparent in the words of Pliny, speaking of *Babylon Chaldaicarvm gentivm capvt* ('Babylon, capital of the Chaldeans': Plin. *Nat.* 6.30.121). Babylon fell to Cyrus the Great in 539. It was probably in this period that the priests of Babylon became known as 'Chaldeans' (Hdt. 1.181, 183). The study of astronomy and astrology was developed in this period, and 'Chaldean' came to mean simply 'astrologer', as occasionally in the book of Daniel (see, for example, 2:2–11) and among the Greeks and Romans: Cicero, for example, used it for 'soothsayer' (Cic. *Div.* 1.1.2). The different meanings of the word 'Chaldean' are well reflected in Str. 16.1.6/739. See also Aaboe 1991 for the nature of Babylonian ('Chaldean') astronomy; and see Oelsner 1996; Maul 1996.
⁸⁶ For a modern attempt at reconstruction see Pedersén 2011. See also Boncquet 1987: 91–5.
⁸⁷ Of these statues, Zeus would represent Marduk and Hera Sarpanîtu, at Babylon frequently called Erûa, the consort of Marduk (Wetzel and Weissbach 1938: 84). As for Rhea, the association below with lions might indicate that Ištar or another deity like Cybele could be meant. However, the image of a triad complicates matters, as Eck 2003: 127 *ad* p. 21 note 4 states: it might reflect an ancient tradition (though not specific to Mesopotamia), but might as well be merely a *topos* recurring in Greek descriptions. Boncquet 1987: 90 points out that it is unlikely that the temple *on* the ziggurat housed three statues, but feasible that they sat in *Esagila*, the great temple *next* to the ziggurat. Diodorus omits to mention the great bed, referred to by both Herodotus (1.181) and the Babylonian *Esagila* tablet (see also Wetzel and Weissbach 1938: 84).
⁸⁸ Assuming the weight was given in Babylonian talents – a *Biltu* (c. 30 kg). An Attic/Euboic *talent* weighed about 25.86 kg.

each one weighing thirty talents [c. 900 kg]. (6) The statue of Hera was also standing and weighed eight hundred talents [c. 24,000 kg]. In her right hand she held a snake by the head and in her left a sceptre studded with precious stones. (7) A common table for all three stood in front of them, made of hammered gold, forty feet long [c. 12.4 m], fifteen wide [c. 4.65 m], and weighing five hundred talents [c. 15,000 kg]. Upon it were two drinking cups, weighing thirty talents [c. 900 kg]. (8) There were censers as well, also two in number, weighing three hundred talents [c. 9,000 kg] each, and also three gold mixing bowls, of which the one belonging to Zeus weighed twelve hundred Babylonian talents [c. 36,000 kg] and the other two six hundred [c. 18,000 kg] each. (9) But these objects[89] were later carried off as spoil by the kings of the Persians, while as for the palaces and the other buildings, time has either entirely effaced them or left them in ruins.[90] In fact, merely a small part of Babylon itself is inhabited nowadays, and most of the area within its walls is being used for agriculture.[91]

(2.10.1) There was also, next to the acropolis, the Hanging Gardens, as they are called, which were not built by Semiramis, but by a later Assyrian king to please one of his concubines.[92] It is told that the latter was a Persian by race and that because she longed for the meadows of her mountains, she asked the king to imitate the distinctive landscape of Persis by means of a planted garden. (2) The park extended four *plethra* [c. 124 m] on each side, and because the approach to the garden sloped like a hillside and the several parts of the structure rose from one another, tier on tier, the appearance of the whole resembled that of a theatre. (3) When the ascending terraces had been built, galleries had been made underneath

---

[89] Eck 2003: 22 note 2 points out that ταῦτα ('these objects') is vague and offers little help in assessing what was taken by the kings of the Persians. Xerxes especially has been blamed for having inflicted quite considerable damage on Babylon: see also Boncquet 1987: 91 note 385.

[90] It is unclear whether Ctesias or, probably, another author is Diodorus' source and where precisely that source's information started: see also Eck 2003: 127–8 *ad* p. 22 note 3.

[91] See Curt. 5.1.27. See also Str. 16.1.5/738 who, like Plin. *Nat.* 6.30.122, considers the ascent of Seleucia as a (major) cause for Babylon's descent.

[92] See also Str. 16.1.5/738 (who considers them as one of the marvels of the world); Curt. 5.1.32–5; J. *AJ* 10.226–7, *Ap.* 1.141. Herodotus remains silent on these Gardens. Allegedly, Josephus based his account on Berossus, Q. Curtius Rufus on Clitarchus, and Strabo presumably on Onesicritus. In the Babylonian sources themselves there is, to the best of my knowledge, no allusion at all to such Gardens as are described here (which, naturally, does not mean there were no (royal) gardens in Babylon). Dalley 1994 suggests the Hanging Gardens did exist, though not in Babylon but in Nineveh, a suggestion she elaborated in Dalley 2013. See also Eck 2003: 128–9 *ad* p. 22 notes 5 and 6. Boncquet 1987: 95 argues that Diodorus based the description of the Hanging Gardens not upon Ctesias but on Clitarchus (Eck, though, does believe Ctesias was Diodorus' source: Eck 2003: 130 *ad* p. 22 note 8). See Boncquet 1987: 95–8 for his discussion on the evidence of the Gardens.

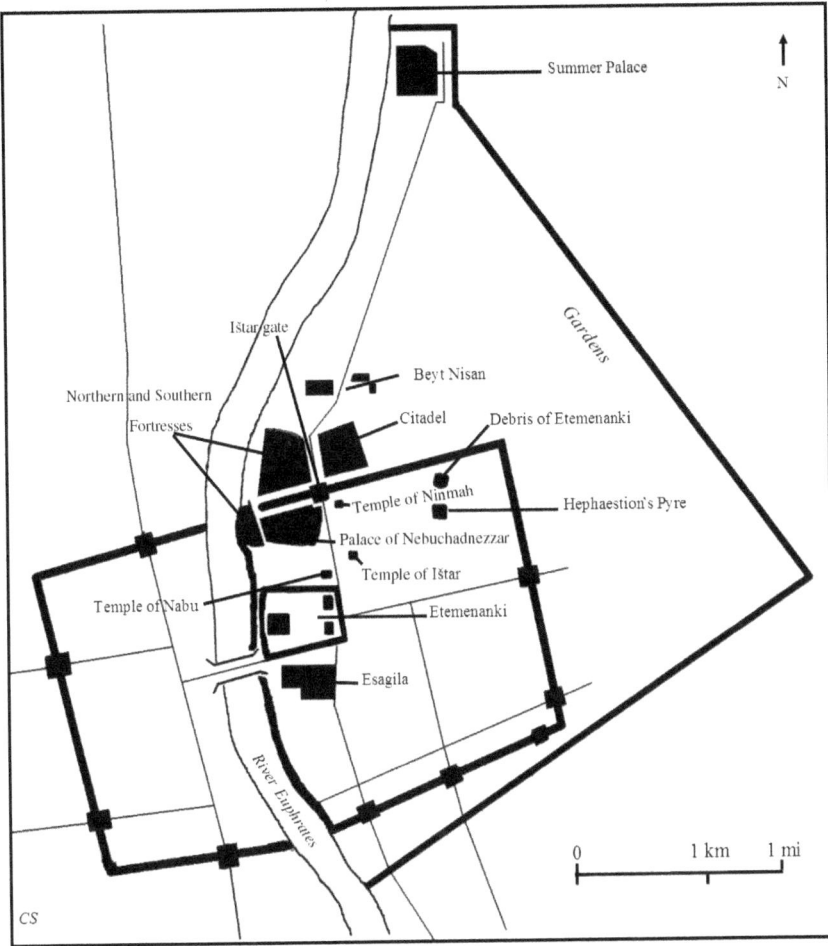

Fig. 2.3. Simplified plan of the city of Babylon (situation c. 323).

that carried the entire weight of the planted gardens and rose little by little one above the other along the approach. The uppermost gallery, which was fifty cubits [c. 22.5 m] high, bore the highest surface of the park,[93] which was made level with the circuit wall of the battlements of the city. (4) Furthermore, the walls, which had been constructed at great expense, were twenty-two feet [c. 6.80 m] thick, while the passageway between each two walls was ten feet

---

[93] Eck 2003: 130 *ad* p. 22 note 8 rightly remarks that the term παράδεισος ('park') is here hardly appropriately used by Diodorus, as the word in its Iranian origin rather suggests a vast domain. What is described here constitutes no more than a, perhaps elaborate, κῆπος ('garden').

[c. 3.10 m] wide. The roofs of the galleries were covered over with beams of stone sixteen feet [c. 5 m] long, inclusive of the overlap, and four feet [c. 1.25 m] wide. (5) The roof above these beams had first a layer of reeds, laid in great quantities of bitumen. Over this layer were two courses of baked brick bonded with cement,[94] and as a third layer a covering of lead, to the end that the moisture from the soil might not penetrate beneath. On all this again earth had been piled to a depth sufficient for the roots of the largest trees. The ground, which was levelled off, was thickly planted with trees of every kind that, by their great size or any other charm, could give pleasure to the beholder. (6) And because each of the galleries, each projecting beyond another, received the light, they contained many royal lodgings of every description. There was one gallery which contained openings leading from the topmost surface and machines for supplying the garden with water, the machines raising the water in great abundance from the river,[95] although no one outside could see it being done. Now this park, as I have said, was a later construction.[96]

Expedition against Armenia:

(2.11.1) Semiramis founded other cities as well, along both the Rivers Euphrates and Tigris. In these cities she established trading posts for the merchants who brought goods from Media, Paraetacene,[97] and all the neighbouring region. For the Euphrates and Tigris, the most notable, one might say, of all the rivers of Asia after the Nile and Ganges,[98] have their sources in the mountains of Armenia and

---

[94] The Greek γύψος can mean here either the mineral gypsum itself or products like plaster of Paris and perhaps even a kind of cement made of it: I opted here for the last, because of its apparent adhesive qualities. See also: 'ἐν γύψῳ κείμενος, embedded in cement, D.S. 2.10<.5>, Arr. *An.* 2.21.4': *LSJ s.v.* As a matter of fact, in Diodorus it reads δεδεμένην, not κείμενος, but the gist is the same.

[95] Perhaps to be considered as a kind of κοχλίαι, Archimedes' screw: see Eck 2003: 134 *ad* p. 23 note 9.

[96] According to Koldewey 1931: 39, a vaulted construction in a corner of the *Südburg*, the palace of Nebuchadnezzar II, might be identified as this garden.

[97] Paraetacene is here the name given to the border region of Persia adjoining Media (Ptol. *Geog.* 6.4.3) and leading eastward to Ecbatana, modern Isfahan. The name Paraetacene – and presumably at least part of the area – is identified with modern Faridān, the uplands west of the Esfahān plain (see also *RE Supp.* X: cols. 478–82). Although the Paraetaceneans are styled as a Median tribe by Herodotus (Hdt. 1.101), the land was later attributed to Persis and to Elymaïs (see 19.34.7; Str. 16.1.17–18/744). As a matter of fact, there are two more regions that go by the name of Paraetacene, one a district behind Bactria and Sogdia, another the 'Oasenland' between Arachosia and Drangia (see Herrmann 1949).

[98] For the Nile, see 1.32–3; for the Ganges, see 2.37.1–3, 17.93.2, 18.6.1. It is unlikely that Ctesias was Diodorus' source here: it may have been Megasthenes (see *FGrH/BNJ* 715 FF 9a & 9b). As a matter of fact, in 2.35.1 the Indus is styled as the greatest river after the Nile.

are two thousand five hundred *stadia* [c. 462.5 km] apart at their origin.[99] (2) After flowing through Media and Paraetacene they enter Mesopotamia,[100] which they enclose between them, thus giving the country this name. Having passed Babylonia in this manner, they empty into the Persian Gulf.[101] (3) Moreover, because they are great streams and traverse a spacious territory, they offer many advantages to men who have a trading profession. Therefore the regions along their banks are full of prosperous trading posts which contribute greatly to the fame of Babylonia. (4) Semiramis quarried out a stone from the mountains of Armenia which was one hundred and thirty feet [c. 40.3 m] long and twenty-five feet [c. 7.75 m] wide and thick. (5) Having hauled this stone to the river by means of many multitudes of yokes of mules and oxen, she loaded it on to a raft and after she had brought it on the raft, she transported it down the stream to Babylon.[102] After it had arrived, she set it up beside the most famous street, an astonishing sight to all who passed by. <This stone is called by some an obelisk after its shape, and it is counted among the seven wonders of the world.>[103]

Wonders of Babylonia:
(2.12.1) Though there are many unique sights in Babylonia, the enormous amount of bitumen which the country produces is especially

The total length of the Euphrates is c. 2,760 km, that of the Tigris c. 1,850 km. See Boncquet 1987: 98–9.
[99] In reality the distance between the two sources is about 370 km. This distance does not help to solve a textual problem. Like Str. 11.12.3/521 and Curt. 5.1.13, MS D^a reads σταδίους δισχιλίους καὶ πεντακοσίους ('two thousand five hundred *stadia*', c. 462.5 km), while MSS C, V, and L read σταδίους χιλίους καὶ πεντακοσίους ('fifteen hundred *stadia*', c. 277.5 km). As both traditions are roughly a hundred kilometres off, I have followed the option preferred by Vogel, Oldfather, and Eck.
[100] In fact, neither river flows through Media or Paraetacene, but the Tigris does flow along them. The term Μεσοποταμία is, to the best of my knowledge, first attested with certainty in Arist. *Mir.* 149 = 845b8, later also used in Plb. 5.44.6 and Str. 11.12.2/521 *sq*. If the text does go back to Ctesias, it would have been the first time the word was used. Here, Babylonia and Mesopotamia are clearly distinguished, but the precise borders of Mesopotamia remain blurred: see also Eck 2003: 134 *ad* p. 24 note 3.
[101] In many Greek texts the term Ἐρύθρα θάλασσα, literally 'Red Sea', includes the Red Sea proper, the northern part of the Sea of Oman, and the Persian Gulf. I have translated according to the (modern) geographical nomenclature.
[102] Though the majority of the manuscripts and editions read here μέχρι τῆς Βαβυλωνίας, I have followed the reading of manuscript V, *Vaticanus gr.* 996, μέχρι τῆς Βαβυλῶνος. The reason for doing so is the context, where we are told that the stone was erected beside the most famous street: it can, in my opinion, only indicate that the stone was intended for the city she had constructed to win repute for herself, Babylon. To transport the stone to Babylon makes, therefore, more sense than to raft it to Babylonia.
[103] Eck 2003: 135 *ad* p. 24 note 9 argues after Eichstädt that the phrase ὅν τινες ... καταριθμοῦσιν is, in fact, a double interpolation and that, once removed, the transition between 2.11.5 and 2.12.1 is more understandable. As I find the argument convincing, I have placed the sentence between angled brackets.

wonderful;[104] so great is the supply of this commodity that not only does it suffice for their buildings, which are numerous and large, but the common people, gathering at the place, collect it without any restriction as well, and burn it instead of wood after they have dried it.[105] (2) And although the number of people who mine it is enormous, the amount remains undiminished, as if it originates from some immense source. Moreover, there is a vent-hole near this source, small in size but of remarkable potency. For it emits a heavy, sulphurous vapour that brings death to all living creatures approaching it, and they meet with a swift and strange end. For after being subjected for a time to the retention of the breath they are killed, as if the expulsion of the breath is prevented by the force which has attacked the processes of respiration. The body swells and blows up immediately, particularly in the region about the lungs. (3) And there is also across the river a lake whose edge offers solid footing, and if any man, unacquainted with it, enters it, he swims for a short time, but as he advances towards the centre he is dragged down as though by a certain force. When he begins to help himself and makes up his mind to turn back to shore again, it appears as if he is hauled back by something else, in spite of the fact that he struggles to help himself out. He becomes numb, first in his feet, then in his legs as far as the groin, and finally, overcome by numbness in his whole body, he sinks to the bottom, and is cast up dead a little later.[106] Now as regards the wonders of Babylonia, let what has been said suffice.

Achievements of Semiramis in Media:

(2.13.1) After Semiramis had concluded her works in Babylon she set forth towards Media with a great force. And when she had

---

[104] We have already encountered bitumen as a building material. For a thorough review of the use of bitumen one should still always consult Forbes 1964. Boncquet 1987: 100 indicates that the main source of bitumen was situated near modern Hit or Id, c. 200 km north-west of Babylon. Hdt. 1.179 mentions a city called Is, eight days' journey from Babylon, on a river also called Is, a tributary of the Euphrates: according to Eck 2003: 25 note 2 and Boncquet (ibid.), that might be the very place intended by τὸν τόπον ('the place') in the following sentence. See also Forbes 1964: 16. For additional references from antiquity see also Boncquet 1987: 100 note 427.

[105] Forbes 1964: 85 asserts that bitumen was rarely used as a fuel. Diodorus (or for that matter Ctesias), however, may have been wrong-footed by the fact that at places one particular form of natural bitumen, called *naft*, is very volatile and can ignite easily. Normally, though, the smell of burning bitumen should forbid its use as an ingredient to make fire.

[106] See the comments by Eck 2003: 26 note 1, believing the description shows Ctesias' hand. On the other hand, Boncquet 1987: 101 is sceptical, suggests the sulphuric vapour is an 'exotic addition', and believes it feasible that Clitarchus' work lies at the basis of *capita* 11 and 12 as well.

Ancient History: Assyrians, Chaldeans, and Medes   109

arrived at the mountain known as Bagistan [Bisitun], she encamped near it and laid out a park.[107] This park had a circumference of twelve *stadia* [c. 2.2 km] and since it was situated in the plain it had a great well by means of which her plantings could be irrigated. (2) The Bagistan Mountain is sacred to Zeus and on the side facing the park its sheer cliffs rise to a height of seventeen *stadia* [c. 3.15 km].[108] The lowest part of this she smoothed off and engraved thereon an image of herself with a hundred spearmen at her side. Besides, she also put this inscription on the cliff in Syrian letters:[109] 'Semiramis, with the pack-saddles of the beasts of burden in her army, built up a mound from the plain and thereby climbed this precipice, even to its very ridge.' (3) After she had set forth from there and had arrived at the city of Chauon in Media,[110] she noticed on a high plateau a rock striking as regards both its height and size. Therefore she laid out there another park of exceeding size and put the rock in the middle of it. To satisfy her taste for luxury {τρυφή}, she erected on the rock some very costly buildings, from which she used to look down both upon her plantings in the park and on the whole army, encamped on the plain. (4) In this place she passed a long time to enjoy everything that suited her love of luxury {τρυφή}. She did, however, not want to marry lawfully, because she was afraid that she might be deprived of her power. Instead, she chose the most handsome of the soldiers to have sex with and next made all who had slept with her disappear.[111] (5) After her stay in Chauon, she advanced in the direction of Ecbatana [modern Hamadān] and arrived at a

---

[107] The earliest reference in Greek historiography to Bisitun. There, King Darius describes his rise to power and subsequent exploits (see Figure 3.2 below; Kent 1953: 116 *sqq*.; Brosius 2000: 28–40; a new publication on the inscription is forthcoming). The actual inscription of Darius at Bisitun is not easily accessible (Kent 1953: 107). Therefore, Ctesias might have been excused for not having read this text, if it was readable at all in his days (Sancisi-Weerdenburg 1999: 91; also Wiesehöfer 1978: 5 note 2). Weissbach 1896 remarks that some twenty-five to thirty metres below the monument of Darius remains of a Greek inscription can be discerned. The Greek inscription in its turn had replaced seven pre-Achaemenid sculptures of human figures: it might account for the description below, '[t]he lowest part (namely of this cliff)'. In combination with the local name of the mountain, Mt Simirria, the entirety may have suggested 'Semiramis' to Ctesias, or its Aramaic equivalent, 'Šamiram', to speakers of that language: see also Phillips 1968: 167; *ARAB*, vol. 2: 73–99; also: Luschey 1974: 118; Boncquet 1987: 101–2. For the park, see Balcer 1972: 119 note 59.
[108] The Persian *bagistana* means 'sojourn of the gods'. The rock is, in fact, c. 166 m high.
[109] Like Herodotus, Ctesias of Cnidus might have referred to this writing as being in Ἀσσύρια γράμματα (see, for example, Hdt. 3.87.1). However, because of the MSS, Vogel 1985a: 190; Oldfather 1968: 392–3; and Eck 2003: 26 all read Συρίοις γράμμασιν, I have followed their lead. Moreover, it is not absolutely clear whether Aramaic (no cuneiform) or Akkadian (or any other language in cuneiform) was originally intended by Diodorus or his source.
[110] The name of the city, or region, is problematic: see Eck 2003: 136 *ad* p. 26 note 8.
[111] Semiramis' alleged sexual appetite is also referred to by Euph. 26 (fr. C), col. i, lines 9–10 (ed. Lightfoot); D.Chr. 47.24; and Oros. *Hist.* 1.3.7.

mountain range called the Zarcaeus.[112] As this range extended many *stadia* and was full of cliffs and chasms, it required a long detour, which is why she conceived the ambition both to leave an immortal monument of herself and at the same time to make a direct route. Therefore, cutting through the cliffs and filling up the crevices, she built a direct and valuable road, which to this day is called the road of Semiramis.[113] (6) Upon arriving at Ecbatana, a city which lies on the plain, she built an expensive palace in it and in every other way gave rather exceptional attention to the region.[114] Because the city had no water supply and since there was a spring nowhere close, she made the whole of it well watered by bringing an abundance of the purest water to it at the cost of much hardship and expense.[115] (7) About twelve *stadia* [c. 2.2 km] from Ecbatana is a mountain, which is called Orontes [modern Alvand Kūh] and is unusual for its ruggedness and enormous height, since the ascent, straight to its summit, is twenty-five *stadia* [c. 4.6 km]. Because there was a great lake, which emptied into a river, situated on the other side of that mountain, she cut through the very mountain down to the base.[116]

---

[112] Like Herodotus, Ctesias of Cnidus referred to this city as Ἀγβάτανα ('Agbatana'), a rendition of the OP name of the city, $Ha^m gmatāna$ (≈ 'City of Gatherings': see Kent 1953: 212 s.v.); see Stephen of Byzantium FGrH/BNJ 688 F 42; see also Stronk 2010: F. 1iα: 161, 254–5). Diodorus usually refers to this city as Ecbatana and on this issue I shall follow him. As regards the name of the mountain, it is usually assumed that the Zagros is intended; Eck 2003: 136–7 *ad* p. 27 note 2 is much less sure regarding this identification, but offers no alternative. See also Boncquet 1987: 104–5. For the Zagros see also Treidler 1967a.

[113] Eck 2003: 27 note 3 suggests that, if one adheres to the belief that the Zarcaeus represents the Zagros (see Treidler 1967c), this road might be the pass that is called the 'Median Gate' in Str. 11.13.8/525. See also Eilers 1971: 19–20. The pass mentioned by Strabo is likely to be a different one from the Ζάγρου πύλαι ('Zagros' Gates') mentioned in Ptol. Geog. 6.2.7 (see also Treidler 1967b). According to the latter, Strabo intended to refer to a pass near the River Dyala, Ptolemy to a more northerly pass, near the River Amardus (modern Safidrud ['White River']). Looking at the situation, it seems the route Semiramis is said to have followed is rather that along the Dyala. See also Boncquet 1987: 104–5.

[114] Ecbatana is situated on a plateau, c. 1,800 m high, at the base of the eastern slope of the Alvand range (the classical Mt Orontes, the 'Iasonius mons' of Ammianus Marcellinus 23.6.39). The city controls the major east–west route through the central Zagros, the so-called High Road. The palace is referred to by Herodotus (1.98) and Polybius (10.27.7–13). According to Calmeyer, a palace has been located (Calmeyer 1975: 66). Most remains from the Median and Achaemenid periods (a citadel and 'royal construction' respectively) have, so far, been retrieved from the north-east quarter of Sar-qal'a, on a mound 30 m high, called Tell Hagmatana. As a matter of fact, the ancient city is largely covered by the present agglomeration. See also Boncquet 1987: 105–6.

[115] This appears to be in contradiction to the current situation. Brown 2011 describes it as follows: 'On the wide, well-watered, fertile plain to the east, fruits and vegetables were traditionally cultivated near the city, while cereal production predominated in the next zone and pastoralism in the extensive periphery. In antiquity, the area was famed for its horses and wheat (Plb. 5.44.1). Nearby reserves of graphite, gold, platinum, antimony, iron, and various mineral salts were evidently not exploited in antiquity.'

[116] As regards the origin of the name of the mountain, Boncquet 1987: 106 refers to OP *Aruanda* (see Kent 1953: 170 s.v. '*aruvasta*'). As regards its height, Diodorus (or his source)

(8) The canal was fifteen feet [c. 4.6 m] wide and forty feet [c. 12.5 m] high. Redirecting the river that ran from the lake through the canal, she provided the city with water. Now, this is what she did in Media.

Other achievements of Semiramis in Asia:
(2.14.1) After this, she visited both Persis and every other country over which she ruled throughout Asia. Cutting through the mountains and the precipitous cliffs everywhere, she constructed very costly roads, while on the plains she made mounds. One time she constructed them as tombs for those of her generals who died, another time she founded cities on their tops.[117] (2) It was also her custom, whenever she made camp, to build little mounds from which she could look down upon all the encampment, after she had pitched her tent. As a consequence, many of the works she built throughout Asia remain to this day and are called works of Semiramis.

Semiramis in Egypt and Ethiopia:
(2.14.3) After this, she visited all of Egypt.[118] She also went to the oracle of Ammon, after she had subdued most of Libya, to inquire of the god about her own end.[119] It is told that the oracular utter-

---

is only 5 *stadia* off the mark: it is in fact 3,745 m high. The canal Semiramis is claimed to have devised is, according to König 1972: 145 note 1, the upper and lower canal of Aranzias, in which 'Aranzias' could represent the pre-Iranian name of the Alvand. After Forbes 1964: 156–63, the information bears on irrigation by so-called *qanats*, small subterranean canals, invented in the kingdom of Urartu, and utilised by the Assyrians from the times of Sargon II (c. 721–c. 705) onwards. Briant 1984: 30 believes these *qanats* go no further back than the Median–Achaemenid period. In July 2015, attempts were started to give Zarach *qanat* World Heritage Site status by UNESCO. This *qanat* is believed to be up to three thousand years old (and could, therefore, predate Briant's limit) and has a length of 120 kilometres. For details see <http://blog.persiaport.com/en/3-millenia-old-zarach-qanat-to-get-world-heritage-status/>.
[117] See Hdt. 1.184; Str. 16.1.2/737. According to Syncellus' reading of Ctesias, these mounds were the tombs of her lovers buried alive: Syncell. *Chron.* p. 119, 11 [= Ctes. *Pers.* F. 1i; see Stronk 2010: 254–5]. Eilers 1971: 22–3 believes the sentence reflects on the countless numbers of *tells* or *kurds* (or whatever name is attributed to them) in the Kurdistan–Luristan region.
[118] Semiramis' journey to Egypt is also casually referred to in 1.56.5: οὐκ ἀγνοῶ δ' ὅτι περὶ τῶν εἰρημένων πόλεων Κτησίας ὁ Κνίδιος διαφόρως ἱστόρησε, φήσας τῶν μετὰ Σεμιράμιδος παραβαλόντων εἰς Αἴγυπτόν τινας ἐκτικέναι ταύτας, ἀπὸ τῶν ἰδίων πατρίδων θεμένων τὴν προσηγορίαν ('I am not unaware that, regarding the cities named above, Ctesias of Cnidus has given a different account, saying that some of those who had come into Egypt with Semiramis founded them, calling them after their native lands'). The *capita* further deal with the Egyptian King Sesoösis and are not relevant for us.
[119] Previously (2.2.3), Diodorus had already informed the audience that Ninus had conquered Egypt. The oracle probably reflects the oracle of Ammon at the Siwa oasis (see 17.50.1–7), consulted by many, including Alexander the Great (17.49.2–51.4). Though Eck states that 'many' (without producing names) consider this a kind of reversed *imitatio Alexandri*, he also observes that no evidence for this theory has, so far, been adduced: see Eck 2003: 137–8 *ad* p. 28 note 4. Boncquet 1987: 107 reveals that among those who believe in an intermediate source between Ctesias and Diodorus is Goossens. Goossens suggests that Ctesias

ance was given her that she would disappear from among men and receive undying honour among some of the peoples and tribes of Asia, and that this would take place when her son Ninyas would conspire against her.[120] (4) Having returned from these regions, she visited most of Ethiopia, subdued it as she went,[121] and inspected the wonders of the land. For in that country, they say, there is a square lake with a perimeter of about hundred and sixty feet [c. 50 m], and its water is like vermilion in colour and its odour is sweet in the superlative degree, not unlike that of old wine.[122] Moreover, the lake has a remarkable power: for they say that whoever has drunk of it falls into a frenzy and accuses himself of every sin he had secretly committed before.[123] However, a man may not readily agree with those who tell such things.

(2.15.1) In the burial of their dead the inhabitants of Ethiopia follow customs peculiar to themselves. After they have embalmed the body and have poured a heavy coat of glass over it, they place it on a pillar, so that the body of the dead man is visible through the glass to those who pass by.[124] This is the statement of Herodotus.[125] (2) But Ctesias of Cnidus himself, declaring that Herodotus invents a tale, states that the body is indeed embalmed, but that no glass is

has been 'reworked' about 300, during the Seleucid Empire, and that Diodorus must have had a copy of this work (perhaps next to a copy of Ctesias' work?) (Goossens 1940: 38–44). Emphatically *contra*: Boncquet 1987: 107–8. See also below, Chapter 10.
[120] This preludes 2.20.1, below.
[121] This contradicts the statement of Diodorus in 3.3.1 (see below, S. 2), that Semiramis abstained from a campaign against the whole nation of the Ethiopians. The source of that paragraph is not given.
[122] See, for this rendering of the colour, Chantraine 1968: 533 *s.v.* 'κιννάβαρι'. Apparently the colour was regarded as important for Ethiopian dignitaries (Plin. *Nat.* 33.36.112, included in a treatise on the colour that runs from 33.36.111 to 33.41.124), but also seems to feature more or less prominently in India (see either *FGrH/BNJ* 688 or Lenfant 2004 F 45: §§ 8, 15, 39, and 45). Though stories regarding the lake (or the source: other evidence refers to a κρήνη) were copied by different authors, none of them provides an explanation for the colour (see Stronk in preparation, *ad loc.*).
[123] In India too there exists a source, though not with vermilion water, that has an almost identical effect on the drinker: see *FGrH/BNJ* 688 or Lenfant 2004 F 45 § 31. Herodotus mentions a source in Ethiopia that can cause the longevity of Ethiopians (Hdt. 3.23). For the 'truth serum', see also Ov. *Met.* 15.317–21; Sen. *Nat.* 3.20.5.
[124] Possibly 'glass' is the most likely translation of ὕελος: though the exact meaning of the word is uncertain, ὕελος apparently represents a transparent material (see 3.9.3; also Hdt. 3.24) and is initially, equally apparently, very hot (2.15.2). The latter point makes some of the solutions suggested in Boncquet 1987: 111 note 492 unlikely.
[125] The statement is a misrepresented paraphrase of Hdt. 3.24, perhaps partly caused by a shift of meaning (or perhaps a multiple meaning) of the word ὕελος, used by both authors. As Boncquet 1987: 112 remarks, Diodorus neglected to consult Herodotus' work itself. In fact, neither Herodotus' nor Ctesias' description does proper justice to the actual process of mummification: see Dodson and Ikram 1998. Müller 1844: 27 suggests that Ctesias may have read γυμνώσαντες ('being stripped naked') instead of Herodotus' γυψώσαντες ('rubbed with chalk'), (partially) explaining the vehemence of his attack: see also Eck 2003: 138 *ad* p. 29 note 6.

Ancient History: Assyrians, Chaldeans, and Medes   113

poured over the naked bodies. If they did so, these bodies would be burned and, being disfigured, eventually lose their likeness. (3) Therefore, they fashion a hollow statue in gold and when the corpse has been put into it, they pour the glass over the statue. When the statue is then placed on the tomb, one can see through the glass the image of the deceased in gold. (4) The rich among them are buried in this manner, Ctesias says, but those leaving a smaller estate get a silver statue, and the poor one made of earthenware. Regarding the glass there is enough of it for everyone, since it occurs in great abundance in Ethiopia and is quite current among the inhabitants.[126] (5) With regard to the habits that are most prominent among the Ethiopians and the other features of their country, we shall expound a little later [in 3.2.1–10.6][127] those most important and worth mentioning, when we shall recount their early deeds and their mythology as well.

Expedition of Semiramis against India:
(2.16.1) After Semiramis had settled the affairs of Ethiopia and Egypt, she returned with her force to Bactra in Asia. Because she had a great army and she had been at peace for a long time, she became eager to do something brilliant in the field of war. (2) After she had been told that the Indian people was the largest one in the world[128] and also possessed both the most extensive and the most beautiful country,[129] she conceived the idea of waging an expedition against India.[130] Stabrobates was king of India at that time and he had an uncountable multitude of soldiers.[131] He also had many elephants at his disposal, fitted out in an exceedingly splendid fashion to strike terror in those opposing them in war.[132] (3) For

---

[126] See Eck 2003: 138–9 *ad* p. 30 note 1.
[127] Apparently Agatharchides is Diodorus' guide there: see also Eck 2003: 139 *ad* p. 30 note 2.
[128] See Hdt. 3.94, 5.3; Str. 2.5.32/130, though Diodorus describes it as an amalgam of tribes and peoples: 2.38.1.
[129] According to Ctesias (*Ind. FGrH/BNJ* 688, Lenfant 2004: F 49 a & b), India was as large as the rest of Asia combined.
[130] Boncquet 1987: 113 parallels Semiramis' expedition against India with those of Achaemenid kings (notably Cyrus the Great and Darius I). See also below, Chapter 10. Eck 2003: 31 note 3 emphatically denies that Semiramis' expedition mirrors Alexander's march against India. I agree (see Chapter 10).
[131] As regards the name of the Indian king there are some issues, but it is the best rendering based upon the MSS. See Eck 2003: 139–40 *ad* p. 30 note 5 for a discussion; also Boncquet 1987: 114.
[132] This, too, appears to mirror the expedition of Alexander the Great, where the elephants of Poros are described in similar fashion (see 17.87.4). As a matter of fact, the mention of elephants ranged against Semiramis looks like a double anachronism: no Assyrian king or queen made war on India, and elephants were not used in warfare, and definitely in substantial

India is a land of unusual beauty, and since it is traversed by many rivers, it is supplied with water over its whole area and yields two harvests each year. Consequently, it has such an abundance of the necessities of life that it favours its inhabitants with a superfluous enjoyment of them at all times. And it is said that because of the favourable climate in those parts, the country has never experienced a famine or a destruction of crops. (4) It has an incredible number of elephants as well, which both in courage and in strength of body surpass those of Libya [that is: the African forest elephant] by far,[133] and likewise gold, silver, iron, and copper. Furthermore, within its borders one may find great quantities of precious stones of every kind and of practically all other things that contribute to luxury and wealth. After Semiramis had received a detailed account of these facts, it induced her to start a war against the Indians, although no injustice had been done to her.[134] (5) As she saw that she would need an exceedingly great force in addition to the one she already had, she despatched messengers to all the satrapies and commanded the commanders to conscript the bravest of the young men.[135] She set their quota in accordance with the size of each of the peoples and tribes. Further, she ordered them all to make new suits of armour and to be on hand, brilliantly equipped in every other respect, at Bactra on the third year thereafter.[136] (6) She also summoned ship-wrights from Phoenicia, Syria, Cyprus, and from the rest of the lands along the sea.[137] After she had shipped to those areas an abundance of timber, she ordered them to build river boats that could be disassembled.[138] (7) Because the River Indus was the largest in

---

numbers, before the sixth to fourth centuries: see Daman Singh 1989: 2, 80, 81, 84. The weapon of choice until then was generally the war chariot.

[133] This type of elephant is, indeed, smaller than the Indian elephant, whereas the African bush elephant is bigger: see Gowers 1948; also Charles 2008: 338.

[134] This description is a prelude to 2.35–42, which is apparently primarily based upon Megasthenes (see *FGrH/BNJ* 715 F 4). These paragraphs may also, perhaps (at least partly) go back to Megasthenes: see Boncquet 1987: 114–15. *Contra*: Eck 2003: 140 *ad* p. 31 note 2.

[135] Here too Diodorus (Ctesias?) has used confusing terminology: σατραπείαι ('satrapies') and ἔπαρχοι ('commanders') instead of ὕπαρχοι. Instead of σατραπείας ('satrapies', a conjecture going back to at least Dindorf and adapted by successive editors), Eck 2003: 31 l. 14 reads, as do the MSS, στρατοπεδείας ('camps'). In spite of the MS tradition I prefer to deviate here from Eck because of the more or less standard method of conscription by region.

[136] The preparation period of three years has also been adopted in the *Suda*, *s.v. sigma*,220 (Σεμίραμις, 'Semiramis').

[137] The traditional suppliers of ships of the Achaemenid kings, augmented in the *Suda* with Egyptians and Cilicians. See also 18.4.4, for Alexander's plans for a fleet.

[138] Though Curt. 8.10.3 relates that Alexander also wanted to have demountable ships, Casson 1971: 136 demonstrates that constructing and using such ships was no exceptional feat in the ancient Near East and had, for example, already been practised by Ramesses III.

Ancient History: Assyrians, Chaldeans, and Medes 115

that region and was the boundary of her kingdom,[139] it required many boats, both to cross the river and to defend it against those of the Indians who crossed it. However, as there was no timber near the river, the boats had to be brought from Bactria by land. (8) Because Semiramis observed that she was at a great disadvantage because of her shortage of elephants, she conceived the plan of making dummies of these animals.[140] By doing so, she hoped that the Indians would be struck with terror, since the Indians believed that there lived no elephants whatsoever apart from those found in India. (9) After she had selected three hundred thousand black oxen, she distributed their meat among her craftsmen and the men who had been ordered to make the figures. The hides, however, she made to be sewn together and stuffed with straw. In this manner she made dummies, copying in every detail the natural appearance of elephants. Inside each dummy was a man to take care of it as well as a camel[141] and, when the camel moved, it was for those who saw it from a distance as if they watched a real elephant.[142] (10) The craftsmen who were making these dummies for Semiramis performed their jobs in a court. It was surrounded by a wall with carefully guarded gates. In this manner neither could one of the workers within pass out, nor could anyone from outside come in to them. Semiramis did this to ensure that neither would anyone from

---

[139] Ctesias pays specific attention to the Indus in his *Indica*: see *FGrH/BNJ* 688, Lenfant 2004: F 45 §§ 1, 14, 46, and F 45r. See also 2.35.1; Hdt. 4.44. Previously Diodorus mentioned the Ganges as the main river of Asia (2.11.1), but that passage probably does not go back to Ctesias. As a matter of fact, the Indus is c. 200 km longer than the Ganges.

[140] The MSS read here τι κατασκευάζειν ιδίωμα, a sentence that hardly makes any sense in translation in the context of Diodorus' story. I will follow the solution adapted by Vogel 1985a: 196, Oldfather 1968: 402, and Eck 2003: 32, which is to athetise τι and to replace ιδίωμα with εἴδωλα, following a conjecture by Henlein. The result is a phrase that both makes sense and corresponds to the story as related in 2.16.9 and 2.17.2.

[141] See also *Suda, s.v. sigma*,220 ('Σεμίραμις'): ὅτι ἡ αὐτὴ ὁρμῶσα ἐπ᾽Ἰνδοὺς εἴδωλα ἐλεφάντινα ξύλινα συμπήγνυται εἰς μυριάδας κ᾽, ἃ ἔμελλον οἴσειν αἱ κάμηλοι, τὰ ἐντὸς ἐμπεπλησμένα φρυγάνου καὶ φορυτοῦ, ὡς εὐβάστακτα εἴη· τὰ δὲ ἔξωθεν αὐτῶν περιεβύρσωσεν· ἐπιβάτας δὲ ἐφ᾽ἑκάστην κάμηλον δύο ἔταξεν Αἰθίοπας τοξεύειν καὶ ἀκοντίζειν. ('Thereupon she herself, having set out against the Indians, constructed twenty thousand wooden dummies of elephants, which the camels would carry, being filled inside with brushwood and woodchips, so that they would be easy to bear. The outside of them she made cover with leather; she stationed two Ethiopian soldiers in each camel to shoot arrows and hurl javelins'). It seems a rather twisted, and anyway much more aggressive, version of the account presented by Diodorus (Ctesias).

[142] Though it should again be stressed that this expedition was a fiction, it should also be remarked that the Assyrians were not totally unfamiliar with elephants: see, for example, Scullard 1974: 28–9; Salonen, A. (1956: 90–2; also Collon 1977: 219. See also Collon's remark on the hunting of elephants by Assyrian kings and the presence of hides and ivory: ibid.: 220. Salonen also remarks that the two-humped Bactrian camel was introduced in Mesopotamia at the beginning of the first millennium, the one-humped Arabian camel (dromedary) in the ninth century, and that both types of animal were used in warfare: ibid.: 84–7. See also Mitchell 2000. The Persepolis reliefs also feature a two-humped camel (presented by Bactrians).

the outside see what was happening nor would any report about the dummies leak to the Indians.

(2.17.1) After the boats and the dummies had been prepared in the two allotted years, she summoned her forces the third year from everywhere to Bactria. And the number of the assembled army, as Ctesias of Cnidus has recorded, was three million infantry, two hundred thousand cavalry, and one hundred thousand chariots. (2) In addition to that, there were also men mounted on camels, carrying swords four cubits [c. 1.8 m] long, as many in number as the chariots.[143] Semiramis had ordered the construction of two thousand river boats that could be disassembled, for which she had summoned camels to carry the vessels overland. Camels also bore the dummies of the elephants, as has been mentioned. The soldiers taught their horses, by bringing them up to these camels, not to fear the fierce nature of camels.[144] (3) ... (4) When Stabrobates, the king of the Indians, learned of both the size of the forces mentioned and the exceedingly great preparation Semiramis had made for the war, he exerted himself to surpass Semiramis in every respect. (5) First of all, then, he made four thousand river boats out of bamboo. For along its rivers and marshy places, India produces an abundance of bamboo, so thick that a man would not easily be able to embrace one.[145] People say, moreover, that ships built of this bamboo are exceedingly serviceable, since this wood does not rot. (6) After he had very carefully prepared his arms and had visited all of India, Strabrobates gathered a force far greater than the one assembled by Semiramis. (7) Furthermore, after Strabrobates had gone on a hunt of wild elephants and had multiplied by many times the number already at his disposal, he equipped them all splendidly with such things as would strike terror in war. (8) Consequently, it

---

[143] The numbers presented in the *Suda*, *sigma*,220, are even more excessive: 3 million infantry; 1 million horsemen; 100,000 scythed chariots; 100,000 camel riders; 200,000 other camels; 30,000 ships; and 200,000 elephant dummies. Such numbers are totally irrational: no ruler could have mustered a force larger than at best 10 per cent of the force mentioned by Diodorus – let alone such fantastic numbers as given in the *Suda*.

[144] The story goes at least back to Hdt. 1.80.4: κάμηλον ἵππος φοβέεται, καὶ οὐκ ἀνέχεται οὔτε τὴν ἰδέην αὐτοῦ ὁρέων οὔτε τὴν ὀδμὴν ὀσφραινόμενος ('horses fear camels and can endure neither the sight nor the smell of them'). Though horses, typical flight animals, are shy and skittish by nature – probably also as regards camels – their extreme fear of camels looks like a, firmly established, urban myth.

[145] In his commentary on Ctesias' *Indica*, Nichols 2011: 102–4 suggests, after Lassen, that the plant κάλαμος refers to is (a species of) bamboo, a translation also adopted by Eck: see Eck 2003: 142 ad p. 33 note 3. According to Nichols, bamboo with extreme properties also features in Indian literature, like the *Mahābhārata* and the *Rāmāyana*. For the sizes bamboo could reach, see Ctes. *Ind.* (FGrH/BNJ 688, Lenfant 2004): F 45 § 14; see also Str. 15.1.56/710–11, based upon Megasthenes.

Ancient History: Assyrians, Chaldeans, and Medes   117

appeared, when they advanced to the attack, both because of their number and the towers upon their backs,[146] that it was beyond human nature to withstand these elephants.
(2.18.1) When he had prepared everything for the war, he despatched messengers to Semiramis, who was already on her way. He argued that she had started the war though she had not been slighted. Next he slandered her in the course of his letter as if she were a slut and, calling upon the gods as witnesses, threatened her with impalement once he had defeated her. (2) When she read the letter, however, Semiramis laughingly dismissed its content and remarked that it would be in deeds that the Indian would make trial of her *aretē*. And when her advance brought her with her force to the River Indus, she found the boats of the enemy ready for battle. (3) Therefore, after she had hastily assembled her boats and manned them with her best marines, she joined battle on the river, while the infantry, drawn up along the banks, also eagerly participated. (4) The battle lasted for a long time and both sides fought spiritedly, but Semiramis was finally victorious. She destroyed about a thousand of the enemy boats, and also took many prisoners. (5) Elated by her victory, she reduced to slavery the islands in the river and the cities on them and gathered more than one hundred thousand captives. After these events the king of the Indians led his force away from the river. He feigned to retreat out of fear, but actually intended to lure his enemies into crossing the river. (6) Because affairs prospered according to her plan, Semiramis crossed the river after she had constructed a costly and large bridge. After she had sent all her forces across it, she left sixty thousand men to guard it and advanced with the rest of her army in pursuit of the Indians. The dummy elephants led the way to ensure that the enemy's spies would report to the king the multitude of these animals in her army. (7) At least in this hope she was not deceived. On the contrary, when those who had been despatched to spy on her reported to the Indians the number of elephants among the enemy, they were all at a loss to discover from where so many beasts as accompanied her could have come. (8) However, the deception did not remain hidden too long. Some of Semiramis' troops were caught at night in the camp because they neglected their watch.

---

[146] Goukowsky 1972 shows that the use of towers on the backs of elephants is a Hellenistic invention, to be dated somewhere between 300 and 280, probably in the entourage of King Pyrrhus of Epirus. Here, therefore, is another anachronism, but it is difficult to indicate who is to blame: Diodorus (whether or not using another source) or someone who reworked Ctesias' *Persica*. It should, though, be obvious this passage cannot be attributed to Ctesias himself (Goukowsky 1972: 475 note 10). Boncquet 1987: 120 attributes the remark to Diodorus.

In fear of the consequent punishment, these soldiers deserted to the enemy and pointed out to them their mistake regarding the nature of the elephants. Encouraged by this information, the king of the Indians told his army that the elephants were dummies and, having deployed his forces, turned about to face the Assyrians.

(2.19.1) Semiramis likewise marshalled her forces, and as the two armies approached each other, Stabrobates, the king of the Indians, sent his cavalry together with the chariots far in advance of the line of battle. (2) But the queen stoutly withstood the attack of the cavalry. The elephants which she had fabricated had been deployed at equal intervals in front of the line of battle, and it now occurred that the horses of the Indians shied at them. (3) From a distance the dummies looked like the actual animals. The horses of the Indians were acquainted with elephants and charged boldly enough. However, as they came closer both the odour struck them as unfamiliar, and all the other differences, which taken all together were very great, threw the cavalry into utter confusion as well. Consequently some of the Indians were thrown to the ground, while it happened that others, because their animals would not obey the reins, were carried with their horses into the midst of the enemy. (4) Then Semiramis, who was in the battle with a select band of soldiers, made skilful use of her advantage and put the Indians to flight. While these Indians were fleeing towards their line of battle,[147] King Stabrobates, undismayed, brought on the companies of the infantry. He directed the elephants to the front, while he himself, positioned on the right wing and fighting from the most powerful of the beasts,[148] charged in terrifying fashion upon the queen, who was by chance positioned opposite him. (5) Because the rest of the elephants also charged, the force that joined Semiramis withstood the attack of the beasts for only a short time. By virtue of their extraordinary courage and the confidence that they felt in their power, the elephants easily destroyed everyone who tried to withstand them. (6) That is why there was widespread slaughter, which was effected in various ways. Some soldiers were trampled beneath the elephants' feet, others ripped up by their tusks,

---

[147] MS D^a reads here: ὧν φυγόντων πρὸς τὴν [τῶν Ἰνδῶν] φάλαγγα. In this context the addition τῶν Ἰνδῶν is superfluous and therefore omitted from the text in the main editions. One might, perhaps, add instead αὐτῶν, but the intention of the sentence is so obvious that this is also unnecessary.

[148] The position of Stabrobates on the right wing *might* suggest the use of an oblique phalanx, first used in the Battle of Leuctra and later quite characteristic of both Alexander and the Diadochs, but unknown to Ctesias (see Goossens 1940: 41–2). I think Eck 2003: 142–3 *ad* p. 37 note 1 is right and that in fact tactics played no role at all in this fantasy that was designed to place both commanders opposite each other.

a number tossed into the air by their trunks. Since a large mass of corpses lay piled up and the danger caused huge consternation and fear in those who faced it, no one dared to remain at his position any longer. (7) After he had turned the entire multitude in flight, the king of the Indians pressed his attack upon Semiramis herself. First he shot at her with his bow and struck her on the arm with an arrow. Next he threw his javelin and pierced the queen's back, but only with a glancing blow. Therefore Semiramis, suffering nothing serious, rode swiftly away, the pursuing beast being much inferior in speed. (8) But because everybody fled to the pontoon bridge and so many forced their way into a single and narrow space, some of the queen's soldiers perished because they were trampled upon by one another and because cavalry and infantry were mixed together in unnatural confusion. When the Indians pressed hard upon them, a violent jostle took place on the bridge because of their terror, so that many being pushed to either side of the bridge fell into the river.[149] (9) When the majority of the survivors of the battle had found safety by putting the river behind them, Semiramis cut the fastenings which held the bridge together. When these were loosened, the pontoon bridge, having been broken apart at many points and bearing great numbers of the pursuing Indians, was carried down in haphazard fashion by the violence of the current and caused the death of many of the Indians. For Semiramis it procured considerable safety, because she had prevented the enemy from crossing over against her. (10) After these events, the king of the Indians remained inactive, because heavenly omens appeared to him that his seers interpreted to mean that he must not cross the river. After Semiramis had exchanged prisoners she returned to Bactra, having lost two-thirds of her force.[150]

---

[149] Eck 2003: 143 *ad* p. 38 note 2 reminds readers of the reliefs in the palace of Sennacherib at Nineveh, showing the victory of Asurbanipal against the Elamites at the River Ulai: see Barnett and Forman 1958: plates 120, 125, 129.
[150] According to Nearchus (*FGrH/BNJ* 133 F 3a & b = Str. 15.1.5/686) the natives (ἐπιχώριοι) recounted that Semiramis was able to save herself with only twenty men. Megasthenes (*FGrH/BNJ* 715 F 11b § 7 = Arr. *Ind.* 5.7; see Str. 15.1.6/686) relates that: Σεμίραμιν δὲ τὴν Ἀσσυρίην ἐπιχειρέειν μὲν στέλλεσθαι εἰς Ἰνδούς, ἀποθανεῖν δὲ πρὶν τέλος ἐπιθεῖναι τοῖς βουλεύμασιν ('Semiramis the Assyrian made preparations for an expedition to India, but died before she was able to complete her plans'). The context makes clear that, according to him, she had not even started the invasion of India before she died. Semiramis allegedly did marginally better than Cyrus, who returned from India with only seven soldiers (Str. 15.1.5/686), but considerably less than the Egyptian Sesoösis (Sesostris in Strabo), who, according to Diodorus, conquered India (1.55.4). Megasthenes (ibid.), on the contrary, stresses that, apart from Heracles and Dionysus, no army had ever subjugated or even invaded India before Alexander. Bichler emphasises, as regards Strabo's remarks, that Alexander vied with both Semiramis and Cyrus, wishing to outperform them: Bichler 2014: 59–60. See also below, Chapter 10.

Death of Semiramis:

(2.20.1) Some time later, after she had been conspired against by her son Ninyas through the agency of a certain eunuch and because she remembered the prophecy given her by Ammon, she did the conspirator no harm. On the contrary, after she had handed over to him the kingdom and having ordered the governors to obey him,[151] she made herself at once unseen,[152] as if having ascended to the gods as the oracle had predicted. (2) Some, telling stories, say that she turned into a dove and that she flew off in the company of many birds that had gathered in her house,[153] and therefore, they say, the Assyrians worship the dove as a god, thus deifying Semiramis. This very woman, after she had been queen over all Asia with the exception of India, passed away in the manner mentioned above, at the age of sixty-two years, of which she reigned forty-two.[154] (3) Such, then, is the account that Ctesias of Cnidus has given about Semiramis; but Athenaeus[155] and certain other historians say that she was a beautiful courtesan and because of her beauty was loved by the king of the Assyrians.[156] (4) Now at first she was only granted a moderate welcome in the palace, but later, when she had been proclaimed a

---

[151] This version differs drastically from that presented by Nicholas of Damascus, allegedly also based upon Ctesias' account: see FGrH/BNJ 90 F 1 = Stronk 2010: 162, 254–7 = Fr. *1|δ [L] (see also Lenfant 2004: 68–9). In Nicholas' next fragment Ninyas is the ruling king. Two other fragments confuse matters more, both ascribed to Cephalion, namely from Eus. (Arm.) Chron. (= FGrH/BNJ 93 F 1a) and from Syncellus' Ecloga chronographica (FGrH/BNJ 93 F 1b). In F 1a it is mentioned that Semiramis killed a son; in 1b that she killed 'sons', but was herself killed by Ninus (Ninyas?). Version 1b might well come nearest to Ctesias' original account, as is suggested in a fragment of the Anon. De mul. 1 = Ctes. Pers. Fr. 1c (see Stronk 2010: 159–60, 248–9; Lenfant 2004: 64). Boncquet 1987: 121 stresses that the emphasis of the story as related by Nicholas is different from Diodorus'. Considering the textual evidence, Boncquet 1987: 121–3 opts for Diodorus as the best representation of Ctesias' account.

[152] Eck 2003: 144 ad p. 38 note 7 remarks that the use of the form ἠφάνισεν ἑαυτήν underlines the voluntary character of Semiramis' action.

[153] As to this alleged event Athenag. Pro Christ. 30 = Ctes. Pers. Fr. 1m (see Stronk 2010: 162, 256–7; Lenfant 2004: 69) remarks: τὸ γὰρ ἀδύνατον, εἰς περιστερὰν μετέβαλεν ἡ γυνή. ὁ μῦθος παρὰ Κτησίᾳ ('it is impossible that a woman transformed into a dove. The story is from Ctesias').

[154] If Semiramis is based upon the Assyrian Queen Šammu-ramat, this number is way too high: her alleged regency may have lasted no more than five or six years (see also below, Chapter 10).

[155] This author should not be confused with Athenaeus of Naucratis, who flourished in the late second to early third century AD! This specific author is unknown beyond this and is dated tentatively by Jacoby (FGrH/BNJ 681) to the second first century. I believe the date might even be extended to fourth–first century. It might be conceivable that Ἀθήναιος here is an ethnicon ('the Athenian': see above, Chapter 1), corresponding to a proposal suggested by Marquart and supported by Krumbholz (though negated by Boncquet 1987: 124–5), to read here [Ἀπολλόδωρος δ' ὁ] Ἀθηναῖος ('[Apollodorus of] Athens').

[156] See the remark by Plin. Nat. 35.36.78: Aetionis svnt nobiles pictvrae ..., Semiramis ex ancilla regnvm apiscens, ... ('famous paintings by Aetion are ...,"Semiramis the slave girl rising to the throne", ...'), underlining Semiramis' doubtful lineage, which is also referred to in the following paragraphs.

Ancient History: Assyrians, Chaldeans, and Medes   121

lawful wife, she persuaded the king to yield royal power to her for a period of five days.[157] (5) And when Semiramis received the sceptre and the regal garb, she held a great festival and gave a magnificent banquet on the first day, at which she persuaded the commanders of the military forces and all the greatest dignitaries to co-operate with her. On the second day, while the people and the most notable citizens were paying her their respects as queen, she arrested her husband and put him in prison.[158] Because she was by nature a woman of great designs and bold as well, she seized the throne and while she remained queen until old age, she accomplished many great things. Such, then, are the conflicting accounts which may be found in the historians regarding the career of Semiramis.

Ninyas and the successors of Semiramis:
(2.21.1) After Semiramis' death, Ninyas,[159] the son of Ninus and Semiramis, took over the kingship and ruled peacefully, in no respect emulating his mother's love for war and risky bravura. (2) In the first place he spent all his time in the palace, seen by no one but his concubines and the eunuchs who attended him. He devoted his life to luxury {τρυφή} and idleness and the consistent avoidance of any suffering or anxiety, assuming that the aim of a happy reign was to enjoy immoderately every kind of pleasure.[160] (3) With regard to the safety of his kingship and the fear he felt with reference to his subjects, he used to send for a fixed number of soldiers and a general from each people or tribe every year.[161] (4) He kept this army, gathered from

---

[157] We find an identical period in Dinon (see *FGrH/BNJ* 690 F 7 = Ael. *VH* 7.1), while Plu. *Amat.* 753DE limits it to one day only. See also Eck 2003: 144 *ad* p. 39 note 4; Boncquet 1987: 125–7, who stresses that he believes this version does not go back to Ctesias, even though the latter left room for such a suggestion before: see Boncquet 1981: 28 note 11.
[158] Both Dinon and Plutarch (see preceding note) report she ordered her husband to be executed. Boncquet 1987: 126–7 suggests that this version of the Semiramis story might be a rationalisation of an ancient substitution rite, perhaps connected with the so-called *Sacaea* festival.
[159] This name also derives from the name of the city of Nineveh, in fact coming closer to its Assyrian name of 'Ninua'.
[160] Eck 2003: 40 note 1 points out that this is a recurring *topos* in Greek literature regarding the Oriental despot: see below, 2.23.1–3 (on Sardanapallus); Ctesias (F.1n = Ath. 12.528EF; see Stronk 2010: 258–9); also X. *Cyr.* 8.8.1–27. See also Boncquet 1987: 128 notes 568 and 569 for further references and Morgan 2016 for Greek notions of such behaviour among Persians.
[161] Though we lack definite evidence for later periods, Florence Malbran-Labat asserts that among the Assyrians the existence of a permanent army in the capital as well as permanent units in the province is well attested (see Malbran-Labat 1982: 60). However, Boncquet 1987: 128 suggests that it might reflect a practice in the Achaemenid Empire. Goossens 1940: 42 suggests the passage on this army refers to the time of the Diadochs. Bigwood 1980: 199 and note 17 remarks, as regards the word διοικητάς, that 'although the language of his [Diodorus'] source may make an impression on him, *he* [Diodorus] *writes by and large in his own style and uses his own terminology* [my emphasis], as is often forgotten'. See also Grayson 1991b: 203.

all his subject peoples and tribes, outside the city, and appointed as commander of each people or tribe the most trustworthy of the men in his service. At the end of the year he would again send for an equal number of soldiers from the peoples or tribes and dismiss the former to their homelands. (5) The result of this scheme was that all those subject to his rule were filled with awe, because they saw at all times a great host encamped in the open and punishment ready to fall on anyone who rebelled or would not yield obedience. (6) This annual change of the soldiers was conceived by him to ensure that all generals and all the other commanders of the army would be back in their own countries before they got too well acquainted with each other. Long service in the field gives commanders both experience in the arts of warfare and proud designs, and, moreover,[162] it offers great opportunities to rebel and plot against their rulers. (7) The fact that he was seen by no one outside the palace made everyone ignorant of the luxury {τρυφή} of his manner of life. Because of their fear of him, as of an unseen god, nobody dared to show disrespect of him even in word. So by appointing generals, satraps, financial officers, and judges for each people or tribe and arranging all other matters as he felt at any time to be to his advantage, he remained for his lifetime in Nineveh.[163] (8) The rest of the kings followed his example, son succeeding father to the throne, and thirty generations reigned down to Sardanapallus. Under this ruler the empire of the Assyrians fell to the Medes, after it had lasted more than thirteen hundred and sixty years,[164] as Ctesias of Cnidus writes in his second book.[165]

Assyrian assistance to the Trojans:
(2.22.1) To write all the names of the kings and the number of years each of them reigned is not urgently required because nothing worth mentioning was done by them.[166] The only event that has been recorded is the despatch by the Assyrians to the Trojans of an

---

[162] See for the stylistic problems the phrase τὸ μὲν πλεῖστον offers Eck 2003: 41 note 2. I have opted for the rendering 'moreover', as this covers best, in my opinion, the situation Diodorus wants to convey.
[163] And not in the city his mother had founded, as Boncquet 1987: 129 points out.
[164] πλείω τῶν χιλίων καὶ τριακοσίων [ἔτι δ' ἑξήκοντα]. Though present in all manuscripts, ἔτι δ' ἑξήκοντα was deleted by Dindorf (and Syncellus). Vogel 1985a: 205 maintained the phrase between square brackets, but Oldfather 1968: 422 deleted it completely, referring to a parallel remark in 2.28.8. However, as Eck 2003: 145 note 1 argues, there is no absolute need at all to delete these words. I will, therefore, follow the manuscript tradition and Eck.
[165] On the division of books in Ctesias' *Persica*, see, for example, Boncquet 1987: 129–31.
[166] Here we meet again with Diodorus' focus on things 'worthy to remember', referred to in my Introduction. Ctesias, on the other hand, had a different view, presenting his audience with a list of kings from Ninus and Semiramis down to Artaxerxes II: see Eus. (Arm.) *Chron.* 29,10–26 = Ctes. *Pers.* F 10; Ctes. *Pers.* F 33 = Phot. *Bibl.* [72] 45a1–4.

Ancient History: Assyrians, Chaldeans, and Medes   123

allied force, under the command of Memnon the son of Tithonus.[167] (2) During the reign of Teutamus over Asia – he was the twentieth in succession from Ninyas the son of Semiramis – they say that the Greeks set out on an expedition against Troy with Agamemnon, at a moment when the Assyrians had controlled Asia for more than a thousand years. People also tell that Priam, who was hard pressed by the war and ruled the Troad, sent messengers to Teutamus requesting aid, because he was a vassal of the king of the Assyrians. Teutamus despatched ten thousand Ethiopians and an equal number of men from Susa along with two hundred chariots, after he had appointed as commander Memnon the son of Tithonus.[168] (3) Tithonus, who was at that time commander of Persis, was the most highly esteemed of the governors at the king's court and Memnon, who was in the bloom of manhood, was distinguished both for bravery and for brilliancy of mind. He also built the palace in the citadel of Susa, which stood until the time of the Persian Empire, and was called after him 'Memnonion'.[169] Moreover, he constructed through the country a highway named the Memnonian to the present day.[170] (4) The Ethiopians who border upon Egypt, however, dispute this, maintaining that this man was a native of their country, and they point out an ancient palace that, they say, is called 'Memnonion' to this very day.[171] (5) Anyway, the story is told that Memnon went to the aid of the Trojans with twenty thousand infantry and two

---

[167] For Tithonus, Eos, and their son Memnon, see, for example, Stronk, *BNJ* (643), F 1. Elsewhere Diodorus succinctly tells another story of Memnon: 4.75.4. See also Eck 2003: 145–6 *ad* p. 42 note 4. Boncquet 1987: 136 and note 615 believes the story told here by Diodorus originated in an Assyrian environment sometime during the seventh century. As it seems, knowledge of the gist of (part of) the story of alleged Assyrian support for Troy was not restricted to Ctesias (Diodorus' source), as becomes clear from a passage in Pl. *Lg.* 685CD: καθάπερ οἱ περὶ τὸ Ἴλιον οἰκοῦντες τότε, πιστεύοντες τῇ τῶν Ἀσσυρίων δυνάμει τῇ περὶ Νίνον γενομένῃ, θρασυνόμενοι τὸν πόλεμον ἤγειραν τὸν ἐπὶ Τροίαν. . . . τῆς ἀρχῆς γὰρ τῆς ἐκείνων ἦν μόριον ('Just as the former dwellers around Ilium, relying on the Assyrian power as it had been in the reign of Ninus, were emboldened to engage the Trojan War. . . . For their country was part of the Assyrians' realm'). Whether, or to what extent, Ctesias – or for that matter Diodorus – has expanded and/or embellished the original story eludes us. See also Stronk in preparation, *ad loc.*
[168] The location of the Ethiopians was, obviously, a problem. Homer distinguishes 'Ethiopians of the West' and 'Ethiopians of the East' (living in Asia, undetermined where precisely): Hom. *Od.* 1.22–4. Susa is here, apparently, connected with the Eastern Ethiopians. As a matter of fact, Hesiod was the first to refer to Memnon as the king of Ethiopia: Hes. *Th.* 984–5; see also Pi. *N.* 3.61–3, *P.* 6.31.
[169] Hdt. 5.53–4, 7.151, also writes about a palace of Memnon, making Susa the city of Memnon: Str. 15.3.2/728 informs us that Susa was said to have been founded by Tithonos, who gave the citadel its name Μεμνόνιον. See also Dossin 1972; Boncquet 1987: 133–4.
[170] After Forshaw 1977, Eck 2003: 43 note 3 suggests this might refer to the Achaemenid Royal Road between Susa and Sardis.
[171] This might refer to the mortuary temple of Amenhotep III in Thebes (= Luxor) West, of which the remaining statues are known to this very day as 'the colossi of Memnon'. See also Gardiner 1961. See also Eck 2003: 146 *ad* p. 43 note 4; Boncquet 1987: 134–6.

hundred chariots. He was admired for his bravery and killed many of the Greeks in the battles, but he was finally ambushed by the Thessalians and killed. After the Ethiopians had recovered the body, they burned the corpse and sent the bones back to Tithonus. The Persians say that such is the account concerning Memnon given in the royal records.[172]

Usages of Sardanapallus:
(2.23.1) Sardanapallus,[173] the thirtieth in succession from Ninus,[174] the founder of the empire, and the last king of the Assyrians,[175] outdid all his predecessors in self-indulgence and complacency. For not to mention the fact that he was not seen by any man residing outside the palace, he lived the life of a woman, and he spent his days in the company of his concubines spinning purple garments and working the softest of wool. He had assumed female garb and so covered his face and indeed his entire body with whitening cosmetics and the other unguents used by courtesans that he rendered it more delicate than that of any luxury-loving woman. (2) He also took care to make even his voice like a woman's. At his carousals, he not only indulged regularly in those drinks and dishes that could offer the greatest pleasure, but also pursued the delights of love with men as well as with women. He practised sexual intercourse of both kinds without restraint and did not show the least concern for the disgrace of such conduct. (3) He went to such an excess of indulgence and of the most shameless sensual pleasure and intemperance that he made an elegy for himself and instructed his successors upon the throne to

---

[172] Unlike many scholars, including Eck 2003: 147 *ad* p. 43 note 5, I do not believe that this phrase suggests that Ctesias consulted the royal archives himself. Taken literally, it merely states that *the Persians said* (my Italics) – to Ctesias or whomever – that the royal archives preserve this account of Memnon, *not* that Ctesias read (or even saw) it there. We may only surmise that Diodorus took the reference from Ctesias' *Persica* (who, therefore, not unlike Herodotus, based (parts of) his story on hearsay), but even that may well be only a conjecture (see also Boncquet 1987: 138).
[173] Apparently a name based upon that of either Ašurbanipal, c. 668–c. 627, in fact one of the stronger kings of the Neo-Assyrian Empire (see, for example, Grayson 1991a and parts of Oates 1991), or a combination of the names of Esarhaddon, who ruled from c. 681–c. 669, and Ašurbanipal. Herodotus was the first, to the best of our knowledge, to refer to King Sardanapallus not for the quality of his rule but for his wealth (Hdt. 2.150). Diodorus' source (Ctesias?) goes, as it seems, at least a step further, making this king as a literary creation the archetype of the effeminate and debauched Oriental ruler (see Boncquet 1987: 139–40). As such, Sardanapallus subsequently figured in the works of several classical authors (see Eck 2003: 44 note 1; Morgan 2016: *passim*).
[174] See Eck 2003: 147 *ad* p. 44 note 2.
[175] Ašurbanipal was certainly not the last king of the Assyrians: three more kings (one with a co-regent) followed, the last being *Aššur-uballit* II (who ruled from 612 to 609, lastly in Harran, having fled Nineveh in 612). See, though, Drews 1974: 393 note 31, stating these last kings did not live on in memory, making Ašurbanipal the last Assyrian king to be remembered.

Ancient History: Assyrians, Chaldeans, and Medes   125

inscribe it upon his tomb after his death. It was composed by him in a foreign language, but was afterwards translated by a Greek:

Knowing well you are born mortal, enjoy and feast!
Death offers pleasures no more;
Reduced to ashes am I, once ruling mighty Nineveh.
But all this is mine: the food I ate, my wantonness, and love's
Delights. Only property and gold are left behind.[176]

(4) Because he was a man of such a character, he not only ended his own life in a disgraceful manner, but caused the total destruction of the Assyrian Empire that had lasted longer than any other known in history.

Conspiracy against Sardanapallus:
(2.24.1) A certain Arbaces,[177] a Mede by descent and conspicuous for his bravery and brilliancy of mind, was the commander of the contingent of Medes, which was sent to Nineveh as it was every year. After he had become acquainted with the commander of the Babylonians during this service, he was urged by him to overthrow the empire of the Assyrians. (2) This man's name was Belesys and he was the most distinguished of those priests whom the Babylonians call Chaldeans.[178] Because he had, therefore, the fullest experience of both astrology and divination, he was accustomed to predict the future unerringly to the people in general. Therefore, as he was greatly admired for those acts, he also predicted to the commander of the Medes, who was his friend, that it was certainly fated for him to be king over all the territory that was held by Sardanapallus at

---

[176] This poem or epitaph poses some problems. Several Greek authors have been suggested as its source, ranging from Hellanicus of Lesbos (for a prose version) to Choerilus of Samos (for a poetic one), both dating to the fifth century. In Athenaeus 8.335F–336B we encounter a slightly enlarged version of this epitaph. Usually these verses are attributed to Choerilus: see Lloyd-Jones and Parsons 1983: no. 335 (pp. 155–8). There are parodies by Chrysippus (ibid.: no. 338, pp. 158–9; different from the rendering in Athenaeus) and Crates (ibid.: no. 355, p. 167). Whence Diodorus' version of these lines originates, I have been unable to trace. Diodorus' lines were copied by Tz., *H.* 3.453–7. As regards the lines in Diodorus, I have chosen to follow the rendition of the epitaph by Vogel, Oldfather, and Eck. See also Boncquet 1987: 141–52 for an elaborate discussion on several versions of the epitaph.

[177] Arbaces is an attested and correct Median name (*Arbaku*): see Boncquet 1987: 160 with several references; the name Belesys also occurs as that of a functionary in the times of Artaxerxes II, namely as satrap of Syria (16.42.1; X. *An.* 1.4.10) or Syria and Assyria (X. *An.* 7.8.25): it seems unlikely that the names of the real *dramatis personae* (if, indeed, there were any) were recorded by Ctesias if he was – as seems likely – Diodorus' source. Oldfather 1968: 429 remarks that the 'kernel of truth' in this story is 'that Nineveh fell before the combined attacks of the Median Cyaxares and the Chaldaean Nabopolassar'.

[178] For Chaldeans and the connection with priests, see above, note 85. See, for a slightly different version of this story, Nicholas of Damascus (*FGrH/BNJ* 90 F 3 = Ctes. *Pers.* F. *1pε [L]; Stronk 2010: 262–7).

that moment. (3) Arbaces, commending the man, promised to give him the satrapy of Babylonia once the affair was brought to completion. For his part, like a man elated by a message from some god, he both bonded with the commanders of the other nations and assiduously invited them all to banquets and social gatherings and thereby established a friendship with each of them. (4) He was also resolved to watch the king face to face and to observe his whole manner of life. That is why, after he had given one of the eunuchs a golden bowl as a present, he gained admittance to Sardanapallus. As he observed from nearby both the king's luxuriousness {τρυφή} and his love of effeminate pursuits and practices, he despised him as worthy of no consideration and was led all the more to cling to the hopes which had been brought to him by the Chaldean. (5) Finally he struck up a conspiracy with Belesys, whereby he himself should move the Medes and Persians to revolt. Belesys should persuade the Babylonians to join the enterprise and should secure the help of the commander of the Arabs,[179] who was his friend, for the attempt to secure supreme control. (6) When the one-year term of their service in the king's army had passed and another force had arrived to replace them, the men who had been relieved were dismissed to their homes as usual. Thereupon Arbaces persuaded the Medes to attack the Assyrian kingdom and the Persians to join in the conspiracy, on the condition of receiving their freedom. Belesys, too, in similar fashion both persuaded the Babylonians to claim their freedom, and, sending an embassy to Arabia, won over the commander of the people of that country, a friend and guest-friend of his, to join in the attack. (7) And in a year's time all these leaders gathered a multitude of soldiers and came with all their forces to Nineveh, ostensibly to bring up replacements, as was the custom, but actually with the intention of destroying the empire of the Assyrians. (8) When, thus, the forces of these four peoples had gathered into one place, the whole number of them amounted to four hundred thousand men. After they had assembled into one camp, they deliberated together what to do next.

Uprising against Sardanapallus:
(2.25.1) As soon as Sardanapallus became aware of the revolt, he led forth against them the contingents that had come from the other peoples and tribes. And at first, when battle was joined on the plain, those who were revolting were defeated. After heavy losses they

---

[179] In the past there had been (friendly) relations between Assyrians and Arabs (see above, 2.1.8–9, 3.2), but the collaboration referred to here is nowhere attested.

were pursued to a mountain seventy *stadia* [c. 13 km] distant from Nineveh. (2) Afterwards, when they came down again into the plain and were preparing for battle, Sardanapallus, who had deployed his own army against them, despatched the heralds to the camp of the enemy to make this proclamation: 'Sardanapallus will give two hundred talents of gold to him who kills Arbaces the Mede,[180] but to him who delivers him alive he will make a present of twice that amount and will also appoint him governor over Media.' (3) Likewise he promised to reward those who would either kill Belesys the Babylonian or take him alive. But since no one paid any attention to the proclamations, he joined battle, killed many of the rebels, and pursued the remainder of the multitude into their encampment in the mountains. (4) The people around Arbaces, having lost heart because of these defeats, now convened a meeting of his friends and called upon them to consider what should be done. (5) Now the majority said that they should retire to their respective countries, seize strong positions, and as far as possible prepare there whatever else would be useful for the war. Belesys the Babylonian, however, after he had maintained that the gods signalled them that after labours and hardship they would finally achieve their goal, encouraged them in every other way as much as he could and persuaded them all to remain to face further perils. (6) Then, after a third battle had occurred, the king was victorious again, and both captured the camp of the rebels and pursued the defeated as far as the boundaries of Babylonia. It also happened that Arbaces himself, who had fought most brilliantly and had killed many Assyrians, was wounded. (7) As the rebels had suffered such decisive defeats one following upon the other, their commanders, despairing of victory, prepared to disperse each to his familiar place. (8) But Belesys, who had passed a sleepless night in the open and had devoted himself to the observation of the stars, spoke to those who had lost hope in their cause. He said that if they would wait five days, help would come of its own accord, and that there would be a mighty turnaround in the whole situation. Thanks to his knowledge of the stars, that was what the gods announced to them. And he appealed to them to wait that many days and test his own skill and the goodwill of the gods.

---

[180] In weight about 6,000 kg of gold. In fact, the Babylonian *monetary* system divided one talent (*biltu*) into 60 *mina* (*manū*), each of which was subdivided into 60 shekels (*šiqlu*), each shekel weighing c. 8.33 g of silver (for comparison: an Attic *drachma* weighed c. 4.17 g of silver): a *biltu* therefore weighed about 30 kg. The king, in fact, offered the betrayer the weight in gold instead of in silver, about tenfold in worth.

(2.26.1) So they were all called back and waited the stipulated time, when a messenger arrived with the news that a force which had been despatched from Bactria to the king was near at hand, advancing with all speed. (2) Arbaces' companions accordingly decided to go and meet their commanders as quickly as possible. They took along the best and most agile of the troops, so that, in case they should be unable to persuade the Bactrians by arguments to join in the revolt, they might resort to arms to force them to share with them in the same hopes. (3) But the outcome was that the newcomers gladly listened to the call to freedom, first the commanders and then the entire force, and they all encamped in the same place. (4) It then occurred that the king of the Assyrians, unaware of the defection of the Bactrians and elated over his past successes, turned to indulgence and divided among his soldiers animals and great quantities of both wine and all other provisions for a feast. Because the whole army was therefore carousing, Arbaces' companions, who had learned from some deserters of the relaxation and drunkenness in the camp of the enemy, attacked it unexpectedly in the night. (5) Falling upon them as organised men upon disorganised and as ready men upon unprepared, they both won possession of the camp and, after killing many of the soldiers, pursued the rest of them as far as the city. (6) After this the king, having named as the chief command Salaemenes,[181] his wife's brother, gave his own attention to the affairs within the city. But the rebels, having deployed their forces in the plain before the city, overcame the Assyrians in two battles. They both killed Salaemenes and cut down some of the opposing forces in their flight, and others, who had been shut out from entering the city and forced to leap into the River Euphrates,[182] they destroyed almost to a man. (7) So great was the multitude of the killed that the water of the stream, mingled with blood, was changed in colour over a considerable distance. Next, because the king was enclosed under siege, many of the peoples revolted, going over to the side of liberty in each case. (8) Because Sardanapallus realised that his entire kingdom was in the greatest danger, he sent his sons, three in number, and two daughters together with much of his treasure to Paphlagonia to the governor,

---

[181] Though Vogel 1985a: 213 and Oldfather 1968: 436–7 maintain the form of MS D^a, Γαλαιμένην, I follow Eck 2003: 50, who after MSS C and V opts for Σαλαιμένην. This form comes close to Assyrian *Salāmānu*, Iranian *salamanah-*, and Elamite *šá-la-ma-na*: see Eck 2003: 50 note 1; Boncquet 1987: 162–3 and notes 754–6.

[182] Obviously a mistake, though a repeated one: Nineveh was situated on the east bank of the Tigris.

Cotta,[183] who was the most loyal of his subjects. Meanwhile he himself, despatching letter-carriers to all his subjects, summoned forces and made preparations for the siege. (9) Now there was a prophecy, which had come down to him from his ancestors, that no enemy would ever take Nineveh by storm unless the river should first become hostile to the city. Assuming, therefore, that this could never be, he held out in hope, his thought being to endure the siege and await the troops that would be sent by his subjects.

Death of Sardanapallus and the end of the Assyrian Empire: (2.27.1) The rebels, elated at their successes, pressed the siege, but because of the strength of the walls they were unable to do any harm to the men in the city, for neither catapults, nor shelters for sappers, nor battering rams designed to break walls had yet been invented in those days.[184] Moreover the inhabitants of the city had a great abundance of all provisions, since the king had taken thought on that score. Therefore the siege dragged on, and they pressed their attack for two years, made assaults on the walls and prevented the inhabitants of the city from going out into the country. In the third year,[185] after there had been heavy and continuous rains, it occurred that the Euphrates, bursting its banks, both overflowed a portion of the city and broke down the walls for a distance of twenty *stadia* [c. 3.7 km]. (2) Consequently the king, believing that the oracle had been fulfilled and that the river had plainly become hostile to the city, abandoned hope of saving himself. And to avoid falling into the hands of the enemy, he built an enormous pyre in his palace. He heaped upon it all his gold and silver as well as the entire royal wardrobe. Next he shut his concubines and eunuchs inside the room that had been built in the middle of the pyre and set fire, with them all inside, to both himself and his palace.[186]

---

[183] Other names as governor of Paphlagonia instead of Cotta's have been proposed: see Eck 2003: 150 note 5; Boncquet 1987: 163 and note 758.
[184] Though Diodorus' remark here underlines later statements on the invention and/or use of war machines (see 12.28.3; 14.42.1, 50.4; 17.42.7, 45.2), most of these machines were, in fact, well known to the Assyrians: see Boncquet 1987: 164–5 and his notes 762 and 764; Eck 2003: 151 *ad* p. 51 note 2; especially De Backer 2013.
[185] ANET 303–5 and ABC no. 3, telling the story of the *Chronicle of the Fall of Nineveh*, mention as the duration of the siege of Nineveh a period of three months.
[186] MacGinnis 1988 believes that Ctesias here transmitted a Babylonian source and combined two events by incorporating elements from the siege and fall of Babylon in 650–648 into the story of the fall of Nineveh in 612. As it stands, Diodorus abridged Ctesias' version of Sardanapallus' pyre: Ctes. *Pers.* F 1q = Stronk 2010: 266–7. See also Berossus' version, *FGrH/ BNJ* 680 F 7d, of the death of Saracus (*Sin-šarra-iškun*); and ABC: 94 *ad* line 44. Clitarchus, *FGrH/BNJ* 137 F 2, relates a totally different story of the death of Sardanapallus.

Accession to the throne of the Mede Arbaces:

(2.27.3) When the rebels learned of the death of Sardanapallus, they took the city by forcing an entrance where the wall had fallen, and clothing Arbaces in the royal garb saluted him as king and put into his hands the supreme authority.

(2.28.1) Then, after the new king had distributed gifts among the commanders who had aided him in the struggle corresponding to their several merits and was appointing satraps over the peoples and tribes, Belesys the Babylonian, the one who had foretold to Arbaces that he would be king of Asia, came to him. He both reminded Arbaces of his good services and asked to be given the governorship of Babylon, as had been promised at the outset. (2) Belesys also explained that, when their cause was endangered, he had made a vow to Belus that, if Sardanapallus were defeated and his palace went up in flames, he would bring its ashes to Babylon. He said that he had promised the god that he would deposit those ashes near the river and the sacred precinct of the god,[187] and that he would construct a mound which would stand as an eternal memorial of the man who had overthrown the rule of the Assyrians for all who sailed down the Euphrates. (3) This request he made because he had learned of the facts regarding the silver and gold from a certain eunuch, who had made his escape and come to Belesys and was kept hidden by him. (4) Because Arbaces knew nothing of these things, due to the fact that all present in the palace had been burned along with the king, he allowed him both to carry the ashes away and to hold Babylon without the payment of tribute. Thereupon Belesys, after he had procured boats, immediately sent off to Babylon most of both the silver and the gold along with the ashes. After the king had been informed of the act in which Belesys had been caught red-handed, he appointed as judges the commanders who had served with him in the war. (5) And after the perpetrator had acknowledged his guilt, the court sentenced him to death. The king, however, being magnanimous and wishing to celebrate the beginning of his rule with moderation, both freed Belesys from the danger threatening him and allowed him to keep the silver and gold which he had carried off. Likewise, he did not even take from him the governorship over Babylon that had originally been given to him, saying that his former services were greater than his subsequent misdeeds. (6) When this act of clemency was noised about, he won

---

[187] τοῦ τεμένους τοῦ θεοῦ καὶ τοῦ ποταμοῦ καταθέμενον. Three manuscript traditions (C, V, and L) omit καὶ τοῦ ποταμοῦ, but since it clearly appears to be connected with the previous part of the story (the flooding and the destruction of the walls), I have followed Vogel, Oldfather, and Eck, who all retained the phrase.

Ancient History: Assyrians, Chaldeans, and Medes   131

extraordinary loyalty from his subjects as well as renown among the peoples and tribes, because all judged that the man who conducted himself in this manner towards sinners was worthy of the kingship. (7) Showing clemency towards the inhabitants of the city, Arbaces settled them in villages and returned to each man his personal possessions, but the city he levelled to the ground. Next he sent away to Ecbatana in Media both the silver and the gold that had been left in the pyre, which amounted to many talents. (8) Thus the rule of the Assyrians, which had endured from the time of Ninus through thirty generations, for more than one thousand three hundred years, was destroyed by the Medes in the aforementioned manner.

S. 2:
3.3.1:

Semiramis campaigns against the Ethiopians:
(3.3.1) ... Semiramis also, who through the magnitude of her plans and acts has become renowned, gave up her campaign against the whole nation after she had advanced a short distance into Ethiopia; ...

S. 3:
7.15.1 (= Eusebius, *Chronographia Armenica* [ed. Karst: 107.18–19]):

Sardanapallus' death ends the Assyrian Empire:
(7.15.1) After the rule of the Assyrians came to an end with the death of their last king, Sardanapallus, the period of the Macedonians followed.[188]

B. THE CHALDEAN HISTORY

S. 4:
2.29.1–31.10:

Education of the Chaldeans and Greeks:
(2.29.1) But it seems appropriate to us to speak briefly of the Chaldeans of Babylon and of their antiquity, in order to omit nothing worthy of record.[189] (2) Now because the Chaldeans belong to the

---

[188] It appears that 'Macedonians' is written here mistakenly instead of 'Medes': see Cohen-Skalli 2012: 269 *ad* note 132.
[189] See for the Chaldeans above, note 85. See also Diodorus' observations on them in 1.28.1, 81.6; 3.1.2; 15.50.3; 17.112.1–6, 116.4; 19.55.8–9. See Boncquet's discussion on these *capita*, Boncquet 1987: 170–3. The first reference to the '*Kaldu*' dates to the beginning of the ninth

most ancient inhabitants of Babylonia, they have about the same position as regards the divisions of the state as the priests of Egypt occupy.[190] For because they have been assigned to the service of the gods, they spend their entire life in study, their greatest renown being in the field of astrology. They spend a lot of time in soothsaying as well, as they make predictions about future events, and they attempt to effect the aversion of evil things and the fulfilment of the good, in some cases by purifications, in others by sacrifices, and in others by some other sung charms. (3) They are also experienced in soothsaying by the flight of birds, and they give out interpretations of both dreams and portents. They also show a distinct skill in divining from the observation of the entrails of animals, deeming that in this branch they are eminently successful. The training in these skills they receive is not the same as that of the Greeks who apply themselves to such practices.[191] (4) For among the Chaldeans the methodical treatment of these skills is passed down in the family, and son takes it over from father, exempted from all other official duties. Moreover, because they have their parents for teachers, they are not only taught everything ungrudgingly, but at the same time they pay attention to the precepts of their teachers, whom they trust more certainly as well. Next, because they have been raised with these teachings from childhood, they attain a great skill in them, both because of the ease with which youth is taught and because of the great amount of time devoted to the study. (5) ... (6) Therefore the Chaldeans, because they always stick to the same things, have a firm hold on everything, ...

Views of the Chaldeans:
(2.30.1) Well now, the Chaldeans say that the world is by its nature eternal, and neither had a first beginning nor has ever suffered destruction.[192] They also say that both the disposition and the

---

century, in an inscription from Assurnasirpal II (c. 883–c. 859). After the fall of the Assyrian Empire, the Chaldeans succeeded, to create a Chaldean dynasty in the Neo-Babylonian Empire, with kings like Nabopolassar (625–605, the Belesys of Hellenistic authors), Nebuchadnezzar II (604–562), and Nabonidus (555–539).

[190] In 1.28.1, 81.6, Diodorus recounts that the Chaldeans came as colonists from Egypt, having the same duties as Egyptian priests, who had taught them their skills. Like these, the Chaldeans were exempt from other official duties (below, 2.29.4).

[191] For the comparison between Chaldeans and Greeks and Diodorus' view in this, see Boncquet 1987: 175–6.

[192] The presentation of the Chaldeans' view has been appreciated differently: see Boncquet 1987: 176–7 and notes 823–4. For the common translation that 'the world is by its nature eternal, and neither had a first beginning nor will at a later time suffer destruction', see Burton 1972: 44. However, the meaning of Diodorus' text is enhanced, as MSS D^{a}L have it, by inserting the aorist form ἐπιδέξασθαι for the future ἐπιδέξεσθαι of most editors (see Vogel 1985a: 219; Oldfather 1968: 448; and, indeed, Burton): in this way the message corresponds to the

Ancient History: Assyrians, Chaldeans, and Medes 133

orderly arrangement of the universe have originated thanks to a divine providence. Finally they assert that everything that happens now in heaven does not originate at haphazard nor by virtue of any spontaneous action, but by a fixed and firmly determined divine decision. (2) Because they have observed the stars over a long time and have noted both the movements and the influences of each of them with the greatest precision of all men, they foretell to mankind many things that will take place in the future. (3) Most important, they say, is the study of the influence of the five stars known as planets,[193] which they call 'Interpreters' when they speak of them as a group. If they refer to them singly, the one named Cronus [the planet Saturn] by the Greeks, which is the most conspicuous and presages more events and those that are of greater importance than the others, they call the star of Helius,[194] whereas the other four they designate, as do our astrologers, as the stars of Ares, Aphrodite, Hermes, and Zeus.[195] (4) The reason why they call them 'Interpreters' is that, whereas all the other stars are fixed and follow a singular circuit in a regular course, these alone, by virtue of following each its own course, point out future events, thus interpreting to mankind the design of the gods. Sometimes by their risings, sometimes by their settings, and again by their colour, the Chaldeans say, these stars give signs of coming events, announcing to mankind the favour of the gods.[196] (5) For at one time they predict the size of storms, at another the excesses of rains or heat, at times the appearance of comets, also eclipses of both sun and moon, and earthquakes, and in general all the conditions

---

Babylonian *Enūma Eliš*: Eck 2003: 56 note 2, 156 *ad* p. 56 note 1. For the *Enūma Eliš* see, for example, Talon 2005. Despite this, some texts in the Babylonian corpus do speak of a massive destruction caused by a flood, the most notable of these texts being the Epic of Gilgameš. This dichotomy underlines Bottéro's statement, quoted by Eck 2003: 156 *ad* p. 56 note 1, that 'le domaine de la cosmogonie en Mésopotamie ne connaisse ni orthodoxie, ni doctrine normative'. In fact, neither view corresponds to the Stoic concept of a dynamic world (see above, Chapter 1, note 4).

[193] See Sen. *Nat.* 2.32.7: *Qvinqve stellarvm potestates Chaldaeorum observatio excepit* ('The Chaldeans confined their observation to the powers of five "stars"'), who shows himself in the sequel critical of the custom of limiting observation to merely these five 'stars'. For a detailed discussion of the Chaldeans' astronomical observations: Boncquet 1987: 176–84.

[194] That the Sun (Sol, Helius) and Saturn are related is suggested in *caput* 2.42 of Hyg. *Astr.*: *... secvnda stella dicitvr Solis, qvam alii Satvrni dixervnt. ...* ('the second star, which some have said to be of Saturn, is said to be of Sol').

[195] Respectively the planets Mars, Venus, Mercury, and Jupiter.

[196] Here again discussion is possible as regards the meaning of the text. On the basis of the text published by Vogel 1985a: 219 and Oldfather 1968: 450, both reading here ἔννοιαν 'intent', first suggested by Dindorf, one might translate here 'making clear the intent of the gods to the people'. Eck 2003: 56, though, reads here εὔνοιαν 'favour', as all MSS do: doing so, the sentence becomes as I translated it. I have opted to follow Eck because of the unanimity in the MS tradition and in view of 2.25.8 (where the εὐεργεσία, 'goodwill', of the gods is spoken of), in spite of the following paragraph that is hardly understandable as a 'favour'.

which owe their origin to the atmosphere and cause both benefits and harm, not only to whole peoples or regions, but also to kings and to commoners.[197] (6) They state that under the course in which these planets move, thirty stars are situated, which the Chaldeans designate as 'counselling gods'. One half of these oversee the regions above the earth and the other half those beneath the earth, which take care of the affairs of mankind and likewise those of the heavens. Every twelve[198] days one of the stars above is sent as a messenger, so to speak, to the stars below, and again in like manner one of the stars below the earth to those above, and this movement of theirs is fixed and determined by means of an orbit which is unchanging. (7) Twelve of these gods, they say, are the chiefs, and to each of these the Chaldeans assign a month and one of the signs of the zodiac, as they are called. Through the midst of these signs, they say, both the sun and moon and the five planets make their course, the sun completing his cycle in a year and the moon traversing her circuit in a month.
(2.31.1) They say that each planet has its own particular course, and that its velocities and periods of time are subject to change and variation. These stars exert the greatest influence on the births of people for both good and evil. Chiefly from the nature of these planets and the study of them they know what is in store for mankind. (2) They say they have made predictions not only to several other kings, but also to Alexander,[199] who defeated Darius, and to Antigonus[200] and Seleucus *Nicator*,[201] who became kings afterwards, and in all their prophecies they believe they have been right. On these matters we will write the particulars on a more appropriate occasion. (3) They also foretell commoners what will occur to them,[202] and with such accuracy that those who have tried them are amazed as regards the feat and believe that it transcends the power of man.[203] (4) Beyond the circle of the zodiac they designate twenty-four stars, of which one half, they say, are situated in the northern parts and one half in the southern. Of these, those that are visible they assign to belong to the living, those invisible they regard as being adjacent to the dead, and address them as 'Judges of the Universe'. (5) Below all the aforementioned stars the moon takes her way, they say, as she is nearest

---

[197] See, for example, Reiner and Pingree 1975–2005; see also Sachs and Hunger 1988–.
[198] Twelve is an emendation suggested by Boll: see Eck 2003: 57 notes 5 and 6.
[199] See 17.112.2–3.
[200] See 19.55.7.
[201] Though announced in 19.55.9, this prediction itself is lost, as is much of book 21.
[202] See Sachs 1952: he dates the first horoscope to 410 (pp. 52–7).
[203] Boncquet 1987: 186 and notes 885–9 points out that the most ancient individual horoscopes date to c. 400 (see note 202 above).

to the earth because of her weight, completing her course in a very brief period of time, not because of her great velocity, but thanks to the shortness of her orbit. (6) They agree with the Greeks that her light is a reflection of the sun's and that her eclipses are due to the shadow of the earth.[204] As regards the eclipse of the sun they adduce the weakest explanations and do not presume to predict it or to determine the times of its event with precision.[205] (7) In connection with the earth they make extremely peculiar assertions, saying that it is shaped like a bowl[206] and hollow. They offer many plausible arguments about both the earth and all other bodies in the firmament, on which to digress in particular we think would be alien to the present research. (8) However, this point someone might fittingly maintain, that the Chaldeans have the greatest grasp of astrology of all men, and that they have spent the greatest care on the study of it. (9) As regards the number of years they say that the order of the Chaldeans has spent on the study of the bodies of the universe, nobody could easily believe them: for they reckon that, down to Alexander's crossing over into Asia, it has been four hundred and seventy-three thousand years since they began in early times to make their observations of the stars.[207] (10) So far as the Chaldeans are concerned we will be satisfied with what has been said, that we may not stray too far from the matter proper to our research. As regards the kingdom of the Assyrians, how it was destroyed by the Medes as related before, we will return to the point at which we digressed.

C. THE MEDIAN HISTORY

Mythical origins (eponymous founders) of the Medes:

S. 5:
4.55.5:
(4.55.5) At Athens, as some say, Medea[208] married Aegeus and gave birth to Medus, who was later king of Media.

---

[204] See Eck 2003: 160 *ad* p. 59 note 1.
[205] Though the Chaldeans were able to predict eclipses of the moon accurately, they were – otherwise than as asserted in 2.30.5 – unable to predict solar eclipses: see Boncquet 1987: 187–9.
[206] See *LSJ* s.v. 'σκαφοειδής'. The translation of Oldfather 1968: 455 and Eck 2003: 59 and 161 *ad* p. 59 note 4, referring to the earth as being in the shape of a boat, though understandable in view of Assyrian reliefs, might well be untenable. See also Boncquet 1987: 189–90 and notes 912–14; Eck 2003: 161 *ad* p. 59 notes 4 and 5.
[207] See Boncquet 1987: 191–2 for comments on the duration of observations.
[208] Medea might well be in origin an Iranian name (see Mayor et al. 2014: 451).

S. 6:

4.55.7:

(4.55.7) From Phoenicia Medea journeyed into the interior regions of Asia and married a certain king of renown, to whom she bore a son Medus; and the son, succeeding to the throne after the death of the father, was greatly admired for his courage and named the people Medes after himself.

S. 7:

4.45.1:

(4.45.1) It is said that Helius had two sons, Aeëtes and Perses, Aeëtes being king of Colchis and the other king of the Tauric Chersonese, and that both of them were exceedingly cruel.

S. 8:

4.56.1–2:

(4.56.1) ... Medea took that Medus whom she bore to Aegeus and got off safe to Colchis. At that time Aeëtes, who had been forcibly driven from the throne by his brother Perses, had regained his kingdom, Medus, Medea's son, having killed Perses. Afterwards Medus, securing the command of an army, advanced over a large part of Asia (2) which lies above the Pontus and secured possession of Media, which has been named after this Medus.

S. 9:

2.32.1–34.7:

Dark age between the rule of Assyrians and that of the Medes:
(2.32.1) Since the earliest writers of history are at variance as regards the greatest empire of the Medes,[209] we feel that it is proper for those who want to write the history of events with a love for truth to place the different accounts of the historians side by side. (2) Herodotus,

---

[209] Whether there has ever been a Median *Empire* is still a matter under debate. Sancisi-Weerdenburg, 1987b and 1988, argues that neither literary sources nor archaeological evidence prove that such an empire ever existed (see also Kuhrt 1995: 654–6). The several contributions in Lanfranchi et al. 2003 offer no conclusive answer, but often add to the problem. Tuplin 2004: 243 prefers to speak of a Median 'domination' rather than of an 'Empire'. Ultimately, it is a matter of asymmetrical evidence: archaeological evidence does not correspond to what the texts claim. The problem is which type of evidence to prefer. In this maximalist/minimalist debate (that is: the attribution of value to the texts), it well might be too early to take too firm a stand on this issue. Meanwhile, it might be sensible to remember that the idea of the continuity of empire was a valid *topos* – and little more – among Greek authors (see, for example, Liverani 2003: 1–2). The issue of a Median Empire has been neatly summarised in a paper by Nijssen 2015/16.

who lived in the time of Xerxes,[210] writes that after the Assyrians had ruled Asia for five hundred years they were conquered by the Medes.[211] Thereafter no king arose for many generations to lay claim to supreme power, but the city-states, which kept themselves to themselves, were administered democratically.[212] But finally, after many years, a man distinguished for his justice, named Cyaxares, was chosen king among the Medes.[213] (3) He was the first to try to attack the neighbouring peoples and tribes and became for the Medes the founder of their universal empire. Next, his descendants extended the kingdom by continually adding a great deal of the adjoining country, until the reign of Astyages, who was conquered by Cyrus and the Persians.[214] We have for the present given only the headlines and shall later describe particulars in detail when we come to the proper periods. For it was in the second year of the seventeenth Olympiad [711/10], according to Herodotus, that Cyaxares was chosen king by the Medes.[215]

Wars between the Medes and the Cadusians:
(2.32.5) This is Ctesias' account: after the destruction of the Assyrian Empire the Medes were the chief power in Asia under their king Arbaces, who conquered Sardanapallus, as has been told before. When Arbaces had ruled twenty-eight years, his son Maudaces[216] succeeded to the throne, who reigned over Asia fifty years. After him Sosarmus ruled for thirty years, Artycas for fifty,[217] the king known as Arbianes for twenty-two, and Artaeus for forty years.[218]

---

[210] A vague attribution, because he appears to have lived during the majority of Artaxerxes' reign as well. It seems that Herodotus was born somewhere between 490 and 480 and died after 430, perhaps even as late as after the Archidamian War (431–421): Fornara 1981.
[211] For Herodotus' period of 520 years of Assyrian rule, see, for example, Boncquet 1987: 194–5. Eck 2003: 60 note 1 states that Diodorus here made a double mistake as regards Herodotus' text.
[212] Contradicting Herodotus' remarks: Hdt. 1.96; see also Boncquet 1987: 195; Eck 2003: 161 ad p. 60 note 2.
[213] Again a misrepresentation of Herodotus by Diodorus: see Eck 2003: 161 ad p. 60 note 3: Herodotus' first Median king was Deioces.
[214] See Hdt. 1.107–30, and especially 1.127–9, for a full account of this story. The relevant part of the *Bibliotheca* is largely lost. The date of Astyages' defeat is generally put around 550.
[215] In fact, Herodotus dates the accession of Deioces (apparently Diodorus' Cyaxares) to c. 709: Hdt. 1.96–9, 101–2. Herodotus' Cyaxares is the grandson of the man who united the Medes: Hdt. 1.103, 106–7. Diodorus' statement (or probably rather Ctesias') and Herodotus' are here completely at odds: see Boncquet 1987: 195–6 and 196–200. See also below, 8.16.1, which seems more in line with Herodotus.
[216] Μανδάκην, the form of MS Dᵃ, transcribes Iranian *maudaka-*, possibly derived from *Mu-da-ba-'ka'* mentioned on the Persepolis tablets: see Hinz et al. 1975: 162; also Eck 2003: 61 note 4.
[217] Schmitt 1979: 127 states that Artycas, together with Ἀρτούχας (Artouchas: X. *An.* 4.3.4, *Cyr.* 5.3.38), might well transcribe OP *Ṛt-uka-*.
[218] In total, in this paragraph and in 2.34.6, Diodorus (Ctesias) counts nine Median kings, more or less doubling the number Herodotus presents, necessary because Ctesias puts the fall

(2.33.1) During the reign of Artaeus a great war broke out between the Medes and the Cadusians for the following reasons. Parsondes the Persian, admired for his *aretē* and intelligence and every other virtue, was both a friend of the king and the most influential of the members of the royal council. (2) Feeling himself aggrieved by the king in a certain decision,[219] he fled with three thousand infantry and a thousand horsemen to the Cadusians, to one of whom, the most influential man in those parts, he had given his sister in marriage. (3) Now that he had become a rebel, he persuaded the entire people to vindicate their freedom and was chosen commander because of his valour. Next, after he had been informed that a great force had been gathered against him, he armed the whole nation of the Cadusians and pitched his camp before the passes leading into the country, with no fewer than two hundred thousand men together. (4) Though the king Artaeus advanced against him with eight hundred thousand soldiers, Parsondes defeated the king in battle and killed more than fifty thousand of his followers and drove the rest of the army out of the country of the Cadusians. For this exploit, he was so much admired by the people of the land that he was chosen king, and he plundered Media constantly and laid waste every district.[220] (5) After he had attained great fame and was about to die of old age, he called to his side his successor to the throne and required of him an oath that the Cadusians should never put an end to their enmity towards the Medes: if ever peace were made with them, it would mean the destruction of both his line and the whole race of the Cadusians. (6) These, then, were the reasons why the Cadusians were always inveterate enemies of the Medes, and had never been subjected to the Median kings up to the time when Cyrus transferred the empire of the Medes to the Persians.

---

of Nineveh around c. 880, much earlier than the much more realistic date of Herodotus; see also Eck 2003: 162–4 *ad* p. 61 note 3. The romantic stories of Parsondes (more extensively preserved by Nicholas of Damascus, *FGrH/BNJ* 90 F 4 = Stronk 2010: F. *6b [L], pp. 272–83) and of Zarinaea moreover suggest an artificial construction. See also Boncquet 1987: 205–7. Meyer 1896 refers to the story of Parsondas as an 'orientalisches Märchen'. Diodorus' version is much more down to earth than Nicholas'. Artaeus is a (form and a) name that also occurs in Herodotus (7.22, 66: indicating other persons) and Nicholas of Damascus (*FGrH/BNJ* 90 F 4 = Stronk 2010: 272–83). See also Hinz et al. 1975: 217.

[219] For Parsondas' reasons to be aggrieved, see Nicholas of Damascus, *FGrH/BNJ* 90 F 4 = Stronk 2010: 272–83.

[220] Nic.Dam. *FGrH/BNJ* 90 F 66.15 = Stronk 2010: 290–311 at 296–7 on the Cadusians: Πέρσας μὲν γὰρ φιλοῦσι, Μήδους δὲ πάνυ μισοῦσι ('they love the Persians, but hate the Medians very much'). The theme recurs below in 2.33.6. For the Cadusians, see X. *HG* 2.1.13; Syme 1988. See also Eck 2003: 63 note 1.

War between the Medes and the Scythians; Queen Zarinaea of the Scythians:[221]

(2.34.1) After the death of Artaeus, Artynes ruled over the Medes for twenty-two years, and Astibaras for forty.[222] During the reign of the latter the Parthians revolted from the Medes and entrusted both their country and their city into the hands of the Scythians. (2) They thereby caused a war between the Scythians and the Medes, which took both many years and no small number of battles. After many lives on both sides had been lost, they finally agreed to conclude peace on the following terms, that the Parthians were to be subject to the Medes, but that each should be forever friend and ally to the other and should retain his former possessions. (3) At that time the Scythians were ruled by a woman by the name of Zarinaea,[223] who was devoted to warfare and was both in daring and in efficiency by far the foremost of the women of the Scythians. This people, indeed, generally has courageous women who share with their husbands the dangers of war. She, however, it is said, was the most conspicuous of them all for her beauty and remarkable as well in respect of both her designs and whatever she undertook.[224] (4) For, after she had subdued such of the neighbouring foreign peoples or tribes as had become proud because of their boldness and were trying to enslave the people of the Scythians, she introduced into much of her own

---

[221] In Diodorus' text this people is called the Saceans (Σάκαι), reminiscent of their Persian name. According to Herodotus (7.64), the Persians called all Scythians by the name *Sakas* (see also Eck 2003: 164–5 *ad* p. 63 note 4). Pliny the Elder provides another explanation, stating that the Persians gave the name *Sacae* to the Scythian tribes 'nearest to them' (Plin. *Nat.* 6.19.50). Persian inscriptions mention four groups of Scythians: the *Sakā paradraya* 'Saka beyond the sea', apparently the Black Sea (see, for example, *DNa* 28f; *DSe* 29; *XPh* 24); the *Sakā tigraxaudā* 'Saka with pointed hats/caps' (see, for example, *DB* V 21–2; *XPh* 26–7); the *Sakā haumavargā* 'haoma-drinking Saka' (Amyrgians, the *Saka* tribe in closest proximity to Bactria and Sogdia: see, for example, *XPh* 26); and the *Sakā para Sugdam* 'Saka beyond Sogdia', that is, at the River Yaxartes (see, for example, *DPh* 5–6). See also Kent 1953: 209 *s.v.* On the ancient Iranian sources for the names 'Scythian', 'Sogdian', and 'Saka', see Szemerényi 1980. Though technically not completely correct, here and elsewhere I have translated *Sacae* as 'Scythians'.

[222] The name Astibaras (see also Nicholas of Damascus, *FGrH/BNJ* 90 F 5 = Stronk 2010: 286–9) corresponds to Iranian *ṛstibara-* (see Hinz et al. 1975: 207) and the name *Iš-ti-ba-ra* on the Persepolis tablets. The meaning of the name is given as 'He who carries a lance': see Eck 2003: 63 note 3.

[223] In *P.Oxy.* 2330, on Ctesias, the name of the queen is presented as Zarinaea. Because this may well have been the correct spelling of her name, as the work of Nicholas of Damascus also suggests (see *FGrH/BNJ* 90 F 5; Stronk 2010: 171, 286–9; Stronk 2008/9: 219–22), I therefore emend the rendering by Diodorus. For this queen see also Anon. *De Mul.* 2; Demetr. *Eloc.* 213 = Ctes. *Pers.* F 8a (Stronk 2010: 284–5). Also Boncquet 1987: 209–11; Eck 2003: 165 *ad* p. 63 note 5.

[224] Eck 2003: 64 note 1 makes some interesting observations comparing Zarinaea with Semiramis; Sparethra (Ctes. *Pers.* F. 9(3) = Stronk 2010: 312–15); Tomyris (Hdt. 1.205–14); and the Amazons; see also Gera 1997: 84–100.

realm civilised life, founded many cities, and made the life of her people altogether happier. (5) Which is why her countrymen after her death, in gratitude for her benefactions and in remembrance of her *aretē*, built her a tomb far exceeding those existing in their land. They erected a triangular pyramid, making the length of each side three *stadia* [c. 550 m] and the height one *stadium* [c. 185 m], and brought it to a point at the top. On the tomb they also placed a colossal gilded statue of her and accorded to her the honours belonging to heroes, and all the other honours they bestowed upon her were more magnificent than those which had fallen to the lot of her ancestors. (6) After Astibaras, the king of the Medes, had died of old age in Ecbatana, his son Aspandas, whom the Greeks call Astyages,[225] succeeded to the throne. When he had been defeated by Cyrus the Persian, the kingdom passed to the Persians. Of them we shall give a detailed and exact account at the proper time.[226] (7) As regards the kingdoms of the Assyrians and of the Medes and the disagreement of the historians, we believe that enough has been said. . . .

S. 10:
8.16.1 (= *Const. Exc.* 2(1): 215, Fr. 36):[227]

Rule of King Deioces:
(8.16.1) *Deioces,[228] the king of the Medes, practised justice and the other *aretae* despite the prevailing great lawlessness.

S. 11:
9.23.1 (= *Const. Exc.* 2 (1): 219, Fr. 54):[229]

Mutiny arises against Astyages:
(9.23.1) *When Astyages, the king of the Medes, had been defeated and was in disgraceful flight,[230] he vented his wrath upon his soldiers. He displaced all who had been assigned positions of command,

---

[225] Ctesias' form of this king's name, Ἀστυίγας probably comes closer to the original form than Diodorus': Schmitt 1979: 123–4; Krumbholz 1886: 332. Aspandas is a *hapax* and does not correspond to any known Iranian form.

[226] Below, 9.22–4. Regrettably book 9 is only fragmentarily transmitted.

[227] According to the editions by Vogel 1985b: 159 and Oldfather 1970a: 406–7; Cohen-Skalli 2012: 107 counts it as Fr. 21.

[228] See Cohen-Skalli 2012: 300–1 *ad* p. 107 note 67.

[229] According to the editions by Vogel 1985b: 183 and Oldfather 1970b: 30–3; Cohen-Skalli 2012: 150 counts it as Fr. 35.

[230] Astyages' defeat took place c. 550. The role of Harpagus is absent in this fragment. See, for a more detailed account, Hdt. 1.125–9; see also Eck 2003: 162–4 *ad* p. 61 note 3; Cohen-Skalli 2012: 349 *ad* p. 150 note 72.

appointing others in their lieu. He also selected all responsible for the flight and put them to the sword, thinking that by punishing them in that way he could force the rest to show themselves brave fighters in times of danger, as he was a cruel man and, by nature, hard.[231] Nevertheless, the people were not dismayed at the harsh treatment he meted out. Because every man, on the contrary, hated his violent and lawless manner, they longed for a change in affairs. As a result there were gatherings of small groups and seditious conversations, the larger number exhorting one another to take vengeance on him.

---

[231] Astyages' cruelty is also referred to by Herodotus, for example Hdt. 1.130.1 (referring to the events related in Hdt. 1.118–19).

3 The Persians and the Greek Wars

A. THE ARIANS AND GENERAL CUSTOMS OF THE PERSIANS

S. 12:
1.94.2:

Zoroaster, one of the inspired lawgivers:
(1.94.2) ... It is recorded that among the Arians Zathraustes [Zoroaster] claimed that the Good Spirit gave him his laws,[1] ... They all did this either because they believed that a conception that would help humanity was marvellous and wholly divine, or because they held that the common crowd would be more likely to obey the laws if their view were directed towards the majesty and power of those to whom their laws were ascribed.

S. 13:
5.55.3:

Qualities of the Persian Magi:
(5.55.3) And men say that the Telchinians[2] were also wizards and could summon clouds and rain and hail at their will and likewise could even bring snow; these things, the accounts tell us, they could do even as could the *Magi* of Persia; and they could also change their natural shapes and were jealous of teaching their arts to others.

---

[1] Zathraustes as a form is a *hapax*. See further Bertrac and Vernière 1993: 173 note 1.
[2] For the Telchinians see, for example, Str. 10.3.7/466, 19/472; 14.2.7/654.

S. 14:
5.77.8:

'Persian Artemis':
(5.77.8) This goddess is held in special honour among the Persians, and the barbarians hold mysteries which are performed among other peoples even down to this day in honour of the Persian Artemis.[3]

S. 15:
10.31.1 (= Tz. H. 1,585–7):[4]

Persian marriage customs:
(10.31.1) *...
   This Cimon was married to his own sister Elpinice
   As Ptolemy at a later time to Berenice,
   And Zeus to Hera before them, and at present the Persians do.[5]

B. CYRUS THE GREAT (C. 576/5–530)[6]

S. 16:
9.2.3–4 (= *Const. Exc.* 4: 281):[7]

Cyrus and Croesus:
(9.2.3) *... And at a later time, when Croesus had been taken prisoner by Cyrus and was about to be burned upon a great pyre,[8] he recalled the answer Solon had given him. And so, while the fire was already blazing about him, he kept on calling the name of Solon.

---

[3] The subject is Artemis, Persian Anaïtis or Anahita, a chief deity of Zoroastrianism (Mazdaism). For an introduction, see Boyce 2011.
[4] According to Oldfather 1970b: 100–1 and Vogel 1985b: 216–17; Cohen-Skalli 2012: 212–13 counts this as Fr. 64.
[5] For this custom see also Hdt. 3.31. Ctesias allegedly remarked that the Persians had sex with their mothers: FF. *44a–b, both from Tertullian (Stronk 2010: 192, 392–3). As, *inter alios*, the Lagides would show, marriages between brother and sister were not at all uncommon during the Hellenistic period and at least in Egypt went much further back in time. I am not at all sure whether the reference 'at present' really means 'in Tzetzes' days': the Qur'an chapter 4 verse 23 explicitly forbids such alliances, though relations between cousins are allowed, sometimes even encouraged.
[6] For a succinct review of Cyrus' career, see for example Briant 2002: 31–50.
[7] According to the editions by Vogel 1985b: 170–1 and Oldfather 1970b: 4–7; Cohen-Skalli 2012: 135–6 counts it as Fr. 4.
[8] See Hdt. 1.86.3–6 and the comments of Asheri et al. 2007: 142–3.

(4) And Cyrus sent men to find out why he kept on calling the name of Solon. When he heard the truth, Cyrus changed his plans, and because he believed that Solon's reply was the truth, he ceased to regard Croesus with contempt, put out the pyre, saved Croesus, and counted him henceforth as one of his friends.[9]

S. 17:
9.21.1 (= Eus. *PE* 10.10.4/488C):[10]

Start of Cyrus' reign:
(9.21.1) * ***[11] Cyrus became king of the Persians in the year of the fifty-fifth Olympiad [560/59], as may be found in Diodorus' *Bibliotheca* and in the histories of Thallus, Castor, Polybius, Phlegon, and all others who have used the reckoning by Olympiads. For all these authors agree on the date.

S. 18:
9.22.1 (= *Const. Exc.* 2 (1): 219):[12]

Education of Cyrus the Great:
(9.22.1) *Cyrus, the son of Cambyses and Mandane, the daughter of Astyages[13] who was king of the Medes, was first among the men of his time in bravery, wisdom, and the other *aretae*. This was due to his father, who had brought him up in a kingly way and had made him zealous to emulate the best men. And it was clear that he would be capable of stout actions, because he revealed an *aretē* beyond his years.[14]

---

[9] See Cohen-Skalli 2012: 329 *ad* p. 138 note 12.

[10] According to the editions by Vogel 1985b: 182–3 and Oldfather 1970b: 30–1; Cohen-Skalli 2012: 149 counts it as Fr. 33.

[11] 'After the seventy years of the Captivity' is added in Eusebius' text, not in Diodorus' fragments.

[12] According to the editions by Vogel 1985b: 183 and Oldfather 1970b: 30–1; Cohen-Skalli 2012: 150 counts it as Fr. 34.

[13] In agreement with Hdt. 1.107.2–108.1 and X. *Cyr.* 1.2.1; *contra* Ctes. *Pers.* F. 8d* = Nic. Dam. *FGrH/BNJ* 90 F 66(3) (Stronk 2010: 290–311 *ad* 290–1) and F. 9(1) = Phot. *Bibl.* [72] 36a9–37a25 (Stronk 2010: 312–19 *ad* 312–13); see also Cohen-Skalli 2012: 348 *ad* p. 150 note 70.

[14] As Cohen-Skalli 2012: 348–9 *ad* p. 159 note 71 observes, it appears that Diodorus treats Cyrus' *aretē* as one of the central themes in this book.

The Persians and the Greek Wars 145

S. 19:
9.24.1 (= *Const. Exc.* 2 (1): 219):[15]

Aretae of Cyrus the Great:
(9.24.1) *Cyrus, we are told, was not only a courageous man in war, but was also considerate and humane in his treatment of his subjects. And it was for this reason that the Persians called him 'Father'.[16]

S. 20:
9.31.1–3 (= *Const. Exc.* 4, p. 289–90):[17]

Croesus goes to war against Cyrus:
(9.31.1) *When Croesus was about to take the field against Cyrus the Persian, he asked the oracle of Delphi. And the answer ran: 'By crossing the Halys, Croesus will destroy a mighty realm.'[18] Interpreting the ambiguous answer of the oracle in the light of his own purpose, he came to grief. (2) *Croesus asked a second time whether he was to have the power a long time. And the oracle spoke the following verses:[19] 'The day a mule becomes the king of Medes, / Then, tender-footed Lydian, along the pebble-laden Hermus / You must flee and not stay, and not be ashamed to be deficient.' *By a 'mule' Cyrus was meant, because his mother was a Mede and his father a Persian.[20] (3) *Cyrus, the king of the Persians, having appeared with his complete army at the passes of Cappadocia,[21] sent messengers to Croesus,[22] both to spy out his power and to declare to him that Cyrus would forgive his previous misdeeds and appoint him satrap of Lydia, if he presented himself at Cyrus' court and acknowledged, as others did, that he was Cyrus' servant. But Croesus answered the messengers that it would be more fitting if Cyrus and the Persians should submit to be the servants of Croesus. He reminded them that in the period before they had been subordinates of the Medes and that he himself never had obeyed another.

[15] According to the editions by Vogel 1985b: 183 and Oldfather 1970b: 32–3; Cohen-Skalli 2012: 150 counts it as Fr. 36.
[16] See Cohen-Skalli 2012: 349 *ad* p. 150 note 75.
[17] According to the editions by Vogel 1985b: 188–9 and Oldfather 1970b: 40–3; Cohen-Skalli 2012: 155–6 counts it as Frr. 42–5.
[18] Similar to the oracle as rendered in Hdt 1.53.3. See Cohen-Skalli 2012: 353 *ad* p. 155 note 90 for further references.
[19] See Cohen-Skalli 2012: 353 *ad* p. 155 note 91.
[20] See S. 18 above.
[21] Croesus started the hostilities, Cyrus reacted: see Hdt. 1.75–91.
[22] According to Herodotus, Cyrus sent messengers to the Ionian cities, to persuade them to defect from Croesus: Hdt. 1.76.3.

S. 21:
9.32.1 (= *Const. Exc.* 2 (1): 220):²³

Mission of Eurybatus:
(9.32.1) *Croesus, the king of the Lydians, under the guise of sending him to Delphi, dispatched Eurybatus of Ephesus to the Peloponnesus, after he had given him money with which to recruit as many mercenaries as he could from among the Greeks.²⁴ But this agent of Croesus defected to Cyrus the Persian and revealed everything to him. Therefore the wickedness of Eurybatus became a byword among the Greeks. Whenever, to this day, a man wants to cast another's knavery in his teeth he calls him a Eurybatus.²⁵

S. 22:
9.33.1–4 (= *Const. Exc.* 4: 290–1):²⁶

Words and actions of Croesus:
(9.33.1) [[*Though evil men may for the moment avoid punishment at the hands of those whom they have wronged, yet the evil report of them is preserved for all time and punishes them as far as possible even after death.]] (2) *We are told that Croesus, on the eve of his war with Cyrus, dispatched ambassadors to Delphi to inquire by what means it would be possible for his son to speak. The Pythia replied: 'O Lydian by birth, of many kings, great fool Croesus, / You do not want to hear what you most want in your halls / When your son speaks. For you, it might be well best that he remains apart / For you shall hear him for the first time on a wretched day.' [[(3) *A man should bear good fortune with moderation and not put his trust in the human successes that can take great changes with a slight turn of the scale.²⁷]] (4) *After Croesus had been taken prisoner and the pyre had been quenched, he asked Cyrus,²⁸ seeing that the city was being plundered and that, apart from other things,

---

²³ According to the editions by Vogel 1985b: 189 and Oldfather 1970b: 42–3; Cohen-Skalli 2012: 156 counts it as Fr. 46.
²⁴ This story is absent in Herodotus. As such, Diodorus' account might be true, because notably Arcadia and Achaea were increasingly becoming (from at least the seventh century) a vast reservoir of mercenaries. See also Cohen-Skalli 2012: 354 *ad* p. 156 note 96.
²⁵ See Cohen-Skalli 2012: 354 *ad* p. 156 note 97.
²⁶ According to the editions by Vogel 1985b: 189–90 and Oldfather 1970b: 44–5; Cohen-Skalli 2012: 157–8 counts it as Frr. 48–50.
²⁷ The two passages in these paragraphs enclosed in double square brackets clearly show some of Diodorus' moral views. In view of the context I have maintained them. See also Cohen-Skalli 2012: 355 *ad* p. 157 notes 98–9.
²⁸ See Hdt. 1.88.2.

much silver and gold was carried off, what the soldiers were doing. After Cyrus laughingly replied: 'They are making plunder of your wealth', Croesus said: 'Not so, by Zeus, but yours, for Croesus has no longer a thing of his own.' And Cyrus, pondering his words, at once changed his plans, and having put a stop to the plunder of the soldiers, he took the possessions of the inhabitants of Sardis to the royal treasury.[29]

S. 23:
9.34.1 (= *Const. Exc.* 2 (1): 220):[30]

Croesus honoured by Cyrus:
(9.34.1) *Because Cyrus believed that Croesus was a pious man because a rainstorm had burst and quenched the flame, and keeping in mind the reply of Solon, he kept Croesus at his side in a position of honour. He gave him a place in his council as well, because he believed that Croesus was a wise man because he had convened with many men of learning and wisdom.

S. 24:
9.35.1–36.1 (= *Const. Exc.* 4: 290):[31]

Encounters with the Greeks:
(9.35.1) *Harpagus had been appointed commander of the regions[32] by the sea by Cyrus the Persian, and when the Greeks of Asia Minor sent an embassy to Cyrus to conclude a treaty of friendship with him, Harpagus remarked to them that what they were doing was very much like a former experience of his own. (2) Once when he wanted to marry, he had asked a girl's father for the hand of his daughter. At first, however, her father decided that Harpagus was not worthy to marry his daughter and betrothed her to a man of higher position. Later, however, when he saw that Harpagus was being honoured by the king, he offered Harpagus his daughter. Harpagus

---

[29] See Hdt. 1.88.2–3.
[30] According to the editions by Vogel 1985b: 190 and Oldfather 1970b: 45–6; Cohen-Skalli 2012: 158 counts it as Fr. 51.
[31] According to the editions by Vogel 1985b: 190–1 and Oldfather 1970b: 46–9; Cohen-Skalli 2012: 158 counts it as Frr. 52–3.
[32] Oldfather 1970b: 47 translates Harpagus' appointment as 'commander on the sea'. Persia, though, did not yet have a fleet at that time (see Briant 2002: 37) and therefore the solution by Cohen Skalli 2012: 158 (after a suggestion by P. Goukowsky: see *apparatus* p. 159) looks much more attractive, namely to insert τῶν, in fact thus relating it to the later (see 14.9.2) attested function of ὁ τῶν ἐπὶ θαλάττης σατραπειῶν ἡγούμενος ('commander of the satrapies by the sea').

Fig. 3.1. Pasargadae, Persis. Tomb of Cyrus the Great. Photo © Jona Lendering <http://www.livius.org>.

then replied that he would no longer have her as his wife, but would consent to take her as a concubine. (3) By such words he made clear to the Greeks that before, when Cyrus had urged them to become friends of the Persians, they had been unwilling. Now, after matters had taken a different turn, they were anxious to agree upon relations of friendship. Cyrus would make no terms with them as with allies, but he would receive them as subordinates if they would surrender themselves to the word of honour of the Persians.³³

(9.36.1) *When the Lacedaemonians learned that the Greeks of Asia Minor were in peril, they sent a message to Cyrus that the Lacedaemonians, being kinsmen of the Greeks of Asia Minor, forbade him to subdue the Greek *poleis*. And Cyrus, marvelling at such words, remarked that he would judge their *aretē* when he sent one of his own subordinates to subdue Greece. [**The Greek *poleis* of Asia Minor came under Persian authority about 547.**]

---

³³ For the career of Harpagus, see Hdt. 1.80–176 *passim*; I agree with Cohen-Skalli 2012: 356 *ad* p. 159 note 107 that Diodorus' account of the embassy, inserting a stay with Harpagus, is more plausible than Herodotus'.

S. 25:
10.13.1 (= *Const. Exc.* 4: 296):³⁴

Cyrus' ambitions:
(10.13.1) *After Cyrus, the king of the Persians, had conquered the land of the Babylonians and the Medes, he was encompassing in his hopes the whole inhabited world.³⁵ Because he had subdued these powerful and great nations, he thought that there would be no king or people or tribe that could withstand his might; [[since some of those who have irresponsible power are unable to bear their good fortune as human beings should.³⁶]]

C. CAMBYSES II (?–523/2)³⁷

S. 26:
10.14.1–3 (= *Const. Exc.* 2 (1): 224–5):³⁸

Nature of Cambyses:
(10.14.1) *Cambyses was by nature manic and mentally disturbed, and the greatness of his kingdom made him much more cruel and arrogant.³⁹ (2) *Because Cambyses the Persian could not bear his luck as men should, he excavated, after the capture of Memphis and Pelusium [in 525], the tomb of Amasis, a former king of Egypt. When he found his mummy in the coffin, he outraged the body of the dead man, and after he had committed every violation of the senseless corpse, he finally ordered it to be burned.⁴⁰ Because the

---

³⁴ According to the editions by Vogel 1985b: 204 and Oldfather 1970b: 74–5; Cohen-Skalli 2012: 199 counts it as Fr. 28.
³⁵ For a review of Cyrus' successes, see the introductory sections of Ambler 2001: 4–11; see also Ctes. *Pers.* FF. *8d–*9e (Stronk 2010: 290–321). It seems that Ctesias was not followed by Diodorus for this part of his account, but we cannot be absolutely certain because parts of this book have not been transmitted, like the siege and fall of Babylon (only briefly referred to; see for a fuller account Hdt. 1.188–91; X. *Cyr.* 8.6).
³⁶ Diodorus again inserts his moral views on human behaviour, as he does in the second sentence of the following section.
³⁷ For this king see, for example, Briant 2002: 49–61, 97–9, 101–5.
³⁸ According to the editions by Vogel 1985b: 204–5 and Oldfather 1970b: 74–7; Cohen-Skalli 2012: 199–200 counts it as Frr. 29–31.
³⁹ Asheri et al. 2007: 397 asserts that the personality of Cambyses in Herodotus does change for the worse after the conquest of Egypt (Hdt. 3.1–14), especially after his return from Ethiopia.
⁴⁰ Both Herodotus and Ctesias present a cause for the Persians' invasion of Egypt. Though the reasons differ, certainly in Herodotus' view Amasis II is, more or less, held accountable for deceiving the Persians: Hdt. 3.1–2; Ctes. *Pers.* F. 13(10). It seems that Diodorus may have been influenced by Herodotus' view and not that of Ctesias. However, no one explains Persia's conquest of Egypt in the light of its desire (or even ideological need; see below, Chapter 10) to expand. At the time of Cambyses' expedition, Amasis II had already been dead about a year

natives were not used to consign the bodies of their dead to the fire, he supposed that in this fashion as well he would offend him who had been long dead.[41] (3) *When Cambyses was about to march against Ethiopia, he sent part of his army against the inhabitants of Ammonium, giving orders to the commanders to plunder and burn the oracle and to enslave all who lived near the temple.[42]

S. 27:
10.15.1 (= *Const. Exc.* 1: 397):[43]

Cambyses' power in North Africa:
(10.15.1) *After Cambyses, the king of the Persians, had mastered the whole of Egypt [in 525],[44] the Libyans and Cyrenaeans,[45] who had been allies of the Egyptians, sent presents to him and declared their willingness to obey his every command.[46]

S. 28:
3.3.1:

Cambyses makes war against the Ethiopians:
(3.3.1) Cambyses, for instance, they say, who made war upon the Ethiopians with a great force, both lost all his army and was himself exposed to the greatest peril; ...

---

and had been succeeded by Psammeticus III. (It seems unlikely that Cambyses destroyed the mummy of Amasis I: he was the founder of the 18th dynasty, died about 1520 BC, and was buried in Thebes West: his mummy was recovered from the Deir el-Bahri cache in AD 1881.)

[41] Schwartz 1949: 66 refers to an Egyptian text, called 'The appeal of Thoth to Re-Harakhte', full of descriptions of the devastation of sanctuaries in the time of Cambyses. The text may well have been pure propaganda and not reflected reality at all.

[42] 'Inhabitants of Ammonium' might well suggest the people around the oracle of Ammon at the Siwa oasis (see Hdt. 3.25). Herodotus writes that this army was lost in the desert due to a sandstorm (Hdt. 3.26). Research at Amheida, in the Thoth temple of the Dakhla oasis, suggests that this oasis was the basis for a second rebellion against the Persians (after the one led by Psammeticus III in 524), led by one Petubastis III (between 522 and 520), who claimed full royal titles and had himself crowned Pharaoh in Memphis, Egypt's capital. Olaf Kaper suggests that Cambyses sent out his army to deal with the army of Petubastis IV but was defeated. The story as Herodotus tells it would be due to the workings of Darius the Great, who adapted the story to his purposes after ending Petubastis' revolt with much bloodshed two years after Cambyses' defeat: see Kaper 2015.

[43] According to the editions by Vogel 1985b: 205 and Oldfather 1970b: 76–7; Cohen-Skalli 2012: 200 counts it as Fr. 32.

[44] Polyaenus claims that, besieging the important city of Pelusium, Cambyses positioned (sacred) animals (dogs, cattle, cats, ibises) in front of his army. Terrified of hurting these animals, the Egyptians ceased their (fierce) resistance and surrendered, enabling Cambyses to enter Egypt (Polyaen. *Strat.* 7.9.1).

[45] See Hdt. 3.13.3–4; the accounts of Herodotus and Diodorus differ, though, for the moment both peoples surrendered to the Persians.

[46] See Cohen-Skalli 2012: 383 *ad* p. 200 note 61.

D. DARIUS THE GREAT (C. 550–486)[47]

S. 29:
1.33.9:

Darius contemplates digging a canal in Egypt:
(1.33.9) [[The first to undertake the construction of this was Necho II, the son of Psammeticus I.]] After him Darius the Persian made progress with the work for some time, but finally left it unfinished. In fact, he had been informed by some people that if he dug through the isthmus he would be responsible for the submergence of Egypt because they pointed out to him that the Red Sea was situated higher than Egypt.[48]

S. 30:
1.58.4:

Darius desires a statue in Memphis:
(1.58.4) So great became the fame of Sesoösis and so enduring through the ages that when, many generations later, Egypt fell under the power of the Persians and Darius, the father of Xerxes, was bent upon placing a statue of himself in Memphis before that of Sesoösis, the chief priest opposed it in a speech made in an assembly of the priests, making it clear that Darius had not yet surpassed the deeds of Sesoösis. The king was not even nearly angered, but, on the contrary was pleased with his frankness, said that he would strive not to be found less than Sesoösis after having lived the same time, and asked to compare the deeds achieved at the same age because that would provide the most just view of their *aretē*.

S. 31:
1.95.4–5:

Aretae of Darius as king of Egypt:
(1.95.4) A sixth person, people say, to be familiar with the laws and customs[49] of the Egyptians was Darius, the father of Xerxes. Because

---

[47] For Darius I the Great see, for example, Briant 2002: 107–61 and *passim*.
[48] In fact the canal was dug (or at least reopened) by Darius in 497, as he testifies in an inscription found in Suez: apparently this canal ran from around Bubastis on the Nile to the Red Sea: see Kent 1953: 147 (*DZc*). See also Ruzicka 2012: 24–5.
[49] As the context shows, *nomoi* means here more than merely 'laws': hence a more embracing translation. For Darius and Egypt see Briant 2002: 472–84.

he was appalled by the lawlessness which had occurred against the sanctuaries throughout Egypt by his predecessor Cambyses,[50] he sought to live a suitable and godly life. (5) He associated himself, indeed, with the priests in Egypt themselves and they made him familiar with both the theology and the activities described in the holy books. When he learned from these books of the greatness of mind of the ancient kings and their care for their subjects, he imitated their way of life. He was, therefore, given such honour that he alone of all Great Kings was addressed by the Egyptians as a god while he was alive, but after he had died he received the same honours as the ancient kings of Egypt who had most strictly observed the laws and customs.[51]

S. 32 (cf. F. 1 ad 2.5.5):
2.5.5:

Size of Darius' army during the Scythian campaign:
(2.5.5) For if one forgets the campaign of Darius against the Scythians with eight hundred thousand men ... and looks at the events that have taken place in Europe only yesterday or the day before, one would be readier to come to regard the statement as credible.[52]

S. 33:
10.19.2–6 (= *Const. Exc.* 4: 297–8):[53]

Darius enlarges his power; Darius' ambitions:
(10.19.2) *Megabyzus, who was also called Zopyrus[54] and was a friend of King Darius, had scourged himself and cut off the extremities of his face,[55] because he had resolved to become a deserter and betray Babylon to the Persians. We are told that Darius was deeply moved and declared that he would rather have Megabyzus whole again, if it were possible, than bring ten Babylons under his power,

---

[50] See above, notes 40–1, 44.
[51] See also Ruzicka 2012: 23–4.
[52] Diodorus refers to expeditions by Dionysius I of Syracuse and Rome, expounded in 2.5.6–7.
[53] According to the editions by Vogel 1985b: 209–10 and Oldfather 1970b: 82–7; Cohen-Skalli 2012: 203–5 counts it as Frr. 41–5.
[54] Seemingly, Diodorus here combines two versions of the story. The story is also related by Herodotus 3.153–160: he, however, calls Zopyrus (who cut off his nose and ears) the son of Megabyzus. Ctesias, *Pers.* F 13(26), mentions Megabyzus as the one responsible for the betrayal of Babylon. See also Asheri et al. 2007: 522–3 on 150–60.
[55] That is, his nose and ears. See Hdt. 3.154, 157.

The Persians and the Greek Wars 153

although his wish could not be achieved.[56] (3) *The Babylonians chose Megabyzus to be their commander, being unaware that the service he would render them would be a kind of bait to entice them to the destruction which was soon to follow. (4) *The successful outcome is sufficient proof of the prophecies.[57] (5) *After Darius had made himself master of practically the whole of Asia, he wanted to subdue Europe.[58] Because the desires he had for further possessions were boundless and he had confidence in the greatness of the power of Persia, he was determined to bring the inhabited world under his command. He thought it a disgrace that, though the kings before his time had inferior resources, they had conquered the greatest nations in war, whereas he, who had forces greater than any man before him had ever acquired, had accomplished no deed worthy of mention. (6) When the Tyrrhenians left Lemnos, because of their fear of the Persians, they claimed that they were doing so because of certain oracles, and they gave the island over to Miltiades.[59] The leader of the Tyrrhenians in this affair was Hermon, and as a result presents of this kind have from that time been called 'gifts of Hermon'.[60]

S. 34:
12.68.1:

Aristagoras of Miletus founds Amphipolis:
(12.68.1) ... Aristagoras of Miletus had undertaken to found this city [Amphipolis] earlier,[61] when he was fleeing [in 497] from Darius, the king of the Persians.

---

[56] Diodorus more or less follows here the story told in Hdt. 3.151–9; Asheri et al. 2007: 523 refers to epic as the basis of this account, *inter alia* connecting this story of (auto-)mutilation with that of Sinon, hero of the *Iliupersis* (and probably of a play by Sophocles: *TGF* [vol. 4, Radt], FF. 542–4).
[57] Hdt. 3.151.2 refers to a prophecy that 'Babylon would be taken when mules bear offspring', an event taking place a while later and related in 3.153.1. Again, Herodotus seems to be Diodorus' main source here.
[58] Darius' first effort had been directed against the Scythians: 2.5.5; Hdt. 4.118–44; Ctes. *Pers.* F. 13(20–1). It appears that his next move was directed against Greece: Hdt. 6.*passim*; Ctes. *Pers.* 13(22); below, 11.2.2. Diodorus describes it primarily as a punitive expedition, though perhaps some traces of attempts to enlarge Persian domination come to the fore as well. Herodotus, on the contrary, accentuates the latter aspect. In this paragraph Diodorus also underlines the latter aspect. Balcer 1995: 327–31 is more cautious, as is Briant 2002: 156–61.
[59] See Hdt.6.137, 140. Cohen-Skalli 2012: 388–9 *ad* p. 205 note 82 believes this passage goes back to Ephorus (and, perhaps, to Hecataeus of Miletus) rather than to Herodotus, in whose version Miltiades is more a conqueror than an upgraded protector.
[60] See Cohen-Skalli 2012: 205 note 83.
[61] See Hdt. 5.126.

154 *Semiramis' Legacy*

Fig. 3.2. Bisitun, Media. Monumental relief of Darius I the Great, representing the king's victory over the usurper Gaumāta (Smerdis) and the nine rebels. Photo © Jona Lendering <http://www.livius.org>.

S. 35:
10.25.1–4 (= *Const. Exc.* **4: 298–301):**[62]

Beginning of the Greek Wars; activities of Persians in Asia Minor:
(10.25.1) * The Persians learned from the Greeks to burn temples, repaying in kind those who had been the first to offend justice [in 498, at Sardis].[63] (2) *When the Carians were becoming exhausted in their struggles with the Persians, they asked the oracle about an alliance, whether they should take the Milesians to be their allies.[64] And the oracle replied: 'Once upon a time the Milesians

---

[62] According to the editions by Vogel 1985b: 213–14 and Oldfather 1970b: 92–5; Cohen-Skalli 2012: 203–5 counts it as Frr. 53–6.
[63] Revenge for setting fire to the temple of Cybele at Sardis (see Hdt. 5.102.1) is a recurrent theme in descriptions of the Greek Wars (I take this term from the book by Cawkwell 2005), possibly in Ctes. *Pers.* 13(30, 31), certainly in Hdt. 7.11.2, and Diodorus. See also Briant 2002: 158. The theme is reversed during the march of Alexander III the Great, when – allegedly – Persepolis was set aflame in retribution for the burning of the acropolis of Athens (below, 17.72.6).
[64] According to Hdt. 5.119.2–120.1, the Milesians (and their allies) came out to help the Carians anyway, with devastating result, not only for the Carians but certainly for the Milesians themselves.

were mighty men.' (3) *But the fear situated nearby made them forget the rivalry towards each other and compelled them to man the *triereis* with all speed.[65] (4) *Hecataeus of Miletus, whom the Ionians dispatched as an ambassador,[66] asked why Artaphernes[67] had no faith in them. When Artaphernes replied that he was afraid that they would harbour resentment because of the injuries they had received during their defeat,[68] Hecataeus said, 'Well then, if suffering ill treatment has caused bad faith, receiving goodness will surely make our *poleis* well disposed towards the Persians.' And Artaphernes, approving the statement, restored to the *poleis* their laws and taxed them with fixed tributes according to their capacity.

S. 36:
10.27.1–3 (= *Const. Exc.* 4: 298–301):[69]

First Greek War; Datis demands Athens surrender itself to him:
(10.27.1) *Because Datis, the commander of the Persians and a Mede by descent, had received from his ancestors the tradition that the Athenians were descendants of Medus, who had established the kingdom of Media,[70] he sent a message to the Athenians making clear that he had come with an army to demand the return of the ancestral sovereignty. In fact Medus, he said, who was the most ancient of his own ancestors, had been deprived of the kingship by the Athenians, and having arrived in Asia had founded the kingdom of Media. (2) If they returned the kingship to him, he would forgive them for this guilty act and for the campaign they had made against Sardis [in 498], but if they opposed him, they would suffer a worse fate than the Eretrians.[71] (3) Miltiades replied, contrary to the opinion of the ten *strategoi*, that according to the statement of the envoys it was more appropriate for the Athenians to rule over the empire of the

---

[65] I have stuck to the Greek word because of the remark in Morrison and Williams 1968: 3 referred to above, Chapter 2, note 36.
[66] See the remarks by Cohen-Skalli 2012: 398 *ad* p. 209 note 106.
[67] The brother of Darius I the Great and at the time of the Ionian Revolt the satrap at Sardis.
[68] The defeat refers to the Battle of Lade, a naval engagement in 494 in which the fleet of the revolting Ionian cities had been defeated by a 'Persian' fleet consisting of Phoenician, Egyptian, Cilician, and Cypriot ships.
[69] According to the editions by Vogel 1985b: 214–15 and Oldfather 1970b: 96–7; Cohen-Skalli 2012: 210 counts it as Fr. 58.
[70] See also Apollod. 1.9.28; Str. 11.13.10/526, 14.14/531.
[71] See Hdt. 6.101.

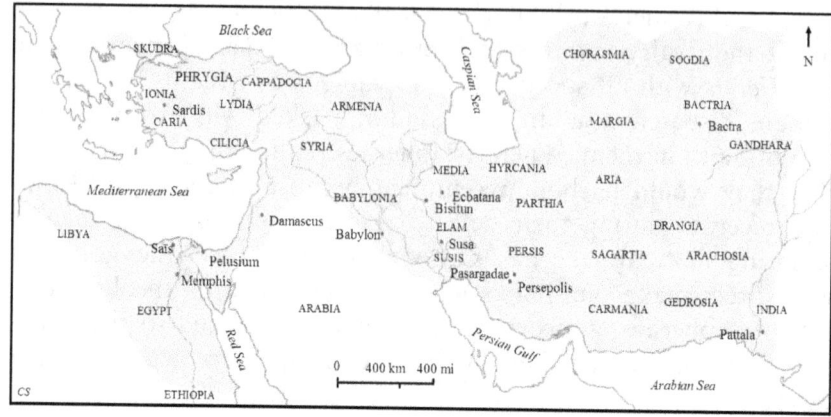

Fig. 3.3. Regions of the Achaemenid Persian Empire.

Medes than for Datis over the *polis* of the Athenians;[72] for it was an Athenian who had established the kingdom of the Medes, whereas no man of Median descent had ever controlled Athens. After he had heard this reply, Datis made ready for battle [at Marathon, probably August or September 490].[73]

E. XERXES I (C. 519–465)[74]

S. 37:
2.5.5:

Second Greek War; the size of Xerxes' army:
(2.5.5) For if one forgets ... the crossing made by Xerxes against Greece [in 480] with a host beyond number, and looks at the events that have taken place in Europe only yesterday or the day before, one would be readier to come to regard the statement as credible.

---

[72] Diodorus' version is ambiguous due to his use of the word ἀπό, which can indicate here both 'contrary to' and 'based upon' (for the latter see *LSJ, s.v. ad* III.6). As Hdt. 6.109–10 makes it clear that the *strategoi* were divided among themselves, I have translated the phrase accordingly.

[73] Diodorus is silent here on the outcome of this battle. The Athenians celebrated it as a huge triumph – a tendency copied by later authors in a variety of Europe-centric countries – but for the Persians it was probably, as Briant phrases it, 'a minor engagement that had no effect whatever on the Aegean strategy defined by Darius. This was surely the version found in Achaemenid propaganda (cf. Dio Chrys. XI.148)' (Briant 2002: 160–1; see also Stronk 2014/15: 226).

[74] For Xerxes see, for example, Briant 2002: 515–68; Bridges 2014; Stoneman 2015.

S. 38:
5.63.1:

Temple at Castabus remains intact:
(5.63.1) And most important of all, when the Persians were the dominant power in Asia and were plundering all the temples of the Greeks, the precinct of Hemithea was the sole shrine on which they did not lay hands.[75]

S. 39:
10.32.1–34.13 (= *Const. Exc.* 4: 301–2):[76]

On the eve of Xerxes' invasion of Greece:
(10.32.1 = 11.1.1)
(10.33.1) *When Xerxes was about to cross over into Europe, all the Greeks sent an embassy to Gelo [the ruler of Gela and tyrant of Syracuse] to strike up an alliance. He replied that he would not agree to an alliance and would not supply them with provisions, unless they assigned to him the supreme command, either on land or at sea ...[77]
(10.34.1) *Though the supremacy which the Persians enjoy entails, for the satisfaction of cupidity, the gifts they require, the greed of a Tyrant does not overlook even any small gain.[78] ... (2) ... (3) ... (4) ... (5) ... (6) ... (7) ... (8) ... (9) ... (10) *I deny being dismayed as regards the magnitude of the army of the Persians. For a war is decided by valour, not numbers.[79] (11) *The inheritance they have received from their fathers is to keep themselves to themselves, to die in response to the need of their fatherland. (12) *Why should we fear the gold with which they cover themselves going into battle, as women do for marriage, since victory will give us as a result as prize not only glory but also riches? For valour fears not gold, which the sword has ever taken captive, but the generalship of those in command. (13) *For every army that exceeds the proper proportion

---

[75] This story refers to the reign of Xerxes: see Cic. *Leg.* 2.26. The temple intended is in Castabus on the Cherronesus. See also above, note 63.
[76] According to the editions by Vogel 1985b: 217–19 and Oldfather 1970b: 102–7; Cohen-Skalli 2012: 213–16 counts it as Frr. 65–79.
[77] See also Hdt. 7.153, 157–63; below, 11.26.4–5, Diodorus returns to the issue.
[78] The 'supremacy' intended here is that in (financial) resources, a recurring *topos*: it allows the Persians to buy assistance whenever need arises and/or to honour those who had served the Great King well: see, for example, Briant 2002: 302–54.
[79] This paragraph and the following ones contain some (moral) observations by Diodorus that might be connected with the imminent invasion of Greece by the Persians.

mostly carries in itself its own demise. For before the ranks hear the commands, we will act first, doing what we want to.

S. 40:
11.1.1–19.6:

Preparations for the Second Greek War:
(11.1.1) The preceding book, being the tenth of our narrative, closed with the events of the year just before Xerxes' crossing into Europe and the deliberations held in the general assembly of the Greeks in Corinth on the alliance between Gelo and the Greeks.[80] In this book we will detail the further course of the history, beginning with Xerxes' campaign against the Greeks, and we will continue until the year preceding the Athenians' campaign against Cyprus under the leadership of Cimon.[81] (2) While Calliades was *archon* in Athens [480/79], the Romans made Spurius Cassius and Proclus Verginius Tricostus consuls[82] and the Eleians celebrated the seventy-fifth Olympiad, in which Astylus of Syracuse won the *stadium* race. It was in this year that King Xerxes made his campaign against Greece, for the following reason. (3) Mardonius the Persian was a cousin of Xerxes and related to him by marriage,[83] and because of his sagacity and courage greatly admired by the Persians.[84] This man, being elated by pride and at the height of his physical vigour, was eager to be the leader of great forces. Therefore he persuaded Xerxes to enslave the Greeks, who had always been hostile to the Persians.[85] (4) Xerxes, persuaded by him and desiring to make all

---

[80] Diodorus appears here to be (deliberately?) ambiguous: Herodotus (7.157–62) states that contacts between Gelo and the Hellenic ambassadors took place on Sicily, but Timaeus (*FGrH/ BNJ* 566 F 94) makes Sicilian ambassadors respond at Corinth. Baron suggests that Diodorus followed that suggestion, but I believe Diodorus leaves this matter completely open: see Baron 2013: 111 and note 104.

[81] In fact, the story of Cimon's expedition against Cyprus only starts in 12.2–3.

[82] It appears that Diodorus knew his list of *archons* better than his list of consuls. Basically, I will follow names and years as presented by Broughton 1951. Broughton reckons the years in the Varronian chronology (after Marcus Terentius Varro). I shall indicate these as years vc. According to the Varronian chronology, the consuls of 486 vc were Sp. Cassius Vicellinus and Proculus Verginius Tricostus Rutilus: Broughton 1951: 20. Diodorus is, therefore, seven years ahead of the Varronian chronology, a distance he maintains through to *caput* 11.41.1 and again from 11.91.1 onwards.

[83] Through his mother, Mardonius was a nephew of Darius I the Great.

[84] Diodorus' portrait of Mardonius only partly corresponds to that by Herodotus, the latter's description of his activities displaying little of Mardonius' intelligence and courage. It seems that Mardonius was born about 520 and therefore flourished at the time of the invasion of Greece.

[85] Probably a reference to the Ionian Revolt and the support for it by some of the Greek *poleis*. However, as Morgan 2016 points out, in the archaic period the Greeks above all saw the Persians as noble warriors.

The Persians and the Greek Wars

the Greeks homeless,[86] sent an embassy to the Carthaginians about collaboration with him and closed an agreement with them that he would make war against the Greeks who lived in Greece, while the Carthaginians should at the same time gather great forces and subdue those Greeks who lived in Sicily and Italy.[87] (5) In accordance, then, with their agreements, the Carthaginians, having collected an amount of money, gathered mercenaries from both Italy and Liguria and also from Galatia and Iberia. In addition to these troops they enrolled citizen forces from the whole of Libya and Carthage. Finally they collected, after spending three years in constant preparation, more than three hundred thousand soldiers[88] and two hundred warships.

(11.2.1) Xerxes, vying with the zeal displayed by the Carthaginians, surpassed them in all his preparations to the degree that he surpassed the Carthaginians in the multitude of peoples at his command. And he began to make ships built along the whole coast that was subject to him, both Egypt and Phoenicia and Cyprus, moreover Cilicia and Pamphylia and Pisidia, and also Lycia, Caria, Mysia, the Troad, and the cities on the Hellespont, and Bithynia, and Pontus.[89] Preparing during three years,[90] like the Carthaginians, he made ready more than twelve hundred warships.[91] (2) He was helped in this by his father Darius, who before his death had made ready great forces.[92] Darius did so because he harboured a continuous grudge against the victorious Athenians, after Darius had, under the command of Datis, been defeated by the Athenians at Marathon. Darius now, when about to cross over against the Greeks, was stopped by death, but Xerxes, because of both the design of his father and the counsel of Mardonius, as already written, determined to make war against the Greeks.

---

[86] As Haillet 2002: 119 *ad* p. 5 note 2 observes, an exaggeration that was at variance with the traditional Persian policy in Asia Minor towards the Greeks.

[87] Though the Persian–Carthaginian treaty is far from accepted historically, Haillet 2002: 120 *ad* p. 5 note 3 refers to several classical sources that believed it was/had been a reality.

[88] Infantry is suggested by Dindorf (πεζῶν), but land forces (infantry *and* cavalry combined) seems to me to be another, and more plausible, option in the light of the use of this word in Diodorus' account. With respect to these two options, I think 'soldiers' is a fair compromise. As a matter of fact, the number was probably considerably lower than the 300,000 mentioned here. See also below, notes 115 and 116. For the preparations made by Carthage, then at the height of its power, see also Hdt. 7.165.

[89] See Hdt. 7.88–9.

[90] After he had crushed a revolt in Egypt that had raged from 486 to 484 and revolts in Babylon in 484 and again in 482, during which his satrap Zopyrus was killed. See also Hdt. 7.20.

[91] Unlike the size of the armies, this number of ships may well be feasible: see also Haillet 2002: 121 *ad* p. 5 note 7.

[92] Diodorus appears here to follow Herodotus' account: see Haillet 2002: 121 *ad* p. 6 note 1.

160   *Semiramis' Legacy*

Xerxes leaves Susa for the invasion:
(11.2.3) When all preparations for the campaign had been completed, Xerxes commanded his admirals to assemble the ships at Cyme and Phocaea, and he himself led forth from Susa, having collected the infantry and cavalry forces from all the satrapies. When he had arrived at Sardis, he dispatched heralds to Greece, commanding them to go to all the *poleis* and to demand of the Greeks water and earth.[93] (4) Then, dividing his army, he sent in advance a sufficient number of men both to bridge the Hellespont and to dig a canal through Athos at the neck of the peninsula, at the same time making the passage safe and short for his forces and simultaneously hoping to strike the Greeks with terror before his arrival by the greatness of his acts.[94] Now the men who had been sent to make ready these works completed them quickly because of the high number of workers.

Greek poleis gather and contemplate their defence:
(11.2.5) When the Greeks learned of the great size of the forces of the Persians, they sent ten thousand hoplites into Thessaly to seize the passes of Tempe. Evaenetus[95] commanded the Lacedaemonians and Themistocles the Athenians. These commanders sent ambassadors to the *poleis* with a request to send soldiers for the common defence of the passes. They eagerly desired all the Greek *poleis* to have a share in the defence and collaborate in the war against the Persians. (6) But since most of the Thessalians and other Greeks who lived near the passes had given water and earth to the envoys of Xerxes when they arrived,[96] the two commanders gave up the intention of defending the Tempe passes and returned home.
(11.3.1) It is useful to distinguish those of the Greeks who chose the side of the Persians, to ensure that, having suffered reproach here, their defamation may deter those who might become traitors to

---

[93] That is, to surrender to his authority.
[94] See also Herodotus 7.22–4 and 7.117. For this canal, of which traces can be found between the modern villages of Nea Roda to the north and Tripiti to the south, see also Isserlin 1994. It seems likely that the construction of the canal was at least started well before Xerxes arrived in Sardis: see also Haillet 2002: 121 *ad* p. 6 note 4, who points out that Herodotus' version of Xerxes' preparations is to be preferred to Diodorus'.
[95] The form as given in Hdt. 7.173 of the name of the Lacedaemonian commander, Evaenetus, is according to Haillet 2002: 122 *ad* p. 6 note 5 to be preferred to that of the MSS, Synetus. See also Hdt. 7.172–4.
[96] Herodotus, apparently Diodorus' source here, shows himself biased against the Thessalians: see Haillet 2002: 7 note 1. Moreover, it seems Thessalian Medism only arose after the forces at Tempe had returned home.

the common freedom.⁹⁷ (2) The Aenianians, Dolopians, Melians,⁹⁸ Perrhaebians, and Magnetans took the side of the Persians even while the defending guard was still present at the Tempe passes, and after it had left, the Achaeans of Phthia, Locrians, Thessalians, and most of the Boeotians went over to the Persians. (3) The Greeks who were convening at the Isthmus decreed by vote that, if they prevailed in the war, the Greeks who had voluntarily chosen the cause of the Persians should pay a tithe to the gods, and decreed to send ambassadors to those who were neutral to urge them to join in the struggle for the common freedom.⁹⁹ (4) Some of these truly joined the alliance, others delayed for a considerable time, merely clinging to their own safety and waiting for the outcome of the war.¹⁰⁰ The Argives, however, sending ambassadors to the common congress, announced that they would join the alliance if the congress gave them some share in the command. (5) To them the representatives declared plainly that, if they thought it worse to have a Greek as commander than a Persian as master, they were right to remain neutral, but if they were ambitious to take the lead among the Greeks, so they said, it was necessary that the Argives first accomplished deeds deserving of this leadership and then sought such an honour.¹⁰¹ Afterwards, when the ambassadors sent by Xerxes arrived in Greece and demanded earth and water, all the *poleis* pointed out the pursuit of the common freedom in the replies.

Xerxes leaves Sardis heading for Greece; review of army and fleet:
(11.3.6) When Xerxes learned that the Hellespont had been bridged and the Athos had been cut through, he left Sardis [in the spring of 480] and made his way towards the Hellespont. When he had arrived at Abydus, he led his force over the bridge into Europe.¹⁰² And as he advanced through Thrace, he added many soldiers from both the Thracians and their neighbouring Greeks.¹⁰³ (7) When he arrived at the city called Doriscus, he ordered his fleet to come there, in order to gather both arms of his forces in one place. And

---

⁹⁷ See the remarks of Haillet 2002: 122 *ad* p. 7 note 3.
⁹⁸ Here not the inhabitants of the island of Melos, but the inhabitants of Melis (or Malis) in southern Thessaly: Diodorus could well have made the distinction more clearly. The reading of the MSS, Μιλήσιοι ('Milesians'), is out of order because of the geography implicated in Diodorus' description. For the position of the Boeotians, also see Stronk 2014/15: *passim*.
⁹⁹ See Haillet 2002: 123 *ad* p. 7 note 7 on the events during the Congress of Corinth.
¹⁰⁰ See Hdt. 7.168: probably Corcyra notably showed itself not willing to decide.
¹⁰¹ See Hdt. 7.148–52.
¹⁰² See, for example, Stronk 1998/9: 57 *sqq*.
¹⁰³ See Hdt. 7.108–10.

he also made there the review of the entire army. The number of his soldiers was over eight hundred thousand men,[104] all together his ships of war exceeded twelve hundred, of which three hundred and ten were Greek,[105] the Greeks providing the complement of men, the king supplying the vessels. All the remaining ships they reckoned as non-Greek. Of these the Egyptians supplied two hundred, the Phoenicians three hundred, the Cilicians eighty, the Pamphylians forty, the Lycians the same number, the Carians moreover eighty, and the Cypriots one hundred and fifty. (8) Of the Greeks, the Dorians who dwelt off Caria, together with the Rhodians and Coans, sent forty ships; the Ionians, together with the Chians and Samians, one hundred; the Aeolians, together with the Lesbians and Tenedans, forty; the peoples of the region of the Hellespont, together with those who live along the shores of the Pontus, eighty; and the inhabitants of the islands fifty; for the king had won over to his side the islands lying within the Cyanean Rocks and Triopium and Sunium.[106] (9) *Triereis* made up the multitude we have listed; the transports for the cavalry numbered eight hundred and fifty, and the triaconters[107] three thousand. So Xerxes spent his time at Doriscus with the review of the forces.[108]

The Greeks react:

(11.4.1) When word came to the Greeks who were in assembly that the Persian forces were near, they decided to send the naval force speedily to Artemisium in Euboea, recognising that this place was well situated for them to go out and meet the enemy, and a sufficient body of hoplites to Thermopylae to seize the passes at the narrowest part of the defile in advance and to prevent the Persians from advancing against Greece. They hastened to protect within their defences those who had chosen the cause of the Greeks and to preserve the allies to the best of their ability.[109] (2) The leader of the entire fleet

---

[104] Possibly estimated several times too high (see also below, note 115). Even so, a force of 180,000 soldiers, or even more, was for those days an incredibly formidable army.
[105] Though the MSS read τριακόσιαι καὶ εἴκοσι ('320'), the enumeration of ships in 11.3.8 points out that τριακόσιοι καὶ δέκα ('310') is likely to be the correct number.
[106] Effectively, therefore, all Aegean islands to the north of a line between Rhodes, Naxos, and south Attica.
[107] Galleys provided with thirty banks of oars. Apparently neither these nor the transports were seen as warships.
[108] See the remarks by Haillet 2002: 123–4 *ad* p. 9 note 1.
[109] See Hdt. 7.175–8, who mentions the reasons to opt for Artemisium and Thermopylae. See further for Thermopylae Stronk 2014/15, discussing the geography, the archaeology, and the ancient sources on the events that took place there in 480.

was Eurybiades the Lacedaemonian,[110] and Leonidas the king of the Spartiates was the leader of the troops sent to Thermopylae, a man who took pride in courage and generalship. When Leonidas received the appointment, he announced that only one thousand men should follow him on the campaign. (3) And when the ephors said that he was leading altogether too few soldiers against a great force and ordered him to take along a larger number, he replied to them in secret that to prevent the Persians getting through the passes they were few, but many for the task to which they were now setting out. (4) Because this reply appeared to be enigmatic and obscure, he was asked again whether he believed he was about to lead the soldiers to an undemanding task. He replied that in name he was leading them to guard the passes, but in fact they were going to die for the common freedom. Therefore, if a thousand were to go, Sparta would be the more famous when they had died, but if the Lacedaemonians in their entirety took the field, Lacedaemon would be utterly destroyed, for no one of them would dare to flee, in order to save his life. (5) There were, then, of the Lacedaemonians one thousand, and with them three hundred Spartiates;[111] of the rest of the Greeks who were sent with them to Thermopylae there were three thousand. (6) Thus, Leonidas advanced with four thousand soldiers to Thermopylae, but the Locrians, who lived near the passes, had already given earth and water to the Persians and had promised that they would seize the passes in advance. When they learned that Leonidas had arrived at Thermopylae, they changed their minds and changed sides to the Greeks. (7) And there gathered at Thermopylae also a thousand Locrians, an equal number of Melians,[112] and almost one thousand Phocians, and likewise some four hundred Thebans of the other party,[113] for the inhabitants of Thebes were divided amongst each other regarding the alliance with the Persians. The Greeks who were drawn up with Leonidas for battle, being as many in number as has been elaborated, passed their time around Thermopylae, awaiting the arrival of the Persians.

(11.5.1) After Xerxes' review of his forces, he pushed on with the entire army, and the whole fleet accompanied the advancing land

---

[110] Στόλος might be interpreted differently: it may indicate both 'expedition' and 'army', as well as 'sea-force, fleet' (see *LSJ, s.v.*). I have opted here for 'fleet' to underline the separate responsibilities of Eurybiades and Leonidas.

[111] For σὺν αὐτοῖς ('with them') see Stronk 2014/15: 176–7.

[112] See above, note 98.

[113] In Thebes was a division among the inhabitants regarding the support for Persia (according to Herodotus the view of its leaders at least) and those supporting 'the Greek cause', assembled at Thermopylae: see also Stronk 2014/15: 177–80, 195–7.

force as far as the *polis* of Acanthus, and from there the ships passed quickly and safely through the newly dug canal into the other sea.[114] (2) When Xerxes arrived at the Gulf of Melis, he learned that the enemy had already seized the passes. Therefore, after he had restored his force there, he summoned his allies from Europe, a little less than two hundred thousand men, so that he now possessed in all not less than one million soldiers exclusive of the naval contingent.[115] (3) And the total mass of those on the warships and transports of the food and general equipment was not less than that of those we have mentioned, and therefore the account of the multitude gathered by Xerxes is not amazing at all. People say that the ever-flowing rivers ran dry because of the close order of the multitude,[116] and that the seas were hidden by the sails of the ships. The greatest forces of those recorded in historical memory were those which accompanied Xerxes.

Battle of Thermopylae:[117]

(11.5.4) After the Persians had encamped on the River Spercheius [in south Thessaly], Xerxes dispatched envoys to Thermopylae and at the same time to find out how the Greeks felt about the war with him. He commanded the envoys to announce that King Xerxes ordered that the Greeks should all lay down their weapons, to depart unharmed to their native lands, and to be allies of the Persians. He announced that he would give all Greeks who would do so more and better lands than they now possessed. (5) But when those around Leonidas heard the envoys, they replied that they would be more useful as allies of the king with weapons, and if forced to make war they would fight for freedom better with them.[118] As for the land which he promised he would give, they replied that it was customary for the Greeks to gain lands not by cowardice but by *aretē*.

---

[114] 'The other sea' refers to the Gulf of Singus, situated south of the Athos promontory.

[115] Again an estimation that is many times too high. A force of the size described by many ancient authors, including Herodotus and Diodorus, simply could not be sustained by the lands the army crossed, quite apart from the insurmountable logistical problems both the 'market' and the gear such an army required would encounter. How and Wells (1964, vol. 2, app. XIX: 366–8) have argued that the *total* field army of Persia amounted to 360,000 soldiers, 300,000 of them infantry, commanded by 30 ἄρχοντες ('captains'), and that for Xerxes' force here '180,000 may be taken as the irreducible minimum of the Persian force, apart from European contingents.... Nevertheless the total must have fallen short of the 300,000 assigned to Mardonius at Plataea' (ibid.: 368).

[116] See Hdt. 7.109, 187; the troops recruited by Xerxes in Europe Herodotus refers to as being 300,000 in number with 120 ships: Hdt. 7.185.

[117] For an elaborate review of the events before and during the Battle of Thermopylae, including a comparison between the accounts of Herodotus and Diodorus and other classical sources, see Stronk 2014/15.

[118] According to Plu. *Apopht.Lac.* 225D, Leonidas merely responded to the demand to hand over the weapons Μολὼν λαβέ ('Come and get them').

(11.6.1) After the king heard the replies of the Greeks from his envoys, he sent for Demaratus, a Spartiate who had fled from his fatherland to him,[119] and jeering at the replies he asked the Laconian, 'Will the Greeks flee more swiftly than my horses can run, or will they dare to face such forces in battle?' (2) And Demaratus, people say, replied, 'You yourself know the courage of the Greeks well, for you make war with Greek forces against those of your subordinates[120] who revolt. Do not think, therefore, that those who fight better than the Persians to maintain your sovereignty will risk their lives less bravely against the Persians to maintain their own freedom.'[121] But Xerxes, jeering at him, ordered Demaratus to stay by his side, in order to witness the Lacedaemonians in flight. (3) Taking with him his army, Xerxes came against the Greeks at Thermopylae, having deployed the Medes in front of all the other peoples, either preferring them because of their courage or wishing to destroy them all. After all, the Medes still retained a proud spirit, the supremacy which their ancestors had exercised having been overthrown only recently. (4) He designated together with the Medes the brothers and sons of those who had fallen at Marathon as well, believing that they would most vehemently avenge themselves upon the Greeks. The Medes, thus, drawn up in the manner we have described, fell upon the defenders of Thermopylae. Leonidas, who had prepared well, gathered the Greeks together in the narrowest part of the pass.
(11.7.1) Because the ensuing fight was fierce, on the one hand because the Persians had the king as a witness of their *aretē*, on the other hand because the Greeks kept their liberty in mind and were exhorted to the contest by Leonidas, it followed that the venture was amazing. (2) Because the men stood shoulder to shoulder in the fighting and the blows were struck at close range, the lines, moreover, densely packed, the battle was evenly balanced for a long time. Because the Greeks had the upper hand in *aretae* and in the great size of their shields, the Medes gradually gave way. In fact, many of them were killed and not a few heavily wounded. The Cissians and Scythians, kept as a reserve, selected for their *aretē*, relieved the Medes in the fight. Joining the struggle as fresh troops, opposite men who were worn out, they withstood the battle for a short while, but being killed by the soldiers of Leonidas, they gave way under

---

[119] For Demaratus see Hdt. 6.50–70; Hofstetter 1978: 45–6, no. 77.
[120] Literally βάρβαροι, foreigners, that is, Persians: in the context of the conversation 'your subordinates' seemed, however, to be the more appropriate translation.
[121] See also Hdt. 7.209 for a conversation between Xerxes and Demaratus, though in different circumstances and with a different tenor.

the pressure. (3) For the Persians, using small round shields and *peltae*,[122] enjoyed an advantage in open fields, due to their mobility. In narrow places, however, they could not easily inflict wounds upon an enemy formed in close ranks and their entire bodies protected by large shields. Being disadvantaged because of the lightness of the protective armour, they came to grief by numerous wounds. (4) When Xerxes finally saw that the entire area about the passes was strewn with dead bodies and that the Persians were not holding out against the *aretē* of the Greeks, he sent forward the picked Persians known as the 'Immortals' and reputed to be pre-eminent among the entire host for bravery.[123] When these also fled after only a brief resistance, then only did the Greeks cease to fight, as night fell, the Persians having lost many dead and the Greeks a small number.
(11.8.1) Because the battle had taken an unexpected outcome, Xerxes the following day chose from all peoples those reputed to be outstanding in bravery and daring. And having begged much of them, he announced in advance that he would give notable gifts to those who would force their way through, but that the punishment would be death for those who fled. (2) Though these men hurled themselves as one mighty mass and with great violence upon the Greeks, the soldiers of Leonidas, then closing their ranks and making their formation like a wall, took up the struggle with ardour. And so far did they go in their eagerness that the lines which were used to join by turns in the battle would not withdraw, but by their continuance of the hardship getting the better they killed many of the picked Persians. (3) Spending the day in combat, they vied with one another: the older soldiers challenged the vigour of the young, the younger vied with both the experience and fame of the elders. When finally the picked Persians also turned in flight, those of the Persians stationed in reserve closed their ranks and would not permit the picked soldiers to flee. Therefore they were compelled to turn back again and do battle. (4) While the king was in a state of dismay and believed that no man would have yet the courage to go into battle, there came to him a certain Trachinian, a native of the region, who was familiar with the

---

[122] Light shields, shaped more or less like an ivy leaf, notably used by Thracians: see further esp. Best 1969.

[123] For the so-called Immortals: Hdt. 7.83; perhaps Herodotus (possibly here Diodorus' source) has misunderstood his source (or the source himself or herself was mistaken) and understood OP *anauša* (from *a[n]*, negating prefix, and *auša*, 'death') 'immortal' instead of *anušiya* 'companion', a much more common denomination for such units in literature. See: Dandamaev and Lukonin 1989: 227–8. See also Kent 1953: 168 s.v. '*Anušiya*'. The so-called 'Immortals' were a vital part of the *spāda*, the standing force of the Achaemenids: Charles 2011: 114.

mountainous area. Approaching Xerxes, this man announced that he would conduct the Persians by way of a narrow and precipitous path, so that the men who accompanied him would get behind the men around Leonidas, and having put them in the middle in this manner, these would be easily annihilated. (5) The king was delighted and, after heaping presents upon the Trachinian, he dispatched twenty thousand soldiers with him under cover of night. From among the Persians was someone by the name of Tyrrhastiadas, a Cymean by birth, who was honourable and upright in his ways.[124] Deserting from the camp of the Persians in the night he came to the men with Leonidas, and revealed to the unknowing the situation concerning the Trachinian.

(11.9.1) Having heard this, the Greeks gathered together about the middle of the night and conferred about the perils which were bearing down on them. Some said that they must abandon the pass immediately and come safely through to the allies. They argued that it would be impossible for those who stayed to come off unscathed. Leonidas, the king of the Lacedaemonians, who was very ambitious to confer honour upon both himself and the Spartiates, ordered that all the other Greeks should depart and save themselves, in order to fight together with the Greeks in the battles which still remained. The Lacedaemonians themselves, he said, had to remain and not abandon the guard of the pass, for it was fitting that those who were the leaders of Hellas should gladly die, striving for the first prize. (2) Immediately, then, all the rest departed, but Leonidas together with his fellow citizens performed heroic and astounding deeds. Though the Lacedaemonians were but few (he detained only the Thespians)[125] and he had all told not more than five hundred men, he was ready to meet death on behalf of Hellas. (3) After this, the Persians who were led by the Trachinian, after making their way around the difficult terrain, suddenly trapped Leonidas in the middle. The Greeks, giving up any thought of their own safety and choosing renown instead, with one voice asked their commander to lead them against the enemy before the Persians learned of the successful detour of their own men. (4) And Leonidas, welcoming the eagerness of the soldiers, ordered them to prepare their breakfast

---

[124] Here it looks as though Ephorus was Diodorus' source. Ephorus was known to exalt his home town of Cyme; see, for example, Str. 13.3.6/622.
[125] The Thespians appear here for the first time in Diodorus' account; Herodotus tells us that Lacedaemonians, Thespians, and Thebans (the last against their wish) remained behind: Hdt. 7.222 and Stronk 2014/15: 177–80.

quickly, since they would dine in Hades.[126] He himself, in accordance with the order he had given, took food, believing that in this way he could keep his strength for a long time and retain his endurance in the combat. When they had hastily refreshed themselves and all were ready, he ordered the soldiers to attack the encampment, killing anyone they came across, and to strike for the very tent of the king.

(11.10.1) The soldiers, then, in accordance with the orders, having formed in a compact body, fell by night upon the encampment of the Persians, Leonidas leading the attack.[127] Because of the unexpectedness of the attack and not knowing what happened to them, the Persians ran together from their tents with great tumult and in disorder, and thinking that the soldiers who had set out with the Trachinian had perished and that the entire force of the Greeks was present, they were struck with terror. (2) Therefore many were killed by the troops of Leonidas, but even more died by the hands of their comrades as if by enemies, due to their ignorance. For both the night prevented any understanding of the real situation, and the confusion, which extended throughout the entire encampment, probably caused great slaughter. For they kept killing one another, because the conditions did not allow a meticulous assessment because there was no order from a commander nor any demanding of a password nor, in general, any recovery of reason. (3) Truly, if the king had remained in the royal tent, he could easily have been killed by the Greeks as well and the whole war might have reached a quick conclusion. Now, however, Xerxes had rushed out to the tumult, and the Greeks storming into the tent massacred nearly all whom they caught in it. (4) While the night lasted they wandered throughout the entire camp, with good reason looking for Xerxes. However, when morning had broken and the entire state of affairs had become clear, the Persians, observing that the Greeks were few in number, came to their senses.[128] They did not, however, join battle face to face, fearing their *aretē*, but deployed on their flanks and

---

[126] A remark absent in Herodotus' account, but quoted elsewhere: for example, Aristides of Miletus (but Jacoby believes it might have been Agatharchides of Cnidus), *FGrH/BNJ* 286 FF 20 a & b; Cic. *Tusc.* 1.42.101; Plu. *Apopht.Lac.* 225D; see also Ceccarelli, commentary on F 20, stating that this remark might well go back to Ephorus.

[127] Diodorus' version here significantly differs from Herodotus 7.223, which has, more or less, become the established view. See notably Stronk 2014/15: *passim*.

[128] Αὐτῶν: *delevi*. In context, contempt (καταφρονέω + gen., here αὐτῶν) makes no immediate sense, but after the previous panic, to come to one's senses does (see for this meaning *LSJ s.v.* III); and the sequel does not appear to be contradict my intervention. On the contrary: you are not afraid of the courage of people you despise or have contempt for. See also 11.16.1.

The Persians and the Greek Wars   169

rear, and shooting arrows and hurling javelins at them from every direction, they killed all of them. Such then was, for the soldiers of Leonidas who guarded the passes of Thermopylae, the end of their lives.

[[11.11.1–6 is a *caput* with eulogies on the Lacedaemonians, also showing Diodorus' moral values.]]

Aftermath of the Battle of Thermopylae:
(11.12.1) Now that we have spoken enough of the *aretē* of these men, we will resume the course of our narrative. After Xerxes had gained the passes in the manner we have described and had won, as the proverb goes, a 'Cadmeian victory',[129] he had destroyed only a few of the enemy, but he had lost great numbers of his own. After he had mastered the passes by his soldiers, he decided to test battles at sea.[130] (2) After he had, therefore, immediately summoned Megabates,[131] the commander of the fleet, he ordered him to sail against the naval force of the Greeks and to try, with all his fleet, a sea-battle against them. (3) And Megabates, in accordance with the king's orders, set out from Pydna in Macedonia[132] with all the fleet and put in at a promontory of Magnesia which bears the name of Sepias.[133] After a great wind arose here, he lost over three hundred warships and great numbers of cavalry transports and other vessels.[134] When the wind had ceased, he weighed anchor and put in at Aphetae in Magnesia.[135] From here he dispatched two hundred *triereis*, ordering the captains to take a roundabout course and, by keeping Euboea on the right, to encircle the enemy.[136]

---

[129] A reference to the victory of the Thebans over the 'Seven' (see also 4.65). We might prefer the term 'Pyrrhic victory'. For 'Cadmeian victory' see also Hdt. 1.166; Pl. *Lg.* 641C.
[130] According to Hdt. 8.15 the battles of Thermopylae and Artemisium took place on the same day; Lys. *Epit.* 31 mentions the battles took place κατὰ τὸν αὐτὸν χρόνον ('around the same time').
[131] Hdt. 7.97 mentions four admirals in the 'Persian' fleet: Ariabignis, the son of Darius and Gobryas' daughter (commanding the Ionian and Carian fleets); Prexaspes, the son of Aspathines; Megabazus, the son of Megabates; and Achaemenes, the son of Darius – and a full brother of Xerxes (commanding the Egyptian fleet).
[132] Apparently the Persian fleet had already rounded the whole of Chalcidice.
[133] See also Hdt. 7.188. Pritchett 1963: 3–5, asserts that an identification of Cape Sepias is difficult unless the beach (of which Herodotus writes) is taken into account as well. Pritchett (p. 5) believes the present-day beach of Koulouri qualifies best, meaning that Cape Sepias should be identified as modern Cape Pori (ibid.). See also Hignett 1963: 371–85.
[134] Hdt. 7.188–93 reports that the storm lasted during three days and that the Persian fleet lost 400 warships.
[135] This is a promontory in Magnesia opposite Artemisium (see Hdt. 7.193–4).
[136] The same manoeuvre and the same number of ships are mentioned by Hdt. 8.7: the aim is to cut off the connection between Euboea and mainland Greece.

Naval battle at Artemisium:

(11.12.4) The Greeks were moored at Artemisium in Euboea and had in all two hundred and eighty *triereis*. Of these ships one hundred and forty were Athenian, the remainder those of the other Greeks.[137] Their admiral was Eurybiades the Spartiate, but Themistocles the Athenian supervised the affairs regarding the fleet. Because of his sagacity and skill as a commander, the latter enjoyed great favour not only with the Greeks throughout the fleet but also with Eurybiades himself, and all men giving heed to him readily listened to him. (5) When a meeting of the captains of the ships was convened regarding the naval battle, the rest of them all favoured waiting quietly for the enemy attack. Themistocles alone, though, expressed the opposite opinion, arguing that it would be of use to sail against the enemy with the whole fleet deployed, because they would in this way have the upper hand, attacking with their collected ships an enemy whose battle order was broken up by disorder, as might be expected for a force issued from many harbours at some distance apart. Finally the Greeks attacked the enemy with the entire fleet in agreement with Themistocles' view.[138] (6) Because the enemy put out from many harbours, the followers of Themistocles, engaging with the scattered Persians, sank many ships at the outset, and forcing many to flee, they pursued them as far as the land. Afterwards though, after the whole fleet had gathered and a fierce naval battle had ensued, each of the sides had the upper hand in one part of the line, but neither side winning a complete victory, the engagement was broken off at nightfall.[139]

(11.13.1) After the naval battle a great storm arose and destroyed many ships moored outside the harbour, so that divine intervention appeared to take sides with the Greeks to ensure, the multitude of the enemy ships having been lessened, that the Greek force became a match for them and strong enough for the naval battles.[140] This is why the Greeks grew ever bolder, whereas the enemy became ever more timorous as regards the risks. Nevertheless, having recovered themselves from the shipwreck, they put out with all their ships against the enemy. (2) And the Greeks, with fifty Attic *triereis* added

---

[137] See also Hdt. 8.1–2; Isoc. *Paneg.* 90; D. 14.29, 18.238; Nep. *Them.* 7.3; Aristid. *Or.* 1.219, 2.252; Paus. 2.29.5; a detailed account can be found in Labarbe 1952: 386–92.
[138] A more detailed account of the meeting can be found in Hdt. 8.4–9.
[139] Hdt. 8.9–11 tells a roughly similar story.
[140] It seems the storm mainly struck the Persian fleet: Hdt. 8.12–13; Labarbe 1952: 404 note 2. As Haillet 2002: 129 *ad* p. 22 note 1 observes, the ratio of Persian to Greek ships was, after the storm, still (over) 10:1.

to their number, deployed themselves opposite the enemy. The naval battle that followed was much like the battles around Thermopylae: the Persians were resolved to overwhelm the Greeks and force their way through the Euripus, while the Greeks, blocking the narrows, were fighting to protect their allies in Euboea. A fierce battle having ensued, many ships were lost on both sides, and nightfall compelled them to return to their naval bases. The most valorous, it is reported, in both battles were the Athenians among the Greeks and the Sidonians among the foreigners.[141]

Athenians retreat to Salamis and Xerxes marches south:
(11.13.3) Afterwards the Greeks, having heard what had happened around Thermopylae and discovering that the Persians were advancing by land against Athens, became dispirited. Therefore, having sailed off to Salamis, they occupied themselves there.[142] (4) The Athenians, surveying the dangers threatening the whole population of Athens, having put on boats their children and wives and every useful article they could, brought them to Salamis.[143] (5) When the Persian admiral learned of the enemy retreat, he set sail for Euboea with his entire fleet, and having subdued and plundered the city of the Histiaeans, he ravaged their territory.[144]
(11.14.1) As this happened, Xerxes, after he set out from Thermopylae, advanced through the territory of the Phocians, sacking the *poleis* and destroying the property in the countryside. The Phocians, having chosen the cause of the Greeks and seeing they were no military match, deserted the *poleis* en masse and took refuge in the rugged regions on Parnassus. (2) Afterwards the king, passing through the territory of the Dorians, did it no harm: they were, after all, allies of the Persians. He separated a portion of his force and ordered it to proceed to Delphi, to burn down the precinct of Apollo and to carry off the votive offerings,[145] but he himself, having advanced into Boeotia with the other Persians, set up his camp. (3) The soldiers dispatched to sack the oracle had proceeded

---

[141] Diodorus' second battle is described by Hdt. 8.15–18 as the third battle; see also Aristid. *Or.* 2.251, who also mentions that Greeks and Persians at Artemisium fought δυοῖν ναυμαχίαιν ('in two battles').
[142] See Hdt. 8.18–23; see also Haillet 2002 129 *ad* p. 22 note 3.
[143] See Hdt. 8.40–1; Ctes. *Pers.* F. 13(26); Lys. *Epit.* 34; Isoc. *Paneg.* 96; Plu. *Them.* 10.1–10; Aristid. *Or.* 2.256; Just. 2.12.16; Labarbe 1952: 407–9; see also Haillet 2002: 129–30 *ad* p. 22 note 4.
[144] See Hdt. 8.23.
[145] Retribution for setting the temple at Sardis in fire: see above, note 63.

as far as the shrine of Athena *Pronoia* ('forethought'),[146] but there, incredibly, while great thunderstorms and many thunderbolts burst from the atmosphere and moreover while the storms wrenched loose huge rocks onto the army of the Persians, it occurred that many of the Persians were killed and that all, dismayed at the intervention of the gods, fled the region. (4) Thus the oracle of Delphi, with the aid of divine care, escaped pillage.[147] The Delphians, wishing to leave to succeeding generations an everlasting memorial of the appearance of the gods, erected a trophy beside the temple of Athena *Pronoia*, on which they inscribed the following elegiac couplet:

> Both as a memorial of war and witness of victory,
> The Delphians erected me, grateful to Zeus
> And Phoebus, who warded off the city-sacking files of Medes
> And delivered the bronze-crowned shrine.[148]

(5) While passing through Boeotia, Xerxes laid waste the territory of the Thespians and burned Plataea, which was without habitants. The people who lived in these two *poleis* had all fled to the Peloponnesus. Afterwards, entering Attica, they ravaged the countryside, then razed Athens to the ground, and sent up in flames the temples of the gods. While the king occupied himself herewith, his fleet sailed from Euboea to Attica, having sacked on the way both Euboea and the coast of Attica.[149]

(11.15.1) Meanwhile the people of Corcyra, who had fitted out sixty *triereis*, were waiting off the Peloponnesus, as they themselves claim, unable to round the promontory at Malea, according to the story of some historians,[150] anxiously awaiting the outcome of the war to ensure, if the Persians prevailed, giving them water and earth, but, if the Greeks were victorious, getting the credit of having come to their aid. (2) When the Athenians, who were waiting around Salamis, saw Attica being burnt down and heard that the precinct of Athena had been razed, they were terribly disheartened. Likewise great fear gripped the other Greeks who, driven from every quarter, were now

---

[146] I follow all MSS and Paus. 10.8.6–7, even though most editors, following Hdt. 8.37, read here *Pronaea* ('Foretemple').

[147] See also Hdt. 8.35–9 for the failed raid on Delphi. Haillet 2002: 23 note 2 believes this episode may well have been forged by the Delphic priests to make people forget the oracle's ambiguity and immunity during the invasion, facilitated by the fact that thunderstorms and landslides are not uncommon in the region.

[148] See Haillet 2002: 130 *ad* p. 24 note 1. Ebert believes the trophy and its epigram were only erected a century later: Ebert 1982: 36.

[149] See also Hdt. 8.27–39, 50–5, 66; Ctes. *Pers.* F. 13(26); Hignett 1952: 193–201.

[150] See also Hdt. 7.168 with a similar statement. Diodorus is here tantalisingly vague on his sources. See above, Chapter 1.

cooped up in the Peloponnesus alone. Therefore they decided that all who had been charged with command should convene and deliberate which places would be suited to do naval battle.

Preparations for the naval battle at Salamis:[151]

(11.15.3) Many and various views were exchanged. The Peloponnesians, only giving heed to their own safety, declared that the contest should be held in the region of the Isthmus: because it had been well provided with a wall, the defeated would be able to withdraw to a safe haven very near by, namely the Peloponnesus, if something should go wrong around the naval battle. If they locked themselves up, however, on the little island of Salamis, they would encounter perils from which it would be difficult to be rescued. (4) Themistocles advised, though, making the contest of the ships around Salamis. He did so because he believed that those who had few ships to fight with would have many advantages in the narrows of Salamis against a vastly superior number of vessels. In general, he showed that the region about the Isthmus would be altogether unsuitable for the naval battle. In fact, the contest would take place on the open sea and because of the room for manoeuvring the Persians would easily subdue the small force of ships by their superior numbers.[152] And by presenting in like fashion many other facts pertinent to the occasion, he persuaded all present to cast their votes with him for the plan he recommended.[153]

(11.16.1) When at last a decision was reached by all to fight the sea-battle around Salamis, the Greeks set about making the preparations necessary to meet the Persians and the battle. Accordingly, Eurybiades together with Themistocles undertook to encourage the crews and incite them to face the impending struggle. However, the crews would not heed them; indeed, nobody paid attention to the commanders because all were terrified of the magnitude of the Persian forces, but everyone kept on urging sailing out from Salamis to the Peloponnesus. (2) Not at all less alarmed by the forces of the enemy was the army of the Greeks on land. Both the loss of their most illustrious men around Thermopylae caused consternation, and the events everywhere in Attica before their very eyes were filling the

---

[151] Essentially, the classical authors' views on the preparations and this battle do not differ very much. See Roux 1974: *passim*. See also Wallinga 2005 for a different approach to the battle, *inter alia* with a much more positive view of the role of the Corinthian ships.
[152] Different views of the actual situation are represented by Labarbe 1957 and Wallinga 1993: esp. 148–64.
[153] Diodorus is here much more concise than Herodotus: Hdt. 8.58–63.

Greeks with utter despair. (3) Because the members of the congress of the Greeks saw the unrest of the masses and the total consternation, they voted to build a wall across the Isthmus. Though the works were completed speedily because of the enthusiasm and the multitude of the workers, the Peloponnesians strengthened the wall, and they extended it to forty *stadia* [c. 7.4 km], from Lechaeum to Cenchreae, while those who spent their time at Salamis with the entire fleet were terrified to such an extent that they no longer obeyed their commanders.

Battle of Salamis and its aftermath:
(11.17.1) Because Themistocles perceived that the admiral Eurybiades was unable to overcome the mood of the people, and recognised that the straits at Salamis could contribute greatly to achieving the victory, he contrived something like the following. He persuaded a certain man to defect to Xerxes and to convince him that the ships at Salamis were going to slip away from that region and assemble at the Isthmus.[154] (2) Therefore the king, because he believed the man because of the plausibility of what he reported, made haste to prevent the naval forces of the Greeks making contact with the armies on land. Thus, he at once dispatched the Egyptian fleet, having ordered it to block the passage between Salamis and the territory of Megaris.[155] The rest of his ships, the majority, he dispatched to Salamis, having ordered it to make contact with the enemy and to decide the war in naval battle. The *triereis* were drawn up by peoples one after another, to ensure that, because they spoke the same language and knew one another, they would help each other actively. (3) When the fleet had been deployed in this manner, the right wing was held by the Phoenicians, the left by the Greeks who served under the Persians. The commanders of the Ionians sent a man of Samos to the Greeks to inform them of the king's decisions and of the entire deployment, and to say that in the course of the battle they were going to desert from the Persians. (4) And when the Samian had secretly swum across and had informed Eurybiades' staff about this plan, Themistocles, realising that his stratagem had worked out as he had planned, was overjoyed and summoned the people to the fight. The Greeks were emboldened by the promise of

---

[154] Though Hignett 1963: 403–8 doubts the historicity of this ruse, it is referred to in Hdt. 8.74–6; Plu. *Them.* 12, *Arist.* 8.2–5, who also provide the (alleged) name of the messenger, namely Sicinnus. Most modern historians seem to accept the story, for example Roux 1974: 61.
[155] See also Roux 1974: 61; Bengtson, 1971.

the Ionians, and though the circumstances forced them to a naval battle against their own preference, they eagerly came down together from Salamis for the sea-battle.[156]
(11.18.1) Finally, when Eurybiades and Themistocles[157] had completed the deployment of their forces, Athenians and Lacedaemonians held the left wing, being to be positioned opposite the squadron of the Phoenicians. The Phoenicians had, in fact, a great superiority because of both their number and the experience in seamanship inherited from their ancestors. (2) Aeginetans and Megarians formed the right wing. Indeed, they were considered to be the best seamen after the Athenians and would be most eager for a good result, because they alone of the Greeks would have no hide-out if any adversity should occur over the sea-battle. The centre was held by the remaining force of the Greeks. Deployed in this way, the Greeks sailed out, and they occupied the narrows between Salamis and the Heracleium.[158] (3) The king gave orders to his admiral to advance against the enemy, but he himself moved to a spot directly opposite Salamis from which he could watch the course of the naval battle.[159] (4) As the Persians advanced at the beginning, they could maintain their line because they had plenty of space. However, when they came to the narrow spot, they were compelled to withdraw some ships from the line, and caused much disorder.[160] (5) The Persians' admiral, who was leading the way before the line and was the first to begin the fighting, was killed after having fought brilliantly. When his ship went down, disorder seized the enemy fleet. Indeed, there were many issuing orders, but not everyone issued the same commands. Therefore they ceased to sail ahead, and having brought their ships to a halt, they moved back to the spacious part.[161] (6) When the Athenians saw the disorder among the enemy, they charged upon the enemy, and some they struck with the rams, from others they swept off the rows of oars. When the oarsmen could no longer do their work, many Persian *triereis*, having got into transverse positions,

---

[156] See Hdt. 8.76–84; Plu. *Them.* 12.6–8, Arist. 8.4; A. *Pers.* 386–95.
[157] Here, as elsewhere, Diodorus uses the construction οἱ περὶ to indicate the persons themselves, a construction not uncommon among Hellenistic authors.
[158] Possibly a temple at the foot of Mt Aegaleus (alt. 468 m) in Attica, a ridge, running south-west to north-east, that separates the plains of Athens and Eleusis: see, for example, Leake 1841: 34. In general, the description by Hdt. 8.85 looks slightly more precise than Diodorus'; see also Roux 1974: 75.
[159] See A. *Pers.* 467; Hdt. 8.90; Plu. *Them.* 13.1; D. 24.129; Roux 1974: 86.
[160] From no ancient author has any more-or-less satisfactory account of this battle in its entirety been transmitted: see the remarks of Roux 1974: 51 on this issue. In that context, Diodorus' remarks stand out as relatively systematic: see also Roux 1974: 80–5.
[161] See the remarks by Haillet 2002: 133 *ad* p. 28 note 3.

were frequently struck by the battering rams. Consequently they ceased merely backing water,[162] but turned about and fled head over heels.[163]

(11.19.1) While the Phoenician and Cypriot ships were being taken by the Athenians, the vessels of the Cilicians and Pamphylians, and also of the Lycians, which followed in their wake, were at first holding out stoutly, but when they saw the strongest ships taking flight they also abandoned the fight. (2) On the other wing the battle was stubbornly fought and for some time the struggle was evenly balanced. However, when the Athenians had pursued the Phoenicians and Cypriots to the shore and then turned back, the enemy, being forced out of line by the Athenians, turned about and lost many of their ships.[164] (3) Gaining the upper hand in this manner, the Greeks conquered the enemy in a very brilliant naval battle. During the fight forty of the Greeks' ships were lost, of the Persians' more than two hundred, not counting those taken with their crews.[165] (4) The king, defeated against his hopes, put to death those of the Phoenicians most responsible for beginning the flight, and threatened to visit upon the rest the punishment they deserved. Fearing his threats, the Phoenicians first set sail to Attica, but when night had fallen they escaped to Asia.[166] (5) Themistocles, who was credited with having brought about the victory, devised another stratagem no less clever than the former. Because, indeed, the Greeks were afraid to fight on land against so many myriads of Persians, he greatly reduced the number of the troops in the following manner. He sent the attendant of his own sons to Xerxes to inform him that the Greeks were about to sail to the bridge of boats and to destroy the causeway.[167] (6) Because the Great King believed the words because of their plausibility, he became very afraid that he would be robbed of the escape to Asia, because the Greeks controlled the sea, and decided to cross as soon as possible from Europe to Asia Minor, leaving Mardonius behind in Greece with the best of both the cavalry and infantry, the total number of whom was not less than four hundred thousand. Thus Themistocles by the use of two

---

[162] For πρύμνην ἀνακρούεσθαι: *LSJ* s.v. 'πρύμνα'; see also Hdt. 8.84.
[163] Haillet 2002: 133 *ad* p. 28 note 4 observes that Diodorus' words imply that the Athenians employed the tactic of the διέκπλους ('breakthrough'): see especially Lazenby 1987.
[164] See Haillet 2002: 134 *ad* p. 28 note 5.
[165] See Haillet 2002: 29 note 1.
[166] See Hdt. 8.80.
[167] See Hdt. 8.108–10; Th. 1.137; Plu. *Them.* 16, Arist. 9.5–6; Haillet 2002: 134 *ad* p. 29 note 3 remarks that doubts exist as regards the historicity of this stratagem, but there is, to the best of my knowledge, no evidence on this matter and I believe that we, therefore, for the time being have to accept it until such evidence emerges.

stratagems caused great advantages for the Greeks. These were the events that took place in Greece at this time.[168]

S. 41:
11.20.1:

Reminder of Persian–Carthaginian alliance:
(11.20.1) As we know, the Carthaginians had agreed with the Persians to make war against the Greeks on Sicily at that very same time . . . .

S. 42:
11.23.2:

Result of Xerxes' presence in Europe:
(11.23.2) . . . With the Persians it occurred that the king managed to escape from Greece and many myriads with him . . . .[169]

S. 43:
11.23.3:

Fate of Themistocles:
(11.23.3) . . ., Themistocles was driven from the whole of Greece and fled for refuge to his arch-enemy, Xerxes, and spent his life until he died in Xerxes' debt.[170] . . .

S. 44:
11.34.1:

Simultaneity of battles of Himera (Sicily) and Thermopylae:
(11.34.1) Thus it occurred on the same day that Gelo was victorious and Leonidas and his soldiers were fighting against Xerxes around Thermopylae, ...[171]

---

[168] As in most Greek accounts, in Diodorus' too the retreat of Xerxes is celebrated as a great feat. The vicissitudes of the Persian army, however, were not really disastrous. The fact that Xerxes retreated to Asia (Minor) may well have been due as much to the advanced time of the year (late September; see Haillet 2002: 29 note 1) as to the result of Salamis, the more so because his march appears to have been orderly and reasonably slow: Hdt. 8.115; Dumortier 1963: 359: 'les Perses se sont retirés selon un plan préconçu et qu'ils pouvaient d'autant mieux exécuter que les Grecs ne les poursuivaient pas'. See also the observations by Briant 2002: 531.
[169] As discussed above, note 168, rather an overstatement.
[170] For the vicissitudes of Themistocles in the Persian Empire see below, S. 52.
[171] Baron believes that Diodorus may have been tempted to present this synchronism by the works of Timaeus: see Baron 2013: 111 and note 103.

S. 45:
11.26.4–5:

Gelo plans to intercede in the Greek Wars:
(11.26.4) In fact, he was making preparations to sail to Greece and to join the Greeks in their war against the Persians. (5) He was already about to make the crossing,[172] when some people from Corinth put in at Syracuse and brought the news that the Greeks had been victorious in the naval battle at Salamis, and that Xerxes with part of his force had retreated out of Europe. . . .

S. 46:
11.27.1:

Persian fleet after the Battle of Salamis:
(11.27.1) While Xanthippus was *archon* in Athens [479–478], the Romans elected as consuls Quintus Fabius Silvanus and Servius Cornelius Tricostus.[173] At this time the Persian fleet apart from the Phoenicians, defeated after the naval battle that occurred at Salamis, resided around Cyme. Having spent the winter there, when the summer arrived it sailed down to Samos, keeping guard on Ionia. The total number of ships present at Samos was more than four hundred. Because the Ionians allegedly harboured hostile sentiments, the ships were there to keep an eye on their cities.[174]

S. 47:
11.27.2:

Exploit of Aminias of Athens, the brother of the poet Aeschylus:
(11.27.2) . . . for Aminias had been the first, while commanding a *trieris*, to ram the flagship of the Persians and sank it and killed the admiral.[175]

---

[172] See, for example, Hdt. 7.157–67; Ephorus *FGrH/BNJ* 70 F 186; Timaeus *FGrH/BNJ* 566 F 94.

[173] Broughton 1951: 21 presents as consuls for 485 vc (at this stage Diodorus' chronology is still seven years ahead of the Varronian chronology) Quintus Fabius Vibulanus and Ser. Cornelius Maligunensis.

[174] See also Hdt. 8.130, who also states that the Persian fleet counted 300 ships that, moreover, did not dare go further west beyond Samos.

[175] See Hdt. 8.93, 123; Plu. *Them.* 14.3–4, 17.1; Aristid. 46.218. The fact that Aminias was Aeschylus' brother is attested in the *Suda s.v. alphaiota*,357, even though *Suda s.v. alpha*,1571 notices it was a common name: in Athens alone more than fifty are known (see *LGPN*, vol. 2 (1994): *Attica*).

S. 48:
11.28.1–33.1:

Friction between Athens and the rest of the coalition; Mardonius offers benefits to Athens:
(11.28.1) When the estrangement of the Athenians from the rest of the Greeks became noised abroad, there came to Athens ambassadors from Persians and from Greeks.[176] Those who, thus, had been dispatched by the Persians said that Mardonius the general had sent the Athenians the message that, if they chose the cause of the Persians, he would give them whatever territory of Greece they wished, would rebuild their walls and temples, and would allow the *polis* to live under its own laws.[177] Those who had been sent from the Lacedaemonians begged the Athenians not to yield to the Persians, but to remain loyal to the Greeks, who were both kindred and of the same speech.[178] (2) The Athenians replied to the Persians that the Persians possessed no such territory or sufficient gold for which the Athenians, receiving it, would abandon the Greeks. To the Lacedaemonians they said that they themselves would endeavour to continue hereafter too the same care for Greece which they had displayed formerly, but asked the Lacedaemonians to come with all speed to Attica together with all their allies, because it was obvious that Mardonius, since the Athenians had declared themselves against him, would advance with his force against Athens.[179] And this is what actually happened. (3) Mardonius, indeed, who stayed in Boeotia with all his forces, tried at first to make some of the *poleis* in the Peloponnesus defect, having distributed money among the leading men of the *poleis*. Afterwards, having learned the reply of the Athenians and being enraged, he led his entire force into Attica. (4) In fact, apart from the army Xerxes had given him, Mardonius himself had gathered many other soldiers from Thrace and Macedonia and the other allied *poleis*, more than two

---

[176] See also in general Hdt. 8.126–9.18; Plu. *Arist.* 10. For Mardonius' rapprochement with Athens see Hdt. 8.140. Haillet 2002: 41 note 1 points to a revolt in Babylon in 479 (led by one Šamaš-erība) as the main reason Xerxes did not return to Greece, but at the time Ionia and the islands were also far from quiet: see Briant 2002: 534–5; see also Ctes. *Pers.* 13(26) (it seems that Ctesias mixes up his dates and/or the order of events: his switching the order of the battles of Thermopylae and Plataea has become notorious).
[177] See Hdt. 8.136–44; Isoc. *Paneg.* 94; Plu. *Them.* 10.1–2 It appears (see Hdt. 8.136.1) that Alexander I of Macedon (r. 498–454) acted as intermediary: see also Cole 1978: 40, also 42 note 9, 44–5.
[178] Hdt. 8.141–2; Plu. *Arist.* 10.3.
[179] Hdt. 8.143–4; Plu. *Arist.* 10.4–6. The Athenian answer to Mardonius as rendered by Diodorus comes close to Herodotus' version.

hundred thousand men. (5) Because he led so large a force into Attica, the Athenians dispatched couriers bearing letters to the Lacedaemonians, asking for their aid. Because the Lacedaemonians still loitered and the Persians had already crossed the border of Attica, the Athenians were dismayed, and again, taking their children and wives and whatever else they were able to carry off in their haste, they left their fatherland and together fled again to Salamis.[180] (6) And Mardonius was so angry with them that he ravaged the entire territory, razed the city to the ground, and utterly destroyed the temples that were still left.

Battle of Plataea:

(11.29.1) After Mardonius with his force had returned to Thebes,[181] the delegates in congress of the Greeks decided to associate with the Athenians and, advancing to Plataea in a body, to make a conclusive fight for liberty, and they also decided to make a vow to the gods that, if they were victorious, the Greeks would celebrate Liberty together on that day and would hold the Freedom Games in Plataea.[182] (2) And when the Greeks were assembled at the Isthmus, all of them agreed to swear an oath about the war, one making their concord staunch and compelling them to endure perils nobly. (3) The oath ran as follows: 'I shall not hold life dearer than liberty, nor shall I desert the leaders, whether they be living or dead, but I shall bury all the allies who have perished in the battle. If I conquer the Persians in the war, I shall not destroy any of the *poleis* participating in the struggle.[183] And of the sanctuaries which have been burnt or demolished I shall rebuild none, but I shall let them be and leave them as a reminder to coming generations of the impiety of the Persians.'[184] (4) After they had sworn the oath, they marched to Boeotia through the pass of Cithaeron, and descending to the foothills near Erythrae, they pitched camp there. Aristides commanded the Athenians, but

---

[180] Hdt. 9.4–11; Lys. *Epit.* 44–6; Plu. *Arist.* 10.7–10. Hdt. 9.4–5 records a second offer by Mardonius to the Athenians on Salamis. Diodorus omits this offer.

[181] In Hdt. 9.2 we are told that the Thebans had advised Mardonius ὡς οὐκ εἴη χῶρος ἐπιτηδεότερος ἐνστρατοπεδεύεσθαι ἐκείνου ('that there was no region more suitable to pitch camp than that'), meaning Boeotia. Though all MSS read here Ἀθήνας ('Athens'), the emendation by Dindorf, Θήβας ('Thebes'), is an obvious one.

[182] Str. 9.2.31/412; Paus. 9.2.6; Plu. *Arist.* 21.1; Aristid. *Panath.* 13.148. The games are celebrated in honour of Zeus *Eleutherius* ('Zeus the Redeemer').

[183] Lycurg. *Leocr.* 81 presents us with a nearly identical oath, only showing some slight variations, though adding at this point: 'and I will exact a tithe of all who have chosen the part of the Persian'. This part seems to be a reminder of Diodorus' statement above in *caput* 3.3.

[184] See the comment on this oath by Haillet 2002: 140–1 *ad* p. 43 note 1 and by Cartledge 2013: 12–40. Both believe the oath not to be authentic.

The Persians and the Greek Wars 181

Pausanias, who was the guardian of the son of Leonidas, had the overall command.
(11.30.1) When Mardonius learned that the enemy force was advancing in the direction of Boeotia, he came forth from Thebes.[185] Having arrived at the River Asopus, he made an encampment, which he strengthened by means of a deep ditch and surrounded with a palisade.[186] The total number of the Greeks was close to one hundred thousand men, of the Persians close to five hundred thousand.[187] (2) The first to open the battle were the Persians, who had poured out upon the Greeks by night and charged with all their cavalry upon the camp. Because the Athenians observed them in time and boldly advanced to meet them with their army in battle formation, a mighty battle ensued. (3) Finally all the rest of the Greeks put to flight the Persians deployed against them. The Megarians alone, facing the commander of the cavalry and the best horsemen the Persians had,[188] though being pressed hard in the fight, did not leave their formation but, having sent some of their men as messengers to the Athenians and Lacedaemonians, asked them to come and help with all speed. (4) After this, Aristides quickly sent the picked Athenians around him, and these, having formed themselves into a compact body and having fallen on the Persians, rescued the Megarians from the perils which threatened them. Killing both the commander of the cavalry himself and many others of the Persians, they put the remainder to flight. The Greeks, having shown their superiority so brilliantly in a kind of preliminary contest,[189] had good hope of a decisive victory. Afterwards they moved their camp from the foothills to a place better suited in view of a complete victory. (5) It was so because on the right was a high hill, on the left the River Asopus. The space in between was held by the camp, fortified by the nature and the impregnability of the terrain.[190] (6) The limited space, therefore, contributed much to the victory of the Greeks, who had laid their plans wisely, because it was impossible to extend the battle-line of the Persians much lengthwise: the result was that it became evident that the many

---

[185] Hdt. 9.1–15 more or less suggests that Mardonius was afraid and hesitant. See also Hignett 1963: 289–301.
[186] For a detailed map of the terrain see plate 1 in Pritchett 1979: 148–9.
[187] As usual these numbers (and those in Herodotus) appear to be considerably exaggerated: see Haillet 2002: 141 *ad* p. 43 note 5.
[188] According to Hdt. 9.20 this commander of the cavalry was Masistius. Paus. 1.27.1 reports that his cuirass was preserved in Athens.
[189] See also Hdt. 9.19–25; Plu. *Arist.* 14.
[190] After the Greeks had repositioned (if only to have access to water), Hdt. 9.25, eleven days of inactivity followed (Plu. *Arist.* 15.1), omitted by Diodorus. See also Hignett 1963: 301–32.

myriads of the Persians were useless. Consequently, Pausanias and Aristides, having placed their confidence in their position, led the army out to battle. Having deployed themselves in a manner suitable to the terrain, they led on towards their enemy.[191]

(11.31.1) Because Mardonius had been forced to make his line a deep one, he deployed his troops in the way that he thought would be to his advantage and raising the battle-cry he opposed the Greeks. With the best soldiers about him he led the way against the Lacedaemonians deployed opposite him. Fighting gallantly, he killed many of the Greeks. With the Lacedaemonians stoutly drawn up opposite him, willingly enduring every peril of battle, there occurred a great slaughter of the Persians.[192] (2) As long as the situation was that Mardonius and his picked soldiers continued to bear the brunt of the fighting, most Persians endured with good spirit. However, when both Mardonius fell, fighting ardently, and of the picked troops some were killed and others wounded, their minds upset, they turned to flee.[193] (3) When the Greeks pressed hard upon them, most of the Persians fled to the palisade, but of the others the Greeks serving with Mardonius withdrew to Thebes; of the remainder, over four hundred thousand in number, Artabazus took command, a man of repute among the Persians, who fled in the opposite direction, and withdrew by forced marches towards Phocis.[194]

Aftermath of the Battle of Plataea:
(11.32.1) Though the Persians were thus separated in their flight, the main body of the Greeks was similarly divided. Indeed, the Athenians, Plataeans, and Thespians chased after those who had set out for Thebes. The Corinthians, Sicyonians, Phliasians, and some others pursued the forces which were fleeing with Artabazus. The Lacedaemonians together with the rest followed the soldiers who had taken refuge within the palisade and trounced them spiritedly. (2) The Thebans, having received the fugitives and having added them to their forces, set upon the pursuing Athenians. When a sharp

---

[191] See Hdt. 9.41–57; Plu. *Arist.* 15–17. It seems that Diodorus rather simplifies the developments leading up to the actual battle.

[192] See Hdt. 9.58–75; Lys. *Epit.* 46–7; Plu. *Arist.* 16.8–19.4. Also: Hignett 1963: 332–44; Balcer 1995: 284–7. Here, too, Diodorus oversimplifies the events.

[193] Diodorus and Hdt. 9.63–4 agree that Mardonius was killed in battle, a view shared by Aristodem. *FGrH/BNJ* 104 F 1(2.5); Plu. *Arist.* 19.1; and Paus. 1.27.1. Ctes. *Pers.* Fr. 13(28) reports that Mardonius, being wounded, fled. Just. 2.14 tells a similar story.

[194] Haillet 2002: 142 *ad* p. 45 note 2 stresses that there were essentially two directions to flee: north, to Thebes, or north-west, to Haliartus and from there to Phocis. Like Diodorus, Hdt. 9.66–9 adds, it appears, a third direction, namely to the fortified camp. See also Plu. *Arist.* 19.3–6.

battle took place before the walls, in which the Thebans fought brilliantly, many fell on both sides, but finally this body, forced by the Athenians, again took refuge within Thebes. (3) After this the Athenians, withdrawing to the Lacedaemonians, joined them in an assault on the walls against those who had fled into the camp of the Persians. After a vigorous contest had started on both sides, though the Persians fought bravely from the fortified positions they held when the Greeks stormed the palisade, many were wounded as they fought desperately, while not a few also, being crippled by the multitude of missiles, awaited death with stout hearts. (4) Nevertheless, neither the constructed wall nor the mass of Persians was a match for the onset and power of the Greeks, but every resistance was forced to give way. In fact, the foremost peoples of Greece vied with each other, the Lacedaemonians and the Athenians, buoyed up by reason of their former victories and supported by confidence in their own *aretē*.[195] (5) In the end the Persians, vanquished and taken prisoner, asked to be left alive, but they found no mercy. Indeed, the commander of the Greeks, Pausanias, observing how superior the Persians were in number, took care that nothing unlooked for could occur, because the Persians were many times more numerous than the Greeks. Because he therefore had given orders to take no man prisoner, there soon arose an incredible mass of the dead. Finally, when the Greeks had slaughtered more than one hundred thousand of the Persians, they reluctantly ceased killing the enemy.

(11.33.1) After the battle had thus ended, the Greeks buried their fallen, of which there were more than ten thousand.[196] And after dividing the booty according to the number of the soldiers,[197] they made their decision as to the awards for valour, and on the urging of Aristides they decided that Sparta was the best *polis*, Pausanias the Lacedaemonian the best man.[198] Artabazus though, with as many as four hundred thousand of the fleeing Persians, making his way through Phocis into Macedonia, availed himself of the quickest routes, and got back safely, together with the soldiers, into Asia Minor.[199]

---

[195] See also Hdt. 9.65–70; Plu. *Arist.* 19.1–4.
[196] The number of Greek casualties mentioned by Hdt. 9.70 is not realistic, even though it only counts the losses of three contingents; the losses recorded by Plu. *Arist.* 19.5–6 seem slightly less unrealistic.
[197] See Hdt. 9.80–2.
[198] See Hdt. 9.64, 70–5; Plu. *Arist.* 20.1–3.
[199] See Hdt. 9.89. Artabazus crossed not the Hellespont but the Bosporus (by boat), having lost, according to Herodotus (ibid.), many men on his way through Thrace to both the Thracians and hunger and weariness.

S. 49:
11.34.1–37.6:

Developments in Ionia:
(11.34.1) Also concerning Ionia, the Greeks fought a great battle with the Persians on the same day as the one that took place at Plataea, and since we intend to describe it, we will take up the account of it from the beginning.[200] (2) Leotychides the Lacedaemonian and Xanthippus the Athenian, the commanders of the naval force, sailed to Delos with two hundred and fifty *triereis*, having collected the fleet after the naval battle of Salamis in Aegina and after spending some days there. And while they lay at anchor in Delos, ambassadors came to them from Samos asking them to liberate the Greeks throughout Asia Minor. (3) Leotychides took counsel with the commanders and, after they had heard all the Samians had to say, they decided to liberate the *poleis* and speedily sailed forth from Delos.[201] When the admirals of the Persians, who were then at Samos, learned that the Greeks were sailing against them, they withdrew from Samos with all their ships. Putting into port at Mycale in Ionia they hauled up their ships, because they saw that the vessels were unable to do naval battle,[202] and threw about the ships a palisade and a deep ditch.[203] Moreover, they summoned land forces from Sardis and the neighbouring cities and gathered in all about one hundred thousand men.[204] Furthermore, they made preparation of all the other equipment useful in war, believing that the Ionians would defect to the enemy as well.

Battle of Mycale:
(4) As Leotychides sailed with the whole fleet set in array against the enemy at Mycale, they dispatched in advance a ship with a herald who had the loudest voice of anyone in the fleet. This man had been ordered to sail up to the enemy and to announce in a loud voice that the Greeks, after having been victorious over the Persians, were now present to liberate the Greek cities of Asia Minor. (5) Leotychides did so, believing that the Greeks in the army of the Persians would defect

---

[200] See the remarks on *capita* 34–6 by Haillet 2002: 144 *ad* p. 48 note 2.
[201] Diodorus omits quite a few steps: see Labarbe 1957: 192–3; Hignett 1963: 240–63. The actual strength of the Greek fleet at Mycale is still a matter of contention: see also Haillet 2002: 145 *ad* p. 48 note 4.
[202] Probably because the ships were waterlogged and therefore too heavy to manoeuvre.
[203] See also Hdt. 9.96; Hignett 1963: 255–6.
[204] Both the number of Persians mentioned here by Diodorus and the number in Hdt. 9.96 (namely 60,000 men) are rejected by Hignett 1963: 250, 254–5, as exaggerated.

The Persians and the Greek Wars 185

from the Persians and that great confusion would arise in the camp of the Persians, which is what happened. Indeed, when the herald approached the ships that had been beached and made the announcement as he had been ordered, it occurred that the Persians lost confidence in the Greeks within the Persian army and that the Greeks began to agree among themselves to defect.[205]

(11.35.1) After the Greeks under Leotychides had found out the situation they were in, they disembarked their forces. On the following day, while they were preparing for battle, the rumour came to them that the Greeks had been victorious over the Persians at Plataea. (2) Therefore Leotychides, after calling an assembly, exhorted the troops to the battle, both adducing the other considerations and re-enacting the victory of Plataea, by which he surmised he would make those who were about to fight more confident. The outcome was marvellous, indeed. In fact, it appears that the battles occurred on the same day, both the one fought at Mycale and the one which occurred at Plataea.[206] (3) Apparently, therefore, Leotychides had not yet learned of the victory, inventing the military success, and did so as a stratagem. In fact, the great distance made it obvious that the announcement was impossible.[207] (4) The leaders of the Persians, distrusting the Greeks in their army, disarmed them and handed the arms over to their own friends. After calling everyone together and announcing that Xerxes in person would come to their aid with a great force, they made everyone of good courage regarding the battle.

(11.36.1) When both sides had deployed the armies in formation and were advancing against each other, the Persians, observing the enemy were few in number, came to their senses[208] and bore down on them with great shouting. (2) Because the Samians and Milesians had unanimously decided beforehand to support the Greeks, they hastily pushed forward all together. As their advance brought them in sight of the Greek army, the Ionians thought that the Greeks

---

[205] Hdt. 9.98 tells us that Leotychides only hesitantly sailed to Mycale. Hdt. 98–100 presents us with an account of the preparations. Hignett 1963: 259 believes Diodorus' version relies upon Ephorus, who rationalised Herodotus' story.
[206] See the comment by Haillet 2002: 145 *ad* p. 49 note 2.
[207] Perhaps Leotychides referred not to the success of the final battle but to the propitious outcome (possibly somewhat enhanced) of the first engagement between Greeks and Persians at Plataea: see, for example, above, 11.30.2–4.
[208] Αὐτῶν: *delevi*. As before, despising the enemy (suggested by the combination καταφρονέω + gen.) is no realistic interpretation of the situation as described by Diodorus (or his source): at first the Persians were terrified to meet the Greeks in combat, then their commanders raised their spirits by announcing the Great King was about to come, and finally they saw the Greeks were few in number. Now they had every reason to come to themselves, find courage, and attack – but no realistic ground (as yet, anyway), under the given circumstances, to despise the Greeks. Hence my emendation. See also above, 11.10.4.

would be encouraged, but the opposite proved to be. (3) Indeed, because the troops of Leotychides thought that Xerxes had come from Sardis with his army, they were filled with fear. After disorder had arisen in the army, they quarrelled with each other: some said that they needed to leave for their ships with all speed, others that they should stay and confidently hold their lines. While they were still in this disturbed state, the Persians appeared, strikingly equipped and assaulting them with shouting. (4) The Greeks, having no respite whatsoever to deliberate, were compelled to withstand the Persians' attack. Because both sides fought stoutly at first, the battle was indecisive and many fell on both sides. However, when the Samians and Milesians made their appearance, the Greeks took courage, but the Persians, panic-stricken, broke in flight. (5) After a great slaughter had followed, the troops of Leotychides and Xanthippus, pressing upon the defeated, pursued the Persians as far as the encampment. Aeolians also participated, after the battle had already been decided, as well as many of the others from all over Asia Minor. Indeed, a huge desire for liberty entered the *poleis* throughout Asia Minor. (6) Therefore nearly all of them gave no thought either to hostages or to oaths,[209] but with the other Greeks they killed the Persians in their flight. While the Persians suffered defeat in this manner, more than forty thousand were killed. Of the survivors some fled into the camp, others withdrew to Sardis.[210] (7) When Xerxes learned of both the defeat at Plataea and the rout of his own troops at Mycale, he left a portion of his force in Sardis to carry on the war against the Greeks, but he himself, highly disturbed, set out with the rest of his army, making his way to Ecbatana.

(11.37.1) Leotychides and Xanthippus, sailing back to Samos, made allies of the Ionians and Aeolians, and then they tried to convince them to abandon Asia Minor and to resettle in Europe. They promised to expel the peoples who had collaborated with the Persians[211] and to give their lands to them. (2) In general, thus, they announced, remaining in Asia Minor, they would always have the enemy as neighbours, far superior in military strength, while their allies,

---

[209] Most subordinate Greek *poleis* had delivered hostages to the Persians as a guarantee of their sworn loyalty to the Persians.

[210] Hdt. 9.102–6 paints a vivid picture of the battle, in which (as might be expected) the Athenians featured prominently. Diodorus' account is succinct. Hignett 1963: 257 believes that it 'combines incongruously items borrowed from Herodotus with others invented by Ephoros, some of which are clearly inspired by a desire to enhance the share of the Asiatic Greeks in Leotychidas' triumph'. I believe that, as regards this issue, Hignett's criticism of Ephorus is as biased as his praise of Herodotus.

[211] Literally, the Medes. Medising ('Μηδίζω') is the usual term for this kind of collaboration.

living across the sea, would be unable to give them timely assistance. Having listened to these professions, the Aeolians and Ionians resolved to take the Greeks' advice and started to prepare to sail with them to Europe. (3) But, changing their minds to the opposite view, the Athenians advised them to stay, saying that even if no other Greeks should come to their aid, the Athenians, being kinsmen, would do so. They reasoned that, if the Ionians were to be resettled by the Greeks in common, they would no longer look upon Athens as their mother-city. Therefore the Ionians changed their minds and decided to remain in Asia Minor.[212] (4) It happened hereafter that the force of the Greeks was divided: the Lacedaemonians sailed back to Laconia but the Athenians weighed anchor for Sestus, together with the Ionians and the people from the Aegean islands. (5) Immediately after disembarkation Xanthippus took Sestus, having assaulted the city, and, after establishing a garrison in it, he discharged the allies and himself with his fellow citizens returned to Athens.[213] (6) Such was the end of the Median War, as it has been called [by the Greeks], after lasting two years. . . .

S. 50:
11.44.1–5:

Liberation of Cyprus; Pausanias prepares a Persian connection:
(11.44.1) After the Lacedaemonians had appointed Pausanias, who had held the command at Plataea, as admiral of their fleet, they instructed him to liberate such Greek *poleis* as were still guarded by Persian garrisons.[214] (2) With fifty *triereis* from the Peloponnesus and having summoned from the Athenians thirty more, under the command of Aristides, he first of all sailed to Cyprus and liberated those *poleis* which still had Persian garrisons. (3) Having sailed after this beyond[215] the Hellespont, he took Byzantium, which was held by Persians. Killing some of the other Persians, expelling others, he liberated the *polis*. After capturing many important Persians

---

[212] See also Hdt. 9.106; Th. 1.89.2. The historicity of the (Lacedaemonian) suggestion is still debated (see Will 1994: 127), though there were other plans for resettlement of Greeks from Asia Minor as well: see Hignett 1963: 260.
[213] See Hdt. 9.114–21; Th. 1.89.2; Aristodem. *FGrH/BNJ* 104 F 1(4.1). Regarding the capture of Sestus too, Diodorus oversimplifies. See, for this period, Hammond 1973: 315–21; Hereward 1974.
[214] See Th. 1.94.1–2, 128.5–6; Nep. *Paus.* 2.1–2, *Arist.* 2.2; Paus. 3.4.9; Just. 2.15.13–14. See also Hammond 1973: 321–5.
[215] Since Byzantium is situated on the Bosporus, I have opted for this, less usual, meaning of ἐπί: see *LSJ s.v. ad* G.I.2.f.

in the *polis*, he handed the men over to Gongylus of Eretria to guard,[216] in name to keep them for punishment, in fact to get them safely off to Xerxes. Indeed, Pausanias had secretly made a pact of friendship with the king and was about to marry Xerxes' daughter, which is why he was betraying the Greeks. (4) The man who was negotiating these things was general Artabazus,[217] and he secretly supplied Pausanias with large sums of money with which to corrupt the fit and proper among the Greeks. The scheme, however, was brought to light and punished in the following way. (5) As he imitated the luxuriousness {τρυφή} of the Persians and behaved like a tyrant ...

S. 51:
11.46.2–3:

Pausanias falls victim to Persian luxuries:
(11.46.2) .... By his love of the wealth and luxury {τρυφή} of the Persians, Pausanias betrayed the good name he had achieved before. (3) Indeed, elated by his successes he came to abhor the Laconian manner of life but started to imitate the licentiousness {ἀκολασία} and luxury {τρυφή} of the Persians, he who least of all had reason to emulate the customs of the Persians. Indeed, he was not aware of them from others, but he knew by personal experience how much his ancestors' way of life, with respect to *aretē*, surpassed the luxury {τρυφή} of the Persians.[218]

S. 52:
11.56.5–58.3:

Themistocles is accused of treason and escapes to Lysithides in Asia Minor:
(11.56.5) Lysithides happened to be a friend of Xerxes the Great King and on the occasion of Xerxes' passage through Asia Minor

---

[216] On Gongylus: Th. 1.28.6; X. *An.* 7.8.8, *HG* 3.1.6; Nep. *Paus.* 2.2; see also Stronk 1995: 292 *ad* (5); Hofstetter 1978: 70–1.
[217] Artabazus, son of Pharnaces (*Parnaka*) the son of Arsames, who belonged to a minor branch of the Achaemenid family. Pharnaces became one of the most important courtiers. Artabazus himself was appointed satrap of Hellespontine Phrygia in 477, founding there a local dynasty that ruled the region until in the fourth century. See also below, note 218.
[218] Diodorus refers here to the passage in Hdt. 9.82. However, Diodorus' story of Pausanias' ambitions finds a source in Hdt. 5.32: there, though, Pausanias betrothed himself to the daughter of General Megabates, a member of the Achaemenid family and related to King Darius and his satrap of Ionia, Artaphernes. See also: Lazenby 1975; Haillet 2002: 151 *ad* p. 63 note 1.

had entertained the entire Persian host.[219] Being, therefore, intimately acquainted with the Great King but because of compassion wishing to save Themistocles, he promised to assist him in procuring everything he wanted. (6) When Themistocles asked him to lead him to Xerxes, he demurred at first, explaining that Themistocles would be punished because of his past activities against the Persians. Later, though, perceiving the profit, he acceded and incredibly and safely he got him through into Persia. (7) Indeed, it was a custom among the Persians that the man who conducted a concubine to the Great King brought her hidden in a wagon. No passer-by who was encountered interfered or came face to face with the passenger. It occurred that Lysithides availed himself of this means of transport for his enterprise.

Themistocles appears at the Persian court:
(8) Indeed, having had the wagon prepared, embellished with costly hangings, he put Themistocles in it. Having got Themistocles through in all safety, Lysithides met the Great King. Having conversed guardedly with Xerxes, he received pledges from him that he would do Themistocles no wrong. Introducing him to the king, and after the latter had allowed Themistocles to speak and learned that he had done nothing wrong, he absolved him from punishment.
(11.57.1) As it seemed that his life had unexpectedly been saved by an enemy, he fell again into even greater dangers for the following reasons. Mandane was the daughter of Darius I the Great, the killer of the *Magi*, and the full sister of Xerxes, and she enjoyed high esteem among the Persians. (2) Having lost her sons at the time Themistocles had defeated the fleet of the Persians in the sea-battle at Salamis, she found the death of her children hard to bear, and because of her great affliction she was the object of the people's pity. (3) When she learned of the presence of Themistocles, she went into the palace clad in raiment of mourning and with tears begged her brother to wreak vengeance upon Themistocles. When he paid no heed to her, she went round along the noblest of the Persians asking for and, speaking generally, spurring on the people to vengeance upon Themistocles. (4) When the mob rushed to the palace and with loud shouts demanded vengeance upon Themistocles, the Great King

---

[219] Plu. *Them.* 26 calls him Nicogenes; Hdt. 7.27 mentions the name of the man who entertained Xerxes' army as Pythius; Thucydides does not mention him at all. At least as important as the name of Themistocles' guest-friend is the name of the actual Persian king at this moment, namely Xerxes or Artaxerxes: see the discussion by, for example, Haillet 2002: 75 note 2. For at least convenience's sake I will here stick to the name of Xerxes.

replied that he would compose a court out of the noblest Persians and that its verdict would be carried out.

Themistocles is acquitted and receives honours:
(5) After this decision was approved by all, and after sufficient time was given for the preparations for the trial, Themistocles was acquitted of the charges, having learned the Persian language and using it during his defence.[220] (6) Because the Great King was overjoyed as to the rescue of Themistocles, he honoured him with great gifts. Indeed, he gave him in marriage a Persian woman, outstanding in both birth and beauty and, besides, praised for her *aretē*,[221] and he gave a multitude of household slaves for their service but also drinking cups of every kind and such other furnishings as comport with a life of pleasure and luxury. (7) He made him a present also of three *poleis*, well suited for support and enjoyment, namely Magnesia upon the Maeander, which had more grain than any *polis* of Asia Minor, for bread; Myus for the fish on his table, since the sea there abounded in fish; and Lampsacus, which had many estates planted with vines, for wine.[222]

(11.58.1) Themistocles, free of the fear he had among Greeks, and incredibly, on the one hand, driven into exile by those on whom he had bestowed the greatest benefits and, on the other, benefited by those who had suffered the most grievous things, spent his life in the *poleis* we have mentioned, having plenty of all the good things that bring pleasure. After he died, he had a notable funeral in Magnesia and a monument that stands even to this day.[223] (2) Some of the historians say that Xerxes, desiring to lead an expedition against Greece again, invited Themistocles to take command of the war, and that he agreed to do so and received from the Great King guarantees under oath that he would not march against the Greeks without Themistocles.[224] (3) After a bull had been sacrificed and the oaths assented to, Themistocles, after filling a cup with its blood, emptied it and immediately died.[225] They add that

---

[220] For Themistocles' (alleged) trial: Th. 1.137.4–138.3; Aristodem. FGrH/BNJ 104 F 1(10.3–5); Nep. *Them.* 9–10; Plu. *Them.* 28–9.5. The main stories differ significantly: neither Thucydides nor Plutarch mentions a trial, and in Thucydides Themistocles first sends a letter to the Persian king.

[221] Except for this passage, there is, to the best of my knowledge, no reference at all in Greek historiography to such a marriage.

[222] See Haillet 2002: 160 *ad* p. 76 note 1. See also Stronk 1995: 15–16 and note 1.

[223] See Haillet 2002: 160–1 *ad* p. 76 note 2.

[224] See Haillet 2002: 76 note 3.

[225] In several Greek works, *inter alia* including Ctesias' *Persica*, bull's blood is described as a hugely effective poison. The background of this is explained in Arist. *HA* 3.19/520b26–7:

Xerxes thereupon relinquished that plan, and that Themistocles by his own death left the greatest apology; that is, that he had excellently behaved as a proper citizen as regards the matters pertaining to the Greeks.

S. 53:
11.60.1–62.2:

Campaigns by Cimon the Athenian:
(11.60.1) When Demotion was *archon* in Athens [470/69], the Romans elected as consuls Publius Valerius Publicola and Gaius Nautius Rufus.[226] In this year the Athenians, electing as *strategos* Cimon the son of Miltiades and giving him a worthwhile force, sent him to the coast of Asia Minor to help the allied *poleis* and to liberate those which were still held by Persian garrisons.[227] (2) After he had received the fleet which was at Byzantium[228] and putting in at the city which is called Eion,[229] he took it from the Persians who were holding it and captured by siege Scyros, inhabited by Pelasgians and Dolopes. Having appointed an Athenian as the founder of a colony, he portioned out the land in allotments.[230] (3) After this, with a mind to begin greater enterprises, he sailed south to the Piraeus, and having added more *triereis* and arranged the other supplies for war on a notable scale, he at that time put to sea with two hundred *triereis*. Later on, having called for complements from the Ionians and all the others, he had in all three hundred *triereis*. (4) Having sailed thus with the entire fleet to Caria, he at once succeeded in persuading those of the coastal *poleis* that had been settled from Greece to secede from the Persians. Against the *poleis* whose inhabitants spoke two languages[231] and still had Persian garrisons, he applied force and laid siege to them. After having brought over to his side the *poleis* of Caria, he likewise won over by persuasion those of

---

τάχιστα δὲ πήγνυται τὸ τοῦ ταύρου αἷμα πάντων ('the quickest of all to congeal is bull's blood'). The idea is that, once having drunk the bull's blood, the blood congeals (coagulates) and chokes the drinker. In reality, of course, this does not work at all: it is an ancient urban myth. See also Haillet 2002: 161 *ad* p. 76 note 4.

[226] According to Broughton 1951: 27 the consuls for 475 vc (Diodorus is now six years ahead of it) were P. Valerius Poplicola and C. Nautius Rutilus.

[227] On the basis of Plu. *Cim.* 6.1, 7.1, it stands to reason to suggest that Cimon's mission took off shortly after the (Second) Greek War.

[228] See Th. 1.131.1; *P.Oxy.* 1610 F 6 (ascribed by Grenfell and Hunt to Ephorus); Plu. *Cim.* 6.6; Just. 9.1.3. See also Will 1994: 135 and note 3.

[229] For references see Haillet 2002: 162 *ad* p. 78 note 6.

[230] See Haillet 2002: 79 note 1.

[231] Most likely Carian (an Anatolian language, probably related to, *inter alia*, Luwian and Lycian) and Greek (see Abe 2014/15) or, in my view less likely, Doric and Ionic.

Lycia.[232] (5) Also, by adding ships from the allies, who were continually coming in, he still further increased the size of his fleet. Now the Persians had composed their land forces from their own peoples, but their navy they had gathered from Phoenicia, Cyprus, and Cilicia. The commander of the Persian forces was Tithraustes, an illegitimate son of Xerxes.[233] (6) When Cimon learned that the Persian fleet was lying off Cyprus, having sailed to the Persians, he engaged them in a naval battle with two hundred and fifty ships against three hundred and forty.[234] After a sharp struggle took place and both fleets fought brilliantly, the Athenians were victorious in the end. They destroyed many of the enemy ships and captured more than one hundred together with their crews. (7) After the rest of the ships escaped to Cyprus, their crews left them and fled on land. The ships, being deprived of defenders, were captured by the Athenians.[235]

(11.61.1) Thereupon Cimon, not satisfied with such a great victory, set sail at once with his entire fleet against the land army of the Persians, encamped on the bank of the River Eurymedon. Intending to outwit the Persians, he manned the captured ships with the best men of the Greeks, giving them tiaras and clothing them in additional Persian outfits. (2) Directly when the fleet approached, the Persians were deceived by the Persian ships and garb and presumed the *triereis* to be their own. They received the Athenians therefore as if they were friends. When night had fallen, Cimon disembarked his soldiers, and though he had been welcomed as a friend, he fell upon the encampment of the Persians. (3) After a great tumult had arisen among the Persians, the soldiers of Cimon killed everyone they happened to encounter. They killed one of the two commanders of the Persians, Pherendates, a nephew of the Great King, after capturing him in his tent. Of the rest of the Persians, some they killed, others they wounded, but all of them they forced to flee, because of the unexpectedness of the attack. In short, consternation mixed with such bewilderment gripped the Persians that most of them did not even know who on earth was attacking them. (4) In fact, they had

---

[232] See *P.Oxy.* 1610 F 8 (see note 228 above); Plu. *Cim.* 12.1–4. Diodorus follows the author of *P.Oxy.* 1610 here closely.

[233] Plu. *Cim.* 12.4 merely mentions that Ephorus stated that Tithraustes was the commander of the Persian fleet: I can find no reference in Ephorus that Tithraustes was the illegitimate son of Xerxes, as Haillet 2002: 162 *ad* p. 79 note 3 might suggest.

[234] Plu. *Cim.* 12.5 gives 350–600 ships as the Persians' strength; in Plu. *Cim.* 12.2 the Greek strength is reported to have been 200 *triereis*: ὥρμησαν ἄρας ἀπὸ Κνίδου καὶ Τριοπίου διακοσίαις τριήρεσι ('they set sail from Cnidus and Triopium with two hundred *triereis*').

[235] See the remarks by Haillet 2002: 162 *ad* p. 79 note 5. One should not confuse the naval victory off Cyprus with that at the River Eurymedon.

no idea that the Greeks had come against them with a force, believing these had no land army whatsoever. They assumed the Pisidians, who dwelt in neighbouring territory and were hostile to them, had come to attack them. Thinking, therefore, that the enemy attack came from the mainland, they fled to their ships as if these were in friendly hands. (5) Because the night was moonless and dark, this contributed to increase the bewilderment much more so that nobody could see the truth. (6) After a great slaughter had occurred, therefore, through the disorder among the Persians, Cimon, who had previously given orders to the soldiers to assemble at the torch that would be raised, had the signal raised beside the ships, having a care that nothing unexpected occurred because the soldiers had become scattered and turned to plunder. (7) After all the men had been gathered at the torch and had stopped plundering, they then retreated into the ships, but on the following day, having erected a trophy, sailed off to Cyprus, having won two most glorious victories, the one on land, the other at sea. Indeed, never before has there been recorded the occurrence of such unusual and important actions on the same day by an army both afloat and on land.[236]

(11.62.1) After Cimon had succeeded in achieving great things through his own skill and *aretē*, his fame was noised abroad not only among his fellow citizens but among all other Greeks as well. Indeed, he had captured three hundred and forty ships, more than twenty thousand men, and a considerable amount of money. (2) The Persians, having met with so great reverses, built other *triereis* in greater number, being afraid of the growth of the Athenians. . . .

---

[236] Unless Diodorus has a very wide concept of περὶ τὴν Κύπρον ('off Cyprus': 11.60.6), it seems less than likely that Cimon achieved victory in a naval battle there and arrived at the Eurymedon, 200-odd miles distant, on the very same day. See, for example, the remarks of Haillet 2002: 162–3 *ad* p. 79 note 5.

4 Revolt and Sedition

S. 54:
11.69.1–6:

Xerxes is murdered and finally succeeded by Artaxerxes I:[1]
(11.69.1) With the passing of this year, Lysitheus was *archon* in Athens [465/4], and in Rome the consuls elected were Lucius Valerius Publicola and Titus Aemilius Mamercus.[2] During this year, in Asia Artabanus,[3] a Hyrcanian by birth, who enjoyed the greatest influence on King Xerxes and was commander of the royal bodyguard, decided to kill Xerxes and transfer the kingship to himself. Having communicated the plot to Mithridates the eunuch, who was the chamberlain of the king and enjoyed his supreme confidence, but simultaneously also a relative of Artabanus and his friend, Mithradates agreed to the plot. (2) Led by him at night into the bedchamber, Artabanus, after killing Xerxes, set out after the sons of the king. These were three in number, Darius the eldest and Artaxerxes, who both stayed at the palace, and the third, Hystaspes, who happened to be away from home at the time: he held the satrapy of Bactria. (3) Artabanus, thus, having come to Artaxerxes while it was yet night, told him that his brother Darius had become the murderer of his father and was shifting the kingship to himself.

---

[1] For the death of Xerxes and the succession by Artaxerxes I, see Depuydt 2008: 9–12.
[2] According to Broughton 1951: 31 the consuls for 470 vc (Diodorus is still six years ahead of it) were L. Valerius Potitus and Ti. Aemilius Mamercus.
[3] Not the Artabanus who features a few times in the account of Herodotus, but perhaps the person who received Themistocles (Plu. *Them.* 27.2–8) and features in Ctes. *Pers.* F. 13(33) as Artapanus. However, Ctesias referred to one Aspamitres, a eunuch, as Artapanus' co-conspirator. In Ctes. *Pers.* F. 14(34) Megabyzus is also mentioned as being aware of Artapanus' plot. See also Haillet 2002: 169 *ad* p. 91 note 1.

(4) He advised him, therefore, before Darius should seize the throne, to see to it that he should not become a subordinate through indifference but that he should assume the kingship after punishing the murderer of his father. He promised him to provide the bodyguard of the king as his helpers. (5) After Artaxerxes was convinced and had killed his brother Darius at once, with the help of the bodyguard, Artabanus, seeing that his plan was prospering and calling his own sons to his side and crying out that now was his time to win the kingship, struck Artaxerxes with his sword. (6) As Artaxerxes was merely wounded and not seriously hurt by the blow, he held off Artabanus and, as he dealt him a fatal blow, killed him. Saved in an incredible manner and having taken vengeance upon the murderer of his father, Artaxerxes took over the kingship of the Persians. Thus Xerxes died in the manner we have discussed, after he had ruled the Persians for more than twenty years, and Artaxerxes, successor to the kingship, ruled for forty years.[4]

A. ARTAXERXES I (?–424)[5]

S. 55:
11.71.1–6:

First regal year of Artaxerxes I; Egypt revolts:
(11.71.1) When Tlepolemus was *archon* in Athens [463/2], the Romans elected as consuls Titus Quinctius and Quintus Servilius Structus.[6] This year Artaxerxes, the king of the Persians, who had recently assumed the kingship, after he had first of all punished the conspirators of the murder of his father, organised the affairs of the kingdom as he saw fit. (2) In fact, of the serving satraps he dismissed those who were unfavourably disposed to him and, having chosen from his companions the competent ones, he gave them the satrapies. He also concerned himself with both the revenues and the preparation of forces, and because he was in general governing the whole kingdom moderately, he enjoyed great approbation among the Persians. (3) When the inhabitants of Egypt learned of the death of Xerxes, though, and of the general conspiracy and disorder in the kingdom of the Persians, they decided to claim their liberty. At

---

[4] See also Haillet 2002: 91 note 2.
[5] See Briant 2002: 569–87.
[6] Diodorus is still six years ahead of the Varronian chronology. Broughton 1951: 32 presents as the consuls of 468 vc T. Quinctius Capitolinus Barbatus and Q. Servilius Structus Priscus.

once, then, having mustered an army, they defected from the Persians and, after expelling the tax-collectors of the Persians in Egypt, they installed as king a man by the name of Inarus.[7] (4) He at first recruited soldiers from the natives, but also gathering afterwards mercenaries from the other nations, he amassed a considerable force. He also sent ambassadors to the Athenians regarding an alliance, promising them that, if they liberated the Egyptians, he would give them a share in the kingdom and grant them favours many times greater than their good service. (5) After the Athenians had decided that it was to their advantage to humble the Persians as far as they could and to attach the Egyptians closely to themselves against the unpredictable shiftings of Fate, they voted to help the Egyptians with three hundred *triereis*. (6) With great enthusiasm the Athenians, therefore, set about the preparation of the expedition. When Artaxerxes learned of the revolt of the Egyptians and their preparations for war, he concluded that he must surpass the Egyptians in the size of his forces. So at once he began to enrol soldiers from all the satrapies, build ships, and make every other preparation his concern. These were the events of this year in Asia and Egypt.

S. 56:
11.74.1–75.4:

Egyptian revolt continues:
(11.74.1) When Conon was *archon* in Athens [462/1], in Rome the consulship was held by Quintus Fabius Vibulanus and Tiberius Aemilius Mamercus.[8] This year Artaxerxes, the king of the Persians, appointed Achaemenes, who was a son of Darius and his own uncle, commander in the war against the Egyptians.[9] Having provided him with more than three hundred thousand soldiers, both cavalry and infantry, he ordered him to subdue the Egyptians. (2) When Achaemenes, thus, had entered Egypt, he pitched his camp near the Nile. After he had restored his force after the march, he prepared everything for the battle. The Egyptians, though, having gathered their force from Libya and Egypt, were awaiting the auxiliary force from

---

[7] For this revolt see also Ruzicka 2012: 30–2. Th. 1.110.2 mentions as Inarus' co-commander one Amyrtaeus (of Saïs), possibly the grandfather of the later Egyptian King Amyrtaeus (r. 404–399). See also Haillet 2002: 170 *ad* p. 93 note 1.
[8] Still six years ahead of the Varronian chronology: Ti. Aemilius Mamercus and Q. Fabius Vibulanus were the consuls of 467 vc, according to Broughton 1951: 32.
[9] Achaemenes had been a satrap of Egypt under his brother Xerxes, but had returned to Persia after Xerxes had been murdered: see Ruzicka 2012: 28; Hdt. 7.1.

the side of the Athenians. (3) After the Athenians had arrived in Egypt with two hundred ships and had deployed in battle order with the Egyptians against the Persians, a mighty struggle developed. And for a time the Persians, having the benefit of superior numbers, maintained the advantage, but later, after the Athenians had seized the initiative and had put to flight those deployed opposite them, killing many, the remainder of the Persians massively turned to flight.[10] (4) After much bloodshed had occurred during the flight, the Persians finally found refuge in the White Fortress,[11] as it is called, having lost the larger part of their army, but the Athenians, who had won the victory by their own prowess, pursued the Persians as far as the aforesaid place and did not hesitate to besiege it. (5) When Artaxerxes learned of the defeat of his troops, he at first sent some of his friends with a large sum of money to Lacedaemon and asked the Lacedaemonians to make war upon the Athenians, believing that in this manner the Athenian troops who had won the victory in Egypt would sail back to Athens to defend their native city. (6) When the Lacedaemonians, however, neither accepted money nor otherwise paid any attention to the requests of the Persians,[12] despairing to receive aid from the Lacedaemonians, Artaxerxes began to prepare other forces. After placing in command of them Artabazus and Megabyzus, men of outstanding *aretē*, he dispatched them to make war upon the Egyptians. (11.75.1) When Euthippus was *archon* in Athens [461/0], the Romans chose as consuls Quintus Servilius and Spurius Postumius Albinus.[13] During their term of office, in Asia Artabazus and Megabyzus, who had been dispatched to the war against the Egyptians, set out from Persia with more than three hundred thousand soldiers,[14] both cavalry and infantry. (2) When they had arrived in Cilicia and Phoenicia, they restored their land forces after the journey and ordered the Cypriots, Phoenicians, and inhabitants of Cilicia to equip ships. And when three hundred *triereis* were ready, they fitted them out with the ablest marines, weapons, and missiles and everything else useful

---

[10] Ctesias distinguishes two battles, one on land and another at sea, which was won by the Athenian Charitimides: Ctes. *Pers*. F 14(36). He also mentions the killing of Achaemenes by Inarus and the latter's return of Achaemenes' body to Artaxerxes.

[11] The 'White Fortress' was apparently Memphis (see below, 11.75.4). It seems to be identical with 'the White Walls', one of the names (in translation) of the Egyptian city of Memphis: see below, note 210.

[12] See Th. 1.109.1–3. At that time, the Lacedaemonians had to deal with a revolt of helots, following the earthquake of 464.

[13] Diodorus is still six years ahead of the Varronian chronology. Broughton 1951: 33 lists as consuls for 466 vc Q. Servilius Priscus and Sp. Postumius Albus Regillensis.

[14] Here as well the number seems far too high to be realistic. Possibly 'multiplication by a factor ten' is in order here too. See also Haillet 2002: 172 *ad* p. 97 note 2.

in naval warfare. (3) These commanders were, thus, busy with their preparations, gave their soldiers training, and accustomed all to the practice of warfare, and with these things they spent almost the year under scrutiny. (4) The Athenians in Egypt, though, continued to besiege the troops that had fled near Memphis into the White Fortress. Unable to seize the place, because the Persians were putting up a stout defence, they remained for the year in the siege.

S. 57:
11.77.1-5:

End of the Egyptian revolt; Athenians return home:
(11.77.1) When Phrasiclides was *archon* in Athens [460/59], the eightieth Olympiad was celebrated, in which Toryllas the Thessalian won the *stadium* race, and the Romans elected as consuls Quintus Fabius and Titus Quinctius Capitolinus.[15] During their term of office, in Asia, the Persian commanders who were staying in Cilicia made ready three hundred ships, competently equipped for warfare, but with their land army they marched through Syria and Phoenicia. As the fleet sailed alongside the land army, they arrived at Memphis in Egypt.[16] (2) First of all they broke the siege of the White Fortress, having struck the Egyptians and the Athenians with terror. Afterwards, though, adopting a prudent course, they avoided a frontal encounter and strove to end the war by operating cleverly. Because the Attic ships lay moored at the island known as Prosopitis,[17] they made the island, therefore, part of the mainland by diverting the river, which flowed around it, by means of canals. (3) After the ships had thus suddenly come to sit on dry land, the Egyptians, in alarm, left the Athenians alone and came to terms with the Persians. The Athenians, being without allies and seeing that their ships had become useless, set fire to them to ensure that they would not fall into the hands of the enemy. They themselves, not alarmed at the enormity of the circumstances, started to exhort one another to do nothing unworthy of the fights they had won in the past. (4) Surpassing in acts

---

[15] Diodorus is still six years ahead of the Varronian chronology. The consuls for the year 465 vc were Q. Fabius Vibulanus and T. Quinctius Capitolinus Barbatus: Broughton 1951: 33.

[16] As Memphis is quite far away from the sea (in fact the whole Delta is in between them), the description by Diodorus seems inaccurate. Several options are possible: for example, fleet and army had been detached at this stage, another place is intended, or (preferably; see below, 14.19.6) 'Memphis in Egypt' should here simply be read as 'Egypt'.

[17] An island in the western Nile Delta, situated between the Saïtic and the Sebennytic branches, apparently deeply dedicated to warfare (see Hdt. 2.165). Several cities were situated on this island with its periphery of c. 90 km, including its capital Atarbechis and, perhaps, a city by the name of Prosopis. The island's precise location has as yet to be determined. See also Hdt. 2.41; Th. 1.109; St.Byz. s.v. 'Προσοπίς'.

of *aretē*, therefore, those who perished in Thermopylae in defence of Greece, they stood ready to engage the enemy. The commanders of the Persians, though, Artabazus and Megabyzus, observing the exceptional courage of their foes and therefore reasoning that it would be impossible to annihilate them without sacrificing many myriads of their own, solemnly concluded a truce with the Athenians whereby these, with impunity, had to depart from Egypt. (5) Thus the Athenians, having saved their lives by their own *aretē*, departed from Egypt, and, having made their way through Libya to Cyrene, made it safely back to their native land, contrary to all expectations.[18]

S. 58:
12.3.1–4.6:

Expedition led by Cimon to Cyprus:
(12.3.1) When Euthydemus[19] was *archon* at Athens [450/49], the Romans elected as consuls Lucius Quinctius Cincinnatus and Marcus Fabius Vibulanus.[20] In their term of office the Athenians, who had been at war with the Persians on behalf of the Egyptians and had lost all their ships at the island which is known as Prosopitis, after a short time, decided again to go to war against the Persians on behalf of the Greeks in Asia Minor. After equipping a fleet of two hundred *triereis* and choosing Cimon, the son of Miltiades, as commander, they ordered him to sail to Cyprus and make war on the Persians. (2) After Cimon had taken the fleet, which had been furnished with crews excelling in *aretē* and abundant supplies, he sailed to Cyprus. At that time the commanders of the Persian forces were Artabazus and Megabyzus.[21] Artabazus, who held the supreme command, stayed in Cyprus with three hundred *triereis*, and Megabyzus was encamped in Cilicia with the land forces, of which the number was three hundred thousand men. (3) Having sailed to Cyprus and being

---

[18] According to Thucydides οἱ δὲ πλεῖστοι ἀπώλοντο ('most of them perished': Th. 1.110.1). For Athenian policy in Egypt see also, for example, Hammond 1967: 296–6.
[19] The name was Euthynus: see *SEG* 37, 1987, 4; also Kirchner *PA*: no. 5654.
[20] This consulship is unknown beyond this in historical tradition: see Perl 1957: 108. However, for the year 458 vc L. Quinctius Cincinnatus was appointed dictator, while Q. Fabius Vibulanus, a legate, was also the *praefectus urbi*. If we accept this combination, Diodorus would be eight years ahead of the Varronian chronology here: see Broughton 1951: 39–40. However, Broughton 1951: 41 and note 2 inserts the names of L. Quinctius Cincinnatus and M. Fabius Vibulanus between the consular pairs of 457 and 456 vc, if only because Diodorus mentions them; nevertheless, Diodorus is seven years ahead of the Varronian chronology here.
[21] A proven combination of commanders that already had performed in Egypt. Possibly this Artabanus is the same as Pharnaces' son who participated in Xerxes' invasion of Greece in 480, as did this Megabyzus. After the Egyptian War the latter became satrap of Syria until 448.

master of the sea, Cimon took Citium and Marium[22] by siege and treated the conquered in humane fashion. When, after this, *triereis* from Cilicia and Phoenicia bore down upon the island, Cimon, having set out to sea against them and forcing battle upon them, sank many of the ships. He captured one hundred together with their crews, and pursued the rest as far as Phoenicia. (4) Now the Persians fled from the ships that were left and sought refuge on the mainland, in the region where Megabyzus lay encamped with the land force. The Athenians, sailing up and disembarking the soldiers, joined battle, during which Anaxicrates, one of the two commanders of the Athenians, having fought brilliantly, ended his life heroically. The rest, having been victorious in the battle and after killing many, returned to the ships. After this the Athenians sailed off again to Cyprus. This happened in the first year of the war.

(12.4.1) When Pedieus was *archon* in Athens [449/8], the Romans elected as consuls Marcus Valerius Lactuca and Spurius Verginius Tricostus.[23] During their term of office Cimon, the *strategos* of the Athenians, being master of the sea, was engaged to subdue the cities of Cyprus. Because there was a large Persian garrison in Salamis and because the city was filled with missiles and all kinds of arms, and also with grain and supplies of every other kind, he decided that it would be to his advantage to reduce it by siege. (2) In such a manner, indeed, he argued, he would in the easiest way both become master of all Cyprus and confound the Persians, who were unable to come to the aid of the Salaminians because the Athenians were masters of the sea, and who would be despised because they had left their allies in the lurch. In short, he argued that the entire war would be decided if all Cyprus were taken by force. And that is what actually happened. (3) The Athenians, having begun the siege of Salamis, were making daily assaults, but the soldiers in the city, possessing missiles and equipment, were easily warding off the besiegers from the walls.

Artaxerxes strives for peace; Peace of Callias:
(4) When Artaxerxes the king, however, learned of the losses at Cyprus, and having taken council of war with his trustees,[24] he decided that it was to his advantage to conclude a peace with the Greek. Accordingly,

---

[22] See for Marium: Casevitz 2002: 95 *ad* chap. 3.3. See also Hammond 1967: 302–3.
[23] The consuls of 456 vc are listed as M. Valerius Maxumus Lactuca and Sp. Verginius Tricostus Caeliomontanus. Diodorus is now eight years ahead of the Varronian chronology.
[24] 'Φίλοι' should be read here in a sense that is more common in Hellenistic usage, namely as 'companions' or 'trustees': see Dreyer 2011.

he wrote to the commanders in Cyprus and to the satraps the conditions on which they were allowed to conclude an agreement with the Greeks. (5) Artabazus and Megabyzus therefore sent ambassadors to Athens who were to discuss a settlement. Because the Athenians were favourable and dispatched ambassadors plenipotentiary, the leader of whom was Callias the son of Hipponicus, the Athenians and their allies concluded with the Persians a treaty of peace.[25] The principal terms of this treaty run as follows: all the Greeks *poleis* throughout Asia Minor are to live under their own *nomoi*; the satraps of the Persians are not to come nearer to the sea than a three days' journey; and no Persian warship is to sail between Phaselis and the Cyanean Rocks;[26] if these terms are observed by the king and his commanders, the Athenians are not to make expeditions into the territory over which the Great King is ruler. (6) After the treaty had been solemnly concluded, the Athenians withdrew their forces from Cyprus, having won a brilliant victory and having concluded most noteworthy terms of peace. It also happened that Cimon during his stay in Cyprus died of an illness.

S. 59:
12.26.2:

Persian treaty with the Lacedaemonians conflicting with the Peace of Callias:
(12.26.2) While these events were taking place [in 442/1], the greater number of the nations of the inhabited world were quiet, practically all of them being at peace.[27] Indeed, the Persians had two treaties with the Greeks, one with the Athenians and their allies in which the Greek *poleis* throughout Asia Minor were to live under their own *nomoi*, but they concluded one later with the Lacedaemonians, in which the opposite had been written, namely that the Greek *poleis* throughout Asia Minor were to be subject to the Persians.[28] Likewise the Greeks were also at peace with one another, the Athenians and Lacedaemonians having concluded a truce of thirty years [**concluding the 'First Peloponnesian War' in 446/5**].

---

[25] Though Habicht 1961: 13, 19, 25–6 is somewhat sceptical on this treaty, others believe it was a real treaty: see for example Hammond 1967: 303 and Raubitschek 1964: 151–2.
[26] In fact the whole Aegean was, therefore, prohibited for Persian warships. For the 'three days' limit' see also Andrewes 1961: 16–18.
[27] See the remarks by Casevitz 2002: 105 *ad* p. 27 chap. 26.2.
[28] I have found no indication of such a treaty for this date in other Greek sources; see also Hammond 1967: 451.

S. 60:
12.27.3:

Pissuthnes, the Persian satrap, interferes in Samian politics:
(12.27.3) When in Samos civil disturbance arose, because some preferred democracy, others willing it to be an aristocracy, the city was very tumultuous. When the opponents of democracy crossed to Asia Minor and travelled to Sardis to Pissuthnes, the satrap of the Persians, to ask for help, Pissuthnes gave them seven hundred soldiers, hoping that he would master Samos in this manner,[29] ...

B. XERXES II (?–423)[30]

S. 61:
12.64.1:

Death of Artaxerxes I, succession of Xerxes II:
(12.64.1) Artaxerxes, the king of the Persians, died having reigned forty years [in 424], but Xerxes, after he had succeeded to the throne, ruled for a year. ...

C. SOGDIANUS (?–423)

S. 62:
12.71.1:

Death of Xerxes II, succession of Sogdianus, who is killed by Darius II:
(12.71.1) In Asia King Xerxes died after a reign of one year, or, as some write, two months. Having succeeded to the kingship, his brother Sogdianus ruled for seven months. Having killed the latter, Darius reigned nineteen years.[31]

---

[29] If not factually then in spirit violating the Peace of Callias.
[30] For the transitions from Artaxerxes I to Darius II (424/3), see Depuydt 2008: 13–34.
[31] The year discussed is 424. In fact, Sogdianus ruled probably only for 45 days. See also Andrewes 1961: 1–2. 'Xerxes and Sogdianos were not recognised in Babylon, so the ultimate source is not simply Babylonian, but if this source used the Babylonian calendar Xerxes was on the throne on 22 April 424, so that Dareios could hardly have established himself before the beginning of December 424. It is consistent with this that Babylonian documents still date by Artaxerxes' "41st year" as late as 24 December 424, and date by Dareios' accession-year as early as 13 February 423.'

D. DARIUS II (?-404)[32]

S. 63:
13.22.1-3:

Fragment of a speech by Nicolaus of Syracuse, 413:
(13.22.1) ... What destroyed the rule of the Medes? Their brutality towards the weaker. (2) Indeed, after the Persians revolted from them, most of the peoples also started to draw together in revolt. Indeed, how did Cyrus the Great from being a private citizen come to rule over all of Asia? By his considerateness towards the conquered. Indeed, having taken King Croesus captive, he not only did him no injustice, but even became his benefactor. In much the same way did he also approach the other kings as well as other peoples. (3) Therefore, when his gentleness had become known to every region, all the inhabitants throughout Asia, vying with one another in entering into alliance with the king, came to his side.

S. 64:
13.36.5:

Balance of power in Greece shifts; Darius helps the Lacedaemonians:
(13.36.5) ... Because Darius, the king of the Persians, was an ally of the Lacedaemonians, Pharnabazus,[33] who had the military command of the regions by the sea, supplied money to the Lacedaemonians. He also summoned the three hundred *triereis* from Phoenicia, thinking to dispatch them to the Lacedaemonians for assistance.

S. 65:
13.37.4-5:

Alcibiades intervenes, 411/10:
(13.37.4) Because Alcibiades was, thus, on friendly terms with Pharnabazus,[34] the satrap of Darius, and saw that he was on the point of sending three hundred ships to the Lacedaemonians in support, he

---

[32] See Briant 2002: 588-611; Depuydt 2008: 17-34.
[33] Diodorus here confuses Tissaphernes (who was the στρατηγὸς τῶν ἐπὶ θαλάττης 'commander of the regions by the sea' and satrap of Lydia and Caria) and Pharnabazus, who was the satrap of Bythinia and Phrygia, a territory run by him and his ancestors from 477 onwards.
[34] Again Diodorus mixes up Pharnabazus and Tissaphernes.

persuaded him to abstain from this action. Indeed, he pointed out to him that it would not be to the advantage of the Great King to make the Lacedaemonians too powerful. In fact, he said, it would be harmful for the Persians. A better policy, therefore, would be to observe the combatants as long as they were equally matched, to ensure that they would struggle with each other as long as possible. (5) Thereupon Pharnabazus, believing that Alcibiades was talking sense, sent the fleet back to Phoenicia. On that occasion, thus, Alcibiades deprived the Lacedaemonians of so great an allied force. . . .

S. 66:
13.38.4–5:

Lacedaemonian admiral learns of Alcibiades' intervention:
(13.38.4) Mindarus, though, the Lacedaemonian admiral, remained some time at Miletus, expecting the aid promised by Pharnabazus. In fact, when he heard that three hundred *triereis* had arrived from Phoenicia, he was buoyed up in his hopes, believing he would destroy the Athenians' supremacy with so great a fleet. (5) When he shortly after heard from some people that Pharnabazus, convinced by Alcibiades, had sent the fleet back to Phoenicia, he gave up the hopes he had placed in him. . . .

S. 67:
13.40.6:

Polis of Cyzicus revolts to Pharnabazus:
(13.40.6) . . . . Thrasybulus and the Athenians set sail to Cyzicus with the entire fleet. In fact, before the sea-battle [in the Hellespont, between Abydus and Sestus, 411] this very city had revolted to Pharnabazus, the governor of Darius, and to Clearchus, the Lacedaemonian commander. Finding the city unfortified, the Athenians easily achieved their end, and having exacted money from the Cyzicenes they sailed off to Sestus.

S. 68:
13.42.4:

Antandrians revolt from Persia with Lacedaemonian support:
(13.42.4) About the same time [410/9] the Antandrians, who were held by a garrison,[35] sent for Lacedaemonian soldiers, with whose aid expelling the guard, they made their country a free place. Indeed,

---

[35] Of Persians (see Th. 8.108).

the Lacedaemonians, charging Pharnabazus with the sending back of the three hundred ships to Phoenicia, gave their aid to the inhabitants of Antandrus.

S. 69:
13.45.6:

Pharnabazus supports Dorieus the Rhodian and Mindarus near the Hellespont:
(13.45.6) ... The land army of Pharnabazus was also there [at the Dardanian Promontory, about ten miles inside the Hellespont on the Asian side], supporting the Lacedaemonians.

S. 70:
13.46.5–6:

After a naval defeat in the Hellespont, the Lacedaemonians seek refuge:
(13.46.5) Finally the Lacedaemonians, having gained the shore, fled to the land army of Pharnabazus. The Athenians, though, at first tried to drag the Lacedaemonian ships from the shore and started to put up a reckless fight. Being, however, checked by the Persian army, they sailed off to Sestus. (6) In fact, Pharnabazus, wishing to make a good defence before the Lacedaemonians against the charges they adduced, put up a pretty vigorous fight against the Athenians. Simultaneously, though, he explained as regards the sending off the three hundred *triereis* to Phoenicia that he had done so having been told that both the king of the Arabs and the king of the Egyptians plotted against the developments affecting Phoenicia.[36]

S. 71:
13.47.2:

Lacedaemonians plan to lay siege to poleis in Asia Minor:
(13.47.2) Having set out to Abydos about the first watch of the night, Mindarus both repaired the damaged ships and sent word to the Lacedaemonians for army and naval reinforcements.

---

[36] Apparently Diodorus is still conflating two satraps, namely Pharnabazus and Tissaphernes. The 'king of the Arabs' is most likely to be the ruler of the Qedarite Arab coalition, whose realm stretched from north-west Arabia into southern Palestine and the Sinai: see Ruzicka 2012: 36, who appears to view Pharnabazus' decision feasible.

In fact, he had in mind, while the materials for the fleet were being made ready, to lay siege with the army together with Pharnabazus to the *poleis* throughout Asia Minor that were allied with the Athenians.

S. 72:
13.49.4:

Mindarus lays siege to Cyzicus:
(13.49.4) Having sailed to Cyzicus, Mindarus, the Lacedaemonian admiral, disembarked his whole force and surrounded the *polis*. Pharnabazus was also there with a large army and with his aid Mindarus, having laid siege, took Cyzicus by storm.

S. 73:
13.50.4–51.8:

Athenians outmanoeuvre Mindarus; Mindarus seeks safety:
(13.50.4) ... Because the Athenians, finally, were appearing from every direction and had blocked the Peloponnesians from their approach to the city, Mindarus was forced to flee from his position to Cleri, as it is called, where Pharnabazus also had his force. (5) ... (6) And when the infantry of Pharnabazus rushed to the aid of the Lacedaemonians, it caused great bloodshed, since the Athenians, because of their advantage, fought rather boldly than smartly, though the Peloponnesians outnumbered them by far. In fact, the army of Pharnabazus supported the Lacedaemonians and making the fight from land it held the safer position. (7) ....

Course of the battle:
(13.51.1) While the Athenians busied themselves with reinforcing their troops, Mindarus himself, the Lacedaemonian commander, was fighting with Alcibiades over the ships that were being dragged off, and he sent Clearchus the Spartan[37] with some of the Peloponnesians against the troops with Thrasybulus. With him he

---

[37] Born about the middle of the fifth century, Clearchus the Spartan was sent with a fleet to the Hellespont in 411 and became governor (*harmost*) of Byzantium, of which town he was a *proxenus*. Having lost this *polis* to the Athenian Alcibiades in 409, Clearchus returned to Sparta, asking for a force to protect Byzantium and neighbouring Greek colonies from the Thracians. He got his army but was subsequently outlawed by the Spartans. Finally, after making war against Thracian tribes for a few years, he left Thrace to join Cyrus the Younger. See also, for example, Schmitt 2011a. Also: Hofstetter 1978: 101–4.

Revolt and Sedition

also sent the mercenaries who served in the army of Pharnabazus. (2) Thrasybulus together with the marines and archers at first stoutly withstood the enemy and killed many of them, but also saw that many of his own men fell. When the mercenaries of Pharnabazus were surrounding the Athenians, though, and were crowding about them en masse from every direction, Theramenes[38] appeared with both his own infantry and that of Chaereas.[39] (3) Although the troops of Thrasybulus were exhausted and had given up hope of rescue, their spirits were suddenly revived again when such a strong reinforcement arrived. (4) For a long time a staunch battle ensued. First, though, the mercenaries of Pharnabazus began to flee and the continuity of their battle-line was broken. Finally the Peloponnesians who had been left behind with Clearchus, having both inflicted and suffered much, were expelled. (5) After the Peloponnesians had been defeated, the troops of Theramenes rushed to help those fighting under Alcibiades. Although the forces had rapidly assembled at one point, Mindarus was not dismayed by the attack of those under Theramenes. After dividing the Peloponnesians, he deployed half of them against the advancing enemy; the other half, which he himself commanded, having first called upon each soldier not to disgrace the reputation of Sparta, moreover in a fight on land, he positioned against the troops of Alcibiades. (6) Putting up a heroic battle about the ships, fighting in person before all his troops, he killed many of the opponents, but was finally killed, battling nobly for his fatherland, by the troops of Alcibiades. When he had fallen, both the Peloponnesians and all the allies banded together and broke into terror-stricken flight. (7) The Athenians pursued the enemy for a distance, but when they learned that Pharnabazus was hurrying up at full speed with a strong force of cavalry, they returned to the ships, took Cyzicus, and set up two trophies for each one of the victories, one for the sea-battle at the island of Polydorus, as it is called, and one for the land-battle where they forced the first flight of the enemy. (8) Thus the Peloponnesians in the *polis* and all the fugitives from the battle fled to the camp of Pharnabazus. The Athenian commanders not only captured all the ships, they also collected many prisoners and an immeasurable quantity of booty,

---

[38] Theramenes was an Athenian oligarchy-oriented politician and general. See, for example, Hornblower 2011: 99, 184–5, 187–8, 203.
[39] Chaereas, son of Archestratus of Athens. In 411/10 he was co-commander in Samos, sent to Athens on the *Paralus* (Athenian state vessel), but able to return (Th. 8.74.1–3; 86.3). In 410 he was a commander at Cyzicus: see Hornblower 2011: 185.

since they had won the victory at the same time over two forces of such size.[40]

S. 74:
13.52.4:

From a speech by the Spartiate ambassador to Athens, Endius, 410/9:
(13.52.4) ... For us, the richest of the kings all over the world is the sponsor[41] of the war, ...

S. 75:
13.63.3:

Hermocrates the Syracusan returns to Sicily from Asia Minor:
(13.63.3) Having himself, from the campaign, friendship with Pharnabazus, the satrap of the Persians, he took from him a great sum of money, with which, after he had sailed down to Messene [Sicilian Messina], he had five *triereis* constructed and hired one thousand soldiers.

S. 76:
13.64.4:

Athenian expedition against Pharnabazus' territory:
(13.64.4) And Alcibiades, after splitting up[42] with Thrasybulus[43] with the thirty ships, sailed to the territory held by Pharnabazus, and when they had together laid waste a great amount of that territory, they not only richly provided the soldiers with plunder but also themselves realised money from the booty, wishing to relieve the Athenian people of the property taxes [levied for the prosecution of the war].

---

[40] The despair of the Lacedaemonians after such a disaster is reflected in the letter from Hippocrates, the vice-admiral, to Sparta, intercepted by Athens and presented in X. *HG*, 1.1.23, which ran as follows: 'The ships are gone. Mindarus is dead. The men are starving. We know not what to do.'
[41] Endius uses, according to Diodorus, the word χορηγός, originally the person who defrays the costs to produce a chorus. The word is here used metaphorically.
[42] Problems may arise from the word ἀπολύσας: for my translation 'splitting up', I have let myself be led by the story as we find it in X. *HG* 1.2.15 *sqq.*, stating that the troops of Alcibiades refused at first to join with those of Thrasyllus (*Thrasybulus*), but later agreed to the union of the two armies. What Alcibiades probably did was to send Thrasyllus ahead, and the generals operated separately for a time.
[43] X. *HG* 1.2.6 *sqq.* names him Thrasyllus.

S. 77:
13.66.6:

Byzantium changes sides while its harmost[44] is with Pharnabazus:
(13.66.6) ... When the *harmost* left the *polis* to visit Pharnabazus to get money, thereupon certain of the Byzantines, hating the severity of his rule (for Clearchus was a harsh man), agreed to deliver up the city to Alcibiades.

S. 78:
13.70.3:

Lysander (Mindarus' successor) meets with Cyrus the Younger:
(13. 70.3) .... Having heard that Cyrus the Younger, the son of King Darius, had been dispatched by his father to go to war together with the Lacedaemonians,[45] Lysander[46] went to him at Sardis, and stirring up the youth's[47] enthusiasm for the war against the Athenians, he received on the spot ten thousand *dareikoi*[48] for the pay of his soldiers. As regards the future, Cyrus told him to ask without restriction. In fact, he had orders from his father to supply the Lacedaemonians with whatever they wanted.

S. 79:
13.73.6:

Alcibiades is accused of conspiring with Pharnabazus:
(13.73.6) ... In fact, some of the Athenian soldiers at Samos, being at odds with him, sailed to Athens and accused Alcibiades in the Assembly of being minded towards the cause of the Lacedaemonians and having a friendly relation with Pharnabazus, by which he hoped to rule over the citizens of Athens when the war was over.

---

[44] The customary title of the Spartan governors. 'Manager' might be an appropriate translation of this word, though it is generally translated as 'governor'.
[45] Cyrus had been appointed στρατηγὸς πάντων ὅσοι ἐν Καστωλοῦ πεδίον ἀθροίζονται (X. *An.* I.1.2), 'commander of all the forces that muster in the plain of Castolus' (meaning all Persian forces of western Asia Minor).
[46] Lysander the son of Aristoclitus was a member of the Spartan Heraclid family, claiming descent from Heracles. He was appointed Spartan *navarch* (admiral) for the Aegean Sea in 407. During his term of office he befriended Cyrus the Younger, a son of Darius II and Parysatis, and acquired his financial support (for Sparta) as well.
[47] Allegedly Cyrus the Younger was at that moment, 408/7, seventeen years of age.
[48] One *dareikos* – weighing about 8.4 g of nearly pure gold, worth 20 (silver) *sigloi*, each weighing about 5.5 gr – had the (changing) value of 20-6 Attic *drachmae*: Stronk 1995: 194 ad (1). For a review of Achaemenid coinage see Tuplin 2014.

S. 80:
13.104.3–6:

Lysander talks with Cyrus the Younger before the latter leaves for Persis, 405:
(13.104.3) Lysander, the admiral of the Lacedaemonians, having collected thirty-five ships from the neighbouring allies of the Peloponnesus, sailed up to Ephesus. Having also summoned the fleet from Chios, he made it ready. He also went inland to Cyrus, the son of King Darius, and received from him a great sum of money for sustenance and support of his soldiers. (4) Because Cyrus' father was summoning him to Persis, Cyrus turned over to Lysander the authority over the cities[49] under his command and ordered them to pay the tribute to him. Lysander, then, being well supplied with every means for making war, returned to Ephesus.

Meanwhile an oligarchic coup d'état takes place in Miletus:
(5) ... (6) The most respectable of those supporting the *demos*, being no less than one thousand in number, fearing the state of affairs, fled to Pharnabazus, the satrap. He, receiving them in a friendly way and handing over to each a gold *stater* [possibly Diodorus means a *dareikos*], resettled them in Blauda, a fortress in Lydia.

S. 81:
13.108.1:

Death of Darius:
(13.108.1) Not long after the peace [between Athens and Sparta, 404] Darius, the King of Asia, died after a reign of nineteen years, and Artaxerxes, his eldest son, succeeded to the throne and reigned for forty-three years. . . .

E. ARTAXERXES II *MNEMON* (C. 436–358)[50]

S. 82:
2.32.4:
Ctesias of Cnidus, now, lived during the period in which Cyrus the Younger made war with his brother Artaxerxes II, and after Ctesias had been captured and had been picked by the Great King

---
[49] Probably both the Greek *poleis* and non-Greek cities.
[50] See, for example, Briant 2002: 612–80; Depuydt 2008: 35.

because of his medical skill, he spent seventeen years at court honoured by him.[51]

S. 83:
14.11.1–4:

Death of Alcibiades and rumours of conspiracy:
(14.11.1) While these events were taking place, Pharnabazus, the satrap of King Darius, having seized Alcibiades the Athenian, put him to death, wishing to please the Lacedaemonians.[52] However, because Ephorus has written that Alcibiades' death was sought for other reasons, I think it not to be without use to provide the plot against him as the historian[53] Ephorus of Cume has described it. (2) In fact, he states in the seventeenth book[54] that Cyrus and the Lacedaemonians were scheming in secret to make war together against Cyrus' brother Artaxerxes; that Alcibiades, learning of Cyrus' purpose from undisclosed persons, went to Pharnabazus and told him of it in detail; and that he asked him for a guide to Artaxerxes, because he wished, indeed, to be the first to disclose the plot to the king. (3) Pharnabazus, though, he states, on hearing the story, wanted to make the report his own and sent trusted men to disclose the matter to the Great King. Because Pharnabazus did not provide the escorts to the palace, he writes that Alcibiades set out to the satrap of Paphlagonia in order to make the trip with his assistance, but that Pharnabazus, fearing lest the Great King should hear the truth of these events, sent men after Alcibiades to assassinate him on the road.[55] (4) They came upon him, having taken shelter in a village of Phrygia,[56] and in the night enclosed the place with a mass of wooden logs. After a great fire was kindled, Alcibiades tried to

---

[51] See, for Ctesias' career at Artaxerxes' court and the circumstances that may have led to his capture, Stronk 2004/5.
[52] See also Isoc. *Bigis* 40; Lys. 14.27; Ath. 13.574E; Plu. *Alc.* 37.6-8, 38.4-5; Nep. *Alc.* 10.2-6. Fear of Alcibiades among members of the Thirty at Athens is referred to as a motive for asking for Alcibiades' death, just as his (sexual) behaviour is mentioned as a cause, and here his enmity with (certain) Lacedaemonians.
[53] For 'historian' Diodorus uses here the more or less customary word συγγραφεύς (generally a 'writer of contemporary history': see *LSJ*), suggesting that a term like ἱστοριογράφος or even ἱστορικὸς, more or less advocated by Aristotle and used a few times since, had not yet found widespread acceptance in Diodorus' days: see, for example, Stronk 2010: 36–43. Apparently this term still had the notion of 'chronicler', for example like Hecataeus.
[54] See *FGrH/BNJ* 70 F 70; also Nep. *Alc.* 10.
[55] Nep. *Alc.* 10.3 and Plu. *Alc.* 39.1 provide their names: Bagaeus (half-brother) and Susamithres (uncle) of Pharnabazus.
[56] Ath. 13.574E appears to provide the name of the village: Melissa (essentially it is the place where one Theodote buried him); see also the comment by Bonnet and Bennett 2002: 164 *ad* p. 18 note 3.

save himself, but died subdued by the fire and those hurling javelins at him.[57]

S. 84:
14.12.7–9:

Clearchus, (former) Spartiate commander at Byzantium, flees to Ionia and Cyrus:
(14.12.7) ... Having become fearful afterwards [after accusations as regards his brutality had been brought forward], he stole away at night and sailed down to Ionia. Having become there familiar with Cyrus, the brother of the king, he became his military commander. (8) In fact, Cyrus, who had been appointed supreme commander of the satrapies lying by the sea and was full of ambition, was planning to go to war against his brother Artaxerxes. (9) Seeing, thus, that Clearchus possessed daring and a blunt rashness, he gave him money and ordered him to enlist as many mercenaries as possible, believing that he would have an apt partner for his bold undertakings.

S. 85:
14.19.1–27.7:

Cyrus' campaign against Artaxerxes II; Cyrus assembles his army:
(14.19.1) At the close of the year Exaenetus[58] was *archon* in Athens [401/0], and in Rome six *tribuni militum* took over the highest authority: Publius Cornelius, Caeso Fabius, Spurius Nautius, Gaius Valerius, Manius Sergius <, and Gnaeus Cornelius>.[59] (2) At this time Cyrus, who was commander of the satrapies by the sea, had been planning for a long time to make war against his brother Artaxerxes. Indeed, the young man was full of ambition[60] and was continuously eager for the contests of war. (3) When a sufficient number of mercenaries had been collected for him and all preparations for the campaign had been completed, he did not reveal the truth to the troops,

---

[57] A very different account of the circumstances of the murder of Alcibiades is given by Plu. *Alc.* 38.3–4; see also the remarks by Bonnet and Bennett 2002: 164 *ad* p. 18 note 4.
[58] Xenaenetus, according to the list of *archons*: see Kirchner *PA*, 11174.
[59] Broughton 1951: 81 lists C. Valerius Potitus Volusus, M'. Sergius Fidenas, P. Cornelius Maluginensis, Cn. Cornelius Cossus, K. Fabius Ambustus, and Sp. Nautius Rutilus as six military tribunes with consular power for the year 404 vc: Diodorus is now four years ahead of the Varronian chronology. Oldfather 1963: 61 note 1 rightly observes that, instead of Gn. Cornelius, several MSS add the name of Iunius Lucullus.
[60] Copied, almost to the letter, from 14.12.8 above. For Cyrus the Younger's motives for attacking his brother see, for example, X. *An.* 1.1.1–4; also Stronk 1995: 15–16.

Revolt and Sedition 213

but kept saying that he was leading the force to Cilicia against the despots who were in rebellion against the Great King.[61] (4) He sent, though, ambassadors to the Lacedaemonians as well, who were to remind them of his services during the war against the Athenians and to urge them to join him as allies.[62] Because the Lacedaemonians believed that the war would be to their advantage, they decided to help Cyrus and forthwith sent ambassadors to their admiral, named Samus,[63] with instructions that he should carry out whatever Cyrus might order. (5) Samus had twenty-five *triereis*. Having sailed with these to Ephesus to Cyrus' admiral, he stood by to co-operate with him in every respect. The Lacedaemonians also sent eight hundred infantry, instating Chirisophus as commander. The commander of the Persian fleet was Tamos,[64] who had fifty *triereis* which had been fitted out at great expense. After the Lacedaemonians had arrived, the fleets put out to sea, following a course for Cilicia.

The march inland starts:
(6) After Cyrus had gathered to Sardis both the levies of Asia and thirteen thousand mercenaries, he appointed as governors of Lydia and Phrygia Persians related to him, but of Ionia, Aeolis, and the neighbouring territories Tamos, who was a trusted friend, a native of Memphis [that is: an Egyptian] of descent. He himself with the army advanced in the direction of Cilicia and Pisidia, spreading the word that some of those settling there had revolted. (7) From Asia Minor he had in all seventy thousand troops, of whom three thousand were cavalry, from the Peloponnesus and the rest of Greece thirteen thousand mercenaries. (8) Clearchus the Lacedaemonian led the soldiers from the Peloponnesus, with the exception of the Achaeans, Proxenus of Thebes those from Boeotia, Socrates the Achaean the Achaeans, and Menon of Larissa those from Thessaly.[65] (9) Persians were in charge of the Persians as regards minor commands, and of the whole army Cyrus himself was commander-in-chief. He had

---

[61] X. *An.* 1.2.1 refers to Pisidians as the alleged target of Cyrus (see also below, 14.9.6).
[62] Something similar is indicated by X. *An.* 3.1.5, *HG* 3.1.1. For Cyrus' help see, for example, above, 13.70.3.
[63] X. *HG* 3.1.1 calls him Samius. In X. *An.* 1.4.2 we are told that the contingent of Peloponnesian ships to Cyrus was commanded by the Lacedaemonian *navarch* Pythagoras.
[64] An Egyptian (see below, 14.19.6), who – according to X. *An.* 1.4.2 – commanded twenty-five *triereis*. In Diodorus' account Cyrus' fleet consisted of seventy-five ships, as against sixty in Xenophon's version.
[65] See X. *An.* 1.2.3. Three names mentioned there are lacking in the *Bibliotheca*, namely Xenias of Arcadia, Sophaenetus of Stymphalus (possibly even a source-author of Diodorus; see Chapter 1), and Pasion of Megara. According to Xenophon, Menon joined Cyrus' troops only in Colossae in Phrygia, not at Sardis.

made clear to the commanders that he was marching against his brother,[66] but kept this concealed from the troops for fear that they would leave his enterprise stranded because of the size of his expedition. Therefore along the march, by way of providing for the coming occasion, he curried favour with the troops by affability and by providing abundant markets [supplies of provisions].

(14.20.1) After Cyrus had traversed Lydia and Phrygia as well as the regions bordering on Cilicia, he arrived at the boundaries of Cilicia and the entrance at the Cilician Gates. This pass is narrow and precipitous, twenty *stadia* [c. 3.7 km] in length, and bordering it on both sides are exceedingly high and inaccessible mountains. Walls stretch down on each side from the mountains as far as the roadway, where gates have been built across it.[67] (2) Having led the force through these gates, Cyrus entered a plain second to no plain in Asia in beauty, advancing through which to Tarsus, the largest of the cities of Cilicia, he speedily mastered it. When the[68] Syennesis, the lord of Cilicia, heard of the size of the enemy force, he was in dire straits, being no match in battle. (3) After Cyrus had sent for him and given pledges, he went to him, and on learning the truth about the war he agreed to join him as an ally against Artaxerxes. One of his sons he sent along with Cyrus, giving him suitable companions for the Cilicians' expedition.[69] Being by nature unscrupulous and having adjusted himself to the uncertainty of Fate, he dispatched his other son secretly to the Great King, both to reveal to him the forces gathered against him and to assure him that he took the part of Cyrus out of necessity, but that he was still faithful to the Great King and, when the opportunity arose, would desert Cyrus and join the army of the Great King. (4) Cyrus rested his force twenty days in Tarsus. When he, after this, was about to resume the march, the troops suspected that the campaign was against Artaxerxes. And as each man calculated the length of the roads and the multitude of hostile peoples and tribes through which it was necessary to make their way,

---

[66] X. *An.* 2.1.19 suggests that only Clearchus had been informed.

[67] The description of the geography differs from that in X. *An.* 1.2.21–2. Combined, they offer a good picture of the situation.

[68] Though 'Syennesis' is generally considered as a personal name (as it seems to be by Diodorus), it might equally be the title used to designate the ruler (dynast) of Cilicia in Tarsus, a suggestion first made by Paul Masqueray in his edition of the *Anabasis* for Les belles lettres (Paris, 1932, vol. 1, p. 52 note 1) and adopted by me: see also Casabonne 1995: 147–8; Ruzicka 2012: 104.

[69] Diodorus probably follows here the account of Ctes. *Pers.* F. 17b [S] (Stronk 2010: 362–3), certainly not that of X. *An.* 1.2.12–27, where it is suggested that Epyaxa, the wife of the Syennesis, was intimate with Cyrus and worked to make her husband support him.

he was taken with anxiety.⁷⁰ In fact, the word had got about that the road to Bactra⁷¹ was a four months' march for an army and that a force of more than four hundred thousand soldiers had been mustered for the Great King. (5) Being therefore most fearful, Cyrus' soldiers shuddered and, in anger at their commanders, attempted to kill them on the ground that the commanders had betrayed them. When Cyrus entreated all of them, though, and assured them that he was leading the army not against Artaxerxes but against a certain satrap of Syria, the soldiers yielded, and when they had received more pay, they resumed their former loyalty.⁷²

Chirisophus arrives; the army passes the Cilician Gates:
(14.21.1) As Cyrus marched through Cilicia he arrived at the town of Issus, which lies on the sea, being the last settlement of Cilicia. At the same time the fleet of the Lacedaemonians also put in there. The commanders went ashore, met with Cyrus, and reported the goodwill of the Spartans towards him and, having disembarked the eight hundred infantry under the command of Chirisophus, they put them under his command. (2) They pretended that the friends of Cyrus sent these mercenaries, but in fact everything was done with the consent of the ephors. The Lacedaemonians had not yet openly entered upon the war, but were concealing their purpose, awaiting the turn of the war. Cyrus abandoned camp with his force, making his way towards Syria, and ordered the admirals to accompany him by sea with all the ships. (3) When he arrived at the Gates, as they are called, and found the place without guards, he was elated. In fact, he was greatly concerned that some might have occupied them beforehand. The nature of the place is narrow and precipitous, so that it can be easily guarded by few. (4) Indeed, two mountains lie near each other, the one jagged and with great crags; from the very road starts the other mountain, the largest in those regions, bearing the name Amanus,⁷³ and it extends along Phoenicia. The

---

⁷⁰ Parallel to X. *An.* 1.3.1.
⁷¹ The modern-day city of Balkh in what is currently northern Afghanistan.
⁷² See X. *An.* 1.3.2–21 for a detailed account.
⁷³ The manuscripts read here, wrongly, Λίβανος: the Libanon is situated further to the south, as Diodorus himself clearly acknowledges (19.58.2–3). Mt Amanus is, though, situated at the Gates referred to (probably not the Cilician Gates proper, situated north of Tarsus: at least at present, the 'Cilician Gates' is generally the name given to the pass north of Tarsus, at Gülek Bogazi, that is, the access to Cilicia from Cappadocia). The pass intended may well have been either the present-day Belen Pass (the Assyrian Gates), the Bahçe Geçidi (Bahçe Pass) – modern Amanian Gates – north of the Belen Pass, or – less likely, because primarily leading south – the pass near the modern 'Pillar of Yunus', all more or less in the region of the modern city of İskenderun. Wesseling believes the error should be attributed to a somnolent copyist.

space between the mountains, some three *stadia* [about 550 m] in length, is altogether provided with a wall with closed gates, to allow a narrow passage. (5) Having passed these safely, thus, Cyrus sent off the remainder of the fleet to return to Ephesus: in fact, it was of no further use to him now that he would be travelling inland. After a march of twenty days he arrived at the town of Thapsacus,[74] which lies on the River Euphrates. (6) Remaining here five days, and after appropriating the force to himself both by abundant supplies and by booty from foraging, he had an assembly convened and disclosed the truth about his campaign. When the soldiers received his words unfavourably, he besought all not to leave him, promising, besides other great rewards, that, when they came to Babylon, he would give every man of them five *minas* of silver [that is, a value of 500 *drachmae* of silver]. The soldiers, accordingly, soaring in their expectations, were convinced to follow him.

Cyrus enters Mesopotamia; deployment of the opposing forces:
(7) When Cyrus crossed the Euphrates with his army, he pressed on without delays, and as soon as he reached the borders of Babylonia he rested his troops.[75]

(14.22.1) King Artaxerxes had learned some time before from Pharnabazus that Cyrus was secretly collecting an army to lead against him, and when he now learned that Cyrus was on the march, he summoned his forces from everywhere to Ecbatana in Media. (2) Since those from both the Indians and some other peoples were delayed because of the remoteness of those regions, Artaxerxes set out to meet Cyrus with the army that had been assembled. He had in all not less than four hundred thousand soldiers, including cavalry, as Ephorus states.[76] (3) When Artaxerxes arrived on the plain of Babylonia, he pitched camp beside the Euphrates, intending to leave his baggage in it. In fact, Artaxerxes had learned that the enemy was not far distant and was apprehensive of their reckless daring. (4) Having ordered, therefore, the digging of a trench sixty feet wide

---

[74] Thapsacus' precise location is unknown and there are several different locations identified as its site. One possibility is a location close to Carchemish, which now lies in Turkey, on its border with Syria. Karkamış and Jarabulus are the closest modern towns in Turkey and Syria respectively. More recently it has been suggested that Thapsacus was renamed Seleucia at the Zeugma, which lies further upstream on the Euphrates than Carchemish. See, for example, Farrell 1961; Engels 1978: 64–5.
[75] A very succinct summary of X. *An.* 1.4.3–6.11.
[76] Numbers given vary hugely: X. *An.* 1.7.11 mentions 1,200,000 men (without 6,000 horsemen); Plu. *Art.* 7.4 gives 900,000 but in *Art.* 13.3 reduces the number to 400,000, referring to Ctesias (F. 22), adding that the number given by Dinon was much higher. Apparently Ephorus here followed Ctesias' lead.

Revolt and Sedition

[c. 17.75 m] and ten deep [c. 3 m],[77] Artaxerxes encircled the camp with the baggage wagons of his train like a wall. Having left behind in the enclosure the baggage and the attendants who were of no use in the battle, he appointed an adequate guard for it, and leading forward his force in person and unencumbered, he advanced to meet the enemy which was near at hand. (5) When Cyrus saw the king's army advancing, he at once drew up his own army in battle order. The right wing, which rested on the Euphrates, was held by infantry composed of Lacedaemonians and some of the mercenaries, all under the command of Clearchus the Lacedaemonian. Helping him in the fight were the cavalry brought from Paphlagonia, more than a thousand. The left wing was held by the troops from both Phrygia and Lydia, moreover about a thousand of the cavalry, under the command of Aridaeus.[78] (6) Cyrus himself had taken a station in the centre of the battle-line, together with the best troops from both the Persians and the other foreigners, about ten thousand strong. Leading the van before him were the best-equipped cavalry, a thousand, armed with breastplates and Greek *machaerae*.[79] (7) Artaxerxes stationed before the whole battle-line scythe-bearing chariots in no small number. As commanders of the wings he assigned Persians, while he himself took his position in the centre with no less than fifty thousand of the elite troops.

Battle of Cunaxa:[80]
(14.23.1) When the forces were about three *stadia* [about 550 m] apart from each other, the Greeks, having struck up the paean, at first advanced at a slow pace. When they were within range of missiles, however, they began to run at great speed.[81] Clearchus the Lacedaemonian had given orders for them to do this. In fact, by not running from a great distance he wanted to keep the fighters fresh in body for the fray, while if they advanced on the run when at close quarters, he believed, it would make the missiles shot by bows and other means fly over. (2) When the troops with Cyrus approached the Great King's army, such a multitude of missiles was hurled upon them

---

[77] Here, too, numbers considerably vary: see Bonnet and Bennett 2002: 171 *ad* p. 34 note 5.
[78] In X. *An.* 1.8.5 this friend and lieutenant of Cyrus is called Ariaeus.
[79] X. *An.* 1.8.6, 25 refers to 600 cavalry. Essentially the *machaera* is a sword with a single, curved cutting edge. Bonnet and Bennett 2002: 35 note 3, though, regard it here as a straight sword. According to X. *Eq.* 12.11 it was, together with two light javelins, the offensive weapon of choice for the horseman.
[80] For the name see Plu. *Art.* 8.2; also X. *An.* 1.10.5–19.
[81] A traditional manoeuvre: see also Hdt. 6.112.1–3.

as was likely to be discharged from a host composed of four hundred thousand. Nevertheless, having fought for only a very short time with javelins, they engaged hand to hand for the remainder of the fight. (3) The Lacedaemonians and the rest of the mercenaries from the very first contact struck terror into the opposing foreigners both by the splendour of their arms and by their skills. (4) These foreign forces were, in fact, protected by small shields, their divisions mostly being equipped with light arms, moreover inexperienced in the perils of war. The Greeks, however, having been in constant battle by reason of the length of the Peloponnesian War, were far superior in experience.[82] Thus, having straight away put their opponents to flight, they pursued them and killed many of the enemy. (5) It so happened that both contenders for the kingship were positioned in the centre of the lines.[83] Therefore, becoming aware of this fact, they dashed against each other, eagerly wanting to decide the battle by their own hands. Indeed, Fate, as it appears, brought the rivalry of the brothers over the throne to culmination in single combat as if in true imitation of that ancient rash struggle between Eteocles and Polynices, resonating in tragedy.[84] (6) Acting first, Cyrus hurled his javelin from a distance and, hitting the Great King, brought him to the ground. The latter's attendants, quickly recovering him, carried him out of the battle. Tissaphernes, a Persian, now succeeding to the supreme command of the Great King, both rallied the troops and himself fought in splendid fashion. Fighting back against the reverse caused by the wounding of the Great King and turning up everywhere with his elite troops, he killed many of the opponents, so that his presence was conspicuous from afar. (7) Cyrus, elated by the success of his forces, rushed boldly into the midst of the enemy and at first killed many, setting no bounds to his daring. Later, though, fighting too imprudently, being struck by a passing Persian, he fell mortally wounded.[85] Upon his death the Great King's soldiers gained confidence for the battle and in the end, by both number and daring, wore down their opponents.

(14.24.1) On the other wing Aridaeus, the satrap of Cyrus to whom the command had been entrusted, at first withstood the enemy charge

---

[82] Whether this really was the case may well be a matter of contention, as the majority of the Greek hoplites had already been stationed in Asia Minor for quite some time: see, for example, Stronk 1995: 16(1).

[83] In the words of Diodorus it appears a coincidence that both Cyrus and Artaxerxes II were in the centre: in fact, X. *An.* 1.8.22 describes it as the customary position of the commander-in-chief in Persian armies.

[84] Notably in the so-called Theban cycle: see also Bonnet and Bennett 2002: 36 note 2.

[85] For the duel between Artaxerxes II and Cyrus the Younger: X. *An.* 1.8.26–7; Plu. *Art.* 10–11.

stoutly. Later, being encircled by the far-extended line of the enemy and having learned of Cyrus' death, he fled with his own soldiers to one of his stations, which had a suitable place of refuge.[86] (2) When Clearchus observed that both the centre and the other parts of his allies had been routed, he stopped his pursuit, and having called back the soldiers, set them in order. He feared, indeed, that if the entire force of Artaxerxes should turn against the Greeks, they would be surrounded and all would be killed. (3) After the Great King's troops had put their opponents to flight, they first plundered Cyrus' baggage train. Next, when night had already set in, having gathered, they attacked the Greeks. When these met the attack valiantly, the Persians withstood them only a short while, but after a little turned in flight, having been overcome by the Greeks' deeds of valour and skills. (4) After the troops of Clearchus had killed many of the foreigners, when it was already night, retracing their steps, they set up a trophy, and about the second watch got safe to their camp.[87]

Aftermath of the Battle of Cunaxa:
(5) After the battle had had such an end, more than fifteen thousand of the army of the Great King were killed,[88] most of whom both Lacedaemonians and mercenaries under the command of Clearchus killed. (6) On the other side some three thousand of Cyrus' soldiers fell. Of the Greeks they say that no one was killed, though a few were wounded. (7) When the night was past, Aridaeus, who had fled to the stopping-place, dispatched messengers to Clearchus, urging him to lead his soldiers to him and to make a safe return together to the regions on the sea. In fact, now that Cyrus had been killed and the king's forces had the upper hand, deep concern had seized those who had dared to take the field to relieve Artaxerxes' kingship.
(14.25.1) After Clearchus had called together both the commanders and captains, he conferred with them on the present situation. While they were discussing it, ambassadors arrived from the Great King, the chief of whom was a Greek, Phalynus by name,[89] a Zacynthian

---

[86] X. *An.* 1.9.31, 2.1.3; also below, 14.24.7.
[87] Regarding the night, three and five watches have been mentioned in Greek literature (*LSJ* s.v. 'φυλακή 4'). Assuming night watches usually ran from c. 6 p.m. till c. 6 a.m., the troops may have returned to camp somewhere between 8.30 p.m. and 10.00 p.m. For the whole episode see also X. *An.* 1.10.5–19.
[88] The number of dead varies: Plu. *Art.* 13.4 quotes Ctesias (F. 22), stating that reports were made to the Great King that from his army 9,000 had been killed, but that it seemed to Ctesias there were no fewer than 20,000. Diodorus gives here an average number of dead.
[89] Xenophon calls him Phalinus (see, for example, X. *An.* 2.1.7), a form one also encounters in MS F of the *Bibliotheca*; Plutarch mentions him as Phallynos: see Plu. *Art.* 13.5.

by origin. Having been introduced to the council they said: 'King Artaxerxes says: Since I have been victorious, killing Cyrus, surrender your arms, come to my doors, and seek how you may appease me and gain favour.'[90] (2) To these words each of the commanders gave a reply similar to that of Leonides [sic!] at the time, when he was guarding the Pass of Thermopylae, that Xerxes sent messengers ordering him to lay down his arms. (3) Indeed, Leonides at that time instructed them to report to the king: 'We believe that if we become friends of Xerxes, we shall be better allies if we keep our arms, and if we are forced to make war against him, we shall fight better if we keep them.'[91] (4) After Clearchus had replied something close to these words, Proxenus the Theban said: 'Now we have lost nearly everything, and all that is left to us is both our *aretē* and our arms. We believe, therefore, that if we guard our arms, our *aretē* also will be useful to us, but if we give them up, then not even *aretē* will be of any help to us.' Therefore he ordered them to say to the Great King, 'If he is plotting some evil against us, with our arms we will fight him for his own possessions.'[92] (5) It is said that Sophilus, one of the commanders, also said that he was surprised at the words of the king. 'Indeed, if he believes that he is stronger than the Greeks, he should, having come with his force, take our arms. If he wishes to use persuasion, he should say what favour of equal worth he will grant us in exchange.' (6) After these speakers Socrates the Achaean said that the Great King certainly behaved surprisingly towards them. 'What he wishes to take from us, he requires at once, while what he will grant us in return, he commands us to request of him at a later time. Summarising, if in ignorance, he orders the victors to obey his command as though we were defeated, he should learn to which of us belongs the victory by showing up with his numerous host. However, if, knowing well enough that we are the victors, he is deceiving us, how shall we trust his later promises?' (7) After the messengers had received these replies, they departed. Clearchus and his men, though, marched to the stopping-place where the troops who had escaped the battle [the troops under Aridaeus] had retired to. When the entire force had gathered in the same place, they debated together how they should make their way back to the sea and by what route.

---

[90] One of the characteristics of *koinē* Greek is that, as here, αὐτοῦ and αὐτὸν are used as *pronomina reflectiva* of the first person.
[91] Above, 11.5.5.
[92] Though the MSS read here τῶν ἀγαθῶν τῶν κοινῶν, the rendering of the speech in X. *An.* 2.1.12: τῶν ὑμετέρων ἀγαθῶν) suggests that Bezzel's emendation, τῶν ἀγαθῶν τῶν ἐκείνου, is here feasible: also because of the implicit threat it contains, I find this emendation attractive.

(8) They decided that they should not return by the same way they had come. In fact, much of it was wasteland, where they could not expect provisions to be available, while a hostile army was on their heels.[93] They resolved, therefore, to make for Paphlagonia, and set out for Paphlagonia with the army,[94] proceeding at a leisurely pace to be able to gather provisions as they marched.

The Greeks retreat; Artaxerxes awards prizes:
(14.26.1) As the Great King, recovering from his wound, learned that his opponents were withdrawing, believing they were fleeing, he set out in haste after them with his force. (2) As soon as he had overtaken them because of their slow progress, he made camp nearby for the moment, since it was night. When day came, as the Greeks were deploying their army for battle, having sent messengers to them, he made for the time being a truce of three days. (3) During these they agreed, the Great King that he would assure that his territory was friendly, that he would provide them with guides for their journey to the sea, and would supply them with a market to buy provisions on the way; the mercenaries under Clearchus and all the troops under Aridaeus, that they would pass through his territory without doing any injury.[95] (4) After this they started on their journey, but the king led his force to Babylon. There, according fitting honours to each of those who had shown courage during the battle in agreement with his merit, he judged Tissaphernes to have been the bravest of all.[96] Honouring him, therefore, with rich gifts, he gave him his own daughter in marriage, and henceforth continued to hold him as his most trusted companion. He also gave him the command over the satrapies by the sea which Cyrus had held. (5) Because Tissaphernes saw that the king was angered at the Greeks, he promised him that he would destroy them all, if the king would give him forces and come to terms with Aridaeus.[97] In fact, he believed the Greeks would be betrayed by him in the course of the march. The Great King, readily

---

[93] The 'market' had been a structural weakness in Cyrus' plans from the beginning: see X. *An.* 1.5.5–6, 2.2.11 (words of Ariaeus).
[94] That is, to move northward along the Tigris, through Armenia, to the Black Sea.
[95] Diodorus is here very succinct: see X. *An.* 2.3.1–16, 17–29.
[96] For rewards and punishments see Plu. *Art.* 14 (who does not mention the name of Tissaphernes here). X. *An.* 2.3.17–19 presents a slightly different picture. As I have expressed previously (Stronk 2010: 188), I believe it feasible that Ctesias' account, whether or not through Ephorus, was Diodorus' main source here, as it would be later for Plutarch (see Ctes. *Pers.* FF. 26 and *26a [S] = Stronk 2010: 372–9).
[97] After this passage, Aridaeus disappears from Diodorus' account; in X. *An.* 2.6.35–40 we read that he did betray the Greeks.

accepting this suggestion, allowed him to select from his entire army as many of the best troops as he chose. <...> (Tissaphernes proposed to Clearchus and the) <...>⁹⁸ (6) rest of the commanders to come to him and hear face to face what he had to say. Therefore, together with Clearchus nearly all the commanders and some twenty captains went to Tissaphernes.⁹⁹ About two hundred of the common soldiers, who wanted to go to the market, accompanied them.

Several Greek commanders are taken captive by Tissaphernes:
(7) Tissaphernes invited the commanders into his tent and the captains waited at the entrance. After a little time, after a red flag had been raised from Tissaphernes' tent, he seized the commanders within; some killed the captains as they had been ordered to, after having attacked them, and others killed the soldiers who had come to the market.¹⁰⁰ Of the last, one made his escape to his camp and revealed the catastrophe.¹⁰¹

(14.27.1) When the soldiers learned what had taken place, they were panic-stricken at the moment itself and all rushed to arms in great disorder, since there was no one to command them. Afterwards, because no one disturbed them, they elected several commanders but entrusted the supreme command to one, namely Chirisophus the Lacedaemonian.¹⁰² (2) The commanders, deploying the army for the march on the route they thought best, led forth towards Paphlagonia. Tissaphernes sent the commanders in chains to Artaxerxes. The latter executed the others but spared Menon alone. In fact, Artaxerxes believed that Menon alone, having fallen out with his fellow commanders,¹⁰³ would betray the Greeks.

---

⁹⁸ About one line of text appears to be missing from the MSS. X. *An.* 2.4.1–5.25 presents us with a detailed picture of the events.
⁹⁹ See for the names of the commanders X. *An.* 2.5.31.
¹⁰⁰ X. *An.* 2.5.32 also mentions a prearranged signal, without stating what it was. Sherylee Bassett argues that Tissaphernes set out from the beginning to destroy the Greek army, but that the Greeks (notably Chirisophus and some of his men) played into his hands by foraging outside the 'market', thereby violating the oaths Tissaphernes and the Greeks had sworn in concluding the agreement: Bassett 2002: 460.
¹⁰¹ See X. *An.* 2.5.33, who calls him Nicarchus, an Arcadian.
¹⁰² See X. *An.* 3.1.15–25, 32–47.
¹⁰³ The MSS read here συμμάχους, 'allies', but Vogel suggests reading συνάρχοντας, 'fellow commanders': in view of the situation as described by Xenophon (for example X. *An.* 2.5.28), I find this a feasible suggestion and have adopted it. Xenophon's picture of Menon is not flattering at all: X. *An.* 2.6.29. See also Ath. 11.505AB; Plu. *Art* 18.1–5; it appears that Menon's relations with the Great King were already established. In one of Plato's dialogues Socrates remarks on Menon: χρυσίον δὲ δὴ καὶ ἀργύριον πορίζεσθαι ἀρετή ἐστιν, ὥς φησι Μένων ὁ τοῦ μεγάλου βασιλέως πατρικὸς ξένος ('to procure gold and silver is an *aretē*, according to Menon, the ancestral guest-friend of the Great King': Pl. *Men.* 78D).

The Greeks seem to escape:
(3) Tissaphernes, following with his army, clung to the Greeks, but he did not dare to meet them face to face in battle, being afraid of the courage and recklessness of desperate men. Although harrying them in convenient places, he was unable to do them any great harm: he followed them, causing slight difficulties, until the country of the people known as the Carduchi.[104] (4) Because Tissaphernes was unable to accomplish anything more, he set out with his army for Ionia. The Greeks went through the mountains of the Carduchi for seven days,[105] suffering greatly at the hands of the natives, who were both warlike and well acquainted with the region. (5) These were enemies of the Great King, free, and practised in the arts of war, and especially trained to hurl the largest stones they could with slings and to use enormous arrows, by which they killed many and seriously injured not a few, wounding the Greeks from high positions. (6) In fact, the missiles were more than two cubits long [c. 0.9 m] and pierced both the shields and breastplates, so that no armour could withstand their force. They say that they used such large arrows that the Greeks, having wound thongs about the missiles shot at them, used them as javelins to hurl back. (7) Having thus traversed with difficulty the country we have mentioned, they arrived at the River Centrites.[106] Crossing this river they entered Armenia. Of this region Tiribazus was the satrap. Having concluded a truce with him, they passed through the region as friends.[107]

[[From 14.28.1 to 14.31.5 Diodorus continues with the retreat of the 'Ten Thousand'. Since he does not provide data relating to Persian history proper in these paragraphs, I have left them out of this account.]]

S. 86:
14.35.1–37.4:

Tissaphernes returns to Asia Minor:
(14.35.1) At the close of this year, Laches was *archon* in Athens [400/399] and in Rome the highest authority was administered by

---
[104] For the Carduchi, allegedly a Median people, see: Stronk, 'Sophainetos Stymphalikos (109)' F 1.
[105] See X. *An.* 3.5.16.
[106] A tributary of the Tigris, bordering the lands of the Carduchi and the Armenians.
[107] In fact not quite so friendly: see X. *An.* 4.4.17 *sqq*.

military tribunes: Manius Claudius, Marcus Quinctius, Lucius Julius, Marcus Furius, and Lucius Valerius.[108] The ninety-fifth Olympiad was held, in which Minos of Athens won the *stadium* race. (2) In these times Artaxerxes, the king of Asia, after he had been victorious over Cyrus, had dispatched Tissaphernes[109] to take control over all the satrapies which bordered on the Sea. Therefore, the satraps, *poleis*, and towns which had allied themselves with Cyrus were in great anxiety whether they would be punished for their offences against the Great King. (3) All the other satraps, thus, having sent ambassadors to Tissaphernes, paid court to him and arranged their affairs to suit him, as much as was in their power. Tamos, though, the most powerful among them and in command of Ionia, embarked in the *triereis* with his possessions and all his sons except one, whose name was Glos,[110] who some time later became commander of the royal forces. (4) Tamos then, being wary of Tissaphernes, sailed off with his fleet to Egypt and fled to Psammeticus, the king of the Egyptians, a descendant of Psammeticus.[111] Because of a favour he had done to Psammeticus in the past,[112] Tamos believed that he would find in him

---

[108] Liv. 5.1 gives the names as M'. Aemilius Mamercus, L. Valerius Potitus, Ap. Claudius Crassus, M. Quinctilius Varus, L. Iulius Iulus, M. Postumius, M. Furius Camillus, and M. Postumius Albinus. More or less the same names are presented by Broughton 1951: 81–2. He adds that Mamercus also might be Mamercinus, that Ap. Claudius' full cognomen was Crassus Inregilensis, that the cognomen of L. Iulius was Iullus, and that the full cognomen of M. Postumius Albinus was Albinus Regillensis. The last functionaries are indicated by Broughton with a question mark. M. Postumius Albinus Regillensis was, by the way, also the censor for this year. Diodorus is here still four years ahead of the Varronian chronology, 403 vc.

[109] All manuscripts read Pharnabazus here, and Pharnabazus and Tissaphernes have also been confused prior to this. In the light of actual events I shall henceforth (after Wesseling), whenever Tissaphernes is intended, adopt his name in my translation. Though this detracts, admittedly, from the picture drawn in the manuscripts of the *Bibliotheca*, it provides a better picture of *ta genomena*.

[110] Though all MSS read Γάου, Wesseling rightly emended this into Γλοῦ: see also Bonnet and Bennett 2002: 52 note 4 and *apparatus*, line 26.

[111] Ruzicka 2012: 38 believes there may have been some dealings between Cyrus the Younger and Amyrtaeus, a ruler in the Egyptian Delta (possibly a grandson of the Amyrtaeus who had allied with Inarus and who was mentioned as such in Th. 1.110.2: see above, note 7; see Ruzicka 2012: 37), who had revolted against the Persians in 406/5. The latter Psammeticus is Psammeticus or Psamtek I (664–610), founder of the 26th or Saïte dynasty. The former was, if he lived at all, to the best of my knowledge, not a king of Egypt: in the times of the events described here, Egypt was ruled by King Amyrtaeus (for this king, see Pasek 2016 and Perdu 2010: 153–7), who ruled from 404 to 398 (28th dynasty) and was defeated and succeeded by King Nepherites I (398–393), founder of the 29th dynasty, who was in his turn succeeded by a King Psammuthis, who ruled less than a year. It may, therefore, be surmised that Diodorus (or his sources) may have mixed up here some names, dates, and relationships, though Ruzicka 2012: 38 and note 11 points to the possibility that Amyrtaeus took the name Psammeticus as a throne name. So far, to the best of my knowledge, this has not yet been established in the archaeological and historical evidence.

[112] Possibly as an intermediary between Amyrtaeus and Cyrus the Younger. As an Egyptian by birth Tamos would have been the man for such a role. See Ruzicka 2012: 38–9. It is noteworthy that Diodorus remains silent regarding the Persian army under Abrocomas, intended to crush Amyrtaeus' revolt.

Revolt and Sedition   225

a haven, as it were, from the perils of the Great King. (5) Psammeticus, however, completely ignoring both the favour and the sacred duty due to suppliants, put his suppliant and friend to the sword, together with his children, in order to become master of both his possessions and his fleet. (6) When the Greek *poleis* of Asia Minor learned that Tissaphernes was on his way to the coast, being concerned for their fate, they dispatched ambassadors to the Lacedaemonians, begging them not to allow them to be laid waste by the Persians. Having promised to help them, the Lacedaemonians sent ambassadors to Tissaphernes to ask him not to commit aggression against the Greek *poleis*. (7) Tissaphernes, however, advancing with his force against the *polis* of the Cymeans first, both plundered its entire territory and got possession of many captives. Having afterwards enclosed the *polis* proper by siege, he released the captives for a heavy ransom and raised the siege when winter approached, because he was unable to capture the *polis*.

The Lacedaemonians react:
(14.36.1) Having appointed Thibron as commander of the war against the Great King, the Lacedaemonians gave him a thousand soldiers from their citizens,[113] and ordered him to enlist as many troops from their allies as would seem fit to him. (2) Having gone to Corinth and having summoned to that city soldiers from the allies, Thibron set sail for Ephesus with not more than five thousand troops.[114] Having enrolled there some two thousand soldiers both from their own *poleis* [which had appealed to Sparta] and the other ones, he marched forth with a total of over seven thousand. Having advanced about one hundred and twenty *stadia* [about 22 km], he came to Magnesia,[115] which was under the government of Tissaphernes. After taking this *polis* at the first assault and advancing speedily to Tralles in Ionia, he began to lay siege to the *polis*. Because he was unable to achieve any success, though, due to its strength, he returned to Magnesia. (3) Because this *polis* was without walls, and

---

[113] X. *HG* 3.1.4 reports that the Lacedaemonian contingent consisted of *neodamodeis*, emancipated Helots.
[114] See X. *HG* 3.1.4.
[115] The distance covered (about 22 km) clearly suggests that the Magnesia intended was Magnesia ad Maeandrum and not Magnesia ad Sipylum (situated to the north-east of Smyrna). This account appears to contradict Xenophon's, who states that Thibron undertook no significant action before he was joined by the remaining soldiers of the 'Ten Thousand' (see X. *HG* 3.1.5). Of Tralles it is sometimes written that it was situated in Ionia (see, for example, Str. 14.1.42/648–9), sometimes that it was in Caria (see, for example, X. *HG* 3.2.19; 19.75.5). This *polis* lies about 140 *stadia* (25 km) from Magnesia.

therefore afraid that at his departure Tissaphernes would master it, Thibron transferred it to a neighbouring hill, which men call Thorax. He himself, however, invading the enemy territory, glutted his soldiers with booty of every kind. Being on his guard, he withdrew to Ephesus when Tissaphernes arrived with strong cavalry.

(14.37.1) About this same time [late 400] some of those who had been on expedition with Cyrus and had got back safe to Greece [the Greek world, including the *poleis* in Asia Minor] went off to their own home towns,[116] but the larger part of them, being about five thousand in number, accustomed to live a soldier's life, chose Xenophon as their commander [as a kind of *condottiere* of a mercenary army].[117] (2) ... (3) ... (4) After this [an expedition against Salmydessos in (European) Thrace during the winter of 400/399, hinted at in the previous paragraphs], when Thibron sent for the soldiers announcing that he would give them pay, they withdrew to him and with the Lacedaemonians started to make war against the Persians.[118]

S. 87:
14.38.1–3:

The Lacedaemonians replace Thibron with Dercylidas:
(14.38.1) At the end of the year in Athens Aristocrates entered the office of *archon* [399/8] and in Rome the highest authority was taken over by six military tribunes, Gaius Servilius, Lucius Verginius, Quintus Sulpicius, Aulus Mutilius, and Manius Sergius.[119] (2) After these magistrates had entered office, the Lacedaemonians, learning that Thibron was conducting the war badly,[120] dispatched Dercylidas as commander to Asia Minor. Having taken over the force, he advanced against the *poleis* in the Troad. (3) Acting thus, he took Hamaxitus, Colonae, and Arisba at the first assault. Afterwards he took possession of Ilium, Cerbenia, and all the rest of the *poleis* of the Troad, some by craft, the others by force. After this he concluded an armistice of eight months with Pharnabazus and advanced against

---

[116] See X. *An.* 7.2.3: as indicated, 'in Greece' should not be taken too literally.
[117] See Stronk 1995: *passim*. Though Diodorus used Xenophon's *Anabasis* as one of his sources for the parts of the *Bibliotheca* on the march of Cyrus the Younger and the retreat of the Greeks, he mentions Xenophon here for the first time.
[118] In the spring of 399: see Stronk 1995: 250 (1), 251–3 (5); see also Stronk 1990/1: 128–30.
[119] There are only five names and the MSS vary greatly. Liv. 5.8 lists Gaius Servilius Ahala, Quintus Servilius, Lucius Verginius, Quintus Sulpicius, Aulus Manlius, and Manius Sergius. Broughton 1951: 82–3 lists for 402 vc C. Servilius Ahala, Q. Servilius Fidenas, L. Verginius Tricostus Esquilinus, Q. Sulpucius Camerinus Cornutus, A. Manlius Vulso Capitolinus, and M'. Sergius Fidenas. Diodorus is still four years ahead of the Varronian chronology.
[120] See X. *HG* 3.1.8.

the Thracians who were dwelling at that time in Bithynia [in Asia Minor]. ...

S. 88:
14.39.1–6:

Pharnabazus takes action and goes to the king:
(14.39.1) After the truce had been made with the Lacedaemonians, Pharnabazus went inland to the Great King and convinced him to prepare a fleet and to appoint Conon the Athenian as its admiral. Conon was, indeed, experienced in military operations and especially in combat with the Lacedaemonians. Although he excelled in warfare, he was at the time in Cyprus at the court of King Evagoras.[121] After he had persuaded the Great King, Pharnabazus, receiving five hundred talents of silver [c. 13,000 kg],[122] prepared to fit out a fleet. (2) Having thus sailed across to Cyprus, he ordered the kings there[123] to prepare one hundred *triereis*. Having discussed the command of the fleet with Conon, he appointed him commander at sea, conjuring up great hopes for Conon in the name of the Great King. (3) At the same time hoping to go and recover the leadership in Greece for his native *polis*, if the Lacedaemonians were subdued in war, and that he would himself win great renown as well, Conon accepted the command. (4) Even before the entire fleet had been made ready, he sailed across to Cilicia with the forty ships that were at hand and there began preparations for the war.[124] Having gathered soldiers from their own satrapies, Pharnabazus and Tissaphernes marched out, making their way towards Ephesus, because their enemy had their force there. (5) Twenty thousand infantry and ten thousand cavalry accompanied them.[125] When he heard of the approach of the Persians, Dercylidas, the commander of the Lacedaemonians, led out his force, having in all not more than seven thousand men. (6) When, though, the armies had got near each other, they concluded a truce

---

[121] After the Athenian defeat at Aegospotami in 405/4, Conon fled to Evagoras, the king of Salamis on Cyprus, the most important city in Cyprus at that moment: X. *HG* 2.1.29.

[122] Assuming Diodorus used here the Attic talent of 25.992 kg.

[123] On Cyprus there resided nine kings. 'In Cyprus were nine important cities; beside them existed small towns which were dependent on the nine cities. Each of these cities was ruled by a king, but they were, all of them, subject to the king of the Persians' (16.43.4; see also Plin. *Nat.* 5.35.129).

[124] In Xenophon's account of this period, Conon is not referred to until the Battle of Cnidus in 394: X. *HG* 4.3.11 *sqq*.

[125] Proportionately a huge number of cavalry, as X. *HG* 2.2.15 also underlines: τὸ ἱππικὸν μάλα πολύ ('the cavalry was very large'). Bonnet and Bennett 2002: 179 *ad* p. 57 note 4 state that, in Greece, 10 per cent of cavalry was a common rate in armies.

and marked out a period, during which Pharnabazus should send word to the Great King regarding a treaty, if he was willing to end the war, but Dercylidas should explain these matters to the Spartans. In such manner, thus, these commanders disbanded the armies.[126]

S. 89:
14.79.1–80.8:

Agesilaus prepares to take command of the troops in Asia Minor:
(14.79.1) In Greece, because the Lacedaemonians foresaw the size of their war with the Persians, they appointed [in 396/5] one of their two kings, Agesilaus, commander of the war. After he had levied six thousand soldiers and constituted a council of thirty of his foremost fellow citizens, he transported the force from Aulis to Ephesus.[127] (2) Having enlisted four thousand soldiers here, he led his army, which numbered ten thousand infantry and four hundred cavalry, into the open field. They were also accompanied by an equally numerous throng of low fellows[128] attracted by the hope of plunder. (3) While traversing the plain of the Cayster,[129] he laid waste the territory held by the Persians until he arrived at Cyme. Operating from there, during the larger part of the summer, he ravaged Phrygia and neighbouring territory.[130] Having sated his force with pillage, he returned in the course of the autumn to Ephesus. (4) While these

---

[126] In spite of all feints by the Persian leaders, the main interest of Artaxerxes II was to secure control of the eastern Mediterranean basin and 'the middle territory', that is, Phoenicia and Palestine. Nevertheless, western Anatolia was too important for the Persians not to take care of. It had to be secure before Artaxerxes could focus on the *reconquista* of Egypt. See also Ruzicka 2012: 43–8.

[127] As a born-again Agamemnon, in a new 'Trojan War': Plu. *Ages.* 6.4–6; X. *HG* 3.4.3, 5.5. The reading constitutes some problems: MSS PAH read Ἀσίας ('from Asia', which hardly makes any sense in the context); other MSS read Εὐρώπης ('from Europe', which is slightly better, but rather general); Bonnet and Bennett suggest Εὐβοίας ('from Euboea', which is very acceptable and based upon X. *HG* 3.1.4: see Bonnet and Bennett 2002: 199 *ad* p. 106 note 3); Αὐλίδος ('from Aulis'), finally, is suggested by Vogel: in a context in which the contest between Greeks and Persians is/was frequently seen as a kind of continuation of the Trojan War, I prefer this solution.

[128] For this meaning of ἀγοραῖος, see Ar. *Ra.* 1015; Pl. *Prt.* 347C; Thphr. *Char.* 6.2; see also LSJ *s.v.* ἀγοραῖος II.

[129] Modern Küçük Menderes, 'Little Meander'. The Cayster, a relatively short river (about 115 km), generally flows westward from modern Beydağ and empties into the Aegean near the modern town of Selçuk. The *polis* of Ephesus (now some 5 km from the coast) was once the main port on the Cayster. Agesilaus therefore basically went northward from Ephesus, crossing part of the plain through which the river flows, to Cyme, which is situated just north of the River Hermus, modern Gediz Nehri, a river that flows (about 100 km to its north) almost parallel to the Cayster.

[130] See X. *HG* 3.4.27, more or less confirming that (the region of) Cyme was used as Agesilaus' base. It appears that Ephorus of Cyme was Diodorus' source here. Diodorus is here, again, very succinct: see Bonnet and Bennett 2002: 200 *ad* p. 106 note 5.

events were taking place, the Lacedaemonians dispatched ambassadors to Nephereus,[131] the king of Egypt, regarding an alliance. In place of the aid requested, he made the Spartans a gift of equipment of one hundred *triereis* and five hundred thousand units of grain.[132] Pharax, the *navarch* of the Lacedaemonians, having left Rhodes with one hundred and twenty ships, sailed down to Sasanda in Caria, a citadel one hundred and fifty *stadia* [about 28 km] from Caunus. (5) Operating from there he laid siege to Caunus and blockaded Conon, the commander of the royal fleet, who lay at Caunus with forty ships. When Artaphernes and Pharnabazus came with a strong force to help the Caunians, though, Pharax lifted the siege and sailed off to Rhodes with the entire fleet. (6) After this Conon, having gathered eighty *triereis*, sailed to the Chersonesus. The Rhodians, however, having expelled the Peloponnesian fleet, revolted from the Lacedaemonians and received Conon, together with his entire fleet, into their *polis*. (7) The Lacedaemonians, accompanying the gift of grain from Egypt and unaware of the defection of the Rhodians, approached the island in full confidence. The Rhodians and Conon, the Persian admiral, though, putting the ships in to the harbours, stocked the *polis* with grain. (8) There also came to Conon ninety *triereis*, ten of them from Cilicia and eighty from Phoenicia, of which the lord of the Sidonians had the command.[133]

(14.80.1) After this Agesilaus, leading out his army into the plain of the Cayster and the country around the Sipylus,[134] ravaged the possessions of the inhabitants. Tissaphernes, having gathered ten thousand cavalry and fifty thousand infantry, followed close on the Lacedaemonians and cut down any who became separated from the main body while plundering. Having deployed his soldiers in a square, Agesilaus clung to the foothills of the Sipylus, awaiting a favourable opportunity to attack the enemy. (2) Assailing the countryside as far as Sardis, he ravaged both the orchards and Tissaphernes' formal garden, artistically laid out at great expense with plants and all other things that contribute to luxury {τρυφή} and the enjoyment in peace of good things. Next, having turned back, when he was midway between Sardis and Thybarnae, he dispatched

---

[131] King Nepherites, founder of the 29th dynasty. See also above, note 111.
[132] Diodorus remains silent on the nature of the unit intended. The usual unit in such situations is the *medimnos*, c. 52.4 litres: in that case the Spartans would have received the staggering amount of c. 26,000,000 litres of grain.
[133] See also *Hell.Oxy.* 9.2. This event can be dated to late 396/early 395. See also Ruzicka 2012: 51 and note 3.
[134] Modern Mt Spil (Spil Daği), c. 1,500 m high, near the modern city of Manisa in the heartland of the Lydians.

the Spartan Xenocles by night, with fourteen hundred soldiers, to a thickly wooded place to set an ambush for the Persians. (3) He himself started to move forward at daybreak with his army. When he had passed the place of ambush while the Persians, advancing without battle order, harassed his rearguard, to their surprise he suddenly turned about on the Persians. After a sharp battle had started, the signal was raised to the soldiers in ambush; these, chanting the paean, charged the enemy. The Persians, seeing they were caught in the middle, were struck with dismay and turned at once in flight. (4) Pursuing them for some distance, Agesilaus' men killed over six thousand, gathered a great multitude of prisoners, and pillaged their camp, stored with many riches. (5) Astounded by the daring of the Lacedaemonians, Tissaphernes withdrew from the battle to Sardis. Agesilaus was about to attack the satrapies farther inland, but led his force back to the sea when he could not obtain favourable omens from the sacrifices.[135] (6) Having learned of the defeats and being alarmed by the war with the Greeks, Artaxerxes, the king of Asia, was angry at Tissaphernes. In fact, he considered him to be the person responsible for the war. Artaxerxes had, moreover, also been asked by his mother, Parysatis, to grant her revenge upon Tissaphernes: she bore immense hatred against him, indeed, for denouncing her son Cyrus, when he was about to make his expedition against his brother.[136] (7) Having thus appointed Tithraustes commander, he ordered him to arrest Tissaphernes and sent letters to the *poleis* and the satraps that all should do for him whatever he commanded. (8) Upon arrival at Colossae in Phrygia, Tithraustes, with the aid of Ariaeus, a satrap,[137] arrested Tissaphernes while the latter was bathing and, having cut off his head, sent it to the Great King. Tithraustes himself, having persuaded Agesilaus to enter into negotiations, concluded a truce of six months.[138]

---

[135] For different accounts of the Battle of Sardis: X. *HG* 3.4.21–4; *Hell.Oxy.* 6.1–4; the observation of the offerings is reminiscent of Pausanias at Plataea (Hdt. 9.61–2), Dercylidas (X. *HG* 3.1.17–19), and Xenophon at Calpes Limen (X. *An.* 6.4.9, 13–16, 19–20). At Calpes Limen, Neon ignored the result of the sacrifices and suffered terrible losses.

[136] Parysatis was the widow of King Darius II Ochus. Bonnet and Bennett 2002: 109 note 2 adduce still another cause for Parysatis' hatred towards Tissaphernes, he being the brother of Terituchmes (their father being Idernes [Hydarnes]), the satrap of Armenia: see Schmitt 2012: *ad* 3), who had attempted to kill Amestris, a daughter of Parysatis (see Ctes. *Pers.* F. 15(55–6)). Lewis 1977: 84 notes 13–14, seriously doubts this connection.

[137] Perhaps the same man who (as Arhidaeus) joined Cyrus the Younger in his expedition: see above.

[138] According to Isoc. *Paneg.* 153, the truce was concluded for eight months.

S. 90:
14.81.4–6:

Conon meets with Artaxerxes II:
(14.81.4) Conon, the *navarch* of the Persians, put the Athenians Hieronymus and Nicophemus[139] in charge of the fleet, but he himself, eager to meet with the Great King, sailed along the coast of Cilicia. Having travelled from there to Thapsacus in Syria, he then sailed down the River Euphrates to Babylon. (5) Meeting the king there, he promised that he would destroy the Lacedaemonians at sea, if the king was willing to provide him with money and other supplies, according to his plan. (6) After approving Conon's plans and honouring him with rich gifts, Artaxerxes appointed a paymaster[140] who should supply such amount of funds as Conon might order. He also gave him authority to take as his co-leader for the war whichever Persian he might choose. Having selected the satrap Pharnabazus, Conon returned to the sea, having arranged everything according to his intentions.

S. 91:
14.83.1–85.4:

The Lacedaemonians call back Agesilaus:
(14.83.1) When they saw [in 395/4] that the greatest of the *poleis* of Greece were uniting against them, the Lacedaemonians voted to summon both Agesilaus and his army from Asia Minor. ... (2) ... (3) After Agesilaus had brought over his army from Asia Minor to Europe, he was victorious in battle over certain Thracians who at first opposed him with a large force, and he killed the majority of the Thracians.[141] Then he made his way through Macedonia, passing through the same region as Xerxes did when he made his campaign against the Greeks.

While Conon proceeds:
(4) ... Conon the Athenian and Pharnabazus were in command of the royal fleet and stayed at Loryma on the Chersonesus[142] with

---

[139] Though all MSS read Νικόδημον ('Nicodemus'), his correct name is given in X. *HG* 4.8.8; Lys. 19.7; *Hell.Oxy.* 10.1; see also Kirchner *PA*, 11066. Conon's journey to the Great King was necessary because his war chest had been drained due to a mutiny described in *Hell. Oxy.* 14–15; Isoc. *Paneg.* 142; Just. 6.2.11.
[140] Possibly Tiribazus, as Ruzicka suggests: Ruzicka 2012: 61. For Tiribazus, see further below.
[141] According to Plu. *Ages.* 16.1, these Thracians were of the tribe of the Trallians.
[142] The *polis* was situated on the Carian coast, opposite the island of Rhodes.

more than ninety *triereis*. (5) Learning that the enemy fleet was at Cnidus, they prepared as necessary for battle. Pisander [the half-brother of Agesilaus],[143] the admiral of the Lacedaemonians, set out from Cnidus with eighty-five *triereis* and put in at Physcus of the Chersonesus [near modern Marmaris, in fact, calculating from Cnidus, past Loryma].[144] (6) Having set out from there, he fell in with the fleet of the king, and engaging the ships under the command of Conon, he won the advantage over them. When the Persians[145] came, however, to help out with their *triereis* in close formation and seeing that all his allies fled to the land, Pisander turned his own ship against them, believing ignoble flight to be disgraceful and unworthy of Sparta. (7) After fighting brilliantly and killing many of the enemy, he was killed in the end, fighting in a manner worthy of his native *polis*. Conon's men, pursuing the Lacedaemonians as far as the land, made themselves master of fifty of their *triereis*. Most of the crews, having leapt overboard, escaped by land, but they captured about five hundred men. The rest of the *triereis* found safety at Cnidus.

(14.84.1) ... (2) ... (3) After the naval battle Pharnabazus and Conon put out to sea with all their ships against the allies of the Lacedaemonians. First of all they induced the people of Cos to secede, and then those of Nisyros and of Telos.[146] After this the Chians, expelling their garrison, joined Conon's men. Similarly, Mytilenaeans, Ephesians, and Erythraeans also changed sides. (4) A similar eagerness for change got hold of the *poleis*, of which some expelled the garrisons of the Lacedaemonians and maintained their freedom, others attached themselves to Conon. The Lacedaemonians from this time lost the sovereignty of the sea. Conon, having decided to sail with the entire fleet to Attica, put out to sea, and after bringing over to his cause the islands of the Cyclades, he sailed against the island of Cythera.[147] (5) Having mastered it at once on the first assault, he sent the Cytherians under a truce away to Laconia, himself leaving an adequate garrison for the *polis*, and sailed off for Corinth. After putting in there, he discussed with the delegates of the council

---

[143] X. *HG* 3.4.29 remarks that Pisander was inexperienced.

[144] Ruzicka 2012: 56 believes that Diodorus misnames Pisander's destination: he believes Pisander remained at the western side of the Loryma peninsula, possibly at or near Bybassus.

[145] The part of the fleet led by Pharnabazus, as we read in X. *HG* 4.3.11–12.

[146] Though most of the MSS suggest it might be the island of Teos, Robert, 1934 points out that geographically Telos suits the description better.

[147] Situated just off the Laconian Gulf and strategically of the utmost importance. See Hdt. 7.235; Th. 4.53.1–56.2; X. *HG* 4.8.7; Paus. 1.27.6.

whatever they wanted, and having made an alliance with them, left them money, but himself sailed off to Asia.[148] (6) ...
(14.85.1) At the conclusion of the year, Eubulides was *archon* in Athens [394/3] and in Rome the highest authority was administered by six military tribunes: Lucius Sergius, Aulus Postumius, Publius Cornelius, and Quintus Manlius.[149] (2) At this time Conon, who held the command of the royal fleet, putting in at the Piraeus with eighty *triereis*, promised the citizens that he would rebuild the fortifications of the city.[150] ... (3) ... (4) Tiribazus,[151] though, who commanded the land forces in Asia, was envious of Conon's successes. On the pretext that Conon used the royal forces to win the cities for the Athenians, having persuaded him to come to Sardis, he arrested him and, having put him in irons, imprisoned him.[152]

S. 92:
14.98.1–99.3:

Developments on Cyprus, 391/0; Evagoras tries to expand his power:
(14.98.1) In Cyprus, Evagoras of Salamis, who was of very noble descent, being a scion of the founders of the *polis*,[153] ... drove out Abdemon of Tyre,[154] the ruler of the *polis* [Cyprian Salamis], who was a friend of the king of the Persians. ... (2) Having subdued some of the *poleis* by force, and won over others by persuasion, Evagoras easily gained control of the other *poleis*. The peoples of Amathus, Soli, and Citium, however, resisted him with arms and dispatched ambassadors to Artaxerxes the king of the Persians for

---

[148] These negotiations – and the harsh conditions – were in fact the work of Pharnabazus, who was in supreme command of the fleet (X. HG 4.8.6–8) and who alone could speak for the king of Persia.
[149] Liv. 5.16.1 has A. Manlius instead of Q. Manlius, and adds Lucius Iulius and Lucius Furius. Broughton 1951: 86–7 lists as the military tribunes with consular power for 397 vc: L. Iulius Iulius, L. Furius Medullinus, L. Sergius Fidenas, A. Postumius Albinus Regillensis, P. Cornelius Maluginensis, and A. Manlius Vulso Capitolinus. Diodorus is still four years ahead of the Varronian chronology.
[150] The *polis* encompasses the whole of Attica: the walls are, therefore, those of the *city* of Athens and Piraeus.
[151] Originally subordinate satrap of Western Armenia, succeeded Tithraustes as satrap of Lydia: the date of succession remains in the dark, but, apparently, must have been effectuated before the current event, perhaps in gratitude for his support to Artaxerxes during the Battle of Cunaxa (see X. *An.* 4.4.4).
[152] Again Diodorus appears to be too succinct: see Bonnet and Bennett 2002: 203–4 *ad* p. 117 note 1.
[153] See Paus. 1.3.2, 8.15.7: Evagoras traced his descent to Teucer, the founder of Cyprian Salamis.
[154] At the latest the expulsion took place in 411: Lys. 6.28; Isoc. *Evag.* 19–28.

help. They accused Evagoras of having killed King Agyris,[155] an ally of the Persians, and declared themselves ready to help the Great King to acquire the island. (3) The king decided to accept the alliance, both because he did not wish Evagoras to become any stronger, and because he appreciated the strategic position of Cyprus and its having a great naval force, by which it would be able to make war in defence of Asia. He dismissed the ambassadors, but himself sent letters to the *poleis* situated by the sea, and to the satraps in command of the *poleis*, to construct *triereis* and to prepare with all speed everything the fleet might need. He also ordered Hecatomnus, the ruler of Caria, to make war upon Evagoras.[156] (4) Having traversed the towns of the satrapies inland, Hecatomnus crossed over to Cyprus with great forces. (5) Such was the state of affairs in Asia. . . .

And the Lacedaemonians are having problems as well:
(14.99.1) At the close of this year Demostratus was *archon* in Athens [390/89], and in Rome the consuls Lucius Lucretius and Servilius[157] took office. At this time Artaxerxes sent Struthas as commander to the coast with an army to make war on the Lacedaemonians.[158] When the Spartans learned of his presence, they dispatched Thibron as commander to Asia. He seized the stronghold of Ionda and a high mountain, Cornissus, forty *stadia* [c. 7 km] from Ephesus.[159] (2) He then advanced with eight thousand soldiers including the troops gathered from Asia, pillaging the territory of the Great King.

---

[155] We have few details of the growth of the domination of Evagoras over the rest of Cyprus. We read in Ctesias (F. 30(72): Stronk 2010: 386–7) of a conflict of Evagoras with Anaxagoras, 'some king of the Cyprians', probably identical with the person Diodorus mentions here as Agyris (in his *Ctesiae . . . Fragmenta*, Müller (1844: 77) had already explained the name of Agyris here as a mistake by Diodorus). It appears that this Anaxagoras was an ally of the Persians. The Persians' interest in Cyprus is explained in the following lines. The figure of Agyris is, to the best of my knowledge, not attested in any of the Cypriot sources.

[156] According to Theopompus, the new satrap of Lydia, Autophradates, was charged with the conduct of the war, while Hecatomnus was the admiral of the fleet: see *FGrH/BNJ* 115, F 103.4 (= Phot. *Bibl*. [176] 120a23–5). Evagoras had been king of Salamis previously, had been expelled, but had regained the city from Abdemon of Tyre in 411: see 14.98.1; Isocr. *Evag*. 26–32.

[157] According to Liv. 5.29.2, Servilius is mistakenly used for Servius Sulpicius Camerinus. However, it appears (see Broughton 1951: 91) that both L. Lucretius Tricipitinus Flavus and Ser. Sulpicius Camerinus were only the *consules suffecti* for 393 vc, the actual consuls being L. Valerius Potitus and P. (or Ser.) Cornelius Maluginensis. Diodorus is still four years ahead of the Varronian chronology. As a matter of fact, Diodorus mentions Lucius Lucretius and Servius Sulpicius as the names of his college of consuls in 15.8.1 for the year 385/4.

[158] See also X. *HG* 4.8.17. Struthas was satrap of Ionia, replacing Tiribazus. Tiribazus had resumed support for Sparta, out of fear of renewed Athenian imperialism. Nevertheless, it appears that Artaxerxes II intended to put an end to the wars with Greek *poleis*. See also Ruzicka 2012: 63.

[159] Meritt et al. 1939: 493 suggests we should read here Isinda and Solmissus.

Struthas, with a strong force of Persian cavalry, five thousand hoplites, and more than twenty thousand light-armed troops, pitched camp not far from the Lacedaemonians. (3) Finally, when Thibron once had set out with part of his troops and had seized much booty, Struthas, having attacked him, both killed Thibron in battle and massacred most of the soldiers, and took captive others, while but few found safety in Cnidinium, a fortress [probably near Ephesus].[160]

S. 93:
14.110.1–5:

Sparta has to sue for peace; terms of the Peace of Antalcidas:
(14.110.1) At the conclusion of these events the year came to an end, and among the Athenians Theodotus was *archon* [387/6] and in Rome the highest authority was held by six military tribunes, Quintus Caeso Sulpicius, Aenus Caeso Fabius, Quintus Servilius, and Publius Cornelius.[161] (2) After these men had taken office, the Lacedaemonians, being distressed by their war both against the Greeks and against the Persians, sent their *navarch* Antalcidas off to Artaxerxes to discuss peace.[162] (3) After he had discussed with him as well as he could the subject of his mission, the Great King agreed to make peace on the following terms: that the Greek *poleis* of Asia Minor would be subject to the Great King, but that all the other Greeks were to be independent, and that he would make war through the aid of those who consented against those who refused compliance and did not accept these terms.[163] (4) The Lacedaemonians thus consented to the terms and offered no opposition, but the Athenians, Thebans, and some of the other Greeks felt weighed down by the abandoning of the *poleis* in Asia Minor. However, being no match in war by themselves, they consented of necessity and accepted the

---

[160] Diodorus describes the role of Thibron much more benevolently than X. *HG* 4.8.17–19, who blames Thibron for lack of organisation and discipline. Thibron was replaced by Diphridas, who succeeded in preserving the *poleis* that had allied themselves with Sparta: X. *HG* 4.8.21–2.

[161] Instead of Caeso Sulpicius, Liv. 5.36.11 gives Q. Sulpicius Longus, and instead of P. Cornelius he gives P. Servilius. Moreover, both he and the *Fasti Capitolini* add two more sons of M. Fabius Ambustus to the four men mentioned here. The college of the six military tribunes with consular power for 390 vc is presented by Broughton 1951: 94 as follows: Q. Fabius Ambustus, K. Fabius Ambustus, N. Fabius Ambustus, Q. Sulpicius Longus, Q. Servilius Fidenas, and P. Cornelius Maluginensis. Broughton moreover records a dictator, namely M. Furius Camillus. Diodorus is still four years ahead of the Varronian chronology.

[162] Here, too, Diodorus omits some events that contributed to Sparta's plight: see Bonnet and Bennett 2002: 213 *ad* p. 142 note 2.

[163] See, for a fuller account of the terms of the treaty, X. *HG* 5.1.31. In fact, the terms were similar to those originally proposed by Sparta in 392: see X. *HG* 5.1.25.

peace. (5) After his difference with the Greeks was resolved, the Great King prepared his forces for the Cypriot War. In fact, Evagoras had got hold of nearly the whole of Cyprus and gathered strong forces, because of Artaxerxes' being distracted by the war against the Greeks.

S. 94:
15.2.1–4.3:

Artaxerxes II prepares to go to war against Evagoras:
(15.2.1) When Mystichides was *archon* in Athens [386/5], the Romans elected in place of consuls three military tribunes, Marcus Furius, Gaius, and Aemilius.[164] This year Artaxerxes, the king of the Persians, made war upon Evagoras, the king of Cyprus.[165] Spending much time on the preparations for the war, he organised a large force, both naval and land. In fact, his land force consisted of three hundred thousand men including cavalry, and he equipped more than three hundred *triereis*. (2) As commanders Artaxerxes appointed of the land force his son-in-law Orontes,[166] of the naval force Tiribazus, a man who happened to be in high favour among the Persians. Having taken over the forces in Phocaea and Cyme, these commanders came down to Cilicia, and having passed over to Cyprus, they prosecuted the war with vigour.[167]

Countermeasures by Evagoras:
(3) Evagoras made an alliance with Acoris,[168] the king of the Egyptians, who was hostile to the Persians, and received a strong

---

[164] I am unable to match these names with actual functionaries. Broughton too offers no direct solution: he refers, however, to the college of military tribunes of 394 vc (Broughton 1951: 90 note 1).
[165] According to Ruzicka 2012: 79–82, Artaxerxes' decision fits in with the Persian strategy of the time, namely to neutralise the Aegean theatre and to remove outspoken Athenophile leaders, like Evagoras, from the eastern Mediterranean basin, at the same time appeasing Athens by stressing its access to the Black Sea grain route through the terms of the Peace of Antalcidas. All this was conceived so that he would have a free hand to engage in an expedition against Egypt. As regards the date for (the beginning of) the war, discussion is ongoing: see Vial 2002: 121 ad chap. 2.1.
[166] After the Battle of Cunaxa, Orontes had been given Rhodogune, a daughter of Artaxerxes II by a concubine, as wife: see X. *An.* 2.4.8; *OGIS* 391.7–9 and *OGIS* 392.10–15 and notes relevant to these lines; also Plu. *Art.* 27.
[167] Ruzicka 2012: 89–90 argues that Diodorus misrepresents the events: to ensure success in Cyprus, the Persian commanders first had to secure Cilicia, notably the coastal cities opposite Cyprus, as well as the coast of Syria, Phoenicia, and Palestine. This operation may have taken some time.
[168] The third king of the 29th dynasty, Hakor(is), who claimed to be a grandson of Nepherites I, defeated the usurper Psammuthis in 393 and ruled Egypt from 393 to 380.

force from him.[169] From Hecatomnus, the lord of Caria,[170] who was secretly co-operating with him, Evagoras got a large sum of money to support his mercenary troops. Likewise he also allured the others who were at variance with the Persians, either secretly or openly, to join the war with Persia. (4) He was master of practically all the cities on Cyprus, of Tyre and some others in Phoenicia. He also had ninety *triereis*, of which twenty were provided by Tyre and seventy Cypriot, six thousand soldiers of his own subjects, and many more than this number from his allies.[171] In addition to these Evagoras had enlisted many mercenaries, because he had money in abundance. The king of the Arabs sent many soldiers, as did some others who had ill feelings towards the king of the Persians.[172]

War begins:
(15.3.1) Since Evagoras had such advantages, he entered the war with confidence. First, because he had many pirate ships, he lay in ambush for the suppliers of goods for the enemy. Some of them he sank at sea, others he drove off, and yet others he captured. Because the merchants therefore did not dare to transport food to Cyprus and because large forces had been gathered on the island, the army of the Persians soon suffered from lack of food. (2) When the want of food led to revolt, the mercenaries of the Persians, attacking their officers, killing some of them, filled the camp with disorder and revolt. With difficulty the commanders of the Persians and the leader of the naval armament, known as Glos,[173] put an end to the mutiny. (3) Sailing off with their entire fleet and transporting more than enough grain from Cilicia, they provided a great abundance of food. King Acoris transported a sufficient amount of grain from Egypt to Evagoras as well as sending him money and all other adequate supplies.[174] (4) Because Evagoras saw that he was much inferior in naval strength, he fitted out sixty other ships and sent for fifty from Acoris in Egypt,

---

[169] Ruzicka 2012: 66–7 believes Persia had fought a failed Egyptian campaign from 390/89 to 388/7: see also Isoc. *Paneg.* 140–1.
[170] By this time, Hecatomnus must already have been appointed satrap of Caria (see 14.98.3–4 and note).
[171] Though Isoc. *Paneg.* 141 states Evagoras only had 3,000 peltasts, Vial 2002: 122 *ad* chap. 2.4 believes the number Diodorus presents is much more realistic, the rhetor's only (or main) purpose being to accentuate the Great King's ultimate weakness.
[172] Most probably (including) the king of the Qedarite Arab coalition, whose realm stretched from north-west Arabia into southern Palestine and the Sinai: see Ruzicka 2012: 36, 42, 84.
[173] Γλῶς in Polyaenus (7.20), Γλοῦς in X. *An.* 1.4.16, 2.1.3 (in both cases as commander of a detachment of the troops of Cyrus the Younger), and Aen.Tact. 31.35 (as admiral of the Great King).
[174] Ruzicka 2012: 86 points to King Acoris as the real instigator and organiser of the revolt in the eastern Mediterranean basin.

so that he had in total two hundred *triereis*. Having these fitted out in an amazing way for a sea-battle and performing continuous trials and exercises, he got ready for a naval battle. Therefore, when the Great King's fleet sailed past towards Citium,[175] approaching the ships unexpectedly, he had a great advantage over the Persians. (5) Indeed, with his ships in battle order he attacked ships in disorder, and fighting with men whose plans were prepared against men caught by surprise, he prepared the victory beforehand at once at the first encounter. In fact, attacking with his *triereis* in close order against scattered and confused ones, he sank some and captured others. (6) As yet, because both *navarch* Glos of the Persians and the other commanders faced the enemy excellently, a fierce naval battle developed in which at first Evagoras held the upper hand. Later, however, when Glos attacked with a strong force and excellently put up a fight, the result was that Evagoras' men turned in flight and lost many of their *triereis*.[176]

Persians gain the upper hand; Evagoras escapes from Cyprus:
(15.4.1) Having won the sea-fight, the Persians gathered both their sea and land forces at the city of Citium. Sallying from there, they organised a siege of Salamis and beleaguered the *polis* both by land and by sea. (2) Meantime Tiribazus, having crossed over to Cilicia after the sea-fight and from there making the journey to the Great King, both reported the victory and carried back two thousand talents for the war. Before the sea-fight Evagoras, having met on land with a body of the Persian infantry near the sea, defeated it and had been confident of success. When he suffered defeat in the sea-fight, though, and found himself besieged, he lost heart. (3) Nevertheless, deciding to continue the war, Evagoras left his son Pnytagoras[177] behind, having appointed him commander of all forces in Cyprus, and himself eluded his enemies, taking with him ten *triereis*, sailing off from Salamis. Having travelled to Egypt and meeting with Acoris, he urged him to continue the war energetically and to consider the war against the Persians a common undertaking.[178]

---

[175] Probably already at that time (see 15.4.1) the site of the Persians' headquarters for the Cypriot War. See also the remarks of Vial 2002: 7 note 1.
[176] Ruzicka 2012: 91 suggests Evagoras led his fleet in person and was therefore 'responsible for the "flight" that Diodorus reports'. I cannot find any confirmation for such a suggestion in Diodorus' words.
[177] For this name see also Theopompus: *FGrH/BNJ* 115, F 103(12).
[178] Ruzicka 2012: 91 dates Evagoras' mission to Acoris to 381. Obviously, this is at variance with the date Diodorus provides for Evagoras' return after his visit to Acoris (see 15.8.1).

S. 95:
15.8.1–11.2:

Evagoras returns to Cyprus; the war continues:
(15.8.1) When Dexitheus was *archon* in Athens [385/4], the Romans elected as consuls Lucius Lucretius and Servius Sulpicius.[179] This year Evagoras, the king of the Salaminians, arrived in Cyprus from Egypt, bringing money from Acoris,[180] the king of Egypt, though it was less than he had expected. Comprehending that Salamis was vigorously besieged, and deserted by his allies, he was forced to negotiate a settlement. (2) Tiribazus, who held the supreme command, said he would agree to a settlement if Evagoras would withdraw from all other cities on Cyprus; if, being king of Salamis alone, he would pay the Persian king a fixed annual tribute; and if he would do as he was told to do, as a subject obeys his superior.

Orontes accuses Tiribazus in a letter to the king:
(3) Although the conditions were hard, Evagoras agreed to them all except performing as subject the orders of his superior, but said that he should be subordinate as king to king. When Tiribazus would not agree to this, Orontes, the other commander, being envious of Tiribazus' reputation, secretly sent letters to Artaxerxes against Tiribazus.[181] (4) He denounced him first on the grounds that, though Tiribazus was able to take Salamis, he was not doing so, but was receiving embassies from Evagoras and conferred with him on a common enterprise and in like manner also contrived a private alliance with the Lacedaemonians, being their friend. He also wrote that Tiribazus had sent some people to Pytho,[182] who were to inquire of the god regarding Tiribazus' plans for revolt. The most important allegation was, though, that he was winning for himself the commanders of the forces, bringing them over by benevolences, honours, gifts, and promises.

Orontes continues the Cypriot expedition:
(5) Having taken notice of the letter and believing the slanders, the Great King wrote to Orontes to arrest Tiribazus and dispatch

---

[179] They are the same as those mentioned for 390/89: see 14.99.1. Though Liv. 5.29.2 states otherwise, we have to deal with *consules suffecti* (see also Broughton 1951: 91).
[180] Though Theopompus remarks (FGrH/BNJ 115 F 103(10) that the Egyptian king was Nectanebo (I), this is impossible, as Nectanebo only became king in 379/8.
[181] Theopompus interprets the events quite differently, emphasising on the one hand the enmity between Evagoras and Tiribazus and on the other an entente between Evagoras and Orontes: see FGrH/BNJ 115, F 103(9) = Phot. Bibl. 176 120a32–4.
[182] That is, the oracle of Apollo at Delphi.

the latter to him. When the order had been carried out,[183] Tiribazus, having been brought to the Great King and having asked for a trial, was for the time being incarcerated. Because after this the king was engaged in a war with the Cadusians[184] and the trial postponed, the affairs of the court of justice were deferred.

(15.9.1) Orontes succeeded to the command of the forces in Cyprus. When he saw, however, that Evagoras again bore the siege boldly and, furthermore, because the soldiers found the arrest of Tiribazus difficult to accept and thereby were insubordinate and abandoned the siege, Orontes became afraid of the unpredictability of the situation. He sent men to Evagoras to discuss a settlement and to urge him to agree to a peace on the same terms Evagoras had agreed to with Tiribazus. (2) Evagoras, thus, was surprisingly able to dispel the menace of his arrest and agreed to peace, on the conditions that he should be king of Salamis, should pay the fixed tribute annually, and should obey as a king the orders of the Great King. So the Cypriot War, lasting approximately ten years, but with the larger part of the time spent in preparations, making continuous war last only two years in all, came in this way to an end.[185]

Glos secedes and turns to Acoris and the Lacedaemonians:
(3) Glos, who was in command of the fleet, having been married to the daughter of Tiribazus, fearful that it might be thought that he had co-operated with Tiribazus in his plan and that he would be punished by the Great King, resolved to safeguard his own situation by a fresh approach. Because he was well supplied with money[186] and soldiers, moreover having won the commanders of the *triereis* to him by favours, he resolved to revolt from the king. (4) At once, thus, having sent ambassadors to Acoris, the king of the Egyptians, he concluded an alliance with him against the Great King. Writing moreover to the Lacedaemonians,[187] he incited them against the Great King,

---

[183] See also Polyaen. *Strat.* 7.14.1; Plu. *De Superst.* 168E.

[184] The Cadusians were a nomad tribe, living in the western Elburz Mountains between Media and the Caspian Sea. See for this tribe Str. 11.7.1/508. Probably Plu. *Art.* 2.24–5 describes this war: surprisingly, there is in this account a role for Tiribazus (in Plutarch he is called Teribazus) in ending the war.

[185] In 14.98 Diodorus announced the beginning of the war: a ten-year duration would mean the war ended in 381/0, a date that seems feasible (see also the remarks above, on 15.2.1: the 'active' war would therefore have lasted from 382 to 380).

[186] Possibly part of the two thousand talents his father-in-law Tiribazus had collected during his trip to Artaxerxes (see above, 15.4.2).

[187] Whether or not through the Laconophile Tiribazus or through his participation in Cyrus the Younger's expedition, Glos may well have been personally acquainted with several Lacedaemonians, like Antalcidas.

Revolt and Sedition 241

and announced that he would give lots of money and made other great promises, pledging himself to co-operate with them regarding matters in Greece and that he would restore their ancestral supremacy. (5) Even before this, the Spartiates had made up their minds to rebuild their supremacy. At the time they were already stirring up the poleis and it was evident to all that they were trying to enslave them. Moreover, being in bad repute, because it was believed that in the agreement they had made with the Great King [the Peace of Antalcidas] they had delivered up the Greeks throughout Asia Minor, they repented their actions and sought a plausible excuse for a war against Artaxerxes. Therefore they were glad to enter the alliance with Glos.

Trial of Tiribazus:
(15.10.1) After Artaxerxes had concluded the war with the Cadusians, he set himself to the trial of Tiribazus and assigned three judges from the most highly esteemed among the Persians.[188] At this time other judges who were believed to have been corrupt were flayed alive and their skins were stretched tight over judicial benches.[189] Having before their eyes an example of the punishment meted out to corrupt decisions, the judges rendered their decisions sitting on these benches. (2) The accusers, thus, having read out the letter sent by Orontes, declared that it contained sufficient elements for an accusation. Against the charge regarding Evagoras, Tiribazus presented the agreement Orontes had made, namely that Evagoras should give ear to the Great King as a king. He stated that he himself, though, had agreed upon a peace on the terms that Evagoras should obey the Great King as a subject does his superior. Regarding the oracle he stated that the god in general does not prophesy about death, and to the truth of this he invoked all the Greeks present as witnesses. As for the friendship with the Lacedaemonians, he replied in defence that he had made the friendship not for any personal benefit, but for the profit of the Great King. He pointed out that due to this friendship, the Greeks of Asia Minor were detached from the Lacedaemonians and delivered defenceless to the Great King.[190] At the conclusion of his apology he reminded the judges of his earlier actions of which the king was the beneficiary. (3) It is related that he pointed out many other services to the king, the greatest, though, one, through which he was honoured

---

[188] For Persian judges see also Hdt. 3.31.
[189] Hdt. 5.25 tells almost the same story.
[190] According to X. *HG* 5.1.25, 30, Tiribazus played a significant role around the conclusion the Peace of Antalcidas.

and became a very great friend. It happened that during a hunt, as the Great King was riding in a *quadriga*, two lions attacked him and tore two of the horses of the four-in-hand to pieces, then made a charge upon the king himself. At that very moment, however, Tiribazus, appearing, killed the lions, and rescued the king from the danger. (4) In wars also, people say that he excelled in bravery, and in council his judgement was so good that when the king used Tiribazus' advice he never went astray. Using such a defence, Tiribazus was unanimously cleared of the charges by all judges.

(15.11.1) Summoning the judges one by one, the king asked upon which principles of justice each cleared the accused. The first said that he observed the charges to be debatable, the benefactions, however, uncontested. The second said that, even when the charges were granted to be true, nevertheless the benefactions exceeded the offence. The third stated that he did not take into account the benefactions, because Tiribazus had received from the king in return for them favours and honours many times as great, but that when the charges were examined apart by themselves, the accused did not appear to be guilty of them. (2) The Great King praised the judges for having decided justly and bestowed upon Tiribazus the customary highest honours. After he had condemned Orontes, however, as one who had fabricated a false accusation, he both struck him from his companions, and subjected him to the utmost deprivation of privileges. Such was the state of affairs in Asia.

S. 96:
15.18.1–19.1:

Glos is assassinated and succeeded by Tachos; troubles in Asia Minor, 383–2:
(15.18.1) In Asia, Glos, the *navarch* of the Persians in the Cypriot War, a deserter from the Great King, who had called to his aid both the Lacedaemonians and the king of the Egyptians for the war against the Persians, did not achieve his goal, being assassinated by certain persons.[191] Having taken over Glos' affairs after his death, Tachos [Glos' son] gathered a force about him and founded, on a cliff near the sea, a *polis* by the name of Leuce, housing a sacred shrine of Apollo. (2) Shortly after Tachos died, a dispute over this city arose between the inhabitants of Clazomenae and Cyme. At first, the *poleis* attempted

---

[191] Ruzicka 2012: 97 suggests Glos' murder may have been connected with Tiribazus' acquittal and (alleged) subsequent overtures between Glos and Artaxerxes II.

Revolt and Sedition 243

to settle the matter by war. Later, though, after someone suggested asking the god which one of the two *poleis* he judged should be master of Leuce, the Pythia judged that the *polis* should be master which first might be able to offer sacrifice in Leuce. They should start from their own *polis* at the rising of the sun on a day upon which both should agree. (3) When the day was set, the Cymeans assumed that they would have the advantage because their *polis* lay the nearer, but the Clazomenians, being a greater distance away, contrived the following scheme to get the victory. Choosing by lot colonists from among themselves, they founded near Leuce a *polis*, starting from which at the rising of the sun they forestalled the Cymeans in performing the sacrifice. (4) Having become masters of Leuce by this cunningly devised trap, they decided to hold an annual eponymous festival, naming the feast the *Prophthasia* ('Anticipation').[192] After these events the rebellions in Asia came to an end of themselves.
(15.19.1) After the death of Glos and Tachos, the Lacedaemonians renounced their enterprises in Asia Minor [that is, to conclude the Peace of Antalcidas], having seized control throughout Greece: winning over some of the *poleis* by persuasion, getting others into their hands by force through the return of the exiles, they began openly to bring into their own hands the supremacy of Greece from this point, contrary to the common agreements adopted in the time of Antalcidas after intervention by the king of the Persians.

S. 97:
15.23.5:

Consequences of Spartan superiority in Greece:
(15.23.5) Consequently [that is, in 380/79] the then greatest rulers – I mean the king of the Persians and the tyrant of Sicily, Dionysius – paid court to the supremacy of the Spartans and attempted to strike an alliance with them.

S. 98:
15.29.1–4:

Preparations for war in Egypt:
(15.29.1) While these things were going on [in 377/6], Acoris, the king of the Egyptians,[193] being hostilely disposed towards the

---

[192] This festival is only referred to in this text.
[193] There is a major problem here regarding the dates. Though these events may have

Persian king, collected large mercenary forces. In fact, offering high wages to those who enrolled, showing kindness to many, he had quickly won over many of the Greeks to enrol in the army.[194] (2) However, because he had no capable commander, he sent for Chabrias the Athenian, a man distinguished for both his prudence and his military knowledge, who had also won great repute for personal *aretē*. Chabrias, thus, without awaiting the judgement of the Athenian people, accepted the appointment and took command of the forces in Egypt and with great haste made preparations to make war against the Persians.[195] (3) However, having been appointed by the Great King as commander of the Persian force, Pharnabazus stockpiled large supplies of the materials useful for war. Moreover, he also sent ambassadors abroad to Athens, denouncing Chabrias, who would, by commanding the Egyptians, alienate the Great King's goodwill from the people of Athens, and inviting them to give him Iphicrates as commander. (4) The Athenians quickly both recalled Chabrias from Egypt[196] and dispatched Iphicrates[197] as commander to act in alliance with the Persians, because they were eager to procure the favour of the Persian king and to win over Pharnabazus.

---

stretched to 377/6, this does not go for King Acoris. According to the available data he died in 380 and cannot possibly have been active in 377/6 (see Shaw and Nicholson 2008: 351 *sub* Late Period, *sub* 29th dynasty). Moreover, Chabrias was elected as a *strategos* in Athens in the year 379 and had to return to that *polis* before that date. Accepting 380 as the real date of these events makes the situation (described in the following note) more plausible.

[194] This war between the Persians and the Egyptians (see Isoc. *Paneg.* 140 *sq.*; D. 20.76; Nep. *Cha.* 2.1) most likely belongs to an earlier period, namely to the years 385–383, and is, therefore, misdated by Diodorus.

[195] See Nep. *Cha.* 2.3. Here, again, discussion on the dates is possible. Views vary from c. 386–384 (when Chabrias was in charge of the Athenian army which was recalled from Cyprus) to 377. A convenient discussion of dates is found in Parke 1970: 59–62. As for the preparations: Chabrias appears to have protected (some of) the mouths of the Nile by a palisade, the Χαβρίου χάραξ ('palisade of Chabrias': see Str. 16.2.33/760). Strabo also mentions a Χαβρίου κώμη ('village of Chabrias') near Lake Mariout (ancient Mareotis, situated near modern Alexandria): Str. 17.1.22/803; see also Str. 16.2.33/760; Plin. *Nat.* 5.14.68.

[196] The recalling of Chabrias had probably already occurred in the winter of 380/79, since in the next winter he held the Athenian frontier against Cleombrotus (X. *HG* 5.4.14) and in the early summer of 378 he helped defend Thebes against Agesilaus. He was probably elected *strategos* in the spring of 379 (see also above, note 192). Ruzicka 2012: 105–6 suggests Chabrias may well have shared intelligence regarding Egypt's defensive system with Iphicrates and/or the Persians.

[197] Iphicrates was probably sent out to Persia (see Nep. *Iph.* 2.4) about the time Chabrias was elected *strategos*, and he returned from Persian service to Athens in 373. He was a master of light-armed tactics and a most able *condottiere* (see, *inter alia*, Nep. *Iph. passim*).

S. 99:
15.38.1-3:

Artaxerxes II urges the settling of differences between Greek poleis; mixed result:
(15.38.1) When Hippodamas was *archon* at Athens [375/4], the Romans elected four military tribunes in the place of the consuls, namely Lucius Valerius, Lucius Manlius, Servius Sulpicius, and Lucretius.[198] During their term of office Artaxerxes, king of the Persians, intending to make war on the Egyptians and being busily engaged in organising a considerable mercenary army, decided to put an end to the wars going on in Greece.[199] In fact, he particularly hoped that in this way the Greeks, released from their domestic wars, would be more willing to be recruited into mercenary service. Therefore he sent out ambassadors to Greece appealing to the *poleis* to conclude a general peace. (2) As the Greeks gladly accepted his proposal,[200] because they wearied of the uninterrupted series of wars, they all agreed to make peace,[201] stating that all the *poleis* would be independent and free from garrisons. The Greeks appointed overseers who, visiting *polis* after *polis*, proceeded to march out all the garrisons. (3) Because only the Thebans would not agree that the ratification of the peace was to be made *polis* by *polis*, ... ; all the other Greek states harmoniously agreed on the terms, but the Thebans alone were refused participation in them.[202] As Epaminondas inspired

---

[198] Liv. 6.21.1 mentions two additional tribunes, namely L. Aemilius and L. Trebonius: unlike Diodorus, he names one of the tribunes Aulus Manlius instead of Lucius Manlius. Broughton also lists six military tribunes with consular power for the year 383 vc: L. Valerius Poplicola, A. Manlius (Capitolinus), Ser. Sulpicius Rufus, L. Lucretius Flavus Tricipitinus L. Aemilius Mamercinus, and M. Trebonius: Broughton 1951: 103. Diodorus is here nine years ahead of the Varronian chronology.

[199] Diodorus more or less repeats this fragment (= 15.38.1-39.2), regarding a treaty in 375/4, discussing a treaty in 371 (15.50.4-51.1). The latter fragment is, however, shorter and somewhat more precise: the motives of the Greeks for agreeing, the conditions, and the debates are absent. Diodorus seems to be aware of the fact that the events he describes for 371 are very much *like* those he describes here. It might explain his phrase in 15.50.4: ὥσπερ καὶ πρότερον ('like before'). See also Lauffer 1959; *contra*: Stylianou 1998: 325-6. See also Cawkwell 1963, who places the peace late in 375 (in the autumn) rather than in 374. See also Philochorus, *FGrH/BNJ* 328, F 151. In general, Hornblower 2011: 246, in my view understandably, calls 15.38 'a muddled chapter'.

[200] Notably, the Athenians did so: Philochorus *FGrH/BNJ* 328 F 151; Isoc. *Antid.* 109-10; also Hornblower 2011: 246.

[201] The so-called *koinē eirēnē* ('common peace') of 375: see also Hornblower 2011: 247.

[202] Isoc. *Plat.* 14 indicates that Diodorus is wrong on this point: though the Thebans were excluded from the treaty in 371, they were not excluded from the treaty in 375. Moreover, in 373/2 Thebes was still an active member of the Athenian League, as is shown by *IG* II², 1607.49.

his fellow citizens with proud designs by his own personal *aretē*, these were emboldened to resist the decision of all.

S. 100:
15.41.1–43.6:

The Egyptian War begins:
(15.41.1) When Socratides was *archon* at Athens [374/3], instead of consuls the Romans elected four military tribunes, namely Quintus Servilius, Servius Cornelius, and Spurius Papirius.[203] During their term of office King Artaxerxes sent an expedition against the Egyptians, who had revolted from Persia.[204] The commanders of the forces were Pharnabazus of the Persian contingent and Iphicrates the Athenian of the mercenaries, who numbered twenty thousand.[205] The latter, who had been sent for the command by the Great King, was assigned because of his *aretē* in generalship. (2) After Pharnabazus had lost several years making preparations, Iphicrates, seeing that Pharnabazus was formidable in talk, but sluggish in action, frankly told him that he marvelled that Pharnabazus was so sharp in speech but so dull in action. Pharnabazus replied that it was because he himself was master of his words but the Great King master of his actions. (3) When the Persian army had assembled at the city of Ace [modern Akko], it numbered two hundred thousand Persians, who were under the command of Pharnabazus; of the twenty thousand [?] Greek mercenaries Iphicrates was the commander. The ships numbered three hundred *triereis* and two hundred triaconters. The number of ships conveying food and other supplies was great. (4) At the beginning of the summer[206] the Great King's commanders moved off with the entire army, and accompanied by the fleet, sailing along the coast, they proceeded to Egypt. When they came near the Nile, they found on arrival that the Egyptians

---

[203] Liv. 6.22.1 mentions three additional names, namely Lucius Papirius, Gaius Sulpicius, and Lucius Aemilius. Broughton 1951: 103 mentions as the six military tribunes with consular power for 382 vc: Sp. Papirius Crassus, L. Papirius (Mugillanus), Ser. Cornelius Maluginensis, Q. Servilius Fidenas, C. Sulpicius (Camerinus), and L. Aemilius Mamercinus. Diodorus is still nine years ahead of the Varronian chronology.

[204] Additional accounts of this expedition are to be found in Nep. *Iph.* 2.4; Trog. *Prol. ad* 10; Plu. *Art.* 24; Polyaen. 3.9.38, 56, 59.

[205] According to Nep. *Iph.* 2.4, the number of mercenaries was 12,000 instead of Diodorus' 20,000.

[206] In a time reckoning like Thucydides', using two seasons per year, 'summer' usually starts in spring, which is late March or early April. See also 15.43.4, also suggesting a date of the spring of 373, at least some time before the flooding of the Nile, which usually heralded the 'real' summer. *Caput* 15.43.5–6, moreover, indicates that by autumn of that very year, Iphicrates was back in Athens.

had manifestly prepared for the war. (5) Indeed, Pharnabazus made the expedition a slow one and had given the enemy ample time for preparation. In fact, this usually occurs with the Persian commanders: not being independent in the general conduct of war, they refer all matters to the Great King and await his replies concerning each of those matters.

(15.42.1) The king of the Egyptians, Nectanebo,[207] learned the size of the Persian forces, but was confident, chiefly from the strength of the country, because Egypt is extremely difficult of approach, and second from the thorough blockage of all points of invasion from land or sea. (2) Indeed, because the Nile empties into the Egyptian Sea through seven branches,[208] at each branch a city had been established with great towers on each bank of the stream and a wooden bridge commanding its entrance. He fortified the Pelusian branch especially, because it is the first one encountered by those approaching from Syria and it seemed that enemies would most likely make their approach by way of that branch. (3) He fenced this branch off with a canal, cut off and fortified with a wall the entrances for ships at the most suitable places, inundated the approaches by land, and blocked the navigable approaches with embankments. Therefore it was not easy either for the ships to sail in, or for the cavalry to approach, or for the infantry to proceed. (4) Pharnabazus' staff officers, finding the Pelusian branch excellently fortified and guarded by a multitude of soldiers, utterly rejected forcing a way through it, but decided to make the invasion by way of another branch. Therefore, sailing on the open sea to avoid the ships being sighted by the enemy, they put in by way of the branch known as Mendesian,[209] which had a beach stretching over a considerable space. Disembarking on that beach with three thousand men, both Pharnabazus and Iphicrates pushed forward to the walled town on the branch. (5) The Egyptians made a sally with three thousand men, both horse and infantry. A violent battle ensued, while many men had come from their ships to increase the number of the Persians. The Egyptians were surrounded, many died, and not a few were captured alive. The remainder were driven in confusion into the city. Dashing in with the defenders

---

[207] Nectanebo (I) [Νεκτάνεβις], founder of the 30th dynasty, ruled Egypt from 380 to 362.
[208] Diodorus uses here the word τὸ στόμα, generally meaning 'the mouth'. In view of both the geographical situation and the archaeological evidence I find it more convenient to translate it here generally as 'the branch'. As for the archaeological evidence: though for all branches a city upstream can be attested, this is not (yet?) the case with all mouths, which is why I opt to be not too specific.
[209] The third branch counting from the east, the first being the Pelusian, the second the Saïtic.

inside the walls and taking possession of the fortress, Iphicrates' men razed it and enslaved the inhabitants.

(15.43.1) After this, discord set in amongst the commanders, causing the failure of the enterprise. Iphicrates, indeed, learning from the captives that Memphis,[210] the most important city of those all over Egypt, was undefended, advised sailing immediately up to Memphis before the forces of the Egyptians arrived there. However, Pharnabazus believed they should await the entire force of the Persians, because the expedition against Memphis would be safer.[211] (2) When Iphicrates asked to be given the mercenaries that were on hand and promised that he would capture the city with them, Pharnabazus became suspicious of both his boldness and his *aretē*; that is, that he might take possession of Egypt for himself. Because Pharnabazus, therefore, would not yield, Iphicrates protested, saying that if they let slip such a critical moment, they would make the whole campaign unavailing. Some Persian captains,[212] thus, bore a grudge against him and were creating unfounded prejudices. (3) Meanwhile the Egyptians, benefiting from the long delay, dispatched an adequate garrison into Memphis, and then, coming to the ravaged fortress at the Mendesian branch of the Nile with all their forces and being now at a great advantage owing to the strength of their position, fought constant engagements with the enemy. Growing ever stronger, they killed many of the Persians and behaved boldly against their enemy. (4) As the campaign around this fortress lingered on, and when the Etesian winds had already set in, the Nile, filling up and flooding the whole region with the abundance of its waters,[213] made Egypt daily more secure. As the circumstances became increasingly harder to manage, the commanders of the Persians decided to withdraw from Egypt. (5) Therefore, when they were on their way back to Asia and a disagreement arose between Pharnabazus

---

[210] Memphis was the first capital of a united Egypt. It was situated on the border between Upper and Lower Egypt, some 20 km south of modern Cairo, where the Nile branches out, on the west bank of the river. One of the other names the city was known by was *Inebu-Hedju* ('White Walls'). Especially important during the period of the Old Kingdom, it retained much of its importance (mainly as a religious centre) during succeeding periods, but saw a renewed political importance during the reign of Nectanebo I, which lasted more or less until the rise of Alexandria under the Ptolemies.

[211] This suggests that Iphicrates and Pharnabazus had advanced with a vanguard (probably consisting mostly of the Greek mercenaries), and that the remainder of the Persian force had pitched camp near Pelusium, both attending the outcome of the operation and pinning down a substantial part of the Egyptian army.

[212] In the MSS there is a lacuna preceding ἐφθόνουν ('bore a grudge'), containing the verb's subject. In view of the context, the present conjecture seems appropriate.

[213] Generally the flood of the Nile started about May and, having flooded the country to the desert's edges, returned to normal level in late September (see also Hdt. 2.97.1; 1.36.7–12). A similar situation to that here is described regarding the invasion of Egypt by Antigonus Monophthalmus in 306: see 20.73–6 (not included in this account).

Revolt and Sedition 249

and Iphicrates, Iphicrates decided to flee secretly from the camp, suspecting that he might be arrested and punished, as Conon the Athenian had been.[214] This is why he sneaked away at night, having secured a ship and reaching port at Athens. (6) Pharnabazus, having dispatched ambassadors to Athens, accused Iphicrates of being responsible for not capturing Egypt.[215] The Athenians, though, gave the Persians for answer that if they found that he had done wrong, they would punish him as he deserved, but they themselves shortly afterwards appointed Iphicrates as *strategos* in command of their fleet.

S. 101:
15.50.4:

Artaxerxes tries again to establish peace in Greece:[216]
(15.50.4) At this time [mid-371: see Plu. *Ages.* 28.5], King Artaxerxes, seeing that Greece was again in turmoil, sent ambassadors,[217] exhorting the Greeks to settle their intestine wars and establish a common peace in accordance with the covenants that had formerly been made. Because all the Greeks welcomed his words gladly, all the *poleis* agreed to a general peace except Thebes.[218] ...

S. 102:
15.70.2:

Artaxerxes sends Philiscus[219] *to Greece, 368:*
(15.70.2) After this [the performance of Sicilian troops in Greece in support of the Lacedaemonians in 368, against the Boeotians], Philiscus, sent by King Artaxerxes, sailed to Greece, exhorting the Greeks to resolve their wars and to conclude a general peace. All

---

[214] When Antalcidas visited Tiribazus in 392, asking for Persian assistance against Athens, Tiribazus arrested Conon, in spite of the fact that Conon was supported by Pharnabazus. Some say Conon was killed in prison, others relate he fled to Evagoras and died there of illness. See also X. *HG* 4.8.16; see also above, 14.85.4.

[215] Ruzicka 2012: 119–20 convincingly argues that Pharnabazus did not intend to abort the expedition but only to retreat a little, to resume the invasion in full force after the Nile had resumed its pre-flood level. Diodorus leaves us in the dark about the position of the Greek mercenary force, trained by Iphicrates. Possibly Pharnabazus' sending ambassadors to Athens may have served yet another end, namely finding a successor to Iphicrates in the person of Timotheus: see Ruzicka 2012: 123.

[216] This paragraph in more than one respect continues the story from 15.38.1–39.2. Moreover, Artaxerxes still needed Greek mercenaries, as he was about to renew his attack on Egypt: see Ruzicka 2012: 125.

[217] See D.H. *Lys.* 12; X. *HG* 6.3.12, 6.5.1. See also Vial 2002: 64–5, note 1.

[218] See X. *HG* 6.3.1–19; see also Plu. *Ages.* 28.

[219] Philiscus of Abydus was an agent of Ariobarzanes, the satrap of Hellespontine Phrygia: see, for example, Hornblower 2011: 259.

250   *Semiramis' Legacy*

others complied gladly,[220] but the Thebans, adhering to their own design to bring all Boeotia into one confederation, were excluded from the agreement. Because the general peace was not agreed to, Philiscus, leaving for the Lacedaemonians two thousand picked mercenaries with their wages, returned to Asia Minor.

S. 103:
15.76.3:

Artaxerxes finally succeeds in bringing peace in Greece:
(15.76.3) While these things were going on [in 366/5], the king of the Persians, having sent envoys, persuaded the Greeks to resolve their wars and conclude a general peace with one another.[221] Therefore the so-called Laconian–Boeotian War was resolved after lasting more than five years, having started with the Battle of Leuctra.

S. 104:
15.90.1–93.6:

'Great Satraps' Revolt' against Artaxerxes II starts; Egypt joins the revolt:[222]
(15.90.1) When Molon was *archon* at Athens [362/1], Lucius Genucius and Quintus Servilius were elected as consuls in Rome.[223] During their term of office the inhabitants of the coast of Asia Minor revolted from Persia,[224] and some of the satraps and military commanders, who had risen in insurrection, made war on Artaxerxes. (2) Simultaneously, Tachos,[225] the king of the Egyptians, having

---

[220] See X. *HG* 7.1.27: he believes that not Thebes but Messene was the problem at the Delphi convention. See also, for a succinct view, Hornblower 2011: 266–7
[221] See X. *HG* 7.4.6–11; see also: Ryder 1957; 1965: Appendix VII, pp. 137–9; Cawkwell 1961.
[222] For this 'Revolt', if it ever was that, see Weiskopf 1989.
[223] See Liv. 7.1.7. Broughton 1951: 115–16 lists as the consuls for 365 vc L. Genucius Aventinensis and Q. Servilius Ahala. Diodorus is here four years ahead of the Varronian chronology.
[224] Diodorus relates the whole 'Great Satraps' Revolt' (if it ever occurred) under one year, 362/1. In fact, the first steps in this whole enterprise were taken several years earlier, at least as early as 366, by Datames and Ariobarzanes, while the affair lasted beyond the end of the year under Diodorus' scrutiny, in 360. In practice, we have here a textbook example of time compression or telescoping (for the term and an explanation, see for example Stronk 2011: 120 and note 3). For a thorough account of this alleged revolt see Weiskopf 1989. Some short notes are to be found in Hornblower 2011: 266.
[225] Tachos (also known as Takhor, Teos, or Zedhor) had been the co-ruler of Egypt with his father Nectanebo I from c. 365, and became single ruler in 363/2. He was forced to flee Egypt (to Persia) in 360, due to a rebellion led by Nectanebo II, his cousin, who was supported by Agesilaus (see further below). Nectanebo II ruled to 342/1 (when Egypt was taken again by the Persians) and would be the last king of the 30th dynasty.

decided to fight the Persians, both prepared ships and gathered infantry forces. Having procured many mercenaries from the Greek *poleis*, he persuaded the Lacedaemonians also to ally themselves with him. In fact, the Spartans had distanced themselves from Artaxerxes because the Messenians had been ranked by the Great King on the same terms as the other Greeks in the common peace.[226] Because the general uprising against the Persians reached such large proportions, the Great King began to prepare the things necessary for the war as well. (3) For at one and the same time he had to fight the Egyptian king, the Greek *poleis* throughout Asia Minor, the Lacedaemonians, and the allies of these, namely satraps and commanders, governing the coastal districts and agreeing to make common cause with them. Of these the most distinguished were Ariobarzanes, satrap of Phrygia, who at the death of Mithridates had taken possession of his kingdom,[227] and Mausolus, overlord of Caria and master of many strongholds and notable *poleis* of which the hearth and mother city happened to be Halicarnassus, boasting a famous acropolis and the palace of Caria. Apart from these two, there were Orontes, satrap of Mysia, and Autophradates, satrap of Lydia. Among the peoples revolting were Lycians, Pisidians, Pamphylians, and Cilicians, moreover Syrians, Phoenicians, and practically all the coastal peoples. (4) Because the revolt was so extensive, half of the revenues of the Great King were cut off, and what remained was insufficient for the expenses of the war.

Treason in the ranks of those revolting against the king:
(15.91.1) Those who had revolted from the Great King chose Orontes as their commander in charge of everything. Having taken over the command and funds to recruit mercenaries – that is, a year's pay for twenty thousand men – he became the betrayer of those who trusted him. Indeed, he suspected that he would both obtain from the Great King great rewards and also succeed to the satrapy of the entire coastal region if he delivered the rebels into the hands of the Persians. First he arrested those who brought the money and dispatched them to Artaxerxes. Next he handed over many of the *poleis* and the

---

[226] See X. *HG* 7.1.33–40; Plu. *Pel.* 30; Isoc. *Archid.* 27. Two inscriptions testify to the fact that the insurgents also tried to win the *poleis* of mainland Greece for their cause, namely Dittenberger *Syll.*³ 182, an inscription from Argos in which the Greeks refuse to engage with the revolting satraps, and *IG* II².119, from Athens dated to 364/3, honouring Tachos' ambassadors. Possibly this embassy is related to events described in X. *Ages.* 2.27.

[227] Diodorus here makes a shambles of different characters by the name of Ariobarzanes and Mithradates: see, for a convenient review, Sherman 1963: 202–3 note 1; also Vial 2002: 113 note 1.

mercenary soldiers to the officers who had been sent by the Great King. (2) Similarly, betrayal occurred all over Cappadocia as well, where something strange and unexpected occurred. After Artabazus, the Great King's commander, had invaded Cappadocia with a large force, Datames, the satrap of the country, pitched camp opposite him, for he had collected many horsemen and had twenty thousand mercenary infantry serving with him.[228] (3) But Datames' father-in-law,[229] who commanded the cavalry, wishing to acquire favour and at the same time thinking of his own safety, having deserted at night, rode off with the cavalry to the enemy, having the day before made arrangements with Artabazus for his betrayal. (4) Entreating his mercenaries and promising presents, Datames launched an attack upon the deserters. Overtaking them when they had already joined the enemy, and himself attacking Artabazus' men and the horsemen at the same time, he killed whoever came close. (5) Because he was at first unaware of the truth and suspecting that the man who had deserted Datames was effecting a counter-betrayal, Artabazus ordered his own men to kill all the horsemen who approached. Mithrobarzanes was in a predicament, being caught in the middle, as some were seeking revenge against him as a traitor, others were trying to punish him for counter-betrayal. Because his predicament did not allow him time to deliberate, he turned to force, and fighting against both parties he made many victims. After, finally, more than ten thousand had been killed, Datames, having put the rest of Mithrobarzanes' men to flight and killed many of them, called back with the *salpinx*[230] his soldiers who had gone in pursuit. (6) Of the surviving cavalrymen some, returning to Datames, asked to be pardoned. The rest kept quiet, having nowhere to turn, and finally, surrounded and being about five hundred in number, were shot down by Datames. (7) Datames, thus, who even before this was admired for his generalship, got far greater acclaim at that time for both

---

[228] Possibly mercenaries who had served under him when he commanded the Persian army, preparing to resume action against Egypt at Ace (Akko): see Nep. *Datam.* 8.2; see also Ruzicka 2012: 127.

[229] Namely Mithrobarzanes: see Nep. *Datam.* 6; Polyaen. 7.21.7.

[230] The classical Greek *salpinx* or 'trumpet' was a narrow cylindrical tube leading to a bell (the κώδων): on vase paintings the bell's shape varies from a ball to a bulb to a cone. Each of these shapes may have affected the instrument's timbre. The mouthpiece of the *salpinx* opens only slightly, lacking a mouthpiece such as modern trumpets have. With its piercing sound and loud volume the *salpinx* appeared the instrument best suited for military use, though its use was not general. I have left *salpinx* untranslated. A comparison might be made with the 'trumpets' found in the tomb of King Tut-ankh-amun: they were blown for the first time again in 1939 by James Tappern for a live BBC radio broadcast from the Cairo museum: the preserved soundtrack does indeed reveal, for both 'trumpets', a piercing sound.

Revolt and Sedition 253

his courage and his sagacity in the conduct of war. However, when King Artaxerxes learned about Datames' exploit as general, eagerly seeking to have him removed, he got him murdered by means of a plot.[231]

Events in Egypt:
(15.92.1) While these things were going on, Rheomithres,[232] who had been sent by the insurgents to King Tachos in Egypt and had received from him five hundred talents of silver and fifty warships, sailed to Asia Minor to the aforementioned Leuce.[233] After summoning many leaders of the insurgents to this city and arresting them, he sent them in irons to Artaxerxes. Though he himself had been an insurgent, he became reconciled with the Great King by the gifts springing from his betrayal. (2) In Egypt King Tachos, having completed his preparations for the war, now had two hundred *triereis* expensively adorned,[234] ten thousand picked mercenaries from Greece, and besides these eighty thousand Egyptian infantry. He gave the command of the mercenaries to the Spartiate Agesilaus, who had been dispatched by the Lacedaemonians with a thousand hoplites to fight as an ally,[235] a man capable of commanding soldiers and admired because of his courage and his strategic sagacity. (3) The command of the naval contingent he put in the hands of Chabrias the Athenian, who had not been dispatched officially by his country, but had been privately convinced by the Egyptian king to join the war.[236] Tachos himself, having command of the Egyptians and being commander-in-chief of the whole force, did not follow Agesilaus' advice to remain in Egypt and conduct the war by means of his commanders, though the advice was sound. In fact, when the force had advanced quite far and was encamped in the neighbourhood of

---

[231] Allegedly executed by Ariobarzanes' son Mithradates: see also X. *Cyr.* 8.8; Arist. *Pol.* 5.1312a*; Harp. *s.v.* 'Ἀριοβαρζάνης'; Nep. *Dat.* 10–11; Polyaen. 7.29.1.
[232] See X. *Cyr.* 8.8.4. Stylianou 1998: 541 might suggest that Orontes and Rheomitres acted in concord. This is likely to be correct.
[233] See 15.18.2, 4.
[234] [Arist.] *Oec.* 1353a18–24 (2.37) reports that Chabrias prepared 120 ships, though he only needed sixty.
[235] Probably only after the Battle of Mantinea, which probably took place in the period between midsummer and early autumn of 362. Whether the time of year allowed him then to set sail for Egypt is hard to determine: I believe, therefore, he might have arrived in Egypt as late as spring 361. At the time of these events, Agesilaus was already over eighty years old. The alliance between Tachos and Sparta is likely to have been sealed during the embassy sent by Tachos to Greece in 364/3: see 15.90.2 and note 225. See also X. *Ages.* 2.28–30; Plu. *Ages.* 37.1–2. See also Ruzicka 2012: 137–9.
[236] See Plu. *Ages.* 37.5; Nep. *Cha.* 2.3; Polyaen. 3.11.7.

Phoenicia,[237] the commander left in charge of Egypt revolted from the king,[238] and having sent a message to his son Nectanebo, and convincing him to claim the kingship in Egypt, he kindled a great war. (4) In fact, Nectanebo, who had been appointed commander of the soldiers from Egypt by Tachos, and had been sent from Phoenicia to besiege the cities in Syria, after assenting to his father's designs, influencing the officers with bribes and the common soldiers with promises, persuaded them to be his accomplices. (5) After Egypt was finally seized by the insurgents,[239] Tachos, panic-stricken, dared to go up to the Great King through Arabia[240] and asked to be pardoned for his past errors. Artaxerxes not only cleared him of the charges against him but even appointed him commander in the war against the Egyptians.

F. ARTAXERXES III OCHUS (425–338)[241]

(15.93.1) Shortly later, the king of the Persians died after ruling forty-three years.[242] Ochus, who assumed a new name, that is Artaxerxes, succeeded to the kingdom and ruled twenty-three years. Indeed, because Artaxerxes II *Mnemon* had ruled well and had shown himself to be altogether peace-loving and successful, the Persians changed the names of those who ruled after him and prescribed that they should bear that name.[243]

---

[237] Ruzicka 2012: 145–6 believes the Egyptian army pitched camp at Akko. It is obvious that Tachos' intent was to secure the 'middle territory', Phoenicia and Palestine, before taking further action. At the same time, with Akko as his base, he could secure the southerly route to Egypt from there.

[238] Probably one Tamos, Tachos' own brother: see De Meulenaere 1963; see also Ruzicka 2012: 147–8. Ruzicka remarks that this points to an intra-dynastic conflict, which contradicts a remark in Plu. *Ages.* 37.2–38.2, mentioning one 'Mendesian' not mentioned by name. Mendes was the home of the 29th dynasty (displaced by Tachos' father): this rather suggests an inter-dynastic conflict. If Tamos really took action, it may have been, therefore, a preemptive strike to safeguard the kingship for the family.

[239] According to the chronological data, which are absolutely solid for the 30th dynasty, Tachos lost his kingdom in 359/8. Contrary to Diodorus, who imputes Tachos' flight to a revolution, Plutarch maintains that Tachos' retreat was caused by Agesilaus' siding with Nectanebo II (Plu. *Ages.* 37.3–38.1; see also X. *Ages.* 2.28–31).

[240] Arabia here probably means no more than 'east of the River Jordan', through the region later known as Arabia *Petraea*. See Stylianou 1998: 546; X. *An.* 1.5.1.

[241] For the succession by Artaxerxes III *Ochus*, see Depuydt 2008: 37; for *Ochus*' reign see Briant 2002: 680–90.

[242] Here too Diodorus struggles a bit with chronology: it appears that Artaxerxes II died between November 359 and November 358 after a reign of forty-six years (see, for example, as well as Depuydt 2008: 37, Vial 2002: 164, note *ad* chap. 93.1). So far, the placement of Artaxerxes' death in relation to developments in Egypt is largely correct.

[243] This seems incorrect: after both Artaxerxes I and Artaxerxes III, Persian kings with a different name ruled the country.

Revolt and Sedition 255

Revolt in Egypt continues; Agesilaus saves the new Egyptian king:
(2) When King Tachos[244] [**Nectanebo**] had returned to the army of Agesilaus, Nectanebo [**a pretender**], who had collected more than a hundred thousand men, stood up against Tachos [**Nectanebo**] and challenged him to fight for the kingship. Agesilaus, thus, observing that the king was terrified and did not dare to run all risks, exhorted him to be of good courage, because, indeed, the victory would not end up with those who had the advantage of numbers, but with those who excelled in bravery. Since Nectanebo paid no heed to Agesilaus, Agesilaus was obliged to withdraw with Nectanebo to a large city.[245] (3) The insurgents at first started to besiege them once Agesilaus, Nectanebo, and their men were trapped inside. However, after the rebels had lost many men in their attacks on the walls, they began to surround the city with a wall and a ditch. Because the works were rapidly nearing completion due to the multitude of workmen and because their provisions were exhausted, Tachos [**Nectanebo**] despaired of his safety, but Agesilaus, encouraging the men and attacking the enemy by night, unexpectedly succeeded in saving all the men. (4) Because the Egyptians had pursued them closely and the district was flat, the Egyptians believed that they had the enemy surrounded by their numbers and would utterly destroy all of them. Agesilaus, though, seizing a position which had on each side a handmade canal that was fed by the river, halted the enemy attack. (5) Having deployed his force as the terrain required and having protected his army by the river channels, he joined battle. Because the superior numbers had become useless for the insurgents, the Greeks, who surpassed them in *aretē*, killed many of the Egyptians and forced the rest to flee. (6) After these events Tachos [**Nectanebo**] easily recovered the Egyptian kingly office, but Agesilaus, as the one who all alone had restored his dominion, was honoured with

---

[244] Vial 2002: 117 note 1 rightly remarks that Diodorus loses his footing here entirely: the battles described in the sequel are not between Tachos (though he may have returned to Egypt for a short time, accompanying an unsuccessful Persian force, in late 360 or early 359, led by Ochus 'while his father Artaxerxes still lived': Syncellus, *Ecloga Chronographica* 487; Trogus, *Prol.* 10) and Nectanebo II, but between Nectanebo II and another pretender to the throne, based in Mendes, the Greek name for the Egyptian city of *Djedet* (modern Tell el-Ruba), the capital of Egypt during the 29th dynasty, situated in the eastern part of the Nile Delta. Where Diodorus writes 'Tachos' we should read 'Nectanebo', and where he writes 'Nectanebo' we should read 'a Mendesian' or 'a pretender'. Ruzicka 2012: 152 at first opts to follow Diodorus' text to the letter and cannot but conclude '[t]his is not at all what happened, but it has some elements of truth in it', though on the same page he notices further Diodorus' confusion of the names. A more detailed (and different) account of this conflict can be found in Plu. *Ages.* 38–9. Agesilaus' role and/or position are described entirely differently in X. *Ages.* 2.28–31, Plu. *Ages.* 36–40, and Nep. *Ag.* 8.
[245] Ruzicka 2012: 152 surmises this city may have been Pelusium.

appropriate gifts. On his journey back to his native land by way of Cyrene Agesilaus died, and after his body was conveyed to Sparta packed in honey,[246] he received both a kingly burial and honour. So far did events in Asia proceed to the end of the year.

S. 105:
16.22.1–2:

Artabazus is temporarily supported by Chares; Athens withdraws its support:
(16.22.1) Having succeeded to the command of the whole fleet [in 356/5] and eager to relieve the Athenians of its expense, Chares undertook a hazardous operation. In fact, Artabazus had revolted from the Great King [in 356] and with only a few soldiers was about to take the field against the satraps, who had seventy thousand. Because Chares with his whole force fought together with Artabazus and was victorious over the force of the Great King, Artabazus, out of gratitude for his kindness, made him a present of a large sum of money, from which it was possible to pay his entire force.[247] (2) The Athenians at first approved the action of Chares, but later, after the Great King had sent ambassadors and denounced Chares, they held the opposite view. In fact, a rumour had been spread that the Great King had announced to the enemies of the Athenians that he would join them in their war against the Athenians with three hundred ships. Afraid of such an action, thus, the Assembly decided to end the war against those [of their allies] who had revolted. When the Assembly found that these desired peace as well, it easily came to terms with them.[248] The Social War, thus, as it is called, came to such an end, having lasted four years.

S. 106:
16.34.1–2:

Artabazus' revolt continues, now with help from Thebes:
(16.34.1) While these things were going on [in 353/2], Artabazus, being in revolt from the Persian king, continued the war against the

---

[246] Both Plu. *Ages.* 40.3 and Nep. *Ag.* 8.7 report that the body of Agesilaus had been enclosed in melted wax because there was no honey available.
[247] See below, 16.34.1; Isoc. *Areop.* 8, 10, 81; Plu. *Arat.* 16; Schol. Demosthenes 4.19.
[248] See 15.26; Isoc. *Pax* 16 *et passim*. Diodorus omits the fact that the Second Athenian League was considerably weakened, as Chios, Cos, and Rhodes were allowed to withdraw from it and Athens had to recognise the independence of Byzantium as well.

satraps who had been dispatched by the Great King to make war against him. At first, when Chares the commander of the Athenians was fighting with him, Artabazus resisted the satraps vigorously, but after Chares had left, being without support, he convinced the Thebans to send him an auxiliary force. They, now, choosing Pammenes as commander and giving him five thousand soldiers, dispatched him to Asia Minor. (2) By supporting Artabazus and by defeating the satraps in two great battles, Pammenes won great glory for both himself and the Boeotians. In fact, it seemed amazing that the Boeotians sent armies across the sea into Asia Minor and for the most part proved successful in the battles, after the Thessalians had abandoned them, and while the Phocian War was adding serious dangers.

S. 107:
16.36.2:

Mausolus dies and is succeeded by Artemisia:
(16.36.2) About the same time [in 353/2] Mausolus, the tyrant of Caria, died, having ruled for twenty-four years. Artemisia, his sister and wife, having succeeded him, ruled for two years.

S. 108:
16.40.1–52.8:

Artaxerxes III goes to war against Egypt:
(16.40.1) When Theellus was *archon* in Athens [351/0], the Romans elected as consuls Marcus Fabius and Titus Quintius.[249] During their term of office the Thebans, growing weary of the war against the Phocians and finding themselves short of funds, sent ambassadors to the king of the Persians beseeching him to furnish the city with a large sum of money. (2) Artaxerxes, readily acceding, made them a gift of three hundred talents of silver.[250] Between the Boeotians and the Phocians skirmishes and raids on each other's territory occurred,

---

[249] Broughton 1951: 124 lists as consuls for 354 vc M. Fabius Ambustus and T. Quinctius Poenus Capitolinus Crispinus. In some annals M. Popillius Laenas is listed instead of Quinctius. Diodorus is four years ahead of the Varronian chronology. As for the name of the Athenian *archon*, all MSS read Θεσσαλοῦ (or in the case of PX Θεσσάλου) 'Thessalus', but all Attic inscriptions give the *archon*'s name as Θέελλος, a reason to prefer that name here as well.

[250] Artaxerxes III was anything but an altruist: it appears that this paragraph is a prelude to 16.44.2, in which Diodorus relates Theban support for Artaxerxes III in his Egyptian campaign. Artaxerxes' gesture becomes, therefore, an obvious *quid pro quo*. Artabazus understood the implications and arrested Pammenes before Pammenes could betray him: see Polyaen. 7.33.2.

but no actions worth mentioning took place during this year. (3) In Asia, the king of the Persians had been unsuccessful, having, in the period treated above, made an expedition into Egypt with vast multitudes of soldiers. In the period under scrutiny he again made war on the Egyptians and, having achieved some remarkable feats by his own forceful activity, regained possession of Egypt, Phoenicia, and Cyprus.[251] (4) To ensure we make clear the history of these events, we shall first expound the causes of the war, briefly reviewing the period these events belong to. Indeed, when the Egyptians revolted from the Persians earlier, Artaxerxes, surnamed *Ochus*, being himself unwarlike, remained inactive. Though sending out armies and commanders many times, he remained unsuccessful because of the cowardice and inexperience of the commanders.[252]

The Egyptian revolt spreads to Phoenicia and Cyprus:
(5) Though regarded with contempt by the Egyptians, *Ochus* was compelled to be patient because of both his own inertia and his peace-loving nature. However, because the Phoenicians and the kings in Cyprus had imitated the Egyptians and in contemptuous disregard of him initiated revolt in the period under scrutiny, *Ochus*, enraged, decided to make war upon the insurgents. (6) He rejected, thus, the sending out of commanders, and decided that he would perform in person the struggles over his kingdom. Therefore, having made great provision of arms, missiles, food, and forces, *Ochus* assembled three hundred thousand infantry, thirty thousand cavalry, three hundred *triereis*, and five hundred merchantmen and other ships to carry the supplies.

(16.41.1) *Ochus* also began to make war on the Phoenicians for the following reasons. In Phoenicia there is an important city called Tripolis, of which the name matches its nature, for there are in it three quarters,[253] at a distance of a *stadium* [c. 185 m] from one another. Of these one is called the quarter of the Aradians, another that of the Sidonians, the third that of the Tyreians.[254] This city

---

[251] It appears that Diodorus, once again, has got his facts mixed up here. It seems that the conquest of Egypt was achieved only in 342/1, but *Ochus*' 351/0 expedition (the period this part of the *Bibliotheca* is dealing with) ended in failure.

[252] As far as we now know, this statement is valid for Artaxerxes II *Mnemon*, but Artaxerxes III *Ochus* is credited with himself having led (after the unsuccessful attempt in 360/59: see above) the, also unsuccessful, 351 expedition against Egypt. The picture painted here by Diodorus owes a great deal to Isoc. *Phil.* 101–2.

[253] Diodorus calls them πόλεις, cities. In view of the geographical evidence (see below, note 254), I prefer, however, the term 'quarter'.

[254] The city of Tripolis (modern Tripoli), situated by the sea in the northern foothills of the Lebanon Mountains, sits at the end of an excellent route towards the interior of Syria. It is

enjoys the highest repute amongst the cities of Phoenicia, and in it, as it happens, the Phoenicians hold their common council and deliberate on the greatest subjects.

Sidon revolts:
(2) Because the Great King's satraps and commanders resided in the city of the Sidonians and behaved insolently and arrogantly towards the Sidonians in ordering things to be done, those maltreated, who found the conduct hard to bear, decided to revolt from the Persians.[255] (3) After they had also persuaded the other Phoenicians to cling to their independence, they sent ambassadors to Nectanebo, the king of the Egyptians. He was hostile to the Persians, and after persuading him to accept them as allies, they began to prepare for the war. (4) Because Sidon stood out for its prosperity and because its private citizens had amassed great wealth from its trade by sea, many *triereis* were quickly equipped and a multitude of mercenaries quickly gathered, and, besides, arms, missiles, food, and all the other materials useful in war were immediately prepared. (5) Beginning the hostilities, they cut down and destroyed the royal park in which the Persian kings were used to take their recreation. Next they burned the fodder for the horses, stored up by the satraps for the war. Finally, having apprehended Persians who had committed acts of insolence, they took vengeance upon them. (6) After the war against the Phoenicians had had such a beginning, the Great King, having learned of the insurgents' effrontery, issued threatening warnings to all the Phoenicians and in particular to the people of Sidon.
(16.42.1) In Babylon the Great King, after assembling his infantry and immediately raising cavalry forces, advanced against the Phoenicians. While he was still on the way, Belesys, the satrap of Syria,[256] and Mazaeus, the ruler of Cilicia,[257] having joined forces,

---

some 80 km north of present Beirut (which is north of both Sidon and Tyre, though south of Aradus (modern Ruad), an island nowadays situated in Syria), and consisted of three quarters, allegedly founded by these three cities, namely Aradus, Sidon, and Tyre. See Rey-Coquais 1976.

[255] Diodorus is here quite hazy in what he intends to convey, including by his use of the term πόλεις for the quarters of Tripolis. From the context (esp. 16.42.2) it becomes clear that he is now referring to the city of Sidon itself, as Tennes (*Tabnit* in Phoenician) is mentioned as the city's king. Tennes ruled the city of Sidon until he was killed at *Ochus*' orders in 346/5 (see, for example, Markoe 2000).

[256] He was also the satrap of 'Beyond the River', the trans-Euphrates region, including Phoenicia.

[257] Numismatic evidence suggests that Mazaeus officially had supervision over the Persians' Phoenician affairs, issuing *inter alia* Sidonian coinage, with some interruptions (notably for 347 and 346, suggesting this may have been the date of the Sidonian revolt) from c. 353 to 333, when Alexander the Great took over: see Ruzicka 2012: 159, 165.

opened the war against the Phoenicians. (2) Tennes, the king of Sidon, acquired from the Egyptians four thousand Greek mercenary soldiers, under the command of Mentor the Rhodian.[258] Having engaged the aforementioned satraps with these and the citizen soldiers, Mentor defeated them and drove the enemy out of Phoenicia.

Cyprus revolts:
(3) While these things were going on, a war broke out in Cyprus as well, of which the actions were interwoven with the war in question in Egypt. (4) In fact, in this island there were nine substantial *poleis*,[259] and under these were ranged small towns which belonged to the nine *poleis*. Each of these *poleis* had a king as ruler of the *polis*, but subject to the king of the Persians. (5) All these kings in common agreement and in imitation of the Phoenicians revolted and, after having made preparations for the war, made their own kingdoms independent. (6) Incensed at these actions, Artaxerxes wrote to Idrieus,[260] ruler of Caria, who had only recently come to power [in 351/0] and was a friend and ally of the Persians of old,[261] to collect both an infantry force and a navy to carry on a war with the kings in Cyprus. (7) Idrieus, now, having immediately equipped forty *triereis* and eight thousand mercenary soldiers, sent them to Cyprus, having assigned as commanders Phocion the Athenian and Evagoras,[262] who had formerly been king in the island. (8) These two, thus, having

---

[258] The brother-in-law of Artabazus.

[259] They are Salamis, Citium, Paphos, Curium, Amathus, Marium, Soli, Lapethus, and Ceryneia: see Maier 1994: 327.

[260] Here, too, we encounter some problems. Regarding problems in Cyprus in 346, Isoc. *Phil.* 103 discusses Idrieus, satrap of Caria since 351/o, after Mausolus' death and the two-year reign of Artemisia, as a *potential* rebel. Idrieus himself died in 344 (see, for example, Hornblower 2011: 283). Either Isocrates' discourse is vain and void or the action Diodorus refers to in this paragraph must have taken place between 346 and 344, which seems to agree with modern ideas that place this expedition in 344: see also Sherman 1963: 355 note 1. Either way, Diodorus' description here, compressing all the events within the description of one year, looks again like telescoping (see above, note 224). For Maus(s)olus see Ruzicka 1992: 90–9; for Artemisia and Idrieus see ibid.: 100–19.

[261] Diodorus appears to omit the fact that Mausolus, briefly as it may have been, had joined a revolt against the Persian king (see 15.90.3), as Isoc. *Phil.* 103 also points out.

[262] This Evagoras should not be confused with the Evagoras who ruled Salamis between 411 and 373 and had previously been in conflict with Artaxerxes II (see 14.98.3; 15.2.1–4.3; and 15.8.1–11.2). That Evagoras had been murdered in 373, and succeeded by Nicocles (almost certainly a son of his). This Nicocles had, probably in 361, been succeeded by his son Evagoras II, who – according to the coins issued in his name – ruled between 361 and 351: he is the Evagoras this paragraph appears to refer to (see Theopomp.Hist. *FGrH/BNJ* 115 F 111; also Arist. *Pol.* 5.1311B; Isocr. *Cypr.* 31–47, *Evag.* 72). This Evagoras II, in his turn, was – again, this is on the basis of numismatic evidence – succeeded by Pnytagoras, who ruled between 351 and 332. Diodorus' text might imply (see 16.46.2, below) that the succession had already taken place some time before 351 and was the consequence of a *coup d'état*: see also Maier 1994: 329.

Revolt and Sedition 261

sailed to Cyprus, at once led their force against Salamis, the largest of the *poleis*. After erecting a palisade and fortifying the encampment, they began to besiege the Salaminians simultaneously by land and sea. Because the whole island had enjoyed peace for a long time[263] and because the territory was wealthy, the soldiers, who had possession of the open country, gathered much booty. (9) When their affluence was bruited around, many from the opposite coast of both Syria and Cilicia voluntarily flowed together as soldiers towards the hope of gain.[264] Finally, after the army with Evagoras and Phocion had doubled in size, the kings throughout Cyprus fell into anxiety and very great fear. Such was the situation in Cyprus.

Artaxerxes III marches into Phoenicia:
(16.43.1) After this, the king of the Persians, who had begun his expedition from Babylon, led forth his army against Phoenicia. After he had learned the size of the force of the Persians and believing that the insurgents were no match for this, Tennes,[265] the ruler of Sidon, decided to provide for his personal safety. (2) Therefore he sent out the most loyal of his servants, Thettalion, to Artaxerxes, without the knowledge of the people of Sidon, reporting to *Ochus* that he would betray Sidon, would make war against Egypt with him, and would contribute great services, as he was familiar with the geography of Egypt and knew the landing-places along the Nile accurately. (3) When the Great King heard these particulars from Thettalion, he was especially pleased and said that he would free Tennes of the charges relative to the revolt, and he promised that he would give rich rewards if Tennes performed all that he had agreed upon. However, when Thettalion added that Tennes asked him also to give pledges to confirm his promise, the Great King, flying into a rage at these words at the thought that he was not trusted,[266] handed Thettalion over to his attendants and gave them orders to behead him. (4) When Thettalion was being led off to his punishment, he said as follows: 'You, o king, will do as you please, but Tennes will assuredly not perform any of his promises because you refuse the

---

[263] At least over some thirty years, from 383.
[264] This seems to contradict the statement in Isoc. *Phil.* 102 that Artaxerxes had lost Cilicia. The remark may have been valid, though, for some cities.
[265] All MSS read here, instead of Τέννης ('Tennes'), Μέντωρ ('Mentor'). However, at least from Wesseling onward, all editors have emended this.
[266] The Great King operated within a religious and ethical system that expressly forbade lies, deceit, and the breaking of oaths (see also Herodotus' remark that the essence of Persian education was 'to ride, to shoot, and to tell the truth': Hdt. 1.136). See also Hirsch 1985: 18–19 on Tissaphernes.

pledge, though he is able to achieve complete success.' After he heard these things, the Great King changed his mind again and, recalling the attendants, charged them to release Thettalion and gave him his right hand: this is the surest pledge amongst the Persians. Thettalion, thus, returning to Sidon, reported what had happened to Tennes without the knowledge of the people of Sidon.

(16.44.1) As the Great King put the conquest of Egypt as a high priority in view of his former defeat,[267] he sent out envoys to the greatest *poleis* of Greece, requesting them to make war against the Egyptians together with the Persians. Now the Athenians and the Lacedaemonians said they would observe their friendship towards the Persians, but oppose sending allied troops. (2) However, after they had chosen Lacrates as commander, the Thebans dispatched him with a thousand hoplites. The Argives sent three thousand men, but they themselves did not choose a commander. After the Great King had asked by name for Nicostratus as commander, though, they assented. (3) In fact, Nicostratus was good both in action and in counsel, but there was madness mingled with his intelligence. Being exceptional in bodily strength, he used to imitate Heracles when on a campaign and dressed in a lion's skin and carried a club in battle. (4) Like these *poleis*, the Greeks who inhabited the sea-coast of Asia Minor dispatched six thousand men, making the total of Greeks becoming allies ten thousand. Before their arrival, the Great King, after he had traversed Syria and reached Phoenicia, pitched camp not far from Sidon.

Artaxerxes III attacks Sidon:
(5) Because the Great King had been slow to move, the Sidonians made the preparation of food, armour, and missiles their prime concern. Likewise they had surrounded their city with huge triple ditches and constructions of lofty walls. (6) They also had a sufficient number of citizen soldiers, well trained in exercises and hard work and superior in the vigour and strength of their bodies. In wealth and in other resources the city far exceeded the other cities of Phoenicia and had, as main asset, more than a hundred *triereis* and *penteres*.[268]

---

[267] Diodorus juggles with his facts in this paragraph. *Ochus* conquered Egypt in 341, while he was defeated in 351/0 – the very year described in this and the following *capita*. There is, therefore, no *prior* defeat, at least not by *Ochus*, to be accounted for in this part of the history.

[268] The *penteres* is credited to the invention of Dionysius I of Syracuse in or shortly after 398 (see 14.42.2). Afterwards, this type of ship gradually appeared in the eastern Mediterranean too. Due to their relations with Carthage, the Phoenicians may have employed this type of ship even before the *poleis* of mainland Greece (see Morrison and Williams 1968: 249). As regards the configuration of the *penteres* there is, to the best of my knowledge, as yet no solid evidence.

(16.45.1) After Tennes had confided his treason to Mentor, the commander of the mercenaries from Egypt, he left him to guard a portion of the city and to collaborate with those handling the treason. He himself marched out of the city with five hundred men, pretending that he was going to a common meeting of the Phoenicians. He took with him the most distinguished of the citizens, one hundred men, under the guise of advisers. (2) When they were near the Great King, Tennes delivered the hundred men to Artaxerxes after he had suddenly seized them. The Great King, who welcomed him as a friend, had the hundred shot as if they were guilty of the revolt. When five hundred of the foremost Sidonians approached *Ochus* like suppliants, he summoned Tennes and asked him whether he was able to deliver the city to him. In fact, *Ochus* was very eager not to get hold of Sidon by surrender, since his aim was to overwhelm the Sidonians with a merciless disaster and to strike terror into the other cities by their punishment. (3) When Tennes had assured him that he would hand over the city, the Great King, maintaining his implacable rage, had all five hundred, still holding the supplicant branches, shot down. Next Tennes, going to the mercenaries from Egypt, convinced them to lead both him and the Great King inside the walls. (4) Thus Sidon was delivered to the Persians by such treason.[269] Believing Tennes was of no further use to him, the Great King put him to death. The people of Sidon burned all their ships before the arrival of the king, to ensure that none of the people in the city would be able to procure personal safety by sailing out.[270] However, when they saw the city and that the walls were captured and swarming with many myriads of soldiers, after shutting themselves, their children, and their women up in their houses, they set them in flames. (5) The word is that those who were then killed in the fire, including the domestics, were more than forty thousand. After this disaster had befallen the Sidonians and the whole city together with its inhabitants had been consumed by the fire, the Great King sold the burnt ruins for many talents.[271]

---

[269] ABC: 114 [9] (also Glassner, 2004: 240 no. 28) dates the arrival of prisoners from Sidon to Babylon (and Susa) between 11 October and 9 November of the year 14 of Artaxerxes, which is 345. 345 may therefore well have been the year of the sack of Sidon. *Contra*: Stevenson 1997: 134 and n. 17.

[270] It seems, rather, a precautionary measure instigated by Mentor, after being informed of Tennes' treason, to prevent these ships being used by Artaxerxes III to invade Egypt. See Ruzicka 2012: 171.

[271] In spite of this description, Arr. *An.* 2.20–1 and Curt. 4.1.15 discuss Sidon, at the time of Alexander the Great, as an important harbour, if not a large and powerful city, hardly two decades after the events described here by Diodorus. It leaves one wondering whether the destruction by Artaxerxes was as thorough as Diodorus pretends, or whether Arrian and

(6) In fact, as a result of the prosperity of the residents there was found a vast amount of both silver and gold massed together by the fire. Thus the disasters which had befallen Sidon had such a fateful conclusion, and the other cities in Phoenicia, terrified, went over to the Persians. (7) Shortly before this time Artemisia, the ruler over Caria, passed away after having ruled two years,[272] and Idrieus, her brother, succeeded her and ruled seven years. (8) ... (9) ...

The Cypriot War comes to an end:
(16.46.1) When Apollodorus was *archon* in Athens [350/49], the Romans elected as consuls Marcus Valerius and Gaius Sulpicius.[273] During their term of office, the rest of the cities in Cyprus all became subject to the Persians,[274] while the people of Salamis were being besieged by Evagoras II and Phocion, and Pnytagoras, the king of Salamis, alone continued to endure the siege.[275] (2) Evagoras was trying to retrieve the ancestral rule over the Salaminians and tried to make his return to the kingship through the king of the Persians. Later, though, after he had been falsely accused to Artaxerxes and the Great King was supporting Pnytagoras, Evagoras, having put his return out of his mind and having made his defence against the accusations brought against him, was deemed worthy of another and higher command in Asia.[276] (3) However, after he had administered his office badly, he fled again to Cyprus and, after being arrested, duly received punishment. After Pnytagoras had voluntarily submitted to the Persians, he thenceforth confidently continued to rule Salamis.

Artaxerxes III enters Egypt:
(4) After the capture of Sidon, after his allies from Argos and Thebes and the Greek cities throughout Asia Minor had arrived, having

---

Curtius exaggerated the significance of Sidon at Alexander's time to some extent, either to do justice to the city's reputation or to make Alexander shine out.

[272] She ruled 353–351, succeeding her husband Mausolus. In itself Diodorus places Artemisia's death in the right year: above (16.42.6–7) he described Idrieus as being already in position, having succeeded Artemisia: it adds to the confused picture Diodorus creates by placing the (successful) expedition against Egypt here.

[273] For the year 353 vc, Broughton 1951: 125 lists as consuls C. Sulpicius Peticus and M. Valerius Poplicola, as dictator T. Manlius Imperiosus Torquatus. Diodorus is four years ahead of the Varronian chronology.

[274] Ruzicka 2012: 174 surmises the surrender of the rebellious Cypriot *poleis* really took place in 344/3.

[275] Pnytagoras had succeeded Evagoras II after a *coup d'état*, possibly because of Evagoras' pro-Persian attitude. See Maier 1994: 329. Possibly Pnytagoras at this stage feared a similar fate to that of Tennes after a surrender.

[276] As Maier 1994: 330 remarks, numismatic evidence suggests this command may well have been the kingdom of Sidon, from 344/3 to 342/1. See also Ruzicka 2012: 175 and note 29.

Revolt and Sedition 265

assembled his whole force, the king of the Persians advanced against Egypt. (5) As he came to the great marshy lake where the *Barathra* ['the Pits'] are,[277] as they are called, Ochus lost a portion of his force through his unfamiliarity with the region.[278] Having discussed the nature of the marshy lake before and the peculiar mishaps which occur there in the first book,[279] we shall forbear to discuss the same subjects twice. (6) Having passed through the *Barathra* with his force, the Great King came to Pelusium. This is a city at the first branch through which the Nile empties into the sea. The Persians pitched camp at a distance of forty *stadia* [c. 6.5 km] from Pelusium, but the Greeks close to the town itself. (7) Because the Persians had given them much time for preparation, the Egyptians already had all the mouths of the Nile well fortified, especially that near Pelusium because that was the first and the most advantageously situated. (8) Five thousand soldiers garrisoned the town, under the command of Philophron the Spartiate. Because the Thebans were eager to show themselves the best of the allied Greeks, they recklessly tried, first and unsupported, to cross through a narrow and deep canal. (9) After they had passed through it and were assaulting the walls, the garrison of Pelusium sallied forth from the city and engaged the Thebans in battle. As the engagement proved severe because of mutual rivalries,[280] they were separated by the night, having spent at that time the whole day in the battle.

Artaxerxes III splits the Persian army:
(16.47.1) After the Great King on the next day divided the Greek force into three parts, each contingent had a Greek as commander, and stationed along beside him a Persian as partner in command, the most eminent for both *aretē* and loyalty. (2) The Boeotians held the forward line, which had as commander Lacrates of Thebes and as Persian captain Rhoesaces. The latter was a descendant of one of the seven Persians[281] who deposed the *Magi* and was satrap of Ionia and Lydia. He was accompanied by a large cavalry and no small infantry army of the Persians. (3) The second contingent was the line

---

[277] (Lake) Sirbonis, at present Lake Bardawil, a salty marshland. See also, for example, 1.30.4–9; Hdt. 2.6; Str. 16.2.32–3/760.
[278] Ruzicka 2012: 162, 182, suggests this episode might in reality have been part of the 351 expedition against Egypt. It seems unlikely that, with Mentor at his side, Artaxerxes III would not have avoided this trap.
[279] 1.30.4–9.
[280] Both sides essentially consisting of Greek mercenaries.
[281] Namely Darius the Great and his accomplices: see, for example, Hdt. 3.76–9; also Ctes. *Pers.* F 13(16–17).

of the Argives under the command of Nicostratus and with him as Persian fellow commander Aristazanes. The latter was an usher of the Great King and the most trusted of his friends after Bagoas. Five thousand elite soldiers and eighty *triereis* were assigned to him. (4) Of the third contingent Mentor was commander, who had betrayed Sidon, with the mercenaries that were formerly under his command. Together with him campaigned Bagoas, exceptionally daring and unrestrained, whom the king trusted most. He had the Great King's Greeks and a sufficient number of Persians and many ships. (5) *Ochus* himself with the remainder of the force held himself in reserve for the whole action. This was the distribution of the army on the Persian side. The king of the Egyptians, Nectanebo, was worried neither by the multitude of the enemy nor by the total deployment of the Persians forces, though his numbers were far less. (6) In fact, he had twenty thousand Greek mercenaries, about the same number of Libyans, and sixty thousand Egyptians known amongst them as 'the warriors',[282] and besides these an incredible number of river vessels suited for the fights and engagements on the Nile. (7) The bank of the river facing Arabia had also been strongly fortified by him, being a region crowded with towns and, besides, all intersected by walls and ditches. Although he had all the other preparations which were adequate for the war ready as well, he completely fell down because of his own poor judgement.[283]

(16.48.1) The reason for his defeat was above all his lack of experience in commanding an army and the fact that the Persians had been defeated by him in the previous expedition. (2) In fact, he had had as the commanders of the day men who were distinguished and outstanding both in *aretē* and in sagacity in the art of war, namely Diophantus the Athenian and Lamius the Spartiate, through whom everything was accomplished successfully. However, now assuming that he was an accomplished commander, he did not want to share the command with anyone, and because of his inexperience he was unable to perform any of the useful manoeuvres in this war.

---

[282] See Ruzicka 2012: 4–5 and note 8, 17–22. For these *machimoi* see also Fischer-Bovet 2013.

[283] Diodorus makes, once more, a mess of his chronology. Though he claims to describe events in 351/0, the actual defeat of Egypt occurred at the latest in 341. That Diodorus may well have been acutely aware of the actual course of events is suggested in his following sentence. See also Lloyd 1994: 349: 'the second [attempt to recapture Egypt], apparently in 351, is alleged to have failed through the cowardice and inexperience of its leaders and seems to have made Artaxerxes something of a laughing-stock . . . . The third was an altogether different matter. After the most meticulous preparation, Artaxerxes marched south again in 343/2, and in 341, thanks to the military incompetence of Nectanebo and treachery within the Egyptian forces, the country was once more in Persian hands.'

(3) Interspersing sufficient garrisons among them, he guarded the towns closely; he himself remained in reserve with thirty thousand Egyptians, five thousand Greeks, and half the Libyans, to defend the most exposed approaches.

Part of the Persian army attacks an Egyptian stronghold:
While this was the deployment of the forces on both sides, Nicostratus, the commander of the Argives, with Egyptian guides whose children and wives were held as hostages by the Persians, sailed by with his fleet through a canal into a hidden place and, after disembarking his men and fortifying a site for an encampment, pitched camp there. (4) When the mercenaries of the Egyptians, who were guarding the neighbouring district, observed the presence of the enemy, they straightway made a sally, being in number not less than seven thousand. (5) Clinius the Coan, their commander, deployed his force to fight.[284] After those who had sailed in were drawn up opposite, a desperate battle ensued in the course of which the Greeks serving with the Persians, fighting brilliantly, both killed the commander Clinius and cut down more than five thousand of the rest of the soldiers. (6) When Nectanebo, the Egyptian king, heard of the loss of his men, he was panic-stricken, thinking that the rest of the force of the Persians would also easily cross the river. (7) Because he assumed that the enemy with their entire army would come to Memphis itself, he decided to provide for this city in particular. Accordingly he returned to Memphis with the army he had retained and began to prepare for the siege.

Siege of Pelusium:
(16.49.1) Lacrates the Theban, who was in command of the first contingent, started the siege of Pelusium. After he had diverted the stream of the canal in other directions and had filled it with earth when the channel had become dry, he brought siege engines against the city. When a large portion of the walls fell, the garrison in Pelusium quickly built others instead and raised up huge towers of wood. (2) As the battle for the walls continued for several days running, the Greeks in Pelusium at first vigorously warded off the besiegers. When, however, they learned of the king's withdrawal to Memphis, terror-stricken they sent envoys to arrange a

---

[284] Ruzicka 2012: 186 surmises this force was located at Daphnae, 'an important part of the 26th (Saïte) dynasty's eastern defense line (Hdt. 2.154)', halfway between Bubastis and Pelusium.

settlement. (3) Because Lacrates gave them pledges backed by oaths that if they surrendered Pelusium, they would all be conveyed back to Greece with whatever they could carry off, they surrendered the garrison. (4) After this, Artaxerxes dispatched Bagoas[285] with Persian soldiers to take over Pelusium. When the Persian soldiers arrived at the place as the Greeks [who had been in Egyptian service] were issuing forth, they seized many of the articles the Greek soldiers were carrying out. (5) When the victims of this injustice were angered and called loudly upon the gods who were guardians of their oaths, Lacrates, becoming incensed, put the Persians to flight, and, slaying a number of them, stood by those who suffered from the broken oaths. (6) After Bagoas [**Rhoesaces**] had fled to the Great King and had accused Lacrates, Artaxerxes decided that Bagoas' [**Rhoesaces'**] contingent had met with their just deserts and put to death the Persians who were responsible for the robbery. This was, thus, the fashion Pelusium was delivered to the Persians.

Bubastis is taken too:
(7) Mentor, who was in command of the third contingent and had captured Bubastis[286] and many other cities, made them subject to the Great King by a single stratagem. Because all the cities were garrisoned by two peoples, both Greeks and Egyptians, Mentor passed the word around to the soldiers that King Artaxerxes had decided to treat those who voluntarily surrendered their cities magnanimously, but to mete out the same penalty as he had imposed on the people of Sidon to those who were overcome by force. He also instructed those who guarded the gates to permit passage to those who wished to desert from the other side. (8) Because the captured Egyptians, therefore, were leaving their quarters without hindrance, the aforementioned word was quickly spread throughout all the cities of Egypt.[287] Immediately, thus, the mercenaries of Nectanebo were everywhere at variance with the natives and the cities were filled with strife. In fact, each and every one was privately eagerly trying to surrender

---

[285] More likely Rhoesaces, as Bagoas was engaged at Bubastis with Mentor. I believe in the rest of this episode too Rhoesaces should be read for Bagoas.
[286] Though Diodorus calls the city 'Bubastus', I prefer here to use its proper name of Bubastis, a city in the eastern Nile Delta. See, for a summary view and main literature, Shaw and Nicholson 2008: 54–5 *s.v.* 'Basta, Tell'. Strategically and politically Bubastis was of prime importance: see also Ruzicka 2012: 188.
[287] The retreat of Nectanebo II to Memphis meant that Egypt's defensive forces throughout the Nile Delta had to sustain the chances of war without the likelihood of the arrival of the relief force led by the Egyptian king. For the mercenaries an additional setback became the uncertainty of pay, now the position of the king was insecure.

their posts and nursing private hopes of gain in exchange for this favour, which is what actually happened first in the case of the city of Bubastis.
(16.50.1) When, namely, the forces of Mentor and Bagoas had pitched camp near it, the Egyptians, without the knowledge of the Greeks,[288] sent someone to Bagoas, offering to surrender the city if he would consent to their safety. (2) When the Greeks became aware of the mission, they overtook the envoy and, threatening him, learned the truth. Consequently, they attacked the Egyptians in great anger, killed some, wounded others, and herded the rest into a quarter of the city. (3) The beaten men, after notifying Bagoas of what had taken place, asked him to come with all speed to receive the city from them. After the Greeks had secretly been exchanging messages with Mentor, he covertly encouraged them to attack the Persians, as soon as Bagoas should enter Bubastis.

Mentor and Bagoas strike up a friendship:
(4) Afterwards, when Bagoas with the Persians was entering the city without the sanction of the Greeks and when a portion of his men had got inside, the Greeks, having suddenly closed the gates, attacked those who were inside the walls, and, having killed them all, they took Bagoas himself prisoner. (5) The latter, seeing that his hopes of safety lay in Mentor, begged him to save him and promised in future to do nothing without his advice. (6) Mentor, convincing the Greeks to set Bagoas free and to arrange the surrender through himself, won credit for his success. Having become responsible, though, for the rescue of Bagoas, he made an agreement with him for common action, and after an exchange of pledges on this matter, kept the agreement faithfully till the end of his life. (7) Therefore it occurred that these men, co-operating in the service of the Great King, achieved later on the greatest power of all the friends and relatives at Artaxerxes' court.[289] In fact, Mentor, having been appointed chief commander in the coastal districts of Asia, performed great services for the Great King, gathering mercenaries from Greece and sending them to Artaxerxes, and in the course of his activities administering all his duties courageously and loyally. (8) As for Bagoas, after he had administered all the Great King's affairs in the upper

---

[288] Diodorus refers here to the Greek mercenaries of Nectanebo II, recruited to defend the city and, most likely, a combination of Egyptian *machimoi*, 'warriors', and civilians, likewise enclosed within Bubastis.
[289] In this case possibly, or even probably, not (all) real relatives. As *LSJ*, *s.v.*, rightly remarks, συγγενής 'represented a title bestowed at the Persian court by the king as a mark of honour'.

satrapies,²⁹⁰ he rose to such power because of his partnership with Mentor that he was master of the kingdom, and Artaxerxes did nothing without his advice. And after Artaxerxes' death he designated in every case the successor to the throne and enjoyed all the functions of kingship save the title. But of these matters we shall record the details in their proper chronological sequence.

Nectanebo flees; aftermath of the expedition:
(16.51.1) At that time, after the surrender of Bubastis, the remaining cities, terror-stricken, were surrendered to the Persians by capitulation. But King Nectanebo, while still staying at Memphis and perceiving the trend of the cities towards betrayal, did not dare to engage the fights for his dominion. So giving up hope of his kingship and taking with him the greater part of his possessions, he fled to Ethiopia.²⁹¹ (2) After Artaxerxes had taken over all Egypt and demolished the walls of the most important cities,²⁹² he gathered a vast quantity of both silver and gold by plundering the shrines, and he carried off the records from the ancient temples, which later on Bagoas returned to the priests of the Egyptians for a vast ransom.²⁹³ (3) After he had rewarded those of the Greeks who had accompanied him on the campaign with lavish gifts, each according to his deserts, he dismissed them to their native lands. Having installed Pherendates as satrap of Egypt,²⁹⁴ he returned with his force to Babylon, bearing many possessions and spoils and having won great renown by his successes.

---

[290] These were the satrapies in the interior of the empire.

[291] Most likely this means he made a tactical retreat into Nubia, very much as the 25th dynasty King Taharqa had done, faced with the Assyrian conquest of Egypt, hoping to return later: see also Ruzicka 2012: 193.

[292] Most likely Diodorus means here the cities in the Delta. There is no indication that the Persian army advanced further south than Memphis: see Ruzicka 2012: 201–2; in Edfu (between Asswan and Egyptian Thebes), for example, there is an inscription dating to the eighteenth year of Nectanebo II, 342/1, a year after Artaxerxes' victory.

[293] It appears, thus, that Artaxerxes III *Ochus*, unlike Cambyses and Darius, tried to dismantle Egypt's religious and political system: see also Ruzicka 2012: 195 and notes 18 and 19. Schwartz 1949: 68–70 remarks that the story of Cambyses and the Apis bull really took place during the rule of *Ochus*. Nevertheless, this paper is less than positive regarding Cambyses' attitude towards the Egyptians.

[294] Of this Pherendates no personal data are known. Perhaps he was a descendent of the Pherendates mentioned in 11.61.3, who was a nephew of Xerxes I: if so, he belonged to the Achaemenid family. Pherendates ruled for some years, probably until the murder of Artaxerxes III in 338. It seems likely that in his absence one Khabash, also known as Chababash, revolted and took the kingship of Egypt for about two years, ruling from Saïs: he is mentioned on the so-called *Satrap Stela* of Ptolemy *Lagides*, lines 35, 80 (translated by Ritner 2003; see also Ritner 1980). Darius III restored order and instated Sabaces as satrap about 335. Sabacus joined Darius III at Issus in 333: his position in Egypt was (with Sabacus' consent?) taken by Mazaeus (sometimes also called Mazaces), who was there in 332 (Arr. *An.* 2.11.8; also Curt. 3.11.10, 4.1.28; below, 17.34.5).

Mentor is rewarded for his services:
(16.52.1) When Callimachus was *archon* at Athens [349/8], the Romans elected as consuls Gaius Marcius and Publius Valerius.[295] During their term of office Artaxerxes, seeing that Mentor the general had performed great services for him in the war against the Egyptians, advanced him more than any of his companions. (2) Assessing the man on his qualities, *Ochus* gave him a hundred talents [3,000 kg or c. 2,600 kg, depending on whether measured in Babylonian or in Attic talents] of silver and also the best of expensive decorations. He appointed him satrap of the coast of Asia Minor and placed him in charge of the war against the rebels, having designated him commander-in-chief. (3) And since Mentor was related to Artabazus and Memnon,[296] both of whom had made war against the Persians in the preceding times, at that time having fled from Asia and residing at the court of Philip, he requested the Great King and prevailed upon him to dismiss the charges against them. Immediately afterwards he also summoned them both to come to him with all their families. (4) In fact, Artabazus had got by the sister of Mentor and Memnon eleven sons and ten daughters. Being delighted with the large number of children, Mentor promoted the boys, giving them the most distinguished commands in the armed forces. (5) He made his first campaign against Hermias the tyrant of Atarneus, who had revolted from the Great King and was master of many fortresses and *poleis*.[297] (6) After he had promised Hermias that he would convince the Great King to dismiss the charges against him as well, he met to speak with him and, after deceiving him, arrested him. After Mentor had got possession of Hermias' signet ring and had written to the *poleis* that Hermias had reconciled with the Great King through Mentor, and after Mentor had sealed the letters with Hermias' ring, he sent the letters together with men who were to take over the districts. (7) The people of the *poleis*, trusting

---

[295] Broughton 1951: 125 lists as consuls for 352 vc P. Valerius Poplicola and C. Marcus Rutilius, as dictator C. Iulius (Iullus?). Diodorus is four years ahead of the Varronian chronology.
[296] Artabazus was his brother-in-law, Memnon his brother; see below, paragraph 4.
[297] Apparently Diodorus' chronology is still a mess. The *successful* conclusion of the Egyptian War, after which Mentor could be relieved of those duties, was no earlier than 342, some six years after Callimachus was Athens' *archon*. The war against Hermias was also not before 342: after Plato's death (348/7), Aristotle lived at least three years at Hermias' court (see also Stronk, *BNJ* 77 F 1; see also Theopompus, *FGrH/BNJ* 115 F 219, and Callisthenes of Olynthus, *FGrH/BNJ* 124 FF 2-3). In the time of Callimachus' archonship, Artaxerxes III *Ochus* was too focused on Egypt, Cyprus, and Phoenicia to worry greatly about Hermias and, more important, Mentor was not yet in his service. Engels 1998 puts Hermias' death at 341. Hermias ruled over several *poleis*, located in the region between Atarneus in Aeolis and Assos in the Troad, including at least both these *poleis*.

the documents and gladly accepting the peace, all surrendered their fortresses and *poleis*. Because Mentor, thus, had recovered the towns of the rebels through deception quickly and without risk, he won great favour with the Great King, who concluded that Mentor was capable of acting prudently as commander. (8) Similarly with regard to the other rulers who were at odds with the Persians, Mentor soon subdued them all, some by force and others by stratagem. Such was then the state of affairs in Asia.

S. 109:
16.56.6–7:

Value of property stolen by Phocians from Delphi (and by Alexander the Great in Persia):
(16.56.6) ... the value of the stolen property surpassed ten thousand talents. (7) Some of the historians say that the pillaged property was not less than the sums acquired by Alexander in the Persian treasuries. ...

S. 110:
16.75.1–2:

Growth of Philip's power alarms the Great King:
(16.75.1) ... Because reports of the increase of power of Philip, the king of Macedon, had been passed on throughout Asia, the Great King, alarmed by Philip's power, wrote to his satraps on the coast to help the Perinthians with all their might. (2) Therefore the satraps after deliberating sent to Perinthus a force of mercenaries, ample funds, sufficient food, missiles, and all the other necessities for military use.

S. 111:
16.89.1–3:

Philip of Macedon announces he wants to invade Persia:
(16.89.1) When Phrynichus was *archon* at Athens [337/6], the Romans installed as consuls Titus Manlius Torquatus and Publius Decius.[298] During their term of office, King Philip, proudly conscious

---

[298] Broughton 1951: 135–6 lists T. Manlius Imperiosus Torquatus and P. Decius Mus as the consuls of 340 vc, L. Papirius Crassus as the dictator. Diodorus is still four years ahead of the Varronian chronology.

Revolt and Sedition 273

of his victory at Chaeronea and seeing that he had dashed the confidence of the most noticeable Greek *poleis*, developed the ambition of becoming the leader of all Greece. (2) Spreading the word that he wanted to make war against the Persians on the Greeks' behalf and to punish the Persians for the profanation of the temples, this won for him the loyal support of the Greeks. He showed a kindly face to all, both in private and in public, and he continued to make clear to the *poleis* that he wished to discuss with them matters of mutual benefit. (3) After, therefore, a general congress had convened at Corinth, speaking about the war against Persia and raising great expectations, he won the representatives over to war. After the Greeks had finally elected him plenipotentiary commander of Greece, he started to make great preparations for the campaign against the Persians. After he had ordered for each *polis* the number of soldiers for the alliance, he returned to Macedonia. This was the state of affairs as regards Philip.

S. 112:
15.90.2:

Ariobarzanes dies, Mithridates succeeds:
(15.90.2) Around this time [337/6] Ariobarzanes II died, having ruled during twenty-six years, and having succeeded him Mithridates ruled for thirty-five years over Cius.[299]

S. 113:
16.91.1–4:

Philip sets in motion his plans to invade Persia:
(16.91.1) When Pythodorus was *archon* at Athens [336/5], the Romans elected as consuls Quintus Publius and Tiberius Aemilius Mamercus, and the one hundred and eleventh celebration of the Olympic Games took place, in which Cleomantis of Cleitor won the *stadium* race.[300] (2) As these events took place, King Philip, having been installed as leader by the Greeks and opening the war with

---

[299] Ariobarzanes II had been the satrap who had revolted against Artaxerxes II *Mnemon* in 362. The dynasty of Cius would later establish the kingdom of Pontus, founded by Mithridates I *Ctistes*, who reigned from 281 to 266.
[300] The *archon*'s name was Pythodelus, and his term ran from July 336 to June 335. The Olympic Games were held in midsummer, 336. The consuls of 339 vc were Ti. Aemilius Mamercinus and Q. Publilius Philo, the dictator Q. Publilius Philo: see Broughton 1951: 137. Diodorus is still four years ahead of the Varronian chronology.

Persia, sent Attalus and Parmenion ahead into Asia Minor, giving them a part of the force and ordering them to liberate the Greek *poleis*. He himself, wanting to enter upon the war with the gods' approval, asked the Pythia whether he would conquer the king of the Persians. She prophesied to him with the oracular utterance: 'Wreathed is the bull. The end is near. He who will perform the sacrifice is present.'[301] (3) Though Philip found this utterance ambiguous, he interpreted the oracle in his own favour, that is, that the response prophesied that the Persian would be slaughtered like a sacrificial victim. The truth did not hold such an outcome, but on the contrary it signalled that Philip in the midst of a festival and holy sacrifices, like the bull, would be slaughtered being decked with a garland. (4) Nevertheless, believing that the gods would fight at his side he was elated that Asia would be made captive under the hands of the Macedonians. . . .

[[Next Diodorus relates how one Pausanias killed Philip. Because that episode falls more or less outside the history of Persia proper, I have left that part out.]]

---

[301] The oracle is cited in the same form by Paus. 8.7.6.

5 Alexander the Great Defeats Darius III

[[The first chapters of book 17 are devoted to the rise of Alexander after the murder of Philip. Since they have no direct relationship with the history of Persia, I have omitted them from this account.]]

A. DARIUS III CODOMANNUS (C. 380–330)[1]

S. 114:
17.4.9:

Alexander is appointed commander plenipotentiary of the Greeks:
(17.4.9) After Alexander had called a meeting at Corinth of both envoys and delegates,[2] and when the usual representatives came, as the king spoke to them using moderate terms, he convinced them to pass a resolution that Alexander be commander plenipotentiary of the Greeks and to join together in an expedition against Persia seeking satisfaction for the offences which the Persians had committed against Greece. Having obtained this tribute, the king returned to Macedonia with his army.

---

[1] For the succession (through Arses) by Darius III see Depuydt 2008: 39–41; for the reign of Darius III see, for example, Briant 2002: 769–872. For the confrontation between Alexander and Darius see the extensive and balanced account of Briant 2003. For the comments on book 17, I made extensive use of Prandi 2013, but will only occasionally refer to it: not to detract from its value, but it is often too detailed for my purpose.
[2] See Arr. *An.* 1.1.2.

276   *Semiramis' Legacy*

S. 115:
17.5.3–7.10:

Developments in the Achaemenid Empire; Artaxerxes III is murdered:
(17.5.3) As we will now discuss the kingdom of the Persians, we must pick up the history a little earlier. In fact, while Philip II was still king, Artaxerxes III *Ochus* ruled the Persians and oppressed his subjects cruelly and harshly.³ Because he was hated for the savagery of his manners, the chiliarch Bagoas,⁴ though being a eunuch in physical fact, but by nature malicious and quarrelsome, killed him by poison administered by a physician and placed upon the throne Arses,⁵ the youngest of the sons of the king. (4) He similarly killed the brothers of the new king, who were barely of age, in order that the young man, being isolated, would be more obedient to him. However, because the young king was disgusted with these outrages against the law and made it clear that he was prepared to punish the author of these crimes, Bagoas, anticipating his intentions, killed Arses and his children in the third year of his reign.⁶ (5) Because the royal house was extinguished and there was no one in the direct line of descent to succeed,⁷ Bagoas, selecting one of his friends, by the name of Darius, secured the throne for him.⁸ He was the son of Arsanes,⁹ the son of Ostanes, who was a brother of Artaxerxes II, king of the Persians. (6) As to Bagoas, something peculiar happened to him and worth remembering. Pursuing his habitual savagery he attempted to murder Darius by poison. Because he was informed of the plan, the Great King, as if out of courtesy calling upon Bagoas

---

³ See 15.93.1; 16.40.3, 45.4–6, 51.2.
⁴ For Bagoas, see 16.47.4. For the career of Bagoas see Badian 1958. The **hazāra-patiš* ('master of a thousand') or chiliarch commanded the royal bodyguard and all court security and enjoyed the complete confidence of the ruler, controlling access to his person through the protocol of the royal audience, making him *de facto* in power second only to the Great King. See Keaveney 2010; see also Llewellyn-Jones forthcoming; Benveniste 1966: 50–68; Collins 2001.
⁵ Plu. *De Alex. Fort.* 336D also mentions the name of Oarses. The MSS of the *Bibliotheca* appear to favour Arses.
⁶ Arses ruled from 338 to 336, but was formally in his third regnal year. While Diodorus describes Artaxerxes III as a victim of a palace coup initiated by Bagoas, a Babylonian document simply states: 'Month Ulul [August/September]: *Umakuš* [Artaxerxes III] (went to his) fate. His son Aršu sat on the throne.' See *BM* 71537; see also Walker 1997: 22. The expression 'to go to one's fate' is a standard phrase to express someone's death by natural causes.
⁷ According to Arr. *An.* 3.19.4, one son of *Ochus* survived, Bisthanes, who joined Alexander. Just. 10.3 attributes the extermination of the royal family (largely) to *Ochus* himself: see also Curt. 10.5.23.
⁸ For Bagoas' role in the accession of Arses and Darius III, see also Curt. 6.3.12 and Str. 15.3.24/736.
⁹ As MS F reads; MS R gives Ὀαρσάνης ('Oarsanes') as the name of Darius' father. Though Goukowsky 2002a: 13 prefers the latter, I follow Fischer 1985d: 151.

and handing him his own cup,[10] forced him to drink the poison. (17.6.1) Darius was deemed worthy of the kingship because he was known to be the first of the Persians in bravery. Once when King Artaxerxes *Ochus* was making war against the Cadusians,[11] one of the Cadusians with a wide reputation for strength and courage challenged a volunteer among the Persians to fight in single combat with him. No one else dared accept but Darius alone, and after entering the fight he killed the challenger and was honoured by the Great King with rich gifts, and among the Persians he was conceded the first place in bravery. (2) Being thought worthy of the kingship because of this prowess, he succeeded at about that time in which, after the death of Philip, Alexander became king. (3) Since Fate had selected such a man to be the antagonist of Alexander's *aretē*, it occurred that they opposed one another in many and great struggles for the supremacy.[12] About these we will describe the events in each case in detail. And we will now return to the line of our story.

(17.7.1) In fact, Darius who had become king before the death of Philip, strove eagerly to turn the coming war back upon Macedonia. When Philip died, Darius was relieved of his anxiety because he thought slightly of the youth of Alexander. (2) However, when Alexander's energy and rapidity of action had secured for him the leadership of all Greece and the *aretē* of the young man became evident, then Darius, warned by the facts, began to pay serious attention to his own forces.[13] He fitted out a large number of *triereis*, assembled numerous strong armies, and chose the best commanders, among whom was also Memnon of Rhodes, outstanding in courage and in strategic grasp. (3) The Great King, giving him five thousand mercenaries, ordered him to march to the *polis* of Cyzicus and to try to get possession of it.[14] Therefore he marched with this force across

---

[10] According to Ath. 11.503F, the king drank from a special egg-shaped cup: naturally Bagoas should have been flattered by the king's courtesy. See also Curt. 6.4.10.
[11] The Cadusians, also known as Gelae, lived near the south-western coast of the Caspian Sea, in the region still named after them, namely Ghīlān: see Anon. (1940), *RE* Suppl. VII, cols. 316–17 *s.v.* Καδουσίοι.
[12] See Arr. *An*. 3.22.2 for his similar synchronism.
[13] See Aeschin. 3.163: ἤκμαζε δ' ὁ τῶν Περσῶν βασιλεὺς καὶ ναυσὶ καὶ χρήμασι καὶ πεζῇ στρατιᾷ, ἄσμενος δ' ἂν ἡμᾶς εἰς τὴν συμμαχίαν προσεδέξατο διὰ τοὺς ἐπιφερομένους ἑαυτῷ κινδύνους ('The king of Persia was at the height of his power, with ships, money, and infantry, and he would gladly have received us into an alliance because of the dangers he was facing'). Goukowsky 2002a: 15 note 3 believes that the infantry hinted at by Aeschines was 'evidently formed by Greek mercenaries'. Though it seems likely, there is no 'evidence'.
[14] See also Polyaen. 5.44.4, who mentions 4,000 soldiers. Memnon's task becomes understandable through Polyaen. 5.44.5, strongly suggesting Cyzicus (the name of the *polis* is not uncontested) had made an alliance with the Macedonians. The conjecture by Curt. 5.11.5, namely 50,000 soldiers in Memnon's force, seems unrealistic for the job at hand.

the Ida range. (4) ... (5) ... (6) ... (7) ... (8) Having traversed this mountain range, Memnon suddenly fell upon the *polis* of Cyzicus and failed to take it by a whisker. Failing to obtain it, he wasted their territory and collected much booty. (9) While these events took place, Parmenion, having taken the *polis* of Grynium by storm,[15] sold its inhabitants as slaves, but when he besieged Pitane, Memnon broke the siege, appearing and frightening the Macedonians. (10) Afterwards Callas,[16] with a force of Macedonians and mercenaries, joined battle in the Troad against the Persians, who were many times more numerous, and, finding himself inferior, fell back on the promontory of Rhoetium.[17] That was the situation in Asia.

S. 116:
17.14.2–4:

Discussion of the fate of Thebes after its capture by the Macedonians:

(17.14.2) When the discussion was opened, certain men who were hostile to the Thebans began to recommend that these should be visited with the direst penalties, and they pointed out that the Thebans had taken the side of the Persians against the Greeks.[18] They did so, because in the time of Xerxes the Thebans had actually joined forces with the Persians and campaigned against Greece and, alone of the Greeks, were honoured as benefactors by the kings of the Persians, so that the ambassadors of the Thebans were seated on thrones set in front of the kings.[19] (3) Relating many other details of similar tenor, they so aroused the feelings of the council against the Thebans that it was finally voted[20] to raze the city, to sell the captives, to outlaw the Theban exiles from the whole of Greece, and to allow no Greek to offer shelter to a Theban. (4) The Macedonian king, destroying the city in accordance with the decree of the council, caused aspiring rebels among the Greeks great fear.[21] By selling off the prisoners he realised a sum of four hundred and forty talents of silver.[22]

---

[15] An Aeolian *polis* in Asia Minor on the Bay of Elaea, like Pitane (near modern Çandarlı). See Bean 1967: 110–12, 115–17. For Parmenion, see Heckel 2009: 190–2 s.v. 'Parmenion'.
[16] For Callas see Heckel 2009: 74–5 s.v. 'Calas'.
[17] At the Hellespont, north of Ilium.
[18] See, *inter alia*, Arr. *An.* 1.9.6–7; *P.Oxy.* 13 (= *FGrH/BNJ* 153 F 1).
[19] For the meaning of thrones in Persian court etiquette see, for example, Hdt. 8.67.
[20] See Just. 11.4.
[21] See, for Alexander's potential afterthoughts, Plb. 38.1.
[22] An amount of 2,640,000 *drachmae*. For 30,000 prisoners, that would mean an average price of 88 *drachmae* per head: see Ducrey 1968: 252 and note 3. Goukowsky 2002a: 176 considers this a realistic price.

Alexander the Great Defeats Darius III 279

B. ALEXANDER'S EXPEDITION UP TO THE END
OF THE BATTLE OF ISSUS

S. 117:
17.16.1–49.2:

Alexander's expedition against the Persian Empire; preparation:
(17.16.1) Thereupon the king, having returned with his army to Macedonia, assembled his military commanders and the noblest of his friends[23] and laid on the table the plan for crossing over to Asia, when the campaign should be started, and how the war should be conducted. (2) Antipater and Parmenion advised him to produce an heir first and then to turn his hand to so ambitious an enterprise, but Alexander, eager for action and opposed to any postponement, contradicted them. In fact, he made it clear that it would be a disgrace for the man who had been appointed by Greece commander of the war, and who had inherited his father's invincible forces, to sit at home celebrating a marriage and awaiting the birth of children.[24] (3) In fact, after showing them where their advantage lay and by his words arousing their enthusiasm for the contests, he made lavish sacrifices to the gods at Dium in Macedonia and held dramatic contests for Zeus and the Muses, which Archelaus, one of his predecessors, had instituted.[25] (4) He celebrated the festival for nine days, appointing to each of the Muses an eponymous day. Having erected a tent to hold a hundred couches,[26] he invited both his companions and his officers, as well as the ambassadors from the *poleis*, to the banquet. Employing great magnificence and entertaining great numbers, besides distributing to his entire force sacrificial animals and all else suitable for the festive occasion, he restored his army.

---

[23] For the figure of the royal 'friend' – apparently the second closest group of the king's trustees, directly after the 'relatives' (συγγενεῖς) – both in Alexander's times and later, under the Diadochs, see Dreyer 2011. See also above, Chapter 4, note 289, and below, notes 44 and 164.
[24] In book 29.2 Diodorus reproaches King Antiochus III for precisely such acts: Ὅτι Ἀντίοχος ... τῆς μὲν περὶ τὸν πόλεμον παρασκευῆς ἠμέλησε, παρθένου δὲ εὐπρεποῦς ἐρασθεὶς ἐκάθητο τοὺς ταύτης ἐπιτελῶν γάμους καὶ πανηγύρεις λαμπρὰς συνῆγαγε ('Antiochus ... neglected to prepare for the war, but having fallen in love with a beautiful girl, wasted the time in celebrating his marriage with her and held brilliant feasts').
[25] See Arr. *An.* 1.11.1 for a sacrifice to Olympian Zeus. He adds, though, 'that others say he held games for the Muses', suggesting this information was lacking in his primary sources, namely Ptolemy and possibly Aristobulus.
[26] Typical of Macedonian banquets: Tomlinson 1970: 310.

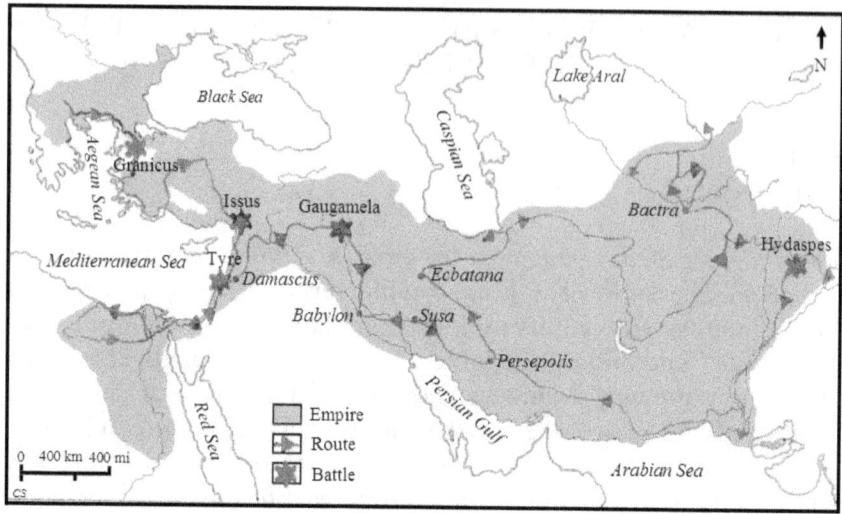

Fig. 5.1. Outline of the expedition of Alexander the Great, 334–323 BC.

(17.17.1) When Ctesicles was *archon* at Athens [334/3], the Romans elected as consuls Gaius Sulpicius and Lucius Papirius.[27] Having advanced with his army to the Hellespont, Alexander transported the force from Europe to Asia. (2) After personally sailing with sixty warships to the Troad,[28] he flung his spear from the ship, fixing it in the ground, and then also personally leaping ashore first of the Macedonians, he made clear that he received Asia from the gods as a spear-won prize.[29]

Composition of Alexander's force:
(3) He likewise honoured the tombs of the heroes Achilles, Ajax, and the other heroes with offerings for the dead and other proper acts of honour,[30] and then proceeded to make an accurate count of his accompanying force personally. There were found to be, of

---

[27] C. Sulpicius Longus is listed as one of the consuls of 337 vc, together with P. Aelius Paetus and with C. Claudius Inregillensis as dictator: Broughton 1951: 138–9; L. Papirius Crassus is listed as one of the consuls of the year 336 vc (together with K. Duillius). Diodorus is four or three years ahead of the Varronian chronology.

[28] Just. 11.6.2 writes that Alexander had in total 182 warships, though Arr. *An.* 1.18.4 counts only 160 warships. The remaining part of the fleet, under the command of Parmenion, dropped anchor at Abydus, while Alexander re-enacted the landing of the Achaeans starting the Trojan War (see Arr. *An.* 1.17.6). For Alexander's campaign at sea and the Persian response see also Grainger 2011: 1–10.

[29] At least according to Macedonian law: see, for example, Schmitthenner 1968: 32–8. See also the remark in 21.5 by Seleucus.

[30] See Just. 11.6.2; Plu. *Alex.* 15.4; Arr. *An.* 1.11.7.

infantry, twelve thousand Macedonians, seven thousand allies, and five thousand mercenaries, all of whom were under the command of Parmenion. (4) Odrysians, Triballians, and Illyrians accompanied him to the number of seven thousand; and of archers and the so-called Agrianians[31] one thousand, making up a total of thirty-two thousand foot soldiers. Of cavalry there were eighteen hundred Macedonians, under the command of Philotas, the son of Parmenion, eighteen hundred Thessalians, commanded by Callas, the son of Harpalus, six hundred from the rest of Greece under the command of Erigyius, and nine hundred Thracian and Paeonian scouts with Cassander in command, making a total of four thousand and five hundred cavalry. These were the men who crossed with Alexander to Asia.[32] (5) The soldiers who were left behind in Europe, of whom Antipater held the command, numbered twelve thousand foot and fifteen hundred horse.[33] (6) As the king began his march out of the Troad and came to the sanctuary of Athena,[34] the sacrificing priest, named Aristander,[35] noticed in front of the temple a statue of Ariobarzanes, a former satrap of Phrygia, lying fallen on the ground, together with some other favourable omens that occurred. He approached the king and affirmed that he would be victor in a great cavalry battle and especially if he happened to fight in Phrygia. (7) He added that the king with his own hands would kill in battle a distinguished commander of the enemy. Those things, he said, the gods disclosed to him, and particularly Athena, who would help him in his success as well. (17.18.1) Welcoming the seer's prediction, Alexander made a splendid sacrifice to Athena and dedicated his own shield to the goddess,

---

[31] A Balkan people allied with the Macedonians: see Launey 1949: 404–7. Together with the aforementioned tribes they were probably counted as skirmishers.

[32] Just. 11.6.2 mentions 32,000 foot, 4,500 horse; Plu. *Alex*. 15.1 30,000–43,000 foot and 4,000–5,000 horse; Arr. *An*. 1.11.3 'not much more than' 30,000 foot and 5,000 horse; Ptolemy 30,000 foot and 5,000 horse; Anaximenes 43,000 foot and 5,500 horse. Plu. *De Alex. Fort*. 327D writes that Aristobulus provided 30,000 foot and 4,000 horse. Diodorus' is the most elaborate enumeration of all, though his maths are wrong: in total he mentions 5,100 horse.

[33] Nowhere else in our sources, to the best of my knowledge, are these figures present. It seems that Alexander had left about half of Macedonia's military potential behind for Antipater: see Momigliano 1935: 11.

[34] In line with his re-enactment in setting foot on Asian soil, the alleged site of the Trojan War was a necessary stop for Alexander, the 'Second Achilles': the sanctuary of Athena is the temple at Ilium. The remains of a temple of Athena (though of somewhat later date) are still visible there. Moreover, Athena – in the shape of Athena *Alcidemus* – is the protector of the Macedonian kings (see Plin. *Nat*. 35.114) and adorns the gold staters of Alexander.

[35] Though all MSS read 'Alexander', Freinsheim has emended this into 'Aristander' (see Goukowsky 2002a: *apparatus a.l.*). Since nowhere is it stated that the priest belonged to the temple, I believe it feasible that one of the priests joining the army performed the sacrifice: therefore I follow this emendation. Aristander of Telmessus, born into a family of seers, served Philip of Macedon first, next the latter's son Alexander: see Laumonier 1958: 613.

Fig. 5.2. Bed of the River Granicus (modern Biga Çayi), site of the battle. Photo © Jona Lendering <http://www.livius.org>.

but taking the finest of the shields deposited in the temple, he appropriated it to himself and used it in his first battle.[36] Deciding this through his own personal prowess, he won a resounding victory. But this did not take place until a few days later.

Persian defence; first battle, at the River Granicus:
(2) The Persian satraps and commanders were too late to prevent the Macedonians' crossing,[37] but after mustering their forces they started to deliberate how they should oppose Alexander. Memnon of Rhodes, famed for his military competence, advocated not engaging in a face-to-face battle, but stripping the countryside and preventing the Macedonians through the shortage of supplies from advancing further, but also making both naval and land forces cross to Macedonia and transferring the whole war to Europe. (3) This man advocated the best measures, as became obvious from after-events,

---

[36] Arr. *An.* 1.11.7–8 records only that he had it carried in front of him. See also below, 17.21.2.

[37] Persian forces were notorious for coming late into action, *inter alia* because all plans and actions had to be consented to by the Great King. See, for example, 15.41.5 and 16.44.5; also Ruzicka 2012: 119 regarding the 373 Persian campaign against Egypt.

though he failed to convince the other commanders, allegedly because he advocated actions unworthy of the lordliness of the Persians.[38] (4) Therefore, after the opinion for fighting it out had prevailed, these commanders advanced to Hellespontine Phrygia after they had summoned their forces from every quarter, heavily outnumbering the Macedonians. They pitched camp by the River Granicus, using the bed of the aforementioned river as a line of defence.

(17.19.1) When Alexander learned of the concentration of the Persian forces, he took the initiative and, having advanced rapidly, encamped opposite the enemy, so that the Granicus flowed between the encampments.[39] (2) Resting on high ground, the Persians made no move, determined to fall upon the foes as they crossed the river. They surmised they could easily have the upper hand in the fight when the Macedonian phalanx was scattered and in disorder. (3) Alexander, though, boldly bringing his army across the river at dawn, surprised the enemy, deploying his force fitly for the battle. The Persians positioned their mass of horsemen all along the front of the Macedonians and had resolved to decide the battle with these. (4) Memnon of Rhodes and the satrap Arsamenes held the left wing, each with his own cavalry; next Arsites was stationed with the horsemen from Paphlagonia; then came Spithrobates, the satrap of Ionia, commanding Hyrcanian cavalry.[40] The right wing was held by a thousand Medes and the two thousand horse with Rheomithres as well as Bactrians of like number.[41] Horsemen from the other national contingents occupied the centre, numerous and picked for their *aretē*. In

---

[38] According to Just. 11.6.8–9 Darius objected to such stratagems and wanted a battle. Arr. *An.* 1.16.3, though, reports that the satrap of the region, Arsites, refused to allow scorched-earth politics on the territory he had received from the Great King: after the Battle of the Granicus, Arsites committed suicide, and his son, Mithropastes, was banished to an island in the Persian Gulf: Str. 16.3.5–7/766–7.

[39] For a different account see Arr. *An.* 1.13.3–7 and Plu. *Alex.* 16.2–3.

[40] Hyrcania was the name of a satrapy located in the territories of modern Gīlān, Māzandarān, and Golestān provinces of Iran and part of Turkmenistan, lands south of the Caspian Sea (the 'Hyrcanian Sea' for Greeks), regions famous for both horses and horsemen. Here, though, it may well be that Hyrcanians from Lydia are intended, referred to by Str. 13.4.13/629: εἶτα τὸ Ὑρκάνιον πεδίον, Περσῶν ἐπονομασάντων καὶ ἐποίκους ἀγαγόντων ἐκεῖθεν ('Then comes the Hyrcanian Plain, a name given it by the Persians, who brought Hyrcanian colonists there'). As a matter of fact: Spithridates, not Spithrobates, was the satrap of Ionia (and Lydia): see Arr. *An.* 1.12.15–16; below, note 41. It seems, moreover, that Diodorus possibly confounds Spithrobates with Mithridates, the son-in-law of Darius, and Spithridates with his brother Rhoesaces in his account of the battle: see Heckel 2009: 254–5 *s.v.* 'Spithridates'; below, note 43.

[41] Arsites was at that time the satrap of Hellespontine Phrygia, Spithridates of Lydia and Ionia (see Arr. *An.* 1.12.8). Arsamenes (Curt. 3.4.3, Arr. *An.* 2.4.5: Arsames) was the satrap of Cilicia. For Rheomitres see 15.92.1. In his list Arrian adds Petines and Niphates, though omitting to describe the Persian line-up. On the other hand he does present that of the Macedonians (1.14.1–3), which, in its turn, is disregarded by Diodorus.

all, the cavalry amounted to more than ten thousand. (5) The Persian infantry were not fewer than one hundred thousand,[42] but being posted behind the line they stayed put, since the cavalry was thought to be sufficient to crush the Macedonians. (6) As the horse of each side joined battle spiritedly, the Thessalian cavalry, posted on the left wing under the command of Parmenion, gallantly met the attack of the troops posted opposite them. Alexander, who had the finest of the riders with him on the right wing, first charged upon the Persians and, engaging the enemy, began to cause great carnage.

(17.20.1) As the Persians resisted bravely and opposed their spirit to the Macedonian *aretē*, Fate brought together in one and the same place the finest fighters to dispute the victory. (2) The satrap of Ionia, Spithrobates, a Persian by descent, son-in-law of King Darius,[43] of superior courage, hurled himself at the Macedonian lines with a large force of cavalry. At his side fought forty 'Royal Relatives'[44] of outstanding *aretē* and he pressed hard on the opposite line and, attacking fiercely, killed some of his opponents, and wounded others. (3) As the force of this attack seemed very dangerous, Alexander turned his horse towards the satrap and rode at the Persian. The Persian believed that this opportunity for a single combat was god-given. Perhaps his individual prowess might relieve Asia of its worst fears, the renowned daring of Alexander be arrested by Spithridates' own hands, and the glory of the Persians saved from disgrace.[45] He hurled his javelin first at Alexander with so mighty an impulse and so powerful a cast that he pierced Alexander's shield and right shoulder protector and drove through the breastplate.[46] (4) The king

---

[42] Just. 11.6.11 states the Persians were 600,000 strong, which seems highly overstated (as Diodorus' number looks exaggerated), Arr. *An.* 1.14.4 that there were on the Persian side 20,000 foot and 20,000 horse.

[43] As to the actual events some discrepancy is present. Spithridates was a satrap of Lydia and Ionia under Darius III, and one of the Persian commanders. Arr. *An.*1.15.8 reports that while Spithridates was aiming a blow from behind at Alexander the Great, his arm was cut off by Clitus, son of Dropides. Diodorus, however, mentions that the person this fate befell was Spithrobates, whom he, moreover, appears to confound with Mithridates, the son-in-law of Darius (Arr. *An.* 1.15.7): Mithradates was 'hurled to the ground' in the battle by Alexander personally. On the other hand, what Arrian tells of Spithridates is recorded by Diodorus of his brother Rhoesaces (see 17.20.1–6; also Plu. *Alex.* 16, *De Alex. Fort.* 326F–327A).

[44] Probably not (all) real relatives. As LSJ, *s.v.*, remarks, συγγενής 'represented a title bestowed at the Persian court by the king as a mark of honour.' See Chapter 4, note 289.

[45] This translation is based upon the text as adapted by, *inter alios*, Welles. It is a merger of what different MSS present. No MS has a full text here. See also Goukowsky 2002a: 32 lines 15–20 and *apparatus*.

[46] This description may create some confusion regarding the trajectory of the javelin and whether Alexander carried the shield himself. Was it the shield taken from Ilium? Was it carried before him by an attendant as Arr. *An.* 1.11.7–8 suggests? Does such a gesture make sense in a battle? Apparently Alexander was not wounded (see Plu. *Alex.* 16.5), though by all accounts it must have been a powerful cast.

shook off the projectile dangling by his arm, then urged his horse forward and, employing the favouring momentum of his charge, drove his lance into the middle of the satrap's chest. (5) When this happened, adjacent ranks in both armies cried out at the superlative display of prowess. As the point, however, snapped off against the breastplate and the broken shaft recoiled, the Persian, having drawn his sword, drove at Alexander.[47] The king, however, recovering his grip upon his lance, thrust at the man's face and drove the blow home. (6) Just at this moment, Rhoesaces, the brother of the fallen man, galloping up, brought his sword down on Alexander's head with such a fearsome blow that it split his helmet and inflicted a slight scalp wound.[48] (7) As Rhoesaces aimed another blow at the same break, Clitus, surnamed the Black, dashing up on his horse, cut off the Persian's arm.[49]

(17.21.1) The 'Relatives' now assembled in a solid body about Spithridates and Rhoesaces. At first they threw their javelins at Alexander, then, fighting closely together, went all out to kill the king. (2) Though he was exposed to many and fierce attacks, he was nevertheless not vanquished by the numbers of the foes, but taking two blows on the breastplate, one on the helmet, and three on the shield which he had brought from the temple of Athena, he still did not give in. Being borne up by an exaltation of the spirit, he surmounted every danger. (3) After this, several of the other noble Persians fighting against him also fell, of whom the most illustrious were Atizyes, Pharnaces, brother of Darius' queen, and also Mithrobuzanes who commanded the Cappadocians.[50] (4) Because many of their commanders had been killed and all the Persian squadrons were worsted by the Macedonians, those facing Alexander were forced to flee first. When, next, the others also turned around, the king by common consent won the palm for bravery and was regarded as the chief cause of the victory. Next to him, the Thessalian cavalry won a great reputation for valour because of the skilful handling of their squadrons and their unmatched fighting quality. (5) After the rout of the cavalry, the foot soldiers, engaging one another, fought briefly. The Persians, indeed, dismayed by the rout of the cavalry and shaken in

---

[47] Again a version deviating from Arrian's: see Arr. *An.* 1.15.7–8; see also Plu. *Alex.* 16.4.
[48] See Plu. *De Alex. Fort.* 327A.
[49] See Curt. 8.1.20. Goukowsky 2002a: 32 note 3 surmises this was Clitarchus' version.
[50] A list of prominent Persians killed in the Battle of the Granicus is presented in Arr. *An.* 1.16.3, in which Pharnaces and Mithrobuzanes do figure, but Atizyes does not. Diodorus has Atizyes killed a second time during the Battle of Issus (17.34.5, below), this time confirmed by Arr. *An.* 2.11.8 and Curt. 3.11.10.

spirit, were quick to flee.[51] (6) The total of the Persian infantry killed was more than ten thousand, of the cavalry not less than two thousand, and over twenty thousand were taken captive. After the battle the king buried the dead magnificently, striving eagerly by this sort of honour for the soldiers to prepare with greater enthusiasm to face the hazards of battle.

Alexander marches southward; sieges of Miletus and Halicarnassus: (7) Recovering his forces, Alexander led them down through Lydia and took over both the city of the Sardians and the citadels, and moreover the treasures stored therein, because Mithrines the satrap surrendered them without resistance.[52]

(17.22.1) Because the Persian survivors of the battle, together with their commander Memnon, had taken refuge in Miletus, the king, after setting up camp near the city,[53] made assaults on the walls in relays every day.[54] (2) At first the besieged easily defended themselves from the walls, for many soldiers were gathered in the city, and they had abundant provision of missiles and other things useful for the emergency. (3) However, when the king, in a more determined fashion, both battered the walls with siege engines and pressed the siege very actively both by land and by sea,[55] and the Macedonians forced an entry through the crumbling walls, then at last, yielding to superior force, they took to flight. (4) Immediately the Milesians, falling before the king with supplicant olive boughs, surrendered themselves and their *polis*. Some of the Persians were killed by the Macedonians, others fled, having escaped the city, and all the remainder were taken captive.[56] (5) Alexander treated the Milesians kindly, but sold all the rest as slaves. Because the naval force was now useless and entailed great expense, he dismissed the fleet except for a few ships which he employed for the transport of his siege engines.[57] Among these were the twenty allied ships of the Athenians.

(17.23.1) Some say that Alexander thought strategically of the dismissal of his fleet. Darius was, indeed, still to be reckoned with

---

[51] On this part of the battle Diodorus, and/or his source, remains largely silent. However, the figures indicate carnage. See, for a fuller account, Arr. *An.* 1.16.2; also Plu. *Alex.* 16.6–7.
[52] See Plu. *Alex.* 17.1; Arr. *An.* 1.17–18.2 is a fuller account.
[53] Opposite the island of Lade.
[54] For this method of siege warfare, see Sinclair 1966.
[55] Arr. *An.* 1.18.4–5, 19.3 refers to the occupation of Lade.
[56] On the fate of the garrison, referred to by Arrian as 'Greek mercenaries', see Arr. *An.* 1.19.4–6; they were commanded by the *phrourarchos* Hegisistratus (Arr. *An.* 1.18.4).
[57] Vitr. 10.13.3 refers to Diades of Pella, stating the Macedonians had demountable siege engines: their transport across the sea is referred to, for example, as having occurred between Tyre and Gaza (see Arr. *An.* 2.27.3).

and there was bound to be a great battle, and he judged that the Macedonians would fight more ardently if he took away all hope of escape by flight. (2) He had done the same thing at the battle of the Granicus. In fact, he had placed the stream at his rear, for no one could think of flight because the destruction of any who were followed into the bed of the river was obvious. . . . (3) . . . (4) After the capture of Miletus, the bulk of the Persians and mercenaries, as well as the most enterprising of the commanders, flocked together at Halicarnassus. This was the largest *polis* in Caria, containing the palace of the kings of the Carians, and well provided with fortresses. (5) About the same time Memnon sent both his wife and children to Darius,[58] because he calculated that leaving them in the Great King's care was a good way to ensure their safety, while at the same time the Great King, now that he had good hostages, would be more willing to entrust Memnon with the supreme command. And so it turned out. (6) In fact, Darius straightaway sent letters to those who dwelt next to the sea, directing them all to obey Memnon. Therefore he, having assumed the supreme command, made all the necessary preparations for a siege in the city of the Halicarnassians.

(17.24.1) King Alexander had his siege engines and provisions conveyed by sea to Halicarnassus, but he himself with all his army marched into Caria and won over the cities en route by kind treatment. He was particularly generous to the Greek *poleis*, granting them independence and exemption from taxation, adding that because of the freedom of the Greeks he had taken upon himself the war against the Persians.[59] (2) On his journey he was met by an elderly woman, named Ada, who belonged in descent to the ruling house of Caria.[60] When she presented a petition to recover the position of her ancestors and requested his assistance, he gave orders that she should become the ruler of Caria and won the support of the Carians by the favour that he bestowed on this woman. (3) Indeed,

---

[58] Memnon's wife, Barsine, the daughter of Artabazus, was captured at Damascus after the Battle of Issus and allegedly afterwards bore Alexander a son by the name of Heracles. Tarn is sceptical (see Tarn 1921), but perhaps unnecessarily so. See also Goukowsky 2002a: 184–5.

[59] Only Greek *poleis* were nominally exempted from taxation, instead paying a *syntaxis* ('contribution') to conduct the war. For non-Greek cities and countryside nothing changed.

[60] See Arr. *An.* 1.23.7–8. Ada, the daughter of Hecatomnus and sister of, *inter alios*, Mausolus and Artemisia, had ruled Caria as 'dynast' after the death of Idrieus, her older brother and husband and successor of Artemisia (see 16.69.2), but had been ousted by her younger brother Pixodarus (see 16.74.2). Surprising in this sentence is the use of (τι) γύναιον instead of the more common word γυνή. Due to its precise meaning, it might indicate a pejorative intent in Diodorus' account or in that of his source, accentuated by the use of the word τι ('some'), though I think Goukowsky 2002a: 37 solved the problem elegantly with 'vieille femme'. For Ada, see also Ruzicka 1992: 123–6, 139–40, 143–6, 153–4.

straightaway all the cities, sending embassies, honoured the king with golden crowns and announced they would do everything in unison with him. Having pitched camp near the city, Alexander set in motion an active and formidable siege.[61] (4) At first he made, in relays, continued assaults on the walls and spent whole days in active fighting. Having deployed later all sorts of engines of war and filled in the trenches in front of the city with the aid of protective sheds for the workers, he battered the towers and the curtain-walls in between with the battering rams. Whenever he overthrew a portion of the wall, he attempted to force entry into the city through the breach by hand-to-hand fighting. (5) Memnon, though, at first easily beat off the Macedonians assaulting the walls, because there were many soldiers in the city. As regards the attacks of the siege engines, making a sortie from the city at night with many soldiers he set fire to the machines. (6) When fierce fights occurred in front of the city, the Macedonians had considerable advantage through their *aretē*, but the Persians had the larger scale of numbers and of armaments. Indeed, men who fought from the walls supported them, and killed some of their enemies and disabled others using sharp-pointed projectiles.

(17.25.1) At the same moment, the *salpinxes*[62] sounded the battle signal on both sides and exhortations came from all parts as the soldiers applauded in concert the braveries on either side. (2) Some tried to extinguish the fire that rose high among the siege engines; others joined with the foe in close combat and caused slaughter; others again erected within the fallen walls new walls instead, much heavier in construction than the preceding ones. (3) After Memnon and the commanders had taken their places in the front and had offered great rewards to those who distinguished themselves in prowess, an unsurpassable desire for victory rose on both sides. (4) There could be seen some encountering frontal wounds and being carried unconscious out of the battle; others standing over the fallen bodies and organising great fights for the recovery of them; others again, on the brink of yielding to the storm of terrors, being again put in good heart by their officers' appeals and being renewed in spirit.[63] (5) Finally, some

---

[61] For a detailed account of this siege see Arr. *An.* 1.20.4–23.6.
[62] For the *salpinx*, see above Chapter 4, note 230.
[63] The accounts of Diodorus and Arr. *An.* 1.20.9–10 differ: as Goukowsky 2002a: 38 notes 1 and 2 remarks, what is basically a skirmish in Arrian turns into a pitched battle in Diodorus; again, the number of casualties mentioned by Arrian (170 among the besieged, 16 Macedonian dead and 300 wounded) suggests a serious confrontation, not a major battle. Moreover, in Arrian's account Memnon does not participate himself and the Macedonian goal is not attained.

Alexander the Great Defeats Darius III 289

of the Macedonians were killed at the very gates, among them an officer, Neoptolemus, a man of distinguished family.[64] Afterwards, after two towers were levelled to the ground and two curtain-walls overthrown, some of Perdiccas' soldiers, being drunk, made a wild night attack on the walls of the citadel.[65] Memnon's men noticed the awkwardness of these attackers and, issuing forth themselves in considerably larger numbers, routed the Macedonians and killed many of them. (6) As this situation became known, large numbers of Macedonians rushed up to help and a great struggle took place, and when Alexander and his staff came up, the Persians, forced back, were confined within the city, and the king through a herald asked for a truce to recover the Macedonians who had fallen in front of the walls. Ephialtes and Thrasybulus, the Athenian allies of the Persians, advised not giving up the deceased for burial, but Memnon granted the request.

(17.26.1) After this, when the commanders conferred, Ephialtes advised them not to wait until they found themselves captives after the city was taken, but that the leaders themselves, braving the danger in front of the mercenaries, should attack the enemy. (2) Because Memnon saw that Ephialtes was driven to *aretē* and had great hopes of him because of his courage and bodily strength, he allowed him to do as he wished. (3) With two thousand picked men, giving half of them lighted torches and positioning the others so as to meet the enemy, he suddenly threw all the gates wide open.[66] Sallying out at daybreak with them, he made the first group set fire to the siege engines, causing a great conflagration to flame up at once. (4) He personally led the rest in a dense phalanx many ranks deep and charged the Macedonians as they issued forth to help. When the king saw what was happening, he placed the best fighters of the Macedonians in front and stationed picked men in reserve. Behind these he deployed as a third group others who had a good record for

---

[64] According to Arr. *An.* 1.20.10, Neoptolemus, the son of Arrabaeus and brother of the Amyntas mentioned in 17.48.2–5 below (not to be confused with another Amyntas, the son of Andromenes, mentioned in 17.45.7 below, one of Alexander's staff officers), had deserted to the Persians. Though Arrian also concedes that Neoptolemus died during the attack on Halicarnassus, Arrian and Diodorus hold opposite views on the circumstances: Diodorus seems to believe Neoptolemus fought in the Macedonian ranks, a view shared by Welles 1970: 188–9 note 1. He, however, appears to confuse the two 'Amyntae'.

[65] Arrian reports it was two men only of Perdiccas' battalion and that this attack took place some days later (Arr. *An.* 1.21.1).

[66] Arr. *An.* 1.21.5–6, 22.1–3 mentions two sallies by the besieged. It is unclear which of them, if either, can be identified with that described by Diodorus. It might be the latter because of the massiveness of the sortie, but in Arrian's account Ephialtes plays no role whatsoever. As Goukowsky 2002a: 186 *ad* 26.2 suggests, Diodorus may have used an Athenophile source here.

stout fighting. Taking command at the head of all, he himself made a stand against the enemy, who believed themselves unconquerable because of their abundance. He also sent men out to extinguish the fire and to rescue the siege engines. (5) As at the same time both violent shouts arose on both sides and the *salpinxes* sounded the attack, a terrific contest ensued because of the *aretē* of the contestants and their consummate fighting spirit. (6) The Macedonians prevented the fire from spreading, but Ephialtes' men had the advantage in the battle. He himself, indeed, who had far greater bodily strength than the rest, killed many of those who came to blows with him. Soldiers standing on the top of the recently erected replacement wall killed many by the use of close-packed missiles. In fact, a wooden tower had been erected, a hundred cubits high [c. 45 m], filled with *euthytona*.[67] (7) As many Macedonians fell and the rest recoiled before the mass of missiles, and as Memnon threw himself into the battle with heavy reinforcements, the king himself also fell into dire trouble.[68]

(17.27.1) Just at that moment as the men from the city were prevailing, the tide of battle was surprisingly reversed. Indeed, the oldest Macedonians, who were exempt from combat duty by virtue of their age, had served with Philip on his campaigns and had been victorious in many battles. (2) They were roused by the emergency to show their valour, and, being far superior in pride and war experience, sharply rebuked the faint-heartedness of the youngsters who wished to avoid the battle. Having closed ranks and overlapping their shields, they confronted those who thought themselves already victorious. (3) Finally, killing both Ephialtes and many others, they forced the rest to take refuge in the city. (4) Night had already fallen as the Macedonians pushed within the walls along with the fleeing men. However, when the king ordered the recall to be sounded, they withdrew to their camp.[69] (5) When, however, the commanders and

---

[67] Arr. *An.* 1.23.2 mentions such a tower, but fails to present its dimensions. Both the *euthytona* and *palintona* (referred to later in Diodorus' account) used as siege machines technically count as *ballistae*. Diodorus clearly differentiates between the two, as did Hero Mechanicus in his *Belapoeica*: τὰ μὲν εὐθύτονα ὀϊστοὺς μόνους ἀφίησι, τὰ δὲ παλίντανα ἔνιοι καὶ λιθοβόλα καλοῦσιν διὰ τὸ λίθους ἐξαποστέλλειν· πέμπει δὲ ἤτοι ὀϊστοὺς ἢ <λίθους ἢ> καὶ συναμφότερα ('the *euthytona* only shoot arrows, the *palintona* some also call "stone-throwers" because they throw stones; they shoot either arrows or <stones or> even both': *Bel.* 3). I have translated henceforth according to these denominations. For these machines see also: Campbell 2011; for *euthytona* and *palintona* see esp. ibid.: 685–9.

[68] See also Arr. *An.* 1.22.1–2. This suggests two separate sorties at the same time, causing Alexander problems.

[69] According to Arr. *An.* 1.22.7, Alexander did so to save the civil population if they still surrendered amicably.

Alexander the Great Defeats Darius III 291

satraps around Memnon assembled,⁷⁰ they decided to abandon the *polis*. Having installed the best of the soldiers in the acropolis with sufficient provision, they sent off the rest of the army and the war chest to Cos. (6) When Alexander learned what had taken place at daybreak, he razed the city and surrounded the citadel with a formidable wall and trench. He dispatched a portion of his force with its commanders into the interior of Caria with orders to subdue the neighbouring tribes. These commanders, campaigning vigorously, subdued the whole region as far as greater Phrygia, providing their men with food at the expense of the land.⁷¹

The Macedonian army goes east:
(7) Alexander, for his part, having overrun the littoral as far as Cilicia, acquired many cities and having besieged strong points quite energetically he subdued them by force. Among those he captured one surprisingly, which it is not right to omit due to the peculiarity of the sudden reversal of circumstances.⁷²

(17.28.1) The Marmarans,⁷³ as they are called, inhabit a great rock fortress of unusual strength near the frontiers of Lycia. As Alexander marched by, these people attacked the Macedonian rearguard and, killing many, carried off numerous men and pack animals. (2) Enraged at this, the king laid a siege and exerted every effort to take the place by force. The Marmarans, being outstanding in bravery and being confident in the strength of their fortifications, stoutly faced the siege. For two whole days, thus, there were constant assaults and it was clear that the king would not leave until he had captured the rock fortress. (3) First, then, the older men of the Marmarans advised their younger countrymen to end their resistance and make peace with the king on whatever terms possible. When they did not listen, however, but all were eager to die together simultaneously with the end of the freedom of their state, the elders

---

⁷⁰ Arr. *An.* 1.23.1 states that the decision was taken by Memnon and Orontopates, the satrap.
⁷¹ The cheapest way by far to 'provide a market' for the soldiers, simultaneously harming the enemy; see also Arr. *An.* 1.23.3; also Briant 1973: 43–4.
⁷² Diodorus here abbreviates the story of Alexander considerably, omitting large parts of the Pisidian campaign, including – most notably – the tale of the Gordian knot. These are to be found in Arr. *An.* 1.24.3–2.4.6, Curt. 3.1, Just. 11.7.4–15, and Plu. *Alex.* 17–18.2, largely based upon the story as related by Aristobulus (*FGrH/BNJ* 139 FF 7a and 7b). See also: Franck 1966: 109–10.
⁷³ We find neither this episode nor this people anywhere else in the accounts of Alexander's expedition. Goukowsky 2002a: 188 *ad* 28.1 refers to a paper by Radet 1903 in which the latter expresses his view that the rock of the Marmarans may have been the rock of Saradjik, which is 1,300 m high.

urged upon them that they should kill with their own hands their children and wives and aged relatives, and those who were strong enough to save themselves should break out through the midst of the enemy at night and take refuge in the neighbouring mountain. (4) After the young men agreed and consequently gave orders to go each to his own house and there, enjoying the best of food and drink with their families, to await the dread event, the young men – they were about six hundred – decided to abstain from killing their relatives with their own hands, but to set fire to the houses and issuing forth from the gates to withdraw to the mountain. (5) Carrying out their decision, these men caused each family to be entombed at its own hearth, but they themselves, having escaped through the midst of the enemy encamped about them, fled to the nearby hills when it was still night.[74] This is what happened in this year.

Meanwhile Darius attempts to move the war to Greece:
(17.29.1) When Nicocrates was *archon* at Athens [333/2], Caeso Valerius and Lucius Papirius[75] became consuls at Rome. In this year Darius sent much money to Memnon and appointed him commander of the whole war. (2) Having gathered a force of mercenaries and manned three hundred ships, Memnon pursued the affairs of the conflict vigorously. He secured Chios, and then, sailing to Lesbos, easily mastered Antissa, Methymna, Pyrrha, and Eressus. Mytilene also – large and with rich stores of supplies as well as plenty of fighting men – he nevertheless captured with difficulty by assault after a siege of many days and with the loss of many of his soldiers.[76] (3) Immediately when the general's activity was bruited about, most of the Cycladic islands sent missions to him. As rumour spread to Greece that Memnon was about to sail to Euboea with his fleet,[77] the *poleis* of that island became alarmed, but those Greeks who were friendly to Persia, among them the Spartans, were buoyed up with hopes of a political change. (4) Corrupting them

---

[74] Goukowsky 2002a: 43 note 1 remarks that Diodorus seems to have a special interest in collective suicides (though I doubt this case entirely qualifies as such), as is also clear from 18.22.1–8 (Isaurians) and 25.17.1 (the city of Victomela in Liguria: not included in this book).

[75] Diodorus has probably made a mistake somewhere: he has already (wrongly) mentioned L. Papirius Crassus as consul in 17.17.1. His colleague as consul in his proper year of office (336 vc) is listed as K. Duillius: See Broughton 1951: 139. Diodorus is here four years ahead of the Varronian chronology.

[76] Arr. *An.* 2.1.3 reports that Mytilene was not captured until after Memnon's death.

[77] Euboea was strategically of the utmost importance: see also 19.78.2 (centred on the *polis* of Chalcis): ἐπίκαιρος γὰρ ἡ πόλις ἐστὶ τοῖς βουλομένοις ἔχειν ὁρμητήριον πρὸς τὸ διαπολεμεῖν περὶ τῶν ὅλων ('the city is well situated for anyone wishing to have a base to carry through a war for supremacy [in Greece]'); see also Plb. 18.11.4–6; Liv. 32.37.3.

with bribes,[78] Memnon convinced many Greeks to share the Persian hopes. However, Fate did not allow his *aretē* to last longer. Indeed, falling into an illness and detained by a perilous malady, Memnon died and with his death Darius' case also collapsed.

New plans by Darius; he decides to lead his army westward in person:
(17.30.1) The Great King had counted on Memnon to transfer the whole war from Asia into Europe. However, when he learned of Memnon's death, he convened his Council of Trustees[79] and gave them the opportunity to counsel whether it was necessary to send commanders with an army down to the coast or whether the king should march down with all his force to fight against the Macedonians. (2) Some said that the king himself must join in battle, and they made it plain that the Persians would fight better. Charidemus, however, the Athenian, a man generally admired for his bravery and skill as a commander (he had made expeditions with the Great King[80] and had led or counselled all his successes), recommended Darius not to risk his throne head over heels, but to keep the reserve strength and the control of Asia in his own hands and to send to the war a commander who had given proof of his *aretē*. (3) One hundred thousand men would be an adequate force, of which a third should be Greek mercenaries, and Charidemus indicated that he would bring that plan to a successful end. (4) At first, the king was moved by his arguments. Later, though, the Great King's friends opposed them violently and brought Charidemus under suspicion of wanting to get the command in order to surrender the leadership of the Persians to the Macedonians. Blinded by anger, Charidemus, too readily upbraided, made free with slurs on Persian lack of manliness, with his words offending the Great King even more. Darius, whom wrath had made forget his interests, seized Charidemus by the girdle according to the custom of the Persians, turned him over to the

---

[78] Plu. *De Alex. Fort.* 327C may allude to this period: τὸ δὲ Περσικὸν χρυσίον διὰ τῶν ἑκασταχοῦ δημαγωγῶν ῥέον ἐκίνει τὴν Πελοπόννησον ('The Persian gold, flowing through the hands of the demagogues everywhere, roused the Peloponnesus'). See also Arr. *An.* 2.14.6.
[79] See above, note 23, and Chapter 4, note 289.
[80] Though all MSS read here 'king Philip', this seems hardly possible and I believe Goukowsky 2002a: 44 line 23 is right to delete Philip's name here and interpret τῷ βασιλεῖ as referring to the Great King. Charidemus is mentioned by Demosthenes (D. 23.103) as ἡγούμενος τῶν Κερσοβλέπτου πραγμάτων ('administering the affairs of Cersobleptes'). As a brother-in-law of Cersobleptes (the Thracian king of the Odrysians), Charidemus advocated a fiercely anti-Macedonian policy. After the Thracian defeat against Macedonia in 335, he fled to Persia, to Darius III. See, for example, Tuplin 2012.

attendants and ordered him put to death.[81] (5) As Charidemus was led away to his death, he shouted that the Great King would soon change his mind and would receive a prompt requital for this unjust punishment, when he would witness the overthrow of the kingdom. [[Charidemus' prospects had been high, but he missed their fulfilment because of his ill-timed frankness and he ended his life in this fashion.]] (6) Once his passion had cooled, the Great King promptly regretted his act and reproached himself for having made very great mistakes, but all his royal power, indeed, was unable to undo what was done. (7) Because he was haunted by dreams of Macedonian *aretē*, and visualising Alexander's operations, he searched for a competent commander to take over Memnon's command. Because he could find no one, he felt compelled to go down to the war for his kingdom himself.

(17.31.1) Immediately he summoned his forces from everywhere and ordered them to muster in Babylon.[82] He also selected the fit and proper persons among his companions and relatives,[83] to some of whom he allotted suitable commands, and ordered others to fight at his side. (2) When the time set for the march had come, they had all arrived in Babylon. The number of the soldiers was over four hundred thousand infantry and not less than one hundred thousand cavalry.[84]

Darius sets out from Babylon:

This was the force with which Darius marched out of Babylon in the direction of Cilicia, having with him both his wife and children (a son and two daughters) and his mother.[85] (3) Alexander had learned how, prior to his death, Memnon had won over Chios and the cities in Lesbos and had taken Mytilene by storm. Moreover, he had learned that Memnon wanted to carry the war into Macedonia with three hundred ships of war and a land army, and that the greater part of the Greeks were ready to revolt. This caused him no little anxiety.

---

[81] See, for example, X. *An.* 1.6.10. After Widengren, Goukowsky 2002a: 45 note 2 explains that the girdle represents the bond between the vassal and his lord. By taking his vassal by the girdle, the lord declares the bond to be broken.

[82] This seems slightly overstated: troops from the eastern satrapies had not been recruited, because these could never be in Babylon in time for the relatively quick reaction that was needed in these circumstances. See also Marsden 1964: 3.

[83] Possibly, or even probably, not (all) real relatives. See note 23 and Chapter 4, note 289.

[84] Just. 11.9.1 also reports 400,000 foot and 100,000 horse. Arr. *An.* 2.8.8 does not differentiate and only mentions the total strength of Darius' force, which he believed to have been 600,000, as does the anonymous author on Alexander preserved in *P.Oxy.* 1798 [= *FGrH/BNJ* 148] F 44 col. 2 l. 3.

[85] See Curt. 3.3.8–9.

(4) When, though, some people came reporting Memnon's death, he was relieved of much of this fear. However, falling rather seriously ill shortly thereafter and being afflicted by severe pain, he sent for his physicians. **(5)** Each of the others was hesitant to treat him, but Philip, an Acarnanian by descent, familiar with risky but quick-acting remedies, offered to stop the illness with drugs. **(6)** The king accepted gladly, because it was being said that Darius had already left Babylon with his force.[86] The physician gave him a drug to drink and, aided by the nature of the patient and by Fate, promptly relieved Alexander of the illness. The latter, recovering astonishingly and honouring the physician magnificently, assigned him to the most loyal of his companions.

(17.32.1) Alexander's mother wrote to him both other useful advice and that he should beware of the Lyncestian Alexander.[87] The latter, being distinguished for bravery and a high spirit, accompanied the king with the other companions in a trusted capacity.[88] **(2)** Because there were, though, many other plausible circumstances joining to support the charge, having been arrested and bound, he was placed under guard, until he should face court.

Battle of Issus:
Learning that Darius was only a few days' march away, Alexander sent off Parmenion with his force to seize the passage of the so-called 'Gates'.[89] The latter, reaching the place and forcing out the Persians

---

[86] Diodorus is, here again, extremely succinct and down to earth: see Aristobulus (*FGrH/BNJ* 139 F 8); Curt. 3.5.2–3; Plu. *Alex.* 19.1; Just. 11.8.3–6; Arr. *An.* 2.4.7. Diodorus seems here to remain close to Aristobulus' account.

[87] According to Just. 11.7.1–2 and Arr. *An.* 1.25, the plot of this Alexander of Lyncestis (Lyncestis is a district in Upper Macedonia) was revealed by a Persian captive and should be dated to an earlier stage of the expedition. Though Alexander the Great had executed two brothers of this Lyncestian Alexander, the man himself had always behaved like a loyal and trusted companion of the king, in the expedition under discussion as commander of the Thessalian cavalry. Being a possible rival for the throne of Macedonia, he was no doubt closely watched by Olympias, the mother of Alexander the Great. Though the following paragraph mentions that the Lyncestian Alexander was arrested in order to face court, a proper trial is not reported. At the time of Philotas' conspiracy, about 329/8 (see below, 17.80.2), Lyncestian Alexander was, after a more or less summary conviction, executed. See also Kärst 1893; Carney 1980; Ellis 1971: esp. 23–4.

[88] See above, note 23, and Chapter 4, note 289.

[89] Diodorus does not inform us which Gates are intended here. On the basis of Curt. 3.7.6 we might surmise the Gates in question could be the modern pass of Kara Kopou, between Tarsus and Issus. The suggestion of Arr. *An.* 2.5.1 and Callisthenes (preserved in Plb. 12.17.2), that the Cilician Gates (about 20 km south of Issus) between Cilicia and Syria are intended, might well be a bit too far ahead in respect of Alexander's route. See also Goukowsky 2002a: 189–90 *ad* 32.2. At least at present, the 'Cilician Gates' is generally the name given to the pass north of Tarsus, at Gülek Bogazi; that is, the access to Cilicia from Cappadocia. The pass intended may well have been either the present-day Belen Pass (the Assyrian Gates) or the pass near the modern 'Pillar of Yunus', both in the region of the modern city of İskenderun.

who were holding the pass, became master of it. (3) Deciding to make his army mobile, Darius diverted his baggage train and the non-combatants to Damascus in Syria. Learning that Alexander was holding the passes and thinking that he would never dare to fight in the plain, he made his way quickly to meet him. (4) The locals, who had little respect for the small numbers of the Macedonians, but were much impressed with the great size of the Persian army, abandoned Alexander and came over to Darius. They brought the Persians both food and other materials with great goodwill, and in their own judgement assigned the victory to the Persians. Alexander, however, occupied Issus, a considerable city, which was terrified into submission. (17.33.1) When the scouts reported to Alexander that Darius was only thirty *stadia*[90] away and was advancing, strikingly, with his forces deployed, he grasped that this was a god-given opportunity to destroy the power of the Persians in a single victory. He exhorted his soldiers with the appropriate words for the decisive battle and deployed the battalions of foot and the squadrons of horse as the present location required. He positioned the cavalry along the front of the whole army, and ordered the infantry phalanx to form the reserve behind it.[91] (2) Having with him the best of the cavalry, he himself, commanding the right wing, advanced to the enemy. The horsemen of the Thessalians, far exceeding the rest in both prowess and skill, held the left wing. (3) When the armies were within missile range, the Persians launched such a barrage of missiles at Alexander's force that because of the denseness of the missiles they collided with one another and made the impact weaker. (4) As the trumpeters signalled the attack on both sides, the Macedonians, crying aloud, gave a violent war cry, and because after that the Persians raised a shout in reply, the whole nearby hillside echoed back the sound: the volume of this roar surpassed the Macedonian shouting, as if five hundred thousand men shouted with one voice. (5) Casting his glance in all directions, striving to see Darius, Alexander with his cavalry drove immediately at the Great King himself when he had identified him, not so much in an attempt to defeat the Persians as to win the victory with his own hands.[92] (6) Since by now all the other horsemen were

---

[90] That is, c. 5.5 km. As regards the precise distance and the different problems involved in Diodorus' account, see Goukowsky 2002a: 190–1 *ad* 33.1 and *ad* 33.5.

[91] As Goukowsky 2002a: 191 *ad* 33.1 (second remark) also notes, Diodorus confounds marching order and battle order here: see Plb. 12.20.8; Curt. 3.11.4; Arr. *An.* 2.8.2–4. The battle took place near the River Payas, ancient River Pinarus: see Hammond 1992: 395 with reference. As Hammond asserts, Diodorus' geography here is a mess, unlike Arrian's account.

[92] A romanticised version, compared with the more factual account of Arr. *An.* 2.11.1–4. From a military point of view I prefer the latter account.

Fig. 5.3. The River Payas (ancient River Pinarus), site of the Battle of Issus. Photo © Jona Lendering <http://www.livius.org>.

engaged in fighting with each other and there was much slaughter, the battle could have turned in any direction because of the evenly matched *aretae* of the fighting men, the scales inclining now one way, now another, as the lines swayed alternately forward and backward. (7) Indeed, everyone either throwing a javelin or thrusting a sword hit a target, as if the crowd offered a ready target. Many fell with wounds received as they faced the enemy and, preserving their fury to the last breath, life failed them sooner than *aretē*.
(17.34.1) Fighting valiantly at the head of their men, the officers of each unit by their personal *aretē* inspired courage in the ranks. One could see many forms of wounds inflicted, furious struggles of all sorts inspired by the will to win. (2) When the Persian Oxathres,[93] a brother of Darius and a man highly praised for his fighting qualities, saw Alexander uncontrollably riding at Darius, he aspired to share his brother's fate. (3) Taking with him the best of the horsemen in his company to follow him, he threw himself with them against Alexander's group, thinking that this demonstration of

[93] See also Curt. 3.11.8–9.

brotherly love would bring him high renown among the Persians. He took up the fight directly in front of Darius' *quadriga* and, expertly and courageously engaging the enemy, killed many of them there. (4) Because the bravery of Alexander's group was superior, many bodies quickly lay piled high about Darius' *quadriga*. Indeed, because all the Macedonians wanted to strike the Great King, the combatants fought among each other very vehemently and took no thought for their lives. (5) Many of the distinguished Persian nobles fell in this struggle, among them Atizyes, Rheomithres, and Sabaces, the satrap of Egypt.[94] While many of the Macedonians had likewise fallen, it happened that even Alexander himself had been wounded in the thigh,[95] as the enemy pressed about him. (6) The horses which were harnessed to the yoke of Darius' *quadriga*, covered in wounds and terrified by the piles of the dead about them, violently shaking off their bits, nearly carried off Darius himself into the midst of the enemy. The Great King himself, in extreme peril, caught up the reins, forced to abandon the dignity of his position and to violate the ancient custom of the Persian kings. (7) Another *quadriga* was brought up for Darius by his adjutants and, in the confusion as he changed over to it, Darius fell into terror and fear in the face of constant attack. As the Persians saw their king in such disorder, they turned to flee.[96] Because the horsemen of adjacent units did the same, soon all were in full retreat. (8) Because their flight took place in narrow and rugged terrain, they clashed and trampled on one another and many died without an enemy blow. In fact, men lay piled up together, some without armour, others retaining their panoply. Some, retaining their drawn swords, killed

---

[94] Atizyes had already, probably wrongly, been assumed killed at the Granicus (see 17.21.3 above), unless some otherwise unknown Antixyes is intended here (see MSS; *contra, inter alios*, Wesseling, Goukowsky). Rheomithres is mentioned as a cavalry commander at the Granicus (see 17.19.4 above). Curt. 3.11.10 mentions among the Persian dead Atizyes, Rheomithres, and Sabaces. Arr. *An.* 2.11.8 mentions Arsames, Rheomithres, Atizyes, Sabaces, and Bubaces. Though the MS tradition of Diodorus gives the name of the satrap of Egypt here as Tasiaces, the name should be Sabaces, as appears not only from the testimonies of the other authors, but also from numismatic evidence (see Newell 1938: 62, 68–9).

[95] Allegedly by Darius himself, as one source (Chares, *FGrH/BNJ* 125 F 6) states: see also Plu. *De Alex. Fort.* 341B. Alexander's wound is further mentioned in Curt. 3.11.10; Just. 11.9.9; Plu. *Alex.* 20.5, referring to a letter from Alexander to Antipater, in which Alexander reports having been wounded by a dagger; and Arr. *An.* 2.12.1.

[96] Though it seems that Darius, one way or another, ceased to participate in the battle, there is no actual flight as yet: that is only reported in 17.37.1 below. With regard to Darius' past (see 17.6.1 above), fleeing from the battlefield seems rather out of character (though fitting in with Greek propaganda-fuelled views of effeminate and cowardly Persians!). His flight after the battle was clearly lost, however, was not out of character: it was his only chance to regroup and continue his defence of the empire.

those who searched about that pile.⁹⁷ Most of the cavalry, however, bursting out into the plain of Issus and forcibly driving their horses through the plain, fled to the allied cities.⁹⁸ (9) The Macedonian phalanx and the Persian infantry remained in battle a short time, because, indeed, the rout of the cavalry had been, as it were, a prelude to the whole victory.⁹⁹ Since all of the Persians were soon in retreat and so many tens of thousands were making their escape through narrow passes, the whole countryside was soon filled with bodies.

Alexander is victorious; Macedonian troops take the Persian camp:
(17.35.1) When night fell, the remainder of the Persian army easily succeeded in scattering in various directions, while the Macedonians gave over the pursuit and turned to plunder and were especially attracted by the royal pavilions because of the amount of extravagance. (2) Therefore they carried off from the royal treasure much silver, no little gold, and vast numbers of costly clothes.¹⁰⁰ Likewise no mean amount of wealth was taken belonging to the Great King's companions, relatives,¹⁰¹ and military commanders. (3) In fact, not only the ladies of the royal house but also those of the Great King's relatives and companions, borne on gilded chariots,¹⁰² had accompanied the army, according to an ancestral custom of the Persians.¹⁰³ (4) Each of them, in keeping with their vast wealth and luxury {τρυφή}, had brought with her a store of rich furniture and feminine adornment. The lot of these captured women was pathetic in the extreme. (5) They, who previously from daintiness had only with reluctance been conveyed in luxurious {τρυφή} carriages and had exposed no part of their bodies unveiled, now burst wailing out of

---

⁹⁷ See Arr. *An.* 2.11.3 and Curt. 3.11.16–19. According to Arr. *An.* 2.11.8, Ptolemy declared that he saw a ravine filled with bodies (see *FGrH/BNJ* 138 F 8).

⁹⁸ See Curt. 3. 11.18.

⁹⁹ The infantry were notably the 30,000 Greek mercenaries in Persian service. See also comments of Plb. 12.17–18 on this battle (and notably Callisthenes' report); Curt. 3.9.2, 11.8; Arr. *An.* 2.10.5–11.3; Plu. *Alex.* 20.3–5; and the anonymous author on Alexander (*P.Oxy.* 1798 [= *FGrH/BNJ* 148] F 44, col. 3 lines 1–2: εἰς φυγὴν ὥρμη]σαν οἱ Πέρσαι, εἶτα τὸ λοιπὸν τῶν βαρβάρων πλῆθος, μεθ' οὓς οἱ ξένοι ('the Persians turned to flee, next the remaining mass of the Persians, including the mercenaries')).

¹⁰⁰ This paragraph and the following ones obviously relate to a slightly later stage, namely the capture of the non-combatants and all other things that were not needed in battle, dispatched by Darius to Damascus (see 17.32.3 above).

¹⁰¹ See also note 23 and Chapter 4, note 289.

¹⁰² Elsewhere in classical literature such luxurious, roofed and curtained, four-wheeled wagons have been well described. For references see, for example, Goukowsky 2002a: 52 note 1. Also above, Chapter 3, 11.56.8.

¹⁰³ Diodorus might hint here at the nomadic origin of the Persians that may have lasted until c. 550: see, for example, Sancisi-Weerdenburg 1980: 246–7.

the tents, clad only in a single *chiton*, rending their garments, calling on the gods, and falling at the knees of the conquerors. (6) Flinging off their jewellery with trembling hands and with their hair flying, they ran over rugged ground and, huddling together, called for help to those who were themselves in need of help from others. (7) Some dragged these unfortunates by the hair, others drove them on, having ripped off their clothing, striking them with blows of their hands or spear butts against their naked bodies and outraging the dearest and proudest of the Persian possessions by virtue of Fate's generosity.[104] (17.36.1) Now the most prudent of the Macedonians, looking at this reversal of Fate, were compassionate and felt pity for the case of those who had seen their former lot so violently changed. Decency and status were far removed from them, while the foreign and hostile was nearby: the women were herded off into a luckless and humiliating captivity.[105] (2) Especially Darius' mother, wife, two daughters of marriageable age, and son, a child as regards his age, moved those present to tears and pity. (3) Indeed, as one observed their change in fortune and the magnitude of their unlooked-for misfortunes, this spectacle made those who beheld it sympathise with good reason. (4) In fact, the women and children knew nothing of Darius, whether he lived and survived or had perished in the general disaster as well. They saw, however, armed hostile men plundering their tent, unaware of the identity of their captives, committing many improper acts through ignorance. They saw the whole of Asia taken prisoner with them, and had no possibility of helping any of the wives of the satraps who fell at their feet and implored their help,[106] but they themselves as well sought the assistance of the others in their own misfortunes. (5) Taking over the tent of Darius,[107] the royal pages prepared the latter's bath and dinner and, lighting a great blaze of torches, waited for Alexander, so that he, after returning from the pursuit and finding ready for him all the riches of Darius, might

---

[104] Goukowsky 2002a: 192 *ad* 35.7 remarks that this description 'must' be based upon Clitarchus. See also Curt. 3.11.21–2. Plu. *Alex.* 24.2 states that the Macedonians developed a taste for money and women after Issus, a theme based upon or derived from (at least regarding the women) Isoc. *Ep.* 9.9–10. Diodorus' description also shares many traits with this passage.

[105] Though the sentence as it is does make some sense, there seems to be something missing. The chapter begins with 'the most prudent of the Macedonians' and therefore one would expect an antithesis, telling how others felt about these women. The MS tradition, however, offers no clues on this matter.

[106] Though Curt. 3.11.25 also mentions *nobiliarvm feminarvm tvrba* ('a great throng of high-born women'), he acknowledges further on (Curt. 3.13.12–14) that these were in fact in Damascus (see also Plu. *Alex.* 21.4, 24.1). Arr. *An.* 2.11.9 only refers to τῶν ὁμοτίμων γυναῖκες οὐ πολλαί ('some women of noble birth'), adding that most other (well-born) Persians had sent their womenfolk to Damascus.

[107] For Darius' tent and its symbolism, see Goukowsky 2002a: 193 *ad* 36.5.

Alexander the Great Defeats Darius III 301

take it as an omen for his rule of the whole of Asia. (6) In the course of the battle there died on the Persian side more than one hundred thousand infantry and not less than ten thousand cavalry. On the Macedonian side there died three hundred infantry and one hundred and fifty cavalry. This was the conclusion of the battle at Issus of Cilicia.[108]

C. FROM ISSUS TO GAUGAMELA

Darius tries to accommodate the new situation; Alexander refuses: (17.37.1) Of the kings, however, Darius, being decisively defeated,[109] fled head over heels and, mounting in turn one after another of his best horses, galloped on at top speed, desperately seeking to escape from Alexander's hands and planning to reach the upper satrapies. (2) Alexander made the pursuit with the companion cavalry [the royal horse guards] and the best of the other horsemen, eager to get hold of Darius. Having continued on for two hundred *stadia* [c. 38 km], he turned back to the encampment about midnight. Having dispelled the fatigue of his strain in the bath, he turned to relaxation and to dinner. (3) Someone, approaching Darius' wife and mother, told them that Alexander had come back from the pursuit after stripping Darius of his arms. After a great outcry and lamentation had risen among the women, and the rest of the captives, joining in their sorrow at the news, sent up a loud wail, the king, having heard of the emotion among the women, sent Leonnatus, one of his companions. He had to make the uproar end and to reassure Sisyngambris[110] and her entourage and to explain that Darius was still alive, but that Alexander would show them the proper consideration and therefore would come in the morning both to address them and to demonstrate his kindness by deeds. (4) As they heard this welcome and

---

[108] Other authors report other figures: Curt. 3.11.27 mentions a loss of 100,000 foot and 10,000 horsemen on the Persian side and 4,500 wounded and 302 soldiers (officially missing) and 150 horsemen killed on the Macedonian side; Just. 11.9.10 gives 61,000 infantry and 10,000 cavalry as well as 40,000 captives on the Persian side, 130 infantry and 150 cavalry on the Macedonian; the anonymous author on Alexander (*P.Oxy.* 1798 [= *FGrH/BNJ* 148] F 44 col. 4 ll. 9–18) reports on the Persian side the death of 50,000 foot and 3,000 horse, and of the mercenaries a number that has disappeared into a lacuna of the text, and on the Macedonian side 1,000 foot and 200 horse. Arr. *An.* 2.11.7–8 mentions the loss of 90,000 foot and 10,000 horse on the Persian side and 120 on the Macedonian; and Plu. *Alex.* 20.5, finally, only reports Persian casualties, which he gives as 110,000 men in total.
[109] Diodorus' description of the behaviour of Darius III and Alexander is quite tendentious and represents Greek propaganda more than a balanced view of the events.
[110] Usually written as Sisigambis (see, for example, Curt. 3.3.22) or Sisygambis. See Wiesehöfer 2001.

altogether unexpected good news, the captive women both hailed Alexander as a god and ceased from their wailing. (5) So at daybreak, the king, taking with him one of his companions, the highly valued Hephaestion, came to the women.[111] Though they were both dressed alike, Hephaestion was taller and more handsome. Sisyngambris took him for the king and did him obeisance.[112] Because the others present made signs to her and pointed to Alexander with their hands, Sisyngambris, embarrassed by her mistake, again from the beginning did obeisance to Alexander. (6) The king, however, lifting her up, said: 'Never mind, Mother, for actually he too is Alexander.'[113] Truly, by addressing the aged woman as 'Mother', he gave through this kindliest of appellations the promise of coming benefactions to those who had been wretched before. Assuring her that she would be his second mother, he immediately confirmed in deeds what he had just announced in words.

(17.38.1) He both bestowed on her royal jewellery and restored her previous dignity with its proper honours. Indeed, he transmitted to her all the retinue of servants which she had been given by Darius and personally added a supplementary one not less in number than the preceding. He also announced he would provide for the daughters' marriage even more generously than the choice of Darius and would bring up the boy as his own son and show him royal honour. (2) As he saw that, having called the boy to him and kissed him, the boy looked fearless and not in the least scared, he remarked to Hephaestion that the boy, though six years old and showing a courage beyond his years, was much braver than his father. As to Darius' wife and her dignity, he said that he would take care that she would suffer nothing unworthy of her former happiness.[114] (3) Adding many other assurances of consideration and generosity, he made the women burst out into uncontrollable tears because of the size of the unhoped-for joy. After he had given them his right hand as pledge of all the aforementioned promises, he not only received commendations from those who had

---

[111] Neither Ptolemy (*FGrH/BNJ* 138 F 7) nor Aristobulus (*FGrH/BNJ* 139 F 9) mentions such a visit. The words of Arr. *An.* 2.2.16: λόγος δ' ἔχει ('word has it') suggest the story may well be apocryphal. Goukowsky 2002a: 193 *ad* 37.3 surmises it might have been invented by Clitarchus.

[112] For obeisance see, for example, Frye 1972.

[113] See D.L. 7.23, on Zeno: ἐρωτηθεὶς τίς ἐστι φίλος, «ἄλλος,» ἔφη, «ἐγώ.» ('To the question "Who is a friend?"' he said "Another I"'). The inventor of the story or indeed Alexander himself through his teacher, Aristotle, may well have been familiar with the ideas and sayings of Zeno (c. 490–after 445).

[114] Plu. *Alex.* 22.2 refers to a letter by Alexander in which he states that he has never seen, or wished to see, Darius' wife. See also Curt. 3.12.21–2, 4.10.22–4, applauding Alexander's continence.

been done well to, but won recognition as well among all his soldiers. (4) ... (5) ... (6) ... (7) ... [[All dedicated to moral observations, notably as regards Alexander.]]

Darius wants to assemble a new army:
(17.39.1) Having hurried to Babylon and gathering the survivors of the battle at Issus,[115] Darius was not crushed in spirit, even though he had just experienced a great mishap. Instead he wrote to Alexander, advising him to bear his success as one who was only human and to release the captives in return for a large ransom. He added that he would yield to Alexander the territory and cities of Asia west of the River Halys, if he would become his friend.[116] (2) Having summoned his companions, Alexander concealed the real letter. Forging another more in accord with his interests, he introduced it to his advisers and sent the envoys away empty handed.[117] (3) Therefore Darius, giving up agreement with Alexander through letters, set to work on vast preparations for war. He re-equipped those who had lost their panoplies in the defeat and after enlisting others he assigned them to military units. He sent for the forces from the upper satrapies, which he had previously left unemployed because of the haste of the campaign. (4) In the end, he took such pains over the constitution of the army that it became twice the size of that which had been engaged at Issus. In fact, there assembled eight hundred thousand infantry and two hundred thousand cavalry, and without reckoning a multitude of scythe-bearing chariots.[118] These were the events of this year.

Alexander sets out for Phoenicia; hostile reception by Tyre:
(17.40.1) When Niceratus was *archon* at Athens [332/1], the Romans elected as consuls Marcus Atilius and Marcus Valerius, and the one hundred and twelfth Olympic Games were held, in which Gryllus of Chalcis was the victor.[119] In this year, Alexander

---

[115] Including 2,000 Greek mercenaries: Curt. 4.1.3; Arr. *An.* 2.13.1.
[116] On this letter and the divergent presentation of its contents, see Goukowsky 2002a: 194–5 *ad* 39.1.
[117] No other author reports a forgery by Alexander, though other letters have been reported. Welles 1970: 228–9 note 1 presents a review of various letters occurring in the various accounts of Alexander's march at this stage. See also Goukowsky 2002a: 57 note 2 and 194–5 *ad* 39.1.
[118] See also Curt. 4.13.1 and below, 17.53.1–2.
[119] The correct name of the *archon* of this year is Nicetes, as appears from numerous inscriptions. See, *inter alia*, IG II², 344–7, 368, most notably in 346, 1544, 4594a: ἐπὶ Νικήτου ἄρχοντος ('under the archonship of Nicetes'). This formula also occurs in some Agora inscriptions, for example Agora 16.78–80, and inscriptions collected by Schwenk 1985. The consuls (of 335 vc) were M. Atilius Regulus Calenus and M. Valerius Corvus, while L. Aemilius

buried the dead after his victory at Issus, including even those of the Persians who had distinguished themselves by prowess. After that, having performed rich sacrifices to the gods and rewarding those who had excelled in *aretē* in battle with gifts appropriate to each, he rested his force for some days. (2) Next, marching on towards Egypt and arriving in Phoenicia, he allied with himself all the other cities, for their inhabitants accepted him willingly. The Tyrians, however, because the king wished to sacrifice to the Tyrian Heracles, overhastily barred him from entering the city.[120] (3) When Alexander became angry and threatened that he would make war against the city, the Tyrians cheerfully faced the prospect of a siege. They wanted at the same time to gratify Darius and keep unimpaired their loyalty to him, and thought that they would receive great gifts from the Great King in return for such a favour. As they would draw Alexander into a protracted and dangerous siege, they would give Darius time for his military preparations, but at the same time they had confidence in the strength of their island and the armaments in it,[121] moreover in their colonists, the Carthaginians.[122]

Siege of Tyre by the Macedonians starts:
(4) The king saw that the city was not to be besieged by sea because of both the engines mounted along its walls and the fleet that it possessed, while from the land it was almost unassailable because it lay four *stadia* [c. 750 m] away from the coast. All the same he determined to run every risk and make every effort to save the Macedonian army from being held in contempt by a single undistinguished city. (5) Immediately demolishing what was called Old Tyre and after setting to work many tens of thousands of men carrying stones, he had a mole constructed two *plethra* [c. 60 m] in width. Having drafted into service the entire population of the neighbouring cities, the project of the works rapidly neared completion due to the many hands set to work.

Mamercinus (Privernas) was that year's dictator: see Broughton 1951: 139–40. Diodorus is still four years ahead of the Varronian chronology. As for the *Olympionikes*, I concur with the emendation of Goukowsky 2002a: 58 *ad* l. 4, Gryllus, based upon a remark in Herod. *Mimes* 1: 50–1: Γρύλλος, ὁ πέντε νικέων ἆθλα ('Gryllus, the winner of five Games').

[120] Curt. 4.2.10 adds that Alexander's demand (Curtius mentions in 4.2.4 an alternative way for Alexander to offer sacrifice to the Tyrian Heracles, more correctly Melqart (see Hdt. 2.44): Milk-Qart ('King of the city' or Ba'l Ṣūr 'Lord of Tyre')) more or less coincided with an annual festival (for the god?).

[121] See Goukowsky 2002a: 195 *ad* 40.3, second remark. Marsden 1964: 7–8 believes Diodorus paints here an accurate picture of the situation, perhaps based on inside information (probably from one of the Great King's Greek mercenaries).

[122] See Curt. 4.2.10; Just. 11.10.13–14.

Alexander the Great Defeats Darius III 305

(17.41.1) At first the Tyrians, sailing up to the jetty, mocked the king: did he believe he would get the better of Poseidon? Then, as the work proceeded with unexpected rapidity, they voted to transport their children, women, and old men to Carthage, assigned the ablebodied of military age to the defence of the walls and made ready for a naval engagement, having eighty *triereis*. (2) In the end, they did succeed in getting some of their children and women to safety with the Carthaginians, but outstripped by the abundance of Alexander's labour force and with their ships insufficient in strength, they were compelled to stand the siege with almost their whole population.

Defensive countermeasures by the Tyrians; the force of omens:
(3) Having a great abundance of catapults and other engines employed for sieges, they had no difficulty in constructing many more because of the engineers and artisans of all sorts who were in the city. (4) Because of their fashioning of all kinds of novel and strange devices, the entire circuit of the walls was covered with machines, especially on that very side where the mole was approaching the city. (5) As the construction made by the Macedonians came within range of their missiles, portents were sent by the gods to them in their danger. Indeed, out of the sea the billow drove a sea-monster of incredible size against the works in progress.[123] It crashed into the jetty but did it no harm, remained resting a portion of its body against it for a long time and caused much fear in those watching the extraordinary event. (6) Then, however, swimming off into the sea again, it induced a religious feeling in both parties. In fact, both parties interpreted the portent to mean that Poseidon was about to come to their aid, fitting their views to their own interests. (7) There were other strange omens

---

[123] Prandi 2013: 67, referring to Curt. 4.2.9 (who mentions the noteworthy depth of the sea, even close to the coast), concludes 'e questo rende possibile e credibile l'avvicinarsi a riva di animali di grandi dimensioni'. Though I am somewhat hesitant as regards its credibility, we might, perhaps, yet think of the presence of a fin whale (*Balaenoptera physalus*), the commonest large whale species in the Mediterranean Sea, which is found mostly in the deep, offshore waters of the western and central portion of the region. It is less frequent elsewhere, though present throughout the region (see <http://www.cetaceanalliance.org/cetaceans/Bp_home.htm>, retrieved 1 July 2015). An alternative would, perhaps, be the appearance of a Mediterranean sperm whale (*Physeter macrocephalus*: see <http://www.cetaceanalliance.org/cetaceans/Pm_home.htm>, retrieved 1 July 2015). These species seem to me the least unlikely candidates matching both description and possibilities. It seems the Greeks were not wholly unfamiliar with sea-monsters (or whales), as appears, for example, from 17.106.6–7, where too the creature is referred to as a κῆτος ('sea-monster' or 'huge fish': see *LSJ s.v.*). As a matter of fact, it is the same word the translators of the *Septuagint* used to describe the fish (whale?) that swallowed Jonah: Καὶ προσέταξεν κύριος κήτει μεγάλῳ καταπιεῖν τὸν Ιωναν· καὶ ἦν Ιωνας ἐν τῇ κοιλίᾳ τοῦ κήτους τρεῖς ἡμέρας καὶ τρεῖς νύκτας ('And the Lord appointed a great fish to swallow up Jonah; and Jonah was in the belly of the [great] fish three days and three nights': Jonah 1:17 (2:1), *RSV*).

too, calculated to spread confusion and terror among people. At the distribution of rations on the Macedonian side, the broken pieces of bread had a bloody look.[124] Someone reported, on the Tyrian side, that he had seen a vision in which Apollo told him that he would leave the city. (8) Because everyone suspected the man had made up the story in order to gratify Alexander, some of the younger citizens therefore set out to stone the man. The latter, however, spirited away by the magistrates and taking refuge in the temple of Heracles, escaped retribution through supplication. The Tyrians, though, being superstitious, tied the image of Apollo to its base with golden cords, preventing, as they thought, the god's departure from the city.

Fighting intensifies:
(17.42.1) After this, the Tyrians, being alarmed at the advance of the jetty, equipped many of the small vessels with *euthytona, palintona*, archers, and slingers, and, sailing towards the workers on the mole, wounded many and killed not a few.[125] (2) As missiles of all sorts in large numbers rained upon unarmed and densely packed men, no soldier missed his mark, since the targets were exposed and unsuspecting. In fact, the missiles struck not only from the front but also from the back, as men were working on both sides of a rather narrow structure and no one could protect himself from those who shot from two directions. (3) Wanting to rectify this unforeseen occurrence quickly, Alexander, manning all his ships and taking personal command of them,[126] sailed with all speed for the harbour of Tyre and tried to cut off the Phoenicians' retreat. (4) Terrified that he, after seizing the harbours, would capture the city while it was empty of soldiers, the Phoenicians rowed back to Tyre as fast as they could. As both fleets touched the surface of the water with their oars at a fast stroke in a fury of determination and the Macedonians were already nearing the harbours, the Phoenicians, by a whisker,

[124] See Goukowsky 2002a: 196 *ad* 41.7, first remark, for a plausible explanation of this phenomenon.
[125] Arrian reports an impressive counteraction by the Tyrians. They filled a cavalry transport ship with dry boughs and other combustible wood, made a construction on the ship with bulwarks from bow to bow and added chips, shavings, torches, pitch, sulphur, and anything else to stir a great blaze. Next they attached cauldrons to yardarms on the masts, filled with anything that could be poured or thrown on to increase the flames, and balanced the ship in such a manner that the weight was aft. When the wind was favourable, they directed the ship to the mole, lit the material, and dashed the ship on to the mole. The final result of the action was huge damage to the mole (Arr. *An.* 2.19.1–5). Curt. 4.3.2–7, 9–11 also relates this and other Tyrian actions, the last against Alexander's measures to strengthen the mole.
[126] Alexander had sent most of his fleet home (above, 17.22.5–23.1), leaving him with few ships, unless we assume he had commissioned a number of ships from the Phoenician cities friendly to him. See also below, note 129.

escaped losing their whole force. Thrusting their way in and losing the ships at the tail of the column, they got safely to the city after all. (5) Having failed in a great attempt, the king pushed on with the jetty, providing safety for his workers with the main body of the ships. As his engines drew close to the city and its capture seemed imminent, a powerful north-west gale rose and ruined a large part of the mole.[127]

Alexander temporarily beaten but not yet defeated:
(6) Falling into helplessness at the destruction of the works caused by nature, Alexander started to regret the siege attempt, but nevertheless, driven by ambition, having felled extremely large trees, he brought them from the mountain and, after digging them into the sea floor branches and all, he broke the force of the waves. (7) After he had restored the collapsed parts of the mole quickly, and pushing on with an ample labour force until within missiles' range, he positioned his engines at the end of the jetty and pelted the walls with his *palintona*, while the *euthytona* kept back those stationed along the battlements. These machines were joined by both the archers and slingers, and they wounded many in the city who rushed to the defence.
(17.43.1) As the Tyrians had bronze-workers and engineers, they contrived ingenious countermeasures. Against the projectiles from the catapults they made wheels with many spokes, and, setting these to rotate by a certain device, they destroyed some of the missiles, deflected others, but broke the force of all.[128] Catching the stones thrown by the *palintona* in soft and yielding materials, they weakened the impact of their force. (2) While this attack was going on from the mole, the king sailed around the city with his whole fleet and inspected the walls,[129] and made it clear that he was about to attack the city alike by land and sea. (3) Because the Tyrians did not

[127] See Curt. 4.3.6–7. This setback occurred while Alexander was in the interior: see Arr. *An.* 2.20.4; Curt. 4.3.1; Plu. *Alex.* 24.6–8 (quoting Chares of Mytilene).

[128] Such wheels have never been described before, though they appear again – in somewhat different shape – below in 17.45.3. It is not easy to present a translation that fits both the Greek and the picture of a functioning device, and I do wonder whether the description originates from Diodorus' source on Alexander or from another source and, in fact, whether Diodorus himself had a clear picture in his mind of such a device. See also Welles 1970: 238–41 note 3 and Goukowsky 2002a: 197–8 *ad* 42.1, second remark (sic!).

[129] Obviously Alexander here had at least some ships at his disposal. In 17.22.5 above, Diodorus reports that Alexander dismissed all his ships apart from a few employed to transport siege engines. Though it may be feasible that those Phoenician or Cypriot cities that had submitted to Alexander provided him with additional ships, Diodorus does not report such an occurrence: Arr. *An.* 2.19.6–20.3, however, does, as does Curt. 4.3.11. Plu. *Alex.* 24.3 merely mentions that Alexander disposed of 200 *triereis*.

dare to put to sea again with their whole fleet but kept three ships moored at the harbour mouth, the king, sailing up to these ships and sinking them all, returned to his camp. Wanting to double the security of their walls, the Tyrians built another wall, ten cubits [c. 4.5 m] in thickness, at a distance of five cubits [c. 2.25 m] within the first, and the space between the walls they filled with stones and earth.[130] (4) Joining the *triereis* together and mounting various siege engines upon them,[131] Alexander overthrew the wall for the space of a *plethrum* [c. 30 m]. Through this breach the Macedonians burst into the city. (5) Pressing the invaders hard with a thick shower of darts, the Tyrians managed to turn them back with toil and pain and, when night came, they rebuilt the fallen part of the wall. Later, when the causeway had reached the wall and had made the city a peninsula, many great fights occurred during the battle for the walls.

Macedonians and Tyrians fight for the walls of Tyre:
(6) Having the present horror before their eyes and imagining the disaster of the capture of the city, the Tyrians were so passionately devoted to the contest that they despised death. (7) When the Macedonians moved up towers of the same height as the walls and from them fastened assault-bridges to the walls and boldly assaulted the battlements,[132] the Tyrians had, due to the ingenuity of their engineers, many countermeasures to defend the wall.[133] (8) Indeed, having forged long tridents armed with barbs, they struck those standing on the towers with these at close range. Because these tridents stuck in the shields and ropes were attached to the tridents, the Tyrians took hold of the ropes and pulled them to themselves. (9) The Macedonians were thus obliged either to let go their shields and expose their bodies to be wounded by the missiles which showered

---

[130] See Aen.Tact. 32.12 for the advice to build in this way.

[131] In Alexander's army were at least two engineers of siegecraft, mentioned by name by Athenaeus Mechanicus (see Whitehead and Blyth 2004), namely Diades and Charias. Apparently they wrote a *Poliorcetica* (*Siegecraft*) together, while Diades is also credited with a Μηχανικός σύγγραμμα (see Ath.Mech. 5, 10; see also Vitr. 10.13.3). From Ath.Mech. 8 we may surmise that the range of the *palintona* may well have been up to 3.5–4 *stadia*, about 700 m, though this distance was here not needed any more. Unfortunately, Athenaeus Mechanicus (or Athenaeus of Seleucia, first century BC) shows little understanding of the machines he describes, though he had been educated by Agesistratus of Rhodes (see Whitehead and Blyth, ibid. pp. 18–20, 34–5).

[132] For the (portable) tower, see Ath.Mech. 10–12; for the assault-bridge: Ath.Mech. 10, 15, 25. See also Vitruvius on the towers (Vitr. 10.13.4–5), on the assault-bridges (*epibathra*), which Vitruvius calls both *ascendens machina* ('climbing machine') and an *accessus* ('entry'): Vitr. 10.13.3, 8.

[133] See also Aen.Tact. 33, 36 for several of these methods.

upon them or to cling to their shields for shame[134] and to fall from the high towers and die. (10) Other Tyrians, casting fishing nets over those Macedonians fighting on the assault-bridges and making their hands helpless, drew them down and rolled them round from the bridge to the earth.

(17.44.1) They conceived yet another ingenious device against the bravery of the Macedonians, by which they inflicted on the bravest of the enemy unavoidable and terrible sufferings. Indeed, having fashioned shields of bronze and iron and filling those with sand, they roasted them continuously over a strong fire and made the sand red hot. (2) By means of a certain apparatus they scattered this sand over those Macedonians fighting most boldly and inflicted upon those struck with it the utmost misery. Sifting down under breastplates and undergarments and scorching the skin with the intense heat, the sand inflicted irremediable disaster.[135] (3) The Macedonian victims shrieked, therefore, all kinds of supplications like those under torture. There was, however, no one to help them, but the excruciating agony made them fall into madness and they died, victims of a pitiable and helpless lot. (4) At the same time, the Phoenicians poured down fire and flung javelins and stones, and by the volume of their missiles weakened the *aretē* of the attackers. They let down long poles or spars equipped with concave cutting edges and cut the ropes supporting the rams, thus rendering these instruments useless.[136] With their fire-throwers they discharged huge, red-hot masses of metal into the mass of the enemy, and because of the density of men they did not miss their mark. With 'crows' and 'iron hands' they dragged over the edge many who were stationed behind the breastworks on the towers.[137] (5) Keeping all the machines busy with many hands at work, they killed many of the besiegers.

Slowly the Macedonians appear to lose faith:
(17.45.1) Though there was extreme terror because of all of this and the fury of the Tyrians' fighting became hardly resistible, the Macedonians did not lose their boldness. Replacing those ever falling,

---

[134] It was considered a disgrace to lose one's shield in battle.
[135] In fact, a form of chemical warfare: see Mayor 2009: 215–17. In another contribution, Mayor 2013 concluded that the effects of the burning sand described by Diodorus were very similar to the effects of white phosphorus, a chemical weapon still used in recent conflicts. See also Curt. 4.3.25–6.
[136] For rams, see Ath.Mech. 9–11, 23–5 and Vitr. 10.13.4, 6.
[137] Both 'crows' and 'iron hands' appear to have been types of grappling hooks. See also Curt. 4.2.23, 3.26.

they were not deterred by the sufferings of their comrades. (2) Having positioned the *palintona* in proper places and throwing large stones, Alexander made the walls rock. With the *euthytona* on the wooden towers maintaining a barrage of all kinds of projectiles, he punished the defenders of the walls terribly. (3) Rigging against these things, the Tyrians positioned marble wheels in front of the walls and causing these to rotate by some mechanisms they shattered the catapults' flying missiles and, deflecting them from their course, made the impact of the projectiles ineffective.[138] (4) In addition, stitching up hides or pairs of skins and stuffing them with seaweed, they took the blows of the *palintona* on these. As these cushions were soft and yielding, the impact of the thrown stones was lessened.[139] (5) In sum, the Tyrians defended themselves vigorously in all respects and, as they were well provided with the means of defence, they resisted the enemy boldly. Leaving the shelter of the walls and their positions within the towers, the Tyrians pressed forward onto the very assault-bridges and set their own *aretē* in opposition to the courage of the enemy. (6) Grappling with the enemy and fighting hand to hand, they put up a stout battle for their home town and some of them chopped off with axes any protruding part of the body of an opponent. There was one of the officers among the Macedonians, named Admetus, outstanding in bravery and physical strength, who withstood the fury of the Tyrians boldly and died heroically there and then, smitten on the middle of his head with an axe.[140] (7) Seeing that the attack turned ugly for the Macedonians, Alexander called his soldiers back with the *salpinx*, as night had already fallen. First he decided to break off the siege and to march on to Egypt, but on second thoughts and reflecting that it would be disgraceful to leave the Tyrians with all the glory of the operation, he turned again to the siege, finding support from only one of his companions, Amyntas the son of Andromenes.

Final push; Alexander is victorious and Tyre is taken:
(17.46.1) Exhorting the Macedonians to dare no less than he, having fitted out all his ships for fighting, he began a furious attack upon the walls by land and sea. Observing that the wall on the side of the naval base was weaker than elsewhere, he brought up to that point his *triereis*, lashed together and supporting his best siege engines.

---

[138] See above, note 128.
[139] Already hinted at above, 17.43.1.
[140] According to Arr. *An.* 2.23.5, 24.4, Admetus, the commander of the *hypaspistae* (infantry of the guard), fell later in the siege, namely during the final attack, struck by a lance and not by an axe.

(2) Now he had the courage to perform a feat which was hardly believable even to those who saw it. Indeed, flinging an assault-bridge across from the wooden tower to the city walls, he crossed by it alone to the wall, neither concerned for the envy of Fate nor fearing the menace of the Tyrians. Having as witness of his personal prowess the great army which had defeated the Persians, he ordered the Macedonians to follow him. Leading the way, he killed some of those who came within reach with his spear, others by a blow of his *machaera*. Knocking down still others with the rim of his shield, he put an end to the high confidence of the enemy. (3) As this happened, in another part of the city the battering ram, put to its work, brought down a considerable stretch of wall. When the Macedonians entered through this breach and Alexander's party poured over the assault-bridge on to the wall, the city was taken. The Tyrians, however, keeping up the resistance and shouting cries of support to each other, blocked the alleys with barricades[141] and all except a few were cut down fighting, in number more than seven thousand. (4) The king sold the women and children into slavery and all the men of military age, not less than two thousand, he crucified. Although most of the non-combatants had been removed to Carthage, those who remained to become captives were found to be more than thirteen thousand.[142] (5) The Tyrians, enduring the siege bravely rather than wisely, thus came into such misfortunes, having been besieged for seven months. (6) Removing the golden chains and fetters from Apollo, the king announced that the god should be called '*Apollo Philalexander*'. Having carried out magnificent sacrifices to Heracles, rewarded those who had distinguished themselves, and lavishly buried his dead, he installed as king of Tyre a man named Abdalonymus,[143] ....

(17.47.1) ... (2) ... (3) ... (4) ... (5) ... (6) ...

---

[141] According to the description of Str. 16.2.23/757, Tyre was well suited for such a defence: see also Curt. 4.4.12–13.
[142] The remark about non-combatants escaping to Carthage contradicts an earlier statement (17.41.2) that only a few could flee to Carthage. Arr. *An*. 2.24.5 remarks that 30,000 Tyrians survived the siege and that 400 Macedonians were killed. Curt. 4.4.15–16 states that the Sidonians, fighting in Alexander's army, saved as many as 15,000 Tyrians, considering them as relatives: *qvippe vtramqve vrbem Agenorem condidisse credebant* ('because they believed that Agenor had founded both cities').
[143] Wesseling, after Q. Curtius Rufus and Justin, who present the man as Abdalonymus (Curt. 4.1.15–26; Just. 11.10.8), a proper Phoenician name, meaning 'Servant of the gods' (see the current Arabic name عبد الله (Abd'allah)). The name suggested by Plu. *De Alex. Fort.* 340CE, Aralynomus, has no such connection, and nor does the name preserved in the MSS of Diodorus, Bal(l)onymus.

Developments in Greece, Cyprus, and Egypt:

(17.48.1) In Europe, Agis, the king of Sparta, engaging the services of those mercenaries who had escaped from the battle at Issus, eight thousand in number, sought to change the political situation in Greece in favour of Darius.[144] (2) Receiving from the latter both ships and a large amount of money, he sailed to Crete and, capturing most of the cities, he forced them to take the Persian side.[145] That Amyntas who had fled from Macedonia and had gone up to Darius had fought on the Persian side in Cilicia.[146] He escaped, however, from the battle at Issus with four thousand mercenaries and, having got to Tripolis in Phoenicia before Alexander's arrival, he chose from the whole fleet ships sufficient for the transport of his own soldiers, and burned the rest. (3) Having sailed over to Cyprus and taken on additional soldiers and ships, he crossed down to Pelusium. Having become master of that city, he proclaimed that he had been sent by King Darius as military commander because the acting satrap of Egypt had been killed fighting at Issus in Cilicia. (4) Sailing up the river to Memphis, he at first defeated the local forces, deployed in front of the city. Afterwards, as his soldiers turned to plunder, the Egyptians, issuing out of the city, attacked his men as they were scattered looting estates located in the countryside, and killed Amyntas and utterly butchered all who were with him. (5) Such was the end of Amyntas, who had set his hand to great undertakings and failed against expectation. Like him, some of the other officers and commanders, who escaped at the head of their military units from the battle at Issus, also remained clinging to the Persian hopes.[147] (6) Some, seizing important cities, held them for Darius; others, raising tribes and furnishing themselves with troops, performed appropriate duties in the time under review.[148] The delegates of the League of Corinth voted to send fifteen envoys, with a golden wreath bestowed as the prize of valour, from Greece to Alexander; they were to congratulate him on his victory in Cilicia.

---

[144] See Curt. 4.2.39–40; see also Badian 1967; Bosworth 1994: 852–3.
[145] Arr. *An.* 2.13.4–6 reports that Agis received ten ships as well as thirty talents (180,000 *drachmae*).
[146] See Ellis 1971: 18–21.
[147] Q. Curtius Rufus is our only source for such a Persian counteroffensive: see Burn 1952: 81–4.
[148] See *inter alia* Arr. *An.* 2.13.2–3; also Anaximenes of Lampsacus (*FGrH/BNJ* 72 F 17).

Alexander the Great Defeats Darius III   313

Alexander invades Egypt and is handed victory by the Egyptians:
(7) Having marched down to Gaza, which was garrisoned by the Persians, and after beleaguering it for two months, Alexander took the city by storm.[149]
(17.49.1) When Aristophanes was *archon* at Athens [331/0], the consuls at Rome were Spurius Postumius and Titus Veturius.[150] During their term of office, King Alexander, having set in order the affairs of Gaza, sent off Amyntas with ten ships to Macedonia, with orders to enlist the young men who were fit for military service. He himself with all his army marched on to Egypt and secured the adhesion of all its cities without striking a blow. (2) Because the Persians had committed impieties against the temples and had governed harshly,[151] the Egyptians in fact gladly welcomed the Macedonians. Having settled affairs throughout Egypt, Alexander proceeded to the temple of Ammon, seeking to consult the god.[152] ...

[[The text of Diodorus continues with the vicissitudes of Alexander in Egypt, most prominently with his dealings with the oracle of Ammon in the Siwa oasis and the founding of Alexandria. As this episode, important as it may be, has no direct bearing upon his struggle against the Achaemenids or upon Persian history proper, I have left this part of Diodorus' story out of this account.]]

S. 118:
17.52.7–73.4:

Expedition of Alexander against Darius continues:
(17.52.7) So, having charged certain of his companions with the construction of Alexandria and having settled everything regarding Egypt, King Alexander returned with his force to Syria.[153]

---

[149] Diodorus is again extremely succinct. See Curt. 4.6.7–30; Arr. *An.* 2.26.2–27.7; Plu. *Alex.* 25.3–4.
[150] The Roman consuls of 334 vc were Sp. Postumius Albinus and T. Veturius Calvinus, the dictator for that year P. Cornelius Rufinus: see Broughton 1951: 140. Diodorus is four years ahead of the Varronian chronology.
[151] This may well refer to different atrocities, allegedly committed by Artaxerxes III *Ochus*, *inter alia* against the Apis bull. Schwartz 1949 attributes these allegations to a bad press that might have been caused by several misunderstandings as well as religious-political propaganda.
[152] The temple intended (as appears from Diodorus' following chapters, not rendered here) is that of the Siwa oasis.
[153] Marsden 1964: 8–9 suspects that Alexander was intending to force Darius to a(nother) decisive battle and hoped to avoid the latter 'follow[ing] a strategy based on a combination of scorched-earth policy and guerrilla-warfare', a strategy that could have cost Alexander dearly. See also Alexander's reported remark in Curt. 4.13.23–4.

(17.53.1) By the time he heard of his arrival, Darius had already assembled his forces from all directions and prepared everything useful for the battle. He had fashioned much longer swords and lances than his earlier types because Darius believed that Alexander had had a great advantage in this respect in the battle in Cilicia. He had also constructed two hundred scythe-bearing chariots, well designed to astonish and terrify the enemy.[154] (2) From each of these long scythes projected out beyond the trace horses by three spans [c. 70 cm], attached to the yoke, and presenting their cutting edges to the front. At the axle housings there were two more scythes, pointing straight out with their cutting edges turned to the front like the others, but longer and broader. Curved blades were fitted to the ends of these.[155] (3) After he had provided the whole force with both shining armour and commanders of *aretae*, the Great King marched out of Babylon with eight hundred thousand infantry and no less than two hundred thousand cavalry.[156] With the Tigris on his right during the march and the Euphrates on the left, he proceeded through a wealthy country able to furnish ample fodder for the animals and supply sufficient food for so many soldiers. (4) In fact, Darius intended to deploy his forces in the vicinity of Nineveh, since the plains around there were excellently suited and provided much open space regarding the size of the forces assembled by him. After he had pitched camp near a village named Arbela, he there drilled his troops daily and made them well disciplined by continued training and practice.[157] In fact, he was most concerned to avoid confusion arising in the battle due to the different ways of speaking of the many peoples and tribes that were assembled.[158]

---

[154] Such chariots have already been described in X. *An.* 1.7.12, 8.10, and notably formed part of Seleucid armies (see Plb. 5.53.10).

[155] See for another description Curt. 4.9.5, though his description of swords projecting from both sides of the yoke seems irreconcilable with Diodorus' description of trace horses.

[156] Various authors provide different numbers: Just. 11.12.5 mentions a total of 500,000 soldiers, Plu. *Alex.* 31.1 a total of 1,000,000. Arr. *An.* 3.8.6 refers to 1,000,000 foot and 40,000 horse, while Curt. 4.12.13 provides – in my view – the least unlikely (though still huge) numbers of 200,000 foot and 45,000 horse.

[157] Diodorus makes it look as though Darius opted for the region around Arbela as the battlefield from the beginning. I believe that Marsden 1964: 12–13, 21, is absolutely right to state it must have been a 'last minute decision' by Darius, only taken after the moment he knew Alexander's chosen route to Babylon after crossing the Euphrates: see also Arr. *An.* 3.7.3.

[158] Though Diodorus does not mention it, Darius at some stage crossed the River Tigris, as both Nineveh (near the modern town of Mosul) and Arbela (modern Erbil) are situated on the eastern bank of the Tigris: Curt. 4.9.7, though, does mention that Darius crossed the Tigris as well as the Upper Zab (Curt. 4.9.9). In fact, it appears that the actual site of the Battle of Gaugamela, as it is commonly known, took place less than the 600 *stadia* (90 km) west of Arbela, close to Nineveh, stated by Arr. *An.* 3.8.7. The most likely place can be traced by combining the data provided by several classical authors: it is near Tel Gōmel (Camel Hill),

Alexander the Great Defeats Darius III 315

(17.54.1) Regarding the cessation of hostilities, he had also previously sent ambassadors to Alexander, offering to concede to him the land west of the River Halys, and beyond that announced that he would give him twenty thousand talents [120,000,000 *drachmae*] of silver. (2) When Alexander did not pay heed to him, Darius again sent other envoys, praising him for his generous treatment of both Darius' mother and the other captives, asking him to become a 'friend'[159] and to receive the territory west of the Euphrates, thirty thousand talents [180,000,000 *drachmae*] of silver, and the hand of one of his daughters. Thus Alexander, having become Darius' son-in-law and occupying the place of a son, would share in the rule of the whole empire.[160] (3) Assembling all his companions in a meeting and taking council on the proposals at hand, Alexander urged each to speak his own mind freely. (4) None of the others, however, dared to give an opinion because of the impact of the question at hand, but Parmenion spoke first: 'If I were Alexander, I would accept what was offered and make a treaty.' (5) Interrupting him, Alexander said: 'So would I, if I were Parmenion.' Thus, using other proud words as well and refuting the arguments of the Persians, preferring glory to the gifts which were extended to him, he gave the envoys as answer that the earth could not preserve both its plan and its order when there were two suns, nor could the inhabited world remain calm and free from war so long as two kings shared the rule. (6) Therefore he told them to report to Darius that, if he desired the supremacy, he should do battle with him regarding the sole rule of everything. But if, despising glory, he preferred profit and luxury {τρυφή} based

---

some 45 km west of Arbela and 10 km due north of the confluence of the River Khāzir (the Bumelus of Arr. *An.* 3.8.7, though the correct name is more likely Bumodus) with the Upper Zab. It should be noted that the Upper Zab flowed between Darius' 'original' campsite near Arbela and the likely location of the battle, indicating – as Marsden 1964: 21 suggests – that Gaugamela was in fact Darius' third choice. See also: Stein 1942: 159–64. For a different view, see Schachermeyr 1973: 270 and note 311. See also Streck 1910; Burn 1952: 87–8. For a recent picture of the probable site of Gaugamela: <https://www.awesomestories.com/asset/view/Gaugamela-Contemporary-View>, retrieved 12 February 2015.

[159] See above, notes 23 and 44, and below, note 163.
[160] Goukowsky 2002a: 78 note 1 believes Darius' step is not at all unusual. It might be explained by unfavourable omens, preserved in the so-called Babylonian astronomical diaries, for example tablets BM 36761 + BM 36390: see Van der Spek 2003: 297–9. On Darius' embassies, see also Goukowsky 2002a: 208–10 *ad* 54.2. The story (along with the following paragraphs) is also related in the *Constantine Excerpts*, 4: 369 = 30.21.4: Ότι Δαρείου μετὰ τὴν πρώτην μάχην ἐκχωροῦντος τοῦ μέρους τῆς βασιλείας καὶ τετρακισμύρια τάλαντα καὶ τὴν θυγατέρα πρὸς γάμον διδόντος, ἀπεκρίθη μήτε τὸν κόσμον ὑπὸ δυεῖν ἡλίων δύνασθαι διοικεῖσθαι μήτε τὴν οἰκουμένην ὑπὸ δυεῖν δεσποτῶν ('When Darius after the first battle proposed to surrender part of his empire and offered to give both forty thousand talents and his daughter in marriage, he was answered by Alexander that neither the universe could be ruled by two suns nor the world by two masters').

on a life of ease, he should follow Alexander's orders, but be a subordinate king ruling others, since this privilege was granted him by Alexander's generosity.[161] (7) Dismissing the meeting and taking up his forces again, he advanced to the camp of the enemy. When all this happened, Alexander, after the wife of Darius had died, gave her a sumptuous funeral.

(17.55.1) Having heard Alexander's answers and abandoning the diplomatic settlement, Darius continued to drill his troops each day and brought their battle discipline to a satisfactory state. He dispatched one of his companions, Mazaeus, with picked soldiers to guard the crossing of the river and to seize and hold the ford.[162] Other troops he sent out to scorch the earth which the enemy needed to cross. In fact, he contemplated using the current of the river as a barrier against the advance of the Macedonians. (2) Of these, because Mazaeus saw that the river was not crossable, because of both its depth and the swiftness of the current, he neglected to guard it. Joining forces, though, with those who were burning the countryside and having wasted a great stretch of territory, he surmised that it would be unusable by the enemy because of the lack of forage. (3) However, when Alexander came to the crossing of the River Tigris and learned of the ford from some of the locals, he transferred his army, not only with difficulty but even at substantial risk. (4) In fact, the depth of water at the ford was above breast high, but the force of the current swept away many who were crossing and deprived them of their footing. Moreover, as the water struck their shields, it both bore many off their course and brought them into extreme danger. (5) Contriving a defence against the violence of the river, Alexander told all to lock arms with each other and to make the whole closeness of their bodies something resembling a bridge. (6) Because the crossing had been hazardous and the Macedonians had had a narrow escape, he rested the force that day. On the following

---

[161] As Welles 1970: 275 note 2, observes, Alexander's answer was consistent with the lines of the Persian feudal state structure. See also Goukowsky 2002a: 79 note 1, 210–11 ad 54.1 (sic!).

[162] It is unclear which river is actually meant. Coming from Syria, Alexander had to cross both the Euphrates and the Tigris, as Arr. An. 3.7.1 and Curt. 4.9.7, 12, appear to acknowledge. It appears that Mazaeus certainly (also) had to guard the Euphrates (Curt. 4.9.12; Arr. An. 3.7.1), and not merely the Tigris, as Diodorus appears to imply here. Marsden 1964: 11 refers to Alexander's crossing the Euphrates near Thapsacus by two bridges constructed by Hephaestion, obviously a feature that should have been noted by Mazaeus (and most likely was noted and subsequently reported to Darius). Probably there has been some 'telescoping' here (see above, Chapter 4, note 224), due to which Diodorus compressed two separate tasks for Mazaeus into one. See also Goukowsky 2002a: 211 ad 55.1. Alexander probably crossed the Tigris at Abū Wajnam, some 95 km north of Nineveh: see Stein 1942: 157–8.

he led his deployed army forward towards the enemy and pitched camp, having come into the proximity of the Persians.

Battle of Gaugamela:
(17.56.1) Recapitulating the massiveness of the force of the Persians and the magnitude of the impending battle, and moreover that the decision of everything was at hand, Alexander lay awake all night occupied with concern for the next day. Falling asleep about the morning watch, he slept so deeply that he could not be wakened when the sun rose. (2) At first his companions[163] observed the whole gladly, thinking that the king would be more energetic for the battle for his thorough relaxation. As time passed, however, but sleep continued to possess the king, Parmenion, the oldest of the companions, on his own authority issued the order to the troops to prepare the necessary things for the battle. (3) Because Alexander did not wake up, the companions, going to him, finally succeeded in awakening him. As all wondered about the occurrence and wanted to hear the cause, Alexander said that Darius by assembling his forces in one place had freed him from all anxiety. (4) A decision of all issues in one day, indeed, would end the toils and long-lasting trials. Nevertheless, having exhorted his officers with the customary words and arraying them, encouraged, in the face of the approaching struggle, he led out his force deployed for battle against the Persians, having posted the cavalry squadrons in front of the infantry phalanx. (17.57.1) On the right wing Alexander stationed the royal squadron, under the command of Clitus the Black (as he was called), and next to this the other companions [the Companion Cavalry] under the command of Philotas, the son of Parmenion, then in succession the other seven squadrons of horse under the same commander. (2) Behind these was stationed the infantry battalion of the Silver Shields,[164] distinguished by both the brilliance of their

---

[163] Alexander's ἑταῖροι or companions. The use of φίλοι, a proper translation for *amici*, by Diodorus *might* suggest a Latin source for at least part of book 17. Welles 1970: 14 note 1 suggests Diodorus' source might be Gn. Pompeius Trogus. Goukowsky, on the other hand, believes that both Trogus (a contemporary of Diodorus) and Diodorus (and to some extent Q. Curtius Rufus and M. Junianus Justinus too) based themselves for the story of Alexander directly on a Hellenistic source now lost, possibly (or even probably) Clitarchus (Goukowsky 2002a: x–xix; Hornblower 2011: 317–18). See also for 'friends' and/or 'relatives' note 23 and Chapter 4, note 289.
[164] The *hypaspistae*. Silver Shields *might* be an anachronism here, as the term was *possibly* only introduced in the time of the Diadochs: see Tarn 1948: 116. His conclusion is, however, not uncontested: see, for example, Roisman 2012: 177. For a more detailed analysis of (the main participants in) the battle see, for example, Burn 1952: 87–90; Marsden 1964: 40–74; Heckel 2009: *svv*.

armour and the *aretē* of the men: they were led by Nicanor, the son of Parmenion. Next to them he positioned the battalion from Elimiotis,[165] as it was called, under the command of Coenus. Next he stationed the battalion of the Orestaeans and the Lyncestians, of which Perdiccas held the command. Meleager commanded the next battalion and Polyperchon the one after that, the people called Stymphaeans being under him. (3) Philip the son of Balacrus held the next command and, after him, Craterus. As for the cavalry, the combined Peloponnesian and Achaean horse continued the line of the aforementioned squadrons, then cavalry from Phthiotis and Malis, then Locrians and Phocians, all under the command of Erigyius of Mytilene. (4) Next were posted the Thessalians, with Philip as commander, and in manliness and horsemanship far superior to the other squadrons. Next to these he stationed the archers from Crete and the mercenaries from Achaea.[166] (5) On both flanks he kept his wings back, so that the enemy with their mass of soldiers could not envelop the inferior number of the Macedonians. (6) Contriving a defence against the use of the scythe-bearing chariots, the king ordered the infantry of the phalanx, when the four-horse chariots came near, to join shields and to beat the shields with their spears, in order that the horses, frightened by the noise, would make a rush backward, but to make openings for those chariots going on, through which openings they could make the passage without risk to the Macedonians.[167] He himself, commanding the right wing and advancing obliquely, planned to settle the whole outcome of the battle by his own actions. (17.58.1) Having drawn up his array of battle according to the extent of the peoples and positioned opposite Alexander,[168] Darius led on against the enemy. As the forces approached each other, the trumpeters on both sides sounded the attack and the troops charged each other with a loud shout. (2) First the scythe-bearing ones of the chariots, swinging into action at full gallop, created great alarm

---

[165] Elimiotis or Elimaea is a region of Upper Macedonia, just like Orestis, Lyncestis, and Tymphaeis (Diodorus' Stymphaeis): the battalions of the Macedonian phalanx appear to have been organised on a territorial basis: see Welles 1970: 281 note 3; also Goukowsky 2002a: 212 *ad* 57.3.

[166] The last group, the mercenaries from Achaea, causes some confusion among the commentators: see Goukowsky 2002a: 212–13 *ad* 57.4.

[167] A tactic also practised by the Greeks in the army of Cyrus the Younger: X. *An.* 1.8.20; Arrian states that Alexander had read Xenophon's *Anabasis*: Arr. *An.* 2.7.8–9.

[168] The Persian order of battle is described by Arrian, on the basis of the report of Aristobulos (Arr. *An.* 3.11.3–7; *FGrH/BNJ* 139 F 17). As all Great Kings used to lead their armies from the centre, the fact that Darius found himself opposite Alexander, who commanded his right wing, may serve to demonstrate the superiority in numbers of the Great King's force over the Macedonian. See also below, note 170.

and terror among the Macedonians, especially because Mazaeus, the commander of the cavalry, with his dense squadrons of horse, joined the attack of the scythe-bearers, making the attack of the scythe-bearing chariots more terrible.[169] (3) As the phalanx joined shields, however, and all beat upon their shields with their spears as the king had commanded, it occurred that much noise was created. (4) As the horses shied away, the majority of the chariots turned about and bore hard with irresistible impact against their own ranks. Because others continued on against the phalanx and the Macedonians opened wide gaps, the chariots were channelled through these. Some horses were killed by javelin casts, others rode through and escaped, but some chariots, using the full force of their momentum and applying their steel blades actively, caused many and various forms of deaths. (5) Indeed, such was the sharpness and force of the weapons wrought to destroy that they severed the arms of many, shields and all; and of many sliced through their necks, and the heads fell to the ground with the eyes still open and the expression of the countenance unchanged; of some they cut through the sides with dangerous incisions and inflicted quick deaths.

(17.59.1) As the main forces now neared each other, they employed bows and slings and threw javelins. When they had expended their missiles, they turned to hand-to-hand fighting. (2) As the cavalry first joined battle and the Macedonians contended on the right wing, Darius, who commanded his own left, had as fellow combatants his kinsman cavalry.[170] These were men chosen for their *aretē* and their loyalty, the whole (ten) thousand[171] included in one squadron. (3) Having the Great King as spectator of their prowess, they cheerfully faced the mass of missiles which were cast in his direction. With them together were the Apple Bearers,[172] outstanding

---

[169] Goukowsky 2002a: 83 note 2 explains that Diodorus here confounds two complementary manoeuvres.

[170] Diodorus is obviously wrong on this issue. In 17.58.1 Diodorus places Darius opposite Alexander (who holds the Macedonian right wing: 17.57.6). Given the vast superiority in number of the Persian army, positioning himself opposite Alexander would most likely imply that Darius, as Arrian also acknowledges (Arr. *An.* 3.11.5), was positioned in the Persian centre, the customary position of Persian kings (see X. *An.* 1.8.21–3).

[171] The MSS are here at variance: MS F reads μυρίους ('ten thousand'), MS RF[2hand] reads χιλίους ('one thousand'); though ten thousand is possible and favoured by Goukowsky 2002a: 84 line 9, I believe one thousand to be probably the more feasible option, but I am insufficiently sure of it not to refer to the alternative version.

[172] That is: the royal foot guards, called 'Apple Bearers' because the butts of their spears were made in the form of a golden apple, and the elite of the 10,000 'Immortals' of the Royal Guard: see Heraclides of Cume, *FGrH/BNJ* 689 F 1 (= Ath. 12.514BC): διὰ τῆς τῶν μηλοφόρων αὐλῆς. ἦσαν δὲ οὗτοι τῶν δορυφόρων καὶ τῶι γένει πάντες Πέρσαι, ἐπὶ τῶν στυράκων μῆλα χρυσᾶ ἔχοντες, χίλιοι τὸν ἀριθμόν, ἀριστίνδην ἐκλεγόμενοι ἐκ τῶν μυρίων Περσῶν τῶν Ἀθανάτων καλουμένων ('through the court of the "apple-bearers". These belonged to his bodyguards and

in prowess and numerous, and in addition to these Mardians and Cossaeans,[173] admired for both their physical strength and distinct daring. (4) Together with them fought both the royal household troops and the best fighters as regards bravery among the Indians. They all, attacking the enemy with a loud battle-cry, engaged them valiantly and by their mass pressed hard upon the Macedonians. (5) Mazaeus, who was in command of the Persian right wing and contending together with the best of the cavalry, killed not a few of his opponents at the first onslaught, but sent off two thousand Cadusians and a thousand picked Scythian horsemen with orders to ride around the enemy's flank and to advance to their camp and capture the baggage.[174] (6) As they carried out their orders immediately and as they burst into the camp of the Macedonians, some of the captives, having seized weapons, aided the Scythians and seized the baggage. There were shouting and confusion throughout the whole camp area at this unexpected event. (7) The other female captives rushed off to welcome the Persians, but the mother of Darius, Sisyngambris, did not heed it when the female captives called upon her, but remained placidly where she was, since she neither trusted the uncertain turns of Fate nor would dishonour her gratitude to Alexander. (8) Finally, after the Scythians had grabbed much of the baggage, they rode off to Mazaeus and reported their success. Simultaneously, some of the cavalry of Darius, continuing to press in superior numbers upon the opposing Macedonians, also forced them to give ground.

(17.60.1) Because this had become a second success for the Persians, seeing that he himself had to rectify the defeat of his forces, Alexander, together with the royal squadron and the rest of the elite horse guards, pushed on against Darius. (2) The king of the Persians, receiving the enemy attack and fighting from a chariot, hurled javelins against his opponents, and many supported him. As the kings approached each other, Alexander, flinging a javelin at Darius, missed him, but striking the driver, standing beside the

---

all were Persians of descent, carrying golden apples on the butts of their spears, one thousand in number, chosen according to merit [or rank] from the 10,000 Persians called "the Immortals"'); also Arr. *An.* 3.11.5, 13.1. See also Charles 2011.

[173] For the Mardians, see below, *caput* 76. The Cossaeans (or Cissaei: 11.7.2; Plb. 5.79.5) lived in the Zagros Mountains. Though they also figure in this battle in Curt. 4.12.10, they are absent in Arrian's report. See also for the Cossaeans below, 17.111.4–6.

[174] For a similar picture see Curt. 4.15.5–18, but Arr. *An.* 3.14.4–6 paints an altogether different image. Plu. *Alex.* 32.4 describes the action from some distance. With such diverging descriptions it is hard to assess the actual events of the day. Burn 1952: 88–90 makes an attempt to do so anyway.

Great King, knocked him to the ground. (3) When those around Darius shouted out loudly, those at a greater distance surmised that the Great King had fallen. After they had started to flee, those next to them followed, and steadily, little by little, the solid ranks of Darius' corps disintegrated. As both flanks became exposed, the Great King himself, alarmed, also started to flee.[175] (4) As these fled in this manner, as dust raised by the Persian cavalry rose to a height, as Alexander's squadrons followed on their heels, it was impossible, because of their numbers and the thickness of the dust, to tell in what direction Darius was fleeing. The air was filled with the groans of the fallen, the rattling of the horses, and the constant sound of lashing of whips.[176] (5) As these things happened, Mazaeus, the commander of the Persian right wing, with the most and the best of the cavalry, was pressing hard on those opposing him. Parmenion, however, with the Thessalian cavalry and the rest of those fighting together with him, resisted the attackers. (6) At first, fighting brilliantly, he had the upper hand thanks to the *aretae* of the Thessalians. Both the weight and numbers, though, of the body of those belonging to Mazaeus' command crushed the cavalry of the Macedonians.[177] (7) As a great slaughter took place and he started to despair of withstanding the Persian strength, Parmenion sent off some of his horsemen to

---

[175] Here, too, Diodorus' version of events is (much) more positive regarding the attitude of Darius III than the accounts of Arrian and even Plutarch (see Arr. *An.* 3.14.3–6; Plu. *Alex.* 33.2–5). Q. Curtius Rufus seems to follow, more or less, the same source as Diodorus, though Darius' attempted suicide, recorded by Curt. 4.15.28–30 and Just. 11.14.3, may well be a later invention. The Babylonian astronomical diaries, no. 330 (consisting of two tablets, *BM* 36761 + *BM* 36390, both only partly preserved, in parts that do not join) obv. lines 15–18 inform us that: '(15) On the 24th <of the month *Ululu*> [1 October 331], in the morning, the king of the world [= Alexander] erected his] standard [. . .] (16) Opposite each other they fought and a heavy defeat of the troops [of the king [= Darius III] he inflicted]. (17) The king [= Darius III], his troops deserted him and to their cities [. . .] (18) [to the l]and of the Gutians [= the mountainous regions east of the Tigris] they fled' (translation Van der Spek 2003: 297–8). This text suggests that the Persian troops fled their king, not the Persian king his troops, as Arrian presents the outcome of the battle: the astronomical diaries appear to support Diodorus' (and Curtius Rufus') version of these events. As a matter of fact, Diodorus does not refer to the lunar eclipse that took place on 20 September 331, recorded on the same tablets, lines 3–5, and considered a bad omen for the reigning king, Darius III. Arr. *An.* 3.7.6, though, does mention the eclipse. See also below, Chapter 6, note 188.
[176] The Scythians at least are known to have used whips (Hdt. 4.3.4), but also Persian commanders of companies: Hdt. 2.223.3; see also Stronk 2014/15: 220.
[177] The Persians used the strength of their type of formation. The differences in fighting method are explained by Asclepiodotus: ταῖς δὲ τετραγώνοις Πέρσαι τε καὶ Σικελοὶ καὶ Ἕλληνες ἐχρῶντο διὰ τὸ ἐν τούτοις δύνασθαι ζυγεῖν τε ἅμα καὶ στοιχεῖν τὰς εἴλας ('the Persians, Sicilians, and Greeks regularly used the square formation since it can hold the squadrons in both rank and file': Ascl. 7.4; also Ael. *Tact.* 18.5–9), whereas τῇ μὲν οὖν ῥομβοειδεῖ τῶν εἰλῶν δοκοῦσι Θετταλοὶ κεχρῆσθαι πρῶτοι ἐν ἱππικῇ πολὺ δυνηθέντες ('it appears that the Thessalians were the first to use the rhomboid formation for their squadrons in cavalry fighting': Ascl. 7.2; also Ael. *Tact.* 18.1–3), expounding in the sequels the use of either method.

Alexander, telling him to come to their support quickly. Because they carried out their orders immediately and learned that Alexander was already in full pursuit at a great distance from the battlefield, they returned without having accomplished their mission.[178] (8) However, Parmenion, handling the Thessalian squadrons with the utmost skill and killing many of the enemy, only just routed the Persians, who were extremely disheartened by the flight of Darius.

(17.61.1) Being an outstanding strategist and benefiting from the mass of dust, Mazaeus did not withdraw like the other Persians. Moving in the opposite direction and keeping his withdrawal hidden by the stirred-up dust, he both got away safely himself and brought all his troops in safety into villages which lay behind the Macedonian position.[179] (2) When finally all the Persians had fled and as the Macedonians kept slaughtering the stragglers, the whole surroundings of the plain were soon covered with the dead. (3) On the Persian side in the battle there fell, cavalry and infantry together, more than ninety thousand. About five hundred of the Macedonians were killed, but there were very many wounded.[180] Among them were some of the most prominent commanders: Hephaestion, the commander of the bodyguards, wounded with a spear thrust in the arm, Perdiccas and Coenus, of the general officers; and moreover Menidas and some others of the prominent commanders. Such was the outcome of the battle near Arbela.[181]

---

[178] Curt. 4.16.2–3; Arr. An. 3.15.1–2; and Plu. Alex. 33.6 (quoting Callisthenes) inform us, though, that Alexander did break off the pursuit to assist Parmenion. Alexander's refusal may have had to do with a previous warning by Parmenion (Curt. 4.15.6–8; Plu. Alex. 32.3–4; Polyaen. 4.3.6) regarding the plundering of the Macedonian camp, which Alexander chose to ignore, Diodorus confounding both appeals.

[179] Due to his locating the battle at Arbela, between the Upper and the Lower Zab, Diodorus is here at fault. An escape in a northerly direction would have been nearly impossible. Instead, Darius probably fled southward, first to Arbela and from there up into the valley of the Lower Zab (which originates in the Zagros Mountains): see Curt. 4.16.8; Arr. An. 3.15.4–5. In spite of the text in the MSS, the move northward should probably not be attributed to Darius but to Mazaeus: Goukowsky 2002a: 87 note 1 believes an error of a copyist, substituting ΔΑΡΕΙΟΣ for ΜΑΖΑΙΟΣ, is responsible for the confusion (see also Curt. 4.16.7). I have opted to follow this suggestion, especially because of the context. The dust Diodorus refers to may have played a part, due to the time of the engagement, probably 1 October; that is, at the end of a long dry season before the autumn rains start: see Stein 1942: 161.

[180] Other authors present different figures. Curt. 4.16.26 mentions 40,000 Persian deaths and less than 300 Macedonian ones, Arr. An. 3.15.6 reports 300,000 Persian casualties and 100 Macedonian, and the anonymous author on Alexander counts 50,000 Persian foot and 3,000 horse killed, 1,000 Macedonian foot and 200 horse (P.Oxy. 1798 [= FGrH/BNJ 148] F 44 col. iv, lines 10–16). Plutarch and Justin present no figures.

[181] Like, for example, Curt. 4.9.9, Diodorus refers to the battle as having taken place near Arbela, but Arr. An. 3.8.7, 6.11.4–6; Plu. Alex. 31.3 make clear the battle site was at Gaugamela.

Alexander the Great Defeats Darius III 323

D. FROM GAUGAMELA TO PERSEPOLIS

Developments in Greece; arrival of fresh troops:
(17.62.1) When Aristophon was *archon* at Athens [330/29], the consular office at Rome was assumed by Gaius Domitius and Aulus Cornelius.[182] When during their term of office word was brought to Greece about the battle near Arbela, many of the cities, having become alarmed at the growth of Macedonian power, decided that they should strike for their freedom as long as the Persian cause was still alive.[183] (2) They believed, indeed, that Darius would help them and send them a large amount of money to enable them to gather great mercenary forces and that Alexander would not be able to divide his forces. (3) If, on the other hand, they watched idly while the Persians were utterly defeated, the Greeks would be isolated and never again be able to think of recovering their freedom. (4) ... (5) ... (6) ... (7) ... (8) ...
(17.63.1) ... (2) ... (3) ... (4) ... [[Developments in Europe following the Battle of Gaugamela.]] (5) Now that we have exposed the events in Europe, we may in turn pass on to what occurred in Asia.
(17.64.1) After his defeat in the battle near Arbela, Darius directed his course to the upper satrapies, seeking by putting distance between himself and Alexander to gain a respite and sufficient time to procure a force. First arriving at Ecbatana in Media,[184] he paused there and picked up the survivors from the flight and rearmed those without weapons.[185] (2) He also summoned soldiers from the neighbouring peoples and tribes and sent messages to the satraps and commanders in Bactria and the upper satrapies, calling upon them to preserve their loyalty to him. (3) Having buried the dead after the victory, Alexander entered Arbela and found there plenty of food, much Persian dress, and treasure, namely three thousand talents of silver [18,000,000 *drachmae*].[186] Inferring the impending deterioration of the air of the region from the multitude of unburied corpses,[187] he moved off immediately and arrived with his whole force at Babylon.

---

[182] The consuls of 332 vc were Cn. Domitius Calvinus and A. Cornelius Cossus Arvina, while M. Papirius Crassus was dictator: Broughton 1951: 141. Diodorus is now three years ahead of the Varronian chronology.
[183] For the following episode in Greece see Bosworth 1994: 853–5.
[184] For Darius' route, see, for example, Herzfeld 1968: 231–8.
[185] In Ecbatana he found, amongst others, the horsemen of Bessus, the 'Royal Relatives', a band of 'apple-bearers', and about 2,000 Greek mercenaries.
[186] Curt. 5.1.10 even mentions a captured amount of 4,000 talents (24,000,000 *drachmae*).
[187] See also Curt. 5.1.11.

(4) Because the local people received him gladly and all over their quarters feasted the Macedonians lavishly, Alexander refreshed his army from its previous labours. He remained more than thirty days in the city, both because the abundance of food was plentiful and because of the hospitality of the local population. (5) After this time he transferred the citadel to Agathon of Pydna to guard, assigning to him seven hundred Macedonian soldiers. He appointed Apollodorus of Amphipolis and Menes of Pella as governors of both Babylonia and the other satrapies as far as Cilicia, and giving them one thousand talents of silver [6,000,000 *drachmae*] ordered them to enlist as many mercenary soldiers as possible. (6) He assigned Armenia as a province to Mithrines, who had surrendered to him the citadel of Sardis.[188] From the captured money he presented to each of the cavalrymen six *minas* [600 *drachmae*], to each of the allies five [500 *drachmae*],[189] and to the Macedonians of the phalanx two [200 *drachmae*], and he gave all the mercenaries two months' pay as an accolade.[190]

(17.65.1) After the king had marched out of Babylon and while he was still on the road, there came to him, sent by Antipater, five hundred Macedonian horse and six thousand foot, from Thrace six hundred horse, three thousand five hundred Trallians, from the Peloponnese four thousand foot and little less than a thousand horse, and from Macedonia, from the companions of the king, fifty sons sent by their fathers for the bodyguard.[191] (2) Welcoming these reinforcements, the king continued his march, and on the sixth day arrived in the province of Sittacene.[192] Because this region had a great abundance of all provisions Alexander stayed several days in it, at once anxious to rest his forces from the fatigue of their long marches and intending to attend to the organisation of his army, realise promotions in the command, and strengthen the forces by both the number and the *aretae* of the commanders.[193] (3) Finishing the things he had resolved upon, making a decision with great care on the rewards of valour, promoting many from a high command to

---

[188] For all names and the problems involved with Diodorus' text, see Goukowsky 2002a: 215–16 *ad* 64.5.
[189] One *mina* had the value of 100 *drachmae*. As IG II².329, lines 8–10 (probably from 336/5), demonstrates, each Athenian *hypaspist* in Alexander's allied troops received at that time for his service a *drachma* a day from the city. Whether such an arrangement was also valid during this expedition cannot be established, to the best of my knowledge.
[190] For the various remunerations see Goukowsky 2002a: 216 *ad* 64.6.
[191] More likely as pages: see Goukowsky 2002a: 91 note 2.
[192] The classical sources locate Sittacene on the east bank of the Tigris, between Mesopotamia and Susis (Susiane): see Plin. *Nat.* 6.31.132; Str. 11.13.6/524; Curt. 5.2.1–9.
[193] See for these reforms, *inter alios*, Goukowsky 2002a: 217 *ad* 65.2.

Alexander the Great Defeats Darius III   325

an even higher responsibility, he thus enlarged the prestige of all commanders and created a strong bond to him personally. (4) He also paid attention to the situation of the individual soldiers and, contriving many things for their utility, he introduced many improvements. After bringing the whole army to an outstanding level in both devotion to its commander and obedience to his commands, exceeding in prowess, Alexander set out to the remaining contests. (5) Having entered Susis[194] without opposition, he took over the fabulous palace of the kings in Susa, after the satrap Abuletes surrendered the city to him voluntarily,[195] as some have written, on the orders of Darius to his trusted officials. They say that the king of Persia acted in this way to ensure that Alexander would be kept busy with dazzling distractions and the acquisition of the most brilliant cities and huge treasures, and that Darius would win time by his flight for the preparation for war.

Alexander enters Susa:
(17.66.1) Taking possession of the city, Alexander found the treasure in the palace included more than forty thousand talents of gold and silver bullion.[196] (2) The Great Kings had accumulated these over a long period of time, unused, leaving them as a last resort against the vicissitudes of Fate. In addition there were nine thousand talents of minted gold in the typical shape of the *dareikos* [daric].[197] (3) A curious thing happened to the king when he was taking over the precious booty.[198] When he went to sit down upon the royal throne, it was larger than the proportions of his body. When one of the pages saw that his feet were a long way from reaching the footstool which

---

[194] Diodorus, being a Hellenistic author, writes Susiane, like, for example, Bactriane for Bactria; I here prefer Susis.
[195] See Arr. *An.* 3.16.6, 9; Curt. 5.2.8 (both referring to the satrap's name as Abulites). MS F of the *Bibliotheca* gives his name as Ἀβουλήτης ('Abuletes'), MS R as Ἀβουλεύτης ('Abuleutes'). Though Fischer 1985d: 236 opts for the latter version, I have chosen (after Plu. *Alex.* 68.4) the name as rendered in MS F. See also Heckel 2009: 2–3 s.v. 'Abulites'.
[196] A Greek (or Attic) talent weighed c. 26 kg, a Babylonian (and by implication a Persian) one c. 30 kg. Diodorus probably uses the Attic measure. Justin and Plutarch also refer to the worth of the booty as 40,000 talents, though Plutarch remarks it was coined money (Just. 11.14.9; Plu. *Alex.* 36.1). Arr. *An.* 3.16.7 and Curt. 5.2.11 mention an amount worth 50,000 talents, but they only refer to silver and not to gold. Polyclites of Larissa remarks (*FGrH/BNJ* 128 F 3a = Str. 15.3.21/735) that precious metal was minted only as need dictated.
[197] The *dareikos* (daric) or 'archer' (after the figure depicted on it, which is the king carrying a bow) was a gold coin, with a purity of 95.83 per cent or even higher, weighing c. 8.4 g. At this time 1 daric was worth about 25 (Attic) *drachmae*. See Alram, M., 'daric', in *Encyclopædia Iranica Online*: <http://www.iranicaonline.org/articles/daric>, published 15 December 1994, updated 17 November 2011, retrieved 15 April 2013. See also *EI*, vol. 7, fasc. 1: 36–40.
[198] Possibly a parallel with Nicholas of Damascus, *FGrH/BNJ* 90 F 66 = Ctesias of Cnidus F. 8d (see Stronk 2010: 171–3, 290–311 at 308–9(45)).

belonged to the throne, he picked up Darius' table and placed it under the dangling legs.[199] (4) As this fitted, the king was pleased by the aptness of him who did it, but one eunuch of those standing by the throne wept,[200] troubled in his heart at this reminder of the changes of Fate. (5) Seeing him, Alexander asked: 'What wrong have you seen that you are crying?' The eunuch replied, 'Now I am your servant, but formerly Darius', and by nature being devoted to my masters, I was grieved at seeing what was most held in honour by him has now become an ignoble piece of furniture.' (6) Because the answer made the king realise the complete change concerning the Persian kingdom, he interpreted it to mean that he had done something arrogant and very much at odds with his gentleness to the captives. (7) Therefore, after he had called the person to him who had placed the table under his feet, he ordered him to remove it again. Then Philotas, who was present, said: 'But this was not *hubris*, for the action was not commanded by you, but it occurred through the providence and design of a good spirit.' Taking this remark for an omen, the king ordered the table to be kept at the foot of the throne. (17.67.1) After this Alexander left Darius' mother, his daughters, and his son in Susa, and appointed for them people to teach them the Greek language, but marching on with his force he reached the River Tigris on the fourth day.[201] (2) This flows down from the mountains of the Uxians and runs at first for a thousand *stadia* [c. 185 km] through rough country breached by great gorges, but then traverses a level plain, becoming ever quieter, and running further empties into the Persian sea after six hundred *stadia* [c. 110 km]. (3) Crossing the Tigris, he entered the country of the Uxians,[202] which was rich, drenched by abundant streams, and producing many and various fruits. At the season when the ripe fruit is dried, the merchants who sail on the Tigris are able to bring down to Babylonia all sorts of confections good for the pleasures of the table.[203] (4) Finding on arrival

---

[199] Representations of enthroned Achaemenid kings always show a footstool under the Great King's feet. Calmeyer suggests the particular 'table' in this story originally had a religious purpose: see Calmeyer 1973: pls. 30–40 at 140–1. For the meaning of thrones in Persian court etiquette see, for example, Hdt. 8.67.
[200] For eunuchs at the Persian court and the various types (as it seems not all eunuchs were castrates), see Pirngruber 2011. See also Jursa, 2011; Llewellyn-Jones 2013: 38–40. A good assessment is Lenfant 2012.
[201] Not the Tigris bordering Mesopotamia, but the River Pasitigris or Karun. See also Curt. 5.3.1: *pervenit ad flumen Tigrim. Pasitigrim incolae vocant*; Str. 15.3.4–5/729; Arr. *An.* 3.17.1.
[202] For this tribe, hitherto not mentioned by Greek authors, see Str. 15.3.4/728; see also Treidler 1967d.
[203] As it appears that Diodorus here confuses Tigris and Pasitigris, we should, in all likelihood, discard the shipping story, as Goukowsky 2002a: 218–19 *ad* 67.3 also suggests.

the approaches guarded by Madetes, a 'relative' of Darius,[204] with a substantial force, Alexander saw at once the difficulty of the place. Though the sheer cliffs offered no passage, a local man, an Uxian by birth, who knew the country, offered to the king to lead soldiers by a narrow and hazardous path, in order to get above the enemy.[205] (5) Accepting the proposal, Alexander sent off the competent soldiers with him, but he himself, expediting the move as far as possible, attacked those posted at the approaches in waves. As the assault was pressed vigorously and the Persians were preoccupied with the struggle, those sent around appeared unexpectedly above the guards of the approaches. Because the Persians were panic-stricken and took to flight, Alexander became master of the pass and soon of all the cities in Uxia.

Alexander and his army march into Persis:
(17.68.1) Moving on from there, he carried on in the direction of Persis and came to the so-called Susian Rocks on the fifth day.[206] These had been taken on beforehand by Ariobarzanes with a force of twenty-five thousand foot and three hundred horse. (2) Believing he would master the gate by force, the king advanced through steep and rugged terrain without opposition.[207] Allowing him to proceed along the pass up to a certain place, the Persians suddenly attacked him when he had come about half-way into the hostile terrain, and rolled down from above boulders that were large enough to load a wagon, which, falling suddenly upon the Macedonians, who were grouped together, killed many of them. Many Persians, throwing javelins down from the cliffs into the crowded Macedonians, did not miss their mark. Still others flinging stones at close quarters pushed back those of the Macedonians who pressed on. The Persians had a tremendous advantage because of the difficulty of the country, and killed many and injured not a few. (3) Because Alexander was unable to avert the horror of the suffering and saw that no one of the enemy was killed or even wounded, but of his own force many were killed and practically all of his attacking force were disabled, he recalled

---

[204] See also note 23 and Chapter 4, note 289.
[205] A reference to the detour of the Persians at Thermopylae?
[206] According to Arr. *An.* 3.18.1-2; Curt. 5.3.16-17, Parmenion had been sent to Persepolis by the 'Royal Road' with the majority of Alexander's force and the baggage, while Alexander himself travelled, together with the light armed force and the Companion cavalry, over the mountain route.
[207] This part of Alexander's march has been identified by Aurel Stein: 'The route from the Pul-i-murd ("Bridge of the myrtles"), through the defiles of the Tang-i-Gerrau, a lower continuation of the Tang-i-Khas, [and] up the very steep slopes above the left bank of the stream [that is: the Ab-i-Laleh] in the latter': Stein 1938: 314–16 at 314 and plates 1 and 2.

the soldiers from the battle with the *salpinx*. (4) Withdrawing from the pass to a distance of thirty *stadia* [c. 5.6 km],[208] he pitched camp and inquired of the natives whether there was any other mountain pass. Though all insisted that there existed no other way through, but that there was a way around the mountains taking several days, Alexander believed it was discreditable to abandon his dead. Seeing that asking for the bodies was also unseemly and implied the acknowledgement of defeat, he ordered all his captives to be brought up. (5) From among these, brought forward in reply, came a man who was bilingual, and familiar with Persian. He identified himself as a Lycian by descent who, having become a captive, had been a shepherd in these mountains several years, which is why he had become familiar with the region and could lead the force through a byway protected by closely grown trees and bring them to the rear of those guarding the pass. (6) After the king had promised that he would honour the Lycian with great gifts, he made his way under the Lycian's direction over the mountain at night, struggling through deep snow, crossing a very broken country, transected by deep ravines and many gorges.[209] (7) Coming in sight of the enemy outposts, he cut down their first line and captured those who were stationed in the second position, then routing the third line he got possession of the passes and killed most of Ariobarzanes' troops.[210] (17.69.1) After these events, setting out to Persepolis, Alexander received a letter from the governor of the city, whose name was Tiridates, while he was on the road. In it was written that if Alexander arrived ahead of those who planned to defend the city for Darius,[211] he would become master of it, because it would be given into his hands by Tiridates. (2) Therefore Alexander led his force on in haste and, after bridging the River Araxes, he brought his men to the other bank. While the king was advancing, he was confronted by a strange and dreadful sight, provoking indignation against the perpetrators and causing sympathetic pity for the unfortunate victims.[212] (3) Indeed, Greeks, who had been deported by the previous kings

---

[208] Though the MSS assert that Alexander withdrew 300 *stadia* (one even mentions 400 *stadia*), Curt. 5.3.23 mentions 30 *stadia*, which is much more realistic under the circumstances: I have therefore emended Diodorus' text on this point and replaced τριακοσίους with τριάκοντα.

[209] See Stein 1938: 316.

[210] Here as well, Diodorus is very succinct: see Goukowsky 2002a: 96 note 2.

[211] Apparently (the troops of) Ariobarzanes: see Curt. 5.4.33-4.

[212] Goukowsky surmises that this whole episode of the mutilated Greeks has been fabricated by Clitarchus. In Arrian's account the whole incident is absent. See Goukowsky 2002a: 97 note 2.

of Persia, came to meet him, bearing branches of supplication. They were about eight hundred in number, most of them elderly. All had had amputations, of some their hands, of others their feet, of again others their ears and noses. (4) Because they had acquired skills or crafts and had made good progress in their instruction, their other extremities had been amputated and only those vital to their profession were left.[213] All the soldiers, seeing the venerability of their age and the losses their bodies had suffered, pitied the wretches' fate, and Alexander himself was especially affected by them and unable to restrain his tears. (5) As they all cried with one voice and asked Alexander for succour in their misfortunes, the king, having called their leaders to him and, worthy of his own greatness of spirit, having greeted them respectfully, promised that he would pay much attention to their being restored to their homes. (6) Gathering to debate the matter, they decided that it would be better for them to remain where they were rather than to return home. In fact, if they were brought back safely, they would be scattered in small groups, and would find their abuse at the hands of Fate an object of reproach as they lived on in their *poleis*. However, living together, sharing the same experiences, they would have consolation for their mutilation in the similarity of the mutilation of the others. (7) So, appearing again before the king and telling him their decision, they asked him to give them help appropriate to this proposal. (8) Applauding their decision, Alexander gave each of them three thousand *drachmae*, five men's robes and the same number for women, two yoke of oxen, fifty sheep, and fifty *medimnoi* [c. 2600 litres] of wheat. He also made them exempt from any royal tax and charged his administrative officials to see that they were harmed by no one. (9) Thus Alexander, in keeping with his virtuousness, tried to rectify the experiences of these unfortunate persons by such benefactions.

Alexander in Persepolis:
(17.70.1) Alexander described Persepolis,[214] the capital city of the Persian kingdom, to the Macedonians as the most hateful of the cities throughout Asia and gave it over to his soldiers to plunder,

---

[213] For Greek artisans working in the Achaemenid Empire, see Boucharlat 2012.
[214] Persepolis is the name invented by the Greeks. In Persian, the name of the city is rendered as *Pārsa*, identical to the name used for the land of Persia (Persis) and for a Persian. In this respect the way Arr. *An.* 3.18.10 described the city, Πέρσαι, is closer to the original. The acts of violence described in the following paragraphs are omitted by Arrian.

Fig. 5.4. Persepolis, Persis: panoramic view on the palace platform from Kuh-e Mehr (Mt Mehr). Photo © Jona Lendering <http://www.livius.org>.

apart from the palaces.[215] (2) Because it was the richest city under the sun and the private houses had been furnished with every sort of wealth over the years, the Macedonians raced into it, murdering all the men, plundering the residences. Many of the houses belonged to the common people but were full of furniture and decoration of all sorts. (3) Here much silver was carried off and no little gold was taken, and many costly dresses, some worked in embroidery with patterns woven in sea purple and others in gold, formed the rewards of the victors. The great palaces, famous throughout the entire inhabited world, fell victim to *hubris* and utter destruction. (4) The Macedonians, spending the whole day in these acts of robbery, could not satisfy their insatiable greed for more. (5) Indeed, so great was the excess of greed concerning the seizure of these objects, that they also fought each other and killed many of those who had appropriated the majority of the booty. Some, cutting through with their swords the richest of the finds, carried away their personal shares. Some cut off the hands of those who were grasping at disputed property, driven mad by their passions. (6) They dragged off women, clothes and all, against their will, converting their captivity into slavery. As much as Persepolis had exceeded the other cities in prosperity, so much it now exceeded the others in misfortunes.

---

[215] This image is most likely created by Clitarchus and echoed in Curt. 5.6.1–8. See also Goukowsky 2002a: 98 note 3.

Alexander the Great Defeats Darius III

(17.71.1) Alexander, ascending to the palatial terrace,[216] took possession of the treasuries on it. These were full of both gold and silver, which had been collected from the state revenues, from Cyrus, the first king of the Persians, until the time under discussion. There was, in fact, found in them one hundred and twenty thousand talents [720,000,000 *drachmae*], when the gold was rated at the value of silver.[217] (2) Because Alexander wanted to take some of the money with him, to meet the costs of the war, and to deposit the rest in Susa and keep it under guard in that city, he sent for a vast number of mules from Babylon and Mesopotamia, as well as from Susa, some pack animals, others to pull carts, and in addition three thousand pack camels.[218] Using these, he had everything carried away to the places selected. (3) Feeling bitter enmity for the inhabitants, he both distrusted them and exerted himself to destroy Persepolis altogether.[219] We believe that it is proper to expand briefly on the palaces in this city because of the extravagance of the construction. (4) As the terrace is important,[220] a triple wall surrounds it,[221] of which the first wall is built on an expensive foundation and is sixteen cubits [c. 7.2 m] in height and is provided with battlements. (5) The second wall is in all other respects constructed identically to the first but twice the height. The third circuit is rectangular in plan, but the wall of this one has a height of sixty cubits [c. 27 m], and is built of a hard, resistant stone for durable continuance in good condition.

---

[216] Though the word ἄκρα may have the specific meaning of citadel (see *LSJ*, *s.v.* ad 5), I doubt whether the situation in Persepolis warrants this translation here, even though the palaces form part of a citadel-like construction on the slopes of the Kōh-e Raḥmat ('Mountain of Mercy'), in total covering some 12 ha of the city's total 50 ha. In this layout, the palaces, the formal halls, the harems, and the treasury were situated on an (elevated) terrace, which is why I have opted for the translation 'palatial terrace'. For a good general yet relatively succinct description see, for example, Mousavi 2012: 9–56.
[217] The Greek gold–silver parity (probably referred to in this paragraph), at this time, is about 1:10 (20 silver *drachmae* (of c. 4.3 g each) was worth 1 gold stater (of c. 8.5 g), at least in Athens): see, for example, Bellinger 1963: 31. Alram (see my note on the *daric*, above, note 197) reckons 25 *drachmae* for one *daric* of c. 8.4 g.
[218] See Goukowsky 2002a: 100 note 1.
[219] Nevertheless Diodorus refers to Persepolis as 'the capital (τὸ βασίλειον) of Persis' in 19.22.2: it might indicate that Alexander wanted to destroy not so much the city of Persepolis as the palatial complex. It makes one wonder, however, whether it was a genuine wish of Alexander's or merely an excuse (classical) authors concocted to explain away an act committed in – or sprung from – a 'Dionysiac delirium': see also Goukowsky 2002a: 100 note 2.
[220] Normally the word ἀξιόλογος only translates as 'important' for people (see *LSJ*, *s.v.*), but I believe the context warrants this translation here as well.
[221] Schmidt 1939: 7 ascribes this reference to Clitarchus. Schmidt notes: 'Particularly if seen from the south or south-west, the defense system of Persepolis would have appeared to consist of three lines, since the wall at the eastern Terrace edge was raised considerably above the sky line of most of the buildings and of the wall at the southern Terrace end. At the northern edge the additional defense wall, now a pronounced mound of debris, was presumably as high as the eastern wall; but the base of the latter was higher up on the slope.'

(6) Each of the sides has bronze gates and beside them bronze poles, twenty cubits [c. 9 m] high, which were intended to catch the eye, but the gates were for security. (7) At the eastern side of the terrace at a distance of four *plethra* [c. 120 m] is the so-called royal hill in which were the graves of the kings. In fact, this was a rock, which was hollowed and with several chambers in the middle, in which were the sepulchres of the dead kings.[222] These have no other access but receive the sarcophagi of the dead which are lifted by certain mechanical hoists.[223] (8) Throughout this terrace were several royal residences and those of the high nobility, luxuriously furnished, and treasuries suitably arranged for the safeguarding of the property.

Persepolis is set on fire; Alexander follows Darius III into Bactria:
(17.72.1) Alexander, holding games in honour of his victories, also performed costly sacrifices to the gods and entertained his companions bountifully. When the companions were feasting and the drinking-bout advanced, a frenzy largely took possession of the minds of the fuddled as the drunkenness progressed. (2) At this point one of the women present, Thaïs by name and Attic in origin, said that it would be the finest of all Alexander's feats in Asia if he, going in festal procession with them, set fire to the palaces, and if women's hands obliterated the famed structures of the Persians in an instant.[224] (3) As these things were said to men who were young and irrationally unsettled with wine, as might be expected someone shouted out to lead on and to kindle torches, and urged all to requite the outrage towards the sanctuaries of the Greeks.[225] (4) Others also took up the cry and said that this deed was for Alexander alone. When the king had caught fire at their words, all got to their feet from the carouse and cheered themselves on to hold a victory

---

[222] That is, the tombs of Artaxerxes II *Mnemon* and Artaxerxes III *Ochus* and the unfinished tomb of Darius III: see Schmidt 1970. Though Diodorus states that the rock at the back of the palaces is so steep that the bodies of the dead kings could only be hoisted to their last resting place, this seems incorrect for the tombs behind Persepolis: one can easily climb or ride up there. However, it is true for the royal tombs at Naqš-e Rustam. It appears, therefore, that Diodorus or his source (Clitarchus?) mixed up his facts. Moreover, the distance between the east wall of the complex and the royal tombs is at most some 65 m.
[223] See Ctesias F. 13(19) (*ad* Darius I); Stronk 2010: 328–9.
[224] Thaïs was the friend – or partner – of Ptolemy and therefore probably slightly more than a casually present courtesan. For the fire as set deliberately see Arr. *An.* 3.18.11–12 and Plu. *Alex.* 38. 4; for the role of Thaïs see Clitarchus (*FGrH/BNJ* 137 F 11), Curt. 5.7.2–11, and Plu. *Alex.* 38.1–3.
[225] Whether this really was the main reason is a matter of contention, as is the role of Thaïs: both might be a (later?) invention. It looks certain, however, certain that Alexander wanted to destroy the structure of power of Persian rule (and, by implication, its symbol), moreover looking not upon Persepolis but upon Pasargadae as the capital of the Persian Empire: see Sancisi-Weerdenburg 1991: 21–2.

procession for Dionysus. (5) After he had quickly gathered several torches and female musicians, present at the carouse, the king led the way for the procession with song and flutes and pipes, Thaïs the courtesan leading the affair. (6) After the king, she was the first to hurl her blazing torch into the palace. As the others all did the same, the entire area around the palace complex was ablaze, so great was the conflagration.[226] The most remarkable thing of all was that one woman, a citizen of the place that had been wronged, as a game, repaid in kind many years later the impious act of Xerxes, king of the Persians, committed against the acropolis of the Athenians.
(17.73.1) When all this was over, Alexander went to the cities of Persis and having captured some by storm and won over others by his own fairness,[227] he set out after Darius. (2) The latter had planned to collect the forces of Bactria and the other satrapies, but being overtaken and directing his flight with thirty thousand men, both Persians and Greek mercenaries, towards the city of Bactra,[228] but, being seized during the retreat, he was murdered by Bessus, the satrap of Bactria. (3) Just after his death Alexander, in pursuit with his cavalry and finding Darius dead, deemed him worthy of a royal funeral. (4) Some, however, have written that Alexander found him still breathing and commiserated with him on his disasters, but being urged by Darius to avenge his death and consenting, he set out after Bessus.[229] Because the latter had a long start and got away into Bactria, Alexander returned to the rest of his troops, giving up the pursuit of the enemy. That was the situation in Asia.

[226] Here, too, there is a problem of asymmetrical evidence. The destruction was apparently less complete than sometimes believed. Archaeological evidence reveals that the *apadāna*, the room of 100 columns, the treasury, and the palace of Xerxes had suffered major damage by fire, but that other parts had remained completely or largely undamaged: see, for instance, Sancisi-Weerdenburg 1991: 13–15, referring to Schmidt 1953.
[227] According to Curt. 5.6.11–20 this expedition took place before the burning of Persepolis.
[228] The modern day city of Balkh in what is currently northern Afghanistan. As for Bactria, see the introduction to the country and its people by Holt 1988. See also Foucher and Bazin-Foucher 1942–7. The volumes show Hellenocentric and supremacist views throughout and are sometimes chatty, but informative as regards, for example, the landscape and climate.
[229] The controversy as to whether Alexander found Darius dead or barely living is a long one (see Goukowsky 2002a: 223 *ad* 73.4; Welles 1970: 328–9 note 1) and was continued into medieval Iranian literature like the *Šāhnāmeh* ('Epic of the Kings') and the *Iskandar-nāmeh* ('Epic of Alexander'): see, for example, Stronk forthcoming.

6 From Persepolis to Babylon

A. ALEXANDER PURSUES BESSUS

S. 119:
17.74.1–83.9:

Alexander in pursuit of Bessus:
(17.74.1) After this year was over, Cephisophon became *archon* at Athens [329/8], and Gaius Valerius and Marcus Clodius consuls in Rome.[1] In their year of office, after Darius' death, Bessus with Nabarzanes,[2] Barzaentes,[3] and many others, escaping from Alexander's hands, got to Bactria. Bessus, having been appointed satrap of this region by Darius and known to everyone because of his administration, now called upon the masses to defend their freedom. (2) He pointed out that their country would assist them very much, as it was hard to invade and had a sufficient number of men to establish their independence. Having proclaimed that he would take command of the war and having convinced the people, he designated

---

[1] The consuls of 331 BC were C. Valerius Potitus and M. Claudius Marcellus, Cn. Quinctius Capitolinus was the dictator: Broughton 1951: 143. Diodorus is three years ahead of the Varronian chronology.
[2] Though the MSS read this name as Ναβάρνου, the genetive form of Ναβάρνης ('Nabarnes'), Rhodoman (Hanover, 1604) emended it to Nabarzanes, a haplography of OP *Nabābrdana* (see Benveniste 1966: 98), at the time acting as the chiliarch. See, however, below 17.76.1 and note 13. See also Heckel 2009: 171 *s.v.*
[3] Though the MSS read this name as Βαρξαεντος and Dindorf emended this to Βαρξαέντου, I prefer to read here Βαρζαέντου, rendering the name of Barzaentes, who was the satrap of Arachosia, the region of modern Kandahar in Afghanistan. We would, then, have to do with a ζ/ξ-shift like the one that may have been the case in 2.6.2 (see also above, Chapter 2, note 40). See also Heckel 2009: 69 *s.v.* 'Barsaentes'.

334

himself Great King.⁴ Thus, he enrolled soldiers, manufactured a stock of weapons, and ambitiously prepared all the other things for the approaching need. (3) Seeing that the Macedonians regarded Darius' death as the end of the campaign and were impatient to return to their homeland, Alexander, having called them all to a meeting and addressing them with proper words,⁵ got them compliant and ready for the remaining part of the expedition. However, assembling the allied troops from the Greek cities and praising them for their services, he released them from their military duty and gave to each of the cavalry a talent [60 *minae* or 6,000 *drachmae*] and each of the infantry ten *minae* [1,000 *drachmae*]. Besides this, he paid them both their due wages and those to cover their march back until they returned to their homes. (4) To each of those who opted to remain in the royal army he gave three talents [18,000 *drachmae*]. He rewarded the soldiers with great gifts not only because he was generous by nature, but also because he had come into possession of very much money during the pursuit of Darius. (5) In fact, he had received from the royal treasurers the sum of eight thousand talents [48,000,000 *drachmae*]. Apart from this, what was distributed to the soldiers, including clothing and goblets, amounted to thirteen thousand talents [78,000,000 *drachmae*]; the stolen or plundered items' value was thought to be even more.

(17.75.1) Having started out for Hyrcania, Alexander encamped on the third day near a city called Hecatontapylus.⁶ Because this

---

⁴ In the summer of 331, Bessus commanded the Bactrian troops as satrap. He was probably, therefore, a close relative of King Darius III: the satrap of Bactria was usually the first in the line of succession, the *maθišta* ('the greatest') – a term first used by Xerxes in the so-called *Harem inscription*, XPf, line 32 (a crown prince would reign in Bactria for a couple of years and a king without grown-up sons would appoint his brother to this satrapy). The situation can, to some extent, be followed in Van der Spek 2003: 301–10, a revised interpretation of *ABC* 112–13, Chronicle 8, presenting a fragment known as *BM* 36304 or the *Alexander Chronicle*. Darius III was killed in July of 330, near Hecatompylus, at the order of Bessus (Arr. *An.* 3.21.9–10; Curt. 5.13.13; Plu. *Alex.* 42). Bessus returned to Bactria and prepared for war against Alexander. He took the royal tiara and declared himself successor to Darius under the throne name Artaxerxes V (Arr. *An.* 3.25.3; Curt. 6.6.13). Lendering observes that, if the *Alexander Chronicle* deals with the dethronement of Darius and the accession of Bessus, it contradicts the European sources (Lendering 2004: 214). Arrian and the other Alexander historians state that Bessus only took the royal title in the autumn of 330, after Alexander's conquest of Hyrcania; the *Alexander Chronicle* suggests that this happened immediately. The latter is the more likely chronology, not only because Bessus as *maθišta* was the presumptive successor to the throne (Sancisi-Weerdenburg 1980: 68–70), but also to avoid any kind of interregnum ('the king is dead, long live the king'). Moreover, as he was probably an Achaemenid, Bessus' claim was not wholly unjustified.

⁵ Here and in the sequel of this *caput* Diodorus is too succinct: see Goukowsky 2002a: 224–5 *ad* 74.3, first remark and third remark. See also Goukowsky 2002a: 104 notes 1 and 2.

⁶ Also known as Hecatompylus. At present the city is known as Šahr-e Qumis, but as Sad Darvāzeh it was the capital of the Parthian Arsacid dynasty, situated in the region known as West Khurāsān in Iran.

was a wealthy city with a profusion of everything contributing to pleasure, he rested his force there for some days. (2) Advancing one hundred and fifty *stadia* [c. 28 km], he encamped near a huge rocky peak. At its base was a marvellous cave, from which flowed a great river, named the Stiboïtes.[7] Tumbling out with a boisterous current for a distance of three *stadia* [slightly over 500 m], this river then divides into two courses on either side of a breast-shaped rocky peak, beneath which there is a gigantic yawning chasm in the earth. Plunging into this chasm with a great roar, foaming from its clash against the rock, the river flows underground over three hundred *stadia* [c. 55.5 km], then again discloses its mouth.[8] (3) Invading the country of the Hyrcanians with his force, Alexander took possession of all the cities in it as far as the so-called Caspian Sea, which some name the Hyrcanian.[9] People say that in this sea are spawned many large serpents and fish of all sorts, quite different in colour from those in our regions.[10] (4) Passing through Hyrcania, he came to the villages called, and verily being, 'Fortunate': as for crops their land far surpasses the crops elsewhere, indeed. (5) In fact, people say that each of the vines produces a *metretes* [slightly less than 40 l] of wine, while some of the fig trees carry a harvest of ten *medimni* [about 50 l] of dried figs. People also relate that the grain, overlooked at the harvest and fallen on the ground, though being unsown, germinates and brings to maturity an abundant harvest. (6) The natives also have a tree very much like an oak in appearance, but from the leaves of which drips honey: and some, collecting this, take their pleasure from it abundantly.[11] (7) There is also in this country a winged animal, which is called *anthredon*; smaller in size than the bee, it has a mottled appearance.[12] In fact, inhabiting the mountains, it forages on all kinds of flowers and, lingering in rocky hollows and

---

[7] The Stiboïtes might be the present-day Chesmeh-i Ali ('Fountain of Ali'): see Pédech 1958: 75–6. See also the extensive note in Goukowsky 2002a: 225–6 *ad* 75.2.
[8] Translated more interpretatively: 'resurfaces to empty into the [Caspian] Sea'.
[9] See above, Chapter 5, note 40. See also the references in Goukowsky 2002a: 105 note 1.
[10] For an analysis see Goukowsky 2002a: 226 *ad* 75.3.
[11] See Goukowsky 2002a: 227 *ad* 75.6.
[12] I follow Goukowsky's text (Goukowsky 2002a: 105): ποικίλην ἔχει τὴν ἐπιφάνειαν ('it has a mottled appearance') rather than Welles' (Welles 1970: 334) μεγίστην ἔχει τὴν ὠφέλειαν ('it is extremely useful'). The text of the MSS reads μεγίστην ἔχει τὴν ἐπιφάνειαν ('with a vast appearance'), which looks not really consistent with the first part of the sentence (even though Tarn opts for it: Tarn 1948: 90). Though neither solution is totally satisfactory (Prandi 2013: 124 *ad* 75.7 remarks that '[n]on risulta del tutto chiaro che cosa volesse dire Diodoro a proposito di questo insetto'), the comparison with the size of the bee in the first part of the sentence induces me to favour Goukowsky's solution, even though Welles' appears to fit in more neatly with the following sentence. I feel there, however, uncomfortable with the word μεγίστην as being overstated, since μεγάλην would suffice in the context. It seems the animal intended is a species of wild bee. The natural wealth of Hyrcania is also alluded to by Str. 2.1.14/73.

lightning-blasted trees, it makes wax cells and prepares a substance of surpassing sweetness, not far inferior to our honey.[13]
(17.76.1) Alexander acquired Hyrcania and the neighbouring tribes in that region. Many of the commanders who had fled together with Darius surrendered themselves.[14] Receiving them kindly, Alexander gained wide repute for fairness. (2) Indeed, to take the first example that occurs, those of the Greeks who had served with Darius, about one thousand five hundred in number, and of outstanding courage, surrendered themselves to Alexander and, thought fit for a pardon, they were incorporated into the units at identical wages. (3) Following the coastline of Hyrcania, Alexander invaded the territory of the people known as Mardians.[15] These, outstanding in prowess, in fact thought little of the increase in power of the king and deemed him worthy of no meeting or honour whatsoever. (4) Having occupied the entranceways in advance with eight thousand soldiers, they confidently awaited the Macedonian approach. Having fallen upon them and joined battle, the king killed most of them and closely pursued those remaining into the inhospitable regions. (5) As he was burning the countryside and the servants who led the royal horses were at a little distance from the king, some of the Mardians, having attacked, stole the best one of the horses. (6) This animal had been presented as a gift to Philip by Demaratus of Corinth and had shared with Alexander all the battles throughout Asia.[16] Without harness he would permit only the groom to mount him, but with the royal horse-trappings he would no longer allow even him, but for Alexander alone stood quietly and even lowered his body to let him mount. (7) Angry, because of the *aretē* of the animal, the king ordered that every tree in the land be felled and that it should be announced to the natives through interpreters that if they did not return the horse, they could well see both the country utterly brought to naught and its inhabitants slaughtered to a man. (8) As he immediately started to carry out these threats, the natives, being terrified, returned the horse and sent with it their costliest gifts and

---

[13] See also Herzfeld 1968: 48.
[14] They included Nabarzanes, Artabazus and his (nine) sons, Phrataphernes, and Autophradates. See Arr. *An.* 3.23.4, 7; Curt. 6.4.23–4, 6.5.1–4, 22–3.
[15] Apparently Alexander went westward. For details of his march and the Mardians, see Goukowsky 2002a: 228 *ad* 76.3 and 229 *ad* 76.4.
[16] Though King Philip does not feature in the MSS of Diodorus, I base my translation upon Gell. 5.2.1, retaining a fragment of Chares of Mytilene (*FGrH/BNJ* 125 F 18), suggesting the following text ἐδόθη δῶρον μὲν Φιλίππῳ ὑπὸ .... Arr. *An.* 5.19.6 places the theft of Bucephalas earlier in time, namely in the country of the Uxians. A wide variety of sources on Bucephalas can be found in Anderson, A. R. (1930), 'Bucephalas and His Legend', *American Journal of Philology* 51:1, pp. 1–21.

moreover also sent fifty men, asking for forgiveness. Alexander took the most important of these men as hostages.[17]

Alexander and Thallestris:
(17.77.1) When Alexander had returned again to Hyrcania, the queen of the Amazons came to him. She was named Thallestris and ruled all the country between the rivers Phasis and Thermodon.[18] She was outstanding both in beauty and in bodily strength, and was admired by her countrywomen for bravery. Having left the bulk of her army on the frontier of Hyrcania, she had arrived with an escort of three hundred Amazons in full armour. (2) Because the king marvelled at both the unexpected arrival and the dignity of the women and had asked Thallestris with what purpose she had come, she replied that she had come in order to get a child. (3) She said that he, indeed, was the best of all men, as his achievements demonstrated, and she was superior to all women in both strength and courage: thus it was likely that the offspring of such outstanding parents would surpass all other mortals in *aretē*. Being delighted at this, having granted her request, after consorting with her for thirteen days, and having honoured her with fine gifts, the king sent her home. (4) As it seemed to Alexander after that that he had accomplished his objective and now held the kingdom uncontested, he began to emulate Persian luxuriousness {τρυφή} and the extravagance of the Asian kings.[19] First he had staff-bearers [ushers?] of Asiatic race in his court; next he ordered the most distinguished of the men to attend as bodyguards, among them Darius' brother Oxathres.[20] (5) Then he both put on

---

[17] On the basis of a mosaic, Fuhrmann, 1931: 133 believes (one of) the gift(s) referred to was the skin of a panther (or leopard).

[18] The River Thermodon, emptying into the Black Sea in modern Turkey, and the adjacent city of Themiscyra were the traditional homeland of the Amazons. See, for example, Stronk, *BNJ* 606 F 1 (commentary). Diodorus is very clear in his statement of the existence of the city of Themiscyra ἐν ᾗ τὰ βασίλεια τῶν Ἀμαζόνων ὑπῆρχε ('in which was the palace of the Amazons': 4.16.1; see also 2.45.2, locating the city at the mouth of the Thermodon. See also Wilson 1976. For the River Phasis (and the city of Phasis), see, for example, Stronk, *BNJ* 171 F 17 (commentary). As regards the etymology of the word 'Amazon', the most frequent version is connected with a remark by Hellanicus of Lesbos (*FGrH/BNJ* 4 F 107; see also Diodorus 2.45.3) that they removed a breast (μαζός or μαστός) to be able to draw the bow more easily (in this case it is noteworthy that in Greek visual arts the Amazons are always represented with two breasts). However, as neither this nor any other Greek etymology (see, for example, Blok 1995: 23) suffices, Frisk's suggestion is perhaps less unsatisfactory, namely to connect the word with the Iranian **ha-mazan* ('warrior': Frisk 1973: 83–4, *s.v.* Ἀμαζών'). See also for Amazons: Toepffer 1894; Ley 1996. For Amazons in general I think the best work is still that by Blok (though there is a more recent work on them: Mayor 2014; see its review by Boliaki 2015. See also Goukowsky 2002a: 107 note 1.

[19] See Curt. 6.2.1–10; Just. 12.3.8–12; *Epit.Mett.* 1; Plu. *Alex.* 45.1–3.

[20] This may have been as well the occasion when Alexander appointed Hephaestion as ἵππαρχος τῶν ἑταίρων (that is, effectively the position of χιλίαρχος, chiliarch, the commander

the Persian fillet[21] around the tiara and dressed himself in the white *chiton*[22] and the Persian belt and everything else except the trousers and the Median upper garment with sleeves. He also distributed to his companions robes with purple borders and provided the horses with Persian harnesses.[23] (6) In addition to all this, he took his concubines everywhere with him in the manner of Darius, in number not less than the days of the year and outstanding in beauty, selected from all the women of Asia.[24] (7) Each night these paraded about the couch of the king, so that he might make the choice of the one who would meet him that night. Alexander, indeed, seldom employed these customs but mostly kept to the pre-existing customs, afraid to offend the Macedonians.

(17.78.1) As many did yet reproach him, he conciliated them with gifts. However, having learned that the satrap of Aria, Satibarzanes, had put to death the soldiers who were left under his command,[25] had conspired with Bessus, and with the latter had decided to attack the Macedonians, Alexander set out against the man. Satibarzanes had collected his forces in Artacoana,[26] the most notable city of the people of that region and outstanding in natural strength. (2) As the king approached, though, Satibarzanes was scared by both the size of the force and the manly virtues of the Macedonians, which had become celebrated. Therefore he rode off with two thousand horsemen to Bessus, asking him to send help with all speed, but told his other followers to seek refuge at a mountain called ...,[27] which offered rough ground and suitable places of refuge for those who did not dare to fight face to face. (3) After they had done as they

---

of the royal guard, the 'apple-bearers'): see 18.3.3: ταύτης [the ἱππαρχία τῶν ἑταίρων] γὰρ Ἡφαιστίων πρῶτος μὲν ἡγήσατο ('Hephaestion was the first commander [of the Companion cavalry]') and 18.48.5. Arr. *An.* 3.27.4, however, places Hephaestion's appointment after the so-called conspiracy of Philotas (see below). For Oxathres see Heckel 2009: 188 *s.v.* 'Oxyathres'.

[21] See Goukowsky 2002a: 229 *ad* 77.5.
[22] See Stronk 2010: 372–3, F. 25a = Hsch. *Lex. s.v.* 'Sarapis'.
[23] See Farkas 1969: 67.
[24] Plu. *Art.* 27.2, refers to a number of 360 concubines, basically the number of days in the regular Persian year. Though Welles 1970: 342–3 note 2 asserts this passage goes back to Ctesias, neither Jacoby (*FGrH* 688), nor Lenfant (2004), nor I (Stronk 2010) have included the fragment in our review of Ctesias' fragments, as any evidence for such an attribution is lacking. Regarding the number of concubines, other classical authors mention there were 365 of them in the royal harem.
[25] For a clearer account see Curt. 6.6.13–21 and notably Arr. *An.* 3.25.1–6.
[26] Though all MSS of Diodorus read here Χορτάκανα, I fully support Goukowsky's emendation (see Goukowsky 2002a: 109 line 12). For Goukowsky's motivation, see Goukowsky 2002a: 230 *ad* 78.1.
[27] None of the MSS provides a name for this mountain, nor does any of the other sources. See, though, Goukowsky 2002a: 231 *ad* 78.2.

had been told to do, the king, using his customary ambition and vigorously besieging those who had sought refuge on a steep and large rocky peak, compelled them to surrender. (4) Having brought into submission, thereafter, within thirty days all the cities of the satrapy, he left Hyrcania and, traversing to the capital of Drangia,[28] he paused there and rested his force.

Conspiracy against Alexander:
(17.79.1) Around this very time Alexander stumbled into a knavish action, foreign to his own goodness. One of the king's companions, named Dimnus,[29] finding fault with the king about some things and in a rash fit of anger, organised a conspiracy against Alexander. (2) Having an *eromenos* named Nicomachus,[30] he persuaded this man to partake in the conspiracy. The latter, still being young, disclosed the affair to his brother Cebalinus, who, fearing that one of those privy to the plan would get ahead and reveal the plot to the king, decided himself to be the informer. (3) Going to the court, meeting Philotas, and talking with him, he urged him to tell the king about the affair as soon as possible. Either because Philotas actually participated in the plot or through indifference, he handled the story told to him idly and, although he visited Alexander and participated in a long and diverse conversation, he said nothing about the things told him by Cebalinus. (4) Returning to Cebalinus, he said that he had no suitable moment to make a clear statement, but reported that he would surely meet the king alone the next day and would tell him all that had been said. Because Philotas did the same thing on the next day as well, Cebalinus, taking precautions so that he would run no risk when someone else was the whistle-blower, dropped Philotas and, approaching one of the royal pages and telling him all that had happened in detail, asked him to report to the king immediately. (5) The page, leading Cebalinus into the armoury, hid him there, but himself, approaching the king as he was bathing,[31] told him the story and for what reason he guarded Cebalinus in the vicinity. Terrified, the king both arrested Dimnus at once and, learning everything from him, sent for both Cebalinus and Philotas. (6) After

---

[28] Though Diodorus writes here 'Drangine', the region's usual name is Drangia (for Hellenistic authors frequently Drangiana). It is the region round modern Lake Hāmūn and the River Helmand in modern Sīstān on the Iran–Afghan–Pakistan border. See also Schmitt 2011b. I have opted for the usual form, as I did with Bactria instead of Diodorus' Bactriane.
[29] See Heckel 2009: 112 *s.v.* 'Dimnus'.
[30] For *eromenos* see, for example, Davidson, 2007: 24–7.
[31] According to Plu. *Alex.* 23.3, Alexander bathed in the evening.

From Persepolis to Babylon 341

all had been interrogated and the fact had been established, Dimnus killed himself, but though Philotas acknowledged his carelessness, he utterly denied the plot.[32] Alexander entrusted the judgement concerning Philotas to the Macedonians.
(17.80.1) After many arguments had been heard, the Macedonians condemned Philotas and the other accused persons to death.[33] Among these was Parmenion, who was believed to be the first of Alexander's companions. Though he was absent at the time, it was thought that he had contrived the conspiracy by means of his son Philotas.[34] (2) Under torture first, Philotas, after confessing to the conspiracy, was executed with the other convicted people in the manner of the Macedonians.[35] The same occurred to Alexander the Lyncestian, who was charged with having plotted against the king and had been kept for three years under guard. Because of his being related to Antipater he had got a delay,[36] but brought for the judgement of the Macedonians at this time, and failing words for his defence, he was executed. (3) Having dispatched men on racing camels, and having outrun the report of Philotas' punishment, Alexander had Philotas' father Parmenion murdered. He had been appointed governor of Media and had been entrusted with the royal treasuries in Ecbatana, holding one hundred and eighty thousand talents [1,080,000,000 *drachmae*]. (4) Alexander selected from among the Macedonians those who made remarks hostile to him, those who were distressed at the death of Parmenion, as well as those who had written in letters sent to Macedonia to their relatives anything contrary to the king's interests. Those people Alexander assembled into one unit, and called it the disciplinary company, so that the rest of the Macedonians might not be corrupted by their improper remarks and criticism.

---

[32] Plu. *Alex.* 49.1 speaks not of a conspiracy by Philotas but of a conspiracy against Philotas, a remark supported by, *inter alios*, Badian 1960: 326, 330–2, 337; Badian surmises that the actual target of the plot may well have been Parmenion, but that the torture of Philotas (see below) did not result in sufficient 'evidence' to charge Parmenion officially. See also Goukowsky 2002a: 231 *ad* 80.2 (sic!), which should be 80.1, third remark.
[33] According to Curt. 6.8.23 there were about 6,000 Macedonians present. For the arguments see Curt. 6.9.2–11.7.
[34] Neither Arrian nor Curt. 6.11.21–34 mention the conviction of Parmenion, though the latter does refer to the fact that Philotas under torture acknowledged the role of his father in the conspiracy.
[35] Arrian and Q. Curtius Rufus disagree on what this method amounted to. Arr. *An.* 3.26.3 relates it meant the victim was killed by throwing lances at him; Curt. 6.11.38 refers to death by stoning *more patrio*.
[36] Alexander the Lyncestian was married to the daughter of Antipater, the regent of Macedonia in the absence of Alexander the Great on expedition, and not related to Antigonus, as the MSS of Diodorus suggest: I have therefore followed Goukowsky's emendation after Johann Freinsheim (see Goukowsky 2002a: 111 *apparatus ad* line 26). Alexander the Lyncestian had been arrested at Phaselis: see above, 17.32.1–2.

Alexander's army marches on:

(17.81.1) Free of this affair and having settled things in Drangia, Alexander marched with his force against a tribe, before called 'Ariaspians'[37] but now for the following reasons 'Benefactors'. Having transferred the rule from the Medes to Persepolis, Cyrus the Great, surviving during an expedition in a desert territory with a total lack of provisions, came into the utmost danger, because the soldiers were forced through the want of food to eat each other's flesh, when the Ariaspians appeared bringing thirty thousand wagons laden with grain. Saved against all expectation, Cyrus honoured the tribe both with exemptions from taxation and with other gifts and, abolishing their former appellation, named them 'Benefactors'. (2) When Alexander led his army into their country at that time and when the natives received him kindly, he honoured the tribe with suitable gifts. Because their neighbours, who were called Gedrosians,[38] did the same, he rewarded these as well with appropriate favours. He gave the administration of these two tribes to Tiridates.[39] (3) While he was occupied therewith, there came some people reporting that Satibarzanes, having returned from Bactria with a large force of cavalry to the tribe of the Arians, had caused the natives to revolt from Alexander. Having heard this news, the king dispatched against Satibarzanes a portion of his army, having put Erigyius and Stasanor in command,[40] while he himself, subduing Arachosia in a few days, subjugated it. (17.82.1) When this year was over, Euthycritus became *archon* at Athens [328/7] and at Rome Lucius Platius and Lucius Papirius became consuls.[41] The one hundred and thirteenth Olympic Games were held.[42] In this year Alexander marched against the so-called

---

[37] In spite of the form Ἀριμάσπους in all of the Diodorus MSS, the correct name appears to have been Ἀριάσπους or Ἀριάσπας, as Arr. *An.* 3.27.4 observes. I think it feasible that the form 'Arimaspians' was inspired by the reference to a one-eyed Scythian people, made known by Aristeas of Proconnesus in the 'Arimaspian Epic' (see Str. 1.2.10/21; see also Hdt. 4.13–15).

[38] For Gedrosia (or Cedrosia: both forms appear to be allowed, the first preferred): Vogelsang 2012.

[39] The former commander of Persepolis (see above, 17.69.1). Arr. *An.* 3.27.5 mentions that the Ariaspians were granted autonomy, Curt. 7.3.4 that Amenides, one of Darius III's courtiers, was appointed as the Ariaspians' ruler.

[40] Neither Arrian nor Q. Curtius mentions the command of Stasanor, though Arr. *An.* 3.29.5 states that Stasanor was later appointed satrap of Aria.

[41] The consuls for 330 vc were L. Papirius Crassus and L. Plautius Venno (or Venox): Broughton 1951: 143–4. Diodorus is three years ahead of the Varronian chronology.

[42] That is, in July 328. Contrary to his habit, Diodorus omits to mention the winner of the *stadium* race: according to Eus. *Chron.* (ed. Schoene-Petermann), p. 205, this was Cliton of Macedonia. There is a rather large discrepancy between Diodorus' chronology of events and that of, for example, Str. 15.2.10/725, who dates the journey through the country of the Paropanisadians ὑπὸ Πλειάδος δύσιν ('at the setting of the Pleiad'), that is, before the winter (of 330/29). Goukowsky 2002a: 233 *ad* 82.1 identifies the Paropanisadians with OP **pari upari*

From Persepolis to Babylon 343

Paropanisadians. (2) Their country lies in the extreme north;[43] its whole is snow-covered and is hard to get at for other tribes because of the extreme cold. The most part of it being a plain and woodless,[44] it is divided up among many villages. (3) The houses in these have tiled roofs, drawn up at the top into a peaked vault. In the middle of each roof an aperture is left, through which smoke escapes, and because the building is enclosed at all sides, the people have much protection.[45] (4) Because of the depth of the snow, the natives spend the largest part of the year indoors, having their own supplies at hand. Heaping up soil about vines and fruit-bearing trees and leaving it for the winter season, they remove the earth again at the time of budding. (5) The whole nature of the land has the appearance of neither green nor cultivation, but is white and dazzling because of the snow and the ice which forms in it. Because, therefore, neither any bird settles nor any animal passes, all parts of the country were unvisited and inaccessible. (6) Nevertheless, in spite of all these obstacles for the army, the king, with his customary boldness and the hardihood of the Macedonians, surmounted the difficulties of the region. (7) Indeed, they left behind, exhausted, many of the soldiers and of the camp followers. Some, too, lost their sight because of the glare of the snow and the hard brilliance of the reflected light. (8) Nothing could be seen clearly from a distance, but the smoke alone revealing the villages allowed the Macedonians to discover where the natives lived, once they were in their proximity. After the villages had been taken by this method, and the soldiers recovered from their hardships through the plentiful provisions, the king quickly made himself master of all the inhabitants.

Alexander enters Bactria; Bessus declares himself Great King: (17.83.1) Advancing after these events, Alexander pitched camp near the Caucasus, which some call Mount Paropanisum [the Hindu Kush].[46] Traversing this range in its breadth in sixteen days, he founded a city in the pass which leads down to Media, calling it Alexandria.[47] In the midst of the Caucasus there is a rocky peak ten

---

sēna, 'people on the other side of the Upari-Sēna' (Hindu Kush), namely the region between Kabul and the Peshawar Valley, usually referred to as Gandhāra. See Herzfeld 1968: 336–7.
[43] Literally: 'under the Bears themselves', meaning Ursa Major and Ursa Minor, the Great Bear and the Little Bear, both constellations of the northern sky.
[44] See Goukowsky 2002a: 234, final remark *ad* 82.2.
[45] See Goukowsky 2002a: 234–5, remark *ad* 82.3.
[46] See Goukowsky 2002a: 236 *ad* 83.1, first remark. See also above, note 42.
[47] For the various problems this passage offers, see Goukowsky 2002a: 236–7 *ad* 83.1, second remark.

stadia [c. 1.9 km] in perimeter and four *stadia* [c. 750 m] in height, in which the cavern of Prometheus was pointed out by the natives, as well as the nest of the eagle in the story and the marks of the chains.[48] (2) Alexander founded other cities as well, at the distance of a day's march from Alexandria. In these he settled seven thousand natives, three thousand of the camp followers, and volunteers from the mercenaries. (3) He himself, taking up his force, marched into Bactria, learning that Bessus had put on the diadem and was enrolling forces.[49] Such was the state of Alexander's affairs. (4) The generals who had been sent to Aria, finding that the insurgents had gathered substantial forces and had as commander Satibarzanes, a man versed in generalship and outstanding in bravery, pitched camp close by the enemy. After there had been frequent skirmishes, they kept to small engagements for a time. (5) After it came to a pitched battle after these encounters and the Persians were making the confrontation an equal battle, Satibarzanes, the commander of the renegades, removing with his hands the helmet on his head and showing himself as he was,[50] challenged any of the generals of the Macedonians who wished to do so to fight with him alone. (6) After Erigyius had accepted and a contest of a heroic nature ensued, it occurred that Erigyius was victorious. The Persians, disheartened at the death of their commander and opting for safety, gave themselves up to the king. (7) Having designated himself Great King, Bessus sacrificed to the gods and, inviting his friends to a banquet, he fell into an argument in the course of the drinking with one of his companions, Bagodaras by name. As the quarrel increased, Bessus, who was losing his temper, attempted to execute Bagodaras, but changed his mind, persuaded by his friends. (8) Saved from this danger, Bagodaras escaped by night to Alexander. Enticed by his safety and the gifts promised by Alexander, the most prominent of the commanders conspired and, after seizing Bessus, carried him off to Alexander.[51] (9) The king honoured them with substantial gifts, but handed Bessus over to the brother and the other relatives of

---

[48] See this story with the comments on this episode by Str. 11.5.5/505–6 and Arr. *An*.5.3.1–4, while Curt. 7.3.22 appears to follow the same source as Diodorus for this episode.

[49] In fact, Bessus had become the Great King directly after he had Darius III killed: see above, note 4. Alexander's route through Bactria (and Sogdia) is notoriously hard to follow: see Rapin 2013: 57–61, 63–9.

[50] See also X. *An*. 1.8.6 for the practice.

[51] Goukowsky 2002a: 238 *ad* 83.8 rightly points to the discrepancies on the topic of Bessus' capture between the two contemporary primary sources we have, namely Aristobulus (*FGrH/BNJ* 139 F 24) and Ptolemy (*FGrH/BNJ* 138 F 14), both referred to by Arrian, as the latter also provides an alternative account of Bessus' punishment (Arr. *An*. 3.29.6–30.5; 4.7.2). Curt. 7.5.19–26 also tells a story different from Diodorus'.

Darius for punishment. Inflicting upon Bessus every humiliation and abuse and cutting his body up into little pieces, they scattered the parts about.

[[After Bessus' death there occurs a long break in the manuscript, in which the latter part of Diodorus' account of Alexander for the year 328/7 and the beginning of 327/6 is lost, including events like the end of the Scythian, Bactrian, and Sogdian campaigns, the quarrel with Clitus, the arrest of Callisthenes, the Pages' Conspiracy, and the marriage with Roxane. The text goes on with events in the autumn of 327.]][52]

B. ALEXANDER'S INDIAN ADVENTURE

S. 120:

17.84.1–89.6:

Alexander prepares to march against King Porus of India:
(17.84.1) A truce was concluded on these terms, and the queen,[53] impressed by Alexander's generosity, sent him valuable gifts and promised to follow his orders in everything. Leaving the city immediately under the terms of the truce and moving on eighty *stadia* [c. 14.5 km], the Indian mercenaries pitched camp without interference, without an inkling of what would happen. (2) Because Alexander nursed an implacable hostility towards the mercenaries, he followed the Indians,[54] with his forces in readiness, and suddenly falling upon them he caused a great slaughter. At first the mercenaries kept shouting that he made war against them in violation of his oaths and they called to witness the gods against whom he had transgressed.

---

[52] Into this period probably also falls the issue of the προσκύνησις ('obeisance'), related in Arr. *An.* 4.10.5–12.2 and Curt. 8.5.5–22. In much of the later literature on Alexander this practice has been referred to as degrading in the eyes of Alexander's companions and countrymen. Bowden 2013 mitigates this picture. For obeisance see also Chapter 5, note 112.

[53] We have to rely here on reports by Arrian, Q. Curtius Rufus, and Justin's *Epitome*. On his way from the Kabul valley to India, arriving in the city of Mazageans (Curt. 8.10.22) or Massagans (Arr. *An.* 4.26.1), in the country of the Assacenians (the modern region of the Swat Valley in northern Pakistan, bordering the Khyber Pass), Alexander captured Queen Cleophis, but reinstated her in her kingdom, a gesture *credidere qvidam plvs formae qvam miserationi datvm* ('some believed granted rather by her beauty than through compassion': Curt 8.10.35; see also Just. 12.7.9–11, and *Epit.Mett.* 39). See also Goukowsky 2002a: 117 note 1.

[54] According to Arr. *An.* 4.26–27.4, the mercenaries came from 'further India': Arrian's story deviates from Diodorus', who apparently follows, like Plu. *Alex.* 59.3–4, a source that is rather critical of Alexander and less 'romantic'. Str. 15.1.6/687, referring to Megasthenes, tells us that the Achaemenid kings recruited mercenaries from India: their serving the Assacenians was, therefore, not out of the ordinary.Tucci 1977: 51 describes the people (and therefore the women) fighting Alexander and his men as Scythians.

Alexander shouted loudly back that he had granted them the right to leave the city, but not to be forever friends of the Macedonians. (3) Undeterred by the greatness of their danger, the mercenaries joined ranks and, forming their line in a full circle, removed both their children and women to the centre, so that they might face those who were attacking from all directions with certainty. Because they were filled with desperate courage and fought stoutly with native toughness and the *aretē* of previous contests, and because the Macedonians were anxious not to show themselves inferior to Indians in fighting ability, the battle was a scene of horror. (4) As they fought hand to hand and as the contestants engaged each other, many and various forms of death and wounds were to be seen. The Macedonians, indeed, penetrating with their long spears[55] the *peltae* of the Indians, pressed the iron points on into their lungs; the mercenaries, flinging their javelins into the close ranks of their enemy, could not miss the mark, so near was the target. (5) As many were wounded and not a few killed, the women, catching up the weapons of the fallen, fought beside their men. Indeed, the acuteness of the danger and the fierceness of the action forced them to join the battle against their nature. Consequently, some of them, clad in armour, sheltered behind the same shields as their husbands, but others rushing in without armour, grasped the opposing shields, and to a large extent hindered their enemy. (6) Finally, all of them, including women, being outnumbered and cut down, chose a glorious death over ignoble attachment to life.[56] Leading off both the useless and unarmed camp followers and the surviving women, Alexander put the cavalry in charge of them.

Alexander besieges the rock fortress of Aornus:
(**17.85.1**) After he had taken many other cities by storm and had slaughtered whoever resisted him, he led the army forth to the rock fortress called Aornus.[57] In this place, indeed, the surviving natives had taken refuge because of its great strength. (2) In fact, it is said that at one time Heracles, intending to besiege this fortress, refrained

---

[55] The long spear was known as the *sarissa*. See Goukowsky 2002a: 118 note 1.
[56] Here too Diodorus' source may well have been the same as that of Plu. *Alex.* 59.7.
[57] Aurel Stein, investigating Gandhāra, the present north-western frontier province of Pakistan, believed that the rock (or steep hill) of Pir-Sar was to be identified as Aornos (Stein 1929: 128–53), an identification questioned by later archaeologists (see Tucci 1977: 52–5), suggesting that the Ilam might equally qualify as the site of Aornos. To the best of my knowledge the latter option is by now the more widely supported. In a review in the *Journal of the Royal Asiatic Society [of Great Britain and Ireland]* of 1931: 938–41 at 940, on the report of two 'tours' by Stein, J. Charpentier points out that Aornos might well translate from Sanskrit *āvaraṇa* or OP *āvarəna*: 'fortification, fort'.

because of the occurrence of some major tremors and divine signs. Having heard of these occurrences, Alexander became even more eager to capture the stronghold and to rival the god's reputation. (3) The rock fortress had a circumference of one hundred *stadia* [c. 18.5 km], and a height of sixteen [c. 3 km]. Its surface was even and circular on all sides. Its southern side was washed by the River Indus, being the largest of those in India. On the other sides it was surrounded by deep gorges and sheer cliffs. (4) After Alexander had surveyed the difficult terrain and decided that its forcible capture was impossible, an old man came to him with two sons.[58] (5) Being extremely poor and having supported himself in the region for a long time, he lived in a cave in which three beds had been cut out of the rock. Living in these conditions with his sons, the old man had come to know the country intimately. He offered, having appeared before the king and having told his story, to guide the king through the difficult terrain and to get him above the people who occupied the rock. (6) After Alexander had promised that he would present him with rich gifts[59] and with the help of the old man as a guide, he first occupied the access road to the rock.[60] Because there was no other egress at all, he thus enclosed the defenders in a hopeless siege. Next, with the help of many workmen filling up the chasm at the foot of the rock,[61] he mounted a vigorous siege, having drawn near to it, assaulting it continuously for seven days and seven nights with relays of troops. (7) At first the Indians had the advantage because they held the higher ground, and they killed many of those who attacked rashly. When, however, the embankment was finished and the dart-throwing catapults and other engines were deployed, and when, moreover, the king made it evident that he would not break off the siege, the Indians were alarmed. Anticipating sensibly what would happen, Alexander removed the guard which had been left in the path, presenting a way out for those who wished to withdraw from the rock.[62] Fearing both the Macedonian *aretae* and the king's ambition, the Indians left the rock at night.

---

[58] The old man and his sons also figure in Curt. 8.11.3, but are absent in the *Epit.Mett.*; Arr. *An.* 4.29.1–4 refers first to locals familiar with the region, subsequently to an Indian deserter with specific knowledge of the place.
[59] According to Curt. 8.11.4 he promised him 80 talents [480,000 *drachmae*].
[60] According to Arr. *An.* 4.29.2, Ptolemy was charged with this task.
[61] According to Stein 1929: 132–3, the ravine was probably that of Burimar Kandao.
[62] Goukowsky 2002a: 120 note 3 rightly points to Polyaen. 3.9.3, relating a similar stratagem employed by Iphicrates, and moreover suggests Diodorus may have been inspired by Iphicrates to insert such a ruse here, not related by our other sources.

Alexander crosses the River Indus:
(**17.86.1**) Having outmanoeuvred the Indians with the false alarms of war, Alexander gained possession of the rock without further fighting. He gave the promised reward to his guide and marched off with his army. (**2**) About this time, a certain Indian, Aphrices,[63] with twenty thousand troops and fifteen elephants, resided in the vicinity. Some of his followers, killing him and bringing his head to Alexander, ensured their own safety by this favour. (**3**) The king both took them into his service and rounded up the elephants, which were wandering about the countryside. He himself now, advancing to the River Indus, and finding both his thirty-oared boats in readiness and fully equipped and the stream spanned by a floating bridge, rested his army for thirty days and, after offering splendid sacrifices to the gods, then moved his army across and experienced a startling fright and relief. (**4**) After Taxiles, the king, had died earlier, his son Mophis had succeeded to the throne.[64] He had sent word to Alexander before, when the latter was in Sogdia, announcing he would join him in a war against those of the Indians who opposed Alexander, and now he stated, having sent messengers, that he surrendered his kingdom to him. (**5**) When Alexander was still forty *stadia* [c. 7.5 km] off, Mophis marched forward surrounded by his companions, having deployed his force as if for war and having adorned his elephants. When Alexander saw that a great army approached in warlike array and, concluding at once that the Indian had deliberately made the announcements in order to attack the Macedonians unprepared, he ordered the trumpeters to sound the call to arms. Having deployed the soldiers, he marched against the Indians. (**6**) When Mophis saw the Macedonians' disturbance, and understanding the cause, he left his army behind and surrendered both himself and his army to the king, having ridden forward with a few men and having corrected the Macedonians' misapprehension.[65] (**7**) Alexander, much relieved, both restored his kingdom to him and thereafter held him as a friend and ally. He also changed his name to Taxiles.[66] That is what happened in that year.

---

[63] For this name and its possible origins: Goukowsky 2002a: 241 *ad* 86.2.
[64] Mophis also is referred to as Motis or Mothis (*Epit.Mett.* 49–51: see *apparatus*); Curt. 8.12.5 calls the heir Omphis; and Arr. *An.* 4.22.6, 5.3.5–6 only uses the name Taxiles, perhaps his dynastic name. The editor of the Metz *epitome*, Thomas, opted for 'Mophis' in the text.
[65] See also Curt. 8.12.7–10 and the *Epit.Mett.* 51–2.
[66] See also Curt. 8.12.4–18; Arr. *An.* 5.3.5–6; and, differently, Plu. *Alex.* 59.1–3.

Alexander faces Porus:
(17.87.1) During the *archon*ship of Chremes at Athens [326/5], the Romans elected as consuls Publius Cornelius and Aulus Postumius.[67] In this year Alexander, after restoring his force in the land of Taxiles,[68] marched against Porus, the king of the neighbouring Indians.[69] (2) The latter had more than fifty thousand infantry, about three thousand cavalry, over a thousand chariots of war, and one hundred and thirty elephants.[70] He had as ally another king of the neighbouring regions, whose name was Abisares.[71] He had an army hardly smaller than that of Porus. (3) When Alexander learned that this king was four hundred *stadia* [c. 75 km] away, he decided to attack Porus before the arrival of his ally. (4) As Alexander approached the Indians, Porus, learning that his enemies were near, deployed his forces promptly. He divided his cavalry over both flanks, and arranged his elephants, rigged out terrifyingly, in a single line at equal intervals along his front. Between these beasts he placed the rest of his infantry, with the order to help the animals and to prevent them being shot at from the sides. (5) His whole array looked very much like a city, indeed: the outfit of the elephants resembled towers, the soldiers between them curtain walls. After viewing the deployment of the enemy, Alexander arranged his own force to cope therewith properly.
(17.88.1) When the battle had begun,[72] first practically all of the Indians' chariots were put out of action by Alexander's cavalry. Next the elephants entered the fight, trained to make good use of their

---

[67] As consuls for the year 328 VC several options are possible but, as Broughton phrases it, 'no choice is certain'. The alternatives are C. Plautius Decianus or P. Plautius Proculus and P. Cornelius Scapula or P. Cornelius Scipio Barbatus: Broughton 1951: 145. A. Postumius is mentioned nowhereother than in Diodorus' remark as magistrate for this year, though a Sp. Postumius Albinus is referred to as a *magister equitum* in 327 VC (Liv. 8.23.14; Broughton 1951: 146). As far as the evidence goes, Diodorus is three years ahead of the Varronian chronology.
[68] For the territory occupied by the country of Taxiles, see Goukowsky 2002a: 242 *ad* 87.1, first remark.
[69] Porus is likely to have been the Greek rendering of the name *Puru*, Sanskrit *Purushottama*, king of Paurava, ancient Punjab: see, for example, Kulke and Rothermund 1986: 57. For the territory of Porus, see Goukowsky 2002a: 242 *ad* 87.1, second remark. Diodorus omits that to attack Porus, Alexander had to cross the River Hydaspes (modern River Jhelum), a huge enterprise (see Arr. *An.* 5.8.5–14.6). See also Rollinger 2013: 10–11. According to Stein 1932: 31 this crossing 'was probably the most hazardous among the many amazing exploits of the great Macedonian's campaigns'.
[70] Generally lower figures are presented in Arr. *An.* 5.15.4, Curt. 8.13.6, Plu. *Alex.* 72.1, and *Epit.Mett.* 54.
[71] Though the MSS present various versions of his name, the correct one seems to be Abisares, king of the Abhisāra region, a mountainous area in modern west Kashmir: see *Epit. Mett.* 53; Arr. *An.* 5.22.2; see also Nilakanta Sastri 1957: 120–1. I have chosen to use that form: see Goukowsky 2002a: 122 note 2.
[72] As Stein 1932: 43 observes, the precise location of the battle cannot be established, but was probably near the small city of Miani, Jhelum district, Punjab Province, Pakistan.

Fig. 6.1. Punjab, Pakistan: the River Jhelum (ancient River Hydaspes). Photo © Jona Lendering <http://www.livius.org>.

height and strength. Some Macedonians were trampled, armour and all, under the beasts and died, their bones crushed; others were caught up by the trunks and, lifted on high, were dashed back down to the ground again, dying a fearful death; many were pierced by the tusks, run through the whole body, and died instantly. (2) Because the Macedonians faced the frightening experience manfully and used their long spears to good effect against those stationed beside the elephants, the battle was in equipoise. (3) Then, when the animals were being struck by the javelins and felt the pain of the number of their wounds, the Indian riders were no longer able to control their movements. In fact, the elephants veered and, no longer manageable, turned upon their own ranks and trampled friendly troops. (4) As his formations grew more confused, Porus,[73] observing the events and being mounted on the largest of the elephants, gathered about him forty of the animals which were not yet out of hand. Attacking

---

[73] Both Diodorus and Curt. 8.14.32, 38, 39–40 put considerable emphasis on the courage (ἀνδραγαθία, ἀνδρεία, ἀριστεῖα) of Porus, while Arr. *An.* 5.18.4–5 merely remarks he fought bravely. It suggests once more that Diodorus and Curtius Rufus may have used a source that was independent of, for example, Arrian's.

his enemies with the combined weight of the elephants, he inflicted many losses, since he also stood out among his followers in bodily strength: in fact he was five cubits in height [c. 2.25 m][74] and as regards the breadth of chest twice that of his mightiest soldiers. (5) Therefore the javelins flung by him had such force that they were little inferior to the darts of the catapults. Because the Macedonians who opposed him were amazed at Porus' bravery, Alexander, having sent for the bowmen and other light-armed troops, ordered them to concentrate their fire upon Porus.[75] (6) The soldiers followed the order promptly and many projectiles flew towards the Indian at the same time, and none missed its mark because of his great size. Though Porus continued to fight heroically, he became drained of blood from his many wounds, collapsed, and having fainted, fell to the ground by his animal. (7) As the word went about that the king was killed, the remaining mass of the Indians began to flee. (17.89.1) After many were killed in their flight, Alexander, victorious in a remarkable battle, called his soldiers back with the *salpinxes*. Of the Indians, there fell in the battle more than twelve thousand, among whom were also two sons of Porus, his commanders, and the most outstanding of the captains.[76] (2) The Macedonians captured alive over nine thousand men and eighty elephants. Porus himself, still breathing, was turned over to the Indians for medical attention. (3) Of the Macedonians there died two hundred and eighty cavalry and more than seven hundred infantry.[77] The king buried the dead, rewarded those who had distinguished themselves in accordance

---

[74] A somewhat comparable height is given in *Epit.Mett.* 54, Arr. *An.* 5.19.1 (who adds that such height was not uncommon among the Indians), and Plu. *Alex.* 60.6. Curt. 8.14.13 only remarks that Porus *hvmanae magnitvdinis prope modvm excesserat* ('had almost exceeded the measure of human stature'). Tarn 1948: 170 believes the source of this information was using a short (Macedonian?) cubit. This seems hardly feasible: most systems using the *cubit*, including the Indian (the *hasta*), reckon with a not very dissimilar length. If Tarn were right, Porus' height would be reduced to about 1.8 m. Actually, Alexander ordered, as a ruse and/or statement, huts to be made with two beds each, five *cubits* long (17.95.2).

[75] See also *Epit.Mett.* 60 and Curt. 8.14.38. This strategy differs considerably from that in Just. 12.8.3–4, in which a duel between Alexander and Porus figures. Luc. *Hist.Conscr.* 12 suggests that the tale of the duel had been invented by Aristobulus (*FGrH*/*BNJ* 139 T4). See also Goukowsky 1972: 479–80; Baynham 1995; see also Lane Fox 1996; Bosworth 1998: 6–8, 167–9. For an exhaustive discussion of how Alexander wished his victory over Porus to be portrayed on the so-called 'elephant medallions', see Holt 2003. On Aristobulus' account of the Battle of the Hydaspes, see the commentary in the *BNJ* 139 to F 35.

[76] *Epit.Mett.* 61 gives about the same numbers of fallen Indians, but Arr. *An.* 5.18.2 states a much higher number of Indian losses: he mentions 20,000 foot and 3,000 horse, all command-ers, many captains, all chariots, and all elephants either killed or captured. Arr. *An.* 5.18.5–6 mentions that Alexander and Porus negotiated a treaty, under the terms of which Porus surren-dered himself. See also *Epit.Mett.* 60.

[77] Here *Epit.Mett.* 61 presents us with a slightly higher count – 900 foot and 300 horse – while Arr. *An.* 5.18.3 reports 80 foot and 230 horse.

with their deserts, and sacrificed to Helius, who had given him the eastern regions to conquer.[78]

Alexander wants to move on:
(4) Since there were mountains not far away which possessed many thriving firs, no little cedar and pine, and an ample supply of other woods suitable for shipbuilding, Alexander had a large number of ships constructed.[79] (5) He did so because he intended, having reached the borders of India and subdued all of its inhabitants, to sail downstream to the ocean.[80] (6) He founded two cities, one beyond the river where he had crossed and the other on the spot where he had defeated Porus.[81] These were built quickly because there was a plentiful supply of labour. When Porus had recovered, Alexander appointed him, in recognition of his *aretē*, king over the country where he formerly ruled.[82] He rested his force for thirty days because there was a vast plenty of provisions.

[[There now follow three paragraphs on natural phenomena of the region, which I shall leave out of this account.]]

S. 121:
17.90.4–111.6:

Alexander continues his expedition; his soldiers are exhausted:
(17.90.4) Alexander forced Abisares,[83] the king who had not moved in time to help Porus in the battle and who was frightened, to accept his orders. He himself, having crossed the river with his force, resumed his march through a region of remarkable quality. (5) It possessed, indeed, strange kinds of trees which reached a height of seventy cubits [c. 31.5 m], were so thick that they could scarcely

---

[78] Goukowsky 2002a: 244 *ad* 89.3, second remark, argues that, regarding the composition of Alexander's army at the time, a sacrifice to the Sun was a likely option.

[79] See the remarks of Goukowsky 2002a: 244 *ad* 89.4.

[80] Miltner 1952 argues that the desire to reach the ocean was the result of an idea, hatched by the Persian kings, that as 'Kings of the four quarters of the World' they (and as a consequence Alexander) had to extend Persian rule to the shores of the (four) oceans. See also Chapter 10.

[81] These were Alexandria Nicaea and Alexandria Bucephala. See also Goukowsky 2002a: 245 *ad* 89.6.

[82] Goukowsky 2002a: 125 note 1(*) remarks that, though Alexander had defeated Porus in a battle, he had not at all conquered Porus' kingdom. Therefore the gesture (which appears to have followed an Indian custom; see Goukowsky's note) seems mainly meaningful for the image of Alexander Diodorus is trying to convey.

[83] As in the case of 17.87.2 (see above, note 71), we encounter several variations on this king's name in the MSS. Consistency has made me opt for Abisares.

From Persepolis to Babylon 353

be embraced by four men, and cast a shadow of three *plethra* [c. 90 m].[84] This country also possessed a multitude of snakes, small in size and variously coloured.[85] (6) In fact, some of them looked like bronze rods, others had thick, shaggy crests, but through their bites they brought sudden death. The person who had been bitten suffered fearful pains and was covered with a bloody sweat. (7) Because the Macedonians were much affected by the bites, they slung their hammocks from trees and remained awake most of the night. Later, however, having learned from the natives the use of a root as an antidote, they were freed from these fears.

(17.91.1) As he continued the march with his force, people came to Alexander to report that King Porus (a cousin of the Porus who had been defeated), leaving his kingdom, had fled to the people of Gandara.[86] (2) Enraged, Alexander sent Hephaestion with an army into his country and ordered that the kingdom be transferred to the friendly Porus. He himself, having campaigned against the people known as the Adrestians,[87] getting possession of their cities, some by force, others by agreement, came into the country of the Cathayans.[88] (3) Among these it was the custom for wives to be cremated together with their husbands.[89] This law had been put into effect by the Cathayans because of one woman who had killed her husband with poison. (4) The king, now, having captured their greatest and strongest city after much fighting, burned it down.[90] When he was in the process of besieging another notable city and the Indians came to him with suppliant branches, he spared them further attack. Next he made an expedition against the cities under the rule of Sopithes,[91]

---

[84] Both Goukowsky 2002a: 126 note 2 and Welles 1970: 382–3 note 1 suggest the tree intended is the banyan (*Ficus benghalensis*). Further references to classical authors on these trees are in those notes.
[85] In 17.90.1 Diodorus had referred to very large snakes, measuring 16 cubits [c. 7.2 m], probably Indian pythons. Goukowsky 2002a: 246 *ad* 90.5 surmises this smaller snake may have been the *Echis carinatus*, the Indian saw-scaled viper, the size of which ranges between 38 and 80 cm in total length, but usually no more than 60 cm.
[86] Though the name resembles that known from Achaemenid inscriptions, the precise situation of this kingdom eludes us. See Goukowsky 2002a: 247 *ad* 91.1.
[87] Certainty regarding the identity of this tribe is lacking: Goukowsky 2002a: 247 *ad* 91.2, first remark, mentions two possibilities, namely the Adrjas from the *Mahābhāratā* or the Arishtas.
[88] The Cathayans, the *Kaṭhas* of Sanskrit sources, a warlike tribe, occupied the region of modern Lahore and Amritsar: see Goukowsky 2002a: 247 *ad* 91.2, second remark.
[89] See also Goukowsky 2002a: 127–8 note 1, for further references.
[90] Probably the city of Sangala, the capital city of the Madras, of which the *exact* location is still disputed, though Law asserts it was situated between the rivers Chenab and Degh in the upper Punjab: Law 1969: 402; the destruction by the Macedonians is referred to by Law on the same page.
[91] See for this king Goukowsky 2002a: 248, first remark.

which were exceedingly well governed. Not only are all the functions of this state directed to the acquiring of good repute, but also beauty is valued more than anything among them. (5) Therefore their children are subjected from birth to a process of selection and those who are well formed and designed by nature to have a fine appearance and bodily strength are reared, while they destroy those who are bodily deficient, believing they are not worth bringing up. (6) Consequently, they also marry without regard to dower or any other financial consideration, only caring for beauty and physical excellence. (7) Therefore most of those living in these cities enjoy a higher reputation than the other Indians. Their king Sopithes, being strikingly handsome and tall beyond the rest, being over four cubits [c. 1.8 m] in height,[92] came out of his capital city, surrendering himself and his kingdom to Alexander, but received it back through the kindness of the conqueror. (8) Sopithes, with great goodwill, feasted the whole army bountifully for several days.

(17.92.1) Presenting Alexander with many impressive gifts, he gave him one hundred and fifty dogs, remarkable for their size and courage and other good qualities, of which people said that they had been crossbred from tigresses.[93] (2) Wishing Alexander to gain experience of the *aretē* of the dogs in action, he brought into a ring a full-grown lion and set two of the poorest of the dogs he had given on the lion. When they were having a hard time with the animal, he released two others to assist them. (3) As, however, the four were getting the upper hand over the lion, someone sent by Sopithes with a scimitar started to separate the right leg of one of the dogs. When Alexander shouted out indignantly and his bodyguards rushed up and seized the arm of the Indian, Sopithes said that he would give three dogs for that one, and the handler, taking a firm grip on the leg, severed it slowly. The dog, uttering neither yelp nor whimper, continued though with his teeth clamped shut until, fainting with loss of blood, it died on top of the lion.

Alexander wants to move on further, but his soldiers refuse to comply:
(17.93.1) While all this was going on, Hephaestion returned with the force that had joined him, having conquered a big piece of India.[94] Alexander praised him on account of his brave actions.

---

[92] Tarn believes Sopithes was about as tall as Porus, but that the cubit used to measure them differed: see Tarn 1948: 170. See also note 72, above.
[93] See Goukowsky 2002a: 248–9 *ad* 92.1.
[94] See for the details Curt. 9.1.35.

He himself, having invaded the kingdom of Phegeus,[95] while its inhabitants gladly accepted the presence of the Macedonians and Phegeus himself met the king with many gifts, allowed Phegeus to keep the kingdom. Being bountifully feasted with the army for two days, he then advanced to the River Hyphasis,[96] the width of which was seven *stadia* [c. 1,300 m], the depth six fathoms [c. 11 m], and the current violent and difficult to cross. (2) He had learned from Phegeus about the country beyond the River Indus that there was a desert to traverse for twelve days,[97] that next there was a river by the name of Ganges, which was thirty-two *stadia* [c. 7 km] in width and the deepest of all the Indian rivers. Beyond this dwelt the peoples of the Prasians and the Gangarids,[98] whose king was Xandrames.[99] The latter had twenty thousand cavalry, two hundred thousand infantry, two thousand chariots, and four thousand elephants equipped for war.[100] Disbelieving this information, Alexander sent for Porus, and asked him about the truth regarding the aforementioned reports. (3) Porus assured him that all the rest of the account was quite correct, but that the king of the Gangarids was utterly common and undistinguished, as he was supposed to be the son of a barber. He added that Xandrames' father, being a handsome man, was greatly loved by the queen and that the kingdom fell to him when the king had been murdered by his wife.[101] (4) Even though Alexander saw that an expedition against the Gangarids would not be easy, he stuck to his ambition. Really confiding in the *aretae* of his Macedonians, he also had confidence in the oracles that he would be victorious over the Gangarids: he did so because

---

[95] Though this is also mentioned in *Epit.Mett.* 68 and Curt. 9.1.36–2.1, it does not occur in Arrian's account. The precise location of Phegeus' kingdom eludes us.
[96] See also Arr. *An.* 5.24.8. Though the river may be identified as the modern Beas (shortly before it empties into the River Sutlej), its precise course in Alexander's time is not determinable.
[97] The only feasible desert in this region is the Thar (or Great Indian) Desert: see Eggermont 1970–1: 91; its location is, however, difficult to match with the description of Alexander's whereabouts at this time. See also Goukowsky 2002a: 249–50 and 93.2.
[98] For the names of these peoples, I shall not follow the renditions in the MSS, but make connections with more probable names, like the Sanskrit *Praçya* ('People of the East'), used by people from the Punjab for those living east of them, to some extent perhaps identical with Gangarids, people from the Ganges area(s).
[99] In Curt. 9.2.3 he is called Aggrammes (Ἀγγράμμης). It might, perhaps, be a play on ἀγραμμάτος ('illiterate'), and as such a pejorative description of the man (see 17.93.3 below). For a different approach to the Gangarids see below, 18.6.1.
[100] See Curt. 9.2.2–4 and *Epit.Mett.* 68. It seems this information is based upon the account of Clitarchus. See also, for example, Meyer 1927; Pfister 1961: 45 and note 45.
[101] Curt. 9.2.6–7 presents us with an account that resembles Diodorus', but shows notable nuances regarding, *inter alia*, the queen's role. For the story of Xandrames (whose real name may have been *Anuruddha*: Eggermont 1970–1: 92–9) see Goukowsky 2002a: 250–1 *ad* 93.3.

the Pythia had called him 'invincible' and Ammon had given him the rule of the whole world.[102]

(17.94.1) Because he observed that his soldiers were exhausted by their constant campaigns and had spent almost eight years among toils and dangers, Alexander understood that it was necessary to persuade the masses with suitable words to undertake the expedition against the Gangarids. (2) There had been many losses among the soldiers and no relief from fighting was in sight. The horses' hooves had been worn thin by steady marching, most of the arms and armour were wearing out, and Greek clothing was quite gone. They had to clothe themselves in foreign materials, remodelling the garments of the Indians.[103] (3) As Fate would have it, heavy rains poured down for seventy days, to the accompaniment of continuous thunder and lightning. Accounting all this adverse to his enterprise, he had only one hope of realising his desire: if he might gain the soldiers' great goodwill through gratitude. (4) Therefore he allowed them to ravage the country along the river,[104] which was full of every good thing. During these days, when the force was busy foraging, after assembling the wives of the soldiers and their children, he offered the wives a monthly ration, and to the children he distributed a service bonus in proportion to the military records of their fathers.[105] (5) When the soldiers returned laden with many goods from their expedition, he brought them together in a meeting. When he delivered a preconceived speech about the expedition against the Gangarids and the Macedonians did not approve it in any wise, he gave up the enterprise.[106]

---

[102] For the remark (in fact not a proper prophecy) of the Pythia, see Plu. *Alex.* 14.4. The Ammon 'present' is preluded in 17.49.2. Ammon's sayings are described in 17.51.2–3.

[103] Goukowsky 2002a: 130 note 1 is adamant these lines are based upon Clitarchus: they return in Coenus' speech as described by Curt. 9.3.2, 10–11 and, less clearly, Arr. *An.* 5.27.2–9.

[104] I opt here to follow Goukowsky's text, following MS F, and read here παραποταμίαν instead of πολεμίαν: see Goukowsky 2002a: 130 *apparatus ad* line 16. Though Goukowsky 2002a: 251 *ad* 94.4 believes that Phegeus' territory is intended, this seems hardly logical given the friendly relations with him (see 17.93.1, above).

[105] This is almost an interpretative translation of ἐπιφορὰς ταγματικάς and συλλογισμούς. Only in Just. 12.4.2–11 do we find an offer by Alexander to provide in some way for the needs of the camp followers at this stage, though Plu. *Alex.* 71.5 mentions such a provision, but only after the mutiny. The story here looks like an adaptation of an account as later related by Arr. *An.* 7.12.1–2.

[106] Though the theme very briefly returns once more in 17.108.3, this is all Diodorus relates about the notorious mutiny of Alexander's troops. See Curt. 9.2.12–3.19; Just. 12.8.10–17; Plu. *Alex.* 62; Arr. *An.* 5.25–8. Diodorus appears to depict Alexander here as a commander who listens to his soldiers, a picture that diverges from Arr. *An.* 5.28.1–4, in which Alexander acts like a spoiled child. Arrian even adds a story by Ptolemy that Alexander ventured to offer sacrifices to cross the river nonetheless, but that the victims proved unfavourable and forced him to alter his plans (Arr. *An.* 5.28.4 = *FGrH*/*BNJ* 138 F 23; see also Str. 15.1.27/697).

Alexander contemplates how to continue:
(17.95.1) Thinking how best to mark the limits of his campaign at this point, he first had altars of the twelve gods of fifty cubits [c. 22.50 m] high[107] erected and then, after tracing the circuit of a camp thrice the size of the existing one, he had a ditch dug fifty feet [c. 15 m] wide and forty feet [c. 12 m] deep. Heaping up the earth inside the ditch, he had a substantial wall constructed out of it. (2) He ordered the infantry to construct huts, each containing two beds five cubits [c. 2.25 m] long,[108] and the cavalry, in addition to this, to build also two mangers twice the normal size and, analogically, also to enlarge everything else that would be left behind. He wanted to do so with the plan of making a camp of heroic proportions and leaving to the natives evidence of men of huge stature, displaying supernatural bodily strength. (3) Marching back with his entire force, after all this had been done, he returned to the River Acesines by the same route by which he had come.[109] Arriving there, he found the ships wrought, and fitting these out he had still others built. (4) About that time, there arrived from Greece allied and mercenary troops under their own commanders, more than thirty thousand infantry and a little less than six thousand cavalry. They brought with them magnificent suits of armour for twenty-five thousand foot soldiers, and a hundred talents [c. 2,600 kg] of medical supplies.[110] These he distributed to the soldiers. (5) When the nautical preparation was completed and two hundred open galleys were ready with eight hundred service ships, he gave names to the two cities which had been founded on either side of the river, calling one of them Nicaea in celebration of his victory in war, and the other Bucephala in honour of his horse that had died in the battle against Porus.

Alexander sets sail down the River Indus:
(17.96.1) After embarking with his companions, he began to make the voyage down the river towards the southern ocean. The bulk of his force marched along the banks of the river, under the command

---

[107] For an elaborate commentary on these altars see Goukowsky 2002a: 252 *ad* 95.1.
[108] Here, as in the preceding paragraph, the issue of the cubits returns: see above, 17.88.4 and note 74.
[109] Modern River Chenab, the *Ashkini* or *Iskmati* of the Vedas. There seems to be some inconsistency here, as Diodorus has previously suggested Alexander founded two cities near the River Hydaspes (see above, 17.89.6 and note 81), where he also ordered the fleet to be made: see Arr. *An.* 6.1.1, quoting Nearchus (see Arr. *Ind.* 18.1 = *FGrH/BNJ* 133 F 1I), the commander of the fleet (Arr. *An.* 6.2.3). See also Arr. *An.* 6.2.4 (referring to Ptolemy) and Curt. 9.3.27 on the Hydaspes fleet. In fact, Arr. *An.* 6.3.1 suggests the Acesines was here very close to the Hydaspes, into which it emptied.
[110] The medical supplies are mentioned by no other source on Alexander's expedition.

of Craterus and Hephaestion.[111] When they came to the junction of the Acesines and the Hydaspes,[112] he led his soldiers, after disembarking them, against the people called Sibians. (2) People say that these Sibians are the descendants of the soldiers who came with Heracles to the rock of Aornus and were unsuccessful in its siege,[113] and were settled in this spot by Heracles.[114] When Alexander had pitched camp beside a very fine city, the prominent figures among the citizens came out. Having met the king and renewing their ties of kinship, they said they would do anything with enthusiasm since they were his relatives, and they also brought him magnificent gifts. (3) Accepting their goodwill and having declared their cities to be free, Alexander marched forth to the neighbouring tribes. Having found the Agalassians,[115] as they were called, drawn up in battle order, forty thousand foot and three thousand horse, engaging in battle with them and victorious over them, he cut down most of them. The rest, having fled to the cities nearby, he sold as slaves after forcing the besieged cities to surrender. (4) When the other natives had collected, he took by storm a large city in which twenty thousand persons had taken refuge. As the Indians had barricaded the streets and fought stoutly from the houses, he lost not a few Macedonians as he was hard pressed. (5) Setting fire to the city in anger,[116] he burned up most of the inhabitants. He pardoned the remaining natives, to the number of three thousand, who had fled to the citadel and appealed for mercy with supplicant branches.

Alexander escapes drowning, but is later severely wounded:
(**17.97.1**) Having embarked again with his companions upon the ships, he continued his voyage down the river until he came to the

---

[111] Arr. *An.* 6.2.2 tells us that Craterus marched on the right bank, Hephaestion on the left. See also Just. 12.9.1; Plu. *Alex.* 63.1; Curt. 9.3.24.

[112] Goukowsky 2002a: 132–3 note 2 is absolutely right in pointing out that the geographical situation has changed considerably since Alexander's day: not only has the bed of these tributaries to the Indus moved to the south-west, but also the confluence of the rivers Chenab and Jhelum (Acesines and Hydaspes) is nowadays tens of kilometres more to the south than it was then.

[113] See above, 17.85.2. Though this episode is lacking in Arrian's account, it is told by Curt. 9.4.1–3 and Just. 12.9.2.

[114] Goukowsky 2002a: 253–4 *ad* 96.1 refers to evidence indicating this legend cannot be true, as the Sibians were most likely a non-Aryan tribe, perhaps originating from Gandhara.

[115] Just. 12.9.2 refers to them as the 'Agensones', while Curt. 9.4.5 simply calls them *alia gens* ('another nation'), though referring to their 40,000 infantry. So far, this tribe, and therefore its habitation(s), have not been identified with any certainty.

[116] Curt. 9.4.6–7, on the other hand, states that the Indians themselves set fire to the city, to avoid subjection. He may have been mistaken and confounded this outcome with that of a 'Brahmin' city mentioned by Arr. *An.* 6.7.6, after his vicissitudes with the Mallians (see below, 17.98–9; also 17.102.7–103.8).

confluence of the aforementioned rivers with the Indus.[117] As mighty streams dashed together at one spot, many dangerous eddies were created, which, uniting, tried to destroy the vessels. Because the force of the current was swift and violent and overcame the skill of the helmsmen, two of the galleys were sunk and not a few of the other vessels ran aground. (2) As Alexander's flagship was swept into a great cataract, the king was brought into extreme danger. Because death was staring him in the eyes, Alexander, flinging off his clothing, clung, naked, to any possible help,[118] but his companions swam alongside the ship, hastening to take up the king when his ship had been wrecked. (3) Though there was much confusion all over the ship and the crew struggled against the might of the current, as the river was superior both to all human skill and to all human power, Alexander and the swimmers got ashore with toil and pain.[119] Having narrowly escaped, he sacrificed to the gods because he had escaped extreme danger and had struggled with a river, like Achilles.[120] (17.98.1) Next, making an expedition against the Sydracians and the people known as Mallians,[121] populous and warlike tribes, he found the natives assembled, over eighty thousand infantry, ten thousand cavalry, and seven hundred chariots. Before the arrival of Alexander they had been at war with each other, but when he approached the country, they patched up their quarrel and, giving and receiving ten thousand young women, settled their differences through

---

[117] Though the rivers joined far more to the north than at present, as noted above (note 112), there is much uncertainty about the exact background of Diodorus' remark: see Goukowsky 2002a: 255 ad 97.1, first remark; also Welles 1970: 399 note 2.

[118] Plu. Alex. 58.4 remarks that Alexander could not swim.

[119] I find appealing an emendation suggested by L. A. Post, mentioned by Welles 1970: 399 note 4, to read, instead of the νεῶν 'ships' of the MSS (or perhaps even νέων 'young men'), νεόντων, 'swimmers', especially in the context of paragraph 2: οἱ δὲ φίλοι παρενήχοντο ('but his companions swam alongside the ship').

[120] See Curt. 9.4.14: cum amne bellum fuisse crederes ('You would have believed that there had been a war with the river'). Though this confluent is obviously no sea, the situation may also have been preserved in Plu. De Alex. Fort. 340E: καὶ θάλατταν μαχομένην ἔπλευσε ('he sailed a battling sea'). The reference to Achilles reflects the latter's struggle with the River Xanthus (see Hom. Il. 21.228–382). Though the connection may well have been made by Clitarchus, it also reflects Alexander as 'the second Achilles'.

[121] The Sydracians of the main MSS of Str. 15.1.8/687, on which Fischer based his emendation, figure in the MSS of Diodorus as the Συρακοῦσαι (other MSS of Strabo, though, read here Ὀξύδρακαι, Σύδρακαι, or Ὀξυδράκαι: as a matter of fact, elsewhere Strabo (Str. 15.1.6/687) refers to the Ὀξύδρακαι (though again in some MSS the Ὕδρακαι; see also Steph.Byz. s.v. 'Ὑδράκαι') as mercenaries in the Achaemenid Persian army). Curt. 9.4.15 calls this tribe by a similar name to that in Strabo's main MSS, 'Sudracians'; but Just. 12.9.3 calls them 'Sugambrians'; Arr. An. 6.4.3 Ὀξυδράκαι'; and Epit.Mett. 75 'Oxydraceans'. As regards their strength, the different descriptions also vary, adding up to 100,000 foot and 20,000 horse in the Metz epitome, while Justin even mentions 60,000 horse and 80,000 foot. As regards the Mallians, their name returns inter alia in the Mahābhārata as Malla/Māla/Mālava, with a warlike connotation: see also Goukowsky 2002a: 255 ad 98.1, second remark.

that intermarriage. (2) They, however, did not come out to fight together, but, quarrelling again over the command, retired into the neighbouring cities.[122] Having approached the first city, Alexander thought to take it by storm.[123] (3) There, then, one of the seers, named Demophon, coming to him, reported that there had been revealed to him by numerous portents that there would be great danger for the king from a wound during the attack. Therefore he begged Alexander to leave that city alone for the present and to turn his mind to other activities. (4) The king scolded him for dampening the *aretē* of those who were about to fight. He himself, having deployed everything for the attack, led the way in person to the city, eager to reduce it by force. As the first man in, breaking open a gate, since the engines of war were slow to come up,[124] and bursting into the city, he struck down many defenders and, driving the others before him, pursued them to the citadel. (5) While the Macedonians were still busy fighting along the wall, seizing a ladder and leaning it against the walls of the citadel, he clambered up, holding a light shield above his head. Because of the quickness of the action he reached the top of the wall before the Indians could forestall him. (6) Since the Indians did not dare to come within his reach, but were flinging javelins and shooting arrows at him from a distance, the king was oppressed by the mass of projectiles. The Macedonians, however, raising two ladders, swarmed up in a mass, but, as both broke down, tumbled back upon the ground. (17.99.1) Bereft of any help, the king boldly took an admirable step, worthy to be remembered. Indeed, judging it unworthy of his personal tradition of success to descend from the wall back to his troops without accomplishing anything, he leapt down, alone with his arms and armour, inside the city. (2) As the Indians thronged about him, he boldly withstood the attack of the Indians. Protecting himself on the right by a tree which grew close by the wall and on the left by the wall itself, he kept the Indians off, displaying such courage as you might expect from a king who had achieved such wondrous acts, being eager that the end of his life should be a supremely glorious conclusion. (3) In fact, he took many blows upon the helmet, not a few upon the shield. At length, being shot below the breast,[125] he fell upon one knee,

---

[122] Arr. *An.* 6.11.3 reports they did agree on a single commander, a Sydracian, but adds that Alexander did not allow them time to effectuate their union.
[123] Goukowsky 2002a: 256 *ad* 98.2, second remark, is right to observe that it is difficult to follow this expedition on the map.
[124] See for these machines and their constructors above, 17.40.4–46.6 and relevant notes on the siege of Tyre, as well as Chapter 5, note 67.
[125] Arr. *An.* 6.10.1, referring to Ptolemy (who was not present during this battle but may have been informed about the events at first hand shortly after his return), states that the arrow

From Persepolis to Babylon 361

overborne by the blow. Straightway after he had shot Alexander, the Indian, thinking that Alexander was helpless, ran up and as the Indian delivered a blow, Alexander thrust his sword up into the man's side and the Indian died, as the wound proved fatal. The king, though, getting hold of a branch close by and getting on his feet, defied the Indians who wished to do so to fight with him.[126] (4) At this point Peucestes,[127] one of his bodyguards, having mounted another ladder, was the first to cover the king with his shield.[128] After him a good many others, appearing and frightening the Indians, saved Alexander. When the city was taken by storm, the Macedonians, in a fury at the injury to their king, killed all they met and filled the city with corpses. (5) As the king lay helpless under his treatment for many days, the Greeks who had been settled in Bactria and Sogdia, who had borne unhappily their settlement among peoples of another race for a while, rose up in revolt against the Macedonians when word came to them that the king after being wounded had died. (6) After assembling in a group of three thousand men and suffering greatly on their homeward route, they were later massacred by the Macedonians after Alexander's death.[129]

Alexander recovers and continues the journey; the army is halted by poisoned arrows:
(17.100.1) Alexander recovered from his wound, sacrificed to the gods, and held a great banquet for his companions.[130] ... (2) ... (3) ... (4) ... (5) ... (6) ... (7) ... (8) ...

---

penetrated Alexander's corslet and that πνεῦμα ὁμοῦ τῷ αἵματι ἐκ τοῦ τραύματος ἐξεπνεῖτο ('breath spouted from the wound together with the blood'), suggesting that Alexander's lung was punctured.
   [126] According to Arr. *An.* 6.11.2, there existed many false accounts on this episode.
   [127] Though accounts vary, Peucestes is generally considered as the man who saved Alexander. Curt. 9.5.14–18 adds the names of Timaeus, Leonnatus, and Aristonus; Plu. *Alex.* 63.4 also names Limnaeus in one work; Arr. *An.* 6.10.1–2 mentions Leonnatus and Abreas as well. In *Epit.Mett.* 76–7 it is related that Alexander climbed (and descended?) the ladder with three men, of whom only Leonnatus is mentioned. Clitarchus (and Timagenes) state(s) that Ptolemy would also have been present, but Ptolemy himself denies this (see Curt. 9.5.21; Arr. *An.* 6.11.8; see also *FGrH/BNJ* 88 F 3, Timagenes; *FGrH/BNJ* 138 F 26, Ptolemy; and *FGrH/BNJ* 137 F 24, Clitarchus). Nevertheless, he is mentioned as Alexander's saviour by Plutarch in his *De Alex. Fort.*, 327B (also mentioning Limnaeus, though omitting Peucestes). Plu. *De Alex. Fort.* 344D refers to Limnaeus, Ptolemy, and Leonnatus, again omitting Peucestes.
   [128] From Diodorus' phrasing, ὑπερήσπισε, it seems appropriate to assume Peucestes used his own shield to protect Alexander, but Arr. *An.* 6.10.2 explicitly states that Peucestes used Alexander's (sacred) shield that he had taken at Ilium.
   [129] Diodorus is probably referring here (mistakenly) to the 20,000 foot and 3,000 horse killed by the soldiers of Peithon, referred to in 18.4.8, 7.1–9; Curt. 9.7.11, though, states the (former) settlers finally made a safe journey to Greece.
   [130] Curt. 9.7.12–15 reports that the banquet was held in honour of Mallian and Sydracian envoys coming to surrender themselves to Alexander; Arr. *An.* 6.14.1 confirms these envoys came and surrendered.

(17.101.1) ... (2) ... (3) ... (4) ... (5) ... (6) ... [[In the paragraphs I have left out, Diodorus tells the story of the single combat between the Macedonian Coragus and the Greek Dioxippus, the Macedonian's defeat, and the subsequent fall of Dioxippus.]]
(17.102.1) Alexander gave orders to the army to march beside the river and escort the ships, but he himself, resuming his river voyage in the direction of the ocean, sailed down to the country of the people called Sambastians.[131] (2) These, in numbers of men and in *aretae*, were inferior to none of the Indian tribes. Living in cities governed in a democratic manner[132] and learning of the arrival of the Macedonians, they assembled soldiers: sixty thousand infantry, six thousand cavalry, and five hundred chariots. (3) When the fleet put in to them, they sent out fifty of their leading citizens as envoys, begging Alexander to treat them kindly, because they were amazed at the strange and unanticipated manner of the fleet's arrival and trembling at the great reputation of the Macedonians, because, moreover, their own older men advised them not to risk a fight. (4) Praising them and agreeing to a peace, the king was showered with both large gifts and heroic honours by the natives. Next Alexander received the submission of those who dwelt on either side of the river, who were called Sodrians and Massanians.[133] In this region he built a city, Alexandria by the river, selecting ten thousand inhabitants.[134] (5) Next, coming to the country of King Musicanus, taking him prisoner, he both killed him and made the tribe subject.[135] Thereafter, invading the kingdom of Porticanus,[136] he took two cities by storm

---

[131] Curt. 9.8.4–7 calls them 'Sabarcians'. Arr. *An*. 6.15.1–4, however, provides us with different names and events. It seems impossible to reconcile both traditions. See also Goukowsky 2002a: 139 and note 1.

[132] Probably merely indicating they were not governed by a king, as Curt. 9.8.4 observes: see Goukowsky 2002a: 139–40 and note 2.

[133] The Sodrians of Diodorus may well be identical with the Sogdians of Arr. *An*. 6.15.4. Arrian does not refer to the Massanians.

[134] This seems not to be Alexandria on the Indus, founded in February 325 on the confluence of the Indus and the Acesines (Chenab) (see also Curt. 9.8.8 and Arr. *An*. 6.15.2, and Goukowsky 2002a: 140 and note 1), probably on the site of an older, Persian settlement, modern Uch in Pakistan, which was settled with Thracian veterans and natives. It had large dockyards, which suggests that it was meant as a commercial centre. The settlement discussed here was probably a temporary military station north of modern Rohri.

[135] Apparently a condensation of events. Arr. *An*. 6.15.5–7, 17.1–2, relates them more elaborately: at first Musicanus came and gave presents to Alexander, but revolted later, a revolt quenched by Pithon. Musicanus was hanged in his own country, together with the Brahmins who had instigated the revolt. Curt. 9.8.8–10, 16 speaks of a tribe called Musicani (perhaps identical with the Mūshikas of the *Mahābhārāta*) and somewhat later mentions that it had revolted. The region is also mentioned by Str. 15.1.34/701–2, providing some of its peculiarities, on the basis of an account by Onesicritus (= *FGrH/BNJ* 134 F 24). See also Goukowsky 2002a: 259 *ad* 102.4, second remark.

[136] See also Curt. 9.8.11–12. Arr. *An*. 6.16.1–2 mentions this king as 'Oxicanus'.

From Persepolis to Babylon 363

and, after allowing the soldiers to plunder the houses, set them on fire. Porticanus himself, who had escaped to a stronghold, Alexander killed, still fighting, after capturing the stronghold. Having taken all the cities subordinated to Porticanus, he destroyed them and induced much fear among the neighbouring tribes. (6) Next, he ravaged the kingdom of Sambus and, after enslaving and destroying most of the cities, he killed more than eighty thousand of the natives.[137] (7) He inflicted a similar disaster upon the tribe of the Brahmins, as they are called. When the survivors came supplicating him with branches, having punished the guiltiest, he freed them of charges. King Sambus, fleeing with thirty elephants into the country beyond the Indus, escaped the danger.

(17.103.1) Because the last city of the Brahmins, which they called Harmatelia,[138] was proud of the valour of its inhabitants and of the rough ground around it, Alexander sent a limited number of light troops with orders to engage the enemy and retire if they came out against them. (2) These, five hundred in number and assaulting the walls, were despised by the Brahmins. When three thousand soldiers issued out of the city, Alexander's light-armed troops started to flee, pretending to be frightened. (3) Presently the king, launching an unexpected attack against the pursuing Brahmins and charging them furiously, killed some of the Brahmins, and captured others. Of the soldiers around the king many who had been wounded met a serious danger.[139] (4) For indeed, the weapons of the Brahmins had been smeared with a drug of mortal force, relying upon which they joined battle. The force of the drug was derived from certain snakes which were caught and killed and left in the sun. (5) When the heat melted the substance of the flesh, it started to liquefy and in this moisture the poison of the animals was secreted. That is why when a man was wounded, the body became immediately numb and sharp pains followed shortly after, and convulsions and shivering shook the whole frame and the skin became cold and livid and bile appeared in the vomit, while a black froth was exuded from the wound and gangrene set in. As this spread quickly and overran to the vital parts of the body, it brought a horrible death to the victim. (6) The same result occurred to those who had received large wounds and to those

---

[137] According to Curt. 9.8.15, this is the number mentioned by Clitarchus. For the Sambians, see also Goukowsky 2002a: 259–60 *ad* 102.6, first remark.

[138] In MSS RX the city is called Ἅρματα, as indeed in Steph.Byz.; the name of the inhabitants in 17.103.8, however, suggests Harmatelia (see MS F) is the correct name. See also Goukowsky 2002a: 260 *ad* 103.1, first remark.

[139] See also Goukowsky 1969: 320–7.

whose wounds were small, or even a mere scratch. As the wounded were dying in this fashion, the king was not so much concerned for the others, but he was distressed for Ptolemy, the future king [of Egypt], who was then greatly beloved. (7) In fact, something interesting and quite extraordinary occurred regarding Ptolemy, which some attributed to the providence of the gods. He was loved by all because of both his *aretē* and the extent of his kindness to all, and he obtained succour appropriate to his good deeds.[140] The king, indeed, saw a vision in his sleep, in which he believed he saw a snake carrying a plant in its mouth, and showing its nature and power and the place where it grew. (8) When Alexander awoke, seeking out the plant, and grinding it up, both plastering it on Ptolemy's body and giving it him to drink, he restored him to health.[141] Since the value of the remedy had been demonstrated, the rest also became well, having received the same therapy. Then Alexander prepared to attack and capture the city of the Harmatelians, which was strong and large, but when the inhabitants came to him with suppliant branches and handed themselves over, he spared them any punishment.

C. THE FINAL PHASE OF THE EXPEDITION

The army and fleet reach the ocean; fleet and army separate:
(17.104.1) After he himself had sailed downstream into the ocean with his companions and had discovered there two islands,[142] he performed magnificent sacrifices on them. He threw many large golden cups into the sea as he poured the libations from them and, after he had erected altars to Tethys and Oceanus, he judged that the projected campaign had come to an end. Setting sail from there,

---

[140] A similar eulogy on Ptolemy is rendered in Curt. 9.8.22–4. Goukowsky 2002a: 142 note 1 is convinced that Clitarchus is the source of the eulogy, showing Providence saved the future king of Egypt – a motive elaborated in Curt. 9.8.25–8 as well as in the sequel of Diodorus' account. Clitarchus was possibly a native of Egypt, or at least spent a considerable time at the court of Ptolemy *Lagides*. See also Prandi 2012 for arguments for a 'high' date for Clitarchus.

[141] This occurrence, seemingly attributing special powers to Alexander, is not mentioned by Arrian. We cannot be sure where Diodorus took it from, though Clitarchus might well come to mind as stated above, note 140. We do know that it is also related by Str. 15.2.7/723; Just. 12.10.3; and Curt. 9.8.22–7, who also explains the relationship between Alexander and Ptolemy. See also Goukowsky 1969: 320–1 note 5. In Goukowsky 2002a: 142 note 2, Goukowsky compares Alexander's dream with that of Pericles in which the goddess Athena led him to a cure, referring to Plu. *Per.* 13.13 and Plin. *Nat.* 22.44.

[142] Curt. 9.10.27 relates that Alexander proceeded about 400 *stadia* (c. 70 km) into the ocean to perform his offerings (see also Arr. *An.* 6.19.5). I believe, though I have no evidence to support my view, that this distance is exaggerated: even 40 stadia (c. 7 km) would have been an achievement. For Alexander's offering see also Ehrenberg 1933. See also Goukowsky 2002a: 260–1 *ad* 104.1, first remark.

he proceeded back up the river to Patala,[143] a remarkable city. (2) It had a political structure organised very much like that of Sparta. In fact, two kings from two houses succeeded in it, always being in command regarding the arrangements concerning war, but the magistracy of the elders was at the head of the whole.[144] (3) Alexander, thus, set fire to the damaged ones among his boats, but handing over the rest of the fleet to Nearchus and some others of his companions, he ordered them to coast along through the ocean and, having observed everything, to meet him at the mouth of the River Euphrates.[145] (4) Having collected his force, he traversed much territory and defeated his opponents, while he received kindly those who submitted. Indeed, he brought over without fight the so-called Arbitans and those who inhabited Gedrosia.[146] (5) Next traversing a long stretch of waterless and largely desert country, he reached the frontiers of Oritis.[147] Dividing his force into three parts, he appointed Ptolemy commander of the first, Leonnatus of the second. (6) He ordered Ptolemy to despoil the region along the sea, Leonnatus to lay waste the interior, but he himself devastated the upper country and the hills.[148] As at one and the same time much land was laid waste, every spot was filled with fire and devastation and great slaughter. (7) Therefore the soldiers soon mastered much booty, and the number of persons killed reached many myriads. All their neighbours, having become terrified by the destruction of these tribes, submitted to the king. (8) Alexander wanted to found a city by the sea and after he had found a sheltered mooring-place with suitable terrain nearby, he founded a city at it, Alexandria.[149]

---

[143] Though the MSS give different readings for the place, Fischer has rightly emended it into Patala. The location of the site is unknown. See Goukowsky 2002a: 261 *ad* 104.1, second remark.

[144] As Goukowsky 2002a: 143 note 1 observes, such comparisons largely go back to Onesicritus (see, for example, *FGrH/BNJ* 134 F 24 on Musicanus).

[145] The fleet under the command of Nearchus would be prevented from sailing due to the monsoon winds for several months: Engels 1978: 114. For Alexander's route and decisions, Engels 1978: 112–17 and 137–43 (largely confirming the observations of Stein 1943).

[146] See Goukowsky 2002a: 143–4 note 3. I opt for the consistent reading of Γεδρωσία; see MS F *ad* 17.105.3. I prefer the reading Arbitans on the basis of Ptol. *Geog.* 6.21.4: τὰ μὲν οὖν ἐπὶ θαλάσσῃ τῆς χώρας κατέχουσιν Ἀρβιτῶν κῶμαι ('in the region by the sea lie the villages of the Arbitans'). Goukowsky 2002a: 143–4 note 3 locates these villages near modern Karachi.

[147] See, for this conquest, the suggestions by Stein 1943 and the critical comments thereon, *inter alia* based upon Strabo, by Strasburger, 1954.

[148] The hills mentioned here probably formed part of the Kirthar Range, which forms the boundary between the Lower Indus Plain (east) and southern Baluchistan (west), Stein's Las Bela. It consists of a series of parallel rock hill ridges rising from c. 1,200 m in the south to nearly 2,500 m in the north. See also, for example, Lambrick 1964: 39–45.

[149] The site of this city has not yet been established with certainty. See also Arr. *An.* 6.21.5 and the comment by Brunt 1983: 164–5 note 5 that Diodorus 'must be wrong in attributing it to a sheltered harbour; none is mentioned in *Ind.* 23'. See also Curt. 9.10.7. The latter's remark

(17.105.1) Advancing into the country of the Oritans through the passes,[150] he quickly brought it all into submission. The Oritans have the same customs as the Indians in other respects, but one which is strange and quite unbelievable. (2) Indeed, naked and carrying spears, the relatives of the dead carry out the bodies. Placing the bodies in the thickets which exist in the country, they remove the clothing from them and leave the body as the prey of wild beasts. After dividing up the clothing of the dead, they sacrifice to the heroes of the nether world and organise a reception of the kinsmen.[151] (3) Next Alexander advanced into Gedrosia, marching to the side of the sea, and encountered a tribe unfriendly and utterly brutish. (4) Indeed, those who dwelt here both let their nails grow from birth to old age and also let their hair be compressed into felt. Their colour is burned black by the heat of the sun, and they clothe themselves in the skins of beasts. (5) They subsist by eating the flesh of stranded whales, and as regards their dwellings, they construct the walls of their houses from shells,[152] the roofs with whale's ribs, from which originate rafters eighteen cubits [c. 8.10 m] in length. In the place of tiles, they cover their roofs with the scales of these beasts.

Alexander's troops enter a desert; narrow escape:
(6) Having passed through this territory with difficulty because of the shortage of provisions, Alexander entered a region which was desert, and lacking in everything which could be used to sustain life. Because many died of hunger not only was the army of the Macedonians disheartened,[153] but also Alexander fell into no ordinary grief and anxiety. Indeed, it seemed a dreadful thing that those

---

on the settlers of this city (*dedvctique svnt in eam [vrbem] Arachosii* ('he [Alexander] colonised it [the city] with Arachosians')) may well refer to the fact that both Oritis and Gedrosia were governed by the satrap of Arachosia from 325/4 onwards (see also Goukowsky 2002a: 262 *ad* 104.8). Arrian attributes the actual responsibility for the construction of the city to Leonnatus: Arr. *An.* 6.22.3.

[150] Goukowsky 2002a: 144 note 1 makes it clear that Diodorus' phrase here indicates that Alexander, travelling from Sind (Hyderabad) to Baluchistan (Las Bela), took the road through the mountains.

[151] Only Diodorus describes the funerary rites of the Oritans. For this tribe, see Stein 1939. See also Goukowsky 2002a: 262 *ad* 105.2.

[152] Fischer suggests this emendation on the basis of Arrian's account (Arr. *An.* 6.23.3), even though it appears that Diodorus may have opted for another material, possibly something whale-related. Diodorus' account is more or less likely on the basis of Nearchus' account (see Str. 15.2.1/720). See also Goukowsky 2002a: 263 *ad* 105.3, second remark. As a matter of fact, proper whales do not have scales.

[153] See Curt. 9.10.13: *famem deinde pestilentia secvta est ... et nec manere sine clade nec progredi poterant* ('next pestilence followed hunger ... and they could neither remain without mortal danger nor advance'). Diodorus' account is quite condensed and frugal compared with Rufus'.

From Persepolis to Babylon 367

who had overcome everyone in *aretē* and in arms should perish ingloriously, being in want of everything in a desert country. (7) Therefore he sent out swift messengers into Parthyaea, Drangia, and Aria and the other areas bordering on the desert, ordering these to bring racing camels and other animals, trained to carry burdens, quickly to the gates of Carmania, after loading them with food and other necessities.[154] (8) These messengers, having hurried to the satraps of these provinces, caused many supplies to be transported to the specified place. Alexander lost many of his soldiers, nevertheless, first because of shortages that were not relieved, and then at a later stage of this march, when some of the Oritans attacked those assigned to Leonnatus and fled to their own country after shooting down many.

Alexander celebrates the crossing of the desert; fleet and army shortly meet:
(17.106.1) So, having passed through the desert with great difficulty, he came into a prosperous[155] country provided with everything needful. After resting his army here, he proceeded with his troops in festive dress for seven days.[156] He himself led a procession for Dionysus, feasting and using strong drink and wine during the journey.[157] (2) After this party was over, having learned that many of his satraps and commanders had violated the law by using their power forcibly and insolently, he punished them.[158] As the word spread of his righteous indignation against his offending subordinates, many of the commanders recalled acts of insolence or illegality which they had performed and became alarmed. Some, who had mercenary troops, revolted against the king; others fled after packing up sums

---

[154] From a geographical point of view probably not a very likely solution to Alexander's direct needs. See Welles 1970: 426–7 note 1.
[155] For this translation of χώρα οἰκουμένα see Stronk 1995: 11, 81. According to Curt. 9.10.18 this country was Gedrosia.
[156] Goukowsky 2002a: 263 *ad* 106.1 states that this happened at Pura, the capital of Gedrosia. Arrian, however, notes that Alexander later celebrated a feast in Carmania, the Σωτήρια, with offerings in honour of several gods, including Apollo *Alexikakos* ('averter of evil'; see Arr. *Ind.* 36.3). Though it may have been celebrated primarily because of the reunion with the fleet under Nearchus, it seems reasonable to surmise that on that occasion Alexander's safe arrival from the desert was (once more) commemorated. My translation is, to some extent, dictated by the data provided by Curt. 9.10.27 and Plu. *Alex.* 67.1.
[157] See Curt. 9.10.21, 24–8, and Plu. *Alex.* 67.1–3 on this celebration, which took place in Carmania. Arr. *An.* 6.28.1–2 states that he does not believe the story and that neither Aristobulus nor Ptolemy relates it. Badian, though, believes these celebrations did take place: Badian 1958: 152. See also Carystius of Pergamum, quoted by Ath. 10.434F.
[158] Being not really straightforward, the sentence as it is has provoked many emendations. So far no one of these, however, is really convincing. For Alexander's measures see Curt. 9.10.20–1, 10.1.1–9; Just. 12.10.8; Plu. *Alex.* 68.2–4; Arr. *An.* 6.27.1–5.

of money. (3) After learning these things, the king wrote to all commanders and satraps throughout Asia to disband all mercenaries immediately, as soon as they had read his letter. (4) As the king was resting in a city, by the name of Salmus, by the sea at this moment and was holding a dramatic contest in the theatre, those sent to sail the coast of the ocean put in and, going directly to the theatre, greeted Alexander and reported what they had done.[159] (5) Being delighted at the arrival of the men, the Macedonians welcomed the occurrence with loud applause and the whole theatre was filled with unsurpassable delight. (6) The seafarers told how they had encountered astonishing tides in the ocean, and that at low tide many large and unsuspected islands appeared along the coast, but that at high tide all the aforementioned places were flooded over,[160] as a copious and strong current bore in towards the land, while the surface of the water was white with much foam; but that the most astonishing thing was to encounter many incredibly big whales. (7) That they had been terrified, at first, and despaired of their lives, thinking that they would be dashed to pieces immediately, ships and all. But that, when they all shouted in unison, beating upon their shields to make a great din, and the *salpinxes* were blown loudly in addition, the beasts were alarmed by the strange noise and plunged into the depths.

(17.107.1) After the king had listened to the end to their story about these events, he ordered his captains of the fleet to sail on to the Euphrates, but he, having gone through a vast area with his force, came to the frontier of Susis. About this time the Indian Calanus,[161] who had advanced far in philosophy and was highly regarded by Alexander, put a remarkable end to his life. (2) ... (3) ... (4) ... (5) ... [[Tells how Calanus committed (assisted) suicide.]]

Events at Susa; developments in Asia:
(6) The king gave Calanus a magnificent funeral and after he had proceeded to Susa, he married Stateira, the elder daughter of Darius, and gave her younger sister Drypetis as wife to Hephaestion.

---

[159] See Arr. *An.* 6.28.5–6, *Ind.* 33.5–35.8; Curt. 10.1.10; Plu. *Alex.* 68.1. The location of Salmus has not (yet) been identified (see Goukowsky 2002a: 264 *ad* 106.2, first remark), but if we may believe Nearchus, *FGrH/BNJ* 133 F 1, the city was situated five days' march from the sea, not by the sea.

[160] The description appears to match that of mangrove banks: see Str. 16.3.6/766–7; Nearchus *FGrH/BNJ* 133 F 27 and F 34 with commentaries.

[161] Though all MSS of Diodorus read here as well as elsewhere Κάρανος, I have followed Goukowsky's emendation and opt for Κάλανος: see Goukowsky 2002a: 264–5 *ad* 107.1 for his motives.

From Persepolis to Babylon 369

He persuaded the most prominent of his companions to marry as well, and gave them in marriage the noblest Persian ladies.[162] (17.108.1) About this time a body of thirty thousand Persians came to Susa, certainly very young of age, selected for the grace and strength of their bodies.[163] (2) Having been enrolled in compliance with certain orders of the king, having been taught under supervisors and teachers of the arts of war for as long as necessary, all splendidly equipped with the full Macedonian armament, they made camp before the city and, after demonstrating to the king their skill and discipline in the use of their weapons, received an exceptional reward. (3) Because the Macedonians had, in fact, not only mutinied against the crossing of the River Ganges,[164] but were frequently unruly when called to assembly,[165] and ridiculed his descent from Ammon,[166] Alexander set up this unit from a single age-group of the Persians, constituted homogeneously, able to become a counterbalance to the Macedonian phalanx. These were the concerns of Alexander. (4) Though Harpalus had been given the custody of the treasury in Babylon and of the revenues which accrued to it, he assumed, that as soon as the king had set out on expedition to India, Alexander would never come back.[167] Giving himself up to comfortable living, though he had been appointed as satrap of a great country,[168] he first occupied himself with the abuse of women and illegitimate amours with the natives and squandered much of the treasure under his control on extremely immoderate pleasure. Fetching a great quantity of fish all the long way from the Persian Gulf and introducing an extravagant way of life, he came under general criticism. (5) Later, moreover,

---

[162] See Curt. 10.3.11–12; Just. 12.10.9–10; Plu. *Alex.* 70.2; Arr. *An.* 7.4.4–8. Plu. *De Alex. Fort.* 329E reports there were 100 couples. Both Justin and Plutarch state that Alexander married Stateira, but Arrian mentions it was Barsine and Parysatis as well (allegedly on the basis of Aristobulus' account (= *FGrH/BNJ* 139 F 52)). The latter marriage is described in Ath. 12.538B–539A, taken from Chares of Mytilene's account (= *FGrH/BNJ* 125 F 4). Altogether, as Arr. *An.* 7.4.8 reports, over 10,000 Macedonians had married Asian women.
[163] Mentioned by other authors as well: Arr. *An.* 7.6.1 also refers to these *Epigoni*, as Alexander called them, as does Plu. *Alex.* 71.1, having already preluded the occurrence in describing events in Hyrcania in 330 (Plu. *Alex.* 47.3), something Curt. 8.5.1 does while accounting for the organisation of Alexander's force in Bactria in 327.
[164] Though, as Goukowsky 2002a: 149 note 1 underlines, most people in Diodorus' age believed that Alexander had advanced as far as the Ganges, the soldiers in fact had (already) refused to cross the River Hyphasis (see above, 17.93.1, 94.5).
[165] For such behaviour, see Plb. 5.27.6. Also Granier 1931: 17.
[166] For these insults, see Arr. *An.* 7.8.3; Just. 12.11.6.
[167] Though the story of Harpalus was well known (see Plu. *Alex.* 41.4, *Phoc.* 21–2, *Dem.* 25–6.3; Just. 13.5.9), only Curt. 10.2.1–3 relates it, like Diodorus, here.
[168] We have no evidence Harpalus really had been officially appointed as a satrap, but his function as keeper of the treasure may have included this role, formally or not: see Goukowsky 2002a: 265–6 *ad* 108.4, second remark.

he sent for the most dazzling of the courtesans from Athens by the name of Pythionice.[169] When she was alive he presented her with gifts worthy of a queen, and after she died he gave her a magnificent funeral and had a costly grave monument erected in Attica.[170] (6) After that, having sent for another Attic courtesan by the name of Glycera, he entertained her in exceeding luxury and with extravagant customs. Providing a shelter, with an eye on the uncertainties of Fate, he did good services to the *demos* of the Athenians. When Alexander after his return from India put many of the satraps who had been charged to death, Harpalus, fearing the punishment and grabbing up five thousand talents of silver [c. 125,000 kg], departed from Asia and sailed across to Attica, after enrolling six thousand mercenaries. (7) Because no one there accepted him,[171] he shipped his troops off to Taenarum in Laconia, but he, keeping some of the money with him, became a supplicant of the Athenian *demos*. As his surrender was asked for by Antipater and Olympias, he stole away, though he had distributed large sums of money to those persons who spoke in his favour, and came down to Taenarum to join his mercenaries. (8) Having sailed from there to Crete, he was murdered by Thibron, one of his friends. Investigating the account of Harpalus' funds, the Athenians convicted Demosthenes and some other *rhetors* of having profited from Harpalus' money.

Events in Greece; further developments in Asia:
(17.109.1) While the Olympic Games were being celebrated,[172] Alexander had it proclaimed in Olympia that all exiles should return to their cities, except those who had been charged with sacrilege or murder.[173] Having selected the oldest of his soldiers who were

---

[169] Though Diodorus refers to her as Pythonice, I have emended this on the basis of, *inter alia*, her name as rendered in Athenaeus. Both she and Glycera feature in Ath. 13.586C, 595A–F, referring to Theopompus and Clitarchus. For courtesans (*hetaerae*) see, for example, Stronk, *BNJ* 171, F 2a with literature. For Pythionice see also Ziegler 1963; for Glycera: *RE* Suppl. III, *s.v.* 'Glykera [3]'. It was she who mediated between Harpalus and the city of Athens to make him send there the corn that earned him Athenian citizenship: Badian 1998; 1961: 24. See also Goukowsky 2002a: 266 *ad* 108.6.

[170] My translation is based, apart from on the Greek (which is slightly ambivalent here), also upon the description of Athenaeus. There it can be read that Harpalus, next to the grave in Babylon, erected a monument (a cenotaph) in Attica: it would have been situated on the Sacred Way between Athens and Eleusis (see McClure 2003, for example, pp. 146–8, in which is referred to Theopompus' *Letter to Alexander* (Theopomp. *FGrH/BNJ* 115 F 253 = Ath. 13.595AB)). See also Paus. 1.37.5; Plu. *Phoc.* 22.2.

[171] The presence of 6,000 mercenaries would have constituted an unacceptable disruption of the equilibrium of power within the city. See also Goukowsky 2002a: 150–1 note 1.

[172] Namely those of 324, celebrated in our months of July or August.

[173] For this announcement and its context see also 18.8.2–6.

Macedonians,[174] he released them from service, ten thousand in number. (2) Having learned that many of them were in debt, he paid their obligations, which were little short of ten thousand talents [60,000,000 *drachmae*], in a single day. Because the Macedonians who remained with him were becoming insubordinate and interrupted him by shouting during the assembly, he boldly denounced them because he was infuriated. Having cowed the throng, having leaped down from the platform, he undertook to hand over the ringleaders of the tumult with his own hands to his attendants for punishment. (3) As this augmented the hostility even more, the king appointed captains from the selected Persians and advanced them to the first rank. Repentant and begging in tears, the Macedonians with difficulty persuaded Alexander to take them back into favour.[175]

(17.110.1) When Anticles was *archon* at Athens [325/4], the Romans installed as consuls Lucius Cornelius and Quintus Popillius.[176] In their term of office Alexander supplemented his army with Persians equal to the number of those he had dismissed, assigned a thousand of them to the bodyguards stationed at the court,[177] and altogether trusted them no less than the Macedonians. (2) Around this time Peucestes arrived as well, with twenty thousand Persian bowmen and slingers. After mixing those with the soldiers already at his disposal, Alexander created by the novelty of this innovation in his whole army a mixture, blended and adjusted to his own idea. (3) Since there were by now sons of the Macedonians born of captive women, he determined the exact number of these. As they were in number about ten thousand, having set aside for all of them suitable arrangements for an upbringing proper for freeborn children, he assigned them teachers to give them their proper training. He himself marched with his force from Susa and after crossing the Tigris, he pitched camp in the villages called Carian.[178] (4) Thence, marching for four days through Sittacene,[179] he came to the place called

---

[174] Diodorus uses the word πολῖται, 'citizens', but the context makes it clear that he intended Macedonians serving as soldiers in his army: see also *LSJ*, *s.v.* 'πολίτης' *ad* II.

[175] For this substantial mutiny, also recorded in our other sources, see Goukowsky 2002a: 267 *ad* 109.2, second remark. See Arr. *An.* 7.11.1–8; Plu. *Alex.* 71.3–5; Just. 12.12.1–6.

[176] The consuls intended are L. Cornelius Lentulus and Q. Publilius Philo, consuls for 327 VC (see Broughton 1951: 145). Diodorus is here three years ahead of the Varronian chronology.

[177] Goukowsky, in my opinion rightly, surmises that Diodorus confounds here two series of events: see Goukowsky 2002a: 267 *ad* 110.1.

[178] These Carian villages were probably established when Darius I settled the Milesians in Mesopotamia: see Hdt. 6.20; also Goukowsky 2002a: 268 *ad* 110.3, second remark.

[179] Sittacene is an emendation by Wesseling after 17.65.2. The MSS read here Σίτταν (RX) or Σίττα (F). See also Plin. *Nat.* 6.31.132.

Sambana. Remaining there for seven days and, after proceeding with his force, he came on the third day to the Celonans, as they are called, in which region dwells down to our time a Boeotian clan, who were moved in the time of Xerxes' campaign, but still have not forgotten their ancestral customs. (5) They are bilingual and speak like the natives in the one language, while in the other they preserve most of the Greek vocabulary, and they maintain some Greek practices.[180] After a stay of ... days,[181] he resumed his march and, having left the beaten track for sightseeing, he entered the region called Bagistane [Behistun aka Bisitun], which is a magnificent country covered with fruit trees and all other things one needs for good living. (6) Next he arrived in a land that could support enormous herds of horses, in which of old they say that there were one hundred and sixty thousand horses grazing, but at the time of Alexander's visit they could count only sixty thousand.[182] Having stayed there for thirty days, he arrived in Ecbatana of Media on the seventh day. (7) They say that its circuit is two hundred and fifty *stadia* [c. 46 km], that it contains the main palace of Media, and treasuries with great wealth. Refreshing his force for some time here, he organised both a dramatic festival and constant drinking-bouts among his companions. (8) In the course of these, Hephaestion, having drunk excessively and fallen ill, died.[183] Being intensely grieved at this occurrence, the king entrusted the body of the deceased to Perdiccas to conduct it to Babylon, intending to celebrate a magnificent funeral for him.
(17.111.1) As these events took place, disturbances and revolutionary movements erupted throughout Greece, from which the so-called Lamian War evolved, for the following reason.[184] Because Alexander

---

[180] Possibly the Eretrians of whom Hdt. 6.119 mentions that they had been deported by Darius I, though these had been reallocated nearer to Susa according to him, or, nearer to Diodorus' observation, the descendants of 400 Thebans who had been with Leonidas at Thermopylae, though apparently not actively fighting; there is, though, no reference known to me that these men had been deported by Xerxes (see Hdt. 7.233) as Cozzoli 1958 appears to believe.

[181] The numeral is missing in this sentence. As the narrative of Q. Curtius Rufus (which most resembles Diodorus' account) is missing here (down to the death of Alexander), no realistic emendation can be suggested.

[182] The region intended appears to have been Nesaea (Nysa, OP *nēsāya) in Media. The number of horses varies slightly in our sources: Arr. *An*. 7.13.1 mentions 150,000 mares there formerly, against 50,000 in Alexander's days (see also, for example, Hdt. 3.106 and Luc. *Hist. Conscr.* 39 for the reputation of these horses).

[183] Plu. *Alex*. 72.1–2 remarks that Hephaestion died because he had not observed the regime prescribed by his physician. See also Arr. *An*. 7.14.1–4; Just. 12.12.11 remains largely silent about the cause of Hephaestion's death.

[184] Diodorus' story here is quite condensed. Mitchel 1964: 16, who believes there is good reason to trust Diodorus' overall story on this issue, summarises Diodorus' account (17.110.1–18.9.5) of the events. Goukowsky 2002a: 153 note 2 believes the prime motive for

From Persepolis to Babylon 373

had ordered all his satraps to disband their mercenaries and they complied with his instruction, all Asia was overrun with soldiers released from service and supplying themselves with the necessary food by plunder. Afterwards they began to assemble from all directions at Taenarum in Laconia. (2) Simultaneously the escapees of the Persian satraps and the other commanders, having collected both funds and soldiers, also sailed for Taenarum and started to assemble a joint force. (3) Ultimately they chose as supreme commander Leosthenes of Athens, a man of unusually brilliant mind and thoroughly opposed to Alexander's cause. He conferred secretly with the *boulē* at Athens and received fifty talents for mercenary wages and an amount of arms sufficient to meet pressing needs. Moreover, he negotiated through ambassadors with the Aetolians, who were unfriendly to the king, regarding an alliance, and prepared everything for war. (4) Leosthenes was, therefore, occupied with such matters, foreseeing the greatness of the conflict. Alexander, though, with a mobile force made an expedition against the Cosseans [Kassites] because they would not submit to him. This tribe, outstanding in valour, inhabits the mountains of Media, relying upon the ruggedness of their country and their *aretae* in war.[185] It had never accepted a foreign master, but had even remained unconquered throughout the Persian kingdom, and at this time had become presumptuous, undeterred by the *aretē* of the Macedonians. (5) Having taken possession of the access routes, ravaging most of Cossea [modern Khūzestān], being superior in every engagement, the king killed many of the Cosseans and captured many times more. Being utterly defeated and distressed at the number of their captives, the Cosseans were forced to exchange the recovery of the prisoners for submission. (6) Placing themselves and their goods, therefore, in the hands of the king, they were granted peace on condition that they should do as the king ordered. Having conquered this tribe in forty days in total and having founded strong cities in the mountainous terrain,[186] Alexander rested his army.

Athens to act as it did was the edict of Alexander regarding the return of the exiles, which would imply for Athens the loss of Samos. For Athens this may have been the main motive, but I am not sure about the reasons for the others to go to war.
[185] This expedition, executed as it appears in winter, against the people in the Zagros Mountains, was a strategic masterpiece, even if it did not last, as the adversity of Antigonus *Monophthalmus* in this region suggests (see 19.19.4–8).
[186] Goukowsky 2002a: 154 note 2 remarks that these cities had disappeared when the army of Antigonus *Monophthalmus* crossed the Zagros Mountains. He presumes the cities were actually fortified camps.

S. 122:
17.112.1–118.4:

Alexander continues his march to Babylon:
(17.112.1) [When ... was *archon* at Athens, the Romans installed as consuls Lucius Cornelius Lentlus and Quintus Popillius.[187] In their term of office] Alexander, after the conclusion of his war with the Cosseans, moved off with his force and marched towards Babylon. He marched at his ease, interrupting the march frequently and resting the army. (2) While he was still three hundred *stadia* [c. 55 km] from the city, the so-called Chaldeans,[188] who have gained a very great reputation in astrology and are accustomed to predict the future through a perpetual surveillance, chose from their number the eldest and most experienced to read the king's horoscope.[189] Knowing through the configuration of the stars that the king's coming death would occur in Babylon, they instructed their representatives to make known to the king the danger and exhort him in no way to make his entry into the city. (3) They said that he could escape the danger if he re-erected the tomb of Belus [Marduk] which had been demolished by the Persians and would bypass the city, abandoning his intended route.[190] The leader of the Chaldean envoys, whose name was Belephantes,[191] did not dare to address the king directly through fear, but securing a private audience with Nearchus, one of Alexander's companions, and informing him in

---

[187] In the MSS we may surmise a lacuna in the archetype, suggested by both the abrupt ending of *caput* 17.111 and the beginning of *caput* 17.112 (starting with the formula where the *archon*'s name is missing and the names of the consuls are repeated from 17.110.1, but with the addition of a *cognomen*, Lentlus, in the name of L. Cornelius). See, however, Perl 1957: 108, who states this was a pseudo-year, inserted by some interpolator. Nevertheless, I have adapted the translation as much as possible to resemble the MS structure, even if fraudulent.

[188] For Chaldea and the Chaldeans see above, Chapter 2, note 85.

[189] Van der Spek discusses an omen from the so-called 29th *ahû* tablet of *Enūma Anu Enlil*, announcing the end of Darius III's reign after the moon's eclipse of 20 September 331. It predicted the victory of an intruder from the west, the escape of Darius III to the east, and that the intruder was expected to rule for eight years (Van der Spek 2003: 294–5). Alexander's return to Babylon more or less coincided with the end of the predicted period of his eight years' rule. See also, in the same paper, pp. 297–9 for text and comments, pp. 332–40 for a discussion on the Chaldeans' position as regards Alexander.

[190] Arr. *An.* 7.17.1–4 paints a different picture, stating that Alexander contemplated entering the city and rebuilding the temple of Bel/Marduk (allegedly razed by Xerxes, although such a destruction is supported by neither cuneiform or archaeological evidence, nor by Herodotus; see Kuhrt and Sherwin-White 1987), but that the Chaldeans wished to prevent such an occurrence, because they received the surplus revenues of the god as long as the temple was not reconstructed, and wanted this to continue. See also Goukowsky 2002a: 271 *ad* 112.3, first remark.

[191] Known from the so-called Babylonian astronomical diaries as Bêl-apla-iddin (^{md}EN-A-MU): see, for example, Boiy 2004: 298; also Van der Spek 2003: 333.

detail, asked him to make it known to the king.¹⁹² (4) Hearing about the Chaldeans' prophecy from Nearchus, Alexander was alarmed, and the more he reflected upon the ability and reputation of these men the more his mind was stirred up. Finally, sending the majority of his companions to the city, he avoided Babylon, altering his own route, and paused, having pitched camp at a distance of two hundred *stadia* [c. 37 km].¹⁹³ Because everyone was astonished, many of the Greeks came to him, including among the philosophers Anaxarchus and his entourage.¹⁹⁴ (5) Discovering the reason for his decision and effectively using arguments drawn from philosophy,¹⁹⁵ they changed him to the extent that he despised all prophetic arts, especially that which was held in high regard by the Chaldeans. Therefore the king, as though he had been wounded in his soul and healed by the words of the philosophers, entered Babylon with his force. (6) Because the inhabitants, as before,¹⁹⁶ received the soldiers hospitably, all turned their attention to relaxation and pleasure, since everything necessary was available in profusion. These were the events of this year.

Alexander's stay in Babylon; he receives various embassies:
(17.113.1) When Agesias was *archon* at Athens [324/3], the Romans installed as consuls Gaius Publius and Papirius, and the one hundred and fourteenth celebration of the Olympic Games took place, in which Micinas of Rhodes won the *stadium* race.¹⁹⁷ About then came ambassadors from practically all the inhabited world, some congratulating Alexander on his successes, some bringing him crowns, others concluding treaties of friendship and alliance, many bringing handsome presents, some to defend themselves against accusations. (2) In fact, apart from the tribes and cities as well as the local rulers

---

¹⁹² Though Aristobulus (*FGrH/BNJ* 139 F 54) states that the Chaldeans addressed Alexander directly, a version rendered by Arr. *An.* 7.16.5 and Just. 12.13.3, who calls them '*Magi*', Goukowsky 2002a: 271 *ad* 112.3, second remark, believes it feasible that Nearchus was indeed the intermediary.

¹⁹³ Arr. *An.* 7.17.5-6 reports that, according to Aristobulus, Alexander did, after all, want to avoid Babylon, but could not pass it due to the marshes and pools surrounding the city.

¹⁹⁴ Anaxarchus of Abdera was a Greek philosopher of the school of Democritus. Together with Pyrrho of Elis, another philosopher, he accompanied Alexander the Great into Asia. The reports of their philosophical views (*inter alia* preserved in D.L. 9.58-108) suggest that they were forerunners of the Greek sceptics.

¹⁹⁵ The main lines of the arguments are rendered by Just. 12.13.5.

¹⁹⁶ Described above, 17.64.4.

¹⁹⁷ The name of the *archon* was Hegesias (see *SEG* 21:292.1, 32:88.1, both elaborating on *IG* II² 547). The consuls of 326 vc were C. Poetelius Libo Visolus and L. Papirius Cursor (see Broughton 1951: 146). MSS of Eus. *Chron.* 205 give the name of the victor of the *stadium* race as Macinnas of Rhodes. The events described actually took place from the spring of 323 onwards, the Olympic Games, however, in the summer of 324: in total, Diodorus' chronology is somewhat confused, here. Diodorus is three years ahead of the Varronian chronology.

of Asia, many of their counterparts in Europe and Libya put in an appearance. From Libya came Carthaginians and Libyphoenicians[198] and all those who inhabit the coast as far as the Pillars of Heracles. From Europe both the Greek cities and the Macedonians sent embassies, as well as the Illyrians and most of those who dwell about the Adriatic Sea, the Thracian tribes and the neighbouring Celts, whose race then first became known in the Greek world.[199] (3) With a list of the embassies, Alexander scheduled to whom he would reply first and then the others in sequence. First he transacted business with those who came on matters concerning religion; second with those who brought gifts; next with those who had disputes with their neighbours; fourth with those who had problems concerning themselves alone; and fifth with those who wished to present arguments against the return of the exiles. (4) He dealt with the Eleans first; then with the Ammonians, the Delphians, and the Corinthians; next with the Epidaurians and the rest, receiving their petitions in the order of the sanctuaries' reputation. Being eager to give gratifying replies, he sent everyone away content, to the best of his ability.

Alexander's stay in Babylon; the funeral of Hephaestion:
(17.114.1) After dismissing the embassies, he occupied himself with the burial of Hephaestion.[200] He showed such zeal about the care of the funeral that it not only surpassed all those previously celebrated throughout the world, but also left no way for future generations to exceed it. He did so because he had loved Hephaestion most of the group of reputed companions, and after Hephaestion's death he honoured him unsurpassably. During Hephaestion's lifetime, Alexander had preferred him above all the companions, even though Craterus had a rivalling friendship. (2) Indeed, when one of the companions said that Craterus was loved no less than Hephaestion, Alexander had answered that Craterus was, in fact, king-loving, but Hephaestion

---

[198] A term Diodorus elaborates in 20.55.4 as people settled along the Libyan coast and intermarrying with the Carthaginians, carrying this name because of the interwoven ties of kinship. Arr. *An.* 7.15.4 doubts as regards a Carthaginian embassy.

[199] Plin. *Nat.* 3.5.57 states that Clitarchus reports that Rome would also have sent an embassy (*FGrH/BNJ* 137 F 31), but Arr. *An.* 7.15.5–6 (who also mentions other historians mentioning such an event) strongly doubts, with arguments, such an embassy. As regards the Celts, Arr. *An.* 7.15.4 links them with the Iberians, suggesting they were Celts from Spain and/or southern France, known to the Greeks since the times of Dionysius the Elder (see 15.70.1), whereas Diodorus places them in a Danubian context, apparently unknown to the Greeks, according to him. See, however, Theopomp. Hist., *FGrH/BNJ* 115 F 40; Polyaen. 7.42. I find Goukowsky's comment on this passage incomprehensible: Goukowsky 2002a: 272 *ad* 113.2.

[200] The story of Hephaestion's burial is lacking in the account of Q. Curtius Rufus. In the accounts of Arr. *An.* 7.14.8–10, Just. 12.12.12, and Plu. *Alex.* 72.2, though much briefer, it is placed in time before the Cossean expedition – if that is mentioned at all.

was Alexander-loving.[201] When the mother of Darius, at their first encounter, did obeisance to Hephaestion as if he were the king and was distressed after the recognition of her mistake, Alexander said: 'Never mind, mother. For actually he too is Alexander.' (3) Indeed, on the whole Hephaestion enjoyed so much power and freedom of speech on the basis of this friendship that, when Olympias was estranged from him because of jealousy and wrote sharp criticisms and threats against him in her letters, he felt strong enough to answer her reproachfully and ended his letter as follows: 'Stop quarrelling with us, do not be angry, and do not menace! If not, we shall not too greatly care. You know that Alexander is superior to everyone.' (4) Thus, as he prepared everything for the funeral, the king ordered the neighbouring cities to contribute to the splendour of the funeral to the best of their ability, and he proclaimed to all living throughout Asia that they should carefully quench the 'sacred fire', as the Persians call it, until such time as the funeral should be ended.[202] This the Persians were wont to do at the deaths of their kings. (5) The people, however, thought that the order was an ill omen, and that the godhead announced the king's death. There were also other strange signs pointing to the death of Alexander, which we will relate a little later, after we have finished the account of the funeral.

(17.115.1) In fact, as each of the generals and companions aimed at obsequiousness to the king[203] and made images of Hephaestion in ivory, gold, and other materials which men hold in high regard, Alexander, having collected artisans and an army of workmen, tore down the city wall to a distance of ten *stadia* [nearly 2 km]. Having collected the baked tiles from the wall and levelled off the place which was to receive the pyre,[204] he constructed a four-sided pyre, each side being a *stadium* [c. 185 m] in length. (2) Dividing up the area into thirty compartments and laying out the roofs upon the trunks of palm trees, he wrought the whole structure into a square.[205]

---

[201] Goukowsky rightly points out that in Macedonian military hierarchy Craterus was, after the death of Parmenion, Alexander's highest-ranking commander, but that Hephaestion, being the chiliarch, was the highest-ranking person after Alexander in the Persian court system adopted by Alexander: Goukowsky 2002a: 272 *ad* 114.2.
[202] See Goukowsky 2002a: 272–3 *ad* 114.4.
[203] For the atmosphere at Alexander's court at this period see, for example, Luc. *Cal.* 17–19.
[204] The Greek is a little ambiguous: πυρά can indicate a grave monument, a tumulus, as well as a pyre (see *LSJ* s.v. *ad* b). The phrasing of 18.4.2 suggests that the former option may well have been intended. Nevertheless, I have opted to follow the traditional lines more or less, and simply rendered it as 'pyre', but *with a neutral connotation*, as in the Greek. It should be noted, moreover, that no source indicates this pyre was lit, seemingly making the colloquial understanding of 'pyre' less likely.
[205] The exact meaning of Diodorus' account is slightly obscure, even though the gist seems more or less clear. See also Goukowsky 2002a: 159 note 1.

Then he applied a decoration to all the exterior walls, of which the golden prows of *pentereis*[206] filled up the foundation, two hundred and forty in number. Each of the cat-heads carried two kneeling archers four cubits [c. 1.80 m] in height, and small statues of armed men, five cubits [c. 2.30 m] high, while dark-red military cloaks made of felt filled the intervening spaces.[207] (3) Above these, torches fifteen cubits high [6.75 m] supported the second floor, with golden wreaths about their handles, perched eagles with outspread wings looking downward at their flaming ends, and serpents looking up at the eagles about their bases.[208] On the third level was carved a multitude of wild animals being pursued by hunters. (4) Next, the fourth level carried a *centauromachy* in gold, the fifth golden lions and bulls alternating. The next higher level was filled with Macedonian and Persian arms, the first testifying to the military prowess, the others to the defeats. On top of all stood Sirens, hollowed out and able to conceal the persons within, singing a dirge for the dead.[209] (5) The total height of the construction was more than one hundred and thirty cubits [c. 58.5 m]. On the whole, because all of the commanders, the soldiers, the envoys, and even the natives rivalled one another as regards the magnificence of the funeral, people say that the total expense came to over twelve thousand talents [72,000,000 Attic *drachmae*].[210] (6) In keeping with this magnificence and among the other marks of honour at the funeral, Alexander decreed that all should sacrifice to Hephaestion as a god coadjutor.[211] And truly, as Fate would have it, Philip, one of the companions, came with an oracle from Ammon to sacrifice to Hephaestion as a god.[212] Being,

---

[206] See above, Chapter 2, note 36, for the use of this word.
[207] For an altogether maritime interpretation of these decorations, see Goukowsky 2002a: 273 *ad* 115.2, fourth remark.
[208] See Goukowsky 2002a: 273 *ad* 115.3.
[209] For the interpretation of the decorations in this paragraph, see Goukowsky 2002a: 273 *ad* 115.4, first and second remarks.
[210] Just. 12.12.12 mentions the same amount, but both Arr. *An.* 7.14.8 and Plu. *Alex.* 72.3 refer to 10,000 talents. Costs for a burial in Greece ranged from 300 *drachmae* (see Lys. 31.21) to 2 *talents* (see D. 45.79), so the amount spent by Alexander seems by all accounts excessive and moreover hard to reconcile with the austerity (at Athens, at least) required by Demetrius of Phalerum, prohibiting extravagance in funerals (see Cic. *Leg.* 2.62–4). Of course, Solon's law applied to humans, not godlike creatures.
[211] Though all MSS read προέδρῳ, Luc. *Cal.* 17 makes clear that the correct reading should be παρέδρῳ.
[212] Both Lucian's paragraph, referred to in the preceding note, and other authors focus on this event: Just. 12.12.12 reports that Hephaestion was to be worshipped *ut devm* ('as a god'); according to Plu. *Alex.* 72.2, Ammon suggested Hephaestion should be honoured as ἥρως, a hero, just as Arr. *An.* 7.23.6 reports, after Ammon had first denied Hephaestion *divine* sacrifices (Arr. *An.* 7.14.7). This suggestion returns in a speech by Hyperides: καὶ [τ]οὺς <τού>των οἰκέτας ὥσπερ ἥρωας τιμᾶν ἡμᾶς ἀναγκαζομένους ('and forcing us to honour the slaves of their household as if they were heroes': Hyp. *Epit.* col. 8, ll. 22–4 [= 6.21]). Goukowsky

From Persepolis to Babylon 379

therefore, delighted at the fact that the god had ratified his own opinion, Alexander was the first to perform the sacrifice, and entertained everybody handsomely, offering ten thousand victims of all sorts in number.

Alexander's stay in Babylon; signs announce his death:
(17.116.1) When the king, after the funeral, turned to amusements and festivals, believing that he was at the peak of his power and good fortune, Destiny cut off the time of living allowed to him by nature. Straightway the divinity began to foretell his death, and many strange portents and signs occurred as well. (2) Indeed, once when the king's skin was being anointed with oil and the royal robe and diadem were lying on a chair, the feet of one of the natives who was kept in bonds were spontaneously freed from their fetters, and he escaped, unnoticed by his guards, through the doors of the palace with no one hindering. (3) Going to the royal throne and putting on the royal dress and the diadem, he seated himself upon the throne and remained quiet.[213] When he learned of this act, the king, being terrified at the odd event, walked to the throne and without showing his agitation asked the man quietly who he was and what he meant by doing this. (4) When the man made no reply whatsoever, Alexander referred the portent to the seers for interpretation and put the man to death in accordance with their judgement, in order to divert onto the man the trouble which was forecast.[214] Picking up the clothing and sacrificing to the gods who avert evil, he continued to be seriously troubled, recalled the prediction of the Chaldeans, and was angry with the philosophers who had persuaded him to enter Babylon. He was impressed anew with the Chaldeans' skill and their insight, and generally railed at those who used specious reasoning to argue away the power of Destiny. (5) A little while later heaven sent him a second portent about his death. Indeed, as he had conceived a desire to see the great swamp of Babylonia and had set sail with his friends in a number of skiffs, he was lost and alone for some days when his vessel became separated from the other ships, and consequently even gave up hope of his safe return. (6) Then, as his craft was proceeding through a narrow channel where the reeds grew thickly and overhung the water, when his diadem was caught and lifted from his head by one of those and then dropped into the swamp, one of the

---

surmises that the idea of the full deification of Hephaestion might go back to Clitarchus: see Goukowsky 2002a: 274–5 *ad* 115.6, first remark.
[213] For the meaning of thrones in Persian court etiquette see, for example, Hdt. 8.67.
[214] See for this episode the comment by Goukowsky 2002a: 276 *ad* 116.4.

oarsmen, swimming after it and wishing to return it safely, placed the diadem on his head and swam back to the boat.[215] (7) After three days and nights of wandering, Alexander found his way to safety, and, as he had again put on his diadem unexpectedly, he turned again to the soothsayers for the meaning of all this.

Alexander's stay in Babylon; his death and its aftermath:
(17.117.1) Though they bade him sacrifice to the gods on a grand scale and with all speed, he was then called away to one of his companions, Medius the Thessalian,[216] to take part in a revel. And there, as he drank much unmixed wine, having at the end filled a big Heraclean beaker,[217] he drained it at a draught. (2) Of a sudden he groaned aloud, howling exceedingly, as if struck by a violent blow, and he was taken away by his companions, who led him by the hand. His chamberlains put him to bed and attended him closely. (3) Because the pain increased and not one of the physicians who were summoned was able to be of any help, as he suffered in great distress and terrible pains, when he despaired of life, having taken off his ring he handed it to Perdiccas. (4) When his companions asked: 'To whom do you leave the kingdom?' he replied: 'To the best',[218] and he added – and these were his last words – that all of his foremost

---

[215] Arr. *An.* 7.22.4–5 reports various accounts, one supported by most Alexander historians telling that the swimmer got a reward of a talent for keenness, but was decapitated for lese-majesty; another by Aristobulus that the swimmer, a Phoenician sailor, got his reward of a talent but was flogged; yet another 'by some' that the diadem was retrieved by Seleucus, presaging both Alexander's death and Seleucus' ascent to power.

[216] Medius, the son of Oxythemis, was a native of Larissa in Thessaly and a companion of Alexander the Great. He is mentioned by Arr. *Ind.* 18 as commander of a *trieres* during the descent of the Indus, but his name does not occur further in Alexander's military operations. Nevertheless, he appears to have enjoyed great favour with the king. After Alexander's death, Medius followed the fortunes of Antigonus *Monophthalmus*, notably as *navarch*. Though Medius is referred to by Str. 11.14.12/530 (= *FGrH/BNJ* 129 T 1) in a manner that might indicate that he left some historical work, we find no further mention of him as an author. See also Welles 1970: 465 note 3; Goukowsky 2002a: 162–3 note 1.

[217] For a different interpretation of ἐπὶ τελευτῆς Ἡρακλέους μέγα ποτήριον πληρώσας ἐξέπιεν see, for example, Welles 1970: 466–7 and note 1. Goukowsky 2002a: 162 simply translates 'il finit par faire remplir une grande "coupe d'Héraclès" qu'il but jusqu'à la dernière goutte', without elaborating on what a 'coupe d'Héraclès' might be. The term also occurs in Plu. *Alex.* 75.3, who refers to a σκύφον Ἡρακλέους ('cup of Heracles') Alexander would have emptied. Perhaps the solution may be found in Ath. 10.434A, stating that Alexander emptied a ποτήριον δίχουν, a drinking cup able to hold nearly 12 pints (c. 7 l). To empty such a cup would be a Herculean task: I have translated the sentence in this vein. As a matter of fact, Plutarch records Aristobulus' account that Alexander drank unmixed wine while he had a fever (Plu. *Alex.* 75.4 = *FGrH/BNJ* 139 F 59). Ephippus of Olynthus (*FGrH/BNJ* 126 F 3 = Ath. 10.434AB) and Nicobule (*FGrH/BNJ* 127 F 1 = Ath. 10.434C and F 2 = Ath. 12.537D) merely indicate that Alexander drank excessively and died of the consequences.

[218] For this translation of κράτιστος (also occurring in Arr. *An.* 7.26.3), see 18.1.4 ('ἄριστος'); Curt. 10.5.5 ('*optimvs*'); Just. 12.15.8 ('*dignissimvs*') and the multiple meanings of the word (see *LSJ, s.v.*).

From Persepolis to Babylon 381

companions should stage a vast funeral contest for him.[219] (5) In the above-mentioned manner he died, after a reign of twelve years and seven months,[220] after achieving the greatest deeds not only of the kings who had lived before him but also of those who were to come later down to our time. Since some historians disagree about the king's death, stating that it was caused by a lethal drug,[221] we believe it to be necessary not to pass over their account.
(17.118.1) They say, indeed, that Antipater, who had been left by Alexander as viceroy in Europe, was at variance with the king's mother, Olympias.[222] At first he did not take her seriously because Alexander did not heed her complaints against him, but later, as their enmity kept growing and the king showed an anxiety to gratify his mother in everything out of piety to the divinity, he gave Antipater many indications of his disaffection. Moreover, because the murder of Parmenion and Philotas struck terror into the king's companions,[223] Antipater gave the king a lethal drug to drink by the hand of Antipater's own son, who was the king's wine-pourer.[224] (2) As he held the highest authority in Europe after Alexander's death, and as afterwards his son Cassander took over the kingdom, they say that many historians did not dare write about the drug. They say that it has become obvious from his own activities that Cassander was a bitter enemy to Alexander's policies: indeed, not only, having murdered Olympias, did he discard her body without burial,[225] but

---

[219] 18.1.4–5 explains this as follows: that Alexander foresaw a struggle between his companions to succeed him.
[220] See Welles 1970: 467 note 5. Alexander died, in our reckoning, on 10/11 June 323; that is, the 29th of the Babylonian month of *Ajara*, the 29th of the Macedonian month of *Daisios*, both in the 1st year of Philip III Arrhidaeus (a half-brother and the direct successor of Alexander). See Sachs 1955: no. 209; Samuel 1965: 8.
[221] See Arr. *An.* 7.27.1–2; Just. 12.13.10–14.8. Goukowsky 2002a: 276 *ad* 117.6 states that it is generally believed that Alexander died of an acute crisis caused by *Malaria tropica*, though Brunt 1983: 295 note 1 rightly remarks that '[m]odern speculations on the cause of death are futile'.
[222] See Goukowsky 2002a: 277 *ad* 162, 118.1. See, for example, also Bosworth 1971: 113.
[223] See, for example Plu. *Alex.* 49.8; Curt. 10.10.15. (I believe the translation by Rolfe for the Loeb Classical Library of the latter passage, taking Alexander as the object, makes no sense in the context.)
[224] Diodorus brings in the story of an alleged poisoning relatively neutral, as does Arr. *An.* 7.27.1–2, though he mentions Cassander, his brother Iollas (Bosworth, surprisingly, uses the name of Iolaus: see Bosworth 1971: 113–14), and possibly even Medius as alleged accomplices. Plu. *Alex.* 77.1–3, who mentions Iolas as alleged accomplice, discards the suggestion of poisoning. Just. 12.14.6–9, however, seems to be a true believer in a poisoning scheme, implicating Antipater's sons Cassander, Iollas, and Philip. The *Epitome Mettensis* also treats Alexander's death as being the consequence of poisoning, administered by Antipater and/or members of his family. Iollas was, indeed, the king's wine-pourer. See also Goukowsky 2002a: 277 *ad* 163, 118.1.
[225] The vicissitudes of Olympias in her struggle against Cassander are described by Diodorus in 19.49–51.

also with great enthusiasm he restored Thebes, which had been destroyed by Alexander.[226] (3) After the king's death Sisyngambris, Darius' mother, grieving much about both Alexander's death and her own solitude, having reached the limit of her life, refrained from food and died on the fifth day, abandoning life painfully but not ingloriously.[227] (4) Having reached the death of Alexander as we proposed to do at the beginning of the book, we shall try to narrate the actions of his successors in the books that follow.

---

[226] The struggle for and destruction of Thebes have been described above, in 17.9–14, the reconstruction in 19.53.3–54.3. It appears that the latter enterprise was a Panhellenic one, not solely Cassander's.

[227] See Curt. 10.5.19–25 for a more elaborate description of Sisyngambris' motives and death.

7 The Period of the Diadochs: The Rift Opens

THE YEARS 323/2–318/17[1]

S. 123:
18.2.1–4.8:

Division of Alexander's empire:
(18.2.1) When Cephisodorus was *archon* at Athens [323/2], the Romans elected Lucius Frurius and Decius Junius consuls.[2] During their term the throne was vacant, because Alexander the king had died childless,[3] and great contention arose over the leadership. (2) The phalanx of the infantry supported Arrhidaeus, son of Philip II, for the kingship, though he was afflicted with incurable mental disorders.[4] The most influential of the companions and of the bodyguard, however, taking counsel together and joining to themselves the corps of horsemen known as the companion cavalry, at first decided not[5] to

---

[1] For a comprehensive view of the period after 323 see, for example, *CAH²*, vol. 7.1; Shipley 2000; and Erskine 2005. For a chronology: Boiy 2008.
[2] L. Furius Camillus and D. Junius Brutus Scaeva were the consuls of 325 vc, L. Papirius Cursor the dictator *rei gervndae causa* ('because of the present situation'), namely the Samnite War. Diodorus is still three years ahead of the Varronian chronology. See Broughton 1951: 147.
[3] Diodorus' statement here is at least remarkable. Roxane, Alexander's wife, was pregnant (Just. 12.15.9), and he had a son, Heracles, with Barsine (Memnon's wife/widow): see above, Chapter 5, note 58 *ad* 17.23.5; also Just. 12.15.9. See also 19.23.3 (mentioning τὸ Ἀλεξάνδρου παιδίον, 'Alexander's son', without further specification) and 19.36.5 (referring to Alexander's son and his mother Roxane).
[4] According to Plu. *Alex.* 77.5, Olympias was to blame for this.
[5] In view of the context (the sending of ambassadors), I concur with the view of Goukowsky 2002b: 106 *ad* <2.2>, third remark, to insert μὴ in front of the verb διαγωνίζεσθαι, leading to the description of a situation that, though extremely tense, is not primarily directed at an armed confrontation. Meleager, though, showed himself intent on another scheme. See also Curt. 10.8.15–18; Plu. *Eum.* 3.2.

383

take up arms against the phalanx and sent envoys chosen from men of rank, of whom the most prominent was Meleager,[6] to the infantry, asking them to submit to their orders. (3) However, when Meleager came to the men of the phalanx, he made no mention of his mission whatsoever but, on the contrary, after praising them for their decisions, sharpened their anger against their opponents. Therefore the Macedonians of the phalanx, after instating Meleager as their leader, advanced under arms against those who disagreed with them. (4) As the bodyguards had withdrawn from Babylon and were making ready for war, the most accomplished of the men persuaded the parties to come to an agreement.[7] Straightaway they instated as king Arrhidaeus, son of Philip II, and changed his name to Philip III, but they instated Perdiccas, to whom Alexander had given his ring as he died, as an *epimeletes* ['curator'] of the kingdom, and they decided that the most important of the companions and of the bodyguard should take over the satrapies and obey both Philip and Perdiccas. (18.3.1) After the latter had assumed the supreme command and had taken counsel with the commanders,[8] he gave Egypt to Ptolemy, son of Lagus; Syria to Laomedon of Mytilene; Cilicia to Philotas; and Media to Peithon.[9] To Eumenes he gave Paphlagonia and Cappadocia and all the lands bordering on these, which Alexander did not invade, having been prevented by the urgency of his affairs when he was carrying on the war with Darius; to Antigonus he gave Pamphylia, Lycia, and what is called Great Phrygia;[10] then to Asander[11] Caria; to Menander[12] Lydia; to Leonnatus Hellespontine Phrygia. These

---

[6] Though at least two more people by this name figure in the different versions of Alexander the Great's expedition, this Meleager was probably the son of Neoptolemus: see Badian 1999.
[7] According to Plu. *Eum.* 3.2, Eumenes had stayed in Babylon, working on a rapprochement between the factions. See also Curt. 10.8.15–23. For the outlines of the arrangement, see Arr. *Succ.* 1.3.
[8] Goukowsky 2002b: 107 *ad* 3.1 rightly stipulates that the action by Meleager must have caused great mutual distrust among the commanders. It is, therefore, understandable that the empire was only divided after the execution of Meleager, referred to below, 19.4.7, and not at the moment alluded to here.
[9] The region of Media intended here is Media Maior: see Str. 11.13.1/522. There is another region by the name of Media as well: see below, paragraph 3 and note 15. See also below, note 35, for Peithon.
[10] For Antigonus *Monophthalmus* and his career, see Billows 1990. See also Briant 1973; Roisman 2012.
[11] In spite of the MS tradition and Fischer, I tend to support Wesseling's emendation of this name to Asander, following *inter alios* Arr. *Succ.* 1.37 = Phot. *Bibl.* [92] 72a9 and Dexipp. [*FGrH/ BNJ* 100] F 8.2 = Phot. *Bibl.* [82] 64a40. Arr. *Succ.* 1.6 = Phot. *Bibl.* [92] 69b1, though, reads Casander. The tradition is, therefore, not at all conclusive enough to be sure as regards Wesseling's emendation, even though Goukowsky, 2002b: 107 *ad* 3.1, remark 5, appears to be so. Nevertheless, I have followed his example, especially on the basis of Dittenberger *Syll.*³ 311, 320.
[12] On the basis of the majority of the classical tradition (Arrian's Τὰ μετὰ [τοῦ] Ἀλεξάνδρου

The Period of the Diadochs: The Rift Opens   385

satrapies, thus, were distributed in that way. (2) In Europe, Thrace and the neighbouring tribes near the Pontic Sea were given to Lysimachus; Macedonia and the adjacent tribes were assigned to Antipater. Perdiccas, however, decided not to disturb the remaining satrapies in Asia, but to leave them subordinate to the same rulers; likewise he determined that Taxiles and Porus should be masters of their own kingdoms as Alexander himself had arranged. (3) To Peithon[13] he gave the satrapy next to the kings connected with Taxiles; the satrapy that lies along the Caucasus [= Hindu Kush], called that of the Paropanisadians, he assigned to Oxyartes the Bactrian, whose daughter Roxane Alexander had married. He gave Arachosia and Gedrosia to Sibyrtius, Aria and Drangia to Stasanor of Soli, Bactria and Sogdia to Philip,[14] Parthia and Hyrcania to Phrataphernes, Persis to Peucestes, Carmania to Tlepolemus, Media to Atropates,[15] Babylonia to Archon, and Mesopotamia to Arcesilaus. (4) He placed Seleucus in command of the cavalry of the companions, a most distinguished office; in fact, Hephaestion commanded them first, Perdiccas after him, and third the aforementioned Seleucus.[16] (5) The transportation of the body of Alexander and the preparation of the vehicle that was to carry the body of the dead king to Ammon they assigned to Arrhidaeus.[17] (18.4.1) Craterus, who was one of the most prominent men, happened to have been previously sent away by Alexander to Cilicia with the men discharged from the army, ten thousand in number.[18] At the same time he had received written instructions which Alexander had

(≈ *History of the Diadochs* = Arr. *Succ.*), Dexippus, Q. Curtius Rufus, and Justin), I have followed Wesseling here, though the MS tradition (and Fischer 1985d: 322) read 'Meleager'.

[13] Though Goukowsky 2002b: 8 leaves it out, Πίθωνι δὲ ('to Peithon') is an emendation based upon 18.39.6 and Dexipp. *FGrH/BNJ* 100 F 8.4: see Geer 1969: 16 note 4. Nevertheless the sentence is not satisfactory, but neither are the translations and/or solutions of Goukowsky and Geer.

[14] Possibly Philip, son of Menelaus, a Macedonian, *hipparch* first of the Thessalian cavalry after 334/3, after 331 of the mercenary horse: see Heckel 2009: 212 *s.v.* 'Philip [4]'.

[15] Atropates, the father-in-law of Perdiccas, had been the satrap of all Media (see Arr. *An.* 4.18.3, 7.4.5). He now got its north-western portion, from then on known as Lesser Media or Media Atropatane. It soon became independent and was ruled by Atropates' descendants for at least three centuries: see Str. 11.13.1–3/523.

[16] For Seleucus, his career, and his successors, see Kosmin 2014, Grainger 1990a, and, for the years 323–223, Grainger 2014. See also Roisman 2012.

[17] Not to be confused with King Philip Arrhidaeus, despite Just. 13.4.6. This Arrhidaeus had been one of the commanders in the army of Alexander the Great. Paus. 1.6.3 states that Alexander's body was to be buried at Aegae in Macedonia, but that Ptolemy persuaded the Macedonians, who had to carry it there, to hand it over to him and consequently buried it in Memphis. Arr. *Succ.* 1.25 (= Phot. *Bibl.* [92] 70b17–22) informs us that, though Perdiccas had ordered otherwise, Arrhidaeus directly transported Alexander's remains, via Damascus, to Egypt, to Ptolemy.

[18] Craterus had received his orders about a year earlier, in the spring of 324. On the, presumed, contents of his orders see, for example, Goukowsky 2002b: 108 *ad* 4.1.

given him to perform. After the death of Alexander, the successors decided not to carry out these plans. (2) ... (3) ... (4) ... (5) ... (6) ... [[In these paragraphs the plans of Alexander are mentioned. They are not relevant to the history of Persia.]] (7) Perdiccas first put to death those of the soldiers who were agitators and most at enmity with himself, thirty in number.[19] After that he also punished Meleager,[20] who had been a traitor during the contention and his mission, using as a pretext a private quarrel and a charge that Meleager was plotting against him. (8) Then, because the Greeks who had been settled in the upper satrapies had revolted and raised a considerable force, he sent one of the nobles, Peithon, to make war against them.[21]

S. 124:
18.5.2–7.9:

Geography of Asia and its satrapies:
(18.5.2) Well then, from the Taurus in Cilicia a continuous range of mountains extends through the whole of Asia as far as the Hindu Kush and the Eastern Ocean [the Bay of Bengal].[22] This range is divided by crests of varying heights, and each part has its proper name. (3) As Asia is thus separated into two parts, one slopes to the north, the other to the south. Corresponding to these slopes, the streams of the rivers flow in opposite directions;[23] some empty into the Caspian Sea, some into the Pontus Euxinus, and some into the Northern Ocean. Of the rivers that lie opposite to these, some flow into the ocean opposite India, some into the ocean that is adjacent to Asia, and some empty into what is called the Red Sea.[24] (4) As the satrapies are divided likewise, some slope towards the north, the others towards the south. The first of those that face the north lie along the River Tanaïs:[25] Sogdia

---

[19] The rest of the transmitted sources put these executions before the distribution of the satrapies and the annulment of Alexander's (megalomaniac) plans.
[20] See above, note 6. See also Goukowsky 2002b: 111–12 ad 4.7. All MSS of Q. Curtius Rufus mention 300 (CCC) as the number of adversary soldiers killed by Perdiccas: Curt. 10.9.18, though Bentley emended that into 30 (XXX). Curtius Rufus also narrates that Meleager was killed in spite of the fact that he had sought refuge in a temple: Curt. 10.9.21.
[21] Though Pompeius Trogus refers to this revolt in the *Prologus* of his book 13 (Seel 1985: 310), Justin does not discuss it.
[22] This division of Asia follows the lines of Eratosthenes; see Str. 2.1.1/67–8, 2.5.31–2/129–30, probably outlined by Dicearchus (see *GGM*, II: 472). See also Goukowsky 2002b: 112–13 ad 5.2.
[23] See the remarks by Goukowsky 2002b: 11–12 note 1.
[24] These waters are the Arabian Sea, the Bay of Bengal (also known as the Eastern Ocean), and the Persian Gulf. ἤπειρος is here used (and translated) in its specific later meaning: see *LSJ*, s.v. ad III.
[25] Usually Τάναϊς is used to indicate the modern Don, but the context makes it clear that only either the Oxus (Ὦξος, modern Amu-Darya) or the Yaxartes (Ἰαξάρτης, modern Syr-

The Period of the Diadochs: The Rift Opens   387

and Bactria; and next to these are Aria, Parthia, and Hyrcania, which surrounds the Hyrcanian Sea,[26] a detached body of water. Next is Media, which has many names of places and is the greatest of all the satrapies. Next are Armenia, Lycaonia, and Cappadocia, all having a very wintry climate. Bordering on them in a straight line are situated both Great Phrygia and Hellespontine Phrygia; to the side are Lydia and Caria; above Phrygia and beside it is Pisidia, with Lycia next to it. (5) In the coastal regions of these satrapies the *poleis* of the Greeks are established; to write their names is not necessary for the purpose under discussion. The satrapies that face the north are situated in the way described.

(18.6.1) Of the satrapies that face the south, the first one along the Hindu Kush is India, a great and populous kingdom, inhabited by many Indian tribes, of which the greatest is the tribe of the Gangarids, against whom Alexander did not make an expedition because of the multitude of their elephants.[27] (2) The River Ganges,[28] which is the deepest of the region and has a width of thirty *stadia*,[29] separates this land from the next part of India. Adjacent to this is the rest of India, which Alexander conquered, irrigated by water from five[30] rivers and most conspicuous for its prosperity, over which ruled, together with several other kingdoms, both the house of Porus and Taxiles. Through it happens to flow the River Indus, from which the country received its name. (3) Next to the Indian satrapy, Arachosia, Gedrosia, and Carmania were marked off, and to the side of them Persis, in which are Susis and Sittacene. Next comes Babylonia, extending to the Arabian Desert. On the other side, in the direction from which we make the march inland, is Mesopotamia

---

Darya) can have been intended here. I know of no distinct cause for this confusion: however, Str. 2.5.31/129 might suggest these rivers were thought to be part of the Don system. See also Goukowsky 2002b: 113–14 *ad* 5.4.

[26] Ὑρκανία θάλαττα is sometimes used in the sense of Caspian Sea; sometimes it merely indicates the eastern part of it. Both Eratosthenes and later geographers believed that the Caspian Sea formed a part of the Northern Ocean (see Str. 2.1.17/74 and most clearly 2.5.18/121), even though Herodotus (Hdt. 1.203.1) had already referred to it as an inland sea. See also the elaborate note of Goukowsky 2002b: 114–16 *ad* 5.4.

[27] No such considerations were mentioned in 17.93.2 *sqq.*, above. There, the reluctance of Alexander's force to proceed is presented as the reason not to attack this tribe. Diodorus' inconsistency on this point is annoying.

[28] Though the MSS omit the name of the river, Wesseling's emendation is surely correct.

[29] In 17.93.2, Diodorus noted that the width of the Ganges was 32 *stadia*, c. 6 km. A quite extreme width for this river was recorded by Megasthenes, stating that its *medium* width was 100 *stadia*, well over 18 km: see Str. 15.1.35/702.

[30] I fully support a suggestion by Goukowsky to insert here πέντε ('five'), prompted by the geographical situation of the Punjab ('Pentepotamia', counting the rivers Jhelum [ancient Hydaspes], Chenab, Ravee, Beas [ancient Hyphasis], and Sutle): see Goukowsky 2002b: 12, note 2 and line 8.

encompassed by two rivers, the Euphrates and the Tigris, through which it got that name. Next to Mesopotamia are Upper Syria,[31] as it is called, and the countries adjacent thereto along the sea: Cilicia, Pamphylia, and Coele Syria,[32] which encloses Phoenicia. Along the frontiers of Coele Syria and along the desert that lies next to it, through which the Nile, making its way, divides Syria and Egypt,[33] the best satrapy of all and one that has the greatest revenues was created, Egypt. (4) All these satrapies are very hot, since the air in the south is different from that which extends to the north. Thus the satrapies that were conquered by Alexander, being situated as described, were distributed to the most noteworthy men.

Expedition against the Greeks in the upper satrapies:
(18.7.1) The Greeks who had been settled by Alexander in the upper satrapies, as they were called, although they longed for the Greek customs and manner of life, being cast away in the most distant part of the kingdom, submitted through fear while the king was alive, but when he was dead they rose in revolt.[34] (2) After they had taken counsel together and elected Philon the Aenianian as general, they raised a considerable force. They had more than twenty thousand infantry and three thousand cavalry, all of whom had many times been tried in the contests of war and were of exceeding courage. (3) When Perdiccas heard of the revolt of the Greeks, he drew by lot from the Macedonians three thousand infantry and eight hundred horsemen. Having chosen as commander of the whole Peithon,[35] who

---

[31] The region between Cilicia, the mouth of the Orontes, and the Euphrates: see Bosworth 1974: 49–50.
[32] It seems the region referred to as Coele Syria varied over the years; here it appears to be that part of the hinterland of Syria situated between the sources of the River Orontes and the Dead Sea: its centre may well have been the modern Beqaa valley in eastern Lebanon. See Bosworth 1974: 48–50.
[33] Apparently Diodorus adheres to the view of some, as related by Str. 1.4.7/65, that the Nile was the boundary between Asia and Africa, even though others believed Egypt to be part of Asia (see Str. 2.5.33/130: μετὰ δὲ τὴν Ἀσίαν ἐστὶν ἡ Λιβύη συνεχὴς οὖσα τῇ τε Αἰγύπτῳ καὶ τῇ Αἰθιοπίᾳ ('after Asia comes Libya, which is a continuation of both Egypt and Ethiopia')), as also Diodorus seems to think as the wording of 18.14.1 suggests κατὰ δὲ τὴν Ἀσίαν ... Πτολεμαῖος μὲν ἀκινδύνως παρέλαβε τὴν Αἴγυπτον ('in Asia ... Ptolemy took over Egypt without difficulty'), and some even denied the existence of continents (see Str. 1.4.7./65–6).
[34] They had already risen in revolt after rumours of Alexander's death in 325: see above, 17.99.5–6.
[35] The MSS and editors are not uniform as regards this name: both πείθων (*inter alios* Berve and Goukowsky), πίθων (most MSS and Fischer 1985d: 328), and πύθων (F and Gn. Pompeius Trogus) are given. Peithon (c. 355–314), the son of Crateuas, had been a bodyguard of Alexander. Though he lacked experience as a commander, he appears to have been very ambitious: apparently Perdiccas noticed that and therefore treated him with some distrust, as the sequel makes clear. See also Ael. *VH* 14.47a; Goukowsky 2002b: 117 *ad* 7.3, second remark (with wrong reference to Aelian). See also Heckel 2009: 195 *s.v.* 'Peithon [3]'.

had been of the bodyguard of Alexander, a man full of spirit and able to command, he assigned to him the troops that had been drawn. After giving him letters for the satraps, in which it was written that they should furnish Peithon ten thousand infantry and eight thousand horsemen, he sent him against the rebels. (4) Peithon, who was a man of great ambition, gladly accepted the expedition, intending to win the Greeks over through kindness, and, after making his army great through an alliance with them, to work in his own interests and become the ruler of the upper satrapies. (5) But Perdiccas, suspecting his design, gave definite orders to kill all the rebels after subduing them and to distribute the spoils to the soldiers. Peithon, setting out with the troops that had been given to him and receiving the auxiliaries from the satraps, came upon the rebels with all his force. Through the agency of a certain Aenianian he corrupted Lipodorus,[36] who had been made a commander of three thousand among the rebels, and won a complete victory. (6) In fact, when the battle had begun and the victory was doubtful, leaving his allies without warning, the traitor withdrew to a certain hill with his three thousand men. The rest, believing that these were bent on flight, were thrown into confusion and, turning about, fled. (7) After his victory in the battle Peithon sent a herald to the conquered, ordering them to lay down their arms and to return to their several colonies after receiving pledges. (8) When oaths to this effect had been sworn and the Greeks were interspersed among the Macedonians, Peithon was greatly pleased, seeing that the affair was proceeding according to his intentions. The Macedonians, however, remembering Perdiccas' orders and regarding the oaths that had been sworn as null and void, broke faith with the Greeks. (9) Indeed, setting upon them unexpectedly and catching them off their guard, they shot them all down with javelins and robbed them from their possessions. Peithon then, cheated of his hopes, returned with the Macedonians to Perdiccas. This was the state of affairs in Asia.

[[In 18.14.1–2, Ptolemy's coming to power in Egypt is related, with Egypt's factual detachment from the former (Achaemenid) empire, just as its European part *de facto* had become detached. In Diodorus' history of Persia, I will focus on the story of the territories which still can be considered as a more or less integral part of an empire that (at least nominally) includes Persis.]]

---

[36] Neither the MSS nor the editors appear to agree on the name of this commander. I follow Goukowsky 2002b: 14 and note 3 and *apparatus* lines 9–10. See also Fischer 1985d: 329, *apparatus ad* line 15.

S. 125:
18.16.1–3:

Perdiccas makes an expedition against Cappadocia:
(18.16.1) While these things were going on, Perdiccas, taking with him King Philip and the royal army, made an expedition against Ariarathes,[37] the ruler of Cappadocia. Indeed, the latter's not attending to the Macedonians had been overlooked by Alexander, owing to the struggle with Darius and its distractions, and Ariarathes had enjoyed a very long respite as lord of Cappadocia. (2) Therefore he had amassed a great sum of money from the revenues and had formed large force, consisting of natives and mercenaries. He was thus prepared to engage Perdiccas in defence of his kingdom, having thirty thousand infantry and five thousand cavalry. Joining battle with him, and, gaining a victory over him in the conflict, Perdiccas killed men to the number of four thousand and took captive more than five thousand, among them Ariarathes himself. (3) The latter and all his relatives, after torture, Perdiccas impaled; but granting immunity to the conquered people, and after putting in order the affairs of Cappadocia, he handed over the satrapy to Eumenes of Cardia,[38] just as it had originally been assigned.

S. 126:
18.22.1–25.6:

Campaign against Pisidia:
(18.22.1) After Perdiccas and King Philip had defeated Ariarathes and delivered his satrapy to Eumenes, they departed from Cappadocia. When they had arrived in Pisidia,[39] they determined that they would lay waste two cities, both that of the Larandeans and that of the Isaureans.[40] In fact, these cities, while Alexander was still alive, had put to death Balacrus the son of Nicanor,[41] who had been appointed

---

[37] Ariarathes (c. 404–322), the son of Ariaramnes the satrap of Cappadocia, ruled there from c. 331 onward and was the first of about ten rulers of Cappadocia of that name. They were loyal supporters first of Artaxerxes III, later of Darius III. See also Goukowsky 2002b: 129 *ad* 16.1; Heckel 2009: 44 *s.v.*
[38] For the life and career of Eumenes, see Anson 2015.
[39] Roughly the territory of the modern district of Antalya, directly to the north of Lycia.
[40] See for these cities Ramsey 1962: 336, 358.
[41] Balacrus, one of Alexander's bodyguards, had been appointed satrap of Cilicia in 332 (see Arr. *An.* 2.12.2), but the sources offer no definite evidence to establish the year of his death, even though the numismatic evidence suggests he ruled for several years, possibly even to 323. See also Heckel 2009: 68–9 *s.v.* 'Balacrus [2]'. *Contra*: Bosworth 1974: 58, who believes Balacrus died in 331.

commander as well as satrap. (2) Having, therefore, taken the city of the Larandeans by storm and after killing the men of fighting age and enslaving the rest of the population, they razed it to the ground. However, after they had vigorosly besieged the city of the Isaureans, which was strongly fortified and large and moreover was filled with stout warriors, for two days, and had lost many of their own men, they withdrew. (3) Indeed, the inhabitants, who were well provided with missiles and other things needed to withstand a siege and were enduring the dreadful ordeal with desperate courage in their minds, died willingly to preserve their freedom. (4) On the third day, though, when many had been killed and the walls had few defenders because of the lack of men, the citizens performed a heroic and memorable deed. Indeed, seeing that the punishment that hung over them could not be averted and not having a force that would be adequate to stave the enemy off, they decided not to surrender the city and not to place their fate in the hands of the enemy, because their punishment combined with outrage was certain. At night, seeking noble-minded death, shutting up their children, wives, and parents in their houses, they set the houses on fire, choosing through the fire a common death and burial. (5) As the flame suddenly flared high, the Isaureans threw into the fire their goods and everything that could be of use to the victors. As Perdiccas wondered what was taking place, he stationed his troops about the city and tried vigorously to break into the city on all sides. (6) As the inhabitants defended themselves from the walls and struck down many of the Macedonians, Perdiccas, being confounded, sought the reason why these men, who had given their homes and all else to the flames, defended the walls zealously. (7) Finally, when Perdiccas and the Macedonians withdrew from the city, the Isaureans, throwing themselves into the fire, found burial in their homes along with their families. (8) When the night was over, Perdiccas gave the city to his soldiers for booty. After they had extinguished the fire, they found an abundance of both silver and gold, as one might expect in a city that had been prosperous for many years.

Perdiccas plots his advancement in position:
(18.23.1) After the destruction of the cities there came two women to marry Perdiccas, both Nicaea, the daughter of Antipater, whom Perdiccas himself had sought in marriage, and Cleopatra, the legitimate sister of Alexander, daughter of Philip son of Amyntas.[42] (2)

---

[42] For a potential background to these marriages see, for example, Goukowsky 2002b: 134–5 *ad* 23.1.

Perdiccas had formerly planned to collaborate with Antipater and therefore asked her to marry him even though his position was not yet firmly established. However, when he had gained control of both the royal forces and the guardianship of the kings,[43] he changed his calculations. (3) Since he was now reaching out for the kingship, he was eager to marry Cleopatra, believing that he could use her to persuade the Macedonians to help him gain supreme power. But not wishing as yet to reveal his design, he married Nicaea for the time being, in order to avoid making Antipater hostile to his own undertakings. Afterwards, however, when Antigonus learned Perdiccas' intentions and because Antigonus was a friend of Antipater and, moreover, the most energetic of the commanders, Perdiccas decided he would put Antigonus out of the way. (4) Thus, by bringing false slanders and unjust charges against him,[44] it was obvious that he would bring him down. As Antigonus, however, excelled in keenness and daring, he let it be known outwardly that he wished to defend himself against these charges, but secretly he made arrangements to flee and he escaped notice, with his personal friends and his son Demetrius, embarking on the Attic ships at night.[45] And having been brought to Europe in these, he travelled on to join forces with Antipater.

Expedition against the Aetolians:
(18.24.1) About this time, Antipater and Craterus had started an expedition against the Aetolians with thirty thousand foot and two thousand and five hundred horse.[46] In fact, the Aetolians alone had remained unconquered of those who had taken part in the Lamian War.[47] (2) Although such great forces were sent against them, they were in no panic-stricken mood, but having gathered all who were in the full vigour of manhood to the number of ten thousand, they retired to the mountainous and rough places, in which they placed the children, the women, the old, and the greater part of their wealth. They abandoned the *poleis* that could not be defended, but securing

---

[43] By now Roxane had given birth to Alexander's son, whom the army had acclaimed as king as well: Arr. *Succ.* 1.8 = Phot. *Bibl.* [92] 69b16–17.

[44] See Arr. *Succ.* 1.20 = Phot. *Bibl.* [92] 70a30–2; see also Plu. *Eum.* 3.3 for (a cause of) enmity between Antigonus and Perdiccas. See also Goukowsky 2002b: 37 note 1.

[45] Goukowsky 2002b: 37 note 2 suggests these ships, perhaps, might have been sent from Athens to collect κληροῦχοι ('settlers') from Samos.

[46] This expedition is not corroborated in our other sources. Though it is usually dated to the autumn of 322, Goukowsky 2002b: 38 note 1 believes it only took off in the summer of 321. I think the weather conditions described for the expedition appear to plead against this suggestion.

[47] A useful review of this war is Schmitt 1992.

those excelling in strength each with a considerable garrison they boldly awaited the approach of the enemy.
(18.25.1) Invading Aetolia and finding the *poleis* which were easy to capture deserted, Antipater and Craterus moved against the men who had withdrawn into the difficult regions. At first, then, violently attacking positions that were strongly fortified and in broken terrain, the Macedonians lost many of their soldiers. Indeed, the courage of the Aetolians joined with the strength of their positions easily turned back men who rushed headlong into dangers beyond reach of succour. Afterwards, though, when Craterus had built shelters and was forcing the enemy to stay through the winter and to hold out in regions that were covered with snow and lacking in food, the Aetolians came into the greatest dangers. (2) In fact, they had either to come down from their mountains and fight against forces many times as large and famous commanders, or to remain and be utterly destroyed by want and cold. When they were already giving up hope of salvation, some relief from their troubles appeared of its own accord, as though one of the gods had been moved to pity by their good courage. (3) Indeed, Antigonus, who had fled from Asia, joining Antipater, told him the whole of Perdiccas' plot, and that, after marrying Cleopatra, he would come at once with his force to Macedonia as king and deprive them of the supreme command.[48] (4) Dumbfounded by the unexpected news, Craterus and Antipater met in council with their commanders. After a debate had been conducted on these affairs, it was unanimously decided to make peace with the Aetolians on whatever terms were possible, to transport the armies with all speed to Asia, to assign the command of Asia to Craterus and that of Europe to Antipater, and also to send an embassy to Ptolemy to discuss a joint action, because he was utterly hostile to Perdiccas but friendly to them, and he together with them was an object of the plot. (5) Therefore they at once made a treaty with the Aetolians, firmly resolved to conquer them later and to move them all with their entire households to the desert and the most distant region of Asia. Having recorded a decree embodying these plans, they prepared the things necessary for the campaign.
(6) Having gathered his friends and generals, Perdiccas asked them for counsel whether it was better to march against Macedonia or first to take the field against Ptolemy. When all were in favour of defeating Ptolemy first, to ensure they would have no obstacle in

---

[48] See also Arr. *Succ.* 1.26 = Phot. *Bibl.* [92] 70b22–9. Antigonus' arrival in Macedonia was probably somewhere in the middle of 321.

the way of their Macedonian campaign, he sent Eumenes off with a considerable force, ordering him to watch over the region of the Hellespont and to prevent a crossing. Perdiccas himself, taking the army from Pisidia, proceeded against Egypt. Such, then, were the events of this year [323/2].

[[*Capita* 18.26-8 relate the description of the wagon to transport Alexander's body to Egypt, his coffin, and the burial in Alexandria. As this does not directly bear on the history of Persia, I leave it out, in spite of its significance.]]

S. 127:
18.29.1–33.1:

Open confrontation between Perdiccas and his opponents begins:
(18.29.1) Indeed, Perdiccas, who saw with suspicion Ptolemy's increase in power, decided that he himself and the kings would conduct a campaign against Egypt with the larger part of the army, but he sent Eumenes to the Hellespont in order to prevent Antipater and Craterus crossing into Asia Minor,[49] giving him a suitable force. (2) He also sent with him sufficient well-reputed commanders, of whom the most prominent were his brother Alcetas and Neoptolemus, and he ordered them to obey Eumenes in all things, because of both his skill as general and the firmness of his loyalty. (3) Going to the Hellespont with the forces that had been given him and having prepared beforehand a large body of cavalry from his own satrapy, Eumenes marshalled his army, which had previously been deficient in that branch.[50] (4) When Craterus and Antipater had brought their forces across from Europe, Neoptolemus, who was jealous of Eumenes[51] and had a considerable number of Macedonians in his following, secretly entered into negotiations with Antipater and, having come to an agreement with him, plotted against Eumenes.[52] Being exposed and forced to fight, he was

---

[49] See above, 18.25.6. Also Arr. *Succ.* 1.26–7 = Phot. *Bibl.* [92] 70b29–71a9; Just. 13.8.1–9; Plu. *Eum.* 4–7. The Paros fragment of the *Marmor Parium* (11–13) dates this event to 321/0 ('when Archippus was *archon* at Athens'), and thus probably (early) summer 321.

[50] Diodorus, resuming here the account from 18.25, omits several relevant events and diverges at times substantially from the story presented in Arrian's fragments, as is notably apparent in Photius' *Bibliotheca* (*codex* 92). However, as I have argued before, Photius is not a very diligent excerpter (Stronk 2010: 141–6). See also Goukowsky 2002b: 142 *ad* 29.3.

[51] See, for example, Plu. *Eum.* 1.6–7, 4.1–2.

[52] According to Arr. *Succ.* 1.26 = Phot. *Bibl.* [92] 70b32–4, the initiative for the rapprochement between Neoptolemus and Antipater and Craterus was taken by the latter two: πρεσβεύονται δὲ καὶ πρὸς Εὐμένη καὶ πρὸς Νεοπτόλεμον τοὺς ὑπὸ Περδίκκαι· καὶ Νεοπτόλεμος μὲν πείθεται, Εὐμένης δὲ οὐκ ἀνέχεται ('they also sent messages to Eumenes and to Neoptolemus, Perdiccas' lieutenants, and Neoptolemus let himself be convinced, but Eumenes did not

himself in danger of being killed and he lost almost all his forces.[53] (5) Eumenes, indeed, after he had been victorious and had killed many, both won over most of the remaining soldiers and increased his own power, not only by the victory but also by having acquired a large number of stout Macedonians. (6) Neoptolemus, then, who had saved himself from the battle with three hundred horsemen, rode off with them to Antipater.[54] Holding a council of war, these decided to divide the forces into two parts and that Antipater with one part should set out for Cilicia, to fight against Perdiccas, and Craterus was to attack Eumenes with the other part and, after defeating these, return to Antipater. In this way, when they had combined their forces and when Ptolemy had been added to the alliance, they might be able to outmatch the royal forces.

Eumenes is victorious:
(18.30.1) As soon as Eumenes heard that the enemy was advancing upon him, he collected his forces, particularly his cavalry, from all sides.[55] In fact, since he could not equal the Macedonian phalanx with his foot soldiers, he prepared a substantial corps of horsemen,[56] by means of whom he hoped to defeat his opponents. (2) When the forces were near each other, Craterus, summoning the whole army to an assembly and spurring them to battle with suitable words, said he would give them, if the soldiers were victorious in battle, all the baggage of the enemy to plunder. (3) When all had become eager for battle, he deployed his force, himself taking command of the right wing, and giving the command of the left one to Neoptolemus. (4) He had in all twenty thousand infantry, of which the most part were Macedonians famed for their courage, on whom in particular he placed his hopes of victory. More than two thousand horsemen served as auxiliaries. (5) Eumenes had twenty thousand foot, men of every race, and five thousand horse, through whom he had resolved to decide the fight. After both leaders had distributed their cavalry over the wings and had ridden far in advance of the line of battle of the infantry, Craterus, charging first upon the enemy with his picked

---

accept'). Plu. *Eum.* 5.4 follows the same story-line as Diodorus. In his account, Antipater and Craterus only sent word to Eumenes after Neoptolemus' defeat: Plu. *Eum.* 5.6–8.

[53] See Plu. *Eum.* 5.5 for our only testimony, to the best of my knowledge, on this fight.

[54] For Neoptolemus' flight to Craterus (not to Antipater): Plu. *Eum.* 5.6; Arr. *Succ.* 1.27 = Phot. *Bibl.* [92] 70b36–8; Just. 13.8.5 relates that Neoptolemus fled to Polyperchon. For the latter's distinguished career see Heckel 2009: 226–31 *s.v.* 'Polyperchon'.

[55] Apparently Eumenes' forces were dispersed, which might explain his flight from Sardis when Antigonos approached.

[56] See above, 18.29.3, relating the collecting of the Cappadocian cavalry by Eumenes.

troops, fought admirably.⁵⁷ As his horse stumbled he fell to the ground, and trampled under foot he ended his life ingloriously,⁵⁸ unrecognised in the confusion and dense array of those riding against each other. (6) Because Eumenes' men had taken courage from Craterus' death and rushed upon the mass from every side, a great slaughter ensued. The right wing, crushed in this way, overwhelmingly defeated, was compelled to flee to the phalanx of the infantry.

Neoptolemus is killed:
(18.31.1) On the left wing, however, since Neoptolemus was arrayed against Eumenes himself, there occurred a great display of ambitious rivalry when the leaders rushed full at each other. (2) Indeed, as soon as they recognised one another from both their horses and other insignia, they engaged each other in single combat and made the victory depend upon the duel between themselves.⁵⁹ After the opening exchange of sword strokes, then, they engaged in a strange and most extraordinary combat. Indeed, carried away by their anger and their hatred against each other, letting the reins fall from their left hands they grappled with each other. When this happened, their horses ran out from under them by their own momentum, and the men themselves fell to the ground. (3) Although it was difficult for either of them to get up because of the suddenness and force of the fall, especially as the armour hampered their bodies, Eumenes rose up first and forestalled Neoptolemus by striking him in the back of the knee. (4) Because the gash proved to be severe and his legs gave way, the stricken man lay disabled, prevented by his wound from rising to his feet. Yet, as his courage overcame the weakness of his body, he wounded his opponent with three blows on the arm and the thighs, resting on his knees. (5) As none of these blows was fatal and the wounds were still fresh, Eumenes killed Neoptolemus, striking him in the neck with a second blow.

(18.32.1) Meanwhile, the remaining part of the cavalry, having joined battle as well, was making great slaughter. Therefore, while some fell and others were wounded, the battle at first was even, but later, when the death of Neoptolemus and the rout of the other wing

---

⁵⁷ Plu. *Eum.* 7.1–4 presents a quite different version of the battle, if only because in his version Eumenes charges first.
⁵⁸ There exist at least several other, different, versions of Craterus' death: see Goukowsky 2002b: 142–3 *ad* 30.5.
⁵⁹ See also Arr. *Succ.* 1.27; Plu. *Eum.* 7.7–12; Nep. *Eum.* 4.1–2; Just. 13.8.7–8. Goukowsky 2002b: 143 *ad* 31.2 observes that this is less a 'heroic duel' than a scene to show the mutual hatred between the contestants.

The Period of the Diadochs: The Rift Opens 397

had become obvious, all started to flee to the phalanx of their infantry as if it were a strong wall.

Neoptolemus' soldiers fool Eumenes and join Antipater:
(2) Eumenes, being satisfied with his advantage and master of the bodies of both enemy commanders, called back his soldiers with the *salpinx*. After he had set up a trophy and buried the dead,[60] he sent a messenger to the phalanx of the vanquished, inviting them to unite with him and giving permission to as many as wanted to beat a retreat.[61] (3) When the Macedonians had accepted the terms of surrender and had pledged their faith by oaths, they received permission to go for food to certain villages that lay near.[62] And they deceived Eumenes: for after they had lifted themselves up and had collected the supplies, they set out at night and went off secretly to Antipater. (4) Eumenes attempted to punish the faithlessness of these men who had violated their oath and to follow at the heels of the phalanx. However, unable to do anything, because of both the *aretae* of those who were retreating and the loss of strength caused by his wounds, he gave up the pursuit. Being victorious in a notable battle and killing two mighty leaders, Eumenes acquired a great reputation. (18.33.1) When Antipater had received and enrolled those who had escaped the rout, he went on to Cilicia, making haste to go to the aid of Ptolemy. . . .

[[This *caput* continues, as do the following ones, with Perdiccas' expedition to and in Egypt and his death in a revolt (320/19: this has, however, no significance for the history of Persia. It is notable, though, that after Perdiccas' demise, Arrhidaeus and Peithon became the guardians of the kings.]]

---

[60] According to Paus. 9.40.7–9, the Macedonians did not usually raise trophies: οὐ γάρ τι Μακεδόσιν ἱστάναι τρόπαια ἦν νενομισμένον ('in fact, it was not considered something for Macedonians to raise trophies'), a custom started by a king by the name of Caranus and continued at least through the reign of Alexander the Great. However, the Greeks did raise trophies and Eumenes was, after all, a Greek (from Cardia in the Thracian Chersonesus). Whether Eumenes breaks with the Macedonian rule here or just follows traditional Greek habits, or Diodorus is mistaken in his remark, cannot be ascertained.

[61] Accepting that papyrus *PSI* 1284 bears on this encounter, the name of Eumenes' envoy to these soldiers may well have been Xennias (see line 6; Heckel 2009: 271 *s.v.*). However, Bosworth 1978: 230–1 thinks it feasible that this fragment does not refer to the battle under scrutiny.

[62] The text of papyrus *PSI* 1284 implies, on the contrary, that Eumenes did not allow them to replenish their provisions (see lines 8–9): παρακολουθῶν δὲ . . . εἴρξοι αὐτοὺς τῶν ἐπιτηδείων ('[he declared that] . . . following them . . . he would bar them from provisions'). Naturally, this may have been part of Eumenes' negotiation strategy to force his opponents into submission, allowing them after they had done so to collect supplies, but as it is we only have a text contradicting Diodorus' statement. Note, however, Bosworth's observation (note 61, above).

S. 128:
18.39.1–7:

Negotiations at Triparadisus; the empire is divided anew:
(18.39.1) In Asia, Arrhidaeus and Peithon, the guardians of the kings, setting out from the Nile with the kings and the force, came to Triparadisus in Upper Syria.[63] (2) Because Eurydice, the queen,[64] was interfering there in many matters and working against the efforts of the guardians, Peithon was distressed and, seeing that the Macedonians were paying more and more attention to her commands, he summoned a meeting of the assembly and laid down the guardianship. The Macedonians now elected Antipater guardian with full power. (3) When the latter arrived at Triparadisus a few days later, he found Eurydice stirring up discord and turning the Macedonians away from Antipater.[65] (4) As there was great disorder in the army and a general assembly was called, Antipater put an end to the tumult by addressing the crowd and, thoroughly frightening Eurydice, he persuaded her to keep quiet. (5) Thereafter he distributed the satrapies anew and assigned to Ptolemy what he already ruled. It was, by all means, impossible to displace him, since he seemed to be holding Egypt by virtue of his own prowess, as if it were a prize of war. (6) He gave Syria to Laomedon of Mytilene and Cilicia to Philoxenus. Of the upper satrapies, Mesopotamia and Arbelitis were given to Amphimachus; Babylonia to Seleucus; Susis to Antigenes, because he had been foremost in making the attack on Perdiccas; Persis to Peucestes; Carmania to Tlepolemus; Media to Peithon; Parthia to Philip; Aria and Drangia to Stasander of Cyprus; Bactria and Sogdia to Stasanor of Soli, who was from that same island. He added the country of the Paropanisadians to the domain of Oxyartes, the father of Alexander's wife Roxane; and the part of India bordering on the country of the Paropanisadians to Pithon, son of Agenor. Of the two neighbouring kingdoms, the one along the

---

[63] The precise location of this site (Triparadisus or Paradisus) still eludes us. Str. 16.2.19/756 tells us that it was situated in the proximity of the sources of the River Orontes; Polyaen. 4.6.4 that this river flowed between the camps of the royal army and that of Antipater.

[64] Eurydice (II, died 317), birthname – as it seems – Adea (see Arr. *Succ.* 1.23 = Phot. *Bibl.* [92] 70b6), was the daughter of Amyntas IV, son of Perdiccas III, king of Macedon, and Cynane, a daughter of Philip II and his first wife Audata. See for her career Heckel 2009: 4–5 *s.v.* 'Adea'.

[65] It seems the cause of discontent was the failure to produce the payments promised by Alexander. Eurydice joined the (verbal) attack on Antipater in a speech, partly composed by the scribe Asclepiodorus, which was seconded by Attalus: see Arr. *Succ.* 1.32–3 = Phot. *Bibl.* [92] 71a39–71b8. The order of events as presented by Arrian appears somewhat more rational than that in Diodorus' account. See also Polyaen. 4.6.4.

The Period of the Diadochs: The Rift Opens 399

River Indus was assigned to Porus, that along the Hydaspes to Taxiles (for it was not possible to remove these kings without employing a royal army and an outstanding commander). Of the satrapies that face the north, Cappadocia was assigned to Nicanor; Great Phrygia and Lycia to Antigonus as before; Caria to Asander; Lydia to Clitus; and Hellespontine Phrygia to Arrhidaeus.[66] (7) As commander of the royal army he appointed Antigonus, to whom was assigned the finishing of the war against both Eumenes and Alcetas. Antipater, though, attached his own son Cassander to Antigonus as chiliarch, in order to prevent the latter pursuing his own ambitions undetected. Antipater himself, with the kings and his own army, went on into Macedonia, escorting the kings to their fatherland. [[It appears that at about this point there may well be a lacuna in the text of considerable length: see Geer 1969: 124–5 note 1 and references. Goukowsky 2002b, though, does not refer to a lacuna.]]

S. 129:
18.40.1–43.2:

War against Eumenes continues:
(18.40.1) Antigonus, who had been designated general of Asia, and who was carrying on the war with Eumenes, collected his troops from their winter quarters.[67] After making preparations for the battle, he set out against Eumenes, who was still in Cappadocia. (2) Because one of Eumenes' excellent captains, named Perdiccas,[68] had deserted him and was encamped at a distance of three days' march with the soldiers who had joined him in the mutiny (three thousand foot and five hundred horse), Eumenes sent Phoenix of Tenedos against him with four thousand picked infantry and a thousand horsemen. (3) Taking advantage of a forced night march, Phoenix fell unexpectedly on the deserters at about the second watch of the night.[69] Having caught them asleep, he took Perdiccas alive and

---

[66] In this list of (re)appointments, Sibyrtius, the satrap of Arachosia, is missing: he occurs, though, in the list as presented in Arr. *Succ.* 1.36 = Phot. *Bibl.* [92] 71b36–7. Arrian's list is more complete than Diodorus'.
[67] Meaning the winter of 321/0.
[68] Not further known. In Plu. *Eum.* 9.2 treason is hinted at, but Bernadette Perrin, the editor of the *Eumenes* for the Loeb series of Plutarch's *Lives* (vol. 8, 1919, repr. 1989, pp. 104–5 note 2), refers to the traitor (immediately preceding and during the battle) as Apollonides, not Perdiccas. I think she may well be right and Goukowsky 2002b: 58 note 2 wrong: events described here took place longer before the Battle of Orcynia. I find Engel 1971: 229–30 not really helpful in solving this issue.
[69] Basically, the Greeks divided the night (sunset to sunrise) into three or five watches (see *LSJ*, *s.v.* 'φυλακή' *ad* 4): 'at about the second watch' would, therefore, probably indicate that

secured control of his troops. (4) Eumenes executed the leaders who had been most responsible for the desertion; by distributing the common soldiers among the other troops and by treating them with kindness, he secured himself their loyalty. (5) Thereafter Antigonus, sending messages to a certain Apollonides, who commanded the cavalry in the army of Eumenes, by great promises secretly persuaded him to become a traitor and to desert during the battle. (6) While Eumenes was encamped on a plain in Cappadocia well suited for cavalry fighting, Antigonus, falling upon him with all his men, took the skirts of the mountain range that commanded the plain. (7) Antigonus had more than ten thousand foot soldiers at that time, half of whom were Macedonians admirable for their hardihood, two thousand horsemen, and thirty elephants. Eumenes, though, commanded not less than twenty thousand infantry and five thousand cavalry. (8) But when the battle of Orcynia had become violent and Apollonides with his cavalry unexpectedly deserted his own side, Antigonus gained the victory and killed as many as eight thousand of the opponents. He also became master of the entire supply train, as a consequence of which Eumenes' soldiers were dismayed by the defeat and despondent at the loss of their supplies.

Eumenes retreats into a fortress:
(18.41.1) After this Eumenes tried to flee into Armenia and to add some of the inhabitants of that land to his alliance.[70] As he was being overtaken, however, and saw that his soldiers changed sides to that of Antigonus,[71] he occupied a stronghold that was called Nora.[72] (2) This fortress was very small, as it had a circuit of not more than two *stadia* [less than 400 m], but of wonderful strength. In fact, its buildings had been constructed close together on the top of a high rock, and it had been marvellously fortified, partly by nature, partly by the work of men's hands. (3) It also held stores with much grain, wood, and salt, in order to be able to supply everything during many years for those who had found refuge in it. Together with Eumenes

---

the attack took place somewhere between 9 p.m. and 2 a.m. It seems the watches were not functioning properly.

[70] Only Diodorus reports this. However, Eumenes apparently kept up relations with Orontes, the satrap of Armenia: see Polyaen. 4.8.3; see also 19.23.1–3, which starts to assert the letter was false/deceptive (ψευδεῖς ἐπιστολάς), but continues to state it came from Orontes.

[71] According to Plu. *Eum.* 10.1 and Just. 14.2.3, at least partly on Eumenes' own initiative.

[72] See, for example, Plu. *Eum.* 9–11; Just. 14.2.1–4; Str. 12.2.6/537. I have not found this episode in Arrian's *Successors*. Though Goukowsky 2002b: 149 *ad* 41.1, second remark still states the site has not been identified, Mitchell 1994: 130 convincingly argues Nora should be identified as Gelin Tepe at Sivrihisar, on the northern slopes of Melendiz Dağ.

had fled those of his friends who were exceptionally loyal and had determined to die along with him if it came to the worst. Altogether, both cavalry and infantry, there were about six hundred people. (4) Now that Antigonus had taken over the army that had been with Eumenes and had become master of Eumenes' satrapies together with their revenues, and moreover had seized a great sum of money, he aspired to greater things. Indeed, there was no longer any commander throughout Asia who had an army sufficient in strength to compete with him for supremacy. (5) Therefore, Antigonus made believe for the time that he was friendly to Antipater, but he had decided, as soon as he had made his own position secure, to take orders no longer either from the kings or from Antipater. (6) Thus, he first surrounded those who had fled to the stronghold with double walls, ditches, and amazing palisades. Later, then, parleying with Eumenes and recalling to memory their former friendship, he tried to persuade him to collaborate with him. Eumenes, however, well aware that Fate tends to change quickly, asked for greater concessions than his existing circumstances justified. (7) In fact, his object was to be given back the satrapies that had been originally assigned to him and acquittal of all charges. Antigonus, however, referred these matters to Antipater, and then, after leaving a sufficient guard about the fortress, he set out to meet those enemy commanders who had survived and had troops, both Alcetas, the brother of Perdiccas, and Attalus, who commanded the whole fleet.[73]

Eumenes negotiates terms for surrender:
(18.42.1) Eumenes later sent envoys, of whom Hieronymus, who wrote the *History of the Successors*, was the leader, to Antipater to discuss the terms of surrender.[74] Eumenes himself, who had experienced many and various changes in the circumstances of his life, was not cast down in spirit, knowing sufficiently well that Fate makes sudden changes in both directions. (2) In fact, he saw that though the kings of the Macedonians held an empty pretence of royalty, many men of great ambitions were succeeding to the positions of command, and that each of them wished to act in his own interests. He hoped, thus, as truly happened, that many would have need of him because of

---

[73] Attalus, Perdiccas' brother-in-law and commander of his fleet, had apparently retained the fleet, and moreover had 10,000 foot and 800 horse. He had started (unsuccesful) operations against Cnidus, Caunus, and Rhodes: see Arr. *Succ.* 1.39 = Phot. *Bibl.* [92] 72a31–35. See also Van Dessel and Hauben 1977: 317–18.
[74] That is, Hieronymus of Cardia, *FGrH/BNJ* 154; see: Hornblower 1981; Roisman 2010: 135–50; Heckel 2009: 139–40 *s.v.* See also Just. 14.2.4.

both his judgement and his experience in warfare, and even more his unusual steadfastness in loyalty. (3) Seeing that the horses, unable to exercise themselves because of the roughness of their confined space, would become unfit for use in mounted battle, he devised a certain strange and extraordinary exercise for the horses.[75] (4) Attaching their heads by ropes to beams or pegs and lifting them two or three *dichadeis*,[76] he forced them to rest their weight upon their hind feet, as their forefeet were just clearing the ground. At once each horse, in an effort to find footing for its forefeet, began to struggle with its whole body and with its legs, all its members sharing in the exertion. As they had such an activity, sweat poured freely from their bodies, and due to the exceptional quality of the exercises he achieved perfect training for the animals. (5) He gave the same ration to all the soldiers, he himself sharing in the simplicity of it, and by his unchanging affability he gained great goodwill for himself and secured harmony among all his fellow refugees. Such was the situation of Eumenes and his fellow refugees on the rock.

(18.43.1) ... Seeing, though, that Phoenicia and Coele Syria,[77] as it was called, were favourably situated north of Egypt, Ptolemy *Lagides* made a great effort to annex these regions.[78] (2) He thus dispatched a sufficient force and a commander, selecting Nicanor, one of his friends. The latter, having marched into Syria, took the satrap, Laomedon, captive and subdued the whole of Syria. Having similarly secured the allegiance of the cities throughout Phoenicia and having provided these with garrisons, he returned to Egypt, having made a short and effective campaign.

S. 130:
18.44.1–47.5:

Antigonus sets out against Alcetas and Attalus:
(18.44.1) When Apollodorus was *archon* at Athens [319/18], the Romans elected Quintus Popillius and Quintus Poplius to

---

[75] See also Anderson 1961: 94.
[76] The *dichas* (διχάς, also known as ἡμιπόδιον), double palm (or half-foot), was a measure of about 15 cm. The word in the MSS, δοκίδας, was deleted by Goukowsky 2002b: 61, line 22, but he offers no alternative. For *dichadeis* see Geer 1969: 131 note 4 after Fischer. In view of the description and the goal intended, the measure seems quite high, making the passage rather enigmatic.
[77] On Coele Syria, see above, note 32.
[78] Such an annexation was obviously a flagrant violation of the Triparadisus distribution of regions. The *Marmor Parium* line B.12 (see Jacoby 1904: 22) places this event directly after the death of Antipater: this looks a more sensible chronology than Diodorus'.

The Period of the Diadochs: The Rift Opens 403

the consulship.[79] During their term Antigonus, who had defeated Eumenes, decided to make war against Alcetas and Attalus. In fact, these two had remained from the friends and household of Perdiccas, noteworthy commanders with sufficient soldiers to dispute power. Therefore Antigonus, setting out with all his forces from Cappadocia, pushed on towards Pisidia, where Alcetas and his army were staying.[80] (2) Making a forced march that strained the endurance of his men to the utmost, he traversed two thousand five hundred *stadia* [over 450 km] in seven days and the same number of nights, reaching Cretopolis, as it is called.[81] Escaping the notice of the enemy because of the rapidity of his march and drawing close to them while they were still ignorant of his presence, he stole a march on them by occupying certain rugged ridges.[82] (3) As soon as Alcetas learned that the enemy were at hand,[83] he quickly drew up the phalanx and, attacking the troops that were holding the ridge with a mounted force, he tried with all his might to get the best of them by force and hurl them from the hill. (4) As a stubborn battle was waged and many fell on both sides, Antigonus launched a violent charge against the phalanx of the adversaries with six thousand horsemen in order to cut off the retreat to the phalanx of those surrounding Alcetas. (5) When this manoeuvre had been successfully completed, the forces on the ridge, who were far superior in number and also had an advantage from the difficulty of the terrain, routed the attackers. Alcetas, whose retreat to the infantry had been cut off, being caught in the middle by the sheer number of the enemy, faced imminent destruction. Though survival itself had therefore become difficult, Alcetas, abandoning many of his men, barely escaped to the phalanx of the footmen. (18.45.1) Antigonus, however, leading both his elephants and his whole army down from higher positions, struck panic into his opponents, who were far inferior to him in number. In fact, they were in all sixteen thousand foot and nine hundred horse, while Antigonus,

---

[79] The consuls for 320 vc were Q. Publilius Philo (third time) and L. Papirius Cursor (second time); C. Maenius (who had to abdicate), L. Cornelius Lentulus, and T. Manlius Imperiosus Torquatus (perhaps to hold elections) were the dictators: see Broughton 1951: 152–3. Diodorus is now two years ahead of the Varronian chronology.
[80] It seems Alcetas may well have formed his own territory in Pisidia: see Briant 1972: 63.
[81] Cretopolis, modern Yüreğil, some 27 km south of the modern city of Bucak, an identification made by Mitchell 1994: 129–36. See also Sekunda 1997. As a matter of fact, the distance between Nora and Cretopolis is 452 km (Mitchell 1994: 130), a testimony to the reliability of Diodorus' source. Its site also makes Diodorus' description of the events thoroughly feasible, probably apart from the speed of Antigonus' march (Mitchell 1994: 130–2).
[82] See, for the Battle of Cretopolis: Engel 1972b, comparing Diodorus' account with Polyaenus'.
[83] According to Polyaen. 4.6.7, this was thanks to the bellowing and trumpeting of (an) elephant(s).

apart from the elephants, had more than forty thousand infantry and above seven thousand horsemen. (2) As the elephants were at the same time attacking from the front, and the horsemen because of their number were pouring about them on all sides, and moreover a force of infantry, which far outnumbered them and also surpassed them in *aretae*, was holding a position above them, tumult and panic began to get hold of Alcetas' soldiers. Because of the great rapidity and force of the attack, Alcetas was unable to draw up the phalanx properly. (3) As the rout was complete, Attalus, Docimus,[84] Polemon, and many of the renowned officers were taken captive, but Alcetas, accompanied by his own guards and attendants, escaped with his Pisidian allies to a Pisidian city by the name of Termessus.[85]

After Alcetas' defeat; Antigonus' position is enhanced:
(4) Antigonus, having obtained these commanders by negotiation with the soldiers,[86] enrolled the rest of the soldiers in his own ranks and, treating them kindly, he augmented his force not inconsiderably. (5) The Pisidians, however, who numbered six thousand and were of outstanding prowess, admonished Alcetas to be of good courage, promising that they would in no way fail him. Indeed, they were exceedingly well disposed to him for the following reasons.

(18.46.1) Because Alcetas did not have supporters in Asia after the death of Perdiccas, he decided to show kindness to the Pisidians, thinking that he would thus secure as allies men who were warlike and who possessed a country difficult to invade and well supplied with strongholds. (2) Therefore he honoured them exceedingly above all the allies during the campaigns and distributed to them spoils from the hostile territory, giving them half of the booty.[87] By employing the friendliest language in his conversation with them, by each day inviting the most important of them in turn to his table at banquets, and moreover by honouring many of them with notable gifts, he secured them as loyal supporters. (3) As Alcetas, therefore, kept his hopes in them even at this time, they did not disappoint his

---

[84] Docimus, a brother of Attalus, has not been mentioned anywhere as a captain or commander under Alexander. Nevertheless, Perdiccas had instated him as satrap of Babylonia in 321. See also Heckel 2009: 115 *s.v.*

[85] Termessus was situated about 30 km north-west of modern Antalya, on a natural platform in the Taurus Mountains. It sat on the top of modern Güllük Dağı (ancient Solymus), soaring to a height of 1,665 m from among the surrounding mountains of Antalya, which average only 200 m above sea level. See also Arr. *An.* 1.26.6; Str. 12.8.5/573, 13.4.16/630.

[86] For this construction see Goukowsky 2002b: 152 *ad* 45.4. It is not a very good-looking solution, but one that fits the textual problems raised by the Greek.

[87] Goukowsky 2002b: 65 note 1 suggests this remark implies a prolonged stay by Alcetas in Pisidia.

hopes. In fact, when Antigonus pitched camp near Termessus with all his army and demanded Alcetas, even when the older men advised that he be surrendered, the younger, opposing their parents together, voted to meet every danger in the interest of his safety. (4) The older men at first tried to persuade the younger not to watch their native land become the spoils of war for the sake of a single Macedonian. When they saw, though, the youngsters' determination was not to be shaken, they sent, after deliberating in secret, an embassy to Antigonus by night, promising to surrender Alcetas either alive or dead. (5) They asked Antigonus to attack the city for a number of days and, drawing the defenders forward by skirmishing with light-armed troops, to withdraw as if in flight. Indeed, they said that, when this had happened and the young men were engaged in the battle at a distance from the city, they would seize a suitable occasion for their own undertaking. (6) Antigonus, convinced by them and shifting his camp far from the city, by skirmishing lured the young men to battle outside the city. (7) When the older men saw that Alcetas had been left alone, and selecting the most trustworthy of the slaves and those of the citizens in the prime of life who were not working for Alcetas, they made their attempt in the absence of the young men. They did not now succeed in taking him alive, for he committed suicide first, in order not to fall into the hands of his enemies alive, but laying his body on a bier and covering it with a coarse cloak, they carried it out through the gates and delivered it to Antigonus without attracting the attention of the skirmishers.

(18.47.1) By delivering their home town from danger by their own inventiveness, they did avert the war, but they did not escape estrangement from the younger men.[88] Indeed, these, returning from the fight and hearing what had happened, became enraged at their kinsfolk because of their own excessive devotion to Alcetas. (2) First gaining possession of part of the town, they voted to set the houses on fire; then, rushing from the town under arms and keeping to the mountains, to plunder the country that was subject to Antigonus; but later, changing their minds, they refrained from burning the city, but, devoting themselves to brigandage and raids, ravaged much of the hostile countryside. (3) As for Antigonus, having received the body of Alcetas and maltreated it for three days and, as the corpse began to decay, throwing it out unburied, he departed from Pisidia. But the young men of Termessus, still maintaining their goodwill for the victim, both recovered the body and attended to it splendidly. [[Thus

[88] See for this, for example, Robert 1966: 55 note 8; Briant 1972: 64 note 3.

kindness in its very nature possesses the peculiar power of a love charm on behalf of benefactors, preserving unchanged men's goodwill towards them.]] (4) Antigonus, thus, setting out from Pisidia, marched towards Phrygia with all his force. When he had come to Cretopolis, Aristodemus of Miletus met him with the news that Antipater had died, but that the supreme command and the guardianship of the kings had fallen to Polyperchon the Macedonian. (5) Being delighted at what had happened, he was carried away by hope and made up his mind to get hold of the government throughout Asia and to yield the rule of that continent to no one. This was the situation as regards Antigonus.

S. 131:
18.48.4-5:

Antipater appoints Polyperchon as guardian, Cassander as chiliarch:
(18.48.4) ... Antipater, who was already at the point of death,[89] appointed as guardian of the kings and supreme commander Polyperchon, who was almost the oldest of those who had campaigned with Alexander and was held in honour by the people throughout Macedonia. Antipater made, though, his own son Cassander chiliarch and second in power. (5) The position and rank of chiliarch had first been brought to fame and honour by the Persian kings, and afterwards under Alexander it gained great power and glory at the time when he became an admirer of all other Persian customs as well. Antipater, therefore, following the same course, appointed his son Cassander, though he was young, to the office of chiliarch.[90]

S. 132:
18.50.1-53.7:

Antigonus' schemes; vicissitudes of Arrhidaeus:
(18.50.1) As soon as the death of Antipater was noised abroad throughout Asia, there was the first stirring of revolution, since each of those in power undertook to work for his own ends. Antigonus, as foremost of these, already victor over Eumenes in Cappadocia

---

[89] Explained in 18.48.1: 'After Antipater had been struck by a rather serious illness, which old age was tending to make fatal'.
[90] Goukowsky 2002b: 153 *ad* 48.4 puts forward some of the reasons Antipater may have had for this appointment. As the sequel of Diodorus' work shows (not rendered in this account), Cassander was, nevertheless, not too pleased with the new situation.

The Period of the Diadochs: The Rift Opens 407

and having taken over his army, annihilator of Alcetas and Attalus in Pisidia and annexationist of their troops, moreover, being chosen supreme commander of Asia by Antipater, and at the same time appointed commander of a great army, was filled with pride and haughtiness. (2) Already hopefully aspiring to the supreme power, he decided to take orders neither from the kings nor from their guardians.[91] In fact, he took it for granted that he himself, since he had a better army, would be master of the treasures throughout Asia,[92] as there was no one able to stand against him. (3) Indeed, he had sixty thousand foot soldiers, ten thousand horsemen, and thirty elephants at that time. Apart from these forces, he hoped to make ready other forces as well, if need be, since Asia could provide pay without end for the mercenaries he might muster. (4) With these plans in mind he sent for Hieronymus, the author of the *Histories*, a friend and fellow citizen of Eumenes of Cardia,[93] who had taken refuge with Eumenes in the stronghold called Nora. After endeavouring to attach Hieronymus to himself by great gifts, he sent him as an envoy to Eumenes, urging him to forget the battle that had been fought against him in Cappadocia, to become his friend and ally, to receive gifts many times the value of what he had formerly possessed and a greater satrapy, and in general to be the first of Antigonus' companions and his partner in the whole undertaking. (5) Also convening at once a council of his companions and sharing with them his designs about everything, he assigned satrapies to some of his important companions and military commands to others. Offering to all great expectations, he made them eager for his undertakings. Indeed, he had it in mind to go through Asia, remove the existing satraps, and reorganise the positions of command in favour of his companions. (18.51.1) As Antigonus was engaged in these matters, Arrhidaeus, the satrap of Hellespontine Phrygia, discovering his plan, decided to provide for the safety of his own satrapy and also to secure the most considerable cities by means of garrisons. As the *polis* of the Cyzicenes was strategically most important and very large, he set out against it,[94] with more than ten thousand mercenaries as infantry, a thousand Macedonians, five hundred Persian bowmen

---

[91] Namely Polyperchon and Olympias, the mother of Alexander the Great and grandmother of the son of Roxane and Alexander (see 18.49.4).
[92] The main ones were stored in Susa and Ecbatana, but possibly there was also a (temporary?) one stored in Cilicia (see below, 18.52.7).
[93] Hieronymus had been sent by Eumenes to Antipater (see 18.42.1), but after the death of the latter Hieronymus may well have been on his way back to Nora.
[94] According to Ath. 11.509A, quoting Demochares, Arrhidaeus first tried to establish a tyrant who was well disposed towards him, a man by the name of Timaeus. After the latter

and slingers, eight hundred horsemen, all kinds of missiles, *euthytona* and *palintona*, and all the other equipment proper for storming a city. (2) After falling suddenly upon the *polis* and cutting off a great multitude in the outlying territory, he applied himself to the siege and, by terrifying those who were in the city, tried to force them to receive a garrison.[95] Since the attack had been unexpected and most of the Cyzicenes had been cut off in the country, as there were only a few people left in the city, they were completely unprepared for the siege.[96] (3) Deciding, nevertheless, to maintain their freedom, they openly sent envoys to confer with Arrhidaeus about raising the siege. In fact, they said that the city would do anything for him except receive a garrison. Secretly, though, having assembled the young men and having selected suitable slaves, they armed them and manned the wall with defenders. (4) When Arrhidaeus insisted that the city admit a garrison, the envoys said that they wished to consult the people on this. As the satrap agreed, they obtained a truce, and both that day and the following night they improved their preparations for withstanding the siege. (5) Being outwitted, Arrhidaeus, also missing his opportunity, was balked of his expected success. Indeed, since the Cyzicenes possessed a city that was strong and very easy to defend from attacks by land thanks to its being a peninsula, and since they controlled the sea, they easily warded off the enemy. (6) Moreover, they sent for soldiers from Byzantium and for missiles and whatever else was of use against a siege. When the people of Byzantium supplied all this quickly and willingly, the Cyzicenes became confident and set themselves courageously against the danger. (7) Also launching ships of war at once, they sailed along the coast and, recovering those cut off in the country, brought them back. Soon having plenty of soldiers and after killing many of the besieging force, they rid themselves of the siege. Thus Arrhidaeus, outgeneralled by the Cyzicenes, returned to his own satrapy without accomplishing anything.

Vicissitudes of Antigonus; Antigonus revolts:

(18.52.1) Antigonus happened to be staying in Celaenae when he learned that Cyzicus was being besieged. Deciding to get possession of the endangered *polis* in view of his forthcoming designs, he

had been convicted, Arrhidaeus had no option but to attack if he wanted to take control of the *polis*.

[95] This method of attacking cities, when the population is occupied (in agricultural work) outside the walls, is described in Ph. *Bel.* 5.4.3 (Diels and Schramm: 66).

[96] For the *polis* of Cyzicus, see Bryce 2009: 179 *s.v.* 'Cyzicus'; see also Akurgal 1976.

selected the best from all his force, twenty thousand foot and three thousand horse. (2) Taking these, he set out in haste to bring aid to the Cyzicenes.[97] He was a little too late, but he made his goodwill towards the *polis* manifest, even though failing to gain his entire object. (3) He sent envoys to Arrhidaeus, charging him first, that he had dared to besiege a Greek *polis* that was an ally and not guilty of any offence;[98] next that he had shown he intended to rebel and to convert his satrapy into a private domain; finally, he ordered him to abandon his satrapy and, retaining a single city as a residence, to retire. (4) Arrhidaeus, however, after listening to the envoys and censuring the arrogance of their words, refused to abandon his satrapy, and said that in occupying the cities with garrisons he was trying to decide the contest against Antigonus with the implements of war. In accordance with his answers, after making the cities secure, he sent away a part of his force as well as a commander at its head. He ordered the latter to get in touch with Eumenes, relieve the fortress from the siege, and, when he had freed Eumenes from danger,[99] make him an ally. (5) Antigonus, who was anxious to retaliate upon Arrhidaeus, sent a force to carry on the war against him, but he himself with a sufficient army set out for Lydia, from which he wanted to expel its satrap, Clitus. (6) He, however, foreseeing Antigonus' attack, secured the more important cities with garrisons, but he himself went by ship to Macedonia to reveal both to the kings and to Polyperchon the boldness and defection of Antigonus and to beg them to come to help him. (7) Antigonus took Ephesus at the first assault with the aid of some collaborators from the *polis*.[100] After this, when Aeschylus of Rhodes[101] arrived by sea in Ephesus, conveying in four ships six hundred talents of silver [c. 15,600 kg] from Cilicia that were being sent to Macedonia for the kings, Antigonus took hold of it, saying that he needed it to pay his mercenaries. (8) By doing this, he made it clear that he had begun to act for his own ends and was opposing the kings. Then after storming Cyme,[102] he

---

[97] It enabled him, moreover, to pose as a προστάτης τῆς Ἑλλάδος ('protector of Greece'), specifically of the rights of Greek *poleis*, which would be a recurring theme of his politics. By his action he probably went beyond the mandate he had as 'Commander of Asia', which was directed against Eumenes: see Goukowsky 2002b: 73 note 1.
[98] Cyzicus was already an ally of the Macedonians before 336/5: see above, Chapter 5, 17.7.3 and note 14.
[99] Just. 14.2.4 reports that Antipater had already sent help to Eumenes, by which Antigonus had been forced to lift the siege of Nora.
[100] In 320, Antigonus had stayed some time at Ephesus (see, for example, Goukowsky 2002b: 142 *ad* 29.3), where he may well have forged some useful relationships.
[101] See Heckel 2009: 6 *s.v.* 'Aeschylus'.
[102] The text is corrupt: Cyme looks like the best conjecture available.

advanced against the cities one after another, taking some by force, winning others by persuasion.

Vicissitudes of Eumenes:
(18.53.1) Having disclosed the activities of Antigonus, we shall turn our narrative to the fortunes of Eumenes. This man, experiencing great and incredible reversals of fortune, continually had a share in good and evil beyond expectation. (2) For example, in the period preceding these events, when he was fighting for both Perdiccas and the kings, he had received as his satrapy Cappadocia and the adjacent regions, in which, having become master of great armies and much wealth, his good fortune became famous. (3) He defeated, indeed, Craterus and Neoptolemus, famous commanders in charge of the invincible forces of the Macedonians, in a pitched battle and killed them during the battle. (4) But although he won the reputation of being irresistible, he experienced such a change of fortune that he was defeated by Antigonus in a great battle and was compelled to take refuge with a few friends in a very small spot. Shut up there and surrounded by the enemy with a double wall, he had no one to help in his own misfortune. (5) When the siege had lasted a year and hope of being rescued had been abandoned, there suddenly appeared an unexpected deliverance from his misfortunes. Indeed, Antigonus, who was besieging Eumenes and aiming to kill him, changed his plan, invited him to share in his own undertakings, and after receiving an oath-bound pledge,[103] freed him from the siege. (6) Thus unexpectedly saved after a considerable time, he then spent his time in Cappadocia, gathering again his former friends and those wandering about the country of those who had once served under him. Since he was highly esteemed, he quickly found many men sharing the same expectations and ready to enlist for the campaign with him. (7) In the end, within a few days, in addition to the five hundred friends who had been besieged in the fortress with him, he had over two thousand soldiers,[104] who followed him of their own free will. Because Fate helped him, he achieved so great an increase in power that he took over the royal forces and stood up for the kings against those who had boldly tried to end their rule. But we shall relate these events in more detail a little later in their proper place.

---

[103] See Plu. *Eum.* 12.1–3 for the oath; also Nep. *Eum.* 5.7. For a comment see Goukowsky 2002b: 155 *ad* 53.5.
[104] Plu. *Eum.* 12.5–6 reports that Eumenes gathered 1,000 additional horsemen.

S. 133:
18.58.1–63.6:

Kings entrust Eumenes with extensive powers:
(18.58.1) When Archippus was *archon* of Athens [318/17], the Romans elected Quintus Aelius and Lucius Papirius consuls.[105] While these held office, Eumenes, just after he had made good his retreat from the fortress, received the letters that had been dispatched by Polyperchon, in which was written, apart from what has been told above,[106] the statement that the kings were giving him a gift of five hundred talents [c. 13,000 kg <of silver?>] as recompense for the losses that he had experienced.[107] To effect this, they had written to the commanders and treasurers in Cilicia in order to give him the five hundred talents and whatever additional money he requested for raising mercenaries and for other pressing needs. They also wrote to the commanders of the three thousand Macedonian Silver Shields,[108] ordering them to place themselves at the disposal of Eumenes and in general to co-operate wholeheartedly with him, since he had been appointed supreme commander of all Asia. (2) There came to him also a letter from Olympias, in which she begged and besought him to aid the kings and herself. She wrote that, indeed, he alone was left, the most faithful of her friends and the one able to set right the isolation of the royal house. (3) Olympias asked him to advise her whether he thought it better for her to remain in Epirus and place no trust in those who were for the time being supposed to be guardians of the kings,[109] but were in truth trying to transfer the kingdom to themselves, or to return to Macedonia. (4) Eumenes at once replied to Olympias, advising her to remain in Epirus for the present, until the war should come to some decision. As for himself, since he had always observed the most unwavering loyalty towards the Kings, he decided not to take orders from Antigonus, who was trying to appropriate the kingship for himself. Because, however, the son of

---

[105] As the consuls for 319 vc, Broughton 1951: 54 lists L. Papirius Cursor and Q. Aulius Cerretanus. Diodorus is two years ahead of the Varronian chronology.
[106] Decisions outlined in 18.57.2–3.
[107] As Goukowsky 2002b: 80 note 2 rightly remarks, the sum was huge and seems more intended to buy Eumenes' services than a realistic compensation for his losses.
[108] Survivors of the corps of *hypaspists*, who had changed their name to the *Argyraspides* ('Silver Shields') whilst in India under Alexander (Arr. *An.* 7.11.3). Having been demobilised in 324, they had not followed Craterus into Macedonia for the Lamian War. Although most of them were at that time already over sixty, they were feared and revered due to their battle skills and experience. Later, the Seleucid kings of Syria employed an infantry corps of the same name. See also Goukowsky 2002b: 160 *ad* 58.1.
[109] In fact, she was herself one of the guardians of the kings; see above 18.49.4.

Alexander was in need of help because of his orphaned state and the greediness of the commanders, he believed that it was fitting for himself to run every risk for the safety of the kings.[110]
(18.59.1) Immediately, therefore, Eumenes, bidding his men to break camp, departed from Cappadocia with about five hundred horsemen and more than two thousand infantry. Indeed, he did not have time to wait for the laggards among those who had promised to join him, because of the approach of a considerable force, sent from Antigonus under the commander Menander[111] to prevent Eumenes from staying in Cappadocia, having become an enemy of Antigonus' men. (2) In fact, when this army arrived three days later, although it had missed its opportunity, it undertook to follow those who had gone with Eumenes. When it was not able to come up with them, it returned to Cappadocia. (3) Making forced marches and quickly passing over the Taurus, Eumenes entered Cilicia. Antigenes and Teutamus, the leaders of the Silver Shields, complying with the letters of the kings, with their companions, came from a considerable distance to meet Eumenes.[112] After bidding him welcome and congratulating him on his unexpected escape from the greatest dangers, they promised to co-operate willingly with him in everything. The Macedonian Silver Shields, about three thousand in number, likewise met him with both friendship and zeal. (4) All wondered at the incredible fickleness of Fate, seeing that a little while before both the kings and the Macedonians had condemned Eumenes and his friends to death, but now, forgetting their own decision, had not only let him off punishment scot-free, but also entrusted to him supreme command over the entire kingdom. (5) And it was with good reason that all who then beheld the reversals in Eumenes' fortunes shared these emotions. . . . (6) . . . [[personal moral observations by Diodorus.]]

Eumenes takes charge of his forces, remaining cautious:
(18.60.1) Eumenes, who at this time also kept these things in mind, prudently made his own position secure, for he foresaw the reversal of Fate. Perceiving that he himself was a Greek and had no claim

---

[110] See also Nep. *Eum.* 6.2, which follows more or less the same tradition.
[111] Though Goukowsky 2002b: 82 note 1 asserts this Menander is not identified, it seems he was identical with Alexander's *hetairos*, mentioned in Arr. *An.* 3.6.7–8, 7.23.1. Later, at the settlement in Babylon, he was confirmed as satrap of Lydia (see above 18.3.1; Arr. *Succ.* 1.6 = Phot. *Bibl.* [92] 69b1). See also Heckel 2009: 163 *s.v.* 'Menander [1]'.
[112] See Plu. *Eum.* 13.2–3; Just. 14.2.6–12; also Goukowsky 2002b: 82 note 2; Heckel 2009: 30–1 (*s.v.* 'Antigenes [1a]'), 262 ('Teutamus'). As a matter of fact, according to Polyaen. 4.8.2, both commanders of the 'Silver Shields' were far from pleased to have to deal with Eumenes.

at all to the royal power, that the Macedonians who were now subject to him had previously decreed his death,[113] and that those who occupied the military commands were filled with arrogance and were aiming at great affairs, he understood that he would soon be despised and at the same time envied, and that his life would eventually be in danger. He sensed that, indeed, no one would willingly carry out orders given by those whom he regarded as his inferiors, or be patient when he had over him as masters those who ought themselves to be subject to others.[114] (2) Reasoning about these matters with himself, when the five hundred talents for refitting and organisation were offered to him in accordance with the kings' letters, he said he would not accept them: in fact, that he had no need of such a gift, just as he had no ambition to receive a command. (3) Even now, he said, it was not of his own will that he had yielded with respect to his present office, but he had been compelled by the kings to undertake this great task.[115] In fact, because of his continuous military service, he was no longer able to endure the skirmishes and wanderings, especially since no magistracy was in prospect for one who was an alien, excluded from the national rights of the Macedonians. (4) He revealed, however, that in his sleep he had seen a strange vision,[116] which he considered necessary to disclose to all; in fact, that he thought that it would contribute both to harmony and the general good. (5) He said that, in fact, in his sleep he had seemed to see Alexander the king, alive and clad in his kingly garb, presiding over a council, giving orders to the commanders, and actively administering all the affairs of the monarchy. (6) 'Therefore I think that we must fetch a golden throne from the royal treasury, on which the diadem, the sceptre, the crown, and the rest of the insignia should be placed. All the commanders must burn incense to Alexander in the presence of the throne at daybreak, hold

---

[113] Probably because he was linked to Perdiccas. 18.37.2 reports that the Macedonians sentenced Eumenes and fifty of his chief followers to death, following Eumenes' victory over Craterus and Neoptolemus, and more or less connects it with Perdiccas' death. Also, 'After Perdiccas' defeat and murder in Egypt, Eumenes and the remnants of the Perdiccan party were outlawed': Heckel 2009: 121.

[114] See Westlake 1969: 315 and note 8, who asserts that in this kind of passage Diodorus preaches 'his own uninspired theory of history'. I disagree with the latter view.

[115] Plu. *Eum.* 13.2 phrases it as follows: Πολυσπέρχοντος δὲ καὶ Φιλίππου τοῦ βασιλέως κελευόντων Ἀντιγόνῳ πολεμεῖν ('because Poly[s]perchon and King Philip ordered him to make war against Antigonus').

[116] Plu. *Eum.* 13.5–6 has a different version of the dream, but Polyaen. 4.8.2 comes close to Diodorus: moreover it underlines the stratagem of this action μηδὲν τῶν κοινῶν καὶ βασιλικῶν διοικεῖν ἔξω τῆς βασιλικῆς σκηνῆς ('not to do any public or royal business outside the royal tent'). Applying this course of action, Eumenes more or less returns to the idea of a centralised and controlled state. Neither Cornelius Nepos nor Justin reports the dream.

the meetings of the council in its presence, and receive their orders in the name of the king just as if he were alive and at the head of his own kingdom.'

(18.61.1) Because all agreed to his proposal, everything needed was quickly prepared for use, since the royal treasure was rich in gold. Straightaway then, after a magnificent tent had been set up, the throne was placed with the diadem, the sceptre, and the armour that Alexander had been wont to use. Then after a brazier with a fire[117] on it had been put in place, all the commanders made a sacrifice from a golden casket, both frankincense and the most costly of the other kinds of incense, and made obeisance to Alexander as to a god. (2) In accordance with this ritual those who exercised command sat down in the many chairs that had been placed about and, taking counsel together, they deliberated on the matters that from time to time required their attention. By placing himself as an equal with the other commanders in all the matters that were discussed and by seeking their favour through the most friendly intercourse, Eumenes both wore down the envy with which he had been regarded and secured for himself a great deal of goodwill among the commanders. (3) As their reverence for the king grew stronger, they were all filled with good hopes, just as if some god were leading them. And by conducting himself towards the Macedonian Silver Shields in a similar way, Eumenes gained great favour among them as a man worthy of the solicitude of the kings. (4) Selecting the most able of his companions and giving them ample funds, he sent them out to engage mercenaries, having determined a notable rate of pay. Some of them, going straight to Pisidia, Lycia, and the adjacent regions, zealously enrolled troops. Others travelled through Cilicia, others again through Coele Syria and Phoenicia,[118] some through the *poleis* in Cyprus. (5) As the news of this levy spread widely and the pay offered was worthy of consideration, many reporting voluntarily even from the *poleis* of Greece were enrolled for the campaign. In a short time more than ten thousand infantry and two thousand horsemen were gathered together, apart from the Silver Shields and those who had accompanied Eumenes.

---

[117] See for the use of an ἐσχάρα, for example, Stronk, *BNJ* 171 F 7. As a matter of fact, I will not exclude the possibility that Diodorus (or his source) played a game in this passage with a line from Aeschylus' *Eumenides*: ἐπ' ἐσχάραι πυρὸς ἔθυον ('they offered on braziers of fire'): A. *Eu.* 108–9. Though Goukowsky 2002b: 163 *ad* 61.1, fourth remark, suggests the ceremony was altogether based upon Persian objects, I cannot see sufficient evidence for this suggestion.

[118] Goukowsky 2002b: 164 *ad* 61.4 rightly points out that this remark indicates that Ptolemy's hold on Phoenicia was all but firm.

Eumenes' position is threatened, but he seems to emerge victorious:
(18.62.1) At Eumenes' unexpected and sudden rise to power, Ptolemy, having sailed to Zephyrium in Cilicia with a fleet, kept sending messages to the commanders of the Silver Shields, exhorting them not to turn to Eumenes, whom all the Macedonians had condemned to death. (2) Likewise he sent to those who had been placed in command of the garrisons in Cynda,[119] begging them earnestly to give nothing of the money to Eumenes, and promised to provide for their safety. But no one paid any attention to him because the kings and Polyperchon, their guardian, and also Olympias, the mother of Alexander, had written to them that they should serve Eumenes in every way, since he was the commander-in-chief of the kingdom. (3) The advancement of Eumenes and the magnitude of the power that was being concentrated in him displeased Antigonus in particular. In fact, Antigonus assumed that Eumenes was being prepared by Polyperchon as the strongest rival of himself now that he had become a rebel against the monarchy. (4) Deciding, therefore, to organise a plot against Eumenes, Antigonus selected from his friends Philotas and gave him a letter that he had written both to the Silver Shields and to the other Macedonians with Eumenes. With Philotas he also sent thirty other Macedonians, of the meddlesome and talkative kind, who were instructed to meet separately with Antigenes and Teutamus, the commanders of the Silver Shields, and through them to organise a plot against Eumenes by promising both great gifts and greater satrapies. Antigonus told them also to get in touch simultaneously with their acquaintances and fellow citizens among the Silver Shields and seduce them with presents to partake in the plot against Eumenes. (5) Although they were unable to persuade any others, Teutamus, the leader of the Silver Shields, was bribed and undertook to persuade his fellow commander, Antigenes, to share in the enterprise. (6) Antigenes, however, who was outstanding in shrewdness and stability of loyalty, not only spoke in opposition, but even won back the man who had been corrupted beforehand. In fact, he showed him that it was preferable that Eumenes rather than Antigonus should remain alive. (7) The latter, indeed, if he became

---

[119] See 20.108.2; Str. 14.5.10/672. Cynda was a fortress in Cilicia where (part of) the royal treasure had been deposited, a tradition that had probably started as early as the Assyrian King Esarhaddon, who also used Cilician Kundi as a treasury: see Bing 1973: 346 and note 3. See also Simpson 1957. The precise location of Cynda is, to the best of my knowledge, not yet established, but it should be in western Cilicia, between the town of Soli (in the close proximity of modern Mersin) and the mouth of the River Cydnus (modern River Berdan, also known as the Tarsus), probably not too far from the sea: see ibid.: 503.

more powerful, would take away their satrapies and set up some of his companions in their places but Eumenes, since he was not a Macedonian,[120] would never dare to advance his own interests, but, remaining a commander-in-chief, would treat them as friends and, if they co-operated with him, would protect their satrapies for them and perhaps give them others also. Therefore those who were contriving plots against Eumenes met with failure in the aforementioned way.

(18.63.1) When, however, Philotas gave the commanders the general letter, both the Silver Shields and the other Macedonians came together privately without Eumenes and ordered the letter to be read.[121] (2) In it was written an accusation against Eumenes, appealing to the Macedonians to seize Eumenes quickly and put him to death. If they did not do this, Antigonus said that he would come with his whole force to make war against them, and that upon those who refused to obey he would inflict suitable punishment. (3) When they had taken notice of this letter, the commanders and all the Macedonians fell into great embarrassment. Indeed, it was necessary for them either to side with the kings and receive punishment from Antigonus, or to obey Antigonus and be chastised by Polyperchon and the kings. (4) While the troops were in this confused state, Eumenes entered and,[122] after taking notice of the letter, urged the Macedonians to act according to the decisions of the kings and to take no heed of one who had become a rebel. (5) Discussing many matters pertinent to the subject, Eumenes not only freed himself from the imminent dangers, but also gained greater favour with the men than before. (6) Eumenes thus again, having fallen into unforeseen danger, unexpectedly made his own power greater. Therefore, ordering the soldiers to break camp, he led them to Phoenicia, desiring them to gather ships from all the cities and to assemble a considerable fleet, in order to enable Polyperchon, by adding the Phoenician ships, to become master of the sea and, whenever he would wish, be able to transfer the Macedonian forces safely to Asia against Antigonus. Accordingly Eumenes remained in Phoenicia preparing the naval force.[123]

---

[120] Literally a ξένος ('foreigner').
[121] Above, 18.60.1, Eumenes himself had indicated already that he, being Greek instead of Macedonian, had no real say in either Macedonian counsels or, for that matter, Macedonian politics in general.
[122] Why Eumenes entered and on what conditions remains unclear.
[123] If Polyaen. 4.6.9 is right, it may reflect on the Phoenician fleet under the command of Sosigenes (formerly *navarch* of Perdiccas: see Heckel 2009: 253 *s.v.*), anchored at the harbour of Rhosius in Cilicia.

The Period of the Diadochs: The Rift Opens   417

S. 134:
18.73.1–4:

Antigonus sets out against Eumenes; Eumenes escapes to Persis:
(18.73.1) By inflicting so disastrous a blow upon the enemy,[124] Antigonus acquired a great reputation for generalship and sagacity. He now set out to gain command of the sea and to place his control of Asia beyond dispute. Selecting, therefore, from his entire force twenty thousand lightly equipped infantry and four thousand cavalry, he set out for Cilicia, hoping to annihilate Eumenes and his men before he should gather a more abundant force. (2) Having learned about Antigonus' efforts, Eumenes set himself to recover Phoenicia for the kings, as it had been unjustly occupied by Ptolemy,[125] but being forestalled by events, he moved from Phoenicia and marched with his army through Coele Syria, intending to join with the so-called upper satrapies. (3) As some locals attacked him near the River Tigris by night, however, he lost some of his soldiers. Similarly in Babylonia, when Seleucus attacked him near the River Euphrates, Eumenes was in danger of losing his whole army.[126] When a canal was breached, his entire camp was inundated, but yet by a piece of strategy of his own, escaping to a mound and redirecting the canal again, he saved both himself and his army. (4) Thus unexpectedly escaping the hands of Seleucus, he arrived in Persis with his force, which was fifteen thousand infantry and thirty-three hundred cavalry.[127] After letting the soldiers recover from their hardships, he sent a message to both the satraps and commanders in the upper satrapies, requesting both soldiers and money. And the affairs of Asia progressed to such a point during this year.

---

[124] Namely the naval victory in the Hellespont, gained by Nicanor, the *navarch* of Antigonus, over the fleet of Clitus, the *navarch* of Polyperchon, after an initial victory for Clitus. See also Polyaen. 4.6.8. Polyaenus adds that, subsequently, Nicanor sailed back to Cilicia and there took Eumenes' fleet (not least due to the treason of Eumenes' sailors, committed as Sosigenes watched helplessly from the coast) and his treasure: Polyaen. 4.6.9. Diodorus omits this. For a review of Antigonus' maritime campaigns: Grainger 2011: 19–26.
[125] Immediately after the Triparadisus conference, Ptolemy seized the Phoenician towns. Together with Cyprus and Cyrenaica, they were a protective belt around his main possession, Egypt. It was, however, a violation of the Triparadisus agreement. After Alexander, Phoenicia was, thus, controlled by a succession of Greek or Macedonian rulers, (nominally) residing in Tyre: Laomedon (323–320), Ptolemy I (320–315), Antigonus (315–301), Demetrius (301–296), and Seleucus (296–286). Between 286 and 197, the largest part of Phoenicia fell to the Ptolemies.
[126] This incident occurred by the River Tigris instead of the Euphrates: Diodorus is here obviously mistaken. See below, 19.13.2–6; also Goukowsky 2002b: 169–70 *ad* 73.3.
[127] As regards the number of horsemen the MSS are in discord: MS F mentions χιλίους καὶ τριακοσίους ('1,300'), MS R τρισχιλίους καὶ τριακοσίους ('3,300'). As most editors follow the lead of MS R here, I have believed it right to do the same.

8 The Period of the Diadochs: The Rift Deepens

THE YEARS 317/16-311/10

S. 135:
19.12.1-34.8:

Eumenes seeks support; he directs his course towards Susa:
(19.12.1) In Asia,[1] Eumenes with the Macedonian Silver Shields and their commander Antigenes wintered [winter of 318/17] in the villages of Babylonia known as the villages of the Carians.[2] He sent embassies to Seleucus and Peithon asking them to aid the kings and to join him in the struggle against Antigonus. (2) Of these men, Peithon had been appointed satrap of Media and the former had been named satrap of Babylonia at the time when the second distribution of satrapies was made at Triparadisus. Seleucus said that he was willing to be of service to the kings, but that he would nevertheless never consent to carry out the orders of Eumenes, whom the Macedonians in assembly had condemned to death. After deliberating much regarding this principle, they sent an ambassador from themselves to Antigenes and the Silver Shields, asking them to remove Eumenes from his command. (3) Since the Macedonians did not comply with these words, Eumenes, after praising their loyalty, set out with the force and pitched camp on reaching the River Tigris,

---

[1] Continued from and partly repeating, partly elaborating, the story above, last at 18.73.4.
[2] These villages are also mentioned in 17.110.3, during Alexander's expedition. They should not be confused with the Carae (τῶν ἐν Κάραις κατισκωμένων [Μακεδόνες] ('[the Macedonians] who were settled at Carae')) of 19.91.1 (see below), which appears to have to be identified as the city of Carrhae.

The Period of the Diadochs: The Rift Deepens   419

at a distance of three hundred *stadia* [slightly over 55 km] from Babylon. His purpose was to march to Susa, intending to summon the armies from the upper satrapies and to use the royal treasury for his urgent needs. (4) He was forced, though, to cross the river because the country behind him had been plundered, whereas that on the other side was untouched and able to furnish abundant food for his army. (5) After Eumenes had gathered, thus, ships from all sides for the crossing, Seleucus and Peithon sailed down with two *triereis* and a fair number of punts. In fact, these vessels still survived from those that had been built by Alexander near Babylon.[3]

(19.13.1) Directing these craft to the landing place, Seleucus and Peithon attempted again to persuade the Macedonians to remove Eumenes from his command and not to promote against their own interests a Greek and the killer of very many Macedonians. (2) But when Antigenes and his men were in no way persuaded, Seleucus sailed off to a certain ancient canal to clear its intake, which had been filled up in the course of time. Because the camp of the Macedonians was washed all round and the neighbouring land was inundated on all sides, the entire encampment was in danger of being destroyed by the flood.[4] (3) The Macedonians, then, remained inactive that day, being at a loss how to deal with the situation. On the next day, though, after bringing up the punts, about three hundred in number, they carried the best part of the army across as no one hindered them during the evacuation. Indeed, Seleucus had cavalry only and that too far inferior to the opponents' as regards number. (4) But when night was overtaking them, Eumenes, being anxious about the baggage, made the Macedonians transfer back again and, under the guidance of one of the local people, began to clear out a certain place, through which it was easy to turn the canal and make the neighbouring land passable. (5) As Seleucus saw this and wishing them to get out of his satrapy as soon as possible, he sent envoys to propose a truce, conceding to Eumenes his passage across the river. Forthwith, though, they also sent letter-carriers into Mesopotamia to Antigonus, asking him to come as soon as possible with his force,

---

[3] See Arr. *An.* 7.19.4. He mentions, though, no punts, but 17.116.5 (see above) records the story that Alexander wanted to explore the swamps around Babylon and used some skiffs for that purpose. Diodorus does not, however, state whether these had been constructed recently or not.
[4] It might be that this episode is alluded to in a Babylonian chronicle, as Momigliano 1932: 475–6 suggests. However, even though Geer 1969: 263 note 1 alludes to events therein, its date (autumn 318) hardly fits with the events described here. Moreover, it deals with the capture of the acropolis/citadel of Babylon, which is not related at all by Diodorus. See also Bizière 2002: 153 *ad* 13.2.

before the satraps of the upper satrapies came from the inland with their forces. (6) Eumenes, however, having crossed the Tigris and arrived in Susis, divided his army into three parts because of the dearth of food. Marching through the country in separate columns, he was completely without grain, but he distributed to his soldiers rice, sesame, and dates, since the land produced such fruits as these in plenty. (7) He had already sent to the commanders of the upper satrapies the letter from the kings[5] in which it was written that they should obey Eumenes in every way, and at this time again he sent letter-carriers bidding them all to present themselves with their separate forces in Susis. But it happened at this very time that they, too, had mobilised their forces and had assembled because of other reasons, with which it is necessary to deal first.

Eumenes' forces are supplemented by those from the upper satrapies:
(19.14.1) Peithon had been appointed satrap of Media, but having become commander of all the upper satrapies, he put to death Philotas, the former commander of Parthia, and installed his own brother Eudamus in his place.[6] (2) At this, all the other satraps joined forces, fearing that they might suffer a similar fate, since Peithon was seditious and had included great undertakings in his plans.[7] Prevailing over him in a battle and killing many of his supporters, they drove him out of Parthia. (3) At first he withdrew to Media, but having arrived at Babylon after a little, he exhorted Seleucus to help him and to share in his expectations. (4) Because the upper satraps had for these reasons concentrated their armies in a single place, the letter-carriers from Eumenes found the forces ready. The most eminent of the commanders and the one who, by common consent, had assumed command of all the forces was Peucestes, who had been a bodyguard of Alexander and had been promoted by the king because of his courage.[8] (5) He had held the satrapy of Persis for many years [from 324 onwards] and had gained great favour with

---

[5] Actually Polyperchon's letter on behalf of the kings.

[6] During the distribution of posts at Triparadisus, Peithon was appointed satrap of Media, but Philip as satrap of Parthia (see 18.39.6, above). How and when Peithon obtained the title/function of commander of the upper satrapies is unknown. Diodorus does not make it clear whether Philip still remained satrap. Heckel believes that Diodorus' text is corrupt and that instead of Philotas we should here read Philip: Heckel 2009: 214 s.v. 'Philip [10]'. The context, notably the following sentence, lends credibility to this suggestion.

[7] See above, 18.7.4.

[8] For Peucestes' courage, see above, 17.99.4. Peucestes had been appointed as satrap by Alexander (see Arr. *An.* 6.30.2–3) and was confirmed in his position by Perdiccas (18.3.3) and at Triparadisus (18.39.6).

The Period of the Diadochs: The Rift Deepens   421

the local population. They say that for this reason Alexander permitted him alone of the Macedonians to wear Persian raiment,⁹ wishing to please the Persians and believing that through Peucestes he could keep the nation obedient in all respects. At this time Peucestes had ten thousand Persian archers and slingers, three thousand men of every origin equipped for service in Macedonian array,¹⁰ six hundred Greek and Thracian cavalry, and more than four hundred Persian horsemen. (6) Tlepolemus the Macedonian,¹¹ who had been appointed satrap of Carmania, had one thousand five hundred foot and seven hundred horse. Sibyrtius, the commander of Arachosia,¹² brought a thousand foot and six hundred and ten horse. Androbazus had been dispatched from Paropanisadae, of which satrapy Oxyartes was ruler, with twelve hundred infantry and four hundred cavalry. (7) Stasander, the satrap of Aria and Drangia,¹³ bringing the troops from Bactria as well, had fifteen hundred infantry and a thousand horse. (8) From India came Eudamus with five hundred horsemen, three hundred footmen, and one hundred and twenty elephants. These beasts he had secured after the death of Alexander, after treacherously killing King Porus.¹⁴ In all, there were assembled with the satraps more than eighteen thousand seven hundred infantry and four thousand six hundred cavalry.¹⁵

Discussions regarding the command:
(**19.15.1**) When the satraps had come into Susis and had joined Eumenes, they called together a general assembly¹⁶ in which there was found to be much rivalry regarding the chief command. Peucestes,

---

⁹ However, 17.77.5 suggests Alexander gave Persian clothes to several of his companions. See also, though, Plu. *Alex.* 45.
¹⁰ That is, as heavy infantry. Perhaps they belonged to the young Persians mentioned in 17.108.1–2, above.
¹¹ The MSS read here Πολέμων, but Τληπόλεμος in 18.39.6 and 19.28.3. Hence Wesseling made this emendation.
¹² Appointed as such by Alexander (see Arr. *An.* 6.27.1) and confirmed in his position by Perdiccas (18.3.3) and at Triparadisus (Arr. *Succ.* 1.36). In 18.39.6 his name is omitted.
¹³ See Heckel 2009: 255 *s.v.* Stasander also commanded the troops of Bactria, of which Stasonor of Soli had been appointed satrap at Triparadisus (see above, 18.39.6).
¹⁴ Arr. *An.* 6.27.2 relates that Alexander left Eudamus as Macedonian supervisor, with satrap Philip son of Machatas, with Taxiles. After Philip was murdered, Alexander appointed Eudamus as satrap (see Curt. 10.1.21). Of the murder of King Porus, Taxiles' enemy, there are no further reports known to me. This Eudamus should obviously not be confused with Peithon's brother. See also Heckel 2009: 120 *s.v.* 'Eudamus [2]'.
¹⁵ The numbers do not add up correctly, but it may that the troops of Amphimachus from Mesopotamia, who was present at Gabiene (below, 19.27.4), account for the difference. Moreover, the text in the MSS regarding paragraph 6, on the number of horsemen of Sibyrtius, is corrupt: see Bizière 2002: 26 *apparatus* line 7, 154 *ad* 14.8.
¹⁶ An expression with a double meaning: it indicates not only an assembly composed from different army groups (see 18.39.4; 19.51.1, 61.1), but also the assembly of a federal state (19.67.4): see Bizière 2002: 154 *ad* 15.1.

indeed, because of the number of soldiers who followed him on the campaign and because of his high rank under Alexander, thought that he should have the supreme command. (2) Antigenes, though, who was commander of the Macedonian Silver Shields, said that the right to make the selection ought to be granted to his Macedonians, since they had conquered Asia with Alexander and had been unconquered because of their *aretē*. (3) Fearing that through their rivalry with each other they would become an easy prey for Antigonus, Eumenes advised them not to appoint one commander, but that all the satraps and commanders who had been selected by the mass of the army, convening in the royal tent each day, should take counsel together about the matters at hand. (4) For a tent had been erected for Alexander, although he was dead, and in the tent a throne, before which they, having offered, were used to deliberate about pressing issues. As all approved his proposal as made in the general interest, he called a council each day in the manner of some *polis* ruled on democratic principles.[17] (5) Later, when they had arrived in Susa, Eumenes received from those in charge of the treasury a sum of money sufficient for his needs. Indeed, the kings had ordered them in their letter to give to him alone whatever sum he should ask. After paying the Macedonians for six months, he gave two hundred talents [1,200,000 *drachmae*] to Eudamus, who had brought down the elephants from India, in name for the cost of maintaining the animals, in reality wheedling the man by this gift. In fact, which of the rivals he might attach himself to would make a very great impact, since the employment of the beasts strikes terror. Of the other satraps, each maintained the troops who had followed him from the territory under his command. (6) Eumenes, then, remaining in Susis, refreshed his forces. Antigonus, though, who had wintered in Mesopotamia,[18] had at first planned to follow close on Eumenes' heels before he increased his strength. However, when he heard that the satraps and their forces had joined the Macedonians, he checked his speed and began both to refresh his forces and to enrol additional soldiers. Indeed, he perceived that the war would require large armies and no chance preparation.

Imprisoned commanders try to escape from Antigonus:
(**19.16.1**) While these things were happening, Attalus, Polemon, and Docimus, as well as Antipater and Philotas, the commanders who

---

[17] See the comment by Bizière 2002: 154 *ad* 15.4.
[18] The winter intended is always still that of 318/17.

The Period of the Diadochs: The Rift Deepens 423

had been captured along with the army of Alcetas, were being kept under guard in an exceedingly strong fortress.[19] However, hearing that Antigonus was leading an expedition into the upper satrapies, believing that they had a favourable opportunity, they persuaded certain of their custodians to release them. Having gained possession of arms, they set upon the guard at about midnight. Though they themselves, then, numbered only eight and were guarded by four hundred soldiers, but excelling in daring and dexterity thanks to their service with Alexander,[20] after getting hold of him, they threw Xenopithes, the captain of the garrison, from the wall at a point where the cliff was a *stadium* high [c. 185 m]. Slaughtering some of the other guards, casting down others, they set fire to the buildings. (2) From those who had been standing aside to observe the outcome they increased their number to fifty. Because the fortress held a large amount of grain and other provisions, they took counsel together whether they should stay and use the strength of the location, waiting for aid from Eumenes, or fleeing as quickly as possible should wander about the country, waiting for a change in the situation. (3) As there was a considerable argument, Docimus advised leaving the place, but Attalus declared he was not able to endure hardship because of his bad condition contracted through imprisonment. But while they were disputing with each other, troops appeared, assembling from the adjacent fortresses, more than five hundred infantry and four hundred horsemen, apart from those from the native peoples, others, men of every kind, more than three thousand, who, having selected a commander from their own ranks, encamped about the stronghold. (4) When they had unexpectedly been shut in again, Docimus, learning that a certain way of descent was unguarded, sent an ambassador to Antigonus' wife Stratonice,[21] who was in the neighbourhood. Having escaped himself with a second man by arrangement with her,[22] he himself was given no protection but was handed over to a guard. The man, however, who had gone out with him, having become a guide for the enemy, conducted many of them into the stronghold, and occupied one of the peaks.

---

[19] Possibly a fortress in the neighbourhood of Celaenae (later Apamia) in Phrygia (see Stillwell 1976: 445 *s.v.* 'Kelainai'), as suggested by Heckel 2009: 258 *s.v.* 'Stratonice'. This episode resumes that of 18.45.3–4.
[20] Bizière 2002: 28 note 2 rightly underlines that here as elsewhere the superior qualities of Alexander's veterans are stressed.
[21] For the position of Macedonian wives, see the reference of Bizière 2002: 152 *ad* 11.9.
[22] Though the sentence is grammatically correct and does make sense, in context, Bizière believes, nevertheless, that the construction is faulty or not precise (she calls it 'maladroite'): see Bizière 2002: 154–5 *ad* 16.4.

(5) Although Attalus and his colleagues were far outnumbered, they held their ground through their *aretae*, and keeping up the fight day after day they resisted stubbornly. However, after they had been besieged for a year and four months, they were they taken by assault.

Antigonus joins forces with Seleucus and Peithon:
(19.17.1) When Democlides was *archon* at Athens [316/15], the Romans elected Gaius Junius and Quintus Aemilius consuls.[23] This was the one hundred and sixteenth celebration of the Olympic Games, at which Dinonmenes the Laconian won the *stadium* race.[24] (2) About this time, Antigonus setting out from Mesopotamia came into Babylonia and there he made an agreement for common action with Seleucus and Peithon. Having received soldiers from them as well, he made a ship-bridge over the River Tigris and, having taken his force across, set out against the enemy. (3) When Eumenes learned what had taken place, he ordered Xenophilus, who was guarding the citadel of Susa, not to give any of the money to Antigonus or to have any conference with him. He himself, taking with him his forces, set out for the River Pasitigris,[25] which is a day's march from Susa at the place where it flows out of the mountainous country that is occupied by the independent tribesmen they call the Uxians. Its width in many places is three *stadia* [c. 550 m], and in some places even four [nearly 750 m]. In the middle of the stream the depth is about the height of the elephants. After flowing along for some seven hundred *stadia* [c. 129 km] from the mountains, it empties into the Persian Gulf. It holds abundant salt-water fishes as well as marine predators,[26] which appear especially about the time of the rising of the Dog Star [Sirius].[27] (4) Keeping this river in front of him and holding the bank from its source to the sea with pickets, he awaited the enemy onset. Because the guard, because of the length it covered, required many soldiers, Eumenes and Antigenes asked Peucestes to summon ten thousand bowmen from Persis. (5) At first he paid no heed to them, because

---

[23] C. Iunius Bubulcus Brutus and Q. Aemilius Barbula were the consuls of 317 vc: Broughton 1951: 155. Diodorus is two years ahead of the Varronian chronology.

[24] According to Paus. 6.16.8 and an inscription from Olympia (Dittenberger and Purgold 1896: no. 171; also SEG 29.419), the name of the victor was Dinosthenes (Δεινοσθένης).

[25] Diodorus here appears to confuse (again) the rivers Tigris and Pasitigris. From Susa to the Pasitigris (modern River Karun) was earlier described as a four days' march (17.67.1), which seems more realistic. The march led eastward: Eumenes and his men are postponing a confrontation with Antigonus. Remarkably, Diodorus changes between the names Pasitigris and Tigris, most obviously below, 19.18.3-4.

[26] Both Geer 1969: 277 and Bizière 2002: 30 note 5 believe that Diodorus intended sharks. I prefer to keep it relatively neutral. However, sharks are known to (have) visit(ed) the Karun.

[27] About the latter part of our month of June.

The Period of the Diadochs: The Rift Deepens 425

he still bore a grudge at not having received the command, but later, reasoning with himself, he admitted that, when Antigonus was victorious, he himself would be in danger of losing his satrapy and in danger of his life. (6) Being anxious, then, about himself and thinking that he would gain the command sooner if he had as many soldiers as possible, he brought up ten thousand bowmen as they had asked. Although some of the Persians were distant a thirty days' journey, they all heard the message on that very day, through the skilful arrangement of the posts of the guard, which it is not well to pass over. (7) Indeed, as Persis is cut by many narrow valleys and possesses lookout posts which are high and close together, those of the inhabitants who had the loudest voices had been stationed on these. In fact, since these posts were separated from each other by the distance at which a man's voice can be heard, those who received the message passed it on in the same way to others, next those again to others, until the message had been delivered at the border of the satrapy.[28]

Battle at the River Coprates and its aftermath:
(19.18.1) While Eumenes and Peucestes were engaged in these matters, Antigonus, advancing with his force, came to Susa, the capital. He appointed Seleucus as satrap of that country[29] and, giving him troops, ordered him to lay siege to the citadel because Xenophilus, the treasurer, did not co-operate. He himself with his army marched on against the enemy, even though the road was very hot and very dangerous for a foreign force to traverse. Therefore they were forced to march at night and make camp near the river before sunrise. (2) Nevertheless, he was not able to escape altogether untouched by the hardships inherent in the country. Even though doing everything to the best of his ability, he lost a large number of men because of the extreme heat, for it was the time of the year when the Dog Star rises. (3) When he reached the River Coprates,[30] he began to make the preparations for crossing. This river, running from a certain mountainous region, enters the Pasitigris, which was at a distance of about eighty *stadia* [nearly 15 km] from Eumenes'

---

[28] A similar system is described by Cleomedes as being employed by Xerxes during the Greek war: ὁ Πέρσης ἡνίκα ἐπὶ Ἑλλάδα ἐστράτευε, λέγεται διαστῆσαι ἀνθρώπους ἀπὸ Σούσων μέχρις Ἀθηνῶν, ὡς δύνασθαι διὰ φωνῆς δηλοῦσθαι τὰ γινόμενα ὑπ' αὐτοῦ ἐν Ἑλλάδι τοῖς ἐν Πέρσαις ('when the Persian made an expedition against Greece, he is said to have deployed people from Susa to Athens, in order to make known through their voice what he achieved in Greece to the people in Persis': Cleom. 2.156–83 at 156–9).
[29] That is, Susis: see, for example, Heckel 2009: 246–8 s.v. 'Seleucus' at 248. As commander of Asia, Antigonus may have had the authority to do this.
[30] The modern River Dez, a tributary of the Karun, emptying into it on its western side.

camp and is about four *plethra* [c. 150 m] in width, but since it is swift in current, it required boats or a bridge. (4) Seizing a few punts, he sent some of the infantry across in them, ordering them to dig a moat and build a palisade in front of it to receive the rest of the army. But when Eumenes heard from scouts of his enemies' attempt, crossing the bridge over the Pasitigris with four thousand infantry and thirteen hundred horsemen, he surprised the soldiers of Antigonus who had crossed – more than three thousand foot soldiers, four hundred cavalry, and of those soldiers who were in the habit of crossing in scattered groups in search of forage not less than six thousand.[31] (5) Falling suddenly upon them while they were in disorder, Eumenes routed the rest at once, but overcoming those of the Macedonians who resisted by his onset and by numbers, he compelled them all to flee to the river. (6) As they all rushed to the boats, these were submerged by the number of the men embarking, and most of those who ventured to swim, being carried away by the current, died, few saving their lives. (7) Those who did not know how to swim, preferring captivity to death in the river, were taken prisoners, being four thousand. Although he saw that such a great number of his men was being destroyed, Antigonus was unable to help because of his lack of boats.

(19.19.1) Believing that the crossing was impossible, Antigonus set out towards the city of Badace, which is situated on the bank of the River Eulaeus.[32] Since the march was scorching because of the burning heat, many soldiers perished and the army fell into despair. (2) Nevertheless, after staying in the above-mentioned city for a few days and letting the army recover from its sufferings, he decided it was best to march to Ecbatana in Media and, setting out from there, to gain control of the upper satrapies. There were two roads leading into Media, each with some disadvantage. In fact, the road leading to Calo[33] was a good royal highway, but hot and long,

---

[31] These soldiers of Antigonus were, thus, caught in the fork between the rivers Karun and Dez, as Antigonus stood on the western bank of the Dez, unable to help. See also Plu. *Eum.* 14.2, who appears to locate the confrontation on the banks of the Pasitigris (Karun) rather than the Coprates (Dez).

[32] The Eulaeus is mentioned by Strabo as one of the rivers contributing to the Pasitigris: Str. 15.3.4/728–9; he also states that its water was very light in weight: Str. 15.3.22/735. A precise equation with a present-day river in Iran seems not to be feasible, due to the fact that the hydrographic situation has changed too much since antiquity. As for the site of Badace, this is also still in need of identification.

[33] After MS F and Bizière 2002: 33 *apparatus* line 5. The name is somewhat confusing, resembling names like Καλλωνῖτις (Plb. 5.54.7), Καλωνῖτις, or Χαλωνῖτις (Str. 16.1.1/736), and the phrase εἰς τοὺς Κέλωνας (17.110.4), all as it seems relating to the same geographical entity in or near the Zagros Mountains.

The Period of the Diadochs: The Rift Deepens 427

extending for almost forty days' march, but the road through the Cossaean tribes was difficult, narrow, precipitous, passing through enemy territory, and moreover lacking in supplies, but it was short and cool. (3) It is not easy for an army to follow this route without having gained the consent of the people who inhabited the mountain ranges. Indeed, being independent from ancient times, they live in caves, eating acorns and mushrooms, and also the smoked flesh of wild beasts. (4) Antigonus regarded it as beneath his dignity to persuade these people or to make them presents when he had so great an army following him. Selecting the finest of the peltasts and dividing the bowmen, the slingers, and the other light-armed troops into two bodies, he gave one part to Nearchus, ordering him to go on ahead and occupy in advance the places that were narrow and difficult; but deploying the others along the entire route, he himself advanced with the phalanx, but put Peithon in command of the rearguard. (5) Nearchus' detachment, then, which had been sent ahead, occupied a few of the lookouts, but being too late for most, and the most important, locations, they lost many men and barely made their way through with the Cossaeans pressing upon them. (6) As for the troops led by Antigonus, whenever they came to these difficult places, they fell into dangers without help. Indeed, the natives, who were familiar with the region and had occupied the heights first, kept rolling great rocks in quick succession upon the marching troops. Shooting, at the same time, arrows thick and fast, they wounded men unable either to ward off or avoid the missiles because of the difficulties of the terrain. (7) Since the road was precipitous and nearly impassable, it happened that both the elephants and the cavalry, and even the heavy-armed soldiers, were in dire peril and toiled hard, without being able to help themselves. (8) Caught in such toils, Antigonus regretted that he had not heeded Peithon, when he advised him to purchase the right of passage with money. Nevertheless, after losing many men and endangering the others, with toil and pain he reached the settled part of Media safely on the ninth day.

Antigonus restores his army; Eumenes heads for Persepolis:
(19.20.1) However, because of the continuation of their misfortunes and their own extreme misery, the soldiers of Antigonus blamed him so that offensive words were let fall.[34] Indeed, they had met with three great disasters in forty days. Nevertheless, by mingling with the

---
[34] See also 18.36.2–4, where Perdiccas suffered similar treatment.

soldiers on friendly terms and by making ready an abundant supply of all provisions, Antigonus restored the army from its miserable state. (2) He sent Peithon out, ordering him to go through all Media and gather as many horsemen and war horses as he could, next to a multitude of baggage animals. (3) Easily accomplishing his mission, because that region always abounds in four-footed beasts, Peithon returned with two thousand horsemen, more than a thousand horses with their trappings, of the beasts of burden such a number that they could equip the entire army, and above that five hundred talents [3,000,000 *drachmae*] of the royal treasure. (4) Antigonus organised the horsemen in troops, and handing over horses to men who had lost their own and distributing most of the pack animals as presents, he restored the goodwill of the soldiers.

(19.21.1) When the satraps and commanders with Eumenes learned that the enemy was encamped in Media, they disagreed among themselves. Indeed, Eumenes, Antigenes, the commander of the Silver Shields, and all those who had made the march up from the sea believed that they should go back to the coast, but those who had come down from the upper satrapies, anxious about their own possessions, stated it was essential to maintain control of the upper country. (2) As the disagreement became more violent, Eumenes, seeing that, if the army were divided, neither part would be capable of fighting by itself, deferred to the wishes of the satraps who had come from the interior. Leaving the Pasitigris, then, they proceeded to Persepolis, the capital of Persis, being a march of twenty-four days. The first part of the road as far as the so-called Ladder was through an enclosed valley, scorching, and lacking in provisions, but the rest was over high land, blessed with a very healthful climate and full of seasonal fruits. (3) Indeed, there were both numerous shady glens, diverse plantings of gardens,[35] as well as natural converging glades full of trees of every sort and streams of water, so that travellers lingered with delight in the most pleasant places for repose. There was a mass of various flocks and herds as well, which Peucestes, gathering it from the inhabitants, distributed without stint to the soldiers, seeking their goodwill. Those who inhabited this region were the most warlike of the Persians, all being bowmen and slingers, and in density of population it happened that this country far surpassed the other satrapies as well.

---

[35] For such gardens see, for example, X. *Oec.* 4.13. The word derives from OP *paradayadām*, perhaps 'pleasant retreat', basically referring to a space confined by a wall: see Kent 1953: 195 *s.v.* See also Fakour 2012.

(19.22.1) When they had arrived in Persepolis, the capital, Peucestes, who was commander of this region,[36] performed a magnificent sacrifice to the gods, Alexander, and Philip. Having gathered from almost the whole of Persis a multitude of sacrificial animals and of whatever else was needed for festivities and religious gatherings, he gave a feast to the force. (2) With the company of those participating he filled four circles, one within the other, with the largest circle enclosing the others. The circuit of the outer ring was of ten *stadia* [c. 1,850 m], which both the mercenaries and the mass of the allies filled; the circuit of the second was of eight *stadia* [c. 1,480 m], and in it were both the Macedonian Silver Shields and those of the companions who had fought under Alexander;[37] the circuit of the next was of four *stadia* [c. 740 m] and its area was filled with reclining men – both the commanders of lower rank, the friends and commanders who were unassigned, and the cavalry;[38] lastly in the inner circle with a perimeter of two *stadia* [c. 370 m] each of the commanders and hipparchs, with the addition of the most honoured Persians,[39] occupied his own couch. (3) In the middle of these there were altars for the gods, Alexander, and Philip. The couches were formed of heaps of leaves covered with hangings and rugs of every kind, because Persis furnished in plenty everything needed for luxury {τρυφή} and enjoyment. The circles were at such a distance from each other that the banqueters should not be crowded but have all the provisions near at hand.

Eumenes gets the upper hand in 'his' army:
(19.23.1) After all had been duly served, the crowd applauded the generosity of Peucestes, and it was clear that he had made a great advance in popularity. Seeing this and reasoning that Peucestes showed public spirit to the crowd as he reached out for the chief command, Eumenes fabricated a false letter,[40] through which he both made the soldiers confident of the outcome of the battles and,

---

[36] Though previous editors had added σατράπης καὶ ('satrap and') before στρατηγός ('commander'), Fischer decided, following the MSS, to remove this addition. I have, like Geer and Bizière, followed his lead.
[37] Bizière 2002: 36 note 1 believes these ἑταῖροι ('companions'), normally cavalry guardsmen, were in fact *pezetairoi*, Macedonian infantry. See also Robert, and Holleaux 1942: 10.
[38] The Macedonian cavalry, possibly including those who had survived from the ἑταῖροι ('companions') proper.
[39] As Bizière rightly remarks, this position seems to indicate that at least Peucestes had not (yet) deviated dramatically from Alexander's policy towards non-Greeks and/or non-Macedonians: Bizière 2002: 156 *ad* 22.2, fourth remark.
[40] See also Polyaen. 4.8.3.

by lowering the pomp and pretension[41] of Peucestes, improved his own standing and increased his prospects of success in the eyes of the crowd. (2) The point of the letter was that Olympias, associating Alexander's son with herself, had recovered firm control of the kingdom of Macedonia, because Cassander was dead,[42] and that Polyperchon had crossed into Asia against Antigonus with the strongest part of the royal force and the elephants and was already advancing in the neighbourhood of Cappadocia.[43] (3) The letter, written in the Syrian writing,[44] was sent by Orontes, who held the satrapy of Armenia and who was a friend of Peucestes. Because the letter was believed, due to the previous friendship between the satraps, Eumenes ordered it to be carried around and to be shown both to the commanders and also to most of the other soldiers. The sentiment of the entire encampment was changed and all began to turn their attention to Eumenes' prospects: that he would be able, through the kings, both to promote whomever he wished and to exact punishment from those who wronged him. (4) After the feast Eumenes, in his desire to overawe those who did not obey him or who craved the command, brought to trial Sibyrtius, who was satrap of Arachosia and a very close friend of Peucestes, having sent some horsemen into Arachosia without Sibyrtius' knowledge. By ordering the seizure of his baggage, he brought him into such danger that, if he had not escaped secretly, he would have been condemned to death by the assembly.[45]

(19.24.1) After Eumenes had frightened the others in this manner and had surrounded himself with great pomp and pretension, he changed once more and, having won Peucestes over with kind words and great promises, he made him loyal to himself and eager to join in the struggle on behalf of the kings. (2) Desiring to exact even from the other satraps and commanders something like hostages, to prevent their deserting him, he pretended to be in need of money and called on each of them to lend to the kings according to ability.

---

[41] Literally pretension and pomp, but for reasons of rhythm I found it better to reverse it.
[42] In fact, Cassander was very much alive and busy: see, for example, 19.35.1–36.1, 49.1–51.5; see also, for a summary review of his activities after Triparadisus, Heckel 2009: 79–81 at 80–1.
[43] Like the previous statement, this one too was not even close to the truth, Polyperchon being heavily involved in problems inside Greece and Macedonia.
[44] Most likely intended to mean written in Imperial Aramaic: see also Deshayes, 1969: 512.
[45] It appears, though, from 19.48.3 that Sibyrtius, if not in fact, remained in fact satrap of (Gedrosia and) Arachosia: see, for example, Heckel 2009: 248–9 s.v. The translation of τὸ πλῆθος offers some problems: the word may denote 'the assembly', as I have read it (like Geer 1969: 293 and Bizière 2002: 38), but equally plausibly 'the mob', namely the rank and file of the army.

The Period of the Diadochs: The Rift Deepens 431

(3) Taking four hundred talents [2,400,000 *drachmae*] from those leaders from whom he considered it expedient, he converted men whom he had formerly suspected of conspiring or abandoning him into most faithful guards of his person and his associates.[46]

Eumenes' army sets out against Antigonus; Antigonus sends messengers:
(4) While he was making these strategic moves with an eye to the future, there came some men from Media, saying that Antigonus and his force had set out for Persis. When he heard this, he also set out, having made up his mind to meet the enemy and risk the issue. (5) On the second day of the journey he performed a sacrifice to the gods and, entertaining the army sumptuously, enticed the large majority into loyalty. However, he himself, being led on during the drinking bout by those of the invited guests who were eagerly engaged in drinking, became ill.[47] Therefore he delayed the march for some days, being overcome by the ailment. The army was disheartened, because the enemy were expected to engage them shortly, while the ablest of their commanders was oppressed by his illness. (6) Nevertheless, when he recovered little by little after the illness had passed its crisis, he advanced with the force while Peucestes and Antigenes were leading; he himself, carried in a litter, followed the rearguard so that he might not be disturbed by the confusion and the congestion of the road.
(19.25.1) When the armies were a day's march from each other, they both sent scouts and, after learning the size and the intentions of the enemy, they both prepared for the battle, but they separated without a fight.[48] (2) In fact, both deployed their forces keeping a river and a ravine before them, and were unable to engage battle because of the difficulty of the terrain. Pitching camp three *stadia* [c. 550 m] from each other, they spent four days skirmishing and plundering the country, for they were entirely without supplies. On the fifth day, though, Antigonus sent envoys to both the satraps and the Macedonians, urging them not to obey Eumenes but to trust in himself.[49] (3) He said, indeed, that he would allow the satraps to keep their own satrapies, that to some of the other men he would give a large

---

[46] According to Plu. *Eum.* 13.6 this incident took place earlier. I cannot but agree with Geer's statement that '[i]n general Plutarch's account of the last campaigns of Eumenes is of little value': Geer 1969: 295 note 1.
[47] See Plu. *Eum.* 14.3–5.
[48] See Plu. *Eum.* 15.2–3 for an altogether different account of this encounter.
[49] According to 18.62.4–63.2, Antigonus had already sent a letter to the satraps and to the Macedonians.

amount of land, would send back others to their fatherlands with honours and gifts, but would to each of those who wanted to take service with him assign appropriate posts. (4) When the Macedonians paid no heed to these offers but even threatened the envoys, Eumenes, coming forward, both praised them and told them a tale, one of the traditional and ancient stories, but one not unsuited to the situation. (5) He said, indeed: 'A lion, having fallen in love with a maiden, spoke to the girl's father about marriage. The father said that he was ready to give her to him, but that he was afraid of the lion's claws and teeth, that after he had married her and losing his temper about something, he might turn on the maiden in the manner of a beast. (6) When, however, the lion had pulled out both his claws and his teeth, the father, perceiving that the lion had thrown away everything which had made him formidable, killed him easily, beating him with a club. Antigonus, then, is doing something quite similar. (7) He will, in fact, keep his promises, until he becomes master of the army, and in that very moment will execute its leaders.' While the crowd was shouting approval and saying 'Right', he dismissed the assembly.

Battle of Paraetacene;[50] *preliminary movements:*
(19.26.1) When the night had come, however, there came some deserters from Antigonus' army, saying that Antigonus had given his soldiers orders to break camp at about the second watch.[51] Considering the matter, Eumenes assumed rightly that the enemy intended to withdraw into Gabene.[52] (2) This place, indeed, which was about a three days' march away, had not been plundered and was filled with grain, fodder, and in general with that which could amply supply the provisions for a great army. (3) Furthermore, the terrain itself added to these benefits, having rivers and ravines that were hard to cross. Anxious, then, to anticipate the enemy, he practised the same method as theirs. He sent off some of the mercenaries, whose consent he had won by money, as if they were deserting, with an order to say that Eumenes had decided to attack the entrenched camp during the night. He himself, however, sent

---

[50] Paraetacene is a mountainous area in western Iran, enclosed to the north and east by Media, Aria, and Carmania and to the south-west by Susis. Strabo describes the Paraetaceneans as a predatory mountain people (Str. 15.3.12/732). See also above, Chapter 2, note 97.
[51] See above, 18.40.3, and Chapter 7, note 70.
[52] A region at the borders of Susis. The orthography of this region is inconsistent: see Str. 16.1.18/744–5, who calls it a province of Elymaea and one of the entries to Seleucia in Mesopotamia, on the west bank of the Tigris, opposite the town of Ctesiphon; Polyaen. 4.6.13; Ptol. Geog. 6.2.13, who lists it as one of the πόλεις καὶ κῶμαι ('cities and villages') of Media; and Plu. *Eum.* 15.4, who mentions the residents as οἱ Γαβηνοί ('the Gabenans').

the baggage ahead and ordered the soldiers to break camp as soon as possible after having taken a meal. (4) While all this was swiftly accomplished, Antigonus, who had heard from the deserters that the enemy had decided to fight during the night, postponed his departure and deployed his force for the battle. (5) As he was distracted by these operations and concentrating on the coming battle, Eumenes sneaked away and marched at top speed for Gabene. Antigonus kept his force under arms for some time. However, when he learned from his scouts the departure of his opponents, although he knew that he had been outmanoeuvred, he nevertheless held to his original plan. (6) So, ordering his soldiers to break camp, he led them on a forced march that resembled a pursuit. As Eumenes, however, had a start of two watches, Antigonus, understanding that it was not easy to overtake with his whole army a force that was so far ahead, contrived the following stratagem. (7) Handing over the rest of the army to Peithon he ordered him to follow at leisure, but he himself with the cavalry pursued at full gallop, and overtaking the rearguard of the enemy at daybreak just as it was coming down from hilly country, he took position on the ridges, being visible to his opponents. (8) When Eumenes saw their enemies' horsemen from a considerable distance and supposed that the entire army was near, he halted the march and deployed the army as if there would be an engagement immediately. (9) Thus the commanders of both armies outmanoeuvred each other in the manner described, as if they were taking part in a preliminary contest of skill and showing that each placed his hope of victory in himself. (10) Antigonus, then, by this plan prevented the enemy moving forward, giving himself a respite to bring up his army; and when the army arrived, he deployed it all for battle and marched down terrifyingly, all arrayed against the enemy.

Battle of Paraetacene; the battle:
(19.27.1) Including the reinforcements brought by Peithon and Seleucus, Antigonus had in all more than twenty-eight thousand infantry, eight thousand five hundred horsemen, and sixty-five elephants. The commanders employed different formations, vying with each other with regard to their competence in tactical skill as well. (2) Indeed, on his left wing Eumenes stationed Eudamus, who had brought the elephants from India, with his corps[53] [division?] of

---

[53] The word ἄγημα can, according to *LSJ*, be translated as 'corps' or 'division'. In view of the relatively fixed meaning of 'division' in military terminology, I have opted here primarily for 'corps'.

horsemen, one hundred and fifty in number, and as an advance guard for them two companies[54] of selected mounted lancers, fifty horsemen strong.[55] (3) He positioned them in contact with the higher land of the base of the hill, and next to them he deployed Stasander, the commander, with his own cavalry of nine hundred and fifty. (4) After them he stationed Amphimachus, the satrap of Mesopotamia, whom six hundred horsemen followed, and in contact with these were the six hundred horsemen from Arachosia, whom Sibyrtius formerly led, but, because of the latter's flight, Cephalon had assumed command of them. (5) Next were five hundred cavalry from Paropanisadae and an equal number of Thracians from the colonies of the upper country.[56] In front of all these he deployed forty-five elephants in a curved line, with the competent bowmen and stone-slingers in the spaces between the animals. (6) Having strengthened the left wing in this way, he linked the phalanx to it. The outer end of this was taken by the mercenaries,[57] who numbered more than six thousand, with next to them those equipped in the Macedonian way, though being mixed in origin – about five thousand men.

(19.28.1) After them the Macedonian Silver Shields were positioned, more than three thousand in number, undefeated and through their *aretē* causing the enemy much fear; and finally the men from the *hypaspists*, more than three thousand, with Antigenes and Teutamus leading both them and the Silver Shields. (2) In front of the whole phalanx he placed forty elephants, filling the spaces between them with platoons of light-armed soldiers.[58] (3) On the right wing he stationed the rest of the cavalry: next to the phalanx, eight hundred from Carmania, led by the satrap Tlepolemus, then the nine hundred called the Companions and the corps of Peucestes and Antigenes, which contained three hundred horsemen arranged in a single

---

[54] In Greek εἶλαι. Technically, in modern armies a company is a military unit, typically consisting of 80–250 soldiers. Though εἶλαι stands for 'companies', I am not absolutely certain it should be regarded here as the correct interpretation of the deployment. In 19.28.3, below, the number of 50 is given for each of six εἶλαι, though 300 for another.

[55] Bizière 2002: 42 line 21 reads here, after the MSS, βάθος, 'depth'. After Geer 1969: 302 (who in his turn follows Post), I prefer, however, πλῆθος, which I have translated rather freely as 'strong'. The reason for deviating from the text of the MSS is that a line of fifty deep, especially of horsemen, is unmanageable.

[56] The (military) colonies founded by Alexander, as described in 17.83.2, above.

[57] As Bizière 2002: 157 *ad* 27.6 rightly observes, Diodorus indiscriminately uses both μισθοφόροι and ξένοι to indicate mercenaries, though technically there used to be some distinction between the two: apparently the difference was lost on Diodorus (or even his source).

[58] Diodorus uses here the word τάγμα. According to the *LSJ*, this normally translates as 'division' or 'brigade'. However, as Latin counterparts both *manipulus* and *legio* are mentioned. With reference to the meaning of *manipulus*, I have opted here for the translation 'platoon', though perhaps even the word 'section' might qualify.

company. At the outer end of the wing was Eumenes' corps, with the same number of horsemen, and as an advance guard for them two companies of Eumenes' pages,[59] each composed of fifty mounted men, and guarding the flanks outside the wing were four companies, in which there were two hundred selected horsemen. (4) Apart from these, Eumenes stationed three hundred men selected for swiftness and strength from all the hipparchies behind his own corps. Along the whole of the wing he deployed a forward line of forty elephants. The entire force of Eumenes consisted of thirty-five thousand foot, sixty-one hundred horse, and one hundred and fourteen elephants.[60] (19.29.1) As Antigonus looked down from a high position on the battle-line of his enemy, he positioned his own force accordingly. In fact, seeing that the right wing of the opponents had been strengthened with both the elephants and the strongest of the cavalry, he deployed against it the lightest of his horsemen, who, drawn up in open order, were to avoid a frontal action but maintain a battle of wheeling tactics and in this way make unprofitable that part of the enemy forces in which they had the greatest confidence. (2) On this wing he stationed both the mounted archers and lancers from Media and Parthia, a thousand in number, men well trained in the execution of the wheeling movement, and next he placed the twenty-two hundred Tarentines[61] who had come up with him from the sea, men selected for their skill in ambushing, and very well disposed to himself; the thousand cavalry from Phrygia and Lydia; the fifteen hundred with Peithon; the four hundred lancers with Lysanias; and in addition to all these, the cavalry who are called the 'two-horse men',[62] and the eight hundred cavalry from the colonists established in the upper *satrapies*.[63] (3) The left wing was made up of these cavalrymen, of all of whom Peithon had the command. Of the infantry, the mercenaries were placed first, more than nine thousand in number, with next to them three thousand Lycians and Pamphylians, then more than eight thousand mixed troops in Macedonian equipment, and finally the nearly eight thousand Macedonians, whom Antipater had given

---

[59] I prefer this description to Geer's translation 'slaves': Geer 1969: 305. See also Bizière 2002: 43 note 5.
[60] See Geer 1969: 307 note 1 as well as Bizière 2002: 44 note 1 for these figures.
[61] Cavalrymen equipped with javelins. As Geer 1969: 307 note 2 rightly remarks, the connection with Tarentum is obscure, even though Tarentine coins show such troops. Bizière 2002: 44 note 4 remarks that these men were not necessarily from Tarentum: Vigneron 1968: 261; Bikerman 1938: 59.
[62] Seemingly men who came to the army with two horses. Geer 1969: 308–9 note 1 rightly points to Liv. 35.28.8, describing Tarentines with two horses following Philopoemen during the battle near the Barnosthenes in Lacedaemon in 192. See also Ael. *Tact.* 2.4.
[63] Apparently not all the people from the upper satrapies supported Eumenes.

him at the time when he was appointed guardian of the kingdom [in 321]. (4) Of the horsemen, the first on the right wing adjacent to the phalanx were five hundred mercenaries of mixed origin, then a thousand Thracians, five hundred from the allies, and next to them the thousand known as the Companions with Demetrius the son of Antigonus as commander, who was now about to fight in company with his father for the first time. (5) At the outer end of the wing was the corps of three hundred horsemen with whom Antigonus himself was entering the battle. As an advance guard for these there were three companies from his own pages, and parallel to them were as many companies, reinforced by a hundred Tarentines. (6) Along the whole wing he drew up the strongest thirty of the elephants, making a curved line, and he filled the interval between them with selected light-armed men. Most of the other elephants he placed before the phalanx, but a few were with the cavalry on the left wing. (7) Having deployed the army in this fashion, he advanced downhill against the enemy, keeping an oblique formation. In fact, he thrust forward the right wing, in which he had most confidence, and held the other back, having determined to avoid battle with the one and to engage the battle with the other.

(19.30.1) When the armies were close to each other and the signal had been raised in both of them, the forces shouted the battle-cry alternately several times and the trumpeters sounded the signal for battle. First Peithon's cavalry, who had neither stability nor any advance guard worth mentioning, but were superior to their adversaries both in numbers and in mobility, started to try to make use of their own advantages. (2) In fact, they did not consider it safe to make a frontal attack against elephants, but by riding out around the wing and making an attack on the flanks, they kept inflicting wounds with repeated flights of arrows, suffering no harm themselves because of their mobility but causing great damage to the beasts, which because of their weight could neither pursue nor retire whenever the moment demanded. (3) When Eumenes observed that the wing was hard pressed by the multitude of mounted archers, he summoned the most lightly equipped of his cavalry from Eudamus, who had the left wing. (4) Leading his small body of soldiers[64] in

---

[64] Geer 1969: 312 reads here τὴν ὅλην τάξιν ('the whole body of soldiers'), after a conjecture by Wesseling, also followed by Fischer, whereas Bizière 2002: 46 line 23 reads here τὴν ὀλίγην τάξιν ('the small body of soldiers'), following the text of the MSS. Both readings are perfectly feasible, though depending on the meaning one gives to τάξις (admittedly a term with diverse meanings). Nevertheless, because there is no real need to emend the text as Wesseling did, I tend to support the choice made by Bizière, albeit that in the translation I have altered the

a flanking movement, he attacked his opponents with light-armed soldiers and the most lightly equipped of the cavalry. Easily routing Peithon's forces, because the elephants followed as well, he pursued them to the foothills. (5) At the same time that this was going on, it so happened that the infantry for a considerable time had been engaged in a battle of phalanxes with each other, but finally, after many had fallen on both sides, Eumenes' men got the upper hand because of the *aretae* of the Macedonian Silver Shields. (6) Indeed, these men were already well on in years,[65] but due to the number of battles they had fought they stood out in hardihood and skill, so that no one confronting them could withstand their might. Therefore, although there were then only three thousand of them, they had become, so to speak, the spearhead of the whole army. (7) Although he saw both that his own left wing had been put to flight and that the entire phalanx had been defeated, Antigonus paid no attention to those who advised him to retire to the mountains and collect those who escaped from the rout, keeping the part of the force under his command intact, but, cleverly using the opportunity offered by the situation, he both saved the fugitives of his own forces and gained the victory. (8) In fact, as soon as Eumenes' Silver Shields and the remaining body of his infantry had routed their adversaries, they pursued them as far as the nearer hills.[66] (9) When a break was thus caused in the line of his enemy, Antigonus, charging through with a detachment of cavalry, struck on the flank the troops who had been stationed with Eudamus on the left wing. (10) Because the attack was unexpected, quickly putting to flight his opponents and killing many, he sent out the swiftest of his horsemen and by means of them he assembled those fleeing and once more formed them into a line of battle along the foothills. In fact, when Eumenes learned of the rout of his own soldiers, he recalled the pursuers by a signal of the *salpinx*, eager to help Eudamus.

Battle of Paraetacene; the aftermath:
(19.31.1) Although it was already lamp-lighting time, both began to deploy their entire force once more, having called back their fleeing troops: such zeal for victory filled not only the commanders but also

---

article into a combination of article and *pronomen possesivum*, resulting in 'his small body of soldiers': after all Eudamus commanded not more than 200 soldiers, next to the elephants and their mahouts.

[65] As 19.41.2 (below) points out, they all were at least sixty years old, most about seventy, some even older.

[66] As the following paragraph shows, a grave tactical error which one would not expect of such seasoned warriors as the 'Silver Shields', understandable as the action might have seemed at the moment.

the mass of the contestants. (2) Because the night was clear and with a full moon and the armies were positioning parallel to each other at a distance of about four *plethra* [c. 120 m], the clatter of arms and the whinnying of the horses seemed close at hand to all the contestants. But as they were being deployed, about thirty *stadia* [c. 5.5 km] away from those who had fallen in the battle, the hour of midnight overtook them, and both armies were so exhausted through both the march and their suffering in the battle, and moreover from the lack of food, (3) that they were forced, giving up the battle, to go into camp. Eumenes, then, tried to march back to the dead, desiring to control the disposal of the bodies and to put his claim to victory beyond dispute.[67] Because, though, the soldiers would not listen to him, but shouted to return to their own baggage train, which was some distance away, he was forced to yield to the mass. (4) Indeed, neither was he able to punish the soldiers severely, because there were many who disputed his right to command, nor was the time right, he saw, to chastise those who disobeyed. Antigonus, on the contrary, who held the command firmly without need of courting popular favour, forced his army to make camp by the bodies. Having become master of their burial, he claimed the victory, declaring that to possess the fallen is to be victorious in battle. (5) In this battle three thousand seven hundred foot and fifty-four horse of the soldiers of Antigonus were killed and more than four thousand men were wounded. Of the soldiers of Eumenes there fell five hundred and forty infantry and very few of his cavalry, and more than nine hundred men were wounded.

(19.32.1) When, after his departure from the battle, Antigonus saw that his men were disheartened, he decided to move as far as possible from the enemy with the utmost speed. Wishing to have the army well equipped for the retreat, he sent the wounded men and the heaviest part of the baggage ahead to one of the neighbouring cities. Beginning to bury the dead at dawn and detaining the herald who had come from the enemy for the recovery of the bodies,[68] he ordered his men to eat dinner at once.[69] (2) When the day had passed he sent the herald back, assigning the removal of the bodies to the next morning. He himself, however, moved forward with the whole force

---

[67] See 17.68.4 (above). See also Just. 6.6.10; X. *HG* 7.5.26. Again, the 'Silver Shields' should have known this and should have supported Eumenes. The fact they did not, might cast some doubt as regards their absolute loyalty to him.

[68] Polyaen. 4.6.10 argues that Antigonus acted like this to conceal from Eumenes that Antigonus' losses were (far) greater than his.

[69] And not, as was usual, when night had fallen.

The Period of the Diadochs: The Rift Deepens   439

at the beginning of the first watch and by making forced marches withdrew a long distance from the enemy. He gained an undamaged country to refresh the army. In fact, he went as far as Gamarga in Media,[70] the region that was subject to Peithon and able to supply great armies abundantly with everything needed for their support. (3) Learning through scouts of Antigonus' departure, Eumenes refrained from following him because his own soldiers were also hungry and heavily battered. He attended, however, to the taking up of the dead and saw to it that they received a magnificent burial. Then an event took place that was amazing and very different from Greek custom.

(19.33.1) Ceteus, the commander of the soldiers who had come from India, was killed in the battle after fighting brilliantly, but he left two wives who had accompanied him in the army, one of them a bride, the other married to him some years before, but both of them loving him deeply. (2) ... (3) ... (4) ...
(19.34.1) ... (2) ... (3) ... (4) ... (5) ... (6) ...[[In these paragraphs Diodorus tells the story of the two wives of Ceteus, vying with each other to be burned on the pyre together with their deceased husband.]] (7) When Eumenes had completed the burial of the dead, he moved the army from the Paraetacene into Gabene, which was untouched and capable of supplying everything in abundance for the armies. (8) This region happened to be situated a twenty-five days' march from Antigonus' army if one went through inhabited country, but if through a waterless desert,[71] a march of nine days. Eumenes' and Antigonus' armies passed the winter [of 317/16] at this distance from each other and in such places, and at the same time they refreshed their men.

S. 136:
19.37.1–44.5:

Antigonus leaves camp for a new confrontation:
(19.37.1) In Asia, Antigonus, who was wintering in Gadamala in Media[72] and saw that his force was weaker than that of his enemies,

---

[70] The name occurs in some variety: see below, 19.37.1; Polyaen. 4.6.10. It might be the region of modern Qom.
[71] Though some 23 per cent of modern Iran consists of deserts and identification is, therefore, difficult, the description Diodorus provides here and in the following fragment might suggest that the desert intended is the Dašt-e Kevir or Kevir Desert between Qom and Esfahān (Isphahan).
[72] Probably Diodorus intends to indicate here the same location as in 19.32.2 above, where he mentions it as Gamarga. Though neither precise location nor the correct form of the name is certain, it might refer to modern Qom.

was anxious to attack them unexpectedly and defeat them. His enemies happened to have their winter quarters split up in many parts, so that some were six days' march distant from others.[73] (2) Antigonus, then, disapproved of the idea of marching through inhabited country because the route was both long and easily observed by the enemy, but decided to venture on the difficult journey through the waterless desert, the most suitable for the attack that he had planned. In fact, it was not only possible to go quickly by that route, but also easy to escape attention and fall unexpectedly upon an army that, ignorant of his movements, would be scattered among villages and at its ease. (3) Having formed this plan, he ordered the soldiers to be ready to break camp and to prepare ten days' supply of food that would not require cooking. He himself, spreading the story that he would set out against Armenia, suddenly and contrary to the assumption of all set out across the desert, it being about the time of the winter solstice.[74] (4) He gave orders to make fires in the camps by day, but to extinguish them completely at night, in order to avoid someone seeing them from the higher ground and announcing to the enemy what was happening. (5) Indeed, almost the entire desert was a plain, but it was surrounded by high hills from which it was easy to see the bright light of fire from a great distance. After the army had been marching five days with great suffering, the soldiers, both because of the cold and to satisfy their urgent needs, lighted fires in the camps both by day and by night. (6) On seeing this, certain of those who lived near the desert sent men on running camels to report it on the same day to Eumenes and Peucestes.[75] In fact, a running camel can travel continuously for almost fifteen hundred stadia [c. 275 km].[76]

(19.38.1) When Peucestes learned that the camp had been seen in the middle of the route, he decided to withdraw to the most distant part of the territory in which he was wintering, afraid that he might be overtaken by the enemy before his allied force had assembled from all directions. (2) When he saw their lack of spirit, Eumenes urged him

---

[73] Though problems in acquiring sufficient food may well have caused this spreading out of the army, Plutarch blames it on indiscipline among the soldiers: Plu. *Eum.* 15.4.
[74] That is, the latter part of December 317.
[75] See Plu. *Eum.* 15.7–8; Nep. *Eum.* 9.1; Polyaen. 4.6.11.
[76] According to Str. 15.2.10/724, men on running camels could complete in eleven days a journey of thirty to forty days. At present, most camel races are performed on one-humped animals, but Diodorus' account does not make clear whether these men here used one- or two-humped animals, the latter indigenous in Central Asia. Goukowsky 1967 believes it was one-humped animals (therefore proper dromedaries), confirmed by Plu. *Eum.* 15.8, who refers to them as ἱππάστριαι κάμηλοι ('dromedaries'): see *LSJ* s.v. 'ἱππάστριαι'.

to take courage and to remain on the borders of the desert. In fact, he said that he had found a method by which he would delay Antigonus by three or four days.[77] In that case, their own force could easily be assembled, but the enemy would be delivered into their hands, being utterly worn out and lacking everything. (3) As all were wondering at this strange promise and were trying to learn whatever it might be that could prevent the opponents from advancing, he ordered all the commanders to follow him with their own soldiers bringing fire in many jars. Having selected a place on the higher ground facing the desert and well situated to be clearly visible from every direction, and setting up markers, he enclosed a circumference of seventy *stadia* [c. 13 km]. Assigning areas to each of those who followed him, he ordered them to light fires about twenty cubits [c. 9 m] apart at night and to keep the flames bright during the first watch, as if men were still awake and busy with the care of their bodies and the preparation of food, but dimmer during the second watch, and in the third watch to leave only a very few, so that to those who watched from a distance it would seem to be a genuine camp. (4) As the soldiers carried out the directions, some of those who pastured flocks on the hills opposite and who were friendly to Peithon, the satrap of Media, noticed the fires. Believing that this truly was a camp, hurrying down into the plain, they announced the news to Antigonus and Peithon. (5) Being astonished at this unexpected news and halting the march, they took counsel how they should use this information. Indeed, it was dangerous to engage an army that had been undergoing hardship and was in need of everything with enemies that were already assembled and were well provided with everything. (6) Assuming that there had been treachery and that the enemy had assembled because they knew in advance what was going to happen, they gave up the plan of going straight forward and, turning to the right, went to untouched parts of the inhabited country, wishing to restore the force after its hardships.

Battle of Gabene; preliminary actions:
(19.39.1) Having outmanoeuvred the enemy in the manner described, Eumenes called together from all sides those of his soldiers who had been widely scattered while wintering in the villages. After building a palisade and strengthening the encampment with a deep ditch, he received those of the allies who came down from time to time, and he filled the camp with all the necessary supplies. (2) Antigonus,

---

[77] See Plu. *Eum.* 15.7–8; Nep. *Eum.* 9.3–5; Polyaen. 4.8.4.

however, having got across the desert and learning from the inhabitants that almost all the rest of his army had joined Eumenes, but that the elephants were still destined to go there from their winter quarters and were near at hand, cut off from all assistance, he sent against them two thousand mounted Median lancers, two hundred Tarentines, and all his light infantry. (3) In fact, he hoped that, by attacking the elephants when they were isolated, he could both easily master them and deprive the enemy of the strongest element in his force. Guessing what was about to happen, however, Eumenes sent to the rescue the strongest fifteen hundred horsemen and three thousand light infantry. (4) Because Antigonus' soldiers arrived first, the commanders of the elephants, having arranged the animals in a square, continued to advance, having put the baggage train in the centre and, in the rear, with the cavalry, not more than four hundred men, as allies. (5) As the enemy fell upon them with all their weight and pressed ever more heavily, the cavalry was routed, overwhelmed by numbers. Those who were in charge of the elephants, though, resisted at first and held firm even though being wounded from all directions, unable to hurt the enemy at all. (6) When they were already becoming exhausted, the troops sent by Eumenes, suddenly appearing, rescued them from their danger. A few days later, when the armies were encamped opposite each other at a distance of forty *stadia* [nearly 7.5 km], both commanders drew up their army for battle, expecting this would be decisive.[78]

Battle of Gabene:
(19.40.1) Antigonus, then, placing his cavalry on the wings, gave the command of the left to Peithon and that of the right to his own son Demetrius, together with whom he himself decided to fight. Having positioned the infantry in the centre, he deployed the elephants along the whole force, filling the spaces between them with the light-armed troops. The total number of his force was twenty-two thousand foot, nine thousand horse, including the extra conscripted ones from Media, and sixty-five elephants. (2) Having learned that Antigonus had taken his place on the right with his best cavalry, Eumenes himself also deployed the force in his turn, stationing his best troops on the left wing. In fact, he placed there most of the satraps with the selected bodies of cavalry that accompanied them in battle, and he himself intended to take part in the fight with them. There was also present with them Mithridates, a man of outstanding courage and

[78] See Just. 14.3.3–5.

The Period of the Diadochs: The Rift Deepens   443

trained from childhood as a soldier, the son of Ariobarzanes and a descendant of one of the seven Persians who put down together the *magus* Smerdis.[79] (3) In front of the whole wing Eumenes drew up in a curved line the sixty strongest of the elephants and interspersed the intervals with light troops. Of the foot soldiers he positioned first the *hypaspistoi*,[80] then the Silver Shields, and finally the mercenaries and those of the other soldiers who were armed in the Macedonian fashion, and in front of them elephants and an adequate force of his light troops. (4) Having positioned on the right wing the weaker of the cavalry and of the elephants, he appointed Philip as commander of them all. He ordered the latter to avoid battle and to observe the outcome on the other wing. Altogether there were in Eumenes' army at that time thirty-six thousand seven hundred foot, six thousand horse, and one hundred and fourteen elephants.

(19.41.1) A short time before the battle Antigenes, the commander of the Silver Shields, sent one of the Macedonian horsemen towards the phalanx of the opponents, ordering him to draw near to it and make a proclamation.[81] This man, riding up alone to within earshot, opposite the position where the phalanx of Antigonus' Macedonians was stationed, shouted: 'Miscreants, are you fighting against your fathers, who conquered the whole world under Philip and Alexander? You shall see them in a little while, worthy both of the kings and of their own past battles.'[82] (2) In fact, it happened at this time that the youngest of the Silver Shields was about sixty years old, most of the others about seventy, and some even older, but all of them irresistible because of experience and strength: such was their skill and daring acquired through the unbroken series of their battles. (3) After the proclamation was delivered as related above, there arose from the soldiers of Antigonus angry cries, stating that they were being forced to fight against their kinsfolk and their elders, but from the ranks of

---

[79] Smerdis was subdued in the conspiracy that led to the enthronement of Darius I, not further transmitted in the fragments of Diodorus' account we have. See, for example, Hdt. 3.67–79; Ctes. *Pers*. F. 13(15–18); and the inscription of Darius at Bisitun (*DB*, column I, §§10–14; column IV, §68): Kent 1953: 119–20; 132. In MS R the name of Smerdis is omitted, though Bizière 2002: 59 believes it is less an omission in R than a gloss in MS F. This Mithridates is omitted by Heckel 2009, but if Diodorus is correct, he may well have been a nephew of the Mithridates who died at the Granicus (17.21.3) and a grandson of Darius III (see Heckel 2009: 44–5 *s.v.* 'Ariobarzanes [1]').

[80] That is, nearest to the left wing.

[81] See Plu. *Eum*. 16.8, who mentions that the 'Silver Shields' shouted shortly before they attacked ἐπὶ τοὺς πατέρας ἁμαρτάνετ' ὢ κακαὶ κεφαλαί ('you are sinning against your fathers, miscreants!').

[82] Even though the Greek switches in these two sentences from the direct to the indirect mode, I have opted to consider them as part of the same challenge and translated them accordingly.

Eumenes there came a cheering and a cry to lead them against the enemy as soon as possible. When Eumenes saw their eagerness, he gave the sign by which he directed the trumpeters to sound the signal for combat, the whole force to raise the battle-cry.

(19.42.1) The first to join in battle were the elephants, and after them the main body of the cavalry. Because the plain was of great extent and entirely uncultivated because of the salt that permeated it, such a cloud of dust was raised by the cavalry that from a little distance nobody could easily see what was happening. (2) When Antigonus noticed this, he dispatched the Median cavalry and an adequate force of Tarentines against the enemy's baggage. In fact, he hoped, as came true, that this manoeuvre would be undetected because of the dust, but that by the capture of the baggage he would conquer the enemy without effort.[83] (3) Those sent out, riding around the flank of their opponents and without being noticed, attacked the baggage train, which was about five stadia [c. 900 m] distant from the battle. Finding it packed with a multitude of persons who were useless for fighting but had few defenders, and quickly defeating those who resisted, they captured all the others. (4) As this was happening, Antigonus joined battle with his adversaries and appearing with a large number of cavalry struck panic into Peucestes, satrap of Persis, who, retiring from the dust cloud with his own cavalry, drew away fifteen hundred others as well. (5) Left unsupported at the extremity of the wing with a few supporters, Eumenes regarded it as shameful to yield to Fate and flee. Preferring to die while upholding with noble resolution the trust given by the kings, he forced his way towards Antigonus himself. (6) When a fierce cavalry battle ensued, and Eumenes' men were superior in spirit but those of Antigonus had the advantage in number, many men died on both sides. At this time it occurred that, as the elephants were also struggling against each other, Eumenes' leading elephant fell, having come to blows with the strongest of those arrayed against it. (7) Therefore, seeing that his forces were everywhere having the worst of it, Eumenes led what remained of the cavalry out of the battle and, going around to the other wing, he assumed command of those troops whom he had assigned to Philip and had ordered to avoid fighting. This, then, was the outcome of the cavalry engagement.

---

[83] As usual, ὄχλος, 'baggage', is an encompassing notion: it includes not only material luggage, but also non-fighting elements connected to the army, including wives, children, 'the market', et al.

Battle of Gabene; infantry; its aftermath:
(19.43.1) As for the infantry, the Silver Shields in close order, falling heavily upon their adversaries, killed some of them in hand-to-hand fighting, and forced others to flee. Being unstoppable in their charge and engaging the entire opposing phalanx, they showed themselves so superior in skill and strength that of their own men they lost not one, but killed of those who opposed them over five thousand[84] and routed all the foot soldiers, who were many times their number. (2) When Eumenes learned that his baggage train was taken but that the horsemen of Peucestes were nearby, he tried to collect all his mounted men and renew the cavalry battle against Antigonus. He hoped, indeed, if victorious in battle, not only to save his own baggage, but also to capture that of the enemy. (3) When Peucestes, however, would not comply with him, but on the contrary retired still further to a river,[85] and because at the same time night was coming on, Eumenes was forced to yield at the time. (4) Antigonus, dividing his cavalry into two bodies, lay himself with one in wait for Eumenes, watching for his first move, but handing over the other to Peithon, he ordered him to attack the Silver Shields, who had been cut off from their cavalry support. (5) Though Peithon promptly carried out his orders, the Macedonians, forming themselves into a square, withdrew safely to the river and accused Peucestes of being responsible for the defeat of the mounted forces. After Eumenes joined them at about the time for lighting lamps, they took counsel together what should be done. (6) The satraps, indeed, said that it was necessary to retire to the upper satrapies as rapidly as possible, but Eumenes declared that they should stay and fight it out, because the phalanx of the opponents had been shattered and the cavalry forces on the two sides were equal. (7) The Macedonians, however, said they would comply with neither of them, because their baggage had been taken, and their children, their wives, and many other kinsfolk were in the hands of the enemy. (8) At that moment, then, they broke up the meeting, without having adopted any generally approved plan. Afterwards the Macedonians, secretly entering into negotiations with Antigonus, surrendered Eumenes, having seized him,[86] and recovering their baggage

---

[84] See also Polyaen. 4.6.13.
[85] Even though the main MSS have (a variant of) τόπον 'place', like Fischer and Bizière, I nevertheless opt to follow the suggestion by Geer 1969: 346, and read here ποταμόν, 'river'. The situation described below, paragraph 5, especially suggests to me Geer's conjuncture may well be right.
[86] The story as told by Plutarch, Nepos, and Justin is much more dramatic than Diodorus' matter-of-fact account.

and after receiving pledges, they were enrolled in Antigonus' army. (9) Very much in the same way the satraps and most of both the other commanders and the soldiers, deserting their commander, only thought of their own safety.[87]

(19.44.1) Now that Antigonus had unexpectedly mastered Eumenes and all the army that had been opposing him, having seized Antigenes, the commander of the Silver Shields, and having thrown him into a pit, he burned him alive and killed Eudamus, who had brought the elephants from India, and Celbanus,[88] as well as certain others of those who had always been hostile to him. (2) Putting Eumenes under guard, he considered how he might best be of use to him. He wished, indeed, to have at his side a good commander and one who would be under obligations to him, but certainly did not trust Eumenes' promises because of the latter's loyalty to Olympias and the kings. In fact, before, having been spared by Antigonus at Nora in Phrygia, Eumenes had none the less supported the kings most wholeheartedly. When Antigonus saw also that the ardent desire of the Macedonians for the punishment of Eumenes was not to be turned aside, he put the man to death. But because of his former friendship for him, having cremated his body and after placing his bones in an urn, he sent them to his relatives. (3) Among the wounded there was also brought in as a captive the historian Hieronymus of Cardia, who formerly spent his time held in honour by Eumenes, but after Eumenes' death enjoyed the favour and confidence of Antigonus. (4) After Antigonus had taken his entire army into Media, he himself spent the winter[89] in a village that is near Ecbatana, where the capital of this region is situated, but he distributed the soldiers throughout the entire satrapy and particularly in the eparchy[90] called Rhagae, which had received this name from a catastrophe that had occurred there in former times.[91] (5) Indeed, having the most, and most prosperous, cities of the lands in that

---

[87] See Plu. *Eum.* 17–19; Just. 14.3–4. Plu. *Eum.* 16.1–5 even relates that before the battle most of his generals and satraps, incited by Antigenes and Teutamus, had already decided to get rid of Eumenes, but only after his insight had procured them another victory. Warned by Eudamus and Phaedimus, Eumenes had put all his business in order before the battle began.

[88] Further unknown. However, there is, to the best of my knowledge, no need for a conjecture that identifies this man with Cebalinus, the man who exposed a conspiracy against Alexander by Dimnus (see above, 17.92.2).

[89] That is, the remaining part of the winter of 317/16.

[90] An administrative subdivision of a satrapy.

[91] Diodorus assumes here an etymology (the name of the city being related to Greek ῥαγάς 'fissure' or ῥῆγμα 'breakage, fracture'), occurring also in Duris and Posidonius (both according to Str. 1.3.19/60; 11.9.1/514), which is unlikely to be correct, even though the region is indeed prone to earthquakes.

part of the world, it had suffered such violent earthquakes that both the cities and all inhabitants vanished, and, in general, the land was altered and new rivers and marshy lakes appeared in place of the former ones.

S. 137:
19.46.1–48.8:

Antigonus rids himself of Peithon and the latter's supporters:
(19.46.1) Antigonus, who was wintering[92] in Media and was informed that Peithon was winning the support of many of the soldiers in the winter quarters by promises and gifts, and that he planned to revolt, concealed his own intention, pretending not to believe those who were spreading the charges, and rebuked them for trying to disrupt his friendship, while many listened, and caused the rumour to be spread that he was about to leave Peithon as commander of the upper satrapies with an army sufficient for their safety. (2) He even wrote to Peithon himself a letter, asking him to come as soon as possible, so that he, having discussed the necessary matters face to face, could quickly make his journey to the sea. He devised this plan, wishing to prevent Peithon's suspecting Antigonus' real intention, to persuade him to come within reach on the assumption that he was about to be left behind as satrap. It was, indeed, no easy matter to arrest a man by force who had gained preferment for *aretē* while serving under Alexander, and who at that very time was satrap of Media and had curried favour with the entire army. (3) Peithon happened to be wintering in the most distant parts of Media but, though having already corrupted a large number who promised to join him in the revolt, he came to Antigonus, deceived by empty expectations, because his friends wrote to him about Antigonus' plans and hinted at his own great prospects. (4) Antigonus, when he had gained possession of his person and had accused him before the members of the council,[93] easily won a conviction and had him executed at once. (5) Gathering the army into one place, he appointed Orontobates the Mede as satrap of Media,[94] but Hippostratus as commander with an

---

[92] The winter of 317/16. The events described here start in early 316.
[93] See Polyaen. 4.6.14, informing us that Peithon was tried ἐς τὸ κοινὸν τῶν Μακεδόνων ('in the assembly of the Macedonians'). As regards the precise content of the charges, both Diodorus and Polyaenus remain silent.
[94] It cannot be established whether this Orontobates was a relative of the Orontobates who was a prominent member of the elite of Darius III: see Heckel 2009: 186 *s.v.* 'Orontopates', 323 *ad* note 490.

infantry force of thirty-five hundred mercenaries....⁹⁵ (6) Antigonus himself moved to Ecbatana with his force. From there, having taken possession of five thousand talents of silver in bullion [c. 130,000 kg], he led the army into Persis, the march lasting about twenty days to the capital, which is called Persepolis.

(19.47.1) While Antigonus was on the march, Peithon's friends who had shared in his conspiracy, of whom the most notable were Meleager and Menoetas, collected the scattered comrades of both Eumenes and Peithon, about eight hundred horsemen. (2) At first they plundered the territory of those Medes who refused to join the revolt, but afterwards, learning that both Hippostratus and Orontobates were encamped without regard for precautions, they attacked the camp by night. They almost made good their attack,⁹⁶ but overcome by numbers and after winning some soldiers to join the revolt, they withdrew again. (3) As they were without heavy equipment and were all mounted, they made their raids unexpectedly and filled the region with confusion. After some time, however, being enclosed in a narrow place surrounded by cliffs, some of them were killed, others were taken alive. (4) Of their captains, Meleager and Ocranes the Mede, and some of the outstanding men, were killed while resisting the attack. Such was the outcome of the revolt in Media.

Antigonus solidifies his position further:
(19.48.1) As soon as Antigonus came into Persis, he was granted the dignity of kingship by the inhabitants as if he was the acknowledged lord of Asia.⁹⁷ He himself, sitting in council with his companions, considered the question of the satrapies. He permitted Tlepolemus to retain Carmania, and likewise Stasanor to retain Bactria: it was, indeed, not easy to remove them by sending a message, since they had conducted themselves well towards the inhabitants and had many

---

⁹⁵ As Fischer records in the *apparatus ad loc.*: *eqvitum nvmervs lacvna periit* ('the number of horsemen has been lost in a lacuna'). Dindorf, however, adds ἱππεῖς δὲ ('and horsemen') before πεντακοσίους ('five hundred'), resulting in a force of three thousand foot and five hundred horse. Though both versions are feasible, I have decided to follow Fischer's lead.

⁹⁶ The MSS and Fischer read here (forms of) ἐπιβολῆς ('attack'). Following the text of the MSS, the meaning of 'make good' for κρατέω comes to mind: see *LSJ, s.v. ad* VI. However, the context also offers another option. It concerns a conjecture made by Capps and followed by Geer 1969: 356, namely περιβολῆς (to be translated as 'outer works'), especially because of the connotation of κρατέω ('master', 'conquer', etc.): in that case the translation would run: 'They almost took the outer works...'. I generally prefer to stay as close as possible to the text of the MSS, unless of course the context and/or logic forces me to deviate. I have, therefore, opted to follow Fischer's text.

⁹⁷ Formally, that position still belonged to Alexander's direct heirs.

supporters. (2) He sent Evitus to Aria,[98] but, when he died soon afterwards, he put Evagoras in his place, a man admired for both courage and shrewdness. He permitted Oxyartes, the father of Roxane, to keep the satrapy in Paropanisadae as before: in fact, it was impossible to remove him without a long campaign and a strong army as well. (3) From Arachosia he summoned Sibyrtius, who was well disposed to him, and both permitted him to retain the satrapy and assigned to him the most turbulent of the Silver Shields, in name because of their use in the war, but in reality to ensure their destruction. In fact, he privately directed the satrap to send them, little group by little group at a time, on missions without the possibility of returning alive.[99] (4) Among them also happened to be those who had betrayed Eumenes, so that punishment for their treachery to their general came upon them speedily. ... (5) Antigonus, then, seeing that Peucestes happened to enjoy great favour among the Persians, first took his satrapy away from him. Because the Persians were angry and Thespius, one of their leading men, even frankly said that the Persians would not obey anyone else, Antigonus had this man killed and instated Asclepiodorus as governor [hyparch] of Persis and gave him a sufficient number of soldiers. Leading Peucestes on to hope for other things and elevating him with vain expectations, Antigonus removed him from the country.[100] (6) While Antigonus himself was making the journey to Susa, he was met at the River Pasitigris by Xenophilus, the supervisor of the treasury at Susa,[101] who had been sent by Seleucus with orders to do all he was told by Antigonus. Receiving him, then, he pretended to honour him among the closest of his friends, taking care lest he change his mind and shut him out again. (7) When he himself had occupied the citadel of Susa, he found in it the golden climbing vine[102] and a great number of other objects of art, weighing all told fifteen thousand talents [c. 390,000 kg]. (8) There was also collected for him another great amount of treasures, both from the crowns and the other gifts, and also from the spoils. This amounted to five thousand talents [c. 130,000 kg], and there was another equal

---

[98] Previously (see 18.39.6, above), Antipater had assigned Aria and Drangia to Stasander: however, the latter had supported Eumenes (see above, 19.14.7), as allegedly Tlepolemus, Sibyrtius, and Oxyartes had done as well. As becomes obvious, though, their position was judged differently.
[99] See Plu. *Eum.* 19.3 and Polyaen. 4.6.15.
[100] Though it seems that Peucestes outlived Antigonus, he never appears in the sources, to the best of my knowledge, in a really leading role. However, Phylarchus reports (*FGrH/BNJ* 81 F 12 = Ath. 14.614F) that Peucestes was among those favoured by Antigonus' son Demetrius. See also Heckel 2009: 203–5 s.v. 'Peucestas [2]'.
[101] For Xenophilus see also above, 19.17.3, 18.1.
[102] For the golden vine (and the golden plane tree) see Hdt. 7.27; Ath. 12.514F.

amount in Media apart from the treasury in Susa, so that in all twenty-five thousand talents [c. 650,000 kg] were gathered together. Such was the state of Antigonus' affairs.

S. 138:
19.55.1–62.9:

Antigonus confronts Seleucus over Babylonia; Seleucus flees:
(19.55.1) When this year had passed, Praxibulus was *archon* at Athens [315/14] and in Rome Nautius Spurius and Marcus Poplius were consuls.[103] While these held office, Antigonus left Aspisas, one of the natives, as satrap of Susis.[104] He himself, having decided to bring down all the money from the inland to the sea, prepared wagons and camels and after that, taking the treasure, set out for Babylonia with the army. (2) After he had arrived in twenty-two days in Babylon, Seleucus, the satrap of the region, both honoured him with gifts suitable for a king and feasted the whole army. (3) When Antigonus, however, demanded an accounting for the revenues, Seleucus answered that he was not bound to undergo a public investigation of his administration of this region, which the Macedonians had given him in recognition of his services rendered while Alexander was alive.[105] (4) As the dispute grew more serious each day, Seleucus, reasoning from the fate of Peithon, feared that Antigonus would someday seize a pretext and murder him. Antigonus seemed, indeed, eager to put out of the way all of his associates who were of high rank and were capable of claiming a share in the government. (5) To avoid this, then, Seleucus fled with fifty horsemen, intending to make his way to Egypt, to Ptolemy. In fact, word had spread abroad of Ptolemy's kindness and of his cordiality and friendliness to those who fled to him. (6) When Antigonus learned of the flight, he was pleased, since it seemed that he was not forced to lay hands upon a man who had been his friend and had actively co-operated with him, and that Seleucus, by condemning himself to flee, had surrendered his

---

[103] Sp. Nautius Rutilus and M. Popillius Laenas were the consuls of 316 VC, while L. Aemilius Mamercinus Privernas held the function of dictator (Broughton 1951: 155–6). Diodorus is still two years ahead of the Varronian chronology. However, in spite of the date presented by Diodorus, the events described in this chapter and the following one still belong to the year 316.

[104] Replacing Antigenes (above, 18.39.6). Though Geer believes this Antigenes may well have been a different person from the commander of the 'Silver Shields' (see Geer 1969: 381, note 3), Heckel believes they are one and the same: see Heckel 2009: 30–1 *s.v.* 'Antigenes [1a]' at 30. The death of the commander of the 'Silver Shields' was described above, 19.44.1.

[105] In fact, the satrapy had been awarded by Antipater, but the latter had been appointed by the Macedonian assembly.

The Period of the Diadochs: The Rift Deepens 451

satrapy without struggle or danger. (7) However, when the Chaldeans came to him later and foretold that if he let Seleucus escape from his hands, the consequence would be that all Asia would become subject to Seleucus and that Antigonus himself would lose his life in a battle against him,[106] repenting his former course, he sent out men in pursuit. They, though, after tracking him for a certain distance, returned unsuccessful. (8) Although Antigonus on other occasions was accustomed to despise such prophecies, he was not a little disturbed at this time, being struck by the men's reputation. Indeed, it appears they possess great experience and make most exact observations of the stars. In fact, they declare that for many myriads of years the study of these matters has been pursued among them. It is also believed that they foretold to Alexander that, if he entered Babylon, he would die.[107] (9) And just as was the case with the prophecy about Alexander, it happened that this prophecy with regard to Seleucus was fulfilled according to these men's assertion. Of this we will speak in detail when we come to the proper period.[108]

Seleucus teams up with Ptolemy, Lysimachus, and Cassander:
(19.56.1) After arriving safely in Egypt, Seleucus received nothing but kindness from Ptolemy. He bitterly accused Antigonus, saying that Antigonus had determined to remove from their satrapies all who were men of rank and in particular those who had served under Alexander. As examples of this he mentioned the killing of Peithon, the removal of Peucestes from Persis, and his own experiences. (2) In fact, all were not only guiltless of wrongdoing, but also, having performed many great services out of friendship, had been patiently awaiting a reward for *aretē*. He reviewed too the magnitude of Antigonus' armed forces, his vast wealth, and his recent successes, and went on to intimate that in consequence he had become arrogant and had encompassed in his ambitious plans the entire kingdom of the Macedonians. (3) Having induced Ptolemy through such arguments to prepare for war, he sent certain of his friends to Europe, directing them to try to convert both Cassander and Lysimachus[109] into enemies of Antigonus by similar arguments. (4) Because they

---

[106] Hinting at the Battle of Ipsus in 301. For Chaldeans and prophecies, see above, 2.29.1–31.9, 17.112.2, and relevant notes.
[107] See above, 17.112.2.
[108] Book 21, however, which would deal with these events, is only extant in fragments: see below.
[109] Lysimachus had received, after Alexander's death, the authority over Thrace, now detached from Macedonia. See also Heckel 2009: 153–5 *s.v.* 'Lysimachus [2]'.

quickly carried out their instructions, the seed of a quarrel and of great wars began to grow. But Antigonus, who had deduced Seleucus' course by reasoning from probabilities, sent envoys to Ptolemy, Lysimachus, and Cassander, urging them to maintain the existing friendship. Having next established as satrap of Babylonia that Pithon who had come from India,[110] setting out with his army, he marched towards Cilicia. (5) When he arrived at Malus,[111] he divided the army, after the setting of Orion,[112] for passing the winter. He also took the money at Cyinda,[113] ten thousand talents [60,000,000 *drachmae*]. Apart from this there fell to him from the annual revenue eleven thousand talents [66,000,000 *drachmae*]. It therefore happened that he was fear-inspiring both because of the size of his armies and because of the amount of his wealth.

(**19.57.1**) While Antigonus was going into Upper Syria, envoys arrived from Ptolemy, Lysimachus, and Cassander. When they had been brought into the council, they demanded that Cappadocia and Lycia be given to Cassander,[114] Hellespontine Phrygia to Lysimachus, all Syria to Ptolemy, and Babylonia to Seleucus, and that Antigonus should divide the treasures that he had seized after the battle with Eumenes: they too had, in fact, had a share in the war. They said that if he would do none of these things, they would all join in waging war on him. (2) Because Antigonus answered rather harshly and told them to make ready for war, the envoys went away with their mission unaccomplished. After this, Ptolemy, Lysimachus, and Cassander, after making a mutual alliance, both gathered their forces and prepared stocks of arms, missiles, and the other needful things.[115] (3) Antigonus, seeing that many men of great repute had combined against him, and computing the size of the approaching war, summoned the tribes, cities, and rulers to join him in alliance. (4) He sent Agesilaus to the kings in Cyprus, Idomeneus and Moschion to Rhodes, and his own nephew Polemaeus[116] with an

---

[110] Pithon, the son of Agenor, appointed satrap of India by Antipater (see 18.39.6).
[111] Malus or Mallus, a city in Cilicia by the River Pyramus: see Str 14.5.16/675. To the best of my knowledge the exact location of the site has not yet been established.
[112] That is, in November 316.
[113] See above, 18.62.2, Chapter 7, and note 120.
[114] It might be that, in fact, Asander is meant here, the satrap of Caria (19.62.2), and that instead of Lycia either Cilicia or Lydia should be read: see Bizière 2002: 81 note 1.
[115] See App. *Syr.* 53; Just. 15.1.1–5.
[116] On the basis of *IG* II².469 line 3 from 306/5, Fischer in his *apparatus* suggests reading Πολεμαῖον (Polemaeus) here, a suggestion followed by Bizière 2002: 81 (*apparatus ad* l. 19–20). The inscription unmistakably links a Polemaeus with Antigonus and his son Demetrius. I will, therefore, follow Fischer and Bizière's lead, in spite of the fact that MSS R and F consistently read his name as Πτολεμαῖον ('Ptolemaeus').

The Period of the Diadochs: The Rift Deepens   453

army to Cappadocia to lift the siege of Amisus, to drive out all who
had been sent by Cassander into Cappadocia, and finally having
arrived on the Hellespont to lie in wait for Cassander, if he should
try to cross over from Europe. (5) He sent Aristodemus of Miletus
to the Peloponnesus with a thousand talents [6,000,000 *drachmae*].
Him he instructed to establish friendship with Alexander[117] and
Polyperchon and, after raising an adequate force of mercenaries,
to carry on the war against Cassander. He himself established, at
intervals throughout all that part of Asia of which he was master,
a system of fire-signals and dispatch-carriers, by means of which he
expected to be served quickly in all matters.[118]

Antigonus tries to acquire a naval force in Phoenicia:
(19.58.1) After attending to these matters, Antigonus set out for
Phoenicia, hastening to organise a naval force. In fact, his enemies
then ruled the sea with many ships, but he had, altogether, not even
a few. Pitching camp in Old Tyre in Phoenicia and intending to
besiege Tyre, he called together the kings of the Phoenicians and the
governors [hyparchs] of Syria. (2) He instructed the kings to assist
him in building ships, since Ptolemy was holding all the ships from
Phoenicia in Egypt with their crews. He ordered the governors to
prepare quickly four and a half million *medimnoi* of wheat...,[119] for
such was the annual consumption. He himself, having collected lum-
berjacks, sawyers, and shipwrights from all sides, had wood from
the Lebanon carried to the sea, while there were eight thousand
men employed in cutting and sawing the timber and one thousand
pairs of draught animals in transporting it. (3) This mountain range
[the Lebanon] extends along the territory of Tripolis, Byblus, and
Sidon, and is covered with cedar and cypress trees, wonderful in
both beauty and size. (4) He allocated three shipyards in Phoenicia,
at Tripolis, Byblus, and Sidon, and a fourth in Cilicia, for which the
wood was brought from Mount Taurus. (5) There was also another
in Rhodes, where the *demos* agreed to make ships from imported
wood. While Antigonus was busy therewith and after he had established his camp near the sea, Seleucus arrived from Egypt with a

---

[117] The Alexander meant here is the son of Polyperchon: see 19.61.1 and Arr. *Succ.* 1.38; also Heckel 2009: 20 *s.v.* 'Alexander [6]'.
[118] A similar system, apparently, to that employed by the Achaemenid kings: see Arist. *Mu.* 398a32–5. A different system was described above, 19.17.7 and note 28.
[119] Fischer indicates here a lacuna. Four and a half million *medimnoi* of wheat equals about 119,000,000 litres of wheat, though Bizière calculates an amount of 25 to 30 million litres: I am not sure where the mistake lies. Geer 1969: 391 note 3 adds that a quantity of barley, to feed the horses, was probably lost from the text.

hundred ships, royally equipped and sailing adequately. After he had sailed contemptuously along past the very camp, both the men from the allied cities and all who were co-operating with Antigonus were downhearted. (6) It was, indeed, very clear that the enemy, being masters at sea, would wreak havoc upon those who aided their opponents out of friendship for Antigonus. Antigonus, however, bade them carry on, having affirmed that in that very summer he would take the sea with five hundred vessels.

(19.59.1) While Antigonus was thus engaged, Agesilaus, the envoy who was sent to Cyprus, arrived with the information that Nicocreon and the most powerful of the other kings had made an alliance with Ptolemy,[120] and that those of Cition, Lapithus, Marion, and Cerynia had concluded a treaty of friendship with him. (2) On learning this, Antigonus left three thousand soldiers with Andronicus as commander to continue the siege, but he himself, setting out with his force, took by storm both Joppa and Gaza, cities that had refused obedience. The soldiers of Ptolemy whom he captured, he distributed among his own ranks, but he placed in each city a garrison to force the inhabitants to obey him. (3) He himself, going back to the camp at Old Tyre, made preparations for the siege. At this time Ariston, who had been entrusted by Eumenes with the bones of Craterus, gave them for burial to Phila, who had formerly lived in wedlock with Craterus, but at this time with Demetrius, the son of Antigonus. (4) This very woman seems to have been of exceptional sagacity. Indeed, she would quell the trouble-makers in the camp by dealing appropriately with each individual; she would arrange marriages at her own expense for the sisters and daughters of the poor; and she would free from jeopardy many who had been trapped by false accusations. (5) It is even said that her father Antipater, who is reputed to have been the wisest of the rulers of his age, used to consult with her about the most important matters even when she was still a maiden. (6) But the character of the woman will be more clearly revealed as the story proceeds and by the events that brought change and a final crisis to the reign of Demetrius.[121] This was the situation of the affairs of Antigonus and of Phila, the wife of Demetrius.

---

[120] Nicocreon was the king of Cyprian Salamis and had concluded a treaty of alliance with Ptolemy as early as 321 (see Arr. *Succ.* 24.6 [= *Cod. rescr. Vatic. gr.* 495 fol. 230, 235]) and later governed the whole island for him (see below, 19.79.5).

[121] Unfortunately that part of Diodorus' *Library* is lost. It appears that Phila played a very important role after the Battle of Ipsus: see, for example, Wehrli 1964: 143.

The Period of the Diadochs: The Rift Deepens 455

Antigonus acquires allies in Greece and Asia Minor:
(19.60.1) Of the commanders who had been sent out by Antigonus, Aristodemus, having sailed to Laconia, and with permission from the Spartans to recruit mercenaries, enrolled eight thousand soldiers from the Peloponnesus. Meeting Alexander and Polyperchon, he established friendship with them on behalf of Antigonus and appointed Polyperchon commander of the Peloponnesus, but persuaded Alexander to sail to Antigonus in Asia. (2) The other commander, Polemaeus, proceeding with his force to Cappadocia and finding Amisus under siege by Asclepiodorus, a commander of Cassander, delivered the city from danger and restored the satrapy after dismissing Asclepiodorus and his men under a truce. (3) Thereafter advancing through Bithynia and finding Zibytes, the king of the Bithynians, laying siege to both the *polis* of the Astacenians[122] and that of the Calchedonians, he forced him to abandon the siege. After making alliances both with these *poleis* and with Zibytes, and moreover taking hostages, he proceeded towards Ionia and Lydia. In fact, Antigonus had written to him to go quickly to the support of the coast, because Seleucus was about to make a naval expedition there. (4) As he finally drew near to the aforementioned regions, it happened that Seleucus laid siege to Erythrae,[123] but when he heard that the force of his enemies was near, he sailed away empty-handed. (19.61.1) After Polyperchon's son Alexander had come to him, Antigonus made a treaty of friendship with him. Calling a general assembly both of the soldiers and of those who sojourned there,[124] Antigonus laid charges against Cassander, bringing forward the murder of Olympias and the treatment of Roxane and the king.[125] (2) Moreover, he said that Cassander had married Thessalonice by force, and was clearly trying to establish his own claim to the Macedonian throne. Moreover that, although the Olynthians were very bitter enemies of the Macedonians, Cassander had re-established them in a city called by his own name and had rebuilt Thebes, which had been razed by the Macedonians. (3) When the crowd showed that it

---

[122] Astacus was situated on a bay of the same name, some 50 km south-east of Calchedon. For Calchedon see, for example, Stronk 1995: 134, 156–8 *ad* (3).
[123] A Ionian city, one of the original twelve Ionian *poleis* in Asia Minor, situated on a peninsula directly opposite the island of Chios: see also Paus. 7.3.7; Str. 14.1.3/633.
[124] That is, Macedonians not enlisted in Antigonus' army, as appears from the text in 19.62.1, which refers to 'a decree of the Macedonians'. See also the comments in Bizière 2002: 162–3 *ad* 61.1, second remark.
[125] They were discussed in 19.51.5 (murder of Olympias, apparently not by Cassander himself, but not without his consent) and 19.52.4 (capture and putting under custody of Roxane and Alexander IV).

shared his wrath, he introduced a decree according to which it was voted that Cassander was to be an enemy unless he both destroyed these *poleis* and, releasing the king and his mother Roxane from imprisonment, restored them to the Macedonians, and, in general, yielded obedience to Antigonus, the duly established commander who had succeeded to the guardianship of the throne. It also stated that all the Greeks were free,[126] not subject to foreign garrisons, and autonomous. When the soldiers had voted in favour of these measures, Antigonus sent men in every direction to carry the decree. (4) He believed, indeed, that through their hope of freedom, he would gain the Greeks as eager participants with him in the war, and that the commanders and satraps in the upper satrapies, who had suspected that he was determined to depose the kings who inherited from Alexander, would, now he publicly took upon himself the war on their behalf, all change their minds and promptly obey his orders. (5) Having finished these matters, he gave Alexander five hundred talents [3,000,000 *drachmae*] and, after leading him to hope for great things to come, sent him back to the Peloponnesus. He himself, after summoning ships from Rhodes and equipping most of those that had been built, sailed against Tyre. Though he was master at sea and prevented food from being brought in, he pressed the siege with vigour for a year and three months, reducing the besieged to extreme want, but he permitted the soldiers who had come from Ptolemy to depart each with his own possessions; but taking the city by capitulation, he introduced into it a garrison to watch it closely.[127]

Confrontation between Antigonus and Ptolemy:
(19.62.1) While these things were going on, Ptolemy, who had heard the decisions of the Macedonians with Antigonus regarding the freedom of the Greeks, wrote a similar decree himself, wishing the Greeks to know that he was no less interested in their autonomy than Antigonus. (2) Each, indeed, perceiving that it was a matter of no little moment to gain the goodwill of the Greeks, rivalled the other in conferring favours upon this people. Ptolemy also brought into his alliance Asander,[128] satrap of Caria, who was strong and had

---

[126] Continuing his policy previously practised in Cyzicus. See above, Chapter 7, 18.52.1-2 and note 97.
[127] In 314.
[128] Though the MSS and Fischer read Κάσανδρος here (and elsewhere) for this functionary, I have nevertheless opted here to follow the lead of Wesseling, supported, *inter alios*, by Geer and Bizière, and read Ἀσανδρος.

The Period of the Diadochs: The Rift Deepens 457

a considerable number of *poleis* subject to him.[129] (3) Having dispatched beforehand three thousand soldiers to the kings on Cyprus, he now sent out a strong army, anxious to force those who were opposing to carry out his commands. (4) He sent, then, Myrmidon the Athenian with ten thousand men, Polyclitus with a hundred ships, and Menelaus, his own brother, as commander of the whole force. These, having sailed to Cyprus and having found Seleucus and his fleet there, met together, considering what they should do. (5) They decided, then, that Polyclitus should sail to the Peloponnesus with fifty ships and carry on the war against those supporting Aristodemus,[130] Alexander, and Polyperchon; that Myrmidon and the mercenaries should go to Caria to help Asander and his men, under attack by Polemaeus the commander; and that Seleucus and Menelaus and their men, left in Cyprus with King Nicocreon and the other allies, should carry on the war against their adversaries. (6) After the force had been divided in this way, Seleucus and his men took Ceryneia and Lapithus by siege, secured the support of Stasioecus, king of the Marienses, forced the ruler of the Amathusians to give a guarantee, and laid unremitting siege with the whole force to the city of the Citienses, unable to induce it to join. (7) About this time forty ships under the command of Themison sailed down to Antigonus from the Hellespont, and likewise Dioscurides put in with eighty vessels from the Hellespont and Rhodes. (8) The first of the completed ships that had been constructed in Phoenicia were also at hand, fully equipped; including those captured at Tyre, they were one hundred and twenty, so that in all there were gathered together about Antigonus two hundred and forty fully equipped ships of war. Of these there were ninety *tetrereis*, ten *pentereis*, three *ennereis*, ten *dekereis*, and thirty undecked boats.[131] (9) Dividing the fleet, he sent fifty ships to the Peloponnesus, and, having instated his nephew Dioscurides as *navarch* of the other ships, he ordered him to sail round, both providing safety to the allies and winning the support of the islands that had not yet joined the alliance. Such was the state of Antigonus' affairs.

---

[129] What mattered most to Ptolemy were the Greek *poleis* in Caria and to a much lesser extent the non-Greek settlements in this region: hence this translation.
[130] Antigonus had sent Aristodemus of Miletus to the Peloponnesus: see above, 19.57.5.
[131] Only 143 ships have been listed so far. If we accept the number of 240 ships gathered, it could be assumed the rest of the ships were *triereis*, more or less the standard ship of war at the time. As regards the division of oars and/or people handling the oars, especially concerning the *dekereis*, *ennereis*, *pentereis*, and *tetrereis*, views differ. See, for example, Blackman and Rankov et al. 2013: 81: '[t]hese new types would still have been rowed at either two or three levels: ... [m]ore than three levels would have been impractable'. See also Casson 1971: 137 and Murray 2012.

S. 139:
19.68.2–69.3:

Cassander tries to get hold of Asia Minor; Antigonus counters:
(19.68.2) When Cassander had arrived in Macedonia and heard that war was being waged on all the *poleis* in Caria that were allied to Ptolemy and Seleucus, he sent a force into Caria, wishing to aid his allies, and at the same time eager to force Antigonus into distracting undertakings so that he might not have the opportunity to cross over into Europe. (3) He also wrote to Demetrius of Phalerum[132] and to Dionysius, who commanded the garrison on Munychia,[133] ordering them to dispatch twenty ships to Lemnos. Though they at once sent the ships, with Aristotle as *navarch*, the latter, having sailed to Lemnos and having summoned Seleucus with his fleet, undertook to persuade the Lemnians to revolt from Antigonus. Because they did not assent, he both ravaged their land and began a siege, after surrounding the city with a stockade. (4) Later, however, Seleucus sailed off to Cos, and Dioscurides, who had been appointed as *navarch* by Antigonus, on learning of Seleucus' departure, swooped on Lemnos and drove Aristotle himself from the island, and captured most of his ships together with their crews. (5) Asander and Prepelaus were in command of the force sent by Cassander into Caria and, on being informed that Polemaeus, the commander of Antigonus, had divided his army for wintering[134] and was himself engaged in burying his father, they sent Eupolemus to lie in wait for the enemy near Caprima in Caria.[135] They sent with him eight thousand foot soldiers and two hundred horse. (6) But at this time Polemaeus, who had heard the enemy's scheme from some deserters, gathered from the troops who were wintering nearby eight thousand three hundred infantry and six hundred horse. (7) Falling unexpectedly upon the palisaded camp of the opponents about midnight and catching them off guard and asleep, he both captured Eupolemus himself alive and forced the soldiers to give themselves up. This, then, is what befell the generals who were sent by Cassander into Asia.
(19.69.1) When Antigonus saw that Cassander was trying to win Asia for himself, he left his son Demetrius in Syria,[136] ordering him to

---

[132] Demetrius of Phalerum, c. 350–c. 280, an Athenian orator, originally from Phalerum, was appointed by the Macedonian king Cassander to rule Athens, a task he performed from 317 to 307.
[133] Munychia is a steep hill (86 m high) in Piraeus, Athens, known today as Kastella.
[134] The winter of 314/13.
[135] To the best of my knowledge Caprima is otherwise unknown.
[136] See Plu. *Demetr.* 5.2; App. *Syr.* 9.54.

The Period of the Diadochs: The Rift Deepens 459

lie in wait for Ptolemy, whom he suspected of intending to advance from Egypt with a force against Syria. With Demetrius he left an infantry force consisting of ten thousand mercenaries, two thousand Macedonians, five hundred Lycians and Pamphylians, and four hundred Persian archers and slingers, five thousand horsemen, and forty-three elephants. He assigned to him four counsellors: Nearchus of Crete; Pithon, son of Agenor, who had returned a few days before from Babylon; and moreover Andronicus of Olynthus and Philip, men advanced in years and having accompanied Alexander on his whole campaign. Demetrius, indeed, was still young, being twenty-two years of age. (2) Antigonus himself took the rest of the army and, first trying to cross the Taurus Range and encountering deep snow, lost large numbers of his soldiers. Turning back therefore into Cilicia and seizing another opportunity, he crossed the aforesaid range in greater safety. On reaching Celaenae in Phrygia, he divided his army for wintering.[137] (3) Thereafter he summoned his fleet from Phoenicia under the command of Medius, who fell in with the ships of the Pydnaeans,[138] thirty-six in number, and after defeating them in an engagement, he captured the vessels together with their crews. This was the situation in Greece and in Asia Minor.

S. 140:
19.75.1–6:

Antigonus gets hold of Caria:
(**19.75.1**) In Asia Minor,[139] Asander, the ruler of Caria, being hard pressed by the war, came to terms with Antigonus, on condition that he would transfer all his soldiers to Antigonus, would leave the Greek *poleis* autonomous, and would keep as a grant the satrapy that he had formerly had, remaining a steadfast friend of Antigonus. (2) Having given his brother Agathon as a hostage for these terms and then after a few days having repented of the agreement, he stole and carried away his brother from custody and, sending envoys to Ptolemy and Seleucus, asked them to help him as soon as possible. (3) Enraged at this, Antigonus dispatched a force, both by sea and by land, for the liberation of the *poleis*, appointing Medius *navarch* of the fleet and instating Docimus as commander of the army. (4) Having arrived at the *polis* of the

---
[137] Also referring to the winter of 314/13.
[138] Pydna, a city in Macedon, had been taken by Cassander in 316.
[139] The events described in this *caput* are dated to 313.

Milesians, these men both encouraged the citizens to free themselves and, after taking by siege the citadel, which was held by a garrison, made the government return to autonomy. (5) While they were thus engaged, Antigonus besieged and took Tralles.[140] Next, proceeding to Caunus[141] and summoning the fleet, he captured that *polis* also except for its citadel. After encircling this with a palisade, he kept making continuous attacks on the side where it was most easily assailed. Polemaeus, who had been sent to Iasus[142] with an adequate force, compelled that city to side with Antigonus. (6) In this way, then, these *poleis* in Caria were made subject to Antigonus. When ambassadors came to the latter from the Aetolians and the Boeotians a few days later, he made an alliance with them. However, when he entered into negotiations with Cassander about peace in the Hellespontine region, he remained unsuccessful, because they could in no way agree. Therefore Cassander, despairing of a solution, decided to cling to the affairs of Greece once more.

S. 141:
19.79.4–86.5:

Ptolemy tries to capture Cyprus:
(19.79.4) When the matter of Cyrene had been disposed of according to his wishes,[143] Ptolemy crossed over with a force from Egypt into Cyprus against the kings who refused to obey him. Finding that Pygmalion was negotiating with Antigonus, he put him to death. He arrested Praxippus, king of Lapithia and ... (?) ruler of Cerynia,[144] whom he suspected of being ill-disposed to himself, and also Stasioecus, ruler of Marion:[145] he destroyed the city and trans-

---

[140] The modern city of Aydın. The city is located at the heart of the lower valley of the River Büyük Menderes (ancient Maeander) in Caria, in a commanding position for the region extending from the uplands of the valley down to the seacoast. During the Seleucid period, it received the name Ἀντιόχεια, 'Antiochia'. At other times it was also called 'Seleucia ad Maeandrum' and 'Erynina'. In Roman and Byzantine times, it was known as Tralles or Τραλλεῖς, and was one of the larger Aegean *poleis* in antiquity. See also Smith 1854: *s.v.*

[141] Another city in Caria, some km west of the modern city of Dalyan: see, for example, Smith 1854: *s.v.*

[142] A Greek *polis* in Caria located on the Gulf of Iasos (present-day Gulf of Güllük), opposite the modern town of Güllük. It was originally situated on an island, but is now connected to the mainland.

[143] The story starts still in 313. In the summer of that year the people of Cyrene had revolted from Ptolemy, but, largely thanks to Ptolemy's commander Agis, the sedition was quickly suppressed.

[144] Fischer suspects that after καί ('and') a proper name has been lost from the MSS, leaving us without the name of the ruler of Cerynia. Both Lapithia and Cerynia were situated near the middle of the north coast of Cyprus.

[145] Stasioecus had first supported Antigonus, then Ptolemy (see 19.62.6, above), and is now

The Period of the Diadochs: The Rift Deepens 461

ported the inhabitants to Paphos.[146] (5) After accomplishing these things, he appointed Nicocreon as commander of Cyprus, giving him both the *poleis* and the revenues of the abolished kings.[147] (6) He himself, though, having sailed with his army towards Upper Syria, as it is called, captured and plundered Posidium and Potami Caron.[148] Having sailed without delay to Cilicia, he took Malus and sold as booty those who were captured there. He also plundered the neighbouring countryside and, after sating his army with spoil, sailed back to Cyprus. (7) He played up to the soldiers in this way, calling forth their enthusiasm in the face of the battles to come.

(19.80.1) Antigonus' son Demetrius was still staying on in Coele Syria, lying in wait for the Egyptian armies. But when he heard of the capture of the cities, he left Pithon as commander in charge of the region, giving him the elephants and the heavy-armed units. He himself, with both the cavalry and the light-armed units, moved rapidly to Cilicia, to help those who were in danger. (2) Arriving after the critical moment and finding that the enemy had sailed away, he went rapidly back to his camp, having lost most of his horses during the march. In fact, he covered twenty-four stages towards Malus in six days,[149] so that due to the excessive hardship neither any porter nor the grooms were able to follow.

Ptolemy in Coele Syria; Demetrius' countermeasures:
(3) Because his affairs had turned out as he intended, Ptolemy now sailed away to Egypt, but after a little while, spurred on by Seleucus because of his hostility to Antigonus, he decided to make a campaign into Coele Syria and take the field against Demetrius. (4) Having gathered, then, his forces from all sides, he marched from Alexandria to Pelusium with eighteen thousand foot and four thousand horse. Of them some were Macedonians, others mercenaries, but the majority Egyptians, of whom some carried the missiles and

---

suspected of having left Ptolemy's side again. The *polis* of Marion was situated on the west coast of Cyprus.
[146] Paphos was situated on the south-western coast of Cyprus. Though Geer 1962: 53 note 2 finds the text of this sentence unsatisfactory and suspects a lacuna, neither Fischer nor Bizière appears to share his view. I must admit I do not understand Geer's problem.
[147] Nicocreon was the king of Salamis, situated on the south coast of Cyprus and already mentioned as a supporter of Ptolemy in 19.59.1, above.
[148] Posidium was situated south of the mouth of the River Orontes, at the foot of Mount Cassios. To the best of my knowledge Potami Caron has not yet been identified.
[149] It seems impossible to calculate the distance covered, because we know neither where Demetrius' journey started nor what value should be attributed to a *stathmos* ('stage'): however, Bizière believes a distance of 430 km feasible (Bizière 2002: 112 note 1), Geer believes that the distance was 'very much less' than 400 miles (c. 650 km; Geer 1962: 54–5 note 1).

the other baggage, others were armed and serviceable for battle.[150] (5) Marching through the desert from Pelusium, he pitched camp nearby the enemy near Old Gaza in Syria.[151] Demetrius, similarly gathering his soldiers from everywhere from their winter quarters[152] to Old Gaza, awaited the approach of his opponents.

(19.81.1) Though his friends advised him not to take the field against so great a commander and a superior force, Demetrius paid no heed to them, but confidently prepared for the battle, even though he was very young and was about to engage in so great a battle without his father.[153] (2) When he had called together an assembly under arms and, anxious and agitated, had taken his position on a raised platform, the crowd shouted with a single voice, bidding him carry on and, before the herald bade the shouting men cease their tumult, they all became silent. (3) Indeed, because he had just been placed in command, neither soldiers nor civilians had for him any ill will. [[That usually develops against seasoned commanders when at a particular time many minor irritations are combined in a single mass grievance. In fact, the multitude becomes exacting when it remains under the same authority and every group that is not preferred welcomes change.]] Because his father was already an old man, the hopes of the kingdom,[154] centring upon his succession, were bringing him the command and at the same time the goodwill of the multitude. (4) ... (5) In fact, he was about to engage a decisive battle not only against superior numbers, but also against commanders who were almost the greatest: Ptolemy and Seleucus. Indeed, these generals, who had shared all his wars with Alexander and had often led forces independently, were unconquered up to this time. (6) Demetrius, then, addressing the crowd with suitable words and promising that he would both give gifts according to merit and yield the booty to the soldiers, deployed his army for the battle.[155]

---

[150] According to Briant, this was the last time the Lagids employed Egyptian soldiers until 217: see Briant 1972: 61.

[151] Though Str. 16.2.30/759 asserts that Alexander the Great had destroyed Gaza completely and left it uninhabited, it appears the site retained some importance after all, if only as a fortress (see Arr. *An.* 2.26-7).

[152] For the winter of 313/12. The ensuing Battle of Gaza is dated on the *Marmor Parium* to the second half of 312 (see Jacoby 1904: 22: B16, 128 with parallel sources). Jacoby, though (*FGrH*, vol. IIC [Kommentar]: 700), places the battle in spring ('Frühjahr') 312.

[153] When Demetrius was sent to Coele Syria, in the summer of 314, he was 22 years of age (see 19.69.1). See for the ensuing battle Plu. *Demetr.* 5; Just. 15.1.6-9.

[154] For Diodorus' terminology (notably as regards βασιλεία, 'kingship') see the remarks by Bizière 2002: 68 note 1 *ad* 19.48.1.

[155] See also Just. 15.1.6-9; Plu. *Demetr.* 5.3-4.

Battle of Gaza:
(19.82.1) On the left wing, where he himself was going to partake in the battle, he first deployed the two hundred selected horsemen of his guard, among whom were not only all his other friends but also Pithon, who had campaigned with Alexander and had been appointed joint commander and partner in the whole undertaking by Antigonus. (2) As an advanced guard he drew up three companies[156] of cavalry and the same number as guards on the flank, and in addition to these, and stationed separately outside the wing, three companies of Tarentines,[157] so that those positioned about his person were five hundred horsemen armed with the lance and one hundred Tarentines. (3) Next he posted those of the cavalry who were called the Companions, eight hundred in number, and after them no less than fifteen hundred horsemen of all kinds. In front of the whole wing he stationed thirty of his elephants, and he filled the intervals between them with platoons of light-armed men, of whom a thousand were javelin-throwers and archers and five hundred Persian slingers. (4) In this fashion, then, forming the left wing, he intended to decide the battle with it. Next to it he drew up the phalanx of the infantry, composed of eleven thousand men. Of these two thousand were Macedonians, one thousand Lycians and Pamphylians, and eight thousand mercenaries. On the right wing he deployed the rest of his cavalry, fifteen hundred men, of whom Andronicus had the command. This officer was ordered to hold his line back at an angle and avoid fighting, awaiting the outcome of the conflict fought by Demetrius. The remaining thirteen elephants he stationed in front of the phalanx of the infantry, with sufficient light-armed troops positioned in the intervals. In this manner, then, Demetrius arrayed his army.

(19.83.1) Ptolemy and Seleucus at first made strong the left part of their line, not knowing the intention of their opponents. However, learning the formation Demetrius had adopted from scouts, they quickly repositioned their force in such a way that their right wing had the strength and greatest power to decide the contest against those arrayed with Demetrius on his left. They deployed on this wing the strongest three thousand of their cavalry, among whom they themselves had decided to fight as well. (2) In front of this position they placed the men who were to handle the iron crowfeet,[158]

---

[156] For the terminology, see above, 19.27–8 and the relevant notes.
[157] See above, 19.29.2 and note 61.
[158] The usual (military) meaning of χάραξ is a pointed stake to make a palisade or the very palisade itself (see *LSJ*, s.v. II, 1 and 2). The context of 19.84.1–2, however, makes it clear that

connected by chains, which they had prepared against the attack of the elephants. Indeed, when this device had been placed, it was easy to prevent the beasts from moving forward. (3) In front of this wing they also stationed their light-armed platoons, ordering both the javelin-men and archers to shoot continuously at the elephants and at those who were mounted upon them. Having strengthened their right wing in this manner and deploying the rest of their force to the best of their abilities, they advanced upon the enemy with a great shout. As their opponents also advanced, there first took place a cavalry battle on the extreme wings between the forward horsemen, in which the men of Demetrius had much the better of it. (4) Shortly after, though, when the men of Ptolemy and Seleucus had ridden around the wing and charged upon them more heavily with the companies drawn up in column, there occurred very severe fighting because of the zeal of both sides. (5) In the first charge, then, fighting with spears, most of these were shattered and not a few of the warriors were wounded. However, during the second round, they moved in to do battle at sword's point, and, being engaged in close fight, killed many of each side. The very commanders, fighting in front of all, encouraged those under their command to withstand the danger stoutly, and the horsemen upon the wings, all of whom had been selected for *aretē*, vied with each other, having their commanders, who shared the battle with them, as witnesses of their valour.

(19.84.1) After the cavalry battle had continued for a long time on equal terms, the elephants, urged on into the combat by their mahouts,[159] advanced for a certain distance in a way to inspire terror, as if no one was going to withstand them. When, however, they came up to the crowfeet, the host of javelin-throwers and archers, constantly shooting, began to wound seriously the bodies of the elephants and those mounted upon them. (2) While the mahouts were forcing the beasts forward and chastising them, one of the elephants was pierced by the cleverly devised crowfeet and, suffering great pain from its wounds[160] and from the frequency of the projectile hits, began to cause disorder. (3) Indeed, on smooth and yielding ground this kind of animal displays in direct onset a might that is irresistible,

---

these χάρακες were intended to be laid on the ground (whether or not covered with sand, as during the defence of Megalopolis against Polyperchon by Damis: 18.71.2–6) and be stepped upon by the elephants, to wound them. This led to Kromayer's writing 'Fußangeln' (Kromayer and Veith 1928: 141) and to my translation of 'crowfeet' (though 'caltrop' perhaps might serve as well).

[159] Diodorus uses here the word Ἰνδός, which can mean here both 'Indian' and 'mahout': see *LSJ*, s.v. In view of the context I have opted for the latter meaning.

[160] See 18.71.6 for the meaning 'wound' for πληγή.

The Period of the Diadochs: The Rift Deepens 465

but on terrain that is rough and difficult their strength is completely useless because of the tenderness of their feet. (4) Therefore, on this occasion, because Ptolemy shrewdly foresaw what would result from use of the crowfeet, he made the power of the animals useless. The final outcome was that, after most of the mahouts had been shot down, all the elephants were captured. (5) When this happened, most of Demetrius' horsemen were panic-stricken and rushed into flight. He himself, being left with a few and begging each to stand and not to desert him, when no one paid attention, was forced to leave with the rest. (6) As far as Gaza, then, most of the cavalry who were following with him listened to orders and remained in formation, so that not one of those who were pursuing at random lightly risked attacking. In fact, the plain, being open and yielding, was favourable to men who wished to withdraw in formation. (7) There followed too those of the infantry who preferred to leave their lines and, without their heavy arms, save themselves by travelling light. But as Demetrius was passing Gaza at about sunset, some of the cavalry, dropping out, entered the city, wishing to carry away their baggage. (8) Then, when the gates were opened and a large number of pack animals were gathered together, and moreover when each man tried to lead out his own beasts first, there arose such confusion around the gates that, when the troops of Ptolemy came up, no one was able to close the gates in time. Therefore, when the enemy dashed within the walls, the city came into the possession of Ptolemy.

Demetrius tries to carry on, but Ptolemy enlarges his power:
(19.85.1) After the battle had ended in this fashion, Demetrius reached Azotus[161] about the middle of the night, covering two hundred and seventy *stadia* [c. 50 km]. From there he sent a herald about the burial of the dead, being anxious to honour the dead in any way with the funeral they had deserved. (2) In fact, it happened that most of his friends had fallen, of whom the most distinguished were Pithon, who had shared the command on equal terms with himself, and Boeotus, who for a long time had lived with his father Antigonus and had shared in all his state secrets. (3) Throughout the battle there had fallen more than five hundred men,[162] the majority of whom were cavalry and men of distinction, while over eight thousand had been captured. Ptolemy and Seleucus permitted the recovery of the dead, and they sent to Demetrius without ransom

---

[161] The modern city of Ashdod.
[162] Plu. *Demetr.* 5.3 reports that 5,000 men had been killed.

both the captured royal baggage and those of the prisoners who had been used to employ themselves at the court. They said, indeed, that it was not about these that they were at variance with Antigonus, but because, although he and they had made war together, first against Perdiccas and later again Eumenes, he had not turned over to his companions their share of the captured territory, and again because, though concluding friendship[163] with Seleucus, he had nevertheless taken away from him his satrapy of Babylonia, contrary to all right. (4) Sending the captured soldiers off into Egypt, Ptolemy ordered their distribution among the *nomes*.[164] He himself, however, after magnificently burying all those of his own men who had died in the battle, went with his force against the cities of Phoenicia, besieging some of them, winning others by persuasion. (5) As he did not have a sufficiently strong army, Demetrius sent a letter-carrier to his father, asking him to help as quickly as possible. He himself, moving to Tripolis in Phoenicia, summoned both the soldiers from Cilicia and those of his other men who were guarding cities or strongholds far removed from the enemy.

(19.86.1) After he had gained control of the open country, Ptolemy won Sidon to his side. After he had pitched camp near Tyre, though, he summoned Andronicus, the commander of the garrison, to surrender the city, and he promised to give him both gifts and abundant honours. (2) He, however, saying that he would in no wise betray the trust that had been placed in him by Antigonus and Demetrius, vulgarly insulted Ptolemy. Later, when his soldiers had mutinied, expelled from Tyre and fallen into the hands of Ptolemy, he expected to receive punishment both for the insults and for his unwillingness to surrender Tyre. But in truth Ptolemy bore no malice, but on the contrary, giving him gifts, he kept him in his court, making him one of his companions and advancing him in honour.[165] (3) For indeed, this ruler was exceedingly gentle and forgiving, and moreover beneficent, which is what most increased his power and made many men desire to share his friendship. (4) For example, he generously received Seleucus, who had been expelled from Babylonia, and

---

[163] Though Fischer and Bizière follow here the text of the MSS and read πάλιν, 'again', the context nevertheless entices me to follow Geer, following Hertlein, and read φιλίαν, 'friendship'.

[164] A *nomos*, 'district', was the key element in the administrative division of ancient Egypt. For most of Egypt's history, there were 42 *nomes*. The word in the MSS here, ναυαρχίας, 'maritime commandments', makes little or no sense in context, whereas νομαρχίας, '*nomes*', a suggestion by Wesseling, does.

[165] Behaviour that deviates from that displayed by Demetrius in Greece, described by Diodorus in 20.103.5–6.

he used to share his own prosperity with both him and his other friends. (5) Therefore on this occasion also, when Seleucus asked him to give him soldiers for an expedition into Babylonia, he readily consented, and in addition, he promised to help him in every way until he regained the satrapy that had formerly been his. Such was the situation of affairs in Asia.

S. 142:
19.90.1–94.1:

Seleucus regains Babylonia:
(19.90.1) In Asia, after the defeat of Demetrius at Gaza in Syria, Seleucus, receiving from Ptolemy no more than eight hundred foot soldiers and about two hundred horse,[166] set out for Babylon.[167] He was elevated with great expectations to such an extent that, even if he had had no force whatsoever at all, he would have made the expedition into the interior with his friends and his own servants. Indeed, he assumed that the Babylonians, on account of the goodwill that had previously existed, would promptly join him, and that Antigonus, by withdrawing to a great distance with his force, had provided him with a suitable opportunity for his own enterprises. (2) Though his own enthusiasm was so great, those of his friends present, seeing that the men who were making the campaign with them were very few and that the enemy against whom they were going possessed large armies ready for service, magnificent resources, and a host of allies, were not a little disheartened. (3) Seeing that they were terror-stricken, Seleucus encouraged them, saying that men who had campaigned with Alexander and had been advanced by him because of their *arete* ought not to rely solely on armed force and wealth when confronting difficult situations, but upon experience and skill, through which Alexander himself had accomplished his great deeds, admired by everyone. Seleucus added that they also should believe the oracles of the gods,[168] namely that the end of his campaign would be worthy of his purpose. (4) In fact, when he had consulted the oracle in Branchidae, the god had greeted him as King Seleucus, and Alexander standing beside him

---

[166] App. *Syr.* 9.54 states Seleucus got 1,000 foot and 300 horse.
[167] Though Geer 1962: 77–9 *in margine* still puts the events described here in 312, they belong, according to the *Marmor Parium*, to the spring of 311: see Jacoby 1904: 22, B16 (but still to the office of Polemon as *archon* of Athens [312/11]). Given the context, though, I believe 312 is the correct year.
[168] See Hadley 1969: 144.

in a dream had given him a clear sign of the future leadership that was destined to fall to him in the course of time.[169] (5) Moreover, he made clear that everything that is good and admired among men is gained through toil and danger. But he also sought the favour of his fellow soldiers and put himself on an equality with them all, so that everyone respected him and willingly accepted the risk of the daring venture.

(19.91.1) When in his advance he entered Mesopotamia, he persuaded some of the Macedonians who were settled at Carae[170] to join his forces, and compelled others. When he pushed into Babylonia, most of the inhabitants came to meet him, and, siding with him, said they would do anything together with him, whatever he decided. (2) Indeed, when he was satrap of that country for four years, he had shown himself generous to all, winning the goodwill of the common people and long in advance securing men who would assist him, if an opportunity should ever be given to him to dispute supreme power. (3) Polyarchus, who had been placed in command of a certain district,[171] joined him as well, with more than a thousand soldiers. When those remaining loyal to Antigonus saw that the impulse of the people could not be checked, they took refuge together in the citadel, of which Diphilus had been appointed keeper. (4) But Seleucus, by laying siege to the citadel and taking it by storm, recovered his friends and servants, who had been placed there under guard by the order of Antigonus after Seleucus' own departure from Babylon to Egypt. (5) When he had finished this, he enlisted soldiers, and, having brought up horses, he distributed them to those who were able to use them. Associating in a friendly way with all and raising high hopes in all, he kept his fellow adventurers ready and eager under every condition. In this way, then, Seleucus regained Babylonia.

---

[169] That is, the oracle at Didyma, in Asia Minor near Miletus. Until its destruction by the Persians in 494, Didyma's sanctuary had been administered by the family of the Branchidae. A priestess, seated above the sacred spring, would give utterances that were interpreted by the Branchidae. Callisthenes reports that the spring began to flow again after Alexander passed the site in 334 (FGrH/BNJ 124 F 14a = Str. 17.1.43/814). Alexander reinstated the oracle, but placed its administration in the hands of the city, where the priest in charge was annually elected. See, for example, Hammond 1998: 339. Other signs and omens regarding Seleucus' rise to power are presented in App. Syr. 9.56. For the excellent relationship of Seleucus and Seleucids with this sanctuary, see Meijering 2014/15.

[170] Not the Carae mentioned in 17.110.3 and 19.12.1, but probably the inhabitants of Carrhae, apparently situated somewhere near the upper course of the Euphrates.

[171] The word διοίκησις generally has a financial connotation, for example for taxation: see LSJ, s.v.

Seleucus moves further eastward and takes, inter alia, Susis and Media:
(19.92.1) But when Nicanor, the commander in Media,[172] gathered about him soldiers from Media and Persis and the neighbouring lands, more than ten thousand foot and about seven thousand horse, Seleucus set out at full speed to oppose the enemy. (2) He had in all more than three thousand foot and four hundred horse.[173] Crossing the River Tigris and learning that the enemy were a few days' march distant, he hid his soldiers in the adjacent marshes, intending to make his attack a surprise. (3) When Nicanor arrived at the River Tigris and did not find the enemy, he pitched camp near a royal station, believing that they had fled further away. When night was come and Nicanor's men were keeping a perfunctory and negligent guard, Seleucus, suddenly falling on them, caused great confusion and panic. (4) In fact, when the Persians had joined battle, it happened that their satrap, Evager,[174] fell together with some of the other captains. When this occurred, most of the soldiers, some being frightened at the danger, others because they were offended by the conduct of Antigonus, went over to Seleucus. (5) Being left with only a few men and afraid that he would be delivered to the enemy, Nicanor fled with his friends through the desert. But Seleucus, now being master of a large army and behaving graciously to all, easily won over both Susis, Media, and some of the adjacent lands. He wrote to Ptolemy and his other friends about his achievements, already possessing a king's stature and a reputation worthy of royal power.[175]

Demetrius recovers from the defeat at Gaza:
(19.93.1) Meanwhile Ptolemy remained in Coele Syria, having been victorious over Demetrius, Antigonus' son, in a great battle. Having learned that Demetrius had returned from Cilicia and camped in Upper Syria, he chose from the friends who were with him Cilles the Macedonian. (2) Giving him an adequate army, he ordered him to drive Demetrius completely out of Syria or, after enclosing him, to shatter him. While Cilles was on the way, Demetrius, hearing from

---

[172] See the remark by Bizière 2002: 166 *ad* 92.1.
[173] See App. *Syr.* 55.
[174] Possibly identical with Evagoras, who has been mentioned as satrap of Aria in 19.48.2.
[175] See *Suda*, *s.v. beta*,147 [2]: Βασιλεία. οὔτε φύσις οὔτε τὸ δίκαιον ἀποδιδοῦσι τοῖς ἀνθρώποις τὰς βασιλείας, ἀλλὰ τοῖς δυναμένοις ἡγεῖσθαι στρατοπέδου καὶ χειρίζειν πράγματα νουνεχῶς· οἷος ἦν Φίλιππος καὶ οἱ διάδοχοι Ἀλεξάνδρου ('Neither nature nor justice gives kingdoms to men, but to those who are able to lead an army and to handle affairs intelligently; such as Philip was, and the successors of Alexander').

scouts that Cilles camped carelessly at Myus,[176] left his baggage behind but, with his soldiers in light equipment, made a forced march and, suddenly falling upon the enemy during the early morning watch,[177] he not only captured the army without a battle but also took the commander himself prisoner. By achieving such a success he believed that he had wiped out the defeat.[178] (3) Nevertheless, assuming that Ptolemy would march against him with all his army, he went into camp, using as the outworks of his defence swamps and marshes. He also wrote to his father about the success that had been gained, urging him either to send an army as soon as possible or to cross over into Syria himself. (4) Antigonus happened to be in Celaenae in Phrygia and, on receiving the letter, he rejoiced exceedingly that his son, though he was young, seemed to have got out of his difficulties by himself and to have shown himself worthy to be a king.[179] He himself with his army set out from Phrygia, crossed the Taurus, and within a few days joined Demetrius. (5) However, when Ptolemy heard of the arrival of Antigonus and having called together his captains and companions, he took counsel whether it was better to remain and reach a final decision in Syria or to withdraw to Egypt and carry on the war from there as he had formerly done against Perdiccas. (6) All, then, advised him not to wage a war against a force that was many times stronger and had a larger number of elephants, and moreover an unbeaten commander. It would, indeed, be much easier to settle the war in Egypt, where he both had plenty of supplies and could trust to the difficulty of the terrain. (7) Deciding, therefore, to leave Syria, he razed the most noteworthy of the cities that he had captured: Ake in Phoenician Syria, and Ioppe, Samaria, and Gaza in Syria; and with his force and what of the booty it was possible to drive or carry, he returned into Egypt.[180]

Expedition against the Nabataeans:
(19.94.1) After regaining the whole of Syria and Phoenicia without problems, Antigonus planned an expedition against the region of the Arabs who are called Nabataeans.[181] Considering this tribe to be hostile to his interests, he chose from his companions Athenaeus,

---

[176] Myus in Syria is, to the best of my knowledge, further unknown.
[177] That is, the last watch of the night, probably between 4.30 and 7.00 a.m.
[178] Pausanias minimises Demetrius' victory: καί τινας τῶν Αἰγυπτίων λοχήσας διέφθειρεν οὐ πολλούς ('and after surprising some of the Egyptians, he killed a few of them': Paus. 1.6.5). According to Plu. *Demetr.* 6.3, Demetrius returned Cilles and his staff to Ptolemy.
[179] See the remarks of the *Suda* above, note 175.
[180] See Paus. 1.6.5.
[181] The region of Petra in modern Jordan. For this tribe see Hammond 1973.

The Period of the Diadochs: The Rift Deepens 471

giving him four thousand light-armed troops and six hundred horsemen capable of moving very quickly, and ordered him to attack the Nabataeans by surprise and to appropriate all flocks and herds. [[Now follow some paragraphs giving information on Nabataean habits, followed in the next *capita* by Athenaeus' vicissitudes, orders to Demetrius to conquer the Nabataeans, Demetrius' vicissitudes, and the final failure of the expedition.]]

S. 143:
19.100.3–7:

Antigonus sends Demetrius to Babylon; Demetrius captures the city:
(19.100.3) ... In fact, there came to Antigonus at this time[182] a letter-carrier with a letter from Nicanor, the commander of both Media and the upper satrapies. In this letter was written both about Seleucus' march inland and of the disasters that had occurred concerning him. (4) Therefore Antigonus, worried about the upper satrapies, sent Demetrius, his son, with five thousand Macedonian and ten thousand mercenary infantry and four thousand horse.[183] Antigonus ordered him to go up to Babylon and, after recovering the satrapy, to come down to the sea immediately. (5) Demetrius, then, having set out from Damascus in Syria, carried out his father's orders with zeal. When Patrocles, the man who had been appointed commander of Babylonia by Seleucus, learned that the enemy were on the frontiers of Mesopotamia, he did not dare await their arrival, since he had few men with him. He ordered the civilians to leave the city, some of them crossing the Euphrates to flee to the desert, others to go into Susis to Euteles[184] and the Persian Gulf, after passing over the Tigris. (6) He himself with what soldiers he had, using river courses and canals as defences, kept moving about in the satrapy, watching the enemy and at the same time sending word into Media to Seleucus about all that was taking place and urging him to help as soon as possible. (7) When Demetrius on his arrival at Babylon found the city abandoned, he began to besiege the citadels. Having

---

[182] The events described should still be dated to 312.
[183] See for this expedition Plu. *Demetr.* 7.2–3. Perhaps the expedition itself should be dated to 311, but this does not appear absolutely certain. See also Momigliano 1932: 477.
[184] The phrase πρὸς Εὐτελῆ ('to Euteles') is omitted in MS F. Therefore many editors in the past deleted it, but Fischer restored it (see his *apparatus a.l.*) 'because it appears he was the *praefectus* when Seleucus took Susis (19.92.5)'. Like Geer and Bizière, I follow Fischer's example.

taken one of these, he delivered it to his own soldiers for plundering. Having besieged the other for a few days, he left, since the capture required time, Archelaus, one of his friends, as commander for the siege, giving him five thousand infantry and one thousand cavalry. He himself, because the time was near at which he had been ordered to return, made the march down to the sea with the rest of his army.

9 The Vicissitudes of the Diadoch Kingdoms: The Final Years of Diodorus' Persian Account

A. THE YEARS 311/10–280/79

[[By this time there were four main actors in the former empire of Alexander: Cassander, ruler of Macedon; Ptolemy I *Soter Lagides*, ruler of Egypt, the Cyrenaica, Cyprus, and parts of Cilicia; Antigonus *Monophthalmus*, ruler of the larger part of Phoenicia, Syria, and Anatolia; and Seleucus, ruler of the rest of Alexander's former empire, though the formal ruler of the *whole* empire still was Alexander IV (with his custodian, Roxane). For the history of Persia especially the confrontation between Antigonus and Seleucus became increasingly important.]]

S. 144:
19.105.1–4:

Reshuffling power; Roxane and her son are murdered:
(19.105.1) When Simonides was *archon* in Athens [311/10], the Romans elected to the consulship Marcus Valerius and Publius Decius.[1] While these held office, Cassander, Ptolemy, and Lysimachus [he ruled Thrace] came to terms with Antigonus and made a treaty. In this it was provided that Cassander would be commander of Europe until Alexander, the son of Roxane, should come of age; that Lysimachus would rule Thrace; Ptolemy Egypt and the cities adjacent thereto in Libya and Arabia; that Antigonus

---

[1] The consuls of 312 vc were M. Valerius Maximus (Corvinus) and P. Decius Mus, while C. Sulpicius Longus and/or C. Iunius Bubulcus Brutus was/were the dictator(s): see Broughton 1951: 159. Diodorus is still two years ahead of the Varronian chronology.

would command all Asia; and that the Greeks would be autonomous. They did not, however, stick to these agreements, but each of them, putting forward plausible excuses, kept seeking to increase his own power. (2) Seeing that Alexander, the son of Roxane, was growing up and that word was being spread throughout Macedonia by certain men that it was fitting to release the boy from custody and give him his father's kingdom, Cassander, fearing for himself, instructed Glaucias, who was in command of the guard over the child, to murder Roxane and the king and conceal their bodies, but to disclose to no one of the others what had been done. (3) After Glaucias had carried out the instructions, Cassander, Lysimachus, and Ptolemy, and Antigonus as well, were freed of their anticipated danger from the king. (4) Because there was no longer anyone to inherit the realm for the future, each of those who had rule over nations or cities entertained hopes of royal power and held the territory that had been placed under his authority as if it were a kingdom won by the spear. This was the situation in Asia, Greece, and Macedonia.

S. 145:
20.19.2–5:

Antigonus encounters some problems but resolves them:
(20.19.2)... Polemaeus, the commander of Antigonus, who had been entrusted with forces but had taken offence at his prince because, as he said, he was not being honoured according to his deserts, revolted from Antigonus and made an alliance with Cassander.[2] Having left as governor of the satrapy along the Hellespont one of his most faithful friends, Phoenix, Polemaeus sent soldiers to him, bidding him guard the forts and the cities carefully and not to obey Antigonus. (3) Because the agreements agreed upon by the leaders provided for the liberation of the Greek *poleis*,[3] Ptolemy, the ruler of Egypt, charged Antigonus that he had occupied some of the *poleis* with garrisons, and prepared to go to war. (4) Sending his army and Leonides as its commander, Ptolemy subdued the cities in Cilicia Trachea[4] which were subject to Antigonus. He sent also

---

[2] This occurred in 310.
[3] See above, 19.105.1.
[4] Cilicia Trachea ('rugged Cilicia') is a mountain district formed by the spurs of the Taurus, which often terminate in rocky headlands with small, sheltered harbours. The district is watered by the Calycadnus (modern River Göksu; see Wainwright 1956: 205–6) and was covered in ancient times with forests that supplied timber to Phoenicia and Egypt. Its most

The Vicissitudes of the Diadoch Kingdoms 475

messages to the *poleis* and cities that were controlled by Cassander and Lysimachus, asking them to co-operate with him and prevent Antigonus from becoming too powerful. (5) But Antigonus sent Philip, the younger of his sons, to the Hellespont to fight it out with Phoenix and the rebels and he sent Demetrius to Cilicia, who, carrying on the campaign with vigour, defeated the commanders of Ptolemy and recovered the cities.

S. 146:
20.21.1-3:

Developments on Cyprus:
(20.21.1) When Ptolemy, however, who was master of the *poleis* of Cyprus, learned from certain persons that Nicocles,[5] the king of Paphos, had secretly and privately formed an alliance with Antigonus, he dispatched two of his companions, Argaeus and Callicrates, ordering them to kill Nicocles. Ptolemy was, indeed, taking all precautions to prevent some of the others hastening to shift allegiance as well, seeing that those were left unpunished who had previously rebelled. These two men, then, after sailing to the island and obtaining soldiers from Menelaus the commander, surrounded the house of Nicocles and, after making the decisions clear to the king, ordered him to take his own life. (2) At first he tried to defend himself against the charges, but when no one heeded him, he killed himself. After Axiothea, the wife of Nicocles, heard of her husband's death, she killed her daughters, who were unwed, in order that no enemy might possess them; and she urged the wives of Nicocles' brothers to choose death along with her, although Ptolemy had given no instructions with regard to the women, but had agreed to their safety. (3) When the palace had thus been filled with bloodsheds and unforeseen disasters, the brothers of Nicocles, after fastening the doors, set fire to the building and killed themselves. Thus, the house of the kings of Paphos, after meeting such tragic suffering, was brought to its end in the way described.

---

important *polis* became Seleucia *ad Calycadnum*, modern Silifke. See also Str. 14.5.4/670; Bean and Mitford 1970.
[5] Nicocreon of Salamis (see above, 19.59.1, 62.5, 79.5) should not be confused with Nicocles of Paphos: see Arr. *Succ.* 24.6. However, in this passage Diodorus appears to have done just that: the fate he describes here for Nicocles was that suffered by Nicocreon, according to the *Marmor Parium*, Jacoby 1904: 22-3, 128-9, B17, regarding 311/10 (Simonides *archon* of Athens).

S. 147:
20.27.1-3:

Ptolemy on the offensive:
(20.27.1) When Demetrius of Phalerum was *archon* in Athens [309/8], in Rome Quintus Fabius received the consulship for the second time and Gaius Marcius for the first.[6] While these were in office, Ptolemy, the king of Egypt, learning that his own commanders had lost the cities of Cilicia, having sailed with a force to Phaselis, took this city. Having crossed into Lycia, he took by storm Xanthus, which was garrisoned by Antigonus. (2) Having sailed next to Caunus, he won the city. Violently attacking the citadels, which were held by garrisons, he destroyed the *Heracleum*, but he gained possession of the *Persicum* when its soldiers delivered it to him. (3) Having sailed thereafter to Cos, he sent for Polemaeus, who, although he was the nephew of Antigonus and had been entrusted by him with an army, had deserted him and offered co-operation to Ptolemy. After Polemaeus had sailed from Chalcis and had come to Cos, Ptolemy at first received him graciously. Then, seeing that he had become presumptuous and was trying to win over the captains to himself by conversing with them and giving them gifts, fearing that he might devise some plot, acting first he arrested him and compelled him to drink hemlock juice.[7] As for the soldiers who had followed Polemaeus, after winning their favour through promises, Ptolemy distributed them among the men of his own army.

S. 148:
20.37.3-6:

Antigonus conspires to murder Cleopatra, Alexander's sister:
(20.37.3) While Cleopatra was meanwhile[8] quarrelling with Antigonus, inclining to cast her lot with Ptolemy, she started from Sardis in order to cross over to him. She was the sister of Alexander, the conqueror of Persia, and daughter of Philip, son of Amyntas,

---

[6] The consuls for 310 vc were Q. Fabius Maximus Rullianus and C. Marcius Rutilus (Censorinus), the dictator was L. Papirius Cursor: see Broughton 1951: 161–2. Diodorus is still two years ahead of the Varronian chronology.

[7] Unlike elsewhere in Diodorus (18.67.6), all MSS read here κώνιον (litt. 'pine-cone') instead of the more usual κώνειον ('hemlock (juice)').

[8] These events took place in 308, when Charinus was *archon* in Athens [308/7]. In the preceding paragraphs Diodorus relates Ptolemy's actions on the Aegean islands, the isthmus, and mainland Greece.

The Vicissitudes of the Diadoch Kingdoms   477

and had been the wife of the Alexander who made an expedition into Italy.[9] (4) Because of the distinction of her descent, then, Cassander and Lysimachus, as well as Antigonus and Ptolemy and in general all the leaders who were most important after Alexander's death, sought to marry her. In fact, each of them, hoping that the Macedonians would follow the lead of this marriage, clung to the royal house, in order to gain supreme power for himself. (5) The governor of Sardis, who had orders from Antigonus to watch Cleopatra, prevented her departure. Later, though, on the orders of his lord, he treacherously murdered her with the help of certain women. (6) Since Antigonus did not wish the murder to be ascribed to him, he punished some of the women for having plotted against her, and took care that the funeral should be conducted in royal fashion. Thus Cleopatra, after having been the prize in a contest among the most eminent leaders, met this fate before her marriage was concluded.

S. 149:
20.46.5–53.4:

Antigonus wants to finish the war in Cyprus:
(20.46.5) Antigonus wrote to his son Demetrius, ordering him to call together counsellors from the allied cities who should counsel in common what was advantageous for Greece,[10] and to sail himself with his force to Cyprus and finish the war with the commanders of Ptolemy as soon as possible. (6) Demetrius, promptly doing all according to his father's orders and having moved to Caria, summoned the Rhodians for the war against Ptolemy. Because they did not obey but preferred to maintain a common peace with all, this became the beginning of the hostility between that people and Antigonus.
(20.47.1) After sailing along the coast to Cilicia and assembling additional ships and soldiers there, Demetrius crossed to Cyprus with fifteen thousand infantry and four hundred horsemen, more than one hundred and ten swift *trieres*, fifty-three heavier troopships, and freighters of every kind sufficient for the strength of his

---

[9] For the marriage of Cleopatra and Alexander I of Epirus (her uncle), where Philip II was murdered: see 16.91.4–6. Alexander of Epirus died in 326 and Cleopatra then made overtures to Leonnatus (Plu. *Eum.* 3.9). After he died, in 322, she proposed that Perdiccas become her husband (Arr. *Succ.* 1.26): he died in 321, while invading Egypt. For Cleopatra see also Heckel 2009: 90 *s.v.* 'Cleopatra [2]'.
[10] This took place in 307.

cavalry and infantry.[11] (2) First he pitched camp on the coast of Carpasia,[12] and after beaching his ships, he strengthened his encampment with a palisade and a deep moat. Next, making raids on the peoples who lived nearby, he took by storm Urania[13] and Carpasia, and leaving a sufficient guard for the ships, he marched on with his force against Salamis. (3) Menelaus, who had been appointed commander of the island by Ptolemy, gathering his soldiers from the garrisons, was waiting in Salamis. However, when the enemy were forty *stadia* [nearly 7.5 km] away, he came out with twelve thousand foot and about eight hundred horse. In a battle of short duration which occurred, the forces of Menelaus, being overwhelmed, were routed. Demetrius, pursuing the enemy into the city, took prisoners numbering not much less than three thousand and killed about a thousand. (4) Initially, freeing the captives of all charges, he distributed them among the units of his own soldiers. However, because they ran off to Menelaus because their baggage had been left behind in Egypt with Ptolemy, recognising that they had not changed sides, he forced them to embark on his ships and sent them off to Antigonus in Syria. (5) The latter was tarrying in Upper Syria at this time, founding a city on the River Orontes, which he called Antigonia after himself.[14] He laid it out lavishly, making its perimeter seventy *stadia* [nearly 13 km]. The location was, indeed, by nature well adapted to keep watch over both Babylon and the upper satrapies, and again over Lower Syria and the satrapies off Egypt.[15] (6) However, it happened

---

[11] Diodorus' text here is confusing, at least if we read it with the text of 20.50.1–3 in mind. There, it is reported that Demetrius, after leaving 10 *pentereis* at Salamis, still had 10 *pentereis*, 10 *hexereis*, and 7 *heptereis* in his left wing alone. The usual nautical meaning of στρατιῶτις is 'troopship', but because of the information provided in 20.50.1–3 we might argue that βαρύτεραι στρατιώτιδες could mean here something else than 'heavier troopships'. It might suggest that βαρύτεραι στρατιώτιδες was used here by Diodorus for 'heavy ships of war', namely anything heavier than a *trieres*. An additional problem in the sentence under scrutiny is posed by the word τριήρεις ('*triereis*'): Henlein has, as indicated by Fischer in his *apparatus*, 'ordered' its deletion. It would leave us with the construction that Demetrius gathered soldiers, ναῦς ταχυναυτούσας, ... ('swift-going ships') etc.: these might as well include, for example, the *tessereis* mentioned in 20.50.3. Another question might be, though, whether Diodorus does not exaggerate Demetrius' strength: Polyaen. 4.7.7 only mentions that Demetrius had 170 *triereis*. See also the comments on this sentence by Geer 1962: 270–1 note 2.

[12] On the north coast of Cyprus.

[13] The location of this city is, to the best of my knowledge, still unknown.

[14] The city of Antigonia was situated some 7 km north-east of the modern city of Antakya, Turkey. See also Benzinger 1894.

[15] Though all MSS read ταῖς ἀπ'Αἰγύπτου σατραπείαις ('the satrapies off Egypt'), Reiske proposed reading here ταῖς περὶ Αἰγύπτου σατραπείαις ('the satrapies near Egypt'), a suggestion followed by Geer 1962: 272, while Madvig even proposed ταῖς ἀπ' Αἰγύπτου στρατείαις ('the expeditions leaving from Egypt'). Geer 1962: 273 note 3 adds another alternative: τοῖς περὶ Αἰγύπτου πράγμασι ('and affairs in Egypt'). The last option I find the least attractive, since much would then have been misread by the copyists. The other options are all feasible, but I have opted to follow the lead of the MSS (and Fischer).

The Vicissitudes of the Diadoch Kingdoms   479

that the city did not exist very long, because Seleucus dismantled it and transported it to the city which he founded and called Seleucia after himself.[16] But we will make these matters clear in detail when we come to the proper time.[17] (7) As to affairs in Cyprus, Menelaus, having been defeated in the battle, had missiles and engines brought to the walls and, assigning positions on the battlements to his soldiers, he prepared for the fight, seeing that Demetrius was making preparations for the siege as well. (8) Menelaus sent messengers to Egypt to Ptolemy who were to inform him about the defeat and to ask him to help, as his interests on the island were in danger.

(20.48.1) Seeing that the city of the Salaminians was not to be despised and that a large force was in the city defending it, Demetrius decided to prepare siege engines of very great size, *euthytona*, different kinds of *palintona*, and other equipment that would strike terror.[18] He also sent for skilled workmen from Asia and for iron, and moreover for a large amount of wood and for convenient assets of other supplies. (2) After everything was quickly made ready for him, he constructed a device called the '*helepolis*', which had a length of forty-five cubits [c. 20.25 m] on each side and a height of ninety cubits [c. 40.5 m]. It was divided into nine storeys, and the whole was mounted on four solid wheels, each eight cubits [c. 3.60 m] high. (3) He also had constructed very large battering rams and two protecting sheds to carry the rams. On the lower levels of the *helepolis* he mounted all sorts of *palintona*, of which the largest could hurl three talents [c. 90 kg]. On the middle levels he placed the largest *euthytona*, and on the highest both his lightest catapults and a large number of *palintona*, as well as more than two hundred men to operate these engines in the proper manner. (4) Having brought the engines up to the city and hurling a shower of missiles, he cleared the battlements with the *palintona* and shattered the walls with the rams. (5) Because those within the city resisted boldly and opposed his engines of war with other devices, the battle was doubtful for some days, both sides suffering hardships and severe wounds. When finally the wall was falling and the city was in danger of being taken by storm, the assault was interrupted by

---

[16] Diodorus is here at fault. The new city founded by Seleucus was called Antiochia, after Seleucus' father (as is also reflected in a conjecture by Dindorf). As a matter of fact, Antigonia appears not to have been abandoned completely, as it is referred to as if it still existed in 51: D.C. 40.29.1. See also Tomaschek 1894
[17] Sadly, these references are missing in the transmitted parts of Diodorus' *Bibliotheca*.
[18] See Plu. *Demetr.* 15–17. For Demetrius' operations against Cyprus and succeeding ones, see also Grainger 2011: 32–44.

the coming of night. (6) Clearly seeing that the city would be taken unless he tried something new, Menelaus gathered a large amount of dry wood, threw this upon the siege engines of the enemy at about midnight, and at the same time all shooting down fire-bearing arrows from the walls, set on fire the largest of the siege engines. (7) When the fire suddenly blazed high, Demetrius tried to come to the rescue, but because the fire was accelerating it occurred that the engines were completely burnt down and many of those who manned them were lost. (8) Disappointed in his hopes, Demetrius did not stop but persistently carried on the siege by both land and sea, believing that he would overcome the enemy in time.

(20.49.1) When Ptolemy heard of the defeat of his men,[19] he sailed from Egypt with a considerable force, both land and sea. Reaching Cyprus at Paphos, he received ships from the *poleis* and sailed along the coast to Citium, which was distant from Salamis two hundred *stadia* [c. 37 km].[20] (2) He had in all one hundred and forty ships of war,[21] of which the largest was a *penteres*, the smallest a *tetreres*. More than two hundred troop-transports followed, carrying no less than ten thousand foot soldiers. (3) Ptolemy sent some men to Menelaus by land, directing him, if possible, to send him quickly the ships from Salamis, which numbered sixty. In fact, he hoped that, if he received these, he would easily be superior in the naval engagement, engaging the battle with two hundred ships. (4) Learning of his intention, Demetrius left a part of his force for the siege. Having completely manned all his ships and having embarked upon them the best of his soldiers, he equipped them with missiles and *palintona* and mounted on the prows a sufficient number of *euthytona* to shoot bolts three *spithamae* [spans] in length [c. 69 cm]. (5) After making the fleet ready for a naval battle in every way, he sailed around the city and, anchoring at the mouth of the harbour just out of range of projectiles, spent the night, simultaneously preventing the ships from the city joining the others, watching for the arrival of the enemy, and being ready for battle. (6) When Ptolemy sailed up towards Salamis, the service vessels following at a distance, his fleet was awe-inspiring to behold because of the multitude of its ships.

---

[19] That is, the defeat described above in 20.47.3.

[20] As Geer 1962: 278–9 note 1 rightly points out, this is about the distance as the crow flies, but by sea the distance is certainly at least twice as great due to the circumnavigation of Cape Pedalium, protruding from the south-east into the Mediterranean.

[21] Plu. *Demetr.* 16.1 mentions that the strength of his fleet was 150 ships.

The Vicissitudes of the Diadoch Kingdoms 481

Sea-fight off Cyprian Salamis and its aftermath:
(20.50.1) When Demetrius observed Ptolemy's approach,[22] he left the *navarch* Antisthenes with ten of the *pentereis*, to prevent the ships in the city leaving it for the battle, since the harbour had a narrow exit. He ordered the horsemen to patrol the shore so that, if any misfortune should occur, they might rescue those who swam across to the land. (2) Having deployed his ships, he moved against the enemy with one hundred and eight ships in all, including those that had been provided with crews from the captured towns.[23] The largest of the ships were *heptereis*, most of them *pentereis*. (3) The left wing was composed of seven *heptereis* of Phoenicians and thirty *tetrereis* of the Athenians, Medius the *navarch* having the command. Sailing behind these he deployed ten *hexereis* and as many *pentereis*, having decided to reinforce this wing, where he himself was going to fight the decisive battle. (4) In the middle of the line he positioned the lightest of his ships, which Themison of Samos and Marsyas, who compiled the *History of Macedonia*,[24] commanded. The right wing was commanded by both Hegesippus of Halicarnassus and Plistias of Cos, who was the chief pilot of the whole fleet. (5) At first, while it was still night, Ptolemy sailed for Salamis at top speed, believing that he could beat the enemy in gaining an entrance. However, as day broke, the fleet of the opponents in battle order was seen close by, and Ptolemy prepared for the sea-fight as well. (6) He ordered the supply ships to follow at a distance and, effecting a suitable formation of the other ships, he himself took command of the left wing, as the largest warships engaged together with him. After the fleet had been disposed in this way, both sides prayed to the gods, as was the custom, the boatswains[25] leading and the crews joining in the response.

---

[22] For the strength of Demetrius' fleet see above, 20.47.1 and note 11.
[23] This number contradicts numbers presented previously (20.47.1) by Diodorus himself and by other authors, namely Plu. *Demetr.* 16, who mentions 180 ships, and Polyaen. 4.7.7, giving a total of 170 ships. The solution, presented in note 11 above, of considering the βαρύτεραι στρατιώτιδες as heavy warships, might solve part of the riddle, unsatisfactory as the artifice may appear.
[24] For Marsyas, see, for example, *Suda, s.v. mu*,227: Μαρσύας, Περιάνδρου, Πελλαῖος, ἱστορικός. οὗτος δὲ ἦν πρότερον γραμματοδιδάσκαλος, καὶ ἀδελφὸς Ἀντιγόνου τοῦ μετὰ ταῦτα βασιλεύσαντος, σύντροφος δὲ Ἀλεξάνδρου τοῦ βασιλέως. ἔγραψε Μακεδονικὰ ἐν βιβλίοις δέκα· ἤρξατο δὲ ἀπὸ τοῦ πρώτου βασιλεύσαντος Μακεδόνων, καὶ μέχρι τῆς Ἀλεξάνδρου τοῦ Φιλίππου ἐπὶ τὴν Συρίαν ἐφόδου, μετὰ τὴν Ἀλεξανδρείας κτίσιν· Ἀττικὰ ἐν βιβλίοις ιβ΄· καὶ αὐτοῦ Ἀλεξάνδρου ἀγωγήν ('Son of Periander, from Pella, an historian. This man was formerly a schoolmaster, and brother to the Antigonus who later became king. He grew up in company with King Alexander. He wrote a *History of Macedonia* in ten books, which began with the first king of Macedon and extended as far as the attack against Syria by Alexander, Philip's son, after the foundation of Alexandria; a *History of Attica* in twelve books; and an *Education of Alexander Himself*). See also FGrH/BNJ 135.
[25] The primary task of the boatswains was to give the time for the rowers, but it appears they had a leading role in (religious) ceremonies before battle as well.

(20.51.1) Because the lords were about to fight for their lives and their all, they were in much anxiety. When Demetrius was about three *stadia* [c. 550 m] distant from the enemy, he raised the battle signal that had been agreed upon, a gilded shield, visible to all by relays. (2) Because Ptolemy also gave a similar signal, the distance between the fleets was rapidly reduced. When both the *salpinxes* sounded the battle and both forces raised the battle-cry, all the ships rushed to the encounter in a terrifying manner. At first using their bows and their *palintona*, next their javelins in a shower, the men wounded those who were within range. Then, when the ships had come close together and a violent encounter was about to take place, those on the decks crouched down and the oarsmen, spurred on by the boatswains, bent more desperately to their oars. (3) As the ships drove together with force and violence, some swept off each other's oars so that the ships became useless for flight or pursuit, and the men who were on board, though eager for a fight, were prevented from joining in the battle; others, having met prow to prow with their rams, drew back for another charge; and those on board wounded each other, since the mark was close for each party. Some, when their *trierarchs* had delivered a broadside blow and the rams had become firmly fixed, leaped aboard the enemy ships, receiving and giving severe wounds. (4) Indeed, some, after grasping the rail of a ship that was drawing near, missed their footing, fell into the sea, and at once were killed with spears by those who stood above them; others, making good their intent, killed some of the enemy and drove others into the sea, forcing them along the narrow deck. As a whole, the fighting was varied and full of surprises: because frequently those who were weaker got the upper hand thanks to the height of their ships, and because those who had the upper hand were foiled through their inferiority of position and by the irregularity with which things happen in such fights. (5) In contests on land, indeed, *aretē* is made clearly evident, since it is able to gain the upper hand when nothing external and fortuitous interferes; in naval battles, however, there are many causes of various kinds that, contrary to reason, defeat those who would properly gain the victory through prowess.
(20.52.1) Demetrius fought most brilliantly of all, having taken his stand on the stern of his *hepteres*. When, in fact, a crowd of men rushed upon him, he killed some by hurling his javelins at them, others by striking them at close range with his spear. Though many missiles of all sorts were aimed at him, he avoided some that he saw in time, and received others upon his defensive

armour. (2) Of the three men who protected him with shields, one fell, struck by a lance, and the other two were severely wounded. Finally Demetrius, driving back his opponents and creating a rout in the right wing, forthwith forced even the ships next to the wing to flee. (3) Ptolemy, with the heaviest ships and the strongest men with him, easily routed those stationed opposite him, sinking some of the ships and capturing others with their crews. Turning back from that victorious action, he expected to subdue the others easily too. However, when he saw that the right wing of his forces had been shattered and all those next to that wing driven into flight, and moreover that Demetrius was pressing on with full force, he sailed back to Citium. (4) After winning the victory in the naval battle, Demetrius gave the troopships to Neon and Burichus, ordering them to pursue and pick up those who were swimming in the sea. He himself, decking his own ships with bow and stern ornaments and towing the captured crafts, sailed to his camp and his home port. (5) At the time of the naval battle Menelaus, the commander in Salamis, having manned his sixty ships, sent them as a reinforcement to Ptolemy, instating Menoetius as *navarch*. When a battle occurred at the harbour mouth with the ships on guard there and the ships from the city pressed forward vigorously, Demetrius' ten ships fled to the camp of the army. Menoetius, however, after sailing out and arriving a little too late for the battle, returned to Salamis. (6) During the naval battle, of which the conclusion was as stated, more than a hundred of Ptolemy's supply ships were taken, upon which were almost eight thousand soldiers; of the warships forty were captured with their crews, and about eighty were disabled, which the victors towed, full of seawater, to the camp before the city. Twenty of Demetrius' ships were disabled, but all of these, after receiving proper care, continued to perform the services for which they were suited.

(20.53.1) Thereafter Ptolemy, abandoning the fight in Cyprus, returned to Egypt. After he had taken over all the *poleis* of the island and their garrisons, Demetrius enrolled the men in his regiments, in total marshalling sixteen thousand foot and about six hundred horse. He at once sent people to his father to inform him of the successes, embarking them on the largest ship. (2) When Antigonus heard of the victory that had been gained, elated by the magnitude of his good fortune, he assumed the diadem and from that time on used the title of king, allowing Demetrius as well to assume the same appellation and honour. (3) Ptolemy, however, not at all humbled in spirit by his defeat, also assumed the diadem and always signed himself king.²⁶ (4) Like these, the remaining rival rulers also called themselves kings: Seleucus, who had recently gained the upper satrapies, Lysimachus, and Cassander, who still retained the territories originally allotted to them.

[[This also formally ends the (alleged) collaboration between the Diadochs and the pretence of (some form of) unity.]]

S. 150:
20.73.1–76.7:

Antigonus plans to invade Egypt and collects his army:
(20.73.1) When this year had passed, Coroebus became *archon* in Athens [306/5], and in Rome Quintus Marcius and Publius Cornelius succeeded to the consulship.²⁷ While these held office King Antigonus, after the younger of his sons, Phoenix, had died,²⁸ buried this son royally. Having summoned Demetrius from Cyprus, Antigonus collected his forces in Antigonia. He had decided to make a campaign against Egypt. (2) He himself, then, taking command of the land army, advanced through Coele Syria with more than eighty thousand foot, about eight thousand horse, and eighty-three elephants. Giving the fleet to Demetrius, he ordered him to sail along the coast next to the army as it advanced. In all, there had been made ready a hundred and fifty warships and a hundred troop-carriers, in which a large number of projectiles were being conveyed. (3) Because the pilots thought that it was necessary to heed the setting of the Pleiades,²⁹ which was expected to take place after eight days, Antigonus charged them with being men afraid of danger. He himself, having pitched camp at Gaza, and eager to anticipate Ptolemy's preparations, ordered his soldiers to provide themselves with ten days' rations, and loaded on the camels, which had been gathered together by the Arabs, one hundred and thirty thousand *medimnoi*³⁰ of grain and a good stock of fodder for the quadrupeds. Carrying his projectiles in wagons,

---

[26] According to the *Marmor Parium* [Jacoby 1904: 24 B23], Ptolemy assumed the diadem in 305/4.
[27] The consuls of 306 vc were P. Cornelius Arvina and Q. Marcius Tremulus: see Broughton 1951: 167–8. By omitting the 'dictator year', 309 vc, Diodorus' chronology henceforth more or less corresponds to the Varronian chronology, as it does here.
[28] An error, by either Diodorus or a copyist: the name of Antigonus' son who died was Philip: see above 20.19.5; also Plu. *Demetr.* 2.1.
[29] About the first days of our month of November.
[30] Taking 52.4 litres as the basic amount of the dry measure of a *medimnos*, that is 6,812,000 litres of grain.

The Vicissitudes of the Diadoch Kingdoms 485

he advanced through the desert with great hardship, because many places in the region were swampy, particularly near the spot called *Barathra*.[31]

Antigonus and Demetrius take the offensive:
(20.74.1) After setting sail from Gaza at about midnight, since the weather at first was calm for several days, Demetrius had his troop-carriers towed by the swifter ships. Next, when the setting of the Pleiades overtook them and a north wind arose, many of the *tetrereis* were driven dangerously to the town of Raphia by the storm,[32] a place that affords no anchorage and is surrounded by shoals. (2) Of the ships carrying his projectiles, some, overwhelmed by the storm, were destroyed, others turned back to Gaza. However, pressing on with the strongest of the ships, he held his course as far as Casium.[33] (3) This place is not very distant from the Nile, but it has no harbour and in the stormy season it is impossible to make a landing here. They were, therefore, compelled to ride at anchor, after casting their anchors, at a distance of about two *stadia* [c. 370 m] from the land, at once encompassed by many dangers. Because, indeed, the surf was breaking rather heavily, they were at risk of the ships foundering with their crews, and because the shore was harbourless and in enemy hands, neither could a ship approach without danger, nor could the men swim ashore; but worst of all, the drinking water had given out and they were reduced to such straits that, if the storm had continued for a single day more, all would have perished of thirst. (4) As all were in despair and already expecting death, the wind fell, and Antigonus' force, which had come up, pitched camp near the fleet. (5) Disembarking, then, and recuperating in the camp, they waited for those vessels that had become separated. In this exposure to the waves three ships of the *pentereis* were lost, but some of the men from these swam to the shore. Next, Antigonus, leading his force near to the Nile, pitched camp at a distance of two *stadia* [c. 370 m] from the river.

---

[31] 'The Pits' is the region of quicksands and marshes between the Sirbonian Lake and the Mediterranean: see also, for example, 1.30.4–9; 16.46.4–5.
[32] Raphia, the modern town of Rafah, is situated about a day's march south of Gaza. Later (217), Raphia was also the site of a major battle between Ptolemy IV *Philopator* and Antiochus III the Great over the sovereignty of Coele Syria.
[33] Casium is to be found in the Nile Delta on Lake Sirbon, where the border between Egypt and Syria ran (Hdt. 2.158.4): see Niehr 1999.

Ptolemy waits and takes defensive action:
(20.75.1) Having occupied the most strategic points with trustworthy guards in advance, Ptolemy sent some men in small boats, ordering them to approach the landing-place and proclaim that he would pay any who deserted Antigonus two *minae* [200 *drachmae*] to each of the ordinary soldiers and one talent [6,000 *drachmae*] to each man who had been assigned to a position of command. (2) When, then, proclamations to that effect had been made, an urge to change sides fell upon the mercenaries of Antigonus, and it occurred that many even of their captains were inclined for one reason or another to desire a change. (3) Because many were going over to Ptolemy, Antigonus, stationing bowmen, slingers, and many of his catapults on the edge of the river, drove back those who were drawing near in their punts. Capturing some of the deserters, he tortured them frightfully, wishing to intimidate any who were contemplating a similar attempt. (4) Having added to his fleet the ships that were late in arriving, he sailed to the place called *Pseudostomon*,[34] believing that he would be able to disembark some of the soldiers there. Finding, however, a strong garrison at that place and held in check both by bolts and by other missiles of every kind, he sailed away as night was closing in. (5) Next giving orders to the pilots to follow the commander's ship, keeping their eyes fixed on its light, he sailed to the mouth of the Nile called the Phatnitic.[35] However, when day had broken, since many of the ships had missed their course, he was forced to wait for these and to send out the swiftest of those that had followed him to search for them.

(20.76.1) Because this caused considerable delay, Ptolemy, hearing of the enemy's arrival, came quickly to help and after drawing up his army, stationed it along the shore. Demetrius, though, having failed to make this landing also and hearing that the adjacent coast was naturally fortified by swamps and marshes, retraced his course with his whole fleet. (2) When next a strong north wind burst upon them and the billows rose high, three ships of his *tetrereis* and one of the troop-carriers were cast violently upon the land by the waves and fell into the hands of Ptolemy. The other ships, however, since the crews had kept them from the shore by main force, reached the

---

[34] Pseudostomon (lit. 'False Mouth') is recorded among the towns in the Delta on the map on the floor of the mid-sixth-century ad church at Madaba (Jordan): see Piccirillo and Dailey 1993: 28, 81–95, pl. 74.

[35] The Phatnitic mouth is where the second largest branch of the Nile (after the Canopic branch), namely the Damiette branch, emptied into the Mediterranean. The city of Busiris, situated on this branch, was close by.

The Vicissitudes of the Diadoch Kingdoms 487

camp of Antigonus in safety. (3) Since Ptolemy, however, had already occupied every landing-place along the river with strong guards, since many river boats had been made ready for him, and since all of these were equipped with projectiles of every kind and with men to use them, Antigonus was in no little difficulty. (4) In fact, his naval force was of no use to him since the Pelusiac mouth of the Nile had been occupied in advance by the enemy, and his land forces found their advance thwarted, being checked by the width of the river; but above all, because many days had passed, both food and fodder for the beasts were falling short. (5) Since, then, his forces for these reasons were disheartened, Antigonus, calling together the army and its captains, laid before them the question of whether it was better to remain and continue the war or to return now to Syria and make a campaign later, with better preparation at a time at which the Nile was supposed to be lowest. (6) Because all inclined to the quickest possible withdrawal, he commanded the soldiers to break camp and speedily returned to Syria, as the whole fleet coasted along beside him. After the departure of the enemy Ptolemy, rejoicing greatly and having made a thank-offering to the gods, entertained his friends lavishly. (7) He also wrote to Seleucus, Lysimachus, and Cassander about his successes and about the large number of men who had deserted to him. He himself, having finished the second struggle for Egypt[36] and convinced that the country was his as a prize of war, returned to Alexandria.

[[As the struggle for Rhodes, 20.81.1–88.9 and 20.91.1–100.4, does not relate any more directly to the vicissitudes of the empire, interesting as the story may be, I have left it out of this account.]]

S. 151:
20.107.2–109.7:

Further confrontation between Lysimachus and Antigonus:
(20.107.2) Crossing with his army from Europe to Asia Minor,[37] Lysimachus left free the inhabitants of Lampsacus and Parium, who came over to him willingly, but when he took Sigeum by force, he installed a garrison there. Next, giving his commander Prepelaus six thousand foot and a thousand horse, he sent him to win over the *poleis* throughout both Aeolis and Ionia. He himself first attempted

---
[36] The first struggle was the attack by Perdiccas: 18.33–5.
[37] These events are dated to 302.

to lay siege to Abydus and set about preparing missiles, engines, and the other equipment. (3) However, when there arrived by sea a large body of soldiers sent by Demetrius to assist the besieged, sufficient to secure the safety of the city, Lysimachus gave up this attempt, but having won over Hellespontine Phrygia he also laid siege to the city of Synnada,[38] which possessed a great royal treasure. (4) At this very time even persuading Docimus, the commander of Antigonus, to collaborate with him, he took by his aid Synnada and some of the strongholds that held the royal wealth. Prepelaus, the commander who had been sent by Lysimachus to Aeolis and Ionia, mastered Adramyttium[39] as he passed by, and then, laying siege to Ephesus and frightening its inhabitants, he took the city. The hundred Rhodian hostages[40] whom he found there he sent back to their native land, and he left the Ephesians free under a treaty,[41] but burned all the ships in the harbour, because the enemy were masters at sea and the whole outcome of the war was unclear. (5) After this he secured the adherence of the people of Teos and of Colophon, but since reinforcements came by sea to Erythrae and Clazomenae, he could not capture these *poleis*, but, after plundering their territory he set out for Sardis. Having there persuaded Antigonus' commander Phoenix to desert the king, he gained control of the city except the acropolis. In fact, Philip,[42] one of the friends of Antigonus, who was guarding the citadel, held firm his loyalty to the man who had placed trust in him. The affairs of Lysimachus were in this position.

(20.108.1) Having made preparations to celebrate great games and a festival in Antigonia, Antigonus collected from all sides the most famous athletes and artists to compete for great prizes and fees. However, when he heard of the crossing of Lysimachus and the desertion of his generals, he abandoned the games, but distributed to the athletes and artists not less than two hundred talents [1,200,000 *drachmae*] as wages. (2) He himself set out from Syria with his army, making a rapid march against the enemy. Arriving at

---

[38] Synnada, on the site of the modern city of Şuhut, was situated in Upper Phrygia (and not in Hellespontine Phrygia), which lends credibility to a conjecture by Fischer: καὶ <ἐπὶ τὴν ἄνω Φρυγίαν προάγων> Σύνναδα ('and advancing to Upper Phrygia, [he laid siege to] Synnada'), unless we suppose an error by Diodorus (or an early copyist).

[39] Situated some 11 km south of modern Edremit (see also Stronk 1995: 290).

[40] In 20.99.3 Diodorus recorded that, after a prolonged siege of the *polis* of Rhodes, the Rhodians and Demetrius agreed on a treaty, one of the conditions being that Demetrius could select 100 Rhodians as hostages.

[41] This addition is based upon a conjecture by Hertlein, and supported by Fischer (see his *apparatus a.l.*), of inserting ὑποσπόνδους before ἀφῆκε.

[42] Possibly the same Philip who had been instated as adviser to Demetrius in 314: see above, 19.69.1.

Tarsus in Cilicia, he paid the army for three months from the money he had brought down from Cynda.[43] (3) Apart from this money, he was carrying three thousand talents [18,000,000 *drachmae*] with the army, in order that he might have this provision whenever he had need of money. Next, crossing the Taurus, he marched towards Cappadocia and, advancing upon the deserters in Upper Phrygia and Lycaonia, he brought them back again into the former alliance. (4) At this very time Lysimachus, learning of the presence of the enemy, held a council, deliberating how they should deal with the approaching dangers. (5) He decided not to engage battle until Seleucus came down from the upper satrapies, but to occupy strong positions and, after making their encampment safe with palisade and ditch, to await the enemy attack. They, then, carried out their decision with vigour. However, when he came near his enemies, Antigonus, having deployed his army, challenged them to battle. (6) As no one dared to issue forth, he himself occupied certain places through which the provisions of his opponents needed to be transported. Lysimachus, fearing that, when their food supply was cut off they would be in the power of the enemy, broke camp at night and, after making a forced march of four hundred stadia [c. 74 km], pitched camp near Dorylaeum.[44] (7) In fact, the stronghold had an ample store of both grain and other supplies and a river running by it, able to provide safety to those who camped beside it. After pitching their camp, they strengthened the encampment with a deep ditch and a triple palisade.

(20.109.1) Learning of the enemy departure, Antigonus at once pursued them and, having come close to their encampment, when they did not come out for battle, started to surround their camp with a trench and sent for *palintona* and missiles, intending to storm it. When shots were exchanged round the ditch and Lysimachus' men tried to drive away with missiles those who were working, Antigonus' men in every case had the better of it. (2) Then as time passed and the work was already nearing completion, because food was growing scarce for the besieged, Lysimachus, after waiting for a stormy night, setting out from the camp, retreated through the higher land to go into winter quarters. When, though, Antigonus saw the enemy's departure at daybreak, he himself marched parallel with them through the plains. (3) Because great rainstorms occurred and

---

[43] For the treasury there see Chapter 7, 18.62.2 and note 120; 19.56.5.
[44] Situated at the site of modern Karaca Hisar, c. 10 km south-west of the modern city of Eskişehir.

the country was deep-soiled and very muddy, Antigonus lost both a considerable number of his pack animals and a few of his men, and in general the whole army was in serious difficulty. (4) Therefore Antigonus, both because he wished to restore his soldiers after their sufferings and because he saw that the winter season was at hand, gave up the pursuit, but selecting the places best suited for wintering, he divided his force into sections. (5) Learning, though, that Seleucus was coming down from the upper satrapies with a great force, he sent some of his friends into Greece to Demetrius, exhorting him to come to him with his force as soon as possible. In fact, because all the kings had united against him, he was taking every precaution not to be forced to decide the whole war in battle before the force from Europe had come to join him. (6) Similarly Lysimachus also divided his army in order to go into winter quarters in the plain called that of Salonia.[45] Large supplies were sent to Lysimachus from Heraclea, having made a connection by marriage with the Heracleotes. (7) He had, indeed, married Amestris, the daughter of Oxyartes and niece of King Darius III. She had been the wife of Craterus, given him by Alexander, and at the time in question was ruler of the city.[46] Such was the situation in Asia.

S. 152:
20.111.1–4:

Demetrius prepares to go to Asia Minor; rise of Mithridates:
(20.111.1) While affairs in Thessaly were in this state,[47] the messengers sent by Antigonus came to Demetrius, accurately detailing his father's orders and exhorting him to take his army across into Asia Minor as quickly as possible. (2) Because Demetrius regarded it as necessary to obey his father, he made a settlement with Cassander, making the condition that the settlement would only be valid if it should be acceptable to his father, knowing with certainty that his

---

[45] Though the MSS read here Σαλμωνίας, Fischer follows an emendation by Wesseling, conjecturing here Σαλωνίας, based upon Str. 12.4.7/565 (not 12.5.7 as in Fischer's *apparatus*: that section is non-existent) and Steph.Byz. s.v. 'Σαλώνεια' *inter alia*. This place, rich in pasture, is situated in Bithynia.

[46] Amestris had been given in marriage in 324 by Alexander to Craterus, who left her to marry Phila (18.18.7). Next she married the ruler of Heraclea (Pontica), Dionysius (see Str. 12.3.10/514), in 322/1. After he died (306/5), she continued to rule the city as regent for her children, at that time still minors, and then (302) married Lysimachus, with whom she resided in Sardis. However, he left her as well, apparently amicably, in 300/299, to marry Arsinoe, the daughter of Ptolemy. See also Heckel 2006: 21 s.v. 'Amastris'.

[47] The events described still date to 302. The preceding chapter describes the stalemate in Thessaly between Demetrius and Cassander.

father would not accept it, because he had definitely decided to bring the war that had set in to an end by force of arms, wishing, though, to make his withdrawal from Greece dignified and not something like a flight. Indeed, it was written among other conditions in the agreement that the Greek *poleis* were to be free, not only those throughout Greece, but also those throughout Asia.[48] (3) After this, Demetrius, after preparing transports for the passage of the soldiers and the equipment, set sail with his whole fleet and, going through the islands, put in at Ephesus. Having disembarked his force and having pitched camp near the walls, he forced the city to return to its former status.[49] He dismissed on terms the garrison that had been introduced by Prepelaus, Lysimachus' commander, and after stationing his own garrison on the acropolis, went on to the Hellespont. He also recovered Lampsacus[50] and Parium,[51] likewise some of the other *poleis* that had changed sides, and when he arrived at the entrance of Pontus, he constructed a camp beside the shrine of the Calchedonians[52] and left three thousand infantry and thirty warships to guard the region. Dividing the rest of his force over the *poleis*, he sent them to winter quarters. (4) At about this time also Mithridates,[53] who was subject to Antigonus but appeared to be shifting his allegiance to Cassander, was killed at Cius in Mysia after having ruled that city and ...[54] for thirty-five years. Mithridates,[55] succeeding to power, added many new subjects and ruled Cappadocia and Paphlagonia for thirty-six years.

---

[48] I have no means of determining whether Asia here is, in fact, only Asia Minor or whether the Greek settlements founded further to the east–, for example, during Alexander's expedition – might also have been intended (though, thanks to Demetrius' intentions as described by Diodorus, the treaty appears in fact to have been stillborn).
[49] To return to the side of Antigonus (and Demetrius).
[50] Modern Lapseki, on the north end of the eastern shore of the Hellespont. See Stronk 1995: 284.
[51] Parium, near the modern village of Kamares, was a Greek *polis* in Mysia on the Hellespont. Located near Lampsacus, it was a colony probably founded by Eretria and Paros. Like Lampsacus, it had temporarily been controlled by Lysimachus.
[52] I here follow MSS RX (Καλχηδονίων) rather than the frequently used (*inter alios* by Geer) Χαλκηδονίων: the latter form is predominantly used in Athenian sources, but the first is the correct form: see also Stronk 1995: 134 *ad* (4), 156 *ad* (3). The form of MS F, Καρχηδονίων ('Carthaginians') is manifestly wrong. The shrine of the Calchedonians might be the same as Hieron, mentioned in 19.73.6, though absolute certainty is lacking.
[53] This was Mithridates II, who ruled Cius in Bithynia from 337 onward, succeeding Ariobarzanes II, possibly his brother. At the time of his murder, Mithradates appears to have been at least 84 years old: see Luc. *Macr.* 13.
[54] I have opted to leave the name of this place open, as neither the MSS nor the editors agree: see Fischer, *apparatus a.l.*
[55] Mithridates III of Cius. If he is identical with the Mithridates mentioned in 19.40.2 and Plu. *Demetr.* 4, he is also Mithridates I of Pontus and son of an Ariobarzanes, who might well be the brother of his predecessor as ruler of Cius.

S. 153:
20.113.1–5:

The kings gather their forces for a final battle:
(20.113.1) During these same days, King Ptolemy, setting out from Egypt with a considerable force, made all the cities of Coele Syria subject. As he was besieging Sidon, though, certain men came to him, falsely reporting that when a battle had taken place between the kings, Lysimachus and Seleucus, having been defeated, had withdrawn to Heraclea, and that Antigonus, after being victorious, advanced with a force against Syria. (2) Deceived, then, by them and believing that their report was true, Ptolemy made a four-months' truce with the Sidonians and, securing the subjugated cities with garrisons, went back to Egypt with his force. (3) At the same time as this was taking place, some of the soldiers of Lysimachus, having left their winter quarters as deserters, went over to Antigonus, namely two thousand Autariates[56] and about eight hundred Lycians and Pamphylians. Antigonus, then, receiving these men benevolently, not only gave them the pay that they said Lysimachus owed them, but also honoured them with gifts. (4) At this time Seleucus arrived as well, having crossed over from the upper satrapies into Cappadocia with a large army and, after making huts for the soldiers, he went into winter quarters nearby. He had about twenty thousand foot, about twelve thousand horsemen including his mounted archers, four hundred and eighty elephants, and more than a hundred scythed chariots. (5) In this way, then, the forces of the kings were being gathered together, because they all had determined to decide the war by arms during the coming summer. We, though, as we proposed in the beginning, will make the war that these kings waged against each other for supreme rule the beginning of the following book.

[[In 301, the Battle of Ipsus (a village in Phrygia) was fought between, on the one hand, Antigonus I *Monophthalmus* and his son Demetrius *Poliorcetes* and, on the other, the coalition of three other companions of Alexander: Cassander, ruler of Macedon; Lysimachus, ruler of Thrace; and Seleucus I *Nicator*, ruler of Babylonia and Persia. A description, rather romanticised, can be read in Plutarch's *Life of Demetrius*: Diodorus' account is lost. During the battle Antigonus was killed and the Antigonid battle-line was dissolved. Demetrius managed to recover 5,000 foot and

---
[56] An Illyrian tribe.

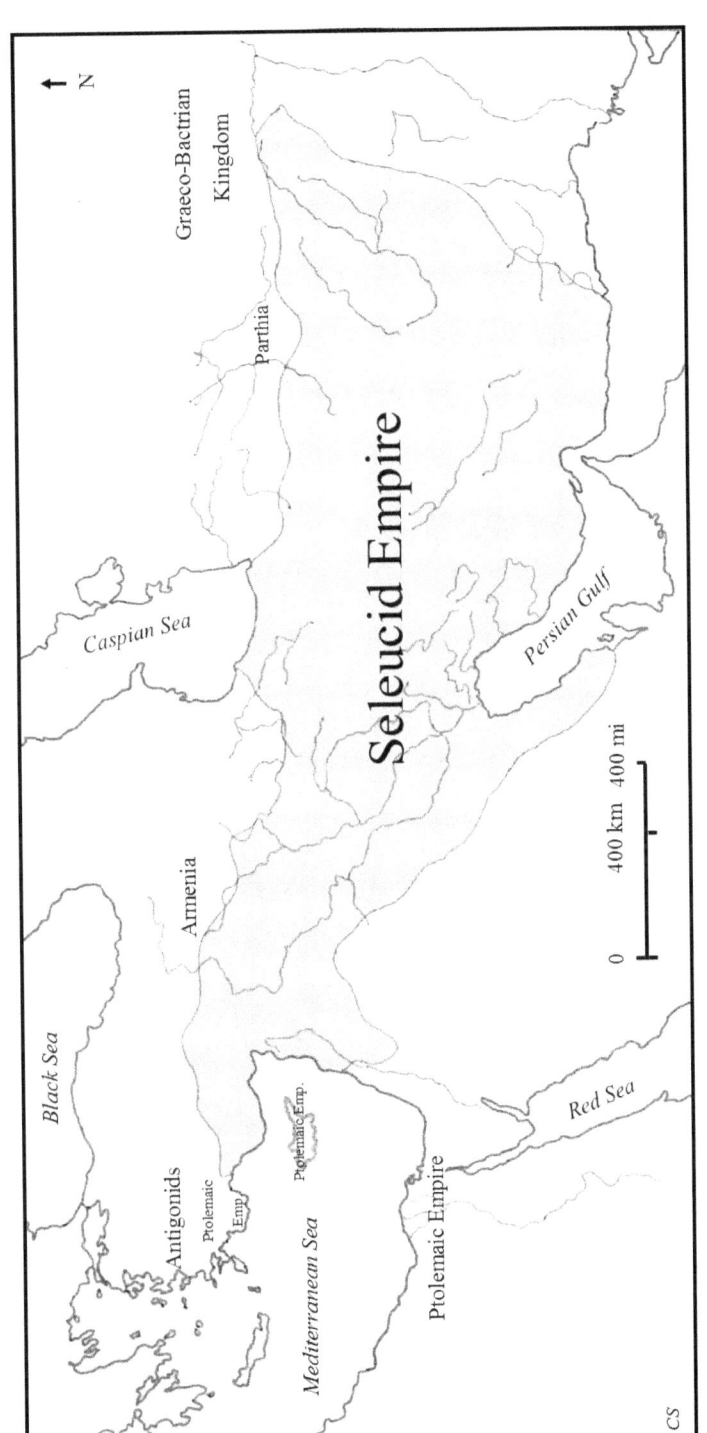

Fig. 9.1. Outline of the extent of the Seleucid Empire, c. 200 BC.

Table 9.1. List of Seleucid kings.

Name of king	Period of kingship
Seleucus I *Nicator*	Satrap 311–305, king 305–280
Antiochus I *Soter*	Co-regent from 291, king 280–261
Antiochus II *Theos*	261–246
Seleucus II *Callinicus*	246–225
Seleucus III *Ceraunus Soter*	225–223
Antiochus III the Great	223–187
Seleucus IV *Philopator*	187–175
Antiochus IV *Epiphanes*	175–164
Antiochus V *Eupator*	164–162
Demetrius I *Soter*	162–150
Alexander I *Balas*	154–145
Demetrius II *Nicator*	145–138[a]
Antiochus VI *Theos Dionysus Epiphanes*	145–141
Diodotus *Tryphon*	141–138
Antiochus VII *Euergetes Sidetes*	138–129
Demetrius II *Nicator* (again)	129–126
Alexander II *Zabinas*	129–123
Cleopatra *Thea*	126–123
Seleucus V *Philometor*	126–125
Antiochus VIII *Grypus*	125–96
Antiochus IX *Cyzicenus*	114–96
Demetrius III *Eucaerus Philopator*	97/6–88
Seleucus VI *Epiphanes Nicator*	96–94
Antiochus XI *Epiphanes Philadelphus*	95–93/2
Philip I *Philadelphus*	c. 95–75
Antiochus X *Eusebes Philopator*	95–88
Antiochus XII *Dionysus*	87–83/2
[Tigranes II of Armenia	74–69][b]
Antiochus XIII *Asiaticus*	69–64
Philip II *Philoromaeus*	67/6–64

[a] Numismatic evidence suggests that *Tryphon* was sufficiently powerful from at least 144 onwards to be represented on Seleucid coins struck at Antioch, perhaps even operating as co-regent.

[b] Tigranes II or Շհզnաh Մեծ (Tigran Mets = Tigran the Great), king of Armenia and member of the Artaxiad royal house and as such not a proper Seleucid king, ruled the Seleucid Empire during the period 74–69.

4,000 horse and with them escaped to Ephesus. The Battle of Ipsus finalised the breakup of the empire, from which the Seleucid Empire (officially 311–64) emerged as that encompassing most of the former Achaemenid Empire. However, not Persis but Syria was from now on seen as the 'homeland' of the new rulers (see Kosmin 2014: 93–119); see also Hammond and Hammond 1988: 123–98; Shipley 2000: 44–5.]]

S. 154:
21.1.1–6 [various sources]:

Outcome of the Battle of Ipsus; Demetrius retires to Cyprus; Ptolemy feels slighted:
(21.1.1 = *Const. Exc.* 2(1): 252)[57] *King Antigonus, who rose from private station to high power and became the mightiest king of his day, was not content with the gifts of Fate, but trying to bring unjustly into his own hands the kingdoms of all the others he lost his own dominion and was deprived of life as well.
(2 = *Const. Exc.* 4: 344)[58] *Ptolemy, Seleucus, and Lysimachus united against King Antigonus. Not so much enticed by goodwill towards one another as compelled by the fear each had for himself, they moved readily to make common cause in the supreme struggle. In the battle, the elephants of Antigonus and Lysimachus fought as if nature had matched them equally in courage and strength.
(3) [[= resumé of 19.55.7–9]]
(4b = *Exc. Hoesch.*: 489 W.)[59] *Antigonus, king of Asia, made war against a coalition of four kings, Ptolemy, son of Lagus, king of Egypt; Seleucus, king of Babylonia; Lysimachus, king of Thrace; and Cassander, son of Antipater, king of Macedonia. When he engaged them in battle, he was pierced by many missiles, and was carried from the field and buried with royal honours. His son Demetrius, however, sailed with his mother Stratonice, who had remained in Cilicia with all their valuables, to Salamis in Cyprus, since it was in his possession.[60]

---

[57] According to the editions by Dindorf and Fischer 1969: 282 and Walton 1968: 2–3; Goukowsky 2006: 12 counts this as Fr. 2. (After the introduction, Dindorf and Fischer 1969 starts with pp. 282–407 for books 21–30 (taken from Dindorf's volume 4 from 1868), and continues with the preface to Dindorf's volume 5, followed by pp. 1–186 for books 31–40, pp. 187–9 for some dubious fragments, pp. 190–639 for comments, and an extensive 'index nominum et rerum' prepared by C. Müller.)
[58] According to the editions by Dindorf and Fischer 1969: 282 and Walton 1968: 4–5; Goukowsky 2006: 13 counts this as Fr. 4.
[59] According to the editions by Dindorf and Fischer 1969: 283, line 14 *sqq.* and Walton 1968: 4–7; Goukowsky 2006: 13 counts this as Fr. 3. The letter W in the pages of the *Excerpta Hoescheliana* stands for Wesseling, editor of this work.
[60] For a different account see Plu. *Demetr.* 30.

(5 = *Const. Exc.* 4: 344)[61] [1] *As for Seleucus, after the partition of the kingdom of Antigonus, he went to Phoenicia with his force and tried in accordance with the terms of the agreement to appropriate Coele Syria.[62] [2] Ptolemy, though, had already occupied the cities of that region and denounced Seleucus because, although he was a friend, Seleucus had accepted the assignment to his own share of a district that was already subject to Ptolemy. Moreover, even though he had been a partner in the war against Antigonus, he accused the kings of giving him no part of the conquered territory. To these charges Seleucus replied that it was only just that those who were victorious on the battlefield should dispose of the spoils. As regards Coele Syria, he answered, he would not interfere for friendship's sake for the present, but would consider later how best to deal with friends who chose to claim more than their due.

(6) [[= 20.47.6, above]]

S. 155:
21.20.1 (= *Exc. Const.* 2(1): 256):[63]

Demetrius taken prisoner; Seleucus considers how best to release him:
(21.20.1) *While Demetrius was held under guard in Pella,[64] Lysimachus, having sent ambassadors, asked that Seleucus should in no way let Demetrius out of his hands, because Demetrius was a man of restless ambition and had plotted against all the kings.[65] Lysimachus promised that he would give Seleucus two thousand talents [12,000,000 *drachmae*] to kill him. (2) But the king censured the ambassadors for urging him not only to cancel his assurances but even to incur that pollution in respect of a man allied to him by marriage. Having written to his son Antiochus, however, who

---

[61] According to the editions by Dindorf and Fischer 1969: 283–4 and Walton 1968: 6–7; Goukowsky 2006: 14 counts this as Fr. 6.
[62] See Plb. 5.67.4–9.
[63] According to the editions by Dindorf and Fischer 1969: 297–8 and Walton 1968: 38–9; Goukowsky 2006: 32 counts this as Fr. 34.
[64] This event should be dated after 285. In 294 Demetrius had become king of Macedonia by murdering the son of Cassander, Alexander V, but his kingdom was under continuous threat. Pella, here, is Apamea in Syria (Str. 16.2.10/752): it is the very place where Demetrius died in 282 after an imprisonment of three years (see Plu. *Demetr.* 52.5–6, which also paints quite a different view of the situation described by Diodorus; see also Heckel 2009: 109 *s.v.* 'Demetrius [4]').
[65] Not least thanks to expert use of his fleet: see Grainger 2011: 45–53. After Demetrius' defeat his successor Antigonus II *Gonatas* largely continued this policy.

The Vicissitudes of the Diadoch Kingdoms 497

was in Media, he discussed with[66] him how to deal with Demetrius. (3) In fact, he was determined to release Demetrius and restore him with great pomp to his throne. He wanted, though, that gratitude be given to his son for this kindness,[67] because Antiochus had married Stratonice, the daughter of Demetrius, and had begot children by her.

B. THE YEARS AFTER 280

S. 156:
29.7.1–29.11.1 [various sources]:

Conflict between Antiochus III and the Romans:
(29.7.1 = *Const. Exc.* 1: 398–9)[68] *Antiochus III,[69] learning that the Romans[70] had crossed to Asia Minor, sent Heraclides of Byzantium to the consul to discuss a settlement, conceding that he would pay half the costs of the war and to give up Lampsacus, Smyrna, and Alexandria,[71] through which, it seemed, the war had been set in motion. Of the Greek *poleis* in Asia Minor these had been, in fact, the first to dispatch embassies to the Senate, invoking its aid in behalf of their independence.
(29.8.1 = *Const. Exc.* 1: 398–9)[72] *Antiochus III, in addition, offered Publius Scipio, the senior member of the Senate, the return without ransom of his son, who had been taken prisoner during his stay on Euboea, in addition to a large sum of money, if he would support the peace. Scipio replied as regards the release of

---

[66] Though the MS reads here συνεβούλευσε ('advising'), I think, partly in the context of his son being far away in Media, that I opt for Dindorf's conjecture here (Walton 1968: 38 *ad* 4, not used in Dindorf and Fischer 1969) and read συνεβουλεύσατο ('discussed with').
[67] See Plu. *Demetr.* 51.4; this paragraph of Plutarch suggests that Seleucus was not so much led by real generosity, but by calculation: releasing Demetrius might greatly annoy Lysimachus, whom Seleucus despised.
[68] According to the editions by Dindorf and Fischer 1969: 383 and Walton 1968: 254–5; Goukowsky 2012: 83–4 counts this as Fr. 9.
[69] These events took place in 190; see also Plb. 21.13.1–15.13; Liv. 37.34–6. There had already been some controversy between Antiochus III and the Romans on Lysimachia in Thrace in 196, as told in 28.12.1 (= Goukowsky 2012: 55 Fr. 13), in which the Romans at that time (οὐκ εὐδοκοῦντες, 'ill content') had chosen to opt out and again in 194/3, when an embassy from Antiochus to Rome was told that he was not to meddle in affairs in Europe unless he wanted the Romans to meddle in Asiatic affairs (28.15.1–4 = Goukowsky 2012: 57–8 Fr. 16). At that time, the Senate made clear – after the embassy refused to comply – that Rome would take action against Antiochus III.
[70] Under the command of L. Cornelius Scorpio *Asiaticus*, the consul, and P. Cornelius Scipio *Africanus*. For the role of the Romans henceforth in this region see Eckstein 2008.
[71] That is, Alexandria Troas.
[72] According to the editions by Dindorf and Fischer 1969: 384 and Walton 1968: 254–7; Goukowsky 2012: 84 counts this as Fr. 10.

his son that he would be grateful to the king, but that there was no need of a large sum of money. In return for his kindness, however, he advised Antiochus not to engage the Romans in battle, having experienced their *aretē*. However, because Antiochus imagined that Scipio asked heavier conditions than was fitting, he received the answer unfavourably.

(2 = *Const. Exc.* 4: 362)[73] *With an eye to the surprises of Fate, Antiochus III thought it advantageous to render Scipio's son to Scipio, and sent him away, decked out in rich array.

[[For *caput* 9, see below, after *caput* 10.]]

(29.10.1 = *Const. Exc.* 1: 399–400)[74] *Antiochus III, abandoning the conflict in despair,[75] dispatched an embassy to the consul, asking to be pardoned for his errors and to be granted peace on the best conditions possible. The consul, adhering to traditional Roman fairness and moved by the appeals of his brother Publius, granted peace on the following terms: the king should cede to the Romans his territory and the cities and tribes included therein both in Europe and on this side of the Taurus; he must surrender both his elephants and warships and pay in full the expenses incurred in the war, which were assessed at 15,000 Euboean talents;[76] and he must deliver up Hannibal the Carthaginian, Thoas the Aetolian, and certain others, as well as twenty hostages, whomever the Romans might designate.[77] Accepting all conditions in his desire for peace, Antiochus brought the war to a close.

---

[73] According to the editions by Dindorf and Fischer 1969: 384 and Walton 1968: 254–5; Goukowsky 2012: 84 counts this as Fr. 11.
[74] According to the editions by Dindorf and Fischer 1969: 384–5 and Walton 1968: 254–7; Goukowsky 2012: 84–5 counts this as Fr. 12. Walton 1968: 255 note 2 remarks that he has retained the order of Dindorf's numbering of *capita* 10 and 9, but restored the order in which they appear in the *Excerpta Constantiniana*, based upon the relevant chapters in Polybius and Livy *inter alios*.
[75] 'The conflict' is the Battle of Magnesia ad Sipylum, in Lydia, between the Romans and Eumenes II of Pergamum on one side and Antiochus III the Great, the then ruler of the Seleucid Empire, on the other. Antiochus was defeated.
[76] The Euboean *talent* equals the Attic one: it is a weight unit, based on 25.86 kg of barleycorn and with an equivalent value of 60 *minae* or 6,000 *drachmae*: 15,000 Euboean *talents* would, therefore have had an equivalent value of 90,000,000 *drachmae*.
[77] Plb. 21.16–17 discusses the embassy and the Roman conditions at some length. He mentions that Antiochus III had to pay to the Romans 15,000 Euboean *talents* (500 at once, 2,500 upon the peace being ratified by the Roman people, and the remainder in twelve yearly instalments of 1,000 *talents* each), apart from the 400 *talents* he still owed to Eumenes II and the corn he had not yet delivered according to a preceding agreement with Eumenes' father Attalus. Apart from Hannibal and Thoas, Polybius also mentions that Mnasilochus the Acarnanian, Philon, and Eubulidas of Chalcis were to be delivered. The same conditions are mentioned in Liv. 37.45: neither Polybius nor Livy, however, mentions the surrender of elephants and/or warships.

The Vicissitudes of the Diadoch Kingdoms 499

(29.9.1 = *Const. Exc.* 1: 399–400)[78] *At Rome, before the defeat of Antiochus III,[79] when the envoys from Aetolia were brought before the Senate and said no word of their own shortcomings, but spoke at length of their service to the Romans, a member of the Senate, standing up, asked the envoys whether the Aetolians would put themselves in the hands of the Romans. When the envoys made no reply, the Senate, assuming that the Aetolians still had their hopes pinned on Antiochus, sent them empty-handed back to Greece.

[[For *caput* 10, see above, after *caput* 8.]]

(29.11.1 = *Const. Exc.* 1: 400)[80] *After the defeat of Antiochus III, envoys presented themselves from all the cities and rulers throughout Asia Minor, some about freedom, others about a return for their good services to Rome, having collaborated against Antiochus. The Senate, sketching out great perspectives, told them all to send to Asia Minor ten legates, who together with the commanders in the field were to settle all matters. When the envoys had returned to their homes, and the ten legates had conferred with Scipio and Aemilius,[81] they decided and proclaimed that the territory on this side of the Taurus was Eumenes' as were the elephants; to Rhodes they added Caria and Lycia; the cities that had previously paid tribute to Eumenes were to be subject to Eumenes;[82] and any that still paid tribute to Antiochus were relieved of all levies.

S. 157:
29.15.1 (= *Const. Exc.* 2(1): 273):[83]

Antiochus pillages the temple of Bel:
(29.15.1) *Antiochus III, pressed for funds and hearing that the temple of Bel in Elymaïs had a large store of silver and gold, derived

---

[78] According to the editions by Dindorf and Fischer 1969: 384 and Walton 1968: 256–7; Goukowsky 2012: 85 counts it as Fr. 13.
[79] The context of Livy's account (37.49; that is, after the account of the Battle of Magnesia and the ensuing agreement but before the news of these events reached Rome [Liv. 37.51.8]) suggests the order of these chapters. Livy dates the appearance of the Aetolians in the Senate to the consular year of 189.
[80] According to the editions by Dindorf and Fischer 1969: 385 and Walton 1968: 256–9; Goukowsky 2012: 86 counts it as Fr. 14.
[81] This is probably L. Aemilius Regillus, the victor of Myonnesus, a promontory in Ionia near the *polis* of Teos, where a combined Roman and Rhodian fleet defeated the fleet of Antiochus III under Polyxenidas in September 190. The context seems to suggest that the meeting between the ambassadors, Scipio, and Regillus took place in Rome.
[82] The text of Polybius suggests that the first instance of Eumenes should be read as Attalus: see Plb. 21.45.2.
[83] According to the editions by Dindorf and Fischer 1969: 386 and Walton 1968: 258–61; Goukowsky 2012: 87 counts this as Fr. 18. The event should be dated to 187.

from the dedications, resolved to pillage it. He went to Elymaïs and, after accusing the inhabitants of having begun a war, pillaged the temple, but though he amassed much wealth he speedily received becoming punishment from the gods.[84]

S. 158:
29.29.1 (= *Const. Exc.* 4: 364):[85]

Ptolemy on Coele Syria and his 'friends':
(29.29.1) *When King Ptolemy[86] was asked by one of his companions why he neglected Coele Syria, though it was rightfully his, he replied that these matters were frequently in his thoughts. When the companion continued and asked where he would find sufficient money for the war, the king pointing to the courtiers, said: 'Look, my walking money-bags.'

S. 159:
29.24.1 (*Const. Exc.* 2(1): 274?):[87]

Seleucus advances but comes to his senses:
(29.24.1) *Seleucus,[88] with an army of considerable size, advanced as if intending to cross the Taurus in support of Pharnaces. Taking note, though, of the treaty that his father had made with the Romans, the terms of which forbade ...

---

[84] His punishment is preluded in 28.3.1: Ἀντίοχος δὲ τὸ κατὰ τὴν Ἐλυμαΐδα τέμενος τοῦ Διὸς συλᾶν ἐπιβαλόμενος τρέπουσαν τὴν καταστροφὴν εὗρε τοῦ βίου, μετὰ πάσης τῆς δυνάμεως ἀπολόμενος ('As for Antiochus, his project of plundering the sanctuary of Zeus [that is, Bel] at Elymaïs brought him to appropriate disaster, and he perished with his entire force').
[85] According to the editions by Dindorf and Fischer 1969: 392 and Walton 1968: 270–1; Goukowsky 2012: counts this as Fr. 32.
[86] King Ptolemy is here Ptolemy V *Epiphanes*. The story is dated to 181/0. Coele Syria had been taken by the Seleucids about 200 and ruled by them since, at this time by Seleucus IV. Walton 1968: 271 note 1 remarks that Jerome quotes this story from Porphyry: *FGrH/BNJ* 260 F 48, adding that Ptolemy's remark led to him being poisoned. Walton's remark refers to Jer. *In Dan.* 11.20: 'Porphyry, however, claims that it was not this Seleucus who is referred to, but rather Ptolemy Epiphanes, who contrived a plot against Seleucus and prepared an army to fight against him, with the result that he* was poisoned by his own generals. They did this because when someone asked him* where he was going to get the financial resources for the great enterprises he was planning, he answered that his financial resources consisted in his friends. When this remark was publicly noised abroad, the generals became apprehensive that he would deprive them of their property and for that reason killed him by nefarious means.' (Archer 1958: 128, slightly adapted after Hieronymus, *Commentariorum in Danielem Prophetam Liber Unus*, in Migne *PL*, vol. 025, p. 566. Archer gives the name of Seleucus on the places where I, on the basis of both context and Latin, read a *pronomen* referring to Ptolemy (asterisked)).
[87] According to the editions by Dindorf and Fischer 1969: 391 (Fr. number is lacking) and Walton 1968: 272–3; Goukowsky 2012: 93 counts this as Fr. 27. Walton has changed the order of *capita* and I shall follow his example.
[88] The Seleucus intended is Seleucus IV, the successor of Antiochus III. The date is 180.

S. 160:
30.2.1 (= *Const. Exc.* 1: 401–2):[89]

Ptolemy and Antiochus ask Rome to consider Coele Syria:
(30.2.1) *Ptolemy,[90] king of Egypt, knowing that his ancestors had held Coele Syria, made great preparations for disputing this territory. In fact,[91] he hoped to recover justly on the same terms what had been detached before through an unjust war. Learning of this, Antiochus dispatched ambassadors to Rome, commanding them to call the Senate to witness that Ptolemy, without just cause, was bent on making war. The latter, however, also sent off envoys to speak in his defence and to inform the Senate that, because Coele Syria had belonged to Ptolemy's own forebears, Antiochus ruled over it contrary to all justice. He also instructed them to renew friendly relations with the Romans and to try to bring about peace with Perseus.

S. 161:
30.14.1–18.2 [various sources]:

War between Antiochus and Ptolemy:
(30.14.1 = *Const. Exc.* 2(1): 278)[92] *Though Antiochus was in a position to kill the defeated Egyptians,[93] riding about, he called to his men not to kill them, but to take them alive. Soon he reaped the fruits of his shrewdness, because this generosity contributed very greatly to his seizure of Pelusium and after that to the acquisition of all Egypt.

---

[89] Dindorf and Fischer 1969: 395, Walton 1968: 282–5, and Goukowsky 2012: 108–9 all count this as Fragment 2.
[90] The Ptolemy intended is Ptolemy VI *Philometor*, who had just come of age, his antagonist being Antiochus IV *Epiphanes*, whose personal habits were described in 29.32. The year the events of the present chapter are dated to is 170/69. The Perseus of this fragment is Perseus of Macedon (c. 212–166: he succeeded his father, Philip V, in 179), the last king of the Antigonid dynasty, after losing the Battle of Pydna in 168, after which Macedon came under Roman rule. See also Plb. 27.19, 28.1.
[91] On the basis of *Suda*, *s.v.* Ἀμφισβητεῖν, 'to dispute' (*alpha*,1763), I have replaced the 'τε' of the text by Dindorf and Fischer, Walton, and Goukowsky with 'γὰρ', here translated as 'In fact'.
[92] According to the editions by Dindorf and Fischer 1969: 401 and Walton 1968: 296–7; Goukowsky 2012: 116 counts it as Fr. 18.
[93] This refers to the Battle of Mount Casius. Mount Casius, at present known as Ras Kouroun, El-Katieh, or El-Kas, is a small hill, about 100 m high in a rather flat landscape, which marked the boundary between Syria and Egypt in antiquity. It was situated near the marshes of Lake Bardawil, between Gaza and Pelusium. Antiochus IV was here victorious over the forces of Ptolemy VI: see also Porphyry in *FGrH/BNJ* 260 F 49. On Antiochus' attitude: see Mørkholm 1966: 73–4.

(30.15.1 = *Const. Exc.* 4: 367–8)⁹⁴ *The trustees of the young Ptolemy, Eulaeus the eunuch and Lenaeus of Syria, contrived every possible means and device and heaped up silver, gold, and all other kinds of wealth in the royal treasury. Therefore no one should have been surprised if through the efforts of such men in such a short period such great supplies for war⁹⁵ were prepared, or that one, who was a eunuch and had newly laid aside comb and perfume bottles, should exchange the service of Aphrodite for the contests of Ares, or that the man from Coele Syria who was born a slave and from whose hands the abacus had just fallen should have dared to take upon himself the war for Syria, even though Antiochus was second to none as regards both his armies and his other resources. Most importantly, however, they were completely without experience of battles in warfare and lacking either a single competent adviser or a capable commander, yet undertook these great tasks. As might be expected, they themselves soon met with the punishment that their folly deserved, and they brought the kingdom to utter ruin as far as it was in their power.

(30.16.1 = *Const. Exc.* 4: 367–8)⁹⁶ *Having summoned the populace to an assembly, the regents of Ptolemy⁹⁷ promised to bring the war to a speedy end. Proclaiming that, they were at least not in error, since they swiftly succeeded in putting an end both to the war and to themselves. However, because of their inexperience they entertained such high hopes of taking not only Syria but even the whole kingdom of Antiochus that they took with them the greater part of the treasures they had amassed, including the gold plates from the sideboard. They also packed up and carried off from the palace couches, mostly with silver feet, but a few also with feet of gold, and moreover a large quantity of clothes, women's jewellery, and precious stones. These things, they declared, they were taking along for those who would promptly surrender either cities or fortresses to them. This was not to be, but they carried off ready treasure for their own destruction.

[[(30.17.1 = *Const. Exc.* 2(1): 278–9)⁹⁸ *In keeping with our policy

---

⁹⁴ According to the editions by Dindorf and Fischer 1969: 401–2 and Walton 1968: 296–9; Goukowsky 2012: 116–17 counts it as Fr. 19.

⁹⁵ Instead of θεωρίαι ('spectacles'), I prefer, with a view to the context, χορηγίαι, proposed by Van Herwerden 1860 *ad loc.* (primarily discussing the text of MS V, the *Excerpta de Sententiis*).

⁹⁶ According to the editions by Dindorf and Fischer 1969: 402–3 and Walton 1968: 298–301; Goukowsky 2012: 117 counts it as Fr. 20.

⁹⁷ The regents intended were probably Eulaeus the eunuch and Lenaeus of Coele Syria.

⁹⁸ According to the editions by Dindorf and Fischer 1969: 403 and Walton 1968: 300–3; Goukowsky 2012: 118 counts this as Fr. 21.

we could not pass over without comment the ignoble flight of Ptolemy. That he, though standing in no immediate danger and though separated by such a distance from his enemies, would at once and virtually without a struggle abandon his claim to a great and opulent throne can only, it would seem, be regarded as indicating a thoroughly effeminate spirit. Now had Ptolemy been a man endowed by Nature with such a spirit, we might perhaps have found fault with her. But since Nature finds a sufficient rebuttal to the charge in his subsequent actions and has demonstrated that the king was second to none whether in firmness to resist or in energy to act, we are forced to assign the responsibility for his ignoble cowardice on this occasion to the eunuch and to Ptolemy's close association with him. For he, by rearing the lad from boyhood amid luxury {τρυφή} and womanish pursuits, had been undermining his character.[99]]]

(30.18.1 = *Const. Exc.* 2(1): 278–9)[100] *Antiochus showed himself a wise and prudent man and worthy of the royal dignity, except for the stratagem at Pelusium.[101]

(2 = *Const. Exc.* 4: 368–9)[102] *Antiochus got possession of Pelusium by means of a questionable stratagem. Though, in fact, all warfare is an exception to humane standards of law and justice, even so it has certain quasi-laws of its own, such as: a truce should not be broken; heralds should not be put to death; a man who has placed himself under the protection[103] of a superior opponent should not be visited with punishment or vengeance. These and similar matters ... one might fairly say that Antiochus, like the legal swindlers from the courts, held fast to the letter of the law in making the seizure of Pelusium after the truce, but not to the just and good, through which the life of all is bonded. Indeed, being obliged because of kinship,[104] as he said himself, to spare the young man, he tried on the contrary by deceit to bring him to utter ruin after winning his confidence.

---

[99] See Plb. 28.21.2–5. Polybius informs us that the eunuch persuaded Ptolemy to abandon his kingdom and flee to Samothrace, even though Ptolemy showed himself in later life to be steadfast and brave in danger.
[100] According to the editions by Dindorf and Fischer 1969: 403 and Walton 1968: 302–3; Goukowsky 2012: 118 counts this as Fr. 22a.
[101] See Plb. 28.18.
[102] According to the editions by Dindorf and Fischer 1969: 403–4 and Walton 1968: 302–5; Goukowsky 2012: 118–19 counts it as Fr. 22b.
[103] In the MS is a lacuna that might well be filled with the words suggested by Mai, παραδίδοντα μή (rather than Herwerden's παραδόντα μή, favoured by Goukowsky 2012: 119: see Walton 1968: 303, crit. 4).
[104] Antiochus IV was the uncle of Ptolemy VI. See also Jer. *In Dan.* 11.21.

S. 162:
31.1.1–2.2 (= *Const. Exc.* 4: 370-):[105]

Rome forces Antiochus to leave Egypt alone:
(31.1.1) *Antiochus at first posed as a dignified man, asserting that it was not desiring the throne of Egypt for himself that he had prepared large forces for the war, but to assist the elder Ptolemy to regain the ancestral throne.[106] This was by no means true, but he believed that by presiding over a dispute between the youths and making an investment in goodwill he would conquer Egypt without a blow. In fact, when Fate put his policy to the test and deprived him of the aforementioned pretext, he stood revealed as one of the many princes who count no point of honour more important than gain.
(31.2.1) *Antiochus, after greeting them verbally from a distance, stretched out his hand in welcome to the approaching Romans. Popillius,[107] however, who had the document in which the Senate's decision was recorded at hand, held it out and ordered Antiochus to read it. He was thought to act like this because he would not clasp hands as a friend until he knew from Antiochus' decision whether he was a friend or a foe. When the king, after reading the document, said that he would consult with his companions on these matters, Popillius, hearing this, performed an act that seemed offensive and arrogant in the extreme. Having a stick cut from a vine ready at hand, he drew a line about Antiochus with the stick, and directed him to give his answer in that circle. (2) The king, astonished by what had taken place, and awed by the superiority of Rome, having come

---

[105] According to the editions by Dindorf and Fischer 1969: 1–2 (for the pagination of this volume, see above, note 57) and Walton 1968: 312–15; Goukowsky 2012: 140–1 counts it as Fr. 1 and Fr. 2.

[106] The events described took place in 169/8. The elder Ptolemy here is Ptolemy VI *Philometor*. After the capture of Ptolemy VI and all of Egypt, with the exception of the city of Alexandria, by Antiochus, and while Ptolemy VI ruled as a puppet monarch, the people of Alexandria chose his younger brother Ptolemy VIII *Euergetes* II (c. 182–116), aka *Physcon*, as king. After Antiochus withdrew from the area in 168 (see below), *Physcon* agreed to rule Egypt jointly with *Philometor* and Cleopatra II (*Philometor*'s wife and their sister). In 163 *Physcon* became ruler of Cyrenaica and claimed Cyprus, which he tried twice to conquer, failing both times. In the last attempt he was taken prisoner by his brother, who spared him and sent him back to Cyrenaica. When *Philometor* died on campaign in 145, Cleopatra II quickly had her son proclaimed King Ptolemy VII. *Physcon*, however, returned and proposed another joint rule as well as marriage with Cleopatra II: she accepted both proposals. He had the younger Ptolemy VII, his nephew and stepson, assassinated during the wedding feast, and next (144) claimed the throne himself, as 'Ptolemy VIII *Euergetes* II'. For the present fragment see also Plb. 29.26. See also below, 33.4 and note 165.

[107] In 168 the Roman Senate sent out C. Popillius Laenas to settle affairs in Egypt, forcing Antiochus to leave the country. This encounter took place at Alexandria, in a suburb by the name of Eleusis: see also Plb. 29.2.1–4, 27.1–11.

in helplessness and considering all options, said that he would do all that the Romans proposed. Popillius and his colleagues then took his hand and greeted him cordially. The content of the letter was to abandon his war against Ptolemy at once. Obeying the instructions, the king led his forces out of Egypt, panic-stricken by the superiority of Rome, because he had newly had news of the Macedonian collapse.[108] Indeed, had he not known that this had taken place, he would never have accepted the decree of his own free will.

S. 163:
31.17a.1 (= *Const. Exc.* 3: 199–200):[109]

Armenia threatens to break away from the Seleucid Empire:
(31.17a.1) *Artaxias,[110] the king of Armenia, defecting from Antiochus,[111] founded a city named after himself, and assembled a powerful force. Antiochus, whose strength at this period was unmatched by any of the other kings, marched against him and after being victorious forced him to do as he was told.

S. 164:
31.18a.1 (= Jer. *In Dan.* 11.36):[112]

Antiochus tries to despoil the temple of Artemis in Elymaïs:
(31.18a.1) *Polybius and Diodorus, the authors of *Historical Libraries*,[113] relate that Antiochus IV *Epiphanes* not only opposed the god in Judaea but also,[114] inflamed by the fires of avarice, tried

---

[108] Referring to the outcome of the Battle of Pydna (22 June 168), in which the Roman general L. Aemilius Paul(l)us (*Macedonicus*) defeated King Perseus, ending the reign of the Antigonid dynasty over Macedon.
[109] According to the editions by Dindorf and Fischer 1969: 19–20 and Walton 1968: 354–7; Goukowsky 2012: 160 counts this as Fr. 25.
[110] I prefer the form Ἀρταξίας, as used in Dindorf and Fischer 1969: 19 line 31, to the form Ἀρτάξης, used by both Walton and Goukowsky, following the MS, even though both acknowledge in notes that Artaxias was the preferred form (Walton 1968: 355 note 2; Goukowsky 2012: 160 note 84). For this ruler see also Schottky 1989: 139–40. The action is to be dated to 165.
[111] Still referring to Antiochus IV. For his action against Artaxias see also App. *Syr.* 45–6: ἐστράτευσε δὲ καὶ ἐπὶ Ἀρταξίαν τὸν Ἀρμενίων βασιλέα. | Καὶ αὐτὸν ἑλών, ἐτελεύτησεν ('he made an expedition against Artaxias the king of the Armenians. | And after capturing him, he [Antiochus *Epiphanes*] died'; I am not convinced that the punctuation of the Loeb edition is right); and App. *Syr.* 66.
[112] According to the edition by Walton 1968: 360–1; Goukowsky 2012: 162–3 counts this as a testimony and part of Fr. 29. Dindorf and Fischer 1969 omits this fragment/testimony.
[113] Technically Jerome is not totally correct: Polybius' work is known as the *Histories*, Diodorus' as the *Historical Library*. The story is set about 164.
[114] Antiochus IV *Epiphanes* had a garrisoned castle, the Acra, constructed in Jerusalem to the south-west of the Temple Mount terrace in 167 to monitor the city's population: remains

to despoil the temple of Artemis, which was very rich, in Elymaïs.[115] Thwarted by the guardians of the temple and by the neighbouring peoples, he was driven mad by certain apparitions and terrors, and finally died of disease; and they state that this happened to him because he attempted to violate the temple of Artemis.[116]

S. 165:
31.19.1–19a.1 [various sources]:[117]

Pedigree of the Cappadocian kings related to events in Persian history:
(31.19.1 = Phot. *Bibl.* [244] 382a23–383a26)[118] *The kings of Cappadocia say that they trace their ancestry back to Cyrus the Persian, and also assert that they are descendants of one of the seven Persians who killed the *Magus*.[119] Now as to their connection with Cyrus, they count as follows. Cambyses,[120] the father of Cyrus, had a sister, of legitimate birth, Atossa. To her and Pharnaces, king of Cappadocia, was born a son, Gallus. From him sprang Smerdis, from him Artamnes, and from him Anaphas, a man of outstanding bravery and daring, who was one of the seven Persians.[121] (2) Such, then, is the pedigree they trace for their kinship with Cyrus and with Anaphas, to

---

of this castle were reportedly excavated in October/November 2015. See, for example, <http://www.upi.com/Science_News/2015/11/03/Ancient-Greek-stronghold-uncovered-in-Jerusalem/3411446567487/>, consulted 5 November 2015. Antiochus' actions in Judaea earned him in Rabbinical sources the addition הרשע (*harasha*, 'the wicked'): see *Jewish Encyclopaedia* s.v. 'Antiochus IV, Epiphanes' (online version: <http://jewishencyclopedia.com/articles/1589-antiochus-iv-epiphanes>), consulted 14 March 2015.

[115] Elymaïs is the Graecised form of the ancient name of Elam. It was located at the head of the Persian Gulf in the present-day region of Khūzestān, Iran. 'Artemis' was, in fact, the assimilated form of the goddess Nanaia. In App. *Syr.* 66 the temple is referred to as a temple of Aphrodite.

[116] From the spring of 165 onwards, Antiochus IV left Syria to campaign against the Parthians in the eastern part of his kingdom and died there, late in 164. See also Mørkholm 1966: 166–7.

[117] Walton, though retaining the numbering of the fragments as provided by Dindorf and Fischer, has somewhat changed their order. Goukowsky largely follows the order provided by Walton.

[118] According to the editions by Dindorf and Fischer 1969: 21–4 and Walton 1968: 362–71; Goukowsky 2012: 163–5 counts it as a (first) testimony to Fr. 31.

[119] The *Magus*, probably better known as the false Smerdis, who briefly ruled Persia in 522 shortly before and after the death of Cambyses: see Hdt. 3.61–79; Ctes. *Pers.* F. 13(11–16) (Ctesias gives the *Magus* the name of Sphendadates).

[120] That is Cambyses I, the king of Anshan from c. 600 to 559 and the father of Cyrus II the Great: see also Dandamayev 1990.

[121] Herodotus does not mention any Anaphas as one of the seven conspirators against 'Smerdis'. However, one Onaphas is mentioned as one of the 'seven' in Ctes. *Pers.* F. 13(14): he is believed to correspond to Herodotus' Otanes (Hdt. 3.70). Herodotus also mentions another Otanes (Hdt. 7.62), who had a son by the name of Anaphes.

whom, they say, because of his valour the lordship[122] of Cappadocia was granted, with the implication that no tribute would be paid to the Persians. After his death a son of the same name ruled. After his death, leaving two sons, Datames and Arimnaeus, Datames succeeded to the throne, a man who both in war and in the other spheres of royal duty won praise, and who, engaging the Persians in battle, fought brilliantly and died in battle. The kingdom passed to his son Ariamnes, whose sons were Ariarathes and Holophernes.[123] After Ariamnes had ruled for fifty years, and having achieved nothing worthy of memory, he died. (3) Ariarathes I succeeded to the throne, the elder of his sons, who is said to have loved his brother with a surpassing love, and promoted him to the most prominent positions: thus he was sent to aid the Persians in their war against the Egyptians, and returned home laden with honours, which Ochus, the Persian king, bestowed for bravery.[124] He died in his native land, leaving two sons, Ariarathes and Aryses. (4) Now his brother, the ruler of Cappadocia, having no legitimate offspring of his own, adopted Ariarathes, his brother's elder son. At about this time Alexander of Macedon defeated the Persians, and then died. Perdiccas, who at this point held the supreme command, sent Eumenes as military governor of Cappadocia. Because Ariarathes I was defeated and fell in battle,[125] both Cappadocia itself and the neighbouring regions fell to the Macedonians. (5) Ariarathes II, the son of the late king, regarding the situation as hopeless for the present, retired with a few followers to Armenia. Not long after, when Eumenes and Perdiccas had died and Antigonus and Seleucus were elsewhere engaged, having got a force from Ardoates, king of Armenia, he killed Amyntas, the Macedonian general, expelled the Macedonians quickly from the land, and recovered his familiar domain. (6) Of his three sons Ariamnes, the eldest, inherited the kingdom. He concluded a marital alliance with Antiochus II, called *Theos*, whose daughter Stratonice he married to his eldest son Ariarathes III. Being a man unusually devoted

---

[122] In the text the word δυναστεία ('lordship') is given, quite a neutral terminology. Though Walton 1968: 365 interprets it as if Anaphas had been granted the σατραπεία ('office of satrap'), I am, for example because of the exemption of taxes to the Persians, not sure whether Cappadocia was a real satrapy or became *de facto* independent: see also Goukowsky 2012: 164 note 118.

[123] The proper name, as found on coins, as Walton 1968: 365 note 2 observes, is Ariaramnes. The name Holophernes is corrupted: the correct name should probably be Orophernes, which occurs in the ruling class in Cappadocia: see, for example, Dressel 1905: 469–71 on the Cappadocian coins of 158/7.

[124] Referring to the Egyptian Wars of Artaxerxes III Ochus, in 351 and most notably 343–1 (see above, Chapter 4, 16.40.1–52.8).

[125] Previously Diodorus has told us that Ariarathes had been taken prisoner by Perdiccas and, after having been tortured, had been impaled (18.16.1–3).

to his children, he placed the diadem upon his son's head, made him joint ruler, and shared with him on equal terms all the privileges of kingship.[126] On his father's death, Ariarathes became sole ruler, and when he departed this life left the kingdom to his son Ariarathes IV, who was then a mere infant. (7) He in turn married a daughter of Antiochus III, surnamed the Great, Antiochis by name, an utterly wicked woman. Failing to have children, she brought in as her own, her husband being unwitting, two supposititious sons, Ariarathes and Holophernes.[127] After a certain time, however, she ceased to be barren and unexpectedly bore two daughters and a single son, by the name of Mithridates. Thereupon, after revealing the truth to her husband, she arranged for the elder of the supposititious sons to be sent off to Rome with a suitable stipend,[128] and the younger to Ionia, in order to avoid any dispute with the legitimate son over the kingdom. He, they say, changed his name to Ariarathes V after he grew to manhood,[129] received a Greek education, and won commendation as well for his other *aretē*. (8) Now because he was such a filial son, his father made a point of taking a parental interest in return, and their regard for one another reached such a point that the father was bent on retiring from the throne altogether in favour of his son, while the son declared that it was impossible for him to accept such a favour while his parents yet lived. He, though, succeeded to the throne when the fatal day came for his father, showing himself worthy of the highest praise by his whole way of life, and especially by his devotion to philosophy. Consequently, Cappadocia, so long unknown to the Greeks, offered at this time a place of sojourn to men of culture. He also renewed the treaty of friendship and alliance with Rome.[130] So much, then, for the descent from Cyrus of the dynasty which to this point ruled over Cappadocia.

(9 = Sync.: 523 Dind.)[131] *Seven kings of Cappadocia, whose dynasty lasted one hundred and sixty years, began at about this time, as Diodorus writes.[132]

---

[126] Walton 1968: 367 note 4 remarks that Ariarathes III is considered the first king of a sovereign Cappadocia and that this sovereignty may well have been a consequence of Ariarathes' alliance with Antiochus II *Theos*.
[127] For the name Holophernes see above, note 123. The twelfth-century AD lexicographer Zonaras has another story: see Zonar. 9.24.
[128] Liv. 42.19 mentions that he arrived in Rome.
[129] That is, Ariarathes V *Eusebes Philopator*, whose reign lasted from 163 to 130.
[130] See Plb. 31.3.1–3.
[131] According to the editions by Dindorf and Fischer 1969: 24 and Walton 1968: 370–1; Goukowsky 2012: 165 includes it as a separate (second) testimony to his Fr. 31.
[132] Though the so-called Ariarathids ruled Cappadocia technically until at least 36 (the death of Ariarathes X *Eusebes Philadelphus*), their position was more or less that of Roman

The Vicissitudes of the Diadoch Kingdoms   509

(31.21.1 = *Const. Exc.* 2(1): 284–5)¹³³ *Ariarathes, surnamed *Philopator*, succeeding to his ancestral kingdom, first of all buried his father magnificently. Then, when he had paid proper attention to the interests of his friends, those in positions of authority, and the other subordinate officials, he earned great goodwill among the populace.¹³⁴

Events related to Cappadocian rulers:
(31.22.1 = *Const. Exc.* 2 (1): 284–5)¹³⁵ *After Ariarathes had restored Mithrobuzanes to his ancestral domain, Artaxias, the king of Armenia, remainining constant to his original rapacity, sent envoys to Ariarathes, urging him to agree, and proposing that they should each put to death the young man who was at his court, and divide Sophene between them.¹³⁶ Ariarathes, to whom such villainy was completely foreign, rebuked the envoys and wrote to Artaxias, urging him to abstain from such actions. Ariarathes, then, in consequence, when this was achieved in this way, enhanced his own reputation in no slight degree, while Mithrobuzanes, thanks to the admirable loyalty and nobility of his supporter, succeeded to the throne of his fathers.
(31.19a.1 = *Const. Exc.* 3: 200)¹³⁷ *Ptolemaeus,¹³⁸ the governor of Commagene, who even before had shown little respect for the Syrian kings, became a seceder. Because they were busy with their own affairs, he established himself without interference in control of the

---

dependents from c. 95 (the reigns of Ariarathes IX and Ariabarzanes I *Philoromaios*, 95 to c. 63). That would make Ariarathes VIII (101–96) supposedly the last independent king of this family in Cappadocia. Accepting that as a starting point, the 160 years' rule of the family as independent kings of Cappadocia would indeed start with Ariarathes III (255–220): see also above, note 126. Diodorus' account – and therefore this conclusion – seems, however, not above suspicion: part of it rests on the assumption that Diodorus (or his source) took the reign of Ariarathes VIII into account.
   ¹³³ According to the editions by Dindorf and Fischer 1969: 25 and Walton 1968: 370–1; Goukowsky 2012: 166 counts it as Fr. 32.
   ¹³⁴ See also Plb. 31.3.4–5, 7.1–4.
   ¹³⁵ According to the editions by Dindorf and Fischer 1969: 25–6 and Walton 1968: 370–3; Goukowsky 2012: 166 counts it as Fr. 33.
   ¹³⁶ Sophene was an independent region situated between Cappadocia and Armenia, east of the Euphrates. It appears that there were two claimants for the throne of the region (after the death of King Zariadris in 163), one staying with Ariarathes (namely Mithrobuzanes) and one with Artaxias (not named). See also Plb. 31.16.1; Str. 11.14.5/528 (in the Loeb translation assigning the wrong region to the respective rulers); and Goukowsky 2012: 166 note 136.
   ¹³⁷ According to the editions by Dindorf and Fischer 1969: 25 and Walton 1968: 372–3; Goukowsky 2012: 167 counts it as Fr. 34.
   ¹³⁸ Ptolemaeus served as a satrap of Seleucid Commagene between 201 and 163, serving under the Syrian Greek kings Antiochus III the Great, Seleucus IV *Philopator*, Antiochus IV *Epiphanes*, and Antiochus V *Eupator*. When the Seleucid Empire began to disintegrate in 163, Ptolemaeus decided to revolt and make Commagene an independent kingdom.

country, chiefly relying on its natural advantages for defence. Not satisfied with this gain, having raised a force, he invaded Melitene, which belonged to Cappadocia and was subject to Ariarathes, and he won an initial success by occupying the points of vantage. When Ariarathes, however, marched against him with a large force, he withdrew into his own province.

S. 166:
31.27a.1 (= *Const. Exc.* 3: 200–1):[139]

Integrity of the Seleucid Empire is threatened:
(31.27a.1) *When it became known that the Romans were ill disposed towards Demetrius,[140] not only did the other kings despise his kingship, but so did even some of the satraps subject to him, of whom the most outstanding was Timarchus. He was a Milesian by birth, and a friend of the previous king, Antiochus.[141] Having been frequently sent as ambassador to Rome, he had worked serious detriment to the Senate. Providing himself, indeed, with large sums of money, he offered the senators bribes, seeking especially to entice with his gifts the weak in means of living. By gaining in this way a large number of adherents and supplying them with proposals contrary to the public policy of Rome, he debauched the Senate, supported by Heraclides, his brother, who was supremely endowed by nature for such service. Following the same tactics, Timarchus travelled to Rome on the present occasion, being now satrap of Media, and, launching many accusations against Demetrius, he persuaded the Senate to pass the following decision concerning himself:[142] 'To Timarchus, because of ... to be their king.'[143] He now, emboldened by the decision, raised a substantial army in Media. He also concluded an alliance against

---

[139] According to the editions by Dindorf and Fischer 1969: 32–3 and Walton 1968: 386–9; Goukowsky 2012: 174 counts it as Fr. 41.

[140] Demetrius I *Soter*, the son of Seleucus IV *Philopator* and Laodice IV, ruled the Seleucid Empire from 162 to 150, after his escape as political hostage from Rome. The current events should, therefore, be put in this period, probably in the first years of his reign. For Timarchus and Heraclides see, for example, Mørkholm 1966: 103–4; Olshausen 1974: nos. 148, 153; Herrmann 1987: 171–3; Kneppe 1989.

[141] Most likely Antiochus IV *Epiphanes* is intended: see, for example, Walton 1968: 387 note 2.

[142] The text of the MS reads here: δόγμα περὶ αὐτοῦ θέσθαι. I believe it feasible, regarding the context that, instead of αὐτοῦ, we should read here ἑαυτοῦ.

[143] As Goukowsky 2012: 266 *ad* note 179 rightly observes, the excerpter of the *Excerpta Constantiniana* probably only copied the first two and the last two words of the *senatus consultum*: any attempt to reconstitute the text is, therefore, doomed to fail. However, the gist of it might be guessed, following App. *Syr.* 45 (235), mentioning that Timarchus had been appointed satrap of Babylon, and Heraclides treasurer. See also Walton 1968: 388–9 note 1.

Demetrius with Artaxias, the king of Armenia. Having, moreover, intimidated the neighbouring peoples by the strength of his force and having made many of them his subjects, he marched against Zeugma, and eventually gained control of the kingdom.[144]

S. 167:
31.28.1–30.1 [various sources]:

Ariarathes V Eusebes Philopator sends a gift to Rome:
(31.28.1 = *Const. Exc.* 1: 403):[145] *In the one hundred and fifty-fifth Olympiad [160], envoys arrived from Ariarathes, bringing with them a crown of ten thousand gold pieces' worth and giving notice of the benevolence which the king had towards the Roman people, and moreover of his renunciation, on their account, of an alliance of marriage and friendship with Demetrius. Because this was testified to by Gracchus and his fellow commissioners,[146] the Senate, expressing their approval of Ariarathes, accepted the crown and sent him the highest gifts that it was their custom to bestow.[147]

Demetrius also sends an embassy with gifts:
(31.29.1 = *Const. Exc.* 1: 403)[148] *At about the same time the envoys of Demetrius were also introduced. They too brought a crown worth ten thousand gold pieces and had with them, in chains, the men responsible for the murder of Octavius.[149] The Senate was for a long time uncertain how to handle the situation. The Senate accepted the crown, but declined to accept the men, Isocrates and Leptines,[150] handed over together with the crown.

---

[144] As Walton 1968: 389 note 2 rightly observes, Diodorus is here at fault. Though Timarchus was recognised by Rome, he received no material support and was soon defeated by Demetrius and killed, in 161 or 160, trying to cross the Euphrates at Zeugma/Seleucia in order to attack Syria: see Habicht 2006: 210. See also Goukowsky 2012: 266 *ad* p. 174 note 182.

[145] According to the editions by Dindorf and Fischer 1969: 33 and Walton 1968: 388–91; Goukowsky 2012: 175 counts it as Fr. 42.

[146] After Demetrius' escape from Rome, a commission led by Ti. Sempronius Gracchus had been sent to the east in 162: see Briscoe 1969: 52; also Broughton 1951: 443. As a matter of fact: Gracchus was not unsympathetic towards Demetrius, unlike the majority of the Senate.

[147] A sceptre and an ivory *sella curulis*: see Plb. 32.1.3.

[148] According to the editions by Dindorf and Fischer 1969: 33 and Walton 1968: 390–1; Goukowsky 2012: 175 counts it as Fr. 43.

[149] In 163, the Senate sent an embassy to Syria (see Plb. 31.2.9–11), led by Gn. Octavius Gn. f. The mission's purpose was quite harsh and Octavius was (consequently?) murdered by one Leptines: see App. *Syr.* 46 (240). For the sources of the murder see also Broughton 1951: 443. See also Briscoe 1969: 52.

[150] Leptines was the actual murderer of Octavius, this Isocrates an orator who had condoned the murder: for the embassy of Demetrius, led by one Menochares, and its reception in Rome, see Plb. 32.2.1–32.3.13; also App. *Syr.* 47 (243).

(31.30.1 = *Const. Exc.* 4: 375)[151] *When Demetrius sent an embassy to the Romans, the Senate gave him an obscure and enigmatic reply, that he would meet a humane treatment if, as regards exercise of his authority, he gave satisfaction to the Senate.

[[As the developments in Asia Minor from now on clearly appear to belong to the sphere of influence of the Roman Republic and no longer to that of the former Persian Empire, I will from now on no longer pay attention to them.]]

S. 168:
32.4.3:

Observation on the qualities of Alexander the Great:
(32.4.3 = *Const. Exc.* 2(1): 291)[152] *... yet in Alexander's Persian expeditions, using the most reasonable measures towards his prisoners of war, not only by his courage but also by his famous gentleness he made those who lived throughout Asia eager to be ruled by him.

S. 169:
32.9c.1–10.1 [various sources]:

Developments in the Seleucid Empire:
(32.9c.1 = *Const. Exc.* 3: 203–4)[153] *Ptolemy *Philometor* entered Syria supporting Alexander on the grounds of kinship.[154] But on discovering the man's downright poverty of spirit, he transferred his daughter Cleopatra to Demetrius, alleging that there was a conspiracy,[155] and

---

[151] According to the editions by Dindorf and Fischer 1969: 33–4 and Walton 1968: 390–1; Goukowsky 2012: 175 counts it as Fr. 44.

[152] This reference preludes an encomium of P. Cornelius Scipio (later surnamed *Africanus*) in 32.7.1; Goukowsky 2012: 203 Fr. 8.

[153] According to the editions by Dindorf and Fischer 1969: 47–8 and Walton 1968: 444–5; Goukowsky 2012: 214 counts it as Fr. 32. Here as well Walton (and Goukowsky) have changed the order of fragments as presented by Dindorf and Fischer.

[154] Parts of this chapter reflect on 31.32.1 and 31.32a.1, to be dated to c. 158/7 (left out because they predominantly focus on regions in the Roman sphere of influence). Orophernes, supported by Demetrius I, drove Ariarathes V *Eusebes Philopator* from the Cappadocian throne. King Attalus (Diodorus, mistakenly, writes Eumenes) of Pergamum was unhappy with the situation in Cappadocia and had, moreover, reasons of his own to thwart Demetrius. He found in Smyrna a young man who sufficiently resembled the late King Antiochus IV *Epiphanes* to pass as a pretender, ready to claim his 'father's' throne, which he actually took in 154 as Alexander *Balas*, with the support of Ptolemy VI *Philometor*. Alexandar *Balas* next married Ptolemy's daughter. Now (about 145), the reign of Alexander *Balas* is threatened by Demetrius II *Nicator Theos Philadelphus*, who recently succeeded his father, Demetrius I *Soter*. The precise date of Ptolemy's expedition is unknown, but should be between 148/7 and 145. For the episode discussed in this fragment see also J. *AJ* 13.103–15; 1 Maccabees 10:68–9, 11:8–13.

[155] In the account of Josephus a conspiracy against Ptolemy, arranged by Alexander and executed by one Ammonius, is referred to.

The Vicissitudes of the Diadoch Kingdoms 513

after arranging an alliance pledged her to him in marriage. Hierax[156] and Diodotus,[157] despairing of Alexander but afraid of Demetrius because of their misdeeds against his father, aroused the Antiochians to rebellion, and receiving Ptolemy within the city, they bound a diadem around his head and put the kingship in his hands. He, however, was not yearning for the kingly office, but desiring to add Coele Syria to his own realm, and privately arranged with Demetrius a joint plan; that is, that Ptolemy should rule Syria[158] and Demetrius his ancestral domains.
(32.9d/10.1 = *Const. Exc.* 3: 204; Phot. *Bibl.* [244] 377a34–b4)[159]
*Alexander, beaten in battle,[160] fled with five hundred of his men to Abae in Arabia, to take refuge with Diocles, its ruler,[161] in whose care he had earlier placed his infant son Antiochus.[162] Next, the captains Heliades and Casius, who were with Alexander, secretly entered into negotiations for their own safety, offering to assassinate Alexander. When Demetrius consented to their terms, they became not merely traitors to their king but also his murderers. Alexander, then, was thus put to death by his friends.

S. 170:
33.3.1–4a.1 [various sources]:

Vicissitudes of Alexander and Demetrius II:
(33.3.1 = *Const. Exc.* 2(1): 294–5)[163] *In Syria, King Alexander, being unfit to govern a kingdom because of his feebleness of spirit, gave up the government of Antioch to Hierax and Diodotus.

---

[156] A flute player from Antioch, influential with Ptolemy VI first, later with Ptolemy VIII. See Grainger 1997: 94. Not to be confused with King Antiochus III *Hierax*.
[157] Diodotus of Apamea, later to become king as *Trypho*. See below, 33.4a.1. See also Grainger 1997: 69–70.
[158] Though Ptolemy primarily aimed for Coele Syria, he is here said to have ruled Syria entirely, something that appears to be confirmed by Polybius: Πτολεμαῖος ὁ τῆς Συρίας Βασιλεὺς ('Ptolemy, the king of Syria': Plb. 39.7.1).
[159] According to the editions by Dindorf and Fischer 1969: 48 and Walton 1968: 444–7; Goukowsky 2012: 214–15 counts it as Fr. 33.
[160] The joint forces of Ptolemy and Demetrius met Alexander in the Battle of the River Oenoparas (modern River Aphreen), 145.
[161] Goukowsky 2012: 280 *ad* note 101 rightly remarks that the name does not look like Arabic, but rather a name given by Graeco-Macedonian settlers to an unidentified Nabataean settlement. In 1 Maccabees 11:17 its ruler is called Zabdiel. Grainger 1997: 95 mentions two additional names for Diocles: Jamblichus and Malchus; see also Goukowsky 2012: 214 *ad* note 102. Walton's suggestion that the place should be sought in northern Syria looks to me contrary to the literary evidence. See also below, 33.4a.1 and note 176, for another name of a ruler taking care of young Antiochus.
[162] Soon put forward as King Antiochus VI *Theos Dionysus Epiphanes* by Diodotus (see above, 32.9c.1, and below, 33.3.1, 4a.1).
[163] According to the editions by Dindorf and Fischer 1969: 65 and Walton 1967: 6–7; Goukowsky 2014: 19 counts it as Fr. 3.

(33.4.1 = *Const. Exc.* 2(1): 294–5):[164] *Now that the kingdom of Egypt had fallen apart[165] and he alone survived,[166] Demetrius believed himself to be out of all danger. Disregarding, therefore, the customary compliance with the masses and growing every day more and more burdensome in his commands, he fell at length into despotic cruelty and extravagances in all sorts of lawless behaviour. The cause of this disposition was not only his own nature, but also the man who conducted the affairs of the kingdom.[167] In fact, being an impious fellow, he was the reckless instigator of all these evils, flattering the young man and prompting him to the most infamous acts. (2) At first, then, he punished all that had sided against him in the war, not with measured punishments, but visiting them with extraordinary retributions. Afterwards, when the Antiochians acted towards him in their usual manner,[168] he deployed a considerable mercenary force against them and stripped the citizens of their arms. Because they refused to hand them over, he killed some of them as they fell into his hands, others he cut down in their houses, together with their children and wives. After a great uproar rose over the disarmament, he burnt down most of the city to the ground.[169] (3) Putting to death many who were accused of leading the commotion, he confiscated their property for the royal treasury. Through fear and hatred many Antiochians, fleeing out of the city, wandered throughout all Syria, waiting for the right time to attack the king. Demetrius, though, being their enemy, never ceased the slaughters, banishments, and confiscations, far exceeding even his father in harshness and thirst for blood. (4) In fact, the latter, too, striving not after royal virtuousness but after tyrannical lawlessness, had involved his subjects in pernicious evils. As a result, the kings of this family were hated by all because of their lawlessness, but those of the other were loved for their virtuousness. Therefore there constantly arose struggles and continual wars throughout Syria, because the rulers of each house lay again and again in wait for one another.

---

[164] According to the editions by Dindorf and Fischer 1969: 65–7 and Walton 1967: 6–11; Goukowsky 2014: 19–21 counts it as Fr. 4.

[165] Ptolemy VI *Philometor* had died from wounds sustained at the Battle of the Oenoparas. See for the vicissitudes of Philometor's infant son, Ptolemy VII *Philopator Neos*, his mother, Cleopatra II, and Ptolemy VIII *Euergetes II Physcon*, above, note 106. However, Egyptian aspirations for (Coele) Syria were dashed.

[166] That is, of the three contenders for Syria: Alexander *Balas*, Ptolemy VI *Philometor*, and Demetrius II *Nicator*.

[167] 1 Maccabees 11:31–2 and J. *AJ* 13.126–7 mention one Lasthenes, a Cretan, as the king's 'kinsman' and 'father'. Goukowsky 2014: 307 *ad* note 17, however, argues that Ammonius might well have been intended as Demetrius' evil genius.

[168] Antioch had only opted for Demetrius thanks to Ptolemy VI and hardly appears to have supported Demetrius with any zeal: see Downey 1961: 120–3.

[169] See 1 Maccabees 11:44–8; J. *AJ* 13.135–42.

Therefore, the masses welcomed the dynastic changes because of the obsequiousness of the ever-succeeding kings.

(33.4a.1 = *Const. Exc.* 3: 204–5)[170] *When a certain Diodotus, nicknamed *Tryphon*,[171] who had a high reputation amongst the companions of the king, saw the fervour of the masses and the hate towards their ruler,[172] having defected from Demetrius, he soon found many to share in his enterprise. He first enlisted[173] the men of Larissa,[174] noted for their courage and who had been allowed their present settlement as a reward for their prowess. They were settlers from Larissa in Thessaly, and had served[175] as allies to the kings from Seleucus I *Nicator* onwards in the first ranks of the cavalry force. He also made Iamblichus an ally,[176] the ruler of Arabia, who happened to have as ward[177] Antiochus, called *Epiphanes*, a mere child, the son of Alexander *Balas*. Placing, then, a diadem on his head and giving him the retinue suitable for a king, he restored him to his ancestral throne.[178] He assumed, indeed, which was reasonable, that the masses, eager for a change, would willingly receive the boy, because of the virtuousness of the previous[179] kings of this house and the lawlessness of the current ruler. And first, after collecting a moderate host, he pitched camp near the city of Chalcis,[180] situated on the borders of Arabia, capable of supporting forces staying there and of providing safety. From there, moving forward, he won over

---

[170] According to the editions by Dindorf and Fischer 1969: 67–8 and Walton 1967: 10–13; Goukowsky 2014: 23–4 counts it as Fr. 7.

[171] Newell 1918: 68 remarks that all drachms and tetradrachms struck at Antioch in the year 144 (year HΞP = 168 after the foundation of the Seleucid Empire) 'show the three letters TPY of *Tryphon*'s name and so bear witness to the preponderant position this man held in the government'. It appears, moreover, that '*Tryphon*' was less a nickname than a kind of dynastic name Diodotus had assumed.

[172] This episode should probably be placed after the bloodshed at Antioch.

[173] The text of the MS shows here a lacuna, but the context suggests the likely words to be substituted.

[174] The modern town of Shaizar, located somewhat to the north-west of modern Hama, on the River Orontes. It was also a tributary to the city of Apamea, where Diodotus himself originated from: see Str. 16.2.10/752.

[175] Again a small lacuna in the text of the MS and a supplement suggested by the context.

[176] 1 Maccabees 11:39 names this ruler Imalkue (Emalchuel), J. *AJ* 13.131 Malchus. He should not be confused with the Diocles mentioned above in 32.9d/10.1.

[177] Though the MS reads here παραθήκην ('*anything entrusted to* one, *deposit*': see LSJ, s.v.), I endorse, because of the context, the conjecture suggested by Müller and De Boor, namely παρακαταθήκην ('ward').

[178] The first coins I know of struck by Antiochus VI *Epiphanes* (more commonly *Dionysos*) are dated to 144: see Newell 1918: 62–5.

[179] I follow for this lacuna the conjecture by Herwerden, to supply here προτέρων, supplemented by a few words from Feder's suggestion, ἀπὸ ταύτης τῆς οἰκίας ('of this house').

[180] Chalcis *ad Belum*, modern Qinnasrīn, situated on the west bank of the River Queiq, some 25 km south-west of Aleppo and on the border of the desert region: see Mango 1991: 406. See also Grainger 1990b: 161.

the neighbouring peoples and prepared all the necessary supplies for war. At first Demetrius regarded him with contempt as some brigand, and ordered his soldiers to arrest him. Later, though, when *Tryphon* had gathered a force of unexpected size and was using the boy's restoration to the throne as the pretext for his own venture, Demetrius decided to send a commander against him.

[[*Cap.* 33.5.1–6 (Dindorf, Fischer/, and Walton as well as Goukowsky) deals with the struggle between the cities of Aradus (Arwad/Ruad Island/Antiochia in Pieria) and Marathus (Amrith). Though formally pertaining to Syria and therefore the (former) Persian Empire, the story itself is not relevant for our account.]]

S. 171:
33.18.1 (= *Const. Exc.* 2(1): 300):[181]

Parthians present themselves as new rulers:
(33.18.1) *King Arsaces,[182] pursuing virtuousness and humanity, gained an automatic stream of successes, and further enlarged his empire. Indeed, extending his power to India, he conquered the territory once ruled by Porus without a battle.[183] Though raised to such height of royal power, he cultivated not luxury {τρυφή} or arrogance, which usually accompany most ruling families, bur virtuousness towards his subjects, and courage towards his opponents. In short, having subdued many peoples, he made known to the Parthians the best of the customs practised by each.

S. 172:
33.28.1 (= *Const. Exc.* 3: 206):[184]

Diodotus Tryphon succeeds Antiochus VI:
(33.28.1) *In Syria, Diodotus called *Tryphon*, having killed Antiochus VI, the son of Alexander *Balas*, who was being raised to be king though he was a mere child,[185] put on the royal diadem.

---

[181] According to the editions by Dindorf and Fischer 1969: 78 and Walton 1967: 34–7; Goukowsky 2014: 33 counts it as Fr. 22.

[182] Most likely King Mithradates I *Arsaces V* (or possibly even VI) is intended: he ruled from 171 to 138 and appears to have been the first who called himself Šaḫinšaḫ ('King of kings'). See for this king, for example, <http://www.parthia.com/mithradates1.htm>; also Will 1982: 400–1.

[183] See Just. 41.6.6–8; also Oros. 5.4.16 for Arsaces' conquests.

[184] According to the editions by Dindorf and Fischer 1969: 82 and Walton 1967: 44–7; Goukowsky 2014: 26–7 counts it as Fr. 29.

[185] The numismatic evidence of Antioch suggests that *Tryphon* and Antiochus *Epiphanes* were joint rulers until at least 142, this being the earliest date a dethronement might be

The Vicissitudes of the Diadoch Kingdoms   517

Having seized the empty throne, he proclaimed himself king, and tried to make war against the satraps and commanders of the royal lineage.[186] In Mesopotamia there was Dionysius the Mede, in Coele Syria there were Sarpedon[187] and Palamedes, and in Seleucia by the Sea Aeschrio, accompanied by Queen Cleopatra, the wife of Demetrius, who had been captured by Arsaces.

[[In 33.28a.1, Diodorus relates how *Tryphon* tried to obtain a *senatus consultum*, but that the Senate deceived him, inscribing a gift by *Tryphon* with the name of the boy-king he had murdered and therefore denying him their support.]]

S. 173:
34/5.1.1–5 (= Phot. *Bibl.* [244] 379a35–b39):[188]

War against the Jews by King Antiochus VII:
(34/5.1.1) *King Antiochus, Diodorus says, besieged Jerusalem.[189] The Jews withstood the siege for some time, but when all their provisions were exhausted, they were forced to send ambassadors to him for a truce. Most of his companions urged him to take the city by storm and to kill the whole nation of the Jews. In fact, they alone of all peoples have no share in dealings with any other people and supposed all were enemies. *They pointed out that the Jews' -ancestors were driven out of the whole of Egypt, as impious and hateful to the gods.[190] (2) Indeed, by way of purification of the country, having gathered those having white or leprous marks on their bodies, by way of expiation they gathered them all together and drove them out of their county, as being under a curse. Those expelled occupied the region around Jerusalem,

---

suggested (though 141 is generally believed to be the year the young king died). The preserved fragment of Livy's book 55, however, suggests that the murder of young Antiochus took place in 137, when he was 10 years old.
    [186] There were still Demetrius II *Nicator* himself (even though he was held captive at the time by Arsaces V) and his queen, Cleopatra *Thea* (mother of the murdered Antiochus VI through her previous marriage to Alexander *Balas*). The events described should be dated to about 141/0 or slightly later, assuming Diodorus has got his data correct here.
    [187] Sarpedon appears to have met *Tryphon* or at least *Tryphon*'s men in battle on the Phoenician coast near modern Akko: see Str. 16.2.26/758 and Posid. = *FGrH/BNJ* 87 F 29 (= Ath. 8.333BD).
    [188] According to the editions by Dindorf and Fischer 1969: 85–6 and Walton 1967: 52–5; differing from them, Goukowsky 2014 does separate books 34 and 35. In his view this fragment belongs to book 34 and he lists it as Fr. 36a, a testimony, and Fr. 36b (Goukowsky 2014: 105–7).
    [189] The Antiochus intended is Antiochus VII *Euergetes Sidetes*, who ruled from 138 to 129. The events described here should be dated to 134. See also J. *AJ* 236–44 for a more or less parallel account.
    [190] This explanation of the Exodus returns in J. *Ap.* 1.229 and Man. *Hist.* 233–50, 279–87 [= Fr. 54, based upon J. *Ap.* 1.227–87 (equals 1.26–31)].

and having organised the nation of the Jews had made their hatred to mankind a tradition. Therefore they also introduced totally unusual laws: never to share the table with any other race or wish them any prosperity at all. (3) His companions reminded him also of the preceding hatred among his ancestors against this people. Indeed, Antiochus surnamed *Epiphanes*, after subduing the Jews [in 169 BC], had entered the innermost sanctuary of the temple of God, into which only the high priest was allowed to enter.[191] Finding in there the stone statue of a man with a long beard sitting upon an ass,[192] with a book in his hands, he supposed it to be an image of Moses, the founder of Jerusalem and organiser of the people, and moreover the man who established by law all the Jews' misanthropic and lawless customs. *Epiphanes*, detesting their antagonism to all other peoples, strove eagerly to abolish their laws. (4) Having, therefore, sacrificed a great sow at the image of the founder and at the altar of God that stood in the open air, he both sprinkled its blood over them and, having prepared its flesh, commanded that their holy books containing the xenophobic laws should be sprinkled with the broth of the meat. He also commanded them to extinguish the lamp, which they call immortal and which burns continually in the temple,[193] and that the high priest and the other Jews should be compelled to eat of the meat.

*Rehearsing all these events, his friends strongly urged Antiochus to root out the whole nation, or, failing that, to abolish their laws and force them to change their traditions. (5) But the king, being magnanimous and mild-mannered, taking hostages, dismissed the charges against the Jews, having exacted the tribute that was due and having demolished the walls of Jerusalem.

S. 174:
34/5.15.1–19.1 [various sources]:

Antiochus VII Euergetes Sidetes provokes a war with the Parthians:
(34/5.15.1 = *Const. Exc.* 4: 387–8)[194] *When the warm[195] spring heat had begun to melt the snow, and the crops, after the long period

---

[191] See J. *Ap.* 2.104.
[192] J. *Ap.* 2.79–89 pays attention to such allegations, specifically referring to Antiochus *Epiphanes*, notably a story spread by Apion but allegedly authored by Posidonius and/or Apollonius Molo in which an ass's head 'made of gold, and worth a great deal of money' is the prominent figure.
[193] See J. *Ap.* 2.106.
[194] According to the editions by Dindorf and Fischer 1969: 106–7 and Walton 1967: 102–5; Goukowsky 2014: 107 counts it as Fr. 37 of Diodorus' book 34.
[195] The word χλιά ('warm') is a hapax: see *LSJ* s.v.; for the situation see below, note 198.

of frost, were advancing into growth and sprouting, and men were resuming their work, Arsaces,[196] intending to probe his enemies, sent envoys to negotiate the terms of peace. In reply Antiochus said that he would agree to peace if Arsaces, releasing Antiochus' brother Demetrius from captivity, would hand him over, if he would evacuate the territories which he had occupied, and if, retaining his ancestral realm, he would pay tribute to Antiochus. Offended by the harshness of this response, Arsaces marched against Antiochus.
(34/5.16.1 = *Const. Exc.* 4: 387–8)[197] *The friends of Antiochus urged him not to engage battle with the Parthians, who were superior in numbers. In fact, taking refuge in the mountainous terrain that overlooked them, they could, through the difficult ground, neutralise the danger of the cavalry. Antiochus totally disregarded this advice, making it clear that it was shameful that the victors should fear the audacity of those they had previously defeated. Having exhorted, then, his friends to face the battle, he stoutly awaited the attack of the Parthians.[198]
(34/5.17.1 = *Const. Exc.* 4: 387–8)[199] *When the death of Antiochus became known at Antioch, not only did the city go into common mourning, but also every private house was full of dejection and lament, especially the wailing of women, bemoaning their grief.[200] In fact, because three hundred thousand men had been lost, including those who had accompanied the army outside the ranks,[201] there was no household found exempt from misfortune. Of the women, some mourned a brother, others a husband, again others a son, and many

---

[196] That is, Arsaces VI *Phraates II* (ruled c. 138–129/8), assuming the kingship apparently at a young age with his mother, Ri-'nu, acting as regent. The current episode is set in 130/29. The embassy mentioned in this sentence is not referred to by Justin, who paints a different picture (see Just. 38.10.7; see also App. *Syr.* 68 [359]).
[197] According to the editions by Dindorf and Fischer 1969: 107 and Walton 1967: 104–5; Goukowsky 2014: 107–8 counts it as Fr. 38 of Diodorus' book 34.
[198] The Parthian expansion westward had continued: in fact, in the years before these fragments are set, the Parthians had become masters of Media and Persis (as, for example, coins struck at Susa and Ecbatana testify to) as well as of Mesopotamia. In 130 Antiochus VII started a successful campaign against the Parthians (see, for example, Just. 38.10.6). In three battles, such as the Battle of the River Lycus (that is, the Upper Zab), the Parthians were defeated, making it possible for Antiochus VII to join Nearer Iran again to the Seleucid Empire, before taking winter quarters in Media for the winter of 130/29 (see below, the story of Antiochus' commander Athenaeus). In the spring of 129, Arsaces started the counterattack, killing Antiochus in battle and capturing or killing most of Antiochus' soldiers. The place where this battle took place is not mentioned. The reference to the superiority in numbers of Arsaces' army suggests that Antiochus had not yet got all his troops from their winter quarters. See also, for example, Ath. 10.439DE.
[199] According to the editions by Dindorf and Fischer 1969: 107 and Walton 1967: 104–5; Goukowsky 2014: 114 counts it as Fr. 1 of Diodorus' book 35.
[200] Just. 39.1.1 extends the mourning to the whole of Syria.
[201] Diodorus' numbers appear to differ from Justin's: the latter states (Just. 38.10.1–2) that Antiochus had an army of 80,000, accompanied by 300,000 non-combatants including cooks, bakers, and stage-players. Such a ratio seems, at the very least, quite odd and out of order.

girls and boys, having become orphans, wept for their own bereavement, until at last time, the best healer of pain, softened the edge of their grief.

(2 = *Const. Exc.* 2(1): 308)²⁰² *Athenaeus,²⁰³ Antiochus' commander, who had committed many wrongs when he put the army into quarters,²⁰⁴ being the first to flee, forsaking Antiochus, met the end he deserved. Indeed, when he came in his flight to some of the villages which he had mistreated when he quartered his men, nobody would admit him into their home or share food with him, but roaming up and down the country, he died at length from starvation.

Intentions of and measures by Arsaces:
(34/5.18.1 = *Const. Exc.* 4: 388–9)²⁰⁵ *Arsaces, king of the Parthians, after defeating Antiochus planned to invade Syria, hoping to make himself master of it easily. However, he was not able to make this expedition, because due to the magnitude of his accomplishments, Fate confronted him with many times as many dangers and misfortunes. [[I believe, indeed, that the deity does not give to mankind unalloyed blessings, but that the divine power, as if on purpose, adds some misfortune to fortune, some good to evil. And truly, Fate did not forget her proper nature, but as if weary of bestowing continual success, she brought about so great a reversal in the course of the whole war, that those who were previously successful were in the end humbled.²⁰⁶]]

(34/5.19.1 = *Const. Exc.* 4: 388–9)²⁰⁷ *Arsaces, king of the Parthians, was angry with the Seleucians²⁰⁸ and bore them a grudge for the despites and punishments that they had inflicted on his general Enius.²⁰⁹ When the Seleucians sent ambassadors to him, to beg forgiveness for what had happened, and wanted to have an answer, he led the ambassadors to the place where blind Pitthides sat on the

---

²⁰² According to the editions by Dindorf and Fischer 1969: 107–8 and Walton 1967: 104–7; Goukowsky 2014: 114 counts it as Fr. 2 of Diodorus' book 35.
²⁰³ This commander is, to the best of my knowledge, unknown beyond this in historiography.
²⁰⁴ Without mentioning Athenaeus' name, Justin paints a lively picture of the misery for Antiochus' army caused by quartering soldiers in the villages: Just. 38.10.5.
²⁰⁵ According to the editions by Dindorf and Fischer 1969: 108 and Walton 1967: 106–7; Goukowsky 2014: 115 counts it as Fr. 3 of Diodorus' book 35.
²⁰⁶ It is likely that Diodorus preludes here the death of Arsaces VI *Phraates II* in a battle against the Scythians, probably around 128. See also Just. 42.1.1–5; Will 1982: 414–15.
²⁰⁷ According to the editions by Dindorf and Fischer: 108 and Walton 1967: 106–9; Goukowsky 2014: 115 counts it as Fr. 4 of Diodorus' book 35.
²⁰⁸ That is, the people of Seleucia *ad Tigrum*, a city situated on the west bank of the Tigris opposite Ctesiphon.
²⁰⁹ Not known further in classical historiography.

The Vicissitudes of the Diadoch Kingdoms   521

ground, his eyes gouged out.²¹⁰ He ordered them to report to the Seleucians that they would all suffer the same fate. Terrified, they forgot their previous troubles in view of the enormity of the horrors that now threatened: men's new misery, indeed, always tends to obscure prior calamities.

S. 175:
34/5.21.1 (= *Const. Exc.* 2(1): 308–9):²¹¹

Most of the city of Babylon is destroyed:
(34/5.21.1) *Euhemerus,²¹² king of the Parthians, Hyrcanian as regards his descent, exceeded all recorded tyrants in cruelty and used every possible kind of punishment in the book. Enslaving many of the Babylonians along with their whole families for whatever reason he could think of, he sent them to Media with the order they should be sold as booty. He also set fire to the marketplace of Babylon and to some of the temples and destroyed the best part of the city.

S. 176:
34/5.28.1–3 [various sources]:

Vicissitudes of King Alexander II Zabinas:
(34/5.28.1 = *Const. Exc.* 2(1): 309)²¹³ *Alexander,²¹⁴ who had no confidence in the multitude because of both their inexperience of the

---

²¹⁰ Pitthides is probably identical with the Elamite King Pittit. The Arsacid king, Frahād II (= Arsaces VI *Phraates II*), makes clear to the Seleucids what they might expect. The chronology of Diodorus, though, seems a bit suspect. See Shayegan 2011: 117–20 and relevant notes.
²¹¹ According to the editions by Dindorf and Fischer 1969: 109 and Walton 1967: 108–9; Goukowsky 2014: 116 counts it as Fr. 6 of Diodorus' book 35. The events in this fragment should probably be dated to 127/6.
²¹² In other sources this man is known as Himerus. Posidonius calls him the 'tyrant' of the Babylonians and Seleucians: *FGrH/BNJ* 87 F 12 (= Ath. 11.466BC): Ποσειδώνιος δ' ἐν ἰζ̄ τῶν Ἱστοριῶν Λυσίμαχόν φησι τὸν Βαβυλώνιον, καλέσαντα ἐπὶ δεῖπνον Ἵμερον τὸν τυραννήσαντα οὐ μόνον Βαβυλωνίων ἀλλὰ καὶ Σελευκέων ('Posidonius in book 16 of his *Histories* says that Lysimachus the Babylonian invited to dinner Himerus, who had become tyrant not only of the Babylonians but also of the people of Seleucia'); see also Just. 42.1.3: *Igitur Phrahates, cvm adversvs eos proficisceretvr, ad tvtelam regni reliqvit Himervm quendam pveritiae sibi flore conciliatvm, qvin tyrannica crvdelitate oblitvs et vitae praeteritae et vicarii officii Babylonios mvltasqve alias civitates inportvne vexavit* ('So, when Phraates set out against the Scythians, he left in charge of the kingdom one Himerus, who appealed to him for his boyish prettiness, though with tyrannical savagery Himerus forgot both his previous life and his duty as a deputy and inflicted a great deal of trouble on the Babylonians and many other states'). For Himerus see also Otto 1913. See also Will 1982: 416; Boiy 2004: 175–6.
²¹³ According to the editions by Dindorf and Fischer 1969: 111–12 and Walton 1967: 116–17; Goukowsky 2014: 119–20 counts it as Fr. 14 of Diodorus' book 35. The events described should be dated to shortly before or in 122.

hazards of war and also their craving for change, did not venture to join battle. He planned to get together the royal treasures and steal the offerings to the gods, and with these to slip away by night towards Greece. Being detected while attempting, with the help of some of his foreign helpers, to plunder the temple of Zeus, he and his accomplices almost suffered the fitting punishment. However, having managed to escape with a few men, he tried to flee to Seleucia.[215] Because the news outran him, the Seleucians, having heard about the sacrilege, barred him from the city. Having failed in this attempt as well, he hurried to seek refuge at Posidium,[216] keeping to the sea-coast.

(2 = *Const. Exc.* 4: 390–1)[217] *After his sacrilege Alexander fled to Posidium. As it seems, he was pursued by the divine power, invisible, following at his heels, operating to effect his punishment that ensnared him to receive the fitting penalty. In fact, two days after his sacrilege, he was arrested and taken to Antiochus in his camp. . . . Indeed, one moment he was king and led forty thousand soldiers, the next he was led in chains to insult and punishment by his enemies.

(3 = *Const. Exc.* 4: 390–1)[218] *When Alexander, king of Syria, was led in chains through the camp, it seemed incredible, not only to those who heard of it but even to those who saw it. Indeed, the expectation that it could never happen was forcibly reversed by the evidence of their senses. However, when the truth had been confirmed by seeing it, they all turned away from the sight in amaze-

---

[214] Alexander II *Zabinas* was a so-called counter-king, who emerged in the chaos following the Seleucid loss of Mesopotamia to the Parthians. He claimed to be an adoptive son of Antiochus VII *Euergetes Sidetes*, but in fact was said to have been the son of an Egyptian merchant. Nevertheless, several Syrian cities acknowledged the authority of Alexander, even though he was a figurehead of the Egyptian king Ptolemy VIII *Physcon*. Allegedly, the name 'Zabinas' means 'the purchased slave', and is said to have been applied to him because rumour had it that he was bought by Ptolemy as a slave. Having lost the latter's support, Alexander was defeated by Demetrius' son Antiochus VIII *Grypus*. *Zabinas* fled to the Seleucid capital Antioch, where he plundered several temples. Enraged, the Antiochians cast him out of the city. He soon fell into the hands of robbers, who delivered him up to Antiochus, by whom he was put to death in 122: see Just. 39.1.1–2.10; J. *AJ* 13.9 [267–9].

[215] With a view to the context, this Seleucia must have been Seleucia *ad mare* or Seleucia Pieria. Seleucia Pieria (later Suedia) was the capital of Seleucus I *Nicator*, in Syria Prima, and founded c. 300. The city was built slightly north of the estuary of the River Orontes: it functioned as the commercial and naval seaport of the western Seleucid capital of Antioch ad Orontem. See also Str. 16.2.8/751.

[216] Modern Rasel-Bassit, situated somewhat south of the Orontes next to Cape Bassit. See also Str. 16.2.8/751, who calls it a πολίχνη ('small town').

[217] According to the editions by Dindorf and Fischer 1969: 112 and Walton 1967: 116–19; Goukowsky 2014: 120 counts it as Fr. 15 of Diodorus' book 35.

[218] According to the editions by Dindorf and Fischer 1969: 112–13 and Walton 1967: 118–19; Goukowsky 2014: 120–1 counts it as Fr. 16 of Diodorus' book 35.

ment. Some applauded the power of destiny in frequent exclamations of approval; others remarked in various ways on the fickleness of Fate, the reversals in human fortunes, the sudden turns of the tide, and how changeable life could be, far beyond what anyone could expect.[219]

S. 177:
34/5.39a.1 (= *Const. Exc.* 4: 392):[220]

Ptolemy IX stays in Seleucia Pieria:
*When the elder Ptolemy was shut up in the city of Seleucia,[221] a plot against him was formed by one of his companions. Having captured him, Ptolemy punished him, but henceforth he no longer had complete trust in his companions.

[[There are some loose sentences referring to occurrences in Persian history in 37.1.1–4, comparing those with the achievements of the Romans: these sentences are not sufficiently coherent and relevant to Diodorus' account of the history of Persia – in its wider sense – to be incorporated in this review. In the fragments we have, the further emergence of the Parthians has not been preserved, if Diodorus described it at all. However, the end of the Seleucid Empire is alluded to in the following fragment.]]

S. 178:
40.1a.1–1b.1 (= *Const. Exc.* 3: 210–11):[222]

Antiochus XIII faces a revolt:
(40.1a.1) *Some of the citizens of Antioch, feeling contempt for Antiochus because of his defeat,[223] stirred up the masses and

---

[219] For Alexander's fate see, for example, the remarks of Justin and Josephus (see above, note 214). Eusebius, perhaps basing his account upon Porphyry, remarks that Alexander poisoned himself, unable to accept his defeat: FGrH/BNJ 260 F 32.23.
[220] According to the editions by Dindorf and Fischer 1969: 121 and Walton 1967: 140–1; Goukowsky 2014: 129–30 counts it as Fr. 32 of Diodorus' book 35.
[221] The story deals with Ptolemy IX *Philometor Soter*, nicknamed *Lathyrus* ('chickpea'), who fled from his mother, Cleopatra III, in 108/7, found refuge in Seleucia Pieria in 106, and remained there for several years. The events described in this fragment should be dated to about 105/4.
[222] According to the editions by Dindorf and Fischer 1969: 178–9 and Walton 1967: 274–7; Goukowsky 2014: 295–6 counts them as Frr. 2 and 3.
[223] The Antiochus intended is Antiochus XIII *Dionysus Philopator Kallinikos*, also named *Asiaticus* because he was raised in Asia Minor: he ruled the Seleucid Empire from 69 to 64. In 64, Pompey had him deposed and killed by a Syrian chieftain, Sampsiceramus I: see also App. *Syr.* 8.49, 11.70; Just. 40.2.2. Though being briefly succeeded by Philip II *Philoromaeus* (also nicknamed *Barypous*, 'heavy-foot'), Antiochus' death is traditionally said to have ended the

proposed that the king should be banished from the city. After there was a great tumult and the king prevailed, the leaders of the uprising took fright and fled from Syria. After reaching Cilicia, they decided to bring back Philip. He was the son of Philip I *Philadelphus* who was the offspring of Antiochus *Grypus*. After Philip agreed to their proposal, he arranged to meet Azizus the Arab,[224] who willingly received him. Azizus, putting a diadem on Philip's head, restored him to the kingship.

(40.1b.1) *Resting all his hopes on his alliance with Sampsiceramus,[225] he[226] summoned him to come with his forces. Sampsiceramus, who had secretly agreed with Azizus to kill the kings, came with his force and sent for Antiochus. Because the latter complied unawares, Sampsiceramus seized the king, though pretending to be a friend. For the time being he held him captive in chains, but later he killed him. In a similar way Azizus, in accordance with their agreement to divide up the kingdom of Syria, attempted to assassinate Philip. However, having become aware of the plot, Philip fled to Antioch.

[[Philip died in 63, ending the Seleucid family. In 64, Pompey the Great had marched into Syria and constituted this as a Roman province. In 63, he moved south and established Roman supremacy in Phoenicia and Coele Syria.]]

Seleucid dynasty. See also Downey 1961: 136–72. Though the specific context of the defeat Diodorus alludes to eludes us, the events described in the fragments should probably be dated to about 65/4.

[224] Probably the same person as the Arab ruler Zizon mentioned in J. *AJ* 13.384, who (together with troops from the Parthian Empire) helped Philip I *Philadelphus* in his struggle against his brother Demetrius III *Eucaerus Philopator*. The latter was defeated and ended his life in imprisonment in Parthia in 88. It appears that Aziz(us) was the father of Sampsiceranus: see Temporini and Haase 1978: 201.

[225] Sampsiceramus, of Bedouin descent (see Birley 2002: 71), settled in the Orontes Valley and there established the so-called Emesani dynasty, centred on Emesa, modern Homs in Syria.

[226] The context makes it clear that the subject of this sentence is Antiochus XIII.

10 Semiramis' Legacy

Semiramis: general remarks

Having concluded Diodorus' account of the history of Persia (in its wider sense), the time has come to assess the story from its very beginning. The most prominent figure in the early phases in Diodorus' *Library* is doubtless the Assyrian Queen Semiramis (in the Armenian version of her story Շամիրամ (Šamiram)).[1] The way she has been portrayed by Diodorus certainly does not match with the life and actions of an actual historical character. Nevertheless, 'Semiramis' as such is not a *complete* historical fiction,[2] even though Robin Lane Fox describes her as 'an invention of Greek legend only'.[3] Strabo records that

---

[1] The Armenian stories about Semiramis are generally (much) less flattering than the one given by Ctesias/Diodorus. For our discussion here, however, they are not relevant: for those interested a general view may be acquired by notably the second volume of the books that accompanied an exhibition in Berlin: Marzahn et al. 2008.

[2] For clarity's sake I will use Semiramis as the persona in the sources, 'Semiramis' as the idea she represents.

[3] Lane Fox 2008: 187: 'Nearchus recorded that Alexander's march into the dreaded Gedrosian desert in south-east Iran in late 325 B.C. was partly motivated by his rivalry with "Queen Semiramis" and her march into this same region. The locals, he wrote, told of her exploit, but they cannot have said such a thing: Semiramis was an invention of Greek legend only.' Though Lane Fox is largely right, I think he slightly misses the point: the issue is not whether or not the Gedrosians may have said that Semiramis had been there, but that the Greeks firmly believed (or stated they believed) she had, much as they believed that Heracles had been in the region, and tried to emulate their actions. It certainly strengthened their interests in the regions east of Persis. Nearchus' remark is taken from Arr. *An.* 6.24.2 (= *FGrH/BNJ* 133 F 3a). That 'Semiramis' was an invention of Greek legend *only* (my emphasis) seems not to be corroborated by the remarks of Eusebius of Caesarea (Eus. PE 10.9.10–11, 17; the Armenian version of his *Chronicle*), though it is in my view quite feasible that his sources were contaminated. As a matter of fact, in Eus. PE 10.9.17 Eusebius puts the date of Semiramis 800 years before the Trojan War (ἡ δὲ Σεμίραμις τῶν Τρωϊκῶν ὀκτακοσίοις ὅλοις ἔτεσι δείκνυται προγενομένη).

525

καὶ τῆς Σεμιράμιδος χωρὶς τῶν ἐν Βαβυλῶνι ἔργων πολλὰ καὶ ἄλλα κατὰ πᾶσαν γῆν σχεδὸν δείκνυται ὅση τῆς ἠπείρου ταύτης ἐστί, τά τε χώματα ἃ δὴ καλοῦσι Σεμιράμιδος, καὶ τείχη καὶ ἐρυμάτων κατασκευαὶ καὶ συρίγγων τῶν ἐν αὐτοῖς καὶ ὑδρείων καὶ κλιμάκων καὶ διωρύγων ἐν ποταμοῖς καὶ λίμναις καὶ ὁδῶν καὶ γεφυρῶν

('Many other works of Semiramis, besides those at Babylon, are extant in almost every part of this continent [Asia], for example, artificial mounds, which are called mounds of Semiramis; and walls; and fortresses, with subterraneous passages; cisterns for water; roads to facilitate the ascent of mountains; canals communicating with rivers and lakes; roads; and bridges.' Str. 16.1.2/737)[4]

Herodotus mentions Semiramis as the one who constructed the dykes that constrained the Euphrates (Hdt. 1.184) and the one whose name was given to one of the gates of Babylon (Hdt. 3.155.5), and finally we have been able to read in the *Bibliotheca* that Semiramis' name has even been connected with the Bisitun inscription (2.13.1-2), a feat Diodorus appears to record on the basis of the story by Ctesias of Cnidus.[5]

Though Semiramis looks to be, therefore, (largely) a creation of Greek imagination, several places in Assyria, throughout Mesopotamia, Media, Persia, the Levant, Asia Minor, Arabia, and the Caucasus, either bore (or are stated to have borne) the name of Semiramis or in another manner retained it.[6] It has even been asserted that the original name of the city of Van was Šamiramagerd (that is: 'Created by Šamiram'), a name given at the time Armenia was included in the Assyrian Empire.[7] It seems therefore, to some extent at least, possible to suggest that there might have been a real figure hidden behind this literary, if not legendary, character. Even though the number of Assyrian successors after Semiramis was allegedly twenty-nine (see 2.23.1) – suggesting many centuries of rulers – Semiramis looks to have been largely fashioned after two Neo-Assyrian queens.

In all likelihood the literary Semiramis[8] has taken her character and power not only from mortal models (allegedly both the Assyrian Queen Šammu-ramāt and Naqi'a/Zakûtu, the Aramaean wife of

---

[4] All of these elements mentioned by Strabo we have encountered in Chapter 2.
[5] See also Stronk 2010: 22-5; 2014/15: *ad loc.*
[6] See, for example, Plin. *Nat.* 6.3.8, 25.92.
[7] See Smith 1833: 17. The author is heavily guided, as perhaps might be expected, by inspired reading of the Bible.
[8] As we have seen above, Diodorus, basing his account upon Ctesias, is neither the only author nor the first who describes her; see also, for example, Eilers 1971 and especially Pettinato 1988: 305-8. See also the *TLG* *sub* *SEM/IRAMIS and *SEMIR/AMIDOS (both entries in Betacode)] > 'Textual search' for a comprehensive view of authors on Semiramis.

Sennacherib), but also from the immortal Ištar/Astarte/Inanna (see Phillips 1968: 163-4; Gardiner-Garden 1987: 5).[9] Phillips adds that:

> from the Babylonian and Assyrian evidence we gather that the goddess of the [Kassite] country and particularly of Behistun [Bisitun] was Shimaliya, who had much in common with the Babylonian Ishtar, and could, like her, have been later absorbed into the figure of Queen Semiramis. (Phillips 1968: 167)

It appears, therefore, that one might describe the persona Semiramis, portrayed by Ctesias (and consequently Diodorus), as a thoroughly syncretistic (and thus largely fictional) character that, one way or another, has found itself, as such, a position within Greek historiography. I think efforts to connect 'Semiramis' with actual occurrences in Assyrian history are therefore *largely* useless, though it may be relevant to look at how 'Semiramis' was used by Greeks to explain the course of events, notably in the East.

Semiramis: Šammu-ramāt
Though it is, as stated above, *largely* useless to combine 'Semiramis' with actual *events* in Assyrian history, it seems fitting to expound at least the basic outlines of the main personae involved in the creation of 'Semiramis'. The historical Šammu-ramāt was the wife of King Šamši-Adad V, who ruled the Neo-Assyrian Empire from 824 to 811, after the fierce internal struggle following the rebellion of *Ašur-nadin-aplu* against his father Šalmaneser III.[10] After Šamši-Adad V's death, Šammu-ramāt was the regent of the realm during five years, until their son, Adad-nirari III came of age, in or about 806. In her days in power, first as wife and queen, second as regent, the Neo-Assyrian Empire comprised Assyria itself and the

---

[9] One of Astarte's symbols (bull, lioness, and sphinx are among the others) was the dove, and it appears she was also depicted with the dove of wisdom on (Phoenician) coinage (see Walker 1983: 253-4). In itself this reference appears to link Ctesias' story as described in 2.4 rather neatly with Ascalon (and with Aphrodite, who is likewise associated with Astarte). See also Du Mesnil du Buisson 1973: 80, where he describes the dove as the hypostasis of Astarte, then as her attribute; see also pp. 235-40 and figs. 124-7. As regards Semiramis and doves: Assyrian *summatu(m)* means 'dove', but it is a long stretch to connect Semiramis or, for that matter, Šammu-ramāt with *summatu(m)*. For this (or rather, more in general, for Semiramis and the animal world) see also Capomacchia 1986: 57-9. The link with Derceto (and fish) is found in Luc. *Syr.D.* 14, while in Luc. *Syr.D.* 33 the possibility of a statue in the great temple at Hierapolis (in Greek Bambyce, in Syrian Ma(n)bog) of Semiramis with a golden dove on her head is mentioned, while in *Syr.D.* 39 a statue of Semiramis outside this temple is referred to, as is in *caput* 40. In that same *caput* Lucian (who originated from nearby Samosata) also mentions a statue outside the temple showing Sardanapallus dressed as a woman, a feature referred to by Ctesias as well and repeated by Diodorus.
[10] Šalmaneser III ruled from c. 859 to 824. The last years of his reign were marked by a rebellion led by his eldest son, *Ašur-nadin-aplu*. After four years, the rebellion was quashed by Šalmaneser's second son, who as Šamši-Adad V also succeeded Šalmaneser after the latter's death.

neighbouring areas of Mesopotamia (to slightly further south than the city of Babylon), Syria, Asia Minor, and Iran (see Figure 2.1, above). Georges Roux rightly remarks that Šammu-ramāt's reign has left hardly a trace in Assyrian records (Roux 1992: 301 and 476 *ad* chapter 19 note 2). How she acquired her formidable reputation in notably Greek but also Iranian (especially Median) traditions (see Roux 1992: 301-2) cannot be substantiated. However, 'Diodorus' account of the Semiramis legend has met with an enormous success, notably in Western Europe, until the beginning of this century [the twentieth century AD]' (Roux 1992: 302).

The impressive list of Assyrian conquests, ascribed by Ctesias (and Diodorus) to Ninus and Semiramis, in fact really started (again) after the regency of Šammu-ramāt.[11] In 806, Adad-nirari III took the reins of power, invaded the Levant, and subsequently subjugated the Arameans, Phoenicians, Philistines, Israelites, Neo-Hittites, and Edomites. He entered Damascus and extracted tribute from its king Ben-Hadad III. Next, he turned to Iran and subjugated those of the Persians who were not yet under Assyrian rule, Medes, and Manneans,[12] and penetrated as far as the Caspian Sea. His next targets were the Chaldean and Sutu tribes of south-eastern Mesopotamia, whom he conquered and reduced to vassalage as well (see Figure 2.1, above).

Semiramis: Naqi'a/Zakûtu

As indicated, part of 'Semiramis" identity (for lack of a better word) was derived as well from Naqi'a/Zakûtu, the wife of Sennacherib, who was the Assyrian ruler from 704 to 681 and the direct heir of Sargon II. During one of the many rebellions he had to face, he destroyed Babylon, in 689 (see: *ARAB*, vol. 2: §§339-41; *ABC*: 80-1 is less outspoken). The act could be construed (and has been construed) as sacrilege: Sennacherib was duly punished by being

---

[11] At the beginning of the Neo-Assyrian period, c. 900, notably during the reigns of Adad-nirari II (911-891) and Ašurnasirpal II (883-859) there had been a policy of expansion, which was largely abandoned by their successors because these had to cope with various rebellions. Naturally, the Middle Assyrian period (c. 1365-1075 BC) had known a significant territorial expansion as well, but I do not believe that period to have had any relevance to the accounts in Greek historiography, even taking into account Eusebius' remark on 'Semiramis" date referred to above, note 3. Nevertheless, an inscription of Adad-nirari III (*RIMA* 3 A.0.104.3: 7b-10a) confirms that Šammu-ramāt, 'the palace woman', conducted a trans-Euphrates campaign (to the west, therefore) together with Adad-nirari III.

[12] The Manneans (that is, the Minni of the Bible, sometimes equated with Arameans) lived in the territory of present-day north-western Iran, south of Lake Urmia. At that time they were neighbours of the empires of Assyria and Urartu, as well as other small buffer states between the two, such as Musasir and Zikirta.

killed in 681.¹³ One of Sennacherib's major feats is the enlarging, fortifying, and embellishing of the city of Nineveh, turning it – as Roux phrases it – 'into a capital-city worthy of the vast empire it commanded' (Roux 1992: 323; see also pp. 323-4 for a description of the city). During the reign of Esarhaddon, who was the son of Naqi'a/Zakûtu and Sennacherib and the latter's successor, from 681 onwards Naqi'a/Zakûtu supervised the reconstruction of Babylon, the city that had been destroyed by her husband (see Roux 1992: 301, 325-6). We might, therefore, at least suggest that the Sennacherib–Naqi'a/Zakûtu couple at least partly embodies the elements of Nineveh and Babylon in the (Ninus and) Semiramis version as related by Ctesias and after him by Diodorus.

Semiramis in Diodorus' work (1)
At this stage it seems right to me to recapitulate a few of the elements we have established so far:

- We know, if only from his references, that Diodorus knew the work of Ctesias of Cnidus.
- From his references we also know that Diodorus knew the work of Clitarchus and we might possibly infer he knew that of Dinon as well.
- As we have discussed in the relevant chapters, the account of 'Semiramis' by Diodorus contains elements that seem to be linked with the stories of Alexander.
- Nevertheless Diodorus claims that his account of 'Semiramis' is completely based upon Ctesias' story, showing it both by his references and by his use of the indirect form.
- At first sight this appears to be a historical impossibility, a complete anachronism, because the Assyrians never went as far to the East as Alexander did. Nevertheless the remark by Nearchus, referred to by Lane Fox, puts this element in an altogether different perspective. Evidently, Ctesias' (and therewith Diodorus') account is not a matter of historical *fact* but of historical *belief* or perhaps rather of a *concept* of history (see below, 'Semiramis and the East').

In my *Ctesias' Persian History* (Stronk 2010: 64-7) I wrote that like Dinon, Clitarchus may have used and adapted Ctesias' work,

---

¹³ One of his sons murdered him while praying, or, according to another version, he was crushed by the winged bulls that protected the sanctuary where he went to pray: see Roux 1992: 323 and 480 *ad* note 15.

in the process – perhaps – transforming Ninus and Semiramis into the central personae of an already familiar cycle. Diodorus may well have used both Ctesias and the adapted version of his work by Dinon and/or Clitarchus for his own purposes (see also Gardiner-Garden 1987: 8–9 and notes 39 and 40). Notably in this respect, I wrote, Nicholas of Damascus (*FGrH/BNJ* 90 F 1) also refers to an Indian War of Semiramis, indicating either that this war had already been described by Ctesias himself or that Nicholas also used the adapted version of his work by, probably, Dinon and/or Clitarchus. If the former is the case, I then concluded, 'the transformation of Semiramis started at least as early as the last quarter of the 5th century and is correctly reflected by Ctesias and through him by Diodorus' (Stronk 2010).

A particular position in the whole process of transmission may well have been played by Dinon, as both Schwartz (1903b) and Jacoby observe. Jacoby even states that

> Dinon scheint in hellenistischer Zeit allerdings das Hauptbuch gewesen zu sein . . . . Sie fußte in ihren älteren Teilen offensichtlich ganz auf K[tesias], natürlich mit der Maßgabe, daß Dinon ihn in der Richtung effektvoll-rhetorischer Ausgestaltung zu übertreffen suchte, ihn variirte und durch solche Mittel die stoffliche Abhängigkeit verdeckte, ganz wie es K[tesias] selbst mit Herodot gemacht hat. (Jacoby 1922: 2069)

Semiramis and the East

In my 2010 book I stated that I was not yet ready to decide what the relation was between Ctesias, Dinon, Clitarchus, and Diodorus. I think I am now, as I announced in Chapter 1, discussing book 2. The starting point must be, I think, the extent of the Achaemenid Empire in Ctesias' days. Following the (Greek) idea of the continuity of empire (Liverani 2003: 1–2), already fashionable in his days, Ctesias painted an idea of Ninus and Semiramis (the first name eponymous, linked with the city of Nineveh; the second, as discussed, a largely syncretistic character, partly linked with the reconstruction of Babylon) as conquerors of the world more or less known to him, the founders of an all-encompassing empire, as if paving the way for the (real and/or alleged) conquests of Cyrus the Great in the East and the expansion realised by Darius I the Great.[14] The situation looks,

---

[14] See, for example, Plin. *Nat.* 6.18.49 on the town of Panda in Sogdia: *arae ibi svnt ab Hercvle ac Libero Patre constitvtae, item Cyro et Samiramide atque Alexandro: finis omnivm eorvm dvctvs ab illa parte terrarvm, inclvdente flvmine Iaxarte* ('Here are altars set up by Heracles and Dionysus, and also by Cyrus and Samiramis and by Alexander, all of them finding their boundary in this region of the world, confined by the River Yaxartes').

Semiramis' Legacy 531

however, more complex, because, it appears, Ctesias (and therefore Diodorus) does not merely reflect Greek notions. The reliefs on the staircase of the *apadāna* in Persepolis show that at least in the imperial *concept* (my emphasis), or perhaps even the state ideology, of the Achaemenids, notably 'India' (as well as some other contested areas) was part of the realm and therefore, by necessity, all the territory between India and the Persian heartland. Table 10.1 clearly depicts the origin of different delegations depicted on the Persepolis *apadāna* relief, underlining the alleged might of the Achaemenids.

Combining these elements, I think it feasible that Ctesias infers 'Ninus' as the conqueror of Bactria (with 'Semiramis' contributing) who laid the foundation of a large empire, and 'Semiramis' as the one who both completed it, by 'adding' (or at least claiming) India, and underlined its unity by her tour throughout the empire, visiting countries as far away as Egypt and Ethiopia.[15] In his description he almost mirrors the exploits of the Achaemenid kings up to his days. He uses elements more or less known to him, and therefore we need not be surprised, for example, that the Indian king deployed elephants against 'Semiramis' and that 'Semiramis' used a decoy to surprise her adversary – even though the development of using elephants in warfare only took place between the sixth and fourth centuries (see above, Chapter 2, note 132). The necessary next step is to acknowledge that Nicholas of Damascus also includes an invasion by 'Semiramis' in India in his account (see *FGrH* 90 F 1 in Stronk 2010: 254–7): he was a slightly younger contemporary of Diodorus and therefore cannot be regarded as a candidate source-author of Diodorus. His work, however, implies either that Ctesias had incorporated into his *Persica* an invasion by 'Semiramis' in India (I believe he did so, even though I do not know of corroborating evidence: however, see below) or that Nicholas worked not from Ctesias as his source but from Clitarchus and/or Dinon.[16] Taking all this together, I think, the element of continuity of empire

---

[15] Egypt takes a particular place in the list. Though it had been part of the Assyrian Empire (through Adad-nirari II, 911–891, temporarily overthrowing King Osorkon I of the 22nd dynasty), it had freed itself afterwards. Only Esarhaddon succeeded in conquering Egypt again, in 671, chasing Pharaoh Taharqa back to Nubia and thus bringing to an end Nubian-Kushite rule in all Egypt and effectively destroying the Kushite dynasty, which had begun in 760. (Although Taharqa was succeeded by Tantamani, who tried to invade Egypt from Nubia, the dynasty never ruled the whole of Egypt again.) Esarhaddon describes his actions as follows: 'Memphis, his royal city, . . ., I besieged, I captured, I destroyed, I devastated, I burned with fire' and 'The root of Ethiopia (Kush) I tore up out of Egypt and not one therein escaped to submit to me. Over all of Egypt I appointed anew kings, viceroys, governors, commandants, overseers (and) scribes' (*ARAB*, vol. 2, §580).

[16] Whether Nicholas also added some saucy details (whether or not derived from Clitarchus and/or Dinon) to the story is, I think, not relevant to this discussion.

Table 10.1. Provenance of delegations presenting gifts on the relief of the east staircase of the apadāna at Persepolis (based upon Junge 1941; Schmidt 1953; Barnett 1957; Walser 1966; Herzfeld 1968; Roaf 1983; Moorey 1988b).

Delegation number	Suggested provenance	Identification status	Suggested alternatives
I	Media	Undisputed	
II	Elam	Undisputed	
III	Armenia	Disputed	Armenia I (Herzfeld)
IV	Aria	Disputed	Arachosia; Drangia
V	Babylonia	Undisputed	
VI	Syria	Disputed	Lydia (Barnett; Roaf; Moorey)
VII	Arachosia	Disputed	Aria; Drangia (Roaf)
VIII	Assyria	Disputed	Sogdia (Barnett); Cilicia
IX	Cappadocia	Undisputed	
X	Egypt	Undisputed	
XI	Scythia (*Saka*)	Undisputed	
XII	Ionia	Disputed	Lydia (Walser)
XIII	Bactria	Disputed	Parthia
XIV	Gandara	Undisputed (largely)	*Maka*? (suggested by Moorey)
XV	Parthia	Disputed	Bactria
XVI	Sagartia	Disputed	'Doubtful' (Roaf; Moorey); Armenia II (Herzfeld)
XVII	Sogdia	Disputed	Chorasmia
XVIII	India	Undisputed	
XIX	*Skudra* (Thrace)	Undisputed (largely)	(Roaf leaves this open)
XX	Arabia	Undisputed	
XXI	Caria	Disputed	Lydia; Drangia; Akofaciya; Media
XXII	Libya	Undisputed (largely)	Putaiya [Oman] (Herzfeld)
XXIII	Nubia/Ethiopia	Undisputed	

is one of the backbones of Diodorus' history of 'Persia', irrespective of the various embellishments that subsequent authors added. Achaemenid state ideology seems to me to have been a second key element for the construction of Ctesias' account at least.

Semiramis' Legacy

For Greek embellishments we might, perhaps, think of the details of the siege of Bactra (mirroring (alleged) occurrences during the expedition of Alexander) and, possibly, details of Alexander's war against Porus. We only can guess who the *auctores* of those embellishments were, because any firm evidence is lacking.[17] However, as I indicated before, Dinon and/or Clitarchus might be excellent candidates. Both were to some extent familiar with the surroundings described and therefore able to present a sufficiently coherent and/or credible account of events unfolding, perhaps also including a detail like the visit by 'Semiramis' to the oracle of Ammon (probably that of the Siwa oasis) in Egypt (again mirroring an element from the Alexander story).[18] Combining their accounts with Ctesias', Diodorus himself no doubt added yet another layer (in fact, therefore, the third strand) to the first two main themes, namely those of Stoic morality, most significantly the search (or absence of it, for example in a lust for luxuriousness, τρυφή) for *aretē*, and the examples this provided for his audience. Perhaps he also added some parallels between Semiramis and Cyrus and between the ascent to power of Arbaces and that of Cyrus (Stronk in preparation). However, as stated above, I believe such elements, telling as they may be, are probably of somewhat subordinate relevance to the essential themes of first Ctesias and after him Diodorus – who, I now believe, did indeed use Ctesias' *Persica* as his main source for this episode.

Diodorus and the ideologies of empire

The idea of continuity of empire also played an obvious role in (the presentation of) the conquests of Alexander, shown as the rightful successor of the Achaemenids. As such, however, it was also made believe (rightly or not) that his goal was to be *šar kib-rāt erbe-tim* ('king of the four corners [of the earth]'), one of the classic epithets of the Neo-Assyrian kings.[19] For example, Alexander's wish to go to

---

[17] There are several possibilities as to how, for example, the alleged events at Bactra have come to us, including, to name but a few, that Ctesias invented such a story and that it was accepted by Diodorus; or that Alexander was inspired by Ctesias and put into practice the latter's idea, with Arrian modelling his story after Ctesias'; or that the story was invented by Dinon or Clitarchus but was inserted into Ctesias' account by Diodorus and into the story on Alexander by Arrian. Regrettably we will probably never know, unless a complete manuscript of Ctesias' *Persica* emerges. Then the number of possibilities might be reduced.
[18] In Diodorus' account (2.14.3) it is unclear whether he took this visit from Ctesias' *Persica* or inferred it from another source.
[19] The title was used together with the phrase *šar kiššati šar māt Aššur* ('king of the world, king of Assyria': see, for example, inscription *RIMA* 3.A.0.104.2001 of Adad-nirari III). In the Bisitun inscription, Darius phrased it differently but with a similar implication: *adam ... xšāyaϑia: xšāyaϑiy | ānām: xšāyaϑia: Pārsaiy: xšāyaϑia: dahyūnām* ('I am ... King of Kings, | King in Persia, King of countries': *DB*, I.1–2; Kent 1953: 116, 119).

the Indian Ocean was presented as a consequence of this notion (see Chapter 6), but here too 'Semiramis' and Cyrus the Great appear to re-emerge as a source of inspiration (also reflected in Pliny's account; see above, note 14), as indicated by Nearchus' remark referred to by Lane Fox. In Arrian's *Anabasis Alexandri*, the source for Lane Fox's remark, it is stated *expressis verbis*: καὶ ταῦτα Ἀλεξάνδρῳ ἐξαγγελλόμενα ἔριν ἐμβαλεῖν πρὸς Κῦρον καὶ Σεμίραμιν ('And this prompted great rivalry in Alexander with Cyrus and Semiramis': Arr. *An.* 6.24.3). This remark is therefore important, not only because it paints a picture of Alexander's alleged motives, but above all because Nearchus' words – *if presented correctly* – seem to imply that the theme of 'Semiramis'' expansion of empire (and, for that matter Cyrus', as Arrian adds) predates any embellishments in the account by either Clitarchus and/or Dinon. To some extent, one might add, it even fuses the Greek concept and Achaemenid ideology.

It reflects a piece of Achaemenid state ideology, also expressed by Darius' charging Scylax of Caryanda to navigate the River Indus and the Persian Gulf (Hdt. 4.44.1–2), which appears as a mission to reinforce the imperial ideological claim of a more or less universal power.[20] It seems that it is, therefore, an ideology that predates Ctesias and even Herodotus. The fact, moreover, that such an ideology of a 'universal empire' existed – at least among the Assyrians and the Achaemenids – probably means that the concept of continuity of empire was, at least for the Achaemenids, irrelevant: the main focus was on the creation and subsequent establishment of a certain image. The list of peoples bringing tribute to the Achaemenid king referred to above is a potent expression of that image. Within such a framework real historical facts, interesting and important as they may be and are to us, are only of subordinate interest, if of any interest at all (see also Stronk 2014/15: 221–8), probably – I think – for the Achaemenids (sources for their views are still absent) but certainly for the Greeks writing Persian history.

Nevertheless, throughout his work, Shayegan also makes clear

---

[20] 'Herodotus and Ctesias respond to Persian imperial structures, the Alexander Historians to the revitalization of Achaemenid territory': Kosmin 2014: 46. The Seleucids notably attempted to keep this imperial ideology alive, as may appear from both the commission and travels of Megasthenes (a companion of Seleucus I *Nicator* (see *BNJ* 715 T 1) and Sibyrtius (see *BNJ* 715 T 2)) and his *Indica*, which appears to have contained references to the works of Dionysus and Heracles in India (preserved in the *Bibliotheca* 2.38.3; 2.39.1; see also *BNJ* 715 F 4 and commentary; above, note 14). As a matter of fact, according to Greek sources only a few people invaded India: Dionysus, Heracles, Alexander – apart from the contested invasion by Semiramis and the forgotten one by Darius I the Great (see Hdt. 4.44.3): *BNJ* 715 F 11 commentary.

that the Arsacid connection with the Achaemenids 'owed its existence to the permanence of the Babylonian cuneiform tradition ... which held records of Achaemenid history', as he summarises the situation (Shayegan 2011: xiii, elaborated in his chapter 3). This tradition linked both empires (as Assyrians and Achaemenids were also connected, at least in Greek views), creating a sense of historical continuity and notion of empire. For me these are considerations, feeble as they may be, which lead me to believe Nicholas of Damascus did also work primarily from Ctesias' *Persica*. It means too that at least Ctesias' – and therewith Diodorus' – work was less 'one-dimensional' than has frequently been assumed. Finally it suggests that Jacoby's remarks quoted above (Jacoby 1922: 2069), to the effect that Dinon's would have become the main work in the Hellenistic period, can probably be discarded in part or as a whole.

As regards the concept of continuity of empire, one aspect needs to be added. It may have become obvious to the reader from the account as it has been rendered that Diodorus did not believe in an altogether uninterrupted continuum.[21] He appears, though, to believe in a continuous succession of empires, each one characterised by a more or less identical development of rise, apex, and decline. One might, I think, define his description of the occurrences from the beginning of 'empire' to his days – at least in 'Persia' – as one of an almost cyclic development, in which the succession of rulers and centres of power ensures the dynamic element in its history (it is because of that dynamism that I refer to the development as 'almost cyclic'), and the geographical theatre (in spite of occasional changes and/or shifts) ensures the aspect of continuity. Into a basically simple main pattern, in which on the one hand the Medes succeed the Assyrians, the Persians the Medes, the Greeks (Macedonians) the Persians, the Parthians (and partly the Romans) the Greeks, and on the other hand first Assyrian, then Achaemenid state ideology plays its part, Diodorus inserts his strong and strict moral convictions, in which the (lack of) *aretē* guides the actions of the various characters that ultimately take care of the pace of the developments, just as it ultimately determines the fate of the actors and even of

---

[21] To Ctesias' position on this issue we really have no clue, as the number of original fragments by him is extremely limited (*P.Oxy.* 2330 and two passages in Demetrius *On Style*: neither of them addresses this point) and the rest of what can be seen as 'Ctesias' has to be collected from the works of other authors, like Diodorus. Though we might suspect that Ctesias held a similar point of view to that of Diodorus, I believe it to be methodologically incorrect to take this at face value. In fact, a similar statement should be made for Diodorus' other source-authors: of none of them do we know sufficient to make any solid and/or credible statements as regards their view on this question.

states.[22] Though Diodorus also refers to Τύχη ('Fate') on this point, it generally shows that Fate is nearly always at least partly determined by *aretē*. In this respect Diodorus really emerges as a straightforward author (presumably some would prefer the adjective 'simple' for him, and perhaps they are right: finally, it all is a matter of judgement), guided by the Stoic convictions of his age (see Chapter 1, note 5).

Diodorus and the weakness of the Persians
As regards this point one element should be added. At least from Herodotus onward, Greek authors stress differences between Persians and Greeks. A telling example is the following description by Herodotus:

ὡς δὲ κελευόμενοι οὗτοι ἐποίευν ταῦτα, ἐνθαῦτα τὸν Παυσανίην ἰδόντα κλίνας τε χρυσέας καὶ ἀργυρέας εὖ ἐστρωμένας καὶ τραπέζας τε χρυσέας καὶ ἀργυρέας καὶ παρασκευὴν μεγαλοπρεπέα τοῦ δείπνου, ἐκπλαγέντα τὰ προκέμενα ἀγαθὰ κελεῦσαι ἐπὶ γέλωτι τοὺς ἑωυτοῦ διηκόνους παρασκευάσαι Λακωνικὸν δεῖπνον. ὡς δὲ τῆς θοίνης ποιηθείσης ἦν πολλὸν τὸ μέσον, τὸν Παυσανίην γελάσαντα μεταπέμψασθαι τῶν Ἑλλήνων τοὺς στρατηγούς, συνελθόντων δὲ τούτων εἰπεῖν τὸν Παυσανίην, δεικνύντα ἐς ἑκατέρην τοῦ δείπνου παρασκευήν, «Ἄνδρες Ἕλληνες, τῶνδε εἵνεκα ἐγὼ ὑμέας συνήγαγον, βουλόμενος ὑμῖν τοῦδε τοῦ Μήδων ἡγεμόνος τὴν ἀφροσύνην δέξαι, ὃς τοιήνδε δίαιταν ἔχων ἦλθε ἐς ἡμέας οὕτω ὀϊζυρὴν ἔχοντας ἀπαιρησόμενος». ταῦτα μὲν Παυσανίην λέγεται εἰπεῖν πρὸς τοὺς στρατηγοὺς τῶν Ἑλλήνων

('they [that is, the bakers and cooks of the Persian general Mardonius] did as Pausanias had asked. And when Pausanias saw both the well-cushioned gold and silver couches and the gold and silver tables and the magnificent service for the meal, he was amazed at the splendour that was before him and, to have a laugh, asked his own men to prepare a meal Laconian style. When that meal was ready, it was much unlike the other. And Pausanias, laughing, sent for the commanders of the Greeks. When they had assembled, Pausanias said, while he pointed at the way each meal had been prepared: "Men of Greece, I made you assemble here because I wanted to show you

---

[22] In this tale of successions it might be a fascinating exercise to discuss the predecessors in empire of the Assyrians. I believe that Ctesias probably and Diodorus certainly believed that the Assyrians' really was the first empire in Asia ('native rulers'), taking shape directly after the age of gods and heroes but still in the mist of human recollection (much as Herodotus argued for the antiquity of Egyptian civilisation in Africa, asserting that the priests were acutely aware of the seniority of their civilisation: Hdt. 2.2.1, 4–5; Diodorus also confirms the antiquity of Egyptian civilisation: 1.9.6–10.7). As a matter of fact, it is noteworthy that the eponymous 'fathers' of both the Medes and the Persians in Diodorus' account are directly linked to the mythic *Greek* past, taking care of a more or less direct lineage between Medes and Persians on the one hand, the Greeks on the other. As such, it might even be argued that Alexander only took what was rightfully the Greeks'. Remarkable in this respect is Diodorus' statement (1.9.5), especially as regards Ephorus' position: περὶ πρώτων δὲ τῶν βαρβάρων διέξιμεν, οὐκ ἀρχαιοτέρους αὐτοὺς ἡγούμενοι τῶν Ἑλλήνων, καθάπερ Ἔφορος εἴρηκεν ('We shall discuss first of all foreign peoples, not because we believe them to be more ancient than the Greeks, as Ephorus asserted'). These words seem to imply that Ephorus believed that (some) 'foreign' cultures predated the Greek one, a view apparently denied by Diodorus.

Semiramis' Legacy 537

the foolishness of the leader of the Persians. With such a way of life as you see, he came here to take ours, pitiful as it is, away from us." According to the story Pausanias said these things to the commanders of the Greeks.' Hdt. 9.82)[23]

In Xenophon's *Hellenica*, one particular picture (X. *HG* 4.1.30) is slightly more subtle. Agesilaus and a delegation of Lacedaemonians were lying on the ground in a grassy spot, waiting for the arrival of Pharnabazus. Pharnabazus came, dressed very richly. When he saw the Lacedaemonians lying in the grass, he joined them and lay down on the ground without further ado, not using the rugs his attendants were spreading to sit upon comfortably, because (as Xenophon phrases it!) ᾐσχύνθη ἐντρυφῆσαι ('he was ashamed to indulge in luxury'). Whether there was actual αἰσχύνη ('shame') might, however, be a matter of contention (see Tuplin 2010: 201 and note 33), even though Xenophon does bring out the picture quite dramatically. The key element of the latter picture, however, is the Persian τρυφή, *tryphē*, which might be translated as 'softness', 'luxuriousness', 'fastidiousness' and the like (see *LSJ*, *s.v.*). However, not only were the Persians – in the view of (some) Greek literature – prone to this weakness, but also, for example, Sardanapallus was described by Diodorus as being (strongly) afflicted by it (see Chapter 2), just like many other people, both Persians and sometimes even Greeks. However, as Gorman and Gorman (2014: ch. 5) adduce, the picture of Persians as in moral decline and luxury-loving is essentially not the typical traditional Greek image of the Persians (see also Morgan 2016: *passim*), but a *topos* especially engendered at Rome during the late Republic, thenceforth becoming a literary commonplace. By incorporating this theme, Diodorus does not merely show himself a typical author from that era but also probably enhances his picture of *aretē*.

To this observation another should be added, as worded by Bruce Lincoln:

> Obviously enough, foreign authors do not report things from a Persian perspective and one has to guard against naturalizing and reproducing their Orientalist tropes as regards Persian luxury, decadence, despotism, and palace intrigue, to cite some of the most common examples. But if one exercises reasonable caution, there is a wealth of information to be gathered from Herodotus, Aeschylus, Xenophon, Aelian, or Polyaenus, as Pierre Briant has amply demonstrated, and the reporting of even so biased an author as Ctesias can prove useful, particularly if one dispenses with his interpretive

[23] The irony is, of course, as most Greeks who heard or read Herodotus' account knew perfectly well, that this very same King Pausanias ended his life as a 'Mediser', indulging in 'grandiose Persian banquets': see above, 11.46.2–3; also Gruen 2011: 28.

additions. What he – and others – describe with disdain as 'luxury' (Greek *tryphē*, a term that has connotations of wantonness, self-indulgence, softness and effeminacy), for instance, can provide a useful picture not only of Persian wealth, but of the extent to which it was deployed in ritual practice and symbolic displays, the significance of which was utterly lost on outsiders. This is true, for instance, in the case of the Great King's banquet table, which was simultaneously a means of redistribution, a display of royal generosity, and a microcosmic image of the empire at large. (Lincoln 2007: 14; see also 2013: 258)

Accepting the observation as it stands (and it at least looks feasible), this seems to make the *topos* of *tryphē*, therefore, a question not merely of policy, but also of ignorance (or policy grounded in ignorance).[24]

There exists a telling mosaic, to be dated to c. 350–400 AD from Syria, presently housed in the Royal Ontario Museum in Toronto. It depicts TRYPHĒ and BIOS ('life') as an affluent couple, engaged in relaxed conversation on an elegant couch. The female figure is identified as *Tryphē*, meaning luxuriously and leisurely living; the male figure is *Bios*, meaning Life. The allegory implies that life should be accompanied by pleasurable living (see Figure 10.1). The man is shown holding a magic wheel in his right hand. This was a charm used to keep lovers together: its presence further emphasises the idea that Life and Luxury should be inseparable. Such an attitude appears in contrast to, for example, military prowess. It is a powerful image and could be deployed as an equally powerful propagandistic tool. As such it might be used as an invitation to adversaries to act, to impose their *aretē* on their – in that respect – less privileged fellow humans.

An increased sense of Greekness and self-confidence in the early fourth century BC[25] led to Agesilaus' call to enter τὸ μὴ περὶ τῆς Ἑλλάδος, ἀλλὰ περὶ τῆς Ἀσίας τὸν ἀγῶνα καθιστάναι ('on a struggle not to save Greece, but to subdue Asia': X. *Ages.* 1.8; this motive is also hinted at in X. *HG* 3.5.1). Such an attempt was also, some years later, advocated by Lysias and Isocrates, in both the *Panegyricus* and the *Philippus*. That such an enterprise was feasible had already been discussed by Xenophon in the *Anabasis*, where he makes a useful strategic observation: καὶ συνιδεῖν δ' ἦν τῷ προσέχοντι τὸν νοῦν τῇ βασιλέως ἀρχῇ πλήθει μὲν χώρας καὶ ἀνθρώπων ἰσχυρὰ οὖσα, τοῖς δὲ

---

[24] Other examples of Greek ignorance on Persian matters, notably regarding Xerxes' whipping of the Hellespont (see Hdt. 7.35.1–3), explained by Herodotus as *hubris*, are discussed by Daryaee 2016.
[25] See, for example, Stronk 2010/11: 85–7.

Fig. 10.1. Luxuriousness and Life (Τρυφή and Βίος), fourth-century AD mosaic from Syria, currently in the Royal Ontario Museum, Toronto. With the permission of the Royal Ontario Museum © ROM.

μήκεσι τῶν ὁδῶν καὶ τῷ διεσπάσθαι τὰς δυνάμεις ἀσθενής, εἴ τις διὰ ταχέων τὸν πόλεμον ποιοῖτο ('further, for the close observer it was obvious that while the strength of the Great King's empire was in its size and number of inhabitants, its weaknesses were the distances and the fact that its forces were scattered, *if one were able to attack it swiftly*': X. *An.* 1.5.9; my italics). It appears that it was this weakness that was exploited by Alexander.

Diodorus' views

As such, Diodorus' account appears to merge Greek traditions, whether these were based upon facts or on propaganda, Achaemenid ideology, and his Stoic belief augmented by elements typical of the period of the late Republic at Rome, the very period Diodorus lived in and the very place where he wrote most of his work. It seems feasible that at least part of his 'Greek influences' had come to Diodorus through Ephorus from Isocrates (one of the most vehement advocates, as far as we know, of Greek action against Persia), but probably other authors (like Ctesias) also added to Diodorus' views, just as the idea of continuity of empire had already been described by Herodotus. Certainly, Diodorus' work suggests he was anything but an original thinker, even if he ever attempted to be one at all. Nevertheless, in spite of the derogatory remarks by Schwartz referred to in the Introduction, Diodorus had acquired some fame, as the words of Jerome may testify: *Diodorvs Sicvlvs Graecæ scriptor Historiæ clarvs habetvr* ('Diodorus of Sicily, author of a History of Greece, is considered famous').[26] Sulimani (2011: 335) therefore rightly remarks that at least amongst Patristic writers Diodorus' work was considered to be a true reflection of the Hellenistic period: this observation looks like a reflection of Schwartz's remarks.

Greatly as I admire the work Sulimani has written on Diodorus (and I share many – if not most – of her views on Diodorus' methods and qualities), I have nevertheless some problems with her stance towards him. She considers him first and foremost as a historian, a historian moreover (as the title of her work stresses) on a 'pagan mission'. True, her definitions and her division into two levels of Diodorus' work hold water and, indeed, *could* qualify Diodorus as the author of a universal history. However, it is precisely her second level – 'Diodorus' own work, echoing his convictions' (Sulimani 2011: 336), together with some of the very examples she adduces – that makes me feel it is increasingly uncomfortable to look at Diodorus primarily, let alone exclusively, as a historian. More and more I believe he was first and foremost a believer in Stoic doctrines, using – as I phrased it in the Introduction – Clio as his handmaiden, an instrument to instruct his audience that these views were valid throughout the centuries. As we have seen in the Introduction he makes unmistakably clear in various *capita* what

---

[26] Jer. *Chron.* II. Olymp. 182 (Migne *PL*, vol. 027, pp. 429–30). Unless, of course, Jerome is to be taken for one of those 'anspruchslose Christen' (see the remarks by Schwartz 1903a: cols. 663–4, referred to in the Introduction).

both his views and his goals were when composing the *Bibliotheca*. In my view that makes his 'universal history' only a secondary objective, a tool if you like, the propagation of the Stoic principles being the main objective. Combining all the elements discussed so far, I believe it is fair to state that the *Bibliotheca* was interconnected throughout, both philosophically and historically: it represents a Hellenistic view of the world, from its very beginnings to the days of the author himself, a view composed out of both Greek and – in the case of his *capita* on the East – Persian visions, moulded by Stoic convictions.

Diodorus and race
In this respect it may also be useful to have a brief look at Diodorus' view on race. It almost goes without saying that – he himself being Greek – Diodorus distinguishes between Ἑλληνικός ('Greek') and βάρβαρος ('non-Greek') – the latter word having, as I phrased it in the Introduction, a slightly pejorative sound. However, though there occasionally appear to be some elements of a dichotomy between 'East' and 'West' in the *Bibliotheca*, for example in his eulogy on the Lacedaemonians who had perished at Thermopylae (11.11.1–6) and the way Alexander lands in Asia, this dichotomy – in my view – practically never leads to 'racial profiling' (I remember one case that suggests '*Pvnica fides*' (15.16.1: see also Chapter 1, note 33), but that is about all). On the contrary, notable throughout the book is Diodorus' positive appreciation for the 'Otherness' of various peoples (Casevitz and Jacquemin 2015: xxxi). Samiei (2014) addresses the problem of racial profiling, notably as regards Persians, in studies of classical antiquity from the eighteenth century AD to the present day. He notes that in many – if not a majority of – works from this period the Persians of the fifth and fourth centuries BC are described as people that are in every respect inferior to the Greeks. Samiei puts the blame for that attitude on Hellenism, the Hellenists, and an ensuing Hellenocentric view that became more or less dominant in this period. Though in the fourth century BC it is notable that Isocrates and his followers also frequently stress Greek superiority to Persians, it should emphatically be stressed that, in spite of his frequent use of βάρβαροι ('foreigners'), such an attitude largely seems alien to Diodorus' work: as we have been able to see, he especially distinguishes people on the basis of their *aretē*, or its absence, no matter whether it regards Greeks, Persians, or Indians. Even his eulogy on the Lacedaemonians referred to above especially focuses on *aretē*, though he comes close to outright discrimination there.

Semiramis in Diodorus' work (2)

One element that emerges in Sulimani's work still needs to be addressed. To be as concise as possible, I shall quote from her 'Conclusions':

> Each one of the heroes [of the first five books] created an empire, in which various peoples and races coexisted. Each figure conferred benefits upon his subjects and, whenever possible, treated them with clemency. Their actions brought peace and quiet to the world. Diodorus, then, found no fault in the conquest of large parts of the world by a single nation. On the contrary, the creation of an empire was the right thing to do, since the concept of the unity of mankind can be realized within its limits. The ruler in this kind of empire should confer benefits and be merciful. (Sulimani 2011: 347)

As she explains some lines further on, Sulimani believes that one of the empires that inspired Diodorus was that of Alexander. Taking the detail of Diodorus' narrative of Alexander into account, Sulimani's suggestion might well be true. Even so, however, not only Alexander but also all his illustrious – and less illustrious – successors and predecessors in the end only contested Semiramis' legacy, she (and Ninus) being the first to establish – in the views expressed in the *Bibliotheca* – this empire.

Conclusion

Some final remarks seem to be in place. Many people involved in ancient history and classical Greek and/or Latin literature apparently tend to forget that the ancient historians, perhaps with a few exceptions such as Thucydides, who stated that he wrote his work as a κτῆμα ἐς ἀεί ('a possession for all time': Th.1.22), did not write for them but for their contemporaries and, maybe, the next generation at best. All efforts to try and categorise those authors, an activity that I myself occasionally also practise, are, therefore, *ultimately* not really very rewarding. Paraphrasing the words of Schwartz (Schwartz 1903a: cols. 663-4), referred to in the Introduction, I might state that only those writing many centuries after Diodorus were sufficiently arrogant to measure his work (and that of many of his contemporaries) by the standards they should have applied primarily to their own works.

I think that, essentially, it might well be more useful to try and find out what kind of sources our predecessors used, how they used them, and – if at all possible – why they used them as they did, and what their personal beliefs (in the widest sense) were. An additional challenge might well be to try and establish how their efforts were valued, by both their contemporaries and, perhaps, the subsequent generation(s), possibly even (though it certainly seems a long shot) what caused their work(s) to be preserved and that of many others not. Such research might, in the end, force us to take a more humble attitude towards those predecessors, on whose work we have to rely, after all, as one of the very sources for our own studies (along with, for example, archaeological, numismatic, papyrological, and epigraphical sources). Having stated this, I do not want to entice anyone to appreciate an author like Diodorus more than he deserves, though I sincerely believe he deserves (much) better than he got from Schwartz and the latter's followers.

In the words of Averil Cameron, introducing M. J. Wheeldon's contribution '"True Stories": The Reception of Historiography in Antiquity':[1]

> [A]ncient historiography would command the confidence of its readers (or rather, in the ancient context, its hearers, for literary works were published by public *performance*), if they found what they wanted in the texts. Thus the very rhetorical elements ... might actually be the most persuasive for an ancient audience. On the whole, we read the ancient historians for purposes quite other, ..., and while much effort has been expended on 'source-criticism', it is largely with the intent of separating out and disregarding the rhetorical elements which are thought to have 'distorted' the writer's presentation of reality. Wheeldon shows how dangerous it is in fact to lose sight of the closeness of history and oratory in the ancient world.

Though I believe that the oratorical emphasis in Diodorus' *Bibliotheca* is probably somewhat less pregnant than in Herodotus' *Histories* (which we know was performed in public),[2] the conclusion as regards the role of '*Quellenkritik*' in the judgement on ancient authors as worded by Cameron remains, in my view, valid for Diodorus too.

As we have seen, Diodorus has written an account that is to a large extent focused on the rewards of *aretē* – and the disasters that may befall someone if he (or she, naturally) does not strive for it (forcibly worded in 15.1.1, 3–4). In this account, he attributes a significant role to the Persian world – in the wider sense – starting with its mythical roots (Medus and Perses) and what we might call its prehistory: the reign of Ninus and notably Semiramis. The account goes on with stories of the Chaldeans, Scythians, and Medes, followed by quite an extensive account of various aspects of the Achaemenid Empire and a discussion of most of the Great Kings, some briefly, some at length. Next comes a report of the expedition by Alexander III the Great and, after Alexander's death, the struggle between the Diadochs, culminating in the Seleucid Empire, the latter's gradual demise, and the rise of new powers in the East: Rome and the Parthians. Perhaps it is not the best of accounts imaginable,

---

[1] In Cameron 1989: 35.
[2] Herodotus is reported to have read his work in public in 445/4 and allegedly was paid handsomely to do so, according to Diyllus, *FGrH/BNJ* 73 F 3 = Plu. *De Mal. Her.* 862B. As evidence for the reading itself (and some form of tribute) may be adduced Eus. *Chron. ad Olymp.* 83.4 (in the translation into Latin as well as partial revision by Jerome): *Herodotvs cvm Athenis libros svos in concilio legisset, honoratvs est* ('Herodotus was honoured for reading his books in the assembly at Athens').

but it is the only account from antiquity that paints such a comprehensive picture of the Persian world, a picture, moreover, based upon (as even Unger 1880: 305 concedes) 'fast lauter guten, uns verlorenen geschichtschreibern', though admittedly from a definitely Greek point of view.

As such, the value of Diodorus' *Bibliotheca* can, in my view, hardly be overestimated, even taking Diodorus' limitations into account, certainly because he did not limit himself to only a few source-authors but used a wide array of them, some of them sparsely, some quite extensively. Working in this manner, occasionally introducing information gathered by autopsy, occasionally also inventing things, he created what some have regarded as a typical Hellenist universal history. I completely admit the universalistic character of Diodorus' work, but I do not view it as a proper history in the first place, but as a work in which history has become a tool to teach his audience the merits of a life of *aretē*. However, thanks to his use of first-rate source-authors, the *Bibliotheca* remains an important historical source as well, in spite of the fact that its 'internal' emphasis lies elsewhere. As such Diodorus' work is not unique: Plutarch, for example, wrote both his *Lives* and his *Moralia* with similar aims and methods (but with a somewhat different scope), but has gained a much wider audience, again – probably – to a large extent consisting of 'anspruchslose Christen'.[3] Compared with Plutarch's work, the value of Diodorus' is, though, as regards both scope and quality, underestimated. He deserves a much better reputation than the image of a 'naiver Dummkopf' he still has among too many students of antiquity.

---

[3] Again referring to the remarks by Schwartz 1903a: cols. 663–4 on Diodorus. In addition, Plutarch was loved and admired by Christians: Ziegler 1964: 65. 'John Mauropus in the XIth century prays in a poem that Christ, if He will save any pagan from wrath, may exempt Plato and Plutarch, the two who were by nature nearest to the law "in doctrine and in character"' (Russell 1973: 146).

Bibliography

EDITIONS OF TEXTS

Wherever I have not given (a) specific edition(s), I have used the text as presented by the TLG and/or Jacoby's *FGrH*.

Appian

Goukowsky, P. (ed.) (2002c), *Appien: Histoire romaine. Tôme IV, Livre VIII: Le livre africain*, Paris: Les Belles Lettres.

Arrian

Brunt, P. A. (ed.) (1976–83), *Arrian: Anabasis Alexandri and Indica, with an English Translation by P. A. Brunt*, 2 vols, Cambridge, MA/London: Harvard University Press/Heinemann (Loeb Classical Library).
Roos, A. G. and G. Wirth (eds) (1967^2), *Flavii Arriani quae exstant omnia*, 2 vols, Leipzig: Teubner.

Athenaeus Naucratites

Kaibel, G. (ed.) (1923–5), *Athenaei Naucratitae Dipnosophistarum Libri XV, recensuit Georg Kaibel*, 3 vols, Leipzig: Teubner.

Cassius Dio

Cary, E. (ed.) (1968–70), *Cassius Dio, in 9 vols, with an English Translation by Earnest Cary; on the Basis of the Version of Herbert Baldwin Foster*, Cambridge, MA/London: Harvard University Press/Heinemann (Loeb Classical Library).

Ctesias

BNJ 688: Madreiter, I., 'Ktesias of Knidos (688)' (in preparation), in I. Worthington (ed.), *Brill's New Jacoby*, <http://referenceworks.brillonline.com/>.
Lenfant, D. (ed.) (2004), *Ctésias de Cnide: La Perse, l'Inde, autres fragments, texte établi, traduit et commenté par Dominique Lenfant*, Paris: Les Belles Lettres.
Müller, C. (ed.) (1844), *Ctesiae Cnidii et Chronographorum Castoris, Eratosthenis, etc.: Fragmenta, dissertatione et notis illustrata a Carolo Müllero*, Paris: Firmin-Didot.
Stronk, Jan P. (ed.) (2010), *Ctesias' Persian History. Part 1: Introduction, Text, and Translation*, Düsseldorf: Wellem.

Diodorus

Diodore de Sicile: Bibliothèque historique. Texte établi et traduit de [editor], Paris: Les Belles Lettres

Chamoux, F. and P. Bertrac (1993), *Tôme I: Introduction générale*.
Bertrac, P. and Y. Vernière (eds. and trs.) (1993), *Tôme I, Livre I*.
Eck, B. (ed. and tr.) (2003), *Tôme II, Livre II*.
Bommelaer, B. (ed. and tr.) (2002), *Tôme III, Livre III*.
Casevitz, M. (ed. and tr.) and A. Jacquemin (comm.) (2015), *Tôme V, Livre V: Livre des îles*.
Haillet, J. (ed. and tr.) (2002), *Tôme VI, Livre XI*.
Casevitz, M. (ed. and tr.) (2002), *Tôme VII, Livre XII*.
Bonnet, M. and E. R. Bennett (eds. and trs.) (2002), *Tôme IX, Livre XIV*.
Vial, C. (ed. and tr.) (2002), *Tôme X, Livre XV*.
Goukowsky, P. (ed. and tr.) (2002a), *Tôme XII, Livre XVII*.
Goukowsky, P. (ed. and tr.) (2002b), *Tôme XIII, Livre XVIII*.
Bizière, F. (ed. and tr.) (2002), *Tôme XIV, Livre XIX*.
Cohen-Skalli, A. (ed. and tr.) (2012), *Fragments: Livres VI–X*.
Goukowsky, P. (ed. and tr.) (2006), *Fragments: Livres XXI–XXVI*.
Goukowsky, P. (ed. and tr.) (2012), *Fragments: Livres XXVII–XXXII*.
Goukowsky, P. (ed. and tr.) (2014), *Fragments: Livres XXXIII–XL*.

Diodori Bibliotheca Historica, edidit [editor], Leipzig/Stuttgart: Teubner (regarded by Teubner as their third Diodorus edition)

Vogel, F. (ed.) (1985a), vol. I, *Libri I–IV*, Stuttgart, ed. stereotypa (orig. 1888, Leipzig).
Vogel, F. (ed.) (1985b), vol. II, *Libri V–XII*, Stuttgart, ed. stereotypa (orig. 1890, Leipzig).

Vogel, F. (ed.) (1985c), vol. III, *Libri XIII–XV*, Stuttgart, ed. stereotypa (orig. 1893, Leipzig).
Fischer, C. T. (ed.) (1985d), vol. IV, *Libri XVI–XVIII*, Stuttgart, ed. stereotypa (orig. 1906, Leipzig).
Fischer, C. T. (ed.) (1985e), vol. V, *Libri XIX–XX*, Suttgart, ed. stereotypa (orig. 1906, Leipzig).
Fischer, C. T. and L. Dindorf (eds) (1969), vol. VI, *Fragmenta librorum XXI–XL: index nominum*, Stuttgart, ed. stereotypa (orig. part of vol. IV and the whole of vol. V of the second edition of 1866–8, Leipzig).

Diodorus Siculus, in Twelve Volumes, with an English Translation by [editor], Cambridge, MA/London: Harvard University Press/ Heinemann (Loeb Classical Library)

Oldfather, C. H. (ed.) (1968), vol. 1, *Books I and II, 1–34*.
Oldfather, C. H. (ed.) (1967), vol. 2, *Books II, 35–IV, 58*.
Oldfather, C. H. (ed.) (1970a), vol. 3, *Books IV, 59–VIII*.
Oldfather, C. H. (ed.) (1970b), vol. 4, *Books IX–XII, 40*.
Oldfather, C. H. (ed.) (1962), vol. 5, *Books XII, 41–XIII*.
Oldfather, C. H. (ed.) (1963), vol. 6, *Books XIV–XV, 19*.
Sherman, C. L. (ed.) (1963), vol. 7, *Books XV, 20–XVI,. 65*.
Welles, C. B. (ed.) (1970), vol. 8, *Books XVI, 66–95–XVII*.
Geer, R. M. (ed.) (1969), vol. 9, *Books XVIII–XIX. 1–65*.
Geer, R. M. (ed.) (1962), vol. 10, *Books XIX, 66–110–XX*.
Walton, F. R. (ed.) (1968), vol. 11, *Books XXI–XXXII*.
Walton, F. R. (ed.) (1967), vol. 12, *Books XXXIII–XL* (with a general index to Diodorus by R. M. Geer).

Bekker, I. (ed.) (1853–4), *Diodori Bibliotheca Historica, ex recognitione I. Bekkeri*, 4 vols, Leipzig: Teubner (regarded by Teubner as their first Diodorus edition).
Bracciolini, G. F. P. (ed. and tr.) (1472), *Diodori Siculi a Pogio Florentino in latinum traducti de antiquorum gestis fabulosis. Lib. I[-V]*, Bologna: ?
Dindorf, L. A. (ed.) (1826), *Diodori Bibliotheca Historica*, 4 vols, Leipzig: Teubner.
Dindorf, L. A. (ed.) (1866–8), *Diodori Bibliotheca Historica, ex recensione et cum annotionibus Ludovici Dindorfi*, 5 vols, Leipzig: Teubner (regarded by Teubner as their second Diodorus edition).
Estienne, H. (1559), *Diodori Sicvli Bibliothecæ historicæ libri qvindecim de qvadraginta. Decem ex his qvindecim nvnqvam privs fverunt editi*, Geneva: Fugger.
Green, P. (2006), *Diodorus Siculus: Books 11–12.37.1. Greek History, 480–431 BC: The Alternative Version, Translated, with Introduction and Commentary by Peter Green*, Austin, TX: University of Texas Press.

Bibliography 549

Green, P. (2010), *Diodorus Siculus, The Persian Wars to the Fall of Athens, Books 11–14.34 (480–401 BCE), Translated, with Introduction and Notes by Peter Green*, Austin, TX: University of Texas Press.
Rhodoman, L. (ed.) (1604), *Diodori Sicvli Bibliothecæ historicæ libri XV, de XL, graece & latine*, 2 vols, Hanoviae (= Hanover): typis Wechelianus, apud hæredes Joannis Aubri.
Wesseling, P. (1745), *Diodori Siculi bibliothecae historicae libri qui supersunt / interprete Laurentio Rhodomano; ad fidem MSS. recensuit Petrus Wesselingius; atque Henr. Stephani, Laur. Rhodomani, Fulvii Ursini, Henr. Valesii, Jacobi Palmerii & suas adnotationes cum indicibus locupletissimis, adjecit*, 2 vols, Amsterdam: sumptiubus Jacobi Wetstenii.

Epitome Mettensis

Thomas, P. H. (ed.) (1960), *Incerti auctoris Epitoma rerum gestarum Alexandri Magni cum libro de morte testamentoque Alexandri*, Leipzig: Teubner.

Excerpta Constantiniana

Boissevain, U. P., C. G. de Boor, and T. Büttner-Wobst (eds) (1903–10), *Excerpta Historica iussu Imperatoris Constantini [VII] Porphyrogeniti Confecta*, 4 vols. in 6, Berlin: Weidman.

  Vol. 1: Boor, C. G. de (ed.) (1903), *Excerpta de legationibus* (Pars I: *Excerpta de legationibus Romanorum ad gentes*, Pars II: *Excerpta de legationibus gentium ad Romanos*).
  Vol. 2: Büttner-Wobst, T. (ed.) and A. G. Roos (*curavit editionem post mortem editoris*) (1906–10), *Excerpta de virtutibus et vitiis*, 2 vols.
  Vol. 3: Boor, C. G. de (ed.) (1905), *Excerpta de insidiis*.
  Vol. 4: Boissevain, U. P. (ed.) (1906), *Excerpta de sententiis*.

Feder, C. A. L. (ed.) (1848–55), *Excerpta e Polybio, Diodoro, Dionysio Halicarnassensi atque Nicolao Damasceno, e magno Imperatoris digestorum opere libri περὶ ἐπιβουλῶν inscripti reliquiae. E cod. Escurialensi a se transscripta interpretatione latina et observationibus criticis comitatus edidit C. Aug. L. Feder*, 3 vols, Darmstadt: Lesske.
Herwerden, H. van (ed.) (1860), *Spicilegium Vaticanum, continens novas lectiones in Historicorum Graecorum excerpta, quae primus edidit Ang. Maius, prolatas e palimpsesto Vaticano denuo excusso*, Leiden: Brill.
Heyse, T. F. (1840), *Historiarum excerpta gnomica in palimpsesto Vaticano LXIII* [sic!] *Ang. Maii curis resignato / Polybii*, Berlin: Reimer.

Mai, A. (1846), *Historicorum Graecorum, Diodori, Dionis, Eunapii, Polybii, Dionysii et aliorum fragmenta / e Vaticanis codicibus edita ab Angelo Maio*, Rome: Typis Vaticanis.

Valois, H. (ed.) (1634), *Polybii, Diodori Siculi, Nicolai Damasceni, Dionysii Halicarnassii, Appiani, Alexandri, Dionis et Ioannis Antiocheni Excerpta ex collectaneis Constantini Avgvsti Porphyrogenetæ*, Paris: Mathurin du Puis.

Excerpta Hoescheliana

Hoeschel, D. (1603), *Eclogae legationum: Dexippi Atheniensis. Evnapii Sardiani. Petri Patricii et magistri. Prisci Sophistae. Malchi Philadelphenis. Menandri Protectoris. Cum corollario excerptorum e libris Diodori Sicvli, amissu, XXI ... XXVI. / Omnia e MSS. cod. a Davide Hoeschelio edita*, Augsburg (Avgvstæ Vindelicorvm): Typis Ioannis Prætorii.

Florilegium Vaticanum

Mai, A. (1827), *Scriptorum veterum nova collectio e Vaticanis codicibus (Graece et Latine)*, vol. II, Rome: Typis Vaticanis.

Herodotus

Hude, C.,(ed.) (1908a, b), *Herodoti Historiae, recognovit brevique adnotatione critica instruxit Carolus Hude*, 2 vols, Oxford: Clarendon.

Wilson, N. G. (ed.) (2015a, b), *Herodoti Historiae, recognovit brevique adnotatione critica instruxit N. G. Wilson*, 2 vols, Oxford: Oxford University Press.

Wilson, N. G. (2015c), *Herodotea: Studies on the Text of Herodotus*, Oxford: Oxford University Press.

Justin/Pompeius Trogus (see also Cn. Pompeius Trogus)

Seel, O. (ed.) (1985), *M. Iuniani Ivstini Epitoma Historiarum Philippicarum Pompei Trogi*, Stuttgart: Teubner (photomechanic reprint of 1972 edn).

Yardley, J. C. (ed.) (1994), *Justin, Epitome of the Philippic History of Pompeius Trogus, Translated by J. C. Yardley, with Introduction and Explanatory Notes by R. Develin*, Atlanta, GA: Scholars Press.

Marmor Parium

Jacoby, F. (ed.) (1904), *Das Marmor Parium, mit drei Beilagen*, Berlin: Weidmannsche Buchhandlung.

Philo of Byzantium

Diels, H. and E. Schramm (eds) (1919), *Philons Belopoiika (Viertes Buch der Mechanik), mit 8 Tafeln, Griechisch und Deutsch von H. Diels und E. Schramm*, Berlin: Verlag der Akademie der Wissenschaften/Georg Reimer (published 1920).

Photius

Henry, R. (ed.) (1959–78), *Photius: Bibliothèque; texte établi et traduit par René Henry*, Paris: Les Belles Lettres.

Cn. Pompeius Trogus

Seel, O. (ed.) (1956), *Pompei Trogi Fragmenta*, Leipzig: Teubner.

Suda

Adler, A. (ed.) (1928–38), *Suidae Lexicon*, 5 vols, Leipzig/Stuttgart: Teubner (repr. 1967–71).

Tractatus de mulieribus

Gera, D. (ed.) (1997), *Warrior Women: The Anonymous Tractatus de mulieribus claris in bello*, Leiden: Brill.

Tzetzes

Leone, P. A. M. (ed.) (1968), *Ioannis Tzetzae Historiae*, Naples: Libreria Scientifica.

SECONDARY LITERATURE

Aaboe, A. (1991), 'Babylonian Mathematics, Astrology and Astronomy', in CAH^2, vol. 3.2, pp. 276–92.
Abe, T. (2014/15), 'Herodotus' First Language: The State of Language in Halicarnassus', *Talanta* 46/7: 145–64.
Akurgal, E. (1976), 'Kyzikos', in Stillwell 1976: 473–4.
Ambaglio, D., F. Landucci, and L. Bravi (2008), *Diodoro Siculo: Biblioteca storica. Commento storico: Introduzione generale*, Milan: Vita e Pensiero.
Ambler, W. (2001), *The Education of Cyrus, Translated and Annotated by Wayne Ambler*, Ithaca, NY/London: Cornell University Press.

Amiet, P. (1977), *L'art antique du Proche-Orient*, Paris: Éditions d'art Lucien Mazenod.
Anderson, J. K. (1961), *Ancient Greek Horsemanship*, Berkeley, CA: University of California Press.
Andrewes, A. (1961), 'Thucydides and the Persians', *Historia* 10:1, pp. 1-18.
Anson, E. M. (2015²), *Eumenes of Cardia: A Greek among Macedonians*, Leiden: Brill.
Archer, G. L. (tr.) (1958), *St. Jerome: Commentary on Daniel*, Grand Rapids, MI: Baker.
Asheri, D., A. B. Lloyd, and A. Corcella (2007), *A Commentary on Herodotus Books I–IV*, Oxford: Oxford University Press.
Aymard, A. (1938), *Les assemblées de la confédération achaienne: étude critique des institutions et d'histoire*, Bordeaux: Féret (repr. 1967: Rome: L'Erma di Bretschneider).
Backer, F. De (2013), *L'art du siège néo-assyrien*, Leiden: Brill.
Badian, E. (1958), 'The Eunuch Bagoas', *Classical Quarterly* 8:3/4, pp. 144-57.
Badian, E. (1960), 'The Death of Parmenio', *Transactions of the American Philological Association* 91, pp. 324-38.
Badian, E. (1961), 'Harpalus', *Journal of Hellenic Studies* 81, pp. 16-43.
Badian, E. (1967), 'Agis III', *Hermes* 95, pp. 170-92.
Badian, E. (1998), 'Glykera', *DNP* 4, col. 1104.
Badian, E. (1999), 'Meleagros [4]', *DNP* 7, col. 1179.
Balcer, J. M. (1972), 'The Date of Herodotus IV,1: Darius' Scythian Expedition', *Harvard Studies in Classical Philology* 76, pp. 99-132.
Balcer, J. M. (1995), *The Persian Conquest of the Greeks, 545-450 B.C.*, Constance: Universitätsverlag.
Banchich, T. M., 'Artemidoros of Ephesos (438)', in I. Worthington (ed.), *Brill's New Jacoby*, <http://referenceworks.brillonline.com/>.
Barber, G. L. (1935), *The Historian Ephorus*, Cambridge: Cambridge University Press (2nd edn M. C. J. Miller (1993), Chicago, IL: Ares).
Barkworth, P. R. (1993), 'The Organization of Xerxes' Army', *Iranica Antiqua* 27, pp. 149-67.
Barnett, R. D. (1957), 'Persepolis', *Iraq* 19, pp. 55-77.
Barnett, R. D. and W. Forman (1958), *Assyrian Palace Reliefs and their Influence on the Sculptures of Babylonia and Persia*, London: Batchworth Press.
Baron, C. A. (2013), *Timaeus of Tauromenium and Hellenistic Historiography*, Cambridge/New York: Cambridge University Press.
Bassett, S. R. (2002), 'Innocent Victims or Perjurers Betrayed? The Arrest of the Generals in Xenophon's *Anabasis*', *Classical Quarterly* 52:2, pp. 447-61.
Baynham, E. (1995), 'Who Put the "Romance" in the Alexander Romance? The Alexander Romances within Alexander Historiography', *Ancient History Bulletin* 9, pp. 1-13.

Bibliography 553

Bean, G. E. (1967), *Aegean Turkey: An Archaeological Guide*, London/New York: Praeger.
Bean, G. E. and T. B. Mitford (1970), *Journeys in Rough Cilicia, 1964–1968*, Vienna: Akademie Verlag.
Bellinger, A. R. (1963), *Essays on the Coinage of Alexander the Great*, New York: American Numismatic Society.
Beloch, K. J. (1904), *Griechische Geschichte*, Bd. 3: *Die griechische Weltherrschaft*, 2 vols, Strassburg: Trübner.
Bengtson, H. (1971), 'Zur Vorgeschichte der Schlacht bei Salamis', *Chiron* 1, pp. 89–94.
Benveniste, E. (1966), *Titres et noms propres en Iranien ancien*, Paris: Klincksieck.
Benzinger (1894), *RE* 1.2, col. 2404 s.v. 'Antigoneia [1]'.
Berg, P.-L. van (1972), *Corpvs Cvltvs Deae Syriae: Les sources littéraires. Étude critique des sources mythographiques grecques et latines, sauf le De Dea Syria*, Leiden: Brill.
Bergamini, G. (1977), 'Levels of Babylon Reconsidered', *Mesopotamia* 12, pp. 111–52.
Best, J. G. P. (1969), *Thracian Peltasts and their Influence on Greek Warfare*, Groningen: Wolters.
Bichler, R. (2014), 'Semiramis and her Rivals: An Essay', in S. Gaspa et al. (eds), *From Source to History: Studies on Ancient Near Eastern Worlds and Beyond*, Münster: Ugarit-Verlag, pp. 55–72.
Bigwood, J. M. (1976), 'Ctesias' Account of the Revolt of Inarus', *Phoenix* 30:1, pp. 1–25.
Bigwood, J. M. (1978), 'Ctesias' Description of Babylon', *American Journal of Ancient History* 3, pp. 32–52.
Bigwood, J. M. (1980), 'Diodorus and Ctesias', *Phoenix* 34:3, pp. 195–207.
Bikerman, E. (1938), *Les institutions des Séleucides*, Paris: Paul Geuthner.
Billows, R. A. (1990), *Antigonos the One-Eyed and the Creation of the Hellenistic State*, Berkeley/Los Angeles, CA: University of California Press.
Bing, J. D. (1973), 'A Further Note on Cyinda/Kundi', *Historia* 22:2, pp. 346–50.
Birley, A. R. (2002), *Septimius Severus: The African Emperor*, London/New York: Routledge.
Blackman, D. and B. Rankov et al. (2013), *Shipsheds of the Ancient Mediterranean*, Cambridge: Cambridge University Press.
Blok, J. H. (1995), *The Early Amazons: Modern and Ancient Perspectives on a Persistent Myth*, Leiden: Brill.
Boiy, T. (2004), *Late Achaemenid and Hellenistic Babylon*, Louvain: Peeters.
Boiy, T. (2008), *Between High and Low: A Chronology of the Early Hellenistic Period*, Frankfurt: Verlag Antike.
Boliaki, E. (2015), 'Review of Mayor, A. (2014), *The Amazons: Lives and Legends of Warrior Women across the Ancient World*, Princeton/Oxford:

Princeton University Press', *Bryn Mawr Classical Review* 2015.12.05 <http://bmcr.brynmawr.edu/2015/2015-12-05.html>.

Boncquet, J. (1981), 'Klassieke reminiscenties aan een Assyrische ritus: Bedenkingen bij Diodorus Siculus II, 20, 3–5', *Handelingen van de Koninklijke Zuidnederlandse Maatschappij voor Taal- en Letterkunde en Geschiedenis* 35, pp. 25–45.

Boncquet, J. (1987), *Diodorus Siculus (II, 1–34) over Mesopotamië: Een historische kommentaar*, Brussels: Verhandelingen van de Koninklijke Academie van Wetenschappen, Letteren en Schone Kunsten van België, Klasse der Letteren (Jaargang 49, No. 122).

Bosworth, A. B. (1971), 'The Death of Alexander the Great: Rumour and Propaganda', *Classical Quarterly* 21:1, pp. 112–36.

Bosworth, A. B. (1974), 'The Government of Syria under Alexander the Great', *Classical Quarterly* 24:1, pp. 46–64.

Bosworth, A. B. (1978), 'Eumenes, Neoptolemus and *PSI* XII 1284', *Greek, Roman and Byzantine Studies* 19, pp. 227–37.

Bosworth, A. B. (1994), 'Alexander the Great, Part 2: Greece and the Conquered Territories', in CAH^2, vol. 6, pp. 846–75.

Bosworth, A. B. (1998), *Alexander and the East: The Tragedy of Triumph*, Oxford: Oxford University Press.

Botteri, P. (1983), 'Arbitraire d'un éditeur et extraits disparus: Photius, 244, Diodore de Sicile', *Mélanges d'archéologie et d'histoire de l'École française de Rome, série I: Antiquité*, 1983:2, pp. 665–76.

Botteri, P. (1992), *Les fragments de l'histoire des Gracques dans la Bibliothèque de Diodore de Sicile*, Geneva: Droz.

Bottin, C. (1928), 'Les sources de Diodore de Sicile', *Revue Belge de Philologie et d'Histoire* 7:4, pp. 1307–27.

Boucharlat, R. (2012), 'Greece: vii. Greek Art and Architecture in Iran', in *Encyclopædia Iranica Online*, <http://www.iranicaonline.org/articles/greece-vii>, published 15 December 2002, updated 23 February 2012, retrieved 1 March 2013; also published in *EI*, vol. 11, fasc. 3 (2003): 329–33.

Bowden, H. (2013), 'On Kissing and Making Up: Court Protocol and Historiography in Alexander the Great's "Experiment with *Proskynesis*"', *Bulletin of Classical Studies* 56, pp. 55–77.

Boyce, M. (2011), 'Achaemenid Religion', *Iranica Online*, <http://www.iranicaonline.org/articles/achaemenid-religion>, published 15 December 1983, updated 21 July 2011, retrieved 15 March 2014; in print: *EI*, vol. I, fasc. 4, pp. 426–9.

Breisach, E. (2007^3), *Historiography: Ancient, Medieval and Modern*, Chicago: Chicago University Press.

Briant, P. (1972), 'D'Alexandre le Grand aux diadoques: le cas d'Eumène de Kardia. I', *Revue des Études Anciennes* 74, pp. 32–73.

Briant, P. (1973), *Antigone le Borgne: les débuts de sa carrière et les problèmes de l'assemblée macédonienne*, Paris: Les Belles Lettres.

Briant, P. (1984), *L'Asie centrale et les royaumes proche-orientaux du premier millénaire (c. VIIIe–IVe siècles avant notre ère)*, Paris: Éditions Recherche sur les Civilisations.
Briant, P. (2002), *From Cyrus to Alexander: A History of the Persian Empire*, Winona Lake: Eisenbrauns (tr. P. T. Daniels from *Histoire de l'empire perse*, Paris: Fayard, 1996).
Briant, P. (2003), *Darius dans l'ombre d'Alexandre*, Paris: Fayard (tr. 2015 by Jane Marie Todd as *Darius in the Shadow of Alexander*, Cambridge, MA/London: Harvard University Press: *non vidi*).
Bridges, E. (2014), *Imagining Xerxes: Ancient Perspectives on a Persian King*, London: Bloomsbury.
Briscoe, J. (1969), 'Eastern Policy and Senatorial Politics 168–140 BC', *Historia* 18:1, pp. 49–70.
Brosius, M. (2000), *The Persian Empire from Cyrus II to Artaxerxes I*, [London].
Broughton, T. R. S. (1951), *The Magistrates of the Roman Republic. Vol. 1: 509 B.C. –100 B.C*, New York: American Philological Association.
Broughton, T. R. S. (1952), *The Magistrates of the Roman Republic. Vol. 2: 99 B.C.–31 B.C.*, New York: American Philological Association.
Brown, S. E. (2011), 'Ecbatana' <http://www.iranicaonline.org/articles/ecbatana>, orig. 15 December 1997, updated 8 December 2011, retrieved 12 October 2013.
Brunt, P. A. (1962), 'Persian Accounts of Alexander's Campaigns', *Classical Quarterly* 12:1, pp. 141–55.
Bryce, T. (2009), *The Routledge Handbook of the Peoples and Places of Ancient Western Asia: The Near East from the Early Bronze Age to the Fall of the Persian Empire*, London: Routledge.
Burn, A. R. (1952), 'Notes on Alexander's Campaigns (332–330)', *Journal of Hellenic Studies* 72, pp. 81–91.
Burstein, S. M., 'Agatharchides of Knidos (86)', in I. Worthington (ed.), *Brill's New Jacoby*, <http://referenceworks.brillonline.com/>.
Burton, A. (1972), *Diodorus Siculus: Book I, A Commentary*, Leiden: Brill.
Busolt, G. (1890), 'Quellenkritische Beiträge zur Geschichte der römischen Revolutionszeit', *Neue Jahrbücher für Philologie und Pädagogik* 141: pp. 321–49, 405–38.
Calmeyer, P. (1973), 'Zur Genese altiranischer Motive, I, Herrscher über Schützfiguren', *Archäologische Mitteilungen aus Iran*, n.s. 6, pp. 135–52.
Calmeyer, P. (1975), 'Hamadān', *RLA* 4, cols. 64–7.
Cameron, A. (ed.) (1989), *History as Text: The Writing of Ancient History*, London: Duckworth.
Campbell, D. B. (2011), 'Ancient Catapults: Some Hypotheses Reexamined', *Hesperia* 80:4, pp. 677–700.
Capomacchia, A. M. G. (1986), *Semiramis: una femminalità ribaltata*, Rome: L'Erma di Bretschneider.

Carney, E. D. (1980), 'Alexander the Lyncestian: The Disloyal Opposition', *Greek, Roman and Byzantine Studies* 21:1, pp. 23–33.
Cartledge, P. (2013), *After Thermopylae: The Oath of Plataea and the End of the Graeco-Persian Wars*, Oxford: Oxford University Press.
Casabonne, O. (1995), 'Le syennésis cilicien et Cyrus: l'apport des sources numismatiques', in P. Briant (ed.), *Dans les pas de dix mille: peuples et pays du Proche-Orient vus par un Grec*, Toulouse: Presses Universitaires de Mirail, pp. 147–72.
Casson, L. (1971), *Ships and Seamanship in the Ancient World*, Princeton, NJ: Princeton University Press.
Cavallaro, M. A. (1977), 'Un "tendency" industriale e la tradizione storiografica su Agatocle', *Historia* 25:1, 33–61.
Cawkwell, G. L. (1961), 'The Common Peace of 366/5 BC', *Classical Quarterly* 11:1, pp. 80–6.
Cawkwell, G. L. (1963), 'Notes on the Peace of 375/4', *Historia* 12:1, pp. 84–95.
Cawkwell, G. L. (2005), *The Greek Wars: The Failure of Persia*, Oxford: Oxford University Press.
Ceccarelli, P., 'Aristeides of Miletos (286)' in I. Worthington (ed.), *Brill's New Jacoby*, <http://referenceworks.brillonline.com/>.
Champion, C. B., 'Antandros of Syracuse (565)' in I. Worthington (ed.), *Brill's New Jacoby*, <http://referenceworks.brillonline.com/>.
Chantraine, P. (1968), *Dictionnaire étymologique de la langue grecque*, vol. 1, Paris: Klincksieck.
Charles, M. B. (2008), 'African Forest Elephants and Turrets in the Ancient World', *Phoenix* 62:3/4, pp. 338–62.
Charles, M. B. (2011), 'Immortals and Apple Bearers: Towards a Better Understanding of Achaemenid Infantry Units', *Classical Quarterly* 61:1, pp. 114–33.
Christesen, P. (2007), *Olympic Victor Lists and Ancient Greek History*, Cambridge: Cambridge University Press.
Clarke, K. (2007), 'Les fragments de Posidonios chez Athénée', in D. Lenfant (ed.), *Athénée et les fragments d'historiens: Actes du colloque de Strasbourg (16–18 juin 2005)*, Paris: De Boccard, pp. 291–302.
Cole, J. W. (1978), 'Alexander Philhellene and Themistocles', *Antiquité Classique* 47:1, pp. 37–49.
Collins, A. W. (2001), 'The Office of Chiliarch under Alexander and the Successors', *Phoenix* 55:3/4, pp. 259–83.
Collon, D. (1977), 'Ivory', *Iraq* 39:2, pp. 219–22.
Cook, J. M. (1983), *The Persian Empire*, London: Dent.
Cozzoli, U. (1958), 'La Beozia durante il conflitto tra l'Ellada e la Persia', *Rivista di Filologia e d'Istruzione Classica* 86, pp. 264–87.
Dalley, S. (1994), 'Nineveh, Babylon and the Hanging Gardens', *Iraq* 56, pp. 45–58.
Dalley, S. (2013), *The Mystery of the Hanging Garden of Babylon:*

An Elusive World Wonder Traced, Oxford: Oxford University Press.
Daman Singh, S. (1989²), *Ancient Indian Warfare: With Special Reference to the Vedic Period*, Delhi: Motilal Banarsidass Publ.
Dandamayev, M. A. (1990), 'Cambyses', *Iranica Online*, <http://www.iranicaonline.org/articles/cambyses-opers>, published 15 December 1990, retrieved 27 February 2014; in print: *EI*, vol. IV, fasc. 7, pp. 726–9.
Dandamaev, M. A. and V. G. Lukonin (1989), *The Culture and Social Institutions of Ancient Iran*, Cambridge: Cambridge University Press.
Daryaee, T. (2016), 'Whipping the Sea and the Earth: Xerxes at the Hellespont and Yima at the Vara, *Dabir* 1:2, pp. 4–9.
Davidson, J. (2007), *The Greeks and Greek Love: A Radical Reappraisal of Homosexuality in Ancient Greece*, London: Weidenfeld & Nicolson.
Depuydt, L. (2008), *From Xerxes' Murder (465) to Arridaios' Execution (317): Updates to Achaemenid Chronology (Including Errata in Past Reports)*, Oxford: Archaeopress.
Deshayes, J. (1969), *Les civilisations de l'orient ancien*, Paris: Arthaud.
Dessel, P. van and H. Hauben (1977), 'Rhodes, Alexander and the Diadochi from 333/332 to 304 B.C.', *Historia* 26:3, pp. 307–39.
Dillery, J. D. (2015), *Clio's Other Sons: Berossus and Manetho, with an Afterword on Demetrius*, Ann Arbor, MI: University of Michigan Press.
Dittenberger, W. and K. Purgold (eds) (1896), *Die Inschriften von Olympia*, Berlin: Asher.
Dodson, A. (2012), *Afterglow of Empire: Egypt from the Fall of the New Kingdom to the Saite Renaissance*, Cairo: American University in Cairo Press.
Dodson, A. and S. Ikram (1998), *The Mummy in Ancient Egypt: Equipping the Dead for Eternity*, London: Thames & Hudson.
Dossin, G. (1972), 'Memnon, fondateur de Suse', *Bulletin de la Classe des Lettres de l'Académie Royale de Belgique* 58, pp. 324–39.
Dowden, K., 'Poseidonios (87)', in I. Worthington (ed.), *Brill's New Jacoby*, <http://referenceworks.brillonline.com/>.
Downey, G. (1961), *A History of Antioch of Syria from Seleucus to the Arab Conquest*, Princeton, NJ: Princeton University Press.
Dressel, H. (1905), 'Das Tempelbild der Athene Polias auf den Münzen von Priene', in *Sitzungsberichte der königlichen preussischen Akademie der Wissenschaften* (Sitzungsbericht 23, 4. Mai 1905, Vortrag 13. April 1905), Berlin: Georg Reimer, pp. 467–76.
Drews, R. (1962), 'Diodorus and his Sources', *American Journal of Philology* 83:4, pp. 383–92.
Drews, R. (1965), 'Assyria in Classical Universal Histories', *Historia* 14:1, pp. 129–42.
Drews, R. (1969), 'Aethiopian Memnon, African or Asiate', *Rheinisches Museum für Philologie* 112, pp. 191–2.

Drews, R. (1973), *The Greek Accounts of Eastern History*, Cambridge, MA: Harvard University Press.
Drews, R. (1974), 'Sargon, Cyrus and Mesopotamian Folk-History', *Journal of Near Eastern Studies* 33:4, pp. 387–93.
Dreyer, B. (2011), 'How to Become a "Relative" of the King: Careers and Hierarchy at the Court of Antiochus III', *American Journal of Philology* 132:1, pp. 45–57.
Ducrey, P. (1968), *Le traitement des prisonniers de guerre dans la Grèce antique: des origines à la conquête romaine*, Paris: De Boccard.
Dumortier, J. (1963), 'La retraite de Xerxès après Salamine (Eschyle, *Perses*, 480–514)', *Revue des Études Grecques* 76:2, pp. 358–60.
Ebert, J. (1982), 'Zum Perser-Epigramm von Delphi (Diod.XI 14,4)', *Zeitschrift für Papyrologie und Epigraphik* 47, pp. 35–6.
Eckstein, A. M. (2008), *Rome Enters the Greek East: From Anarchy to Hierarchy in the Hellenistic Mediterranean, 230–170 BC*, Malden, MA/ Oxford: Blackwell.
Edelstein, L. and I. G. Kidd (eds) (1989²), *Posidonius. Vol. 1: The Fragments*, Cambridge: Cambridge University Press.
Eggermont, P. H. L. (1970–1), 'New Notes on Aśoka and his Successors (part 3)', *Persica* 5, pp. 69–102.
Ehrenberg, V. (1933), 'Die Opfer Alexanders an der Indusmündung', in O. Stein and W. Gampert (eds), *Festschrift Moriz Winternitz*, Leipzig: Harassowitz, pp. 287–97 (repr. in K. F. Stroheker and A. J. Graham (eds) (1965), *Polis und Imperium: Beiträge zur alten Geschichte*, Zurich/ Stuttgart: Artemis, pp. 449–65).
Eilers, W. (1971), *Semiramis: Entstehung und Nachhall einer altorientalischer Sage*, Vienna: Böhlau.
Ellis, J. R. (1971), 'Amyntas Perdikka, Philip II and Alexander the Great', *Journal of Hellenic Studies* 91, pp. 15–24.
Engel, R. (1971), 'Anmerkungen zur Schlacht von Orcynia', *Museum Helveticum* 28:4, pp. 227–31.
Engel, R. (1972a), 'Zur Geschichtsbild des Hieronymos von Kardia', *Athenaeum* 50, pp. 120–5.
Engel, R. (1972b), 'Die Überlieferung der Schlacht bei Kretopolis', *Historia* 21:3: 501–7.
Engels, D. W. (1978), *Alexander the Great and the Logistics of the Macedonian Army*, Berkeley/Los Angeles: University of California Press.
Engels, D. W. (2011), 'Ein syrisches Sizilien? Seleukidische Aspekte des ersten Sizilischen Sklavenkriegs und der Herrschaft des Eunus-Antiochos', *Polifemo* 11, pp. 233–51.
Engels, J. (1998), 'Hermias [1]', *DNP* 5, col. 435.
Erskine, A. (ed.) (2005), *A Companion to the Hellenistic World*, Malden, MA/Oxford: Wiley/Blackwell.
Evers, E. (1882), 'Ein Beitrag zur Untersuchung der Quellenbenutzung bei Diodor', in *Festschrift zu dem fünfzigjährigen Jubiläum der*

Königstädtischen Realschule zu Berlin, Berlin: Lehrerkollegium der Anstalt, pp. 241–92.

Fakour, M. (2012), 'Garden i. Achaemenid Period', *Iranica Online*, <http://www.iranicaonline.org/articles/garden-i>, published 15 December 2000, updated 2 February 2012, retrieved 8 January 2014; in print: *EI*, vol. X, fasc. 3: 297–8.

Farkas, A. (1969), 'The Horse and Rider in Achaemenid Art', *Persica* 4, pp. 57–76.

Farrell, W. J. (1961), 'A Revised Itinerary of the Route Followed by Cyrus the Younger through Syria, 401 B. C.', *Journal of Hellenic Studies* 81, pp. 153–5.

Fischer-Bovet, C. (2013), 'Egyptian Warriors: The *Machimoi* of Herodotus and the Ptolemaic Army', *Classical Quarterly* 63:1, pp. 209–36.

Fleckeisen, A. and H. Masius (eds) (1871), *Neue Jahrbücher für Philologie und Pädagogik* 41:104, Leipzig: Teubner, pp. 446–8.

Forbes, R. J. (1964), *Studies in Ancient Technology*, vol. 1, Leiden: Brill.

Fornara, C. W. (1981), 'Herodotus' Knowledge of the Archidamian War', *Hermes* 109:2, pp. 149–56.

Forsdyke, E. J. (1956), *Greece before Homer: Ancient Chronology and Mythology*, London: Parrish.

Forshaw, L. H. S. (1977), 'The Memnonian Road', *Classical World* 70:7, p. 454.

Foucher, A. and E. Bazin-Foucher (1942–7), *Vieille Route de l'Inde de Bactres à Taxila*, 3 vols in 2, Paris: Mémoires de la Délégation archéologique française en Afghânistân.

Fowler, R. L. (ed.) (2001–13), *Early Greek Mythography*, 2 vols, Oxford: Oxford University Press.

Franck, L. (1966), 'Sources classiques concernant la Cappadoce', *Revue Hittite et Asianique* 24, pp. 1–186.

Frisk, H. (1973), *Griechisches etymologisches Wörterbuch*, vol. 1, Heidelberg: Carl Winter.

Frye, R. N. (1972), 'Gestures of Deference to Royalty in Ancient Iran', *Iranica Antiqua* 9, pp. 102–7.

Frye, R. N. (1992), 'Assyria and Syria: Synonyms', *Journal of Near Eastern Studies* 51:4, pp. 281–5.

Fuhrmann, H. (1931), *Philoxenos von Eretria: archäologische Untersuchungen über zwei Alexandermosaike*, Göttingen: Dieterichische Universitäts-Buchdrückerei.

Gardiner, A. (1961), 'The Egyptian Memnon', *American Journal of Archaeology* 47:1, pp. 91–9.

Gardiner-Garden, J. R. (1987), *Ktesias on Early Central Asian History and Ethnography*, Bloomington, IN: Indiana University Press.

Gera, D. (ed.) (1997), *Warrior Women: The Anonymous Tractatus de mulieribus claris in bello*, Leiden: Brill.

Glassner, J. J. (2004), *Mesopotamian Chronicles*, Atlanta, GA: SBL Press.

Goossens, G. (1940), 'L'histoire d'Assyrie de Ctésias', *Antiquité Classique* 9, pp. 25–45.
Goossens, G. (1950), 'Le sommaire des Persica par Photius', *Revue Belge de Philologie et d'Histoire* 28, pp. 516–521.
Gorman, R. J. and V. B. Gorman (2014), *Corrupting Luxury in Ancient Greek Literature*, Ann Arbor, MI: University of Michigan Press.
Goukowsky, P. (1967), 'Κάμελος δρομάς', *Revue de Philologie, de Littérature et d'Histoire Ancienne* 41, pp. 247–54.
Goukowsky, P. (1969), 'Clitarque seul? Remarques sur les sources du livre XVII de Diodore de Sicile', *Revue des Études Anciennes* 71, pp. 320–37.
Goukowsky, P. (1972), 'Le roi Pôros, son éléphant et quelques autres (en marge de Diodore, XVII, 88, 6)', *Bulletin de Correspondence Hellénique* 96:1, pp. 473–502.
Gowers, W. (1948), 'African Elephants and Ancient Authors', *African Affairs* 47:188, pp. 173–80.
Grainger, J. D. (1990a), *Seleukos Nikator: Constructing a Hellenistic Kingdom*, London/New York: Routledge (repr. 2013).
Grainger, J. D. (1990b), *The Cities of Seleukid Syria*, Oxford: Clarendon.
Grainger, J. D. (1997), *A Seleukid Prosopography and Gazetteer*, Leiden: Brill.
Grainger, J. D. (2011), *Hellenistic and Roman Naval Warfare 336BC–31BC*, Barnsley: Pen & Sword Maritime.
Grainger, J. D. (2014), *The Rise of the Seleukid Empire (323–223 BC): Seleukos I to Seleukos III*, Barnsley: Pen & Sword History.
Granier, F. (1931), *Die makedonische Heeresversammlung: ein Beitrag zum antiken Staatsrecht*, Munich: Beck.
Graux, C. (1880), *Essai sur les origines du fonds grec de l'Escurial: épisode de l'histoire de la renaissance des lettres en Espagne*, Paris: Bibliothèque de l'École des Hautes Études, Sciences Philologiques et Historiques, fasc. 46.
Grayson, A. K. (1991a), 'Assyria 668–635 B.C.: The Reign of Ashurbanipal', in CAH^2, vol. 3.2, pp. 142–61.
Grayson, A. K. (1991b), 'Assyrian Civilization', in CAH^2, vol. 3.2, pp. 194–228.
Grenfell, B. P. and A. S. Hunt (eds) (1919), *The Oxyrhynchus Papyri*, vol. XIII, London: Egypt Exploration Society.
Gruen, E. S. (2011), *Rethinking the Other in Antiquity: Martin Classical Lectures*, Princeton, NJ/Oxford: Princeton University Press.
Gullini, G. (1979), 'Babylon as Cultural Heritage', *Sumer* 35, pp. 187–90.
Habicht, C. (1961), 'Falsche Urkunden zur Geschichte Athens im Zeitalter der Perserkriege', *Hermes* 89:1, pp. 1–35.
Habicht, C. (2006), *The Hellenistic Monarchies: Selected Papers*, Ann Arbor, MI: University of Michigan Press.
Hadley, R. A. (1969), 'Hieronymus of Cardia and Early Seleucid Mythology', *Historia* 18:2, pp. 142–52.

Haerinck, E. (1973), 'Le palais achéménide de Babylone', *Iranica Antiqua* 10, pp. 108–32.
Hammond, N. G. L. (1937), 'The Sources of Diodorus Siculus XVI', *Classical Quarterly* 31:2, pp. 79–91.
Hammond, N. G. L. (1938), 'The Sources of Diodorus Siculus XVI, part 2', *Classical Quarterly* 32:3/4, pp. 137–51.
Hammond, N. G. L. (1967²), *A History of Greece to 322 B.C.*, Oxford: Oxford University Press.
Hammond, N. G. L. (1973), *Studies in Ancient Greek History*, Oxford: Oxford University Press.
Hammond, N. G. L. (1992), 'Alexander's Charge at the Battle of Issus in 333 B.C.', *Historia* 41:4, pp. 395–406.
Hammond, N. G. L. (1998), 'The Branchidae at Didyma and in Sogdiana', *Classical Quarterly* 48:2, pp. 339–44.
Hammond, N. G. L. and F. W. Hammond (1988), *A History of Macedonia. Vol. 3: 336–167 B.C.*, Oxford: Clarendon.
Hammond, P. C. (1973), *The Nabataeans: Their History, Culture and Archaeology*, Göteborg: Åström.
Harrison, T. (2011), *Writing Ancient Persia*, London: Bristol Classical Press.
Heckel, W. (2009), *Who's Who in the Age of Alexander the Great*, Malden, MA/Oxford/Chichester: Wiley-Blackwell.
Heller, A. (2015), 'Why the Greeks Know so Little about Assyrian and Babylonian History', in R. Rollinger and E. van Dongen (eds.), *Mesopotamia in the Ancient World: Impact, Continuities, Parallels. Proceedings of the Seventh Symposium of the Melammu Project Held in Obergurgl, Austria, November 4–8, 2013*, Münster: Ugarit-Verlag, pp. 331–48.
Hereward, D. (1974), 'Some Notes on Miltiades and Kimon', *Museum Africum* 3, pp. 44–8.
Herrmann, A. (1949), 'Paraitakene [1] & [2]', *RE* 18.3, col. 1182.
Herrmann, P. (1987), 'Milesier am Seleukidenhof: Prosopografische Beiträge zur Geschichte Milets im 2. Jhdt. v. Chr.', *Chiron* 17, pp. 171–90.
Herwerden, H. van (1860), see ad *Excerpta Constantiana*, texts and editions.
Herzfeld, E. E. (1968), *The Persian Empire: Studies in Geography and Ethnography of the Ancient Near East, Edited from the Posthumous Papers by Gerold Walser, Bibliography and Addenda by W. Nagel*, Wiesbaden: Steiner.
Hignett, C. (1963), *Xerxes' Invasion of Greece*, Oxford: Oxford University Press.
Hinz, W. et al. (1975), *Altiranisches Sprachgut der Nebenüferlieferungen*, Wiesbaden: Harrassowitz.
Hirsch, S. W. (1985), *The Friendship of the Barbarians: Xenophon and the Persian Empire*, Hanover, NE /London: University Press of New England.
Hofstetter, J. (1978), *Die Griechen in Persien: Prosopographie der Griechen in persischen Reich vor Alexander*, Berlin: Reimer.

Holt, F. L. (1988), *Alexander the Great and Bactria: The Formation of a Greek Frontier in Central Asia*, Leiden: Brill.
Holt, F. L. (2003), *Alexander the Great and the Mystery of the Elephant Medallions*, Berkeley, CA: University of California Press.
Honigmann, E. (1928), 'Ašqalûna', *RLA* 1, p. 169.
Hornblower, J. (1981), *Hieronymus of Cardia*, Oxford: Oxford University Press.
Hornblower, S. (1996), 'Apollodorus (6) of Athens', in S. Hornblower and A. Spawforth (eds), *The Oxford Classical Dictionary*, 3rd edn, Oxford: Oxford University Press, p. 124.
Hornblower, S. (2011⁴), *The Greek World 479–323 BC*, London/New York: Routledge.
How, W. W. and J. Wells (1964), *A Commentary on Herodotus, with Introduction and Appendixes by W. W. How and J. J. Wells, Reprinted with Corrections*, 2 vols, Oxford: Clarendon (orig. edn 1912).
Hoyos, D. (2001), 'Polybius and the Papyrus: The Persuasiveness of "P. Rylands" III 491', *Zeitschrift für Papyrologie und Epigrafik* 134, pp. 71–9.
[Imhof, A.?] (1871), 'Prof. Dr. Bergmann. Nekrolog', in A. Fleckeisen and H. Masius (eds), *Neue Jahrbücher für Philologie und Pädagogik* 41:104, Leipzig: Teubner, pp. 446–8.
Irigoin, J. (1959), 'Pour une étude des centres de copie byzantins, II : Quelques groupes de manuscrits', *Scriptorium* 13, pp. 177–208.
Isserlin, B. S. J. (1994), 'The Canal of Xerxes on the Mount Athos Peninsula', *Annals of the British School at Athens* 89, pp. 277–84.
Jacobs, B. (2011), 'Ktesias und die Architektur Babylons', in Wiesehöfer et al. 2011: 141–58.
Jacoby, F. (1913), 'Hieronymos [10]', *RE* 8.2, cols. 1540–60.
Jacoby, F. (1921), 'Kleitarchos [2]', *RE* 11.1, cols. 622–54.
Jacoby, F. (1922), 'Ktesias', *RE* 11.2, cols. 2032–73.
Jacoby, F. (1927), 'Silenos [1]', *RE* 3A.1, cols. 53–6.
Junge, P. J. (1941), 'Satrapie und Natio', *Klio* 34, pp. 1–55.
Jursa, M. (2011), 'Höflinge (*ša rēši, ša rēš šarru, ustarbaru*) in babylonischen Quellen der ersten Jahrtausends', in Wiesehöfer et al. 2011: pp. 159–74.
Justi, F. (1895), *Iranisches Namenbuch*, Marburg [repr. Hildesheim: Olms, 1963].
Kaper, O. (2015), 'Petubastis IV in the Dakhla Oasis: New Evidence about an Early Rebellion and its Suppression in Political Memory', in J. M. Silverman and C. Waerzeggers (eds), *Political Memory in and after the Persian Empire*, Atlanta, GA: SBL Press, pp. 125–50.
Kärst, J. (1893), 'Alexandros [12]', *RE* 1.1, col. 1435.
Keaveney, A. (2010), 'The Chiliarch and the Person of the King', in B. Jacobs and R. Rollinger (eds), *Der Achämenidenhof/The Achaemenid Court*, Wiesbaden: Harrassowitz, pp. 499–508.

Keaveney, A. (2011), *The Persian Invasions of Greece*, Barnsley: Pen & Sword Military.
Kent, R. G. (1953²), *Old Persian: Grammar, Texts, Lexicon*, New Haven, CT: American Oriental Society.
Klinkott, H. (2005), *Der Satrap: Ein achaimenidischer Amtsträger und seine Handlungsspielräume*, Frankfurt: Verlag Antike.
Kneppe, A. (1989), 'Timarchos von Milet: ein Usurpator im Seleukidenreich', in H. J. Drexhage and J. Sünskes (eds), *Migratio et Commvtatio: Studien zur alten Geschichte und deren Nachleben*, St. Katharinen: Scripta Mercaturae Verlag, pp. 37–49.
Kock, T. (ed.) (1880), *Comicorum Atticorum Fragmenta,*. Vol. 1: *Antiquae comoediae fragmenta*, Berlin: Teubner (repr. 1976, Utrecht: Hes).
Koldewey, R. J. (1914), *The Excavations at Babylon* (tr. A. S. Johns), London: Macmillan.
Koldewey, R. J. (1925⁴), *Das Wiedererstehende Babylon*, Leipzig: Hinrichs.
Koldewey, R. J. (1931–2), *Die Königsburgen von Babylon*, 2 vols, ed. F. Wetzel: *1. Teil: Die Südburg*; *2. Teil: Die Hauptburg und der Sommerpalast Nebukadnezars im Hügel Babil*, Leipzig: Hinrichs (repr. 1969, Osnabrück: Otto Zeller).
König, F. W. (1972), *Die Persika des Ktesias von Knidos*, Graz: Weidner.
Kosmin, P. J. (2014), *The Land of the Elephant Kings: Space, Territory, and Ideology in the Seleucid Empire*, Cambridge, MA: Harvard University Press.
Kresten, O. (1980), 'Der Schreiber und Handschriftenhändler Darmarios', in D. Harlfinger (ed.), *Griechische Kodikologie und Textüberlieferung*, Darmstadt: WBG, pp. 406–19.
Kromayer, J. and G. Veith (1928), *Heerwesen und Kriegführung der Griechen und Römer*, Munich: Beck, Bd. I: *Die Griechen*.
Krumbholz, P. (1886), 'Diodors assyrische Geschichte', *Rheinisches Museum für Philologie* 41, pp. 321–41.
Krumbholz, P. (1895), 'Zu den Assyriaka des Ktesias', *Rheinisches Museum für Philologie* 50, pp. 205–40.
Krumbholz, P. (1897), 'Zu den Assyriaka des Ktesias', *Rheinisches Museum für Philologie* 52, pp. 237–85.
Kuhrt, A. (1995), *The Ancient Near East*, 2 vols, London: Routledge.
Kuhrt, A. (2007), *The Persian Empire: A Corpus of Sources from the Achaemenid Period*, 2 vols, London/New York: Routledge.
Kuhrt, A. and S. Sherwin-White (1987), 'Xerxes' Destruction of Babylonian Temples', in Sancisi-Weerdenburg and Kuhrt 1987: 69–78.
Kuhrt, A. and H. Sancisi-Weerdenburg (eds) (1988), *Method and Theory: Proceedings of the London 1985 Achaemenid History Workshop* (*AchHist*, vol. III).
Kulke, H. and D. Rothermund (1986), *A History of India*, London: Routledge (5th edn 2010).

Kuyper, J. De (1979), 'Les auteurs grecs et la denomination des regions du Proche-Orient ancien', *Akkadica* 14:5, pp. 16–31.
Labarbe, J. (1952), 'Chiffres et mode de repartition de la flotte grecque à l'Artémision et à Salamine', *Bulletin de Correspondance Hellénique* 76, pp. 384–441.
Labarbe, J. (1957), *La loi navale de Thémistocle*, Paris: Les Belles Lettres.
Lambrick, H. T. (1964), *Sind: A General Introduction*, Hyderabad (2nd edn 1975: Hyderabad/Karachi/London): Sindhi Adabi Board.
Lane Fox, R. J. (1996), 'Text and Image: Alexander the Great, Coins, and Elephants', *Bulletin of the Institute of Classical Studies* 41: 87–108.
Lane Fox, R. J. (2008), *Travelling Heroes: Greeks and their Myths in the Epic Age of Homer*, London: Allen Lane.
Lanfranchi, G. B., M. Roaf, and R. Rollinger (eds) (2003), *Continuity of Empire(?): Assyria, Media, Persia*, Padua: S.a.r.g.o.n. Editrice.
Laqueur, R. (1936), 'Timaeus [3]', *RE* 6A.1, cols. 1076–203.
Laqueur, R. (1958), 'Diodorea', *Hermes* 86:3, pp. 257–90.
Lascaris, C. (1866), *De Scriptoribus Graecis Patria Siculis* 9, in Migne *PG*, t. 161.
Lauffer, S. (1959), 'Die Diodordublette XV 38 = 50 über Friedensschlüsse zu Sparta', *Historia* 8:3, pp. 315–48.
Laumonier, A. (1958), *Les cultes indigènes en Carie*, Paris: De Boccard.
Launey, M. (1949), *Recherches sur les armées hellénistiques. Vol. 1: Recherches ethniques*, Paris: De Boccard.
Law, C. B. (1969), 'Śākala, an Ancient Indian City', *East and West* 19, pp. 401–9.
Lazenby, J. F. (1975), 'Pausanias, Son of Kleombrotos', *Hermes* 103:2, pp. 235–51.
Lazenby, J. F. (1987), 'The Diekplous', *Greece & Rome* 34:2, pp. 169–77.
Leake, W. M. (1841²), *The Topogrophy of Athens: With Some Remarks on its Antiquities*, London: Gilbert & Rivington.
Leick, G. (2001), *Mesopotamia: The Invention of the City*, London: Allen Lane.
Lendering, J. (2004), *Alexander de Grote: De Ondergang van het Perzische Rijk*, Amsterdam: Athenaeum-Polak & Van Gennep.
Lenfant, D. (ed.) (2009), *Les Histoires perses de Dinon et d'Héraclide: fragments édités, traduits et commentés par Dominique Lenfant*, Paris: De Boccard (*Persika* 13).
Lenfant, D. (ed.) (2011), *Les Perses vus par les Grecs: lire les sources classiques sur l'empire achéménide*, Paris: Armand Colin.
Lenfant, D. (2012), 'Ctesias and his Eunuchs: A Challenge for Modern Historians', *Histos* 6, pp. 257–97.
Lenfant, D. (2014), 'Greek Monographs on the Persian World', in Parmeggiani 2014: pp. 197–210.
Lewis, D. M. (1977), *Sparta and Persia*, Leiden: Brill.
Ley, A. (1996), 'Amazones', *DNP* 1, cols. 575–6.

Lincoln, B. (2007), *Religion, Empire, and Torture: The Case of Achaemenian Persia, with a Postscript on Abu Ghraib*, Chicago/London: University of Chicago Press.

Lincoln, B. (2013), 'Religion, Empire, and the Spectre of Orientalism: A Recent Controversy in Achaemenid Studies', *Journal of Near Eastern Studies* 72:2, pp. 253–65.

Liverani, M. (2003), 'The Rise and Fall of Media', in Lanfranchi et al. 2003: pp. 1–12.

Liverani, M. (2014), *The Ancient Near East: History, Society and Economy*, London/New York: Routledge.

Llewellyn-Jones, L. (2013), *King and Court in Ancient Persia, 559 to 331 BCE*, Edinburgh: Edinburgh University Press.

Llewellyn-Jones, L. (forthcoming), 'The Court', in B. Jacobs and R. Rollinger (eds), *A Companion to the Achaemenid Persian Empire*, Malden, MA/Oxford: Wiley-Blackwell.

Lloyd, A. B. (1994), 'Egypt, 404–332 B.C.', CAH^2, vol. 6: pp. 337–60.

Lloyd-Jones, H. and P. Parsons (eds) (1983), *Supplementum Hellenisticum*, Berlin: De Gruyter.

Lobel, E., C. H. Roberts, E. G. Turner, and J. W. B. Barns (eds) (1957), *The Oxyrhynchus Papyri*, vol. XXIV, London: Egypt Exploration Society.

Luschey, H. (1974), 'Bisutun-Geschichte und Forschungsgeschichte', *Archäologischer Anzeiger* 1, pp. 114–49.

Lutz, H. F. (1937), 'The Alleged Robbers' Guild in Ancient Egypt', *University of California Publications in Semitic Philology* 10:7, pp. 231–42.

Maas, P. (1960^4), *Textkritik*, Leipzig: Teubner.

Macdonald, M. C. A. et al. (2015), 'Arabs and Empires before the Sixth Century [AD]', in G. Fisher (ed.), *Arabs and Empires before Islam*, Oxford: Oxford University Press, pp. 11–89.

MacGinnis, J. D. A. (1988), 'Ctesias and the Fall of Nineveh', *Illinois Classical Studies* 13, pp. 37–42.

Maier, F. G. (1994), 'Cyprus and Phoenicia: From the Cypriot War to the Peace of 311 B.C.', in CAH^2, vol. 6, pp. 326–36.

Malbran-Labat, F. (1982), *L'armée et l'organisation militaire de l'Assyrie: d'après les lettres des Sargonides trouvées à Ninive*, Geneva: Droz.

Malitz, J. (ed.) (1983), *Die Historien des Poseidonios*, Munich: Beck.

Mango, M. M. (1991), 'Chalkis ad Belum', in A. P. Kazhdan (ed.), *The Oxford Dictionary of Byzantium*, Oxford: Oxford University Press.

Manni, E. (1957–8), 'Sileno in Diodoro?', *Atti della Academia Palermo* ser. 4a, 18:2, pp. 81–8.

Manni, E. (1966), 'Note siceliote, I: un frammento di Antandro? Sull'itinerario siciliano dei thearodokoi delfici', *ΚΩΚΑΛΟΣ* 12, pp. 163–71.

Markoe, G. E. (2000), *Phoenicians*, London: British Museum Press.

Marsden, E. W. (1964), *The Campaign of Gaugamela*, Liverpool: Liverpool University Press.

Martini, E. (1911), *Textgeschichte der Bibliotheke des Patriarchen Photios von Konstantinopel. 1ster Teil: Die Handschriften, Ausgaben und Ueberträgungen*, Leipzig: Abhandlungen der philologisch-historische Klasse der Königliche Sächsische Gesellschaft der Wissenschaften, 28: 6.
Marzahn, J. et al. (eds) (2008), *Babylon: Mythos und Wahrheit. Bd. 1: Wahrheit; Bd. 2: Mythos* (Katalog zur Ausstellung in Berlin, 26.6.2008–5.10.2008, Staatliche Museen zu Berlin, Pergamonmuseum), Munich: Hirmer.
Maul, S. (1996), 'Chaldaioi', *DNP* 2, cols. 1086–7.
Mayor, A. (2009), *Greek Fire, Poison Arrows, and Scorpion Bombs: Biological and Chemical Warfare in the Ancient World*, London/New York: Duckworth.
Mayor, A. (2013), 'Alexander the Great and the Rain of Burning Sand', *Wonders & Marvels*, <http://www.wondersandmarvels.com/2013/02/alexander-the-great-and-the-rain-of-burning-sand.html>, published 6 February 2013, retrieved 15 February 2013.
Mayor, A. (2014), *The Amazons: Lives and Legends of Warrior Women across the Ancient World*, Princeton/Oxford: Princeton University Press.
Mayor, A., J. Colarusso, and D. Saunders (2014), 'Making Sense of Nonsense Inscriptions Associated with Amazons and Scythians on Athenian Vases', *Hesperia* 83:3, pp. 447–93.
Mayrhofer, M. (1973), *Onomastica Persepolitana: Das altiranische Namengut der Persepolis-Täfelchen*, Vienna: Akademie Verlag.
McClure, L. K. (2003), *Courtesans at Table: Gender and Greek Literary Culture in Athenaeus*, New York/London: Routledge.
McGushin, P. (1992), *Sallust: The Histories. Vol. 1: Books i-ii, Translated with an Introduction and Commentary by Patrick McGushin*, Oxford: Clarendon.
Meijering, R. (2014/15), 'Religious Support and Political Gain: The Seleucids, Miletus, and Didyma, 301–281 BC', *Talanta* 46/7, pp. 237–49.
Meister, K. (1967), *Die sizilische Geschichte bei Diodor von den Anfängen bis zum Tod des Agathokles: Quellenuntersuchungen zu Buch IV–XXI*, dissertation, Universität München.
Meister, K. (1990), *Die griechische Geschichtsschreibung: Von den Anfängen bis zum Ende des Hellenismus*, Stuttgart: Kohlhammer.
Meritt, B. D., H. T. Wade-Gery, and M. F. McGregor (1939), *The Athenian Tribute Lists*, vol. I, Cambridge, MA: Harvard University Press.
Mesnil du Buisson, R. M. E. L. du (1973), *Nouvelles études sur les dieux et les mythes de Canaan*, Leiden: Brill.
Meulenaere, H. de (1963), 'La famille royale des Nectanébo', *Zeitschrift für Ägyptische Sprache und Altertumskunde* 90, pp. 90–3.
Meyer, E. (1896), 'Artaios', *RE* 2, col. 1303.
Meyer, E. (1927), 'Alexander und der Ganges', *Klio* 21, pp. 183–91.
Miller, E. (1848), *Catalogue des manuscrits grecs de la bibliothèque de l'Escurial*, Paris: Notices et extraits des manuscrits de la bibliothèque

nationale et autres bibliothèques, Tôme 31, 2e partie (repr. Amsterdam: Hakkert, 1966).
Miltner, F. (1952), 'Der Okeanos in der persischen Weltreichsidee', *Saeculum* 3, pp. 522–55.
Mitchel, F. W. (1964), 'A Note on *IG* II² 370', *Phoenix* 18:1, pp. 13–17.
Mitchell, S. (1994), 'Three Cities in Pisidia', *Anatolian Studies* 44, pp. 129–48.
Mitchell, T. C. (2000), 'Camels in the Assyrian Bas-Reliefs', *Iraq* 62, pp. 187–94.
Momigliano, A. (1932), 'La cronaca babilonese sui Diadochi. II. Commento storico', *Rivista di Filologia e d'Istruzione Classica*, n.s. 10, pp. 462–84.
Momigliano, A. (1935), 'Re e popolo in Macedonia prima di Alessandro Magno', *Athenaeum* 13, pp. 3–21.
Moorey, P. R. S. (1988), 'The Peoples of the Empire', in J. Boardman (ed.), *CAH²*, *Plates to Volume IV*, Cambridge: Cambridge University Press.
Morgan, J. (2016), *Greek Perspectives on the Achaemenid Empire: Persia through the Looking Glass*, Edinburgh: Edinburgh University Press.
Mørkholm, O. (1966), *Antiochus IV of Syria*, Copenhagen: Gyldendal.
Morrison, J. S. and R. T. Williams (1968), *Greek Oared Ships 900–322 B.C.*, Cambridge: Cambridge University Press.
Mousavi, A. (2012), *Persepolis: Discovery and Afterlife of a World Wonder*, Boston/Berlin: De Gruyter.
Muntz, C. E. (2012), 'Diodorus Siculus and Megasthenes: A Reappraisal', *Classical Philology* 107:1, pp. 21–37.
Murray, W. (2012), *The Age of Titans: The Rise and Fall of the Great Hellenistic Navies*, Oxford: Oxford University Press.
Naas, V. and M. Simon (eds) (2016), *De Samos à Rome: personnalité et influence de Douris*, Paris: Presses Universitaires de Paris-Ouest.
Nefiodkin, A. K. (2004), 'On the Origin of the Scythed Chariots', *Historia* 53:3, pp. 369–78.
Németh, A. (2010), *Imperial Systematization of the Past: Emperor Constantine VII and His Historical Excerpts*, doctoral thesis, Budapest: Central European University.
Newell, E. T. (1918), *The Seleucid Mint of Antioch*, New York: American Numismatic Society.
Newell, E. T. (1938), *Miscellanea numismatica: Cyrene to India*, New York: American Numismatic Society.
Nichols, A. (2011), *Ctesias on India: Introduction, Translation and Commentary*, Bristol: Bristol Classical Press.
Niehr, H. (1999), 'Kasion', *DNP* 6, col. 313.
Nijssen, D. (2015/16), 'The Median Dark Age: Iran on the Eve of Cyrus's Conquests', *Ancient History Magazine* 1:1, pp. 50–5.
Nilakanta Sastri, K. A. (1957), *A Comprehensive History of India: In Twelve Volumes. Vol. 2: The Mauryas and Satavahanas, 325 B.C.–A.D. 300*, Bombay (repr. New Delhi, 1987): People's Publishing House.

Nöldeke, T. (1871), 'ΑΣΣΥΡΙΟΣ ΣΥΡΙΟΣ ΣΥΡΟΣ', *Hermes* 5, pp. 443–68.
Oates, J. (1991), 'The Fall of Assyria (635–609 B.C.)', in *CAH*², vol. 3.2, pp. 162–93.
Oelsner, J. (1996), 'Chaldaia', *DNP* 2, col. 1086.
Olshausen, E. (1974), *Prosopographie der hellenistischer Königsgesandten. Vol. 1: Von Triparadeisos bis Pydna*, Louvain: Peeters.
Otto, W. (1913), 'Himeros [5]', *RE* 8.2, col. 1638.
Palm, J. (1955), *Über Sprache und Stil des Diodoros von Sizilien: Ein Beitrag zur Beleuchtung der hellenistischen Prosa*, Lund: Gleerup.
Parke, H. W. (1970, repr.), *Greek Mercenary Soldiers: From the Earliest Times to the Battle of Ipsus*, Oxford: Oxford University Press.
Parmeggiani, G. (ed.) (2014), *Between Thucydides and Polybius: The Golden Age of Greek Historiography*, Washington, DC: Center for Hellenic Studies.
Pasek, S. (2016), *Pharao Amyrtaios und die Mittelmeerwelt: Die Beziehungen zwischen Ägypten, den Griechen und dem Achaimenidenreich im ausgehenden 5. und beginnenden 4. Jh. v. Chr.*, Munich: Akademische Verlagsgemeinschaft München.
Pédech, P. (1958), 'Deux campagnes d'Antiochus III chez Polybe', *Revue des Études Anciennes* 60, pp. 67–81.
Pédech, P. (1964), *La méthode historique de Polybe*, Paris: Les Belles Lettres.
Pedersén, O. (2011), 'Work on a Digital Model of Babylon Using Archaeological and Textual Evidence', *Mesopotamia* 46, pp. 9–22.
Perdu, O. (2010), 'Saites and Persians (664–332),' in A. B. Lloyd (ed.), *A Companion to Ancient Egypt*, Malden, MA and Chichester, Wiley-Blackwell, pp. 140–58.
Peremans, W. (1967), 'Diodore de Sicile et Agatharchide de Cnide', *Historia* 16:4, pp. 432–55.
Perl, G. (1957), *Kritische Untersuchungen zu Diodors römischen Jahrzählung*, Berlin: Akademie Verlag.
Perlman, P. (1999), 'Krētes aei Lēistai? The Marginalization of Crete in Greek Thought and the Role of Piracy in the Outbreak of the First Cretan War', in V. Gabrielsen et al. (eds), *Hellenistic Rhodes: Politics, Culture and Society*, Aarhus: Aarhus University Press, pp. 132–53.
Pettinato, G. (1988), *Semiramis: Herrin über Assur und Babylon*, Zurich/Munich: Artemis (translation of *Semiramide*, Milan: Rusconi, 1985).
Pfister, F. (1961), 'Das Alexander-archiv und die hellenistisch-römische Wissenschaft', *Historia* 10:1, pp. 30–67.
Phillips, E. D. (1968), 'Semiramis at Behistun', *Classica & Mediaevalia* 29 (publ. 1972), pp. 162–8.
Piccirillo, P. M. and T. A. Dailey (eds) (1993), *The Mosaics of Jordan*, Amman: American Center of Oriental Research.
Pirngruber, R. (2011), 'Eunuchen am Königshof: Ktesias und die altorientalische Evidenz', in Wiesehöfer et al. 2011: pp. 279–312.
Pitra, Giambattista and H. Stevenson Sr. (1885), *Codices manuscripti Palatini Graeci Bibliothecae Descripti*, Roma: Typographeo Vaticano.

Plüer, C. C. (1777), *Reisen durch Spanien: aus dessen Handschriften herausgegeben von C.D. Ebeling*, Leipzig: Weygand.
Potts, D. T. (2014), 'Assyria's Eastern Frontier', in J. Aruz, S. B. Graff, and Y. Rakic (eds), *Assyria to Iberia at the Dawn of the Classical Age*, New York: Metropolitan Museum of Art, pp. 75–8.
Pownall, F., 'Aristodemos (104)', in I. Worthington (ed.), *Brill's New Jacoby*, <http://referenceworks.brillonline.com/>.
Prandi, L. (2012), 'New Evidence for the Dating of Cleitarchus (*POxy* LXXI.4808)?', *Histos* 6, pp. 15–26.
Prandi, L. (2013), *Diodoro Siculo: Biblioteca storica. Libro XVII: Commento storico*, Milan: Vita e Pensiero.
Pritchett, W. K. (1963), 'Xerxes' Fleet at the "Ovens"', *American Journal of Archaeology* 67:1, pp. 1–6.
Pritchett, W. K. (1979), 'Plataiai', *American Journal of Philology* 100:1, pp. 145–52.
Radet, G. (1903), 'Sur un point de l'itinéraire d'Alexandre', *Revue des Études Anciennes* 5, pp. 1–10.
Ramsey, W. M. (1962), *The Historical Geography of Asia Minor*, Amsterdam: Hakkert (repr. of the 1890 edn, London: Murray).
Ranke, F. L. von (1885), *Sämtliche Werke*, Bd. 33/4, Leipzig: Duncker und Humblot.
Rapin, C. (2013), 'On the Way to Roxane. The Route of Alexander the Great in Bactria and Sogdiana (328–327 BC)', in G. Lindström et al. (eds.), *Zwischen Ost und West: Neue Forschungen zum antiken Zentralasien. Wissenschaftliches Kolloquium 30.9.–2.10.2009 in Mannhein*, Darmstadt: Philipp von Zabern, pp. 43–82.
Raubitschek, A. E. (1964), 'The Treaties between Persia and Athens', *Greek, Roman and Byzantine Studies* 5:3, pp. 151–9.
Raun, C. (1868), *De Clitarcho Diodori Curtii Justini auctore*, inaugural dissertation, Bonn: A. Marcus.
Reiner, E. and D. Pingree (1975–2005), *Babylonian Planetary Omens*, 4 vols, Malibu, CA: Undena (vols 1 and 2); Groningen: Styx (vol. 3); Leiden: Brill (vol. 4).
Reinhardt, K. (1953), 'Poseidonios [3]', *RE* 22.1, cols. 558–826.
Revilla, A. (1936), *Catálogo de los Códices Griegos de la Biblioteca de El Escorial*, Tomo 1, Madrid: Patronato de la Biblioteca National.
Rey-Coquais, J. P. (1976), 'Tripolis', in Stillwell 1976: p. 935.
Reynolds, L. D. and N. G. Wilson (1991[3]), *Scribes and Scholars: A Guide to the Transmission of Greek & Latin Literature*, Oxford: Clarendon.
Ritner, R. J. (1980), 'Khababash and the Satrap Stela: A Grammatical Rejoinder', *Zeitschrift für ägyptischen Sprache und Altertumskunde* 107, pp. 136–7.
Ritner, R. K. (2003), 'The Satrap Stela (Cairo JdE 22182)', in W. K. Simpson (ed.), *The Literature of Ancient Egypt*, New Haven/London: Yale University Press, pp. 392–7.

Roaf, M. D. (1983), 'Sculptures and Sculptors at Persepolis', *Iran* 21, pp. 1–159.
Robert, L. (1934), 'Diodore, XIV, 84, 3', *Revue de philologie, de littérature et d'histoire anciennes* 8, pp. 43–8.
Robert, L. (1966), *Documents de l'Asie Mineure méridionale. Inscriptions, monnaies et géographie*, Geneva: Droz.
Robert, L. and M. Holleaux (1942), *Études d'épigraphie et d'histoire grecques. Vol. III: Lagides et Séleucides*, Paris: De Boccard,.
Roisman, J. (2010), 'Hieronymus of Cardia: Causation and Bias from Alexander to his Successors', in E. Carney and D. Ogden (eds), *Philip II and Alexander the Great: Father and Son, Lives and Afterlives*, Oxford: Oxford University Press, pp. 135–50.
Roisman, J. (2012), *Alexander's Veterans and the Early Wars of the Successors*, Austin, TX: University of Texas Press.
Roller, D.W., 'Kallias of Syracuse (564)', in I. Worthington (ed.), *Brill's New Jacoby*, <http://referenceworks.brillonline.com/>.
Rollinger, R. (1993), *Herodots babylonischer Logos: Eine kritische Untersuchung der Glaubwürdigkeitsdiskussion*, Innsbruck: Verlag des Instituts für Sprachwissenschaft der Universität Innsbruck.
Rollinger, R. (2006a), 'Assyrios, Syrios, Syros und Leukosyros', *Die Welt des Orients* 36, pp. 72–82.
Rollinger, R. (2006b), 'The Terms "Assyria" and "Syria" Again', *Journal of Near Eastern Studies* 65:4, pp. 283–7.
Rollinger, R. (2013), *Alexander und die großen Ströme: die Flußüberquerungen im Lichte altorientalischer Pioniertechniken*, Wiesbaden: Harrassowitz (CLeO, vol. 7).
Rosen, K. (1967), 'Political Documents in Hieronymus of Cardia (323–302 B.C.)', *Acta Classica, South Africa*, pp. 41–94.
Rothfield, L. (2009), *The Rape of Mesopotamia*, Chicago: University of Chicago Press.
Roux, G. (1974), 'Éschyle, Hérodote, Diodore, Plutarque racontent la bataille de Salamine', *Bulletin de Correspondence Hellénique* 98, pp. 51–94.
Roux, G. (1992³), *Ancient Iraq*, London: Penguin.
Rubincam, C. (1998), 'How Many Books Did Diodorus Siculus Originally Intend to Write?', *Classical Quarterly* 48:1, pp. 229–33.
Russell, D. A. (1973), *Plutarch*, London: Duckworth.
Ruzicka, S. (1992), *Politics of a Persian Dynasty: The Hecatomnids in the Fourth Century* B.C., Norman/London: University of Oklahoma Press.
Ruzicka, S. (2012), *Trouble in the West: Egypt and the Persian Empire, 525–332 BC*, Oxford: Oxford University Press.
Ryder, T. T. B. (1957), 'The Supposed Common Peace of 366/5 BC', *Classical Quarterly* 7:3/4, pp. 199–205.
Ryder, T. T. B. (1965), *Koine Eirene: General Peace and Local Independence in Ancient Greece*, Oxford: Oxford University Press.

Sachs, A. J. (1952), 'Babylonian Horoscopes', *Journal of Cuneiform Studies* 6, pp. 49–75.
Sachs, A. J. (1955), *Late Babylonian Astronomical and Related Texts*, Providence, RI: Brown University Press.
Sachs, A. J. and H. Hunger (eds) (1988–), *Astonomical Diaries and Related Texts from Babylonia*, 7 vols (by 2016), Vienna: Akademie Verlag.
Sacks, K. S. (1990), *Diodorus Siculus and the First Century*, Princeton, NJ: Princeton University Press.
Salonen, A. (1956), *Hippologica Accadica: Eine lexikalische und kulturgeschichtliche Untersuchung über die Zug-, Trag- und Reittiere, . . .*, Helsinki: Suomalainen Tiedeakatemia.
Samiei, S. (2014), *Ancient Persia in Western History: Hellenism and the Representation of the Achaemenid Empire*, London/New York: I. B. Tauris.
Samuel, A. E. (1965), 'Alexander's Royal Journals', *Historia* 14:1, pp. 1–12.
Sancisi-Weerdenburg, H. (1980), *Yauna en Persai: Grieken en Perzen in een ander perspectief*, dissertation, Rijksuniversiteit Leiden, Groningen: Dijkstra Niemeyer.
Sancisi-Weerdenburg, H. (1987a), 'Decadence in the Empire or Decadence in the Sources? From Source to Synthesis: Ctesias', in H. Sancisi-Weerdenburg (ed.), *Sources, Structures and Synthesis (AchHist*, vol. I), pp. 33–45.
Sancisi-Weerdenburg, H. (1987b), 'Herodotus en de Meden: historiciteit en orale traditie', *Lampas* 20:3, pp. 155–67.
Sancisi-Weerdenburg, H. (1988), 'Was there ever a Median Empire?', in Kuhrt and Sancisi-Weerdenburg 1988: 197–212.
Sancisi-Weerdenburg, H. (1991), *'Den Wereltvorst een vuyle streek aan syn eercleet': Alexander en Persepolis*, Utrecht: Rijksuniversiteit-Letteren (inaugural speech).
Sancisi-Weerdenburg, H. (1999), 'The Persian Kings and History', in C. Shuttleworth Kraus (ed.), *The Limits of Historiography*, Leiden: Brill, pp. 91–112.
Sancisi-Weerdenburg, H. and A. Kuhrt (eds) (1987), *The Greek Sources: Proceedings of the Groningen 1984 Achaemenid History Workshop* (*AchHist*, vol. II).
Schachermeyr, S. (1973), *Alexander der Grosse: Das Problem seiner Persönlichkeit und seines Wirkens*, Vienna: Akademie Verlag.
Schamp, J. (1987), *Photios, Historien des Lettres: la Bibliothèque et ses notices biographiques*, Paris: Les Belles Lettres.
Schmidt, E. F. (1939), *The Treasury of Persepolis and Other Discoveries in the Homeland of the Achaemenians*, Chicago: Chicago University Press.
Schmidt, E. F. (1953), *Persepolis. Vol. I: Structures, Reliefs and Inscriptions*, Chicago: Chicago University Press.
Schmidt, E. F. (1970), *Persepolis. Vol. III: The Royal Tombs and Other Monuments*, Chicago: Chicago University Press.

Schmitt, O. (1992), *Der Lamische Krieg*, Bonn: Habelt.
Schmitt, R. (1979), 'Die Wiedergabe iranischer Namen bei Ktesias von Knidos im Vergleich zur sonstigen griechischen Überlieferung', in J. Harmatta (ed.), *Prolegomena to the Sources on the History of Pre-Islamic Central Asia*, Budapest: Akadémiai Kiadó, pp. 119–33.
Schmitt, R. (2011a), 'Clearchus of Sparta', *Iranica Online*, <http://www.iranicaonline.org/articles/clearchus-of-sparta-b>, published 15 December 1992, updated 21 October 2011; in print: *EI*, vol. V, fasc. 6, pp. 702–3.
Schmitt, R. (2011b), 'Drangiana', *Iranica Online*, <http://www.iranicaonline.org/articles/drangiana>, published 15 December 1995, updated 1 December 2011, retrieved 30 March 2013; in print: *EI*, vol. VII, fasc. 5, pp. 534–7.
Schmitt, R. (2012), 'Hydarnes', *Iranica Online*, <http://www.iranicaonline.org/articles/hydarnes>.
Schmitthenner, W. (1968), 'Über eine Formveränderung der Monarchie seit Alexander der Große', *Saeculum* 19, pp. 31–46.
Schottky, M. (1989), *Media Atropatene und Gross-Armenien in hellenistischer Zeit*, Bonn: Habelt.
Schubert, R. (1914), *Die Quellen zur Geschichte der Diadochenzeit*, Leipzig: Wicher (repr. Aalen: Scientia Verlag, 1964).
Schwartz, E. (1903a), 'Diodorus [38]', *RE* 5.1, cols. 663–704.
Schwartz, E. (1903b), 'Dinon[2]', *RE* 5.1, col. 654.
Schwartz, J. (1949), 'Les conquérants perses et la literature égyptienne', *Bulletin de l'Institut Français d'Archéologie Orientale* 48, pp. 65–80.
Schwenk, C. J. (1985), *Athens in the Age of Alexander: The Dated Laws and Decrees of the 'Lykourgan Era' 338–322 B.C.*, Chicago: Ares.
Scullard, H. H. (1974), *The Elephant in the Greek and Roman World*, London: Thames & Hudson.
Sekunda, V. (1997), 'Nearchus the Cretan and the Foundation of Cretopolis', *Anatolian Studies* 47, pp. 217–23.
Shaw, I. and P. Nicholson (2008²), *The Princeton Dictionary of Ancient Egypt*, Princeton, NJ/Oxford: Princeton University Press.
Shayegan, R. M. (2011), *Arsacids and Sasanians: Political Ideology in Post-Hellenistic and Late Antique Persia*, Cambridge: Cambridge University Press.
Shipley, G. (ed.) (2000), *The Greek World after Alexander, 323–30 BC*, Abingdon/New York: Routledge.
Simpson, R. H. (1957), 'A Note on Cyinda', *Historia* 6:4, pp. 503–4.
Simpson, R. H. (1959), 'Abbreviation of Hieronymus in Diodorus', *American Journal of Philology* 80:4, pp. 370–9.
Sinclair, R. K. (1963), 'Diodorus Siculus and the Writing of History', *Proceedings of the African Classical Association* 6, pp. 36–45.
Sinclair, R. K. (1966), 'Diodorus Siculus and Fighting in Relays', *Classical Quarterly* 16:2: pp. 249–55.

Smith, W. (1854), *Dictionary of Greek and Roman Geography*, London: Walton and Maberly.
Smith, E. (1833), *Researches of the Rev. E. Smith and the Rev. H. G. O. Dwight in Armenia ... in Two Volumes*, Boston/New York, vol. 1.
Spek, R. J. van der (2003), 'Darius III, Alexander the Great and Babylonian Scholarship', in W. Henkelman and A. Kuhrt (eds), *A Persian Perspective: Essays in Memory of Heleen Sancisi-Weerdenburg* (*AchHist*, vol. XIII), pp. 289–346.
Stein, M. A. (1929), *On Alexander's Track to the Indus: Personal Narrative of Explorations on the North-West Frontier of India Carried Out under the Orders of H.M. Indian Government*, London: Macmillan (repr. Chicago: Ares, 1974).
Stein, M. A. (1932), 'The Site of Alexander's Passage of the Hydaspes and the Battle with Poros', *Geographical Journal* 80:1, pp. 31–46.
Stein, M. A. (1938), 'An Archaeological Journey in Western Iran', *Geographical Journal* 92:4, pp. 313–42.
Stein, M. A. (1942), 'Notes on Alexander's Crossing of the Tigris and the Battle of Arbela', *Geographical Journal* 100:4, pp. 155–64.
Stein, M. A. (1943), 'On Alexander's Route into Gedrosia: An Archaeological Tour in Las Bela', *Geographical Journal* 102:5/6, pp. 193–227.
Stein, O. (1939), 'Oreitai', *RE* 18.1, cols. 942–51.
Stevenson, R. B. (1987), 'Lies and Invention in Deinon's Persica', in Sancisi-Weerdenburg and Kuhrt 1987: 27–35.
Stevenson, R. B. (1997), *Persica: Greek Writing about Persia in the Fourth Century BC*, Edinburgh: Scottish Academic Press.
Stijnen, A. (2002), 'De organisatie van Apuleius' rovers: feit of fictie', *Hermeneus* 74:1, pp. 33–8.
Stillwell, R. (ed.) (1976), *The Princeton Encyclopedia of Classical Sites*, Princeton, NJ: Princeton University Press.
Stoneman, R. (2015), *Xerxes: A Persian Life*, New Haven, CT/London: Yale University Press.
Strasburger, H. (1954), 'Zur Route Alexanders durch Gedrosien', *Hermes* 82:2, pp. 251–4.
Strasburger, H. (1965), 'Poseidonios on Problems of the Roman Empire', *Journal of Roman Studies* 55:1&2, pp. 40–53.
Streck (1910), 'Gaugamela', *RE* 7.1, cols. 861–5.
Strommenberger, E. (1980–3): 'Kleidung B', *RLA*, vol. 6, pp. 31–8.
Stronk, Jan P. 'Eumelos (77)', in I. Worthington (ed.), *Brill's New Jacoby*, <http://referenceworks.brillonline.com/>.
Stronk, Jan P., 'Demetrios of Salamis (643)', in I. Worthington (ed.), *Brill's New Jacoby*, <http://referenceworks.brillonline.com/>.
Stronk, Jan P., 'Hegias of Troizen (606)', in I. Worthington (ed.), *Brill's New Jacoby*, <http://referenceworks.brillonline.com/>.
Stronk, Jan P., 'Neanthes the Younger of Kyzikos (171)', in I. Worthington (ed.), *Brill's New Jacoby*, <http://referenceworks.brillonline.com/>.

Stronk, Jan P., 'Sophainetos Stymmphalikos (109)' in I. Worthington (ed.), *Brill's New Jacoby*, <http://referenceworks.brillonline.com/>.
Stronk, Jan P. (1990/1), 'Sparta and Persia 412–386: An Outline', *Talanta* 22/3, pp. 117–36.
Stronk, Jan P. (1995), *The Ten Thousand in Thrace: An Archaeological and Historical Commentary on Xenophon's Anabasis, Books VI.iii–vi– VII*, Amsterdam: Gieben.
Stronk, Jan P. (1998/9), 'Crossing the Straits: The Persians in Thrace', *Talanta* 30/1, pp. 55–72.
Stronk, Jan P. (2004/5), 'Ctesias of Cnidus: From Physician to Author', *Talanta* 36/7, pp. 101–22.
Stronk, Jan P. (2008/9), '*P.Oxy* 2330: A New Collation', *Talanta* 40/1, pp. 219–22.
Stronk, Jan P. (2010/11), '*Philobarbaroi* or *Xenophobetikoi*? Greek Authors on Persia(ns): An Exploration', *Talanta* 42/3, pp. 83–104.
Stronk, Jan P. (2011), 'Herodotus and Ctesias: Translators of the Oriental Past', in S. McElduff and E. Sciarrino (eds), *Complicating the History of Western Translation: The Ancient Mediterranean in Perspective*, Manchester: St Jerome, pp. 118–30.
Stronk, Jan P. (2014/15), 'Thermopylae 480 BC: Ancient Accounts of a Battle', *Talanta* (46/7), pp. 165–237.
Stronk, Jan P. (forthcoming), 'The Perception in Iran in the Medieval and Modern Eras', in B. Jacobs and R. Rollinger (eds), *A Companion to the Achaemenid Persian Empire*, Malden, MA/Oxford: Wiley-Blackwell.
Stronk, Jan P. (in preparation), *Ctesias' Persian History, Part 2: Historical Commentary*.
Stylianou, P. J. (1998), *A Historical Commentary on Diodorus Siculus Book 15*, Oxford: Clarendon.
Sulimani, I. (2011), *Diodorus' Mythistory and the Pagan Mission: Historiography and Culture-Heroes in the First Pentad of the Bibliotheke*, Leiden: Brill.
Syme, R. (1988), 'The Cadusii in History and Fiction', *Journal of Hellenic Studies* 108, pp. 137–50.
Szemerényi, O. (1980), *Four Old Iranian Ethnic Names: Scythian, Skudra, Sogdian, Saka*, Vienna: Akademie Verlag.
Talon, P. (2005), *The Standard Babylonian Creation Myth Enūma Eliš: Introduction, Cuneiform Text, Transliteration, and Sign List with a Translation and Glossary in French*, Helsinki: Institute for Asian and African Studies.
Tarn, W. W. (1921), 'Herakles Son of Barsine', *Journal of Hellenic Studies* 41, pp. 18–28.
Tarn, W. W. (1948), *Alexander the Great. Vol. II: Sources and Studies*, Cambridge: Cambridge University Press.
Temporini, H. and W. Haase (1978), *Aufstieg und Niedergang der römischen Welt: Geschichte und Kultur Roms im Spiegel der neueren Forschung*, Abt. 2, *Principat*: 9, 2, Vol. 8, Berlin.

Toepffer, J. (1894), 'Amazones', *RE* 1.2, cols. 1754–89.
Tomaschek (1894), 'Antiocheia [1]', *RE* 1.2, col. 2442–5.
Tomlinson, R. A. (1970), 'Ancient Macedonian Symposia', *Ancient Macedonia* 1, pp. 308–15.
Treidler, H. (1967a), 'Zagros', *RE* 9A.2, cols. 2283–5.
Treidler, H. (1967b), 'Ζάγρου πύλαι', *RE* 9A.2, cols. 2285–8.
Treidler, H. (1967c), 'Ζαρκαίον ὄρος', *RE* 9A.2: col. 2329.
Treidler, H. (1967d), 'Uxii', *RE* 9A2, cols. 1313–19.
Tucci, G. (1977), 'On Swat: The Dards and Connected Problems', *East and West* 27:1–4, pp. 9–104.
Tuplin, C. (2004), 'Medes in Media, Mesopotamia, and Anatolia: Empire, Hegemony, Domination or Illusion', *Ancient West & East* 3:2, pp. 223–51.
Tuplin, C. (2010), 'Xenophon and Achaemenid Courts: A Survey of Evidence', in B. Jacobs and R. Rollinger (eds), *Der Achämenidenhof/The Achaemenid Court*, Wiesbaden: Harrassowitz, pp. 189–230 (*CLeO*, vol. 2).
Tuplin, C. J. (2012), 'Charidemus', in *OCD*[4], pp. 305–6.
Tuplin, C. (2014), 'The Changing Pattern of Achaemenid Persian Royal Coinage', in P. Bernholz and R. Vaubel (eds), *Explaining Monetary and Financial Innovation: A Historical Analysis*, Cham: Springer, pp. 127–68.
Unger, E. (1970^2), *Babylon, die heilige Stadt nach der Beschreibung der Babylonier*, Berlin: De Gruyter.
Unger, G. F. (1880), 'Die jahrepoche [sic!] des Diodoros', *Philologus* 39:2, pp. 305–25.
Vigneron, P. (1968), *Le cheval dans l'antiquité gréco-romaine (des guerres médiques aux grandes invasions): contributions à l'histoire des techniques*, dissertation, Nancy: Faculté des Lettres et Sciences Humaines.
Vimercati, E. (ed.) (2004), *Posidonio: Testimonianze e frammenti. Testo greco e latino a fronte: introduzione, traduzione, commentario e apparati a cura di Emmanuele Vimercati. Presentazione di Roberto Radice*, Milan: Bompiani.
Vogelsang, W. J. (2012), 'Gedrosia', *Iranica Online*, <http://www.iranicaonline.org/articles/gedrosia>, published 15 December 2000, updated 3 February 2012, retrieved 28 March 2013; in print: *EI*, vol. X, fasc. 4, pp. 390–1.
Volquardsen, C. A. (1868), *Untersuchungen über die Quellen der griechischen und sicilischen Geschichten bei Diodor, Buch XI bis XVI*, Kiel: Schwers.
Vycichl, W. (1984–5), 'Le marché aux voleurs: une institution égyptienne de l'époque ptolémaïque. L'organisation du système', *Bulletin de la Société d'Égyptologie de Genève* 9–10, pp. 337–44.
Wacholder, B. Z. (1962), *Nicolaus of Damascus*, Berkeley/Los Angeles: University of California Press.
Wachsmuth, C. (1895), *Einleitung in das Studium der alten Geschichte*, Leipzig: Hirzel.

Wainwright, G. A. (1956), 'Caphtor – Cappadocia', *Vetus Testamentum* 6:2: pp. 199–210.
Walbank, F. W. (1968–9), 'The Historians of Greek Sicily', *ΚΩΚΑΛΟΣ* 14–15, pp. 476–97.
Walbank F. W. (1979), *A Historical Commentary on Polybius. Vol. 3: Commentary on Books XIX–XL*, Oxford: Oxford University Press.
Walker, B. G. (1983), *The Woman's Encyclopedia of Myths and Secrets*, New York: Harper & Row.
Walker, C. (1997), 'Achaemenid Chronology and the Babylonian Sources', in J. Curtis (ed.), *Mesopotamia and Iran in the Persian Period: Conquest and Imperialism 539–331 BC*, London: British Museum Press, pp. 17–25.
Wallinga, H. T. (1993), *Ships and Sea-Power before the Great Persian War: The Ancestry of the Ancient Trireme*, Leiden: Brill.
Wallinga, H. T. (2005), *Xerxes' Greek Adventure: The Naval Perspective*, Leiden: Brill.
Walser, G. (1966), *Die Völkerschaften auf den Reliefs von Persepolis: historische Studien über den sogenannten Tributzug an der Apadanatreppe*, Berlin: Mann.
Wehrli, C. (1964), 'Phila, fille d'Antipater et épouse de Démétrios, roi des Macédoniens', *Historia* 13:2, pp. 140–6.
Wehrli, F. (1945), *Die Schule des Aristoteles. Heft 2: Aristoxenos*, Basel: Schwabe.
Weidner, E. F. (1936), 'Ninyas', *RE* 17.1, cols. 643–4.
Weiskopf, M. (1989), *The So-Called 'Great Satraps' Revolt', 366–360 B.C.: Concerning Local Instability in the Achaemenid Far West*, Stuttgart: Steiner.
Weissbach (1896), 'Bagistane', *RE* 2.2, cols. 2769–71.
Wendel, C. (1935), 'Mythographie', *RE* 16.2, cols. 1352–74.
Westlake, H. D. (1969), *Essays on the Greek Historians and Greek History*, Manchester: Manchester University Press.
Wetzel, F. (1930), *Die Stadtmauern von Babylon*, Leipzig: Hinrichs.
Wetzel, F. and F. H. Weissbach (1938), *Das Haupttheiligtum des Marduk in Babylon, Esagila und Etemenanki*, Leipzig: Hinrichs (repr. Osnabrück 1967: Otto Zeller).
Wetzel, F., E. Schmidt, and A. Mallwitz (1957), *Das Babylon der Spätzeit*, Berlin: De Gruyter.
Whitehead, D. and P. H. Blyth (eds) (2004), *Athenaeus Mechanicus: On Machines (Περὶ μηχανημάτων)*, Wiesbaden: Steiner.
Wiesehöfer, J. (1978), *Der Aufstand Gaumatas und die Anfänge Dareios' I*, Bonn: Habelt.
Wiesehöfer, J. (2001), 'Sisygambis', *DNP* 11, col. 598.
Wiesehöfer, J., R. Rollinger, and G. B. Lanfranchi (eds) (2011), *Ktesias' Welt/Ctesias' World*, Wiesbaden: Harrassowitz (*CLeO*, vol. 1).
Will, É. (1982²), *Histoire politique du monde hellénistique (323–30 av.*

J.-C.). T. II: Des avènements d'Antiochos III et de Philippe V à la fin des Lagides, Nancy: Presses universitaires de Nancy.

Will, É. (1994⁵), Le monde grec et l'Orient. T. 1: Le Ve siècle (510–403); complements bibliographiques, Paris: Presses Universitaires de France.

Wilson, D. R. (1976), 'Themiskyra', in Stillwell 1976: p. 907.

Wirth, G. (2007), Katastrophe und Zukunftshoffnung: Mutmaßungen zur zweiten Hälfte von Diodors Bibliothek und ihren verlorenen Büchern, Vienna: Akademie Verlag.

Wirth, G. (2008a–b), Diodoros: Griechische Weltgeschichte, Fragmente (Buch XXI–XL): Übersetzt, eingeleitet und Kommentiert von G. Wirth, Erster Halbband: Einleitung und Übersetzung, Zweiter Halbband: Kommentar, Stuttgart: Anton Hiersemann.

Ziegler, K. (1941), 'Photios [13]', RE 20.1, cols. 667–737.

Ziegler, K. (1963), 'Pythionike', RE 24, cols. 564–6.

Ziegler, K. (1964²), Plutarchos von Chaironeia, Stuttgart: Alfred Druckenmüller.

Index of Classical Sources

Ancient and medieval sources referred to and/or discussed in text and notes. Not included are the sections themselves of Diodorus' account of Persian History, translated in Chapters 2 to 9.

A. ACHAEMENID INSCRIPTIONS, ASSYRIAN AND BABYLONIAN TEXTS (IN TRANSLATION), CUNEIFORM TEXTS
Achaemenid inscriptions, following Kent's classification:
DB, I.10–14, 443
DB, I.1–2, 533
DB, IV.68, 443
DB, V.21–2, 139
DNa lines 28–9, 139
DPh.5–6, 259
DSe.29, 139
DZc, 151
XPf, line 32, 335
XPh line 24, 139
XPh line 26–7, 139

Assyrian and Babylonian texts (in translation):
ABC 1, pp. 80–1, 528
ABC 1, p. 85, Col. 4, line 25, 89
ABC 3, p. 94, line 44, 129
ABC 8, pp. 112–13, 335
ABC 9, p. 114, 263
ABC 14, lines 28–9, 89
ANET, pp. 303–5, 129
ARAB, vol. 2, pp. 73–99, 109
ARAB vol. 2, p. 473 s.v. Medes, 87
ARAB vol. 2, p.489 s.v. Urartu, 87
ARAB, vol. 2, §§339–41, 528
ARAB, vol. 2, §580, 531
RIMA 3 A.0.104.3, 7b–10a, 528
RIMA 3 A.0.104.2001, 533

Babylonian so-called Astronomical Diaries (British Museum):
BM 36304, 335
BM 36761 + BM 36390, 315, 321
BM 71537, 276

B. BIBLE AND QUR'AN
Daniel 1:4, 103
Daniel 2:2–11, 103
Daniel 9:1, 103
Genesis 11:28, 103
Genesis 11:31, 103
Jonah 1:17 (2:1), RSV, 305
1 Maccabees 10:68–9, 512
1 Maccabees 11:8–13, 512
1 Maccabees 11:17, 513
1 Maccabees 11:31–2, 514
1 Maccabees 11:39, 515
1 Maccabees 11:44–8, 514
Qur'an chapter 4 verse 23, 143

C. GREEK INSCRIPTIONS
Agora 16.78–80, 303
Dittenberger Syll.³ 182, 251
Dittenberger Syll.³ 311, 384
Dittenberger Syll.³ 320, 384
IG XIV.588, 3
IG I².52, 47
IG I².82, 49
IG I².95–101, 49
IG I².98–9, 47
IG I².397, 47
IG II².40–5, 49
IG II².119, 251
IG II².329, lines 8–10, 324
IG II².344–7, 303
IG II².469 line 3, 452
IG II².547, 375
IG II².1607.49, 245
IG II³.1.43, 49

Marmor Parium B11–13, 394
Marmor Parium B12, 402
Marmor Parium B16, 128, 462, 467
Marmor Parium B17, 475
Marmor Parium B23, 484
OGIS 391, 236
OGIS 392, 236
Satrap Stela, 270
SEG 21.292.1, 375
SEG 29.419, 424
SEG 32.88.1, 375
SEG 37.1987, 199

D. GREEK PAPYRI
P.Oxy. 13, 278
P.Oxy. 1011, 43
P.Oxy. 1610, 11, 83
P.Oxy. 1610 F 6, 191
P.Oxy. 1610 F 8, 192
P.Oxy. 1798 [= FGrH/BNJ 148, Anon. de Alex.] F 44 col. 2, 294
P.Oxy. 1798 [= FGrH/BNJ 148, Anon. de Alex.] F 44 col. 3, 299
P.Oxy. 1798 [= FGrH/BNJ 148, Anon. de Alex.] F 44 col. 4, 301, 322
P.Oxy. 2082, F. 3, 61
P.Oxy. 2330, 139, 535
P.Oxy. 2399, 61
P.Rylands III 491, 67
PSI 1284, 397

E. SIGLA AND MANUSCRIPTS
Diodorus' Bibliotheca books 1–5:
MS C = codex Vaticanus gr. 130, 19, 89, 95, 97, 107, 128, 130
MS D = codex Neopolitanus

578

Index of Classical Sources 579

suppl. gr. 4, 18, 95, 97, 99, 107, 118, 128, 132, 137
MS V = *codex Vaticanus gr.* 996, 19, 89, 95, 97, 107, 128, 130
MS L = *codex Laurentianus* 70,1, 19, 89, 95, 97, 107, 130, 132
MS P. = Poggii versio librorum I–V, 95

Diodorus' Bibliotheca books 11–20:
MS F = *codex Laurentianus* 70,12, 21, 219, 276, 319, 325, 356, 363, 365, 371, 417, 426, 443, 452, 471, 491
MS M = *codex Marcianus gr.* 375, 20
MS P = *codex Patmiacus* 50, 20, 228
MS R = *codex Parasinus gr.* 1665, 21, 276, 319, 325, 363, 371, 417, 443, 452, 491
MS X,[1] 363, 371, 491

Excerpta Constantiniana:
codex Escorialensis I.⊠.4, 23
codex Escorialensis Ω.I.11, 24
codex Turonensis 980, 24
codex Vaticanus *(rescriptus) gr.* 73, 25, 502
Codex Parisinus Graecus 1666, 25

Florilegium Vaticanum:
codex Vaticanus gr. 739, 26

Photius' Bibliotheca:
codex Marcianus gr. 450, 28
codex Marcianus gr. 451, 28
codex Parisinus gr. 1266, 28

F. GREEK AND LATIN AUTHORS
Aelian *Tactica*
Tact. 2.4, 435
Tact. 18.1–3, 321
Tact. 18.5–9, 321
Aelian *Varia Historia*
VH 7.1, 121
VH 14.47a, 388

Aeneas Tacticus
Aen.Tact. 31.35, 237
Aen.Tact. 32.12, 308

Aen.Tact. 33, 308
Aen.Tact. 36, 308

Aeschines *De Falsa Legatione*
Fals.Legat. 26–7, 51
Fals.Legat. 132, 51
Aeschines *In Ctesiphon*
Ctes. 85, 51
Ctes. 97, 51
Ctes. 107–12, 51
Ctes. 163, 277
Aeschines *In Timarchum*
Timarch. 152, 47

Aeschylus *Eumenides*
Eu. 108–9, 414
Aeschylus *Persae*
Pers. 386–95, 175
Pers. 467, 175
Aeschylus *Prometheus*
Pr. 459 sq., 46

Agathemerus
(*GGM*, II: 472 sub 5), 56

Ammianus Marcellinus,
Res Gestae 23.6.39, 110
Ars Rhetorica, 8.3/1429b, 51

Anaximenes of Lampsacus (*FGrH/BNJ* 72)
F 17 (*History of Alexander*), 312

Anonymus, *De mulieribus*
De mulieribus 1, 120
De mulieribus 2, 139

Apollodorus, *Bibliotheca*
1.9.28, 155

Appian *Bella Civilia*
BC 5.109 sqq., 14
Appian *Hispanic War*
Hisp. 42–3, 69
Appian *Macedonian War*
Mac. Fr. 11.9, 70
Appian *Punic War*
Pun. 95–6, 72
Appian *Syrian War*
Syr. 45, 510
Syr. 45–6, 505
Syr. 46, 511
Syr. 47, 511
Syr. 49, 523
Syr. 53, 452
Syr. 54, 458, 467
Syr. 55, 469

Syr. 56, 468
Syr. 66, 505, 506
Syr. 68, 519
Syr. 70, 523
Syr. 146, 68
Syr. 198, 68

Aristides, P. Aelius, *Orationes*
Or. 1.219, 170
Or. 2.251, 171
Or. 2.252, 170
Or. 2.256, 171
Or. 13.148, 180
Or. 46.218, 178

Aristides Milesius (*FGrH/BNJ* 286) FF 20 a & b, 168

Aristophanes *Acharnenses*
Ach. lines 530–1, 47
Ach. line 1094, 47
Aristophanes *Pax*
Pax lines 603–11, 47
Aristophanes *Ranae*
Ra. line 1015, 228

Aristotle *Athenian Constitution*
Ath.Con. 35–7, 48
Aristotle *Historia Animalium*
HA 3.19/520b26–7, 190
Aristotle *Mirabilia*
Mir. 149 = 845b8, 107
Aristotle *De Mundo*
Mu. 398A30–5, 58
Mu. 398a32–5, 453
Aristotle *Politica*
Pol. 5.1311B, 260
Pol. 5.1312a*, 253

[Aristotle] *Oeconomicus*
Oec. 1353a18–24 (2.37), 253

Aristobulus (*FGrH/BNJ* 139)
T4, 351
FF 7a and 7b, 291
F 8, 295
F 9, 302
F 17, 318
F 23, 56
F 24, 344
F 52, 369
F 54, 375
F 59, 380

---

[1] MS X, the *codex Marcianus gr.* 376, 15th century, is an apograph belonging to the family of MS P.

Aristodemus (*FGrH/BNJ*
   104)
F 1, 47
F 1(2.5), 182
F 1(4.1), 187
F 1(10.3-5), 190

Arrian *Anabasis Alexandri*
An. 1.1.2, 275
An. 1.11.1, 279
An. 1.11.3, 281
An. 1.11.7, 280
An. 1.11.7-8, 282, 284
An. 1.12.15-16, 283
An. 1.12.8, 283
An. 1.13.3-7, 283
An. 1.14.1-3, 283
An. 1.14.4, 284
An. 1.15.7, 284
An. 1.15.7-8, 285
An. 1.15.8, 284
An. 1.16.2, 286
An. 1.16.3, 283, 285
An. 1.17.6, 280
An. 1.17-18.2, 286
An. 1.18.4, 280, 286
An. 1.18.4-5, 286
An. 1.19.3, 286
An. 1.19.4-6, 286
An. 1.20.4-23.6, 288
An. 1.20.9-10, 288
An. 1.20.10, 289
An. 1.21.1, 289
An. 1.21.5-6, 289
An. 1.22.1-2, 290
An. 1.22.1-3, 289
An. 1.22.7, 290
An. 1.23.1, 291
An. 1.23.2, 290
An. 1.23.3, 291
An. 1.23.7-8, 287
An. 1.24.3-2.4.6, 291
An. 1.25, 295
An. 1.26.6, 404
An. 1.9.6-7, 278
An. 2.1.3, 292
An. 2.2.16, 302
An. 2.4.5, 283
An. 2.4.7, 295
An. 2.5.1, 295
An. 2.7.8-9, 318
An. 2.8.2-4, 296
An. 2.8.8, 294
An. 2.10.5-11.3, 299
An. 2.11.1-4, 296
An. 2.11.3, 299
An. 2.11.7-8, 301
An. 2.11.8, 270, 285, 298, 299
An. 2.11.9, 300
An. 2.12.1, 298

An. 2.12.2, 390
An. 2.13.1, 303
An. 2.13.2-3, 312
An. 2.13.4-6, 312
An. 2.14.6, 293
An. 2.19.1-5, 306
An. 2.19.6-20.3, 307
An. 2.20.4, 307
An. 2.20-1, 263
An. 2.21.4, 106
An. 2.22.1, 99
An. 2.23.5, 310
An. 2.24.4, 310
An. 2.24.5, 311
An. 2.26.2-27.7, 313
An. 2.26-7, 462
An. 2.27.3, 286
An. 3.6.7-8, 412
An. 3.7.1, 316
An. 3.7.3, 314
An. 3.7.6, 321
An. 3.8.6, 314
An. 3.8.7, 314, 322
An. 3.11.3-7, 318
An. 3.11.5, 319
An. 3.13.1, 319
An. 3.14.3-6, 321
An. 3.14.4-6, 320
An. 3.15.1-2, 322
An. 3.15.4-5, 322
An. 3.15.6, 322
An. 3.16.6, 325
An. 3.16.7, 325
An. 3.16.9, 325
An. 3.17.1, 326
An. 3.18.10, 329
An. 3.18.11-12, 332
An. 3.18.1-2, 327
An. 3.19.4, 276
An. 3.21.9-10, 335
An. 3.22.2, 277
An. 3.23.4, 337
An. 3.23.7, 337
An. 3.25.1-6, 339
An. 3.25.3, 335
An. 3.26.3, 341
An. 3.27.4, 339, 342
An. 3.27.5, 342
An. 3.29.5, 342
An. 3.29.6-30.5, 344
An. 4.7.2, 344
An. 4.10.5-12.2, 345
An. 4.18.3, 385
An. 4.18.4-19.5, 97
An. 4.22.6, 348
An. 4.26.1, 345
An. 4.26-27.4, 345
An. 4.29.1-4, 347
An. 4.29.2, 347
An. 5.3.1-4, 344
An. 5.3.5-6, 348

An. 5.8.5-14.6, 349
An. 5.15.4, 349
An. 5.18.2, 351
An. 5.18.3, 351
An. 5.18.4-5, 350
An. 5.18.5-6, 351
An. 5.19.1, 351
An. 5.22.2, 349
An. 5.24.8, 355
An. 5.25-8, 356
An. 5.27.2-9, 356
An. 5.28.1-4, 356
An. 5.28.4, 356
An. 6.1.1, 357
An. 6.2.2, 358
An. 6.2.3, 357
An. 6.2.4, 357
An. 6.3.1, 357
An. 6.4.3, 359
An. 6.7.6, 358
An. 6.10.1, 360
An. 6.10.1-2, 361
An. 6.10.2, 361
An. 6.11.2, 361
An. 6.11.3, 360
An. 6.11.4-6, 322
An. 6.11.8, 361
An. 6.14.1, 361
An. 6.15.1-4, 362
An. 6.15.2, 362
An. 6.15.4, 362
An. 6.15.5-7, 362
An. 6.16.1-2, 362
An. 6.17.1-2, 362
An. 6.19.5, 364
An. 6.21.5, 365
An. 6.22.3, 365
An. 6.23.3, 366
An. 6.24.2, 525
An. 6.24.3, 534
An. 6.27.1, 421
An. 6.27.1-5, 367
An. 6.27.2, 421
An. 6.28.1-2, 367
An. 6.28.5-6, 368
An. 6.30.2-3, 420
An. 7.4.4-8, 369
An. 7.4.5, 385
An. 7.4.8, 369
An. 7.6.1, 369
An. 7.8.3, 369
An. 7.11.1-8, 371
An. 7.11.3, 411
An. 7.12.1-2, 356
An. 7.13.1, 372
An. 7.14.1-4, 372
An. 7.14.7, 378
An. 7.14.8, 378
An. 7.14.8-10, 376
An. 7.15.4, 376
An. 7.15.5-6, 376

Index of Classical Sources 581

An. 7.16.5, 375
An. 7.17.1-4, 374
An. 7.17.5-6, 375
An. 7.17.6, 99
An. 7.19.4, 419
An. 7.22.4-5, 380
An. 7.23.1, 412
An. 7.23.6, 378
An. 7.26.3, 380
An. 7.27.1-2, 381
Arrian, *Indica*
Ind. 5.7, 119
Ind. 18, 380
Ind. 18.1, 357
Ind. 23, 365
Ind. 33.5-35.8, 368
Ind. 36.3, 367
Arrian, *Successors of Alexander*
Succ. 1.3, 384
Succ. 1.6, 384, 412
Succ. 1.8, 392
Succ. 1.20, 392
Succ. 1.23, 398
Succ. 1.25, 385
Succ. 1.26, 393, 394, 477
Succ. 1.26-7, 394
Succ. 1.27, 395, 396
Succ. 1.32-3, 398
Succ. 1.36, 399, 421
Succ. 1.37, 384
Succ. 1.38, 453
Succ. 1.39, 401
Succ. 24.6, 475
Succ. 24.6 [= *Cod. rescr. Vatic. gr.* 495 fol. 230, 235], 454
Arrian *Tactica*
Tact. 19.4, 94

Asclepiodotus Tacticus
Ascl. 7.2, 321
Ascl. 7.4, 321

Athenaeus Naucratites *Deipnosophistae*
Ath. 6.251EF, 65
Ath. 8.333BD, 517
Ath. 8.335F-336B, 125
Ath. 10.434A, 380
Ath. 10.434AB, 380
Ath. 10.434C, 380
Ath. 10.434F, 367
Ath. 10.439DE, 519
Ath. 11.466BC, 521
Ath. 11.503F, 277
Ath. 11.505AB, 222
Ath. 11.509A, 407
Ath. 12.514BC, 319
Ath. 12.514F, 57, 449
Ath. 12.528EF, 121

Ath. 12.537D, 380
Ath. 12.538B-539A, 369
Ath. 12.542A, 59
Ath. 12.542B, 76
Ath. 13.574E, 211
Ath. 13.586C, 370
Ath. 13.595A-F, 370
Ath. 13.605E, 60
Ath. 14.614F, 449

Athenaeus Mechanicus *Poliorcetica*
Ath.Mech. 5, 308
Ath.Mech. 8, 308
Ath.Mech. 9-11, 309
Ath.Mech. 10-12, 308
Ath.Mech. 23-5, 309

Athanis of Syracuse (*FGrH/BNJ* 562)
F 2, 51

Athenagoras *Pro Christianis*
Athenag. 30, 120

Bato of Sinope (*FGrH/BNJ* 268)
BatoSinop. T1, 65
BatoSinop. F 4, 65

Berossus (*FGrH/BNJ* 680)
Beros. F 7d, 129

Callisthenes of Olynthus (*FGrH/BNJ* 124)
Callisth.Olynth. FF 2-3, 271
Callisth.Olynth. F 14a, 468

Chares of Mytilene (*FGrH/BNJ* 125)
Chares F 4, 369
Chares F 6, 298
Chares F 18, 337

Cicero, M. Tullius, *De Divinatione*
Div. 1.1.2, 103
Cicero, M. Tullius, *De Legibus*
Leg. 2.26, 157
Leg. 2.62-4, 378
Cicero, M. Tullius, *Tusculanae Disputationes*
Tusc. 1.42.101, 168

Cleomedes
Cleom. 2.156-9, 425

Clitarchus of Alexandria (*FGrH/BNJ* 137)
Clitarch. F 2, 129

Clitarch. F 11, 332
Clitarch. F 24, 361
Clitarch. F 31, 376

Ctesias of Cnidus (*FGrH/BNJ* 688/Lenfant 2004), *Indica*
Ind. F 45 § 1, 115
Ind. F 45 § 8, 112
Ind. F 45 § 14, 115, 116
Ind. F 45 § 15, 112
Ind. F 45 § 31, 112
Ind. F 45 § 39, 112
Ind. F 45 § 45, 112
Ind. F 45 § 46, 115
Ind. F 45i, 52
Ind. F 45r, 52, 115
Ind. F 49 a & b, 113
Ctesias of Cnidus, *Persica*
Pers. F. 1a, 95
Pers. F. 1b, 6
Pers. F 1c, 120
Pers. F. 1i, 111
Pers. Fr. *1δ [L], 120
Pers. Fr. 1m, 120
Pers. F.1n, 121
Pers. F 10, 122
Pers. F. *1pε [L], 125
Pers. F 1q, 129
Pers. F. *6b [L], 137
Pers. F 8a, 139
Pers. F. 8d, 144, 325
Pers. FF. *8d-*9e, 149
Pers. F. 9(3), 139
Pers. F. 13(10), 149
Pers. F. 13(11-16), 506
Pers. F. 13(14), 506
Pers. F. 13(15-18), 443
Pers. F 13(16-17), 265
Pers. F. 13(19), 332
Pers. F. 13(20-1), 153
Pers. F. 13(22), 153
Pers. F. 13(26), 152, 171, 172, 179
Pers. F. 13(28), 182
Pers. F 13(30, 31), 154
Pers. F. 13(33), 194
Pers. F. 14(34), 194
Pers. F 14(36), 197
Pers. F. 15(55-6), 230
Pers. F. 17b [L], 214
Pers. FF. 26 and *26a [L], 221
Pers. F. 30(72), 234
Pers. F 33, 122
Pers. FF. *44a-b, 143

Curtius Rufus, Q., *Historia Alexandri*
Curt 8.10.35, 345
Curt. 10.2.1-3, 369

Curt. 10.3.11–12, 369
Curt. 10.5.19–25, 382
Curt. 10.5.23, 276
Curt. 10.5.5, 380
Curt. 10.8.15–18, 383
Curt. 10.8.15–23, 384
Curt. 10.9.18, 386
Curt. 10.9.21, 386
Curt. 10.1.10, 368
Curt. 10.1.1–9, 367
Curt. 10.1.21, 421
Curt. 10.10.15, 381
Curt. 3.1, 291
Curt. 3.3.22, 301
Curt. 3.3.8–9, 294
Curt. 3.4.3, 283
Curt. 3.5.2–3, 295
Curt. 3.7.6, 295
Curt. 3.9.2, 299
Curt. 3.11.4, 296
Curt. 3.11.8, 299
Curt. 3.11.8–9, 297
Curt. 3.11.10, 270, 285, 298
Curt. 3.11.16–19, 299
Curt. 3.11.18, 299
Curt. 3.11.21–2, 300
Curt. 3.11.25, 300
Curt. 3.11.27, 301
Curt. 3.12.21–2, 302
Curt. 3.13.12–14, 300
Curt. 4.1.3, 303
Curt. 4.1.15, 263
Curt. 4.1.15–26, 311
Curt. 4.1.28, 270
Curt. 4.2.4, 304
Curt. 4.2.9, 305
Curt. 4.2.10, 304
Curt. 4.2.23, 309
Curt. 4.2.39–40, 312
Curt. 4.3.1, 307
Curt. 4.3.2–7, 306
Curt. 4.3.6–7, 307
Curt. 4.3.9–11, 306
Curt. 4.3.11, 307
Curt. 4.3.25–6, 309
Curt. 4.3.26, 309
Curt. 4.4.12–13, 311
Curt. 4.4.15–16, 311
Curt. 4.6.7–30, 313
Curt. 4.9.5, 314
Curt. 4.9.7, 314, 316
Curt. 4.9.9, 314, 322
Curt. 4.9.12, 316
Curt. 4.10.22–4, 302
Curt. 4.12.13, 314
Curt. 4.13.1, 303
Curt. 4.13.23–4, 313
Curt. 4.15.28–30, 321
Curt. 4.15.5–18, 320
Curt. 4.15.6–8, 322

Curt. 4.16.2–3, 322
Curt. 4.16.7, 322
Curt. 4.16.8, 322
Curt. 4.16.26, 322
Curt. 5.1.10, 323
Curt. 5.1.11, 323
Curt. 5.1.13, 107
Curt. 5.1.27, 104
Curt. 5.1.32–5, 104
Curt. 5.2.1–9, 324
Curt. 5.2.8, 325
Curt. 5.2.11, 325
Curt. 5.3.1, 326
Curt. 5.3.16–17, 327
Curt. 5.3.23, 328
Curt. 5.4.33–4, 328
Curt. 5.6.1–8, 330
Curt. 5.6.11–20, 333
Curt. 5.7.2–11, 332
Curt. 5.11.5, 277
Curt. 5.13.13, 335
Curt. 6.3.12, 276
Curt. 6.4.10, 277
Curt. 6.4.23–4, 337
Curt. 6.5.1–4, 337
Curt. 6.5.22–3, 337
Curt. 6.6.1–10, 338
Curt. 6.6.13, 335
Curt. 6.6.13–21, 339
Curt. 6.8.23, 341
Curt. 6.9.2–11.7, 341
Curt. 6.11.21–34, 341
Curt. 6.11.38, 341
Curt. 7.3.4, 342
Curt. 7.3.22, 344
Curt. 7.5.19–26, 344
Curt. 7.11, 97
Curt. 8.1.20, 285
Curt. 8.5.1, 369
Curt. 8.5.5–22, 345
Curt. 8.10.3, 114
Curt. 8.10.22, 345
Curt. 8.11.3, 347
Curt. 8.11.4, 347
Curt. 8.12.4–18, 348
Curt. 8.12.5, 348
Curt. 8.12.7–10, 348
Curt. 8.13.6, 349
Curt. 8.14.13, 351
Curt. 8.14.32, 350
Curt. 8.14.38, 350, 351
Curt. 8.14.39–40, 350
Curt. 9.1.35, 354
Curt. 9.1.36–2.1, 355
Curt. 9.2.2–4, 355
Curt. 9.2.3, 355
Curt. 9.2.6–7, 355
Curt. 9.2.12–13.19, 356
Curt. 9.3.2, 356
Curt. 9.3.10–11, 356
Curt. 9.3.24, 358

Curt. 9.3.27, 357
Curt. 9.4.1–3, 358
Curt. 9.4.14, 359
Curt. 9.4.15, 359
Curt. 9.4.5, 358
Curt. 9.4.6–7, 358
Curt. 9.5.14–18, 361
Curt. 9.5.21, 361
Curt. 9.7.11, 361
Curt. 9.7.12–15, 361
Curt. 9.8.4, 362
Curt. 9.8.4–7, 362
Curt. 9.8.8, 362
Curt. 9.8.8–10, 362
Curt. 9.8.11–12, 362
Curt. 9.8.15, 363
Curt. 9.8.22–4, 364
Curt. 9.8.22–7, 364
Curt. 9.8.25–8, 364
Curt. 9.10.13, 366
Curt. 9.10.18, 367
Curt. 9.10.20–1, 367
Curt. 9.10.21, 367
Curt. 9.10.24–8, 367
Curt. 9.10.27, 364, 367
Curt. 9.10.7, 365

Demades, *On the Twelve Years*
Duod. Ann. 9–10, 51

Demetrius, *On Style*
Eloc. 213, 139

Demetrius of Salamis (*BNJ* 643)
Demetr.Sal. F 1, 123

Demosthenes, *Orations* (numbers follow the order suggested by Blass's Teubner edition of 1885)
D. 2.14, 51
D. 4.35, 51
D. 6.20, 51
D. 7.32, 51
D. 8.40, 51
D. 9.65–6, 51
D. 10.34, 51
D. 12.6, 51
D. 14.29, 170
D. 15.26, 51
D. 18.238, 170
D. 18.*passim*, 51
D. 19.193–5, 51
D. 19.*passim*, 51
D. 20.76, 49, 244
D. 20.80–2, 51
D. 23.103, 293
D. 23.108, 51
D. 23.121, 51

Index of Classical Sources

D. 23.157, 51
D. 24.129, 175
D. 45.79, 378

Dexippus (*FGrH/BNJ* 100)
Dexipp. F 8.2, 384
Dexipp. F 8.4, 385

Dicearchus *Fragmenta*
(see *GGM*, II: 472), 386

Dinarchus, *Against Demosthenes*
In Dem. 39, 49
In Dem. 14, 51

Dinon (*FGrH/BNJ* 690), *Persica*
Pers. F 7, 121

Dio Cassius, *Roman History*
D.C. 40.29.1, 479

Dio Chrysostomus, *Discourses*
D.Chr. 11.148, 156
D.Chr. 47.24, 109

Diodorus of Sicily, *Bibliotheca Historica*
D.S. 1.1.2, 34
D.S. 1.2.2, 11
D.S. 1.2.6, 16
D.S. 1.4.2, 74
D.S. 1.4.2–4, 12
D.S. 1.4.3–4, 34
D.S. 1.4.4, 3
D.S. 1.5.1, 5, 34
D.S. 1.7.7, 34
D.S. 1.9.5, 536
D.S. 1.28.1, 131, 132
D.S. 1.30.4–9, 265, 485
D.S. 1.36.7–12, 248
D.S. 1.45.3, 16
D.S. 1.55.4, 119
D.S. 1.55.8, 35
D.S. 1.56.5, 35, 111
D.S. 1.56.6, 39
D.S. 1.63.1, 16
D.S. 1.74.7, 4, 66
D.S. 1.80.1–2, 8
D.S. 1.81.6, 131, 132
D.S. 2.1.5–6, 36
D.S. 2.1.7, 6
D.S. 2.1.8–9, 126
D.S. 2.2.3, 111
D.S. 2.5.5, 153
D.S. 2.5.6–7, 152
D.S. 2.6.2, 334
D.S. 2.6.8, 36
D.S. 2.7.3, 36

D.S. 2.9.5–6, 102
D.S. 2.10.5, 106
D.S. 2.11.1, 36, 115
D.S. 2.11.5, 107
D.S. 2.12.1, 107
D.S. 2.13.1–2, 526
D.S. 2.14.3, 533
D.S. 2.15.2, 112
D.S. 2.16.3–4, 36
D.S. 2.16.9, 115
D.S. 2.17.2, 115
D.S. 2.20.1, 112
D.S. 2.20.3–5, 36
D.S. 2.23.1, 526
D.S. 2.23.1–3, 121
D.S. 2.25.8, 133
D.S. 2.28.8, 122
D.S. 2.29.1–31.9, 451
D.S. 2.29.4, 132
D.S. 2.30.5, 135
D.S. 2.32.2–3, 36
D.S. 2.33.6, 138
D.S. 2.34.3–5, 13
D.S. 2.34.6, 137
D.S. 2.35.1, 106, 115
D.S. 2.35.2, 37
D.S. 2.35–2.42, 37, 114
D.S. 2.36.1–3, 37
D.S. 2.37.1–3, 106
D.S. 2.37.2–3, 37
D.S. 2.37.5–6, 37
D.S. 2.38.1, 113
D.S. 2.38.3, 534
D.S. 2.39.1, 534
D.S. 2.43.6, 37
D.S. 2.45.2, 338
D.S. 2.45.3, 338
D.S. 3.1.2, 131
D.S. 3.2, 126
D.S. 3.3.1, 112
D.S. 3.9.3, 112
D.S. 3.11.2, 38
D.S. 3.11.3, 4, 66
D.S. 3.38.1, 12, 38, 74
D.S. 3.40.8, 38
D.S. 3.52.3, 39
D.S. 3.66.5, 39
D.S. 4.1.3, 39
D.S. 4.2.4, 39
D.S. 4.6.3, 39
D.S. 4.7.2, 39
D.S. 4.16.1, 338
D.S. 4.21.2, 5
D.S. 4.21.7, 39
D.S. 4.22.6, 39
D.S. 4.32.2, 39
D.S. 4.39.3, 39
D.S. 4.49.7, 39
D.S. 4.56.1, 39
D.S. 4.56.3, 39
D.S. 4.75.2, 39

D.S. 4.75.4, 123
D.S. 4.80.2, 39
D.S. 4.85.5, 39
D.S. 4.85.6, 39
D.S. 4.85.7, 39
D.S. 5.1.3, 41
D.S. 5.1.4, 41, 42
D.S. 5.2.1, 40
D.S. 5.2.4, 41
D.S. 5.5.1, 41
D.S. 5.6.1, 41
D.S. 5.7.7, 41
D.S. 5.16.3, 41
D.S. 5.17.1, 41
D.S. 5.21.2, 40
D.S. 5.21.3–4, 40
D.S. 5.22.1, 40
D.S. 5.28.4, 41
D.S. 5.56.7, 41
D.S. 5.64.1, 41
D.S. 5.64.4, 41
D.S. 5.66.6, 41
D.S. 5.69.1, 41
D.S. 5.69.3, 41
D.S. 5.80.4, 41
D.S. 6.1.1, 42
D.S. 6.1.3, 42
D.S. 6.4.1, 42
D.S. 7.1.1, 42
D.S. 7.5.1, 42
D.S. 7.5.4, 42
D.S. 7.8.1, 42
D.S. 7.10.1, 42
D.S. 7.12.1–2, 42
D.S. 7.16.1, 42
D.S. 7.17.1, 42
D.S. 8.8.2, 42
D.S. 8.13.2, 42
D.S. 8.16.1, 137
D.S. 8.17.1–2, 42
D.S. 8.21.3, 43
D.S. 8.23.1–2, 43
D.S. 8.29.1, 43
D.S. 9.3.1–2, 43, 44
D.S. 9.6.1, 43
D.S. 9.10.2, 43
D.S. 9.10.4, 43
D.S. 9.10.5, 43
D.S. 9.16.1, 43
D.S. 9.20.2–3, 43
D.S. 9.22–4, 140
D.S. 9.28.1, 43
D.S. 9.31.1–2, 43
D.S. 9.33.2, 43
D.S. 9.36.2–3, 43
D.S. 10.12, 44
D.S. 10.16, 43
D.S. 10.16.2–3, 44
D.S. 10.18.1, 44
D.S. 10.19.1, 44
D.S. 10.21, 44

D.S. 10.24, 43
D.S. 10.25.1, 43
D.S. 10.25.4, 43
D.S. 10.4, 43
D.S. 10.6.4, 43
D.S. 10.9.8, 43
D.S. 11.2.2, 153
D.S. 11.3.8, 162
D.S. 11.10.4, 185
D.S. 11.5.5, 220
D.S. 11.7.2, 320
D.S. 11.11.1-6, 44, 541
D.S. 11.14.4, 44
D.S. 11.16.1, 168
D.S. 11.26.4-5, 157
D.S. 11.29.3, 44
D.S. 11.30.2-4, 185
D.S. 11.33.2, 44
D.S. 11.37.6, 32
D.S. 11.41.1, 158
D.S. 11.46.2-3, 537
D.S. 11.56.8, 299
D.S. 11.60.6, 193
D.S. 11.61.3, 270
D.S. 11.62.3, 44
D.S. 11.75.4, 197
D.S. 11.91.1, 158
D.S. 12.2-3, 158
D.S. 12.3.3, 44
D.S. 12.10.5, 46
D.S. 12.11.4, 46
D.S. 12.12.1, 46
D.S. 12.13.1, 46
D.S. 12.14.1, 47
D.S. 12.26.1, 3
D.S. 12.28.3, 129
D.S. 12.36.2, 47
D.S. 12.40.6, 47
D.S. 12.45.7, 47
D.S. 12.53.1, 47
D.S. 12.84.1, 47
D.S. 13.36.5, 66
D.S. 13.70.3, 213
D.S. 13.74.3, 47
D.S. 13.90.4-7, 58
D.S. 13.90.7, 11
D.S. 14.9.2, 147
D.S. 14.9.6, 213
D.S. 14.11.1, 32
D.S. 14.12.8, 212
D.S. 14.19.6, 198, 213
D.S. 14.24.7, 219
D.S. 14.42.1, 129
D.S. 14.42.2, 262
D.S. 14.46.6, 32, 36
D.S. 14.50.4, 129
D.S. 14.85.4, 249
D.S. 14.98, 240
D.S. 14.98.1, 234
D.S. 14.98.3, 260
D.S. 14.98.3-4, 237

D.S. 14.99.1, 239
D.S. 15.1.1, 9, 544
D.S. 15.1.1-6, 49
D.S. 15.1.3-4, 544
D.S. 15.2.1, 240
D.S. 15.2.1-4.3, 260
D.S. 15.4.1, 238
D.S. 15.4.2, 240
D.S. 15.8.1, 238
D.S. 15.8.1-11.2, 260
D.S. 15.8.4, 253
D.S. 15.16.1, 49, 541
D.S. 15.18.2, 253
D.S. 15.26, 256
D.S. 15.38.1-39.2, 245, 249
D.S. 15.41.5, 282
D.S. 15.43.4, 246
D.S. 15.43.5-6, 246
D.S. 15.50.3, 131
D.S. 15.50.4, 245
D.S. 15.50.4-51.1, 245
D.S. 15.70.1, 376
D.S. 15.76.4, 32
D.S. 15.89.3, 32
D.S. 15.90.2, 253
D.S. 15.90.3, 260
D.S. 15.92.1, 283
D.S. 15.93.1, 276
D.S. 15.95.4, 49
D.S. 16.3.8, 50
D.S. 16.7.1, 14
D.S. 16.14.5, 61
D.S. 16.34.1, 256
D.S. 16.40.1-52.8, 507
D.S. 16.40.3, 276
D.S. 16.42.1, 125
D.S. 16.42.2, 259
D.S. 16.42.6-7, 264
D.S. 16.43.4, 227
D.S. 16.44.2, 257
D.S. 16.44.5, 282
D.S. 16.45.4-6, 276
D.S. 16.46.2, 260
D.S. 16.46.4-5, 485
D.S. 16.47.4, 276
D.S. 16.51.2, 276
D.S. 16.69.2, 287
D.S. 16.70.2, 51
D.S. 16.70.6, 5
D.S. 16.71.3, 50
D.S. 16.74.2, 287
D.S. 16.76.6, 61
D.S. 16.82.5, 4
D.S. 16.83, 52
D.S. 16.83.3, 4
D.S. 16.88.2, 51
D.S. 16.91.4-6, 477
D.S. 17.5, 36
D.S. 17.6.1, 298
D.S. 17.7.3, 409
D.S. 17.9-14, 382

D.S. 17.17.1, 292
D.S. 17.19.4, 298
D.S. 17.20.1-6, 284
D.S. 17.21.2, 282
D.S. 17.21.3, 298, 443
D.S. 17.22.5, 307
D.S. 17.22.5-23.1, 306
D.S. 17.32.1-2, 341
D.S. 17.32.3, 299
D.S. 17.34.5, 270, 285
D.S. 17.37.1, 298
D.S. 17.40.4-46.6, 360
D.S. 17.41.2, 311
D.S. 17.42.7, 129
D.S. 17.43.1, 310
D.S. 17.45.2, 129
D.S. 17.45.3, 307
D.S. 17.48.2-5, 289
D.S. 17.49.2, 356
D.S. 17.49.2-51.4, 111
D.S. 17.50.1-7, 111
D.S. 17.51.2-3, 356
D.S. 17.52.6, 12, 75
D.S. 17.53.1-2, 303
D.S. 17.57.6, 319
D.S. 17.58.1, 319
D.S. 17.64.4, 375
D.S. 17.65.2, 371
D.S. 17.67.1, 424
D.S. 17.68.4, 438
D.S. 17.71.7, 53
D.S. 17.72.6, 154
D.S. 17.76.1, 334
D.S. 17.76.6, 54
D.S. 17.77.5, 421
D.S. 17.77.6, 53
D.S. 17.80.2, 295
D.S. 17.83.2, 434
D.S. 17.85.2, 358
D.S. 17.87.2, 352
D.S. 17.87.4, 113
D.S. 17.88.4, 357
D.S. 17.89.6, 357
D.S. 17.90.1, 353
D.S. 17.92.2, 446
D.S. 17.93.1, 356, 369
D.S. 17.93.2, 106, 387
D.S. 17.93.2 sqq., 387
D.S. 17.93.3, 355
D.S. 17.94.5, 369
D.S. 17.98-9, 358
D.S. 17.99.4, 420
D.S. 17.99.5-6, 388
D.S. 17.102.7-103.8, 358
D.S. 17.103.8, 363
D.S. 17.108.1-2, 421
D.S. 17.108.3, 356
D.S. 17.110.1-18.9.5, 372
D.S. 17.110.3, 418, 468
D.S. 17.110.4, 426
D.S. 17.111.4-6, 320

Index of Classical Sources

D.S. 17.112.1–6, 131
D.S. 17.112.2, 451
D.S. 17.112.2–3, 134
D.S. 17.115.2, 100
D.S. 17.116.4, 131
D.S. 17.116.5, 99, 419
D.S. 18.1.4, 380
D.S. 18.1.4–5, 381
D.S. 18.2.2–3, 55
D.S. 18.2.4, 55
D.S. 18.3.1, 55, 412
D.S. 18.3.3, 53, 95, 338, 420, 421
D.S. 18.4.2, 377
D.S. 18.4.4, 114
D.S. 18.4.8, 55, 361
D.S. 18.5–6, 56
D.S. 18.6.1, 106, 355
D.S. 18.7, 55
D.S. 18.7.1–9, 361
D.S. 18.7.4, 420
D.S. 18.8.2–6, 370
D.S. 18.8.7, 55
D.S. 18.10.5, 55
D.S. 18.12.1, 55
D.S. 18.13.5, 55
D.S. 18.14.1, 55, 388
D.S. 18.15.3, 55
D.S. 18.15.5, 55
D.S. 18.16.1, 55
D.S. 18.16.1–3, 507
D.S. 18.18.7, 490
D.S. 18.22.1–8, 292
D.S. 18.22.4, 55
D.S. 18.23.1, 55
D.S. 18.25.6, 394
D.S. 18.29.3, 395
D.S. 18.29.4–5, 55
D.S. 18.31.2, 55
D.S. 18.33–5, 487
D.S. 18.35.6, 56
D.S. 18.36.2–4, 427
D.S. 18.37.2, 55, 413
D.S. 18.39.4, 421
D.S. 18.39.6, 385, 420, 421, 449, 450, 452
D.S. 18.40.1, 55
D.S. 18.40.3, 432
D.S. 18.42.1, 55, 407
D.S. 18.45.3–4, 423
D.S. 18.48.1, 406
D.S. 18.48.5, 338
D.S. 18.49.4, 407, 411
D.S. 18.52.1–2, 456
D.S. 18.52.4, 55
D.S. 18.52.7, 407
D.S. 18.57.2–3, 411
D.S. 18.60.1, 416
D.S. 18.61.2, 55
D.S. 18.62.2, 452, 489
D.S. 18.62.4–63.2, 431

D.S. 18.67.6, 476
D.S. 18.71.2–6, 463
D.S. 18.71.6, 464
D.S. 18.72.2, 55
D.S. 18.73.4, 418
D.S. 19.1.9, 57
D.S. 19.2.2–3.2, 58
D.S. 19.2.6–7, 58
D.S. 19.4.7, 384
D.S. 19.5.4, 58
D.S. 19.6.4, 58
D.S. 19.11.1, 58
D.S. 19.11.7, 58
D.S. 19.12.1, 468
D.S. 19.13.2–6, 417
D.S. 19.14.7, 449
D.S. 19.17.3, 449
D.S. 19.17.7, 453
D.S. 19.18.1, 449
D.S. 19.18.3–4, 424
D.S. 19.19.4–8, 373
D.S. 19.22.2, 331
D.S. 19.23.1–3, 400
D.S. 19.23.3, 383
D.S. 19.27.4, 421
D.S. 19.27–8, 463
D.S. 19.28.3, 421, 434
D.S. 19.29.2, 463
D.S. 19.32.2, 439
D.S. 19.34.7, 106
D.S. 19.35.1–36.1, 430
D.S. 19.35.4–36, 58
D.S. 19.36.5, 383
D.S. 19.37.1, 439
D.S. 19.38.2, 58
D.S. 19.40.2, 491
D.S. 19.41.2, 437
D.S. 19.43.7–9, 58
D.S. 19.43.8–9, 58
D.S. 19.44.1, 450
D.S. 19.48.2, 469
D.S. 19.48.3, 430
D.S. 19.48.7, 57
D.S. 19.49.1, 58
D.S. 19.49.1–51.5, 381, 430
D.S. 19.51.1, 421
D.S. 19.51.5, 58, 455
D.S. 19.52.1, 58
D.S. 19.52.4, 58, 455
D.S. 19.52.5, 57
D.S. 19.53.3–54.3, 382
D.S. 19.53.5, 57
D.S. 19.55.7, 134
D.S. 19.55.8–9, 131
D.S. 19.55.9, 134
D.S. 19.56.5, 489
D.S. 19.57.1–3, 58
D.S. 19.57.5, 457
D.S. 19.58.2–3, 215
D.S. 19.59.1, 461, 475
D.S. 19.61.1, 421, 453

D.S. 19.62.1, 455
D.S. 19.62.2, 452
D.S. 19.62.5, 475
D.S. 19.62.6, 460
D.S. 19.67.4, 421
D.S. 19.67.5–6, 58
D.S. 19.69.1, 462, 488
D.S. 19.72.9, 57
D.S. 19.73.6, 491
D.S. 19.75.5, 225
D.S. 19.78.2, 292
D.S. 19.79.5, 454, 475
D.S. 19.81.2–85.3, 58
D.S. 19.81.3, 4
D.S. 19.84.1–2, 463
D.S. 19.86.3, 56
D.S. 19.91.1, 418
D.S. 19.92.5, 471
D.S. 19.98.4, 57
D.S. 19.102.7, 58
D.S. 19.105.1, 474
D.S. 19.105.2, 58
D.S. 19.106.2, 58
D.S. 19.108.1, 58
D.S. 20.14.6, 59
D.S. 20.18.3, 59
D.S. 20.19.1, 59, 60
D.S. 20.19.5, 484
D.S. 20.20.1, 60
D.S. 20.26.3–4, 59
D.S. 20.28.2–3, 60
D.S. 20.40.1, 59
D.S. 20.41.3–42.5, 59
D.S. 20.41.6, 59
D.S. 20.42.3, 59
D.S. 20.43.1–44.6, 59
D.S. 20.47.1, 481
D.S. 20.47.3, 480
D.S. 20.50.1–3, 478
D.S. 20.50.4, 54, 59
D.S. 20.54.1–20.72.5, 60
D.S. 20.54.2, 60
D.S. 20.55.4, 376
D.S. 20.64.1–69.5, 60
D.S. 20.71.3, 58
D.S. 20.73.1–77.1, 60
D.S. 20.73–6, 248
D.S. 20.77.1–20.79.5, 60
D.S. 20.81.1–88.9, 60
D.S. 20.89.1–90.2, 60
D.S. 20.91.1–100.7, 60
D.S. 20.99.3, 488
D.S. 20.101.1–4
D.S. 20.102.1–103.7, 60
D.S. 20.103.5–6, 466
D.S. 20.104.3, 60
D.S. 20.106.1–113.5, 60
D.S. 20.108.2, 415
D.S. 21.5.1, 61
D.S. 21.6.1, 61
D.S. 21.7.1, 61

D.S. 21.8.1, 61
D.S. 21.12d, 62
D.S. 21.16.3, 62
D.S. 21.16.4, 61
D.S. 21.16.5, 59
D.S. 21.17.1, 59
D.S. 21.18, 62
D.S. 21.18.1, 62
D.S. 22.2.2, 63
D.S. 22.3.1, 63
D.S. 22.3.2, 63
D.S. 22.4.1, 63
D.S. 22.6.3, 63
D.S. 22.7.5, 62
D.S. 22.8.1, 63
D.S. 22.8.2, 63
D.S. 22.9.1, 63
D.S. 22.9.2, 63
D.S. 22.9.3, 63
D.S. 22.11.1, 63
D.S. 22.13.7, 62
D.S. 22.13.9, 62
D.S. 23.8.1, 62
D.S. 23.13.1, 63
D.S. 23.14.1, 63
D.S. 24.1.10, 64
D.S. 24.11.2, 64
D.S. 25.17.1, 292
D.S. 26.4.1, 65
D.S. 27.1.1, 66
D.S. 27.3.1, 67
D.S. 27.11.1, 66
D.S. 28.2.1, 68
D.S. 28.2–3, 67
D.S. 28.3.1, 68, 500
D.S. 28.12.1, 497
D.S. 28.15.1–4, 497
D.S. 29.2, 279
D.S. 29.2.1, 68
D.S. 29.8.1, 68
D.S. 29.10.1, 68
D.S. 29.17.1–21.1, 69
D.S. 29.22.1, 69
D.S. 29.23.1–24.1, 69
D.S. 29.26.1, 69
D.S. 29.28.1, 69
D.S. 29.30.1, 70
D.S. 29.31.1–34.2, 69
D.S. 30.1.1, 70
D.S. 30.2.1, 70
D.S. 30.3.1, 70
D.S. 30.4.1, 70
D.S. 30.5.1, 70
D.S. 30.7.1, 70
D.S. 30.7.2, 70
D.S. 30.8.1, 70
D.S. 30.21.3–4, 70
D.S. 30.21.4, 315
D.S. 30.22.1, 70
D.S. 30.23.2, 70
D.S. 31.1.1–2.2, 70

D.S. 31.32.1, 512
D.S. 31.32a.1, 512
D.S. 32.1.1–3.1, 72
D.S. 32.6.1, 72
D.S. 32.9c.1, 513
D.S. 32.9d/10.1, 515
D.S. 32.14.1, 72
D.S. 32.27.3, 14, 80
D.S. 33.3.1, 513
D.S. 33.4.4, 4
D.S. 33.4a.1, 513
D.S. 34/5.2.34, 76
D.S. 37.30.1–3, 79
D.S. 38/9.5.1, 79
D.S. 38/9.6, 95
D.S. 38/9.20, 14
D.S. 40.1a.1, 4

Dionysius of Halicarnassus,
De Lysia
12, 249

Diogenes Laertius, *Lives of Eminent Philosophers*
D.L. 7.23, 302
D.L. 9.58–108, 375

Diyllus of Athens (*FGrH/BNJ* 73)
Diyll. F 1, 57
Diyll. F 3, 544

Duris of Samos (*FGrH/BNJ* 76)
Duris F 17, 59
Duris F 18, 60

Ephippus of Olynthus (Alexander historian) (*FGrH/BNJ* 126)
Ephipp.Ol. F 3, 380

Ephorus of Cyme (*FGrH/BNJ* 70), *Histories*
Ephor. F 42, 62
Ephor. F 70, 211
Ephor. F 186, 178

Epicurus, *Sententiae*
Sent. 17, 64

Epitome Mettensis
Epit.Mett. 1, 338
Epit.Mett. 39, 345
Epit.Mett. 49–51, 348
Epit.Mett. 51–2, 348
Epit.Mett. 53, 349
Epit.Mett. 54, 349, 351
Epit.Mett. 60, 351
Epit.Mett. 61, 351
Epit.Mett. 68, 355

Epit.Mett. 75, 359
Epit.Mett. 76–7, 361

Eumachus of Neapolis (*FGrH/BNJ* 178)
Eum.Neap. F 1, 65

Euphorio
Euph. 26 (fr. C), col. i, lines 9–10, 109

Euripides *Iphegenia Taurica*
IT 625–6, 59
Euripides *Phoenix*
Phoenix (Fr. 812, 7–9 [Nauck]), 47
Euripides
TGF, Euripides, 922, 59

Eusebius of Caesarea, *Chronicon*
Eus. (Arm.) *Chron.* (Karst 28,25 = *FGrH/BNJ* 93 F 1a), 120
Eus. (Arm.) *Chron.* (Karst) 28.28–29.3, 96
Eus. (Arm.) *Chron.* (Karst) 29,10–26, 122
Eus. (*FGrH/BNJ* 260, Porphyry) F 32(23), 523
Eus. *Chron.* 205, 375
Eus. *Chron. ad Olymp.* 83.4, 544
Eusebius, *Praeparatio Evangelica*
PE 10.9.10–11, 525
PE 10.9.17, 525

Flavius Vegetius *De re militare*
De re milit. 3.Praef., 65

Gellius, Aulus *Noctes Atticae*
Gell. 5.2.1, 337

Harpocratio, Valerius *Lexicon*
Harp. s.v. 'Ἀριοβαρζάνης', 253

Hellanicus (*FGrH/BNJ* 4)
Hellanic. F 107, 338

Hellenica Oxyrhynchia (anonymous author)
Hell.Oxy. 6.1–4, 230
Hell.Oxy. 9.2, 229
Hell.Oxy. 10.1, 231
Hell.Oxy. 14–15, 231

Index of Classical Sources 587

Heraclides of Cume (*FGrH/ BNJ* 689)
Heraclid.Cum. F 1, 319

Hero Mechanicus
Belopoeica
Bel. 3, 290

Herodas Mimographus
Mimes 1.50–1, 304

Herodotus of Halicarnassus
Histories
Hdt. 1.7, 90
Hdt 1.53.3, 145
Hdt. 1.75–91, 145
Hdt. 1.76.3, 145
Hdt. 1.80.4, 116
Hdt. 1.80–176 *passim*, 148
Hdt. 1.86.3–6, 143
Hdt. 1.88.2, 146
Hdt. 1.88.2–3, 147
Hdt. 1.96, 137
Hdt. 1.96–9, 137
Hdt. 1.98, 110
Hdt. 1.101–2, 137
Hdt. 1.103, 137
Hdt. 1.105, 37, 92
Hdt. 1.106, 6
Hdt. 1.106–7, 137
Hdt. 1.107.2–108.1, 144
Hdt. 1.107–30, 137
Hdt. 1.118–19, 141
Hdt. 1.125–9, 140
Hdt. 1.127–9, 137
Hdt. 1.130.1, 141
Hdt. 1.135, 96
Hdt. 1.136, 261
Hdt. 1.166, 169
Hdt. 1.178, 6, 90
Hdt. 1.179, 108
Hdt. 1.181, 102, 103
Hdt. 1.181–3, 103
Hdt. 1.183, 103
Hdt. 1.184, 111, 526
Hdt. 1.185–6, 102
Hdt. 1.186, 100
Hdt. 1.188–91, 149
Hdt. 1.191, 102
Hdt. 1.203.1, 387
Hdt. 1.205–14, 139
Hdt. 2.2.1, 536
Hdt. 2.2.4–5, 536
Hdt. 2.41, 198
Hdt. 2.44, 304
Hdt. 2.6, 265
Hdt. 2.97.1, 248
Hdt. 2.150, 124
Hdt. 2.154, 267
Hdt. 2.158.4, 485
Hdt. 2.165, 198

Hdt. 2.223.3, 321
Hdt. 3.1–2, 149
Hdt. 3.13.3–4, 150
Hdt. 3.1–14, 149
Hdt. 3.23, 112
Hdt. 3.24, 112
Hdt. 3.25, 150
Hdt. 3.26, 150
Hdt. 3.31, 143, 241
Hdt. 3.61–79, 506
Hdt. 3.67–79, 443
Hdt. 3.70, 506
Hdt. 3.76–9, 265
Hdt. 3.87.1, 109
Hdt. 3.94, 113
Hdt. 3.106, 372
Hdt. 3.125, 43
Hdt. 3.151.2, 153
Hdt. 3.151–9, 153
Hdt. 3.153–60, 152
Hdt. 3.154, 152
Hdt. 3.155.5, 526
Hdt. 3.157, 152
Hdt. 4.3.4, 321
Hdt. 4.8–12, 37
Hdt. 4.13–15, 342
Hdt. 4.44, 115
Hdt. 4.44.1–2, 534
Hdt. 4.44.3, 534
Hdt. 4.45, 88
Hdt. 4.118–44, 153
Hdt. 5.3, 113
Hdt. 5.25, 241
Hdt. 5.32, 188
Hdt. 5.53–4, 123
Hdt. 5.102.1, 154
Hdt. 5.119.2–120.1, 154
Hdt. 5.126, 153
Hdt. 6.20, 371
Hdt. 6.50–70, 165
Hdt. 6.101, 155
Hdt. 6.109–10, 156
Hdt. 6.112.1–3, 217
Hdt. 6.119, 372
Hdt. 6.137, 153
Hdt. 6.140, 153
Hdt. 7.1, 196
Hdt. 7.11.2, 154
Hdt. 7.20, 159
Hdt. 7.22, 137
Hdt. 7.22–4, 160
Hdt. 7.27, 189, 449
Hdt. 7.35.1–3, 538
Hdt. 7.60, 94
Hdt. 7.62, 506
Hdt. 7.64, 139
Hdt. 7.66, 137
Hdt. 7.83, 166
Hdt. 7.88–9, 159
Hdt. 7.97, 169
Hdt. 7.108–10, 161

Hdt. 7.109, 164
Hdt. 7.117, 160
Hdt. 7.148–52, 161
Hdt. 7.151, 123
Hdt. 7.153, 157
Hdt. 7.157–62, 158
Hdt. 7.157–63, 157
Hdt. 7.157–67, 178
Hdt. 7.165, 159
Hdt. 7.168, 161, 172
Hdt. 7.172–4, 160
Hdt. 7.173, 160
Hdt. 7.175–8, 162
Hdt. 7.185, 164
Hdt. 7.187, 164
Hdt. 7.188, 169
Hdt. 7.188–93, 169
Hdt. 7.193–4, 169
Hdt. 7.209, 165
Hdt. 7.222, 167
Hdt. 7.223, 168
Hdt. 7.233, 372
Hdt. 7.235, 232
Hdt. 8.1–2, 170
Hdt. 8.4–9, 170
Hdt. 8.7, 169
Hdt. 8.9–11, 170
Hdt. 8.12–13, 170
Hdt. 8.15–18, 171
Hdt. 8.18–23, 171
Hdt. 8.23, 171
Hdt. 8.27–39, 172
Hdt. 8.35–9, 172
Hdt. 8.37, 172
Hdt. 8.40–1, 171
Hdt. 8.50–5, 172
Hdt. 8.58–63, 173
Hdt. 8.66, 172
Hdt. 8.67, 278, 326, 379
Hdt. 8.74–6, 174
Hdt. 8.76–84, 175
Hdt. 8.80, 176
Hdt. 8.84, 176
Hdt. 8.85, 175
Hdt. 8.90, 175
Hdt. 8.93, 178
Hdt. 8.108–10, 176
Hdt. 8.115, 177
Hdt. 8.123, 178
Hdt. 8.126–9.18, 179
Hdt. 8.130, 178
Hdt. 8.136.1, 179
Hdt. 8.136–44, 179
Hdt. 8.140, 179
Hdt. 8.141–2, 179
Hdt. 8.143–4, 179
Hdt. 9.1–15, 181
Hdt. 9.2, 180
Hdt. 9.4–5, 180
Hdt. 9.4–11, 180
Hdt. 9.19–25, 181

Hdt. 9.20, 181
Hdt. 9.25, 181
Hdt. 9.41–57, 182
Hdt. 9.58–75, 182
Hdt. 9.61–2, 230
Hdt. 9.63–4, 182
Hdt. 9.64, 183
Hdt. 9.65–70, 183
Hdt. 9.66–9, 182
Hdt. 9.70, 183
Hdt. 9.70–5, 183
Hdt. 9.80–2, 183
Hdt. 9.82, 188, 537
Hdt. 9.89, 183
Hdt. 9.96, 184
Hdt. 9.98, 185
Hdt. 98–100, 185
Hdt. 9.102–6, 186
Hdt. 9.106, 187
Hdt. 9.108–13, 97
Hdt. 9.114–21, 187

Hesiodus *Theogonia*
Th. 984–5, 123

Homer *Iliad*
Il. 2.517–19, 51
Il. 9.404–5, 51
Il. 11.236, 57
Il. 13.6, 62
Il. 13.131–4, 51
Il. 21.228–382, 359
Homer *Odyssey*
Od. 1.22–4, 123

Hyginus *Astronomica*
Astr. 2.42, 133

Hyperides *Epitaphius*
Epit. col. 8, ll. 22–4 [= 6.21], 378

Isocrates *Antidosis*
Antid. 109–10, 245
Antid. 129, 51
Isocrates *Archidamus*
Arch. 27, 251
Arch. 44 sq, 49
Arch. 63, 49
Isocrates *Areopagiticus*
Areop. 8, 51, 256
Areop. 10, 51, 256
Areop. 81, 51, 256
Isocrates *De Bigis (On the Team of Horses)*
Bigis 40, 211
Isocrates *The Cyprians*
Cypr. 31–47, 260
Isocrates *Epistulae (Letters)*
Ep. 9.9–10, 300
Isocrates *Evagoras*

Evag. 19–28, 233
Evag. 26–32, 234
Evag. 72, 260
Isocrates *Panegyricus*
Paneg. 47–50, 46
Paneg. 90, 170
Paneg. 94, 179
Paneg. 96, 171
Paneg. 126, 49
Paneg. 140 sq, 49
Paneg. 140 sq., 244
Paneg. 140–1, 237
Paneg. 141, 237
Paneg. 142, 231
Paneg. 153, 230
Paneg. 161, 51
Isocrates *Pax (On the Peace)*
Pax 16, 51, 256
Pax 99, 49
Isocrates *To Philip (II)*
Phil. 101–2, 258
Phil. 102, 51, 261
Phil. 103, 260
Isocrates *Plataicus*
Plat. 14, 245

Jerome (St) *Chronology*
Chron. II. Olymp. 182, 540
Jerome (St) *Commentary on Daniel*
In Dan. 11.20, 500
In Dan. 11.21, 503

Josephus, Flavius *Antiquitates Judaicae (Jewish Antiquities)*
AJ 10.226–7, 104
AJ 13.103–15, 512
AJ 13.126–7, 514
AJ 13.131, 515
AJ 13.135–42, 514
AJ 13.384, 524
AJ 13.9, 521
AJ 236–44, 517

Josephus, Flavius *Contra Apionem (Against Apion)*
Ap. 1.141, 104
Ap. 1.227–87, 517
Ap. 1.229, 517
Ap. 2.79–89, 518
Ap. 2.104, 518
Ap. 2.106, 518

Justin (Iustinus, M. Iunianius) *Epitome of the Philippic History of Pompeius Trogus*
Just. 1.1.9, 95
Just. 1.2.3, 96
Just. 2.12.16, 171

Just. 2.14, 182
Just. 2.15.13–14, 187
Just. 6.2.11, 231
Just. 6.6.10, 438
Just. 9.1.3, 191
Just. 10.3, 55, 276
Just. 11.4, 278
Just. 11.6.2, 280, 281
Just. 11.6.8–9, 283
Just. 11.6.11, 284
Just. 11.7.1–2, 295
Just. 11.7.4–15, 291
Just. 11.8.3–6, 295
Just. 11.9.1, 294
Just. 11.9.9, 298
Just. 11.9.10, 301
Just. 11.10.2, 60
Just. 11.10.8, 311
Just. 11.10.13–14, 304
Just. 11.12.5, 314
Just. 11.14.3, 321
Just. 11.14.9, 325
Just. 12.3.8–12, 338
Just. 12.4.2–11, 356
Just. 12.7.9–11, 345
Just. 12.8.3–4, 351
Just. 12.8.10–17, 356
Just. 12.9.1, 358
Just. 12.9.2, 358
Just. 12.9.3, 359
Just. 12.10.3, 364
Just. 12.10.8, 367
Just. 12.10.9, 60
Just. 12.10.9–10, 369
Just. 12.11.6, 369
Just. 12.12.1–6, 371
Just. 12.12.9, 55
Just. 12.12.11, 372
Just. 12.12.12, 376, 378
Just. 12.13.3, 375
Just. 12.13.5, 375
Just. 12.13.10–14.8, 381
Just. 12.14.6–9, 381
Just. 12.15.8, 380
Just. 12.15.9, 383
Just. *Prol. lib.* 13, 55
Just. 13.2.7, 60
Just. 13.3.1–3, 55
Just. 13.4, 55
Just. 13.4.6, 385
Just. 13.4.9–23, 55
Just. 13.5.10, 55
Just. 13.5.12, 55
Just. 13.5.4–7, 55
Just. 13.5.9, 369
Just. 13.5.14–16, 55
Just. 13.5.15–16, 55
Just. 13.6.1, 55
Just. 13.6.1–3, 55
Just. 13.6.4–7, 55
Just. 13.6.18, 55

Index of Classical Sources 589

Just. 13.8.1–9, 394
Just. 13.8.3–8, 55
Just. 13.8.5, 395
Just. 13.8.7–8, 396
Just. 13.8.8, 55
Just. 13.8.10, 55
Just. *Prol. lib.* 14, 55
Just. 14.1.6–7, 55
Just. 14.2.1–4, 400
Just. 14.2.3, 400
Just. 14.2.4, 55, 401, 409
Just. 14.2.6–12, 412
Just. 14.2.8–12, 55
Just. 14.3.3–5, 442
Just. 14.3.6–11, 58
Just. 14.3.11–4.21, 58
Just. 14.3–4, 446
Just. 14.5.1–5, 58
Just. 14.5.9–10, 58
Just. 14.6.1–5, 58
Just. 14.6.9–11, 58
Just. 14.6.13, 58
Just. 15.1.1, 60
Just. 15.1.1–5, 58, 452
Just. 15.1.6–9, 58, 462
Just. 15.2.1, 60
Just. 15.2.1–2, 58
Just. 15.2.3, 60
Just. 15.2.5, 58
Just. 15.2.12, 60
Just. 15.2.15, 60
Just. 15.2.17, 60
Just. 16.1.7–8, 61
Just. 18.2.7–8, 63
Just. 22.1.2–6, 58
Just. 22.2.1–7, 58
Just. 22.2.10, 58
Just. 22.3.1–8, 58
Just. 22.3.6, 58
Just. 22.4.1–7.3, 59
Just. 22.7.4, 59
Just. 22.7.5, 59
Just. 22.7.6–11, 59
Just. 22.8.4–15, 60
Just. 22.8.15, 60
Just. 23.2.3–4, 61
Just. 23.2.3–12, 62
Just. 23.2.5, 62
Just. 23.2.13, 62, 63
Just. 23.3.1, 63
Just. 24.4.1, 63
Just. 24.5.5–6, 63
Just. 24.5.12–13, 63
Just. 24.6.1–4, 63
Just. 24.8.11, 63
Just. 24.8.16, 63
Just. 38.10.1–2, 519
Just. 38.10.5, 520
Just. 38.10.6, 519
Just. 38.10.7, 519
Just. 39.1.1, 519

Just. 39.1.1–2.10, 521
Just. 40.2.2, 523
Just. 41.6.6–8, 516
Just. 42.1.1–5, 520
Just. 42.1.3, 521

Leonidas of Tarentum (in *Anthologia Palatina*)
Leon.Tarent. *AP* 6.130, 63

Livius, T. *Ab Urbe Condita*
Liv. 5.1, 224
Liv. 5.16.1, 233
Liv. 5.29.2, 234, 239
Liv. 5.36.11, 235
Liv. 5.8, 226
Liv. 6.21.1, 245
Liv. 6.22.1, 246
Liv. 7.1.7, 250
Liv. 21.38.3–4, 63
Liv. 31.44.9, 68
Liv. 32.37.3, 292
Liv. 35.28.8, 435
Liv. 37.34–6, 497
Liv. 37.45, 498
Liv. 37.49, 499
Liv. 37.51.8, 499
Liv. 42.19, 508
Liv. *Per.* 68.11, 77

Lucian *Calumniae non temere credendum*
Cal. 17, 378
Cal. 17–19, 377
Lucian *Quomodo historia conscribenda sit*
Hist.Conscr. 12, 351
Hist.Conscr. 39, 372
Lucian *Macrobii*
Macr. 13, 491
Lucian *De Syria dea*
Syr.D. 14, 92, 527
Syr.D. 33, 527
Syr.D. 39–40, 527

Lycurgus *In Leocratem*
Leocr. 23, 51
Leocr. 81, 44, 180

Lysias *Orations*
2.31, 169
2.34, 171
2.44–6, 180
2.46–7, 182
6.28, 233
14.27, 211
19.7, 231
31.21, 378

Manetho *Aegyptiaca* (*Egyptian History*)

Man.Hist. 233–50, 517
Man.Hist. 279–87, 517

Medius (*FGrH/BNJ* 129)
Medius T 1, 380

Megasthenes (*BNJ* 715)
Indiaca (*On India*)
Megasth. T 1, 534
Megasth. T 2, 534
Megasth. F 4, 114, 534
Megasth. FF 9a & 9b, 106
Megasth. F 11b § 7, 119
Megasth. F 11 commentary, 534

Menodotus of Samos (*FGrH/BNJ* 82)
Menodot., 65

Nearchus of Lato (Crete) (*FGrH/BNJ* 133)
Nearch. F 1, 368
Nearch. F 1I, 357
Nearch. F 3a, 525
Nearch. F 3a & b, 119
Nearch. F 27, 368
Nearch. F 34, 368

Nepos, L. Cornelius *Agesilaus*
Ag. 8, 255
Ag. 8.7, 256
Nepos, L. Cornelius *Alcibiades*
Alc. 10.2–6, 211
Alc. 10.3, 211
Nepos, L. Cornelius *Aristides*
Arist. 2.2, 187
Nepos, L. Cornelius *Chabrias*
Cha. 1, 49
Cha. 2.1, 49, 244
Cha. 2.3, 244, 253
Cha. 4, 51
Nepos, L. Cornelius *Datames*
Dat. 6, 252
Dat. 8.2, 252
Dat. 10–11, 253
Nepos, L. Cornelius *Dion*
Di. 5, 51
Di. 8–10, 51
Nepos, L. Cornelius *Eumenes*
Eum. 4.1–2, 396
Eum. 5.7, 410
Eum. 6.2, 412
Eum. 9, 58
Eum. 9.1, 440

Eum. 9.3-5, 441
Eum. 10, 58
Nepos, L. Cornelius
  Hannibal
Han. 13.3, 65
Nepos, L. Cornelius
  Iphicrates
Iph. 2.4, 49, 244, 246
Iph. 3.3, 51
Nepos, L. Cornelius
  Pausanias
Paus. 2.1-2, 187
Paus. 2.2, 188
Nepos, L. Cornelius
  Pelopidas
Pel. 4.2, 49
Pel. 5, 49
Nepos, L. Cornelius
  Phocion
Phoc. 2.2, 56
Phoc. 2.4, 56
Phoc. 4.1-2, 56
Phoc. 4.3-4, 56
Nepos, L. Cornelius
  Themistocles
Them. 7.3, 170
Them. 9-10, 190
Nepos, L. Cornelius
  Timoleon
Tim. 3, 51
Tim. 5.4, 51

Nicholas of Damascus
  (FGrH/BNJ 90)
Nic.Dam. F 1, 93, 120, 530, 531
Nic.Dam. F 3, 90, 125
Nic.Dam. F 4, 137, 138
Nic.Dam. F 5, 139
Nic.Dam. F. 9(1), 144
Nic.Dam. F 66, 325
Nic.Dam. F 66(3), 144
Nic.Dam. F 66(15), 138
Nic.Dam. F 138, 4

Nicobule (FGrH/BNJ 127)
Nicob. F 1, 380
Nicob. F 2, 380

Onesicritus (FGrH/BNJ 134)
Onesicr. F 24, 362, 365

Orosius, Paulus Historiae
  adversus paganos
Oros. 1.3.7, 109
Oros. 5.4.16, 516

Ovidius Naso, P.
  Metamorphoses
Met. 4.44-51, 92
Met. 15.317-21, 112

Pausanias Descriptio
  Graecae
Paus. 1.3.2, 233
Paus. 1.6.3, 385
Paus. 1.6.5, 470
Paus. 1.14.7, 92
Paus. 1.27.1, 181, 182
Paus. 1.27.6, 232
Paus. 1.37.5, 370
Paus. 2.29.5, 170
Paus. 3.4.9, 187
Paus. 6.16.8, 424
Paus. 7.3.7, 455
Paus. 8.7.6, 274
Paus. 8.15.7, 233
Paus. 9.2.6, 180
Paus. 9.40.7-9, 397
Paus. 10.8.6-7, 172

Philo Judaeus of Alexandria
  On the Eternity of the
  World
Aetern.Mun. 23-7, 34

Philo Mechanicus
  Belopoieca
Bel. 5.4.3, 408

Philochorus of Athens
  (FGrH/BNJ 328)
Philoch. F 132, 51
Philoch. F 151, 245

Photius, Patriarch
  of Constantinople
  Bibliotheca
Bibl. [70] 35a1-39, 27
Bibl. [70] 36a6-14, 85
Bibl. [72] 36a9-37a25, 144
Bibl. [72] 45a1-4, 122
Bibl. [82] 64a40, 384
Bibl. [92] 69b1, 384, 412
Bibl. [92] 69b16-17, 392
Bibl. [92] 70a30-2, 392
Bibl. [92] 70b6, 398
Bibl. [92] 70b17-22, 385
Bibl. [92] 70b22-9, 393
Bibl. [92] 70b29-71a9, 394
Bibl. [92] 70b32-4, 394
Bibl. [92] 70b36-8, 395
Bibl. [92] 71a39-71b8, 398
Bibl. [92] 71b36-7, 399
Bibl. [92] 72a31-35, 401
Bibl. [92] 72a9, 384
Bibl. [176] 120a23-5, 234
Bibl. [176] 120a32-4, 239
Bibl. [244] 377a25-8
  (Diodorus), 27
Bibl. [244] 377a25-393b5
  (Diodorus), 27
Bibl. [244] 379a35-380a4, 76
Bibl. [244] 383b11-16, 72
Bibl. [244] 384a31-386b10, 76
Bibl. [244] 386b11-391a28, 77
Bibl. [244] 390b28, 77
Bibl. [244] 393a12-b5, 5
Bibl. [250] 460b11-13, 75

Phylarchus (FGrH/BNJ 81)
Phylarch. F 12, 449

Pindar Odes
N. 3.61-3, 123
P. 6.31, 123

Plato Laws
Lg. 641C, 169
Lg. 685CD, 123
Plato Menon
Men. 78D, 222
Plato Protagoras
Prt. 347C, 228

Polybius Histories
Plb. 1.7.2, 62
Plb. 1.10.1-2, 62
Plb. 1.11.7, 62
Plb. 1.31.1-3, 63
Plb. 1.32.4-5, 63
Plb. 1.82.8, 60
Plb. 3.24, 51
Plb. 3.25.1-5, 62
Plb. 4.27.4, 49
Plb. 5.27.6, 369
Plb. 5.44.1, 110
Plb. 5.44.6, 107
Plb. 5.53.10, 314
Plb. 5.54.7, 426
Plb. 5.67.4-9, 496
Plb. 5.79.5, 320
Plb. 7.7.1, 65
Plb. 7.7.4, 65
Plb. 10.27.7-13, 110
Plb. <12.4a.2>, 51
Plb. 12.11.1-2, 16
Plb. 12.17.2, 295
Plb. 12.17-18, 299
Plb. 12.20.8, 296
Plb. 12.25, 58
Plb. 13.6.1-11, 66
Plb. 15.20.1-8, 67
Plb. 16.17.9, 41
Plb. 16.9.8-9, 67
Plb. 18.11.4-6, 292
Plb. 18.28.6, 51
Plb. 21.13.1-15.13, 497
Plb. 21.16-17, 498
Plb. 21.45.2, 499

Index of Classical Sources 591

Plb. 22.7.2–14, 69
Plb. 24.5.1–2, 69
Plb. 27.1–11, 504
Plb. 27.19, 501
Plb. 28.1, 501
Plb. 28.18, 503
Plb. 28.21.2–5, 503
Plb. 29.2.1–4, 504
Plb. 29.26, 504
Plb. 31.16.1, 509
Plb. 31.2.9–11, 511
Plb. 31.3.1–3, 508
Plb. 31.3.4–5, 509
Plb. 31.7.1–4, 509
Plb. 32.1.3, 511
Plb. 32.2.1–32.3.13, 511
Plb. 38.1, 278
Plb. 39.1.1–4, 67
Plb. 39.7.1, 513

Pliny *Natural History*
Nat. 3.5.57, 376
Nat. 5.14.68, 244
Nat. 5.35.129, 227
Nat. 6.3.8, 526
Nat. 6.18.49, 530
Nat. 6.19.50, 139
Nat. 6.25.92, 526
Nat. 6.30.121, 103
Nat. 6.30.122, 104
Nat. 6.31.132, 324, 371
Nat. 22.44, 364
Nat. *Preface*, 25, 16
Nat. 33.36.112, 112
Nat. 35.36.78, 120
Nat. 35.114, 281

Plutarch of Chaeronea
  Agesilaus
Ages. 6.4–6, 228
Ages. 28, 249
Ages. 36–40, 255
Ages. 37.1–2, 253
Ages. 37.2–38.2, 254
Ages. 37.3–38.1, 254
Ages. 37.5, 253
Ages. 38–9, 255
Ages. 40.3, 256
Plutarch of Chaeronea
  Alcibiades
Alc. 37.6–8, 211
Alc. 38.3–4, 212
Alc. 38.4–5, 211
Alc. 39.1, 211
Plutarch of Chaeronea
  Alexander
Alex. 14.4, 356
Alex. 15.1, 281
Alex. 15.4, 280
Alex. 16, 284
Alex. 16.2–3, 283

Alex. 16.4, 285
Alex. 16.5, 284
Alex. 16.6–7, 286
Alex. 17.1, 286
Alex. 17–18.2, 291
Alex. 19.1, 295
Alex. 20.3–5, 299
Alex. 20.5, 298, 301
Alex. 21.4, 300
Alex. 22.2, 302
Alex. 23.3, 340
Alex. 24.1, 300
Alex. 24.2, 300
Alex. 24.3, 307
Alex. 24.6–8, 307
Alex. 25.3–4, 313
Alex. 31.1, 314
Alex. 31.3, 322
Alex. 32.3–4, 322
Alex. 32.4, 320
Alex. 33.2–5, 321
Alex. 36.1, 325
Alex. 38.1–3, 332
Alex. 38.4, 332
Alex. 41.4, 369
Alex. 42, 335
Alex. 45, 421
Alex. 45.1–3, 338
Alex. 47.3, 369
Alex. 49.1, 341
Alex. 49.8, 381
Alex. 58.4, 359
Alex. 59.1–3, 348
Alex. 59.3–4, 345
Alex. 59.7, 346
Alex. 60.6, 351
Alex. 62, 356
Alex. 63.1, 358
Alex. 63.4, 361
Alex. 67.1, 367
Alex. 67.1–3, 367
Alex. 68.1, 368
Alex. 68.2–4, 367
Alex. 68.4, 325
Alex. 70.2, 369
Alex. 71.1, 369
Alex. 71.3–5, 371
Alex. 71.5, 356
Alex. 72.1, 349
Alex. 72.1–2, 372
Alex. 72.2, 376, 378
Alex. 72.3, 378
Alex. 75.3, 380
Alex. 75.4, 380
Alex. 77.1–3, 381
Alex. 77.5, 383
Plutarch of Chaeronea
  Amatorius
Amat. 753DE, 121
Plutarch of Chaeronea
  Apophtegmata Laconica

Apopht.Lac. 225D, 164, 168
Plutarch of Chaeronea
  Aratus
Arat. 16, 256
Plutarch of Chaeronea
  Aristides
Arist. 8.2–5, 174
Arist. 8.4, 175
Arist. 9.5–6, 176
Arist. 10, 179
Arist. 10.3, 179
Arist. 10.4–6, 179
Arist. 10.7–10, 180
Arist. 14, 181
Arist. 15.1, 181
Arist. 15–17, 182
Arist. 16.8–19.4, 182
Arist. 19.1, 182
Arist. 19.1–4, 183
Arist. 19.3–6, 182
Arist. 19.5–6, 183
Arist. 20.1–3, 183
Arist. 21.1, 180
Plutarch of Chaeronea
  Artaxerxes
Art. 2.24–5, 240
Art. 7.4, 216
Art. 8.2, 217
Art. 10–11, 218
Art. 13.3, 216
Art. 13.4, 219
Art. 13.5, 219
Art. 14, 221
Art. 18.1–5, 222
Art. 24, 246
Art. 27, 236
Art. 27.2, 339
Plutarch of Chaeronea
  Cimon
Cim. 6.1, 191
Cim. 6.6, 191
Cim. 7.1, 191
Cim. 12.1–4, 192
Cim. 12.2, 192
Cim. 12.4, 192
Cim. 12.5, 192
Plutarch of Chaeronea *De Alexandri magni fortuna aut virtute*
Mor. (= *De Alex.Fort.*)
  326D–345B, 19
De Alex.Fort. 326F–327A, 284
De Alex.Fort. 327A, 285
De Alex.Fort. 327B, 361
De Alex.Fort. 327C, 293
De Alex.Fort. 327D, 281
De Alex.Fort. 329E, 369
De Alex.Fort. 336D, 276

De Alex.Fort. 340CE,
311
De Alex.Fort. 340E, 359
De Alex.Fort. 341B, 298
De Alex.Fort. 344D,
361
Plutarch of Chaeronea *De malignitate Herodoti*
De Mal. Her. 862B,
544
Plutarch of Chaeronea *De superstitione*
De Superst. 168E, 240
Plutarch of Chaeronea *Demosthenes*
Dem. 25-6.3, 369
Plutarch of Chaeronea *Demetrius*
Demetr. 2.1, 484
Demetr. 4, 491
Demetr. 5.2, 458
Demetr. 5.3, 465
Demetr. 5.3-4, 462
Demetr. 15-17, 479
Demetr. 16, 481
Demetr. 16.1, 480
Demetr. 30, 495
Demetr. 51.4, 497
Demetr. 52.5-6, 496
Demetr. 6.3, 470
Demetr. 7.2-3, 471
Plutarch of Chaeronea *Eumenes*
Eum. 1.6-7, 394
Eum. 3.2, 383, 384
Eum. 3.3, 392
Eum. 3.9, 477
Eum. 4.1-2, 394
Eum. 4-7, 394
Eum. 5.4, 395
Eum. 5.5, 395
Eum. 5.6, 395
Eum. 5.6-8, 395
Eum. 7.1-4, 396
Eum. 7.7-12, 396
Eum. 9.2, 399
Eum. 9-11, 400
Eum. 10.1, 400
Eum. 12.1-3, 410
Eum. 12.5-6, 410
Eum. 13.2, 413
Eum. 13.2-3, 412
Eum. 13.5-6, 413
Eum. 13.6, 431
Eum. 14.2, 426
Eum. 14.3-5, 431
Eum. 15.2-3, 431
Eum. 15.4, 432, 440
Eum. 15.7-8, 440, 441
Eum. 15.8, 440
Eum. 16.1-5, 446

Eum. 16.8, 443
Eum. 17-19, 446
Eum. 19.3, 449
Plutarch of Chaeronea *Lucullus*
Luc. 1.8, 78
Plutarch of Chaeronea *Marius*
Mar. 28.5, 74
Plutarch of Chaeronea *Pelopidas*
Pel. 30, 251
Plutarch of Chaeronea *Pericles*
Per. 13.13, 364
Plutarch of Chaeronea *Phocion*
Phoc. 21-2, 369
Phoc. 22.2, 370
Plutarch of Chaeronea *Themistocles*
Them. 10.1-10, 171
Them. 10.1-2, 179
Them. 12, 174
Them. 12.6-8, 175
Them. 13.1, 175
Them. 14.3-4, 178
Them. 16, 176
Them. 17.1, 178
Them. 26, 189
Them. 27.2-8, 194
Them. 28-9.5, 190

Polyaenus *Stratagems in War*
Polyaen. 3.9.3, 347
Polyaen. 3.9.38, 246
Polyaen. 3.9.56, 246
Polyaen. 3.9.59, 246
Polyaen. 3.11.7, 253
Polyaen. 4.3.6, 322
Polyaen. 4.6.4, 398
Polyaen. 4.6.7, 403
Polyaen. 4.6.8, 417
Polyaen. 4.6.9, 416, 417
Polyaen. 4.6.10, 438, 439
Polyaen. 4.6.11, 440
Polyaen. 4.6.13, 432, 445
Polyaen. 4.6.14, 447
Polyaen. 4.6.15, 449
Polyaen. 4.7.7, 478, 481
Polyaen. 4.8.2, 412, 413
Polyaen. 4.8.3, 400, 429
Polyaen. 4.8.4, 441
Polyaen. 5.44.4, 277
Polyaen. 7.9.1, 150
Polyaen. 7.14.1, 240
Polyaen. 7.21.7, 252
Polyaen. 7.29.1, 253
Polyaen. 7.33.2, 257
Polyaen. 7.42, 376

Polyclitus of Larisa (*FGrH/BNJ* 128)
Polyclit. F 3a, 325

Pompeius Trogus, Cn.
History of Philip (II) of Macedon
Pomp.Trog. *Proleg.* 10, 246, 255
Pomp.Trog. *Proleg.* 24, 63

Porphyry of Tyre (*FGrH/BNJ* 260)
Porph. F 48, 500

Posidonius of Apamea (sometimes called of Rhodes) (*FGrH/BNJ* 87)
Posid. F 12, 521
Posid. F 29, 517

Ptolemaeus *Geographia*
Geog. 6.2.7, 110
Geog. 6.2.13, 432
Geog. 6.4.3, 106
Geog. 6.21.4, 365

Ptolemy (*FGrH/BNJ* 138)
Ptol. F 7, 302
Ptol. F 8, 299
Ptol. F 14, 344
Ptol. F 23, 356
Ptol. F 26, 361

Scholia in Demosthenis Orationes
Schol.D. .19, 256

Seneca, L. Annaeus *Naturales Quaestiones*
Nat. 2.32.7, 133
Nat. 3.20.5, 112

Sophaenetus of Stymphalus (*FGrH/BNJ* 109)
Sophaen. F 1, 48, 223

Sophocles *Oedipus Tyrannus*
OT 465, 67
TGF [vol. 4, Radt] FF. 542-4, 153

Sosylus (of Lacedaemon?) (*FGrH/BNJ* 176)
Sosyl. F 1, 65

Stephan of Byzantium *Ethnica*
St.Byz. s.v. 'Προσοπίς', 198
St.Byz. s.v. 'Σαλώνεια', 490

Index of Classical Sources 593

St.Byz. s.v. 'Ὑδράκαι', 359
St.Byz. in Ctesias (FGrH/
  BNJ 688 F 42), 110

Strabo of Amasea
  Geography
Str. 1.2.10/21, 342
Str. 1.3.19/60, 446
Str. 1.4.7/65, 388
Str. 1.4.7./65–6, 388
Str. 2.1.14/73, 336
Str. 2.1.17/74, 387
Str. 2.5.18/121, 387
Str. 2.5.31/129, 387
Str. 2.5.31–2/129–30, 386
Str. 2.5.32/130, 113
Str. 2.5.33/130, 388
Str. 9.2.31/412, 180
Str. 10.3.19/472, 142
Str. 10.3.7/466, 142
Str. 11.5.5/505–6, 344
Str. 11.7.1/508, 240
Str. 11.9.1/514, 446
Str. 11.11.3/516, 95
Str. 11.12.2/521 sq, 107
Str. 11.12.3/521, 107
Str. 11.13.1/522, 384
Str. 11.13.1–3/523, 385
Str. 11.13.6/524, 324
Str. 11.13.8/525, 110
Str. 11.13.9–10/525–6, 96
Str. 11.13.10/526, 155
Str. 11.14.5/528, 509
Str. 11.14.12/530, 380
Str. 11.14.14/531, 155
Str. 12.2.6/537, 400
Str. 12.3.9/544, 37
Str. 12.4.7/565, 490
Str. 12.8.5/573, 404
Str. 13.3.6/622, 11, 42, 167
Str. 13.4.13/629, 283
Str. 13.4.16/630, 404
Str. 14.1.3/633, 455
Str. 14.1.25/642, 78
Str. 14.1.42/648–9, 225
Str. 14.2.7/654, 142
Str. 14.2.20/653, 36
Str. 14.5.4/670, 475
Str. 14.5.10/672, 415
Str 14.5.16/675, 452
Str. 15.1.5/686, 119
Str. 15.1.6/686, 119
Str. 15.1.6/687, 345, 359
Str. 15.1.8/687, 359
Str. 15.1.27/697, 356
Str. 15.1.34/701–2, 362
Str. 15.1.35/702, 387
Str. 15.1.56/710–11, 116
Str. 15.2.1/720, 366
Str. 15.2.7/723, 364
Str. 15.2.10/724, 440

Str. 15.2.10/725, 342
Str. 15.3.2/728, 123
Str. 15.3.4/728, 326
Str. 15.3.4/728–9, 426
Str. 15.3.4–5/729, 326
Str. 15.3.12/732, 432
Str. 15.3.21/735, 325
Str. 15.3.22/735, 426
Str. 15.3.24/736, 276
Str. 16.1.1/736, 426
Str. 16.1.2/737, 111, 526
Str. 16.1.5/738, 104
Str. 16.1.5/739, 100
Str. 16.1.6/739, 103
Str. 16.1.17–18/744, 106
Str. 16.1.18/744–5, 432
Str. 16.2.8/751, 522
Str. 16.2.10/752, 496, 515
Str. 16.2.19/756, 398
Str. 16.2.23/757, 311
Str. 16.2.26/758, 517
Str. 16.2.10/759, 462
Str. 16.2.32–3/760, 265
Str. 16.2.33/760, 244
Str. 16.3.5–7/766–7, 283
Str. 16.3.6/766–7, 368
Str. 17.1.22/803, 244
Str. 17.1.43/814, 468

Suda Lexicon
Suda (alpha,1571), 178
Suda (alpha,1763), 501
Suda (alphaiota,357), 178
Suda (beta,147 [2]), 469
Suda (delta, 1151), 5
Suda (eta,462), 72
Suda (mu,227), 54, 59, 227, 481
Suda (sigma,220), 114–16

Syncellus, G. Chronologia
Chron. p. 119, 11, 111

Theocritus Hymn to
  Ptolemy Philadelphus
Theoc. Hymn, 56

Theophrastus of Eresus
  Characteres
Char. 6.2, 228
Theophrastus of Eresus
  Historia Plantarum
HP 9.6.1–4, 57

Theopompus (of Chios?)
  (FGrH/BNJ 115)
Theopomp.Hist. F 40, 376
Theopomp.Hist. F 103(9), 239
Theopomp.Hist. F 103(4), 234

Theopomp.Hist. F 103(10), 239
Theopomp.Hist. F 103(12), 238
Theopomp.Hist. F 111, 260
Theopomp.Hist. F 219, 271
Theopomp.Hist. F 253, 370

Thucydides History of the
  Peloponnesian War
Th. 1.22, 543
Th. 1.28.6, 188
Th. 1.89.2, 187
Th. 1.94.1–2, 187
Th. 1.109, 198
Th. 1.109.1–3, 197
Th. 1.110.1, 199
Th. 1.110.2, 196, 224
Th. 1.128.5–6, 187
Th. 1.131.1, 191
Th. 1.137, 176
Th. 1.137.4–138.3, 190
Th. 4.53.1–56.2, 232
Th. 8.74.1–3, 207
Th. 8.86.3, 207
Th. 8.108, 204

Timaeus of Tauromenium
  (FGrH/BNJ 566)
Timae. F 28b.4–5, 58
Timae. F 94, 158, 178

Timagenes of Alexandria
  (FGrH/BNJ 88)
Timag. F 3, 361

Trogus see under Pompeius

Tzetzes, I. Historiae
H. 2.34 sqq., 5
H. 3.453–7, 125

Velleius Paterculus, C.
Vell. 2.16.3, 78

Vitruvius Libri decem de
  architectura
Vitr. 10.13.3, 286, 308
Vitr. 10.13.4, 309
Vitr. 10.13.4–5, 308
Vitr. 10.13.6, 309
Vitr. 10.13.8, 308

Xenophon Agesilaus
Ages. 1.8, 538
Ages. 2.27, 251
Ages. 2.28–30, 253
Ages. 2.28–31, 254, 255
Ages. 26, 49
Xenophon Anabasis
An. 1.1.1–4, 212

An. 1.1.2, 209
An. 1.2.1, 213
An. 1.2.3, 213
An. 1.2.12-27, 214
An. 1.2.21-2, 214
An. 1.3.1, 215
An. 1.3.2-21, 215
An. 1.4.2, 213
An. 1.4.3-6.11, 216
An. 1.4.9, 92
An. 1.4.10, 125
An. 1.4.16, 237
An. 1.5.1, 254
An. 1.5.5-6, 221
An. 1.5.8, 96
An. 1.5.9, 539
An. 1.6.10, 294
An. 1.7.11, 216
An. 1.7.12, 314
An. 1.8.5, 217
An. 1.8.6, 217, 344
An. 1.8.10, 314
An. 1.8.20, 318
An. 1.8.22, 218
An. 1.8.25, 217
An. 1.8.26-7, 218
An. 1.9.31, 219
An. 1.10.5-19, 217, 219
An. 2.1.3, 219, 237
An. 2.1.7, 219
An. 2.1.12, 220
An. 2.1.19, 214
An. 2.2.1, 221
An. 2.3.1-16, 221
An. 2.3.17-19, 221
An. 2.3.17-29, 221
An. 2.4.1-5.25, 222
An. 2.4.8, 236

An. 2.5.28, 222
An. 2.5.31, 222
An. 2.5.32, 222
An. 2.5.33, 222
An. 2.6.29, 222
An. 2.6.35-40, 221
An. 3.1.5, 213
An. 3.1.15-25, 222
An. 3.1.32-47, 222
An. 3.5.16, 223
An. 4.3.4, 137
An. 4.4.4, 233
An. 4.4.17 sqq., 223
An. 6.4.8, 10
An. 6.4.9, 230
An. 6.4.13-16, 230
An. 6.4.19-20, 230
An. 7.2.3, 226
An. 7.8.8, 188
An. 7.8.25, 125
Xenophon *Cyropaedia*
Cyr. 1.2.1, 144
Cyr. 1.3.2, 96
Cyr. 5.3.38, 137
Cyr. 6.1.27, 94
Cyr. 8.1.40, 96
Cyr. 8.6, 149
Cyr. 8.8, 253
Cyr. 8.8.1-27, 121
Cyr. 8.8.4, 253
Xenophon *De equitandi ratio*
Eq. 12.11, 217
Xenophon *Historia Graeca*
HG 1.1.23, 208
HG 1.2.6 sqq., 208
HG 1.2.15 sqq, 208
HG 2.1.13, 138

HG 2.1.29, 227
HG 2.2.15, 227
HG 3.1.1, 213
HG 3.1.4, 225, 228
HG 3.1.5, 225
HG 3.1.6, 188
HG 3.1.8, 226
HG 3.1.17-19, 230
HG 3.2.19, 225
HG 3.4.3, 228
HG 3.4.21-4, 230
HG 3.4.27, 228
HG 3.4.29, 232
HG 3.5.1, 538
HG 3.5.5, 228
HG 4.1.30, 537
HG 4.3.11 sqq., 227
HG 4.3.11-12, 232
HG 4.8.6-8, 233
HG 4.8.7, 232
HG 4.8.8, 231
HG 4.8.16, 249
HG 4.8.17, 234
HG 4.8.17-19, 235
HG 4.8.21-2, 235
HG 5.1.25, 235, 241
HG 5.1.30, 241
HG 5.1.31, 235
HG 5.4.14, 244
HG 6.3.1-19, 249
HG 6.3.12, 249
HG 6.4.35-7, 51
HG 6.5.1, 249
HG 7.1.27, 250
HG 7.1.33-40, 251
HG 7.4.6-11, 250
HG 7.5.26, 438
Xenophon *Oeconomicus*
Oec. 4.13, 428

Index of Modern Authors

An index of all post-medieval authors referred to and/or discussed in text and/or notes.

Abe, T., 191
Adler, A., 27
Akurgal, E., 408
Alram, A., 331
Alram, M., 325
Ambaglio, D., 3, 6, 14, 18, 19, 22
Ambler, W., 149
Amiet, P., 102
Anderson, A. R., 337, 402
Andrewes, A., 201, 202
Anson, E. M., 390
Archer, G. L., 500
Asheri, D., 143, 149, 152, 153
Aymard, A., 69

Backer, F. De, 97, 129
Badian, E., 276, 312, 341, 367, 370, 384
Balcer, J. M., 109, 153, 182
Banchich, T. M., 38
Barber, G. L., 8, 9
Barkworth, P. R., 95
Barnett, R. D., 88, 119
Baron, C. A., 15, 35, 158, 177
Baynham, E., 351
Bazin-Foucher, E., 333
Bean, G. E., 278, 475
Bekker, I., 30, 99
Bellinger, A. R., 331
Beloch, K. J., 54
Bengtson, H., 174
Bennett, E. R., 48, 211, 212, 217, 218, 224, 227, 228, 230, 233, 235
Benveniste, E., 276, 334
Benzinger, 478
Berg, P.-L. van, 92
Bergamini, G., 102
Bergmann, W. R., 18, 20, 30
Bertrac, P., 3, 5-7, 10-12,
17-22, 26-8, 33-5, 42, 43, 46, 48, 49, 52, 54, 56, 59, 62, 75, 142
Bessarion, B., 20
Best, J. G. P., 166
Bichler, R., 119
Bigwood, J. M., 10, 36, 83, 89, 94, 98, 102, 121
Bikerman, E., 435
Billows, R. A., 384
Bing, J. D., 415
Birley, A. R., 524
Bizière, F., 57, 58, 419, 421-4, 426, 429, 430, 434-6, 443, 445, 452, 453, 455, 456, 461, 462, 466, 469, 471
Blackman, D., 457
Blok, J. H., 338
Blyth, P. H., 308
Boissevain, U. P., 22, 23, 25, 26
Boiy, T., 374, 383, 521
Boliaki, E., 338
Bommelaer, B., 38, 39
Boncquet, J., 90, 92, 93, 95–104, 106, 108–14, 117, 120–5, 128, 129, 131–5, 138, 139
Bonnet, M., 48, 211, 212, 217, 218, 224, 227, 228, 230, 233, 235
Bosworth, A. B., 36, 312, 323, 351, 381, 388, 390, 397
Botteri, P., 5, 73, 77, 80
Bottin, C., 57
Boucharlat, R., 329
Boyce, M., 143
Breisach, E., 63
Briant, P., 94, 111, 143, 147, 149, 151, 153, 154, 156, 157, 177, 179, 195, 203, 210, 254, 275, 291,
384, 403, 405, 462, 537
Bridges, E., 156
Briscoe, J., 511
Brosius, M., 109
Broughton, T. R. S., 15, 79, 158, 178, 191, 194–9, 212, 224, 226, 233–6, 239, 245, 246, 250, 257, 264, 271–3, 280, 292, 304, 313, 323, 334, 342, 349, 371, 375, 383, 403, 411, 424, 450, 473, 476, 484, 511
Brown, S. E., 110
Brunt, P. A., 365, 381
Burn, A. R., 312, 315, 317, 320
Burstein, S. M., 38
Burton, A., 6, 8, 10, 34, 132
Busolt, G., 73
Büttner-Wobst, T., 22–4, 26

Calmeyer, P., 110, 326
Cameron, A., 544
Campbell, D. B., 290
Camusat, D. F., 21
Capomacchia, A. M. G., 527
Carney, E. D., 295
Cartledge, P., 180
Cary, E., 26
Casabonne, O., 214
Casaubon, I., 11
Casevitz, M., 17, 40, 41, 46, 47, 200, 201, 541
Casson, L., 114, 457
Cavallaro, M. A., 61
Cawkwell, G. L., 154, 245, 250
Ceccarelli, P., 168
Chamoux, F., 3–6, 10–12, 18–22, 27, 28, 42, 43, 46, 48, 49, 52, 54, 56, 59, 62, 75

595

Champion, C. B., 59
Chantraine, P., 112
Charles, M. B., 114, 166, 320
Charpentier, J., 346
Christesen, P., 34
Clarke, K., 73
Cohen-Skalli, A., 41–3, 131, 140, 143–50, 152–5, 157
Cole, J. W., 179
Collins, A. W., 276
Collon, D., 115
Cook, J. M., 87
Cozzoli, U., 372

Dailey, T. A., 486
Dalley, S., 104
Daman Singh, S., 114
Dandama(y)ev, M. A., 166, 506
Darmarios, A., 23
Daryaee, T., 538
Davidson, J., 340
De Boor, C. G., 22–5, 515
Depuydt, L., 2, 31, 194, 202, 203, 210, 254, 275
Deshayes, J., 430
Dessel, P. van, 401
Diels, H. A., 7, 408
Dillery, J. D., 35, 36
Dindorf, L. A., 20, 21, 27, 30, 64, 71, 76, 79, 114, 122, 133, 159, 180, 334, 448, 479, 495–506, 508–23
Dodson, A., 89, 112
Dossin, G., 123
Dowden, K., 73
Downey, G., 514, 524
Dressel, H., 507
Drews, R., 36, 50, 124
Dreyer, B., 55, 200, 279
Ducrey, P., 278
Dumortier, J., 177

Ebert, J., 172
Eck, B., 20, 35–7, 86–90, 92, 93, 95–116, 118–25, 128–30, 132–5, 137–40
Eckstein, A. M., 497
Edelstein, L., 73
Eggermont, P. H. L., 355
Ehrenberg, V., 364
Eilers, W., 90, 93, 98, 110, 111, 526
Ellis, J. R., 295, 312
Engel, R., 54, 399, 403
Engels, D. W., 76, 216, 271, 365
Erskine, A., 383

Estienne, H., 29
Evers. E., 7

Fabri de Peiresc, N.-C., 24
Fakour, M., 428
Farkas, A., 339
Farrell, W. J., 216
Feder, C. A. L., 25, 515
Fischer, C., 18, 21, 30, 76, 79, 276, 325, 359, 365, 366, 385, 388, 389, 402, 429, 436, 445, 448, 452, 453, 456, 460, 461, 466, 471, 478, 488, 490, 491, 495–506, 508–23
Fischer-Bovet, C., 266
Fleckeisen, A., 18
Forbes, R. J., 108, 111
Forman, W., 88, 119
Fornara, C., 137
Forshaw, L. H. S., 123
Foucher, A., 333
Fowler, R. L., 40, 41
Franck, L., 291
Frisk, H., 338
Frye, R. N., 90, 302
Fuhrmann, H., 338
Furia, F. Del, 21

Garafolo, B., 20
Gardiner, A., 37, 123
Gardiner-Garden, J., 37, 527, 530
Geer, R. M., 54–8, 385, 399, 402, 419, 424, 429, 430, 431, 434–6, 445, 448, 450, 453, 456, 461, 466, 467, 471, 478, 480, 491
Gera, D., 139
Giovannelli-Jouanna, P., 32
Glare, P. G. W., 32
Glassner, J. J., 263
Goossens, G., 39, 111, 118, 121
Gorman, R. J., 14, 46, 537
Gorman, V. B., 14, 46, 537
Goukowsky, P., 5, 7, 26, 30, 52–4, 56, 58, 60–81, 117, 147, 276–8, 281, 284, 285, 287–9, 291–6, 298, 299, 300, 302–4, 306, 307, 315–19, 322, 324, 326, 328, 330, 331, 333, 335–9, 341–9, 351–60, 362–81, 383–92, 394, 396, 399, 400, 402, 404, 406, 409–12, 414, 417, 440, 495–523
Gowers, W., 114

Grainger, J. D., 280, 385, 417, 479, 496, 513, 515
Granier, F., 369
Graux, C., 23
Grayson, A. K., 89, 121, 124
Green, P., 7, 10
Grenfell, B. P., 83, 191
Grotius, H., 24
Gruen, E. S., 537
Gullini, G., 102

Haase, W., 524
Habicht, C., 201, 511
Hadley, R. A., 467
Haerinck, E., 101
Haillet, J., 31, 32, 44, 45, 159–62, 170–2, 175–7, 179–82, 184, 185, 188–97
Hammond, N. G. L., 8, 48, 50, 51, 187, 199–201, 296, 468, 470, 495
Harrison, T., 1
Hauben, H., 401
Heckel, W., 60, 278, 283, 317, 325, 334, 339, 340, 385, 388, 390, 395, 397, 398, 401, 404, 409, 412, 413, 416, 420, 421, 423, 425, 430, 443, 447, 449, 450, 451, 453, 477, 490, 496
Heller, A., 6
Henry, R., 29, 38
Hereward, D., 187
Herrmann, A., 106, 510
Herwerden, H. van, 26, 502, 503, 515
Herzfeld, E. E., 90, 323, 337, 343
Heyse, Th. F., 26
Hignett, C., 94, 169, 172, 174, 181, 182, 184–7
Hinz, W., 88, 137, 139
Hirsch, S. W., 261
Hoeschel, D., 26, 27, 65
Hofstetter, J., 165, 188, 206
Holleaux, M., 429
Holt, F. L., 89, 95, 333, 351
Hornblower, J., 401
Hornblower, S., 7, 34, 207, 245, 249, 250, 260, 317
How, W. W., 164
Hunger, H., 134
Hunt, A. S., 83, 191

Ikram, S., 112
Imhof, A., 18
Irigoin, J., 24

Jacobs, B., 98
Jacoby, F., 7, 9, 36, 44, 52, 54, 56, 94, 120, 168, 339, 402, 462, 467, 475, 484, 530, 535
Jacquemin, A., 17, 40, 41, 541

Kaper, O., 150
Kärst, J., 295
Keaveney, A., 95, 276
Kent, R. G., 109, 110, 139, 151, 166, 428, 443, 533
Kidd, I., 73
Kirchner, J., 199, 212, 231
Klinkott, H., 89
Kneppe, A., 510
Kock, T., 47
Koldewey, R. J., 99–101, 106
König, F. W., 111
Kosmin, P. J., 385, 495, 534
Kresten, O., 23
Kromayer, J., 464
Krumbholz, P., 36, 88, 89, 120, 140
Kuhrt, A., 136, 374
Kulke, H., 349
Kuyper, J. de, 87, 90

Labarbe, J., 170, 171, 173, 184
Lambrick, H. T., 365
Lane Fox, R. J., 351, 525, 529, 534
Lanfranchi, G. B., 136
Laqueur, R., 6, 44
Lascaris, C., 7, 17, 21
Lascaris, J., 21
Lauffer, S., 245
Laumonier, A., 281
Law, C. B., 353
Lazenby, J. F., 176, 188
Leake, W. M., 175
Leick, G., 91, 98
Lendering, J., 335
Lenfant, D., 1, 32, 52, 112, 113, 115, 116, 120, 326, 339
Leone, P. A. M., 28
Lewis, D. M., 92, 230
Ley, A., 338
Lincoln, B., 537, 538
Liverani, M., 93, 98, 136, 530
Llewellyn-Jones, L., 276, 326
Lloyd, A. B., 125, 266
Lloyd-Jones, H., 125
Lobel, E., 61
Lukonin, V. G., 166

Luschey, H., 109
Lutz, H. F., 8

Maas, P., 7
Macdonald, M. C. A., 86
MacGinnis, J. D. A., 129
Mai, A., 26, 27, 503
Maier, F. G., 260, 264
Maisonneuve, C., 32
Malbran-Labat, F., 121
Malitz, J., 74
Mango, M. M., 515
Manni, E., 44, 61
Markoe, G. E., 259
Marsden, E. W., 294, 304, 313, 314–17
Martini, E., 29
Marzahn, J., 525
Masius, H., 18
Masqueray, P., 214
Maul, S., 103
Mayor, A., 135, 309, 338
Mayrhofer, M., 86
McClure, L. K., 370
McGushin, P., 79
Meijering, R., 468
Meister, K., 32, 33, 35, 43, 44, 48
Meritt, B. D., 234
Mesnil du Buisson, R. M. E. L. du, 92, 527
Meulenaere, H. De, 254
Meyer, E., 138, 355
Miller, E., 25
Miller, M. C. J., 9
Miltner, F., 352
Mitchel, F. W., 372
Mitchell, S., 400, 403
Mitchell, T. C., 115
Mitford, T. B., 475
Momigliano, A., 281, 419, 471
Mommsen, Th., 6
Morgan, J., 1, 14, 46, 121, 124, 158, 537
Mørkholm, O., 501, 506, 510
Morrison, J. S., 95, 155, 262
Mousavi, A., 331
Müller, C., 25, 112, 234, 495, 515
Muntz, C. E., 36, 37
Murray, W., 457

Naas, V., 61
Nefiodkin, A. K., 94
Németh, A., 26
Newell, E. T., 298, 515
Nichols, A., 116
Nicholson, P., 244, 268

Niebuhr, B.G., 7
Niehr, H., 485
Nilakanta Sastri, K. A., 349
Nöldeke, T., 90

Oates, J., 124
Oelsner, J., 103
Oldfather, C. H., 5, 8, 10, 11, 14, 33, 34, 39, 40, 42, 43, 47, 92, 98, 99, 107, 109, 115, 122, 125, 128, 130, 132, 133, 135, 140, 143–7, 149, 150, 152, 154, 155, 157, 212
Olshausen, E., 510
Orsini, F., 27, 92

Páez de Castro, J., 23, 24
Palm, J., 82, 83, 84, 85
Parke, H. W., 244
Parsons, P., 125
Pasek, S., 224
Pédech, P., 68, 336
Pedersén, O., 103
Perdu, O., 224
Peremans, W., 39
Perl, G., 45, 57, 199, 374
Perlman, P., 67
Perrin, B., 399
Pettinato, G., 96, 526
Pfister, F., 355
Phillips, E. D., 109, 527
Piccirillo, P. M., 486
Pingree, D., 134
Pitra, G., 19
Plüer, C. C., 25
Poggio Bracciolini, G. F., 20
Potts, D. L., 94
Pownall, F., 47
Prandi, L., 275, 305, 336, 364
Pritchett, W. K., 169, 181

Radet, G., 291
Ramsey, W. M., 390
Ranke, F. L. (von), 7, 9
Rankov, B., 457
Rapin, C., 344
Raubitschek, A. E., 201
Raun, C., 52
Reiner, E., 134
Reinhardt, K., 73
Revilla, A., 23
Rey-Coquais, J. P., 259
Reynolds, L. D., 7, 81
Rhodoman, L., 19, 29, 65, 334
Ritner, R. K., 270
Robert, L., 50, 232, 405, 429

Roisman, J., 317, 384, 385, 401
Roller, D., 59
Rollinger, R., 90, 100, 349
Roos, A. G., 22
Rosen, K., 56
Rothermund, D., 349
Rothfield, L., 98
Roux, G., 89, 173–5, 528, 529
Rubincam, C., 5, 7
Russell, D. A., 81, 545
Ruzicka, S., 151, 152, 196, 205, 214, 224, 228, 229, 231, 232, 234, 236–8, 242, 244, 249, 252–5, 259, 260, 263–8, 270, 282, 287
Ryder, T. T. B., 250

Sachs, A. J., 134, 381
Sacks, K. S., 3–6, 8, 10, 11, 12–14, 16, 66, 73
Salonen, A., 115
Samiei, S., 46, 541
Samuel, A. E., 381
Sancisi-Weerdenburg, H., 13, 109, 136, 299, 332, 333, 335
Saumoise, C., 24
Scaliger, J. J., 24
Schachermeyr, F., 315
Schamp, J., 29
Schmidt, E. F., 331–3
Schmitt, O., 392
Schmitt, R., 137, 140, 206, 230, 340
Schmitthenner, W., 280
Schottky, M., 505
Schramm, E., 408
Schubert, R., 57
Schwartz, E., 6, 7, 16, 17, 36, 52, 54, 56, 64, 67–70, 73, 79, 82, 83, 85, 530, 540, 543–5
Schwartz, J., 150, 270, 313
Schwenk, C. J., 303
Scullard, H. H., 115
Seel, O., 53, 55, 386
Sekunda, V., 403
Shaw, I., 244, 268
Shayegan, R. M., 521, 534, 535
Sherman, C. L., 50, 251, 260

Sherwin-White, S., 374
Shipley, G., 383, 495
Simon, M., 61
Simpson, R. H., 57, 415
Sinclair, R. K., 10, 52, 286
Smith, E., 526
Smith, W., 460
Spek, R. J. van der, 315, 321, 335, 374
Stein, M. A., 315, 316, 322, 327, 328, 346, 347, 349, 365, 366
Stevenson, H., 19
Stevenson, R. B., 1, 49, 263
Stijnen, A., 8
Stillwell, R., 423
Stoneman, R., 156
Strasburger, H., 73, 365
Streck, 315
Strommenberger, E., 96
Stronk, J. P., 2–4, 8–10, 12, 28, 31, 32, 36, 39, 44, 46, 48, 66, 75, 81, 90, 93, 95, 110–12, 120, 121, 123, 125, 129, 137–9, 143, 144, 149, 156, 161–4, 167, 168, 188, 190, 209, 211, 212, 214, 218, 221, 223, 226, 234, 250, 271, 321, 325, 332, 333, 338, 339, 367, 370, 394, 414, 455, 488, 491, 526, 529, 530, 531, 533, 534, 538
Stylianou, P. J., 7, 9–12, 34, 45, 46, 49, 245, 253, 254
Sulimani, I., 540, 542
Syme, R., 138
Szemerényi, O., 139

Talon, P., 133
Tarn, W. W., 52, 287, 317, 336, 351, 354
Temporini, H., 524
Thomas, P. H., 348
Toepffer, J., 338
Tomaschek, 479
Tomlinson, R. A., 279
Treidler, H., 110, 326
Tucci, G., 345, 346
Tuplin, C. J., 136, 209, 293, 537
Turner, E. G., 61

Unger, E., 98
Unger, G. F., 8, 82, 545

Valois, H., 24
Veith, G., 464
Vernière, Y., 33–5, 142
Vial, C., 48, 236–8, 249, 251, 254, 255
Vigneron, P., 435
Vimercati, E., 74
Vogel, F., 18, 21, 30, 92, 98, 99, 107, 109, 115, 122, 125, 128, 130, 132, 133, 140, 143–7, 149, 150, 152, 154, 155, 157, 222, 228
Vogelsang, W. J., 342
Volquardsen, C. A., 44
Vycichl, W., 8

Wacholder, B. Z., 22
Wachsmuth, C., 84
Walbank, F. W., 44, 78
Walker, C., 276, 527
Wallinga, H. T., 173
Walton, F. R., 27, 64, 76, 79, 495–523
Wehrli, F., 43, 454
Weidner, E. F., 98
Weiskopf, M., 250
Weissbach, F. H., 103, 109
Welles, C. B., 51–3, 284, 289, 303, 307, 316–18, 333, 336, 339, 353, 359, 367, 380, 381
Wells, J., 164
Wesseling, P., 5, 19–21, 24, 29, 30, 215, 224, 261, 298, 311, 371, 384, 385, 387, 421, 436, 456, 466, 490, 495
Westlake, H. D., 413
Wetzel, F., 100, 101, 103
Wheeldon, M. J., 544
Whitehead, D., 308
Wiesehöfer, J., 109, 301
Wilamowitz, U. von, 6
Will, É., 165, 187, 191, 516, 520, 521
Williams, R. T., 95, 155, 262
Wilson, N. G., 7, 81, 338
Wirth, G., 74

Yardley, J. C., 55, 56, 60

Ziegler, K., 28, 81, 370, 545

General Index

Achaemenes, 169, 196, 197
Achaemenid, Achaemenids, 2, 6, 12, 31, 48, 86, 89, 92, 109, 110, 113, 114, 121, 123, 156, 166, 188, 209, 270, 276, 313, 326, 329, 335, 345, 353, 359, 389, 453, 494, 530–5, 540, 544
Acoris, 236–40, 243
Adad-nirari II, 89, 528, 531
Adad-nirari III, 527, 528, 533
Aegean, 40, 156, 162, 187, 201, 209, 228, 236, 460, 476
Aelian, 388, 537
Aeschines, 47, 51, 277
Aeschylus, 46, 178, 414, 537
Afghanistan, 95, 215, 333, 334
Africa, 38, 39, 59, 65, 88, 150, 388, 536
Agatharchides (of Cnidus), 35, 37, 38, 54, 57, 75, 83, 113, 168
Agathocles, 15, 55, 56, 58–63
Agesilaus, 228–32, 244, 250, 253–6, 537, 538
Akkadian, 86, 90, 93, 98, 102, 109
Akko, 246, 252, 254, 517
Albinus, A. Postumius, 45, 67, 233
Alcibiades, 203, 204, 206–9, 211, 212
Alexander I *Balas*, 71, 512, 513, 515–17
Alexander II *Zabinas*, 521–3
Alexander III the Great, 1, 2, 6, 13, 16, 31, 36, 52–4, 56, 58, 68, 95, 97, 99, 111, 113, 114, 118, 119, 134, 135, 154, 259, 264,
272, 275–382, 384–6, 388, 389, 391, 397, 406, 407, 413–15, 418–23, 429, 430, 443, 446, 447, 450, 451, 456, 459, 462, 463, 467, 468, 469, 473, 476, 477, 481, 490, 507, 512, 525, 530, 533, 534, 539, 541, 544
Alexander IV, 455, 473, 474
Alexander Polyhistor, 12, 35
Alexander, son of Polyperchon, 453, 455–7
Alexandria, 12, 32, 38, 52, 60, 74, 75, 244, 248, 313, 394, 461, 481, 487, 497, 504
Alimentus, L. Cincius, 45, 63, 65
Amazons, 37, 139, 338
Ammon, 111, 120, 150, 313, 356, 369, 378, 385, 533
Amyntas, 57, 289, 310, 312, 313, 391, 398, 476, 507
Amyrtaeus, 196, 224
Anaxagoras (of Clazomenae), 34, 234
Anaximenes (of Miletus), 33, 49, 51, 281, 312
Antalcidas, 235, 236, 241, 243, 249
Antandrus, 61, 205
Antigonia, 478, 479, 484, 488
Antigonid, 32, 492, 501, 505
Antigonus I (*Monophtalmus*), 54, 60, 134, 248, 341, 373, 380, 384, 392, 393, 399–413, 415–19, 422–8, 430–3, 435–61, 463, 465–71, 473, 474–8, 481, 483–92, 495, 496, 507

Antioch, 4, 513–16, 519, 521–4
Antiochia, 460, 479, 516
Antiochus II, 507, 508
Antiochus III, 67, 68, 279, 485, 497–500, 508, 509, 513
Antiochus IV, 72, 501–6, 509, 510, 512, 518
Antiochus VI, 515–17
Antiochus VII, 76, 77, 517–21
Antiochus VIII, 77, 521, 522, 524
Antiochus of Syracuse, 40, 45, 46
Antipater, 279, 281, 298, 324, 341, 370, 381, 385, 391–9, 401, 402, 406, 407, 409, 422, 435, 449, 450, 452, 454, 495
Aphrodite, 92, 133, 502, 506, 527
Apollodorus (of Athens), 34–6, 42, 44, 47, 71, 120
Appian, 67–70, 72, 79
Apple-bearers, 319, 323, 338
Arabia, Arab, Arabs, 37, 40, 86, 87, 90, 126, 205, 237, 254, 266, 470, 473, 484, 513, 515, 524, 526
Arachosia, 106, 334, 342, 366, 385, 387, 399, 421, 430, 434, 449
Aramaic, 109, 430
Arbaces, 125–8, 130, 131, 137, 533
Arbela, 314, 315, 322, 323
Aretē, 10, 34, 82, 86, 117, 138, 140, 144, 148, 151, 164–6, 168, 169, 183, 188, 190, 193, 197, 199, 220, 222, 244, 246, 248, 255, 265, 266, 277, 283, 284, 288, 289, 290, 293, 294, 297, 304, 309, 310,

599

Aretē (cont.)
318, 319, 337, 338, 346, 352, 354, 360, 364, 367, 373, 422, 434, 447, 451, 464, 467, 482, 498, 508, 533, 535, 536, 537, 538, 541, 544, 545
Aria, Arians, 142, 339, 342, 344, 367, 385, 387, 398, 421, 432, 449, 469
Ariarathes, 390, 507, 508
Ariarathes V, 508, 511, 512
Ariarathes VI, 509, 510
Aridaeus, 217–21
Ariobarzanes, 249–51, 253, 273, 281, 327, 328, 443, 491
Ariobarzanes II, 273, 491
Aristides, 26, 168, 180–3, 187
Aristobulus (of Cassandria), 37, 52, 53, 56, 279, 281, 291, 295, 302, 344, 351, 367, 369, 375, 380
Aristodemus, 47, 406, 453, 455, 457
Aristotle, 34, 48, 52, 56, 58, 107, 211, 271, 302
Armenia, Armenians, 87, 106, 107, 221, 223, 230, 233, 324, 387, 400, 430, 440, 505, 507, 509, 511, 526
Arrhidaeus, 385, 397–9, 406–9
Arrian, 1, 19, 94, 97, 119, 263, 283–6, 288, 289, 296, 306, 318–21, 328, 329, 335, 341, 342, 344, 345, 350, 355, 356, 358, 362, 364–7, 369, 384, 394, 398–400, 533, 534
Arsaces V, 516, 517, 519
Arsaces VI, 519–21
Arsacid, 32, 335, 521, 535
Arses, 275, 276
Artabanus, 194, 195, 199
Artabazus, 182, 183, 188, 197, 199, 201, 252, 256, 257, 260, 271, 287, 337
Artaxerxes I, 137, 189, 194–7, 200, 202, 254
Artaxerxes II, 31, 86, 122, 125, 210–12, 214–22, 224, 228, 230, 231, 233–6, 239, 241, 242, 245, 249–51, 253–5, 258, 260, 273, 276, 332
Artaxerxes III, 49, 254, 255, 257–66, 268–72, 276, 277, 313, 332, 390, 507

Artemidorus, 35, 38, 78
Artemisia, 257, 260, 264, 287
Artemisium (Cape), 162, 169–71
Ascalon, 92, 93, 527
Asia, *passim*
Asia Minor 1, 9, 32, 47, 61, 147, 148, 154, 159, 176, 183, 184, 186–8, 190, 191, 199, 201, 202, 205, 206, 208, 209, 213, 218, 223, 225–8, 231, 235, 241–3, 250, 251, 253, 257, 262, 264, 271, 274, 278, 394, 455, 458, 459, 468, 487, 490, 491, 497, 499, 512, 523, 526, 528
Assyria, Assyrian, Assyrians, 1, 6, 31, 37, 86–90, 92–4, 96–8, 100, 102, 104, 111, 113, 115, 118–31, 135–7, 140, 215, 270, 295, 415, 525–9, 531, 534–6
Astarte, 92, 527
Astyages, 137, 140, 141, 144
Ašurbanipal, 119, 124
Athanis (of Syracuse), 49–51
Athenaeus (of Naucratis), 8, 16, 36, 73, 76, 83, 120, 125, 370
Athenian, Athenians, 8, 15, 66, 68, 44, 95, 120, 155, 156, 158–60, 170–2, 175, 176, 179–84, 186, 187, 191–3, 196–201, 204–9, 211, 213, 227, 231, 233–5, 244–6, 249, 253, 256, 257, 260, 262, 266, 286, 289, 293, 324, 333, 370, 457, 458, 481, 491
Athens, 32, 34, 36, 40, 42, 44, 50, 61, 68, 71, 120, 135, 154–6, 158, 171, 172, 175, 178–81, 187, 191, 194–201, 207–12, 223–6, 233, 234, 236, 239, 243–6, 249–51, 256, 257, 264, 271–3, 280, 292, 303, 313, 323, 331, 334, 342, 349, 370–5, 378, 383, 392, 394, 402, 411, 424, 425, 450, 458, 467, 473, 475, 476, 484, 544
Attalus II (King of Pergamum), 71, 75
Attica, 68, 162, 172, 173, 175, 176, 178, 179, 180, 232, 233, 370, 481

Babylon, 6, 87, 90, 97–9, 101–4, 107, 108, 129–31, 149, 152, 153, 159, 179, 202, 216, 221, 231, 259, 261, 263, 270, 294, 295, 303, 314, 323, 324, 331, 334, 369, 370, 372, 374–6, 379, 380, 384, 412, 419, 420, 450, 451, 459, 467, 468, 471, 478, 510, 521, 526, 528, 529, 530
Babylonia, Babylonian, Babylonians, 6, 37, 87, 89, 92, 98–100, 102–4, 107, 108, 125–7, 129–32, 149, 153, 202, 216, 271, 276, 315, 321, 324–6, 374, 379, 381, 385, 387, 398, 404, 417–19, 424, 450, 452, 466–8, 471, 492, 495, 521, 527, 535
Bactra, 36, 95–7, 113, 114, 119, 215, 333, 533
Bactria, Bactrian, Bactrians, 89, 91, 93–8, 106, 115, 116, 128, 139, 194, 283, 323, 325, 332–5, 340, 342–5, 361, 369, 385, 387, 398, 421, 448, 531
Bagoas, 266, 268–70, 276, 277
Balkh, 95, 215, 333
Barathra, 265, 485
Battle of Cunaxa, 94, 98, 217, 219, 233, 236
Battle of Ipsus, 451, 454, 492, 494, 495
Battle of Leuctra, 118, 250
Belesys, 125–7, 130, 132, 259
Belus, 91, 102, 103, 130, 374, 499, 500
Berossus, 36, 104, 129
Bessus, 323, 333–5, 339, 343–5
Bisitun, 109, 372, 443, 526, 527, 533
Bithynia, 75, 89, 159, 227, 455, 490, 491
Boeotia, Boeotians, 49, 161, 171, 172, 179, 180, 181, 213, 249, 250, 257, 265, 460
Bosporus, 183, 187
Brahmins, 362, 363
Bubastis, 151, 267, 268–70
Byzantium, 22, 110, 187, 191, 206, 209, 212, 256, 408, 497

General Index

Caesar, C. Iulius, 5, 14, 40, 80
Callas, 278, 281
Callias (of Syracuse), 59, 61, 200–2
Callisthenes, 39, 48, 51, 53, 271, 295, 299, 322, 345, 468
Cambyses I, 144, 506
Cambyses II, 149, 150, 152, 506
Camel(s), 115, 116, 331, 341, 367, 440, 450, 484
Cappadocia, 89, 145, 215, 252, 295, 384, 387, 390, 399, 400, 403, 406, 407, 410, 412, 430, 452, 453, 455, 489, 491, 492, 506–10, 512
Caria, Carian, Carians, 89, 154, 159, 162, 169, 191, 203, 225, 229, 231, 234, 237, 251, 257, 260, 264, 287, 291, 371, 384, 387, 399, 418, 452, 456–60, 477, 499
Carrhae, 418, 468
Carthage, Carthaginian, Carthaginians, 16, 48, 49, 58, 60, 62–5, 72, 159, 177, 262, 304, 305, 311, 376, 491, 498
Caspian Sea, 240, 277, 283, 336, 386, 387, 528
Cassander, 61, 281, 381, 382, 399, 406, 430, 451–3, 455, 456, 458–60, 473–5, 477, 484, 487, 490–2, 495, 496
Cassius Dio, 16, 26
Castor (of Rhodes), 34, 35, 39, 45, 80, 144
Caunus, 229, 401, 460, 476
Cephalion, 16, 120
Chabrias, 243, 244, 253
Chaldea, Chaldean, Chaldeans, 6, 86, 103, 125, 126, 131–5, 374, 375, 379, 451, 528, 544
Chares (of Mytilene), 54, 57, 256, 257, 298, 307, 337, 369
Chiliarch, 276, 334, 338, 377, 399, 406
Chirisophus, 213, 215, 222
Cilicia, Cilician, Cilicians, 89, 114, 155, 159, 162, 176, 192, 197–200, 213–15, 227, 229, 231, 236–8, 259, 251, 261, 283, 291, 294, 295, 301, 312, 314, 324, 384–6, 388, 390, 395, 397, 398, 407, 409, 411–17, 452, 453, 459, 461, 466, 469, 473–7, 489, 495, 524
Cilician Gates, 214, 215, 295
Cimon, 143, 158, 191–3, 199–201
Clearchus, 204, 206, 207, 209, 212–14, 217, 219–22
Cleopatra of Macedon, 391–3, 476, 477
Clitarchus (of Alexandria), 32, 36, 37, 52, 53, 98, 99, 104, 108, 129, 285, 300, 302, 317, 328, 330–2, 355, 356, 359, 361, 363, 364, 370, 376, 379, 529–31, 533, 534
Clitus, 284, 285, 317, 345, 399, 409, 417
Coele Syria, 89, 388, 402, 414, 417, 461, 462, 469, 484, 485, 492, 496, 500–2, 513, 517, 524
Colchis, 88, 136
Companion cavalry, 301, 383
Companions (also see s.v. ἑταῖροι), 23, 36, 53, 55, 58, 128, 195, 200, 214, 242, 271, 279, 294, 295, 299, 301–3, 310, 313, 315–17, 324, 332, 339–41, 344, 345, 348, 357–9, 361, 364, 365, 369, 372, 374–8, 380, 381, 383–5, 407, 412, 414, 416, 421, 429, 448, 466, 470, 475, 492, 500, 504, 515, 517, 518, 523
Conon, 196, 227, 229, 231–3, 249
Constantinople, 7, 18
Corinth, Corinthian, 4, 158, 161, 173, 178, 225, 232, 273, 275, 312, 337
Cossea, Cossaean, Cossaeans, 320, 373, 374, 427
Courtesan(s), 120, 124, 332, 333, 370
Craterus, 60, 318, 358, 376, 377, 385, 392–6, 410, 411, 413, 454, 490
Crete, 40, 41, 80, 312, 318, 370, 459
Croesus, 143–7, 203
Ctesias, 1, 6, 13, 31, 32, 35–7, 44, 48, 52, 53, 82, 86, 87, 89, 90, 93–5, 97–101, 104, 106–18, 120–5, 129, 137, 139, 140, 143, 149, 152, 179, 190, 194, 197, 210, 211, 216, 219, 221, 234, 325, 332, 339, 506, 525–37, 540
Cyaxares, 125, 137
Cyprus, Cypriot, Cypriots, 24, 34, 48, 49, 114, 155, 158, 159, 162, 176, 187, 192, 193, 197, 199–201, 227, 233, 234, 236–40, 242, 244, 258, 260, 261, 264, 271, 307, 312, 398, 414, 417, 452, 454, 457, 460, 461, 473, 475, 477–80, 483, 484, 495, 504
Cyrus II the Great, 94, 103, 113, 119, 137, 140, 143–9, 203, 331, 342, 506, 508, 530, 533, 534
Cyrus the Younger, 48, 86, 206, 209, 210–21, 224, 226, 230, 237, 241, 318
Cyzicus, 77, 204, 206, 207, 277, 278, 408, 409, 456

Darius I the Great, 2, 94, 109, 113, 150–3, 155, 156, 158, 159, 169, 188, 189, 265, 443, 530, 534
Darius II, 202, 203, 209–11, 230
Darius III, 134, 270, 275–335, 337, 339, 342, 344, 345, 374, 390, 443, 447, 490
Datames, 250, 252, 253, 507
Datis, 155, 156, 159
Delphi, 42, 63, 145, 146, 171, 172, 239, 250, 272
Demetrius (son of Antigonus I *Monophtalmus*), 54, 392, 417, 436, 442, 449, 452, 454, 458, 459, 461–7, 469–71, 475, 477, 478–86, 488, 490–2, 495–7
Demetrius I *Soter*, 510–12
Demetrius II *Nicator*, 512–17, 519, 521
Demetrius of Phalerum, 458, 476
Democritus, 33, 375
Demophilus, 50, 52
Demosthenes, 47, 49, 51, 256, 293, 370
Derceto, 92, 527
Dercylidas, 226–8, 230

Diadochs, 6, 54, 61, 118, 121, 279, 317, 383, 384, 418, 484, 544
Dicearchus (of Messana), 56, 386
Dinarchus, 49, 51
Dinon, 37, 49, 121, 216, 529-31, 533-5
Diodorus (of Sicily), *passim*
Diodotus *Tryphon*, 515-17
Dionysius, 38, 39, 376
Dionysius I, 48, 95, 152, 243, 262
Dionysus, 119, 333, 367, 523, 530, 534
Diyllus (of Athens), 50, 54, 57, 61, 544
Drangia, 106, 340, 342, 367, 385, 398, 421, 449
Duris (of Samos), 45, 49, 50, 54-7, 59-61, 446

Ecbatana, 106, 109, 110, 131, 140, 186, 216, 323, 341, 372, 407, 426, 446, 448, 519
Egypt, Egyptian, Egyptians, 3, 4, 12, 16, 35, 38, 39, 41, 49, 54, 56, 60, 66, 71, 86, 89, 94, 111, 113, 114, 119, 123, 132, 143, 149, 150-2, 155, 159, 162, 169, 174, 195-9, 205, 213, 224, 228, 229, 236, 237-40, 242-8, 250, 253-5, 257, 258-71, 282, 298, 304, 310, 312, 313, 364, 384, 385, 388, 389, 394, 397, 398, 402, 413, 417, 450, 451, 453, 459-62, 466, 468, 470, 473, 474, 476-80, 483-5, 487, 492, 495, 501, 504, 505, 507, 514, 517, 521, 531, 533, 536
Elephant(s), 113-18, 348-51, 355, 363, 387, 400, 403, 404, 407, 421, 422, 424, 427, 430, 433-7, 442-4, 446, 459, 461, 463-5, 470, 484, 492, 495, 498, 499, 531
Eleusis, 175, 370
Elymaïs, 106, 499, 500, 505, 506
Empedocles, 34, 47
Ephesus, 35, 38, 78, 146, 210, 213, 216, 225-8, 234, 235, 409, 488, 491, 494
Ephorus (of Cyme), 8, 9, 11, 12, 31-4, 39, 41, 42, 44-50, 52, 62, 81-4, 153, 167, 168, 178, 185, 186, 191, 192, 211, 216, 221, 228, 536, 540
Epimenides, 40, 41
Eratosthenes, 34, 35, 37, 56, 57, 386, 387
Eretrians, 155, 372
Esarhaddon, 89, 94, 124, 415, 529, 531
Ethiopia, Ethiopian, Ethiopians, 37, 38, 111-13, 115, 123, 124, 131, 149, 150, 270, 388, 531
Euboea, 162, 169, 170-2, 228, 292, 497
Euhemerus, 40-2
Eumenes, 54, 56-8, 384, 390, 394-7, 399, 400-3, 406, 407, 409-33, 435-46, 448, 449, 452, 454, 466, 507
Eumenes II (king of Pergamum), 69, 498, 499, 512
Eunuch(s), 93, 120, 121, 126, 129, 130, 194, 276, 326, 502, 503
Euripides, 34, 43, 46, 47, 59, 79
Eurydice, 13, 398
Eusebius, 96, 120, 122, 131, 144, 523, 525, 528
Euthytona, 290, 306, 307, 310, 408, 479, 480
Evagoras, 227, 233, 234, 236-41, 249
Evagoras II, 260, 261, 264, 469
Excerpta Constantiniana, 7, 17, 22-4, 26, 43, 60, 76, 77, 498, 510

Fabius Pictor, Q, 42, 45, 48, 57, 62-5
First Punic War, 5, 64
First Servile War, 73, 76, 77

Gabene, 432, 433, 439, 441, 442, 445
Gaugamela, 301, 314, 315, 317, 322, 323
Gaza, 92, 286, 313, 454, 462, 463, 465, 467, 469, 470, 484, 485, 501
Gedrosia, Gedrosians, 342, 365-7, 385, 387, 430, 525
Gelo, 157, 158, 177, 178

Glos, 224, 237, 238, 240-3
Gonatas, Antigonus II, 54, 496
Gracchi, 77, 80
Greece, Greek, Greeks, *passim*
Greek Wars, 142, 154, 178

Hannibal, 65, 95, 498
Harpagus, 140, 147, 148
Harpalus, 281, 369, 370
Hecataeus of Abdera, 33, 35, 37, 80, 81
Hecataeus of Miletus, 40, 43, 153, 155, 211
Hellanicus, 32, 40, 44, 125, 338
Hellenica Oxyrhynchia, 32, 48, 84
Hellenism, 46, 541
Hellenistic, 53, 55, 68, 73, 76, 83, 84, 86, 89, 93, 117, 131, 143, 175, 200, 317, 325, 340, 535, 540, 541
Hellenocentric, 46, 333, 541
Hellespont, 89, 159, 160, 161, 162, 183, 187, 204-6, 278, 280, 394, 417, 453, 457, 474, 475, 491, 538
Hephaestion, 58, 302, 316, 322, 338, 339, 353, 354, 358, 368, 372, 376-9, 385
Heracles, 39, 40, 119, 209, 262, 287, 304, 306, 311, 346, 358, 376, 380, 383, 525, 530, 534
Heraclides *Lembus* (of Oxyrhynchus), 72, 319, 497, 510
Hermias (of Methymna), 49, 271
Herodotus (of Halicarnassus), 1, 2, 6, 32, 35-7, 43-5, 57, 82, 84, 88-90, 93, 94, 99, 100, 103, 104, 106, 109, 110, 112, 116, 124, 136, 137-9, 141, 145, 146, 148-50, 152, 153, 158-60, 163, 164, 166-9, 173, 179, 181, 183, 185, 186, 194, 261, 374, 387, 506, 526, 534, 536-8, 540, 544
Hesiod, 39, 40-2, 123
Hieronymus (of Cardia), 32, 36, 37, 45, 54-9, 61, 62, 87, 401, 407, 446

Hindu Kush, 342, 343, 385, 386, 387
Homer, 34, 39–42, 51, 55, 57, 62, 82, 123
Hyrcania, Hyrcanian, 194, 283, 335–8, 340, 369, 385, 387, 521

Iambulus, 37, 40
Idrieus, 260, 264, 287
Immortals, 166, 319, 320
Inarus, 196, 197, 224
India, Indian, Indians, 2, 7, 36, 37, 52, 53, 89, 112–17, 119, 120, 216, 320, 345, 347–56, 358, 360–2, 366, 368–70, 386, 387, 398, 411, 421, 422, 433, 439, 446, 452, 464, 516, 530, 531, 534, 541
Ionia, Ionian, Ionians, 145, 155, 162, 169, 174, 175, 178, 179, 184–8, 191, 212, 213, 223–5, 234, 265, 283, 284, 455, 487, 488, 499, 508
Ionian Revolt, 155, 158
Iphicrates, 244, 246–9, 347
Isocrates, 8, 32, 44, 46, 47, 49, 51, 85, 260, 538, 540, 541
Issus, 215, 270, 285, 287, 295, 296, 299–301, 303, 304, 312
Ištar, 92, 99, 101–3, 527

Jerome (Saint), 500, 505, 540
Jerusalem, 76, 505, 517, 518
Justin, 55, 56, 58, 61, 63, 64, 77, 311, 322, 325, 345, 359, 369, 384, 386, 413, 445, 519, 520, 523

Lacedaemon, Lacedaemonian, Lacedaemonians, 65, 148, 160, 163, 165, 167, 169, 179–84, 187, 197, 201, 203–6, 208–11, 213, 217–19, 222, 225–32, 234, 235, 239–43, 249–51, 253, 262 435, 537, 541
Lagides, 55, 70, 143, 270, 364, 402, 462
Leonidas, 63, 163–9, 177, 181, 372
Leonnatus, 301, 361, 365–7, 384, 477

Leotychides, 184–6
Livy, 15, 68–71, 79, 498, 499, 516
Lucretius, 33, 234, 239, 245
Lycia, Lycian, Lycians, 89, 159, 162, 176, 191, 192, 251, 291, 328, 384, 387, 390, 399, 414, 435, 452, 459, 463, 476, 492, 499
Lycurgus, 44, 51
Lydia, Lydian, Lydians, 89, 145, 146, 203, 210, 213, 214, 217, 229, 233, 234, 251, 265, 283, 284, 286, 384, 387, 399, 409, 412, 435, 452, 455, 498
Lyncestian Alexander, 295, 341
Lysander, 209, 210
Lysias, 48, 538
Lysimachus, 385, 451, 452, 473, 474, 475, 477, 484, 487–92, 495, 496, 497, 521

Macedonia, Macedonian, Macedonians, 50, 54, 59, 63, 70, 87, 131, 169, 179, 183, 231, 273, 275, 277–91, 293–6, 298–301, 304–6, 308–13, 318–24, 327, 329, 330, 335, 337, 339, 341–4, 346–51, 353, 355, 356, 358, 360–2, 366, 368, 369, 371, 373, 376–8, 381, 384, 385, 388–95, 397–401, 405–7, 409–19, 421–3, 426, 429–32, 434, 435, 437, 443, 445–7, 450, 451, 455, 456, 458, 459, 461, 463, 468, 469, 471, 474, 477, 481, 495, 496, 505, 507, 513, 535
Magi, 142, 189, 265, 375
Magus, 95, 443
Mahābhāratā, 353, 359
Mardonius, 158, 159, 164, 176, 179–82, 536
Marduk, 102, 103, 374
Marsyas (of Pella), 54, 59, 60, 481
Mausolus, 251, 257, 260, 264, 287
Mazaeus, 259, 270, 316, 319–22
Media, Median, Mede, Medes, 2, 6, 31, 86–9, 94, 96, 98, 106–11, 122, 125–7, 130, 131, 135–40, 144, 145, 149, 155, 156,

165, 172, 186, 187, 203, 216, 223, 240, 283, 323, 339, 341–3, 372, 373, 384, 385, 387, 398, 418, 420, 426–8, 431, 432, 435, 439, 441, 442, 444, 446–8, 450, 469, 471, 497, 510, 517, 519, 521, 526, 528, 535, 536, 544
Medius, 380, 381, 459, 481
Medus, 135, 136, 155, 544
Megabates, 169, 188
Megabyzus, 152, 153, 194, 197, 199–201
Megasthenes, 36, 37, 53, 106, 114, 116, 119, 345, 387, 534
Memnon of Ethiopia, 123, 124
Memnon of Rhodes, 277, 278, 282, 283, 286–95, 383
Memphis, 149, 150, 151, 197, 198, 213, 248, 267, 268, 270, 312, 385, 531
Mendesian branch, 247, 248
Menelaus, 385, 457, 475, 478–80, 483
Menon, 213, 222
Mentor, 260, 261, 263, 265, 266, 268–72
Mesopotamia, 12, 103, 107, 115, 216, 324, 326, 331, 371, 385, 387, 388, 398, 419, 421, 422, 424, 432, 434, 468, 471, 517, 519, 521, 526, 528
Miletus, Milesians, 48, 153, 154, 161, 185, 186, 204, 210, 286, 287, 371, 406, 453, 457, 460, 468
Miltiades, 153, 155, 191, 199
Mindarus, 204–9
Mosul, 98, 314
Mycale, 184–6
Mysia, 89, 159, 251, 491

Nabataeans, 87, 470, 471
Nabopolassar, 100, 125, 132
Naqi'a/Zakûtu, 526, 528, 529
Nearchus, 37, 53, 119, 357, 365–8, 374, 375, 427, 459, 525, 529, 534
Nebuchadnezzar II, 100, 106, 132
Nectanebo I, 239, 247, 248, 250

Nectanebo II, 250, 254, 255, 259, 266–70
Nepherites I, 224, 229, 236
Nepos, Cornelius 45, 49, 51, 56, 58, 413, 445
Nicholas (of Damascus), 4, 24, 90, 93, 120, 125, 137–9, 325, 530, 531, 535
Nineveh, 3, 6, 89–91, 93, 98, 104, 119, 121, 122, 124–9, 138, 314, 316, 529, 530
Ninus, 2, 12, 36, 37, 86–91, 93–8, 101, 102, 111, 120–4, 131, 528–31, 542, 544
Ninyas, 2, 98, 112, 120, 121, 123
Nitocris, 100, 102
Northern Ocean, 386, 387

Octavian, 5, 14, 80
Olympiad(s), 5, 14, 15, 137, 144, 158, 198, 224, 511
Olympias, 13, 295, 370, 377, 381, 383, 407, 411, 415, 430, 446, 455
Olympic Games, 273, 303, 342, 370, 375, 424
Onesicritus, 37, 53, 104, 362, 365
Onnes, 93, 97
Orontes (satrap), 236, 239–42, 251, 253, 388, 398, 400, 430, 461, 478, 515, 522, 524
Ovid, 34, 112
Oxatres, 338, 339

Palintona, 290, 306–8, 310, 408, 479, 480, 482, 489
Pamphylia, Pamphylians, 89, 159, 162, 176, 251, 384, 388, 435, 459, 463, 492
Paphlagonia, 128, 129, 211, 217, 221, 222, 283, 384, 491
Paraetacene, 106, 107, 432, 433, 437, 439
Parmenion, 274, 278–81, 284, 295, 315, 317, 318, 321, 322, 327, 341, 377, 381
Parsondes, 137, 138
Parthia, Parthians, 1, 77, 89, 139, 385, 387, 398, 420, 435, 506, 516, 518–21, 523, 524, 535, 544

Parysatis, 209, 230
Pausanias (king of Sparta), 181–3, 187, 188, 536, 537
Peithon, 361, 384–6, 388, 389, 397, 398, 418–21, 424, 427, 428, 433, 435–7, 439, 441, 442, 445, 447, 448, 450, 451
Peloponnesus, 146, 172, 173, 179, 187, 210, 213, 293, 453, 455–7
Pelusium, 149, 150, 248, 255, 265, 267, 268, 312, 461, 462, 501, 503
Perdiccas, 54, 289, 318, 322, 372, 380, 384–6, 388–95, 397–9, 401, 403, 404, 410, 413, 416, 420, 421, 427, 466, 470, 477, 487, 507
Persepolis, 86, 115, 137, 139, 154, 323, 327–34, 342, 427, 428, 429, 448, 531
Perses, 136, 544
Persia, Persian, Persians, Persis, *passim*
Persian Gulf, 38, 86, 107, 283, 369, 386, 424, 471, 506, 534
Petra, 87, 470
Peucestes, 361, 371, 385, 398, 420, 421, 424, 425, 428–31, 434, 440, 444, 445, 449, 451
Pharnabazus, 203–11, 216, 224, 226–9, 231–3, 244, 246–9, 537
Pherecydes, 40, 42
Philinus (of Acragas), 5, 45, 62–4
Philip II of Macedon, 50, 55, 271–7, 281, 337, 383, 384, 391, 398, 443, 469, 476, 477, 481
Philip II *Philoromaeus* (Seleucid king), 523, 524
Philip III Arrhidaeus (of Macedon), 381, 383–5, 390, 413, 429
Philip V (of Macedon), 65, 67–9
Philip, son of Antigonus I *Monophtalmus*, 475, 484
Philiscus, 249, 250
Philistus, 41, 45–9
Philochorus, 51, 245
Philotas, 281, 295, 317, 326, 339–41, 381, 384, 415, 416, 420, 422

Philoxenus, 48, 49, 398
Phoenicia, Phoenician, Phoenicians, 40, 49, 89, 114, 136, 155, 159, 162, 174–6, 178, 192, 197, 198, 200, 203–5, 215, 228, 229, 236, 237, 251, 254, 258–64, 271, 303, 304, 306, 307, 309, 311, 312, 380, 388, 402, 414, 416, 417, 453, 457, 459, 466, 470, 473, 474, 481, 496, 517, 524, 527, 528
Photius (Patriarch of Constantinople), 5, 17, 27, 28, 38, 39, 72, 76–8, 80, 84, 394
Phrygia, 89, 188, 203, 211, 213, 214, 217, 228, 230, 249, 251, 281, 283, 291, 384, 387, 399, 406, 407, 423, 435, 446, 452, 459, 470, 488, 489, 492
Pithon, 362, 398, 452, 459, 461, 463, 465
Plataea, 43, 44, 61, 164, 172, 179, 180, 182, 184–7, 230
Plato, 26, 43, 123, 222, 271, 545
Pliny, 6, 16, 103, 112, 139, 534
Plutarch, 16, 19, 75, 78, 81, 121, 190, 219, 221, 240, 254, 321, 322, 325, 361, 369, 380, 399, 431, 440, 445, 492, 497, 545
Polemaeus, 452, 455, 457, 458, 460, 474, 476
Polyaenus, 150, 237, 403, 417, 447, 537
Polybius, 26, 32, 33, 41, 45, 49, 51, 58, 60, 62–73, 78, 84, 107, 110, 144, 498, 499, 503, 505, 513
Polyclitus, 47, 457
Polyperchon, 60, 318, 395, 406, 407, 409, 411, 415–17, 420, 430, 453, 455, 457, 464
Pompeius Magnus, Cn. (= Pompey), 14, 79. 523, 524
Pompeius Trogus, Cn., 12, 52, 53, 55–63, 75, 77, 81, 317, 386, 388
Pontus, 37, 89, 136, 159, 162, 273, 386, 491
Porus, 113, 345, 349–55, 357, 385, 387, 399, 421, 516, 533

General Index

Posidonius (of Apamea), 33, 37, 40, 41, 45, 46, 72–9, 81, 446, 518, 521
Proxenus, 62, 213, 220
Psammeticus I, 89, 151, 224, 225
Psammeticus III, 149, 150
Ptolemy (I *Soter Lagides*), 53, 55, 56, 63, 71, 72, 75, 110, 143, 270, 279, 281, 299, 302, 332, 344, 347, 356, 357, 360, 361, 364, 365, 367, 384, 385, 388, 389, 393–5, 397, 398, 402, 414, 415, 417, 450–4, 456–67, 469, 470, 473–84, 486, 487, 490, 492, 495, 496, 500
Ptolemy VI, 71, 72, 501–5, 512–14
Ptolemy VIII, 75, 504, 513, 514, 521
Pyrrhus, 15, 62, 63, 117
Pythagoras, 43, 55

Quellenforschung, 7, 72, 73, 83

Red Sea, 107, 151, 386
Rhodes, Rhodians 34, 39, 40, 67, 162, 229, 231, 256, 277, 282, 283, 308, 375, 401, 409, 452, 453, 456, 457, 477, 487, 488, 499
Rhoesaces, 265, 268, 283–5
River Acesines, 357, 358, 362
River Cayster, 228, 229
River Don (Tanaïs), 88, 89, 386, 387
River Euphrates, 90, 98, 100, 101, 103, 106, 108, 128–30, 216, 217, 231, 259, 314–16, 365, 368, 388, 417, 468, 471, 509, 511, 526, 528
River Ganges, 36, 106, 115, 355, 369, 387
River Granicus, 282, 283, 285, 287, 298, 443
River Halys, 145, 303, 315
River Hydaspes, 93, 349, 351, 357, 358, 387, 399
River Hyphasis, 355, 369, 387
River Indus, 106, 114, 115, 117, 347, 348, 355, 357–9, 362, 363, 365, 380, 387, 399, 534

River Maeander, 190, 460
River Nile, 88, 106, 151, 196, 198, 244, 246–9, 255, 261, 265, 266, 268, 388, 398, 485, 486, 487
River Pasitigris, 326, 424–6, 428, 449
River Phasis, 88, 338
River Tigris, 90, 103, 106, 107, 128, 221, 223, 314, 316, 321, 324, 326, 371, 388, 417, 418, 420, 424, 432, 469, 471, 520
River Upper Zab, 315, 519
River Yaxartes, 139, 386, 530
Rome, Roman, Romans, 1, 3–5, 8, 12, 14–16, 34, 45, 48, 49, 53, 56, 57, 62–4, 66, 67, 69, 72–9, 86, 90, 93, 95, 103, 152, 158, 178, 191, 194–200, 212, 223, 226, 233–6, 239, 245, 246, 250, 257, 264, 271–3, 280, 292, 303, 313, 323, 334, 342, 349, 371, 374–6, 383, 402, 411, 424, 450, 460, 473, 476, 484, 497, 498–501, 504, 505, 508, 510–12, 523, 524, 535, 537, 540, 544
Roxane, 58, 95, 97, 345, 383, 385, 392, 398, 407, 449, 455, 456, 473, 474
Royal Relatives, 284, 323
Rufus, P. Rutilius, 67, 72, 74, 77, 78
Rufus, Q. Curtius, 52, 99, 104, 311, 312, 317, 321, 341, 345, 372, 376, 384, 386

Saïte dynasty, 89, 224
Salamis on Cyprus, 171–5, 177, 178, 180, 184, 189, 200, 227, 233, 234, 238–40, 260, 261, 264, 454, 461, 475, 478, 480, 481, 483, 495
Salamis, island of, 171–5, 178, 180, 184, 189
Salpinx, 252, 288, 290, 310, 328, 351, 368, 397, 437, 482
Šammu-ramāt, 120, 526, 527, 528
Sardanapallus, 2, 121, 122, 124–31, 137, 527, 537
Sardis, 91, 123, 147, 154, 155, 160, 161, 171, 184,

186, 202, 209, 213, 229, 230, 233, 324, 395, 476, 477, 488, 490
Sargon II, 111, 528
Satrap(s), 89, 93, 122, 125, 130, 145, 155, 159, 188, 195, 196, 199, 201–3, 205, 208, 210, 211, 215, 218, 223, 224, 230, 231, 233, 234, 237, 249–52, 256, 257, 259, 260, 265, 270, 271–3, 281–6, 291, 298, 300, 312, 323, 325, 333–5, 339, 342, 365–70, 373, 385, 389–91, 399, 400, 402, 404, 407–9, 412, 417, 418, 420–2, 425, 428–31, 434, 441, 442, 444, 446, 447, 449, 450, 452, 456, 468, 469, 507, 509, 510, 517
Satrapies, 55, 114, 147, 160, 195, 196, 212, 221, 224, 227, 230, 234, 270, 294, 301, 303, 323, 324, 333, 384–9, 398, 399, 401, 407, 415–20, 423, 426, 428, 431, 435, 445–8, 451, 456, 471, 478, 484, 489, 490, 492
Scipio *Africanus*, P. Cornelius, 58, 66, 74, 497, 498, 499
Scylax (of Caryanda), 36, 534
Scythian, Scythians, 37, 94, 139, 152, 153, 165, 320, 321, 342, 345, 520, 521, 544
Second Greek War (Second Persian War), 156, 158, 187, 191, 425
Second Punic War, 65–7
Seleucia, 104, 216, 308, 432, 460, 475, 479, 511, 517, 520–3
Seleucid, 31, 76, 77, 111, 314, 411, 460, 494, 498, 505, 509, 510, 512, 515, 519, 521–4, 544
Seleucids, 70, 468, 500, 521, 534
Seleucus (I *Nicator*), 134, 280, 380, 385, 398, 417–20, 424, 425, 433, 449, 450–3, 455, 457–9, 461–9, 471, 473, 479, 484, 487, 489, 490, 492, 495–7, 500, 507, 509, 515, 522, 534
Seleucus IV, 500, 510

Semiramis, 2, 12, 13, 31, 36,
  37, 91, 93–104, 106–23,
  131, 139, 525–31, 533,
  534, 542, 544
Sennacherib, 119, 527–9
Sesoösis, 111, 119, 151
Sicily, Sicilian, 1, 3–5, 8, 12,
  14–16, 47–50, 52, 54–7,
  59, 61, 63, 65, 66, 72, 76,
  77, 158, 159, 177, 208,
  243, 249, 540
Sidon, 258–64, 266, 268,
  453, 466, 492
Silenus (of Cale Acte), 44,
  45, 46, 62–5
Silver Shields, 317, 411,
  412, 414–16, 418, 422,
  428, 429, 434, 437, 438,
  443, 445, 446, 449, 450
Sisenna, L. Cornelius, 78, 79
Sisyngambris, 13, 301, 302,
  320, 382
Sixth Syrian War, 70, 71
Social War, 78, 256
Sogdia, Sogdian, 106, 139,
  344, 345 348, 361, 385,
  386, 398, 530
Solon, 43, 143, 144, 147,
  378
Sophaenetus (of
  Stymphalus), 48, 213
Sophocles, 67, 153
Sosylus (either of Elis or of
  Lacedaemon), 45, 64, 65
Sparta, 46, 49, 163, 183,
  206–10, 225, 232, 234,
  235, 253, 256, 312, 365
Spithridates, 283–5
Spithrobates, 283, 284
Stabrobates, 113, 116, 118
Stoic, 33–5, 44, 74, 82, 132,
  533, 536, 540, 541
Strabo, 11, 36, 37, 99, 104,
  107, 110, 119, 244, 359,
  365, 426, 432, 525, 526
Sulla, L. Cornelius, 74, 78,
  79
Susa, 123, 160, 263, 325,
  326, 331, 368, 369, 371,
  372, 407, 418, 419, 422,
  424, 425, 449, 450, 519
Susis, 89, 324, 325, 368,
  387, 398, 420–2, 425,
  432, 450, 469, 471
Syncellus, 42, 111, 120,
  122, 255
Syria, Syrians, 33, 54, 75, 77,
  80, 89, 92, 93, 114, 125,
  198, 199, 215, 216, 231,
  236, 247, 251, 254, 258,
  259, 261, 262, 295, 296,

313, 316, 384, 388, 398,
  411, 452, 453, 458, 459,
  461, 462, 467, 470, 471,
  473, 478, 481, 485, 487,
  488, 492, 494, 496, 501,
  502, 506, 511–16, 519,
  520, 522, 524, 528, 538

Tachos, 242, 243, 250, 251,
  253–5
Tarentines, 435, 436, 442,
  444, 463
Tarsus, 214, 215, 295, 489
Taxiles, 348, 349, 385, 387,
  399, 421
Telescoping, 250, 260, 316
Tennes, 259–63, 264
Textkritik, 7, 18
Thaïs, 332, 333
Thebes, Thebans, 123, 149,
  163, 167, 169, 180–3,
  213, 235, 244, 245, 249,
  250, 256, 257, 262, 264,
  265, 278, 372, 382, 455
Themistocles, 11, 160, 170,
  173–7, 188–91, 194
Theophrastus, 34, 52, 57
Theopompus, 39, 42, 45,
  47, 48, 50, 51, 53, 234,
  238, 239, 271, 370
Thermopylae, 44, 81,
  162–5, 169, 171, 173,
  177, 179, 199, 220, 327,
  372, 541
Thessaly, Thessalian,
  Thessalians, 124, 160,
  161, 164, 198, 213, 257,
  281, 284, 285, 295, 296,
  318, 321, 322, 380, 385,
  490, 515
Thibron, 225, 226, 234, 235
Thrace, Thracian,
  Thracians, 75, 161, 166,
  179, 183, 206, 226, 227,
  231, 281, 293, 324, 362,
  376, 385, 397, 421, 434,
  436, 451, 473, 492, 495,
  497
Thrasybulus, 204, 206–8,
  289
Thucydides, 15, 32, 33, 44,
  46–8, 82, 84, 189, 190,
  199, 246, 543
Timaeus (of Tauromenium),
  15, 16, 35, 39, 41, 44–51,
  55, 56, 58–60, 62, 158,
  177, 178
Timagenes, 12, 361
Timotheus, 48, 249
Tiribazus, 49, 223, 231, 233,
  234, 236, 238–42, 249

Tissaphernes, 203, 205,
  218, 221–7, 229, 230,
  261
Tithraustes, 192, 230, 233
Triparadisus, 13, 398, 402,
  417, 418, 420, 421, 430
Tripolis, 258, 259, 312,
  453, 466
Troad, 89, 123, 159, 226,
  271, 278, 280, 281
Trojan War, 8, 35, 123,
  228, 280, 281, 525
Troy, Trojans, 57, 122, 123
Tryphē, 538
Tyre, Tyrian, Tyrians, 233,
  234, 237, 259, 286,
  303–11, 360, 417, 453,
  454, 456, 457, 466
Tzetzes, 5, 27, 42, 80, 125,
  143

Urartu, 87, 111, 528

Varro, M. Terentius, 15, 16,
  34, 158
Varronian chronology,
  15, 158, 178, 195–200,
  212, 224, 226, 233–5,
  245, 246, 250, 257, 264,
  271–3, 280, 292, 303,
  313, 323, 334, 342, 349,
  371, 375, 383, 403, 411,
  424, 450, 473, 476, 484

Xanthippus, 63, 178, 184,
  186, 187
Xenophon, 4, 32, 47–9, 51,
  84, 89, 94, 98, 213, 219,
  222, 225–7, 230, 318,
  537, 538
Xerxes, 94, 97, 104, 137,
  151, 156–69, 171, 172,
  174, 176–9, 185, 186,
  188–96, 199, 220, 231,
  270, 278, 333, 335, 372,
  374, 425, 538

Zagros, 3, 94, 110, 320,
  322, 373, 426
Zarinaea, 13, 137, 139
Zeno, 34, 41, 67, 82, 302
Zopyrus, 152, 159
Zoroaster, 96, 142

ἑταῖροι, 53, 55, 317, 429
συγγενής, 269, 279, 284
τρυφή, 2, 14, 46, 73, 82,
  109, 121, 122, 126, 188,
  229, 299, 315, 338, 429,
  503, 516, 533, 537
φίλοι, 53, 55, 317, 359

EU representative:
Easy Access System Europe
Mustamäe tee 50, 10621 Tallinn, Estonia
Gpsr.requests@easproject.com